ts

Highways

Major Attractions

Railroads

Highways in blue are Alaskan; green are Canadian; red are International.

ıtes

Southeastern Alaska

Dall sheep ram photographed in Denali National Park. (Bruce M. Herman)

Key to Highways in *The MILEPOST*®

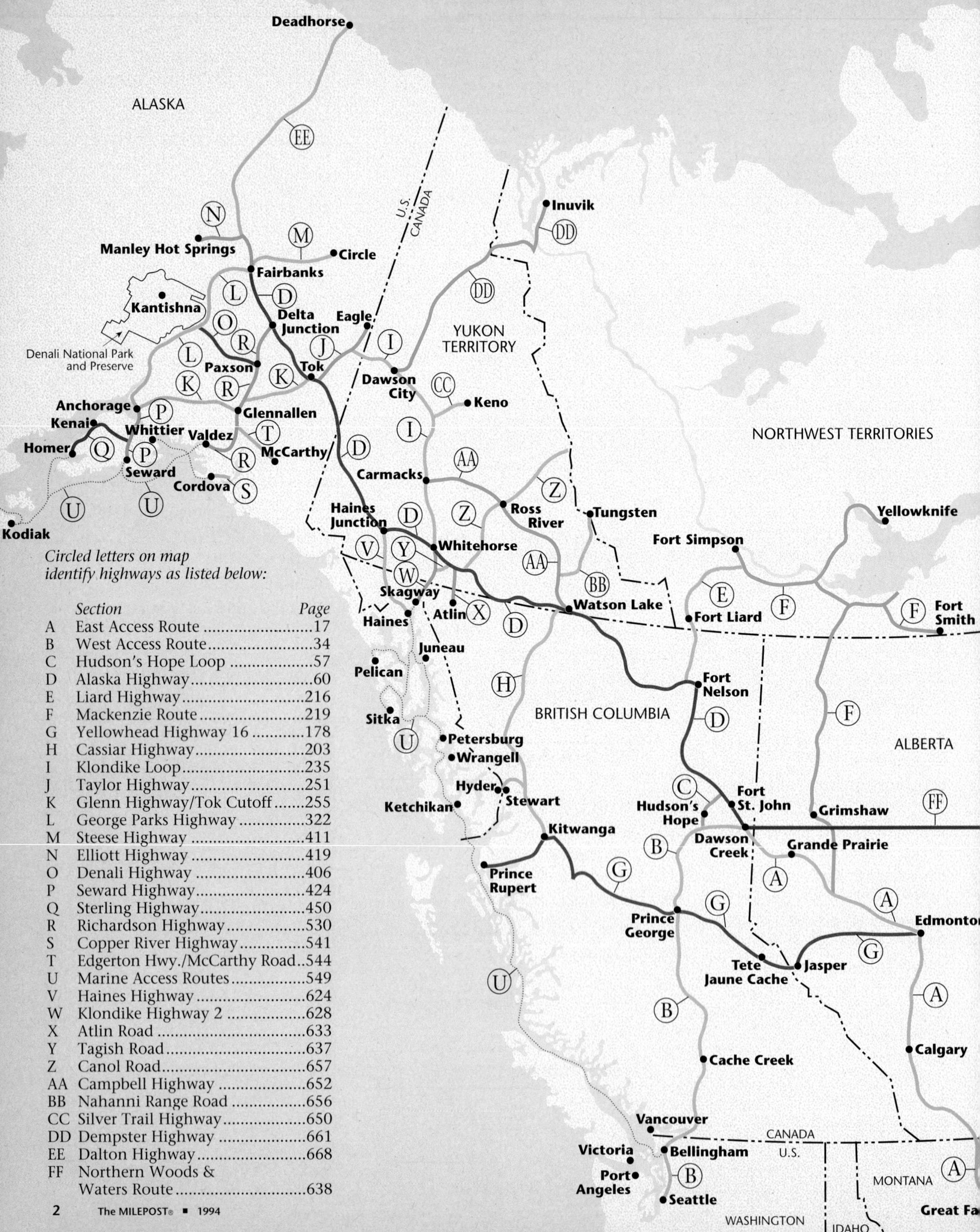

Circled letters on map identify highways as listed below:

Section | *Page*

ISSN 0361-1361 ISBN 1-878425-26-9
Key title: The Milepost
Printed in U.S.A. on recycled stock.

Vernon Publications Inc.
3000 Northup Way, Suite 200
Bellevue, WA 98004
(206) 827-9900
1-800-726-4707
Fax (206) 822-9372

Publishers of:
The MILEPOST®
The MILEPOST® Souvenir Log Book
The ALASKA WILDERNESS GUIDE
NORTHWEST MILEPOSTS®
ALASKA A to Z

COVER: Scenic Tern Lake on the Kenai Peninsula. (© 1993 Ken Graham Photography)
INSET: Brown/grizzly bear with cub. (John W. Warden)

Vernon Publications Inc.
Chairman of the Board, Bill R. Vernon
President/CEO, Geoffrey P. Vernon

How to Use This Guidebook

STEP 1 — Pull out the Plan-A-Trip map for an overview of the North Country and the access routes north.

STEP 2 — Read "Traveling the North Country with *The MILEPOST®*" on page 5 for basic information on planning your trip North and using *The MILEPOST®* on the road. The Key to Highways map on the opposite page will familiarize you with the routes covered in *The MILEPOST®*.

STEP 3 — Read "Welcome to the North Country" on page 9 for highlights of highways and destinations covered in *The MILEPOST®*. Begin a list of places you want to include on your trip.

STEP 4 — Look at the Contents on page 1. Information in *The MILEPOST®* is organized into sections: Highways, Major Attractions, Railroads, Marine Access Routes and Southeastern Alaska. You may also find specific places by checking the Index in the back of the book.

STEP 5 — Look through General Information in the back of the book. This section will answer many of your questions about traveling to Alaska.

STEP 6 — Choose one of the Highways listed on the Contents page and turn to that section. Read the brief description of the highway on the first page of the section; look at the highway strip map; and try reading the highway log. If it seems confusing, go back to page 8 and review "How to Read a Highway Log."

STEP 7 — Start planning your itinerary, referring to appropriate sections in *The MILEPOST®*. If you are driving the Alaska Highway, consult one of the two Access Routes to the Alaska Highway logged in *The MILEPOST®* and the Alaska Highway section. If you are taking the water route to Alaska, refer to the Marine Access Routes section for cruise ship and ferry information; read the descriptions of communities accessible by ferry in the Southeastern Alaska section; and refer to the Haines Highway and Klondike Highway 2 logs for road connections for ferry travelers.

WHAT YOU'LL SEE IN ALASKA WITH PRINCESS

After more than 25 years hosting Alaska vacations, Princess® offers unique experiences in the areas more travelers want to visit.

For example, we've built comfortable hotels and lodges in these popular locations:

Denali Princess Lodge℠, Denali National Park
Kenai Princess Lodge®, Cooper Landing, Kenai Peninsula
Fairbanks Princess Hotel℠, Fairbanks

Each Princess Cruises & Tours℠ Hotel welcomes you to the finest accommodations in its respective area. Featuring scenic riverside settings. Princess' renowned service and superb cuisine. And a friendly tour desk to help you experience the Alaska you've come all this way to discover.

Perhaps you'd like to make the most of your precious vacation time in this vast state. Or you simply want to sit back and enjoy Alaska's magnificent wilderness. Princess offers convenient rail/hotel excursions from both Anchorage and Fairbanks to Denali National Park—home to majestic Mt. McKinley.

You'll board the largest coaches ever built for rail—the elegant ULTRA DOME® railcars of Princess' private *Midnight Sun Express*®. Enjoy 360° views from your reserved seat in the full-length upper lounge. Dine on Alaskan delicacies prepared fresh-to-order by Princess' onboard chefs in elegant lower-level restaurants. Snap that perfect photo from our exclusive fresh-air observation platforms.

HOW YOU'LL FEEL.

At the Park, you'll be whisked to the Denali Princess Lodge. Relax in our open-air hot tubs or view lounge. River raft, flightsee the Denali area, or rent a mountain bike. There's even a convenient free shuttle to the Park Visitors Center.

In Princess' Alaska, we'll show you how to leave the world behind, but not its comforts.

For a free brochure, write Princess Tours, Dept. MP, 2815 Second Avenue, Suite 400, Seattle, WA 98121. Year-round Reservations: **800-835-8907**.

PRINCESS CRUISES® PRINCESS TOURS®

"It's more than a cruise, it's the Love Boat®."

DENALI • KENAI • PRUDHOE BAY • ALASKA'S ARCTIC • CANADA'S YUKON

Traveling the North Country with *The MILEPOST*®

The MILEPOST® has been designed to help you get the most out of your travels in the North. It will help you plan your trip North, and guide you mile-by-mile through the country once you get there. The Key to Highways map on the facing page shows you what highways are covered in *The MILEPOST*®. How to Read a Highway Log (page 8) gives a detailed explanation of the highway logging system.

The first thing to think about in planning your trip North is how you wish to travel — by highway, by ferry, by cruise ship, by airplane, on your own or with a tour. You may want to use more than one form of transportation, such as driving the Alaska Highway one way and taking the Alaska Marine Highway (the state ferry system) the other way.

Regardless of how you travel, *The MILEPOST*® works the same way. Information in *The MILEPOST*® is organized into sections: Highways, Major Attractions, Railroads, Marine Access Routes, Southeastern Alaska and General Information. All sections are listed on the Contents page. If you are driving from Anchorage to Denali National Park, for example, turn to the George Parks Highway section for the log of the highway and the Denali National Park section for a description of the park and its facilities. Pertinent sections are always cross-referenced in capital letters in the log at the appropriate junction. For example, when you reach the turnoff for Denali National Park on the George Parks Highway, the log entry reads "see DENALI NATIONAL PARK section for details."

The quickest way to find another section is to refer back to the Contents page. Place names and highways are also indexed in the back of the book.

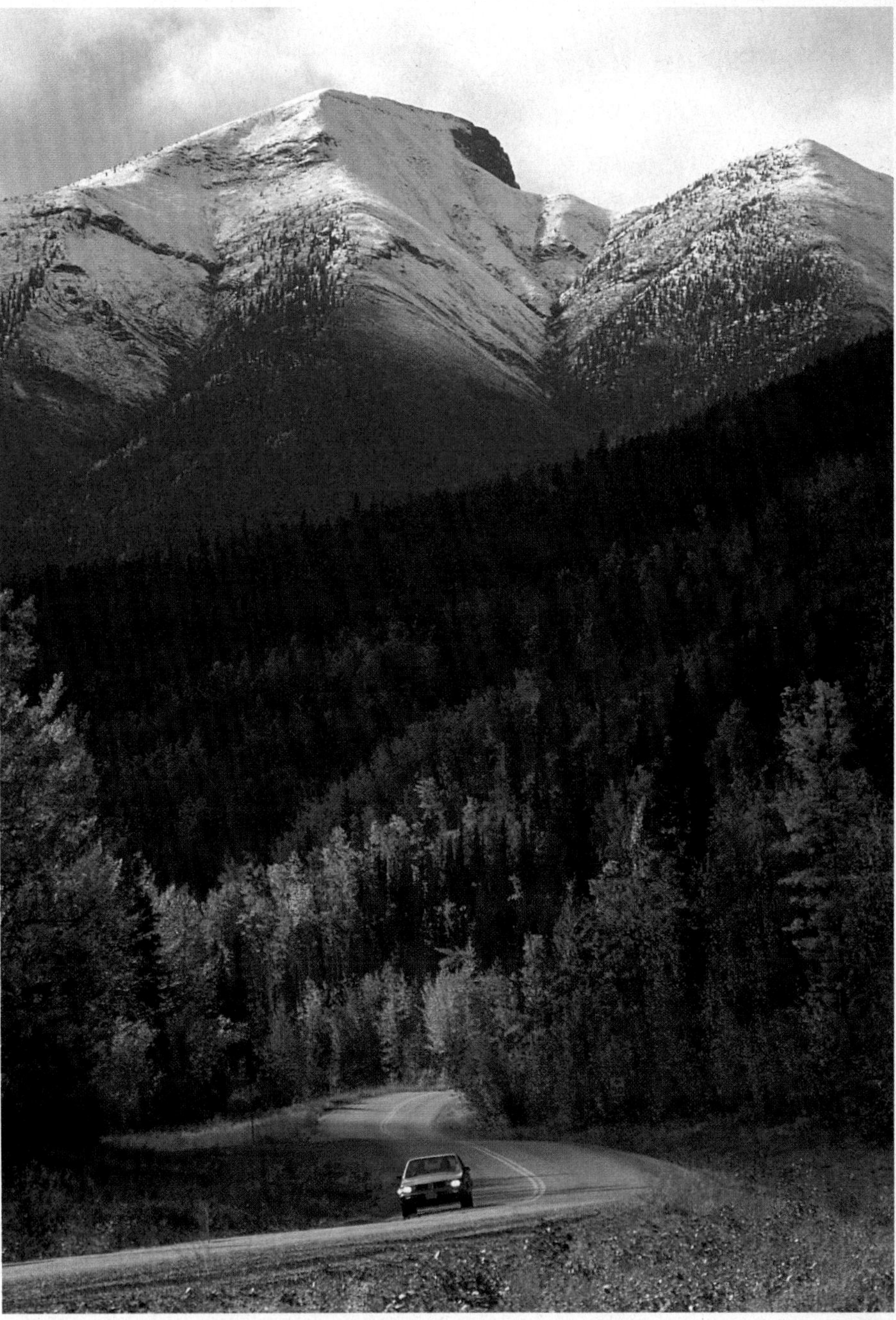

The Alaska Highway near Mile 412 in British Columbia. (Earl L. Brown, staff)

By Highway

For highway travelers, there are mile-by-mile logs and detailed maps of all highways in Alaska and northwestern Canada. The highway logs include campgrounds, businesses offering food, gas, lodging and other services, attractions, fishing spots, and the geography and history of the land. Descriptions of highway communities are included in the highway logs. Highway communities are also indexed in the back of the book.

Whether you are an independent traveler in your own vehicle, or part of a motorcoach tour, you can follow along with these logs. (See How to Read a Highway Log page 8.)

A general description of the highway, including type of surfacing and length in miles, is included in the introduction to each highway section. Mileages are also keyed on the highway strip maps which accompany each highway section.

By Water

Travel to and within Alaska by water is described in *The MILEPOST*®. Major water carriers are the Alaska state ferries, BC Ferries and cruise ships. These are covered in detail in the Marine Access Routes section. There are also numerous charter boat services, private tour boats and some government-operated ferries along the highways; details on these appear in the highway logs.

The Alaska state ferry's Southeastern system connects Bellingham, WA, and Prince Rupert, BC, with southeastern Alaska cities from Ketchikan to Skagway. These communities are covered in detail in the Southeastern Alaska section.

The Alaska state ferry's Southcentral/Southwest system connects Seldovia, Homer, Seward, Whittier, Cordova, Valdez and Kodiak. Homer, Seward and Valdez are accessible by highway. Whittier is accessible by the Alaska Railroad. Seward is covered in the Seward Highway section; Homer and Seldovia in the Sterling Highway section; and Cordova, Valdez and Whittier in the Prince William Sound section. The Southwestern system also has limited summer service to Aleutian Chain communities.

Check the descriptions of attractions along the highways and in the communities for other water carriers. The Prince William Sound community of Valdez, for example, has a number of tour boat operators with sightseeing trips out to see Columbia Glacier. Fishing charter services are also available in Prince William Sound, as well as in Kenai Peninsula communities and Southeastern Alaska communities.

By Air

Air travel is one of the most common forms of transportation in the North. A list of scheduled air operators to and within the North Country is found in Air Travel in the General Information section. Also read the information on air transportation included in each community. There is a vast network of scheduled flights to small communities. These flights, combined with the numerous air charter services, make it possible to visit virtually any spot, no matter how remote.

Check the advertisements in the communities and along the highways for air charter operators offering fly-in hunting and fishing trips, flightseeing and transportation. You may, for instance, take a flightseeing trip out of Anchorage or Talkeetna for a spectacular view of Mount McKinley. From Fairbanks you may fly out to Fort Yukon or Prudhoe Bay for the day, or take an overnight trip to Point Barrow. There are scheduled flights to Glacier Bay out of Juneau which include accommodations; charter planes available by the hour for sightseeing Glacier Bay; and helicopters offering close-up views of Juneau Icefield. These are just a few examples of the variety of air travel available in the North and described in *The MILEPOST®*.

Pilots of private planes can refer to *The MILEPOST®* highway logs, which include the location of airstrips along highways in Alaska and northwestern Canada.

By Rail

No railroads connect Alaska or the Yukon with the Lower 48, but two railroads do operate in the North: the historic White Pass & Yukon Route and the Alaska Railroad.

The White Pass & Yukon Route offers an excursion rail trip to White Pass out of Skagway and through-service to Whitehorse by motorcoach. See the White Pass & Yukon Route section for details.

The Alaska Railroad offers year-round service between Anchorage, Denali Park and Fairbanks, and summer service to Seward. The Alaska Railroad also runs a shuttle service from the Seward Highway to Whittier, port for Alaska state ferries crossing Prince William Sound. See the Alaska Railroad section for more information.

How to Read a Highway Log

Seward Highway Log

ALASKA ROUTE 1
Distance from Seward (S) is followed by distance from Anchorage (A). Physical mileposts show distance from Seward.

S 17.7 (28.5 km) **A 109.3** (175.9 km) Bridge over center channel of Snow River.

S 17 (27 km) **A 110** (177 km) Turn west for Primrose USFS campground, 1 mile/1.6 km from the highway, overlooking Kenai Lake; 10 sites, toilets, dumpsters, tables, firepits, boat ramp, water. ▲

Bridge over south channel Snow River.

S 15 (24.1 km) **A 112** (180.2 km) Watch for moose in ponds and meadows in this area.

S 14 (22.5 km) **A 113** (181.9 km) *CAUTION: Railroad crossing.*

S 11.6 (18.6 km) **A 115.4** (185.7 km) Paved parking area and USFS trail No. 6 to **Golden Fin Lake**, Dolly Varden averaging 8 inches.

S 6.6 (10.6 km) **A 120.4** (193.7 km) **Bear Creek RV and Mobile Home Park.** Good Sam Park has full and partial hookups, dump station, restrooms, showers, cable TV in travelers lounge, propane, laundry, convenience store. Leave your trailer/RV with us, have it serviced or repaired in our RV garage while you explore Seward. [ADVERTISEMENT] ▲

S 3.7 (6 km) **A 123.3** (198.4 km) Turnoff for Exit Glacier Road. This 9-mile/14.5-km dirt road ends at a parking lot at Exit Glacier ranger station. A nature trail leads to base of glacier.

S 3.2 (5.1 km) **A 123.8** (199.2 km) Nash Road.

The White House B&B. See display ad this section.

S 0 A 127 (203.2 km) **Seward**, located on Resurrection Bay.

Illustration by Mark A. Zingarelli

Above is an abbreviated version of part of the Seward Highway log, illustrated to show you how the written log reflects what you will see along the highway. In reading the log, it will help you to know three things: that the boldface letters represent beginning and ending destinations (as explained in the opening boldface paragraph in each log); that the boldface numbers represent the distance in miles from those places, the lightface numbers the metric equivalent in kilometres; and that most highways in *The MILEPOST®* are logged either south to north or east to west. (Exceptions to this rule include the Seward Highway in our example above.) If you are traveling the opposite direction of the log, you will read the log back to front.

It may also help you to know *how* our field editors log the highways. *The MILEPOST®* field editors drive each highway, taking notes on facilities, features and attractions along the way and noting the mile at which they appear. Mileages are measured from the beginning of the highway, which is generally at a junction or the city limits, to the end of the highway, also usually a junction or city limits.

Physical mileposts (usually steel rods with a mileage flag at the top) are found on most highways in Alaska. Kilometreposts are up along most highways in Canada.

Advertising also appears in the highway logs, either as a display advertisement or as a "log" advertisement. Display advertisers are keyed in the log by a boldface entry at their location, followed by the words "see display ad this section." Log advertisements are identified by the boldface name of the business at the beginning of the entry and "[ADVERTISEMENT]" at the end. These log entries are written by the advertiser.

Finally, to determine driving distance between two points, simply subtract the first mileage figures. For example, the distance from the Primrose Campground turnoff at **Milepost S 17** to the trailhead at **Milepost S 11.6** is 5.4 miles.

Welcome to the North Country

The North Country is the land north of 51°16′ latitude. Geographically, it encompasses Alaska, Yukon Territory, western Northwest Territories, northern British Columbia and Alberta. *The MILEPOST®* covers this immense region by exploring its highway system.

Following is an introduction to the highways of the North Country, and some of the sights visitors will see along the way. Highways and destinations covered in *The MILEPOST®* are keyed in **boldface type;** see Contents for page number. We've highlighted here only a few of the top attractions in each area. Read through the individual highway sections in the book for a more complete listing of both attractions and services.

Portage Glacier outside Anchorage is a top attraction. (Ron Levy)

Alaska

Alaska is the most sparsely populated state in the Union. The state's population is 550,043, and its area is 586,412 square miles. That translates into about 1.07 square miles for every person. It became the 49th state in 1959.

Two mountain systems span the Alaskan mainland, and 17 of the 20 highest mountains in the United States are in the 49th state. Above the Arctic Circle is the Brooks Range, a northern extension of the Rocky Mountains and the last major mountain system in North America to be mapped and explored. More massive than the Brooks Range is the Alaska Range, which curves around southcentral Alaska and continues south through southeastern Alaska and Canada as the Pacific Coast ranges. Crowning the Alaska Range is Mount McKinley (also known as Denali), the highest peak in North America.

Roughly six distinct natural regions make up the state of Alaska: the Interior, the Arctic, Southcentral, Southeastern, Western and Southwestern. Each has its own climate, geography, history and industries.

Interior Alaska lies cradled between the Brooks Range to the north and the Alaska Range to the south, a vast area of approximately 166,000 square miles/431,600 square km that drains the Yukon River and its tributaries. It is a climate of extremes, with -40°F temperatures in winter and 90°F days in summer.

Fairbanks is the hub of the Interior, jumping-off point for bush communities in both the Interior and Arctic, and the crossroads of several Interior highways. It is also home to the excellent University of Alaska Museum, Alaskaland and the sternwheeler *Discovery*.

The **George Parks Highway** connects Anchorage and Fairbanks, Alaska's two largest cities, and the smaller communities of Wasilla, Talkeetna, Healy and Nenana. The Parks Highway also provides access to **Denali National Park,** site of Mount McKinley, one of Alaska's top attractions.

From Fairbanks, the **Steese Highway** provides access to two hot springs (Chena Hot Springs and Arctic Circle Hot Springs), Gold Dredge Number 8, and Circle City on the Yukon River. The **Elliott Highway** out of Fairbanks also leads to a hot springs (Manley) and a gold camp (Little El Dorado), and junctions with the Dalton Highway.

The **Alaska Highway** traverses the eastern edge of the Interior, following the Tanana River north from Tok through Delta Junction to Fairbanks. (Although the 98-mile section of road between Delta Junction and Fairbanks is officially designated as part of the Richardson Highway, it is logged in *The MILEPOST®* as a natural extension of the Alaska Highway.) Visitors get their first taste of Alaska in Tok, a bustling community offering traveler ser-

View near Mount Fairplay on the Taylor Highway of Fortymile country. (George Wuerthner)

vices, dog mushing demonstrations and gift shops. Visitors get their first glimpse of the trans-Alaska pipeline at Delta Junction, and a look at Alaska's agriculture. The **Taylor Highway**, which junctions with the Alaska Highway near Tok, leads north past gold mining claims on the Fortymile River to the pioneer community of Eagle on the Yukon River.

Arctic Alaska lies above the Arctic Circle, between the Brooks Range to the south and the Arctic sea coast to the north, and from the Canadian border to the east westward to Kotzebue. Flightseeing trips to two Arctic destinations — Kotzebue and Prudhoe Bay — are popular sightseeing packages offered out of both Anchorage and Fairbanks. The only highway in the region, the **Dalton Highway**, forms a lonely ribbon of road stretching from Fairbanks to Prudhoe Bay on the North Slope. Built in conjunction with the trans-Alaska pipeline, this gravel road is open to public travel to the DOT/PF checkpoint at the top of Chandalar Shelf, just north of the half-way point to Prudhoe Bay. Beyond the checkpoint the highway is restricted to pipeline-related traffic.

The Southcentral region of Alaska curves 650 miles/1046 km north and west from the Gulf of Alaska coast to the Alaska Range. This region has tremendous geographic variety: fertile river valleys, rugged mountain ranges, glaciers, forests, and coastal waters rich in sea life.

Highways in Southcentral reflect this variety. The **Glenn Highway** cuts diagonally across the region. Highlights include magnificent views of the Wrangell and Chugach mountains, Matanuska Glacier, musk oxen and flower gardens at Palmer, and access to Independence Mine State Park. The **Denali Highway**, noted for its scenery and geography, follows the south flank of the Alaska Range to Denali National Park. The **Richardson Highway** offers spectacular views (of Thompson Pass and Worthington Glacier) and access to Valdez, location of the trans-Alaska pipeline terminal and gateway to **Prince William Sound** and Columbia Glacier. The state ferry from Valdez to Cordova is the only way to reach the **Copper River Highway** to the Million Dollar Bridge. The **Edgerton Highway** branches off the Richardson Highway and connects with the McCarthy Road to the historic mining town of Kennicott.

Southcentral includes the **Kenai Peninsula**, a popular spot for sport fisher-

The Glenn Highway winds along the Matanuska River. (Michael DeYoung)

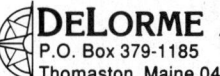

men and outdoorsmen. The **Seward Highway**, one of two major routes on the Kenai, provides access to Alyeska ski resort, Portage Glacier, the Hope Highway, and to Seward, gateway to Kenai Fjords National Park. The **Sterling Highway** follows the Kenai River west to Cook Inlet (waters famous for salmon and halibut), then winds south along the peninsula's west coast to scenic Homer.

Anchorage, Alaska's largest city, is the hub of Southcentral. Anchorage began as a tent city of railroad workers at the head of Cook Inlet during the construction of the **Alaska Railroad** (1915–23). Today, the railroad provides passenger service between Fairbanks, Denali Park, Anchorage and Seward, with a branch line to Whittier, port for cruise ships and the state ferry to Prince William Sound communities. Anchorage offers first-class hotels, shopping, the excellent Anchorage Museum of History and Art, and a variety of other cultural and recreational attractions.

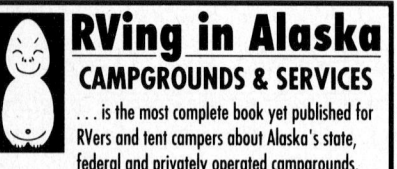

Less than an hour's flight from Anchorage, and about 10 hours by ferry from Homer, is **Kodiak**, the largest island in Alaska and the second largest island in the United States. Kodiak is known for its brown bears, fishing, Russian heritage and WWII historical sites.

Southeastern Alaska is a moist, luxuriantly forested panhandle extending some 500 miles/805 km from Icy Bay on the Gulf of Alaska coast to Dixon Entrance south of Ketchikan. Southeast encompasses both the narrow strip of coast separated from the mainland (and Canada) by the Coast Mountains, and the hundreds of islands that make up the Alexander Archipelago.

The geography of this region prohibits road building, and southeastern communities (with the exception of Haines, Skagway and Hyder) are not connected to any highway system. Transportation is by air or by water, with **Alaska state ferries** providing transport for people and vehicles to more than a dozen communities. Cruise ships also call at mainline ports in Southeast, as well as cruising the waters of Glacier Bay National Park and Preserve. The all-weather **Haines Highway** connects Haines to the Alaska Highway, and also provides access to eagle-viewing areas along the Chilkat River. Scenic **Klondike Highway 2** connects Skagway to the Alaska Highway, cresting the Coast Range at White Pass Summit.

Indian art, Russian architecture, the gold rush, and the lumber and fishing industries make up the sights and sounds of communities in Southeast. A few of the major attractions and events are: the historic **White Pass & Yukon Route** railway at Skagway, the state capitol in Juneau, Sitka National Historic Park, Totem Bight outside Ketchikan, the Little Norway Festival in Petersburg, and the Southeast Alaska State Fair in Haines.

Two of Alaska's regions — Western and Southwestern — are covered in detail in our companion guide — *The ALASKA WILDERNESS GUIDE*. Western Alaska stretches from the head of Bristol Bay north along the Bering Sea coast to the Seward Peninsula near the Arctic Circle and extends inland about 200 miles/322 km from the coast, encompassing the Yukon–Kuskokwim Delta. Probably the region's most popular destination with out-of-state visitors is Nome, with its Native culture and gold rush relics.

The Alaska Peninsula and Aleutian Chain make up Southwestern Alaska. The Alaska Peninsula extends 550 miles/885 km southwest from Mount Iliamna, on the west shore of Cook Inlet, to its tip at False Pass. The Aleutian Islands chain reaches another 1,100 miles/1770 km toward Asia. The volcanic Aleutian Range forms the spine of the peninsula, and the Aleutian Islands are actually crests of an arc of submarine volcanoes. Perhaps one of the best known attractions of this region is Katmai National Park and Preserve, accessible by air from Anchorage to King Salmon.

Yukon Territory

Yukon Territory, shaped somewhat like a right triangle, is bordered on the west by Alaska at 141° longitude and on the south by British Columbia at latitude 60°. The northern boundary is the Beaufort Sea in the Arctic Ocean and the eastern boundary the Mackenzie Mountains that separate Yukon Territory from Northwest Territories.

Yukon Territory is larger than all the New England states combined. It has an area of 186,300 square miles/482,573 square km. The population of Yukon Territory is 29,129.

The **Alaska Highway** crosses the 60th parallel north into Yukon Territory just south of Watson Lake, YT, and travels through the territory for about 580 miles/935 km before reaching the Alaska border. Scenic and historic attractions abound

Distinctive igloo church in Inuvik, Northwest Territories. (Earl L. Brown, staff)

along this pioneer highway: the Watson Lake sign forest, historic Silver City, huge Kluane Lake. The Alaska Highway also provides access to Whitehorse, the territorial capital, home to the SS *Klondike* National Historic Site, the Frantic Follies, Miles Canyon and other attractions.

The **Klondike Loop**, which junctions with the Alaska Highway near Whitehorse, leads north along the Yukon River to the territory's first capital, Dawson City. Yukon's modern history dates from the great Klondike gold rush of 1898, which brought thousands of gold seekers to the Yukon and Alaska. Dawson City, which grew out of that gold rush, is a living history lesson for visitors to the North. The Klondike Loop continues west via the Top of the World Highway to Alaska.

Branching off the Klondike Loop are three Yukon highways: the Silver Trail (Highway 11) and the all-gravel Dempster (Highway 5) and Campbell (Highway 4). The **Silver Trail** leads to the mining communities of Mayo, Elsa and Keno City. The remote **Dempster Highway** starts just south of Dawson City and heads north through magnificent untouched wilderness to Inuvik, NWT. The **Campbell Highway** heads north from Watson Lake through Pelly River country, past the silver–lead–zinc mines at Faro, to Carmack.

Other Yukon routes for the adventurous to explore are: the old **Canol Road**, with its relics from the WWII oil pipeline; the short but scenic **Tagish Road**; and the lonely Nahanni Range Road.

Portions of the **Atlin Road**, **Haines Highway** and **Klondike Highway 2** are also within the Yukon Territory, as are some of the main attractions found along these roads. The Yukon portion of the Haines Highway skirts the eastern boundary of Kluane National Park, and provides access to Kathleen Lake, the only established campground within the park. Klondike Highway 2 passes by Rainbow Lake, one of Yukon's most colorful lakes, and the Carcross desert.

Northwest Territories

Nearly twice the size of Alaska, with a quarter of the population of Anchorage, Canada's Northwest Territories is a vast arctic and subarctic wilderness with only 1,300 miles/2000 km of highway. It has about 54,000 inhabitants (of which one-third live in Yellowknife) and an area of 1,304,903 square miles/3,376,698 square km.

Even its national parks are immense. Wood Buffalo National Park, on Highway 5, is the second largest park in the world with 17,300 square miles/44,980 square km. Nahanni National Park, accessible by air, is 1,840 square miles/ 4765 square km and has one of the

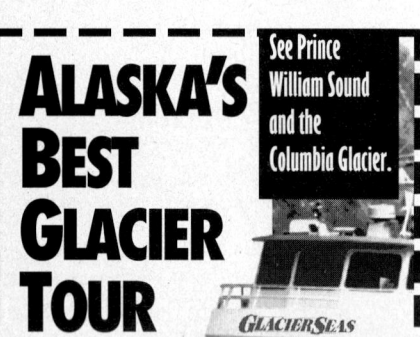

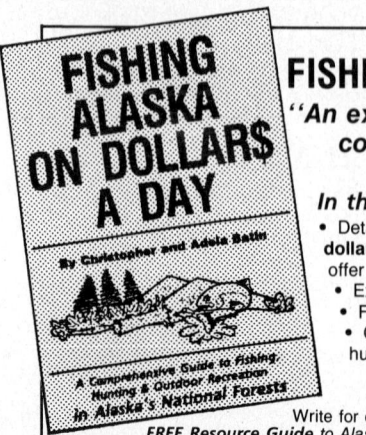

Native crafts on display in Fort Simpson, NT. *(Lyn Hancock)*

world's deepest canyons.

The majority of the population is Native: 16 percent Déné (Indian), 36 percent Inuit (Eskimo), and 8 percent Metis (mixed ancestry). The remaining 40 percent is non-Native. Their unique stone sculpture, carvings, garments and artwork are sold at retail outlets in most cities.

In the southern region of the Northwest Territories, daylight lasts 20 hours in summer, giving visitors long days for driving, fishing, hunting and camping. Average temperature from June to September is 55°F/13°C.

Access to Northwest Territories is from Alberta via the Mackenzie Highway to Fort Simpson. All-weather highways branch off this central highway to Yellowknife, Fort Resolution and Fort Smith. Northwest Territories highways are all covered in the **Mackenzie Route** section of *The MILEPOST®*. Three other highways cross into Northwest Territories: the Dempster Highway to Inuvik; the Nahanni Range Road to Tungsten; and the territory's newest highway, the **Liard Highway**, connecting the Alaska Highway and Mackenzie Highway via Fort Liard.

British Columbia

British Columbia, population 3,185,900, is Canada's most westerly province. It stretches 813 miles/1300 km from its southern border with the United States to the north boundary with Yukon Territory. It is 438 miles/700 km wide, bounded on the east by Alberta and on the west by the Pacific Ocean. Victoria, the capital city, is located on Vancouver Island and is accessible from the mainland by ferry and by air.

British Columbia is where the **Alaska Highway** begins. Mile 0 is at Dawson Creek, BC (not to be confused with Dawson City, YT). The highway crosses the Rocky Mountains at Summit Lake, highest point on the Alaska Highway, before reaching the Yukon Territory border some 600 miles/960 km north of Dawson Creek. Two highlights of the drive are the Stone sheep in Stone Mountain Provincial Park and Muncho Lake Provincial Park.

The **West Access Route** to the Alaska Highway follows Trans-Canada Highway 1 and Provincial Highway 97 from the U.S.–Canada border north along the Fraser and Thompson rivers to Prince George and the junction with Yellowhead Highway 16. There, travelers have a choice: follow the Hart Highway over Pine Pass to Dawson Creek, or go west on **Yellowhead Highway 16** to Prince Rupert, departure point for British Columbia and Alaska state ferries.

Yellowhead Highway 16 also provides access to another scenic road north, the **Cassiar Highway.** This spectacular route follows the Coast Mountains north to the Alaska Highway. There are worthwhile side trips along the way. The Stewart, BC–Hyder, AK, Access Road offers a good view of Bear Glacier. The Telegraph Creek

Fields of bright yellow canola in northern Alberta. (Earl L. Brown, staff)

Road winds its way through the mountains to historic Telegraph Creek.

Other scenic side trips include: the **Hudson's Hope Loop** to W.A.C. Bennett Dam, Peace Canyon Dam and Moberly Lake; and **Atlin Road** to Atlin, the province's most northwesterly town in one of its most memorable settings.

Portions of the Liard Highway, Haines Highway and Klondike Highway 2 also cross into British Columbia.

Alberta

The province of Alberta (population 2,469,800) is known for its great geographical diversity, from the Canadian Rockies, which mark the western border of the province, to the vast wilderness region of lakes, rivers and forests of the northern half of the province. Rolling prairie — and the agricultural heartland of Alberta — stretches from the U.S. border north to Edmonton. Routes west from Edmonton to Dawson Creek, BC, and the start of the Alaska Highway, pass through an area known as the "parkland" — broad valleys, wide ridges, lakes, streams and timberland.

The **East Access Route** to the Alaska Highway crosses both prairie and parkland in its 750-mile/1207-km journey from the southern border of Alberta to Dawson Creek, BC. The Provincial Highway 2 portion of this route, which has served Alaska-bound travelers since the 1940s, also provides access to Calgary and Edmonton. Calgary is perhaps best known for the Calgary Stampede in July, while Edmonton's most famous attraction might be the West Edmonton Mall.

At Edmonton, travelers may turn west on the transprovincial **Yellowhead Highway 16**, which crosses into British Columbia at Yellowhead Pass in the Canadian Rockies. Follow Highway 16 west from Edmonton 906 miles/1,458 km to its end at Prince Rupert, BC, departure point for British Columbia and Alaska ferries.

Another major east-west route is the **Northern Woods & Waters Route**, from the Saskatchewan border to Dawson Creek, BC. This highway junctions with a network of roads in the northern half of the province, including access routes to the Mackenzie Highway to Northwest Territories.

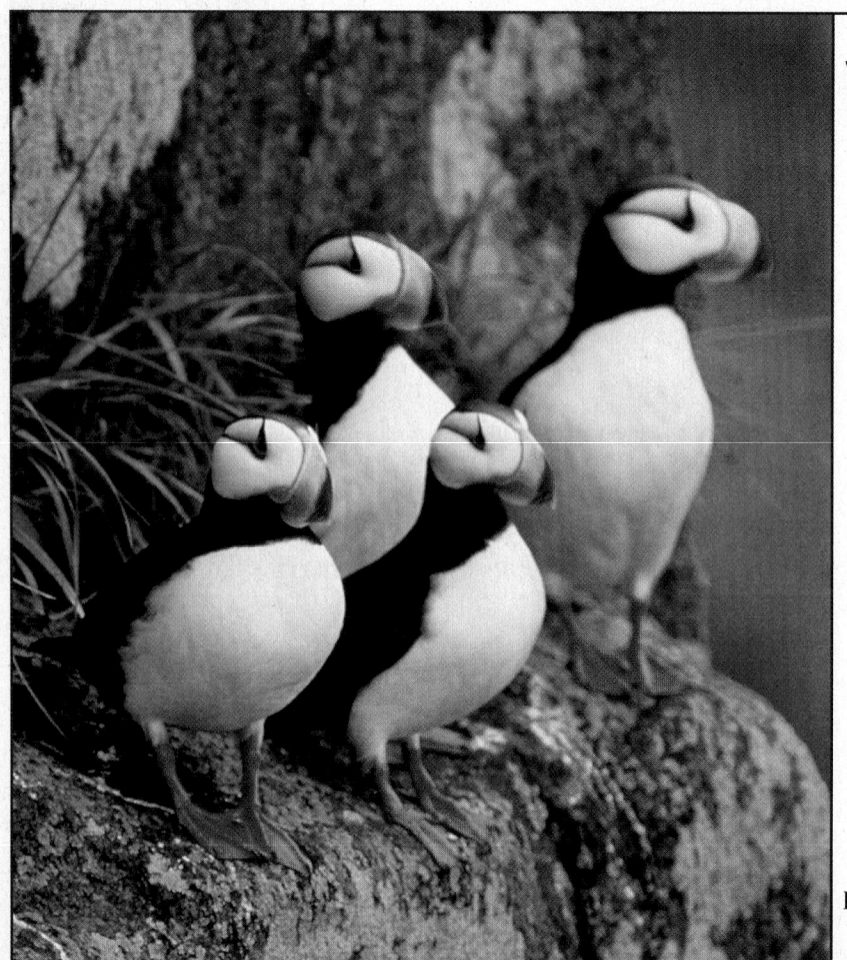

Alaska Highway via
EAST ACCESS ROUTE

Great Falls, Montana, to Dawson Creek, British Columbia via Calgary and Edmonton, Alberta Interstate Highway 15 and Provincial Highways 4, 3, 2, 43 and 34

(See maps, pages 18–19)

The East Access Route is logged in *The MILEPOST®* as one of the two major access routes (the other is the West Access Route) to the Alaska Highway.

When the Alaska Highway opened to civilian traffic in 1948, this was the only access route to Dawson Creek, BC, start of the highway. At that time the route led from Great Falls, MT, through Calgary to Edmonton. From Edmonton, it continued north to Clyde and from there to Athabasca via Highway 2 or Smith via Highway 44. At Triangle, the junction of Highways 2 and 2A (then Highway 34), motorists either headed north to McLennan and Peace River, or south via Valleyview to Grande Prairie, another 110 miles. In late 1955, Highway 43 was completed connecting Edmonton and Valleyview via Whitecourt.

Highways on this route are all paved primary routes, with visitor services readily available along the way. Total driving distance from Great Falls, MT, to Dawson Creek, BC, is approximately 867 miles/1394 km.

INTERSTATE HIGHWAY 15
The East Access Route begins in **GREAT FALLS** (pop. 55,097; elev. 3,333 feet/1,016m), Montana's second largest city. Head north through northcentral Montana on Interstate 15. From Great Falls to the Canadian border it is 117 miles/188.3 km. *The MILEPOST®* log begins at the Canadian border.

Milk River information centre features dinosaur and hoodoos. *(Judy Parkin, staff)*

East Access Route Log

HIGHWAY 4
The East Access Route log is divided into two sections: Canadian border to Edmonton, and Edmonton to Dawson Creek.
This section of the log shows distance from the Canadian border (CB) followed by distance from Edmonton (E).

CB 0 E 382.2 (615 km) U.S.–Canada border, **COUTTS** border crossing; customs and immigration open 24 hours a day. Food, gas and lodging at border. Duty free shop.

CB 11.7 (18.9 km) **E 370.5** (596.2 km) Milk River Travel Information and Interpretive Centre; picnic tables, dump station, souvenir shop, ice cream shop, displays and travel information.

CB 13 (21 km) **E 369.2** (594.1 km) **MILK RIVER** (pop. 900) has food, gas, stores, lodging and a small public campground (six informal sites; no hookups). The eight flags flying over the campground represent seven countries and the Hudson's Bay Co., all of which once laid claim to the Milk River area. Grain elevators are on the west side of the highway, services are on the east side. ▲

CB 13.5 (21.7 km) **E 368.7** (593.3 km) **Junction** with Secondary Road 501 east to Writing-on-Stone Provincial Park, 26 miles/42 km; camping, Indian petroglyphs.

CB 16.3 (26.3 km) **E 365.9** (588.8 km) Stop of interest sign about Milk River Ridge.

CB 24.4 (39.2 km) **E 357.8** (575.8 km) Road west to community of **WARNER** (pop. 434); store, gas, restaurant.

CB 24.6 (39.6 km) **E 357.6** (575.5 km) **Junction** with Highway 36A north to Taber, centre of Alberta's sugar beet industry.

CB 36.8 (59.2 km) **E 345.4** (555.8 km) Small community of New Dayton.

CB 41.5 (66.8 km) **E 340.7** (548.3 km) **Junction** at Craddock elevators with Highway 52 west to Raymond (10 miles/16 km), site of the annual Stampede and Heritage Days; Magrath (20 miles/32 km); Cardston (46 miles/74 km); and Waterton Lakes National Park (74 miles/119 km).

CB 46.1 (74.2 km) **E 336.1** (540.9 km)

EAST ACCESS ROUTE *Great Falls, MT, to Edmonton, AB*

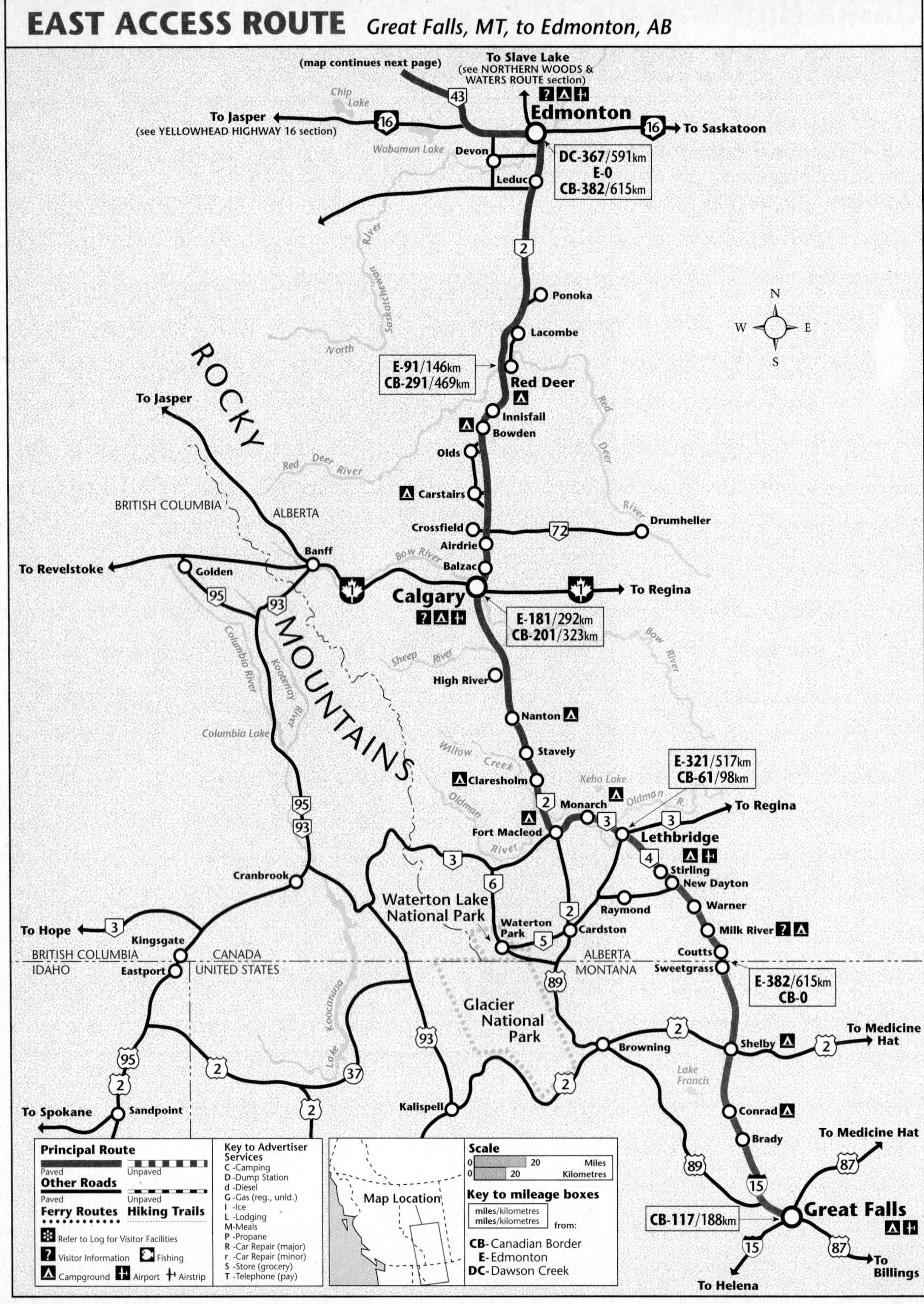

EAST ACCESS ROUTE *Edmonton, AB, to Dawson Creek, BC*

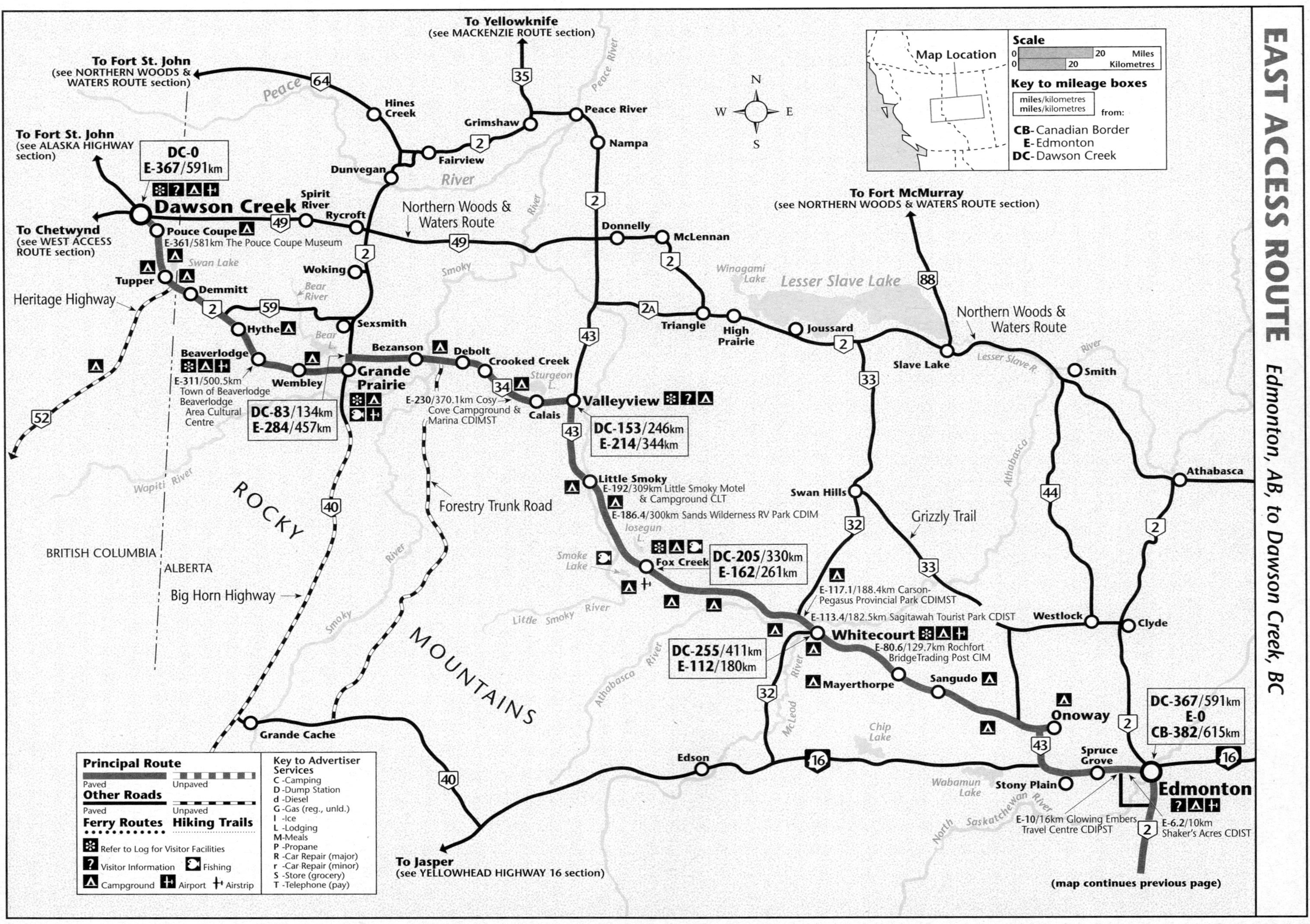

Young visitor to Fort Macleod watches cowboy harness horses. (Judy Purkin, staff)

Small community of Stirling to west; municipal campground with 15 sites, some with power and water, dump station, showers and tennis court. Grain elevators and rail yards alongside highway. ▲

CB 46.6 (75 km) **E 335.6** (540 km) **Junction** with Highway 61 east to Cypress Hills.

CB 57.2 (92.1 km) **E 325** (523 km) Stop of interest sign on west side of road describes how large scale irrigation began in this area in 1901.

CB 61.1 (98.4 km) **E 321.1** (516.7 km) **LETHBRIDGE** (pop. 63,000), Alberta's third largest city, has complete facilities; department stores, shopping malls, a wide choice of hotel/motel accommodations and restaurants. Watch for the tourist information centre (see **Milepost CB 62.9**).

Founded in 1870 on the wealth of nearby coal mines, its economy today is based upon grain, livestock, sugar beets, oil and gas. It is home to Canada's largest agricultural research station. Attractions include Indian Battle Park (exit west on Whoop-up Drive from Highway 4), which contains a replica of Fort Whoop-Up, one of the whiskey-trading posts instrumental in bringing the North West Mounted Police to the west.

Camping at Henderson Lake Park (exit on Mayor McGrath Drive from highway); picnic area, tent and full hookup campsites. Nikka Yuko Japanese Gardens, west end of Henderson Lake, has authentic Oriental gardens. ▲

CB 62.9 (101.3 km) **E 319.3** (513.8 km) **Junction** with Highway 5 south to Cardston and Waterton Park in Waterton Lakes National Park. Mayor McGrath Drive to east provides access to motels, hotels and Henderson Lake Park. Alberta's Waterton Lakes, and adjoining Glacier National Park in Montana, form Waterton–Glacier International Peace Park. The park offers spectacular mountain and lake scenery.

Chinook County Tourist Information Centre, on the north side of the intersection of Highway 4 and Mayor McGrath Drive, has RV parking, restrooms, picnic shelter, dump station and dumpster; open year-round.

CB 66.6 (107.2 km) **E 315.6** (507.9 km) Tourist information centre beside Brewery Gardens.

Highway 4 ends northbound. Route now follows Highway 3 (Crowsnest) West.

HIGHWAY 3

CB 69.5 (111.8 km) **E 312.7** (503.2 km) **Junction** with Highway 25. Access to **Park Lake** Provincial Park (9 miles/14 km north); 53 campsites, swimming, boat launch, fishing, playground. ▲

CB 72 (115.9 km) **E 310.2** (499.2 km) Community of Coalhurst just north of highway; gas station.

CB 73.5 (118.3 km) **E 308.7** (496.8 km) CPR marshalling yards at Kipp.

CB 80.3 (129.2 km) **E 301.9** (485.8 km) **Junction** with Highway 23 north. Continue west on Highway 3 for Fort Macleod.

CB 81.5 (131.2 km) **E 300.7** (483.9 km) Community of Monarch; hotel, gas.

Westbound, the highway enters Oldman River valley. Good view west of the Rockies on a clear day.

CB 96.1 (154.7 km) **E 286.1** (460.4 km) **Junction** with Highway 2 south to the U.S. border and access to Waterton Lakes and Glacier national parks.

Highway 3 continues through **FORT MACLEOD** (pop. 3,100; elev. 3,300 feet/1,006m). There are several hotels and motels, restaurants, shopping facilities and gas stations. This community's main street is a designated historic site. The main attraction in Fort Macleod is the Fort Museum, a replica of the original fort built in 1874, the first outpost of the North West Mounted Police (later the RCMP) in western Canada. During July and August, the museum features re-creation of the Musical Ride: Youth in RCMP uniforms execute drills on horseback in a colorful display. Open daily from May to mid-October; open weekdays except holidays mid-Oct. through April.

CB 99 (159.4 km) **E 283.2** (455.8 km) **Junction** with Highway 2 north to Calgary and Edmonton. Highway 3 (Crowsnest) continues west to Hope, BC. Travel Alberta information office west side of junction; open May to September.

HIGHWAY 2

CB 100 (160.8 km) **E 282.2** (454.1 km) Oldman River bridge. Alberta government campground to southwest with 10 campsites, dump station, playground, fishing and swimming. North of the river is the largest turkey farm in Alberta. ▲

CB 100.4 (161.6 km) **E 281.8** (453.5 km) Side road leads 10 miles/16 km to Head-Smashed-In Buffalo Jump, a World Heritage Site; open 9 A.M. to 8 P.M., May 15 to Labour Day, 9 A.M. to 5 P.M., the remainder of the year. Closed Mondays, Nov. to March. The interpretive centre is built into the cliff and features displays on seven levels.

CB 111.2 (179 km) **E 271** (436.1 km) Road east to Granum, a small settlement dominated by grain elevators. Recreation park in town with 41 campsites. ▲

CB 116.2 (187 km) **E 266** (428 km) Community of Woodhouse.

CB 121.8 (196 km) **E 260.4** (419.1 km) **CLARESHOLM** (pop. 3,500), a prosperous ranching centre with all visitor facilities. The old railway station houses a museum. Camping at Centennial Park; 15 sites, dump station, playground. ▲

CB 125.9 (202.6 km) **E 256.3** (412.5 km) Stop of interest sign commemorating The Leavings, a stopping place on the Fort Macleod–Calgary trail in 1870.

CB 131.3 (211.3 km) **E 250.9** (403.8 km) Community of Stavely to the east.

CB 132.1 (212.6 km) **E 250.1** (402.5 km) Access road west to **Willow Creek** Provincial Park; 150 campsites, swimming, fishing. ▲

CB 138.4 (222.8 km) **E 243.8** (392.3 km) Small settlement of Parkland.

CB 145.9 (234.8 km) **E 236.3** (380.3 km) Nanton campground (75 sites) at junction with Secondary Road 533, which leads west to Chain Lakes Provincial Park. ▲

CB 146.8 (236.3 km) **E 235.4** (378.8 km) **NANTON** (pop. 1,700); all visitor facilities. Nanton is famous for its springwater, which is piped from the Big Spring in the Porcupine Hills, 6 miles/10 km west of town, to a large tap located in town centre. Springwater tap operates mid-May to September. WWII Lancaster bomber on display at Centennial Park.

CB 151.1 (243.2 km) **E 231.1** (371.9 km) **Junction** with Highway 2A, which parallels Highway 2 northbound.

CB 162.8 (262 km) **E 219.4** (353.1 km) **Junction** with Highway 23 west to **HIGH RIVER** (pop. 6,600) located on Highway 2A. All visitor facilities.

CB 164 (264 km) **E 218.2** (351.1 km) Stop of interest commemorating Spitzee Post, built in 1869.

CB 170 (273.6 km) **E 212.2** (341.5 km) Stop of interest sign about cattle brands.

CB 171.6 (276.1 km) **E 210.6** (338.9 km) **Junction** with Highways 2A and 7. Stop of interest commemorating the Turner Valley oil fields.

CB 173.3 (278.9 km) **E 208.9** (336.2 km) Sheep Creek bridge. **Sheep Creek** Provincial Park has a picnic area, playground, swimming and fishing.

CB 188.6 (303.5 km) **E 193.6** (311.6 km) Calgary southern city limits.

NOTE: To bypass downtown Calgary, exit at Marquis of Lorne Trail and continue to Highway 2 (Deerfoot Trail) north.

CB 196.5 (316.2 km) **E 185.7** (298.8 km) Exit for Glenmore Trail, the southwest bypass route that connects with Trans-Canada Highway 1 west to Banff and Vancouver, BC.

Calgary

CB 200.8 (323.1 km) **E 181.4** (291.9 km) Located at the confluence of the Bow and Elbow rivers. **Population:** 720,000. **Elevation:** 3,440 feet/ 1,049m. **Emergency Services:** Phone 911 for emergency services. **Hospitals:** Calgary General, 841 Centre Ave. NE; Holy Cross, 2210 2nd St. SW; Foothills, 1403 29th St. NW; Rockyview, 7007 14th St. SW.; Peter Lougheed Center, 3500 26th Ave. NE.

Visitor Information: In the downtown area at the base of Calgary Tower, and at the Calgary Airport; both are open year-round. Other centres (open summer only) are located on major access routes into the city. Or call Calgary Convention & Visitors Bureau at 263-8510.

This bustling city is one of Alberta's two major population and business centres. The great influx of homesteaders to Calgary came with completion of the Canadian Pacific Railway in 1883. It grew as a trading centre for surrounding farms and ranches. Oil and gas discovered south of the city in 1914 contributed more growth.

Perhaps the city's best known attraction is the annual Calgary Stampede, which takes place at the Exhibition Grounds, July 8–17, 1994. The 10-day event includes a parade and rodeo; phone 1-800-661-1260 for Stampede information and tickets.

Some other major attractions are: Alberta Science Centre and Centennial Planetarium, 11th Street and 7th Avenue; the Glenbow Museum, which presents the culture and history of northwest North America, 130 9th Avenue SE; the Eau Claire Market, adjacent to Prince's Island in the downtown area; the Calgary Chinese Cultural Centre, 197 1st St. SW; the Energeum, at the Energy Resources Bldg., 640 5th Ave. SW; Fort Calgary interpretive centre, 750 9th Ave. SE; Calgary Zoo, off Memorial Drive, has a prehistoric park with life-sized replicas of dinosaurs; and Heritage Park, west of 14th Street and Heritage Drive SW, a re-creation of Calgary's pioneer eras. Visitors may recognize the distinctive Saddledome, located at the Exhibition Grounds, which was the site of the 1988 Winter Olympics skating and hockey events. Olympic Park (site of ski jumping, luge and bobsled) is on Trans-Canada Highway 1, west of Sarcee Trail.

Calgary has large shopping malls, department stores, restaurants and many hotels and motels. Most lodging is downtown or on Highway 2 south (Macleod Trail), Trans-Canada Highway 1 north (16th Avenue) and Alternate 1A (Motel Village). There are several campgrounds in and around the city. ▲

East Access Route Log

(continued)

CB 211.3 (340 km) **E 170.9** (275 km) Calgary northern city limits.

Highway 2 from Calgary to Edmonton bypasses most communities. Except for a few service centres built specially for freeway traffic, motorists must exit the freeway for communities and gas, food or lodging.

CB 211.9 (341 km) **E 170.3** (273 km) Exit to community of **BALZAC**. Private RV park with dump station. ▲

CB 217.9 (350.7 km) **E 164.3** (264.4 km) Road west to **AIRDRIE** (pop. 13,000). Visitor facilities include hotels and motels.

CB 225 (362 km) **E 157.2** (253 km) Dickson–Stephensson Stopping House on Old Calgary Trail; rest area, tourist information.

CB 232.2 (373.6 km) **E 150** (241.4 km) **Junction** with Highway 2A west to Crossfield and Highway 72 east to Drumheller, 60 miles/97 km, site of Alberta's Badlands. The Badlands are famous for the dinosaur fossils found there. Fossil displays at world-renowned Tyrrell Museum of Paleontology in Drumheller.

CB 232.6 (374.4 km) **E 149.6** (240.7 km) Stop of interest sign about the buffalo which once darkened the prairies here. Gas and restaurant at turnout.

CB 235.1 (378.3 km) **E 147.1** (236.7 km) Exit to **CROSSFIELD**; gas, hotel, food.

CB 243.1 (391.2 km) **E 139.1** (223.9 km) Exit west for **CARSTAIRS** (pop. 1,725), a farm and service community with tourist information centre and campground. The campground has 28 sites, electric hookups, hot showers and dump station. Services here include groceries, liquor store, banks, a motel, propane and gas stations. ▲

CB 252.7 (406.6 km) **E 129.5** (208.4 km) **Junction** with Highway 27 west to **OLDS** (pop. 4,888); all visitor facilities, museum and information booth.

CB 268.8 (432.5 km) **E 113.4** (182.5 km) **Junction** with highway west to Bowden and Red Lodge Provincial Park (8.5 miles/14 km); 110 campsites, playground, swimming and fishing. **BOWDEN** (pop. 1,000) is the site of a large oil refinery and Alberta Nurseries & Seeds Ltd., a major employer. Most visitor services available.

Heritage rest area with 24 campsites, dump station and tourist information booth at highway junction. ▲

CB 276 (444 km) **E 106.2** (171 km) **Junction** with Highway 54 west to **INNISFAIL** (pop. 5,500); all visitor facilities. South of Innisfail 3 miles/5 km is the RCMP Dog Training Centre, the only one in Canada; open to the public daily year-round from 9 A.M. to 4 P.M.

CB 278.8 (448.7 km) **E 103.4** (166.4 km) Stop of interest sign about explorer Anthony Henday.

CB 285.6 (459.6 km) **E 96.6** (155.4 km) **Junction** with Highway 42 west to Penhold, a service community for the nearby air force base.

CB 290 (466.8 km) **E 92.2** (148.3 km) Tourist service area with gas stations and restaurants.

CB 290.5 (467.5 km) **E 91.7** (147.6 km) Tourist information booth.

CB 291.4 (468.9 km) **E 90.8** (146.1 km) **Junction** with Highway 2A east to **RED DEER** (pop. 60,000), in the centre of cattle ranching and grain growing, with a burgeoning oil and gas industry and nearby ethylene plants. All visitor facilities available. Camping at Lions Municipal Campground on Riverside Drive; 62 sites, dump station, laundry, picnic area, playground. ▲

CB 298 (479.6 km) **E 84.2** (135.5 km) **Junction** with Highway 11 to Sylvan Lake (10 miles/16 km) and Rocky Mountain House (51 miles/82 km). Sylvan Lake Provincial Park has picnicking and swimming. Private campgrounds and waterslide nearby.

CB 302.5 (486.8 km) **E 80.2** (129.1 km) Access road east to community of **BLACKFALDS** (pop. 1,500). Tourist services and accommodations.

CB 309.1 (497.4 km) **E 73.1** (117.6 km) **Junction** with Highway 12. Exit east for

LACOMBE (pop. 6,000); all visitor facilities. Camping at Michener Park; 21 sites. Site of the Federal Agricultural Research Station; open to the public weekdays, 8 A.M. to 4:30 P.M.

Exit west on Highway 12 for Aspen Beach Provincial Park at Gull Lake (6 miles/10 km); camping, swimming. ▲

CB 325 (524.7 km) **E 56.2** (90.4 km) **Junction** with Highway 53 east to **PONOKA** (pop. 5,000); all visitor facilities. Camping at Ponoka Stampede Trailer Park, May to October. Ponoka's Stampede is held June 29–July 3 at Stampede Park. ▲

CB 340.7 (548.3 km) **E 41.5** (66.8 km) Northbound-only access to Wetaskiwin rest area with picnic tables and information centre (open May to September); restrooms, gas service and groceries.

CB 345.3 (555.7 km) **E 36.9** (59.4 km) **Junction** of Highway 13 east to Wetaskiwin.

CB 356 (572.9 km) **E 26.2** (42.2 km) Turnout to east with litter barrels and pay phone.

CB 366 (589 km) **E 16.2** (26.1 km) Exit for Edmonton bypass route (see NOTE) and access to **LEDUC** (pop. 12,500), founded and named for the Leduc oil well, which blew in on Feb. 13, 1947; all visitor facilities.

NOTE: Northbound motorists wishing to avoid heavy traffic through Edmonton may exit west on Highway 39 for Devon Bypass. Drive 6.8 miles/11 km west on Highway 39, then 20 miles/32 km north on Highway 60 to junction with Yellowhead Highway 16, 10 miles/16 km west of Edmonton (see ***Milepost E 10*** *this section).*

CB 372 (598.6 km) **E 10.2** (16.4 km) **Junction** with Highway 19 west to community of Devon, Devon Bypass and University of Alberta Devonian Botanic Garden, open daily May through September, 10 A.M. to 6 P.M. From Devon continue north on Highway 60 to bypass Edmonton and rejoin this route at **Milepost E 10** on Yellowhead Highway 16 West.

CB 382.2 (615 km) **E 0** Whitemud Drive. Turn east for Highway 16 East, turn west for Highway 16 West (see YELLOWHEAD HIGHWAY 16 section). Continue north for Edmonton city centre (description follows).

Whitemud Drive west continues as Highway 2, crossing the Saskatchewan River, then turns north to become 170 Street. Access to West Edmonton Mall on 170 Street.

Edmonton

E 0 DC 367 (590.6 km) Capital of Alberta, 1,853 miles/2982 km from Fairbanks, AK. **Population:** 618,195; area 831,000. **Elevation:** 2,182 feet/668m. **Emergency Services:** Phone 911 for all emergency services. **Six hospitals:** Charles Camsell, 12804 114th Ave.; General, 11111 Jasper Ave.; Grey Nun's, 34th Avenue and 66th Street; Misericordia, 16940 87th Ave.; Royal Alexandra, 10240 Kingsway Ave.; University, 84th Avenue and 112th Street.

Visitor Information: Edmonton Tourism operates four visitor information centres within the city — Downtown, Highway 2 south, Highway 16 East and Highway 16 West. Hours vary. Write, Edmonton Tourism, Dept. MI 94, 9797 Jasper Ave. N. 104, Edmonton, AB T5J 1N9; phone (403) 496-8400 or toll free (800) 463-4667 for information.

The North Saskatchewan River winds through the centre of Edmonton, its banks lined with public parks. Major attractions include the Edmonton Space & Science Centre, Fort Edmonton Park, Muttart Conservatory, Alberta Legislative Building and the Provincial Museum of Alberta. A shopping centre is also on the list of major attractions for visitors: West Edmonton Mall, dubbed "the world's largest mall," features some 800 stores and services. The mall also has a waterpark, ice arena, aquariums, aviaries and some 110 eating establishments. Located on 170 Street, the shopping mall is open seven days a week.

Known as Canada's festival city, Edmonton hosts a number of events throughout the year. These include: Children's Festival (May 24–28, 1994); Teen Festival of the Arts (May 3–7, 1994); Jazz City International Festival (June 24–July 3, 1994); Street Performers Festival (July 8–17, 1994); Klondike Days (July 21–30, 1994); Heritage Festival (July 31–Aug. 1, 1994); Edmonton Folk Music Festival (Aug. 5–7, 1994); and Fringe Theatre (Aug. 12–21, 1994).

There are 80 hotels and motels in Edmonton and some 2,000 restaurants.

Within the Edmonton vicinity there are several campgrounds. Rainbow Valley public campground has 85 sites, electrical hookups, dump station, laundry facilities and showers; from Highway 2 drive west 2 miles/3.2 km on Whitemud Drive. Klondike Valley Tent & Trailer Park public campground has 160 sites, full hookups, showers, laundry facilities and store. Turn west on Ellerslie Road, take Service Road South; parallel to Highway 2 South. Just west of the city limits off Highway 16 West at the Devon Overpass there is a private campground with 273 sites and all facilities. ▲

East Access Route Log

(continued)

HIGHWAY 16 WEST

This section of the log shows distance from Edmonton (E) followed by distance from Dawson Creek (DC).

Rochfort Bridge is the second longest wooden railway trestle in the world. (Earl L. Brown, staff)

E 0 **DC 367** (590.6 km) Downtown Edmonton. Take Jasper Avenue westbound (becomes 16A then Yellowhead 16 at city limits).

E 6.2 (10 km) **DC 360.8** (580.6 km) Exit 215 Avenue/Winterburn Road.

Shakers Acres Campground. See display ad this section. ▲

E 10 (16 km) **DC 357** (574.5 km) **Junction** of Highways 16 West and 60 (Devon Overpass); access to private campground. ▲

NOTE: Southbound travelers may bypass Edmonton by taking Highway 60 south, then either Highway 19 or 39 east to Highway 2.

Glowing Embers Travel Centre. See display ad this section. ▲

E 18 (29 km) **DC 349** (561.6 km) **SPRUCE GROVE** (pop. 11,343). All visitor facilities including motels, restaurants, grocery stores and gas stations.

E 22 (35.4 km) **DC 345** (555.2 km) **STONY PLAIN** (pop. 4,442). All visitor facilities including hotels, restaurants, supermarket, shopping mall and gas stations with major repair service; RCMP and hospital; swimming pool and golf course. The Multicultural Heritage Centre here has a living museum, art gallery and archives, and serves pioneer food. Open daily 10 A.M. to 4 P.M. Information available at the Old Caboose by the railroad. Lions Campground with 26 sites located nearby. ▲

E 25 (40.2 km) **DC 342** (550.4 km) Turnoff north for Allan Beach recreation area. Resort with RV sites, picnic area, playground and boat rentals. ▲

E 25.6 (41.2 km) **DC 341.4** (549.4 km) Edmonton Beach turnoff to south.

E 26.1 (42 km) **DC 340.9** (548.6 km) Hubbles Lake turnoff to north.

E 27.2 (43.8 km) **DC 339.8** (546.8 km) Restaurant, gas station and store to north.

E 28.4 (45.7 km) **DC 338.6** (544.9 km) Lake Eden Recreation Area to north.

E 31 (49.9 km) **DC 336** (540.7 km) **Junction** of Yellowhead Highway 16 and Highway 43. Turn north onto Highway 43. (If you are continuing west on Yellowhead Highway 16 for Prince George or Prince Rupert, BC, turn to the YELLOWHEAD HIGHWAY section.)

HIGHWAY 43

E 36.9 (59.4 km) **DC 330** (531.2 km) **Junction** of Highways 43 and 33 (Grizzly Trail). The Grizzly Trail junctions with Highway 2; see NORTHERN WOODS & WATERS ROUTE section for logs. Continue on Highway 43.

E 37.3 (60 km) **DC 329.7** (530.6 km) Turnout to east with litter barrel and historical information sign about construction of the Alaska Highway.

E 38.7 (62.3 km) **DC 328.3** (528.3 km) Gas station to east.

E 39.2 (63.1 km) **DC 327.8** (527.5 km) Highway 633 west to Alberta Beach Recreation Area on Lac Ste. Anne.

E 41.6 (66.9 km) **DC 325.4** (523.7 km) **ONOWAY** (pop. 671). Gas, laundromat, restaurants, motel, car wash, post office, pharmacy, RV park with hookups, and other facilities. Information booth and Elks campground with eight sites. ▲

E 45.4 (73.2 km) **DC 321.5** (517.4 km) Alberta government campground with dump station, water, toilets and stoves. ▲

E 45.9 (73.9 km) **DC 321.1** (516.7 km) Restaurant and gas station.

E 48 (77.2 km) **DC 318.9** (513.2 km) **Lessard Lake** county campground; water, stoves, boat launch, fishing for pike and perch. Golf course to west. ▲

E 63.7 (102.5 km) **DC 303.3** (488.1 km) Gas station.

E 72 (115.8 km) **DC 295** (474.8 km) **SANGUDO** (pop. 401) is on a 0.3-mile/0.4-km side road. Restaurant, motel and gas station with garage open seven days a week; grocery store, banks, post office, laundromat and car wash. Public campground at sportsground. ▲

E 74.4 (119.7 km) **DC 292.6** (470.9 km) Pembina River bridge.

E 75.4 (121.3 km) **DC 291.6** (469.3 km) Gas station and restaurant to south.

E 79.5 (128 km) **DC 287.5** (462.7 km) Second longest wooden railway trestle in the world crosses highway and Paddle River. The C.N.R. Rochfort Bridge trestle is 2,414 feet/736m long and was originally built in 1914.

E 80.6 (129.7 km) **DC 286.4** (460.9 km) **ROCHFORT BRIDGE.** Trading post with gas, convenience store, gift shop, restaurant and Lac St. Anne Pioneer Museum. Camping. ▲

Rochfort Bridge Trading Post. See display ad this section.

E 83.1 (133.7 km) **DC 283.9** (456.1 km) Paved turnouts with litter barrels both sides of highway.

E 85 (136.8 km) **DC 282** (453.8 km) **MAYERTHORPE** (pop. 1,615). One mile/1.6 km from the highway on a paved access road. Hotel, motel, restaurant, grocery store, gas stations with repair service, car wash, hospital, laundromat, post office, RCMP and banks. A public campground with 30 sites (no hookups, pit toilets) and nine-hole golf course are located 1 mile/1.6 km south of town. Airstrip located 2 miles/3.2 km southwest of town. ▲

E 87 (140 km) **DC 280** (450.6 km) Gas station and restaurant at junction with Highway 658 north to Goose Lake.

HIGHWAY 43
'THE FLAG ROUTE TO ALASKA'

43 ALBERTA TO ALASKA

VALLEYVIEW

Your introduction to the beautiful Peace River Country, Valleyview welcomes visitors by providing a full compliment of tourist and hospitality services. The friendly, knowledgeable staff at the Tourist Information Centre will be happy to provide you with specific information about the region . . . *plan your next vacation to take you through the "Portal to the Peace", with Valleyview being your first stop.*

Most travellers on their way to Alaska will be choosing Highway 43 as the most direct route to Mile "0" of the Alaska Highway.

FOX CREEK

Fox Creek is a warm, friendly community situated in the heart of Alberta's green belt. A place where industry exists in harmony with nature. The nearby lakes and trails offer sports and fishing enthusiasts recreation in both winter and summer. Hunters, bird watchers, hikers, photographers, cross-country skiers and snowmobilers will be in paradise. *You'll love it here - it's only natural.*

Enjoy the natural beauty of the countryside -the many lakes and streams; the stately forests; radiant yellow fields of canola; lush meadows abounding with wild flowers and berries, fringed with an almost limitless variety of shrubs and other vegetation - truly a naturalist's delight! the woods and grasslands are still a natural haven for deer, moose and bear. Meet the friendly people. Take part in the many community events being hosted enroute. Enjoy the many tourist and hospitality services along Highway 43 including Tourist Information Centres with knowledgeable staff to help you with sightseeing and travel information.

WHITECOURT

Explore the many attractions and the bustling community known as the "forestry centre and snowmobile capital of Alberta". Take a guided tour through the area's four major forest industries to view world-class technology in action. Whether your taste leans towards boating, fishing, camping or cultural events, *Whitecourt is a town for all seasons.*

MAYERTHORPE

Take a relaxing break in the friendly farming community of Mayerthorpe. Visit numerous specialty farms raising buffaloes, wild boar, ostriches, and llamas for unique products. Take in the local rodeo, May Mudfest, and Agricultural Fair in August. Golf a round on our 9-hole course, check out our murals, or shop 7 days a week. Hunting, boating, camping, and fishing are available almost year-round. Tourist Information Center open May through August. Be our guest in Mayerthorpe - where Highways 22 and 43 meet.

IMPROVEMENT DISTRICT NO. 15

I.D. No. 15 is located north of the Athabasca River, west of Whitecourt and north of Vega Ferry. Travel on the historic Klondike Trail through some of the most scenic sand hills in Alberta. Camp and fish in peaceful, attractive surroundings. *Come and share in the abundant natural and recreational resources, and in the beauty of the area.*

SANGUDO

Be sure to turn off Highway No. 43 into Sangudo and take advantage of the services we have to offer which include refreshments and gas stations. Our beautiful campground is located beside the sportsground along the Pembina River. *Stop for a refreshing pause at our friendly little village.*

COUNTY OF LAC STE. ANNE

The County of Lac St. Anne is located northwest of Edmonton. Highway No. 43 dissects the County providing access to Northwest Alberta, the Territories and Alaska. A wide range of recreation facilities including; *ten recreation lakes and rivers, six golf courses, the Paddle river Dam and George Pegg Botanic gardens provides entertainment for both residents and visitors.*

ONOWAY

Onoway, the "Hub of the Highways", is situated at the junction of Highways 37 and 43 (Alaska Highway), close to the Yellowhead Highway (16). With many modern facilities to serve you, Onoway also has a quiet campground equipped with cooking facilities, water well and sanitary dump. There are numerous lakes surrounding Onoway for those interested in fishing and water sports. *Make Onoway your first stop along the Alaska Highway.*

ALBERTA BEACH

Welcome to Alberta Beach, Alberta's largest summer village. Fully equipped campground and clean sandy beaches promise fun in the sun. Our beautiful lake allows exhilarating windsurfing, sailboating, canoeing, fishing and swimming. Farmers market, boat rental, mini-golf and overnight accomodations with dining at its best. *Information on the many facilities is available at the tourist booth for your daily or weekly visits.*

Canada

Alberta, in all her majesty.

FOR MORE INFORMATION CONTACT:

Highway 43 Promotion Committee
c/o Box 515, Whitecourt, Alberta, Canada
T7S 1N6
(403) 778-5362

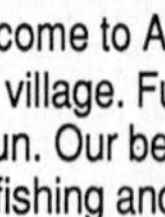

E 109 (175.4 km) **DC 258** (415.2 km) Lions Club Campground; 74 sites, flush toilets, showers, water, tables and firepits. Fee charged. ▲

Whitecourt

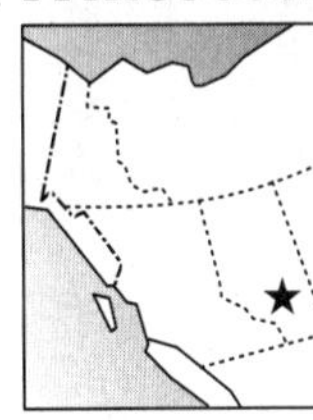

E 111.8 (179.9 km) **DC 255.2** (410.7 km). Located two hours from Edmonton. **Population:** 7,000. **Emergency Services: Police**, phone 778-5454. **Fire Department**, phone 778-2311. **Hospital** located on Hilltop, phone 778-2285. Ambulance service.

Visitor Information: Tourist information booth on Highway 43 west at the traffic lights. The helpful staff will assist with travel plans and directions to Whitecourt sights and activities. The booth is fully stocked with pamphlets and brochures. Open daily, 8 A.M. to 7 P.M., May 1 to Sept. 1; weekdays only, 9 A.M. to 5 P.M., September through April. Free dump station and freshwater fill-up adjacent tourist booth.

Information is also available from the Chamber of Commerce, P.O. Box 1011, Whitecourt, AB T7S 1N9; phone (403) 778-5363.

Elevation: 2,567 feet/782m. **Radio:** 1400 CJYR-AM, 107.5 SKUA-FM. **Television:** 10 channels. **Newspaper:** *Whitecourt Star* (weekly).

Transportation: Air–Whitecourt Airport, 4 miles/6.4 km south on Highway 32, has a 5,800-foot/1,768-m paved runway; all-weather facility, 24-hour flight service station. Avgas and jet fuel, aircraft maintenance available. Local charter air service available; helicopter and fixed-wing aircraft. **Bus**–Greyhound service to Edmonton, Grande Prairie, Peace River and points north.

Located at the junction of Highways 43 and 32, Whitecourt dubs itself the "Gateway to the Alaska Highway and the fabulous North." Established as a small trading, trapping and forestry centre, Whitecourt became an important stop for Alaska Highway travelers when a 106-mile section of Highway 43 connecting Whitecourt and Valleyview was completed in October 1955. This new route was 72 miles shorter than the old Edmonton to Dawson Creek route via Slave Lake.

Several major forest industries operating in and around Whitecourt offer visitors an opportunity to observe state-of-the-art technologies at sawmills, medium density fiberboard production and pulp and paper manufacturing plants. The Eric S. Huestis Demonstration Forest, northwest of town on Highway 32, has 4.3 miles/7 km of self-guided trails with interpretive sites and information signs describing forest management techniques and the forest life-cycle; phone 778-7165.

The Whitecourt Chamber of Commerce has a program of guided industrial tours that are available for visitors. Tours vary from one-and-one-half to two hours in length and reservations are advised; phone 778-5362.

Recreational activities include an excellent 18-hole public golf course and fishing in area creeks, rivers and lakes (boat rentals at Carson Pegasus Provincial Park). Swimming, rollerskating, mini-golf, tennis and

Forestry is a major industry in Whitecourt. (Earl L. Brown, staff)

Explore

WHITECOURT

"Where Even The Rivers Meet"

Renford Inn

DOUBLE ROOM RATE

SAVE $15.00
REG. $50.00

NOW ONLY $35.00
WITH COUPON

MAX. 4 PERSON OCCUPANCY PER ROOM
HIGHWAY 43 SOUTH WEST

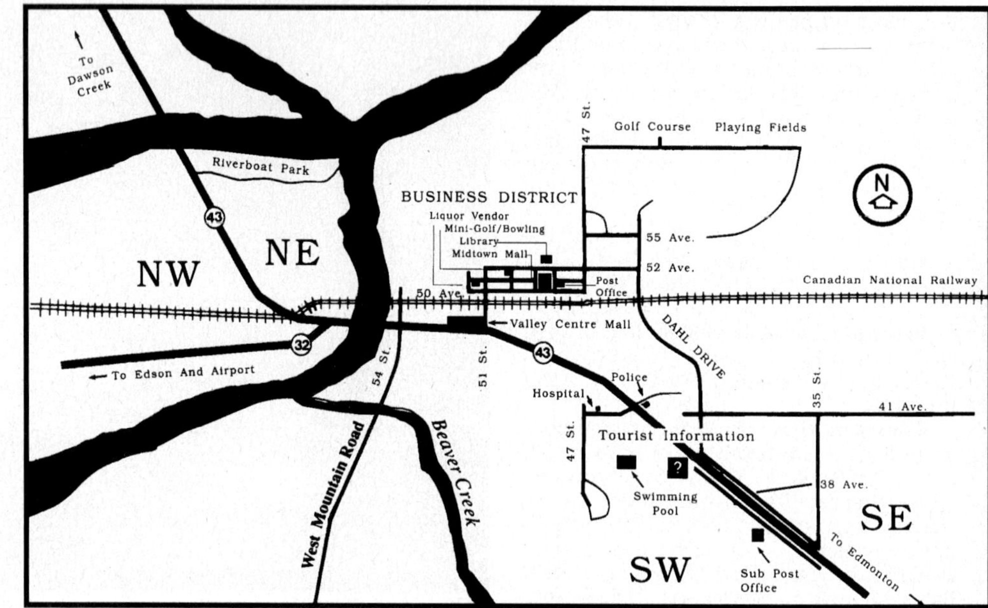

So Much To See & Do . . .

Stop in at our Tourist Information Centre at the corner of Highway 43 & Dahl Drive for info on:

* Nature & Industrial Tours
* Rodeo & River Boat Races
* Sporting & Cultural Events
* Golfing, Swimming, Riding
* Camping, Boating, Fishing
* And Much, Much More . . .

Over 100 merchants with Service, Selection & Smiles
Over 600 Motel Rooms and 275 Shaded Campsites
Make Whitecourt an ideal place for all your needs!

Show your copy of The Milepost to these participating merchants to redeem coupons!

Alberta, in all her majesty. Canada

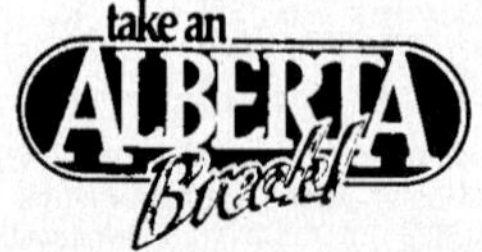

WHITECOURT RESTAURANT GUIDE

Restaurant	OPERATING HOURS	SEATING	CREDIT CARDS: VISA	MASTER CARD	AM. XPRESS	OTHERS	SERVICES: FAST FOOD	TAKE OUT	DRIVE THRU	RESTAURANT	LICENSED	LOUNGE	TAVERN	ENTERTAIN'T	BANQUETS	MEETING RMS	TOUR BUS (Phone Ahead)	DELIVERY	ON LOCATION: HOTEL	MOTEL	SERVICE STN.	RETAIL BUS.
A&W RESTAURANT Hwy 43 sw (403) 778-6611	6 - 10 pm	96						●		●												
GREEN GABLES RESTAURANT Hwy 43 SW (403) 778-3142	6 - 11 pm	110		●				●		●		●								●		
JR'S BURGERS & DELI Hwy 43 SE (403) 778-5450	6 - 10 pm	66		●				●		●												
KENTUCKY FRIED CHICKEN Hwy 43 SE (403) 778-4700	11 - 10 pm	76		●				●		●												
MCDONALD'S RESTAURANT (403) 778-6969 Hwy 43 & Dahl Dr. SE Fax: 779-3088	7-11 p.m.	80						●		●												
MOUNTAIN PIZZA & STEAK HOUSE Hwy 43 SW Info Centre (403) 778-3600	11-12:00 pm	146		●				●		●		●										
RIVERS MOTOR HOTEL RESTAURANT (403) 778-3957 Hwy 43 on McLeod River Fax: 778-6933	6 - Midnite	198		●				●		●		●		●		●						

CAR, TRUCK, TRAILER & R.V. SERVICES

Business	OPEN	CREDIT CARDS: VISA	MASTER CARD	AMERICAN EXP.	OTHERS	FUEL SERVICE: FULL SERVICE	SELF SERVICE	GASOLINE	DIESEL	PROPANE	SPECIAL SERVICES: FRANCHISE CAR	MECHANIC	CAR WASH	TIRE SERVICE	EXHAUST REPAIR	ALIGNMENT	TOWING	WELDING	AUTO PARTS	SANI-DUMP	ON LOCATION: CON. STORE	LOTTERY VENDOR	BANK MACHINE	WHEEL CHAIR	FAST FOOD	BAKERY	RESTAURANT
FAS GAS AM-PM MINI MARKET Hwy 43 SE (403) 778-5541	24 Hours		●		●				●												●		●		●		
HILLTOP TAGS FOOD, GAS & POST OFFICE Hwy 43 SW (403) 778-6088	24 Hours		●		●		●														●		●		●		●
TIMBER TIRE (Kal Tire Assoc.) Hwy 43 SE (403) 778-3863	7-6 p.m.		●		●										●				●								
TIRECRAFT Hwy 43 SW Fax: (403) 778-5224 Tel: (403) 778-4871	7-6 p.m.		●		●										●				●								
MOHAWK WHITECOURT SERVICE 3540 Highway Street (403) 778-3377	7-11 p.m.		●						●				●								●				●		
WHITECOURT SHELL SERVICES Hwy 43 SE (403) 778-2665	7-11 p.m.		●		●				●										●		●						

WHITECOURT ACCOMMODATION GUIDE

Accommodation	NUMBER OF ROOMS	RATES: UNDER $30	$30 - $60	OVER $60	CREDIT CARDS: VISA	MASTER CARD	AMERICAN EXP.	OTHERS	FACILITIES AND SERVICES ON LOCATION: CABLE T.V.	SATELLITE T.V.	HOME MOVIES	KITCHEN	LAUNDROMAT	AIR COND'N	BEER STORE	MEETING ROOMS	WHEEL CHAIR	PETS O.K.	FREE PARKING	NUMBER OF STALLS	RESTAURANT	POWER	SHOWERS	SHELTERS	TABLES	FIREWOOD	BOAT RENTAL	STORE
EAGLE RIVER OUTFITTING 10 KM South Hwy. 32 (403) 778-3251	5		●		●						●								●						●		●	
CARSON-PEGASUS PROV. PARK 12 mi. NW on lake (403) 778-2664					●								●				●		●				●		●		●	
GLENVIEW MOTEL Hwy 43 SW (403) 778-4114 778-2276	31		●		●		●		●		●								●									
GREEN GABLES INN Hwy 43 SW (403) 778-4537 Fax: 778-2510	49		●		●		●		●								●		●		●							
LIONS CLUB CAMPGROUND 1 mi. E. Hwy 43 SW (403) 778-6782					●								●						●				●		●			
RIVERS MOTOR HOTEL (403) 778-3951 Hwy 43 NE (On McLeod River) Fax: 778-6933	70		●		●		●		●						●		●		●		●							
SAGITAWAH TOURIST PARK Hwy 43 NE on Athabasca River (403) 778-3734					●								●				●		●				●		●			
ALASKA HIGHWAY MOTEL & RV PARK Highway 43 SW (403) 778-4156 FAX: 778-5921	36		●		●		●		●								●		●				●		●			
SMITTY'S INN Hwy 43 NW (403) 778-5055	28		●		●		●										●		●		●							
WHITECOURT MOTOR INN (403) 778-2216 Bus. Dist. 5003-50 St. Fax: 778-4733	74		●		●		●		●						●				●		●							

gold panning are also enjoyed in summer. Other attractions available: an exotic animal farm; a guest ranch with arts and crafts; horseback riding; and river boating. In the fall, big game hunting is very popular. During the winter there is ice fishing, snowmobiling and cross-country skiing on area trails, downhill skiing at a local facility, skating and curling, bowling, and swimming at the indoor pool.

There are 14 hotels/motels, 20 restaurants, 14 gas stations, several laundromats, two malls, a liquor vendor and five banks. Most services are located on the highway or two blocks north in the downtown business district. Some gas stations and restaurants are open 24 hours. House Mountain Gallery and Artists' Center, at the corner of Whitecourt Avenue and Sunset Boulevard, features exhibits by local artists.

This full-service community also supports a library and seven churches. The Legion, located in the business district, is open year-round. Service clubs (Lions, Kinsmen) and community organizations (Masons, Knights of Columbus) meet on a regular basis and welcome visitors.

A popular wilderness area nearby is Carson–Pegasus Provincial Park, located 14.6 miles/23.5 km west and north of town on Highway 32 (paved). The park has 182 campsites, electrical hookups, dump station, boat launch, boat rentals, concession, convenience store, hot showers and laundry facilities; open year-round. There are two lakes at the park: **McLeod (Carson) Lake**, stocked with rainbow trout, has a speed limit of 12 kmph for boaters; **Little McLeod (Pegasus) Lake** has northern pike and whitefish, electric motors and canoes only. Eagle River Outfitting, located 7 miles/11.3 km south of town via Highway 32, offers camping and wilderness activities.

Sagitawah Tourist Park. Welcome Campers! We're easy to find as we are located on the north end of Whitecourt, by the Athabasca bridge. You'll be able to park easily in our large pull-through lots. Sit back, relax on our grassed areas. Roast hot dogs and marshmallows by the fire, and later on go for a walk by the river or play a game of horseshoes. We have full hookups, hot showers and laundry as well. The coffee is always on and we welcome back our guests from last year, as well as new travelers to the area. (403) 778-3734. [ADVERTISEMENT]

East Access Route Log

(continued)

E 111.9 (808 km) **DC 255.1** (410.5 km) Beaver Creek bridge.

CAUTION: The highway between Whitecourt and Fox Creek is known locally as "Moose Alley." Several moose-vehicle accidents occur yearly. Northbound travelers, watch for moose on road, especially at dusk and at night.

E 112.4 (180.9 km) **DC 254.6** (409.7 km) McLeod River.

E 112.6 (181.2 km) **DC 254.4** (409.4 km) Railroad crossing.

E 112.7 (181.4 km) **DC 254.3** (409.2 km) **Junction** with Highway 32 South (paved). Access to Eagle River Outfitting, 7 miles/11.3 km south; camping, wilderness activities. Highway 32 leads 42 miles/68 km to Yellowhead Highway 16 (see **Milepost E 99** in the YELLOWHEAD HIGHWAY section).

E 112.9 (181.7 km) **DC 254.1** (408.9 km) Gas stations both sides of highway.

E 113.4 (182.5 km) **DC 253.6** (408.1 km) Turnoff to north for Sagitawah Tourist Park (RV camping) and Riverboat Park, both at the confluence of the McLeod and Athabasca rivers. Riverboat Park has a boat launch, picnic area and toilets.

E 113.6 (182.8 km) **DC 253.4** (407.8 km) Athabasca River bridge.

E 115.6 (186 km) **DC 251.4** (404.6 km) Vehicle inspection station to north.

E 117.1 (188.4 km) **DC 249.9** (402.2 km) **Junction** with Highway 32 North (paved). Access to Eric S. Huestis Demonstration Forest (self-guided trails) and Carson–Pegasus Provincial Park. The provincial park, 9.3 miles/15 km north, is open year-round; 182 campsites, electrical hookups, group camping area, tables, flush toilets, showers, water, dump station, firewood, store, laundromat, playground, boat launch, boat rentals and rainbow trout fishing.

Carson–Pegasus Provincial Park. See display ad this section.

E 117.6 (189.2 km) **DC 249.4** (401.4 km) Alberta Newsprint Co. to south.

E 122 (196.3 km) **DC 245** (394.3 km) Turnout with litter barrel.

E 122.5 (197.1 km) **DC 244.5** (393.5 km) Chickadee Creek government campground; seven sites, pit toilets, water, tables and firepits.

E 124.3 (200 km) **DC 242.7** (390.6 km) Chickadee Creek.

E 131.8 (212.1 km) **DC 235.2** (378.5 km) Turnouts with litter barrels both sides of highway.

E 140.5 (226.1 km) **DC 226.5** (364.5 km) Two Creeks government campground; eight campsites, pit toilets, water, picnic tables and firepits.

E 142.5 (229.3 km) **DC 224.5** (361.3 km) Turnout with litter barrel to south.

E 143 (230.1 km) **DC 224** (360.5 km) Turnout with litter barrel to north.

E 152 (244.6 km) **DC 215** (346 km) Iosegun Creek government campground; 12 sites, pit toilets, water, tables and firepits.

E 159 (255.9 km) **DC 208** (334.7 km) Fox Creek airport.

CAUTION: The highway between Fox Creek and Whitecourt is known locally as "Moose Alley." Several moose-vehicle accidents occur yearly. Southbound travelers, watch for moose on road, especially at dusk and at night.

Fox Creek

E 162 (260.7 km) **DC 205** (329.9 km) **Population:** 2,259. **Emergency Services: RCMP**, phone 622-3740. **Hospital**, phone 622-3545. **Visitor Information:** Tourist Information Centre open in summer; phone (403) 622-3624.

Elevation: 2,800 feet/853m. **Transportation:** Air–Fox Creek airport, 3 miles/4.8 km south on Highway 43; runway length, 2,950 feet/899m; elev. 2,692 feet/821m.

All visitor facilities including a hotel, three motels, gas stations with repair service, a grocery and deli, pharmacy, banks and bank machines, hospital and medical clinic, and a nine-hole golf course with artificial greens. Municipal campground with 17 sites, full hookups. Dump station located at north end of town. Shops open Friday evening, closed Sunday.

Centre of oil and gas exploration and production, North America's largest known natural gas field is here. There are three major gas plants in the area (Amoco, Chevron, Petro–Canada) and a full range of related industrial services.

The Rig Earth Resource Park, with a 151-foot-tall triple drilling rig demonstration and interpretive centre, is scheduled to be completed in 1994.

Fox Creek is in the heart of big game country, and hunting guides are available. Two local lakes popular with residents and visitors are Iosegun and Smoke. Camping, boat launch and fishing at **Iosegun Lake**, 6.8 miles/11 km north on good gravel road; walleye, northern pike and perch. Camping, boat launch and fishing at **Smoke Lake**, 8 miles/13 km southwest; northern pike, perch and pickerel.

East Access Route Log

(continued)

E 167 (268.7 km) **DC 200** (321.9 km) Turnout with litter barrel.

E 169.5 (272.8 km) **DC 197.5** (317.8 km) Turnouts with litter barrels both sides of highway.

E 172 (276.8 km) **DC 195** (313.8 km) Pines government campground; 25 sites, shelter, firewood, pump water, tables and pit toilets.

E 182.1 (293 km) **DC 184.9** (297.6 km) Turnout with litter barrel.

E 186.4 (300 km) **DC 180.6** (290.6 km) **Sands Wilderness R.V. Park.** 24-hour security campground. Power and unserviced sites, tenting area. Water fill-up and dump station. Laundromat, showers. Concession; hot and cold snacks. Horseshoe pits and mini golf. Outdoor adventures — trail rides and raft trips. Your hosts — "Wild Bill" and Agnes Sands, Box 511, Valleyview, AB T0H 3N0. (403) 524-2207, Fax (403) 524-3288. [ADVERTISEMENT]

E 192 (309 km) **DC 175** (281.6 km) **LITTLE SMOKY** (pop. about 50). Motel, RV park, pay phone, propane, grocery store, service station and post office.

Little Smoky Motel & Campground. See display ad this section.

E 192.2 (309.3 km) **DC 174.8** (281.3 km) Little Smoky River bridge.

E 193.5 (311.4 km) **DC 173.5** (279.2 km) Waskahigan (House) River bridge at confluence with Smoky River. Government campground with pit toilets, water, tables and firepits.

E 197 (317 km) **DC 170** (273.6 km) Turnout.

E 204.7 (329.4 km) **DC 162.3** (261.2 km) Gas station, restaurant and grocery; pay phone.

E 206.7 (332.6 km) **DC 160.3** (258 km) Turnout with litter barrel.

E 208.5 (335.5 km) **DC 158.5** (255.1 km) Peace pipeline storage tanks.

E 210.8 (339.2 km) **DC 156.2** (251.4 km) Valleyview Riverside golf course.

E 213.2 (343.1 km) **DC 153.8** (247.5 km) Valleyview tourist information centre; pay phone, picnic tables, flush toilets. Open daily in summer, 8 A.M. to 8 P.M.

E 213.4 (343.4 km) **DC 153.6** (247.2 km) Valleyview airport to west.

Valleyview

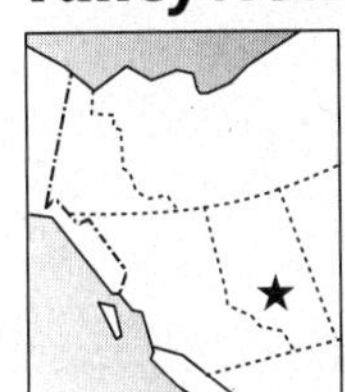

E 214.1 (344.4 km) **DC 152.9** (246.1 km) **Population:** 2,218. **Emergency Services: RCMP,** phone 524-3343. **Fire Department,** 524-3211. **Ambulance,** phone 524-3916. **Hospital,** Valleyview General, 35 beds, phone 524-3356. **Visitor Information:** Major tourist information centre and rest stop located 0.9 mile/1.5 km south of Valleyview on Highway 43. Open 8 A.M. to 8 P.M. May 1 through Labour Day; helpful staff and well stocked with travel information. Phone (403) 524-4129.

Elevation: 2,400 feet/732m. **Newspaper:** *Valley Views* (weekly).

Transportation: Air–Airport 0.7 mile/1.1 km south; length 3,000 feet/914m; paved. **Bus**–Greyhound.

Valleyview, the "Portal to the Peace," is at the junction of Highways 43 and 34. Highway 34 leads west to Grande Prairie and Dawson Creek. Highway 43 continues north to Peace River. From Peace River, travelers have the option of continuing on the Mackenzie Highway to Northwest Territories, or heading west via Highway 64 to Fort St. John. (See the MACKENZIE ROUTE and NORTHERN WOODS & WATERS ROUTE sections for details.)

Highway 43 also connects with Highway 2 east to Athabasca, the Slave Lake route from Edmonton used by Alaska Highway

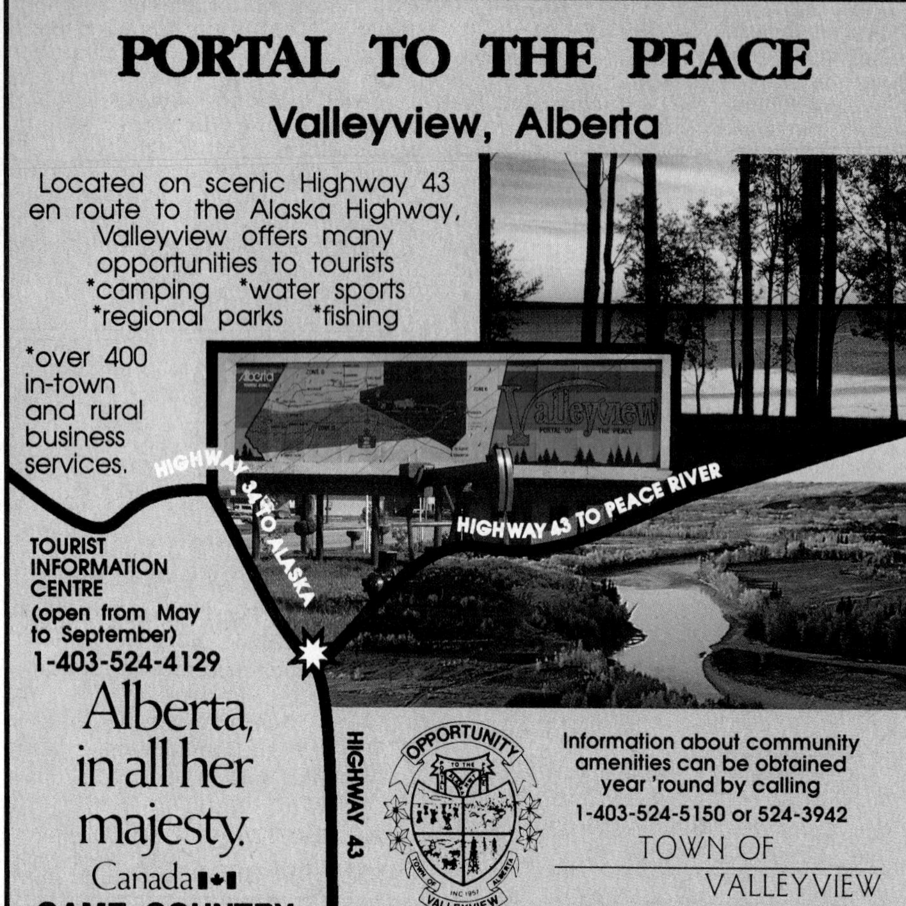

travelers until 1955, when Highway 43 was completed to Whitecourt.

Originally called Red Willow Creek when it was homesteaded in 1916, Valleyview boomed with the discovery of oil and gas in the 1950s, and services grew along with the population. Today, Valleyview's economy is based on both oil and gas and agriculture. Farming consists of grain, oilseed, beef cattle and forage production.

The community has a full range of services, including a library, banks, swimming pool, schools and several churches. The area boasts abundant wildlife.

All visitor facilities including five motels and hotels, restaurants, gas stations (many with major repair service), laundromat, grocery stores, liquor store and a golf course. Some gas stations and restaurants open 24 hours a day.

Horizon Motel & Restaurant. At the Horizon, we have built our business on loyalty and customer satisfaction. An Alberta Best property, clean, well-appointed rooms, several nonsmoking and deluxe family suites available, reasonable rates. Our Westside Cafe, "where to turn when you simply must have a good meal...", tastefully decorated,

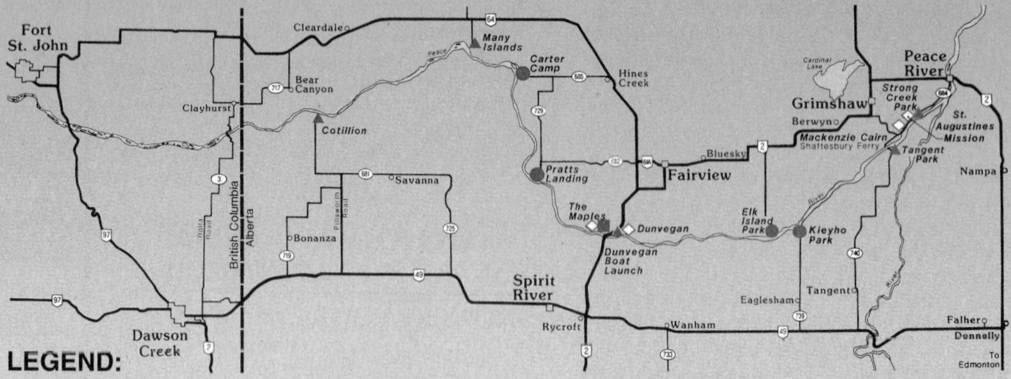

VALLEYVIEW ADVERTISERS

Horizon Motel & Restaurant................Ph. (403) 524-3904
Lion's Den Trailer Park and Campground, The.....W. edge of town
Sherk's R.V. Park..............Ph. (403) 524-4949
Town of Valleyview..........Ph. (403) 524-5150
Valleyview Esso Service....Ph. (403) 524-3504

featuring Western and Chinese menu. Open daily 6 A.M. to 10 P.M. Tour buses welcome. Quality souvenirs and gifts. Bank rate of exchange paid on U.S. funds. We take pride in our service; stop in and experience for yourself! (403) 524-3904. Fax (403) 524-4223. [ADVERTISEMENT]

Lion's Den Campground, west end of town, has 19 sites with hookups, tables, showers and toilets. ▲

Sherk's R.V. Park. (Good Sam). Valleyview's newest and finest. 31 full oversized hookup sites; pull-throughs. R.V. washing facilities. Laundry facilities and clean modern washrooms. Free hot showers. Sheltered BBQ area. Stamps and mail pickup. Relax and enjoy your stay. (See our display advertisement.) Your hosts: Norm and Rose Sherk. Phone (403) 524-4949. [ADVERTISEMENT] ▲

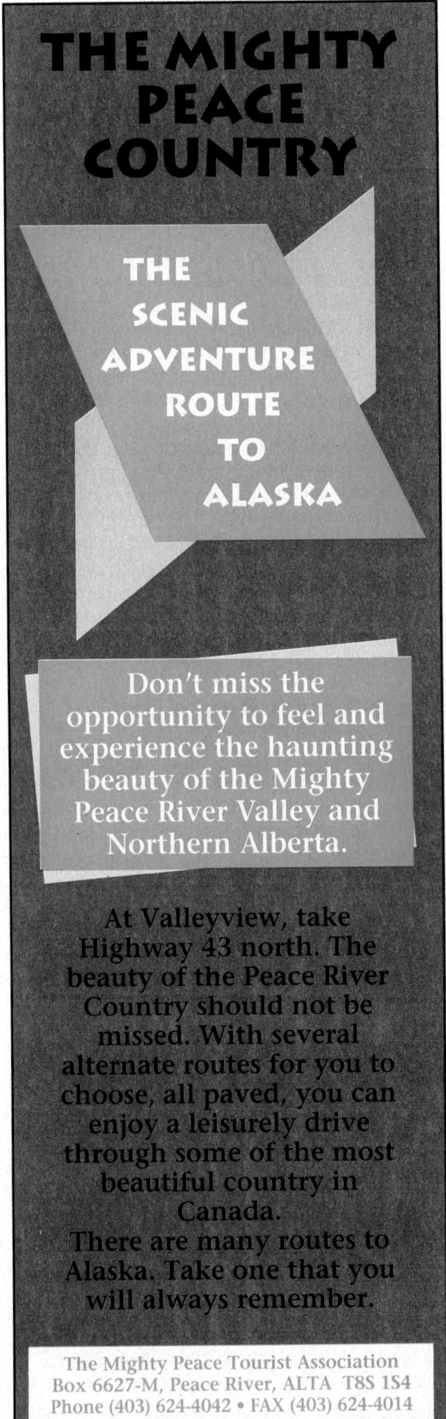

East Access Route Log

(continued)

E 216 (347.6 km) **DC 151** (243 km) Highway 43 continues north 86 miles/138.4 km to **PEACE RIVER** (pop. 6,690). Highway 43 junctions with the Mackenzie Highway 12 miles/19 km west of Peace River. See the MACKENZIE ROUTE section for a description of Peace River and the log of the Mackenzie Highway to Northwest Territories. The Mackenzie Highway is connected to the Alaska Highway via the Liard Highway (see the LIARD HIGHWAY section for details). From Peace River, travelers may also connect with the Alaska Highway at Fort St. John via Highway 64 (see NORTHERN WOODS & WATERS ROUTE section for log.)

Highway 34 begins westbound from Valleyview; continue west on Highway 34.

HIGHWAY 34

E 222.6 (358.2 km) **DC 144.4** (232.4 km) 24-hour convenience store and gas.

E 224.7 (361.6 km) **DC 142.3** (229 km) Access north to Sturgeon Lake; fishing and camping. Williamson Provincial Park (1.2 miles/2 km) has 60 campsites, boat launch, showers and dump station. Sturgeon Lake Campground has 102 sites, some hookups, tables, showers, laundry, dump station and store. Fishing for perch, pickerel, northern pike and whitefish. ▲

E 227 (365.3 km) **DC 140** (225.3 km) **CALAIS** (pop. about 550); post office and grocery store.

E 230 (370.1 km) **DC 137** (220.5 km) Private campground and marina on **Sturgeon Lake**; fishing, boat rentals. ▲

Cosy Cove Campground & **Marina.** See display ad this section. ▲

E 232 (373.3 km) **DC 135** (217.3 km) Sturgeon Heights. Turnoff for Youngs Point Provincial Park, 6 miles/10 km northeast; 94 campsites (some with electrical hookups), firewood, showers, playground, hiking trails, dump station, boat launch, fish cleaning station, beach, fishing in **Sturgeon Lake.** ▲

E 235 (378.2 km) **DC 132** (212.4 km) Turnouts both sides of highway.

E 240 (386.2 km) **DC 127** (204.4 km) **CROOKED CREEK** (pop. 10); gas station, grocery, post office and pay phone.

E 246 (395.9 km) **DC 121** (194.7 km) **DeBOLT**, a small farming community north of highway with a general store and district museum. Garage with gas on highway. Adjacent restaurant serves buffalo burgers.

E 253.8 (408.7 km) **DC 113.2** (181.9 km) **Junction.** Forestry Trunk Road leads 632 miles/1017 km south, intersecting Yellowhead Highway 16 and Trans-Canada Highway 1, to Highway 3.

E 255.2 (410.7 km) **DC 111.8** (179.9 km) Microwave towers to east.

E 259.5 (417.6 km) **DC 107.5** (173 km) Smoky River bridge and government campground; 30 sites, shelter, firepits, firewood, tables, pit toilets, water pump and boat launch. ▲

E 264 (424.9 km) **DC 103** (165.7 km) **BEZANSON.** Post office, gas station with minor repair service, grocery, general store, propane.

E 269 (432.9 km) **DC 98** (157.7 km) Kleskun Hills Park to north 3 miles/5 km. The park features an ancient sea bottom with fossils of dinosaurs and marine life.

E 270.6 (435.5 km) **DC 96.4** (155.1 km) Turnout to north with historical sign about the Kleskun Hills.

E 283.5 (456.2 km) **DC 83.5** (134.4 km) Weigh scales to north.

E 283.8 (456.7 km) **DC 83.2** (133.9 km) Railroad crossing.

E 284 (457 km) **DC 83** (133.6 km) **Junction**, Highways 34 and 2. Westbound travelers turn south for Grande Prairie and Highway 2 to Dawson Creek (log follows). Turn north on Highway 2 for Sexsmith (8.5 miles/13.7 km) and Rycroft (43.2 miles/69.5 km), and Highway 49 west to Dawson Creek (see log in NORTHERN WOODS & WATERS ROUTE section). Continue north from Rycroft on Highway 2 for Highway 64 west to Fort St. John (see log in NORTHERN WOODS & WATERS ROUTE). Continue on Highway 2 north to Grimshaw, to connect with the Mackenzie Highway to Northwest Territories (see MACKENZIE ROUTE section). **SEXSMITH** has a hotel, restaurants, 13-site campground, banks, gas station and golf courses. The Sexsmith Blacksmith Shop is cited as one of the best examples of a working pioneer smithy in Alberta; open daily May to Sept. ▲

HIGHWAY 2

From its junction with Highway 34, Highway 2 leads south into Grande Prairie (description follows). To reach Grande Prairie city centre, keep straight ahead on Highway 2 (Clairmont Road) as it becomes 100th Street and follow it downtown. To skirt the downtown area, take the Highway 2 Bypass. Highway 2 becomes 100th Avenue (Richmond Avenue) on the west side of Grande Prairie.

Grande Prairie

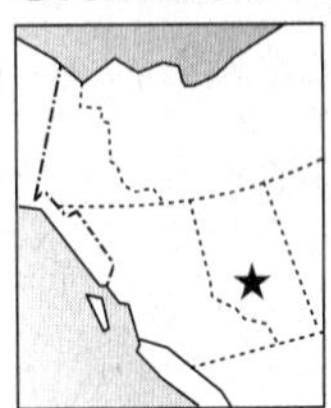

E 288 (463.5 km) **DC 79** (127.1 km). Located at junction of Highways 2 and 34. **Population:** 28,350. **Emergency Services: RCMP**, phone 538-5700. **Fire Department**, phone 532-2100. **Ambulance**, phone 532-9511. **Hospital**, Queen Elizabeth, 10409 98th St., phone 538-7100.

Visitor Information: Chamber of Com-

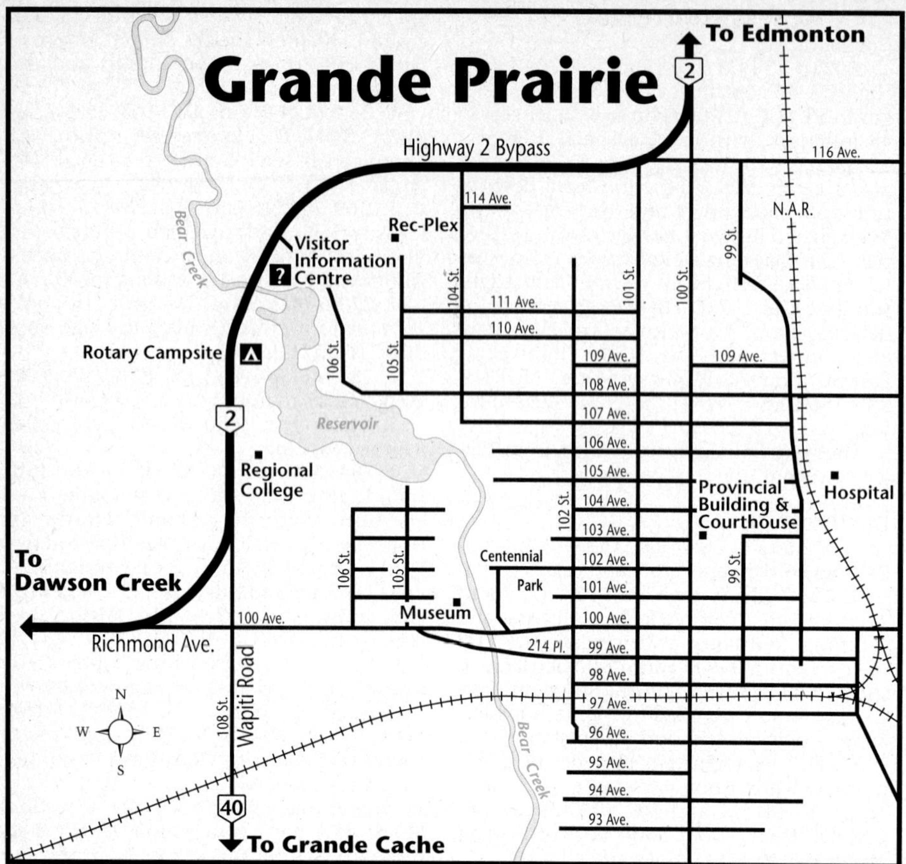

merce office at 10011 103rd Ave., and a visitor information centre off Highway 2 Bypass on 106th Street at Bear Creek Reservoir, open 9 A.M. to 9 P.M. in July and August, shorter hours in June.

Elevation: 2,198 feet/670m. **Climate:** A mild climate with a mean average in summer of 58°F/15°C, and in winter dropping to 10°F/-12°C, with an average of 116 frost-free days annually. Average annual rainfall is 11 inches and snowfall 69 inches.

Radio: CFGP 1050, CJXX 840, CKYL 610, CBC-FM 102.5, CKUA-FM 100.9. **Newspaper:** *Herald-Tribune* (Monday through Friday).

Transportation: Air–Scheduled air service to Vancouver, BC, Edmonton, Calgary, and points north. All-weather 6,500-foot/1,981-m paved runway. **Bus**–Greyhound.

Grande Prairie was first incorporated as a village in 1914, as a town in 1919, and as a city in 1958, by which time its population had reached nearly 8,000. Called "The Commerce Center of the Peace Country," Grande Prairie's economy is based on agriculture (canola, wheat, barley, oats, rye, fescue), forestry (a bleached kraft pulp mill and sawmill are located here), mining, government services, petroleum and natural gas.

There are two shopping malls, a bed and breakfast, and dozens of hotels, motels and restaurants. Recreational facilities include two municipal swimming pools, three 18-hole golf courses, skiing, hockey, skating, broom-ball, curling and tennis facilities, an art gallery and public library, plus theatrical and musical groups and events. Grande Prairie also has many churches, elementary and high schools, and a regional college designed by Douglas Cardinal. The Provincial Bldg. and courthouse are located at Jubilee Park on 100th Street.

Muskoseepi Park encompasses five units along the Bear Creek corridor in town, each offering a variety of facilities and connected by trail. Attractions include a bird sanctuary at Crystal Lake and 9.3 miles/15 km of bike trails. Canoe, paddleboat and mountain bike rentals are available. Easiest access is via 106th Street off the Highway 2 Bypass to Bear Creek Reservoir, which offers bicycling, camping, picnicking, canoeing and tourist information services. Nearby Centennial Park has tennis courts, a playground, lawn bowling and is the site of the Pioneer Museum and Village. Open daily in summer from 10 A.M. to 6 P.M., Pioneer Museum (532-5482) features a log church built in 1911, a one-room schoolhouse and rural post office, and collections of fossils, rocks, mounted wildlife, and implements and tools used by Peace River pioneers. Admission fee charged.

A fairgrounds/rodeo facility at Evergreen Park features a class A track, parimutuel races in July and a farmers market on Saturday mornings.

Rotary Park public campground with 39 sites, hookups and dump station, is located off Highway 2 Bypass at the northwest edge of town next to the college. A private campground is located at the south edge of town. ▲

Wee Links Golf & Campground. Campground, Pitch & Putt Golf Course (grass greens) and driving range at a secluded setting within Grande Prairie city limits. Clean washrooms, hot showers, pay phone, water and power at sites, firepits, snacks, hiking/biking trails. 68 Avenue and 100 Street. VISA and MasterCard. Reservations (403) 538-4501. [ADVERTISEMENT] ▲

Affordable Long Crack Repair. Using a new revolutionary patented process and tools, we inject optically clear resins into the crack or stonebreak, bonding the glass together, restoring your windshield's original strength while removing the annoying light refraction. Fully guaranteed, approved by major insurance companies and highway patrols. 10811 97th Ave. (403) 532-8636 Monday – Friday. [ADVERTISEMENT]

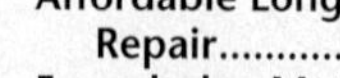

Affordable Long Crack Repair.........................Ph. (403) 532-8636
Econolodge Motor Inn.....Ph. (403) 539-4700
Wee Links Golf & Campground.............S. of Bear Creek Park

East Access Route Log

(continued)

HIGHWAY 2 WEST

E 298 (479.6 km) **DC 69** (111 km) Saskatoon Island Provincial Park is 1.9 miles/3 km north on park road; 96 campsites, dump station, boat launch, swimming, playground; Saskatoon berry picking in July; game preserve for trumpeter swans. ▲

E 299 (481.2 km) **DC 68** (109.4 km) **WEMBLEY** (pop. 1,209), hotel, banking service at hotel, post office, government liquor store, grocery, gas stop, car wash and restaurant. Picnicking at Sunset Lake Park in town. Camping May 1 to Oct. 15 at Pipestone Creek County Park, 9 miles/14.5 km south; 99 sites, showers, flush toilets, dump station, boat launch, firewood, fishing, playground, fossil display and a nine-hole golf course nearby. ▲

Beaverlodge

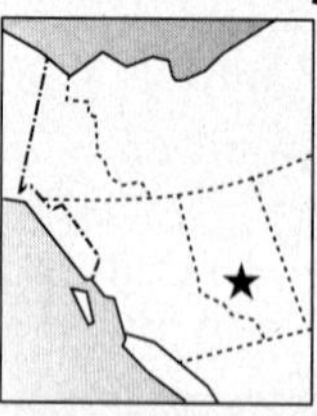

E 311 (500.5 km) **DC 56** (90.1 km) **Population:** 1,808. **Emergency Services: RCMP,** phone 354-2485. **Ambulance,** phone 354-2154. **Hospital,** Beaverlodge Municipal Hospital, phone 354-2136. **Visitor Information:** Located in the restored Lower Beaver Lodge School at Pioneer Campsite on the north side of Highway 2 at the west end of town.

Elevation: 2,419 feet/737m. **Transportation: Air**–Scheduled service to Grande Prairie airport. Beaverlodge DeWit Airpark, length 3,000 feet/914m, paved.

Beaverlodge is a service centre for the area with a provincial courthouse, RCMP, hospital, medical and dental clinic. There are nine churches, schools, a swimming pool and tennis courts.

Visitor services include three motels, eight restaurants and gas stations. There are supermarkets, banks, a drugstore, car wash and sporting goods store. Camping is available at the municipal Pioneer Campsite (19 sites, showers, dump station, electrical hookups, tourist information). The Beaverlodge Airpark, 2 miles/3.2 km south of town, is becoming a popular stopover on the flying route to Alaska. The Airpark has a paved runway and directional beacon. ▲

Beaverlodge is the gateway to Monkman Pass and Kinuseo Falls. Beaverlodge is also home to Canada's most northerly Agricultural Research Station (open to the public), and serves as regional centre for grain transportation, seed cleaning and seed production. Cereal grains, such as wheat, barley and oats, are the main crops in the area.

Beaverlodge Area Cultural Centre. See display ad this section.

Town of Beaverlodge. See display ad this section.

East Access Route Log

(continued)

E 312 (502.1 km) **DC 55** (88.5 km) South Peace Centennial Museum to east, open daily in summer; phone 354-8869. The museum features 15 display buildings and working steam-powered farm equipment from the early 1900s. Open 10 A.M. to 8 P.M., mid-May through mid-October. The annual Pioneer Day celebration, held here the third Sunday in July, attracts several thousand visitors.

E 312.4 (502.7 km) **DC 54.6** (87.9 km) Turnoff for Driftwood Ranch Wildlife Haven, 14.3 miles/23 km west; exotic and domestic wildlife for viewing (phone 356-3769).

E 314.3 (505.8 km) **DC 52.6** (84.8 km) Golf course. This joint project of Hythe and Beaverlodge residents has a clubhouse that was once an NAR station. The nine-hole par 35 course has grass greens. Visitors are welcome; rentals available.

E 320 (515 km) **DC 47** (75.6 km) **HYTHE** (pop. 681) is an agricultural service community and processing center for fruit and berry crops, especially saskatoon berries. Canola is also a major crop. The town has a motel, a bed and breakfast restaurant, laundromat, gas station, tire repair, car wash, outdoor covered heated swimming pool, complete shopping facilities and a hospital. Municipal campground in town with 20 sites, showers, dump station and playground. The information centre is housed in the Tags Food and Gas store. Inquire locally for directions to Riverside Bison Ranch. An old 1910 tack shop, staffed by volunteers in summer, is located between the highway and railroad tracks. ▲

E 329 (529.4 km) **DC 38** (61.1 km) **Junction** with Highway 59 east to Sexsmith.

E 337 (542.3 km) **DC 30** (48.3 km) **DEMMITT**, an older settlement, site of a sawmill (worth a visit), postal service and gas.

E 340 (547.2 km) **DC 27** (43.4 km) Railway crossing.

E 341 (548.8 km) **DC 26** (41.8 km) Public campground to east; 15 sites, shelter, firewood, tables, pit toilets, pump water and playground. ▲

E 341.3 (549.2 km) **DC 25.7** (41.3 km) Vehicle inspection station to west.

E 342 (550.4 km) **DC 25** (40.2 km) Gas station and convenience store.

E 343.3 (552.5 km) **DC 23.7** (38.1 km) Alberta–British Columbia border. Turnout with litter barrels and pay phone.

TIME ZONE CHANGE: Alberta is on Mountain time; most of British Columbia is on Pacific time.

E 345.1 (555.4 km) **DC 21.9** (35.2 km) **Junction** with Heritage Highway 52 (gravel surface) which leads 18.5 miles/30 km south to One Island Lake Park (30 campsites, fee charged, excellent rainbow fishing) and 92 miles/148 km southwest from Highway 2 to Tumbler Ridge townsite, built in conjunction with the North East Coal development. Monkman Provincial Park, site of spectacular Kinuseo Falls, lies south of Tumbler Ridge. A campground with viewing platform of falls is accessible via a 25-mile/40-km road from Tumbler Ridge. Heritage Highway loops north 59.5 miles/96 km from Tumbler Ridge to join Highway 97 just west of Dawson Creek (see **Milepost PG 237.7** in the WEST ACCESS ROUTE section).

E 345.7 (556.3 km) **DC 21.3** (34.3 km) Tupper Creek bridge.

E 347 (558.5 km) **DC 20** (32.1 km) Swan Lake Provincial Park, with 41 campsites, picnic area, playground and boat launch, is 1.2 miles/2 km north of the tiny hamlet of **TUPPER**, which has a general store. ▲

E 347.9 (559.9 km) **DC 19.1** (30.7 km) Sudeten Provincial Park; 15 campsites, eight picnic tables. Plaque tells of immigration to this valley of displaced residents of Sudetenland in 1938–39. ▲

E 348.9 (561.5 km) **DC 18.1** (29.1 km) Tate Creek bridge.

E 349.7 (562.7 km) **DC 17.3** (27.8 km) Side road west to community of Tomslake.

E 356.3 (573.4 km) **DC 10.7** (17.2 km) Turnout to east with litter barrel.

E 358 (576.1 km) **DC 9** (14.5 km) Historic sign tells of Pouce Coupe Prairie.

E 359.4 (578.4 km) **7.6** (12.2 km) Railway crossing.

E 360 (579.3 km) **DC 7** (11.2 km) Weigh scales to east.

E 360.4 (580 km) **DC 6.6** (10.6 km) Bissett Creek bridge. Regional park located at south end of bridge.

E 361 (581 km) **DC 6** (9.6 km) **POUCE COUPE** (pop. 1,200; elev. 2,118 feet/646m). **Visitor Information:** Tourist Bureau Office on Highway 2, open 9 A.M. to 5 P.M., May 15 to Sept. 15.

The Pouce Coupe area was first settled in 1898 by a French Canadian, who set up a trading post in 1908. The Edson Trail, completed in 1911, brought in the main influx of settlers from Edmonton in 1912. Historical artifacts are displayed at the Pouce Coupe Museum, located in the old NAR railroad station, one block south of Highway 2; open 8 A.M. to 5 P.M.

The village has two motels, a hotel, restaurant, post office, gas station, dump station, car wash, garage and food store. Camping at Regional Park, open mid-May to mid-September; hookups. ▲

The Pouce Coupe Museum. See display ad this section.

E 364.5 (586.6 km) **DC 2.5** (4 km) Dawson Creek airport.

E 367 (590.6 km) **DC 0 DAWSON CREEK**, the beginning of the Alaska Highway. For details turn to the ALASKA HIGHWAY section.

Alaska Highway via
WEST ACCESS ROUTE

Seattle, Washington, to Dawson Creek, British Columbia via Cache Creek and Prince George, British Columbia Interstate Highway 5, Trans-Canada Highway 1 and BC Highway 97 *(See maps, pages 35–36)*

The West Access Route links Interstate 5, Trans-Canada Highway 1 and BC Highway 97 to form the most direct route to Dawson Creek, BC, for West Coast motorists. This has been the major western route to the start of the Alaska Highway since 1952, when the John Hart Highway connecting Prince George and Dawson Creek was completed.

The West Access Route junctions with Yellowhead Highway 16 at Prince George. This east–west highway connects with the Alaska State Ferry System and BC Ferries at Prince Rupert, and with the East Access Route to the Alaska Highway at Edmonton. Turn to the YELLOWHEAD HIGHWAY 16 section for a complete log of that route.

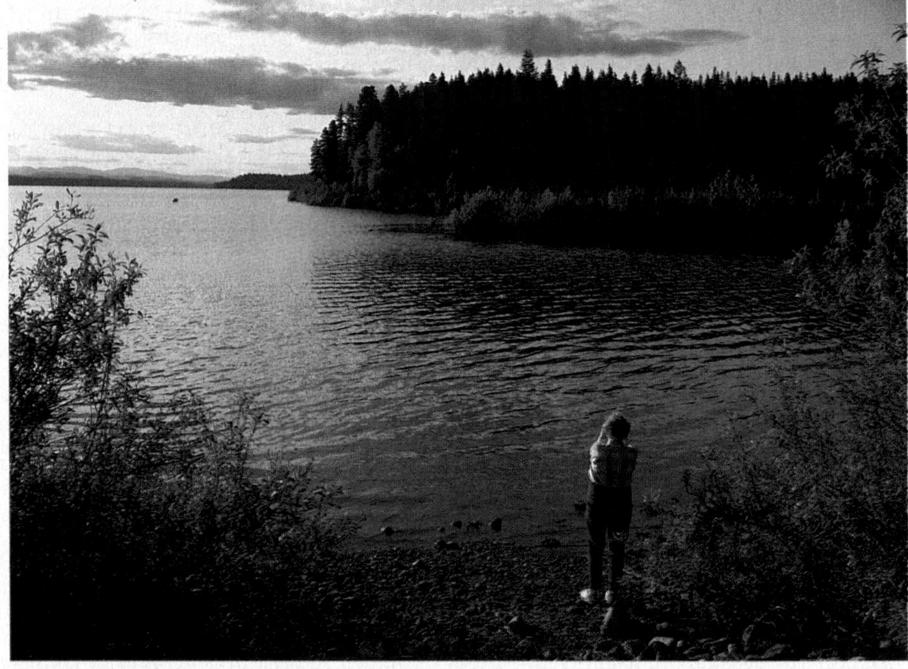

Sunset on McLeod Lake on the Hart Highway northeast of Prince George. (Barb Michaels)

INTERSTATE HIGHWAY 5

The West Access Route begins in **SEATTLE, WA** (pop. 493,846), the largest city in the Pacific Northwest. Seattle has been called the Alaska gateway city since the Klondike gold rush days, when it became the major staging and departure point for most of the gold seekers. Seattle was also southern terminus of the Alaska Marine Highway System until 1989, when the Alaska state ferries moved to the Fairhaven Terminal at Bellingham, WA (Interstate 5, Exit 250). Seattle–Tacoma International Airport is the departure point for jet flights to Alaska. The air terminal is located 10 miles/16 km south of city center via Interstate 5 (Exit 154).

Like most interstate routes in the United States, Interstate 5 has physical mileposts along its route and corresponding numbered exits. From Seattle, drive 92 miles north on Interstate 5 to Bellingham and turn off onto Highway 539 north (Exit 256), which goes north 12 miles to Highway 546, which will take you another 13 miles to Sumas, WA, and the U.S.–Canada border (customs open 24 hours a day). *The MILEPOST®* log begins on Trans-Canada Highway 1 near Abbotsford.

From Seattle to Abbotsford via Sumas it is 120 miles. From Abbotsford to Cache Creek, it is 170 miles; from Cache Creek to Prince George, 277 miles; and from Prince George to Dawson Creek it is 250 miles.

West Access Route Log

TRANS-CANADA HIGHWAY 1

The West Access Route log is divided into three sections: Abbotsford to Cache Creek; Cache Creek to Prince George; and Prince George to Dawson Creek.

This section of the log shows distance from Abbotsford (A) followed by distance from Cache Creek (CC).

A 0 CC 170 (273.6 km) **Junction** of Trans-Canada Highway 1 and Highway 11 south to the international border crossing at Sumas–Huntingdon. Highway 11 north to **ABBOTSFORD** (pop. 60,400), all visitor services. Abbotsford is the "Raspberry Capital of Canada" and is the home of the Abbotsford International Airshow in August.

Bridge over the Fraser River to Mission and Highway 7 to Harrison Hot Springs.

A 1.9 (3 km) **CC 168.1** (270.5 km) Exit 95 to Watcom Road and westbound exit to Sumas River rest area. Access to Sumas Mountain Provincial Park; hiking.

A 5.3 (8.5 km) **CC 164.7** (265.1 km) Exit 99 to Sumas River rest area (eastbound only); tables, toilet, pay phones.

A 8.8 (14.2 km) **CC 161.2** (259.4 km) Exit 104 to small farming community of Yarrow and road to Cultus Lake. The Lower Fraser River Valley is prime agricultural land.

CAUTION: Watch for farm vehicles crossing freeway.

A 15 (24.1 km) **CC 155** (249.4 km) Exit 116 to Lickman Road; access south to tourist infocentre, open daily in summer, and private RV park. Chilliwack Antique Powerland museum located behind infocentre. ▲

Cottonwood Meadows R.V. Country Club. See display ad this section. ▲

A 16.8 (27.1 km) **CC 153.2** (246.5 km) Highway 119B to Chilliwack Airport.

A 17 (27.4 km) **CC 153** (246.2 km) Exit

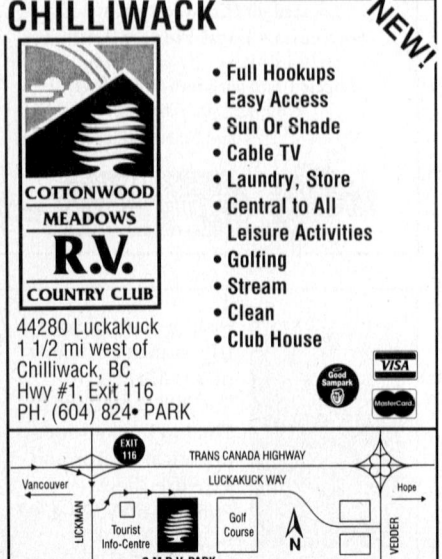

WEST ACCESS ROUTE *Seattle, WA, to Lac La Hache, BC*

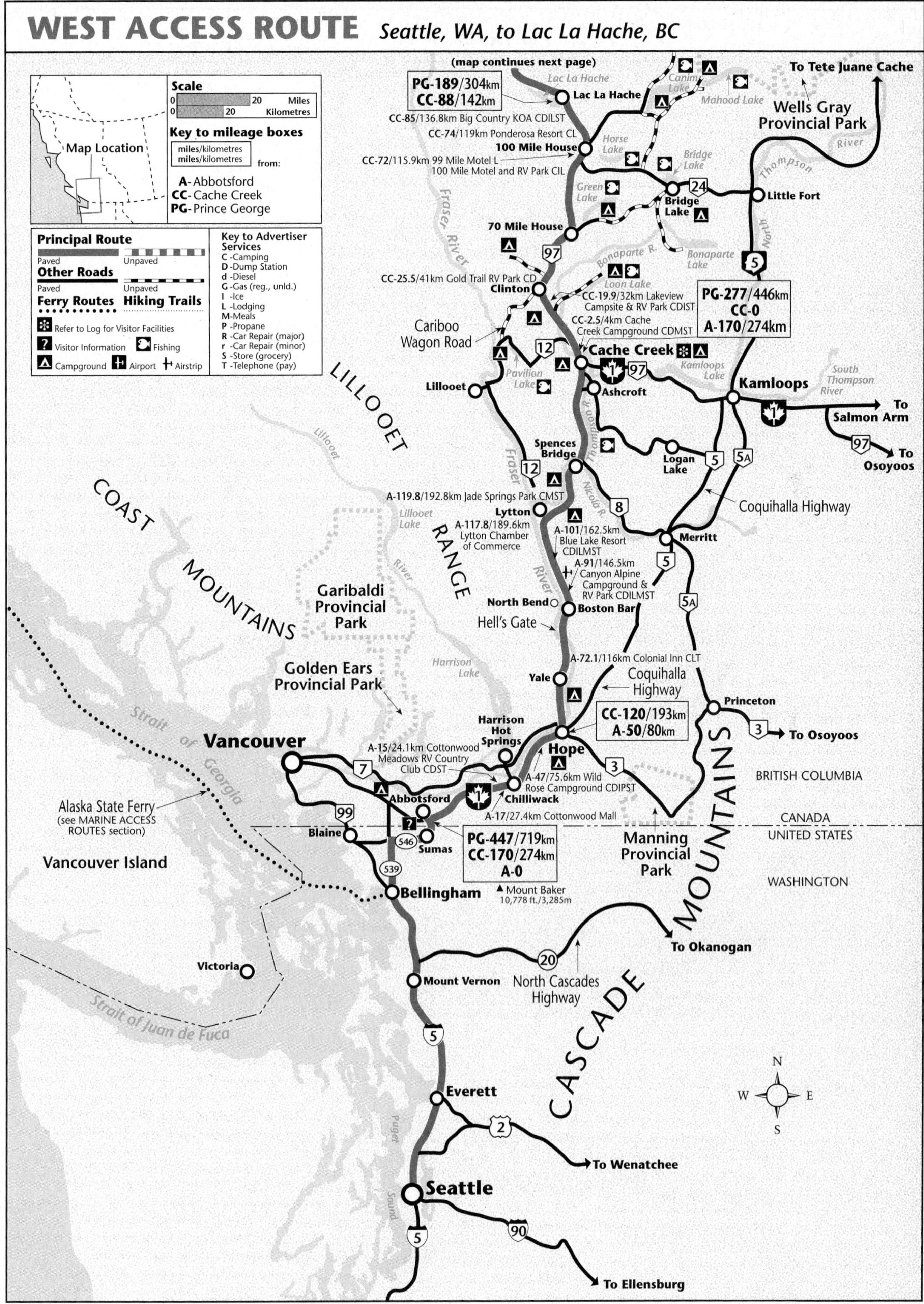

WEST ACCESS ROUTE *Lac La Hache, BC, to Dawson Creek, BC*

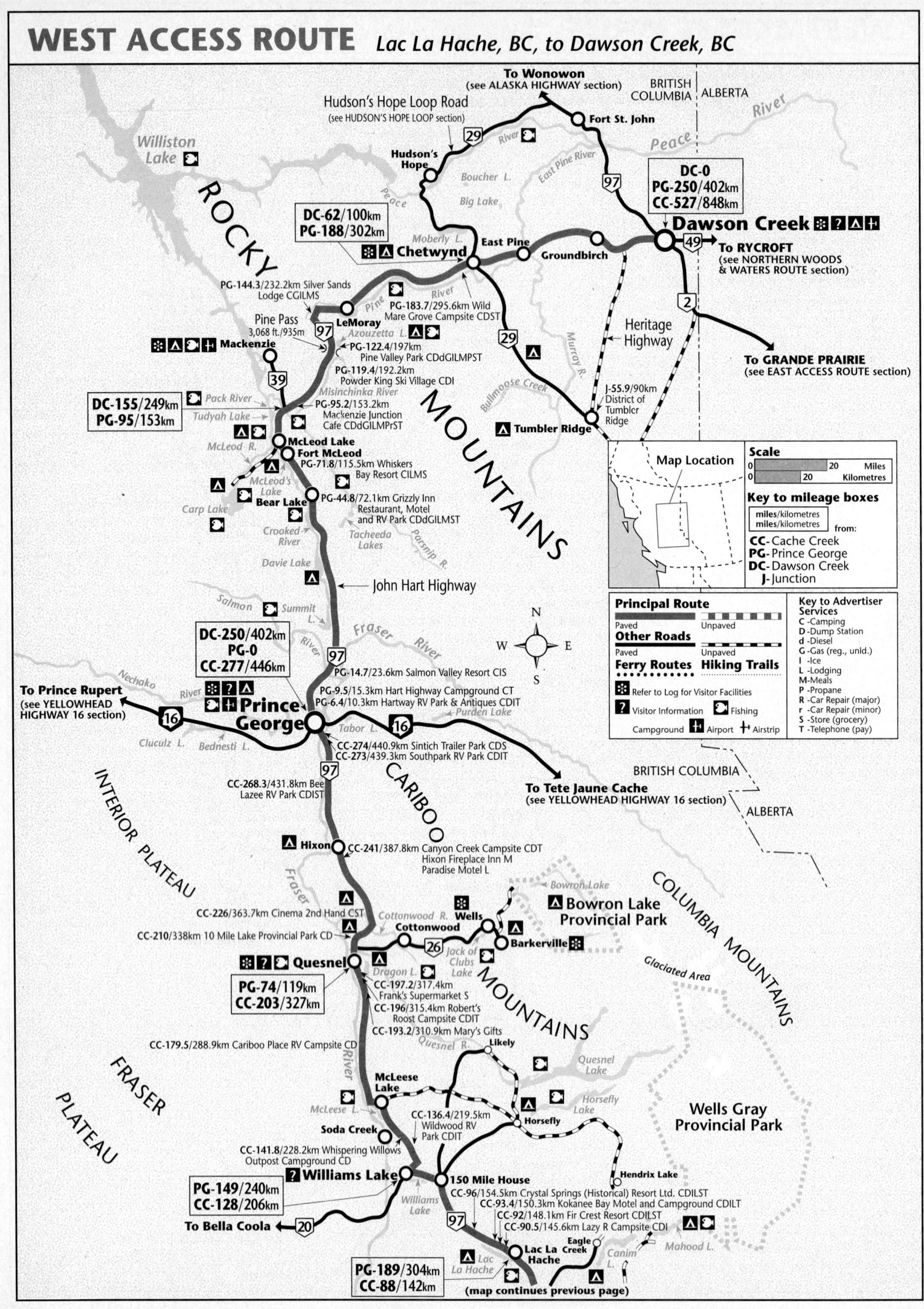

119 (Vedder Road) north to Chilliwack (all services, description follows) and south to Sardis (all services) and Cultus Lake recreation area.

CHILLIWACK (pop. 53,000) has motels, restaurants, shopping malls, banks, gas stations, RV parks and other services. There is a library, movie theatre and arts centre. The Canadian Military Engineers Museum is located off Vedder Road. Recreational attractions include golf and the popular Cultus Lake area with water park, boat rentals, horseback riding and camping. Cultus Lake Provincial Park has 300 campsites. The municipal Sunnyside Campground has 600 sites. ▲

Cottonwood Mall. See display ad this section.

A 18 (29 km) **CC 152** (244.6 km) Exit 123 Prest Road north to Rosedale, south to Ryder Lake.

A 26.5 (42.5 km) **CC 143.5** (230.9 km) Exit 135 to Highway 9 east to Harrison Hot Springs and alternate route Highway 7 to Hope and Vancouver. Westbound exit for Bridal Veil Falls. Also exit here for access to Minter Gardens, which rivals Victoria's famous Butchart Gardens for beauty. The 27 acres of floral displays feature 11 themed gardens, topiary figures and a rare collection of Chinese Penjing Rock Bonsai. Open April to Oct., 9 A.M. to dusk. Entertainment is scheduled Sundays and holidays.

A 27.3 (43.9 km) **CC 142.7** (229.6 km) Exit 138 to Popkum Road. Eastbound access to Bridal Veil Falls Provincial Park to south; picnicking, trail to base of falls. Also access to small community of Popkum and various roadside attractions, including waterslide, Sandstone Gallery rock and gem museum, and Flintstones amusement park. Food, gas and lodging.

Shady park in Hope features wood carving of bear. (Judy Parkin, staff)

A 34.5 (55.5 km) **CC 135.5** (218.1 km) Exit 146 for Herrling Island. Eastbound traffic exit center lane.

A 40.5 (65.2 km) **CC 129.5** (208.4 km) Exit 153 to small community of Laidlaw and Jones Lake.

A 42.5 (65.6 km) **CC 127.5** (205.2 km) Truck weigh scales; public phone.

A 44.7 (71.9 km) **CC 125.3** (201.6 km) Exit 160 to Hunter Creek rest area; tables, toilet, pay phone and tourist information trailer.

A 45.5 (73.2 km) **CC 124.5** (200.4 km) Exit 165 to Flood/Hope Road, access to RV park, Hope (eastbound) and Hope airport. ▲

A 47 (75.6 km) **CC 123** (197.9 km) **Wild Rose Good Sampark**. On Highway 1 east (from Vancouver) 4.8 km (3 miles) west of Hope; take Flood–Hope Road exit 165. On Highway 1 west (from Hope) take Flood–Hope Road exit 168. Full hookups, 15–30 amps, tenting, level grassy sites in parklike setting, 60-foot pull-throughs, free cable TV, free hot showers, laundry, playground, horseshoes, firepits, picnic tables, a limited store. Ice, wood, pay phone, sani-station, near restaurant. Senior citizen discount, weekly rates, MasterCard, VISA. Small pets. Cancellation policy — two days. Open March 15 to Oct. 15. Phone (604) 869-9842. Toll-free reservations in Canada and U.S.A. 1-800-463-7999. [ADVERTISEMENT] ▲

A 48.5 (78.1 km) **CC 121.5** (195.5 km) Exit 168 to Silverhope Creek (eastbound only). Access to RV park. ▲

A 48.7 (78.4 km) **CC 121.3** (195.2 km) Silver Creek, Flood-Hope Road exit.

A 50 (80.5 km) **CC 120** (193.1 km) **Junction** of Trans-Canada Highway 1 and Highway 3 (Crowsnest Highway). Turn north on Trans-Canada Highway 1 for Hope.

Hope

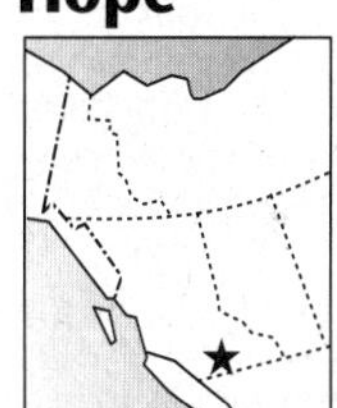

A 50.2 (80.8 km) **CC 119.8** (192.8 km) **Population:** 5,000. **Elevation:** 140 feet/43m. **Emergency Services: RCMP, Fire Department. Ambulance**, phone 911. **Hospital**, 1275 7th Ave., phone 869-5656. **Visitor Information:** Travel Infocentre and museum building, corner of Hudson and Water streets, on the right northbound as you enter town. Open 8 A.M. to 8 P.M. daily in summer.

Hope is on a bend of the Fraser River where it flows through a picturesque gap in the forested Coast Mountains near Mount Hope (elev. 6,000 feet/1,289m). It is a popular tourist stop with complete services. About 20 motels and resorts are in Hope or just outside town on Trans-Canada Highway 1 and on Highway 3. Other facilities include auto body shops, service stations, department stores, restaurants and grocery stores.

The major attraction in the Hope area is the Coquihalla Canyon Provincial Recreation Area, the focus of which is the Othello Quintette Tunnels. The five rock tunnels which cut through the tortuous canyon were part of the Kettle Valley Railway. This stretch of railway has been restored as a walking trail through three of the tunnels and across bridges. The tunnels are accessible from downtown Hope via Kawakawa Lake Road, about a 10-minute drive.

The Coquihalla Highway, completed in 1987, connects Hope with the Trans-Canada Highway just west of Kamloops, a distance of 118 miles/190 km. This is a four-lane divided highway; toll charged.

There are private campgrounds on all roads into town. A town-operated campground on Kawakawa Lake Road has 95 RV sites, 22 tent sites, coin showers and sani-station. ▲

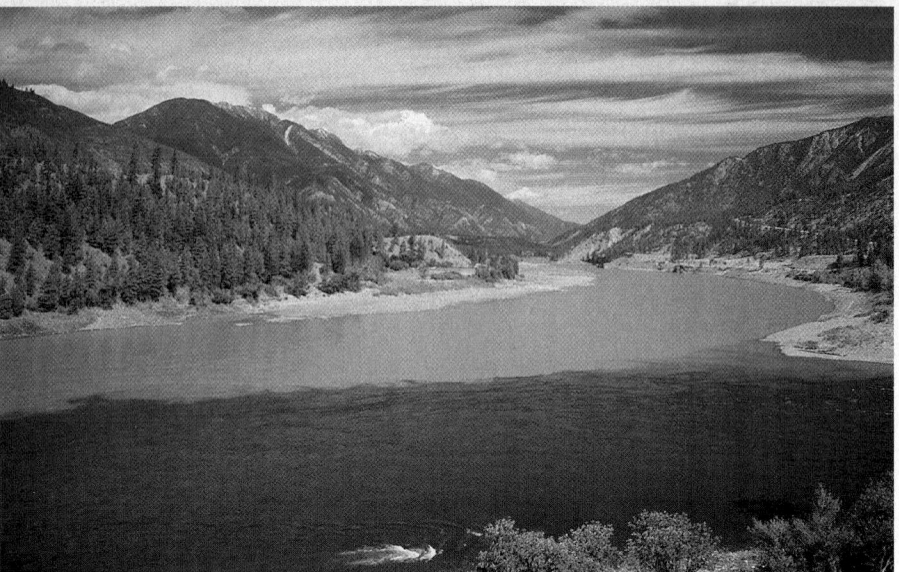

The green Thompson River meets the brown Fraser River in Lytton. (Philip and Karen Smith)

West Access Route Log

(continued)

A 50.7 (81.6 km) **CC 119.3** (191.9 km) Bridge over Fraser River. Turnout at north end, access to pedestrian bridge across the Fraser.

A 51.5 (82.8 km) **CC 118.5** (190.7 km) **Junction** with Highway 7, which leads west to Harrison Hot Springs and Vancouver.

A 53.1 (85.5 km) **CC 116.9** (188.1 km) Rest area (westbound access only) with picnic tables to west by Lake of the Woods.

A 60.8 (97.8 km) **CC 109.2** (175.7 km) Easy-to-miss turnoff (watch for sign 400m before turn) for Emory Creek Provincial Park east of highway. Level gravel sites in trees, water, fire rings, picnic tables, firewood, outhouses and litter barrels. Camping fee May to October. Gold panning in Fraser River. ▲

Very much in evidence between Hope and Cache Creek are the tracks of the Canadian National and Canadian Pacific railways. Construction of the CPR — Canada's first transcontinental railway — played a significant role in the history of the Fraser and Thompson river valleys. Begun in 1880, the CPR line between Kamloops and Port Moody was contracted to Andrew Onderdonk.

A 64.8 (104.3 km) **CC 105.2** (169.3 km) **YALE** (pop. 500; elev. 250 feet/76m). **Emergency Services: Police**, phone 869-5644. **Fire Department**, phone 863-2254. **Ambulance**, phone 863-2300. Visitor facilities include motels, stores, gas stations and restaurants. Travel Infocentre located at the north edge of town, open June 1 to Labour Day; pay phone.

Yale was the head of navigation for the Lower Fraser River and the beginning of the overland gold rush trail to British Columbia's goldfields. The Anglican Church of Saint John the Divine here was built for the miners in 1859 and is the oldest church still on its original foundation in mainland British Columbia. Next to the church is Yale Museum and a bronze plaque honouring Chinese construction workers who helped build the Canadian Pacific Railway. Walking around town, look for the several plaques relating Yale's history.

A 65.6 (105.5 km) **CC 104.5** (168.2 km) Entering Fraser Canyon northbound. The Fraser River and canyon were named for Simon Fraser (1776–1862), the first white man to descend the river in 1808. This is the dry forest region of British Columbia, and it can be a hot drive in summer. The scenic Fraser Canyon travelers drive through today was a formidable obstacle for railroad engineers in 1881.

A 66 (106.2 km) **CC 104** (167.4 km) Yale Tunnel, first of several northbound through the Fraser Canyon.

A 67.3 (108.3 km) **CC 102.7** (165.2 km) Turnout to east with plaque about the Cariboo Wagon Road, which connected Yale with the Cariboo goldfields near Barkerville. Built between 1861 and 1863 by the Royal Engineers, it replaced an earlier route to the goldfields — also called the Cariboo Wagon Road — which started from Lillooet.

A 68.4 (110.1 km) **CC 101.6** (163.5 km) Saddle Rock Tunnel. This 480-foot-/146-m-long tunnel was constructed in 1957–58.

A 72.1 (116 km) **CC 97.9** (157.5 km) **Colonial Inn.** In scenic Fraser Canyon. Cabin-style sleeping and kitchen units with showers and satellite TV. Pay phones. Picnic area with barbecues. Mountain views. Campground with full hookups and showers. For reservations call (604) 863-2277 or write RR #1, Yale, BC V0K 2S0. Stop and smell the flowers. [ADVERTISEMENT] ▲

A 72.3 (116.3 km) **CC 97.7** (157.2 km) Sailor Bar Tunnel. There were dozens of bar claims along the Fraser River in the 1850s bearing colourful names such as Sailor Bar.

A 76.5 (123.1 km) **CC 93.5** (150.5 km) Spuzzum (unincorporated), gas station and food.

A 77.1 (124.1 km) **CC 92.9** (149.5 km) Stop of interest at south end of Alexandra Bridge, the second largest fixed arch span in the world at more than 1,640 feet/500m in length.

A 77.5 (124.8 km) **CC 92.5** (148.9 km) Alexandra Bridge Provincial Park, picnic areas and interpretive displays on both sides of highway. Hiking trail down to the old Alexandra Bridge, still intact. This suspension bridge was built in 1926, replacing the original built in 1863.

A 77.8 (125.2 km) **CC 92.2** (148.4 km) Historic Alexandra Lodge is the last surviving original roadhouse on the Cariboo Wagon Road.

A 79.5 (128 km) **CC 90.5** (145.6 km) Alexandra Tunnel.

A 80.5 (129.5 km) **CC 89.5** (144 km) Rest area by Copper Creek to east.

A 82.6 (133 km) **CC 87.4** (140.7 km) Hells Gate Tunnel.

A 83.3 (134 km) **CC 86.7** (139.5 km) Ferrabee Tunnel.

A 83.6 (134.5 km) **CC 86.4** (139 km) Hells Gate, the narrowest point on the Fraser River and a popular attraction. (Northbound traffic park at lot immediately south of attraction on east side of road; southbound traffic park on west side of road at attraction.) Two 25-passenger airtrams take visitors some 500 feet down across the river to a restaurant and shop complex. Footbridge across river to view fish ladders where some 2 million salmon pass through each year. A display details the life cycle of the salmon, the construction of the International Fishways and the history of Hells Gate. Trams operate daily, mid-April to mid-October. There is also a steep trail down to the fish ladders; strenuous hike.

Hells Gate was well named. It was by far the most difficult terrain for construction of both the highway and the railway. To haul supplies for the railway upstream of Hells Gate, Andrew Onderdonk built the sternwheel steamer *Skuzzy*. The *Skuzzy* made its way upstream through Hells Gate in 1882, hauled by ropes attached to the canyon walls by bolts.

A 85.7 (137.9 km) **CC 84.3** (135.7 km) China Bar Tunnel, built in 1960. It is almost 2,300 feet/700m long, one of the longest tunnels in North America. Point of interest sign at south end about Simon Fraser.

A 91 (146.5 km) **CC 79** (127.1 km) **BOSTON BAR** (pop. 1,000; elev. 400 feet/122m), site of a large mill, has gas stations, cafes, grocery stores, a motel and private RV park. Boston Bar was the southern landing for the steamer *Skuzzy*, which plied the Fraser River between here and Lytton during construction of the CPR.

Canyon Alpine Campground & RV Park. The best kept secret in the Fraser Canyon is under new ownership. It's quickly being discovered and described as "... one of the nicest parks on the Alaskan route." Secure, relaxed tenting and RV parking within easy access of the canyon highway. Roomy pull-throughs, full hookups, fire rings, free firewood, clean washrooms, free, hot showers, flush toilets, children's playground and friendly service. Pets on leash welcome. Adjacent to 24-hour restaurant, store, laundromat and telephones. 10 minutes from world famous Hell's Gate Airtram. Open April 15 to Oct. 15. Visa. MasterCard. 50490 TransCanada Hwy. Phone (604) 867-9734. Hosts: Martha & Fred Jost. [ADVERTISEMENT] ▲

A 101 (162.5 km) **CC 69** (111 km) **Blue Lake Resort.** 1 km off highway on quiet family oriented private trout lake. Wooded RV/tent sites, power and water. Rustic wilderness cabins (need bedding), kitchenettes, central washrooms, free showers. Log lodge, twin or queen bedrooms, shared bathrooms. Family style licensed dining available. Security gate closed 10 P.M.–7 A.M. Swimming, hiking, canoeing, horseback riding. Phone/Fax (604) 867-9246. [ADVERTISEMENT] ▲

A 112.8 (181.5 km) **CC 57.2** (92.1 km) Viewpoint to west overlooking the Fraser River.

A 114.6 (184.5 km) **CC 55.4** (89.2 km) Skupper rest area (northbound only); toilets, tables, litter barrels.

A 117.8 (189.6 km) **CC 52.2** (84 km) **Junction** with Highway 12. Turn west here for community of Lytton (description follows).

LYTTON (pop. 400; elev. 561 feet/171m). **Emergency Services: RCMP**, phone 455-2225. **Fire Department**, phone 455-2333. **Ambulance**, phone 1-374-5937. **Hospital**, St. Bartholomew's, phone 455-2221. **Visitor Information**: Travel Infocentre, 400 Fraser St., phone 455-2523. Located at the confluence of the Thompson and Fraser rivers, Lytton acts as headquarters for river raft trips. All visitor facilities are available. Sand bars at Lytton yielded much gold, and river frontage has been set aside for recreational gold panning. Lytton has recorded the highest temperature in British Columbia, 111°F/44°C.

Lytton. Rafting capital of British Columbia in the scenic Fraser Canyon. Full visitor services. Whitewater rafting on the Thompson River with raft rides through Hells Gate on the Fraser during August and September. Hiker access to the Stein and Botannie valleys. Many other natural attractions from Spences Bridge to Yale. Visit the Infocentre: view the "jellyroll" — a rare geological formation, get highway and local travel information, arrange for sawmill and woods tours. At the confluence of the Thompson and Fraser rivers. Pan for gold at water's edge. Infocentre, 400 Fraser St., phone (604) 455-2523. [ADVERTISEMENT]

A 119.8 (192.8 km) **CC 50.2** (80.8 km) **Jade Springs Park.** Campground, RV park (May–Oct.) 2 km (1.2 miles) east of Lytton on Highway 1. Forest setting, complete washrooms. Hot showers, laundry, full and partial hookups, some pull-throughs. Licensed restaurant, horseshoe pits, phone, river rafting, grocery store, pets. Box 488, Lytton, BC V0K 1Z0. (604) 455-2420. [ADVERTISEMENT] ▲

A 122.8 (197.6 km) **CC 47.2** (76 km) Skihist Provincial Park to east; 68 campsites. Picnic area on west side of highway. ▲

A 134.7 (216.8 km) **CC 35.3** (56.8 km) Goldpan Provincial Park to west alongside river; 14 campsites, picnic area, fishing. ▲

A 140 (225.3 km) **CC 30** (48.3 km) **Junction** with Highway 8 to Merritt and south access to Spences Bridge. Plaque here about the great landslide of 1905.

A 141.2 (227.2 km) **CC 28.8** (46.3 km) North access to **SPENCES BRIDGE** (pop. 300; elev. 760 feet/231m) located at the confluence of the Thompson and Nicola rivers. A record 30-lb., 5-oz. steelhead was caught in the Thompson River in 1984.

Quick Stop Groceries. Spacious parking with shaded picnic area. Groceries and convenience foods. Liquor agency. Ice. Bait and tackle. Fishing and hunting licenses. Video rentals. Daily river rafting May 1 to Sept. 15. Open daily: summer 9–9, winter 10–7. On Frontage Road south. Your hosts Bev and Daryl. [ADVERTISEMENT]

A 153.4 (246.9 km) **CC 16.6** (26.7 km) Viewpoint overlooking Thompson River with plaque about the Canadian Northern Pacific (now the Canadian National Railway), Canada's third transcontinental railway, completed in 1915.

A 158.4 (255 km) **CC 11.6** (18.7 km) Red Hill rest area to east; tables, toilets, litter barrels, pay phone.

A 164.3 (264.4 km) **CC 5.7** (9.2 km) Stop of interest sign to east describes Ashcroft Manor, a roadhouse on the Cariboo Wagon Road. Today, this 19th century roadhouse provides a shady stop for travelers and houses a museum, antique and gift shops, and restaurant. Summer temperatures in this dry and desertlike region typically reach the high 80s and 90s (26°C to 32°C).

A 164.5 (264.7 km) **CC 5.5** (8.9 km) **Junction** with road to **ASHCROFT**, a small village on the Thompson River with full tourist facilities just east of the highway. Historic Ashcroft supplanted Yale as gateway to the Cariboo with the arrival of the Canadian Pacific Railway in 1885. Ashcroft Museum houses a fine collection of artifacts tracing the history of the region. Logan Lake, east of Ashcroft, is the site of the second largest open-pit copper mine in North America (tours available).

A 168.2 (270.7 km) **CC 1.8** (2.9 km) Second turnoff northbound for Ashcroft and road to Logan Lake. Travel Infocentre at junction.

Cache Creek

A 170 (273.6 km) **PG 277** (445.8 km) Located at the junction of Trans-Canada Highway 1 and Highway 97. **Population:** 1,200. **Elevation:** 1,508 feet/460m. **Emergency Services: RCMP**, phone 453-2216. **Ambulance**, phone 1-374-5937. **Hospital**, phone 453-5306.

Visitor Information: Tourist Infocentre located on the west side of Highway 97. Write Box 460, Cache Creek, BC V0K 1H0; phone (604) 457-5306.

Cache Creek has ample facilities for the traveler (most located on or just off the main highways), including motels, restaurants, service stations and grocery store. Private campgrounds are available east of Cache Creek on Trans-Canada Highway 1 (across from the golf course) and just north of town on Highway 97.

A post office and bus depot are on Todd Road. Nearby, a jade shop offers free stone-cutting demonstrations in summer. Public park and swimming pool on the Bonaparte River, east off Highway 97 at the north edge of town.

The settlement grew up around the confluence of the creek and the Bonaparte River. The Hudson's Bay Co. opened a store here, and Cache Creek became a major supply point on the Cariboo Wagon Road. Today, hay and cattle ranching, mining, logging and tourism support the community.

From the junction, Highway 97 leads north 277 miles/445.8 km to Prince George. Kamloops is 52 miles/83.7 km east via Trans-Canada Highway 1. Traveling north from Cache Creek the highway generally follows the historic route to the Cariboo goldfields.

Brookside Campsite. 1 km east of Cache Creek on Highway 1, full (30 amp) and partial hookups, pull-throughs, tent sites, super clean heated wash and laundry rooms, free showers, sani-stations, store, playground, horseshoes, nature path, heated pool, golf

CACHE CREEK ADVERTISERS

Bonaparte Motel	Ph. (604) 457-9693
Brookside Campsite	1 km E. of jct.
Cariboo Jade Shoppe	Ph. (604) 457-9566
Desert Motel	Ph. (604) 457-6226
Wander-Inn Restaurant	Ph. (604) 457-6511

Exterior of doctor's office in Clinton.
(Judy Parkin, staff)

course adjacent, pets on leash, pay phone. VISA, MasterCard, C.P. two days. Good Sam. Box 737, Cache Creek, BC V0K 1H0. Phone: (604) 457-6633. [ADVERTISEMENT] ♿▲

West Access Route Log

(continued)

HIGHWAY 97

From Cache Creek, continue north on BC Highway 97 for Dawson Creek. Highway 97 between Cache Creek and Prince George is called the Cariboo Highway.

This section of the log shows distance from Cache Creek (CC) followed by distance from Prince George (PG).

CC 2.5 (4 km) **PG 274.5** (441.8 km) **Cache Creek Campground,** 3 km north of Cache Creek on Highway 97 north. Full hookups, pull-throughs and tenting, sani-station, store, country kitchen restaurant, laundromat, coin showers, heated washrooms. Outdoor pool and whirlpool (no charge). 18-hole mini-golf, horseshoes, seasonal river swimming and fishing. P.O. Box 127, Cache Creek, BC V0K 1H0. For reservations, phone (604) 457-6414. [ADVERTISEMENT] ▲

CC 7 (11.3 km) **PG 270** (434.5 km) **Junction** with Highway 12 west to Lillooet (46.5 miles/75 km). Drive 0.4 mile/0.7 km west on Highway 12 for historic Hat Creek Ranch, a restored Cariboo Trail roadhouse and farm with reconstructed barn, working blacksmith shop, wagon rides and gift shop. Open daily 10 A.M. to 6 P.M., mid-May to mid-October. Phone (604) 457-9722 for current information.

Marble Canyon Provincial Park, 17.5 miles/28 km west on Highway 12, has 34 campsites, picnicking and hiking trails. ▲

CC 10 (16 km) **PG 267** (430 km) Plaque about the BX stagecoaches that once served Barkerville. Formally known as the BC Express Company, the BX served the Cariboo for 50 years.

CC 13.6 (21.9 km) **PG 263.4** (423.9 km) Gravel road leads east to **Loon Lake,** rainbow fishing, boat launch. Camping at Loon Lake Provincial Park (16 miles/26 km); 14 sites. ▲

CC 16.6 (26.7 km) **PG 260.4** (419.1 km) Rest area.

CC 19.9 (32 km) **PG 257.1** (413.7 km) **Lakeview Campsite & RV Park.** See display ad this section. ▲

CC 25 (40.2 km) **PG 252** (405.5 km) **Junction** with road west to Pavilion via Kelly Lake. Camping at Downing Provincial Park (11 miles/18 km); 25 sites, swimming, fishing. ▲

CC 25.5 (41 km) **PG 251.5** (404.7 km) **CLINTON** (pop. 900, area 4,000; elev. 2,911 feet/887m). All visitor facilities. Originally the site of 47 Mile Roadhouse, a gold rush settlement on the Cariboo Wagon Road from Lillooet. The museum, housed in a red brick building that once served as a courthouse, has fine displays of pioneer tools and items from the gold rush days, and a scale model of the Clinton Hotel. Clinton pioneer cemetery just north of town. Clinton boasts the oldest continuously held event in the province, the Clinton Ball (in May the weekend following Victoria Day), an annual event since 1868.

This community has preserved its frontier heritage — and displays a sense of humour — in its building exteriors. Especially stop and see the doctor's office. Clinton has also started its own sign forest. Visitors may sign a wooden slab (donated by the local sawmill) and add it to the sign forest.

Gold Trail RV Park. Brand new! 30 fully serviced sites with 30-amp power. Pull-throughs. Immaculate. Washrooms with flush toilets, handicap-equipped. Free hot showers for guests. TV. On highway in town; easy walking to all amenities. Well-lit level sites. Grassed and landscaped. Sani-station. Complimentary RV U-wash. 1620 Cariboo Highway North, Clinton, BC V0K 1K0. (604) 459-2519. [ADVERTISEMENT] ♿▲

CC 31 (49.9 km) **PG 246** (395.9 km) Dirt and gravel road leads 21 miles/34 km west to **Big Bar Lake** Provincial Park; 33 campsites, fishing, boat launch. ▲

Rest area to east just north of Big Bar Lake turnoff; toilets, tables, litter barrels.

CC 35 (56.3 km) **PG 242** (389.5 km) Loop road leads east 3 miles/5 km to Painted Chasm geological site and Chasm Provincial Park picnic area.

CC 45 (72.4 km) **PG 232** (373.4 km) **70 MILE HOUSE** (unincorporated), originally a stage stop named for its distance from Lillooet, Mile 0. General store, post office, restaurant, motel, gas station with diesel and bus depot.

A paved road leads east 7.5 miles/12 km to Green Lake Provincial Recreation Area; three campgrounds, boat launch. Rainbow and kokanee fishing at **Green Lake.** Gravel roads lead north to Watch Lake, east to Bonaparte Lake, and northeast to join Highway 24 at Bridge Lake. ▲

CC 66 (106.2 km) **PG 211** (339.6 km) **Junction** with Highway 24 East to Bridge Lake and Little Fort (60 miles/96.5 km) on Yellowhead Highway 5. Highway 24 provides access to numerous fishing lakes and resorts, including **Bridge Lake** Provincial Park (31 miles/50 km east) with 19 campsites. ▲

100 Mile House

CC 72 (115.9 km) **PG 205** (329.9 km) **Population:** 1,900. **Elevation:** 3,050 feet/930m. **Emergency Services: Police,** phone 395-2456. **Ambulance,** phone 1-374-5937. **Hospital,** phone 395-2202. **Visitor Information:** At the log cabin by 100 Mile House Marsh (a bird sanctuary at the south edge of town); phone 395-5353. Look for the 39-foot-/12-m-long skis!

This large bustling town was once a stop for fur traders and later a post house on the Cariboo Wagon Road to the goldfields. In 1930, the Marquis of Exeter established the 15,000-acre Bridge Creek Ranch here. Today, 100 Mile House is the site of two lumber mills, and an extensive log home building industry.

Visitor services include restaurants, motels, gas stations with repair service, stores, a post office, a golf course, government liquor store, supermarket and banks. Shopping malls are located east of the highway and across from Red Coach Inn.

100 Mile House is a popular destination for snowmobiling and cross-country skiing in winter. It is also the jumping-off point for fishermen headed for Canim Lake and Mahood Lake in Wells Gray Provincial Park.

Horse Lake Road leads east from 100 Mile House to **Horse Lake** (kokanee) and other fishing lakes of the high plateau.

99 Mile Motel. Air-conditioned sleeping and housekeeping units. Fridges in all units, housekeeping units with microwave ovens. DD touchtone phones, remote control cable TV, super channel and TSN, courtesy in-room coffee and tea. Carports, winter plug-ins, freezer available for guests, bowling, legion supermarket and cross-country ski trails. Senior citizens discount, commercial rates, wheelchair accessible, small pets. Highway 97, 100 Mile House, BC V0K 2E0. (604) 395-2255 (call collect). [ADVERTISEMENT] ♿

100 Mile Motel and RV Park. 310 Highway 97. Downtown. Ground level sleeping and housekeeping units. DD phones, cable TV, seniors' rates, campground and RV park with hookups, showers, flush toilets, hiking trail, shopping and restaurants nearby. P.O. Box 112, 100 Mile House, BC V0K 2E0. (604) 395-2234. [ADVERTISEMENT] ▲

West Access Route Log

(continued)

CC 74 (119 km) **PG 203** (326.7 km) **Junction** with road east to **Ruth, Canim** and **Mahood lakes.** Resorts and fishing at all lakes. Camping at Canim Beach Provincial Park (27 miles/43 km); 16 sites. Access to spectacular Canim Falls.

Ponderosa Resort. See display ad this section.

CC 78.2 (125.8 km) **PG 198.8** (319.9 km) 108 Mile Ranch, a recreational community built in the 1970s, was once a cattle ranch. Motel and golf course.

CC 80.5 (129.5 km) **PG 196.5** (316.2 km) Rest area to west beside 108 Mile Lake. Alongside is Heritage Centre with some of the original log buildings from 108 Mile Ranch, and others relocated from 105 Mile.

CC 85 (136.8 km) **PG 192** (309 km) **Big Country KOA.** Located on 60 acres of rolling ranchland 3 miles south of Lac La Hache. Heated swimming pool, free showers, store, gift shop, laundromat, games room. Extra-long shady pull-throughs; shaded grassy tent sites; camping cabin. Full hookup facilities, sani-dump, phone. Pets welcome. VISA, MasterCard. (604) 396-4181. Box 68, Lac La Hache, BC V0K 1T0. [ADVERTISEMENT]

CC 88 (141.6 km) **PG 189** (304.2 km) **LAC LA HACHE** (pop. 800; elev. 2,749 feet/838m), unincorporated. Motels, stores, gas stations and a museum with visitor information. Playground adjacent museum. The community holds a fishing derby in July and a winter carnival in mid-February. Lac La Hache is French for "Ax Lake." There are many stories of how the lake got its name, but Molly Forbes, local historian, says it was named by a French–Canadian *coureur de bois* (voyageur) "because of a small ax he found on its shores."

Lac La Hache, lake char, rainbow and kokanee; good fishing summer and winter (great ice fishing).

CC 90.5 (145.6 km) **PG 186.5** (300.1 km) **Lazy R Campsite.** 24 lovely sites right on Lac La Hache. Full and partial hookups. 20-amp service. Shaded tent sites with tables. Free hot showers for campers. Children's playground. Boat launch. Sani-dump. Good fishing in May/June for kokanee, char and rainbow. Box 57, Lac La Hache, BC V0K 1T0. (604) 396-7368. [ADVERTISEMENT]

CC 92 (148.1 km) **PG 185** (297.7 km) **Fir Crest Resort** (Good Sam). Quiet parklike setting just two minutes from Highway 97, but away from traffic noise. Full hookups including pull-throughs, camping and cabins on the lakeshore. Sandy beach, swimming, games room, groceries, sani-dump, laundromat. Full marina with boat, motor, canoe and tackle rentals. Your hosts, Jim and Virginia Wilson. Show this ad for a 10 percent discount. Phone (604) 396-7337. [ADVERTISEMENT]

Canim Lake and other area lakes offer resorts and fishing. (Gerry Deiter)

CC 93.4 (150.3 km) **PG 183.6** (295.4 km) **Kokanee Bay Motel and Campground.** Relaxation at its finest right on the lakeshore. Fish for kokanee and char or take a refreshing dip. We have a modern, comfortable motel, cabins. Full trailer hookups, grassy tenting area, hot showers, laundromat. Aquabike, boat and canoe rentals. Fishing tackle and ice. Phone (604) 396-7345. Fax (604) 396-4990. [ADVERTISEMENT]

CC 96 (154.5 km) **PG 181** (291.3 km) **Crystal Springs Campsite (Historical) Resort Ltd.** Visit the Cariboo's best. (Good Sam), 8 miles north of Lac La Hache. Park-like setting on lakeshore. Showers, flush toilets, laundromat, full (20- and 30-amp pull-throughs) and partial hookups, boat rentals. New log cabins, winterized. Groceries, tackle, camping supplies, handicrafts. Games room, playground, picnic shelter. Pets on leash. Public beach and boat launch adjacent, fishing. BCAA/AAA. Your hosts, Doug and Lorraine Whitesell. Phone (604) 396-4497. [ADVERTISEMENT]

CC 96 (154.5 km) **PG 181** (291.3 km) Lac La Hache Provincial Park; 83 campsites, boat launch, swimming, picnic tables, hiking trail, fishing and sani-station.

CC 104.4 (168 km) **PG 172.6** (277.7 km) Stop of interest sign commemorating the miners, traders and adventurers who came this way to the Cariboo goldfields in the 1860s.

CC 118.5 (190.7 km) **PG 158.5** (255.1 km) **150 MILE HOUSE,** so named because it was 150 miles from Lillooet on the old Cariboo Wagon Road. The post office, which serves about 1,200 people in the area, was established in 1871. Hotel, restaurant, pub, gas station with repair service and a store open daily. Hunting and fishing licenses available at the store.

CC 119.1 (191.7 km) **PG 157.9** (254.1 km) **Junction** with road to **Quesnel** and **Horsefly lakes**. Horsefly Lake Provincial Park (40 miles/65 km) has 22 campsites. Fishing for rainbow and lake trout.

Williams Lake

CC 128 (206 km) **PG 149** (239.8 km) Located at the junction of Highway 97 and Highway 20 to Bella Coola. **Population:** 18,000. **Elevation:** 1,964 feet/599m. **Emergency Services: Police,** phone 392-6211. **Hospital,** phone 392-4411. **Visitor Information:** Travel Infocentre located on east side of highway just south of the junction of Highways 97 and 20; phone 392-5025. Open year-round.

The administrative and transportation hub of the Cariboo–Chilcotin region, Williams Lake has complete services, including hotels/motels, restaurants, an 18-hole golf course and par 3 golf course, a twin sheet arena and pool complex. The airport, 7 miles/11 km north of town on Highway 97, is served by daily flights to Vancouver and other interior communities.

Located on the shore of the lake of the same name, it was named for Shuswap Indian Chief Willyum. The town grew rapidly with the advent of the Pacific Great Eastern Railway (now B.C. Railway) in 1919, to become a major cattle marketing and shipping centre for the Cariboo–Chilcotin. Today the city has the largest and most active cattleyards in the province. Lumber and mining for copper-molybdenum are the mainstays of the economy.

The famous Williams Lake Stampede, British Columbia's premier rodeo, is held here annually on the July 1 holiday. The four-day event draws contestants from all over Canada and the United States. The rodeo grounds are located in the city.

Highway 20 travels west from Williams Lake 288 miles/449 km to Bella Coola, giving access to the Chilcotin country's excellent fishing, Tweedsmuir Provincial Park, and the remote central coast. The highway is paved for the first 112.5 miles/181 km. At Heckman Pass (elev. 5,000 feet/1,524m), 217 miles/349 km west of

Quesnel Rodeo is part of Billy Barker Days celebration in July. (Judy Parkin, staff)

Williams Lake, the highway descends a section of narrow, switchbacked road with an 18 percent grade for about 12 miles/19 km. Beyond "the hill" the road is paved to Bella Coola.

West Access Route Log

(continued)

CC 136.4 (219.5 km) **PG 140.6** (226.3 km) Wildwood Road; gas station, store, access to private campground.

Wildwood RV Park. See display ad this section. ▲

CC 141.3 (227.3 km) **PG 135.7** (218.4 km) Turnout with litter barrel.

CC 141.8 (228.2 km) **PG 135.2** (217.6 km) **Whispering Willows Outpost Campground and Store**. RV pull-throughs, sani-dump. Power and water hookups, free hot showers, flush toilets. Level spacious treed area for camping. Safe firepits, wood available. Teepee for rent. Play area. Pets and horse trailers welcome, corrals available. Deep Creek runs by Whispering Willows Campground, RR 4, Site 12, Comp. 46, Williams Lake, BC V2G 4M8. [ADVERTISEMENT] ▲

CC 145.3 (233.9 km) **PG 131.7** (211.9 km) Turnout with litter barrel.

CC 147.8 (237.9 km) **PG 129.2** (207.9 km) Replica of a turn-of-the-century roadhouse (food and beverage service only) at junction with side road to settlement of **SODA CREEK**. Soda Creek was the transfer point from wagon road to steamboat for miners bound for Quesnel.

CC 155 (249.4 km) **PG 122** (196.4 km) **McLEESE LAKE,** small community with gas stations, cafe, post office, store, pub, private campground and motel on McLeese Lake. The lake was named for a Fraser River steamboat skipper. Mining and logging are the chief industries here. Public tours of Gibraltar Copper Mine, 11 miles/17.7 km east of the highway (watch for sign just north of here), from June to September. ▲

McLeese Lake, rainbow to 2 lbs., troll using a flasher, worms or flatfish lure.

CC 155.3 (250 km) **PG 121.7** (195.8 km) Turnoff to Horsefly and Likely; resorts and active mining area.

CC 155.5 (250.2 km) **PG 121.5** (195.5 km) Rest area to west overlooking McLeese Lake.

CC 160 (257.5 km) **PG 117** (188.3 km) Turnout with litter barrel to west with plaque about Fraser River paddle-wheelers.

CC 167 (268.8 km) **PG 110** (177 km) Free reaction ferry across the Fraser River at Marguerite.

CC 169.8 (273.2 km) **PG 107.2** (172.5 km) Stone cairn commemorates Fort Alexandria, the last North West Co. fur-trading post established west of the Rockies, built in 1821.

CC 179.5 (288.9 km) **PG 97.5** (156.9 km) **Cariboo Place Campsite**. We have the cariboo in the palm of our hands. Beautiful natural park setting. A convenient and delightful stop, just off Highway 97. Pull-through bays for large units, tenters welcome. Exceptionally clean showers and washrooms. Picnic tables and firepits. Sani-dump station. Electrical hookups. Drinking water. Pets welcome but must be leashed. Rates $12 plus tax. Electrical extra. Open 24 hours. [ADVERTISEMENT]. ▲

CC 180 (289.7 km) **PG 97** (156.1 km) Australian rest area to west with toilets, tables and litter barrels. Private campground to east. ▲

CC 188.5 (303.4 km) **PG 88.5** (142.4 km) Kersley (unincorporated), gas and food.

CC 193.2 (310.9 km) **PG 83.8** (134.9 km) **Mary's Gifts,** located 100 yards east of Highway 97 on Dragon Lake Road. Exciting wonderland of Canadian handcrafted gifts. Moccasins, gold and pewter jewellery, gourmet products, pottery and framed prints. Official Bradford Exchange dealer. Canadian souvenirs. Open daily 9 A.M. to 5 P.M. Easy RV access. Mail orders. Box 32, Dragon Lake Road, RR 1, Quesnel, BC V2J 3H5. (604) 747-2993. [ADVERTISEMENT]

CC 196 (315.4 km) **PG 81** (130.4 km) Loop road east to **Dragon Lake,** a small shallow lake popular with Quesnel families. Camping and fishing for rainbow. ▲

CC 196 (315.4 km) **PG 81** (130.4 km) **Robert's Roost Campsite** located 6 km south of Quesnel and 2 km east of Highway 97 in a parklike setting on beautiful Dragon Lake. Grass sites, both partial and fully serviced. 15- and 30-amp service. Sani-dump, fishing, boat rental, swimming, horseshoes, playground, hot showers, flush toilets and laundromat. Can accommodate any length unit. Limited accommodation. Approved by Good Sam and Tourism BC. Hosts: Bob and Vivian Wurm, 3121 Gook Road, Quesnel, BC V2J 4K7. Phone (604) 747-2015. [ADVERTISEMENT] ▲

CC 197.2 (317.4 km) **PG 79.8** (128.4 km) **Frank's Supermarket.** Just about everything for the fisherman and hunter. Extensive selection of fishing tackle and hunting supplies. Hunting and fishing licenses. Tents, backpacks, sleeping bags and camping accessories. Grocery store. Post office. Open daily. Easy RV access on frontage road. 2290 Hydraulic Rd., Quesnel, BC V2J 4C4. (604) 747-2092. [ADVERTISEMENT]

Quesnel

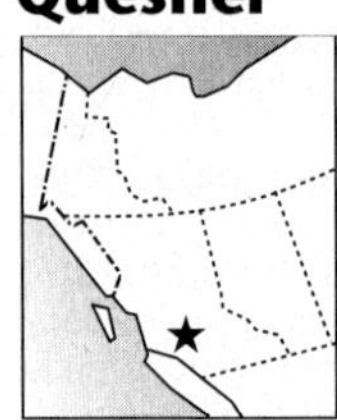

CC 203 (326.7 km) **PG 74** (119.1 km). Located at the confluence of the Fraser and Quesnel rivers. **Population: 8,145. Elevation:** 1,789 feet/545m. **Emergency Services: RCMP,** phone 992-9211. **Ambulance,** phone 992-3211. **Hospital,** phone 992-2181.

Visitor Information: Located on the east side of the highway just north of Quesnel River bridge, in LeBourdais Park. Open year-round. Write Quesnel Travel Infocentre, 703 Carson Ave., Quesnel, BC V2J 2B6; phone 992-8716.

For information on the Cariboo Tourist Region, contact the Cariboo Tourist Assoc., P.O. Box 4900, Williams Lake, BC V2G 2VB; phone toll-free 1-800-663-5885.

Quesnel (kwe NEL) began as a supply town for the miners in the gold rush of the 1860s. The city was named for fur trader

QUESNEL ADVERTISERS

Airport Inn Motel and RV Park .... Ph. (604) 992-5942
Billy Barker Days .... Ph. (604) 992-1234
Dragon Lake Golf Course & Campsite .... Ph. (604) 747-1358
Fountain Motor Motel ...... Ph. (604) 992-7071
Good Knight Inn .... Ph. (604) 992-2187
Mary's Gift Shop .... Dragon Lk. Rd.
Sylvan Motel .... Ph. (604) 992-5611
Tower Inn .... Ph. (604) 992-2201

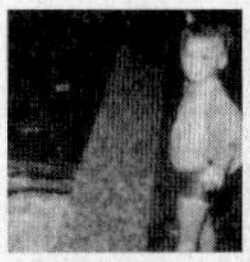

Jules Maurice Quesnel, a member of Simon Fraser's 1808 expedition and later a political figure in Quebec. Today, forestry is the dominant economic force in Quesnel, with two pulp mills, a plywood plant, and five sawmills and planer mills. Check with the Tourist Infocentre about tours.

Accommodations include two hotels, 15 motels, five bed and breakfasts and eight campgrounds. There are gas stations (with diesel), two shopping malls and 45 restaurants offering everything from fast food to fine dining. Golf and a recreation centre with pool are available.

Visitors can take a walking tour of the city along the Riverfront Park trail system. The 3.1-mile/5-km north Quesnel trail starts at Ceal Tingley Park at the confluence of the Fraser and Quesnel rivers. The west Quesnel trail is a 2.7-mile/4.3-km walk through a residential area. Trail information is available at the Tourist Infocentre.

Local attractions include the Quesnel Museum, located adjacent the Tourist Infocentre, which boasts the largest collection of Chinese artifacts west of Ottawa.

There are some interesting hoodoo formations and scenic canyon views a few miles west of town at Pinnacles Provincial Park.

A worthwhile side trip is Highway 26, which intersects Highway 97 at **Milepost CC 206**. This 50-mile/80.5-km paved highway leads to Barkerville Provincial Historic Park, a reconstructed and restored Cariboo gold rush town. (See HIGHWAY 26 side road log opposite page.)

Billy Barker Days, a four-day event held the third full weekend in July, commemorates the discovery of gold at Barkerville in 1858. Held in conjunction with the Quesnel Rodeo, Billy Barker Days is the third largest outdoor family festival in the province. For more information, write Box 4441, Quesnel, BC V2J 3J4.

West Access Route Log

(continued)

CC 206 (331.5 km) **PG 71** (114.3 km) Quesnel airport. **Junction** with Highway 26 to Barkerville and Bowron Lake. See HIGHWAY 26 side road log on pages 45-46.

CC 210 (338 km) **PG 67** (107.8 km) Ten Mile Lake Provincial Park; 142 campsites, picnic area, boat launch, good swimming beach, nature trails, dump station. ▲

10 Mile Lake Provincial Park. See display ad this section. ▲

CC 214.2 (344.7 km) **PG 62.8** (101.1 km) Cottonwood River bridge. Turnout with litter barrels and stop of interest sign at south end of bridge describes railway bridge seen upriver.

CC 218.7 (352 km) **PG 58.3** (93.8 km) Hush Lake rest area to west; toilets, tables, litter barrels.

CC 226 (363.7 km) **PG 51** (82 km) **Cinema 2nd Hand.** General store, groceries. Movie rentals, souvenirs. Local artwork, circle drive. 9 A.M.–9 P.M. every day. Free camping, picnic tables, firepits and wood, toilet, some long pull-throughs, some shady sites, hiking trail, phone, shower available. Welcome to friendly Cinema, BC. [ADVERTISEMENT] ▲

CC 229.6 (369.5 km) **PG 47.4** (76.3 km) Strathnaver (unincorporated), no services.

CC 241 (387.8 km) **PG 36** (58 km) **HIXON** (pop. 1,500) has a post office, two motels, gas stations, grocery stores, two restaurants (one with licensed premises), a pub and private campground. Hixon is the Cariboo's most northerly community. Southbound drivers watch for roadside display about points of interest in the Cariboo region located just north of Hixon. ▲

Hixon Fireplace Inn. See display ad this section.

Paradise Motel. See display ad this section.

Canyon Creek Campsite (Good Sam/CAA). Very long pull-through sites (100 feet) with 30 amps and water. Full hookups. Tent spaces in the trees with firepits. Modern restroom, hot showers, laundromat,

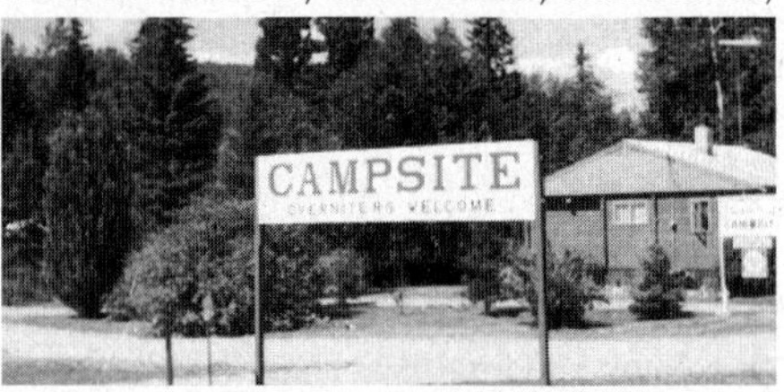

sani-station, children's playground. Grocery stores, restaurant and pub within easy walking distance. Nature trail by the creek. Swimming hole and fishing pools (in season). Pets welcome, even horses. Aussi Tim welcomes you. (604) 998-4307. Box 390, Hixon, BC V0K 1S0. [ADVERTISEMENT] ▲

CC 247.6 (398.5 km) **PG 29.4** (47.3 km) Woodpecker rest area to west; toilets, tables, litter barrels.

CC 257.7 (414.7 km) **PG 19.3** (31 km) Stoner (unincorporated), no services.

CC 261.8 (421.3 km) **PG 15.2** (24.5 km) Red Rock (unincorporated); mini-mart; ice; gas station with diesel; pay phone.

CC 268.3 (431.8 km) **PG 8.7** (14 km) **Bee Lazee RV Park, Campground & Honey Sales.** See display ad this section. ♿▲

CC 270.6 (435.5 km) **PG 6.4** (10.3 km) Junction with bypass road to Yellowhead 16 East. Keep left for Prince George; continue straight ahead for Jasper and Edmonton. If you are headed east on Yellowhead Highway 16 for Jasper or Edmonton, turn to **Milepost E 450** in the YELLOWHEAD HIGHWAY 16 section and read the log back to front.

Highway 26 Log

This 50-mile/80.5-km paved road leads to Barkerville Provincial Historic Park. **Distance from Highway 97 junction (J) is shown.**

J 0 Junction with Highway 97 at **Milepost CC 206.** Highway 26 climbs steeply up through the jackpine forests.

J 15.8 (25.5 km) Cottonwood House Provincial Park, a restored and furnished log roadhouse built in 1864. Picnicking and guided tours by costumed docents; open May to September.

J 21.1 (34 km) Viewpoint to south.

J 26 (42 km) Rest area to north.

J 26.7 (43 km) Historical stop of interest marker for Charles Morgan Blessing's grave. Blessing, from Ohio, was murdered on his way to Barkerville in 1866. His killer was caught when he gave Blessing's keepsake gold nugget stickpin, in the shape of an angel, to a Barkerville dance hall girl. His murderer, John Barry, was the only white man hanged in the Cariboo during the gold rush.

J 27 (43.5 km) Troll's Ski Resort; cross-country and downhill.

J 36.6 (59 km) Stanley Road to south; gold rush cemetery.

J 39.5 (63.5 km) Gravel turnout at start of Devil's Canyon, a narrow winding stretch of road above Chisholm Creek.

J 42 (67.5 km) Rest area at Slough Creek.

J 43.8 (70.5 km) North shore of **Jack of Clubs Lake;** fishing for rainbows, lake trout and Dolly Varden. Picnic tables and boat launch.

J 45.4 (73 km) **WELLS** (pop. 300) offers all visitor facilities, including motels, restaurants, groceries and gas. Wells dates to the 1930s when the Cariboo Gold Quartz Mine, promoted and developed by Fred Wells, brought hundreds of workers to this valley. The mine closed in 1967, but the town has continued as a service center and attraction for tourists. There are numerous art galleries and gift shops, some housed in refurbished 1930s-style buildings. Guided and self-guided tours of the town are available. A museum with displays of local mining history is open daily from June to Sept.

Recreation in the area includes hiking, skiing, curling and snowmobiling. The local Legion hosts horseshoes and bocci tournaments, has a pub, and offers potluck suppers throughout the year.

J 48.5 (78 km) Barkerville Provincial Park Forest Rose Campground to north. Lowhee Campground to south; 170 campsites, picnic areas and dump stations. ▲

J 49 (79 km) Gravel road leads north 11 miles/18 km to Bowron Lakes Provincial Park, noted for its interconnecting chain of lakes and the resulting 72-mile/116-km canoe circuit, which takes from seven to 10 days to complete. Visitor information available at registration centre next to main parking lot where canoeists must register and pay circuit fees. Groups are limited to six people.

There are two private lodges at the north end of the lake with restaurants and canoe rentals. Provincial park campground has 25 sites and a boat

Costumed docents lead guided tours of Cottonwood House. (Tom Parkin)

launch. ▲

J 49.7 (80 km) Road to Barkerville cemetery and access to Government Hill provincial campground. ▲

J 50 (80.5 km) **BARKERVILLE,** a provincial historic park; open year-round. Visitor information at museum.

Barkerville was named for miner Billy Barker, who struck gold on Williams Creek. The resulting gold rush in 1862 created Barkerville. Virtually a ghost town when the provincial government began restoration in 1958, today Barkerville's buildings and boardwalks are faithful restorations or reconstructions from the town's heyday. Visitors can pan for gold, shop at the old-time general store, watch a blacksmith at work, or take in a show at the Theatre Royal. It is best to visit between mid-June and Labour Day, when the Theatre Royal offers performances daily except Fridays, and all exhibits are open.

History comes alive at Barkerville thanks to five performers who each represent an actual citizen of the town in 1870. These street interpreters discuss "current" events with visitors, conduct tours and stage daily dramas throughout the summer.

Beyond Main Street, the Cariboo Wagon Road leads on (for pedestrians only) to Richfield, 1 mile/1.6 km, to the courthouse of "Hanging" Judge Begbie.

Return to Milepost CC 206
West Access Route

CC 273 (439.3 km) **PG 4** (6.4 km) **Southpark RV Park.** See display ad this section. ▲

CC 273.4 (440 km) **PG 3.6** (5.8 km) Access to Prince George airport to east.

CC 274 (440.9 km) **PG 3** (4.8 km) **Sintich Trailer Park.** See display ad this section. ▲

CC 275.2 (442.8 km) **PG 1.8** (2.8 km) Bridge over the Fraser River. Turn right at north end of bridge then left at stop sign for city centre via Queensway. This is the easiest access for Fort George Park; follow Queensway to 20th Avenue and turn east.

Continue straight ahead for Highway 16 entrance to city.

CC 276 (444.1 km) **PG 1** (1.6 km) **Junction** of Highway 97 with Yellowhead 16 West. Description of Prince George follows. If you are headed west on Yellowhead Highway 16 for Prince Rupert, turn to **Milepost PG 0** in the YELLOWHEAD HIGHWAY 16 section. Prince Rupert is port of call for Alaska state ferries and BC Ferries (see MARINE ACCESS ROUTES section for details).

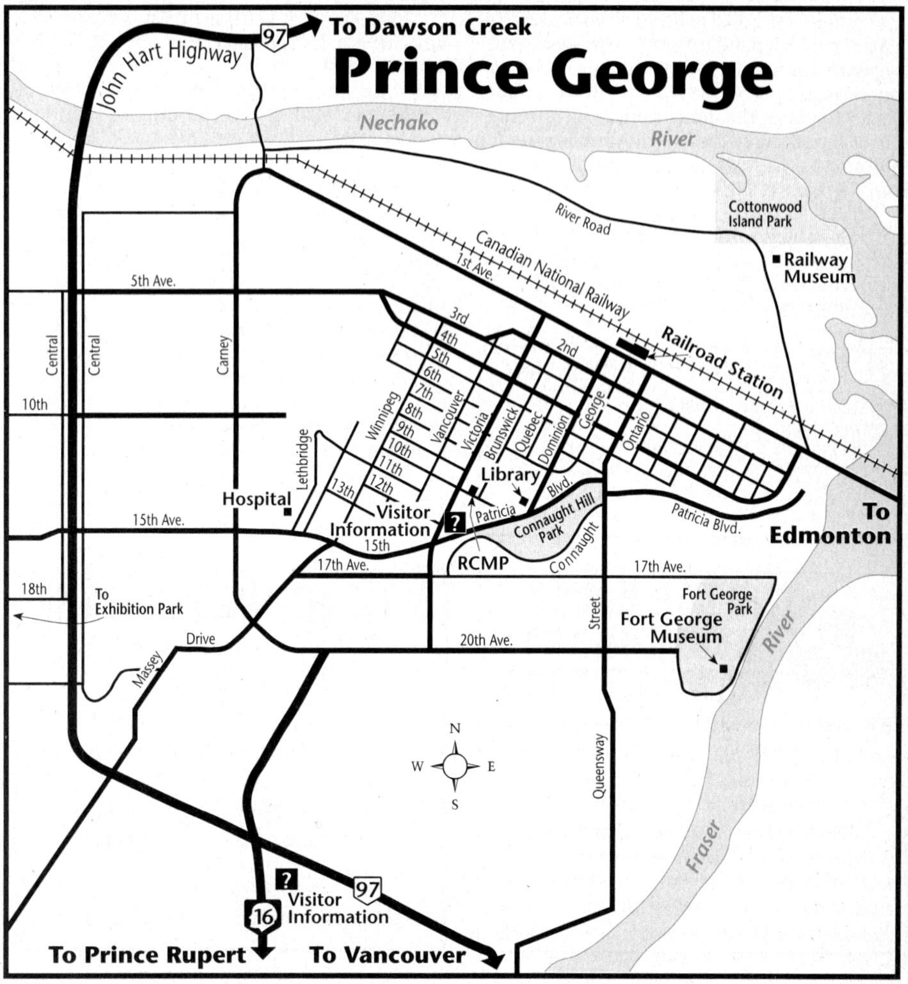

Prince George

CC 277 (445.8 km) **Population:** 71,000, area 160,000. **Emergency Services: RCMP,** phone 562-3371, emergency only, phone 911. **Fire Department,** phone 911. **Ambulance,** 24-hour service, phone 911. **Poison Control Centre,** phone 565-2442. **Hospital,** Prince George Regional, phone 565-2000; emergency, phone 565-2444.

Visitor Information: Tourism Prince George, Dept. MP, 1198 Victoria St., phone 562-3700 or fax 563-3584. Open year-round, 8:30 A.M. to 5 P.M. weekdays September to June, daily in July and August. Visitor centre, junction Yellowhead 16 and Highway 97; open daily mid-May to Labour Day, 9 A.M. to 8 P.M., phone 563-5493.

Elevation: 1,868 feet/569m. **Climate:** The inland location is tempered by the protection of mountains. The average annual frost-free period is 85 days, with 1,793 hours of bright sunshine. Dry in summer; chinooks off and on during winter which, accompanied by a western flow of air, break up the cold weather. Summer temperatures average 72°F/22°C with lows to 46°F/8°C. **Radio:** CKPG 550, CJCI 620, BC-FM 94.3, CBC-FM 91.5, C-101 FM. **Television:** 11 channels via cable. **Newspaper:** *The Citizen* (daily except Sunday); *Prince George This Week* (Wednesday).

Prince George is located at the confluence of the Nechako and Fraser rivers, near the geographical centre of British Columbia. It is the hub of the trade and travel routes of the province, located at the junction of Yellowhead Highway 16 — linking Prince Rupert on the west coast with the Interior of Canada — and Highway 97, which runs south to Vancouver and north to Dawson Creek.

In the early 1800s, Simon Fraser of the North West Trading Co. erected a post here which he named Fort George in honour of the reigning English monarch. In 1906, survey parties for the transcontinental Grand Trunk Pacific Railway (later Canadian National Railways) passed through the area, and with the building of the railroad a great land boom took place. The city was incorporated in 1915 under the name Prince George. Old Fort George is now a park and picnic spot and the site of Fort George Museum.

Prince George
To Dawson Creek
John Hart Highway
Nechako River
River Road
Cottonwood Island Park
Railway Museum
Canadian National Railway
Railroad Station
Hospital
Library
Visitor Information
RCMP
Connaught Hill Park
To Edmonton
Fort George Park
Fort George Museum
Fraser River
To Exhibition Park
Visitor Information
To Prince Rupert
To Vancouver

Prince George is primarily an industrial centre, fairly dependent on the lumber industry, with three pulp mills, sawmills, planers, dry kilns, a plywood plant and two chemical plants to serve the pulp mills. Oil refining, mining and heavy construction are other major area industries. The Prince George Forest Region is the largest in the province.

Prince George is the focal point of the central Interior for financial and professional services, equipment and wholesale firms, machine shops and many services for the timber industry.

Agriculture in central British Columbia is basically a forage-livestock business, for which the climate and soils are well suited. Dairying and beef are the major livestock enterprises, with minor production in sheep and poultry.

ACCOMMODATIONS

Prince George offers five hotels, 17 motels, nine trailer parks and almost two dozen bed and breakfasts. Most accommodations are within easy reach of the business district and the more than 80 restaurants in the downtown area. Most stores are open seven days a week. The usual hours of operation are: Sunday, noon to 5 P.M.; Saturday and Monday through Wednesday, 9:30 A.M. to 6 P.M.; Thursday and Friday, 9:30 A.M. to 9 P.M.

The city campground at 18th Avenue, across from Exhibition Grounds, open mid-May to mid-September, provides trailer spaces, tenting, showers, washrooms and dump station. RV parks are also located just south and north of town on Highway 97, and west and east of town on Yellowhead Highway 16. ▲

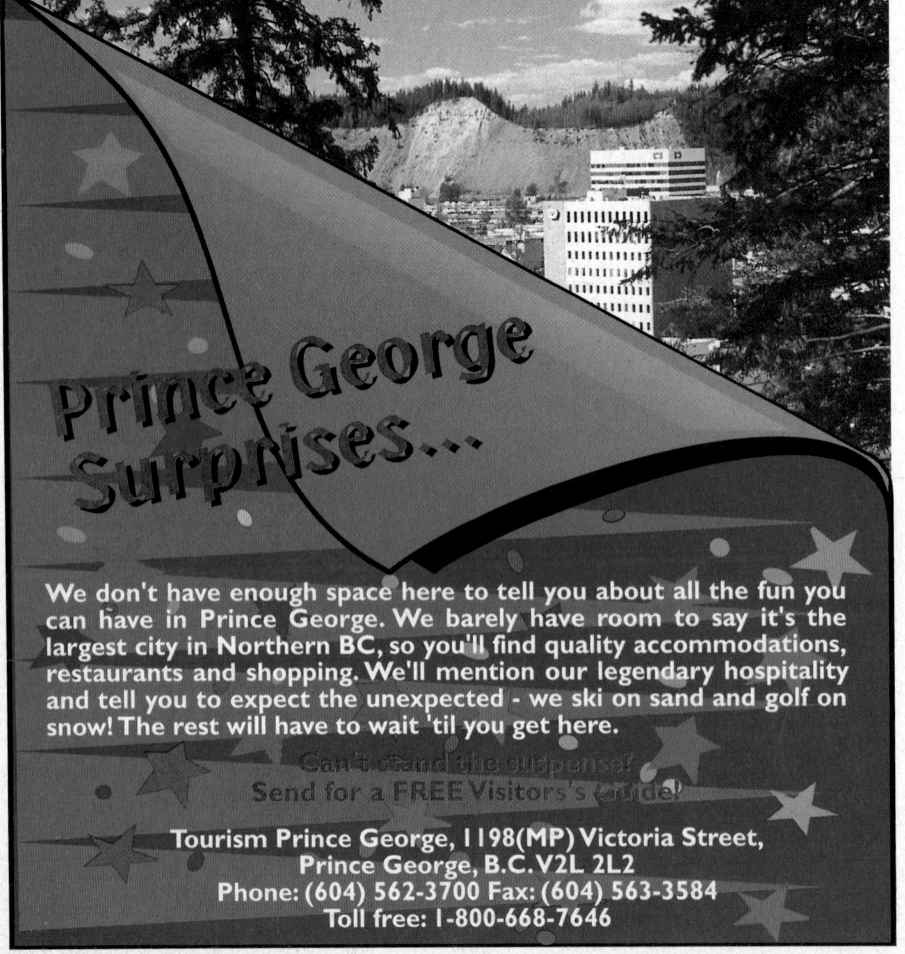

TRANSPORTATION

Air: Prince George airport is southeast of the city, serviced by Canadian Airlines International and Air BC. Limousine service to and from the airport.

Railroad: VIA Rail connects Prince George with Prince Rupert and Jasper, AB. Daily passenger service south to Vancouver via British Columbia Railway.

Bus: Greyhound. City bus service is provided by Prince George Transit & Charter Ltd.

ATTRACTIONS

City View: Follow Connaught Drive to the viewpoint at Connaught Hill Park for a panoramic view of the city.

City Landmarks: Centennial Fountain at the corner of 7th Avenue and Dominion Street depicts the early history of Prince George in mosaic tile. A cairn at Fort George Park commemorates Sir Alexander Mackenzie.

Prince George Art Gallery on 15th Avenue features regional, national and international artists.

Fort George Park is the largest park in Prince George and a good stop for travelers with its playgrounds, picnic tables, barbecue facilities and museum. The Fort George Regional Museum displays artifacts from the pioneer days through 1920. The museum is open daily in summer from 10 A.M. to 5 P.M.; phone 562-1612. The Fort George Railway operates on weekends and holidays at the park from a railway building patterned after the original Grand Trunk Pacific stations.

Cottonwood Island Park, located on the Nechako River (see city map), has picnic facilities and extensive nature trails.

Giscome Portage Regional Park contains the historic Huble Homestead. Tour the Huble House, built in 1912, and the other carefully reconstructed farm buildings in this beautiful setting. Located north of Prince George on Highway 97; turn off highway at **Milepost PG 26.9.**

Prince George Railway Museum, located adjacent Cottonwood Island Park, has an excellent selection of antique rail stock.

PRINCE GEORGE ADVERTISERS

Arctic RV Service Centre.........3323 Hart Hwy.
Big John's R.V. Clinic..888 Lower Patricia Blvd.
Esther's Inn...............10th Ave. & Commercial
Fifth Ave. Bed & Breakfast......................Ph. (604) 562-1315
Grama's Inn..........................901 Central Ave.
Inland Spring and Axle Ltd. ....1852 Quinn St.
Log House Restaurant and R.V. Park, The...........................Tabor Lake
P.G. Hi-Way Motel..................1737 20th Ave.
Prince George KOA Campground.........................3 miles W. on Yellowhead Hwy. 16
Red Cedar Inn & Campground.........................3 miles W. on Yellowhead Hwy. 16
Spruceland Inn Motel........................Hwy. 97 & 15th Ave.
Tourism Prince George..........1198 Victoria St.

Attractions include a 1914 Grand Trunk Railway station and restored dining car.

Golf Courses: Aspen Grove Golf Club is 9 miles/14.5 km south of the city; Yellowhead Grove Golf Club, Pine Valley Golf Club and Prince George Golf and Curling Club are on Yellowhead Highway 16 West.

Swimming: Four Seasons Swimming Pool at the corner of 7th Avenue and Dominion Street has a pool, waterslide, diving tank and fitness centre. Open to the public afternoons and evenings.

Rockhounding: The hills and river valleys in the area provide abundant caches of Omineca agate and Schmoos. For more information, contact Prince George Rock and Gem Club, phone 562-4526; or Spruce City Rock and Gem Club, phone 562-1013.

Tennis Courts: A total of 20 courts currently available to the public at three places — 20th Avenue near the entrance to Fort George Park, at Massey Drive in Carrie Jane Gray Park, and on Ospika Boulevard in the Lakewood Secondary School complex.

Industrial Tours are available from mid-May through August by contacting Tourism Prince George at 562-3700. Tours, which are on weekdays only, include Northwood Pulp and Timber and North Central Plywoods. Tours of Prince George Pulp and Intercon Pulp are available on request. For tours of Pacific Western Brewing Co., phone 562-1131.

Special Events: Elks May Day celebration and the Prince George Regional Forest Exhibition in May; Folkfest on July 1, Canada Day; live theatre through July and August; Simon Fraser Days in late July–early August includes raft races, International Food Festival; Annual Sandblast Skiing in August; Prince George Exhibition in August; Oktoberfest in October; and the winter Mardi Gras Festival in mid-February. Details on these and other events are available from Tourism Prince George.

Side Trips: Prince George is the starting point for some of the finest holiday country

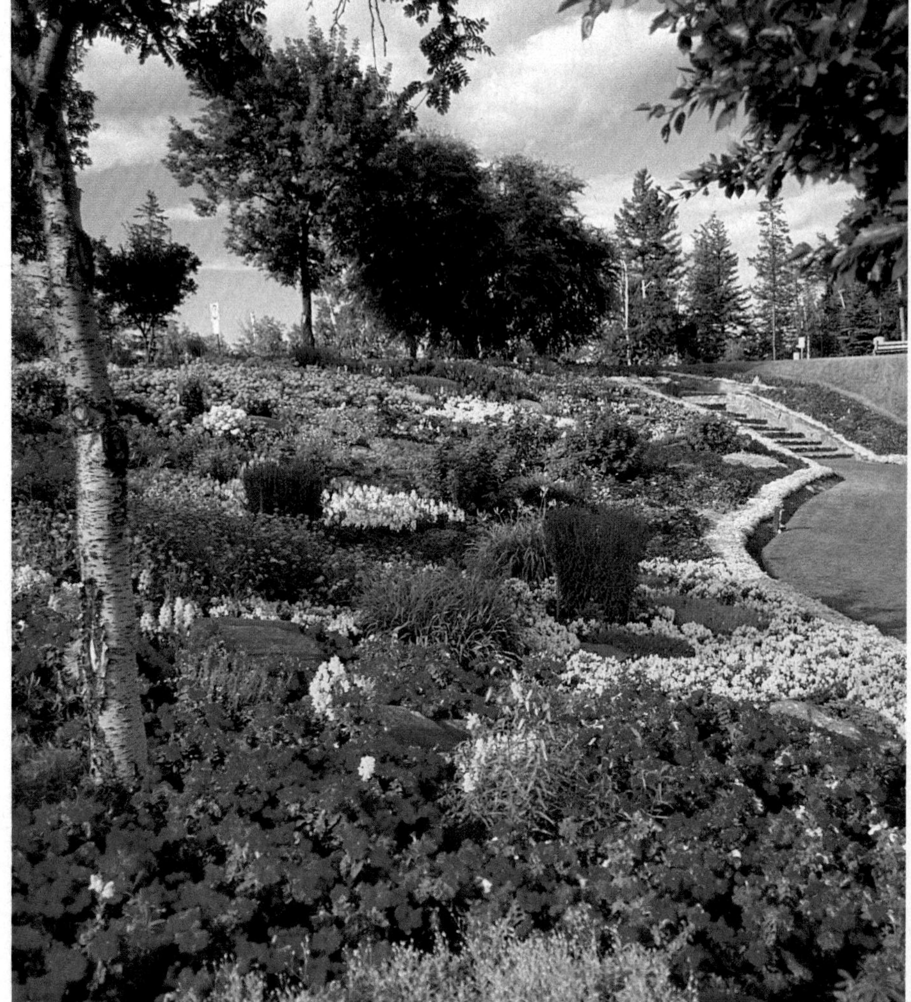

Connaught Hill Park offers floral display and city viewpoint. (Earl L. Brown, staff)

in the province. There are numerous lakes and resorts nearby, among them: Bednesti Lake, 30 miles/48 km west of Prince George; Cluculz Lake, 44 miles/71 km west; Purden Lake, 42 miles/68 km east; and Tabor Lake, 6 miles/10 km east. Day-use only sandy beaches are found at Bear Lake, 40 miles/66 km north, and West Lake, 15 miles/25 km west.

AREA FISHING: Highways 16 and 97 are the ideal routes for the sportsman, with year-round fishing and easy access to lakes and rivers. Hunters and fishermen stop over in Prince George as the jumping-off place for some of North America's finest big game hunting and fishing. For information regarding hunting and fishing contact: Rod & Gun Club, P.O. Box 924, Prince George; Spruce City Wildlife Assoc., in Prince George, phone 564-6859; or Tourism Prince George, phone 562-3700. A comprehensive fishing guide booklet is available from Tourism Prince George.

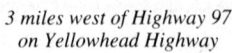

West Access Route Log

(continued)

HIGHWAY 97/HART HIGHWAY

The John Hart Highway, completed in 1952, was named for the former B.C. premier who sponsored its construction. The highway is a two-lane paved highway with both straight stretches and winding stretches.

This section of the log shows distance from Prince George (PG) followed by distance from Dawson Creek (DC).

PG 0 DC 250 (402.3 km) John Hart Bridge over the Nechako River. The four-lane highway extends approximately 6.5 miles/10.5 km northbound through the commercial and residential suburbs of Prince George.

PG 1.5 (2.4 km) **DC 248.5** (399.9 km) Truck weigh scales to west.

PG 2.5 (4 km) **DC 247.5** (398.3 km) RV service centre.

PG 6.4 (10.3 km) **DC 247.5** (243.6 km) **Hartway RV Park**. Shaded, fully-serviced sites. Pull-throughs. Free hot showers, laundromat, 30-amp, cable TV. Groceries nearby. Phone. On-site antique and gift shop. On south Kelly Road adjacent to highway.

Northbound access at stop light (Handlen Road Junction); southbound at off-ramp at RV park. 7729 South Kelly Rd., Prince George, BC V2K 3H5. (604) 962-2465. [ADVERTISEMENT]

PG 6.5 (10.5 km) **DC 243.5** (391.9 km) Two-lane highway (with passing lanes) begins abruptly northbound.

PG 9.5 (15.3 km) **DC 240.5** (387 km) **Hart Highway Campground.** See display ad this section.

PG 14.6 (23.5 km) **DC 235.4** (378.8 km) Salmon River bridge. Litter barrel and river access to west at north end of bridge.

PG 14.7 (23.6 km) **DC 235.3** (378.7 km) **Salmon Valley Resort** campgrounds and convenience store, on over 20 acres along the scenic Salmon River. All facilities are wheelchair accessible including showers. 50 treed sites, 8 pull-throughs, all with fire rings, tables, laundry. Limited water and power 15-30 amp. Swimming and camping on the Salmon that's second to none. Fair fishing for rainbows, grayling and spring salmon. "Home of the Happy Camper." Phone (604) 971-2212. Fax (604) 971-2229. [ADVERTISEMENT]

PG 16.4 (26.4 km) **DC 233.6** (357.9 km) Highway overpass crosses railroad tracks.

PG 22 (35.4 km) **DC 228** (366.9 km) Gravel turnouts both sides of highway.

PG 26.5 (42.6 km) **DC 223.5** (359.7 km) Paved turnout to east with litter barrels and point of interest sign about Crooked River Forest Recreation Area.

PG 26.9 (43.3 km) **DC 223.1** (359 km) Access west to Giscome Portage regional park via Mitchell Road; narrow road. Site of Huble Farm, a 1912 homestead.

PG 28.2 (45.4 km) **DC 221.8** (356.9 km) Turnoff to west for **Summit Lake**, a resort area popular with Prince George residents; lake char and rainbow fishing spring and fall.

PG 29.3 (47.2 km) **DC 220.7** (355.2 km) Westcoast Energy compressor station.

PG 30.7 (49.4 km) **DC 219.3** (352.9 km) Second turnoff to west for Summit Lake.

PG 36.6 (58.9 km) **DC 213.4** (343.4 km) Cottonwood Creek.

PG 38.8 (62.4 km) **DC 211.2** (339.9 km) Paved turnout with litter barrel.

PG 40.6 (65.3 km) **DC 209.4** (337 km) Railroad crossing.

PG 42 (67.6 km) **DC 208** (334.7 km) Slow down for sharp turn across railroad tracks.

PG 43.3 (69.7 km) **DC 206.7** (332.6 km) Turnoff to west for Bear Lake Campground in Crooked River Provincial Park; 90 campsites, flush toilets, tables, firepits, dump station. Also horseshoe pits, volleyball, playground, trails and swimming. Powerboats prohibited. Picnic shelter with wood stove. Fee is $9.50. **Crooked River** and area lakes have fair fishing for rainbow, Dolly Varden, grayling and whitefish.

PG 43.9 (70.6 km) **DC 206.1** (331.7 km) Turnoff to west for Bear Lake picnic area in Crooked River Provincial Park; fishing and swimming. Highway 97 follows the Crooked River north to McLeod Lake.

PG 44.8 (72.1 km) **DC 205.2** (330.1 km) **BEAR LAKE** (unincorporated); gas, diesel, propane, grocery, restaurant, motel, RV park, gift shop, post office and ambulance station. Highway maintenance camp.

Grizzly Inn, Restaurant, Motel & RV Park. See display ad this section

PG 50.7 (81.6 km) **DC 199.3** (320.7 km) Angusmac Creek.

PG 54.2 (87.2 km) **DC 195.8** (315.1 km) Tumbler Ridge branch line British Columbia Railway connects Tumbler Ridge with the B.C. Railway and Canadian National Railway, allowing for shipments of coal from

Tumbler Ridge to Ridley Island near Prince Rupert.

PG 55.6 (89.5 km) **DC 194.4** (312.8 km) Large gravel turnout with litter barrel to west.

PG 56.1 (90.3 km) **DC 193.9** (312 km) Large gravel turnout with litter barrel to west.

PG 57 (91.7 km) **DC 193** (310.6 km) Large gravel turnout with litter barrel to west.

PG 60.8 (97.8 km) **DC 189.2** (304.5 km) Turnout with litter barrel to east.

PG 62.4 (100.4 km) **DC 187.6** (301.9 km) Large gravel turnout with litter barrel to east.

PG 65.2 (104.9 km) **DC 184.8** (297.4 km) Lomas Creek.

PG 67.9 (109.3 km) **DC 182.1** (293 km) Large paved rest area to west beside small lake; litter barrels, picnic tables and pit toilets.

PG 68.8 (110.7 km) **DC 181.2** (291.6 km) 42 Mile Creek.

PG 71.8 (115.5 km) **DC 178.2** (286.8 km) **Whiskers Bay Resort** has beautiful lakeside camping spots on a quiet bay, some with electricity and water. Cabins with showers, fridges and cooking facilities. Fishing is right off our dock or in the many surrounding lakes. Sunsets are sensational and hummingbirds are bountiful. The cafe offers breakfast, lunch, wonderful burgers, homemade pies, soups, the best coffee on the highway, and real northern hospitality. Come visit us! [ADVERTISEMENT] ▲

PG 76.6 (123.3 km) **DC 173.4** (279.1 km) First view northbound of McLeod Lake and view of Whisker's Point.

PG 77.7 (125 km) **DC 172.3** (277.3 km) Turnoff to west for Whisker's Point Provincial Park on McLeod Lake. This is an exceptionally nice campground with a paved loop road, 69 level gravel sites, a dump station, tap water, flush toilets, boat ramp, fire rings, firewood and picnic tables. Also horseshoe pits, volleyball, playground and picnic shelter. Camping fee is $9.50. Boat launch, swimming, changehouse, sandy beach and fishing. ▲

McLeod Lake has fair fishing for rainbow, lake char and Dolly Varden, spring and fall, trolling is best.

PG 81.4 (131 km) **DC 168.6** (271.3 km) Lodge (closed).

PG 84 (135.2 km) **DC 166** (267.1 km) Food, gas, camping and lodging.

PG 84.5 (136 km) **DC 165.5** (266.3 km) **FORT McLEOD** (unincorporated) has a gas station, grocery, motel and cafe. A monument here commemorates the founding of Fort McLeod, oldest permanent settlement west of the Rockies and north of San Francisco. Founded in 1805 by Simon Fraser as a trading post for the North West Trading Co., the post was named by Fraser for Archie McLeod.

PG 84.7 (136.3 km) **DC 165.3** (266 km) **McLEOD LAKE** (unincorporated), post office, store and lodging.

PG 85 (136.8 km) **DC 165** (265.5 km) Turnoff for Carp Lake Provincial Park, 20 miles/32 km west via a gravel road; 105 campsites on Carp and War lakes, picnic tables, firepits, boat launch, fishing and swimming. Also horseshoe pits, playground and picnic shelter with wood stove. Fee is $9.50. Park access road follows the McLeod River to Carp Lake. ▲

Carp Lake, rainbow June through September; special restrictions in effect, check current posted information. **McLeod River**, rainbow from July, fly-fishing only.

PG 85.6 (137.8 km) **DC 164.4** (264.6 km) Paved turnout with litter barrel to west.

PG 87.6 (141 km) **DC 162.4** (261.4 km) Westcoast Energy compressor station and McLeod Lake school.

PG 89.8 (144.5 km) **DC 160.2** (257.8 km) Turnoff to west for Tudyah Lake Provincial Park; 36 campsites, tables, firerings, firewood, pit toilets, drinking water. Also swimming, sandy beach, boat ramp, fishing. Fee is $7. ▲

Tudyah Lake, shore access, rainbow, Dolly Varden and some grayling in summer and late fall. **Pack River** (flows into Tudyah Lake), fishing for grayling, June 1 to July 1; rainbow, June 10 to November; large Dolly Varden, Sept. 15 to Oct. 10, spinning.

PG 89.9 (144.7 km) **DC 160.1** (257.6 km) Bear Creek bridge.

PG 93.9 (151.1 km) **DC 156.1** (251.2 km) Gas, food and lodging.

PG 94.7 (152.4 km) **DC 155.3** (249.9 km) Parsnip River bridge. This is the Rocky Mountain Trench, marking the western boundary of the Rocky Mountains. Northbound motorists begin gradual climb through the Misinchinka then Hart ranges of the Rocky Mountains.

Parsnip River, good fishing for grayling and Dolly Varden, some rainbow, best from August to October; a boat is necessary.

PG 95.2 (153.2 km) **DC 154.8** (249.1 km) **Junction** with Highway 39 (paved), which leads 18 miles/29 km to the community of Mackenzie (description follows). Food, gas, lodging, camping and tourist information at junction. Signed trailheads along Highway 39 are part of the Mackenzie Demonstration Forest. There are eight self-guiding trails in the demonstration forest, each focusing on an aspect of forest management. Interpretive signs are posted along each trail.

Mackenzie Junction Cafe. See display ad this section. ▲

Mackenzie

Located 18 miles/29 km northwest of the John Hart Highway 97 via Highway 39. **Population:** 5,550. **Emergency Services: RCMP,** phone 997-3288. **Hospital,** 12 beds. **Ambulance,** phone 1-563-5433. **Visitor Information:** At the railway caboose located at the junction of Highways 97 and 39. Or write the Chamber of Commerce, Box 880, Mackenzie, BC V0J 2C0; (604) 997-5459.

Elevation: 2,300 feet/701m. **Radio:** CKMK 1240, CKPG 1240; CBC-FM 990. **Television:** Channels 6, 9 and cable.

A large, modern, planned community, Mackenzie was built in 1965. It lies at the south end of Williston Lake, the largest manmade reservoir on the continent. Construction of the new town in what had been just wilderness was sparked by the Peace River Dam project and the need to attract skilled employees for industrial growth. Mackenzie was incorporated in May 1966 under "instant town" legislation; the first residents moved here in July 1966. Industry here includes mining and forestry, with five sawmills, a paper mill and two pulp mills.

On display in Mackenzie is the "world's largest tree crusher." The 56-foot-long electrically powered Le Tourneau G175 tree crusher was used in clearing land at the Peace River Power Project in the mid-1960s.

Attractions include swimming, waterskiing and boating at Morfee Lake, a 10-minute walk from town. There are boat launches on both Morfee Lake and Williston Lake reservoir. Boat rentals and scuba equipment available at Morfee Lake. Good view of Mackenzie and Williston Lake reservoir from the top of Morfee Mountain (elev. 5,961 feet/1,817m); check with Infocentre for directions. There are self-guided hiking trails at John Dahl Regional Park, located behind the recreation centre. The big summer event here is the Blue Grass Festival, held in August.

Mackenzie has all visitor facilities, including motels, restaurants, shopping malls, gas stations, swimming pool, tennis courts, nine-hole golf course and other recreation facilities. There is also a paved 5,000-foot/1,524-m airstrip.

There is a free municipal RV park with 20 sites, flush toilets, showers and sani-dump. Fishing for rainbow, Dolly Varden, arctic char and grayling in **Williston Lake.** ▲

MACKENZIE ADVERTISERS

Alexander Mackenzie Hotel ....Mackenzie Blvd.
District of Mackenzie ....Ph. (604) 997-5459
Paradise Fun Spot! ....At the beach on Morfee Lake

West Access Route Log
(continued)

PG 95.2 (153.2 km) **DC 154.8** (249.1 km) **Junction** with Highway 39 to Mackenzie; food, gas, lodging and tourist booth at junction.

PG 95.5 (153.7 km) **DC 154.5** (248.6 km) Highway crosses railroad tracks.

PG 98.9 (158.2 km) **DC 151.1** (243.2 km) Gravel turnout with litter barrel to east.

PG 106 (170.6 km) **DC 144** (231.7 km) Turnout with litter barrel to east.

PG 108.4 (174.4 km) **DC 141.6** (227.9 km) Highway maintenance yard.

PG 108.5 (174.6 km) **DC 141.5** (227.7 km) Bridge over Honeymoon Creek.

PG 109.6 (176.4 km) **DC 140.4** (225.9 km) Powerlines crossing highway carry electricity south from hydro dams in the Hudson Hope area. (See HUDSON'S HOPE LOOP section.)

PG 110.5 (177.8 km) **DC 139.5** (224.5 km) Slow down for sharp curve across railroad tracks.

PG 112.3 (180.7 km) **DC 137.7** (221.6 km) Bridge over Rolston Creek; dirt turnout by small falls to west.

Watch for frost heaves next 9 miles/14.6 km northbound.

PG 115.3 (185.6 km) **DC 134.7** (216.8 km) Bijoux Falls Provincial Park; pleasant picnic area adjacent falls on west side of highway. This day-use area has paved parking for 50 cars, pit toilets and picnic tables. Good photo opportunity.

Misinchinka River, southeast of the highway; fishing for grayling, whitefish and Dolly Varden.

PG 116.3 (187.2 km) **DC 133.7** (215.2 km) Highway crosses under railroad.

PG 119.3 (191.8 km) **DC 130.8** (210.5 km) Crossing Pine Pass (elev. 3,068 feet/935m), the highest point on the John Hart-Peace River Highway. Beautiful view of the Rockies to the northeast. Good highway over pass; steep grade southbound.

PG 119.4 (192.2 km) **DC 130.6** (210.2 km) Turnoff to Powder King Ski Village. Skiing Nov. to late April; chalet with ski shop, cafeteria, restaurant and lounge, hostel-style hotel. This area receives an annual average snowfall of 495 inches. Campground at Powder King Ski Village, open in summer. ▲

Powder King Ski Village. See display ad this section. ▲

PG 121.4 (195.4 km) **DC 128.6** (207 km) Viewpoint to east with point of interest sign about Pine Pass and view of Azouzetta Lake. Pit toilet and litter barrels.

Watch for frost heaves next 9 miles/14.6 km southbound.

PG 122.4 (197 km) **DC 127.6** (205.3 km) Pine Valley Park, open year-round; gas station, propane, diesel, cafe, lodge, campground on **Azouzetta Lake.** Very scenic spot. Spectacular hiking on Murray Mountain Trail; inquire at lodge for details. A scuba diving school operates at Azouzetta

Lake in summer. Fishing for rainbow (stocked lake) to 1 1/2 lbs., flies or lures, July to October. Boat launch. ▲

Pine Valley Park. See display ad this section. ▲

PG 125.5 (202 km) **DC 124.5** (200.3 km) Microwave station and receiving dish to west.

PG 125.7 (202.3 km) **DC 124.3** (200 km) Westcoast Energy station.

PG 128.7 (207.1 km) **DC 121.3** (195.2 km) Power lines cross highway.

PG 131.1 (211 km) **DC 118.9** (191.3 km) Turnout with litter barrel.

PG 140.6 (226.3 km) **DC 109.4** (176.1 km) Bridge over Link Creek.

PG 141.4 (227.5 km) **DC 108.6** (174.8 km) Gravel turnout with litter barrels.

PG 142.3 (229 km) **DC 107.7** (173.3 km) Bridge over West Pine River.

PG 142.8 (229.8 km) **DC 107.2** (172.5 km) Bridge over West Pine River.

PG 143 (230.1 km) **DC 107** (172.2 km) Paved rest area with litter barrel beside Pine River.

PG 143.4 (230.8 km) **DC 106.6** (171.6 km) Bridge over West Pine River, B.C. Railway overpass.

PG 144.3 (232.2 km) **DC 105.7** (170.1 km) Food, gas, towing, lodging and camping. ▲

Silver Sands Lodge. See display ad this section. ▲

PG 146.1 (235.1 km) **DC 103.9** (167.2 km) Cairns Creek.

PG 146.9 (236.4 km) **DC 103.1** (165.9 km) Gravel access road to Pine River to south.

PG 148.2 (238.5 km) **DC 101.8** (163.8 km) LeMoray (unincorporated). Lodge to north of highway (status of services unknown).

PG 148.3 (238.7 km) **DC 101.7** (163.7 km) Gravel turnout to south.

PG 148.8 (239.5 km) **DC 101.2** (162.9 km) Lillico Creek.

PG 149.7 (240.9 km) **DC 100.3** (161.4 km) Marten Creek.

PG 150.4 (242 km) **DC 99.6** (160.3 km) Big Boulder Creek.

PG 156.2 (251.4 km) **DC 93.8** (151 km) Fisher Creek.

PG 156.9 (252.5 km) **DC 93.1** (149.8 km) Large gravel turnout with litter barrel to south beside Pine River.

PG 159.9 (257.3 km) **DC 90.1** (145 km) Crassier Creek.

PG 161.7 (260.2 km) **DC 88.3** (142.1 km) Westcoast Energy compressor station.

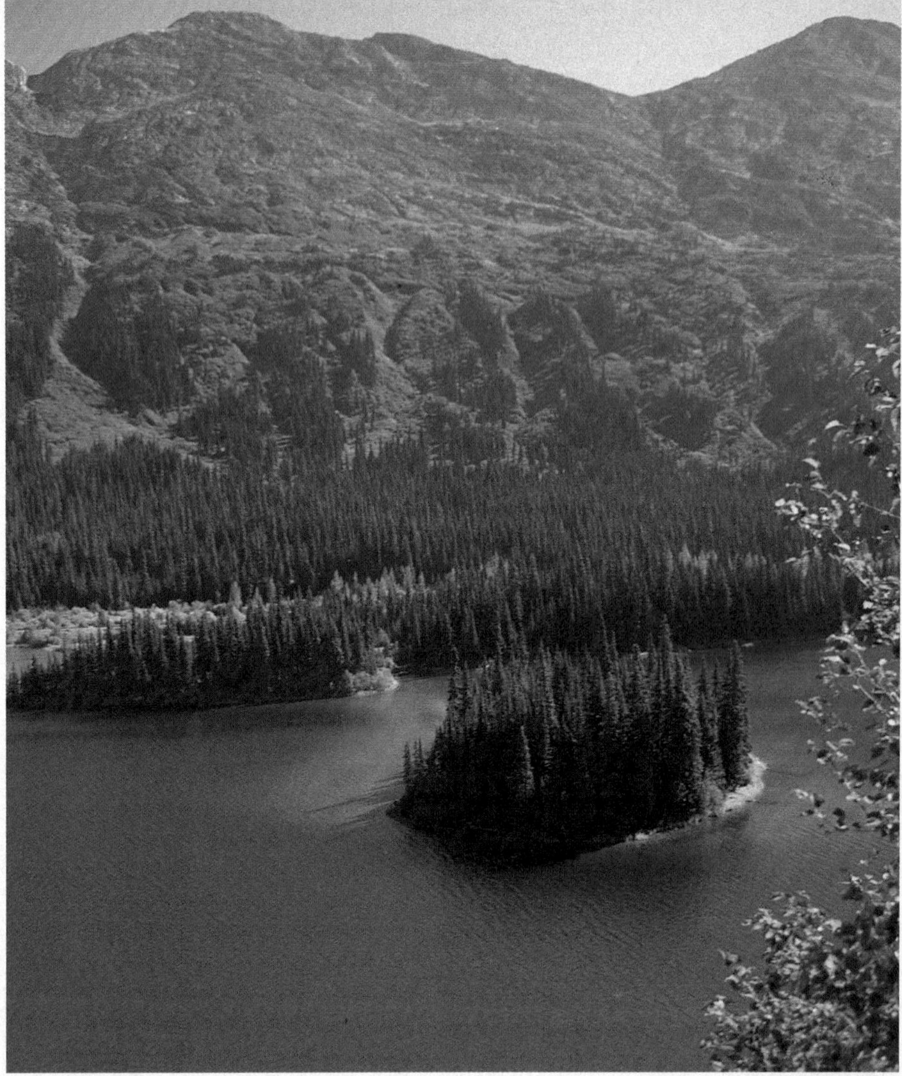

View from Pine Pass of beautiful Azouzetta Lake. (Earl L. Brown, staff)

PG 163.6 (263.3 km) **DC 86.4** (139 km) Pine Valley rest areas, both sides of highway, with picnic tables and pit toilets. View of Pine River to south.

PG 169.5 (272.8 km) **DC 80.5** (129.5 km) Turnout with picnic tables, pit toilets and litter barrel to south overlooking the beautiful Pine River valley.

PG 172.4 (277.4 km) **DC 77.6** (124.9 km) Westcoast Energy (natural gas), Pine River plant. View of the Rocky Mountain foothills to the south and west.

PG 177.4 (285.5 km) **DC 72.6** (116.8 km) Turnout with litter barrel.

Chetwynd is known as the "Chainsaw Carving Capital of the World." (Earl L. Brown, staff)

PG 181.9 (292.7 km) **DC 68.1** (109.6 km) Bissett Creek.

PG 183.6 (295.5 km) **DC 66.4** (106.9 km) Turnout with litter barrels at Wildmare Creek.

PG 183.7 (295.6 km) **DC 66.3** (106.7 km) **Wildmare Grove Campsite.** 50 sites. 32 long pull-throughs, back-ins, tent sites with full hookups, firepits and picnic tables. Quiet, beautifully treed with easy access to and from the highway. Hot showers, flush toilets, sani-station, variety store and pay phone. 3 miles west of Chetwynd on Highway 97. Phone (604) 788-2747. Box 42, Chetwynd, BC V0C 1J0. Enjoy Super, Natural Scenic Adventure. [ADVERTISEMENT] ▲

Chetwynd

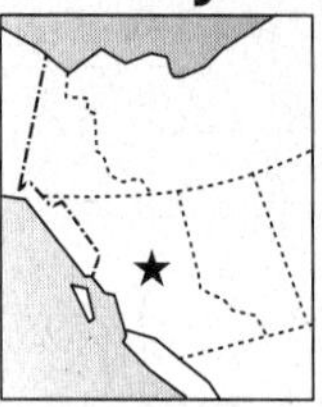

PG 187.6 (301.9 km) **DC 62.4** (100.4 km) Located on Highway 97 at the junction with Highway 29 north to the Alaska Highway via Hudson's Hope, and south to Tumbler Ridge. **Population:** 3,000, area 7,000. **Emergency Services: RCMP**, phone 788-9221. **Hospital, Poison Control Centre** and **Ambulance**, phone 1-562-7241. **Fire Department**, phone 788-2345.

Visitor Information: Chamber of Commerce, open 8 A.M. to 8 P.M. July 1 to Labour Day weekend; open 9 A.M. to 4 P.M. rest of year. Write Box 1000, Chetwynd V0C 1J0, or phone 788-3345 or 788-3655; fax 788-7843. Chetwynd Infocentre is located on Highway 97 near the "Welcome to Chetwynd" sign above the bear sculptures.

The Little Prairie Heritage Museum, located on Highway 97 at the west end of town, features the region's pioneer days; inquire at infocentre for directions. The museum is open from the first Tuesday in July to the last Saturday in August.

Elevation: 2,017 feet/615m. **Radio:** CFGP 105, CISN-FM 102, CJDC 890, CKNL 560, CBC 1170, CFMI-FM 103.9. **Television:** 7 channels (includes CBC, BCTV, ABC, CBS and NBC) plus pay cable.

The town was formerly known as Little Prairie and is a division point on the British Columbia Railway. The name was changed to honour the late British Columbia Minister of Railways Ralph Chetwynd, who was instrumental in the northward extension of the province-owned railway. In recent years, Chetwynd's collection of chainsaw sculptures has earned it the title, "Chainsaw Carving Capital of the World."

Chetwynd lies at the northern end of one of the largest known coal deposits on earth. Access from Chetwynd south to Tumbler Ridge and the resource development known as the North East Coal is via Highway 29 south, a 56-mile/90-km paved road (see HIGHWAY 29 SOUTH side road log on page 56). Forestry, mining, natural gas processing, ranching and farming are the main industries in Chetwynd. Louisiana Pacific has a modern nonpolluting pulp mill here. Free guided tours are available of Canadian Forest Products (788-2231) and Chetwynd Forest Industries (788-2686) soft wood sawmills.

Chetwynd has several large motels, restaurants, banks, post office, laundromat, gas stations, supermarkets, art gallery and golf course. Good traveler's stop with easy access to all services. Chetwynd has a leisure centre with a wave pool; open daily 6 A.M. to 10 P.M., visitors welcome. Chetwynd hosts the annual National Rodeo Assoc. finals in its indoor rodeo arena.

Free municipal campground in town with 20 sites and dump station. There's also a dump station at the 51st Avenue car/truck wash. There are also private tent and trailer parks in town and at Moberly Lake. Moberly Lake Provincial Park is 12 miles/19.3 km north of Chetwynd via Highway 29 north (see **Milepost PG 187.9**) and 1.9 miles/3 km west via a gravel road. The park has 109 campsites, beach, picnic area, playground, nature trail, boat launch and a private marina next door with boat rental and concession. There's good swimming at huge Moberly Lake on a warm summer day. Worth the drive. ▲

Aerial view of Dawson Creek. (Earl L. Brown, staff)

West Access Route Log

(continued)

PG 187.8 (302.2 km) **DC 62.2** (100.1 km) Highway crosses railroad tracks.

PG 187.9 (302.4 km) **DC 62.1** (99.9 km) **Junction** with Highway 29 north, which leads 12 miles/19.3 km to Moberly Lake, 36.5 miles/58.7 km to Peace River Provincial Recreation Area and Peace Canyon dam, and 40.4 miles/64.9 km to community of Hudson's Hope and access to W.A.C. Bennett Dam; Highway 29 north connects with the Alaska Highway 53.7 miles/86.4 km north of Dawson Creek. (See HUDSON'S HOPE LOOP section for details.)

Highway climbs next 12 miles/19 km for Dawson Creek-bound motorists.

PG 189.4 (304.8 km) **DC 60.6** (97.5 km) **Junction** with Highway 29 (paved) south to Gwillim Lake and Tumbler Ridge (see HIGHWAY 29 SOUTH side road log on page 56). Tumbler Ridge is also accessible from **Milepost PG 237.7** via the Heritage Highway.

PG 199.3 (320.7 km) **DC 50.7** (81.6 km) Gravel turnouts with litter barrels both sides of highway.

PG 201.2 (323.8 km) **DC 48.8** (78.5 km) Slow down for sharp curve across railroad tracks.

PG 205.6 (330.9 km) **DC 44.4** (71.5 km) Turnout with litter barrel and a commanding view of the East Pine River valley to the south.

PG 206.5 (332.3 km) **DC 43.5** (70 km) Sharp curves approximately next 2 miles/3.2 km as highway descends toward Dawson Creek. View of Table Mountain.

PG 207.9 (334.6 km) **DC 42.1** (67.7 km) Highway crosses under railroad.

PG 208.1 (334.9 km) **DC 41.9** (67.4 km) Sharp turn to south at west end of bridge for East Pine Provincial Park (0.5 mile on gravel road); picnicking and boat launch on Pine River. Turnout with litter barrel at park entrance.

From East Pine Provincial Park, canoeists may make a two-day canoe trip down the Pine River to the Peace River; take-out at Taylor Landing Provincial Park (at **Milepost DC 34** on the Alaska Highway).

PG 208.2 (335.1 km) **DC 41.8** (67.3 km) Bridge across East Pine River. Railroad also crosses river here.

PG 208.3 (335.2 km) **DC 41.7** (67.1 km) Turnout with litter barrel to south.

PG 209.8 (337.6 km) **DC 40.2** (64.7 km) East Pine (unincorporated) has a store, gas station and distinctive treehouse.

PG 211.7 (340.7 km) **DC 38.3** (61.6 km) Turnout with litter barrel to north.

PG 217.4 (349.8 km) **DC 32.6** (52.5 km) Gas station and store.

PG 221.5 (356.5 km) **DC 28.5** (45.9 km) Turnouts with litter barrels both sides of highway.

PG 222 (357.3 km) **DC 28** (45 km) Groundbirch (unincorporated).

PG 230.7 (371.3 km) **DC 19.3** (31.1 km) Progress (unincorporated), highway maintenance yard, cairn and pay phone.

PG 234.4 (377.2 km) **DC 15.6** (25.1 km) Turnout with litter barrels to north.

PG 237.7 (382.5 km) **DC 12.3** (19.8 km) **Junction** with Heritage Highway, which leads 59.5 miles/96 km south to the community of Tumbler Ridge and access roads to the North East Coal Development. (Tumbler Ridge is also accessible via Highway 29 south from Chetwynd. See side road log this section.) This stretch of the Heritage Highway is paved to Mile 18/29 km, then gravel surfaced to Mile 55/89 km.

From Tumbler Ridge, the Heritage Highway continues 92 miles/148 km east and north to connect with Highway 2 southeast of Dawson Creek. Inquire locally about road conditions.

PG 238 (383 km) **DC 12** (19.3 km) Kiskatinaw River bridge.

PG 240.7 (387.4 km) **DC 9.3** (15 km) Arras (unincorporated), cafe and gas station.

PG 247.9 (398.9 km) **DC 2.1** (3.4 km) Small turnout with litter barrel and point of interest sign to south.

PG 248 (399.1 km) **DC 2** (3.2 km) Private RV Park. ▲

PG 249.9 (402.2 km) **DC 0.1** (0.2 km) Entering Dawson Creek. Private campground on south side of highway; Rotary Lake Park and camping on north side of highway. ▲

PG 250 (402.3 km) **DC 0** **Junction** of the Hart Highway and Alaska Highway; turn right for downtown Dawson Creek. See description of Dawson Creek in the ALASKA HIGHWAY section.

Highway 29 South Log

Highway 29 South is a paved road that leads 55.9 miles/90 km from **Milepost PG 189.4** to the community of Tumbler Ridge. Travelers may return to Highway 97 via Highway 29, or via the Heritage Highway, an all-gravel road that leads 59.5 miles/95 km from Tumbler Ridge to junction with Highway 97 at **Milepost PG 237.7.**

Distance from Highway 97 junction (J) is shown.

J 0 Junction with Highway 97 at **Milepost PG 189.4.**

J 0.1 (0.2 km) Turnout with litter barrels to east.

Highway 29 climbs next 2.3 miles/3.7 km southbound.

J 1.9 (3.1 km) Distance marker indicates Tumbler Ridge 88 km.

J 2.8 (4.5 km) Sign: Trucks check brakes, steep hill ahead.

J 3 (4.8 km) Large gravel turnouts with litter barrels both sides of highway.

J 5.5 (8.8 km) Twidwell Bend bridge.

J 5.6 (9 km) Access road east to Long Prairie (8 miles/12.9 km).

J 6.6 (10.6 km) Highway parallels Sukunka River to west.

J 8.2 (13.2 km) Zonnebeke Creek.

J 9 (14.5 km) Kilometrepost 15.

J 10.6 (17 km) Bridge over Dickebush Creek.

J 11 (17.7 km) Sanctuary River.

J 13.7 (22 km) **Junction** with Sukunka Forest Road, which leads west 11 miles/17.7 km to Sukunka Falls.

J 13.8 (22.2 km) Highway climbs next 3 miles/4.8 km southbound.

J 16.7 (26.9 km) Turnouts with litter barrels both sides of highway.

J 21.6 (34.8 km) Turnout with litter barrels to east.

J 26.9 (43.3 km) Turnouts with litter barrels both sides of highway.

J 28.4 (45.7 km) Paved road leads east 1.2 miles/1.9 km to **Gwillum Lake** Provincial Park (gate closed 11 P.M. to 7 A.M.); 53 campsites, picnic tables, firewood and firepits. Day-use area, boat rentals and boat launch. Fishing for lake trout, grayling and pike. Camping fee $7 to $12. ▲

J 40.8 (65.6 km) Access road leads west 9 miles/14.5 km to Bullmoose Mountain and mine. Mine tours may be available; phone (604) 242-5221 for current information.

J 41.1 (66.1 km) Turnout to east.

J 41.5 (66.8 km) Bridge over Bullmoose Flats River.

J 46.1 (74.2 km) Turnout with litter barrels to east. Phillips Way Summit, elev. 3,695 feet/1,126m.

J 51.4 (82.7 km) Bullmoose Creek bridge.

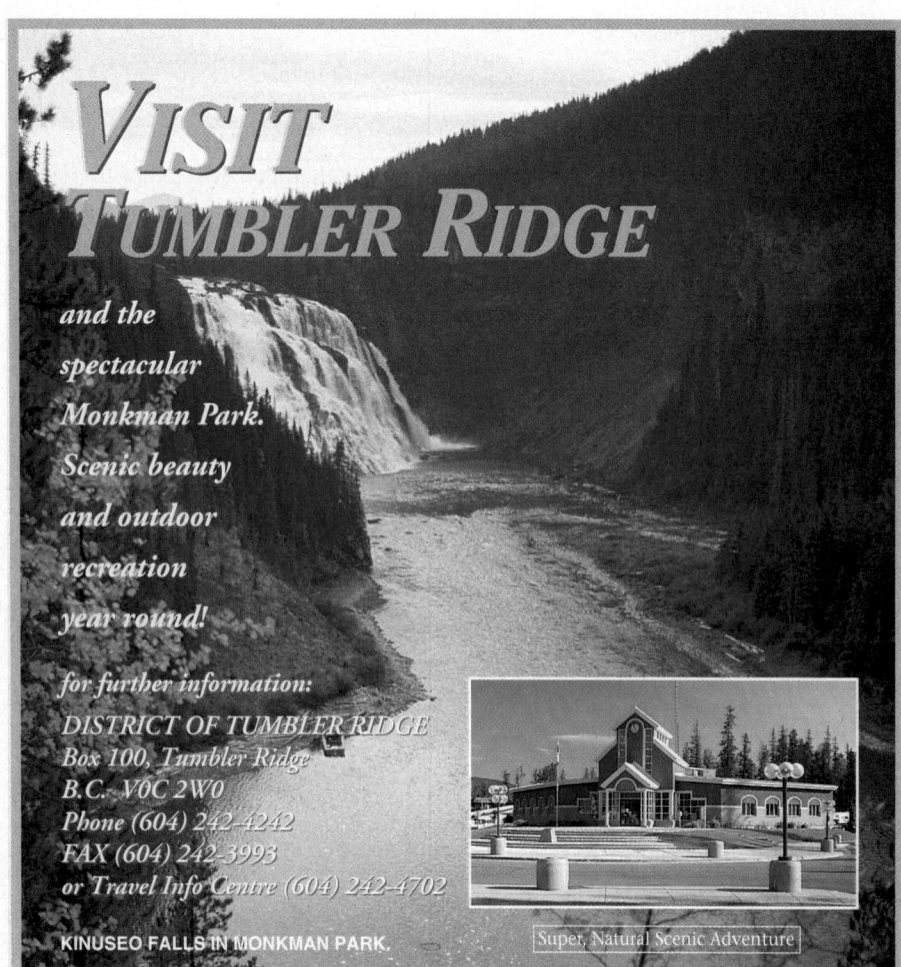

J 52.6 (84.3 km) Wolverine River bridge.

J 54.1 (87 km) Murray River bridge.

J 54.8 (88.2 km) Flatbed Creek bridge.

J 54.9 (88.3 km) Tumbler Ridge Lions campground on the east bank of Flatbed Creek; 33 sites, hookups, water, flush toilets, dump station, picnic tables and showers. Camping fee $10. ▲

J 55.9 (90 km) Turnoff for community of Tumbler Ridge (description follows).

Tumbler Ridge

Located 116.5 miles/187.5 km southwest of Dawson Creek via Highways 97 and 29. **Population:** 4,550. **Emergency Services: RCMP**, phone 242-5252. **Hospital**, phone 242-5271. **Ambulance**, phone 1-562-7241. **Fire Department**, phone 242-5555.

Visitor Information: Located in town at Southgate Road and Front Street, across from the hospital. Open year-round, limited hours in winter. Write the Chamber of Commerce, Box 606, Tumbler Ridge, BC V0C 2W0, or phone (604) 242-4702.

Elevation: 3,000 feet/914m. **Private Aircraft:** 9 miles/15 km south; elev. 3,150 feet/960m, length 4,000 feet/1,218m; asphalt; fuel 80, 100, Jet B.

Tumbler Ridge was built in conjunction with development of the North East Coal resource. Construction of the townsite began in 1981. It is British Columbia's newest community, incorporated June 1, 1984, under instant town legislation. It is nestled in the foothills of the northern Rocky Mountains on a plateau above the confluence of the Murray, Wolverine and Flatbed rivers.

Visitor facilities include a motel, restaurants, retail and grocery outlets, service stations with major repairs, car wash and a laundromat. Recreational facilities include a community center with arena, curling rink, weight room, indoor pool and a library. Outdoor facilities include tennis courts and an 18-hole golf course.

Major attraction in the area is Monkman Provincial Park, site of spectacular 225-foot/69-m Kinuseo (keh-NEW-see-oh) Falls. The falls and a 42-site campground are accessible from Tumbler Ridge via a 37-mile/60-km dirt road (watch for trucks) south from town. Viewing platform of falls is a short walk from the campground. Monkman Park also offers backcountry hiking. For more information on the park, contact BC Parks in Prince George (565-6270), Fort St. John or Tumbler Ridge.

District of Tumbler Ridge. See display ad this section.

Return to Milepost PG 189.4
West Access Route

HUDSON'S HOPE LOOP

Chetwynd, British Columbia, to the Alaska Highway
BC Highway 29
(See map, page 58)

The Hudson's Hope Loop links the John Hart Highway (Highway 97) with the Alaska Highway (also Highway 97). This 86.9-mile/139.8-km paved loop road provides year-round access to the town of Hudson's Hope, W.A.C. Bennett Dam, Peace Canyon Dam and Moberly Lake. Highway 29 is a good scenic two-lane road but steep and winding in places.

A popular side trip with Alaska Highway travelers today, and an alternate access route to the Alaska Highway, Highway 29 was only a 53-mile side road to the Hudson Hope Coal Mines in the 1950s. In the 1960s, with construction of the W.A.C. Bennett Dam under way, Alaska Highway travelers drove the side road to see the Peace River dam site. The highway was completed to Chetwynd in 1968.

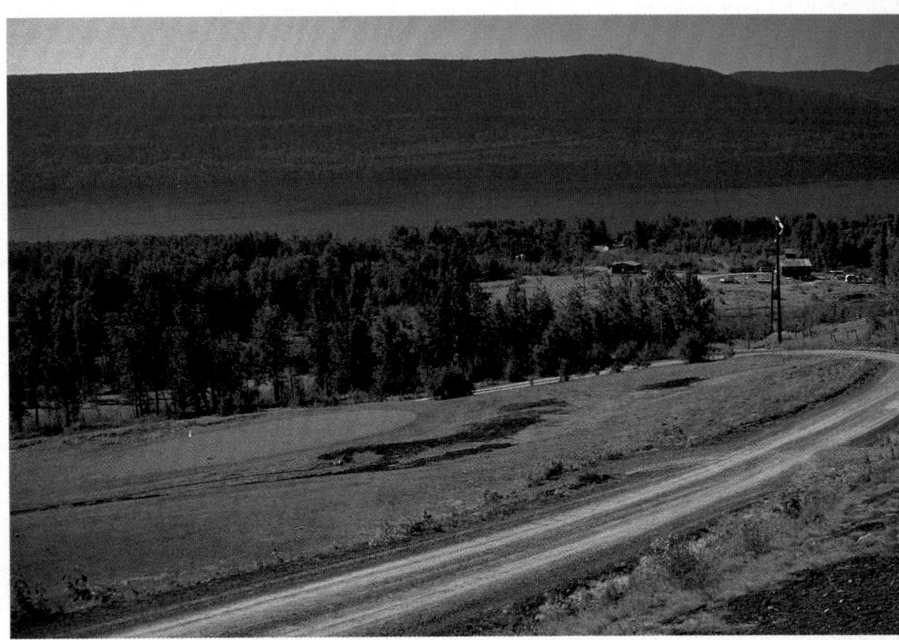

View of Moberly Lake and golf course access road from Highway 29. (Earl L. Brown, staff)

Hudson's Hope Loop Log

Distance from Chetwynd (C) is followed by distance from Alaska Highway Junction (AH).

C 0 AH 86.9 (139.8 km) **Junction** of Highways 29 and 97 at Chetwynd (see **Milepost PG 187.6** in the WEST ACCESS ROUTE section for description of Chetwynd).

C 0.5 (0.8 km) **AH 86.4** (139 km) Truck weigh scales to west.

C 2.3 (3.7 km) **AH 84.6** (136.1 km) Jackfish Road to east.

C 5 (8 km) **AH 81.9** (131.8 km) Turnout with litter barrel to west.

C 12 (19.3 km) **AH 74.9** (120.5 km) Gravel access road leads 2 miles/3.2 km west to **Moberly Lake** Provincial Park on south shore; 109 campsites, swimming, waterskiing, picnicking, drinking water, dump station, boat launch, $9.50 camping fee. Moberly Marina adjacent park. This beautiful 9-mile-/14.5-km-long lake drains at its south end into Moberly River, which in turn runs into the Peace River. Fishing for lake trout, Dolly Varden and whitefish.

C 12.2 (19.6 km) **AH 74.7** (120.2 km) Moberly River bridge; parking area with litter barrel at south end.

C 15.9 (25.6 km) **AH 71** (114.3 km) Highway cairn is memorial to John Moberly, fur trader and explorer who first landed here in 1865.

C 16.4 (26.4 km) **AH 70.5** (113.5 km) Spencer Tuck Provincial Park; picnic tables, swimming, fishing and boat launch.

C 17.4 (28 km) **AH 69.5** (111.8 km) **Harv's Resort,** on the north shore of beautiful Moberly Lake. Treed picnic sites, large grass picnic field, cabins and campsites. Swimming, fishing, pay phone and showers. Store, restaurant and dining room. Gas, oils, propane, hunting and fishing licenses. Boat launch and golf course nearby. Your hosts, Harve and Darlene Evans. Open till 10 P.M. daily. (604) 788-9145. [ADVERTISEMENT]

C 18.3 (29.4 km) **AH 68.6** (110.4 km) **MOBERLY LAKE.** Post office, cafe, store and pay phone.

C 18.5 (29.8 km) **AH 68.4** (110.1 km) Moberly Lake and District Golf Club, 0.7 mile/1.1 km from highway; nine holes, grass greens, rentals, clubhouse, licensed lounge. Open May to September.

C 25.4 (40.9 km) **AH 61.5** (99 km) Cameron Lake camping area; tables, water, toilets, firewood, playground, horseshoe pits, boat launch (no motorboats) and swimming. Camping fee by donation. Fee may be charged in 1994.

C 30.7 (49.4 km) **AH 56.2** (90.4 km) Gravel turnout with litter barrel to east. Highway descends northbound to Hudson's Hope.

C 35.9 (57.8 km) **AH 51** (82.1 km) Suspension bridge over Peace River; paved turnouts at both ends of bridge with concrete totem pole sculptures. View of Peace Canyon Dam.

C 36.5 (58.7 km) **AH 50.4** (81.1 km) Turnoff to west for Dinosaur Lake Campground and B.C. Hydro Peace Canyon Dam. The visitor centre, 0.6 mile/1 km in on paved access road, is open from 8 A.M. to 4 P.M. daily from late May through Labor Day; Monday through Friday the rest of the year (closed holidays). Self-guided tour includes a full-scale model of duck-billed dinosaurs (hadrosaurs), and a tableau portraying Alexander Mackenzie's discovery of the Peace River canyon. A pictorial display traces the construction of the Peace Canyon Dam. You may view the dam spillway from the visitor centre. Get permission before walking across top of dam.

Dinosaur Lake Campground, on Dinosaur Lake, has 30 campsites with firepits, water, toilets and tables. Boat launch and swimming area. Camping fee by donation. Fee

HUDSON'S HOPE LOOP *Chetwynd, BC, to Milepost DC 53.7 Alaska Highway*

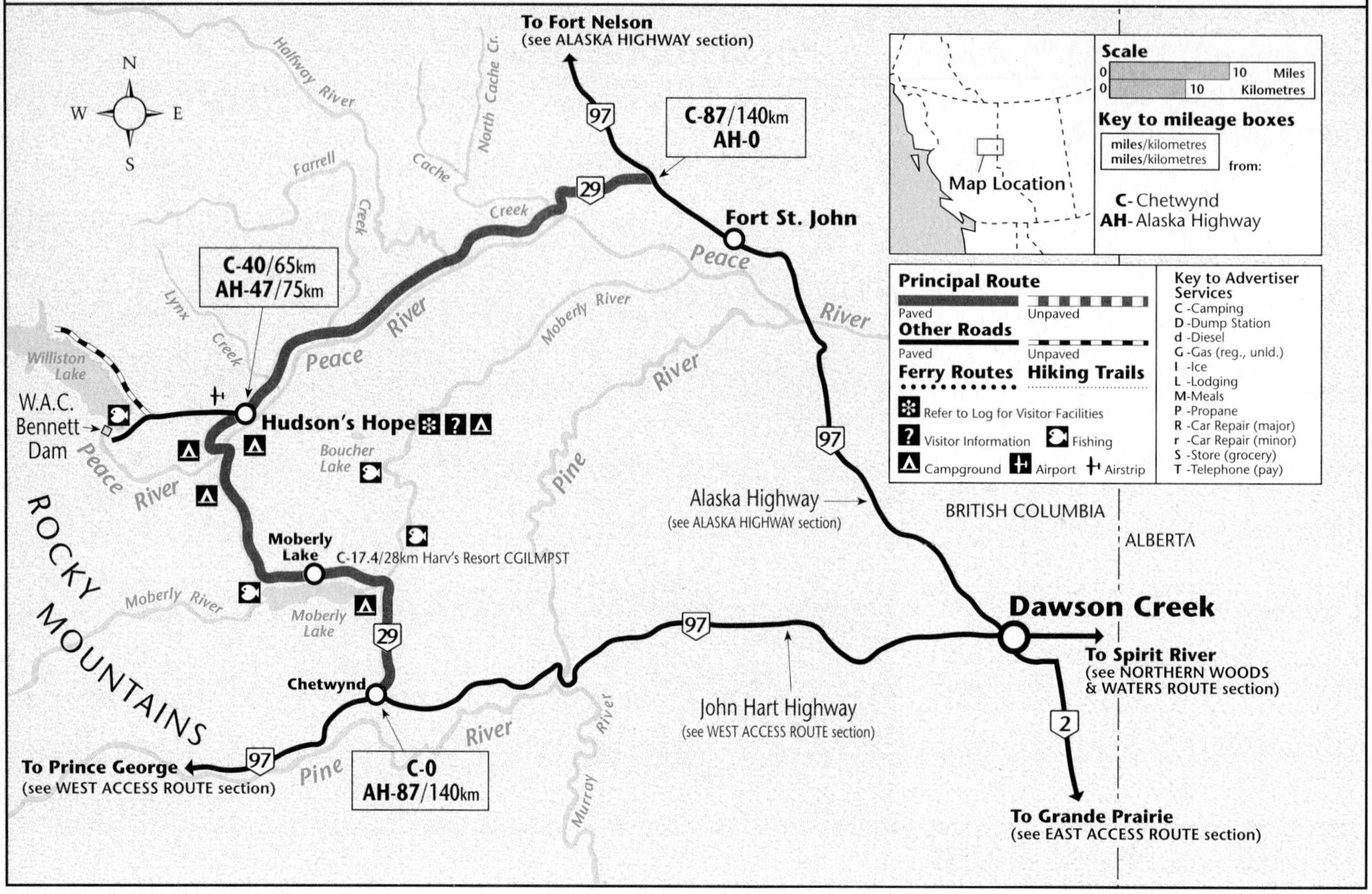

To Fort Nelson (see ALASKA HIGHWAY section)
C-87/140km AH-0
Fort St. John
C-40/65km AH-47/75km
Williston Lake
W.A.C. Bennett Dam
Hudson's Hope
Boucher Lake
ROCKY MOUNTAINS
Moberly Lake
C-17.4/28km Harv's Resort CGILMPST
Chetwynd
To Prince George (see WEST ACCESS ROUTE section)
C-0 AH-87/140km
John Hart Highway (see WEST ACCESS ROUTE section)
Alaska Highway (see ALASKA HIGHWAY section)
Dawson Creek
To Spirit River (see NORTHERN WOODS & WATERS ROUTE section)
To Grande Prairie (see EAST ACCESS ROUTE section)
BRITISH COLUMBIA
ALBERTA
Map Location

Scale: 10 Miles; 10 Kilometres

Key to mileage boxes: miles/kilometres, miles/kilometres from: C-Chetwynd, AH-Alaska Highway

Principal Route: Paved, Unpaved. Other Roads: Paved, Unpaved. Ferry Routes. Hiking Trails.
Refer to Log for Visitor Facilities; Visitor Information; Fishing; Campground; Airport; Airstrip

Key to Advertiser Services: C-Camping, D-Dump Station, d-Diesel, G-Gas (reg., unld.), I-Ice, L-Lodging, M-Meals, P-Propane, R-Car Repair (major), r-Car Repair (minor), S-Store (grocery), T-Telephone (pay)

may be charged in 1994. ▲

C **38.3** (61.6 km) **AH 48.6** (78.2 km) Alwin Holland Memorial Park (0.5 mile/0.8 km east of highway) is named for the first teacher in Hudson's Hope, who willed his property, known locally as The Glen, to be used as a public park. There are 17 campsites, picnic grounds, barbecues and water. Camping fee by donation. Fee may be charged in 1994. ▲

C **38.9** (62.6 km) **AH 48** (77.2 km) Welcome to Hudson's Hope sign.

C **39** (62.8 km) **AH 47.9** (77.1 km) King Gething Park; small campground with 15 grassy sites, picnic tables, cookhouse, flush toilets, showers and dump station east side of highway. Camping fee by donation. Fee may be charged in 1994. ▲

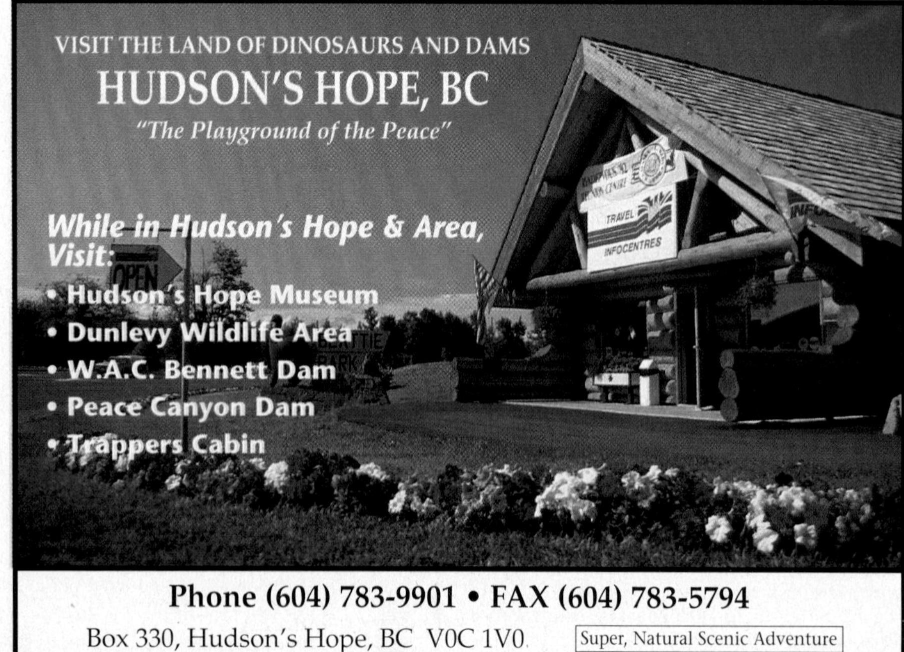
VISIT THE LAND OF DINOSAURS AND DAMS
HUDSON'S HOPE, BC
"The Playground of the Peace"
While in Hudson's Hope & Area, Visit:
• Hudson's Hope Museum
• Dunlevy Wildlife Area
• W.A.C. Bennett Dam
• Peace Canyon Dam
• Trappers Cabin
TRAVEL INFOCENTRES
OPEN
Phone (604) 783-9901 • FAX (604) 783-5794
Box 330, Hudson's Hope, BC V0C 1V0
Super, Natural Scenic Adventure

Hudson's Hope

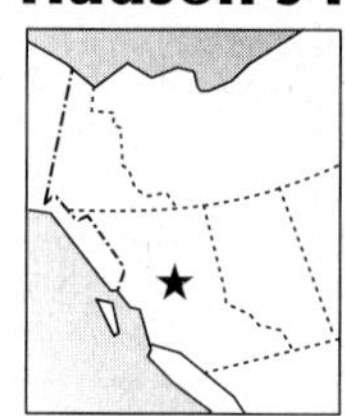

C **40.4** (65 km) **AH 46.5** (74.8 km) **Population:** 985. **Emergency Services: RCMP,** phone 783-5241. **Fire Department,** phone 783-5700. **Ambulance,** phone 112-562-7241. **Medical Clinic,** phone 783-9991.

Visitor Information: A log building houses the tourist information booth at Beattie Park, across from the museum and St. Peter's Anglican United Church. Open daily mid-May to mid-September, hours are 8 A.M. to 8 P.M. Phone 783-9154 or write Box 330, Hudson's Hope, BC V0C 1V0. (Off-season, phone the district office at 783-9901.)

Elevation: 1,707 feet/520m. **Climate:** Summer temperatures range from 60°F/16°C to 90°F/32°C, with an average of 135 frost-free days annually. **Radio:** CBC, CKNL 560, CJDC 870. **Television:** Channels 2, 5, 8, 11 and cable.

Private Aircraft: Hudson's Hope airstrip, 3.7 miles/6 km west; elev. 2,200 feet/671m;

length 5,200 feet/1,585m; asphalt.

Hudson's Hope is the third oldest permanently settled community in British Columbia. The site was first visited in 1793 by Alexander Mackenzie. In 1805 a Hudson's Bay trading post was established here by Simon Fraser. In 1916, after the fur-trading days were over, a major influx of settlers arrived in the area. It was the head of navigation for steamboats on the lower Peace River until 1936, the year of the last scheduled steamboat run. Area coal mines supplied Alaska Highway maintenance camps during the 1940s.

Modern development of Hudson's Hope was spurred by construction of the Peace Power project in the 1960s. Today the area's principal claim to fame is the 600-foot-/183-m-high W.A.C. Bennett Dam at the upper end of the Peace River canyon, 15 miles/24 km west of Hudson's Hope. The 100-million-ton dam is one of the largest earth-fill structures in the world and Williston Lake, behind it, is the largest body of fresh water in British Columbia. Tours of the Gordon M. Shrum generating station are available daily from mid-May through Thanksgiving weekend, weekdays only the remainder of the year (closed holidays). Check with the visitor bureau for tour schedule.

Also of interest is the Hudson's Hope Museum on Highway 29 in town. The museum has a fine collection of artifacts and dinosaur fossils from the Peace District. Souvenir shop in the museum. Next door to the museum is the log St. Peter's Anglican United Church (still in use).

Visitor services in Hudson's Hope include a motel, hotel, three restaurants, two service stations, a laundromat, supermarket, and convenience and hardware stores. There are also a bank, post office, liquor store, community hall, library, swimming pool, tennis courts, and numerous parks and playgrounds. Sightseeing and flightseeing tours are available locally. The main business district is along Highway 29 and adjoining streets. The RCMP office is at the corner of 100th Street and 100th Avenue.

St. Peter's Anglican United Church in Hudson's Hope. (Earl L. Brown, staff)

Hudson's Hope Loop Log

(continued)

C 41.2 (66.3 km) **AH 45.7** (73.5 km) Turnout to north with Hudson's Hope visitor map.

C 44 (70.8 km) **AH 42.9** (69 km) Lynx Creek bridge.

C 48.3 (77.7 km) **AH 38.6** (62.1 km) Pay phone, north side of road.

C 48.4 (77.9 km) **AH 38.5** (62 km) Turnout to north for view of the Peace River.

C 50.9 (81.9 km) **AH 36** (57.9 km) Farrell Creek bridge and picnic site.

C 56.6 (91.1 km) **AH 30.3** (48.8 km) Pull-through turnout with litter barrels. View of Peace River valley.

C 57.1 (91.9 km) **AH 29.8** (48 km) Turnout to south with litter barrels and view of Peace River valley.

C 59.3 (95.4 km) **AH 27.6** (44.4 km) Turnout to south with litter barrels.

C 64.7 (104.1 km) **AH 22.2** (35.7 km) Halfway River.

C 67.2 (108.1 km) **AH 19.7** (31.7 km) Rest area to south with point of interest sign, litter barrel and toilet. A slide occurred here on May 26, 1973, involving an estimated 10 million to 15 million cubic yards of overburden. Slide debris completely blocked the river channel for some 12 hours, backing up the river an estimated 24 feet/7m above normal level.

C 68.4 (110.1 km) **AH 18.5** (29.8 km) Milepost 19.

C 71.1 (114.4 km) **AH 15.8** (25.4 km) Turnout to north.

C 71.4 (114.9 km) **AH 15.5** (24.9 km) Milepost 16.

C 73.5 (118.3 km) **AH 13.4** (21.6 km) Beaver dam to north.

C 74.6 (120.1 km) **AH 12.3** (19.8 km) Cache Creek one-lane bridge. Turnout to north at east end of bridge for picnic area with litter barrels.

C 76.6 (123.3 km) **AH 10.3** (16.6 km) Turnout with litter barrel to north overlooking Bear Flat in the Peace River valley. Highway begins climb eastbound.

C 78.1 (125.6 km) **AH 8.8** (14.2 km) Highest point on Highway 29 (2,750 feet/838m) overlooking Peace River Plateau. Highway descends 10 percent grade westbound.

C 86.9 (139.8 km) **AH 0 Junction** with the Alaska Highway, 6.7 miles/10.8 km north of Fort St. John (see **Milepost DC 53.7** in the ALASKA HIGHWAY section).

ALASKA HIGHWAY

Dawson Creek, British Columbia, to Fairbanks, Alaska
BC Highway 97, Yukon Highway 1 and Alaska Route 2
(See maps, pages 61-65)

The Alaska Highway stretches in a northwesterly direction from Mile 0 at Dawson Creek, BC, through Yukon Territory to Mile 1520 at Fairbanks, AK. Although the Alaska Highway does not compare with highways in the Lower 48, it is no longer a wilderness road but rather a road through the wilderness. The Alaska Highway is driven by thousands of people each year in all sorts of vehicles. The highway is open and maintained year-round.

Aerial view of Muncho Lake, looking south. The Alaska Highway winds up the east side of the lake. (Earl L. Brown, staff)

Road Conditions

All of the Alaska Highway between Dawson Creek, BC, and Fairbanks, AK, is asphalt-surfaced. Repaving and highway improvement continue. Surfacing of the Alaska Highway ranges from poor to excellent.

There are stretches of poor surfacing with many chuckholes, gravel breaks (sections of gravel ranging from a few feet to several miles), hardtop with loose gravel, deteriorated shoulders and bumps. On the northern portion of the highway — in Yukon Territory and on into Alaska — watch for frost heaves. This rippling effect in the pavement is caused by the freezing and thawing of the ground. Drive slowly in sections of frost heaves to avoid breaking an axle or trailer hitch.

Surfacing on much of the highway is fair, with older patched pavement and a minimum of gravel breaks and chuckholes. There are also sections of excellent surfacing where highway maintenance crews have recently upgraded the road.

Travelers should keep in mind that road conditions are subject to change! Weather and traffic may cause deterioration of newer pavement, while construction may improve older sections. Always be alert for bumps and holes in the road and for abrupt changes in highway surfacing. There are stretches of narrow, winding road without shoulders. Also watch for soft shoulders.

Always watch for construction crews along the Alaska Highway. Extensive road construction may require a detour or travelers may be delayed while waiting for a pilot car to guide them through the construction. Motorists may encounter rough driving at construction areas, and muddy roadway if there are heavy rains while the roadbed is torn up.

For current road conditions from Dawson Creek to the BC–YT border, phone the Peace River Alaska Highway Tourist Assoc. in Fort St. John at (604) 785-2544, or the Dawson Creek Tourist Infocentre at (604) 782-9595. The BC Ministry of Highways provides a recorded message on road conditions on the Alaska Highway in BC; phone (604) 774-7447. For a recorded message on road conditions on all other highways in the province, phone 1-800-663-4997 (toll free in Canada) or (604) 525-4997. For recorded message on current road conditions on the Alaska Highway and other highways in Yukon Territory, phone (403) 667-8215 for daily road report.

Detailed weather information for the Canadian portion of the Alaska Highway is available from Atmospheric Environment Service of Environment Canada. For 24-hour recorded weather information between Dawson Creek and Sikanni Chief, phone (604) 784-2244 or 785-7669; for detailed weather information, phone the weather office at (604) 785-4304 between 6:15 A.M. and 4:45 P.M.; or for weather broadcasts, tune to 580 AM. Between Sikanni Chief and the BC–YT border, phone (604) 774-6461 for 24-hour recorded message; for detailed weather information phone (604) 774-2302 between 3 A.M. and 6:15 P.M.; or tune your radio to 590 AM for weather broadcasts. Between the BC–YT border and the YT–AK border, phone (403) 668-6061 for 24-hour recorded message; for detailed weather information phone (403) 667-8464 (24 hours a day); or tune your radio to CBC Yukon (570 AM) for weather broadcasts. Regional weather forecasts are also supplied to local visitor information centres, local hotels and motels, and lodges along the highway.

Road conditions along the Alaska Highway may be summarized as follows. Good pavement first 300 miles/483 km (through Fort Nelson) with recent resurfacing improving some sections. Watch for surface changes and continued construction in some areas. Between Fort Nelson and the BC–YT border, the Alaska Highway crosses the Rocky Mountains, so be prepared for narrow, winding road and some rough spots in surfacing due to deterioration from weather and traffic. Also watch for construction projects on this stretch. Between the BC–YT border and Haines Junction, expect fair to excellent road with a few rough spots and sections of narrow, winding road. From Haines Junction to the YT–AK border, the road is in fair condition with some narrow, winding sections with no shoulders. Between **Historical Mile 1118** (Kluane Wilderness Village) and Beaver Creek there is rough road with some gravel patches and winding road. Travelers with trailers should be especially cautious: Road surface can be hard on trailer hitches. The highway between Beaver Creek and the border was in very poor condition in 1993 due to frost heaving and deterioration; reconstruction is planned for this stretch in 1994. On the

(Continued on page 66)

ALASKA HIGHWAY *Dawson Creek, BC, to Milepost DC 409*

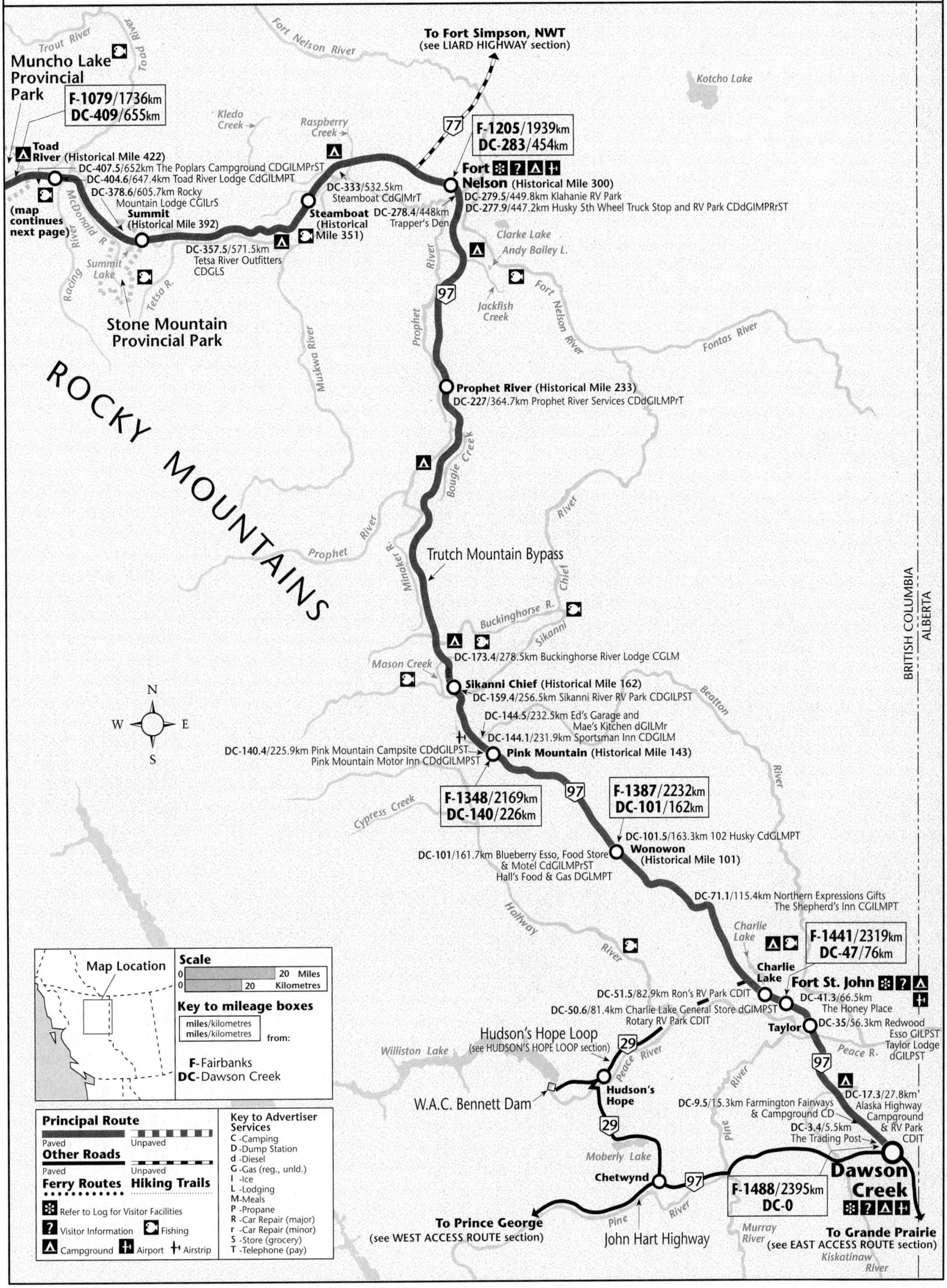

To Fort Simpson, NWT
(see LIARD HIGHWAY section)

Muncho Lake Provincial Park

F-1079/1736km
DC-409/655km

Toad River (Historical Mile 422)
DC-407.5/652km The Poplars Campground CDGILMPrST
DC-404.6/647.4km Toad River Lodge CdGILMPT
DC-378.6/605.7km Rocky Mountain Lodge CGILrS

(map continues next page)

Summit (Historical Mile 392)
DC-357.5/571.5km Tetsa River Outfitters CDGLS

Stone Mountain Provincial Park

Steamboat (Historical Mile 351)
DC-333/532.5km Steamboat CdGIMrT

F-1205/1939km
DC-283/454km

Fort Nelson (Historical Mile 300)
DC-279.5/449.8km Klahanie RV Park
DC-277.9/447.2km Husky 5th Wheel Truck Stop and RV Park CDdGIMPRrST
DC-278.4/448km Trapper's Den

Prophet River (Historical Mile 233)
DC-227/364.7km Prophet River Services CDdGILMPrT

ROCKY MOUNTAINS

Trutch Mountain Bypass

DC-173.4/278.5km Buckinghorse River Lodge CGLM

Sikanni Chief (Historical Mile 162)
DC-159.4/256.5km Sikanni River RV Park CDGILPST
DC-144.5/232.5km Ed's Garage and Mae's Kitchen dGILMr
DC-144.1/231.9km Sportsman Inn CDGILM
DC-140.4/225.9km Pink Mountain Campsite CDdGILPST
Pink Mountain Motor Inn CDdGILMPST
Pink Mountain (Historical Mile 143)

F-1348/2169km
DC-140/226km

F-1387/2232km
DC-101/162km

DC-101.5/163.3km 102 Husky CdGLMPT
DC-101/161.7km Blueberry Esso, Food Store & Motel CdGILMPrST
Hall's Food & Gas DGLMPT
Wonowon (Historical Mile 101)

DC-71.1/115.4km Northern Expressions Gifts
The Shepherd's Inn CGILMPT

F-1441/2319km
DC-47/76km

Charlie Lake
Fort St. John
DC-51.5/82.9km Ron's RV Park CDIT
DC-50.6/81.4km Charlie Lake General Store dGIMPST
Rotary RV Park CDIT
DC-41.3/66.5km The Honey Place
Taylor
DC-35/56.3km Redwood Esso GILPST
Taylor Lodge dGILPST

Hudson's Hope Loop (see HUDSON'S HOPE LOOP section)
Hudson's Hope
W.A.C. Bennett Dam

DC-17.3/27.8km Alaska Highway Campground & RV Park CDIT
DC-9.5/15.3km Farmington Fairways & Campground CD
DC-3.4/5.5km The Trading Post

Dawson Creek
F-1488/2395km
DC-0

Chetwynd
John Hart Highway
To Prince George (see WEST ACCESS ROUTE section)
To Grande Prairie (see EAST ACCESS ROUTE section)

Trout River, Toad River, Fort Nelson River, Kledo Creek, Raspberry Creek, Kotcho Lake, McDonald R., Racing River, Summit Lake, Tetsa R., Muskwa River, Prophet River, Clarke Lake, Andy Bailey L., Jackfish Creek, Fontas River, Bougie Creek, Minaker R., Chief River, Buckinghorse R., Sikanni, Mason Creek, Beatton River, Cypress Creek, Halfway River, Charlie Lake, Williston Lake, Peace River, Pine River, Moberly Lake, Murray River, Kiskatinaw River

BRITISH COLUMBIA
ALBERTA

N E S W

Map Location

Scale: 20 Miles; 20 Kilometres

Key to mileage boxes
miles/kilometres
miles/kilometres
from:
F-Fairbanks
DC-Dawson Creek

Principal Route: Paved, Unpaved
Other Roads: Paved, Unpaved
Ferry Routes
Hiking Trails
Refer to Log for Visitor Facilities
Visitor Information
Fishing
Campground
Airport
Airstrip

Key to Advertiser Services
C -Camping
D -Dump Station
d -Diesel
G -Gas (reg., unld.)
I -Ice
L -Lodging
M -Meals
P -Propane
R -Car Repair (major)
r -Car Repair (minor)
S -Store (grocery)
T -Telephone (pay)

ALASKA HIGHWAY *Milepost DC 409 to Teslin, YT*

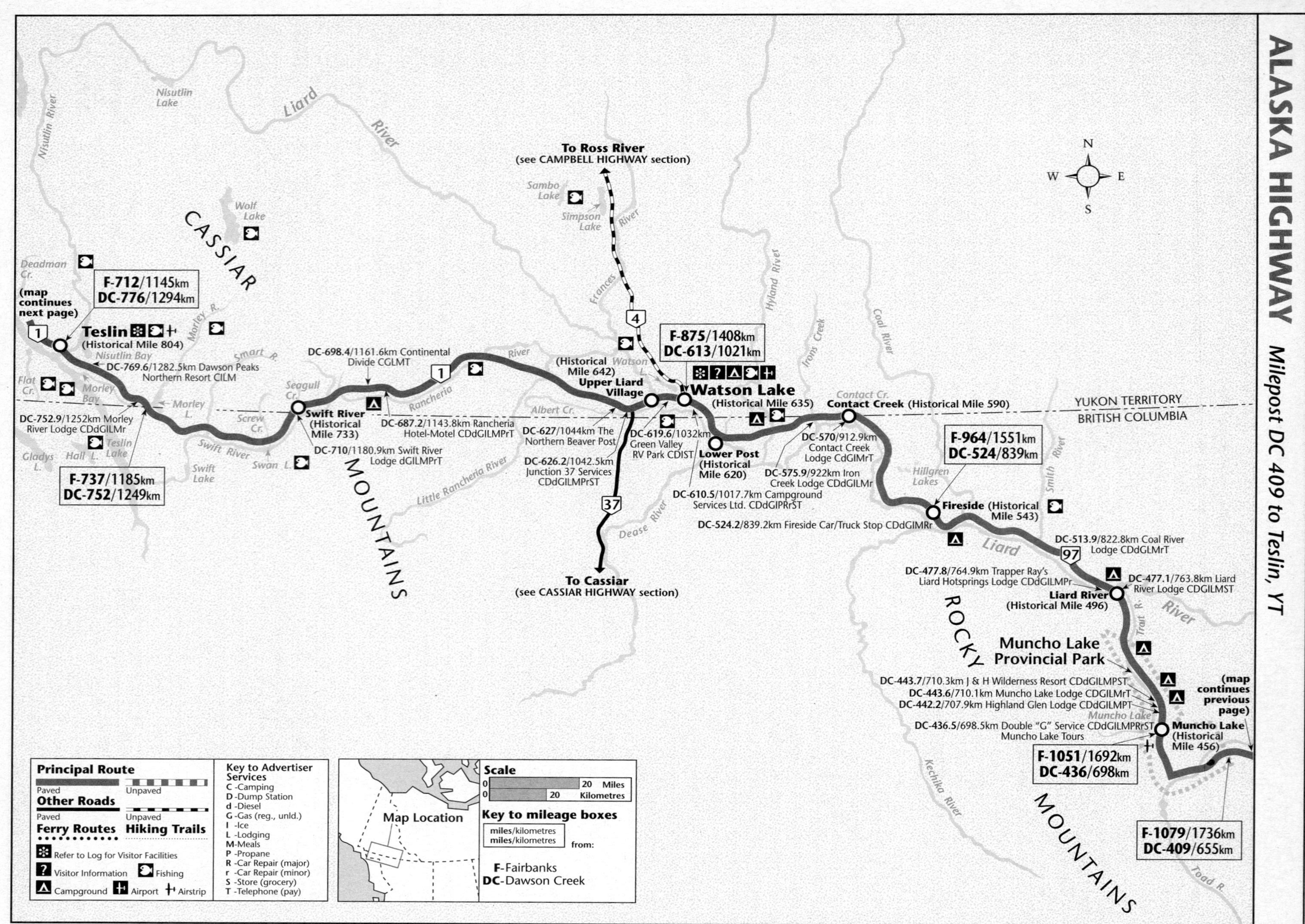

ALASKA HIGHWAY *Teslin, YT, to Milepost DC 1136*

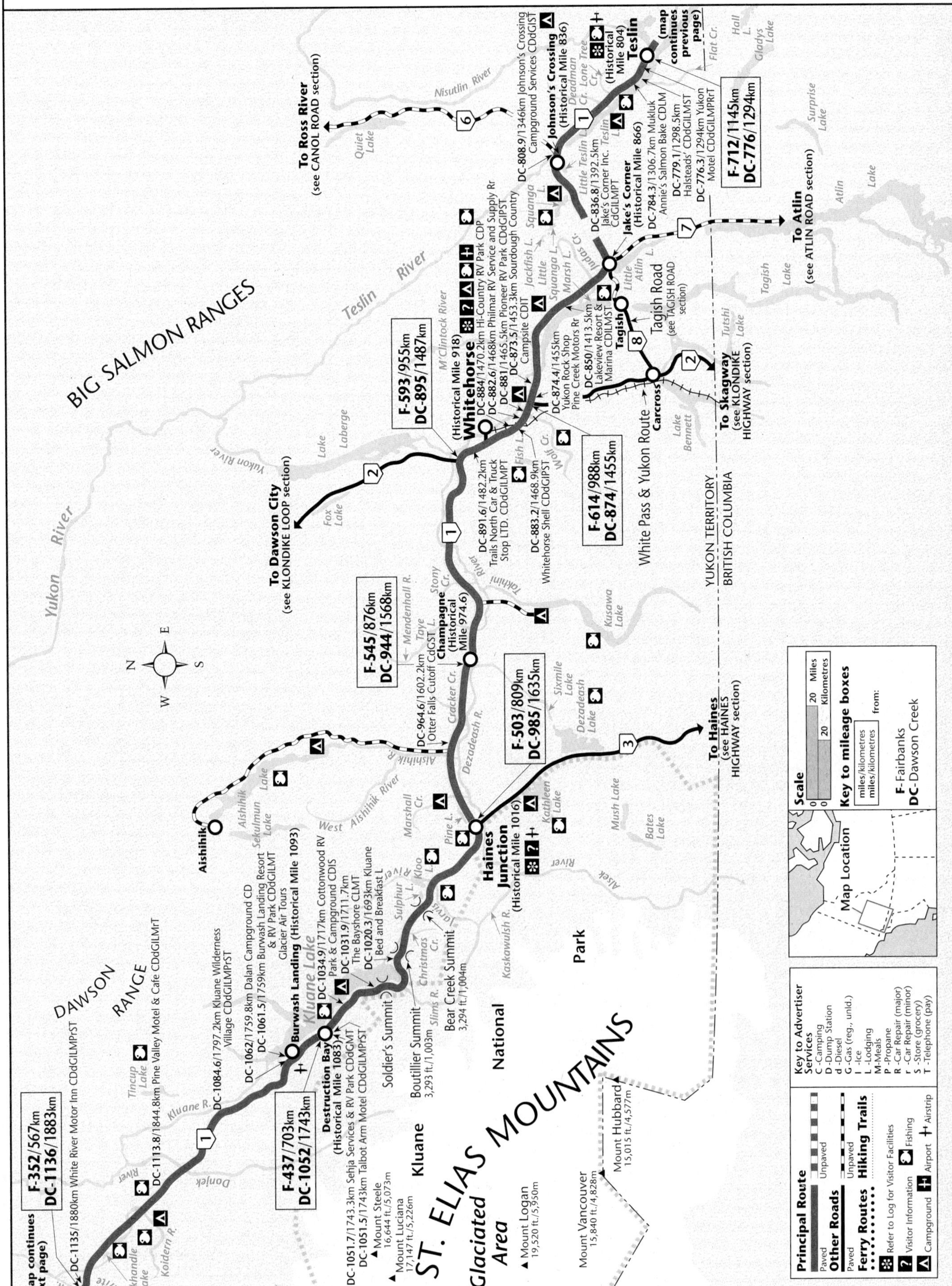

Teslin (Historical Mile 804)

(map continues previous page)

F-712/1145km DC-776/1294km

DC-776.3/1294km Yukon Motel CDdGILMPRrT

DC-779.1/1298.5km Halsteads' CDdGILMST

DC-784.3/1306.7km Mukluk Annie's Salmon Bake CDLM

Johnson's Crossing (Historical Mile 836)

DC-808.9/1346km Johnson's Crossing Campground Services CDdGIST

Jake's Corner (Historical Mile 866)

DC-836.8/1392.5km Jake's Corner Inc. CdGILMPT

To Atlin (see ATLIN ROAD section)

To Ross River (see CANOL ROAD section)

Tagish — Tagish Road (see TAGISH ROAD section)

DC-850/1413.5km Lakeview Resort & Marina CDILMST

DC-874.4/1455km Yukon Rock Shop Pine Creek Motors Rr

F-614/988km DC-874/1455km

Carcross

To Skagway (see KLONDIKE HIGHWAY section)

White Pass & Yukon Route

YUKON TERRITORY

BRITISH COLUMBIA

Whitehorse (Historical Mile 918)

F-593/955km DC-895/1487km

DC-884/1470.2km Hi-Country RV Park CDP

DC-882.6/1468km Philmar RV Service and Supply Rr

DC-881/1465.5km Pioneer RV Park CDdGIPST

DC-873.5/1453.3km Sourdough Country Campsite CDIT

DC-891.6/1482.2km Trails North Car & Truck Stop LTD. CDdGILMPT

DC-883.2/1468.9km Whitehorse Shell CDdGIPST

To Dawson City (see KLONDIKE LOOP section)

BIG SALMON RANGES

Champagne (Historical Mile 974.6)

F-545/876km DC-944/1568km

DC-964.6/1602.2km Otter Falls Cutoff CdGST

F-503/809km DC-985/1635km

To Haines (see HAINES HIGHWAY section)

Haines Junction (Historical Mile 1016)

Aishihik

Burwash Landing (Historical Mile 1093)

DC-1034.9/1717km Cottonwood RV Park & Campground CDIS

DC-1031.9/1711.7km The Bayshore CLMT

DC-1020.3/1693km Kluane Bed and Breakfast L

DC-1062/1759.8km Dalan Campground CD

DC-1061.5/1759km Burwash Landing Resort & RV Park CDdGILMT Glacier Air Tours

DC-1084.6/1797.2km Kluane Wilderness Village CDdGILMPrST

DC-1113.8/1844.8km Pine Valley Motel & Cafe CDdGILMrT

DC-1135/1880km White River Motor Inn CDdGILMPrST

F-352/567km DC-1136/1883km

(map continues next page)

Destruction Bay (Historical Mile 1083)

F-437/703km DC-1052/1743km

DC-1051.7/1743.3km Sehja Services & RV Park CDdGMT

DC-1051.5/1743km Talbot Arm Motel CDdGILMPrST

Soldier's Summit

Boutillier Summit 3,293 ft./1,003m

Bear Creek Summit 3,294 ft./1,004m

DAWSON RANGE

Kluane National Park

ST. ELIAS MOUNTAINS

Glaciated Area

Mount Steele 16,644 ft./5,073m

Mount Luciana 17,147 ft./5,226m

Mount Logan 19,520 ft./5,950m

Mount Vancouver 15,840 ft./4,828m

Mount Hubbard 15,015 ft./4,577m

Kluane Lake · Yukon River · Teslin River · Lake Laberge · Fox Lake · Kusawa Lake · Dezadeash Lake · Sixmile Lake · Kathleen Lake · Mush Lake · Bates Lake · Aishihik Lake · Sekulmun Lake · Pine L. · Kloo L. · Tincup Lake · Pickhandle Lake · Quiet Lake · Nisutlin River · Atlin Lake · Tagish Lake · Tutshi Lake · Lake Bennett · Marsh L. · Little Atlin L. · Jackfish L. · Little Squanga L. · Squanga L. · Little Teslin L. · Teslin L. · Surprise Lake · Gladys Lake · Hall L. · Takhini River · Alsek River · Donjek River · White River · Kluane R. · Koidern R. · Dezadeash R. · Aishihik R. · West Aishihik River · Sulphur L. · Mendenhall R. · Stony Cr. · Cracker Cr. · Marshall Cr. · Christmas Cr. · Slims R. · Jarvis R. · Kaskawulsh R. · M'Clintock River · Wolf Cr. · Fish L. · Judas Cr. · Deadman Cr. · Lone Tree Cr. · Flat Cr. · Taye L.

Key to Advertiser Services

C -Camping
D -Dump Station
d -Diesel
G -Gas (reg., unld.)
I -Ice
L -Lodging
M -Meals
P -Propane
R -Car Repair (major)
r -Car Repair (minor)
S -Store (grocery)
T -Telephone (pay)

Principal Route Paved / Unpaved

Other Roads Paved / Unpaved

Ferry Routes · **Hiking Trails**

Refer to Log for Visitor Facilities · Visitor Information · Fishing · Campground · Airport · Airstrip

Map Location

Scale 0–20 Miles; 0–20 Kilometres

Key to mileage boxes

miles/kilometres miles/kilometres from:

F-Fairbanks
DC-Dawson Creek

ALASKA HIGHWAY *Milepost DC 1136 to Milepost DC 1378*

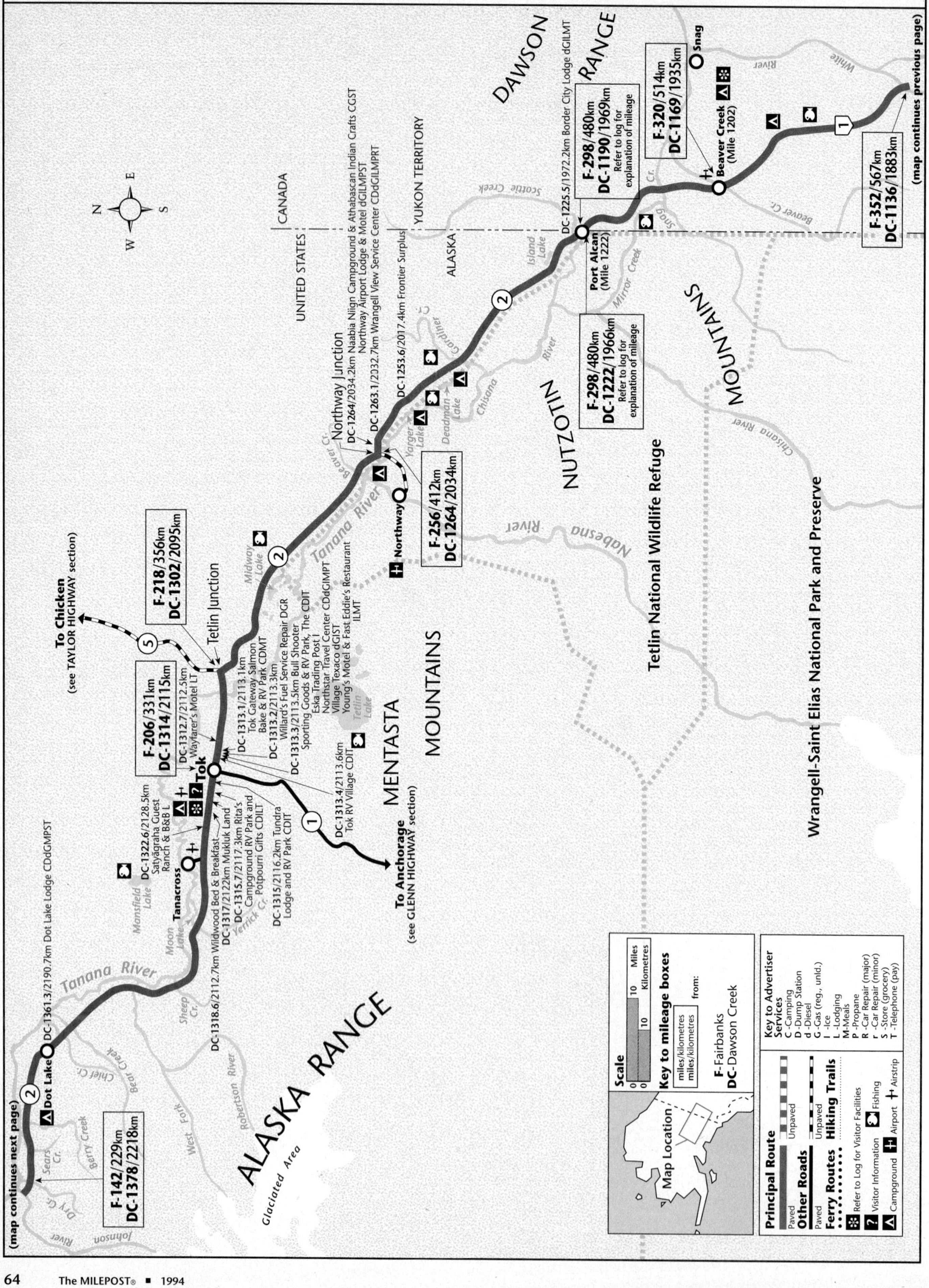

(map continues next page)

F-142/229km
DC-1378/2218km

Dot Lake
DC-1361.3/2190.7km Dot Lake Lodge CDdGMPST

Johnson River
Dry Cr.
Sears Cr.
Berry Creek
Chief Cr.
Bear Creek
Tanana River
West Fork
Robertson River
Sheep Cr.
Moon Lake
Mansfield Lake
Yerrick Cr.

ALASKA RANGE
Glaciated Area

Tanacross
DC-1322.6/2128.5km Satyāgraha Guest Ranch & B&B L

F-206/331km
DC-1314/2115km

Tok
DC-1312.7/2112.5km Wayfarer's Motel LT
DC-1318.6/2112.7km Wildwood Bed & Breakfast
DC-1317/2122km Mukluk Land
DC-1315.7/2117.3km Rita's Campground RV Park and Potpourri Gifts CDILT
DC-1315/2116.2km Tundra Lodge and RV Park CDIT
DC-1313.1/2113.1km Tok Gateway Salmon Bake & RV Park CDMT
DC-1313.2/2113.3km Willard's Fuel Service Repair DGR
DC-1313.3/2113.5km Bull Shooter Sporting Goods & RV Park, The CDIT
Eska Trading Post I
Northstar Travel Center CDdGIMPT
Village Texaco dGIST
Young's Motel & Fast Eddie's Restaurant ILMT
DC-1313.4/2113.6km Tok RV Village CDIT

To Anchorage
(see GLENN HIGHWAY section)

To Chicken
(see TAYLOR HIGHWAY section)

F-218/356km
DC-1302/2095km

Tetlin Junction

Midway Lake
Tetlin Lake

MENTASTA MOUNTAINS

Tanana River
Beaver Cr.

Northway Junction
DC-1264/2034.2km Naabia Niign Campground & Athabascan Indian Crafts CGST
Northway Airport Lodge & Motel dGILMPST
DC-1263.1/2332.7km Wrangell View Service Center CDdGILMPRT
DC-1253.6/2017.4km Frontier Surplus

Northway

F-256/412km
DC-1264/2034km

Yarger Lake
Deadman Lake
Gardiner Cr.
Chisana River

UNITED STATES
CANADA
YUKON TERRITORY
ALASKA

N
W
E
S

Nabesna River

NUTZOTIN MOUNTAINS

Island Lake
Scottie Creek
Mirror Creek
Snag Cr.

DAWSON RANGE

DC-1225.5/1972.2km Border City Lodge dGILMT

Port Alcan
(Mile 1222)

F-298/480km
DC-1222/1966km
Refer to log for explanation of mileage

F-298/480km
DC-1190/1969km
Refer to log for explanation of mileage

F-320/514km
DC-1169/1935km

Snag

Beaver Creek
(Mile 1202)

Beaver Cr.
White River

Tetlin National Wildlife Refuge

Wrangell-Saint Elias National Park and Preserve

F-352/567km
DC-1136/1883km

(map continues previous page)

Map Location

Scale
0 10 Miles
0 10 Kilometres

Key to mileage boxes
miles/kilometres
miles/kilometres
from:
F-Fairbanks
DC-Dawson Creek

Principal Route
Paved
Unpaved
Other Roads
Paved
Unpaved
Ferry Routes
Hiking Trails
Refer to Log for Visitor Facilities
Visitor Information
Fishing
Campground
Airport
Airstrip

Key to Advertiser Services
C -Camping
D -Dump Station
d -Diesel
G -Gas (reg., unld.)
I -Ice
L -Lodging
M -Meals
P -Propane
R -Car Repair (major)
r -Car Repair (minor)
S -Store (grocery)
T -Telephone (pay)

ALASKA HIGHWAY *Milepost DC 1378 to Fairbanks, AK*

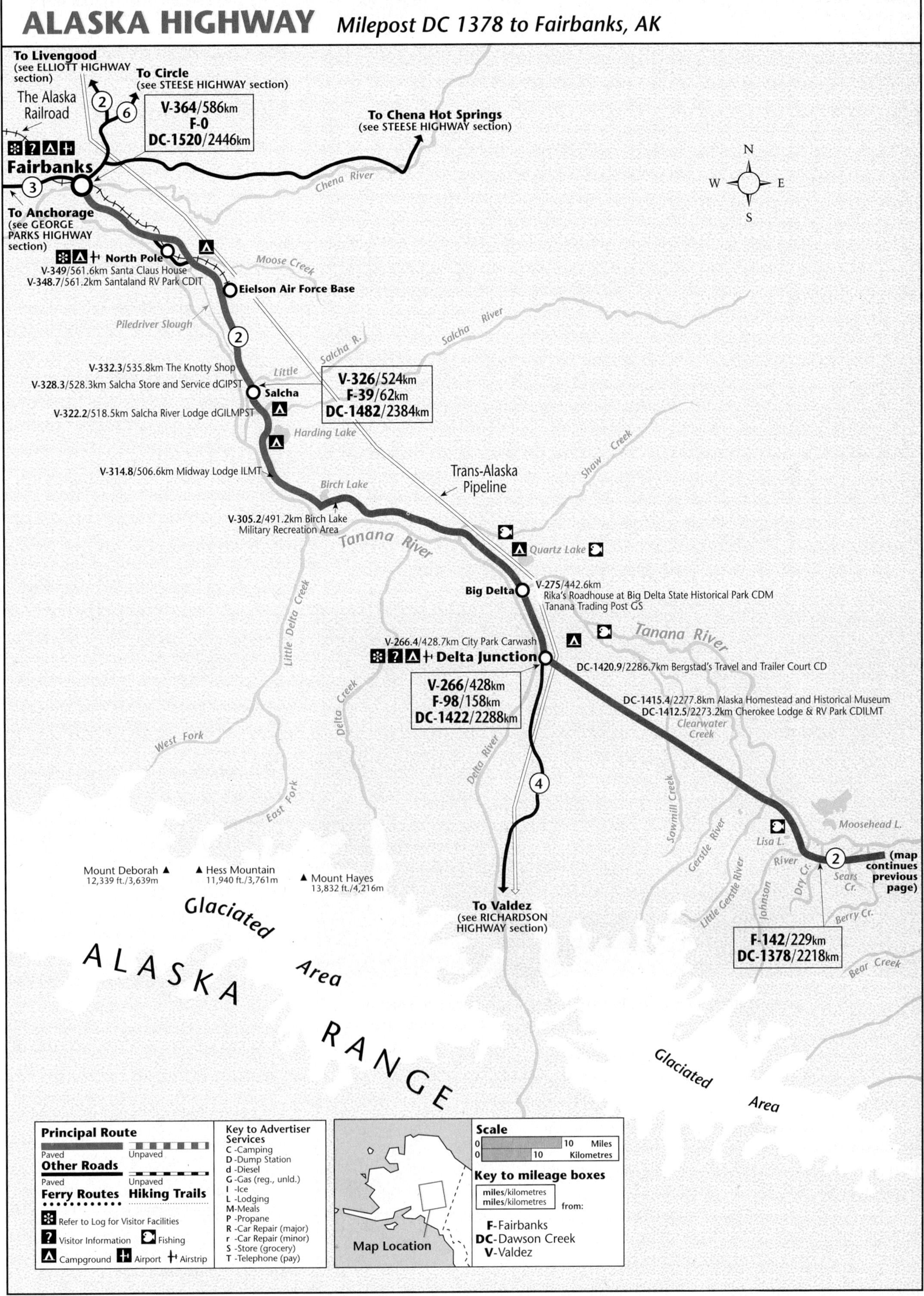

Alaska portion of the Alaska Highway, expect fair to good surfacing, but watch for frost heaves and narrow sections of road without shoulders. Also watch for continued road construction on the highway between the YT–AK border and Tok.

Driving Information

The Alaska Highway is a two-lane highway that winds and rolls across the wilderness. There are sections of road with no centerline and stretches of narrow highway with little or no shoulder. The best advice is to take your time; drive with your headlights on at all times; keep to the right on hills and corners; watch for wildlife on the road; and — as you would on any highway anywhere else — drive defensively.

Dust and mud may be a problem in construction areas and on some stretches of the highway. Gravel road is treated with calcium chloride to keep the dust down. This substance corrodes paint and metal: Wash your vehicle as soon as possible. In heavy rains, calcium chloride and mud combine to make a very slippery road surface; drive carefully! There are relatively few steep grades. The highest summit on the highway is at Summit Lake, elev. 4,250 feet/1,295m. Flying gravel — which may damage headlights, radiators, gas tanks, windshields and paint — is still a problem. There are many sections of hardtop with loose gravel and gravel breaks along the highway. Side roads and access roads to campgrounds and other destinations are generally not paved. Keep in mind that many highways in the Yukon and some highways in Alaska are gravel.

Gas, food and lodging are found along the Alaska Highway on an average of every 20 to 50 miles. (The longest stretch without services is about 100 miles.) Not all businesses are open year-round, nor are most services available 24 hours a day. There are dozens of government and private campgrounds along the highway.

Remember that you will be driving in two different countries that use two different currencies: For the best rate, exchange your money at a bank. There are banks in Dawson Creek, Fort St. John, Fort Nelson, Watson Lake, Whitehorse, Delta Junction and Fairbanks. Haines Junction has banking service at the general store. See GENERAL INFORMATION in the back of the book for details on Customs Requirements, Driving Information, Holidays and Money/Credit Cards.

Mileposts and Kilometreposts

Mileposts were first put up at communities and lodges along the Alaska Highway in the 1940s to help motorists know where they were in this vast wilderness. Today, those original mileposts remain a tradition with communities and businesses on the highway and are still used as mailing addresses and reference points, although the figures no longer accurately reflect driving distance.

When Canada switched to the metric system in the mid-1970s, the mileposts were

Emergency Medical Services

Milepost DC 0 Dawson Creek to **DC 47** Fort St. John. Dawson Creek ambulance 782-2211; RCMP 782-5211.

Milepost DC 47 Fort St. John to **DC 101** Wonowon. Fort St. John ambulance 785-2079; RCMP 785-6617.

Milepost DC 101 Wonowon to **DC 222.3** Bougie Creek bridge. Pink Mountain ambulance 772-3234.

Milepost DC 222.3 Bougie Creek bridge to **DC 373.3** Summit Lake Lodge. Fort Nelson ambulance 774-2344, hospital 774-6916; RCMP 774-2777.

Milepost DC 373.3 Summit Lake Lodge to **DC 605.1** BC–YT border. Toad River ambulance 232-5351; Fort Nelson RCMP 774-2777.

Milepost DC 605.1 BC–YT border to **DC 710** Swift River. Watson Lake ambulance 1-667-3333; RCMP 536-5555 or 1-667-5555.

Milepost DC 710 Swift River to **DC 821** Squanga Lake. Teslin ambulance 1-667-3333; RCMP 390-5555 or 1-667-5555.

Milepost DC 821 Squanga Lake to **DC 936.8** Mendenhall River bridge. Whitehorse ambulance 1-667-3333; RCMP 667-5555.

Milepost DC 936.8 Mendenhall River bridge to **DC 1023.7** Kluane Lake Lodge. Haines Junction ambulance 1-667-3333; RCMP 634-5555 or 1-667-5555.

Milepost DC 1023.7 Kluane Lake Lodge to **DC 1122.7** Longs Creek. Destruction Bay ambulance 1-667-3333; RCMP 643-5555 or 1-667-5555.

Milepost DC 1122.7 Longs Creek to **DC 1189.8** YT–AK border. Beaver Creek RCMP 862-5555 or 1-667-5555; Health Centre 862-7225; Ambulance 862-3333.

Milepost DC 1221.8 YT–AK border to **DC 1314.2** Tok. Northway EMS 778-2211. Port Alcan Rescue Team (Alaska Customs) 774-2252.

Milepost DC 1314.2 Tok to **DC 1361.3** Dot Lake. Tok ambulance 883-2300 or 911.

Milepost DC 1361.3 to **DC 1422** Delta Junction. Delta Rescue Squad phone 911 or 895-4600; Alaska State Troopers 895-4800.

Milepost DC 1422 Delta Junction to **DC 1520** Fairbanks. Dial 911.

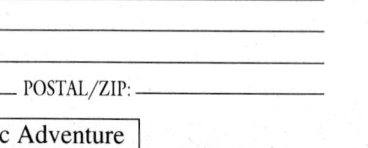

replaced by kilometreposts. These posts are located on the right-hand side of the highway (Alaska-bound). Kilometreposts are up along the British Columbia portion of the Alaska Highway every 3 miles/5 km; reflective white numerals on green signs. In Yukon Territory, white posts with black numerals are up along the highway every 1.2 miles/2 km.

The kilometerage of the British Columbia portion of the Alaska Highway was recalibrated by the government in the fall of 1990, with kilometreposts corrected to reflect current driving distances. As of our press time, kilometreposts along the Yukon Territory portion of the Alaska Highway still reflected the metric equivalent of the historical mileposts. Thus, at the BC–YT border (Historical Mile 627) the kilometerage from Dawson Creek is given as 967.6 km on the BC side and 1009 km on the YT side.

The MILEPOST® log of the Alaska Highway gives distance from Dawson Creek to the AK–YT border as actual driving distance in miles from Dawson Creek followed by kilometre distance based on the kilometreposts. Use our mileage figure from Dawson Creek to figure correct distance between points on the Alaska Highway in Canada. Use our kilometre figure from Dawson Creek to pinpoint location in reference to physical kilometreposts on the Alaska Highway in Canada. On the Alaska portion of the highway, mileposts are based on historical miles, so distance from Dawson Creek in the log is given according to the mileposts up along the road. This figure is followed by the metric equivalent in kilometres.

Traditional milepost figures in Canada are indicated in the text as **Historical Mile**. Where the governments of British Columbia, Yukon and Alaska have installed commemorative mileposts, the text reads **Historic Milepost**. Restored in 1992 to commemorate the 50th anniversary of the construction of the Alaska Highway, many of these historic markers are accompanied by signs and interpretive panels. These mileposts reflect the original or traditional mileage and do not reflect actual driving distance.

A Brief History of the Alaska Highway

Construction of the Alaska Highway officially began on March 8, 1942, and ended eight months and 12 days later on Oct. 25,

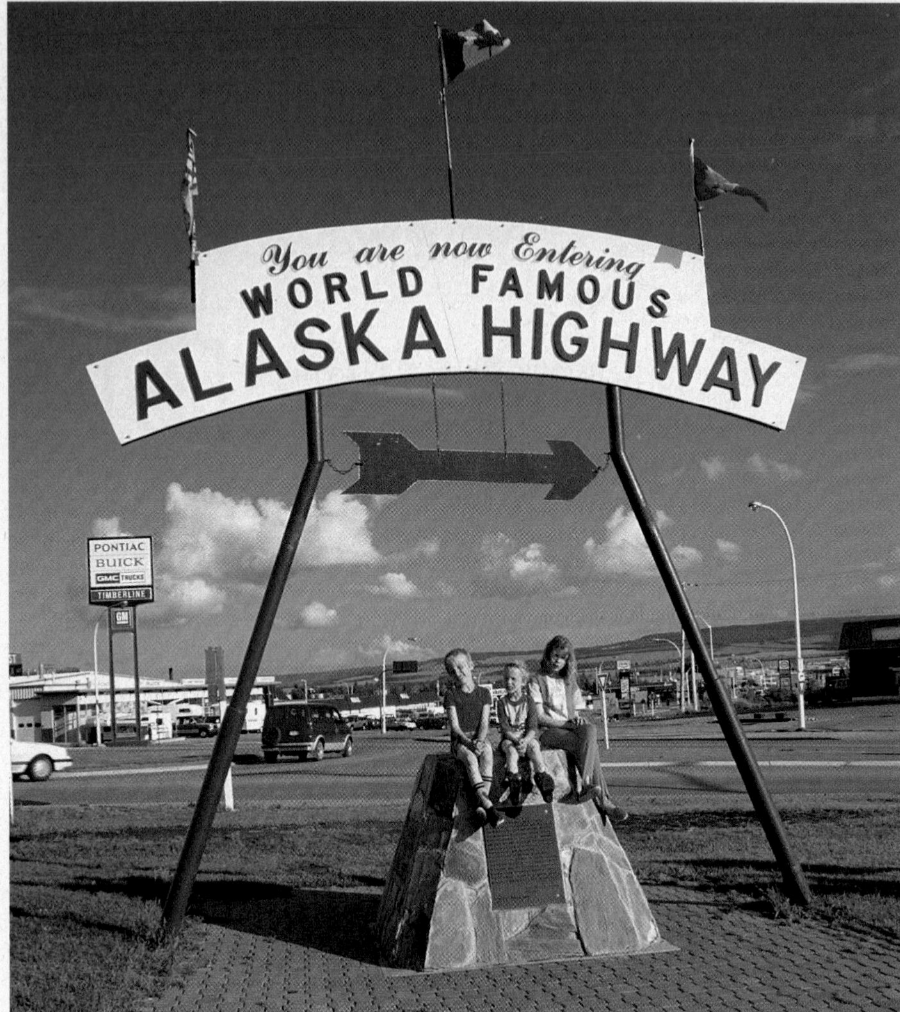

Young travelers have their picture taken at the Alaska Highway cairn in Dawson Creek. *(Earl L. Brown, staff)*

1942. But an overland link between Alaska and the Lower 48 had been studied as early as 1930 under President Herbert Hoover's authorization. It was not until the bombing of Pearl Harbor in December 1941 that construction of the highway was deemed a military necessity. Alaska was considered vulnerable to a Japanese invasion. On Feb. 6, 1942, approval for the Alaska Highway was given by the Chief of Staff, U.S. Army. On Feb. 11, President Roosevelt authorized construction of the pioneer road.

The general route of the highway, determined by the War Department, was along a line of existing airfields from Edmonton, AB, to Fairbanks, AK. This chain of airfields was known as the Northwest Staging Route, and was used to ferry more than 8,000 war planes from Great Falls, MT, to Ladd Air Force Base in Fairbanks, AK, as part of the Russian–American Lend Lease Program. The planes were flown from Fairbanks to Nome, then on to Russia.

In March 1942, rights-of-way through Canada were secured by formal agreement between the two countries. The Americans agreed to pay for construction and turn over the Canadian portion of the highway to the Canadian government after the war ended. Canada furnished the right-of-way, and waived import duties, sales taxes, income taxes and immigration regulations, and provided construction materials along the route.

A massive mobilization of men and equipment began. Regiments of the U.S. Army Corps of Engineers were moved north to work on the highway. By June, more than 10,000 American troops had poured into the Canadian North. The Public Roads Administration tackled the task of organizing civilian engineers and equipment. Trucks, road-building equipment, office furniture, food, tents and other supplies all had to be located and then shipped north.

Road work began in April, with crews working out of the two largest construction camps, Whitehorse and Fort St. John. The highway followed existing winter roads, old Indian trails, rivers and, on occasion, "sight" engineering.

For the soldiers and civilian workers, it was a hard life. Working seven days a week, they endured mosquitoes and black flies in summer, and below zero temperatures in winter. Weeks would pass with no communication between headquarters and field parties. According to one senior officer with the Public Roads Administration, "Equipment was always a critical problem. There never was enough."

In June 1942, the Japanese invaded Attu and Kiska islands in the Aleutians, adding a new sense of urgency to completion of the road. Crews working from east and west connected at Contact Creek on Sept. 25. By October, it was possible for vehicles to travel the entire length of the highway. The official opening of the Alaska Highway was a ribbon-cutting ceremony held Nov. 20, 1942, on Soldier's Summit at Kluane Lake. (A rededication ceremony was held Nov. 20, 1992, as part of the 50th anniversary celebration of the Alaska Highway.)

Dawson Creek

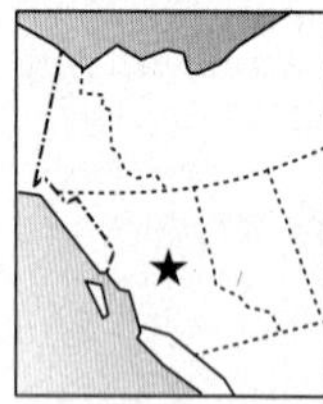

Milepost 0 of the Alaska Highway. **Population:** 12,000, area 66,500. **Emergency Services: RCMP**, phone 782-5211. **Fire Department**, phone 782-5000. **Ambulance**, phone 782-2211. **Hospital and Poison Centre**, Dawson Creek and District Hospital, 11000 13th St., phone 782-8501.

Visitor Information: At NAR (North Alberta Railway) Park on Alaska Avenue at 10th Street (one block west of the traffic circle), in the building behind the railway car. Open year-round, 8 A.M. to 8 P.M. daily in summer, 9 A.M. to 5 P.M. Tuesday through Saturday in winter. Phone 782-9595. Plenty of public parking in front of the refurbished

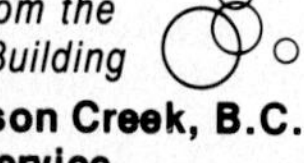

grain elevator which houses the Dawson Creek Art Gallery.

Elevation: 2,186 feet/666m. **Climate**: Average temperature in January is 0°F/-18°C; in July it is 60°F/15°C. The average annual snowfall is 72 inches with the average depth of snow in midwinter at 19.7 inches. Frost-free days total 97, with the first frost of the year occurring about the first week of September. **Radio**: CJDC 890. **Television**: 13 channels via cable including pay TV. **Newspapers**: *Peace River Block News* (daily); *The Mirror* (biweekly).

Private Aircraft: Dawson Creek airport, 2 miles/3.2 km southeast; elev. 2,148 feet/655m; length 5,000 feet/1,524m; asphalt; fuel 100, jet. Floatplane base parallels runway.

Dawson Creek lies 367 miles/591 km northwest of Edmonton, AB, and 250 miles/402 km northeast of Prince George, BC.

Dawson Creek (like Dawson City in the Yukon Territory) was named for George Mercer Dawson of the Geological Survey of Canada, whose geodetic surveys of this region in 1879 helped lead to its development as an agricultural settlement. The open level townsite is surrounded by rolling farmland, part of the government-designated Peace River Block.

The Peace River Block consists of 3.5 million acres of arable land in northeastern British Columbia which the province gave to the Dominion Government in 1883 in return for financial aid toward construction of the Canadian Pacific Railway. (While a route through the Peace River country was surveyed by CPR in 1878, the railroad was

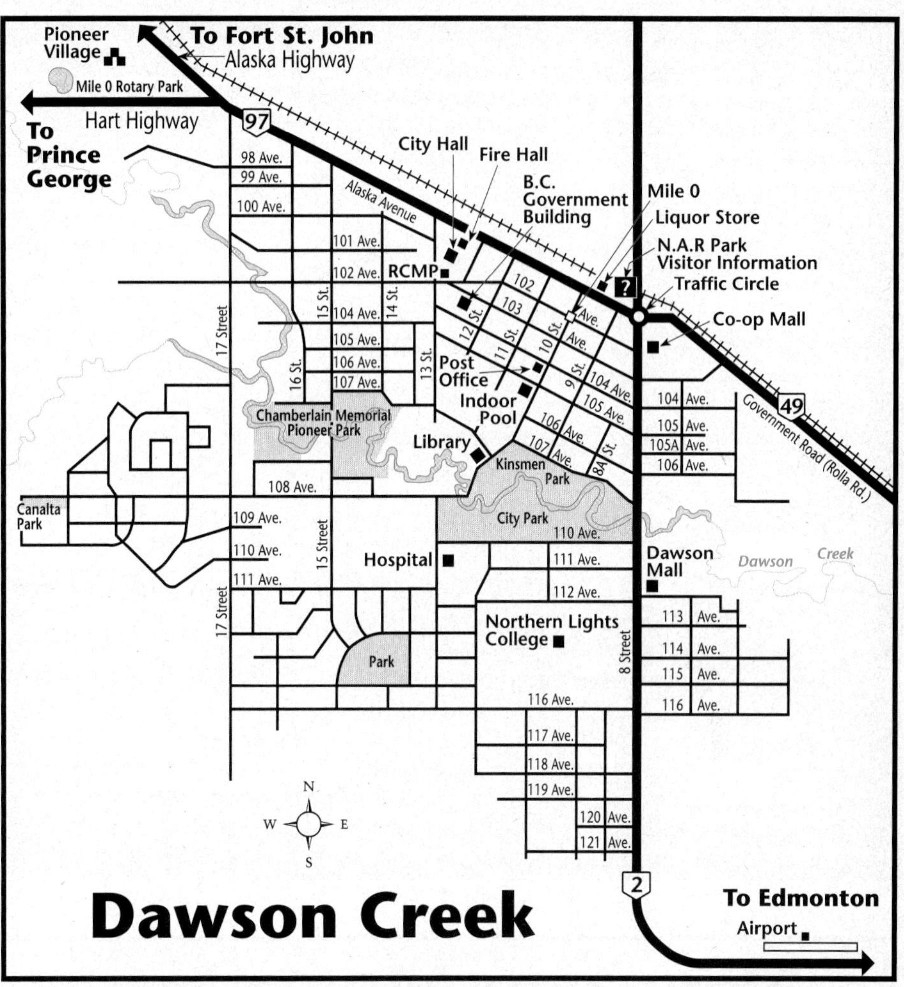

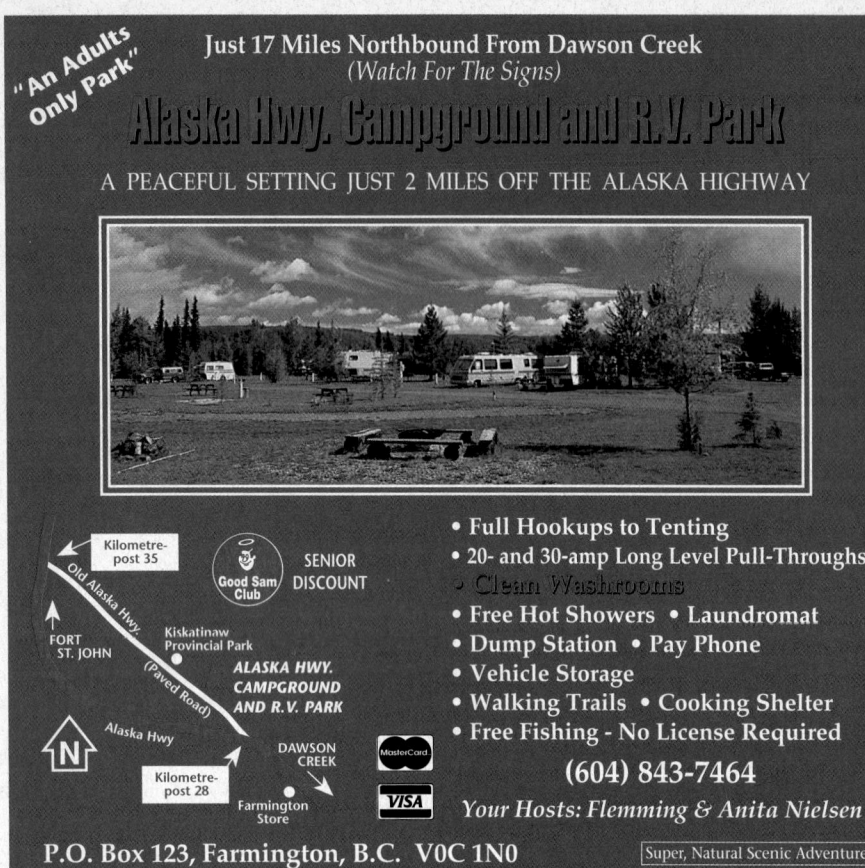

eventually routed west from Calgary through Kicking Horse Pass.) The Peace River Block was held in reserve by the Dominion Government until 1912, when some of the land was opened for homesteading. The federal government restored the Peace River Block to the province of British Columbia in 1930.

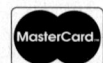

Today, agriculture is an important part of this area's economy. The fields of bright yellow flowers (in season) in the area are canola, a hybrid of rapeseed which was developed as a low cholesterol oil seed. Raw seed is processed in Alberta and Japan. The Peace River region also produces most of the province's cereal grain, along with fodder, cattle and dairy cattle. Other industries include the production of honey, hogs, eggs and poultry. Some potato and vegetable farming is also done here.

On the British Columbia Railway line and the western terminus of the Northern Alberta Railway (now Canadian National Railway), Dawson Creek is also the hub of four major highways: the John Hart Highway (Highway 97 South) to Prince George; the Alaska Highway (Highway 97 North); Highway 2, which leads east to Grande Prairie, AB; and Highway 49, which leads east to Spirit River and Donnelly.

The Northern Alberta Railway reached Dawson Creek in 1930. As a railhead,

DAWSON CREEK ADVERTISERS

Alahart RV Park.....................1725 Alaska Ave.
Alaska Cafe & Pub, The............Half-block S. of Mile 0 Post
Alaska Hwy. Campground and R.V. Park............Mile 17.3 Alaska Hwy.
Bed & Breakfast Inn Margaree.....................Ph. (604) 782-4148
Boston Pizza.........................1525 Alaska Ave.
Carline Rad & Muffler..........1400 102nd Ave.
Corlane Sporting Goods Ltd...............2 blks from Mile 0 Post
Dawson Creek Coin Laundry Ltd..........5 blocks S. of traffic circle
Dawson Creek Tourist Information Bureau.....Ph. (604) 782-9595
Dawson Mall.................On Hwy. 2, 0.75 mile from traffic circle
Econo-Lodge.................1 block E. Co-op Mall
Fynnigan's Pub...................S. entrance to city
King Koin Laundromat.................Across from BC Government Bldg.
Loiselle's Bed & Breakfast......................Ph. (604) 782-4965
Mile 0 Campsite.................Mile 0 Rotary Park
Mile Zero Esso...........................10532 8th St.
Northern Lights Bed & Breakfast...........Ph. (604) 782-3197
Northern Lights R.V. Park Ltd.........1mile from Alaska Hwy. Jct. on Hwy. 97 S.
TLC Carwash.................Across from Northern Lights College
Trail Inn................................1748 Alaska Ave.
Treasure House Imports..........10109 10th St.
Tubby's R.V. Park...................1913 Hart Hwy.
United Spring & Brake Ltd..........Directly behind McDonald's
Voyageur Motor Inn......................Across from Dawson Mall
Walter Wright Pioneer Village..............Mile 0 Rotary Park
Willow Creek Farms Bed and Breakfast.......Ph. (604) 843-7253
Yarn Barn, The....Across from Provincial Bldgs.

Dawson Creek was an important funnel for supplies and equipment during construction of the Alaska Highway in 1942. Some 600 carloads arrived by rail within a period of five weeks in preparation for the construction program, according to a report by the Public Roads Administration in 1942. A "rutted provincial road" linked Dawson Creek with Fort St. John, affording the only approach to the southern base of operations. Field headquarters were established at Fort St. John and Whitehorse. Meanwhile, men and machines continued to arrive at Dawson Creek. By May of 1942, 4,720 carloads of equipment had arrived by rail at Dawson Creek for dispersement to troops and civilian engineers to the north.

With the completion of the Alaska Highway in 1942 (and opening to the public in 1948) and the John Hart Highway in 1952, Dawson Creek expanded both as a distribution centre and tourist destination. Dawson Creek was incorporated as a city in 1958.

The development of oil and natural gas exploration in northeastern British Columbia, and related industries such as pipeline construction and oil storage, has contributed to the economic expansion of Dawson Creek. The city is also one of the major supply centres for the massive resource development known as North East Coal, southwest of Dawson Creek. Access to the coal development and the town of Tumbler Ridge is via the Heritage Highway, which branches off the John Hart Highway just west of Dawson Creek and also branches off Highway 2 southeast of the city. Highway 29 extends south from Chetwynd to Tumbler Ridge.

Louisiana Pacific's waferboard plant, located on the Alaska Highway on the north

edge of town, uses aspen and poplar logs to make sheets of waferboard, which is touted to be stronger than plywood.

Provincial government offices and social services for the South Peace region are located in Dawson Creek. The city has a modern 100-bed hospital, a public library and a college (Northern Lights). There are also an indoor swimming pool, two skating arenas, a curling arena, bowling alley, golf course, art gallery, museum, tennis and racquetball courts. There are numerous churches in Dawson Creek (check at the visitor infocentre for location and hours of worship).

ACCOMMODATIONS

There are 14 hotels/motels, several bed and breakfasts and dozens of restaurants. Department stores, banks, grocery, drug and hardware stores and many specialty shops are located both downtown and in the two shopping centres, Co-op Mall and Dawson Mall. Dawson Mall is considered to be the most modern shopping complex in the Peace River region. Visitors will also find laundromats, car washes, gas stations and automotive repair shops. The liquor store is adjacent the NAR visitor information centre on Alaska Avenue.

There are four campgrounds in Dawson Creek, two located on either side of the Hart Highway at its junction with the Alaska Highway and two located on Alaska Avenue. There is a private campground on the Hart Highway, 2 miles/3.2 km west from the Alaska Highway junction. There are also a private campground and provincial park campground 17 miles/28 km north of Dawson Creek on the Alaska Highway. ▲

The Alaska Cafe and Pub combines the spirit of northern adventure with Old World charm. *Where to Eat in Canada*, which lists the 500 top restaurants, suggests "it is a good idea to start out on the Alaska Highway with a good meal under your belt and there's no better place than the Alaska Cafe." The Cafe also holds membership in World Famous Restaurants International; a definite must to experience! Open daily for brunch, lunch, dinner and snacks. American Express, Visa and MasterCard. Located 55 paces south of the Mile "0" Post. In days of old, the Hotel Alaska proclaimed, "When you drop in to Dawson Creek, do drop in to the Dew Drop Inn." The pub features live entertainment nightly, a hot spot in town. The Alaska's Bed & Breakfast "rooms with charm" have been newly renovated in the "old style" — in addition to original furnishings, the building provides a perfect backdrop for the Kux-Kardos collection of antiques and works of art. At the Alaska, our philosophy is Deluxe Evolutionary ... "Always changing for the better." Phone (604) 782-7998. Enjoy super, natural scenic adventure. [ADVERTISEMENT]

Northern Lights Bed and Breakfast. Make yourself comfortable in our antique-filled home, enjoy the works of local artists and share your travel adventures with us. Scrumptious breakfasts. Centrally located; walking distance to recreational facilities, shopping and bus routes. Your hosts, Lloyd and Shelagh Glibbery. 1501 105th Ave., Dawson Creek, BC V1G 2M5. Phone for reservations (604) 782-3197. [ADVERTISEMENT]

Tubby's R.V. Park. On Highway 97 South (Hart Highway) toward Prince George, three blocks from the junction with the Alaska Highway. Clean, modern restrooms, easy access, full hookups, all level. Picnic tables,

tent sites, laundromat, free hot showers, Good Sam Park. Adjacent to swimming pool; five-bay RV and car wash, 30-amp service, on city bus route. Walking distance to restaurants. Phone (604) 782-2584. [ADVERTISEMENT] ▲

TRANSPORTATION

Air: Scheduled service from Dawson Creek airport to Prince George, Vancouver, Edmonton, Grande Prairie and Calgary via Air BC. The airport is located 3 miles/4.8 km south of the Alaska Avenue traffic circle via 8th Street/Highway 2; there is a small terminal at the airport. There is also a floatplane base.

Railroad: Northern Alberta Railway (now CNR) and British Columbia Railway provide freight service only. B.C. Railway provides passenger service from Vancouver to Prince George.

Bus: Coachways service to Prince George and Vancouver, BC; Edmonton, AB; and Whitehorse, YT. Dawson Creek also has a city bus transit system.

ATTRACTIONS

NAR Park, on Alaska Avenue at 10th Street (near the traffic circle), is the site of the Tourist Information Bureau which is housed in a restored railway station. The tourist bureau offers a self-guided historical walking tour with descriptions of Dawson Creek in the early 1940s during construction of the Alaska Highway.

Also at the station is the Dawson Creek Station Museum, operated by the South Peace Historical Society, which contains pioneer artifacts and wildlife displays.

In front of the station is a 1933 railway car. Adjacent the station is a huge wooden grain elevator which has been refurbished; its annex now houses an art gallery which features art shows throughout the summer. The last of Dawson Creek's old elevators, it was bought and moved to its present location by the art society in 1982.

Recreational facilities in Dawson Creek include a bowling alley, indoor pool, two ice arenas, curling rink, 18-hole golf course, tennis courts, and an outdoor pool at Rotary Lake Park.

Walter Wright Pioneer Village and Mile 0 Rotary Park are a must-see attraction. The pioneer village contains an impressive collection of local pioneer buildings, including a teahouse, photo studio, artist's studio and store. Adjacent the village is Toms Lake Hall, which offers dinner theatre during the summer. The dinner show's theme is the 1940s, when the building of the Alaska Highway forever changed Dawson Creek. Inquire at the Tourist Information Bureau for show times. The village and hall share the same site as Rotary Lake, an outdoor swimming pool.

Tumbler Ridge Side Trip. To reach Tumbler Ridge, drive west from Dawson Creek 12

miles/20 km on Highway 97 to junction with the Heritage Highway (see **Milepost PG 237.7** in the WEST ACCESS ROUTE section), or drive west 60.6 miles/97.5 km to junction with Highway 29 South (see **Milepost PG 189.4** in the WEST ACCESS ROUTE section). Heritage Highway 5 (paved and gravel) leads south 59.5 miles/96 km to the community of Tumbler Ridge. Highway 29 South is paved maintained road all the way to Tumbler Ridge. Tumbler Ridge is the townsite for Quintette Coal Limited's large-scale surface mines, and also serves workers of the Bullmoose Mine. Tours of Quintette and Bullmoose mines are available; inquire at the information centre in Tumbler Ridge. The huge coal processing plant and overhead conveyor are visible from the road. Monkman Provincial Park, site of spectacular 225-foot/69-m Kinuseo (Keh-NEW-see-oh) Falls, lies south of Tumbler Ridge. Contact BC Parks in Prince George (565-6270), Fort St. John or Tumbler Ridge for more information.

At Tumbler Ridge, motorists have a choice: return to Highway 97 via Highway 5; return to Highway 97 via Highway 29 South to Chetwynd; or continue on the Heritage Highway loop 92 miles/148 km via all-gravel road to Highway 2 southeast of Dawson Creek. There are no services on the Heritage Highway except at Tumbler Ridge, which has a motel, campground, bank and shopping. On gravel stretches of the road, watch for poor road conditions in wet weather.

Alaska Highway Log

BC HIGHWAY 97
Distance* from Dawson Creek (DC) is followed by distance from Fairbanks (F). Original mileposts are indicated in the text as Historical Mile.

*Mileages from Dawson Creek are based on actual driving distance. Kilometres from Dawson Creek are based on physical kilometreposts. Please read Mileposts and Kilometreposts in the introduction on page 66 for an explanation of how this highway is logged.

DC 0 F 1488 (2394.6 km) **Mile 0** marker of the Alaska Highway on 10th Street in downtown Dawson Creek.

Northbound: Good pavement approximately next 284 miles/457 km (through Fort Nelson). Watch for road construction and surface changes from Pink Mountain north.

DC 1.2 (1.9 km) **F 1486.8** (2392.7 km) Junction of the Alaska Highway and John Hart Highway.

Prince George-bound travelers turn to the end of the WEST ACCESS ROUTE section and read log back to front. Alaska-bound travelers continue with this log.

DC 1.5 (2.4 km) **F 1486.5** (2392.2 km) Mile 0 Rotary Park, Walter Wright Pioneer Village and Mile 0 Campground to west. ▲

DC 1.7 (2.7 km) **F 1486.3** (2391.9 km) **Historic Milepost 2.** Sign about Cantel Repeater Station. Cantel telephone–teletype lines stretched from Alberta to Fairbanks, AK, making it one of the world's longest open wire toll circuits at the time.

DC 2 (3.2 km) **F 1486** (2391.4 km) Recreation centre and golf course to west. Louisiana Pacific's waferboard plant to east.

DC 2.7 (4.3 km) **F 1485.3** (2390.3 km) Truck scales and public phone to east. Truck stop to west; gas, cafe.

DC 2.9 (4.7 km) **F 1485.1** (2390 km) Northern Alberta Railway (NAR) tracks.

DC 3.3 (5.3 km) **F 1484.7** (2389.3 km) Turnout with litter barrel to east. **Historic Milepost 3;** historic sign marks Curan & Briggs Ltd. Construction Camp, U.S. Army Traffic Control Centre.

DC 3.4 (5.5 km) **F 1484.6** (2389.2 km) **Historical Mile 3. The Trading Post** to east. See display ad this section.

DC 9.5 (15.3 km) **F 1478.5** (2379.3 km) Golf course, driving range and RV park.

Farmington Fairways and Campground. Newly opened (fall 1993), 9-hole par 36 golf course, grass greens, treed fairways. Driving range, club house, rentals available. 28-site shaded campground, firepits, tables, pit toilets and sani-station.

(RV park with 23 pull-through hookups under development.) Camp under the trees and golf at your leisure. (604) 843-7677. (Visa and MasterCard.) Enjoy super, natural scenic adventure. [ADVERTISEMENT] ▲

DC 11.2 (18 km) **F 1476.8** (2376.6 km) Turnout with litter barrels to west.

DC 11.5 (18.5 km) **F 1476.5** (2376.1 km) Turnout with litter barrels to east.

DC 13.1 (21.1 km) **F 1474.9** (2373.5 km) **Historic Milepost 13** "Start of Storms Contracting Co. Ltd. contract."

DC 14.8 (24 km) **F 1473.2** (2370.8 km) Farmington (unincorporated).

DC 15.2 (24.5 km) **F 1472.8** (2370.2 km) Farmington store to west; gas, groceries, phone.

DC 17.3 (27.8 km) **F 1470.7** (2366.8 km) **Alaska Hwy. Campground and R.V. Park.** Turnoff 17 miles north of Dawson Creek onto the Kiskatinaw Provincial Park road (old Alaska Highway, paved). A short 2 miles to a peaceful setting on green grass, surrounded by trees and flowers. A spot for every need and something for every interest. We know you'll enjoy this supervised adults-only RV park, just minutes away from the hectic highway. See advertisement in Dawson Creek section. [ADVERTISEMENT] ▲

DC 17.3 (27.8 km) **F 1470.7** (2366.8 km) Exit east for loop road to private campground and Kiskatinaw Provincial Park. Follow good two-lane paved road (old Alaska Highway) 2 miles/3.2 km for Alaska Hwy. Campgrounds, 2.5 miles/4 km for Kiskatinaw Provincial Park. This side road gives travelers the opportunity to drive the original old Alaska Highway and to cross the historic curved wooden Kiskatinaw River bridge. Sign at bridge notes that this 531-foot-/162-m-long structure is the only original timber bridge built along the Alaska Highway that is still in use today. The provincial park has 28 campsites, drinking water, firewood, picnic tables, fire rings, outhouses, garbage containers, and grayling and Dolly Varden fishing in the **Kiskatinaw River**. Camping fee $7 to $12. ▲

DC 17.5 (28.2 km) **F 1470.5** (2366.5 km) Distance marker indicates Fort St. John 29 miles/47 km.

DC 19.4 (31.2 km) **F 1468.6** (2363.4 km) Large turnout to east.

DC 19.8 (31.9 km) **F 1468.2** (2362.8 km) Highway descends northbound to Kiskatinaw River.

DC 20.9 (33.6 km) **F 1467.1** (2361 km) Kiskatinaw River bridge. *CAUTION: Strong crosswinds on bridge.* Turnout with litter barrel and picnic tables to east at north end of bridge. View of unique bridge support.

DC 21.6 (34.5 km) **F 1466.4** (2359 km) Loop road to Kiskatinaw Provincial Park, Kiskatinaw River bridge and private campground (see **Milepost DC 17.3**).

DC 25.4 (41 km) **F 1462.6** (2353.8 km) NorthwesTel microwave tower to east. Alaska Highway travelers will be seeing many of these towers as they drive north. The Northwest Communications System was constructed by the U.S. Army in 1942–43. This land line was replaced in 1963 with the construction of 42 microwave relay stations by Canadian National Telecommunications (Cantel, now NorthwesTel) between Grande Prairie, AB, and the YT–AK border.

DC 30.5 (49.1 km) **F 1457.5** (2345.5 km) Turnout to east with litter barrels. Turnout to west with litter barrels, pit toilet and historical marker about explorer Alexander Mackenzie.

Historic curved Kiskatinaw River bridge is the only original timber bridge remaining along the Alaska Highway that is still in use. (Earl L. Brown, staff)

Highway begins steep winding descent northbound to the Peace River bridge. *CAUTION: Trucks check your brakes.* Good views to northeast of Peace River valley and industrial community of Taylor. Some wide gravel shoulder next 4 miles/6.4 km for northbound traffic to pull off.

DC 32.1 (51.6 km) **F 1455.9** (2343 km) Large turnout with litter barrels. Viewpoint with information panel.

DC 33.8 (54.4 km) **F 1454.2** (2340.2 km) Pingle Creek.

DC 34 (54.7 km) **F 1454** (2339.9 km) Access to Taylor Landing Provincial Park; boat launch, parking and fishing. A Peace River jet boat outfit operates backcountry tours from here. Also access to Peace Island Regional Park, 0.5 mile/0.8 km west of the highway, situated on an island in the Peace River connected to the south shore by a causeway. Peace Island has 26 shaded campsites with gravel pads, firewood, fire rings, picnic tables, picnic shelter, toilets, pump water, playground and horseshoe pits. There are also four large picnic areas and a tenting area. Camping fee. Open Memorial Day to Labour Day. Nature trail, good bird watching and good fishing in clear water. Boaters should use caution on the Peace River since both parks are downstream from the W.A.C. Bennett and Peace Canyon dams and water levels may fluctuate rapidly. ▲

DC 34.4 (55.4 km) **F 1453.6** (2339.3 km) Peace River bridge. Gas pipeline bridge visible to east.

Bridging the Peace was one of the first goals of Alaska Highway engineers in 1942. Traffic moving north from Dawson Creek was limited by the Peace River crossing, where two ferries with a capacity of 10 trucks per hour were operating in May. Three different pile trestles were constructed across the Peace River, only to be washed out by high water. Work on the permanent 2,130-foot suspension bridge began in December 1942 and was completed in July 1943. One of two suspension bridges on the Alaska Highway, the Peace River bridge collapsed in 1957 after erosion undermined the north anchor block of the bridge. The cantilever and truss type bridge that crosses the Peace River today was completed in 1960.

DC 35 (56.3 km) **F 1453** (2338.3 km) **Historic Milepost 35** at **TAYLOR** (pop. 821; elev. 1,804 feet/550m), on the north bank of the Peace River. **Visitor Information**: On left northbound (10114–100 St.); phone (604) 789-9015. Inquire here about industrial tours of Canadian Forest Products, Fiberco Pulpmill and Greenhouse Complex. Taylor is an industrial community clustered around a Westcoast Energy Inc. gas-processing plant and large sawmill. Established in 1955 with the discovery and development of a natural gas field in the area, Taylor is the site of a pulp mill and plants which handle sulfur processing, gas compressing, high-octane aviation gas production and other byproducts of natural gas. The Westcoast Energy natural gas pipeline reaches from here to Vancouver, BC, with a branch to western Washington.

The fertile Taylor Flats area has several market gardens and roadside stands in summer. A hotel, motels, cafes, grocery store, private RV park, gas station and post office are located here. Free municipal dump station and potable water located behind the Taylor Hotel and Petro–Canada gas station. Taylor holds an annual Class A World Gold Panning Championship in August. Recreation facilities include a motorcross track and recreation complex with swimming pool. ▲

Redwood Esso and Taylor Lodge. See display ad this section.

DC 36.3 (58.4 km) **F 1451.7** (2336.2 km) Railroad tracks.

DC 40 (64.5 km) **F 1448** (2330.3 km) **Historical Mile 41.** Post office; private campground. ▲

DC 40.3 (64.9 km) **F 1447.7** (2329.8 km) Exit east for Fort St. John airport.

DC 40.4 (65 km) **F 1447.6** (2329.6 km) B.C. Railway overhead tracks.

DC 40.9 (65.8 km) **F 1447.1** (2328.8 km) **Historic Milepost 42** "Access Road to Fort St. John Airport."

DC 41.3 (66.5 km) **F 1446.7** (2328.2 km) **Historical Mile 42.3. The Honey Place** to west. See display ad this section.

DC 45.7 (73.5 km) **F 1442.3** (2321.1 km) **Historic Milepost 47**, Fort St. John/"Camp Alcan" sign. In 1942 Fort St. John "exploded." What had been home to 200 became a temporary base for more than 6,000.

DC 45.8 (73.7 km) **F 1442.2** (2320.9 km) South access to Fort St. John via 100th Street. Exit east for visitor information and downtown Fort St. John.

DC 47 (75.6 km) **F 1441** (2319 km) **Historical Mile 48.** North access to Fort St. John via 100th Avenue to downtown. Truck stop with 24-hour gas and food.

Fort St. John

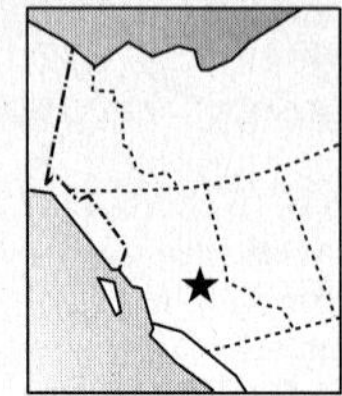

DC 47 (75.6 km) **F 1441** (2319 km) Located approximately 236 miles/380 km south of Fort Nelson. **Population:** 14,000; area 40,000. **Emergency Services: RCMP,** phone 785-6617. **Fire Department:** phone 785-2323. **Ambulance,** phone 785-2079. **Hospital,** on Centre (100th) Avenue and 96th Street, phone 785-6611.

Visitor Information: Travel Infocentre located behind the 150-foot oil derrick in the museum, 9323 100th St. (Fort St. John, BC V1J 4N4); phone (604) 785-3033. Open year-round: 8 A.M. to 8 P.M. in summer, 8:30 A.M. to 5 P.M. the rest of the year. While here, visitors may also contact the Ministry of Environment & Parks, Parks and Outdoor Recreation Division, regarding wilderness hiking opportunities along the Alaska Highway. The Ministry is located at 10003–110 Ave., Room 250, Fort St. John, BC V1J 6M7; phone (604) 787-3407.

Elevation: 2,275 feet/693m. **Radio:** CKNL 560. **Television:** Cable. **Newspaper:** *Alaska Highway News* (daily), *The Northerner* (weekly).

Private Aircraft: Fort St. John airport, 3.8 miles/6.1 km east; elev. 2,280 feet/695m; length 6,900 feet/2,103m and 6,700 feet/2,042m; asphalt; fuel 80, 100. Charlie Lake airstrip, 6.7 miles/10.8 km northwest; elev. 2,680 feet/817m; length 1,800 feet/549m; gravel; fuel 80, 100.

Visitor services are located just off the Alaska Highway and in the town centre, a few blocks north of the highway. Fort St. John is a large modern city with all services available.

Fort St. John is set in the low, rolling hills of the Peace River Valley. The original Fort St. John was established in 1806 on the muddy banks of the Peace River, about 10 miles south of the present townsite, as a trading post for the Sikanni and Beaver Indians. The earlier Rocky Mountain Fort site, near the mouth of the Moberly River, dates from 1794. (The city of Fort St. John plans a 200th birthday celebration in 1994.) A granite monument, located on Mackenzie Street (100th Street) in Fort St. John's Centennial Park, is inscribed to Sir Alexander Mackenzie, who camped here on his journey west to the Pacific Ocean in 1793. Mackenzie was looking for trade routes for the North West fur company. He reached Bella Coola on July 22, 1793.

In 1942, Fort St. John became field headquarters for U.S. Army troops and civilian engineers working on construction of the Alaska Highway in the eastern sector. It was the largest camp, along with Whitehorse (headquarters for the western sector), of the dozen or so construction camps along the highway. Much of the field housing, road building equipment and even office supplies were scrounged from old Civilian Conservation Corps camps and the Work Projects Administration.

As reported by Theodore A. Huntley of the Public Roads Administration, "A narrow winter road from Fort St. John to Fort Nelson, 256 miles north, provided the only access to the forest itself. From Fort St. John north and west for almost 1,500 miles the wilderness was broken only by dog and pack trails or short stretches of winter road, serviceable only until made impassable by the spring thaw.

"But men and machines were arriving by the thousands for its final conquest. Within six months the first vehicle to travel overland to Alaska would roll into Fairbanks.

"Thus was a Highway born."

The Alaska Highway was opened to the

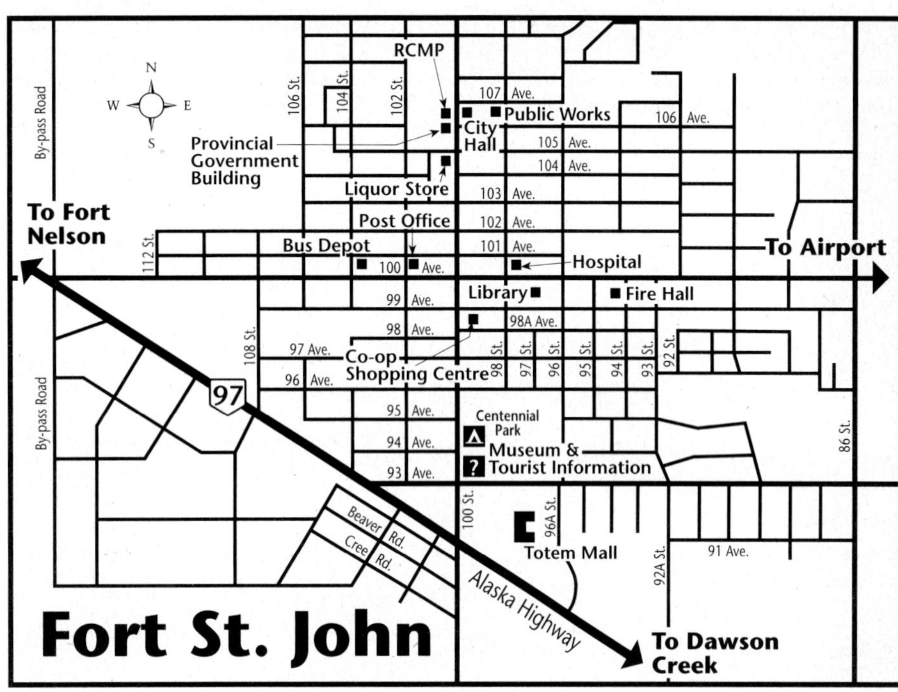

FORT ST. JOHN ADVERTISERS

Alaska Highway Bed & Breakfast ......Ph. (604) 785-3532
Backcountry Adventure Tours ......Ph. (604) 787-5359
Caravan Motel ......Ph. (604) 787-1191
Cedar Lodge Motor Inn ......Ph. (604) 785-8107
City of Fort St. John ......Ph. (604) 785-6037
Eagle "T" Towing ......Ph. (604) 785-4404
Fort St. John Motor Inn ......Behind the courthouse
Fort St. John-North Peace Museum ......Downtown at the derrick
Four Seasons Motor Inn ...Ph. (604) 785-6647
Husky Car and Truck Wash ......Across from McDonald's
North Peace Cultural Centre ......10015 100th Ave.
Northwoods Inn ......Ph. (604) 787-1616
Totem Mall ......Alaska Hwy.

traveling public in 1948, attracting vacationers and homesteaders. An immense natural oil and gas field discovered in 1955 made Fort St. John the oil capital of British Columbia. Land of the New Totems, referring to the many oil rigs, became the slogan for the region.

An extension of the Pacific Great Eastern Railway, now called British Columbia Railway, from Prince George in 1958 (continued to Fort Nelson in 1971), gave Fort St. John a link with the rail yards and docks at North Vancouver.

Today, Fort St. John is a centre for oil and gas exploration, forestry and agriculture. Farms in the North Peace region raise grain and livestock, such as sheep and cattle. Bison are also raised locally. The fields of clover and alfalfa have also attracted bees, and honey is produced for both local markets and export.

TRANSPORTATION

Air: Canadian Regional Airlines and Central Mountain Air to Fort Nelson, Watson Lake, Whitehorse, Vancouver, Grande Prairie, Edmonton and Prince George. **Bus**: Coachways service to Prince George, Vancouver, Edmonton and Whitehorse; depot at 10355 101st Ave., phone 785-6695.

ACCOMMODATIONS

Numerous major motels, hotels, restaurants and full-service gas stations are located on the Alaska Highway and in town. Other services include laundromat, car wash and shops. A large shopping mall is located on the Alaska Highway. Indoor public pool; phone 785-6148 for schedule. The North Peace Cultural Centre has a library.

Alaska Highway Bed & Breakfast. Spacious, comfortable, country-style home on 5 acres, 1 km off and overlooking the Alaska Highway. Great view and wide open feeling. Close to Charlie Lake boat launch and Beatton Provincial Park. Home-cooked delicious breakfasts. Your hosts, Cecilia and Jaye Hetrick. Write: SS #2, Site 7, Comp. 24, Fort St. John, BC V1J 4M7 or phone (604) 785-3532. [ADVERTISEMENT]

Fort St. John RV Park, located at the east end of Centennial Park behind the tourist centre and museum, has 39 sites, showers, a laundry, dump station and hookups; senior citizen rates. Fresh water fill-up and dump station located at the northwest corner of 86th Street and the Alaska Highway. Also camping north of the city at Beatton and Charlie Lake provincial parks, and at private and Rotary campgrounds at Charlie Lake. ▲

ATTRACTIONS

Centennial Park, located on 100th Street, has a museum, the Tourist Information Centre and an RV park. The Fort St. John–North Peace Museum houses more than 6,000 artifacts from the region, including items from Finch's Store (the first store in Fort St. John), an 1806 Fort St. John post, a trapper's cabin and early-day schoolroom. Inquire at the Tourist Information Centre about local hiking trails, trail rides and the lily farm. The tourist centre and museum are open 8 A.M. to 8 P.M. daily in summer.

Directly in front of the tourist centre is a 150-foot oil derrick, presented to the North Peace Historical Society and the people of Fort St. John. The derrick is especially resplendent in winter when it is decorated with Christmas lights, making it the tallest Christmas tree in northern British Columbia. Check with the North Peace Museum (787-0430) about free summer entertainment at the derrick. "Doin's at the Derrick" features volunteer talent shows at 7 P.M. and 9 P.M. daily, mid-June to mid-August.

Play golf. Fort St. John's only in-town golf course is Links Golf Course, just off the Bypass Road at 86 Street; nine holes, pro shop and lounge. Phone 785-9995. The Lakepoint Golf Course, on Golf Course Road at Charlie Lake, is rated as the fifth nicest course in British Columbia. Open 8 A.M. to 7 P.M. daily; 18 holes, pro shop, licensed lounge and restaurant. Phone 785-5566.

Industry and agriculture of the area are showcased for the public at various places. Check with the Infocentre for directions and details. Among those of interest are: Bickford's Buffalo Ranch, phone 781-3507; Canada Forestry Products, 785-8906; and The Honey Place, just south of town on the Alaska Highway, which offers fresh honey for sale and the world's Largest Glass Beehive for viewing year-round.

W.A.C. Bennett Dam is a major attraction in the area. For an interesting side trip, drive north from Fort St. John on the Alaska Highway to **Milepost DC 53.7** and take Highway 29 west 46.5 miles/74.8 km to Hudson's Hope. Highway 29 follows the original Canadian government telegraph trail of 1918. Hudson's Hope, formerly a pioneer community established in 1805 by explorer Simon Fraser, grew with construction of the W.A.C. Bennett Dam, which is located 13.5 miles/21.7 km west of town. B.C. Hydro's Peace Canyon dam is located approximately 4 miles/6.4 km south of Hudson's Hope. Turn to the HUDSON'S HOPE LOOP section for more information.

Alaska Highway Log

(continued)

Distance* from Dawson Creek (DC) is followed by distance from Fairbanks (F). Original mileposts are indicated in the text as Historical Mile.

*Mileages from Dawson Creek are based on actual driving distance. Kilometres from Dawson Creek are based on physical kilometreposts. Please read Mileposts and Kilometreposts in the introduction for an explanation of how this highway is logged.

DC 45.8 (73.7 km) **F 1442.2** (2320.9 km) South access to Fort St. John via 100th Street.

DC 47 (75.6 km) **F 1441** (2319 km) **Mile 48.** North access to Fort St. John via 100th Avenue. Truck stop with 24-hour gas and food.

DC 48.6 (78.2 km) **F 1439.4** (2316.4 km) **Historic Milepost 49** commemorates "Camp Alcan."

DC 49.5 (79.6 km) **F 1438.5** (2315 km) Exit for Beatton Provincial Park, 5 miles/8 km east via paved road; 37 campsites, picnic shelter, wood stove, horseshoe pits, volleyball net, playground, baseball field, sandy beach, swimming and boat launch. Camping fee $7 to $12. Fishing for northern pike, walleye (July best) and yellow perch in **Charlie Lake.** ▲

DC 50.6 (81.4 km) **F 1437.4** (2313.2 km) **CHARLIE LAKE** (unincorporated), gas station, grocery, pub, private RV park and Ministry of Energy, Mines and Petroleum. Access to lakeshore east side of highway; boat launch, no parking. At one time during construction of the Alaska Highway, Charlie Lake was designated Mile 0, as there was already a road between the railhead at Dawson Creek and Fort St. John, the eastern sector headquarters for troops and engineers.

Charlie Lake General Store. See display ad this section.

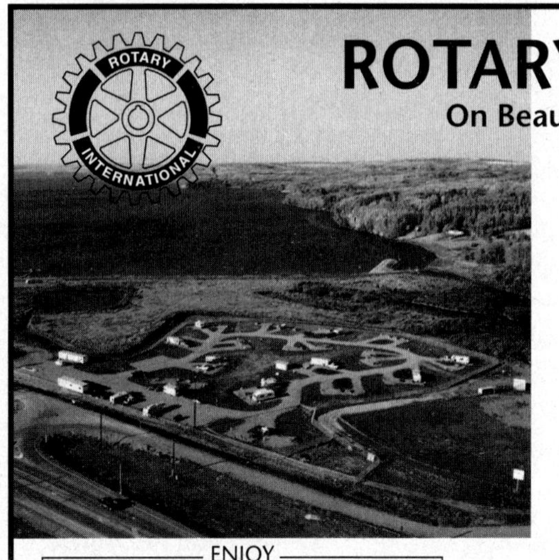

Rotary R.V. Park. Mile 51/km 86 Alaska Highway, Charlie Lake, 6 km north of Fort St. John. 40 serviced sites, full and partial hookups, 30 amp power, coin showers, laundry, washrooms, handicapped facilities, sani-station, pay phone, security fenced, firewood available. Close to Charlie Lake boat ramp and dock, where there is some of the best walleye fishing in BC. Convenience store, service station and landmark Red Barn pub close by. Phone (604) 785-1700 for reservations. Discount rates for caravans. Open May-Sept. Watch for signs "Rotary Park & RV Campground." Visa accepted. Enjoy Super, Natural British Columbia. [ADVERTISEMENT] ♿▲

DC 51.2 (82.4 km) **F 1436.8** (2312.2 km) **Historic Milepost 52.** Charlie Lake Mile 0 Army Tote Road. Site of a major distribution camp for workers and supplies heading north. Twelve American soldiers also drowned here in 1942 while crossing the lake aboard pontoon barges.

DC 51.5 (82.9 km) **F 1436.5** (2311.7 km) **Ron's R.V. Park. Historical Mile 52.** Treed sites with complete RV hookups, shaded lawned tenting areas, picnic tables, firepits, firewood provided. Walking trails, playground, flush toilets, hot showers, laundromat, pay phone, ice, mini-variety store (gift shop). Coffee shop, covered patio seating. Shaded full-hookup pull-throughs, good drinking water. Large boat launching facilities nearby. Boat rentals. Fishing licenses. Quiet location away from hectic city confusion. Post office, golf course, Red Barn Pub nearby. Charlie Lake, world famous for walleye and northern pike fishing. Phone (604) 787-1569. [ADVERTISEMENT] ▲

DC 52 (83.7 km) **F 1436** (2311 km) Exit east on Charlie Lake Road for lakeshore picnicking.

DC 53.6 (86.3 km) **F 1434.4** (2308.4 km) Truck weigh scales east side of highway.

DC 53.7 (86.4 km) **F 1434.3** (2308.2 km) **Junction** with Highway 29, which leads west to Hudson's Hope and the W.A.C. Bennett Dam, then south to connect with the Hart Highway (97) at Chetwynd. (See HUDSON'S HOPE LOOP section.) Truck stop to west.

Turn east for Charlie Lake Provincial Park, just off highway: paved loop road (with speed bumps) leads through campground. There are 58 shaded sites, picnic tables, kitchen shelter with wood stove, firepits, firewood, outhouses, dump station, water and garbage. Level gravel sites, some will accommodate two large RVs. Camping fee $7 to $12. Playfield, playground, horseshoe pits, volleyball net and a 1.2-mile/2-km hiking trail down to lake. Watch for wildflowers: Because of the wide variety of plants here, including some that may not be seen elsewhere along the Alaska Highway, Verna E. Pratt's *Wildflowers Along the Alaska Highway* includes a special list of species for this park. Fishing in **Charlie Lake** for walleye, northern pike and yellow perch. Access to the lake for vehicles and boats is from the Alaska Highway just east of the park entrance. Boat launch and picnic area at lake. ▲

DC 63.6 (102 km) **F 1424.4** (2292.3 km) Microwave tower to east.

DC 65.4 (105 km) **F 1422.6** (2289.4 km) Turnout with litter barrel to west.

DC 71.7 (115.4 km) **F 1416.3** (2279.3 km) **Historical Mile 72.** Food, gas, camping, lodging and crafts store. ▲

Northern Expressions Gifts is a point of interest along the Alaska Highway. It is a log cabin you would expect to see in the Last Frontier. There is easy access for motorhomes, plenty of parking and a nice restful place to stop. The old-fashioned shop will

give you the feeling of old and possibly better days. Come and enjoy our homemade candies and unique selection of gifts including handmade quilts, T-shirts, jewelry, moccasins, stuffed animals and much more! A favorite gift shop on the Alaska Highway! [ADVERTISEMENT]

DC 71.7 (115.4 km) **F 1416.3** (2279.3 km) **The Shepherd's Inn.** We specialize in making folks at home, offering regular and breakfast specials, complete lunch and dinner menu. Low-fat buffalo burgers. Our specialties: homemade soups, home-baked sweet rolls, cinnamon rolls, blueberry and bran muffins, bread, biscuits and trappers bannock. Delicious desserts, rhubarb-strawberry, Dutch apple and chocolate dream pie, cherry and strawberry cheesecake. Hard ice cream. Specialty coffees: Norwegian Mint, Swiss Almond. Herb teas. Refreshing fruit drinks from local fruits: blueberry and raspberry coolers. Caravaners and bus tours ... a convenient and delightful stop on your Alaska Highway adventure! You may reserve your stop – break with us. Full RV hookups, motel service 24 hours. Quality Husky products. Your "Husky Buck" is a great traveling idea. Phone (604) 827-3676. An oasis on the Alcan at Mile 72. [ADVERTISEMENT] ▲

DC 72.7 (117 km) **F 1415.3** (2277.6 km) **Historical Mile 73.** Gas and food to west (closed in 1993, current status unknown).

DC 72.8 (117.1 km) **F 1415.2** (2277.5 km) **Historic Milepost 73** commemorates Beatton River Flight Strip, one of four gravel airstrips built for American military aircraft during WWII. Road to Prespetu and Buick Creek.

DC 79.1 (127.3 km) **F 1408.9** (2267.3 km) **Historical Mile 80** paved rest area to west with litter barrels, picnic tables, water and flush toilets.

DC 91.4 (147.1 km) **F 1396.6** (2247.5 km) **Historical Mile 92.** Westcoast Energy compressor station to west.

DC 94.6 (152.2 km) **F 1393.4** (2242.4 km) Oil pump east of highway behind trees.

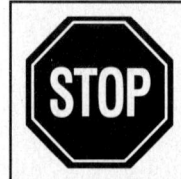

DC 101 (161.7 km) **F 1387** (2232.1 km) **Historic Milepost 101. WONOWON** (pop. 150), unincorporated, has three gas stations, three restaurants, two motels, camping, a food store, pub and post office. Formerly

known as Blueberry, Wonowon was the site of an official traffic control gate during WWII. Wonowon Horse Club holds an annual race meet and gymkhana at the track beside the highway, where the community club holds its annual snowmobile rally in February. ▲

The historic sign and interpretive panel here commemorate Blueberry Control Station, "site of the Blueberry Control Gate, a 24-hour military checkpoint operated by U.S. army personnel through the war years."

The Alaska Highway follows the Blueberry and Prophet river drainages north to Fort Nelson. The Blueberry River, not visible from the highway, lies a few miles east of Wonowon.

Blueberry Esso, Food Store & Motel. See display ad this section.

Hall's Food & Gas. See display ad this section.

DC 101.5 (163.3 km) **F 1386.5** (2231.3 km) Food, fuel (diesel, gas, propane), camping and lodging to east; open year-round. ▲

102 Husky. See display at this section.

DC 103.5 (166.5 km) **1384.5** (2228.1 km) **Historic Milepost 104** marks start of Adolphson, Huseth, Layer & Welch contract during Alaska Highway construction.

DC 114 (183.2 km) **F 1374** (2211.2 km) Paved turnout with litter barrel to east.

DC 124.3 (200 km) **F 1363.7** (2194.6 km) The Cut (highway goes through a small rock cut). Relatively few rock cuts were necessary during construction of the Alaska Highway in 1942–43. However, rock excavation was often made outside of the roadway to obtain gravel fill for the new roadbed.

DC 135.3 (217.7 km) **F 1352.7** (2176.9 km) Gravel turnout to east.

Colourful fireweed is abundant along the highway in summer. (Earl L. Brown, staff)

CAUTION: Northbound travelers watch for moose next 15 miles/24 km, especially at dusk and at night.

DC **140.4** (225.9 km) F **1347.6** (2168.7 km) **Historical Mile 143. PINK MOUNTAIN** (pop. 99, area 300; elev. 3,600 feet/1,097m). Post office, grocery, motels, restaurant, campgrounds, gas stations with minor repair service. Bus depot and ambulance service at Pink Mountain Motor Inn east side of highway.

Pink Mountain Motor Inn. Mile 143, a welcome stopping point for all travelers. 34 fully modern rooms, Get and Go groceries, gift shop, and licensed restaurant with fresh baked pies and pastries (our famed butter tarts) and home-cooked meals. The perfect lunch break stop for bus tours. Ample parking space, picnic tables. For RVs, electric hookups, gravel sites. Treed camping sites with good gravel parking. Picnic tables. Water, hot showers, laundromat. Dump station. Caravans welcome, reservations recommended. Full line of Esso products. We hope you're enjoying your Alaska Highway adventure! Fax (604) 774-1071. Phone (604) 772-3234. [ADVERTISEMENT]

Pink Mountain Campsite, on left northbound. Unleaded gas, diesel, metered propane for RVs and auto. Post office, general store, souvenirs, liquor store, fishing and hunting licenses. Shaded campsites, tents and RVs welcome. Power hookups, water and sani-dump. Cabins available $15–$20. Coin laundromat and showers. Open year-round. VISA and MasterCard. Phone and fax (604) 774-1033. Your hosts, Ron and Pat. Enjoy Super, Natural Scenic Adventure. [ADVERTISEMENT] ▲

DC **144.1** (231.9 km) F **1343.9** (2162.7 km) **Historical Mile 147. Sportsman Inn** to east. See display ad this section. ▲

DC **144.5** (232.5 km) F **1343.5** (2162.1 km) **Historical Mile 147. Mae's Kitchen** and **Ed's Garage** to east. See display ad this section.

DC **144.7** (232.9 km) F **1343.3** (2161.8

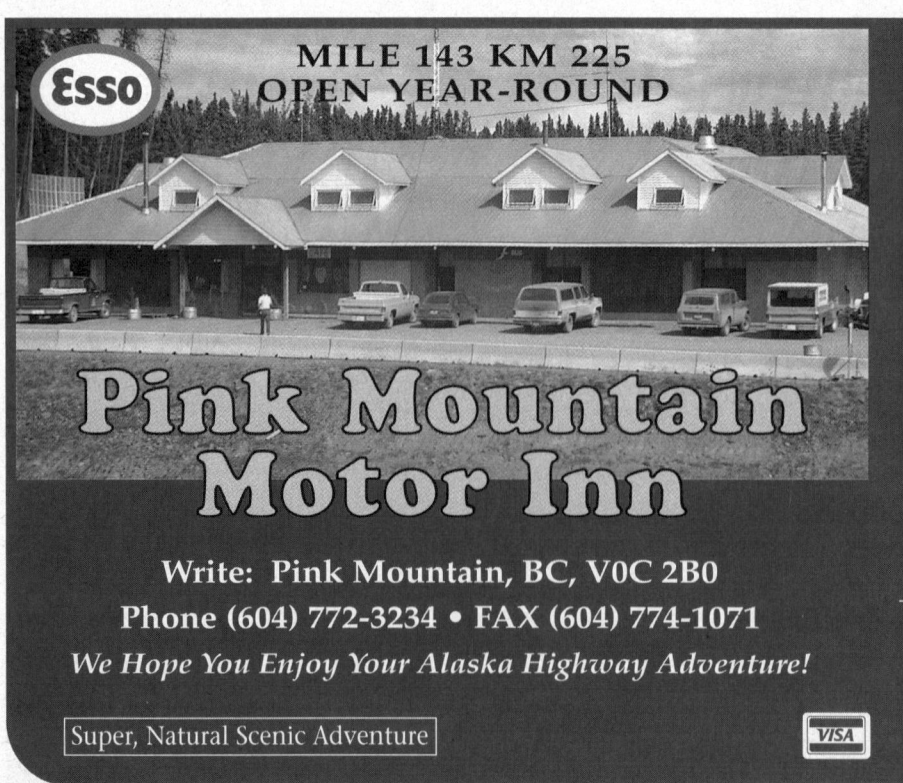

km) **Historic Milepost 148** commemorates Suicide Hill, one of the most treacherous hills on the original highway noted for its ominous greeting: "Prepare to meet thy maker." Beatton River bridge. The Beatton River was named for Frank Beatton, a Hudson's Bay Co. employee. The Beatton River flows east and then south into the Peace River system.

DC 146 (234 km) **F 1342** (2159.7 km) **Private Aircraft**: Sikanni Chief flight strip to east; elev. 3,258 feet/993m; length, 6,000 feet/1,829m; gravel; not maintained in winter, soft in spring. Well-known local pilot Jimmy "Midnight" Anderson used the Sikanni Chief airstrip.

DC 150.3 (241.9 km) **F 1337.7** (2152.8 km) *CAUTION: Southbound travelers watch for moose next 15 miles/24 km, especially at dusk and at night.*

DC 155.6 (250.4 km) **F 1332.4** (2144.2 km) Large gravel turnout with litter barrels. For the next mile northbound, the road makes a brief detour onto the old Alaska Highway. The newer and smoother realigned highway encountered some "bottomless muskeg" here, resulting in about a half-mile of unstable road.

DC 156.6 (252 km) **F 1331.4** (2142.6 km) Sikanni Hill. *CAUTION: Slow down for hill. Watch for road construction northbound to Kilometrepost 258 in 1994.*

DC 159.2 (256.2 km) **F 1328.8** (2138.4 km) Sikanni Chief River bridge (elev. 2,662 feet/811m). To the west you may see steel stanchions, all that remains of the historic wooden Sikanni bridge, which was destroyed by arson July 10, 1992. The original timber truss bridge built across the Sikanni Chief River in the spring of 1943 was the first permanent structure completed on the Alaska Highway. Highway construction crews rerouted much of the pioneer road built in 1942 and replaced temporary bridges with permanent structures in 1943. The Sikanni Chief River flows east and then north into the Fort Nelson River, which flows into the Liard River and on to the Mackenzie River which empties into the Arctic Ocean. Check at the lodge for information on Sikanni River Falls (see **Milepost DC 168.5**).

Sikanni Chief River, fair fishing at mouth of tributaries in summer for pike; grayling to $2^1/_2$ pounds; whitefish to 2 pounds.

DC 159.4 (256.5 km) **F 1328.6** (2138.1 km) **Historical Mile 162. SIKANNI CHIEF.** Food, gas, lodging and camping.

Sikanni River RV Park. Come and enjoy the only riverside RV park in the area. A peaceful, scenic setting to a natural playground for birds and wildlife. 50 supervised sites, picnic tables, fire rings. Free firewood.

Unleaded gas and propane at some of the best prices in the area. Water and dump complimentary for guests. Store, souvenirs, ice, fishing and camping supplies. Munchies. Reasonable rates. Resident owners. Clean, safe and secure. Open 7 A.M. to 9 P.M. daily. See display ad this section. [ADVERTISEMENT] ▲

DC 160.4 (258.1 km) **F 1327.6** (2136.5 km) Section of the old Alaska Highway is visible to east; no access.

DC 168.5 (271.2 km) **F 1319.5** (2123.5 km) Gravel road west to Sikanni River Falls. This private road is signed "Travel at own risk." Drive in 10.5 miles/16.9 km to parking area with picnic tables at B.C. Forest Service trailhead; 10-minute hike in on well-marked trail to view falls. Gravel access road has some steep hills and a single-lane bridge. *CAUTION: Do not travel in wet weather. Not recommended for vehicles with trailers.*

DC 172.5 (277.6 km) **F 1315.5** (2117 km) Polka Dot Creek.

DC 173.1 (278 km) **F 1314.9** (2116.9 km) Buckinghorse River bridge; access to river at north end of bridge.

DC 173.2 (278.2 km) **F 1314.8** (2115.9 km) **Historical Mile 175**. Inn with gas and camping to east at north end of bridge. Also turnoff east for Buckinghorse River Provincial Park. Follow the narrow gravel road past the gravel pit 0.7 mile/1.1 km along river to camping and picnic area. Camping fee $7 to $12. The provincial park has 30 picnic tables, side-by-side camper parking, firewood, fire rings, water pump, outhouses and

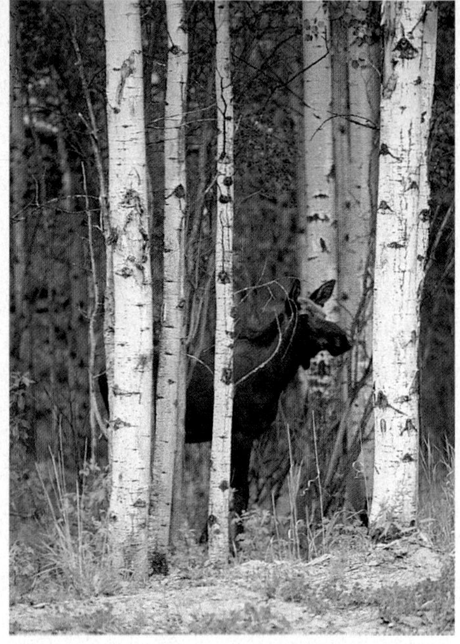

Watch for wildlife along the highway.
(Barb Michaels)

garbage containers. Poor fishing for grayling in **Buckinghorse River**. Swimming in downstream pools.

DC 173.4 (278.5 km) **F 1314.6** (2115.6 km) **Historical Mile 175. Buckinghorse River Lodge**, on left northbound. Motel, cafe with home cooking, ice cream. Bed and breakfast available. Service station, large parking area, free camping. Look forward to our friendly atmosphere. Picnic tables and beautiful scenery. A good spot to take a break to go fishing or walking. Enjoy Super, Natural Scenic Adventure. (604) 773-6468. [ADVERTISEMENT]

DC 176 (283.2 km) **F 1312** (2111.4 km) South end of 28-mile/45-km Trutch Mountain bypass. Completed in 1987, this section of road rerouted the Alaska Highway around Trutch Mountain, eliminating the steep, winding climb up to Trutch Summit (and the views). Named for Joseph W. Trutch, civil engineer and first governor of British Columbia, Trutch Mountain was the second-highest summit on the Alaska Highway with an elevation of 4,134 feet/1,260m. The new roadbed cuts a wide swath through the flat Minaker River valley. The river, not visible to motorists, is west of the highway; it was named for local trapper George Minaker. Trutch Mountain is to the east of the highway. Motorists can see part of the old highway on Trutch Mountain.

DC 182.8 (294.2 km) **F 1305.2** (2100.4 km) Large gravel turnout with litter barrel to west.

DC 204.2 (328 km) **F 1283.8** (2066 km) Beaver Creek. North end of Trutch Mountain bypass. See description at **Milepost DC 176**.

DC 217.2 (349.3 km) **F 1270.8** (2045.1 km) Turnoff to west for Prophet River Provincial Park, 0.4 mile/0.6 km via gravel road. The park access road crosses an airstrip (originally an emergency airstrip on the Northwest Air Staging Route) and part of the old Alaska Highway (the Alcan). This is the first stop on the self-guided Forest Ecology Tours (Ecotours) established by the Fort Nelson Forest District; a pamphlet is available from their office in Fort Nelson (phone 774-3936). This park is noted for its trembling aspen stands and mature white spruce. Side-by-side camper parking (36 sites), picnic tables, firewood, fire rings, water pump, outhouses and garbage containers. Camping fee $7 to $12. ▲

The Alaska Highway roughly parallels the Prophet River from here north to the Muskwa River south of Fort Nelson. *NOTE: Watch for road construction northbound to Kilometrepost 359 in 1994.*

Private Aircraft: Prophet River emergency airstrip; elev. 1,954 feet/596m; length 6,000 feet/1,829m; gravel.

DC **218.2** (350.7 km) F **1269.8** (2043.5 km) View of Prophet River to west.

DC **222.3** (357.2 km) F **1265.7** (2036.9 km) Bougie Creek bridge; turnout with litter barrel beside creek at south end of bridge.

DC **224.8** (360.6 km) F **1263.2** (2032.8 km) Microwave tower to east.

DC **226.2** (363.4 km) F **1261.8** (2030.6 km) Prophet River Indian Reserve to east.

DC **226.5** (363.9 km) F **1261.5** (2030.1 km) St. Paul's Roman Catholic Church to east.

DC **227** (364.7 km) F **1261** (2029.3 km) **Historical Mile 233. PROPHET RIVER,** gas, diesel, propane, food, camping and lodging. Southbound travelers note: Next service 68 miles/109 km. ▲

Prophet River Services. See display ad this section. ▲

DC **227.6** (366.3 km) F **1260.4** (2028.4 km) **Historic Milepost 234**, Adsett Creek Highway Realignment. This major rerouting eliminated 132 curves on the stretch of highway that originally ran between Miles 234 and 275. Turnout with litter barrels.

DC **227.7** (365.9 km) F **1260.3** (2028.2 km) Adsett Creek.

DC **230.7** (366.4 km) F **1257.3** (2023.3 km) Natural gas pipeline crosses beneath highway.

DC **232.9** (374.8 km) F **1255.1** (2019.8 km) Turnout to west with litter barrels.

DC **235.5** (378.4 km) F **1252.5** (2015.6 km) Mesalike topography to the east is Mount Yakatchie.

DC **241.5** (388 km) F **1246.5** (2006 km) Parker Creek.

DC **245.9** (395.7 km) F **1242.1** (1998.9 km) Gravel turnout with litter barrels.

DC **261.1** (420.2 km) F **1226.9** (1974.4 km) Turnout with litter barrels to east.

DC **264.6** (425.2 km) F **1223.4** (1968.8 km) Jackfish Creek bridge.

DC **265.5** (426.5 km) F **1222.5** (1967.4 km) Turnoff to east for Andy Bailey Lake Provincial Park via 6.8-mile/11-km dirt and gravel access road. (Large RVs and trailers note: only turnaround space on access road is approximately halfway in.) The park is located on **Andy Bailey Lake** (formerly Jackfish Lake); side-by-side camper parking (35 sites), tenting and picnic area, picnic tables, fire rings, firewood, water, outhouses, garbage containers, boat launch (no powerboats), swimming and fair fishing for northern pike. Camping fee $7 to $12. Bring insect repellent! ▲

DC **270.8** (435.1 km) F **1217.2** (1958.8 km) Gas pipeline crosses highway overhead.

DC **271** (435.4 km) F **1217** (1958.5 km) Westcoast Energy gas processing plant to east. Petrosul (sulfur processing) to west.

DC **276.2** (443.8 km) F **1211.8** (1950 km) Rodeo grounds to west. The rodeo is held in August.

DC **276.7** (444.6 km) F **1211.3** (1949.3 km) Railroad tracks. Microwave tower at Muskwa Heights.

The Alaska Highway south of Fort Nelson. (Ruth Fairall)

DC **277.5** (446.2 km) F **1210.5** (1948 km) Muskwa Heights (unincorporated), an industrial area with rail yard, plywood plant, sawmill and bulk fuel outlet.

DC **277.9** (447.2 km) F **1210.1** (1947.4 km) Truck stop with gas, restaurant and RV campground.

Husky 5th Wheel Truck Stop and RV Park. See display ad this section. ▲

DC **278.1** (447.5 km) F **1209.9** (1947.1 km) Truck scales to west. Turnoff for Chopstick manufacturing plant. This plant produces six million pairs of chopsticks a day. Tours by appointment only.

DC **278.4** (448 km) F **1209.6** (1946.6 km) **Trapper's Den.** Owned and operated by a local trapping family. Moose horns, diamond willow, northern novelties and books, postcards, souvenirs and professionally tanned furs. Located 300 yards north of

Husky 5th Wheel RV Park on the Alaska Highway. A truly unique souvenir shop. Open 10 A.M. to 8 P.M. daily. John and Cindy Wells. Box 1164, Fort Nelson, BC V0C 1R0; (604) 774-3400. [ADVERTISEMENT]

DC **279.5** (449.8 km) F **1208.5** (1944.8 km) **Klahanie RV Park.** Welcome to Klahanie RV Park. Now under new management. Clean and spacious. Washrooms, coin-op showers and laundry, telephone, picnic tables, firepits. Free solar shower. Screened in gazebo with BBQ. Enjoy an evening meal or just relax and take in a northern sunset overlooking the beautiful Muskwa River Valley. This is a self-register park therefore we offer these low rates. $12 full hookup, $9 overnight camping (plus tax). 10 percent seniors discount. Your choice of open or secluded sites. Box 1164, Fort Nelson, BC. (604) 774-7013. [ADVERTISEMENT] ▲

DC **281** (451.4 km) F **1207** (1942.4 km) Muskwa River bridge, lowest point on the Alaska Highway (elev. 1,000 feet/305m).

The **Muskwa River** flows northeast to the Fort Nelson River. Fair fishing at the mouth of tributaries for northern pike; some goldeye. The Fort Nelson River is too muddy for fishing.

The Alaska Highway swings west at Fort Nelson above the Muskwa River, winding southwest then northwest through the Canadian Rockies.

DC **283** (454.3 km) F **1205** (1939.2 km) Entering Fort Nelson northbound. Fort Nelson's central business district extends along the highway from the private campground at the east end of the city to the private campground at the west end. Businesses and services are located both north and south of the highway.

Fort Nelson

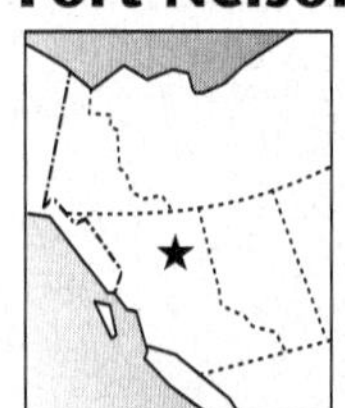

DC **283** (454.3 km) F **1205** (1939.2 km) **Historical Mile 300. Population:** 3,804; area 5,500. **Emergency Services: RCMP,** phone 774-2777. **Fire Department**, phone 774-2222. **Hospital**, 35 beds, phone 774-6916. **Ambulance**, phone 774-2344. Medical, dental and optometric clinics. Visiting veterinarians and chiropractors.

Visitor Information: Located in the Recreation Centre at the west end of town, open 8 A.M. to 8 P.M. Inquire here about local industrial tours, and also about road conditions on the Liard Highway. Fort Nelson Heritage Museum across the highway from the infocentre. Contact the Town of Fort Nelson by writing Bag Service 399, Fort Nelson, BC V0C 1R0; phone (604) 774-6400 (seasonal) or 774-2541 (all year).

Elevation: 1,383 feet/422m. **Climate**: Winters are cold with short days. Summers are hot and the days are long. In mid-June (summer solstice), twilight continues throughout the night. The average number of frost-free days annually is 116. Last frost occurs about May 11, and the first frost Sept. 21. Average annual precipitation of 16.3 inches. **Radio**: CFNL 590, CBC 1610. **Television**: Channels 8, 13 and cable. **Newspaper**: *Fort Nelson News* (weekly).

Transportation: **Air** — Scheduled service to Edmonton, Grande Prairie and Watson Lake, and to Prince George and Vancouver via Canadian Regional Airlines. Charter service available. **Bus** — Greyhound service. **Railroad** — B.C. Railway (freight service only).

Private Aircraft: Fort Nelson airport, 3.8 air miles/6.1 km east northeast; elev. 1,253 feet/382m; length 6,400 feet/1,950m; asphalt; fuel 80, 100, Jet B. Gordon Field, 4 miles/6.4 km west; elev. 1,625 feet/495m approximately; length 2,000 feet/610m; turf; fuel 80.

Fort Nelson is located in the lee of the Rocky Mountains, surrounded by the Muskwa, Nelson and Prophet rivers. The area is heavily forested with white spruce, poplar and aspen. Geographically, the town is located about 59° north latitude and 122° west longitude.

Flowing east and north, the Muskwa, Prophet and Sikanni Chief rivers converge to form the Fort Nelson River, which flows into the Liard River, then on to the Mackenzie River which empties into the Arctic Ocean. Rivers provided the only means of transportation in both summer and winter in this isolated region until 1922, when the Godsell Trail opened, connecting Fort Nelson with Fort St. John. The Alaska Highway linked Fort Nelson with the Outside in 1942.

In the spring, the Muskwa River frequently floods the low country around Fort Nelson and can rise more than 20 feet/6m. At an elevation of 1,000 feet/305m, the Muskwa (which means "bear") is the lowest point on the Alaska Highway. There was a danger of the Muskwa River bridge washing out every June during spring runoff until 1970, when a higher bridge — with piers arranged to prevent log jams — was built.

Fort Nelson's existence was originally based on the fur trade. In the 1920s, trapping was the main business in this isolated pioneer community populated with less than 200 Indians and a few white men. Trappers still harvest beaver, wolverine, weasel, wolf, fox, lynx, mink, muskrat and marten. Other area wildlife includes black bears, which are plentiful, some deer, caribou and a few grizzly bears. Moose remains an important food source for the Indians.

Fort Nelson aboriginal people are mostly Slave (slay-vee), who arrived here about 1775 from the Great Slave Lake area and

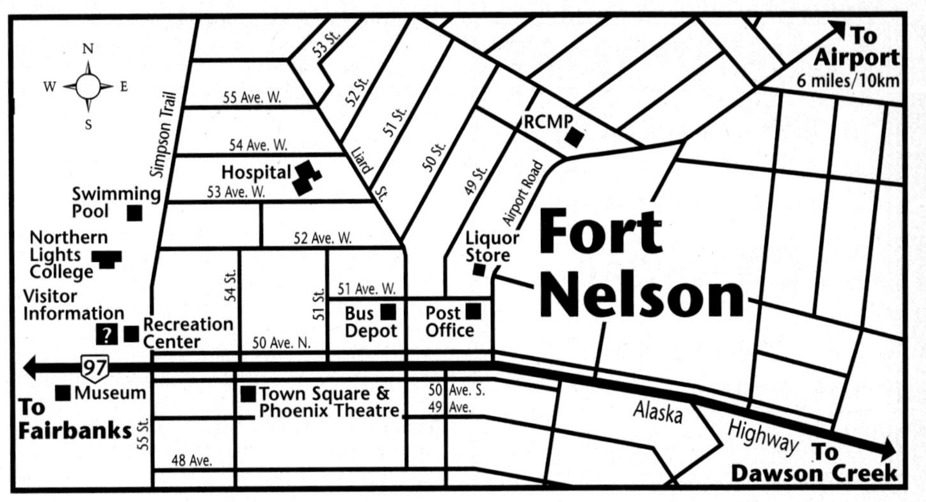

FORT NELSON ADVERTISERS

Bennetts Travel Time Inc..Ph. (604) 774-6144
Blue Bell Motel ....S. end of town
Coachouse Inn ....Ph. (604) 774-3911
Fabric Fun ....Landmark Plaza
Fontas Native Crafts ....5012 Airport Dr.
Fort Nelson Bed & Breakfast.....................Ph. (604) 774-6050
Fort Nelson Esso...........Across from post office
Fort Nelson Heritage Museum ....Across from travel infocentre
Fort Nelson Shell ....S. end of town
Home on the Hill Bed & Breakfast...........Ph. (604) 774-3000
JR Towing..........................Ph. (604) 774-3600
KaCee's Koin Kleeners..Next to IGA Foodstore
Mini-Price Inn ....Ph. (604) 774-2136
Mr. Milkshake...........1 blk. W. of Town Square
Northern Husky.............................Downtown
Northern Lights Deli ....Landmark Plaza
Peter's Place..........Next to Bank of Commerce
Pioneer Motel ....Ph. (604) 774-6459
Poplar Hills Golf and Country Club................4 miles W. of town
Provincial Motel ....S. end of town
Red Rose Convenience Store ....S. end of town
Shannon Motel.......................N. end of town
Town of Fort Nelson ....Town Square
Westend R.V. Campground and Mini-Golf ....N. end of town

speak an Athabascan dialect.

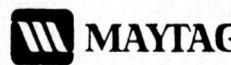

Fort Nelson was first established in 1805 by the North West Fur Trading Co. The post, believed to have been located about 80 miles/129 km south of Nelson Forks, was named for Lord Horatio Nelson, the English admiral who won the Battle of Trafalgar.

A second Fort Nelson was later located south of the first fort, but was destroyed by fire in 1813 after Indians massacred its eight residents. A third Fort Nelson was established in 1865 on the Nelson River's west bank (1 mile from the present Fort Nelson airport) by W. Cornwallis King, a Hudson's Bay Co. clerk. This trading post was built to keep out the free traders who were filtering in from the Mackenzie River and Fort St. John areas. The free traders' higher fur prices were a threat to the Hudson's Bay Co., which in 1821 had absorbed the rival North West Fur Trading Co. and gained a monopoly on the fur trade in Canada.

This Hudson's Bay Co. trading post was destroyed by a flood in 1890 and a fourth Fort Nelson was established on higher ground upstream and across the river, which is now known as Old Fort Nelson. The present town of Fort Nelson is the fifth site.

Fort Nelson saw its first mail service in 1936. Scheduled air service to Fort Nelson — by ski- and floatplane — also was begun in the 1930s by Yukon Southern Air (which was later absorbed by CPAir, now Canadian Airlines International and Canadian Regional Airlines). The Canadian government began construction of an airport in 1941 as part of the Northwest Air Staging Route, and this was followed by perhaps the biggest boom to Fort Nelson — the construction of the Alaska Highway in 1942. About 2,000 soldiers were bivouacked in Fort Nelson, which they referred to as Zero, as it was the beginning of a road to Whitehorse and another road to Fort Simpson. Later Dawson Creek became Mile 0 and Fort Nelson Mile 300.

Fort Nelson expanded in the 1940s and 1950s as people came here to work for the government or to start their own small businesses: trucking, barging, aviation, construction, garages, stores, cafes, motels and sawmills. It is surprising to consider that as recently as the 1950s, Fort Nelson was still a pioneer community without power, phones, running water, refrigerators or doctors. Interesting recollections of Fort Nelson's early days may be found in Gerri Young's book *The Fort Nelson Story*; available at the museum.

Fort Nelson was an unorganized territory until 1957 when it was declared an Improvement District. Fort Nelson took on village status in 1971 and town status in 1987.

Forestry is a major industry here with a veneer plant, plywood plant and sawmill complex. Chopsticks are manufactured at a local plant for export to Asian markets. Check with the infocentre about scheduled industrial tours.

Forestry products are shipped south by truck and by rail. Fort Nelson became a railhead in 1971 with the completion of a 250-mile extension of the Pacific Great Eastern Railway (now British Columbia Railway) from Fort St. John.

Agriculture is under development here with the recent establishment of the 55,000-acre McConachie Creek agricultural subdivision.

Northeastern British Columbia is the only sedimentary area in the province currently producing oil and gas. Oil seeps in the Fort Nelson area were noted by early residents. Major gas discoveries were made in the 1960s when the Clarke Lake, Yoyo/Kotcho, Beaver River and Pointed Mountain gas reserves were developed. The Westcoast Energy natural gas processing plant at Fort Nelson, the largest in North America, was constructed in 1964. This plant purifies the gas before sending it south through the 800-mile-long pipeline which connects the Fort Nelson area with the British Columbia lower mainland. Sulfur, a byproduct of natural gas processing, is processed in a recovery plant and shipped to outside markets in pellet form.

ACCOMMODATIONS

Fort Nelson has nine hotels/motels, three bed and breakfasts, several gas stations and restaurants, a pub, an auto supply store, department stores and other services, most located north and south just off the Alaska Highway. The post office and liquor store are on Airport Drive. There are two banks, both with bank machines, on the business frontage road north of the highway. Fresh

Temperature dips to -38°F/-39°C on a clear but cold winter day in Fort Nelson. (Earl L. Brown, staff)

water fill-up and free municipal dump station adjacent the blue chalet near the museum. Inquire at the infocentre for location of local churches and their hours of worship.

Fort Nelson has four campgrounds: one is located at the north (or west) end of town near the museum; one is at the south (or east) end of town; and the others are in the Muskwa Heights area south of Fort Nelson.▲

Blue Bell Motel. Your first stop in Fort Nelson from the south, has the newest travelers accommodations in town. 46 air-conditioned rooms, kitchenettes and non-

smoking rooms available, direct-dial phones and cable TV. Family restaurant. Full RV and campground facilities, showers, laundromat, dump station, plug-ins. Convenience store. Petro–Canada fuel and products. Open 24 hours, all year long. A family operated business. We look forward to meeting you. (604) 774-6961, fax (604) 774-6983. B.C. Tourism approved accommodation. [ADVERTISEMENT] ▲

Fort Nelson Bed & Breakfast. (Non-smoking). For your convenience and privacy, our B&B is a self-contained unit on one side of our duplex. Rates for full or light breakfast available. Laundry facilities, cable TV. Evening snack provided. "Come and be spoiled." Your hosts, Ken and Ann Muss. Box 58, Fort Nelson, BC V0C 1R0. (604) 774-6050. VISA. Open year-round. (Member — Northern Network of B&B's). [ADVERTISEMENT]

Westend R.V. Campground and Mini-Golf welcome you to Fort Nelson! Located in town, next to the museum, only a few short minutes walk from restaurants, banking, bingo, local stores and services and the free welcome visitors program. Overnight

and extended stay parking with a selection of over 130 sites. Lots of shade and grass, gravelled sites with many full hookups and pull-throughs. Grassy tenting areas with cooking shelter, and a playground for the kids. Caravans welcomed, covered meeting place, handicap facilities, free carwash and firewood. Drinking water, coin-op hot showers and laundry. Pay phones. Good Sam Park, CAA/AAA and Woodall's approved. Confectionary, ice, souvenirs and gift shop with local Indian arts and crafts and tanned furs. Open April 1–Oct. 31. Your hosts, Chris and Sandra Brown, invite you to take a look at their beautiful wild animal displays. We hope you enjoy our northern hospitality. (604) 774-2340. [ADVERTISEMENT] ♿▲

ATTRACTIONS

Fort Nelson offers travelers a free "Welcome Visitor Program" on summer evenings at 6:45 P.M. at the Phoenix Theatre. These interesting and entertaining presentations are put on by local residents and range from slide shows to talks on items of local interest. Check with the travel infocentre or at the Town Square for details.

The Fort Nelson Heritage Museum, across the highway from the travel infocentre, has displays of pioneer artifacts, Alaska Highway history, wildlife (including a white moose), a spruce bark canoe and souvenirs and books for sale. This non-profit museum charges a modest admission fee. Native crafts are displayed at the Fort Nelson–Liard Native Friendship Centre, located on 49th Avenue, and at Fontas Native Crafts, across from the post office on Airport Drive.

The recreation centre, across from the blue chalet, has tennis courts; hockey and curling arena for winter sports. Swimming pool, swirl pool, sauna and gym located in the Aqua Centre on Simpson Trail. For golfers, there is the Poplar Hills Golf and Country Club, just north of town on the Old Alaska Highway. The course has grass greens and is open daily until dark.

A community demonstration forest is open to the public. There is a forest trail (0.6 mile/1 km, half-hour walk) and a silviculture trail (1.9 miles/3 km, 45-minute walk). Located off the Simpson Trail and Mountainview Drive; check at the infocentre for trail guide.

Special Events. Fort Nelson hosts a number of special interest benefits, dances, tournaments and exhibits. Summer events include a rodeo in August. Winter events include the Canadian Open Sled Dog Races in December (with local racers from the well-known Streeper Kennels), and a big cash prize curling bon spiel in February. Trapper's Rendezvous is held in March. Check locally for details and dates on all events.

Fort Nelson Heritage Museum displays road-building equipment. (Earl L. Brown, staff)

Alaska Highway Log

(continued)

Distance* from Dawson Creek (DC) is followed by distance from Fairbanks (F). Original mileposts are indicated in the text as Historical Mile.

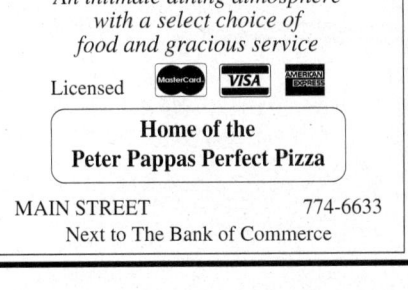

*Mileages from Dawson Creek are based on actual driving distance. Kilometres from Dawson Creek are based on physical kilometreposts. Please read Mileposts and Kilometreposts in the introduction for an explanation of how this highway is logged.

DC 284 (456.4 km) F 1204 (1937.6 km) **Historic Milepost 300**, historic sign and interpretive panel at west end of Fort Nelson. Visitor information in the Recreation Centre north side of highway, log museum south side of highway. Private campground adjacent museum. ▲

Northbound: Watch for sections of rough, narrow, winding road and breaks in surfacing between Fort Nelson and the BC–YT border (approximately next 321 miles/516.5 km).

Southbound: Good pavement, wider road, next 284 miles/457 km (to Dawson Creek).

DC 284.5 (457.5 km) **F 1203.5** (1936.8 km) Fort Nelson Forest District Office to north (phone 774-3936) provides a pamphlet of self-guided Forest Ecology Tours on the Alaska and Liard highways.

DC 284.7 (458.2 km) **F 1203.3** (1936.5 km) **Junction** with south end of Old Alaska Highway (Mile 301–308). The Muskwa Valley bypass between Mile 301 and 308 opened in 1992.

DC 287.9 (462.6 km) **F 1200.1** (1931.3 km) Access to Poplar Hills Golf and Country Club, located on Old Alaska Highway; nine-hole golf course, driving range, grass greens, clubhouse (licensed), golf club rentals. Open 8 A.M. to dusk, May to October.

DC 291 (467.6 km) **F 1197** (1926.3 km) Parker Lake Road. **Junction** with north end of Old Alaska Highway (Mile 308–301).

DC 292 (469.9 km) **F 1196** (1924.7 km) Private airstrip alongside highway; status unknown.

DC 301 (483.5 km) **F 1187** (1910.2 km) Turnoff north for Liard Highway (BC Highway 77) to Fort Liard, Fort Simpson and other Northwest Territories destinations. See LIARD HIGHWAY section and the MACKENZIE ROUTE section for details.

DC 304.1 (489.4 km) **F 1183.9** (1905.3 km) **Historic Milepost 320.** Sign marks start of Reese & Olson contract during construction of the Alaska Highway.

DC 308.2 (495.3 km) **F 1179.8** (1898.7 km) Raspberry Creek. Turnout with garbage barrels to south.

NOTE: Watch for road construction northbound to Kilometrepost 501 in 1994.

DC 316.6 (506.2 km) **F 1171.4** (1885.1 km) Turnout with litter barrel to south.

DC 318.4 (509.1 km) **F 1169.6** (1882.2 km) Kledo Creek bridge.

DC 318.7 (509.5 km) **F 1169.3** (1881.8 km) Kledo Creek wayside rest area to north (unmaintained).

DC 322.7 (516 km) **F 1165.3** (1875.3 km) Steamboat Creek bridge. Highway begins climb northbound up Steamboat Mountain; some 10 percent grades.

DC 329 (526.1 km) **F 1159** (1865.2 km) Pull-through turnout with litter barrel to south.

DC 333 (532.5 km) **F 1155** (1858.7 km) **Historic Milepost 351. STEAMBOAT** (unincorporated), lodge with food, gas, diesel and camping to south; open year-round. Historical sign marks start of Curran & Briggs Ltd. contract during construction of the Alaska Highway. ▲

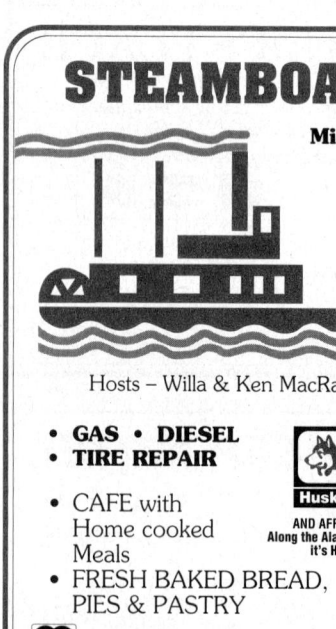

Steamboat at **Historical Mile 351**. Cafe with fresh baked bread, pies and pastry. Husky gas, diesel and oil products. Level pull-throughs, RV parking with a view. Picnic area. Ice, souvenirs and handicrafts. Your hosts, Willa and Ken MacRae and family. Open year-round. (604) 774-1010. [ADVERTISEMENT] ▲

DC 333.7 (533.5 km) F 1154.3 (1857.6 km) Winding road ascends Steamboat Mountain westbound. Views of the Muskwa River valley and Rocky Mountains to the southwest from summit of 3,500-foot/1,067-m Steamboat Mountain, named because of its resemblance to a steamship. Narrow road; watch for sharp curves and rough spots.

DC 334.3 (534.5 km) **F 1153.7** (1856.6 km) Turnout with view and litter barrel to south.

DC 336.7 (538.5 km) **F 1151.3** (1852.8 km) Turnout to south with litter barrels and pit toilets. Highway descends for westbound travelers.

DC 339.1 (542.5 km) **F 1148.9** (1848.9 km) Drinking water to north. *CAUTION: Hairpin curve!*

DC 342.8 (548 km) **F 1145.2** (1843 km) View of Indian Head Mountain, a high crag resembling the classic Indian profile.

DC 343.4 (549 km) **F 1144.6** (1842 km) Turnout with litter barrel, outhouse and point of interest sign to south.

DC 345 (551.5 km) **F 1143** (1839.4 km) Scenic Teetering Rock viewpoint with litter barrel and outhouses to north. Teetering Rock is in the distance on the horizon. Stay on well-marked trails, keep pets on leash; it is easy to get lost in this country.

DC 346.4 (553.9 km) **F 1141.6** (1837.2 km) Mill Creek, which flows into the Tetsa River. The highway follows the Tetsa River westbound. The Tetsa heads near Summit Lake in the northern Canadian Rockies.

Tetsa River, good fishing for grayling to 4 lbs., average 1 1/2 lbs., flies or spin cast with lures; Dolly Varden to 7 lbs., average 3 lbs., spin cast or black gnat, coachman, Red Devils, flies; whitefish, small but plentiful, use flies or eggs, summer.

DC 346.5 (554 km) **F 1141.5** (1837 km) Turnoff to south for Tetsa River Provincial Park, 1.2 miles/1.9 km via gravel road. Grass tenting area, 25 level gravel sites in trees, picnic tables, fire rings, firewood, outhouses, water and garbage containers. Camping fee $7 to $12. ▲

DC 351 (561.2 km) **F 1137** (1829.8 km) *CAUTION: Slow down, dangerous curve!*

DC 357.5 (571.5 km) **F 1130.5** (1819.3 km) **Historical Mile 375.** Gas, store, cabins and private campground. Trail rides and big game outfitting, by reservation; phone (604) 774-1005. ▲

DC 358.6 (573.3 km) **F 1129.4** (1817.5 km) Highway follows Tetsa River westbound. Turnouts next 0.2 mile/0.3 km south to river.

DC 360.2 (575.9 km) **F 1127.8** (1815 km) Turnout with litter barrel, picnic site.

DC 364.4 (582.6 km) **F 1123.6** (1808.2 km) Gravel turnout to south.

DC 365.6 (584.6 km) **F 1122.4** (1806.3 km) Tetsa River bridge No. 1, clearance 17 feet/5.2m.

DC 366 (585.4 km) **F 1122** (1805.6 km) Pull-through turnout with litter barrel to north.

DC 367.3 (587.3 km) **F 1120.7** (1803.5 km) Tetsa River bridge No. 2.

The high bare peaks of the central Canadian Rockies are visible ahead westbound.

DC 371.5 (594.2 km) **F 1116.5** (1796.8 km) South boundary of Stone Mountain Provincial Park.

CAUTION: Northbound, watch for caribou along the highway. Stone sheep on the highway. Stone sheep are indigenous to the mountains of northern British Columbia and southern Yukon Territory. They are darker and somewhat slighter than the bighorn sheep found in the Rocky Mountains. Dall or white sheep are found in the mountains of Yukon, Alaska and Northwest Territories. DO NOT FEED WILDLIFE. Do not stop vehicles on the highway to take photos; use shoulders or turnouts.

DC 372.7 (596 km) **F 1115.3** (1794.9 km) Pull-through turnout with litter barrel to north.

DC 373.3 (597 km) **F 1114.7** (1793.9 km) **Historical Mile 392. SUMMIT LAKE** (unincorporated), lodge with gas, food and lodging. The peak behind Summit Lake is Mount St. George (elev. 7,419 feet/2,261m) in the Stone Mountain range. The Summit area is known for dramatic and sudden weather changes.

DC 373.5 (597.4 km) **F 1114.5** (1793.5 km) Rough gravel side road leads 1.5 miles/2.5 km to Flower Springs Lake trailhead, 4.3 miles/7 km to microwave tower viewpoint. Not suitable for motorhomes, trailers or low clearance vehicles.

DC 373.6 (597.6 km) **F 1114.4** (1793.4 km) Gravel turnout and Summit Lake Provincial campground to south at east end of Summit Lake. **Historic Milepost 392** sign and interpretive panel mark the highest summit on the Alaska Highway, elev. 4,250 feet/1,295m. A very beautiful area of bare rocky peaks (which can be snow-covered anytime of the year). The provincial campground has 28 level gravel sites; picnic tables; water and garbage containers; information shelter; boat launch. Camping fee $7 to $12. Hiking trails to Flower Springs Lake and Summit Peak. Fair fishing for lake trout, whitefish and rainbows in **Summit Lake.** ▲

Watch for Stone sheep. (George Wuerthner)

DC 375.6 (600.8 km) **F 1112.4** (1790.2 km) Turnout to north.

DC 375.9 (601.3 km) **F 1112.1** (1789.7 km) Picnic site to south with tables and litter barrel on Rocky Crest Lake.

DC 376 (601.5 km) **F 1112** (1789.5 km) Erosion pillars north of highway (0.6-mile/1-km hike north); watch for caribou. Northbound, the highway winds through a rocky limestone gorge, before descending into the wide and picturesque MacDonald River valley. Turnouts next 2.5 miles/4 km northbound with views of the valley. Watch for Stone sheep along rock cut.

DC 378.6 (605.7 km) **F 1109.4** (1785.4 km) **Historical Mile 397.** Rocky Mountain Lodge to south; gas, lodging, store and camping. ▲

DC 379.7 (607.4 km) **F 1108.3** (1783.6 km) Turnout to south.

DC 380.7 (609 km) **F 1107.3** (1782 km) North boundary of Stone Mountain Provincial Park. *CAUTION: Southbound, watch for wildlife alongside and on the road. DO NOT FEED WILDLIFE.*

DC 381.2 (611.2 km) **F 1106.8** (1781.2 km) Highway winds along above the wide rocky valley of MacDonald Creek.

MacDonald Creek and river were named for Charlie McDonald, a Cree Indian credited with helping Alaska Highway survey crews locate the best route for the pioneer road. More history on McDonald may be found in *Alcan Trail Blazers* (648th Memorial Fund) and *Northwest Epic — The Building of the Alaska Highway* by Heath Twichell.

DC 382.2 (612.8 km) **F 1105.8** (1779.5 km) Trail access via abandoned Churchill Mines Road (4-wheel drive only beyond river) to Wokkpash Recreation Area, located 12 miles/20 km south of the highway. B.C. Parks is developing hiking trails in this remote area, which adjoins the southwest boundary of Stone Mountain Provincial Park. The area features extensive hoodoos (erosion pillars) in Wokkpash Gorge, and the scenic Forlorn Gorge and Stepped Lakes. Contact the Parks District Office in Fort St. John before venturing into this area; phone (604) 787-3407.

DC 383.3 (614.6 km) **F 1104.7** (1777.8 km) 113 Creek. The creek was named during construction of the Alaska Highway for its distance from Mile 0 at Fort Nelson. While Dawson Creek was to become Mile 0 on the completed pioneer road, clearing crews began their work at Fort Nelson, since a rough winter road already existed between Dawson Creek and Fort Nelson. Stone Range to the northeast and Muskwa Ranges of the Rocky Mountains to the west.

DC 384.2 (615.4 km) **F 1103.8** (1776.3 km) 115 Creek Provincial campground to southwest, adjacent highway; double-ended entrance. Side-by-side camper parking (eight sites), water, garbage containers, picnic tables. Camping fee $7 to $12. Access to the rocky riverbank of 115 Creek and **MacDonald Creek.** Beaver dams nearby. Fishing for grayling and Dolly Varden.

DC 385.4 (615.6 km) **F 1102.6** (1774.4 km) 115 Creek bridge. Turnout to south at east end of bridge with tables and litter barrels. Like 113 Creek, 115 Creek was named during construction of the pioneer road for its distance from Fort Nelson, Mile 0 for clearing crews.

DC 390.5 (624.8 km) **F 1097.5** (1766.2 km) **Historical Mile 408.** MacDonald River Services (closed in 1993; current status unknown).

DC 392.5 (627.8 km) **F 1095.5** (1763 km) MacDonald River bridge, clearance 17 feet/5.2m. Highway winds through narrow valley.

MacDonald River, fair fishing from May to July for Dolly Varden and grayling.

DC 394.8 (631.8 km) **F 1093.2** (1759.3 km) Turnout with litter barrel to east.

DC 396.1 (633.8 km) **F 1091.9** (1757.2 km) Folding rock formations on mountain face to west. The Racing River forms the boundary between the Sentinel Range and the Stone Range, both of which are composed of folded and sedimentary rock.

DC 399.1 (638.6 km) **F 1088.9** (1752.4 km) Stringer Creek.

DC 400.7 (641.1 km) **F 1087.3** (1749.8 km) Racing River bridge, clearance 17 feet/5.2m. River access to north at east end of bridge.

Racing River, grayling to 16 inches; Dolly Varden to 2 lbs., use flies, July through September.

DC 404.6 (647.4 km) **F 1083.4** (1743.5 km) **Historical Mile 422. TOAD RIVER** (unincorporated), situated in a picturesque valley. Highway maintenance camp, school and private residences on north side of highway. Lodge on south side of highway with cafe, gas, propane, camping and lodging. Ambulance service. Toad River Lodge is open year-round. The lodge is known for its collection of hats, which numbers more than 3,600. Also, inquire at the lodge about good wildlife viewing locations nearby.

Toad River Lodge. See display ad this section.

Private Aircraft: Emergency gravel airstrip; elev. 2,400 feet/732m; length 2,300 feet/701m.

DC 405.5 (652.6 km) **F 1082.5** (1742.1 km) Turnout to south with **Historic Milepost 422.** Sign and interpretive panel commemorate Toad River/Camp 138 Jupp Construction.

DC 406.3 (650.1 km) **F 1081.7** (1740.8 km) Turnout with litter barrels to north.

DC 407.5 (652 km) **F 1080.5** (1738.8 km) **Historical Mile 426.** Food, gas and camping south side of highway.

The Poplars Campground. See display ad this section.

DC 409.2 (654.6 km) **F 1078.8** (1736.1 km) South boundary of Muncho Lake Provincial Park.

DC 410.6 (656.8 km) **F 1077.4** (1733.9 km) Turnout with information panel on area geology. Impressive rock folding formation on mountain face, known as Folded Mountain.

DC 411 (657.4 km) **F 1077** (1733.2 km) Beautiful turquoise-coloured Toad River to north. The highway now follows the Toad River westbound.

Toad River, grayling to 16 inches; Dolly Varden to 10 lbs., use flies, July through September.

DC 415.5 (664.7 km) **F 1072.5** (1726 km) 150 Creek bridge. Creek access to south at east end of bridge.

DC 417.6 (668.2 km) **F 1070.4** (1722.6 km) Centennial Falls to south.

DC 419.8 (671.7 km) **F 1068.2** (1719 km) Toad River bridge. Turnout with litter barrel

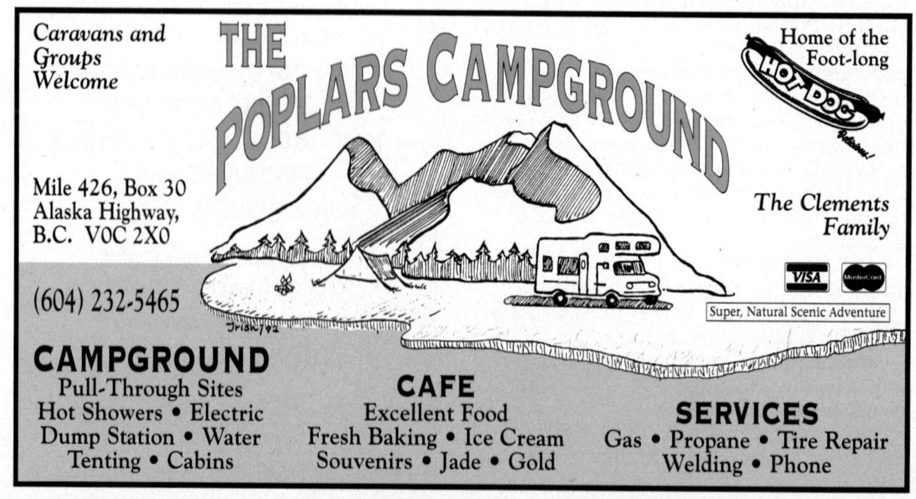

to south at west end of bridge.

DC 422.6 (676.2 km) **F 1065.4** (1714.5 km) Watch for moose in pond to north; morning or evening best.

DC 423 (676.8 km) **F 1065** (1713.9 km) Turnout with litter barrel to north.

CAUTION: Watch for Stone sheep along the highway (or standing in the middle of the highway). DO NOT FEED WILDLIFE. Do not stop vehicles on the highway to take photos; use shoulders or turnouts.

DC 423.1 (677 km) **F 1064.9** (1713.7 km) The highway swings north for Alaska-bound travelers. Highway climbs next 6 miles/9.7 km northbound. For Dawson Creek-bound travelers, the highway follows an easterly direction.

DC 424.1 (678.7 km) **F 1063.9** (1712.1 km) **Historic Milepost 443** at Peterson Creek No. 1 bridge. The creek was named for local trapper Pete Peterson, who helped Alaska Highway construction crews select a route through this area. Historic sign marks start of Campbell Construction Co. Ltd. contract during construction of the Alaska Highway.

DC 429.5 (688.9 km) **F 1058.5** (1703.4 km) Viewpoint to east with information shelter and litter barrels. Information panel on geology of "Sawtooth Mountains."

DC 436.5 (698.5 km) **F 1051.5** (1692.2 km) **Historic Milepost 456.** Entering **MUNCHO LAKE** (pop. 24; elev. 2,700 feet/823m). Muncho Lake businesses extend from here north along the east shore of Muncho Lake to approximately **Milepost DC 443.7.** Businesses in Muncho Lake include four lodges, gas stations with towing and repair, restaurants, cafes and campgrounds. The post office is located at Double G Service. ▲

A historic sign and interpretive panel mark Muncho Lake/Refueling Stop, Checkpoint during Alaska Highway construction. The road around the lake was a particular challenge. Workers had to cut their way through the lake's rocky banks. Horses were used to haul away the rock. The Muncho Lake area offers hiking in the summer and cross-country skiing in the winter. Narrated boat tours of Muncho Lake are available in summer; check with Double G Service. This highly recommended tour highlights the history and geography of the area. Boat rentals are available from J&H Wilderness Resort and Highland Glen Lodge. Flightseeing trips available from Liard Air at Highland Glen Lodge. An annual lake trout derby is held in June; inquire locally for dates.

CAUTION: Watch for Stone sheep and moose on the highway north of here. Please DO NOT FEED WILDLIFE. Please do not stop on the highway to take photos; use shoulders or turnouts.

Muncho Lake Tours. See display ad this section.

DC 436.9 (699.2 km) **F 1051.1** (1691.5 km) Gravel airstrip to west; length 1,200 feet/366m. View of Muncho Lake ahead northbound. The highway along Muncho Lake required considerable rock excavation by the Army in 1942. The original route went along the top of the cliffs, which proved particularly hazardous. The Army relocated the road by benching into the cliffs a few feet above lake level.

Muncho Lake, known for its beautiful deep green and blue waters, is 7 miles/11

km in length, and 1 mile/1.6 km in width; elevation of the lake is 2,680 feet/817m. The colours are attributed to copper oxide leaching into the lake. Deepest point has been reported to be 730 feet/223m, although recent government tests have not located any point deeper than 400 feet/122m. The lake drains the Sentinel Range to the east and the Terminal Range to the west, feeding the raging Trout River in its 1,000-foot/305-m drop to the mighty Liard River. The mountains surrounding the lake are approximately 7,000 feet/ 2,134m high.

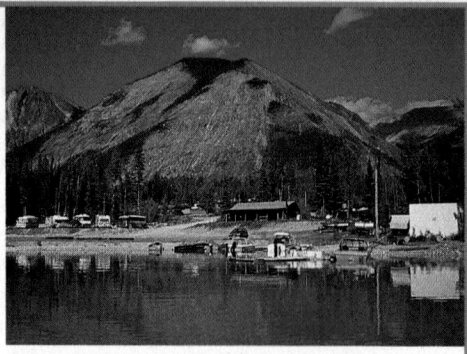

Muncho Lake, fishing for Dolly Varden; some grayling; whitefish to 12 inches; lake trout (record to 50 lbs.), use spoons, spinners, diving plug or weighted spoons, June and July best. The lake trout quota is three trout per person; minimum size 15¾ inches. Make sure you have a current British Columbia fishing license and a copy of the current regulations. Also rainbow trout.

DC 437.7 (700.5 km) **F 1050.3** (1690.2 km) Strawberry Flats Campground, Muncho Lake Provincial Park; 15 sites on rocky lakeshore, picnic tables, outhouses, garbage containers. Camping fee $7 to $12. ▲

CAUTION: Watch for bears in area.

DC 442.2 (707.9 km) **F 1045.8** (1683 km) **Historical Mile 462.** Highland Glen Lodge with cabins, restaurant, gas and camping west side of highway. ▲

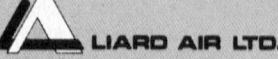

Highland Glen Lodge, Mile 462, Muncho Lake, BC, (604) 776-3481. Individual chalets, licensed dining room, bakery, RV hookups, campground, showers, washrooms, laundromat, Husky service station. Liard Air/Liard Tours offers fly-in fishing trips for arctic grayling, Dolly Varden, rainbow and lake trout, walleye, northern pike, whitefish. Glacier flights to Kwadacha and Stone Mountain provincial parks, Virginia Falls and Headless Valley in famous Nahanni National Park. Bush Pilot Film Festival at Highland Glen Lodge! Free nightly presentations for guests. [ADVERTISEMENT] ▲

DC 442.9 (709 km) **F 1045.1** (1681.9 km) Turnoff to west for MacDonald campground, Muncho Lake Provincial Park; 15 level gravel sites, firewood, picnic tables, outhouses, boat launch, information shelter, pump water, on Muncho Lake. Camping fee $7 to $12. ▲

CAUTION: Watch for bears in area.

DC 443.6 (710.1 km) **F 1044.4** (1680.8 km) **Historical Mile 463.** Muncho Lake Lodge; gas, propane, food, camping and lodging. ▲

Muncho Lake Lodge. See display ad on page 97. ▲

DC 443.7 (710.3 km) **F 1044.3** (1680.6 km) **Historical Mile 463.1.** J&H Wilderness Resort; food, gas, store, boat rentals, tackle, lodging and camping. Open year-round. Muncho Lake businesses extend south to **Milepost DC 436.5.** ▲

J&H Wilderness Resort. See display ad this section. ▲

DC 444.9 (712.2 km) **F 1043.1** (1678.7 km) Muncho Lake viewpoint to west with information panel, litter barrels and outhouses.

NOTE: Watch for Stone sheep on highway next 10 miles/16 km northbound.

DC 453.3 (725.6 km) **F 1034.7** (1665.1 km) Turnout with litter barrel to east.

NOTE: Watch for Stone sheep on highway next 10 miles/16 km southbound.

DC 455.5 (729.2 km) **F 1032.5** (1661.6 km) Turnout with litter barrel and message board to west.

DC 457.7 (732.7 km) **F 1030.3** (1658.1 km) Trout River bridge. The Trout River drains into the Liard River. The highway follows the Trout River north for several miles.

Trout River, grayling to 18 inches; whitefish to 12 inches, flies, spinners, May, June and August best.

DC 458.9 (734.6 km) **F 1029.1** (1656.1 km) Gravel turnout to east.

DC 460.7 (737.4 km) **F 1027.3** (1653.2 km) Prochniak Creek bridge. The creek was named for a member of Company A, 648th Engineers Topographic Battalion, during construction of the Alaska Highway. North boundary of Muncho Lake Provincial Park.

DC 463.3 (741.6 km) **F 1024.7** (1649 km) Watch for curves next 0.6 mile/1 km northbound.

DC 465.6 (745.3 km) **F 1022.4** (1645.3 km) Turnout with litter barrel to east.

DC 466.3 (746.3 km) **F 1021.7** (1644.2 km) *CAUTION: Dangerous curves next 3 miles/5 km northbound.*

DC 468.9 (749.5 km) **F 1019.1** (1640 km) Pull-through turnout with litter barrel to east.

DC 471 (754.1 km) **F 1017** (1636.7 km) First glimpse of the mighty Liard River for northbound travelers. Named by French-Canadian voyageurs for the poplar ("liard") which line the banks of the lower river. The Alaska Highway parallels the Liard River from here north to Watson Lake. The river offered engineers a natural line to follow during routing and construction of the Alaska Highway in 1942.

DC 472.2 (756 km) **F 1015.8** (1634.7 km) Washout Creek.

DC 474.3 (759.5 km) **F 1013.7** (1631.3 km) Turnout with litter barrel to west.

DC 476.7 (763 km) **F 1011.3** (1627.5 km) Lower Liard River bridge. This is the only suspension bridge on the Alaska Highway. The 1,143-foot suspension bridge was built by the American Bridge Co. and McNamara Construction Co. of Toronto in 1943.

The **Liard River** flows eastward toward the Fort Nelson River and parallels the Alaska Highway from the Lower Liard River bridge to the BC–YT border. The scenic Grand Canyon of the Liard is to the east and not visible from the highway. Good fishing for Dolly Varden, grayling, northern pike and whitefish.

DC 477.1 (763.8 km) **F 1010.9** (1626.8 km) **Historical Mile 496. LIARD RIVER** (unincorporated), lodge with gas, store, pay phone, food, camping and lodging to west. ▲

Liard River Lodge. See display ad this section. ▲

DC 477.7 (764.7 km) **F 1010.3** (1625.9 km) **Historic Milepost 496.** Turnoff to north for Liard River Hotsprings Provincial Park, long a favorite stop for Alaska Highway travelers. The park has become so popular in recent years that the campground fills up very early each day in summer. Overflow parking area across highway from park entrance. The park is open year-round. This well-developed provincial park has 53 large, shaded, level gravel sites (some will accom-

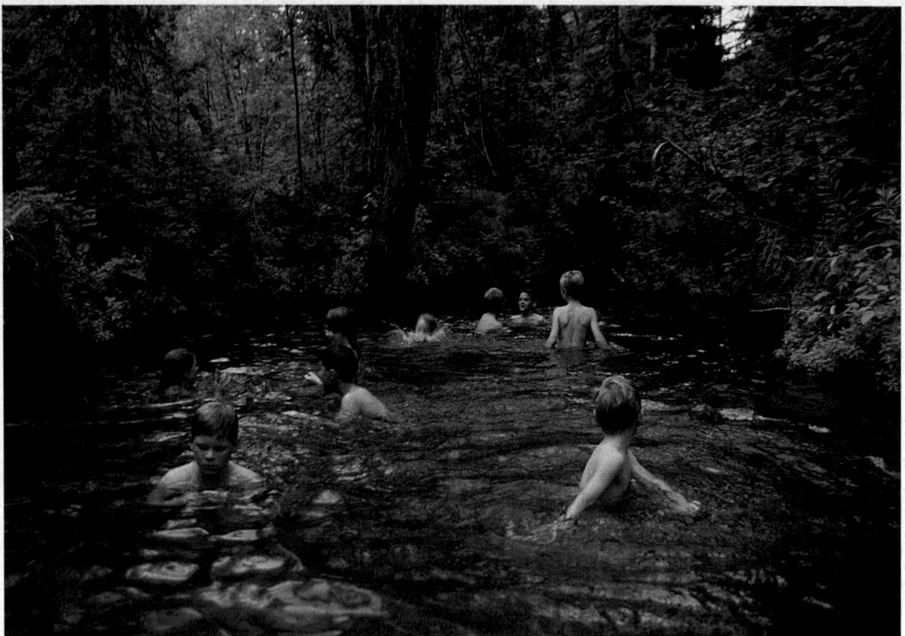

Kids have their own wading pool at Liard River Hotsprings Provincial Park.
(Earl L. Brown, staff)

modate two RVs), picnic tables, picnic shelter, water, garbage containers, firewood, fire rings, playground and heated restrooms with wheelchair accessible toilet. Camping fee $7 to $12. Pay phone at park entrance. ▲

A boardwalk leads to the pools, crossing a wetlands environment that supports more than 250 boreal forest plants, including 14 orchid species and 14 plants that survive at this latitude because of the hot springs. Also watch for moose feeding in the pools. There are two hot springs pools. Nearest is the Alpha pool with a children's wading area. Beyond the Alpha pool is Beta pool, which is larger and deeper. Both have changing rooms. Beta pool is about a 0.4-mile/0.6-km walk. Plenty of parking at trailhead.

Excellent interpretive programs and nature walks in summer; check schedule posted at park entrance and at information shelter near trailhead. Emergency phone at park headquarters. *CAUTION: Beware of bears.*

DC 477.8 (764.9 km) **F 1010.2** (1625.7 km) **Historical Mile 497.** Log lodge (open year-round) with food, gas, lodging and camping. ▲

Trapper Ray's Liard Hotsprings Lodge. See display ad on page 99. ▲

DC 482.8 (772.9 km) **F 1005.2** (1617.7 km) Teeter Creek. A footpath leads upstream (10-minute walk) to falls. Grayling fishing.

DC 486.6 (779 km) **F 1001.4** (1611.6 km) *NOTE: Northbound travelers watch for road construction and some sections of rough surface, gravel breaks and loose gravel next 118.5 miles/190.7 km (to BC–YT border).*

DC 489 (783.6 km) **F 999** (1607.7 km) **Private Aircraft:** Liard River airstrip; elev. 1,400 feet/427m; length 4,000 feet/1,219m; gravel.

DC 495 (792.3 km) **F 993** (1598 km) **Historic Milepost 514. Smith River** bridge, clearance 17 feet/5.2m. Access to river via 1.6-mile/2.6-km gravel road; not recommended for large RVs or trailers or in wet weather. Hiking trail down to two-tiered Smith River Falls from parking area. Grayling fishing.

The historic sign here commemorates Smith River Airport Road. The old airstrip, part of the Northwest Staging Route, is located in a burned over area about 25 miles/40 km from the highway.

DC 509.4 (815.6 km) **F 978.6** (1574.9 km) Large turnout with litter barrel to east.

DC 513.9 (822.8 km) **F 974.1** (1567.6 km) **Historical Mile 533. COAL RIVER,** lodge with gas, diesel, minor repairs, food, camping and lodging. Open year-round. ▲

Coal River Lodge. See display ad this section. ▲

DC 514.2 (823.2 km) **F 973.8** (1567.1 km) **Historical Mile 533.2.** Coal River bridge. The Coal River flows into the Liard River south of the bridge.

DC 514.6 (823.7 km) **F 973.4** (1566.5 km) Improved (1993) highway northbound next 3.7 miles/6 km.

DC 519.5 (831.4 km) **F 968.5** (1558.6 km) Sharp easy-to-miss turnoff to west for undeveloped "do-it-yourself campsite" (watch for sign). Small gravel parking area with outhouse and litter barrels. Beautiful view from here of the Liard River and Whirlpool Canyon (not visible from the highway). ▲

DC 524.2 (839.2 km) **F 963.8** (1551 km) **Historical Mile 543. FIRESIDE** (unincorporated). Truck stop with gas, diesel, major repairs, cafe and RV parking. Open April to Sept. This community was partially destroyed by fire in the summer of 1982. Evidence of the fire can be seen from south of Fireside north to Lower Post. The 1982 burn, known as the Eg fire, was the second largest fire in British Columbia history, destroying more than 400,000 acres.

Fireside Car/Truck Stop. See display ad this section.

DC 527.4 (844.3 km) **F 960.6** (1545.9 km) Good view of Liard River and Cranberry Rapids to west.

NOTE: Watch for road construction northbound to Kilometrepost 864 in 1994.

DC 534.8 (856.3 km) **F 953.2** (1534 km) NorthwesTel microwave tower to east.

DC 535.6 (857.6 km) **F 952.4** (1532.7 km) Large pull-through turnout with litter barrel to east. Northbound trucks stop here and check brakes before descending steep grade.

DC 536.9 (859.7 km) **F 951.1** (1530.6 km) *CAUTION: Slow down! Dangerous curves next 4.4 miles/7.1 km northbound. Watch for loose gravel.*

DC 539 (863 km) **F 949** (1527.2 km) Turnout with litter barrel to west. LeQuil Creek.

DC 540 (864.6 km) **F 948** (1525.6 km) Large pull-through turnout with litter barrel to west.

DC 541.3 (866.7 km) **F 946.7** (1523.5 km) Southbound travelers: *Slow down! Dangerous curves next 4.4 miles/7.1 km.*

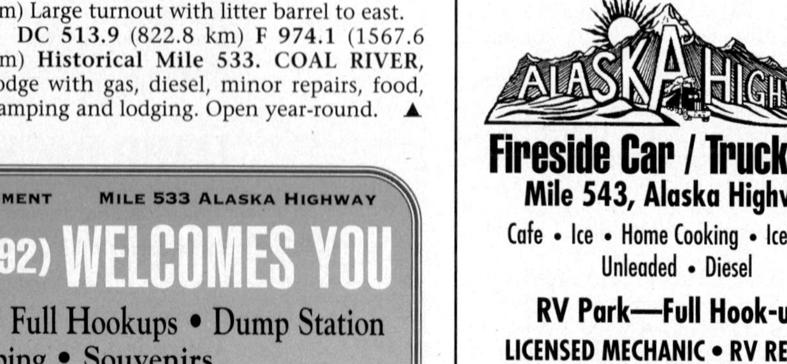

DC 545.9 (874.2 km) F 942.1 (1516.1 km) Turnout with litter barrel to west overlooking the Liard River.

DC 550.9 (882.2 km) F 937.1 (1508 km) **Historical Mile 570.** Allen's Lookout; very large pull-through turnout with picnic tables, outhouse and litter barrel to west overlooking the Liard River. Goat Mountain to west. Legend has it that a band of outlaws took advantage of this sweeping view of the Liard River to attack and rob riverboats of furs and supplies.

DC 555 (888.8 km) F 933 (1501.5 km) Good berry picking in July among roadside raspberry bushes; watch for bears.

DC 556 (890.4 km) F 932 (1499.9 km) Highway swings west for Alaska-bound travelers.

DC 562.5 (900.8 km) F 925.5 (1489.4 km) Large gravel turnout with litter barrel.

DC 567.9 (909.4 km) F 920.1 (1480.7 km) **Historic Milepost 588.** Contact Creek bridge. Turnout to south at east end of bridge with tables, toilets, litter barrels and information shelter. Contact Creek was named by soldiers of the 36th Regiment from the south and the 340th Regiment from the north who met here Sept. 24, 1942, completing the southern sector of the Alaska Highway. Historic sign and interpretive panel.

DC 568.3 (910.2 km) F 919.7 (1480.1 km) First of seven crossings of the BC–YT border. Large gravel turnout to north with point of interest sign about the Yukon Territory. "The Yukon Territory takes its name from the Indian word *Youcon,* meaning 'big river.' It was first explored in the 1840s by the Hudson's Bay Co., which established several trading posts. The territory, which was then considered a district of the Northwest Territories, remained largely untouched until the Klondike gold rush, when thousands of people flooded into the country and communities sprang up almost overnight. This sudden expansion led to the official formation of the Yukon Territory on June 13, 1898."

DC 570 (912.9 km) F 918 (1477.3 km) **Historical Mile 590. CONTACT CREEK,** lodge open year-round with camping, food, gas, diesel, car repair and pay phone. ▲

Contact Creek Lodge. See display ad this section. ▲

DC 573.9 (918.9 km) F 914.1 (1471.1 km) Iron Creek bridge. Turnout with litter barrel to south at east end of bridge.

DC 575.9 (922 km) F 912.1 (1467.8 km) **Historical Mile 596.** Iron Creek Lodge; food, gas, diesel, lodging and camping. Private stocked lake at campground. ▲

Iron Creek Lodge. See display ad this section. ▲

DC 582 (931.8 km) F 906 (1458 km) NorthwesTel microwave tower.

DC 585 (937 km) F 903 (1453.2 km) **Hyland River** bridge; good fishing for rainbow, Dolly Varden and grayling.

NOTE: Watch for logging trucks northbound to Watson Lake.

DC 585.3 (937.2 km) F 902.7 (1452.7 km) **Historical Mile 605.9.** Hyland River bridge. The Hyland River is a tributary of the Liard River. The river was named for Frank Hyland, an early-day trader at Telegraph Creek on the Stikine River. Hyland operated trading posts throughout northern British Columbia, competing successfully with the Hudson's Bay Co., and at one time printing his own currency.

DC 598.7 (957.5 km) F 889.3 (1431.2 km) Access to **LOWER POST** (unincorporated), at **Historical Mile 620,** via short gravel road; cafe and store. A B.C. Forest Service field office is located here. This British Columbia settlement is a historic Hudson's Bay Co. trading post and the site of an Indian village. The Liard and Dease rivers meet near here. The Dease River, named for Peter Warren Dease, a fur trader for the Hudson's Bay Co., heads in Dease Lake to the southwest on the Cassiar Highway.

DC 605.1 (967.6 km) F 882.9 (1420.8 km) **Historic Milepost 627** marks official BC–YT border; Welcome to the Yukon sign. Monitor CB Channel 9 for police. The Alaska Highway dips back into British Columbia several times before making its final crossing into the Yukon Territory near Morley Lake (**Milepost DC 751.5**).

NOTE: Kilometreposts on the Yukon portion of the highway reflect historical mileposts. Kilometreposts on the British Columbia portion of the highway reflect actual driving distance. There is approximately a 40-km difference at the BC–YT border between these measurements.

Northbound: Good paved highway with wide shoulders next 380 miles/611.5 km to Haines Junction, with the exception of some short sections of narrow road and occasional gravel breaks.

Southbound: Watch for rough, narrow, winding road and breaks in surfacing between border and Fort Nelson (approximately 321 miles/516.6 km).

DC 606.9 (1011.9 km) F 881.1 (1418 km) Lucky Lake picnic area to south; ball dia-

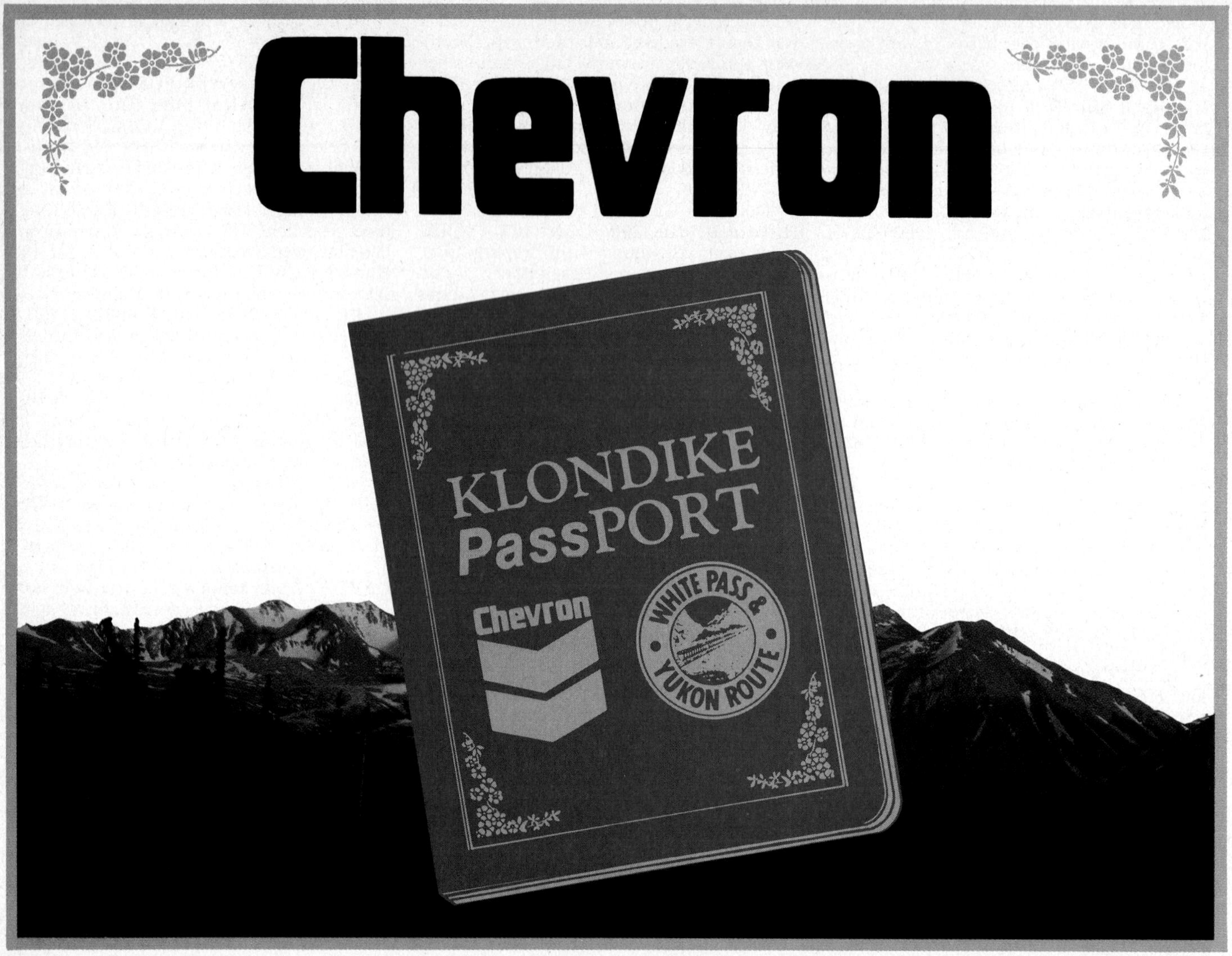

Chevron

KLONDIKE PassPORT

Chevron

WHITE PASS & YUKON ROUTE

VENTURE NORTH TO THE KLONDIKE WITH CONFIDENCE

Be on the lookout for the Chevron sign as you travel Yukon, Atlin B.C., and Haines and Skagway, Alaska and receive your free Klondike PassPORT. It's your passport to quality Chevron products and services; and to the scenic and historic White Pass and Yukon Route Railway, in Skagway.

Pick up your free souvenir KLONDIKE PassPORT at any participating Chevron Dealer, select RV Parks, or at White Pass & Yukon Route Railway Offices in Skagway and Whitehorse.

Have your PassPORT stamped each time you purchase 30 litres or more of fuel at our participating Chevron Dealers. Collect stamps to receive a rail discount or collector series posters that will leave you with an unforgettable memory of your Klondike Adventure.

Chevron — your guarantee of quality products and friendly service.

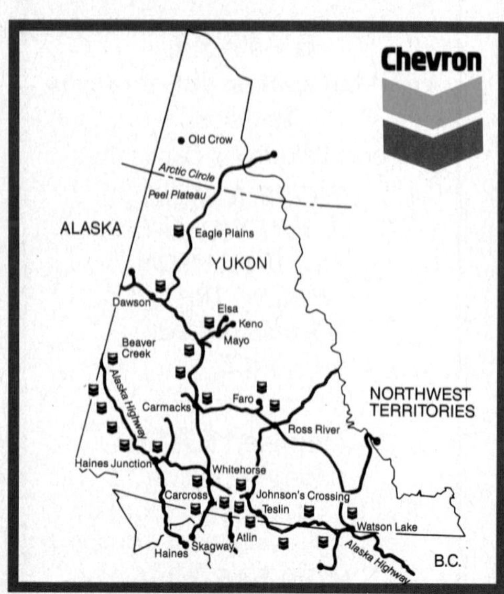

Most major credit cards accepted

CHEVRON PRODUCTS DISTRIBUTED BY

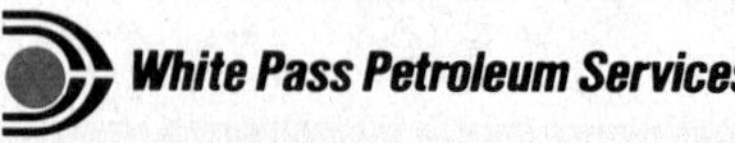

mond, hiking trail to Liard River Canyon (watch for signs). **Lucky Lake** is a popular local swimming hole for Watson Lake residents, who installed a water slide here. Relatively shallow, the lake warms up quickly in summer, making it one of the few area lakes where swimming is possible. Stocked with rainbow trout.

DC 609.2 (1015.5 km) **F 878.8** (1414.3 km) Rest area with litter barrel and outhouses to north.

DC 610.4 (1017.5 km) **F 877.6** (1412.3 km) Weigh station.

DC 610.5 (1017.7 km) **F 877.5** (1412.2 km) **Mile 632.5. Campground Services** at **Mile 632.5** is the largest and best equipped RV park in Watson Lake, the gateway to the Yukon. The park features full or partial hookups and pull-throughs, tent sites, showers, a laundry, car wash and playground, firepits and a screened kitchen. Good Sam Park. A food market stocks groceries, "chester fried" chicken, convenience

items, fishing tackle, licenses and ice. Husky gasoline and diesel and ICG propane are available at the self-serve pumps. A licensed mechanic is available for repairs, alignments, tire changes, etc. Agents for Western Union money transfers. Open for business 12 months a year. Your hosts, Rudi and Hanne Spahmann, serving the traveler's needs for 25 years! Call (403) 536-7448.
[ADVERTISEMENT]

Watson Lake

DC 612.9 (1021 km) **F 875.1** (1408.3 km). **Historic Milepost 635.** "Gateway to the Yukon," located 329 miles/529 km from Fort Nelson, 274 miles/441 km from Whitehorse. **Population:** 1,700. **Emergency Services: RCMP**, phone 536-5555 (if no answer call toll free 1-667-5555). **Fire Department**, phone 536-2222. **Ambulance**, phone 536-3333. **Hospital**, phone 536-4444.

Visitor Information: Located in the Alaska Highway Interpretive Centre behind the signpost forest, north of the Alaska Highway; access to the centre is from the Campbell Highway. Phone (403) 536-7469. The town of Watson Lake provides a toll-free number (Lower 48 only) for information on local attractions; phone 1-800-663-5248.

Elevation: 2,265 feet/690m. **Climate:** Average temperature in January is -15°F/-26°C, in July 57°F/14°C. Record high temperature 93°F/34°C in June 1950, record low -74°F/-59°C in January 1947. Annual snowfall is 90.6 inches. Driest month is April, wettest month is September. Average date of last spring frost is June 2; average date of first fall frost is Sept. 14. **Radio:** CBC 990, CKYN-FM 96.1 (Visitor Radio CKYN is broadcast from the visitor information centre from mid-May to mid-September). **Television:** Channel 8 and cable.

Private Aircraft: Watson Lake airport, 8 miles/12.9 km north of Campbell Highway; elev. 2,262 feet/689m; length 5,500 feet/1,676m and 3,530 feet/1,076m; asphalt; fuel 80, 100, Jet B. Heliport and floatplane bases also located here. The Watson Lake airport terminal building was built in 1942. The log structure has been designated a Heritage Building.

In the late 1800s, Watson Lake was known as Fish Lake. According to one source, the lake was renamed Watson for Frank Watson of Yorkshire, England, who gave up on the gold rush in 1898 to settle here on its shores with his Indian wife. Another source states that Watson Lake was named for Bob Watson, who opened a trading post here in 1936. Whatever its derivation, today Watson Lake is an important service stop on the Alaska and Campbell highways (Campbell Highway travelers fill your gas tanks here!); a communication and distribution centre for the southern Yukon; a base for trappers, hunters and fishermen; and a supply point for area mining and mineral exploration (the Sa Dena Hes Mine is located 27 miles/43.5 km north on the Campbell Highway).

Watson Lake businesses are located along either side of the Alaska Highway. The lake itself is not visible from the Alaska Highway. Access to the lake, airport, hospital and Mount Maichen ski hill is via the Campbell Highway (locally referred to as Airport Road). The ski area is about 4 miles/6.4 km out the Campbell Highway from town.

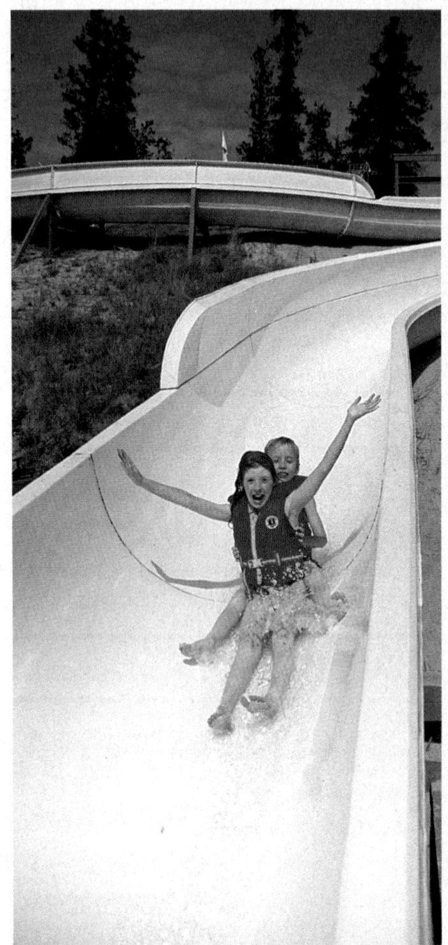

Water slide at Lucky Lake. Both the slide and the lake are popular with local residents. *(Earl L. Brown, staff)*

Watson Lake was an important point during construction of the Alaska Highway in 1942. The airport, built in 1941, was one of the major refueling stops along the Northwest Staging Route, the system of airfields through Canada to ferry supplies to Alaska and later lend-lease aircraft to Russia.

The Alaska Highway helped bring both people and commerce to this once isolated settlement. A post office opened here in July 1942. The economy of Watson Lake is based on services and also the forest products industry. White spruce and lodgepole pine are the two principal trees of the Yukon and provide a forest industry for the territory. White spruce grows straight and fast wherever adequate water is available, and it will grow to extreme old age without showing decay. The lodgepole pine developed from the northern pine and can withstand extreme cold, grow at high elevations and take full advantage of the almost 24-hour summer sunlight of a short growing season.

ACCOMMODATIONS

There are several hotels/motels, two bed and breakfasts, restaurants, and gas stations with regular, unleaded, diesel and propane, automotive and tire repair. There are also department, variety, grocery and hardware stores. A complex on the north side of the highway contains the post office, library, fire hall and government liquor store. The RCMP office is east of town centre on the Alaska Highway. There is one bank in Watson Lake, open Monday through Thursday from 10 A.M. to 3 P.M., Friday 10 A.M. to 6 P.M.; closed holidays. Check at the visitor information centre for locations of local churches. Watson Lake's public swimming pool is open daily in summer; admission fee.

Belvedere Motor Hotel, located in the centre of town, is Watson Lake's newest and finest hotel. It offers such luxuries as Jacuzzi tubs in the rooms, waterbeds, and cable TV, and all at competitive prices. Dining is excellent, whether you decide to try the superb Dining Room Menu, or the Coffee Shop Menu, for those of us on a budget. Drop in for a free coffee ... just show us this editorial. Phone (403) 536-7712, fax (403) 536-7563. [ADVERTISEMENT]

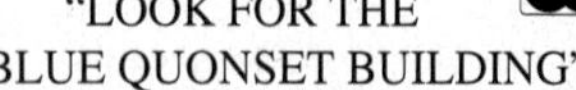

WATSON LAKE ADVERTISERS

Alaska Highway Pavilion ..... 1 blk. N. of signposts
Belvedere Motor Hotel ..... Ph. (403) 536-7712
Ben's Auto Repairs ..... Ph. (403) 536-2720
Big Horn Hotel ..... Ph. (403) 536-2020
Campground Services Ltd. ..... E. edge of town
Canteen Show, The ..... Next to signposts
Cedar Lodge Motel ..... Ph. (403) 536-7406
Downtown R.V. Park ..... Ph. (403) 536-2646
Gateway Motor Inn ..... Ph. (403) 536-7744
Grunow Motors ..... Ph. (403) 536-2272
Jer-Cal Holdings Ltd. ..... Downtown
Napa Auto Parts ..... Ph. (403) 536-2521
O'Neill Repairs ..... 1 blk. S. of signposts
Signpost Services ..... Across from signposts
Town of Watson Lake ..... Ph. (403) 536-7778
Watson Lake Boat Charters ..... Ph. (403) 536-2138
Watson Lake Esso ..... Ph. (403) 536-2545
Watson Lake Hotel ..... Ph. (403) 536-7781

TAKE A BREAK IN WATSON LAKE!

INTERESTED? CALL US TOLL FREE FROM THE LOWER 48: 1-800-663-5248

TOWN OF WATSON LAKE

BOX 590, WATSON LAKE, YUKON YOA 1CO
(403) 536-7778 · FAX (403) 536-7522

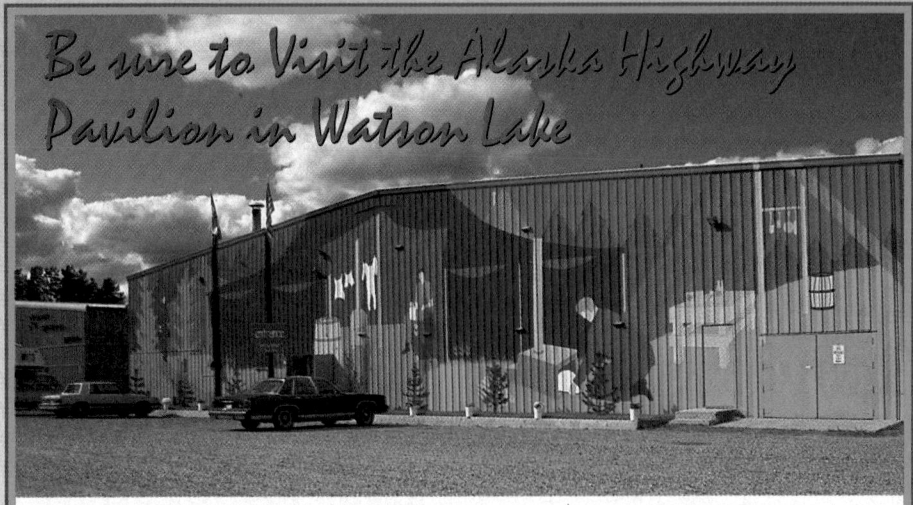

Be sure to Visit the Alaska Highway
Pavilion in Watson Lake

Your chance to discover the many places to see and things to do in Yukon, Northern BC, and Southern Alaska . . . interesting Northern videos, including "Sgt. Preston Of The Yukon." Located in the Johnny Friend Arena, One Block North of the World Famous Sign Post Forest.

For information (403) 536-7778

Show this ad for 25% off your Pavilion Admission!

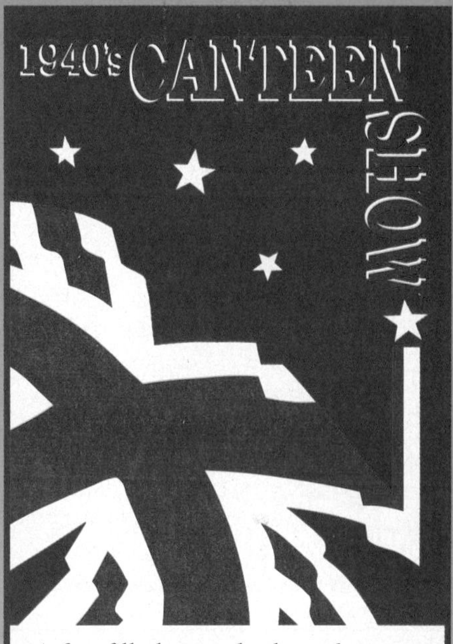

A fun-filled comedy that takes you back to the 40's and a look at the lighter side of the war years during construction of the Alaska Highway.

8:00 P.M. NIGHTLY
JUNE - JULY - AUGUST

Under the big top tent, located next to the world-famous Sign Post Forest
Watson Lake, Yukon, Canada

A Vintage Shows Production
Box 546, Watson Lake
Yukon, Canada Y0A 1C0
Telephone: **(403) 536-7781**
May-August

Be Sure to Bring Your Camera!
(No Video Please)

VISA MasterCard

SAVE MONEY!
Show us this ad and receive $1.00 off each ticket purchased. No other discounts will apply.

Yukon Territory is larger than all the New England states combined.

Big Horn Hotel & Tavern. New in 1993. 29 beautiful rooms. Centrally located on the Alaska Highway in downtown Watson Lake, YT. Our rooms are quiet, spacious, clean and they boast queen-size beds and complimentary coffee. You get quality at a reasonable price. Available to you are king-size motionless waterbeds, Jacuzzi rooms, kitchenette suites. We know you'll enjoy staying with us. Book ahead. Phone (403) 536-2020, Fax (403) 536-2021. [ADVERTISEMENT]

Watson Lake Hotel. The historic "Watson Lake Hotel." We're right in the heart of Watson Lake's historical "Signpost Forest," the Gateway Pavilion and Heritage Museum. Enjoy northern hospitality at its finest. Ample parking on our six acres of property. Quiet outside modern units, (renovated May 1993), complimentary in-room coffee, boardwalk gift shops and espresso bar. Senior, government, military and corporate discounts. Room rates start at $35 to deluxe suites at $129 CAN. Present this editorial for your 5-cent coffee in "Watson's Daytime Grill." (See our display ad). [ADVERTISEMENT]

The turnoff for Watson Lake Yukon government campground is 2.4 miles/3.9 km west of the sign forest via the Alaska Highway; see description at **Milepost DC 615.3.** There is a private campground at **Milepost DC 619.6**, 4.3 miles/6.9 km past the turnoff for the government campground; a private campground 2.4 miles/3.9 km east of the sign forest on the Alaska Highway (see **Milepost DC 610.5**); and an RV park located downtown. ▲

Downtown RV Park, situated in the centre of town. 71 full hookup stalls, 19 with pull-through parking; showers; laundromat. Free truck/trailer, motorhome wash with overnight stay. Easy walking distance to stores, garages, hotels, restaurants, liquor store, banking, churches, information centre and the world-famous signpost forest. Just across the street from Wye Lake Park. Excellent hiking trails. Phone (403) 536-2646 in summer, 536-2224 in winter. [ADVERTISEMENT] ▲

TRANSPORTATION

Air: Scheduled service to Fort Nelson, Fort St. John, Edmonton and Calgary via Time Air. Service to Whitehorse via Air North. Helicopter and fixed-wing aircraft charters available. **Bus:** Scheduled service to Edmonton and Whitehorse via Coachways. **Taxi** and **Car Rental:** Available.

ATTRACTIONS

The **Alaska Highway Interpretive Centre** here is well worth a visit. Excellent slide presentation and displays, including photographs taken in the mid-1940s showing the construction of the Alaska Highway in this area, and a brief Alaska Highway video. A full-scale reproduction of a P-39 Airacobra fighter plane is on display just outside the interpretive centre. Visitor information is available at the Interpretive Centre, which is located behind the sign forest, north of the Alaska Highway. Open 8 A.M. to 8 P.M., May to mid-September. Free admission. Phone (403) 536-7469.

The Alaska Highway Pavilion, located one block north of the signpost forest in the Johnny Friend Arena, has a large map of the Yukon highlighting what to see and do in the territory. Northern videos are available for viewing, including *Sgt. Preston of the Yukon.* A worthwhile stop. Small admission fee charged includes discount coupons for local businesses.

The Watson Lake signpost forest seen at

the north end of town at the junction of the Alaska and Robert Campbell highways, was started by Carl K. Lindley of Danville, IL, a U.S. Army soldier in Company D, 341st Engineers, working on the construction of the Alaska Highway in 1942. (Mr. Lindley made his first visit back to Watson Lake since 1942 for the 1992 Alaska Highway anniversary.) Travelers are still adding signs to the collection, which exceeded 20,000 in 1993.

Canteen Show. The 1940s Canteen Show now in it's seventh season is a definite must see! An award-winning show, this is top-notch, morale-boosting entertainment for all ages. The Canteen Show is unique, differing from other summer productions throughout British Columbia, Yukon and Alaska, as it relates to the building of the "Alcan," rather than the gold rush. This fabulous live show is hilarious, upbeat, full of '40s nostalgia music. Located beside the signpost forest, under the big top. Showtime is 8 P.M. nightly. Show this editorial and receive $1 off each ticket purchased. No other discounts will apply. [ADVERTISEMENT]

Historic Milepost 635 is located at the signpost forest. A sign and interpretive panel explain the Northwest Staging Route.

Heritage House, built in 1948 by the late G.C.F. Dalziel, is the oldest house in Watson Lake and now a wildlife and historic museum. It is located one block north of the sign forest. Dalziel came to this region as a trapper in the 1920s. His heirs opened Heritage House in 1987. Open daily in summer.

Wye Lake Park offers a picnic area and boardwalk trails for viewing birds. There are also a bandshell, kitchen shelter and handicap-accessible restrooms. The lake attracts both migrating birds (spring and fall) and resident species, such as nesting grebes. Native plants and flowers are identified by plaques. The development of this park was initiated by a local citizens group. Further improvements are planned.

Wye Lake Park offers bird watching and picnicking. (Barb Michaels)

Play golf at Upper Liard, 6 miles/9.6 km north of Watson Lake on the Alaska Highway. The nine-hole, par-35 course has grass greens and is open daily May through September. Phone 536-2477.

Wilderness Trips. Outfitters in the area offer guided fishing trips to area lakes. Trips can be arranged by the day or by the week. Check with the visitor information centre.

AREA FISHING: Boat charters available locally. **Watson Lake** has grayling, trout and pike. **McKinnon Lake** (walk-in only), 20 miles/32 km west of Watson Lake, pike 5 to 10 lbs. **Toobally Lake** and string of lakes 14

miles/23 km long, 90 air miles/145 km east, lake trout 8 to 10 lbs.; pike 5 to 10 lbs.; grayling 1 to 3 lbs. **Stewart Lake,** 45 air miles/72 km north northeast; lake trout, grayling.

Alaska Highway Log

(continued)

Distance* from Dawson Creek (DC) is followed by distance from Fairbanks (F). Original mileposts are indicated in the text as Historical Mile.

*Mileages from Dawson Creek are based on actual driving distance. Kilometres from Dawson Creek are based on physical kilometreposts. Please read Mileposts and Kilometreposts in the introduction for an explanation of how this highway is logged.

DC 612.9 (1021 km) **F 875.1** (1408.3 km) Watson Lake signpost forest at the **junction** of the Campbell Highway (Yukon Route 4) and Alaska Highway. The Campbell Highway leads north to Ross River and Faro (see CAMPBELL HIGHWAY section). Campbell Highway travelers should fill gas tanks in Watson Lake. The first 6 miles/9.7 km of the Campbell Highway is known locally as Airport Road; turn here for access to visitor information (in the Alaska Highway Interpretive Centre), airport, hospital and ski hill.

DC 615.3 (1025 km) **F 872.7** (1404.4 km) Turnoff to north for Watson Lake Recreation Park. Drive in approximately 2 miles/3 km for Watson Lake Yukon government campground; 50 gravel sites, most level, some pull-through, drinking water, kitchen shelters, outhouses, firepits, firewood and litter barrels. Camping fee $8. ▲

There is a separate group camping area and also a day-use area (boat launch, swimming, picnicking at Watson Lake). Follow signs at fork in access road. Trails connect all areas.

DC 618.5 (1030 km) **F 869.5** (1399.3 km) Watch for livestock.

DC 619.6 (1032 km) **F 868.4** (1397.5 km) **Green Valley R.V. Park.** Phone (403) 536-2276. Just 7 miles west of Watson Lake, quiet greenbelt area along Liard River. Friendly service, clean facilities. Pay phone. Serviced and unserviced sites, dump station, grassy tent sites, riverside camping, firepits, laundry, showers, grocery, coffee, pastries, ice, souvenirs, free gold panning, game room, fishing licenses and tackle. Fish for grayling and dollies. Pick wild strawberries and raspberries in season. Cold beer and off sales. Bikers welcome. Your hosts: Ralph and Marion Bjorkman. [ADVERTISEMENT] ▲

DC 620 (1032.4 km) **F 868** (1396.9 km) Upper Liard River bridge. The Liard River heads in the St. Cyr Range in southcentral Yukon Territory and flows southeast into British Columbia, then turns east and north to join the Mackenzie River at Fort Simpson, NWT.

Liard River, grayling, lake trout, whitefish and northern pike.

DC 620.2 (1032.7 km) **F 867.8** (1396.5 km) **Historical Mile 642. UPPER LIARD VILLAGE,** site of Our Lady of the Yukon Church. Gas, food, lodging and camping; open year-round.

DC 620.3 (1033 km) **F 867.7** (1396.4 km) Greenway's Greens golf course to south with nine holes, par 35, grass greens, open daily in summer.

DC 620.8 (1033.7 km) **F 867.2** (1395.6 km) Albert Creek bridge. Turnout with litter barrel to north at east end of bridge. A sign near here marks the first tree planting project in the Yukon. Approximately 200,000 white spruce seedlings were planted in the Albert Creek area in 1993.

DC 626.2 (1042.5 km) **F 861.8** (1386.9 km) **Historic Milepost 649. Junction** with the Cassiar Highway, which leads south to Yellowhead Highway 16 (see CASSIAR HIGHWAY section). Services here include gas, store, propane, car repair, car wash, cafe, camping and lodging. ▲

Junction 37 Services. See display ad this section.

DC 627 (1044 km) **F 861** (1385.6 km) **The Northern Beaver Post.** As with trading posts of the past, The Northern Beaver Post is an essential stop for any traveler. Here you will find unique, quality items which are often as useful as they are decorative. In the friendly atmosphere of the Post, discover a fine selection of Native crafts, jewellery, gold, jade, authentic Eskimo carvings, furs, woolens, northern art, tufting, sweatshirts and tees, cards, gifts, and more. Show us this editorial and receive 10 percent off your purchase of a Beaver Post T-shirt or sweat shirt. Open 8 A.M. to 9 P.M. seven days a week, May through September. Free overnight RV parking. Phone (403) 536-2307. [ADVERTISEMENT]

DC 627.3 (1044.5 km) **F 860.7** (1385.1 km) Large gravel turnout and rest area with litter barrels and pit toilets.

DC 630 (1050.8 km) **F 858** (1380.8 km) Several hundred rock messages are spelled out along the highway here. The rock messages were started in summer 1990 by a Fort Nelson swim team.

DC 633 (1055.6 km) **F 855** (1375.9 km) Gravel turnout to north.

DC 637.8 (1063.3 km) **F 850.2** (1368.2 km) NorthwesTel microwave tower access road to north.

DC 639.8 (1066.5 km) **F 848.2** (1365 km) Hill and sharp curve.

DC 647.2 (1078.5 km) **F 840.8** (1353.1 km) Turnout with litter barrel on Little Rancheria Creek to north.

DC 647.4 (1079 km) **F 840.6** (1352.8 km) Little Rancheria Creek bridge. Sign reads: "Northbound winter travelers put on chains here."

NOTE: Watch for road construction northbound to Kilometrepost 1085 in 1994.

DC 650.6 (1084 km) **F 837.4** (1347.6 km) Highway descends westbound to Big Creek.

DC 651.1 (1084.8 km) **F 836.9** (1346.8 km) Big Creek bridge, clearance 17.7 feet/5.4m. Turnout at east end of bridge.

DC 651.2 (1085 km) **F 836.8** (1346.7 km) Turnoff to north for Big Creek Yukon government day-use area, adjacent highway on Big Creek; gravel loop road, outhouses, firewood, kitchen shelter, litter barrels, picnic tables, drinking water.

DC 652.5 (1087.3 km) **F 835.5** (1344.6 km) Sign reads: "Northbound winter travelers chains may be removed."

DC 658.4 (1096.7 km) **F 829.6** (1335.1 km) Pull-through turnout south side of highway.

DC 662.3 (1102.9 km) **F 825.7** (1328.8 km) NorthwesTel microwave tower road to north.

DC 664.1 (1105.8 km) **F 823.9** (1325.9 km) Turnout to north to Lower Rancheria River.

DC 664.3 (1106.2 km) **F 823.7** (1325.6 km) Bridge over Lower Rancheria River. For northbound travelers, the highway closely follows the Rancheria River west from here to the Swift River.

Legendary Northern bush pilot Les Cook was credited with helping General Hoge find the best route for the Alaska Highway between Watson Lake and Whitehorse. According to John Schmidt's *"This Was No ΦΥΧΝΗ Picnic!"*, Cook's Rancheria River route saved engineers hundreds of miles of highway construction over the original plan.

Rancheria River, fishing for Dolly Varden and grayling.

DC 665.1 (1110.4 km) **F 822.9** (1324.3 km) Scenic viewpoint.

DC 667.2 (1113.7 km) **F 820.8** (1320.9 km) Turnout to south.

DC 667.6 (1114.3 km) **F 820.4** (1320.2 km) Turnout with litter barrel to south.

DC 671.9 (1118.7 km) **F 816.1** (1313.3 km) Spencer Creek.

DC 673.4 (1121 km) **F 814.6** (1310.9 km) Steep grade as highway descends westbound. Road narrows. Cassiar Mountains visible ahead for westbound travelers.

DC 677 (1126.9 km) **F 811** (1305.1 km) Turnout with litter barrel to south overlooking the Rancheria River. Trail down to river.

According to R.C. Coutts, author of *Yukon: Places & Names,* the Rancheria River was named by Cassiar miners working Sayyea Creek in 1875, site of a minor gold

The Alaska Highway winds through the Rancheria River valley. (Earl L. Brown, staff)

rush at the time. Rancheria is an old Californian or Mexican miners' term from the Spanish, meaning a native village or settlement. It is pronounced Ran-che-RI-ah.

DC 678.5 (1129.3 km) **F 809.5** (1302.7 km) George's Gorge, culvert.

DC 683.2 (1137 km) **F 804.8** (1295.2 km) NorthwesTel microwave tower to south.

DC 684 (1138.4 km) **F 804** (1293.9 km) Turnout with litter barrel overlooking Rancheria River. *CAUTION: Watch for livestock on or near highway in this area.*

DC 687.2 (1143.8 km) **F 800.8** (1288.7 km) **Historic Milepost 710.** Rancheria Hotel–Motel to south; gas, food, camping and lodging. Open year-round. Historic sign and interpretive panel on highway lodges. ▲

Rancheria Hotel–Motel. See display ad this section. ▲

DC 687.4 (1143.9 km) **F 800.6** (1288.4 km) Turnoff to south for Rancheria Yukon government campground, adjacent highway overlooking Rancheria River; gravel loop road, 12 level sites, outhouses, kitchen shelter, litter barrels, water pump, picnic tables, firepits and firewood. Camping fee $8. ▲

DC 689.2 (1146.6 km) **F 798.8** (1285.5 km) Canyon Creek.

DC 690 (1148 km) **F 798** (1284.2 km) Highway follows the Rancheria River, which is to the south of the road. The Rancheria is a tributary of the Liard River.

DC 692.5 (1152 km) **F 795.5** (1280.2 km) Young Creek.

DC 694.2 (1155 km) **F 793.8** (1277.5 km) **Historical Mile 717.5.** Abandoned building.

DC 695.2 (1156.5 km) **F 792.8** (1275.8 km) Rancheria Falls recreation site has a good gravel and boardwalk trail to the falls; easy 10-minute walk. Parking area with toilets and litter barrels at trailhead.

DC 697.4 (1160 km) **F 790.6** (1272.3 km) Beautiful view of the Cassiar Mountains.

DC 698.4 (1161.6 km) **F 789.6** (1270.7 km) **Historical Mile 721.** Continental Divide; gas, food, camping and lodging. ▲

Continental Divide. See display ad this section. ▲

DC 698.7 (1162 km) **F 789.3** (1270.2 km) Upper Rancheria River bridge, clearance 17.7 feet/5.4m. For northbound travelers, the highway leaves the Rancheria River.

DC 699.1 (1162.8 km) **F 788.9** (1269.6 km) Continental Divide turnout with point of interest sign to north; litter barrels. This marks the water divide between rivers that drain into the Arctic Ocean via the Mackenzie River system and those that drain into the Pacific Ocean via the Yukon River system. All rivers crossed by the Alaska Highway between here and Fairbanks, AK, drain into the Yukon River.

DC 699.6 (1163.3 km) **F 788.4** (1268.8 km) **Historic Milepost 722.** Pine Lake airstrip to north (status unknown).

DC 702.2 (1168 km) **F 785.8** (1264.6 km) Swift River bridge. For northbound travelers, the highway now follows the Swift River west to the Morley River.

NOTE: Watch for road construction northbound to Kilometrepost 1180 in 1994.

DC 706.2 (1174.5 km) **F 781.8** (1258.2 km) Steep hill for westbound travelers.

DC 709.7 (1180 km) **F 778.3** (1252.5 km) Seagull Creek.

DC 709.8 (1180.6 km) **F 778.2** (1252.3 km) Gas and food.

DC 710 (1180.9 km) **F 778** (1252 km) **Historic Milepost 733, SWIFT RIVER.** Lodge with food, gas, lodging, car repair, pay phone and highway maintenance camp. Open year-round.

Swift River Lodge. Friendly haven in a beautiful mountain valley. Tasty cooking with a plentiful supply of coffee. Mouth-watering homemade pies and pastries fresh daily. Wrecker service, welding and repairs. Reasonable rates. Propane. Tempo gas and diesel at some of the best prices on the highway. Clean restrooms, gifts and public phone. [ADVERTISEMENT]

DC 710.5 (1181.5 km) **F 777.5** (1251.2 km) **Historical Mile 733.5.** The highway re-enters British Columbia for approximately 42 miles/68 km northbound.

DC 712.7 (1185 km) **F 775.3** (1247.7 km)

Partridge Creek.

DC 719.6 (1196 km) **F 768.4** (1236.6 km) **Historical Mile 743.** Turnout with litter barrel to south on **Swan Lake.** Fishing for trout and whitefish. The pyramid-shaped mountain to south is Simpson Peak.

DC 724.2 (1203.7 km) **F 763.8** (1229.2 km) Pull-through turnout to south.

DC 727.9 (1209.5 km) **F 760.1** (1223.2 km) Logjam Creek. Litter barrel.

DC 735.8 (1222.5 km) **F 752.2** (1210.5 km) Smart River bridge. The Smart River flows south into the Cassiar Mountains in British Columbia. The river was originally called Smarch, after an Indian family of that name who lived and trapped in this area.

DC 741.4 (1231.7 km) **F 746.6** (1201.5 km) Microwave tower access road to north.

DC 744.1 (1236 km) **F 743.9** (1197.2 km) Upper Hazel Creek.

DC 745.2 (1238 km) **F 742.8** (1195.4 km) Lower Hazel Creek.

DC 746.9 (1240.7 km) **F 741.1** (1192.6 km) Turnouts both sides of highway; litter barrel at south turnout.

DC 749 (1245 km) **F 739** (1189.3 km) Andrew Creek.

DC 751.5 (1249.2 km) **F 736.5** (1185.2 km) Morley Lake to north. The Alaska Highway re-enters the Yukon Territory northbound. This is the last of seven crossings of the YT–BC border.

DC 752 (1250 km) **F 736** (1184.4 km) Sharp turnoff to north for **Morley River** Yukon government day-use area; large gravel parking area, picnic tables, kitchen shelter, water, litter barrels and outhouses. Fishing.

DC 752.3 (1251 km) **F 735.7** (1184 km) Morley River bridge; turnout with litter barrel to north at east end of bridge. Morley River flows into the southeast corner of Teslin Lake. The river, lake and Morley Bay (on Teslin Lake) were named for W. Morley Ogilvie, assistant to Arthur St. Cyr on the 1897 survey of the Telegraph Creek–Teslin Lake route.

Morley Bay and **River**, good fishing near mouth of river for northern pike 6 to 8 lbs., best June to August, use small Red Devils; grayling 3 to 5 lbs., in May and August, use small spinner; lake trout 6 to 8 lbs., June to August, use large spoon.

DC 752.9 (1252 km) **F 735.1** (1183 km) **Historic Milepost 777.7.** Morley River Lodge, food, gas, diesel, camping and lodging. Open year-round. ▲

Morley River Lodge. See display ad this section. ▲

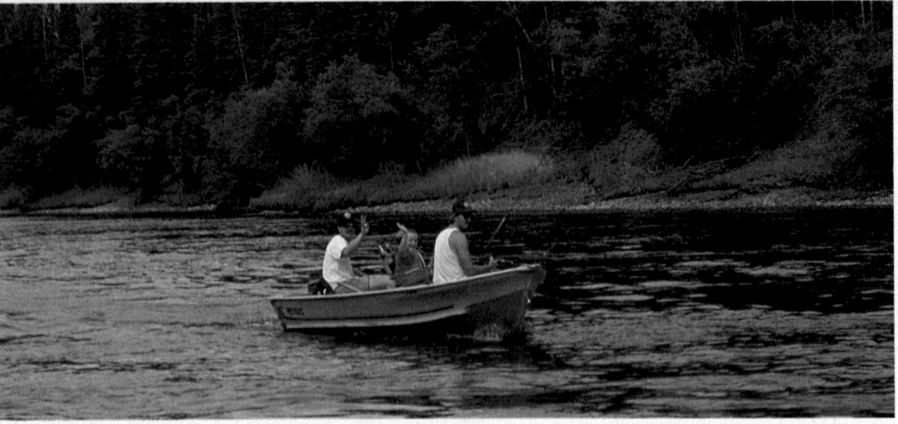

Fishermen head up the Teslin River. *(Earl L. Brown, staff)*

DC 754.8 (1256 km) **F 733.2** (1179.9 km) *CAUTION: Watch for livestock on highway.*

DC 757.9 (1261 km) **F 730.1** (1174.9 km) Small marker to south (no turnout) reads: "In memory of Max Richardson 39163467, Corporal Co. F 340th Eng. Army of the United States; born Oct. 10, 1918, died Oct. 17, 1942. Faith is the victory."

DC 761.5 (1267.9 km) **F 726.5** (1169.1 km) Strawberry Creek.

DC 764.1 (1273.7 km) **F 723.9** (1165 km) Hayes Creek.

DC 769.6 (1282.5 km) **F 718.4** (1156.1 km) **Historical Mile 797.** Food, lodging and camping. ▲

Dawson Peaks Northern Resort. Slow down folks! No need to drive any farther. Fishing's good, coffee's on, camping is easy and the rhubarb pie can't be beat. Couple that with our renowned Yukon hospitality and you'll have one of the best experiences on your trip. We're looking forward to seeing you this summer. See display ad on page 111. [ADVERTISEMENT]

DC 776 (1292 km) **F 712** (1145.8 km) Nisutlin Bay (Nisutlin River) bridge, longest water span on the Alaska Highway at 1,917 feet/584m. The Nisutlin River flows into Teslin Lake here. Good view northbound of the village of Teslin and Teslin Lake. Teslin Lake straddles the BC–YT border; it is 86 miles/138 km long, averages 2 miles/3.2 km across, and has an average depth of 194 feet/59m. The name is taken from the Indian name for the lake — Teslintoo ("long, narrow water").

Turnout with litter barrel and point of interest sign at south end of bridge, east side of highway.

Historic Milepost 804 at the north end of the bridge, west side of the highway; historic sign and interpretive panel, parking area, marina and day-use area with picnic tables and boat ramp. Turn west on side road here for access to Teslin village (description follows).

DC 776.3 (1294 km) **F 711.7** (1145.3 km) Entering Teslin **(Historic Milepost 804)** at north end of bridge. Gas, food, camping and lodging along highway.

Yukon Motel, just right (northbound) on the north side of Nisutlin Bridge. An excellent stop for a fresh lake trout dinner (or full menu), accompanied by good and friendly service topped off with a piece of fantastic rhubarb and strawberry pie (lots of fresh baking). Soft ice cream. Recently renovated. Three satellite TV channels. Open year-round, summer hours 6-11. New lakeshore RV park (mosquito control area), 70 sites, full and partial hookups. "Good Sam Park" — washhouse rated TL 10. A real home away from home on the shore of beautiful Nisutlin Bay. (403) 390-2575. [ADVERTISEMENT] ▲

Teslin

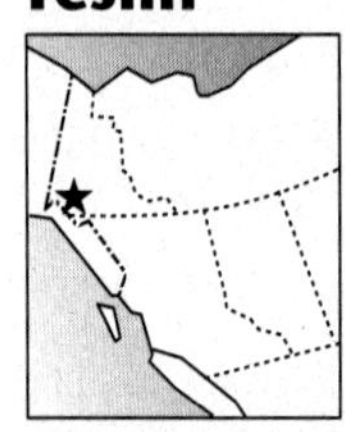

Located at **Historic Milepost 804,** 111 miles/179 km southeast of Whitehorse, 163 miles/263 km northwest of Watson Lake. **Population:** 465. **Emergency Services: RCMP,** phone 390-5555 (if no answer call toll free 1-667-5555). **Fire Department,** phone 390-2222. **Nurse,** phone 390-4444.

Elevation: 2,239 feet/682.4m. **Climate:** Average temperature in January, -7°F/-22°C, in July 57°F/14°C. Annual snowfall 66.2 inches/168.2cm. Driest month April, wettest month July. Average date of last spring frost is June 19; first fall frost Aug. 19. **Radio:**

TESLIN ADVERTISERS

George Johnston Museum	Ph. (403) 390-2550
Nisutlin Trading Post	Ph. (403) 390-2521
Teslin Lake Motors	Ph. (403) 390-2551
Yukon Motel	Ph. (403) 390-2575

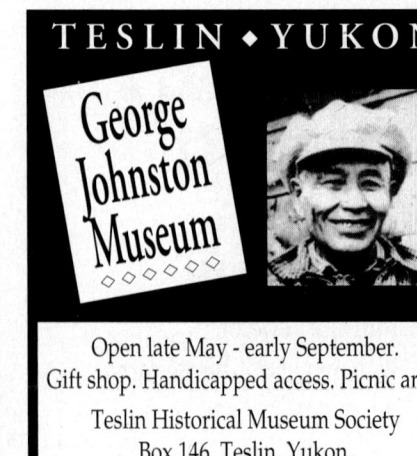

CBC 940. **Television:** Channel 13.

The village of Teslin, situated on a point of land at the confluence of the Nisutlin River and Teslin Lake, began as a trading post in 1903. Today the community consists of a trading post, Catholic church, health centre and post office. There is a three-sheet regulation curling rink and a skating rink.

Teslin has one of the largest Native populations in Yukon Territory and much of the community's livelihood revolves around traditional hunting, trapping and fishing. In addition, some Tlingit residents are involved in the development of Native woodworking craft (canoes, snowshoes and sleds); traditional sewn art and craft items (moccasins, mitts, moose hair tufting, gun cases); and the tanning of moose hides.

George Johnston Museum, renovated in 1991, is located on the right on the way into the village. The museum, run by the Teslin Historical Museum Society, is open daily, 9 A.M. to 7 P.M. in summer; minimal admission fee. Wheelchair accessible. The museum displays items from gold rush days and the pioneer mode of living, Indian artifacts and many items of Tlingit culture. A Tlingit Indian, George Johnston (1884–1972) was an innovative individual, known for his trapping as well as his photography. With his camera he captured the life of the inland Tlingit people of Teslin and Atlin between 1910 and 1940. Johnston also brought the first car to Teslin, a 1928 Chevrolet. Since the Alaska Highway had not been built yet, George built a 3-mile road for his "Teslin taxi." In winter, he put chains on the car and drove it on frozen Teslin Lake. The '28 Chevy has been restored. Write the Teslin Historical Museum Society, Box 146, Teslin, YT Y0A 1B0, or phone (403) 390-2550 for more information.

Teslin is located west of the Alaska Highway, accessible via a short side road from the north end of Nisutlin Bay bridge. Nisutlin Trading Post in the village has groceries and general merchandise. Gas, diesel and propane, car repair, gift shop, restaurants and motels are found along the Alaska Highway. There is one bank, located in the Teslin Village office building; open Wednesday afternoons only in summer. The Teslin area has an air charter service, boat rentals and houseboat tours.

Teslin Lake, fishing for trout, grayling, pike and whitefish. King salmon in August. Guides and boats available locally.

Alaska Highway Log

(continued)

Distance* from Dawson Creek (DC) is followed by distance from Fairbanks (F). Original mileposts are indicated in the text as Historical Mile.

*Mileages from Dawson Creek are based on actual driving distance. Kilometres from Dawson Creek are based on physical kilometreposts. Please read Mileposts and Kilometreposts in the introduction for an explanation of how this highway is logged.

Teslin River bridge is the third longest water span on the highway. (Earl L. Brown, staff)

DC 777 (1295 km) **F 711** (1144.2 km) **Historic Milepost 805. Private Aircraft:** Teslin airstrip to east; elev. 2,313 feet/705m; length 5,500 feet/1,676m; gravel; fuel 80, 100.

DC 779.1 (1298.5 km) **F 708.9** (1140.8 km) **Historical Mile 807.** Halsteads' gas, food, camping and lodging. Microwave tower on hillside to northwest. ▲

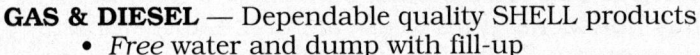

Halsteads'. See display ad this section. ▲

DC 779.5 (1299 km) **F 708.5** (1140.2 km) Fox Creek.

DC 784.3 (1306.7 km) **F 703.7** (1132.5 km) **Historical Mile 812.** Mukluk Annie's; food, lodging and camping. ▲

Mukluk Annie's Salmon Bake. See display ad this section. ▲

DC 785.2 (1308 km) **F 702.8** (1131 km) **Historical Mile 813.** Teslin Lake Yukon government campground to west; 19 sites (some level) in trees on **Teslin Lake**, water pump, litter barrels, kitchen shelter, firewood, firepits, picnic tables. Camping fee $8. Fishing. Boat launch 0.3 mile/0.5 km north of campground. ▲

DC 785.3 (1308.2 km) **F 702.7** (1130.8 km) Tenmile Creek.

DC 788.9 (1314 km) **F 699.1** (1125 km) Lone Tree Creek.

DC 794.6 (1323 km) **F 693.4** (1115.9 km) Deadman's Creek.

DC 800.8 (1333.3 km) **F 687.2** (1105.9 km) Robertson Creek.

DC 801.6 (1334.4 km) **F 686.4** (1104.6 km) **Historic Milepost 829.** Brooks' Brook. According to R.C. Coutts in *Yukon: Places & Names,* this stream was named by black Army engineers who completed this section of road in 1942, for their company officer, Lieutenant Brooks.

DC 808.2 (1345 km) **F 679.8** (1094 km) **Junction** with the Canol Road (Yukon Highway 6) which leads northeast to the Campbell Highway. (See the CANOL ROAD section for details.) Historic sign and interpretive panel about the Canol Project.

The Canol (Canadian Oil) Road was built in 1942–44 to provide access to oil fields at Norman Wells, NWT. Conceived by the U.S. War Dept., the $134 million project was abandoned soon after the war ended in 1945.

DC 808.6 (1345.6 km) **F 679.4** (1093.3 km) Teslin River bridge, third longest water span on the highway (1,770 feet/539m), was constructed with a very high clearance above the river to permit steamers of the British Yukon Navigation Co. to pass under it en route from Whitehorse to Teslin. River steamers ceased operation on the Teslin River in 1942. Before the construction of the Alaska Highway, all freight and supplies for Teslin traveled this water route from Whitehorse.

DC 808.9 (1346 km) **F 679.1** (1092.9 km) **Historic Milepost 836. JOHNSON'S CROSSING** to east at north end of bridge; store, food and camping. One of the original lodges on the Alaska Highway, the history of Johnson's Crossing is related in Ellen Davignon's *The Cinnamon Mine.* Access to Teslin River; boat launch, no camping on riverbank. ▲

Johnson's Crossing Campground Services. Located across the Teslin River bridge, home of the "world famous cinnamon buns," including a small store with a full array of mouth-watering baked goods, souvenirs and groceries. Full-service RV campground facilities include treed pull-throughs, complete laundry and washhouse facilities, Chevron gasoline products, cold beer and ice, and great fishing. Treat yourselves to the historically scenic Km 1347 (Mile 836) Alaska Highway, Yukon Y1A 9Z0. (403) 390-2607. [ADVERTISEMENT] ▲

Teslin River, excellent grayling fishing from spring to late fall, 10 to 15 inches, use spinner or red-and-white spoons for spinning or black gnat for fly-fishing. King salmon in August.

Canoeists report that the Teslin River is wide and slow, but with gravel, rocks and weeds. Adequate camping sites on numerous sand bars; boil drinking water. Abundant wildlife — muskrat, porcupine, moose, eagles and wolves — also bugs and rain. Watch for bear. The Teslin enters the Yukon River at Hootalinqua, an old steamboat landing and supply point (under restoration). Roaring Bull rapids: choppy water. Pull out at Carmacks. Inquire locally about river conditions before setting out.

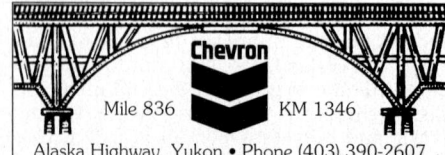

DC 809.1 (1346.5 km) **F 678.9** (1092.5 km) Access road east to the Teslin River. The Big Salmon Range, also to the east, parallels the Teslin. For Alaska-bound travelers, the highway now swings west.

DC 812.8 (1352.5 km) **F 675.2** (1086.6 km) Little Teslin Lake on south side of highway.

DC 819.8 (1364 km) **F 668.2** (1075.3 km) In mid-June, the roadside is a profusion of purple Jacob's ladder and yellow dandelions.

DC 820.3 (1364.8 km) **F 667.7** (1074.5 km) Seaforth Creek bridge.

DC 820.4 (1365 km) **F 667.6** (1074.4 km) Large turnout to south; picnic area.

DC 820.6 (1365.3 km) **F 667.4** (1074 km) Squanga Lake to northwest. Named Squanga by Indians for a type of whitefish of the same name found in the lake. Watch for **Historic Milepost 843,** with historic sign about Squanga Lake flightstrip. Look for the eagle's nest in the old observation tower.

DC 821 (1366 km) **F 667** (1073.4 km) Turnoff to northwest to **Squanga Lake** Yukon government campground: 13 sites, kitchen shelter, drinking water. Small boat launch. Fishing for northern pike, grayling, whitefish, rainbow and burbot.

DC 827.5 (1376.8 km) **F 660.5** (1062.9 km) White Mountain, to the southeast, was named by William Ogilvie during his 1887 survey, for Thomas White, then Minister of the Interior. The Yukon government introduced mountain goats to this area in 1981.

DC 836.8 (1392.5 km) **F 651.2** (1048 km) **Historic Milepost 866. Junction,** commonly known as **JAKE'S CORNER;** gas, food and lodging. There's also a large collection on the premises of artifacts from the Canol Project, Alaska Highway construction, and the gold rush. The Alaska Highway junctions here with Yukon Highway 7 south to Atlin, a very scenic spot that is well worth a side trip (see ATLIN ROAD section). This turnoff also provides access to Yukon Highway 8 to Carcross and Klondike Highway 2 to Skagway, AK. (Klondike Highway 2 junctions with the Alaska Highway at **Milepost DC 874.4.**) Yukon Highway 8 is a scenic alternative to driving the Carcross–Alaska Highway portion of Klondike Highway 2 (see TAGISH ROAD and KLONDIKE HIGHWAY 2 sections for details).

Jake's Corner Inc. See display ad this section.

There are two versions of how Jake's Corner got its name. In 1942, the U.S. Army Corps of Engineers set up a construction camp here to build this section of the Alcan Highway and the Tagish Road cutoff to Carcross for the Canol pipeline. (The highway south to Atlin, BC, was not constructed until 1949–50.) The camp was under the command of Captain Jacobson, thus Jake's Corner. However, another version that predates the Alcan construction is that Jake's Corner was named for Jake Jackson, a Teslin Indian who camped in this area on his way to Carcross.

DC 843.2 (1402.7 km) **F 644.8** (1037.7 km) Judas Creek bridge.

DC 850 (1413.5 km) **F 638** (1026.7 km) Turnoff to west for Lakeview Resort on Marsh Lake; camping, lodging, boat launch.

Lakeview Resort & Marina. See display ad this section.

DC 851.6 (1416 km) **F 636.4** (1024.1 km) Several access roads along here which lead to summer cottages. Marsh Lake is a popular recreation area for Whitehorse residents.

DC 852.7 (1417.8 km) **F 635.3** (1022.4 km) Good view of Marsh Lake to west. The highway parallels this beautiful lake for several miles. Marsh Lake (elev. 2,152 feet/656m) is part of the Yukon River system. It is approximately 20 miles/32 km long and was named in 1883 by Lt. Frederick Schwatka, U.S. Army, for Yale professor Othniel Charles Marsh.

Marsh Lake, excellent fishing for grayling and northern pike.

DC 854.4 (1421 km) **F 633.6** (1019.6 km) **Historic Milepost 883,** Marsh Lake Camp historic sign. Boat ramp turnoff to west.

DC 854.8 (1421.2 km) **F 633.2** (1019 km) Caribou Road leads northwest to Airplane Lake; hiking trail, good skiing and snowmachining in winter. This road was bulldozed out to get men and equipment into a small lake where an airplane had made an emergency landing.

DC 859.9 (1432 km) **F 628.1** (1010.8 km) **Historical Mile 890.** Turnoff to west for Marsh Lake Yukon government campground via 0.4-mile/0.6-km gravel loop road: 47 sites, most level, some pull-

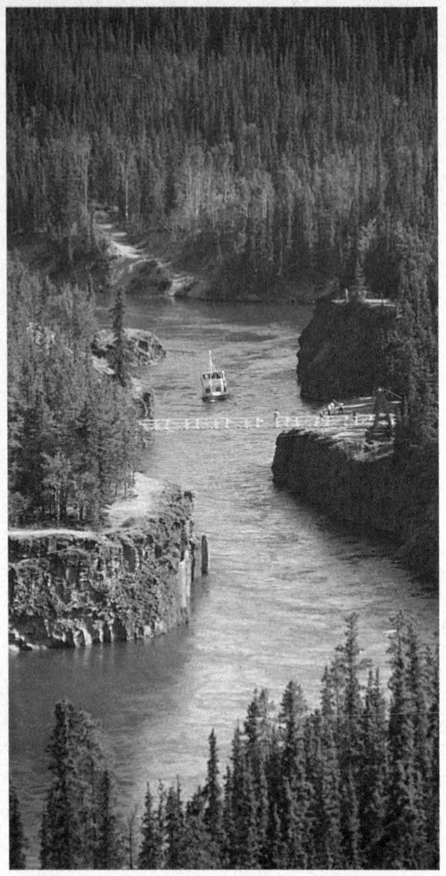

Boat tours of scenic Miles Canyon are available in Whitehorse. (Earl L. Brown, staff)

through; outhouses, firewood, firepits, litter barrels, picnic tables, kitchen shelter, water pump. Camping fee $8. ▲

For group camping and day-use area, follow signs near campground entrance. Day-use area includes sandy beach, change house, picnic area, playground, kitchen shelter and boat launch.

DC 861.1 (1431.8 km) **F 626.9** (1008.9 km) M'Clintock River, named by Lieutenant Schwatka for Arctic explorer Sir Francis M'Clintock. This river flows into the north end of Marsh Lake. Boat ramp turnoff to west at north end of bridge. M'Clintock River is narrow, winding and silty with thick brush along shoreline. However, it is a good river for boat trips, especially in late fall.

DC 864.3 (1437 km) **F 623.7** (1003.7 km) Bridge over Kettley's Canyon.

DC 867.3 (1441.8 km) **F 620.7** (998.9 km) **Historic Milepost 897.** Yukon River bridge. Turnout to north for day-use area and boat launch on **Yukon River** at Marsh Lake bridge near Northern Canada Power Commission (NCPC) control gate. Point of interest sign and litter barrels. From here (elev. 2,150 feet/645m) the Yukon River flows 1,980 miles/3,186 km to the Bering Sea. Good fishing for grayling, jackfish and some trout.

DC 873.5 (1453.3 km) **F 614.5** (988.9 km) **Historical Mile 904.** Sourdough Country Campsite to east. ▲

Sourdough Country Campsite. See display ad this section. ▲

DC 874.4 (1455 km) **F 613.6** (987.5 km) **Historical Mile 905. Junction** with Klondike Highway 2 (Carcross Road) which leads south to Carcross and Skagway. (See KLONDIKE HIGHWAY 2 section.) Food, gas, car repair and rock shop here.

Pine Creek Motors. See display ad this section.

Yukon Rock Shop. See display ad this section.

DC 874.6 (1455.3 km) **F 613.4** (987.1 km) Whitehorse city limits. Incorporated June 1, 1950, Whitehorse expanded in 1974 from its original 2.7 square miles/6.9 square kilometres to 162 square miles/421 square kilometres.

DC 875.6 (1456.9 km) **F 612.4** (985.5 km) Kara Speedway to west.

DC 875.9 (1457.4 km) **F 612.1** (985 km) Cowley Creek.

DC 876.8 (1459 km) **F 611.2** (983.6 km) **Historical Mile 906.** Wolf Creek Yukon government campground to east. An 0.8-mile/1.3-km gravel loop road leads through this campground: 49 sites, most level, some pull-through; kitchen shelters, water pumps, picnic tables, firepits, firewood, outhouses, litter barrels, playground. Wolf Creek self-guiding trail; varied and abundant plant life. Camping fee $8. Fishing in **Wolf Creek** for grayling. ▲

DC 879.4 (1463 km) **F 608.6** (979.4 km) Highway crosses railroad tracks.

DC 879.6 (1463.3 km) **F 608.4** (979.1 km) Point of interest sign about 135th meridian to east; small turnout. Gas station.

DC 879.8 (1463.7 km) **F 608.2** (978.8 km) **Historic Milepost 910.** Historic sign reads: "McCrae originated in 1900 as a flag stop on the newly-constructed White Pass & Yukon Railway. During WWII, this area served as a major service and supply depot, a major construction camp and a recreation centre." McCrae truck stop to east.

DC 880.4 (1464.5 km) **F 607.6** (977.8 km) Turnoff to west for Whitehorse Copper Mines (closed). Road to east leads to Yukon River.

DC 881 (1465.5 km) **F 607** (976.8 km) **Historic Milepost 911.** Site of Utah Construction Co. Camp. Pioneer RV Park, store and self-serve gas to east. ▲

Pioneer R.V. Park. See display ad this section. ▲

DC 881.3 (1466 km) **F 606.7** (976.4 km) White Pass & Yukon Route's Utah siding to east. (WP&YR ceased operation in 1982, but started limited service again in 1988 between Skagway and Fraser. See WHITE PASS & YUKON ROUTE section.) This was also the site of an Army camp where thousands of soldiers were stationed during construction of the Alaska Highway.

DC 881.7 (1466.6 km) **F 606.3** (975.7 km) Sharp turnoff to east (watch for camera viewpoint sign) to see Miles Canyon. Drive down side road 0.3 mile/0.5 km to fork. The right fork leads to Miles Canyon parking lot. From the parking area it is a short walk to the Miles Canyon bridge; good photo spot. Cross bridge for easy hiking trails overlooking Yukon River. The left fork leads to Schwatka Lake Road, which follows the lake and intersects the South Access Road into Whitehorse. Turnouts along road overlook Miles Canyon.

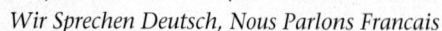

DC 881.9 (1466.9 km) **F 606.1** (975.4 km) Riding stable with daily trail rides in summer.

DC 882.6 (1468 km) **F 605.4** (974.3 km) **Historical Mile 912.** RV service and supply.

Philmar RV Service and Supply. See display ad this section.

DC 883.2 (1468.9 km) **F 604.8** (973.3 km) **Historical Mile 913**. Gas, diesel and mini-mart.

Whitehorse Shell. See display ad this section. ▲

DC 883.7 (1469.7 km) **F 604.3** (972.5 km) Turnout to east with litter barrel, outhouses, pay phone and information sign.

DC 884 (1470.2 km) **F 604** (972 km) **Hi-Country R.V. Park.** Good Sam. New facilities to serve the traveler. Large wooded sites, electric and water hookups, dump station, hot showers. Picnic tables and firepits, gift shop with wildlife display. Propane. Conveniently located on the highway at the south access to Whitehorse, next to beautiful Yukon Gardens. (403) 667-7445, fax (403) 668-7432. [ADVERTISEMENT] ▲

DC 884 (1470.2 km) **F 604** (972 km) First exit northbound for Whitehorse. Exit east for South Access Road to Whitehorse via 4th Avenue and 2nd Avenue. At the turnoff is Yukon Gardens botanical exhibit. At Mile 1.4/2.3 km on this access road is the side road to Miles Canyon and Schwatka Lake; at Mile 1.6/2.6 km is Robert Service Campground (tent camping only) with a picnic area for day use; at Mile 2.6/4.2 km is the SS *Klondike,* turn left for downtown Whitehorse.

DC 885.7 (1472.9 km) **F 602.3** (969.3 km) Yukon Visitors Reception Centre, open mid-May to mid-September, 8 A.M. to 8 P.M. daily; phone 667-2915. Wheelchair accessible. Preview Yukon attractions on laser disc player. Enjoy an outstanding multi-image slide presentation on Yukon National Parks and historic sites. Radio CKYN "Yukon Gold," 96.1-FM, broadcasts from the centre. ♿

DC 885.8 (1473.1 km) **F 602.2** (969.1 km) Yukon Transportation Museum features exhibits on all forms of transportation in the North. A mural on the front of the museum depicts the methods of transportation used in construction of the Alaska Highway in 1942. The 16-by-60-foot/5-by-8-m mural was painted by members of the Yukon Art Society. Open May to September. Admission fee.

DC 886.2 (1473.8 km) **F 601.8** (968.5 km) Turnoff to east for Whitehorse International Airport. Built for and used by both U.S. and Canadian forces during WWII. DC-3 weathervane. (See Attractions in the WHITEHORSE section for details.)

DC 887.1 (1475.2 km) **F 600.9** (967 km) To east, in front of NorthwesTel's maintenance complex, are cairns commemorating 18 years of service on the Alaska Highway (1946–64) by the Corps of Royal Canadian Engineers. At this site, on April 1, 1946, the U.S. Army officially handed over the Alaska Highway to the Canadian Army.

DC 887.4 (1475.6 km) **F 600.6** (966.5 km) Second (and last) exit northbound for Whitehorse. North access road to Whitehorse (exit east) is via Two-Mile Hill and 4th Avenue. Access to private RV park. At Mile 1.2/1.9 km on this access road is Qwanlin Mall.

Alaska Highway log continues on page 131. Description of Whitehorse follows.

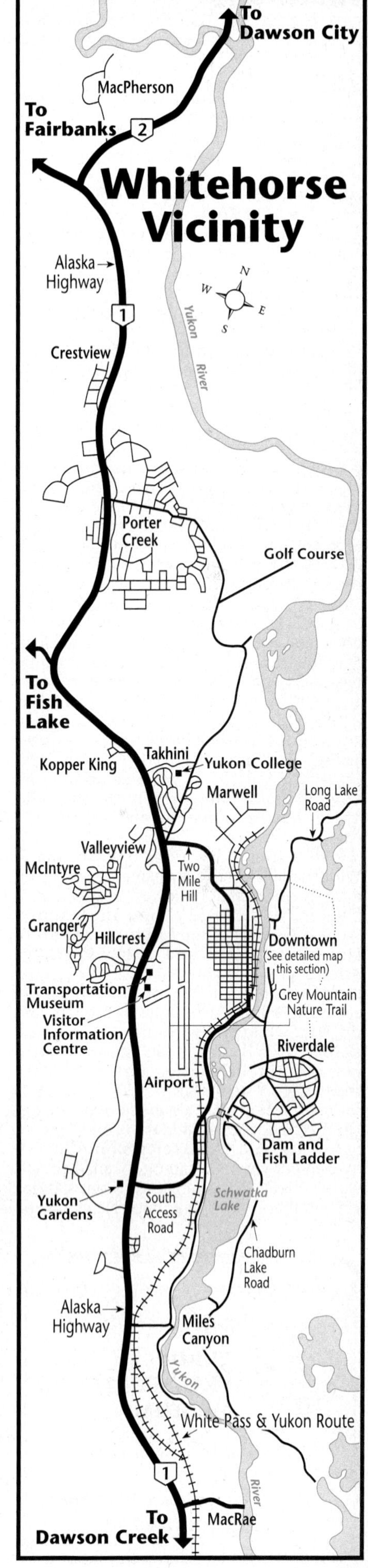

Whitehorse

Historic Milepost 918. Located on the upper reaches of the Yukon River in Canada's subarctic at latitude 61°N. Whitehorse is 100 miles/160 km from Haines Junction; 109 miles/175 km from Skagway, AK; 250 miles/241 km from Haines, AK; and 396 miles/637 km from Tok, AK. **Population:** Approximately 22,000. **Emergency Services: RCMP**, 4100 4th Ave., phone 667-5555. **Fire Department**, 2nd Avenue at Wood Street, phone 667-2222. **Ambulance/Inhalator**, phone 668-3333. **Hospital**, Whitehorse General, phone 668-4444.

Visitor Information: The Visitor Reception Centre is located on the Alaska Highway at **Milepost DC 885.7**, adjacent the Transportation Museum. An excellent multi-image slide presentation on Yukon National Parks and historical sites is presented at the centre, and Yukon attractions can be previewed on a laser disc player. Radio CKYN "Yukon Gold," 96.1-FM, is broadcast from the centre. The centre is open from mid-May to mid-September; phone 667-2915. For additional visitor information contact the Whitehorse Chamber of Commerce, Suite 101, 302 Steele St., Whitehorse, YT Y1A 2C5, phone 667-7545. The chamber is open year-round 9 A.M. to 5 P.M. weekdays, extended hours in summer. Free information is also available from the territorial government by writing Tourism Yukon, Box 2703, Whitehorse, YT Y1A 2C6. Canadian government topographic maps are available at Jim's Toy and Gift on Main Street. Parks Canada is located in the Federal Bldg. at 4th and Main; phone 668-2116. The Parks office has information on hiking the Chilkoot Trail.

Elevation: 2,305 feet/703m. **Climate:** Wide variations are the theme here with no two winters alike. The lowest recorded temperature is -62°F/-52°C and the warmest 94°F/35°C. Mean temperature for month of January is -6°F/-21°C and for July 57°F/14°C. Annual precipitation is 10.3 inches, equal parts snow and rain. On June 21 Whitehorse enjoys 19 hours, 11 minutes of daylight and on Dec. 21 only five hours, 37 minutes. **Radio:** CFWH 570, CBC network with repeaters throughout territory; CBC Montreal; CKRW 610, local; CKYN-FM 96.1, summer visitor information station, "Yukon Gold," broadcasts mid-May to mid-September; CHON-FM 98.1. **Television:** CBC–TV live, colour via ANIK satellite, Canadian network; WHTV, local cable; CanCom stations via satellite, many channels. **Newspapers:** *Whitehorse Star* (weekdays); *Yukon News* (twice-weekly).

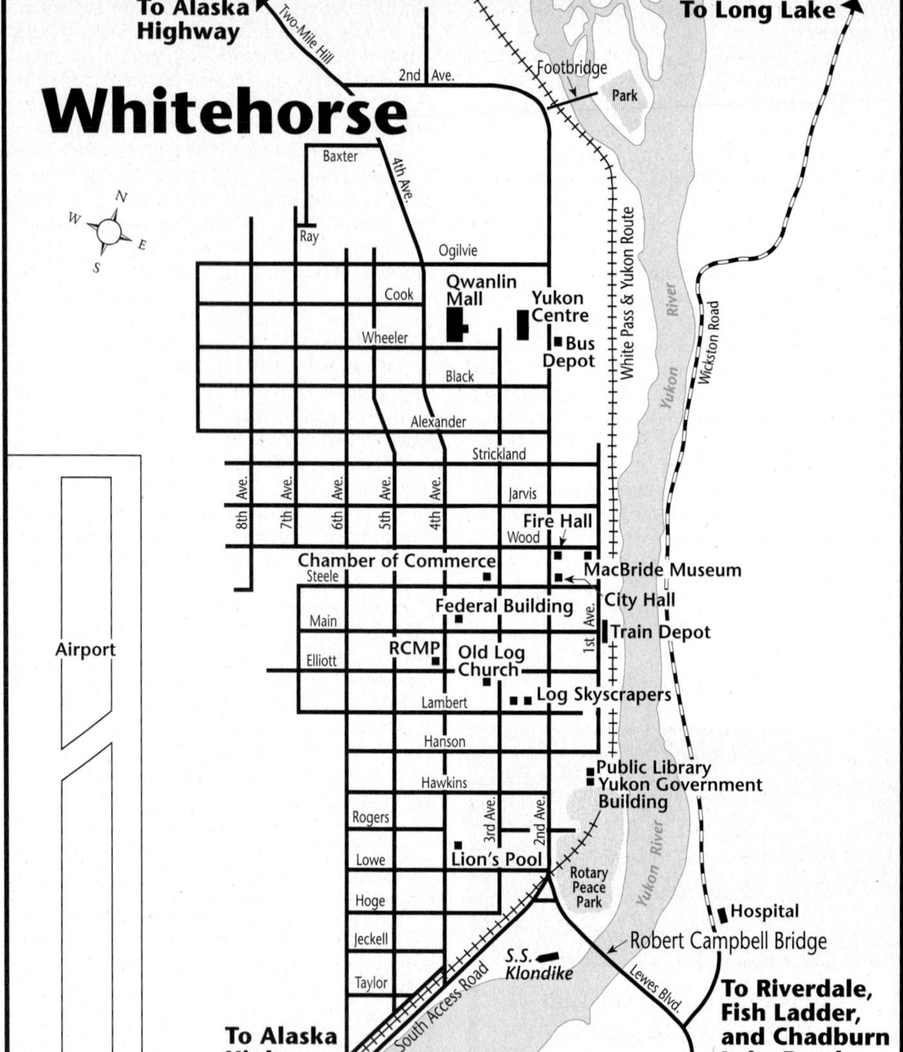

Private Aircraft: Whitehorse International Airport, three runways; has approach over city and an abrupt escarpment; elev. 2,305 feet/703m; main runway length 7,200 feet/2,195m; surfaced; fuel 80/87, 100/130, jet fuel available; AOE.

Floatplane base on Schwatka Lake above Whitehorse Dam (take the South Access Road from Alaska Highway and turn on road by the railroad tracks).

DESCRIPTION

Whitehorse has been the capital of Yukon Territory since 1953, and serves as the centre for transportation, communications and supplies for Yukon Territory and the Northwest Territories.

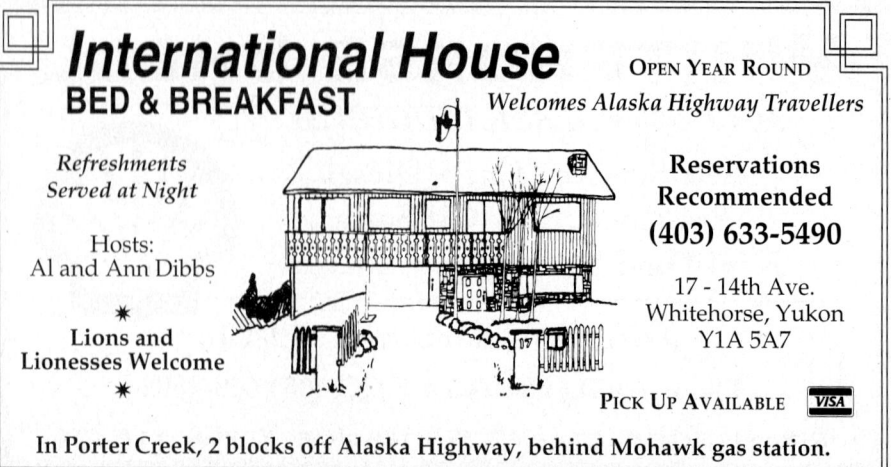

The downtown business section of Whitehorse lies on the west bank of the Yukon River. The Riverdale subdivision is on the east side. The low mountains rising behind Riverdale are dominated by Canyon Mountain, known locally as Grey Mountain. Wolf Creek, Hillcrest and Granger subdivisions lie south of the city; McIntyre subdivision is to the west; and Porter Creek, Takhini and Crestview subdivisions are north of the city. The Takhini area is the location of the Yukon College campus.

Downtown Whitehorse is flat and marked at its western limit by a rising escarpment dominated by the Whitehorse International Airport. Originally a woodcutter's lot, the airstrip was first cleared in 1920 to accommodate four U.S. Army planes on a test flight from New York to Nome. Access to the city is by Two-Mile Hill from the north and by access road from the south; both connect with the Alaska Highway.

In 1974, the city limits of Whitehorse were expanded from the original 2.7 square miles/6.9 square kilometres to 162 square miles/421 square kilometres making Whitehorse at one time the largest metropolitan area in Canada. More than two-thirds of the population of Yukon Territory live in the city.

Today, Whitehorse is the hub of a network of about 2,664 miles/4,287 km of all-weather roads now serving Yukon Territory and is becoming a popular year-round convention centre. A major attraction in winter is the Sourdough Rendezvous, held the last week in February. During this annual event local citizens wear the garb of trappers, miners and saloon hall girls, and menus feature moose stew and sourdough pancakes. Among the many activities are sled dog races, a beard-judging contest and a flour-packing competition.

Whitehorse is also the start and/or finish of the annual Yukon Quest Sled Dog Race in February. This 1,000-mile race between Whitehorse and Fairbanks, AK, takes mushers from 10 to 14 days, with a mandatory 36-hour layover at Dawson City.

A grueling summer race for humans is the 110-mile Klondike Trail of '98 International Road Relay between Skagway, AK, and Whitehorse. Teams of six to 10 runners run 10 legs of varying lengths along Klondike Highway 2.

Whitehorse is the territorial headquarters for the world-famous Royal Canadian Mounted Police. Their office is located at 4th Avenue and Elliott. Responsible for law and order in the Yukon since 1895, today the force relies more on the airplane and automobile than the romantic dog teams that carried mail and the law as far north as Herschel Island off the Yukon's Arctic coast, and across southern Yukon into northern British Columbia. The Royal Canadian Mounted Police will celebrate their 100th anniversary in the Yukon in 1995.

HISTORY, ECONOMY

When the White Pass & Yukon Route railway was completed in July 1900, connecting Skagway with the Yukon River, Whitehorse came into being as the northern terminus. Here the famed river steamers connected the railhead to Dawson City, and some of these boats made the trip all the way to St. Michael, a small outfitting point on Alaska's Bering Sea coast.

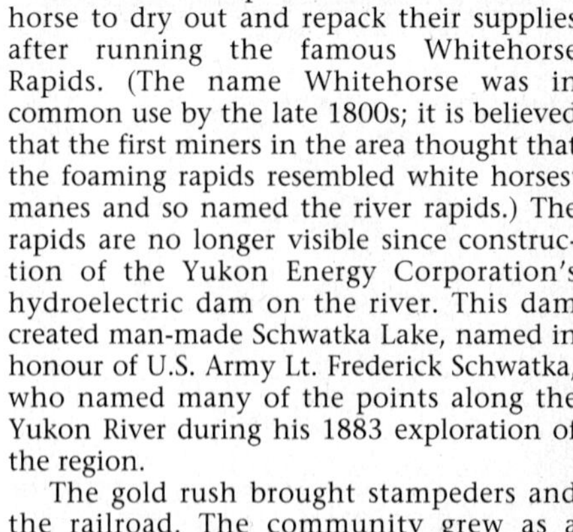

Klondike stampeders landed at Whitehorse to dry out and repack their supplies after running the famous Whitehorse Rapids. (The name Whitehorse was in common use by the late 1800s; it is believed that the first miners in the area thought that the foaming rapids resembled white horses' manes and so named the river rapids.) The rapids are no longer visible since construction of the Yukon Energy Corporation's hydroelectric dam on the river. This dam created man-made Schwatka Lake, named in honour of U.S. Army Lt. Frederick Schwatka, who named many of the points along the Yukon River during his 1883 exploration of the region.

The gold rush brought stampeders and the railroad. The community grew as a transportation centre and transshipment point for freight from the Skagway–Whitehorse railroad and the stern-wheelers plying the Yukon River to Dawson City. The river

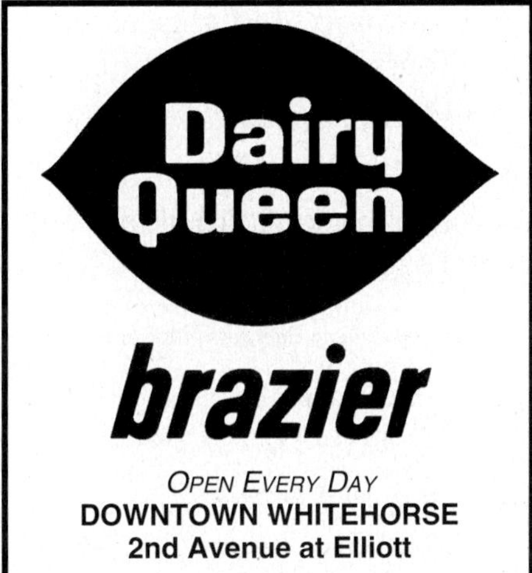

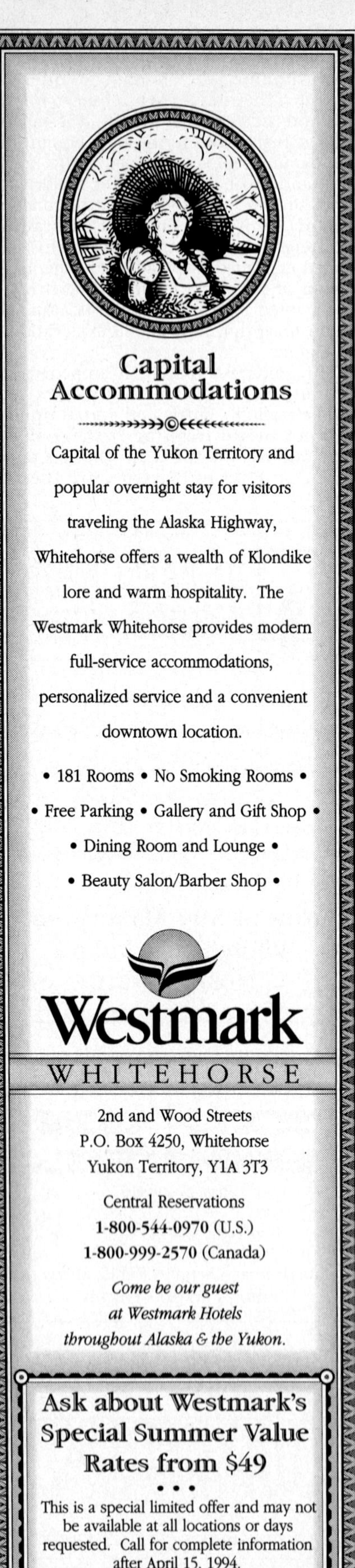

Yukon Territory is larger than all the New England states combined.

was the only highway until WWII, when military expediency built the Alaska Highway in 1942.

Whitehorse was headquarters for the western sector during construction of the Alaska Highway. Fort St. John was headquarters for the eastern sector. Both were the largest construction camps along the highway.

The first survey parties of U.S. Army engineers reached Whitehorse in April of 1942. By the end of August, they had constructed a pioneer road from Whitehorse west to White River, largely by following an existing winter trail between Whitehorse and Kluane Lake. November brought the final breakthrough on the western end of the highway, marking completion of the pioneer road.

During the height of the construction of the Alaska Highway, thousands of American military and civilian workers were employed in the Canadian North. It was the second boom period for Whitehorse.

There was an economic lull following the war, but the new highway was then opened to civilian travel, encouraging new development. Mineral exploration and the development of new mines had a profound effect on the economy of the region as did the steady growth of tourism. The Whitehorse Copper Mine, located a few miles south of the city in the historic Whitehorse copper belt, is now closed. Curragh Resources Mine, located in Faro, produced lead–silver and zinc concentrates until it shut down in 1993. Gold mining activity

WHITEHORSE ADVERTISERS

Airline Inn Hotel ....Across from airport
Ambassador Motorhomes................Ph. (604) 946-3696
Atlas Travel ....Westmark Whitehorse Mall
Baker's Bed & Breakfast....Ph. (403) 633-2308
Barb's Bed & Breakfast.....Ph. (403) 667-4104
Blue Gables Bed & Breakfast.....................Ph. (403) 668-2840
Budget Car and Truck Rental.................Ph. (403) 667-6200
Canada Campers..............Ph. (403) 668-5862
Chilkoot Trail Inn.....Across from Qwanlin Mall
Coffee • Tea & Spice ....Qwanlin Mall
Dairy Queen ....Downtown
Drifters Bed & Breakfast, The.............Ph. (403) 633-5419
Fort Yukon Hotel ....2163 2nd Ave.
Fourth Avenue Residence................(see High Country Inn)
Frantic Follies ....Westmark Whitehorse Hotel
Hawkins House Bed & Breakfast.....................Ph. (403) 668-7638
Hi-Country R.V. Park ...Next to Yukon Gardens
High Country Inn ....4051 4th Ave.
Indian Craft Shop Ltd. ....504 Main St.
International House Bed & Breakfast......................Ph. (403) 633-5490
Klondike Recreational Rentals Ltd. ....29 MacDonald Rd.
Klondike Rib & Salmon BBQ................Ph. (403) 667-7554
Kopper King ....Mile 918.3 Alaska Hwy.
Lapis Art & Artefacts ....3123 3rd Ave.
MacBride Museum ....1st & Wood
MacKenzie's RV Park .....Km 1484 Alaska Hwy.
Mac's Fireweed Books ....203 Main St.
Norcan Car and Truck Rentals ....Ph. (403) 668-2137
Northern Splendor Reindeer Farm ....Mile 10.5 Klondike Hwy.
NorthwesTel ....211 Elliott St.
Pioneer Inn ....Ph. (403) 668-2828
Pizza Hut..........................Ph. (403) 667-6766
Pot O' Gold..........................4th Ave. & Wood
Regina Hotel ....102 Wood St.
Sky High Wilderness Ranches........................Ph. (403) 667-4321
Sourdough City RV Park....................2nd Ave.
Special Discoveries ....206B Main St.
Stop In Family Hotel.........Ph. (403) 668-5558
Tagish Air Service Ltd.......Ph. (403) 668-7268
Tahini-Wud Bed & Breakfast......................Ph. (403) 667-4169
Takhini Hot Springs ....Takhini Hot Springs Rd.
Tamarack Welding & The Spring Shop ....Mile 922 Alaska Hwy.
Tire Town ....2283 2nd Ave.
Town & Mountain Hotel, The...................Ph. (403) 668-7644
Up North Bed and Breakfast ....86 Wickstrom Rd.
Up North Canoe Rentals ....Ph. (403) 667-7905
Westmark Klondike Inn ......Ph. 800-999-2570
Westmark Whitehorse ....Ph. 800-999-2570
White Pass & Yukon Route ....Ph. (403) 668-RAIL
Whitehorse Performance Centre..............................4th Ave. at Jarvis
Wishes Gifts..............................206A Main St.
Yukon Inn ....4220 4th Ave.
Yukon Native Products.............4230 4th Ave.
Yukon Radiator ....108 Industrial Rd.
Yukon Tire Centre Ltd. ....107 Industrial Rd.
Yukon Transportation Museum, The........................At the airport

has been taking place southwest of Whitehorse in the last few years. Stop by the Yukon Chamber of Mines office on Main Street for information on mining and rockhounding in Yukon Territory. The Chamber of Mines log building also houses a mineral display.

Because of its accessibility, Whitehorse became capital of the Yukon Territory (replacing Dawson City in that role) on March 31, 1953.

Bridges built along the highway to Dawson City, after Whitehorse became capital of the territory, were too low to accommodate the old river steamers, and by 1955 all steamers had been beached. After her last run in 1960, the SS *Keno* was berthed on the riverbank in Dawson City where she became a national historic site in 1962. The SS *Klondike* was moved through the streets of Whitehorse in 1966 to its final resting place as a riverboat museum beside the Robert Campbell bridge.

ACCOMMODATIONS

Whitehorse offers 22 hotels and motels for a total of about 840 rooms. Several hotels include conference facilities; most have cocktail lounges, licensed dining rooms and taverns. Rates range from $60 to $150 for a double room with bath. Bed-and-breakfast accommodations are also available.

The city has a reputation for gourmet dining. The 31 restaurants serve meals ranging from French cuisine to fast food; 14 have liquor licenses.

Whitehorse has a downtown shopping district stretching six blocks along Main Street. The Qwanlin Mall at 4th Avenue and Ogilvie has a supermarket and a variety of shops. The Yukon Centre Mall on 2nd Avenue has a liquor store. The Riverdale Mall is located on the east side of the river in the Riverdale subdivision. Another shopping mall is located in the Porter Creek subdivision north of the city on the Alaska Highway.

For travelers phoning home, Northwestel provides a "Phone Home" calling booth at their customer service office (211 Elliott St.). The private and comfortable booth allows callers to pay after they are finished with their call. Northwestel's Customer Service Office is open Monday through Friday, 9 A.M. to 4:30 P.M.; phone 668-8200.

In addition to numerous supermarkets, garages and service stations, there are churches, banks, movie houses, beauty salons and a covered swimming pool.

NOTE: There is no central post office in Whitehorse. Postal services are available in Qwanlin Mall at Coffee, Tea & Spice; The Hougen Centre on Main Street (lower floor below Shoppers Drugs); and in Riverdale and Porter Creek subdivisions. Stamps are available at several locations. General delivery pickup at corner of 3rd Avenue and Wood Street.

Specialty stores include gold nugget and ivory shops where distinctive jewelry is manufactured, and Indian craft shops specializing in moose hide jackets, parkas, vests, moccasins, slippers, mukluks and gauntlets. Inuit and Indian handicrafts from Canada's Arctic regions are featured in some stores.

Baker's Bed & Breakfast. Make Baker's Bed & Breakfast your home away from home. Hosts are longtime residents of Yukon. Friendly, cozy home, decorated with country crafts, and located in quiet area. Enjoy large yard and fireplace. Hearty, variety breakfasts served with fresh fruit. We look forward to sharing our home with you. Phone (403) 633-2308. 84 – 11th Ave., Whitehorse, YT Y1A 4J2. [ADVERTISEMENT]

Blue Gables Bed & Breakfast. Step back in time to the 1890s and savor the luxury of this 1990s Victorian home. Play the piano in the parlour, choose a book from the library or relax in the clawfoot tub. "Set awhile" on the veranda in the Midnight Sun or borrow a bike and take in the sights. Blue Gables is three blocks from city centre on a quiet residential street. Full breakfast. Open year-round. VISA. 506 Steele St., Whitehorse, YT Y1A 2C9. Phone (403) 668-2840, fax (403) 668-7120. [ADVERTISEMENT]

The Drifters Bed & Breakfast. While experiencing Whitehorse and Yukon attractions you will be welcome in our quiet and comfortable home. Hearty and wholesome breakfasts are served. We look forward to your company. Open all year. 44 Cedar Crescent, Whitehorse, YT Y1A 4P3. (403) 633-5419. [ADVERTISEMENT]

Hawkins House Bed & Breakfast. Lavish, spacious and bright best describes our new Victorian home in downtown Whitehorse. Guest rooms have soundproofing, private telephone, bathroom and cable television. Turn-of-the-century charm includes balconies, high ceilings, grand foyer, parlour, and historic and cultural themes. Join our family for sourdough crepes with smoked salmon or homemade pastries. Five minute walk to Main Street shops and restaurants, pool, river, paddlewheeler, 24-hour groceries, etc. Non-smoking. Francais, Deutsch. Reservations, phone (403) 668-7638 or write 303 Hawkins St., Whitehorse, YT Y1A 1X5. Rates start at $80. [ADVERTISEMENT]

High Country Inn. During your stay in Whitehorse, relax and enjoy real northern hospitality at the High Country Inn. The Inn offers over 100 rooms with a wide choice of comfortable, affordable lodging close to downtown and major attractions. Select a single room from $38 to a large deluxe suite, complete with kitchen. Great views, elevators, guest laundry, senior discounts, and the most delightful lobby and restaurant in Whitehorse, just good old-fashioned quality lodgings at surprisingly low prices. (Reservations recommended in the summer.) Phone (403) 667-4471, fax (403) 667-6457, 1-800-554-4471. [ADVERTISEMENT]

Klondike Rib & Salmon BBQ. Located in two of the oldest buildings in Whitehorse at Second and Steele, across from the Frantic Follies and Westmark Hotel. A delicious daily salmon bake, and Texas BBQ ribs, English-style fish and chips, and specialty northern food like musk-ox burgers and fresh baked bannock. Just some of the mouthwatering fare served in a unique historic Klondike Airways Building with historical exhibits as part of the fascinating decor. (403) 667-7554. [ADVERTISEMENT]

Tahini-Wud Bed & Breakfast offers a unique opportunity to experience warm Yukon hospitality in a country setting. Just 25 min. from Whitehorse, 10 min. to Takhini Hot Springs and just 5 min. to Northern Splendor Reindeer Farm and beautiful Lake Labarge. Fishing expeditions and trail rides by horseback are available by reservation. Joanne & Don Flinn, Mile 10, North Klondike Highway. (403) 667-4169. [ADVERTISEMENT]

Up North Bed and Breakfast offers you friendly, family service, a full-cooked breakfast and evening snack. We are located on the Yukon River three minutes from downtown. We have a full canoe rental service for Yukon's rivers and lakes. We look forward to meeting you. Phone Stenzigs (403) 667-7905 or fax (403) 667-6334. Box 5418, 86 Wickstrom Road, Whitehorse, YT Y1A 5H4. [ADVERTISEMENT]

There is a private RV park on the north access road (Two Mile Hill) and on 2nd Avenue downtown. Tent camping only is available at Robert Service Park on the South Access Road. There are three private campgrounds south of downtown Whitehorse on the Alaska Highway (see **Mileposts DC 873.5, 881** and **883.7** in the highway log), and one private campground 6 miles/9.6 km north of the city on the highway (see **Milepost DC 891.9**). Wolf Creek Yukon government campground is 7 miles/11 km south of Whitehorse on the Alaska Highway. A private campground and Yukon government campground are located at Marsh Lake. ▲

IMPORTANT: RV caravans should contact private campground operators well in advance of arrival regarding camping arrangements. At our press time, there was no designated RV parking in downtown Whitehorse.

Viewing platform at Whitehorse Rapids Fishway. (Earl L. Brown, staff)

TRANSPORTATION

Air: Service by Canadian Airlines International and Alkan Air daily to major cities and Yukon communities. Air North to Dawson City, Old Crow, Juneau and Fairbanks, AK. Whitehorse International Airport is reached from the Alaska Highway.

Seaplane dock on Schwatka Lake just above the Whitehorse Dam (take the South Access Road from Alaska Highway and turn right on road by the railroad tracks to reach the base). Flightseeing tours available.

Trans North Air offers helicopter sightseeing tours from the airport.

Bus: Greyhound service to Watson Lake, Dawson Creek, Prince George and other points in southern Canada. Norline serves Mayo and Dawson City. Alaska–Yukon Motorcoaches serves Skagway, Haines, Tok, Anchorage and Fairbanks. Alaska Direct to Anchorage, Skagway and Haines, phone 1-800-288-1305 or contact office at 4th Avenue Residence. North West Stage Lines to Haines Junction, Beaver Creek, Faro, Carmacks and Ross River.

Whitehorse Transit Commission operates bus service around city and suburbs from Qwanlin Mall.

Railroad: Arrangements for White Pass & Yukon Route service between Skagway, AK, and Bennett, BC (with bus service between Bennett and Whitehorse), can be made locally with Atlas Tours at the Westmark Whitehorse Mall, or phone 668-RAIL. (See WHITE PASS & YUKON ROUTE section.)

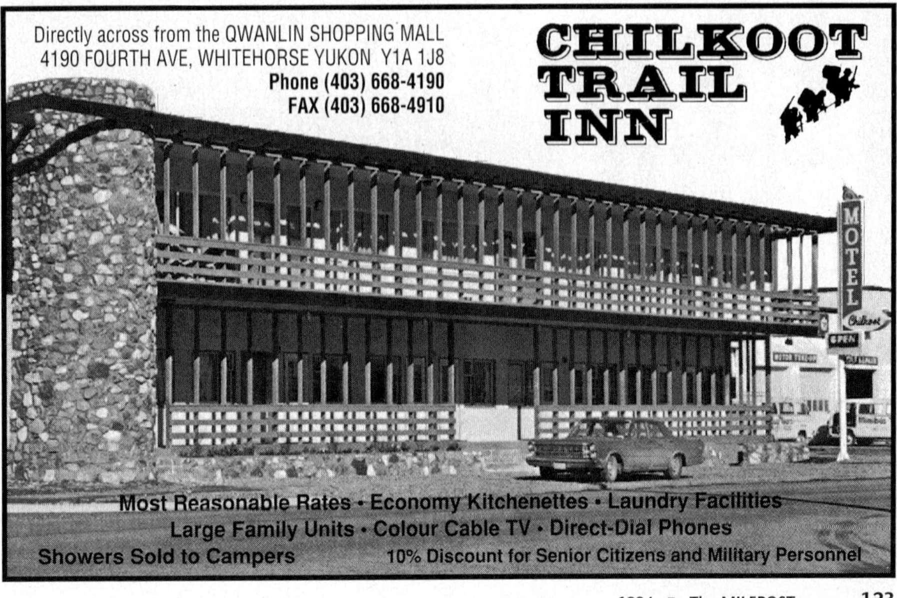

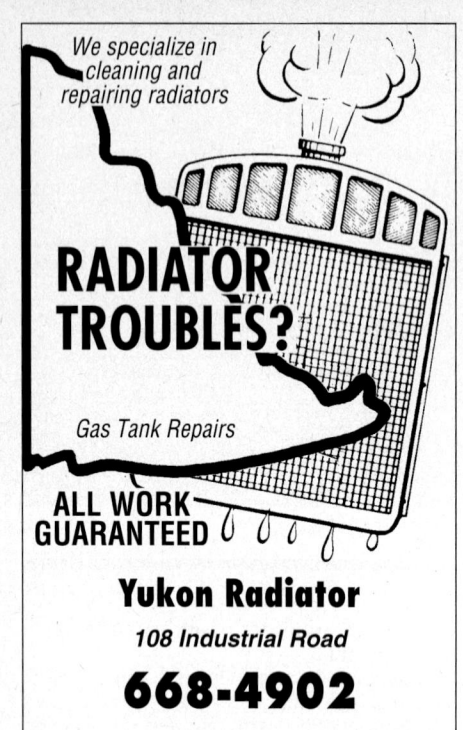

Taxi: Five taxi companies operate in Whitehorse.

Car, Truck and Camper Rentals: Several local and national agencies are located in Whitehorse.

ATTRACTIONS

The SS *Klondike* National Historic Site is hard to miss. This grand old stern-wheeler sits beside the Yukon River near the Robert Campbell bridge. After carrying cargo and passengers between Whitehorse and Dawson City from 1937 until the 1950s, the SS *Klondike* went into permanent retirement on the bank of the Yukon River, donated to the people of Canada by White Pass & Yukon Route. Refurbished by Parks Canada, the stern-wheeler is open to the public. Built by British Yukon Navigation Co., the SS *Klondike* is 210 feet/64m long and 41.9 feet/12.5m wide. Visitor information centre and public parking at the site. A film on the history of riverboats is shown continuously in a tent theatre adjacent the boat. Tours of the stern-wheeler leave on the half hour. The 20-minute film is shown prior to each tour. An admission fee is charged. Large groups are advised to book tours in advance. Contact Yukon National Historic Sites, 300 Main St., Room 205, Whitehorse, YT Y1A 2B5; phone (403) 668-3780, fax (403) 667-3910. The SS *Klondike* visitor centre and stern-wheeler are open from mid-May to Labour Day weekend in September.

Frantic Follies, a very popular vaudeville stage show held nightly June through mid-September at the Westmark Whitehorse Hotel. 1994 marks the 25th season for this almost two-hour show which features entertainers, a high-kicking chorus line, rousing music, hilarious skits from Robert W. Service ballads and plenty of laughs for the whole family. Visitors are advised to get tickets well ahead of time (tickets available at the box office in the Westmark). Be early to get good seats.

Take a hike with the Yukon Conservation Society. Every summer the society offers free guided nature walks, ranging in difficulty from easy to strenuous, from July to late August. Trips are one to six hours in length and informative guides explain the local flora, fauna, geology and history along the trails. For a schedule of hikes, contact the Yukon Conservation Society, at 302 Hawkins St.; phone 668-5678.

World's largest weathervane. Whitehorse International Airport boasts the world's largest weathervane — a Douglas DC-3. This vintage plane (registration number CF-CPY) flew for several Yukon airlines from 1946 until 1970, when it blew an engine on takeoff. The plane was restored by Joe Muff with the help of the Yukon Flying Club and the Whitehorse community. The restored plane was mounted on a rotating pedestal in 1981 and now acts as a weathervane, pointing its nose into the wind.

The Yukon Transportation Museum, located on the Alaska Highway adjacent to the Whitehorse Airport (see **Milepost DC 885.8**), features exhibits on all forms of transportation in the North. Housed in a former RCAF recreation centre, the outside front of the building is covered by an enormous mural depicting methods of transportation used in construction of the Alaska Highway in 1942: a Fairchild '71, P-40s, boats and pack horses. Working from archival photos, the project took almost 2,000 hours to complete and involved nine artists from the Yukon Art Society. Displays inside include the full-size replica of the *Queen of the Yukon* Ryan monoplane, sister ship to Lindbergh's *Spirit of St. Louis;* railway rolling stock; Alaska Highway vintage vehicles, dogsleds and stagecoaches. The museum includes a theatre and small gift shop. Plenty of parking. Admission charged. Open May to September. Write P.O. Box 5867, Whitehorse, YT Y1A 5L6 or phone (403) 668-4792, fax 633-5547.

Historical walking tours of Whitehorse are conducted by the Yukon Historical & Museums Assoc. These free walks take in the city's heritage buildings. Meet at the Donnenworth House, 3126 3rd Ave.; phone 667-4704. There are tours daily from July to the end of August. For self-guided tours, *A Walking Tour of Yukon's Capital* is available from local stores or from the Yukon Historical & Museums Assoc., Box 4357, Whitehorse, YT Y1A 3T5.

MacBride Museum, on 1st Avenue between Steele and Wood streets, features Yukon's cultural and natural history through comprehensive galleries and outdoor displays. *Yukon: The Land and the People* presents 30,000 years of Yukon history from the woolly mammoth to the pioneers. Yukon's wildlife is displayed in the Natural History gallery. Other exhibits include *Ribbon of Change*, the story of Whitehorse, and *The Transition Years*, a series of historical photographs and biographical sketches. Outdoors on the museum grounds, Robert Service's poetry is recited at Sam McGee's cabin, and a telegraph office and steam engine are on display. Facilities include a museum shop and research assistance. Admission charged. Open daily mid-May to

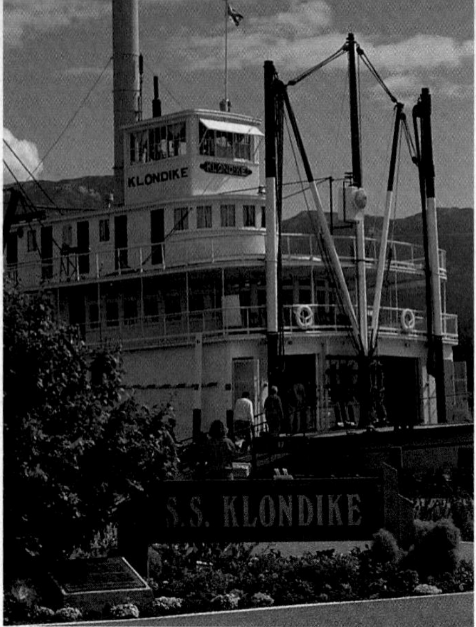

The SS Klondike *National Historic Site is open mid-May to Labour Day weekend.* (Earl L. Brown, staff)

Labour Day. Phone (403) 667-2709, fax (403) 633-6607 or write Box 4037, Whitehorse, YT Y1A 3S9.

Old Log Church, one block off Main on Elliott at 3rd. Built in 1900 by Rev. R.J. Bowen for the Church of England, this log structure and the log rectory next to it have been declared the first territorial historic sites in the Yukon and are being gradually restored. An ecumenical church museum in the log church displays relics of pioneer northern missions; open to the public June to September. Admission fee. Anglican (Episcopal) services held Sunday evenings at 4:30 P.M.

Yukon Government Building, 2nd Avenue and Hawkins, open 9 A.M. to 5 P.M. Administrative and Legislative headquarters of Yukon Territory, the building contains some notable artworks. On the main floor mall is an acrylic resin mural, 120 feet/37m long, which portrays the historical evolution of the Yukon. The 24 panels, each measuring 4 by 5 feet/1.2 by 1.5m, highlight events such as the arrival of Sir John Franklin at Herschel Island in 1825, the Klondike gold rush, and the coming of the automobile. The mural was created by Vancouver, BC, artist David MacLagen.

In the Legislative Chamber, an 18-by-12-foot/5-by-4-m tapestry is an abstraction of the fireweed plant, Yukon's floral emblem. The Yukon Women's Tapestry, five panels each 7 by 13 feet/2 by 4m, hangs in the legislative library lounge. The wool panels portray the role of women in the development of the territory, depicting the five seasons of the North; spring, summer, autumn, winter and "survival," the cold gray season between winter and spring and fall and winter. Begun by the Whitehorse Branch of the Canadian Federation of Business and Professional Women in 1976 to mark International Women's Year, the wall hangings were stitched by some 2,500 Yukoners.

Yukon Gardens, located at the junction of the Alaska Highway and South Access Road, is the only formal northern botanical garden. The 22-acre site features more than 100,000 wild and domestic flowers; vegetables, herbs and fruits; scenic pathways and floral displays; a children's "Old MacDonald's farm"; gift shop; and fresh produce in summer. Open daily in summer. Admission charged.

Whitehorse Rapids Fishway. The fish

ladder was built in 1959 to provide access for chinook (king) salmon and other species above the Yukon Energy Corporation hydroelectric dam. Displays installed and viewing area improved in 1992. Located at the end of Nisutlin Drive in the Riverdale suburb. Open daily, 9 A.M. to 5 P.M. from May 25 to July 1, 8 A.M. to 10 P.M. from July to September. Interpretive displays and viewing decks.

Mountain View Public Golf Course, located in Porter Creek subdivision on the Yukon River, is accessible via the Porter Creek exit off the Alaska Highway or from Range Road. Eighteen holes, grass greens; green fees.

Picnic in a park. Picnicking on a small island in the Yukon River, accessible via footbridge from 2nd Avenue, north of the railroad tracks. Picnic facilities are also available at Robert Service Campground, located on the South Access Road into Whitehorse. Rotary Peace Park is central to downtown and a popular picnic spot.

Whitehorse Public Library, part of the Yukon Government Bldg. on 2nd Avenue, has a room with art displays and books about the Yukon and the gold rush. It features a large double stone and copper fireplace, comfortable chairs, tables and helpful staff. Open noon to 9 P.M. weekdays, 10 A.M. to 6 P.M. Saturday, 1-9 P.M. Sunday and closed holidays.

Yukon Archives is located adjacent Yukon College at Yukon Place. The archives was established in 1972 to acquire, preserve

Whitehorse is home to world-class cross-country skiing facilities.

and make available the documented history of the Yukon. The holdings, dating from 1845, include government records, private manuscripts, corporate records, photographs, maps, newspapers (most are on microfilm), sound recordings, university theses, books, pamphlets and periodicals. Visitors are welcome. Phone (403) 667-5321 for hours, or write Box 2703, Whitehorse, YT Y1A 2C6, for more information.

The Yukon Quest International Sled Dog Race, held in February, is perhaps the major winter event in Whitehorse. This 1,000-mile sled dog race is a grueling 10- to 14-day course between Whitehorse and Fairbanks, AK. The race alternates starting points between the two cities. In 1994, the Yukon Quest starts in Fairbanks and finishes in Whitehorse.

Boat Tours. The MV *Youcon Kat,* docked across from the MacBride Museum, offers two-and-a-half-hour trips down the Yukon River. River Raft Yukon offers four-hour or more river tours. Tours of scenic Miles Canyon aboard the MV *Schwatka* depart from the dock on Schwatka Lake. The cruise takes you up the Yukon River through Miles Canyon and back in about two hours. Phone 668-3161 for more information. Miles Canyon is also accessible by road: take Schwatka Lake Road off the South Access Road into Whitehorse, or turn off the Alaska Highway (see **Milepost DC 881.7**); follow signs.

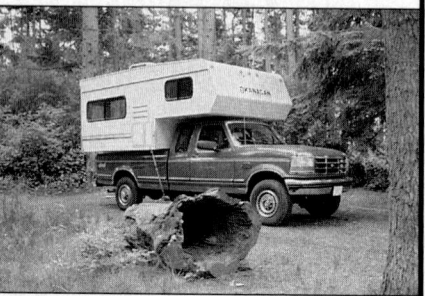

Day trips from Whitehorse. Marsh Lake, 24 miles/39 km south of Whitehorse on the Alaska Highway, and Takhini Hot Springs, 17 miles/27 km north of town via the Alaska and Klondike highways, are within easy driving distance of Whitehorse. The Yukon government day-use area at Marsh Lake offers an excellent sandy beach, picnic area, change house and boat launch. Lakeview Resort at Marsh Lake offers boat rentals. Takhini Hot Springs offers all-day swimming and horseback riding. Beyond Takhini Hot Springs about 7 miles/11 km on the Klondike Loop is a commercial reindeer farm. The farm is open daily in summer, 8:30 A.M. to 9 P.M., and children may pet and feed the reindeer. Admission charged.

Longer trips (which you may want to extend to an overnight) are to Atlin, about two-and-a-half hours by car, and Skagway, three hours by car. Skagway is an old gold rush town and a port of call for both the Alaska state ferries and cruise ships. Atlin, which also dates from 1898, is known for its spectacular scenery. Visitors heading for Skagway should call ahead for accommodations if they expect to overnight. You may make a circle tour, driving down to Skagway then turning off onto the Tagish Road on your way back and continuing on to Atlin via the Atlin Road.

Rockhounding. A wide variety of copper minerals can be found in the Whitehorse area. The following location is suggested by Fred Dorward of the Whitehorse Gem & Mineral Club (26 Sunset Dr. N., Whitehorse, YT Y1A 4M8). Other sources of information for rock hounds include the Yukon Rock Shop, junction of the Alaska Highway and Klondike Highway 2 (Carcross Road), and the Yukon Chamber of Mines on Main Street.

Drive north on the Alaska Highway to the Fish Lake Road turnoff (**Milepost DC 889.4**), located 2 miles/3.2 km from the north entrance to Whitehorse. About 0.5 mile/0.8 km in on Fish Lake Road, park and walk across McIntyre Creek to the old Copper King mine workings. Excellent but small specimens of brown garnet, also serpentine. *IMPORTANT: Rock hounds should exercise extreme caution when exploring. Do not enter old mine workings. Please respect No Trespassing signs.*

Canoe, Raft or Boat to Dawson City. Canoe rentals by the day, week or month, and guide services are available in Whitehorse. From the Yukon River's outlet at Marsh Lake south of Whitehorse to the Alaska border it is 530 river miles/853 km; from Whitehorse to Dawson City it is 410 river miles/660 km. There is a boat launch at Rotary Peace Park, behind the Yukon Government Bldg. You may also launch at Deep Creek Campground on Lake Laberge.

NOTE: Before leaving on any river or other wilderness trip, for your own protection, report your plans and itinerary to the RCMP. Be guided by the advice in government publications regarding travel on the Yukon's rivers and lakes. Do not attempt the Five Finger Rapids on the Yukon River without qualified advice. For more information on wilderness travel, contact Tourism Yukon office, located between 2nd and 3rd on Hawkins; phone 667-5340. Hikers planning to do the Chilkoot Trail should check with Parks Canada, in the Federal Bldg. at 4th and Main; phone 668-2116.

Mount McIntyre Recreation Centre, 0.9 mile/1.5 km west of the Alaska Highway (see **Milepost DC 887.6**), has 70 kilometres of groomed cross-country ski trails (open for hiking, running and mountain biking in summer). Contact Whitehorse Cross-Country Ski Club, P.O. Box 4639, Whitehorse, YT Y1A 3Y7.

Sportsmen can obtain complete information on fishing and hunting in the Whitehorse area by writing Tourism Yukon, Box 2703, Whitehorse, YT Y1A 2C6. They will provide lists of guides and advise what licenses are required.

AREA FISHING: Fish for rainbow and coho salmon in the following lakes: **Hidden, Scout, Long, Jackson** and **McLean.** Inquire locally for directions. Nearby fly-in fishing lakes are accessible by charter plane; see advertisements in this section. **Yukon River,** fish for grayling below the dam and bridge. Fishing below the dam prohibited in August during the salmon run.

Alaska Highway Log

(continued)

Distance* from Dawson Creek (DC) is followed by distance from Fairbanks (F). Original mileposts are indicated in the text as Historical Mile.

*Mileages from Dawson Creek are based on actual driving distance. Kilometres from Dawson Creek are based on physical kilometreposts. Please read Mileposts and Kilometreposts in the introduction for an explanation of how this highway is logged.

DC 887.4 (1475.6 km) **F 600.6** (966.5 km) First exit southbound for Whitehorse. North access road to Whitehorse (exit east) is via Two-Mile Hill and 4th Avenue.

DC 887.6 (1476 km) **F 600.4** (966.2 km) Turnoff to west on Hamilton Boulevard for Mount McIntyre Recreation Centre (0.9 mile/1.5 km); 70 kilometres of cross-country ski trails (summer hiking and biking), chalet for indoor waxing, curling and bonspiels. Truck weigh scales west side of highway.

DC 888.6 (1477.5 km) **F 599.4** (964.6 km) **Historical Mile 918.3.** Turnoff for Kopper King restaurant, grocery and gas.

DC 889.3 (1478.6 km) **F 598.7** (963.5 km) McIntyre Creek.

DC 889.4 (1478.8 km) **F 598.6** (963.3 km) Turnoff to west for Fish Lake Road. Follow paved road west 2.5 miles/4 km to historic information sign about copper mining in this area. Road continues 10.5 miles/17 km (winding gravel) to Jackson Lakes (named Franklin and Louise).

DC 890.1 (1479.9 km) **F 597.9** (962.2 km) Rabbit's Foot Canyon.

DC 890.5 (1480.6 km) **F 597.5** (961.6 km) Turnoff to Porter Creek to east.

DC 891 (1481.4 km) **F 597** (960.8 km) Porter Creek grocery.

DC 891.3 (1482 km) **F 596.7** (960.3 km) **Historical Mile 921**, laundromat, gas and other businesses.

DC 891.5 (1482.3 km) **F 596.5** (959.9 km) Clyde Wann Road. Access to Range Road and Mountain View Golf Course (18 holes).

DC 891.6 (1482.2 km) **F 596.4** (959.8 km) **Historical Mile 922**. Truck stop to west.

Trails North Car & Truck Stop Ltd. See display ad on page 129.

DC 891.8 (1482.5 km) **F 596.2** (959.5 km) MacDonald Road to north; auto repair.

DC 891.9 (1484 km) **F 596.1** (959.3 km) **Historical Mile 922.5.** Access to MacKenzie's RV Park. Azure Road. ▲

DC 894.3 (1486.4 km) **F 593.7** (955.4 km) Turnoff east to Cousins dirt airstrip.

DC 894.5 (1486.7 km) **F 593.5** (955.1 km) Rest area to west with litter barrels, outhouses, information sign and pay phone.

DC 894.8 (1487.2 km) **F 593.2** (954.6 km) **Junction** with Klondike Highway 2 to Dawson City. (See KLONDIKE LOOP section.) Turn off on Klondike Highway 2 for Takhini Hot Springs and reindeer farm. For Alaska-bound travelers, the highway now swings west.

DC 895.5 (1488.3 km) **F 592.5** (953.5 km) Turnoff to south for Haeckel Hill. Not recommended for hiking as this area is used for target practice.

DC 899.1 (1495.4 km) **F 588.9** (947.7 km) Turnoff for 3-mile/4.8-km loop drive on old section of Alaska Highway.

DC 901.6 (1499.3 km) **F 586.4** (943.7 km) Turnoff to north to sled dog track.

DC 905.4 (1507.1 km) **F 582.6** (937.6 km) **Historic Milepost 937.** Camera viewpoint turnout to north with point of interest sign about the old Dawson Trail. There were at least 50 stopping places along the old Dawson Trail winter stagecoach route between Whitehorse and Dawson City, and from one to three roadhouses at each stop. At this point, the stagecoach route crossed the Takhini River. This route was discontinued in 1950 when the Mayo–Dawson Road (now Klondike Highway 2) was constructed.

DC 908.7 (1512.4 km) **F 579.3** (932.3 km) Private farm and windmill; good example of Yukon agriculture. Facilities for overnighting large livestock.

DC 914.7 (1525 km) **F 573.3** (922.6 km) Takhini River bridge. According to R. Coutts in *Yukon: Places & Names,* the name Takhini derives from the Tagish Indian *tahk,* meaning mosquito, and *heena,* meaning river.

DC 922.7 (1535 km) **F 565.3** (909.7 km) Watch for horses and other livestock grazing on open range near highway.

DC 924.5 (1538.4 km) **F 563.5** (906.8 km) Stoney Creek.

DC 924.7 (1538.7 km) **F 563.3** (906.5 km) View of Mount Bratnober.

DC 926 (1540.8 km) **F 562** (904.4 km) Turnout to south with point of interest sign about 1958 burns. More than 1.5 million acres/629,058 hectares of Yukon forest lands were burned in 1958. Campfires were responsible for most of these fires.

DC 927.3 (1542.9 km) **F 560.7** (902.3 km) Turnoff to south for viewpoint (1.9 miles/3 km) and Kusawa Lake Yukon government campground (15 miles/24 km). Access road to campground is a narrow, winding gravel road, very slippery when wet; not recommended for long trailers or heavily loaded vehicles. ▲

Day-use area with sandy beach, boat dock, kitchen shelter and drinking water; boat launch 0.6 mile/1 km south. Campground at north end of lake has 32 sites, kitchen shelter, firepits and drinking water. Camping fee $8.

Kusawa Lake (formerly Arkell Lake), located in the Coast Mountains, is 45 miles/72 km long and averages 2 miles/3.2 km wide, with a shoreline perimeter of 125 miles/200 km. An access road to the lake was first constructed by the U.S. Army in 1945 to obtain bridge timbers for Alaska Highway construction.

Kusawa Lake, lake trout to 20 lbs., good to excellent; also grayling and pike.

DC 936.8 (1558 km) **F 551.2** (887 km) Mendenhall River bridge. A tributary of the Takhini River, the Mendenhall River — like the Mendenhall Glacier outside Juneau, AK — was named for Thomas Corwin Mendenhall (1841–1924), superintendent of the U.S. Coast & Geodetic Survey.

DC 939.5 (1562.3 km) **F 548.5** (882.7 km) View of three prominent mountains northbound (from left to right): Mount Kelvin; center mountain unnamed; and Mount Bratnober.

DC 942.8 (1567.6 km) **F 545.2** (877.4 km) NorthwesTel microwave tower to south.

DC 943.5 (1568.5 km) **F 544.5** (876.3 km) **Historic Milepost 974.** Historic sign and interpretive panel about **CHAMPAGNE.** Originally a camping spot on the Dalton Trail to Dawson City, established by Jack Dalton in the late 1800s. In 1902, Harlow "Shorty" Chambers built a roadhouse and trading post here, and it became a supply centre for first the Bullion Creek rush and later the Burwash Creek gold rush in 1904. The origin of the name is uncertain, although one account is that Dalton's men — after successfully negotiating a herd of cattle through the first part of the trail — celebrated here with a bottle of French champagne. Today, it is home to members of the Champagne Indian Band. There is an Indian cemetery on right northbound, just past the log cabin homes; a sign there reads: "This cemetery is not a tourist attraction. Please respect our privacy as we respect yours."

For northbound travelers, the Alaska Highway parallels the Dezadeash River (out of view to the south) from here west to Haines Junction. The Dezadeash Range is to the south.

DC 955.8 (1588 km) **F 532.2** (856.5 km) First glimpse northbound of Kluane Range.

Flightseeing tour takes in snowy peaks of the Kluane Ranges. (Earl L. Brown, staff)

DC 957 (1590 km) **F 531** (854.5 km) **Historic Milepost 987.** Cracker Creek.

DC 964.6 (1602.2 km) **F 523.4** (842.3 km) **Historical Mile 995.** Otter Falls Cutoff, **junction** with Aishihik Road. Gas station and store to south, Aishihik Road turnoff to north.

Otter Falls Cutoff. See display ad this section.

Aishihik Road leads 84 miles/135 km north to the old Indian village of Aishihik (AYSH-ee-ak, means high place). Northern Canada Power Commission built a 32-megawatt dam at the foot of Aishihik Lake in 1976 to supply power principally to the mining industry. Flow hours for the Otter Falls hydro project are given at the start of Aishihik Road. This is a narrow, gravel road, maintained for summer travel only to the government campground. Aishihik Road is not recommended for large RVs and trailers.

There is a day-use recreation site at Otter Falls, 12.6 miles/20.3 km distance; picnic shelter, tables, outhouses and boat ramp.

The Yukon government Aishihik Lake Campground is located at the south end of Aishihik Lake, approximately 27 miles/43 km distance; 13 sites, drinking water, picnic tables, firepits, kitchen shelter, boat launch and playground. Camping fee $8. ▲

Aishihik Lake, fishing for lake trout and grayling. As with most large Yukon lakes, ice is not out until late June. Low water levels may make boat launching difficult. **Pole Cat Lake,** just before the Aishihik weather station; fishing for pike.

CAUTION: Bears in area. Other wildlife includes eagles, moose and caribou.

DC 965.6 (1603.8 km) **F 522.4** (840.7 km) **Historic Milepost 996.** Turnoff to north at east end of Aishihik River bridge (watch for camera viewpoint sign) to see Canyon Creek bridge. The original bridge was built about 1920 by the Jacquot brothers to move freight and passengers across the Aishihik River to Silver City on Kluane Lake, and from there by boat to Burwash Landing. The bridge was reconstructed in 1942 by Army Corps of Engineers during construction of the Alaska Highway. It was rebuilt again in 1987.

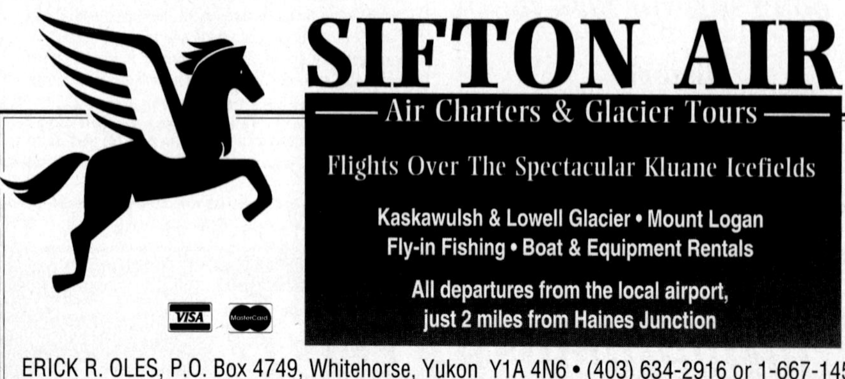

DC 965.7 (1604 km) **F 522.3** (840.5 km) Aishihik River bridge.

DC 966.3 (1605 km) **F 521.7** (839.6 km) View of impressive Kluane Range ice fields straight ahead northbound between Kilometreposts 1604 and 1616.

DC 974.9 (1619 km) **F 513.1** (825.7 km) Turnout to south on Marshall Creek.

DC 977.1 (1622.4 km) **F 510.9** (822.2 km) Turnout to north with information plaques about the Kluane Ranges. The rugged snowcapped peaks of the Kluane Icefield Ranges and the outer portion of the St. Elias Mountains are visible to the west, straight ahead northbound.

The Kluane National Park Icefield Ranges are Canada's highest and the world's largest nonpolar alpine ice field, forming the interior wilderness of the park. In clear weather, Mount Kennedy and Mount Hubbard, two peaks that are twice as high as the front ranges seen before you, are visible from here.

DC 979.3 (1626 km) **F 508.7** (818.6 km) Between Kilometreposts 1626 and 1628, look for the NorthwesTel microwave repeater station on top of Paint Mountain. The station was installed with the aid of helicopters and supplied by the tramline carried by high towers, which is also visible from here.

DC 980.8 (1628.4 km) **F 507.2** (816.2 km) Turnoff to north for Yukon government Pine Lake recreation park and campground. Day-use area has sandy beach, boat launch and dock, group firepits, drinking water and seven tent sites near beach. The Pine Lake Regatta, held here in mid-July, is the "biggest beach party in the Yukon." The campground, adjacent **Pine Lake** with a view of the St. Elias Mountains, has 33 sites, outhouses, firewood, litter barrels, kitchen shelter, playground and drinking water. Camping fee $8. Fishing is good for lake trout, northern pike and grayling. ▲

DC 980.9 (1628.5 km) **F 507.1** (816.1 km) Access road to Sifton Air floatplane dock; flightseeing tours.

DC 982.2 (1630.8 km) **F 505.8** (814 km) Turnoff to north for Haines Junction airport; glacier tours. **Private Aircraft:** Haines Junction airstrip; elev. 2,150 feet/655m; length 6,000 feet/1,839m; gravel.

Highway swings to south for last few miles into Haines Junction, offering a panoramic, close-up view of the Auriol Range straight ahead.

DC 984.8 (1635 km) **F 503.2** (809.8 km) Northbound travelers turn right (southbound travelers turn left) on Kluane Street for Kluane National Park Visitor Centre.

DC 985 (1635.3 km) **F 503** (809.5 km) **Historic Milepost 1016, junction** of Alaska Highway and Haines Highway (Haines Road).

IMPORTANT: This junction can be confusing; choose your route carefully! Fairbanks-bound travelers TURN RIGHT at this junction for continuation of Alaska Highway (Yukon Highway 1); highway log follows description of Haines Junction, YT. Continue straight ahead (south) on the Haines Highway (Yukon Highway 3) for port of Haines, AK; see HAINES HIGHWAY section.

(Haines-bound motorists note: It is a good idea to fill up with gas in Haines Junction. Gas is available en route only at Kathleen Lake Lodge.)

Haines Junction

DC 985 (1635.3 km) **F 503** (809.5 km) **Historic Milepost 1016,** at the **junction** of the Alaska Highway (Yukon Highway 1) and the Haines Highway (Yukon Highway 3, also known as the Haines Road). Driving distance to Whitehorse, 100 miles/161 km; YT–AK border, 205 miles/330 km; Tok, 296 miles/476 km; and Haines, 150.5 miles/242 km. **Population:** 536. **Elevation:** 1,956 feet/596m. **Emergency Services: RCMP**, phone 634-5555. **Fire Department**, phone 634-2222. **Nursing Centre**, phone 634-4444. **Radio:** 890.

Visitor Information: At the Kluane National Park and Yukon government visitor information centre, 0.2 mile/0.3 km east of the junction just off the Alaska Highway. Phone (403) 634-2345. Interpretive exhibits, displays and an outstanding multi-image slide presentation are featured. The centre is open 9 A.M. to 9 P.M., daily from May to September.

Haines Junction was established in 1942 during construction of the Alaska Highway. The first buildings here were Army barracks for the U.S. Army Corps of Engineers. The engineers were to build a new branch road connecting the Alaska Highway with the port of Haines on Lynn Canal. The branch road — today's Haines Highway — was completed in 1943.

The Our Lady of the Way Catholic mission in Haines Junction was built in 1954, using parts from an old Army hut left from highway construction days. The octagonal log St. Christopher's Anglican Church was built in 1987, replacing a 1955 structure built from an old garage used in the pipeline project.

Haines Junction is still an important stop for travelers on the Alaska and Haines highways. Services are located along both highways, and clustered around Village Square at the junction, where a 24-foot monument depicts area wildlife.

Visitor facilities in Haines Junction include motels, restaurants, a bakery, gas stations, a campground, garage services, groceries and souvenirs. There is a full-facility indoor heated swimming pool with showers available; open daily, fee charged. Also here are a RCMP office, Lands and Forest District Office and health centre. The post office and bank are located in Madley's General Store. (Banking service weekdays, 12:30-3:30 P.M.; extended hours on Fridays.) The weigh station is located on the Haines Highway (Kilometre 255.6 Haines Road), 0.2 mile/0.3 km south from the Alaska Highway junction. Across from the weigh station is the Commissioner James Smith Administration Bldg., which contains the government liquor store and public library. The airport is located on the Alaska Highway just east of town (see **Milepost DC 982.2**).

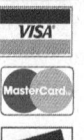

Haines Junction is on the eastern boundary of Kluane National Park. Administration offices and the visitor centre for the park are located in town; the park warden and general works station is located just north of town. Kluane (pronounced kloo-WA-nee) National Park encompasses extensive ice fields, mountains and wilderness. There is

Our Lady of the Way Catholic mission in Haines Junction. (Earl L. Brown, staff)

one campground (Kathleen Lake on the Haines Highway) and there are numerous hiking trails of varying degrees of difficulty. Flightseeing the park (by floatplane or helicopter from Haines Junction; by small plane from Whitehorse and Burwash Landing) is a popular way to see Kluane's scenery.

The park was first suggested in 1942, and in 1943 land was set aside and designated the Kluane Game Sanctuary. A formal park region was established in 1972 and the national park boundaries were official in 1976. In 1980, Kluane National Park, along with Wrangell–St. Elias National Park in

Alaska, became a joint UNESCO World Heritage Site. Kluane has become a world-class wilderness destination among outdoor recreation enthusiasts.

For more information on Kluane National Park, stop by the excellent visitor centre and see the exhibits and the award-winning multi-image slide presentation (shown on the hour and half-hour). Also check at the visitor centre for a schedule of guided activities and nature programs. Contact Kluane National Park at Box 5495, Haines Junction, YT Y0B 1L0, or phone (403) 634-2251, fax 634-2686.

Picnicking available at day-use area on the Dezadeash River, located at the west edge of town on the Haines Highway, which also has a wheelchair accessible trail. Other outdoor recreation available locally includes guided fishing and boating (canoe and boat rentals available).

HAINES JUNCTION ADVERTISERS

Alcan Fuels ....Ph. (403) 634-2268
"The Cabin" Bed & Breakfast ....Ph. (403) 634-2626
Cabin Crafts..............Across from visitor centre
Cozy Corner Motel & Restaurant ....Ph. (403) 634-2511
Gateway Motel ....Ph. (403) 634-2371
Haines Junction Self Serve ....Ph. (403) 634-2246
Kluane Park Inn Ltd. ....Ph. (403) 634-2261
Kluane R.V. Kampground..........Mile 985.3 Alaska Hwy.
Madley's General Store ....Ph. (403) 634-2200
Mountain View Motor Inn ....Ph. (403) 634-2646
North Country Service Centre ....Ph. (403) 634-2505
Sifton Air ....Ph. (403) 634-2916
Village Bakery ....Next to visitor centre
Village of Haines Junction, The ....Ph. (403) 634-2291

A private campground with dump station is located just north of the junction at **Milepost DC 985.3.** Dump stations and water are also available at local service stations. Yukon government campground located 4.2 miles/6.7 km east of junction on the Alaska Highway at Pine Lake. ▲

Alaska Highway Log

(continued)

Distance* from Dawson Creek (DC) is followed by distance from Fairbanks (F). Original mileposts are indicated in the text as Historical Mile.

*Mileages from Dawson Creek are based on actual driving distance. Kilometres from Dawson Creek are based on physical kilometreposts. Please read Mileposts and Kilometreposts in the introduction for an explanation of how this highway is logged.

DC 985 (1635.3 km) **F 503** (809.5 km) **Junction** of the Alaska Highway (Yukon

Highway 1) and the Haines Highway (Yukon Highway 3). Markers indicate distance to Destruction Bay 67 miles/108 km, Beaver Creek 186 miles/299 km.

Northbound: From Haines Junction to the YT–AK border, the Alaska Highway is in fair to good condition but narrow, often without shoulders. Watch for frost heaves north from Destruction Bay.

Southbound: Good paved highway with wide shoulders next 380 miles/611.5 km (from here to Watson Lake) with the exception of some short sections of narrow road and occasional gravel breaks. *NOTE: This junction can be confusing; choose your route carefully!* Whitehorse-bound travelers TURN LEFT at junction for continuation of Alaska Highway (Yukon Highway 1); highway log follows description of Haines Junction. TURN RIGHT for the Haines Highway (Yukon Highway 3) to the port of Haines, AK; see HAINES HIGHWAY section for log. (Haines-bound motorists note: Next gas 119 miles/191.5 km.)

DC 985.3 (1635.9 km) **F 502.7** (809 km) Kluane RV Kampground; RV and tent camping, gas, diesel, dump station, pay phone. ▲

DC 985.8 (1636.5 km) **F 502.2** (808.2 km) **Historical Mile 1017.** Alcan Fuels; gas, diesel, propane, auto repair and towing. Open daily. Open year-round.

DC 986.6 (1637.8 km) **F 501.4** (806.9 km) Highway follows the Kluane Ranges which are to the west. Livestock open range in this area: Watch for horses and cattle!

DC 987.8 (1639.8 km) **F 500.2** (805 km) **Historical Mile 1019.** Kluane National Park warden headquarters. (Visitor information in Haines Junction at the visitor centre.)

DC 988.3 (1640.6 km) **F 499.7** (804.1 km) Rest area to west with pit toilets.

DC 991.4 (1645.6 km) **F 496.6** (799.1 km) Photo stop on right northbound. A short hike up hill leads to lookout and information sign about ancient lakes in the area.

Highway climbs next 9 miles/14.5 km northbound to Bear Creek Summit.

DC 991.6 (1645.9 km) **F 496.4** (798.9 km) **Historic Milepost 1022,** Mackintosh Trading Post historic sign. Lodge to east; food, gas, lodging and camping. Trailhead to west for Alsek Pass trail; 18 miles/29 km long, suitable for shorter day hikes, mountain bikes permitted. ▲

DC 1000.1 (1660 km) **F 487.9** (785.2 km) Bear Creek Summit (elev. 3,294 feet/1,004m), highest point on the Alaska Highway between Whitehorse and Fairbanks.

Glimpse of Kloo Lake to north of highway between Kilometreposts 1660 and 1662.

DC 1003.5 (1665.4 km) **F 484.5** (779.7 km) Jarvis Creek.

DC 1003.6 (1665.6 km) **F 484.4** (779.5 km) **Historic Milepost 1035.** Turnout to west next to Jarvis Creek. Pretty spot for a picnic. Trail rides may be available here.

Jarvis Creek, grayling 8 to 16 inches, good all summer; Dolly Varden 8 to 10 inches, best in early summer.

DC 1013.6 (1682 km) **F 474.4** (763.5 km) Beautiful view to west of the snow-covered Kluane Ranges. For northbound travelers, the Alaska Highway parallels the Kluane Ranges from Haines Junction to Koidern, presenting a nearly unbroken chain of 7,000- to 8,000-foot/2,134- to 2,438-m summits interrupted only by a few large valleys cut by glacier-fed rivers and streams. West of the Kluane Ranges is the Duke Depression, a narrow trough separating the Kluane Ranges from the St. Elias Mountains. Major peaks in the St. Elias (not visible from the highway) are: Mount Logan, Canada's highest peak, at 19,545 feet/5,959m (recalculated in 1992 from 19,520 feet by a scientific expedition); Mount St. Elias, 18,008 feet/5,489m; Mount Lucania, 17,147 feet/5,226m; King Peak, 16,971 feet/5,173m; Mount Steele, Mount Wood, Mount Vancouver and Mount Hubbard, all over 15,000 feet/4,572m.

DC 1016.5 (1686.7 km) **F 471.5** (758.8 km) Turnout to west with view of Kluane Ranges.

DC 1017.2 (1687.8 km) **F 470.8** (757.7 km) Christmas Creek.

DC 1019.8 (1692 km) **F 468.2** (753.5 km) First glimpse of Kluane Lake for northbound travelers at Boutillier Summit (elev. 3,293 feet/1,003m), second highest point on the highway between Whitehorse and Fairbanks.

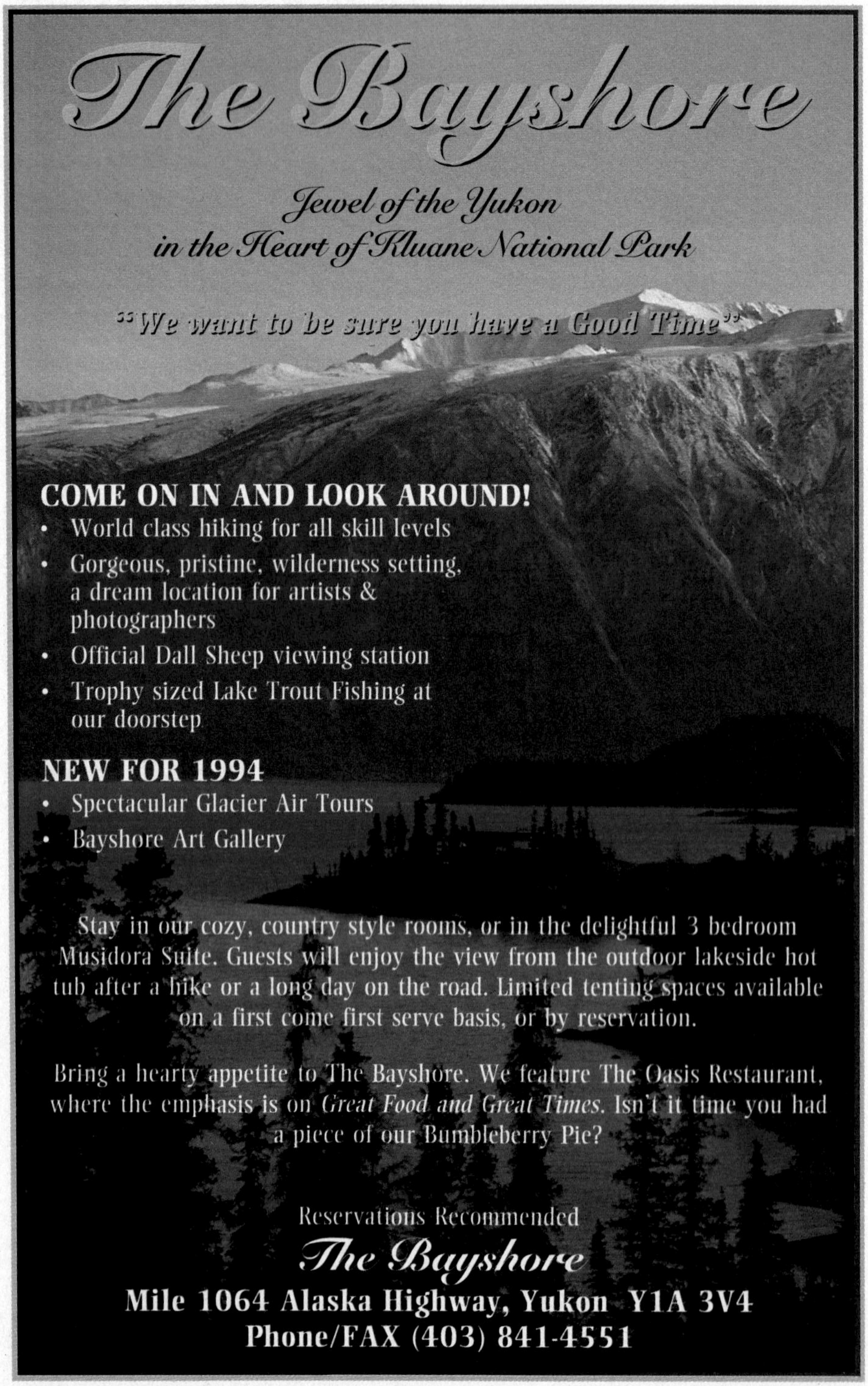

DC 1020 (1692.5 km) **F 468** (753.2 km) Turnout to east with information plaques on area history and geography.

DC 1020.3 (1693 km) **F 467.7** (752.7 km) **Historic Milepost 1053.** Historic sign and interpretive panel at turnoff for Silver City. Access to a bed and breakfast. Follow dirt and gravel road east 3.1 miles/5 km to ruins of Silver City. This old trading post, with roadhouse and North West Mounted Police barracks, was on the wagon road from Whitehorse to the placer goldfields of Kluane Lake (1904–24). Good photo opportunities.

DC 1020.9 (1694 km) **F 467.1** (751.7 km) Silver Creek.

DC 1022.5 (1696.5 km) **F 465.5** (749.1 km) Turnoff to east for Kluane Lake Research Station; station and airstrip are 0.9 mile/1.4 km via a straight gravel road. This research station is sponsored by the Arctic Institute of North America, University of Calgary.

Highway follows west shore of Kluane Lake next 39 miles/63 km northbound to Burwash Landing.

DC 1023.7 (1698.5 km) **F 464.3** (747.2 km) **Historical Mile 1056.** Kluane Camp commemorative plaque. Kluane Lake Lodge (current status unknown).

DC 1026.8 (1703.4 km) **F 461.2** (742.2 km) Slim's River East trail; parking at trailhead.

DC 1027.8 (1705 km) **F 460.2** (740.6 km) Slim's River bridge (clearance 17.7 feet/ 5.4m). Sheep Mountain is directly ahead for northbound travelers. The highway winds along Kluane Lake: Drive carefully!

DC 1029 (1706.8 km) **F 459** (738.7 km) Sheep Mountain visitor information centre. Excellent interpretive programs, laser disk information videos, parking and outhouses are available. Open mid-May to mid-September. Hours are 9 A.M. to 6:30 P.M. June through August, 9:30 A.M. to 5 P.M. in May and September. Stop here for information on Kluane National Park's flora and fauna. A viewing telescope is set up to look for sheep on Sheep Mountain. This is the sheep's winter range; best chance to see them is late August and September, good chance in late May to early June. Slim's River West trail; trailhead adjacent visitor information centre.

The small white cross on the side of Sheep Mountain marks the grave of Alexander Clark Fisher, a prospector who came into this area about 1906.

DC 1030.7 (1709.5 km) **F 457.3** (735.9 km) **Historic Milepost 1061.** Soldier's Summit. The Alaska Canada Military Highway was officially opened with a ribbon-cutting ceremony here on a blizzardy Nov. 20, 1942. A rededication ceremony was held Nov. 20, 1992, commemorating the 50th anniversary of the highway. A trail leads up to the original dedication site from the parking area.

Several turnouts overlooking Kluane Lake next mile northbound. This beautiful lake is the largest in Yukon Territory, covering approximately 154 square miles/400 square km. The Ruby Range lies on the east side of the lake. Boat rentals are available at Destruction Bay and Burwash Landing.

Kluane Lake, excellent fishing for lake trout, northern pike and grayling.

DC 1031.9 (1711.7 km) **F 456.1** (734 km) **Historical Mile 1064. The Bayshore** is a friendly place to be for a few minutes or a few days. Making people feel at home is our specialty. Even if you stop just to take a picture or stretch your legs, feel free to look around. Check out the art gallery with totally unique products at affordable prices. The view is breathtaking from our deck overlooking Kluane Lake. Dall sheep are frequently seen from our yard. Room guests and registered campers relax in our giant lakeside hot tub. Take a spectacular glacier flight for a lifetime of memories. Fish for trophy-sized lake trout in the crystal-clear, glacier-fed waters of Kluane. Enjoy a snack or a meal in the Oasis Restaurant where the emphasis is on great food and great times! Bayshore's bumbleberry pie is legendary. Our charming rooms are well-appointed, comfortable and moderately priced. The deluxe three-bedroom musidora suite will appeal to families and to groups. Reservations recommended. Phone/fax (403) 841-4551. See display ad on page 136. [ADVERTISEMENT] ▲

DC 1034.5 (1715.8 km) **F 453.5** (729.8 km) Williscroft Creek.

DC 1034.9 (1717 km) **F 453.1** (729.2 km) **Historical Mile 1067.** Cottonwood campground to east. ▲

Cottonwood RV Park and Campground. See display ad on page 137. ▲

DC 1039.7 (1724.7 km) **F 448.3** (721.4 km) Congdon Creek trailhead to west; 16-mile/26-km hike to Sheep Mountain.

DC 1039.9 (1725 km) **F 448.1** (721.1 km) **Historical Mile 1072.** Turnoff to east for Congdon Creek Yukon government campground on Kluane Lake. Drive in 0.4 mile/0.6 km via gravel loop road; tenting area, 77 level sites (some pull-through), outhouses, kitchen shelters, water pump, firewood, firepits, picnic tables, sandy beach, interpretive talks, playground, boat launch. Camping fee $8. ▲

DC 1040.4 (1725.6 km) **F 447.6** (720.3 km) Congdon Creek. According to R. Coutts, *Yukon: Places & Names,* Congdon Creek is believed to have been named by a miner after Frederick Tennyson Congdon. A lawyer from Nova Scotia, Congdon came to the Yukon in 1898 and held various political posts until 1911.

DC 1046.9 (1735.3 km) **F 441.1** (709.9 km) Nines Creek. Turnout to east.

DC 1047.3 (1736.2 km) **F 440.7** (709.2 km) Mines Creek.

DC 1048.9 (1739 km) **F 439.1** (706.6 km) Bock's Brook.

DC 1051.5 (1743 km) **F 436.5** (702.5 km) **Historic Milepost 1083. DESTRUCTION BAY** (pop. less than 100). **Emergency Services: RCMP,** phone (collect) 634-5555. **Health clinic,** phone 841-4444; **Ambulance,** phone 841-3333; **Fire Department,** phone 841-2221. Located on the shore of Kluane Lake, Destruction Bay is one of several towns which grew out of the building of the Alaska Highway. It earned its name when a storm destroyed buildings and materials here. Destruction Bay was one of the many relay stations spaced at 100-mile intervals to give truck drivers a break and a chance to repair their vehicles. Historic sign adjacent historic milepost. A highway maintenance camp is located here. Destruction Bay has camping, boat launch, boat rentals and guided fishing tours. A fishing derby is held first weekend in July. Food, gas and lodging at the Talbot Arm, west side of highway; open year-round. ▲

Talbot Arm Motel. See display ad on page 137.

DC 1051.7 (1743.3 km) **F 436.3** (702.1 km) **Sehja Services & RV Park.** When you arrive at Sehja Services and RV Park, treat yourselves to a large steaming bowl of our world-famous whitefish chowder, served with fresh bannock. We serve a full breakfast menu all day long. Your hostess, Ann, has a quality selection of her native crafts available. [ADVERTISEMENT] ▲

DC 1051.9 (1743.6 km) **F 436.1** (701.8 km) Rest area.

DC 1055.1 (1748.8 km) **F 432.9** (696.7 km) Lewes Creek.

DC 1058.3 (1753.9 km) **F 429.7** (691.5 km) Halfbreed Creek trailhead.

DC 1061.5 (1759 km) **F 426.5** (686.4 km) **Historic Milepost 1093.** Turnoff to east for **BURWASH LANDING,** a resort with gas, food, camping and lodging on Kluane Lake. Boat rentals and Kluane Lake fishing trips available. Flightseeing trips of Kluane National Park are available out of Burwash Landing.

Burwash Landing was settled in 1904 by the Jacquot brothers, Louis and Eugene, as a supply centre for local miners. The log mission here, Our Lady of the Holy Rosary, was built in 1944. The historic sign here reads:

A short trail leads up to monument at Soldier's Summit. (Earl L. Brown, staff)

"After months of rough camp life, American soldiers were surprised and delighted when they reached this prosperous little settlement which seemed like an oasis in the wilderness. Burwash also became the home of Father Eusebe Morisset, an Oblate Missionary, who served as an auxiliary chaplain with the American Army."

The highly recommended Kluane Museum of Natural History (renovated in 1992) is located on the east side of highway at the turnoff; open 9 A.M. to 9 P.M. in summer; phone (403) 841-5561. Wildlife, minerals and other natural history exhibits, and a shop. Admission charged. Yukon Passport stamped here.

Burwash Landing Resort & RV Park. See display ad this section. ▲

Glacier Air Tours. See display ad this section.

DC 1062 (1759.8 km) **F 426** (685.5 km) **Dalan Campground.** Turn off north, to Dalan Campground, 1 km off the Alaska Highway on the shores of beautiful Kluane Lake, "largest lake in the Yukon." Owned and operated by Kluane First Nation, this campground offers 25 individual private campsites, RVs welcome! Firewood, water pump, picnic tables, firepits and dump station are available. For additional information, call (403) 841-4274. [ADVERTISEMENT] ▲

DC 1062.7 (1761 km) **F 425.3** (684.4 km) **Historic Milepost 1094. Private Aircraft:** Burwash Yukon government airstrip to north; elev. 2,643 feet/806m; length 6,000 feet/1,829m; gravel.

DC 1067 (1768.8 km) **F 421** (677.5 km) Duke River bridge (clearance 17.7 feet/5.4m). The Duke River flows into Kluane Lake; named for George Duke, an early prospector.

DC 1071.9 (1776.5 km) **F 416.1** (669.6 km) Turnout to north. Burwash Creek, named for Lachlin Taylor Burwash, a mining recorder at Silver City in 1903.

DC 1076.7 (1784.1 km) **F 411.3** (661.9 km) Sakiw Creek.

DC 1078.5 (1787 km) **F 409.5** (659 km) Buildings to west belong to Hudson Bay Mining and Smelting Co.'s Wellgreen Nickel Mines, named for Wellington Bridgeman Green, the prospector who discovered the mineral showing in 1952. During the mine's operation, from May 1972 to July 1973, three shiploads of concentrates (averaging 13,000 tons each) were trucked to Haines, AK. The material proved to be too insufficient to be economical. No facilities or services.

Canada uses the metric system.

DC 1079.4 (1788.5 km) **F 408.6** (657.6 km) Quill Creek.

DC 1080.9 (1791 km) **F 407.1** (655.1 km) Glacier Creek. Kluane River to east of highway.

DC 1083.5 (1795.5 km) **F 404.5** (651 km) **Historic Milepost 1117.** Sign commemorates 1st Lt. Roland Small, of the 18th Engineers Regiment, who died in a jeep accident near this site during construction of the Alaska Highway in 1942.

DC 1084.6 (1797.2 km) **F 403.4** (649.2 km) **Historical Mile 1118.** Kluane Wilderness Village; gas, restaurant, camping and lodging. Open year-round. Viewing platform of: Mount Kennedy, Mount Logan and Mount Lucania. Halfway mark between Whitehorse and Tok. ▲

Kluane Wilderness Village. See display ad this section. ▲

DC 1086.6 (1799.5 km) **F 401.4** (646 km) Swede Johnson Creek. Turnout to east.

DC 1087.4 (1801.7 km) **F 400.6** (644.7 km) *CAUTION: Rough road northbound next 168 km (104 miles), maximum 70 kmph (about 45 mph), some gravel patches, some winding sections. Drive carefully, especially vehicles with trailers. Road surface can be particularly hard on trailer hitches.*

DC 1091.3 (1808 km) **F 396.7** (638.4 km) Buildings to east are a dormant pump station once used to pressure up fuel being transferred from Haines to Fairbanks.

DC 1095 (1814 km) **F 393** (632.4 km) NorthwesTel microwave tower visible ahead northbound.

DC 1095.4 (1814.6 km) **F 392.6** (631.8 km) Abandoned Mountain View Lodge. View of Donjek River Valley.

Alaska Highway workers faced one of their toughest construction jobs during completion of the Alaska Highway in 1943 from the Donjek River to the Alaska border. Swampy ground underlain by permafrost, numerous creeks, lakes and rivers, plus a thick insulating ground cover made this section particularly difficult for road builders.

DC 1096.3 (1816 km) **F 391.7** (630.4 km) Turnout to west with view of Donjek River Valley and the Icefield Ranges of the St. Elias Mountains. Interpretive display.

DC 1099.7 (1819.5 km) **F 388.3** (624.9 km) **Historic Milepost 1130.** Turnout with interpretive panel on the Donjek River bridge. Sign reads: "Glacial rivers, like the Donjek, posed a unique problem for the builders of the Alaska Highway. These braided mountain streams would flood after a heavy rainfall or rapid glacial melt, altering the waters' course and often leaving bridges crossing dry ground."

DC 1100 (1820 km) **F 388** (624.4 km) Donjek River bridge (clearance 17.4 feet/5.3m). Access to river at north end of bridge on west side of highway. This wide silty river is a major tributary of the White River. According to R. Coutts, *Yukon: Places & Names,* the Donjek is believed to have been named by Charles Willard Hayes in 1891 from the Indian word for a peavine that grows in the area.

Watch for breaks in surfacing next several miles northbound.

DC 1113.5 (1844.4 km) **F 374.5** (602.7 km) **Edith Creek** bridge, turnout to west. Try your hand at gold panning here, "colours" have been found. Grayling fishing, June through September.

DC 1113.8 (1844.8 km) **F 374.2** (602.2 km) **Historical Mile 1147. Pine Valley Motel and Cafe.** Thanks to all our customers for your patronage from your hosts Carmen and Dave. Add your card to our collection. The largest collection of business cards in western Canada. We have unleaded and diesel available (seniors gas discount). Tire repairs, towing available, minor repairs and welding. RV park and campground, pull-throughs, water and power hookups, hot showers included, dump station, picnic tables, firepits. Caravan discounts. Gold panning and good fishing at Edith Creek. Motel units, cabins with colour TV. Newly renovated licensed cafe with full menu and bakery, featuring hearty soups, homemade bread, pies and pastries, fresh daily. Enjoy a scenic view of the mountains while our friendly morning cook prepares you up a mean breakfast, or sink your teeth into some of Carmen's wonderful sweet rolls. Take-out for cold beer, wine and spirits. Pay phone, cubed ice, fishing license and tackle, souvenirs. Book exchange available. Fourth annual spring opener on May 28th long weekend. Harleys welcome. Free cup of coffee in the morning to get you going with your overnight stay. MasterCard and VISA. Bonjour et bon vacances! Phone/fax (403) 862-7407. [ADVERTISEMENT] ▲

DC 1118.3 (1852.2 km) **F 369.7** (595 km) Koidern River bridge No. 1.

DC 1118.8 (1853 km) **F 369.2** (594.2 km) **Historical Mile 1152.** Lake Creek Yukon government campground just west of highway; 30 large level sites (six pull-through), water pump, litter barrels, firewood, firepits, picnic tables, kitchen shelter and outhouses. Camping fee $8. ▲

DC 1122.7 (1859.5 km) **F 365.3** (587.9 km) **Historical Mile 1156.** Longs Creek.

DC 1125 (1863.5 km) **F 363** (584.2 km) Turnout to east with litter barrel.

DC 1125.7 (1864.7 km) **F 362.3** (583 km) **Pickhandle Lake** to west, good fishing from boat for northern pike all summer; also grayling, whitefish and lingcod.

DC 1128 (1868.4 km) **F 360** (579.3 km) Aptly named Reflection Lake to west mirrors the Kluane Ranges. The highway parallels this range between Koidern and Haines Junction.

DC 1130.6 (1872.6 km) **F 357.4** (575.2 km) **Historical Mile 1164.** Lodge.

NOTE: Watch for road construction northbound to Kilometrepost 1881.

DC 1130.7 (1872.8 km) **F 357.3** (575 km) Koidern River bridge No. 2.

DC 1133.7 (1877.6 km) **F 354.3** (570.2 km) **Historic Milepost 1167.** Bear Flats Lodge. (Current status unknown.)

DC 1135 (1880 km) **F 353** (568 km) **Historical Mile 1169.** White River Motor Inn; food, gas, lodging and camping. Open year-round. ▲

White River Motor Inn. See display ad this section.

DC 1135.6 (1881 km) **F 352.4** (567.1 km) White River bridge, clearance 17.1 feet/5.2m. The White River, a major tributary of the Yukon River, was named by Hudson's Bay Co. explorer Robert Campbell for its white colour, caused by the volcanic ash in the water. *This river is considered very dangerous; not recommended for boating.*

CAUTION: Slow down for sharp turn in road at north end of bridge.

DC 1141.5 (1890.5 km) **F 346.5** (557.6 km) **Moose Lake** to west, grayling to 18 inches, use dry flies and small spinners, midsummer. Boat needed for lake.

DC 1144.3 (1895 km) **F 343.7** (553.1 km) Sanpete Creek, named by an early prospector after Sanpete County in Utah.

DC 1147.5 (1900.3 km) **F 340.5** (548 km) Dry Creek No. 1. Turnout to east.

DC 1149.8 (1904 km) **F 338.2** (544.3 km) *CAUTION: Slow down for bumpy banked descent to Dry Creek No. 2.*

DC 1150.3 (1904.5 km) **F 337.7** (543.5 km) **Historical Mile 1184.** Dry Creek No. 2. Historical marker to west about the Chrisna gold rush.

DC 1155 (1911.8 km) **F 333** (535.9 km) Small Lake to east.

DC 1155.2 (1913 km) **F 332.8** (535.6 km) **Historical Mile 1188.** Turnoff for Snag Junction Yukon government campground, 0.4 mile/0.6 km in on gravel loop road. There are 15 tent and vehicle sites (some level), a kitchen shelter, outhouses, picnic tables, firewood, firepits and litter barrels. Camping fee $8. Small-boat launch. Swimming in Small Lake. A dirt road (status unknown) connects the Alaska Highway here with the abandoned airfield and Indian village at Snag to the northeast. ▲

DC 1162.1 (1924.5 km) **F 325.9** (524.5 km) Inger Creek.

DC 1165.7 (1930 km) **F 322.3** (518.7 km) View of Nutzotin Mountains to northwest, Kluane Ranges to southwest. On a clear day you should be able to see the snow-clad Wrangell Mountains in the distance to the west.

DC 1167.2 (1932.4 km) **F 320.8** (516.3 km) Beaver Creek plank bridge, clearance 17.1 feet/5.2m.

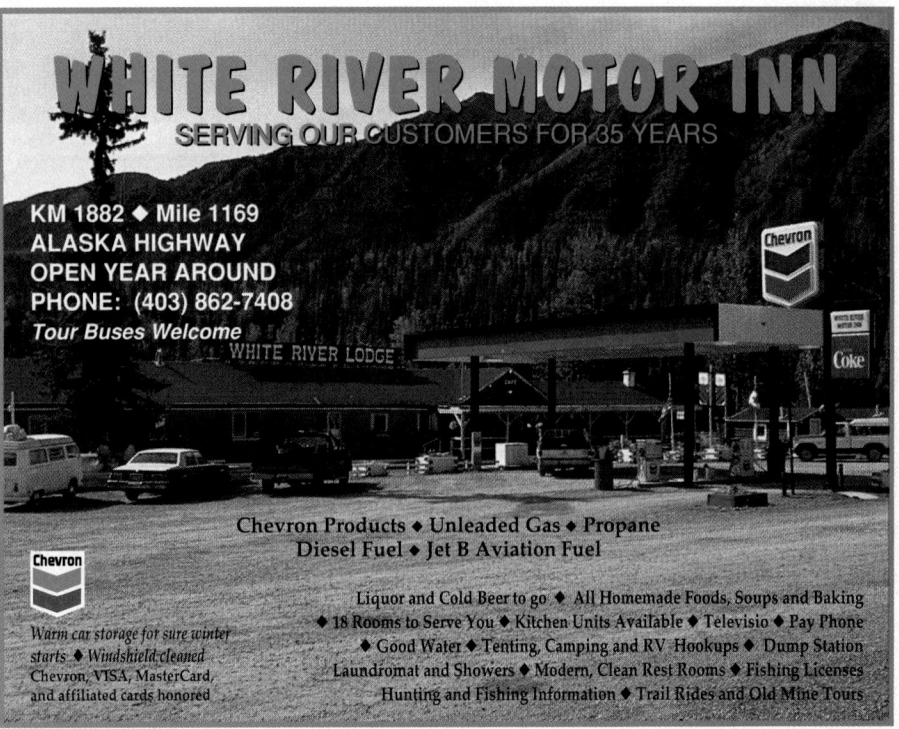

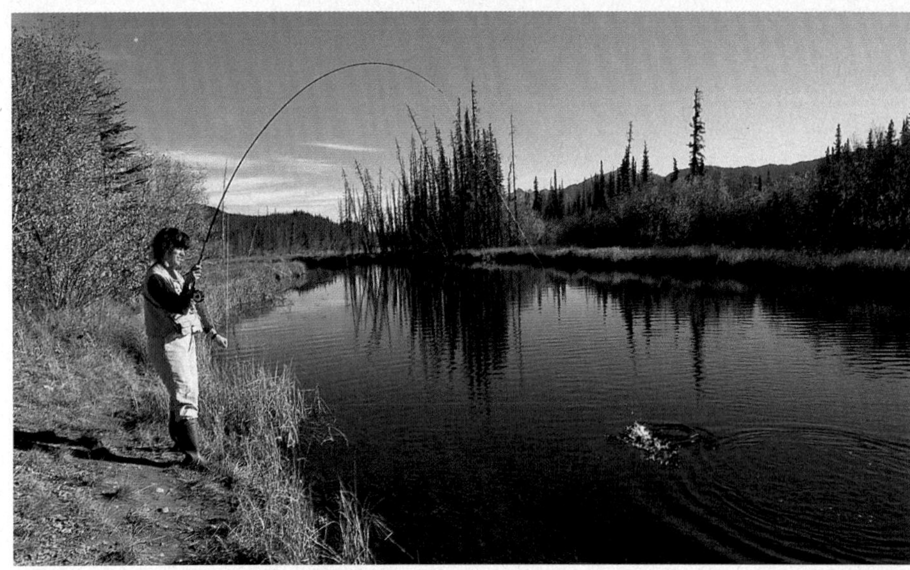

Fly-fishing for grayling at Edith Creek, ***Milepost DC 1113.5.*** *(Michael DeYoung)*

Snowshoe hare are abundant in various areas at different times due to cyclical population highs. (George Wuerthner)

Beaver Creek

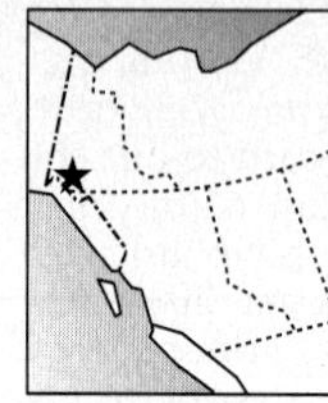

DC 1168.5 (1934.5 km) **F 319.5** (514.2 km) **Historic Milepost 1202.** Driving distance to Haines Junction, 184 miles/295 km; to Tok, 113 miles/182 km; to Haines, 334 miles/537.5 km. **Population:** 106. **Emergency Services: RCMP,** phone 862-5555. **Ambulance,** phone 862-3333. **Visitor Information:** Yukon government visitor information centre open daily 9 A.M. to 9 P.M. late May through mid-September. Phone (403) 862-7321. The visitor centre has a book of dried Yukon wildflowers for those interested in the flora of the territory.

Site of the old Canadian customs station. Local residents were pleased to see customs relocated north of town in 1983, having long endured the flashing lights and screaming sirens set off whenever a tourist forgot to stop.

Beaver Creek is one of two sites where Alaska Highway construction crews working from opposite directions connected the highway. In October 1942, Alaska Highway construction operations were being rushed to conclusion as winter set in. Eastern and western sector construction crews (the 97th and 18th Engineers) pushed through to meet at a junction on Beaver Creek on Oct. 28., thus making it possible for the first time for vehicles to travel the entire length of the highway. East–west crews had connected at Contact Creek on Sept. 24, 1942.

Motels, gas stations with repair service, a post office and licensed restaurants are located here. Beaver Creek is also an overnight stop for bus travelers. Private RV park with hookups, hot showers, store, laundry and dump station. ▲

The interesting looking church here is Our Lady of Grace mission. Built in 1961, it is one of three Catholic missions on the north Alaska Highway (the others are in Burwash Landing and Haines Junction). Services from the last Sunday of May to first Sunday of September. There is a public swimming pool beside the community club. Check with the information centre about the live stage show at the Westmark Inn, evenings in summer; admission charged.

BEAVER CREEK ADVERTISERS

Beaver Creek Motor Inn ...Ph. (403) 862-7600
Doris Johns Arts & Crafts........................Ph. (403) 862-7903
Ida's Motel & Restaurant ....Ph. (403) 862-7223
Westmark Inn ....Ph. 1-800-999-2570

Alaska Highway Log

(continued)

Distance* from Dawson Creek (DC) is followed by distance from Fairbanks (F). Original mileposts are indicated in the text as Historical Mile.

*Mileages from Dawson Creek are based on actual driving distance. Kilometres from Dawson Creek are based on physical kilometreposts. Please read Mileposts and Kilometreposts in the introduction for an explanation of how this highway is logged.

DC 1169.7 (1936.3 km) **F 318.3** (512.2 km) Rest area to west with litter barrels and outhouses.

DC 1170.3 (1937.3 km) **F 317.7** (511.3 km) **Private Aircraft:** Beaver Creek airstrip; elev. 2,129 feet/649m; length 3,740 feet/1,140m; gravel; fuel 100. Airport of entry for Canada customs.

DC 1170.5 (1937.6 km) **F 317.5** (511 km) Beaver Creek Canada customs station. Open 24 hours a day year-round. All traffic entering Canada must stop here for clearance. (See Customs Requirements in the GENERAL INFORMATION section.)

CAUTION: Narrow winding road from here to border northbound (next 19.4 miles/31.2 km). Watch for bad corners and rough spots in road surface. Highway reconstruction and straightening planned for 1994; watch for construction crews and equipment between Beaver Creek and the border.

DC 1175.4 (1945.5 km) **F 312.6** (503.1 km) Snag Creek plank bridge.

DC 1176.3 (1946.9 km) **F 311.7** (501.6 km) Mirror Creek.

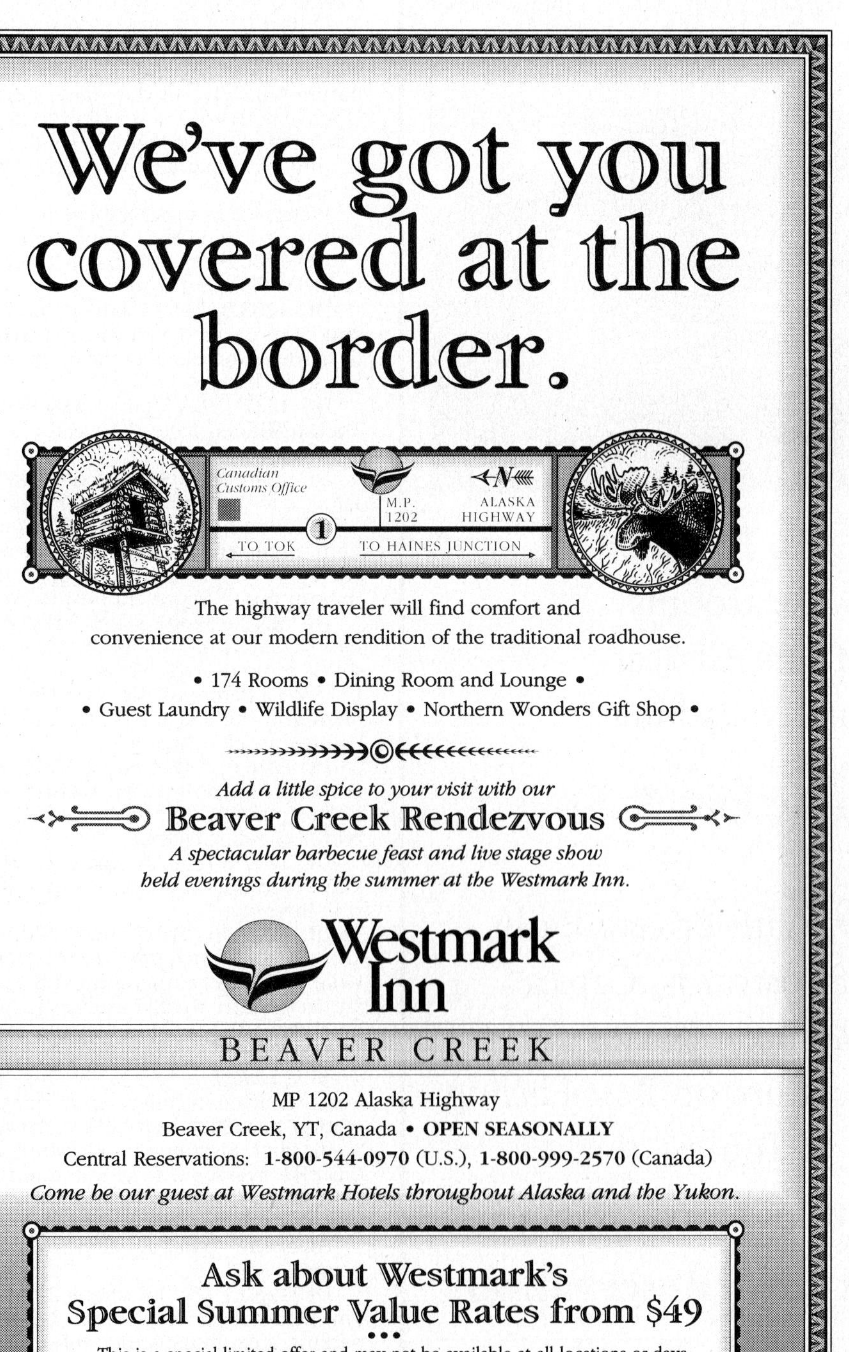

DC 1178.3 (1952 km) **F 309.7** (498.4 km) Lake to east, turnout to west.

DC 1186 (1963 km) **F 302** (486 km) Little Scottie Creek.

DC 1189.5 (1967.5 km) **F 298.5** (480.4 km) **Historic Milepost 1221.** Turnout with plaque and other markers at Canada–U.S. international border. From the viewing decks, note the narrow clearing marking the border. This is part of the 20-foot-/6-m-wide swath cut by surveyors from 1904 to 1920 along the 141st meridian (from Demarcation Point on the Arctic Ocean south 600 miles/966 km to Mount St. Elias in the Wrangell Mountains) to mark the Alaska–Canada border. This swath continues south to mark the boundary between southeastern Alaska and Canada. Portions of the swath are cleared periodically by the International Boundary Commission.

TIME ZONE CHANGE: Alaska observes Alaska time; Yukon Territory observes Pacific time. See Time Zones in the GENERAL INFORMATION section for details.

DC 1189.8 (1968 km) **F 298.2** (479.9 km) **Historical Mile 1221.8.** U.S. customs border station.

IMPORTANT: *The MILEPOST®* log now switches to physical mileposts for northbound travelers. For southbound travelers, the log is based on actual driving distance. The Alaska Highway is approximately 32 miles/51 km shorter than the traditional figure of 1,221.8 miles between Dawson Creek and the YT–AK border. Please read the information on Mileposts and Kilometreposts in the introduction to the Alaska Highway.

Northbound: Fair to good pavement to Fairbanks. Watch for frost heaves, potholes and pavement breaks next 40 miles/64 km. Expect road construction.

Southbound: Narrow, winding road to Haines Junction. Fair to good pavement. Watch for frost heaves and rough spots.

ALASKA ROUTE 2

Distance* from Dawson Creek (DC) is followed by distance from Fairbanks (F).

*Mileages from Dawson Creek and Fairbanks are based on physical mileposts in Alaska. Kilometres given are the metric equivalents of these mileages.

DC 1221.8 (1966.3 km) **F 298.2** (479.9 km) Port Alcan U.S. Customs and Immigration Service border station, open 24 hours a day year-round; pay phone (credit card and collect calls only) and restrooms. All traffic entering Alaska must stop for clearance. Phone (907) 774-2242; emergencies, 774-2252. Read through the GENERAL INFORMATION section for details on alcoholic beverages, holidays, customs requirements, fishing regulations, driving and other aspects of travel in Alaska and Canada.

DC 1222.5 (1967.4 km) **F 297.5** (478.8 km) Tetlin National Wildlife Refuge boundary sign to west.

DC 1222.7 (1967.7 km) **F 297.3** (478.4 km) Border Branch U.S. post office located here; open limited hours.

DC 1223.4 (1968.9 km) **F 296.6** (477.3 km) Scotty Creek bridge.

DC 1224.6 (1970.7 km) **F 295.4** (475.4 km) Double-ended gravel turnout to southwest at Highway Lake with USF&WS interpretive signs on wetlands and peoples. Beaver lodges southwest side of highway.

DC 1225.4 (1972 km) **F 294.6** (474.1 km) Gravel turnout to southwest. Access to

Desper Creek, canoe launch.

DC 1225.5 (1972.2 km) **F 294.5** (473.9 km) **Border City Lodge.** See display ad this section. ▲

DC 1227.8 (1975.9 km) **F 292.2** (470.2 km) Large double-ended paved parking area to southwest with litter barrels and USF&WS interpretive sign on migratory birds and area geography. View to south of lakes in Chisana (SHOE-sanna) River valley along Scotty Creek and west to the Wrangell Mountains. The Chisana gold rush took place in 1913. A mining camp was established on Cross Creek near the Chisana River, 38 miles southeast of Nabesna in the Wrangell Mountains. The settlement's population peaked at 148 in 1920.

DC 1229 (1977.8 km) **F 291** (468.3 km) USF&WS log cabin visitor center to south. (One-way driveway: enter at north end, exit at south.) Viewing deck and outdoor displays on wildlife and other subjects. Indoor wildlife displays and mounts. Deckside nature talks given twice daily. Restrooms. Open 7 A.M. to 7 P.M. Memorial Day to Labor Day. Current highway conditions and fishing information posted on bulletin board.

Watch for frost heaves, patches and potholes northbound and southbound.

DC 1230.9 (1980.9 km) **F 289.1** (465.3 km) View of Island Lake.

DC 1233.3 (1984.7 km) **F 286.7** (461.4 km) Large paved double-ended parking area to northeast on old alignment; litter barrels. Watch for bears.

DC 1237 (1990.7 km) **F 283** (455.4 km) Trail to **Hidden Lake** (1 mile/1.6 km); rainbow fishing.

DC 1240 (1995.5 km) **F 280** (450.6 km) Turnout to west; no easy turnaround.

DC 1240.3 (1996 km) **F 279.7** (450.1 km) Vertical culverts on either side of highway are an experiment to keep ground from thawing and thus prevent frost heaves.

DC 1243.6 (2001.3 km) **F 276.4** (444.8 km) Paved turnout. Scenic viewpoint to south on loop road has a litter barrel and USF&WS interpretive signs on fire management and the effects of forest fires on the natural history of area.

DC 1246.6 (2006.1 km) **F 273.4** (440 km) **Historic Milepost 1248. Gardiner Creek** bridge; parking to west at south end of bridge. Grayling fishing.

DC 1247.6 (2007.8 km) **F 272.4** (438.4 km) Paved double-ended viewpoint to east with litter barrels.

DC 1249.3 (2010.5 km) **F 270.7** (435.6 km) **Historic Milepost 1254. Deadman Lake** USF&WS campground, 1.5 miles/2.4 km in on dirt road. Turnout at highway junction with campground access road. The campground has 18 sites on long loop road, firepits, toilets, picnic tables, no drinking water, boat ramp, interpretive signs, information board and self-guided nature trail. Scenic spot. Swimming and fishing. Northern pike average 2 feet, but skinny (local residents call them "snakes"); use wobbling lures or spinners. ▲

Pavement patches next mile northbound.

DC 1250.1 (2011.8 km) **F 269.9** (434.3 km) Rest area to west. Double-ended paved parking area, four picnic tables, litter barrels, concrete fireplaces, toilets, no water.

DC 1252.2 (2015.2 km) **F 267.8** (431 km) Double-ended gravel turnout to southwest with USF&WS interpretive sign on solar basins (warm ponds and shallow marshes).

DC 1253 (2016.5 km) **F 267** (429.7 km) Views of lakes and muskeg in Chisana River valley.

DC 1253.6 (2017.4 km) **F 266.4** (428.7 km) **Frontier Surplus.** Military surplus goods. Clothing, sleeping bags, extreme cold weather "bunny boots," military tents, ammunition, fishing lures, tanned furs. Alaska T-shirts and caps. Local crafts, shed moose and caribou antlers. Antler products,

belt buckles, earrings, bolo ties, hat racks, handmade ulus. "Moosquitoes," diamond willow lamps and canes, finished or unfinished. Used Alaska license plates, cold pop. Open late every day. Motorhome and RV loop. Phone (907) 778-2274. [ADVERTISEMENT]

DC 1256.3 (2021.7 km) **F 263.7** (424.4 km) Northway state highway maintenance camp; no services.

DC 1256.7 (2022.5 km) **F 263.3** (423.7 km) Lakeview USF&WS campground on beautiful Yarger Lake; eight sites, firewood, no drinking water. *NOTE: No turnaround space. Not recommended for trailers, 5th wheelers or large RVs. (Large vehicles use Deadman Lake Campground at* ***Milepost DC 1249.3****.)* ▲

This is a good place to view ducks and loons. Look for the St. Elias Range to the south, Wrangell Mountains to the southwest and Mentasta Mountains to the west.

Roadside wildflowers include sweet pea, pale yellow Indian paintbrush, yarrow and Labrador tea.

DC 1258 (2024.5 km) **F 262** (421.6 km) Watch for rough patches in pavement.

DC 1260.2 (2028 km) **F 259.8** (418.1 km) 1260 Inn roadhouse (closed in 1993, current status unknown).

Southbound: Watch for frost heaves, potholes and pavement breaks next 40 miles/64 km to border.

DC 1263.1 (2032.7 km) **F 256.9** (413.4 km) **Wrangell View Service Center.** See display ad this section.

DC 1263.5 (2033.4 km) **F 256.5** (412.8 km) Chisana River parallels the highway to the southwest. This is the land of a thousand ponds, most unnamed. Good trapping country. In early June, travelers may note numerous cottony white seeds blowing in the wind; these seeds are from a species of willow.

DC 1264 (2034.2 km) **F 256** (412 km) **Northway Junction.** Campground, gas, laundromat, store and Native arts and crafts shop located at junction. An Alaska State Trooper is also stationed here. ▲

Naabia Niign Campground & Athabascan Indian Crafts. See display ad on page 146. ▲

A 7-mile/11.3-km side road leads south across the Chisana River bridge to the community of Northway (description follows). A boat launch at Chisana River bridge is one of three boat access points to Tetlin National Wildlife Refuge.

Northway

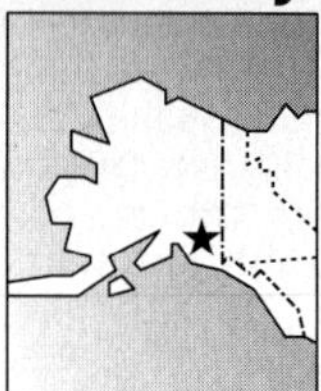

Located 7 miles/11.3 km south of the Alaska Highway via a side road. **Population:** 364 (area). **Emergency Services: Alaska State Troopers**, phone 778-2245. **EMS**, phone 778-2211. **Fire Department, Clinic.**

Elevation: 1,710 feet/521m. **Climate:** Mean monthly temperature in July, 58.5°F/15°C. In January, -21°F/-30°C. Record high 91°F/33°C in June 1969; record low -72°F/-58°C in January 1952.

Private Aircraft: Northway airport, adjacent south; elev. 1,716 feet/523m; length 5,147 feet/1,569m; asphalt; fuel 100LL, Jet B, MOGAS; customs available.

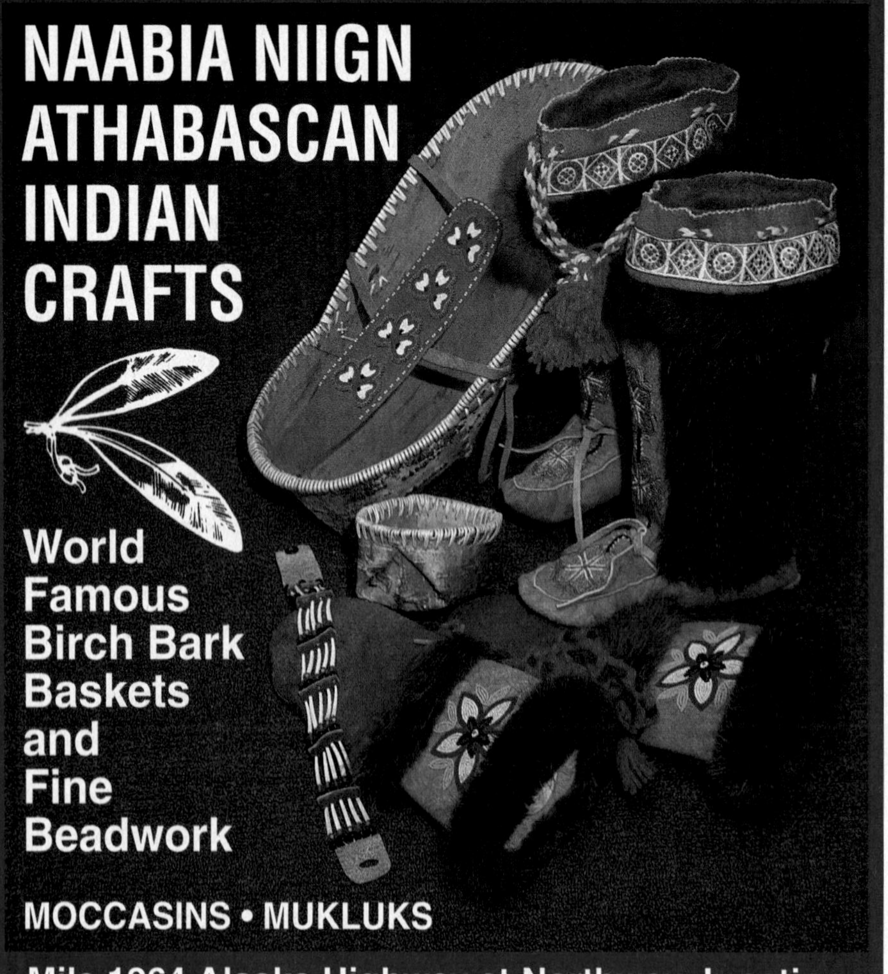

Northway has a community hall, post office and modern school. FAA station and customs office are at the airport. Visitor services include motels, grocery, liquor store, propane, gas stations and air taxi service.

Northway Airport Lodge & Motel. See display ad this section.

Historically occupied by Athabascan Indians, Northway was named to honor the village chief who adopted the name of a river boat captain in the early 1900s. (Chief Walter Northway died in 1993. He was thought to be 117 years old.) The rich Athabascan traditions of dancing, crafts, and hunting and trapping continue today in Northway Village. Local Athabascan handicrafts available for purchase include birchbark baskets, beadwork accessories, and moose hide and fur items such as moccasins, mukluks, mittens and hats.

Northway's airport was built in the 1940s as part of the Northwest Staging Route. This cooperative project of the United States and Canada was a chain of air bases from Edmonton, AB, through Whitehorse, YT, to Fairbanks. This chain of air bases helped build up and supply Alaska defense during WWII and also was used during construction of the Alcan and the Canol project. Lend-lease aircraft bound for Russia were flown up this route to Ladd Field (now Fort Wainwright) in Fairbanks. Northway is still an important port of entry for air traffic to Alaska, and a busy one.

Northway is located within Tetlin National Wildlife Refuge. Established in 1980, the 950,000-acre refuge stretches south from the Alaska Highway and west from the Canadian border. The major physical features include rolling hills, hundreds of small lakes and two glacial rivers (the Nabesna and Chisana) which combine to form the Tanana River. The refuge has a very high density of nesting waterfowl. Annual duck production in favorable years exceeds 90,000. Among the larger birds using the refuge are sandhill cranes, Pacific and common loons, osprey, bald eagles and ptarmigan. Other wildlife includes moose, black and grizzly bear, wolf, coyote, beaver and red fox. Activities allowed on the refuge include wildlife observation, hunting, fishing, camping, hiking and trapping. Check with refuge personnel at the USF&WS office in Tok prior to your visit for more detailed information. Write Refuge Manager, Tetlin National Wildlife Refuge, Box 779, Tok, AK 99780; or phone (907) 883-5312. Information on the refuge is also available at the USF&WS visitor center at **Milepost DC 1229** on the Alaska Highway.

Confluence of Moose Creek and

Chisana River, about 0.8 mile/1.3 km downstream from Chisana River bridge on Northway Road, south side of river, northern pike to 15 lbs., use red-and-white spoon, spring or fall. **Chisana River,** downstream from bridge, lingcod (burbot) to 8 lbs., use chunks of liver or meat, spring. **Nabesna Slough,** south end of runway, grayling to 3 lbs., use spinner or gold flies, late May.

Alaska Highway Log

(continued)

DC 1267.4 (2039.6 km) **F 252.6** (406.5 km) *CAUTION: Slow down for a big bump in the road known as "Beaver Slide." Watch for road construction next 46 miles/74 km southbound in 1994.*

Wonderful view of the Tanana River.

DC 1268.1 (2040.8 km) **F 251.9** (405.4 km) Beaver Creek bridge. The tea-colored water flowing in the creek is the result of tannins absorbed by the water as it flows through muskeg. This phenomenon may be observed in other Northern creeks.

DC 1269 (2042.2 km) **F 251** (403.9 km) **Historic Milepost 1271.** Scenic viewpoint with an interpretive panel about the significance of airfields in the development of the Alaska Highway. Double-ended gravel turnout to west has a litter barrel and USF&WS interpretive sign about the Tanana River, largest tributary of the Yukon River.

DC 1269.1 (2042.4 km) **F 250.9** (403.8 km) Slow down for bad pavement break.

DC 1272.7 (2048.2 km) **F 247.3** (398 km) Scenic viewpoint. Double-ended paved turnout to west with litter barrels. USF&WS interpretive sign on pond ecology and mosquitoes.

To the northwest the Tanana River flows near the highway; beyond, the Kalutna River snakes its way through plain and marshland. Mentasta Mountains are visible to the southwest.

DC 1273.9 (2050.1 km) **F 246.1** (396 km) Paved parking area with litter barrel to west by Tanana River.

In June, wild sweet peas create thick borders along the highway. This is rolling country, with aspen, birch, cottonwood, willow and white spruce.

DC 1275.5 (2052.7 km) **F 244.5** (393.5 km) Slide area next 0.3 mile/0.5 km northbound.

DC 1279 (2058.3 km) **F 241** (387.8 km) Highway cuts through sand dune stabilized by aspen and spruce trees.

DC 1281 (2061.5 km) **F 239** (384.6 km) Rough road, pavement cracks.

DC 1284.2 (2066.7 km) **F 235.8** (379.5 km) Tetlin National Wildlife Refuge boundary sign.

DC 1284.6 (2067.3 km) **F 235.4** (378.8 km) Large double-ended paved turnout to east.

DC 1285.7 (2069.1 km) **F 234.3** (377.1 km) Granite intrusion in older metamorphosed rock is exposed by road cut.

DC 1289 (2074.4 km) **F 231** (371.7 km) First view northbound of 3.4-mile-/5.5-km-long Midway Lake.

DC 1289.4 (2075 km) **F 230.6** (371.1 km) **Historic Milepost 1292.** Turnout uphill on east side of highway with litter barrels, view of Midway Lake and USF&WS interpretive signs on Wrangell-St. Elias National Park and Native peoples. Interpretive panel about Dusenberg Camp No. 2, operated by E.M. Dusenberg Co. of Iowa, one of about 50 civil road construction contractors working on the Alaska Highway in 1943.

NOTE: Difficult access for large vehicles and trailers, easier access from southbound lane.

DC 1290 (2076 km) **F 230** (370.1 km) Beautiful view of Midway Lake southbound.

DC 1292.4 (2079.8 km) **F 227.6** (366.3 km) Paved turnout west side.

DC 1293.7 (2081.9 km) **F 226.3** (364.2 km) Paved turnout west side.

DC 1294.3 (2082.9 km) **F 225.7** (363.2 km) Bad pavement break.

DC 1301.7 (2094.8 km) **F 218.3** (351.3 km) **Historic Milepost 1306. Tetlin Junction,** Alaska Highway and Taylor Highway (Alaska Route 5) junction. 40-Mile Roadhouse; food, gas and lodging. The Taylor Highway (gravel, open summer only) heads northeast via Jack Wade Junction to Eagle (see TAYLOR HIGHWAY section) and to Yukon Highway 9 (Top of the World Highway) to Dawson City. (See KLONDIKE LOOP section for log of Yukon Highway 9 and description of Dawson City.)

NOTE: If you are traveling to Dawson City, keep in mind that both the Canada and U.S. customs stations are closed at night; you CANNOT cross the border unless customs stations are open. Customs hours in summer 1993 were 8 A.M. to 8 P.M. Alaska time, 9 A.M. to 9 P.M. Pacific time on the Canadian side.

DC 1302.7 (2096.4 km) **F 217.3** (349.7 km) Scenic viewpoint at paved turnout to southwest.

DC 1303.4 (2097.5 km) **F 216.6** (348.6 km) Tanana River bridge. Informal parking area and boat launch to east at north end of bridge. Tanana (TAN-uh-naw), an Indian name, was first reported by the Western Union Telegraph Expedition of 1886. According to William Henry Dall, chief scientist of the expedition, the name means "mountain river." The Tanana is the largest tributary in Alaska of the Yukon River. From here the highway parallels the Tanana to Fairbanks. The Alaska Range looms in the distance.

DC 1304.6 (2099.5 km) **F 215.4** (346.6 km) Evidence of 1990 burn from here north to Tok. The Tok River fire occurred in July of 1990 and burned 97,352 acres. The fire closed the Alaska and Glenn highways at times and threatened the town of Tok. There is an interpretive display on the Tok River fire at the Alaska Public Lands Information Center in Tok.

DC 1306.6 (2102.7 km) **F 213.4** (343.4 km) Road east to lake.

DC 1308.5 (2105.7 km) **F 211.5** (340.4 km) Weigh station and turnoff to U.S. Coast Guard loran-C station and signal towers.

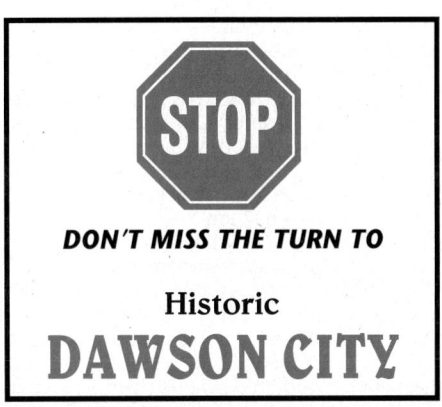

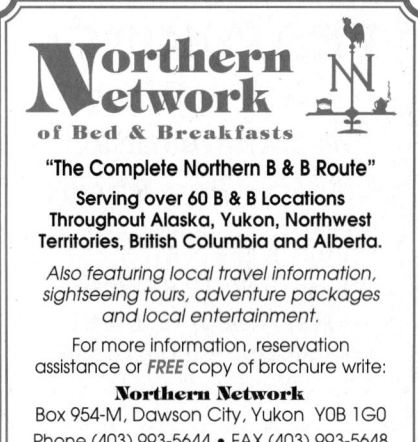

This loran (long range navigation) station is one of seven in Alaska. A series of four 700-foot/213-m towers suspends a multi-element wire antenna used to transmit navigation signals. These signals may be used by air, land and sea navigators as an aid in determining their position. This station is located here as necessary for good geometry with two Gulf of Alaska loran transmitting stations.

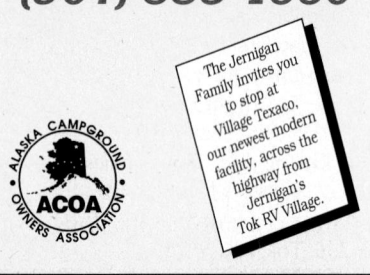

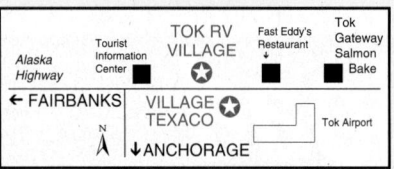

DC 1308.8 (2106.3 km) **F 211.2** (339.9 km) Paved turnout with litter barrels to west.

DC 1309.2 (2106.9 km) **F 210.8** (339.2 km) Tok River State Recreation Site; 25 campsites, overflow parking, tables, firepits, toilets (wheelchair accessible), litter barrels, nature trail and boat launch. Check bulletin board for schedule of interpretive programs. Camping fee $8/night or annual pass. *CAUTION: Swift water.* ♿▲

Annual passes good for unlimited camping at all Alaska state parks within a calendar year are available for $75. Annual boat launch passes for Alaska state parks are $50. Annual daily parking pass is $25. Super Pass (camping, boat launch, parking) is $135 for Alaska residents, $150 for nonresidents. Passes may be purchased at the Alaska Public Lands Information Center in Tok.

DC 1309.4 (2107.2 km) **F 210.6** (338.9 km) Tok River bridge.

DC 1312.7 (2112.5 km) **F 207.3** (333.6 km) Tok community limits. Mountain views ahead northbound.

Wayfarer's Motel. See display ad on page 147.

DC 1312.8 (2112.7 km) **F 207.2** (333.4 km) Tok Dog Mushers Assoc. track and buildings. Paved bike trail from Tok ends here.

DC 1313 (2113 km) **F 207** (333.1 km) Airstrip. See Private Aircraft information in Tok section. Entering Tok (northbound), description follows. Tok is located at the junction of the Alaska Highway and Tok Cutoff (Glenn Highway). Anchorage-bound travelers turn west on the Tok Cutoff (see the TOK CUTOFF/GLENN HIGHWAY section). Fairbanks-bound travelers continue north on the Alaska Highway.

Southbound travelers: Driving distance from Tok to Beaver Creek is 113 miles/182 km; Haines Junction 296 miles/476 km; Haines (departure point for Alaska state ferries) 446.5 miles/718.5 km; and Whitehorse 396 miles/637 km.

DC 1313.1 (2113.1 km) **F 206.9** (332.9 km) **Tok Gateway Salmon Bake and RV Park.** Vacationers should not miss Tok's Gateway Salmon Bake, featuring outdoor flame-grilled Alaska king salmon, halibut, ribs and reindeer sausage. Buffalo burgers. Chowder. Good food, friendly people; casual

dining at its best. Open 11 A.M. to 9 P.M., except Sunday 4-9 P.M. Shuttle bus service from local hotels and RV parks. Wooded RV and tent sites with tables, clean restrooms, dump station and water. Phone 883-5555. [ADVERTISEMENT] ▲

DC 1313.2 (2113.3 km) **F 206.8** (332.8 km) **Willard's Full Service Repair**. See display ad this section.

DC 1313.3 (2113.5 km) **F 206.7** (332.6 km) **Eska Trading Post,** on the left northbound, home of premium quality hand-dipped ice cream, an Alaska-made gourmet treat. Frozen yogurt. Video and Nintendo rentals. Alaska crafts and souvenirs and a large selection of Alaska books. Snacks, cold pop, ice. "Hex" tanning unit. See display ad this section. [ADVERTISEMENT]

DC 1313.3 (2113.5 km) **F 206.7** (332.6 km) **Young's Motel and Fast Eddy's Restaurant.** A touch of Alaskana in a modern setting. Affordable, clean and spacious. We cater to the independent highway traveler. Open year-round with all the

amenities: telephones, private baths, color TV, ample parking. Check in at Fast Eddy's full-service restaurant, open 6 A.M. to midnight. Reserve early! P.O. Box 482, Tok, AK 99780. (907) 883-4411; Fax (907) 883-5023. [ADVERTISEMENT]

DC 1313.3 (2113.5 km) **F 206.7** (332.6 km) **Village Texaco.** See display ad this section.

DC 1313.3 (2113.5 km) **F 206.7** (332.6 km) **Northstar Travel Center.** After your long journey through Canada, you deserve the best. At Northstar you will find reasonable prices for quality goods and services, served to you by friendly individuals who respect your importance to the success of our business. You have endured this long journey to fully enjoy your much-deserved vacation in Alaska. We will endeavor to assist you in every way possible. We want

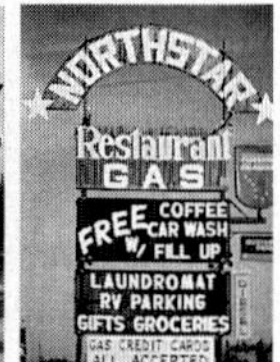

you to return and tell your friends about Northstar. We have carefully chosen the services available to you and carefully selected the caring personnel to assist you in having a pleasant vacation. We appreciate any suggestions you might have while you are here at Northstar. See our display ad for services. Thank you for considering Northstar in your plans for this season. [ADVERTISEMENT] ▲

DC 1313.3 (2113.5 km) **F 206.7** (332.6 km) **The Bull Shooter Sporting Goods & RV Park**, Tok, Alaska. Fishing and hunting licenses and information. Sporting goods. Large selection of fishing gear and tackle. Camping supplies. Guns and ammo. Plan to stay at the Bull Shooter's nice, quiet RV park. 30 spaces, 24 pull-throughs. Full or partial hookups, dump station, good drinking water. Non-metered showers, restrooms, ice and phone. We accept VISA and MasterCard. Welcome to Alaska! We are on the left as you come into Tok. P.O. Box 553, Tok, AK 99780. Reservations accepted; senior discounts. Call (907) 883-5625. See display ad in Tok section. [ADVERTISEMENT] ▲

DC 1313.4 (2113.6 km) **F 206.6** (332.5 km) **Tok RV Village.** Alaska's finest. Good Sam or KOA cards honored. Convenient pull-through spaces with 30-amp power. Full and partial hookups, clean restrooms and showers, dump station, laundry, car wash, picnic tables, public phones. Gift shop. RV supplies, ice. MasterCard, VISA and Discover. Located across highway from Village Texaco/Food Mart. Shopping area with propane, liquor store, restaurant, nightclub, hardware store and video rentals next door. See display ad in Tok section. [ADVERTISEMENT] ▲

DC 1314.1 (2114.8 km) **F 205.9** (331.3 km) Alaska Public Lands Information Center and Tok Mainstreet Visitor Center.

Tok

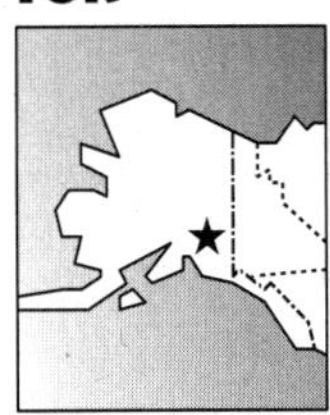

DC 1314.2 (2115 km) **F 205.8** (331.2 km) At the junction of the Alaska Highway and Tok Cutoff (Glenn Highway) between the Tanana River to the north and the Alaska Range to the southwest. **Population:** 935. **Emergency Services: Alaska State Troopers,** phone 883-5111. **Fire Department,** phone 883-2333. **Community Clinic,** across from the fire hall on the Tok Cutoff, phone 883-5855 during business hours. **Ambulance,** phone 883-2300 or 911. EMT squad and air medivac available. **Public Health Clinic,** next to the Alaska State Troopers at **Milepost 1314.1,** phone 883-4101.

Visitor Information: The state-operated Alaska Public Lands Information Center at **Milepost DC 1314.1** offers free coffee and has a public phone and message board. Alaska State Park annual passes may be purchased here. Open 8 A.M. to 8 P.M. daily May through September. Winter hours (Oct. 1 through May 15) are 8 A.M. to 4:30 P.M., weekdays. Write: Box 359, Tok, AK 99780. Phone (907) 883-5667.

The Tok Mainstreet Visitor Center, operated by the Tok Chamber of Commerce, is located at the junction of the Alaska Highway and Tok Cutoff. This huge log building is a center for local and state information, trip planning, art exhibits and shows. The center offers free coffee, public telephones and restrooms, a message board and gift shop. It is open daily 7 A.M. to 9 P.M., May 1 to Oct. 1. Write Box 389, Tok, AK 99780; phone 883-5775 or 883-5887.

The U.S. Fish & Wildlife Service office is located directly across the highway from the Public Lands Information Center. Visitors are welcome. Check with them regarding Tetlin National Wildlife Refuge. Office hours are 8 A.M. to noon and 1-4:30 P.M., weekdays. Write Box 155, Tok, AK 99780, or phone (907) 883-5312.

Elevation: 1,635 feet/498m. **Climate:** Mean monthly temperature in January, -19°F/-29°C; in July 59°F/14°C. Record low was -71°F/-57°C in January 1965; record high, 96°F/36°C in June 1969. **Radio:** FM stations are 90.5, 91.1 (KUAC-FM, University of Alaska Fairbanks) and 101.5. **Television:** Satellite channel 13. **Newspaper:** *Mukluk News* (twice monthly).

Private Aircraft: Tok Junction, 1 mile/1.6 km east; elev. 1,630 feet/497m; length 2,510 feet/765m; asphalt; fuel 100 LL, Jet A; unattended. Tok airstrip, 2 miles/3.2 km south; elev. 1,670 feet/509m; length 1,700 feet/518m; gravel; unattended. Tok NR 2 airstrip, 2 miles/3.2 km south; elev. 1,630 feet/497m; length 2,000 feet/609m; gravel; private, unattended.

Tok had its beginnings as a construction camp on the Alcan Highway in 1942. High-

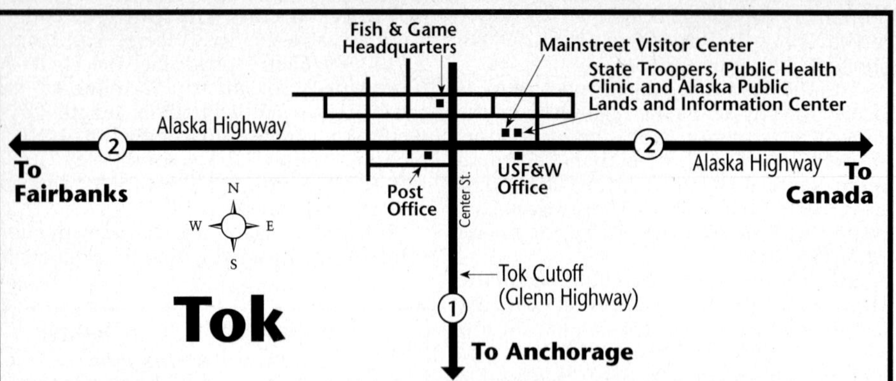

way engineer C.G. Polk was sent to Fairbanks in May of 1942 to take charge of Alaskan construction, and start work on the road between Tok Junction and Big Delta. Work was also under way on the Gulkana–Slana–Tok Junction road (now the Tok Cutoff on the Glenn Highway to Anchorage). But on June 7, 1942, a Japanese task force invaded Attu and Kiska islands in the Aleutians, and the Alcan took priority over the Slana cutoff.

The name Tok is believed to be derived from Tokyo Camp, patriotically shortened during WWII to Tok. But there exist at least three other versions of how Tok (pronounced to rhyme with poke) got its name.

TOK ADVERTISERS

"A Tent in Tok" .... P.O. Box 110
Alaska Territorial Outpost .... Next to Public Lands Information Center
Arctic Gifts in Tok ...... Mile 1313.8 Alaska Hwy.
Bull Shooter Sporting Goods & RV Park, The .... Mile 1313.3 Alaska Hwy.
Burnt Paw .... Adjacent post office
Cheryl's Old Fashion Bed & Breakfast ... Mile 1315.7 Alaska Hwy.
Cleft of the Rock Bed & Breakfast .... Ph. (907) 883-4219
Eska Trading Post ...... Mile 1313.3 Alaska Hwy.
Faith Chapel .... First & Center
Fast Eddy's Restaurant .... Mile 1313.3 Alaska Hwy.
First Baptist Church .... Downtown
Glenwood Bed and Breakfast .... Ph. (907) 883-2707
Golden Bear Motel .... Mile 0.3 Tok Cutoff
Golden Dreams Bed and Breakfast .... Ph. (907) 883-5659
Hayner's Trading Post .... Mile 1.7 Tok Cutoff
Kuebler's Husky Lounge & Liquor .... Ph. (907) 883-2381
Lois's Bed & Breakfast ...... Ph. (907) 883-5647
Mukluk Land .... Mile 1317 Alaska Hwy.
Northern Energy Corp. .... Mile 1314.8 Alaska Hwy.
Northern Wonders Gift Shops .. Westmark Tok
Northstar Travel Center .... Mile 1313.3 Alaska Hwy.
Satyãgraha Guest Ranch B & B .... Ph. (907) 883-5226
Shamrock Hardware .... Ph. (907) 883-2161
Snowshoe Fine Arts and Gifts .... Across from visitor center
Snowshoe Motel ...... Across from visitor center
Sourdough Campground .. Mile 1.7 Tok Cutoff
Sourdough Pancake Breakfast .... Mile 1.7 Tok Cutoff
Stage Stop, The .... Ph. (907) 883-5338
Texaco Truck Stop and Restaurant .... Mile 1313.8 Alaska Hwy.
Tok Chamber of Commerce .... Next to Public Lands Information Center
Tok Gateway Salmon Bake .... Mile 1313.1 Alaska Hwy.
Tok Liquor & Mini-Mart ... Adjacent Tok Lodge
Tok Lodge .... Ph. (907) 883-2851
Tok RV Village .... Mile 1313.4 Alaska Hwy.
Tok Saveway .... Ph. (907) 883-5389
Tundra Lodge and RV Park .... Mile 1315 Alaska Hwy.
Westmark Tok .... Jct. Alaska Hwy. & Tok Cutoff
Wildwood Bed & Breakfast .... Ph. (907) 883-5866
Young's Chevron Service .... Ph. (907) 883-2821
Young's Motel .... Ph. (907) 883-4411

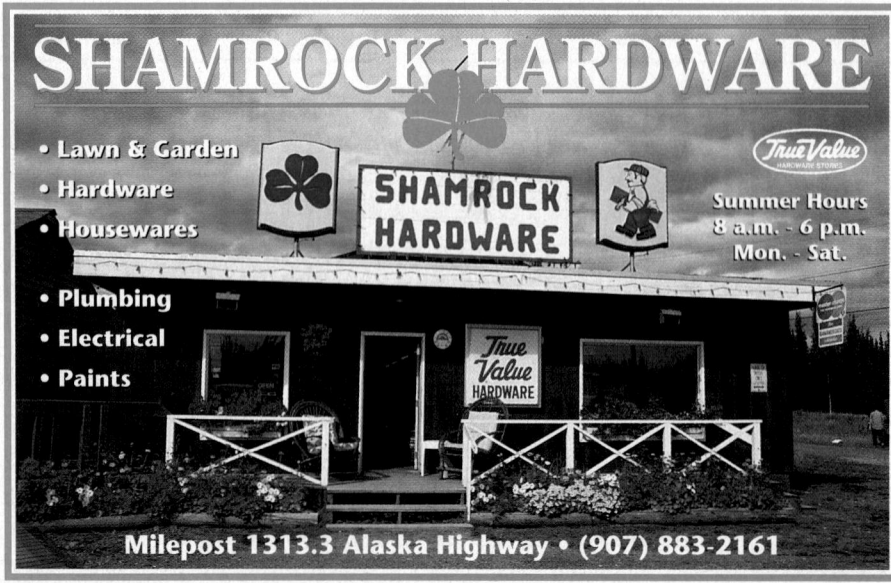

COMCHEK
CCIS
Insta Cash NTS
EFS
MOST GAS
CREDIT CARDS

Discount Fuel • Quality Fuel at Discount Prices
With fill up—Discount on Restaurant and some other services
FREE Coffee, FREE Car Wash, and FREE RV Parking (no hookups)

Extra Special Discounts for Caravans, Buses, and Return Visits

Restaurant • Homestyle Cooking • Daily Specials • Full Menu
Sourdough Pancakes • Halibut & Salmon
Homemade Pies • Ice Cream

RV CAMPGROUND • Pull-through Spaces • Full & Partial Hookups
Dump Station • 2 FREE SHOWERS *(included with full hookup)*
Picnic Area • Tent Sites • Ice • Pay Telephone • Campfire Barbecues and Folk Singing

PROPANE • SHOWERS • GIFT SHOP • GROCERIES • LAUNDROMAT • WESTERN UNION
We Honor KOA and other discount cards • Some Services Seasonal

(907) 883-4501 • Reservations: (907) 883-4631
Mile 1313.3 Alaska Highway • P.O. Box 677, Tok, Alaska 99780

Stop here for Visitor Information and free discount coupons good throughout Alaska

Because Tok is the major overland point of entry to Alaska, it is primarily a trade and service center for all types of transportation, especially for summer travelers coming up the Alaska Highway. A stopover here is a good opportunity to meet other travelers and swap experiences. Tok is the only town in Alaska that the highway traveler must pass through twice — once when arriving in the state and again on leaving the state. The governor proclaimed Tok "Mainstreet

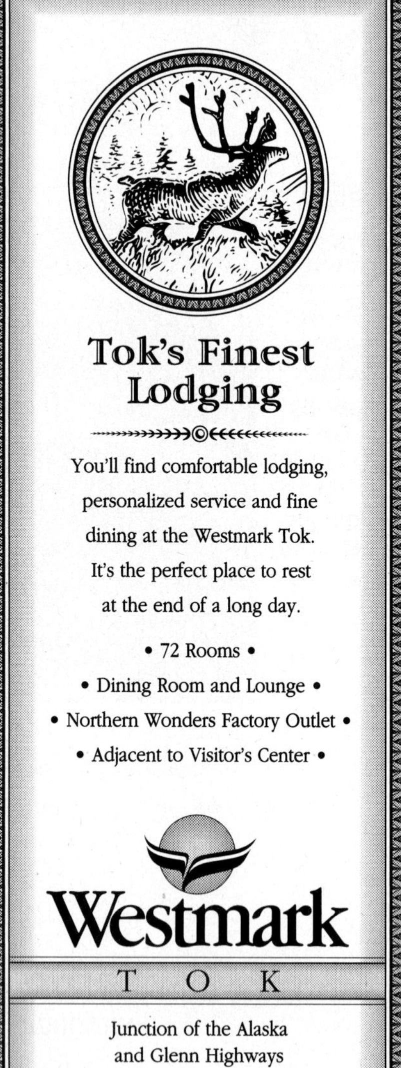
Tok's Finest Lodging
You'll find comfortable lodging, personalized service and fine dining at the Westmark Tok. It's the perfect place to rest at the end of a long day.
• 72 Rooms •
• Dining Room and Lounge •
• Northern Wonders Factory Outlet •
• Adjacent to Visitor's Center •
Westmark
T O K
Junction of the Alaska and Glenn Highways
P.O. Box 130, Tok Alaska 99780
Central Reservations
1-800-544-0970 (U.S.)
1-800-999-2570 (Canada)
Come be our guest at Westmark Hotels throughout Alaska & the Yukon.
Ask about Westmark's Special Summer Value Rates from $49
• • •
This is a special limited offer and may not be available at all locations or days requested. Call for complete information after April 15, 1994.

Alaska" in 1991. Townspeople are proud of this designation and work hard to make visitors happy and to represent their community and state.

Tok's central business district is at the junction of the Alaska Highway and Tok Cutoff (Glenn Highway). From the junction, homes and businesses spread out along both highways on flat terrain dotted with densely timbered stands of black spruce.

Tok has 13 churches, a public library, an elementary school, a four-year accredited high school and a University of Alaska extension program. Local clubs include the Lions, Disabled American Veterans, Veterans of Foreign Wars, Chamber of Commerce, Dog Mushers, Little League, Girl Scouts, PTA, a snowmobile club and a homemaker's club.

ACCOMMODATIONS

There are eight hotels/motels, a variety of restaurants and several gas stations in town, as well as bed and breakfasts both in Tok and just north of Tok Junction along the Alaska Highway. Also here are grocery, hardware and sporting goods stores, bakery, beauty shop, gift shops, liquor stores, auto repair and auto parts stores, wrecker service, laundromats and a post office. The nearest bank is in Delta Junction or Glennallen.

Tok AYH youth hostel is located on Pringle Road, 0.8 mile/1.3 km south of **Milepost DC 1322.6**; phone (907) 883-3745.

There are several private RV parks in Tok. Nearby state campgrounds include: Tok River State Recreation Site at **Milepost DC 1309.2** and Moon Lake State Recreation Site at **Milepost DC 1331.9** Alaska Highway; and Eagle Trail State Recreation Site at **Milepost GJ 109.3** Tok Cutoff (Glenn Highway) 16 miles/25 km west. ▲

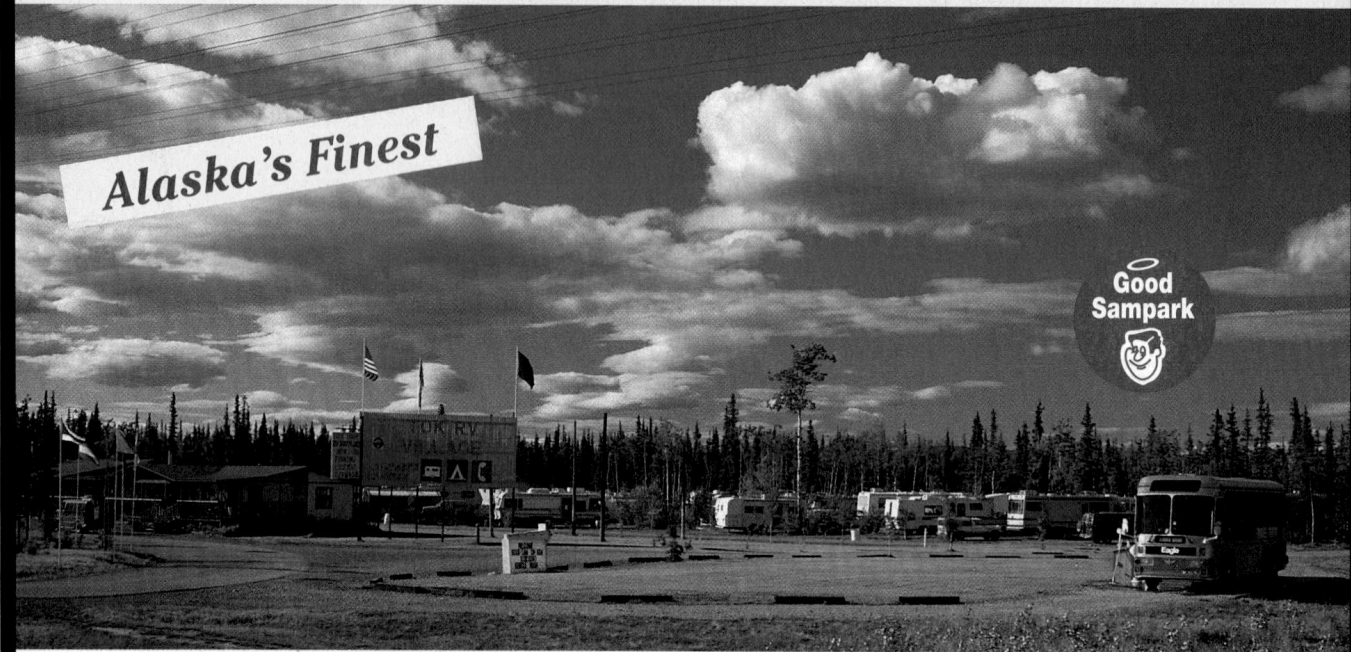

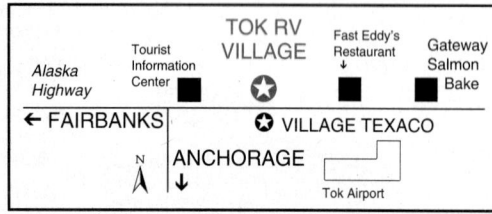

Cheryl's Old Fashion Bed & Breakfast (Mile 1315.7 Alaska Highway) located in Rita's Campground/RV Park, 1.7 miles from Tok toward Fairbanks. Relaxing, comfortable, private log cabin shaded by an Athabascan cache. Enjoy the midnight or contemplate your plans over coffee on the sun porch. Cleanest bathhouse shared with Rita's Campground. Continental breakfast. Use Rita's covered cookout, fireplace, grills and picnic tables. Bring your own steaks or

salmon to grill. Microwave, refrigerator, toaster, coffeemaker available. From humble beginnings, a highway camp bunkhouse evolved into Rita's first private campground office, a gift shop, a residence for Doug and Rita's daughter, Cheryl, before being relocated and remodeled into Cheryl's Bed & Breakfast. Doug and Rita Euers, pioneer Alaskans from Michigan, hosts. Box 599, Tok, AK 99780; (907) 883-4342. [ADVERTISEMENT]

Glenwood Bed and Breakfast in a modern log home. Listen to the sounds of nature. Guided nature walks are available. Enjoy homemade jams and breads with full breakfast. Relax in a comfortable queen-size bed with private bathroom. Mile 1316.6, turn south onto Scoby. Phone (907) 883-2707. (See display ad this section.) [ADVERTISEMENT]

Golden Bear Motel. Quiet location, 62 deluxe units, RV park with wooded pull-through sites, heated bathhouse; fine restaurant with cocktails available. Open 6 A.M. to 10 P.M. Our gift shop carries an extensive selection of Alaskana, jewelry, T-shirts and souvenirs. The friendly atmosphere you came to Alaska to find! See display ad this section. [ADVERTISEMENT] ▲

Golden Dreams Bed and Breakfast will begin your real Alaskan adventure. Let us cheerfully accommodate your need to relax at the end of a long day's journey. Awaiting you in the glow of our family room are personalized photo albums depicting 20 years of gold mining, dog mushing and trapping adventures. Our hot breakfast,

served on fine china and crystal, will leave our guests feeling pampered and loved. Accommodations include Mother Lode (queen bed, private bath); Bonanza, Nugget and Discovery rooms (double beds, shared bath). Reasonable rates. Group and senior discounts available. Warm hospitality with your comfort our priority. Hebrews 13:2. Smoke and alcohol-free environment. Reservations: (907) 883-5659; Box 106, Tok, AK 99780. Mile 1316.7 Alaska Highway, 2.5 miles west of Tok Junction; first left past Scoby. [ADVERTISEMENT]

Sourdough Campground's Pancake Breakfast, served 7-11 A.M. Genuine "Sourdough"! Full and partial RV hookups. Dry campsites. Showers included. High-pressure car wash. Open-air museum with gold rush memorabilia. Evening video program. Located 1.7 miles from the junction toward Anchorage on Tok Cutoff (Glenn Highway). See display ad this section. [ADVERTISEMENT] ▲

The Stage Stop, bed and breakfast for people and horses. Private cabin and three large rooms with king and queen beds, one with private bath, plus full breakfast. Quiet location Mile 1.7 Tok Cutoff highway. New barn and corrals for horses. Reasonable rates from $35. Open all year. Mary Underwood, Box 69, Tok, AK 99780. Phone (907) 883-5338. [ADVERTISEMENT]

Tok Lodge, located on Glenn Highway, one block from junction. Alcan Room serves buses, leaving full-service restaurant open for car traffic. 36 new motel rooms.

Common comments are: "nicest rooms on the highway" and "best meal since leaving home." Locally owned by Pam and Bud Johnson for 22 years. Mini-Mart and liquor store located on premises. See display ad this section. [ADVERTISEMENT]

Tundra Lodge & RV Park offers spacious, tree-shaded camping sites. Full and partial hookups. Tent sites. Pull-throughs. Clean restrooms and showers included in price. Picnic tables, fire rings and wood. Dump station. Laundromat. Vehicle wash. Pay phone. Ice. Lounge and meeting room. See display ad Mile 1315 Alaska Highway. [ADVERTISEMENT] ▲

Wildwood Bed & Breakfast. Clean, newly redecorated cabins and rooms in a wooded setting. Enjoy our pond and garden area and our sled dogs with summer or winter sled rides. Call (907) 883-5866 or in Alaska 1-800-887-5866 for reservations only. [ADVERTISEMENT]

TRANSPORTATION

Air: Charter air service available; inquire at Tok state airstrip (**Milepost DC 1313**). Charter flightseeing and fly-in fishing trips available. Scheduled passenger and freight service between Tok, Delta Junction and Fairbanks four days a week via 40-Mile Air.

Bus: See Bus Lines in the GENERAL INFORMATION section for scheduled service to other communities.

ATTRACTIONS

Alaska Public Lands Information Center has a large floor map, trip-planning center, and a historical timeline room. There is an award-winning interpretive display on the 1990 Tok River fire. Wildlife displays at the museum include an 8-foot grizzly bear, a wolf, wolverine, lynx, walrus, Dall sheep, musk-ox, a caribou head mount and moose rack. Also on display are examples of baleen (part of the food-filtering apparatus of the bowhead whale, from which fine Alaskan jewelry is now made). Restrooms, pay phone and message board located here.

Tok Mainstreet Visitor Center. This 7,000-square-foot building was built using local timber and local labor. Huge natural spruce logs support an open-beamed, cathedral ceiling. Large picture windows frame the Alaska Range. Displays at the center include Alaskan wildlife, waterfowl and Alaska Highway memorabilia. Built in a modified T shape, three of the four wings are devoted to the visitor, with displays, restrooms and trip planning. Tok's community library is housed in the fourth wing.

Donna Bernhardt, an Alaskan writer and TV personality, can frequently be seen in the summer months in live performances at the center.

Local Events: There is a variety of things to do in Tok, thanks to local individuals, businesses and clubs. Local campgrounds offer slide shows, movies, gold panning, a salmon bake, miniature golf and sourdough pancake breakfasts. Sled dog demonstrations are given at Burnt Paw gift shop and at the Westmark.

Other local events include bingo games and softball games at the local field. Visitors are welcome at the senior citizens center. The Tok triathlon (12 miles of biking, 10 of canoeing and five of jogging) and Tok Trot are both held annually. Tok's Fourth of July celebration is a major event, complete with a parade, picnic and games. Check at the

THREE WAYS TO SAVE

AT WAREHOUSE PRICES!

• Groceries • Automotive Needs
• Camping Supplies • Paper • Soda

And Much, Much More!

ANCHORAGE

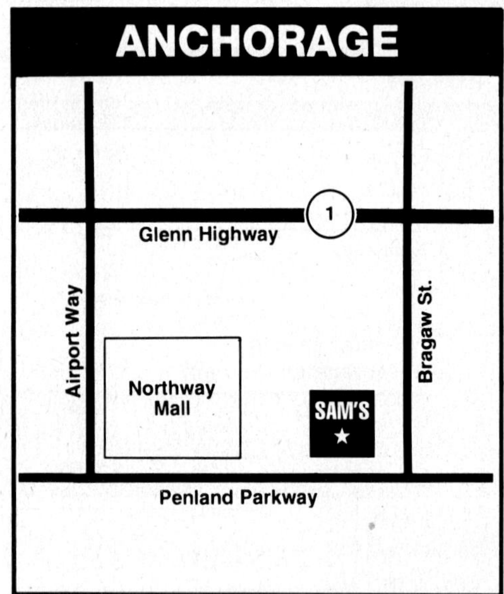

3651 Penland Parkway
276-2996

FAIRBANKS

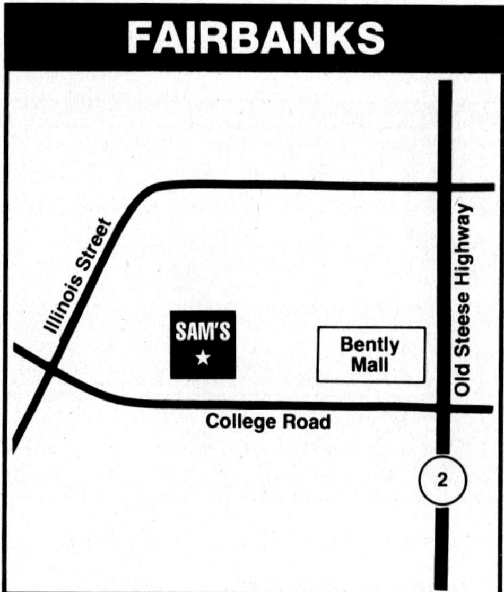

48 College Road
451-4800

SOUTH ANCHORAGE

1
N
Dimond Blvd.
Kmart
SAM'S
Old Seward Hwy.
New Seward Hwy.

8801 Old Seward Hwy.
522-2333

Stock up on wholesale supplies for your trip down the Alaska Highway.

We guarantee low everyday prices on all our products.

A one-day pass is available at our warehouses.

Mainstreet Visitor Center for more information on these local events.

Bike Trail: A wide paved bike trail extends southeast from Tok on the Alaska Highway as far east as the Dog Mushers Assoc. track, and as far west as Tanacross Junction; approximate length is 13.2 miles/ 21.2 km. You may also bike out the Tok Cutoff past Sourdough Campground. Travelers may park their vehicles in and around Tok and find a bike trail nearby leading into or out of Tok.

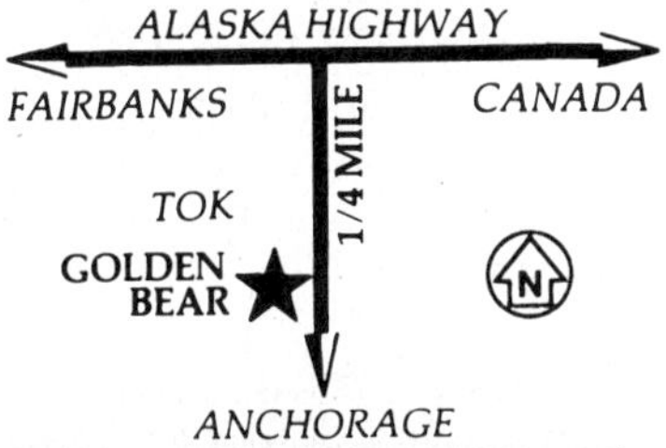

Native Crafts: Tok is a trade center for the Athabascan Native villages of Tanacross, Northway, Tetlin, Mentasta, Dot Lake and Eagle. Several of the Native women make birch baskets, beaded moccasins, boots and beaded necklaces. Examples of Native work may be seen at the Native-operated gift shop

at Northway junction and at several gift shops and other outlets in Tok.

The state of Alaska has a crafts identification program which identifies authentic Native and Alaskan handicrafts. This symbol is of a polar bear.

Birch baskets were once used in the Native camps and villages. Traditionally they had folded corners, would hold water, and were even used for cooking by dropping heated stones into the liquid in the baskets. The baskets are made by peeling the bark from the birch trees, usually in the early summer months. The bark is easiest to work with when moist and pliable. It is cut into shape and sewn together with strips of spruce root dug out of the ground and split. If the root is too dry it is soaked until it is manageable. Holes are put in the birch bark with a punch or screwdriver and the spruce root is laced in and out. Native women dye the spruce root with food coloring, watercolors or berry juice. A few Natives also make birch canoes and birch baby carriers.

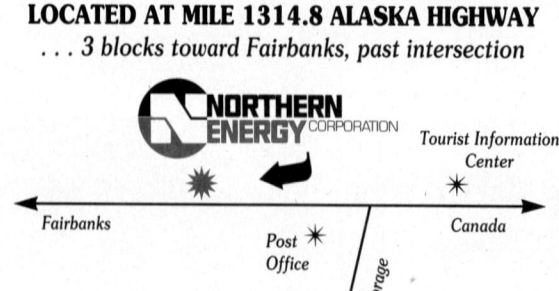

Many of the moccasins and mukluks for sale in Tok are made with moose hide that has the "Native tan." This means moose hide tanned by the Native. First the excess fat and meat is scraped off the hide, then it is soaked in a soap solution (some use a mixture of brains and ashes). After soaking, all the moisture is taken out by constant scraping with a dull knife or scraper. The hide is then scraped again and rubbed together to soften it. Next it is often smoke-cured in rotted spruce wood smoke. The tanning process takes from a few days to a week.

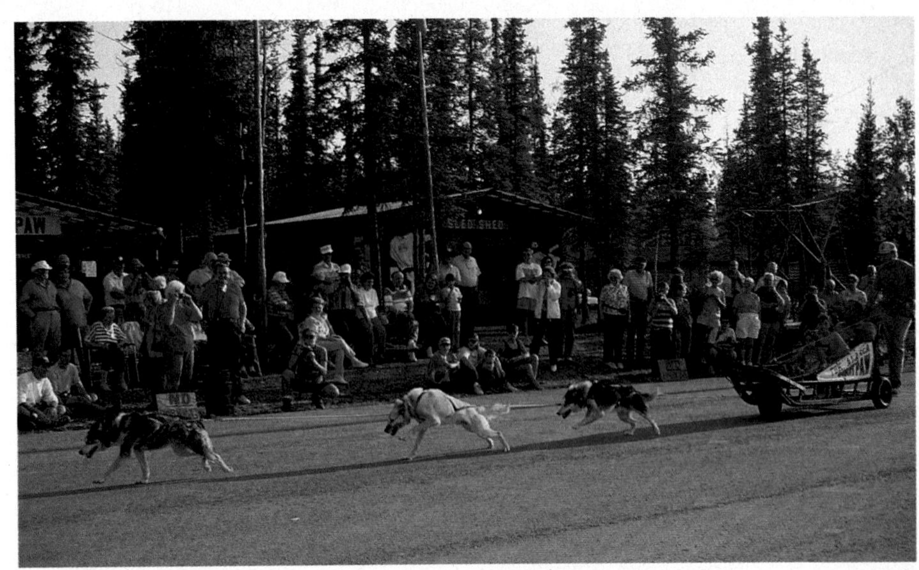

Dog sled demonstration is a popular Tok attraction. (Jerrianne Lowther, staff)

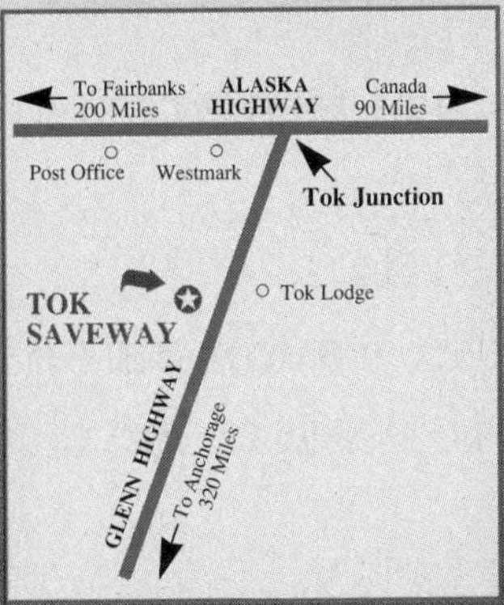

Beading can be a slow and tedious process. Most women say if they work steadily all day they can put the beading on one moccasin, but usually they do their beadwork over a period of several days, alternating it with other activities.

Snowshoe Fine Arts and Gifts invites you to come browse and shop in our gift store. See our gallery of art prints, figurines, Alaska Native-made carvings, masks, dolls, birch and grass baskets and beadwork. Jewelry made of natural Alaska gemstones, ivory and gold nugget. Lots of caps, T-shirts and sweatshirts. Souvenir items and Alaska-made products. Fur hats, earmuffs and bronzes by Alaskan artists Sue and Frank Entsminger. See display ad this section. [ADVERTISEMENT]

Arctic Gifts in Tok. First or last chance for the best buys in Alaska. Alaska's largest gem and mineral store. Garnet, hematite or quartz necklaces, hats, vials of gold — a sourdough's dream, all $5 each. Snack shop. [ADVERTISEMENT]

Sled Dog Breeding and Training: Dog mushing is Alaska's official state sport, and Tok has become known as the "Sled Dog Capital of Alaska," with at least one out of every three people in town involved in some way with raising dogs. Kennels range in size from 100 dogs to a single family pet. Visitors who come to Tok seeking either a pet or a racing sled dog will probably find what they are looking for here.

The Siberian husky is the most popular sled dog and oftentimes has distinctive blue eyes. The Alaskan malamute is much larger than the Siberian and is used for hauling heavy loads at a slower pace. Both breeds are AKC recognized. The Alaskan husky (or husky) is a catchall term for any of the arctic breeds or northern types of dogs and is usually a cross. Sled dogs may be any registered breed or crossbreed, since mushers look for conformation, attitude and speed when putting together a working team rather than pedigrees. Common strains in racing dogs have included Irish setter, Labrador and wolf, among others.

Sled Dog Trails and Races: Tok boasts a well-known and long-established dog mushing trail, which draws many world-class and recreational mushers. The 20.5-mile/33-km trail begins at the rustic log Tok Dog Mushers Assoc. building at **Milepost DC 1312.8**

on the Alaska Highway. The trail is a favorite with spectators because it affords many miles of viewing from along the Alaska Highway.

Racing begins in late November and extends through the end of March. Junior mushers include one-, two-, three- and five-dog classes; junior adult mushers include five- and eight-dog classes. Open (unlimited) classes can run as many as 16 dogs.

The biggest race of the season in Tok is the Race of Champions, held in late March, which also has the largest entry of any sprint race in Alaska. Begun in 1954 as a bet between two roadhouse proprietors, today the Race of Champions includes over 100 teams in three classes competing for prize money and trophies. It is considered to be the third leg of sled dog racing's "triple crown," following the Fur Rendezvous in Anchorage and the Fairbanks North American Championship. Visitors are also welcome to attend the Tok Native Assoc.'s potlatch, held the same weekend as the race, in the Tok school gym.

AREA FISHING: Fly-in fishing to area lakes for northern pike, grayling and lake trout; inquire at Tok state airstrip. There are 43 lakes in the Delta-Tok area that are stocked by the Alaska Dept. of Fish and Game. Lakes are stocked primarily with rainbow trout; other stocked species include arctic grayling, lake trout, arctic char and king salmon. Most of these lakes are located close to the road system, but there are walk-in lakes available as well. Most easily accessible are **North Twin, South Twin** and **Mark Lake.** There is a trailhead 0.5 mile/0.8 km east of the Gerstle River bridge for **Big Donna Lake** (3.5-mile/5.6-km hike) and **Little Donna Lake** (4.5 miles/7.2 km). **Quartz Lake,** north of Delta Junction, is a popular spot for rainbow trout and silver salmon. Consult ADF&G offices in Tok or Delta Junction for other locations.

Alaska Highway Log

(continued)

DC 1315 (2116.2 km) **F 205** (329.9 km) **Tundra Lodge and RV Park.** See display ad this section. ▲

DC 1315.7 (2117.3 km) **F 204.3** (328.8 km) **Rita's Campground RV Park and Potpourri Gifts.** See display ad this section. ▲

DC 1316.6 (2118.8 km) **F 203.4** (327.3 km) Scoby Road, Sundog Trail. Access to bed and breakfast.

DC 1317 (2119.4 km) **F 203** (326.7 km) **Mukluk Land.** See display ad this section.

DC 1318.6 (2122 km) **F 201.4** (324.1 km) **Wildwood Bed & Breakfast.** See display ad this section.

DC 1322.6 (2128.5 km) **F 197.4** (317.7 km) Pringle Road; access to bed and breakfast and youth hostel. Tok youth hostel, housed in a wall tent, is located 0.8 mile/1.3 km south; 10 beds, tent space available.

Satyãgraha Guest Ranch B & B. Mile 1, Pringle Road. Enjoy a true frontier experience with enthusiastic Alaskans Tenny and C. Gordon Pool. Bed and breakfast offers two complete, private, housekeeping cabins in tall spruce. Each cabin sleeps up to five. Also, two fully equipped camper units. Parking for self-contained RVs. Open year-round. We have horses, a sled dog team, canoeing, winter ski-joring; sled dog weight-pulling demonstration on request. Reservations and information (907) 883-5226, P.O. Box 261, Tok, AK 99780. [ADVERTISEMENT]

DC 1324.6 (2131.7 km) **F 195.4** (314.5 km) Tanacross fireguard station.

DC 1324.7 (2131.8 km) **F 195.3** (314.3 km) Gravel access road to Tanacross airstrip. (See also **Milepost DC 1325.7**)

DC 1325.6 (2133.3 km) **F 194.4** (312.8 km) **Historic Milepost 1328.**

DC 1325.7 (2133.4 km) **F 194.3** (312.7 km) **Tanacross Junction.** End of paved bike trail from Tok and access to Tanacross.

Drive in 1.2 miles/1.9 km on gravel road to junction, turn left for village of **TANACROSS** (pop. 106), home of the once numerous branch of the Tanah, or Tinneh, Indians. This village of colorful modern houses is built on a short 0.7-mile/1.1-km loop road. Turn right at junction and drive 0.2 mile/0.3 km for access road to airstrip, or 0.3 mile/0.5 km to reach Tanana River and view across river of the white church steeple in the old village of Tanacross which burned down in 1979. Road eventually dead ends in residential area.

Private Aircraft: Tanacross airstrip; elev. 1,549 feet/472m; two runways, length 5,000 feet/1,524m and 5,100 feet/1,554m; asphalt; unattended.

DC 1327.4 (2136.2 km) **F 192.6** (310 km) Parking area at lake to north.

DC 1328 (2137.2 km) **F 192** (309 km) Watch for sections of patched pavement and frost heaves northbound to Dot Lake.

DC 1330.1 (2140.5 km) **F 189.9** (305.6 km) Paved turnout with litter container to east. View of Alaska Range to the west.

DC 1330.7 (2141.5 km) **F 189.3** (304.6 km) Paved turnout with litter barrels to east.

DC 1331.9 (2143.5 km) **F 188.1** (302.7 km) Moon Lake State Recreation Site, 0.2 mile/0.3 km north off highway; 15 campsites, toilets, tables, water, firepits, swimming (watch for floatplanes). Camping fee $8/night or annual pass. ▲

DC 1333.6 (2146.2 km) **F 186.4** (300 km) **Historic Milepost 1339.** Yerrick Creek bridge.

DC 1335 (2148.4 km) **F 185** (297.7 km) Watch for moose.

DC 1338.2 (2153.5 km) **F 181.8** (292.6 km) Highway crosses Cathedral Creeks three times between here and **Milepost DC 1339.**

DC 1342.2 (2160 km) **F 177.8** (286.1 km) Sheep Creek culvert.

DC 1344.5 (2163.8 km) **F 175.5** (282.4 km) **Historic Milepost 1352.** Double-ended paved parking area with litter barrels to east. Interpretive panel on the "father of the international highway," Donald MacDonald. Mentasta Mountains to the south. Good photo stop.

DC 1347.3 (2168.2 km) **F 172.7** (277.9 km) Entering Game Management Unit 20D northbound, Unit 12 southbound.

DC 1347.5 (2168.5 km) **F 172.5** (277.6 km) Robertson River bridge. The river was named by Lt. Henry T. Allen for a member of his 1885 expedition.

DC 1348 (2169.3 km) **F 172** (276.8 km) Bad frost heaves.

DC 1348.1 (2169.5 km) **F 171.9** (276.6 km) Side road west to parking lot at old Haines pipeline right-of-way. Hike in 0.3 mile/0.5 km for **Robertson No. 2 Lake;** rainbow fishing.

DC 1348.8 (2170.6 km) **F 171.2** (275.5 km) Bad frost heaves.

DC 1350.5 (2173.3 km) **F 169.5** (272.8 km) Double-ended paved turnout with litter barrels to west. Rough road next mile northbound.

DC 1353.7 (2178.5 km) **F 166.3** (267.6 km) Jan Lake Road. Drive in 0.5 mile/0.8 km to parking area with boat launch and toilets. No overnight camping, carry out garbage. **Jan Lake** is stocked with rainbow, use spinners, flies, or salmon eggs with bobber. Dot Lake Native Corp. land, limited public access.

DC 1357.3 (2184.4 km) **F 162.7** (261.8 km) Bear Creek bridge. Paved turnout to west.

DC 1358.7 (2186.6 km) **F 161.3** (259.6 km) Chief Creek bridge. Paved turnout with litter barrel to west at north end of bridge.

DC 1361.3 (2190.2 km) **F 158.7** (255.4 km) **DOT LAKE** (pop. 70). Gas, groceries, lodge restaurant, car wash, motel, camping and post office. Headquarters for the Dot Lake (Athabascan) Indian Corp. Homesteaded in the 1940s, a school was established here in 1952. Dot Lake's historic chapel was built in 1949. ▲

Dot Lake Lodge. See display ad this section. ▲

DC 1361.6 (2191 km) **F 158.4** (254.9 km) **Historic Milepost 1368.** Gravel turnout by lake to east. Rough narrow road northbound.

DC 1370.2 (2205.1 km) **F 149.8** (241.1 km) Double-ended paved parking area with litter barrels to east.

DC 1370.5 (2205.4 km) **F 149.5** (240.6 km) **Historic Milepost 1376.** Alaska Highway interpretive panel on "the Crooked Road."

DC 1371.5 (2207.2 km) **F 148.5** (239 km) Berry Creek bridge. Parking area to west.

DC 1374.2 (2211.5 km) **F 145.8** (234.6 km) Sears Creek bridge. Parking area with litter barrel to west.

DC 1376 (2214.4 km) **F 144** (231.7 km) Entering Tok Management Area, Tanana

State Forest southbound.

DC 1378 (2217.6 km) **F 142** (228.5 km) Bridge over Dry Creek. Evidence of forest fire next mile northbound.

DC 1379 (2219.2 km) **F 141** (226.9 km) Double-ended paved turnout to west with mountain views.

DC 1380.5 (2221.6 km) **F 139.5** (224.5 km) Johnson River bridge. A tributary of the Tanana River, the Johnson River was named by Lt. Henry T. Allen in 1887 for Peder Johnson, a Swedish miner and member of his party. Road narrows northbound.

*NOTE: Watch for road construction northbound to **Milepost DC 1412** in 1994.*

DC 1381.1 (2222.6 km) **F 138.9** (223.5 km) Bumpy paved turnout to west. Access road to **Lisa Lake** (stocked). Watch for patches of rough pavement northbound.

DC 1383.9 (2227.1 km) **F 136.1** (219 km) **Craig Lake** access west side of highway via 0.5-mile/0.8-km trail; rainbow trout fishing.

DC 1385 (2228.9 km) **F 135** (217.3 km) Double-ended gravel turnout.

DC 1388.4 (2234.4 km) **F 131.6** (211.8 km) Little Gerstle River bridge.

DC 1391.9 (2240 km) **F 128.1** (206.2 km) Trailhead to **Big Donna Lake**, 3.5 miles/5.6 km, and **Little Donna Lake**, 4.5 miles/7.2 km; stocked with rainbow.

DC 1392.3 (2240.6 km) **F 127.7** (205.5 km) Cummings Road through Delta barley project. *CAUTION: Watch for buffalo (bison) on highway between here and Delta Junction.*

On the southwest side of the Alaska Highway approaching Delta Junction is the Bison Range. This range provides the bison herd with autumn and winter grazing on over 3,000 acres of grassland. It was developed to reduce agricultural crop depredation by bison.

DC 1392.7 (2241.3 km) **F 127.3** (204.9 km) Gerstle River bridge. The river was named for Lewis Gerstle, president of the Alaska Commercial Co., by Lt. Henry T. Allen, whose 1885 expedition explored the Copper, Tanana and Koyukuk river regions for the U.S. Army Dept. of the Columbia.

DC 1401 (2254.7 km) **F 119** (191.5 km) Double-ended gravel turnout to northeast.

DC 1403.6 (2258.8 km) **F 116.4** (187.3 km) Sawmill Creek Road to northeast. This rough gravel road goes through the heart of the Delta barley fields. A sign just off the highway explains the barley project. Visiting farmers are welcome to talk with local farmers along the road, except during planting (May) and harvesting (August or September) when they are too busy.

DC 1403.9 (2259.3 km) **F 116.1** (186.8 km) Sawmill Creek bridge.

DC 1408 (2265.9 km) **F 112** (180.2 km) Entrance to University of Alaska Agricultural and Forestry Experiment Station. Major research at this facility concentrates on agricultural cropping, fertilization and tillage management.

DC 1410 (2269.1 km) **F 110** (177 km) Access road north to Delta barley project.

DC 1411.7 (2271.8 km) **F 108.3** (174.3 km) Double-ended gravel turnout. Scenic view of Alaska Range to south.

DC 1412.5 (2273.2 km) **F 107.5** (173 km) **Cherokee Lodge & RV Park.** You won't regret this stop! Owned and operated by a lifelong Alaskan, offering true Alaskan hospitality and food. Full menu, including reindeer sausage breakfasts, "blue ribbon chili"! (Winner at Deltana State Fair Chili Cook-off for last two years.) Try our halibut! Hand-picked right off the fishing boats and a favorite among locals, visitors and truckers. Well-stocked cocktail lounge and liquor store. Ice cold beer and spirits "to go." Clean, reasonable rooms, pay phones, ice

and showers. Shaded RV park includes electric hookups, water, dump station, fire pits and picnic tables. See the "Arctic Train" with tires over 9 feet high and 4 feet wide. Want to see Alaska's beauty up close? Do it on horseback! Trail rides available through our neighbors at Rockin G Ranch. Sack lunches made to order for fire fighters, construction crews, bird and bison hunters. Hunters, please call Gary for hunting and weather updates. Open daily June 1–Oct. 1. Winters we are closed Mondays. Your host: Gary Schoening (907) 895-4814. [ADVERTISEMENT] ▲

DC 1413.3 (2274.4 km) **F 106.7** (171.7 km) Grain storage facility.

DC 1414.9 (2277 km) **F 105.1** (169.1 km) Clearwater Road leads north past farmlands to Clearwater State Recreation Site campground and junctions with Remington Road. Stay on pavement leading to Jack Warren

Road, which goes west to the Richardson Highway at **Milepost DC 1424.4 (V 268.4).** Good opportunity to see area agriculture; see Delta Vicinity map this section.

To reach the state campground, follow Clearwater Road 5.2 miles/8.4 km north to junction with Remington Road; turn right and drive 2.8 miles/4.5 km east for Clearwater state campground on bank of stream. There are 15 campsites, toilets, tables, firepits, water and boat ramp. Camping fee $6/night or annual pass. Grocery and lodge nearby. ▲

Delta–Clearwater River (boat needed for best fishing), beautiful spring-fed stream, grayling and whitefish; silver salmon spawn here in October. **Goodpaster River,** accessible by boat via Delta–Clearwater and Tanana rivers; excellent grayling fishing.

DC 1415.4 (2277.8 km) **F 104.6** (168.3 km) Dorshorst Road; access to homestead farm and private museum, open to public June 1 to Sept. 15, admission charged.

Alaska Homestead & Historical Museum. See display ad this section.

DC 1420.2 (2285.5 km) **F 99.8** (160.6 km) Restaurant.

DC 1420.7 (2286.3 km) **F 99.3** (159.8 km) Alaska State Troopers.

DC 1420.9 (2286.7 km) **F 99.1** (159.5 km) **Bergstad's Travel and Trailer Court.** See display ad this section. ▲

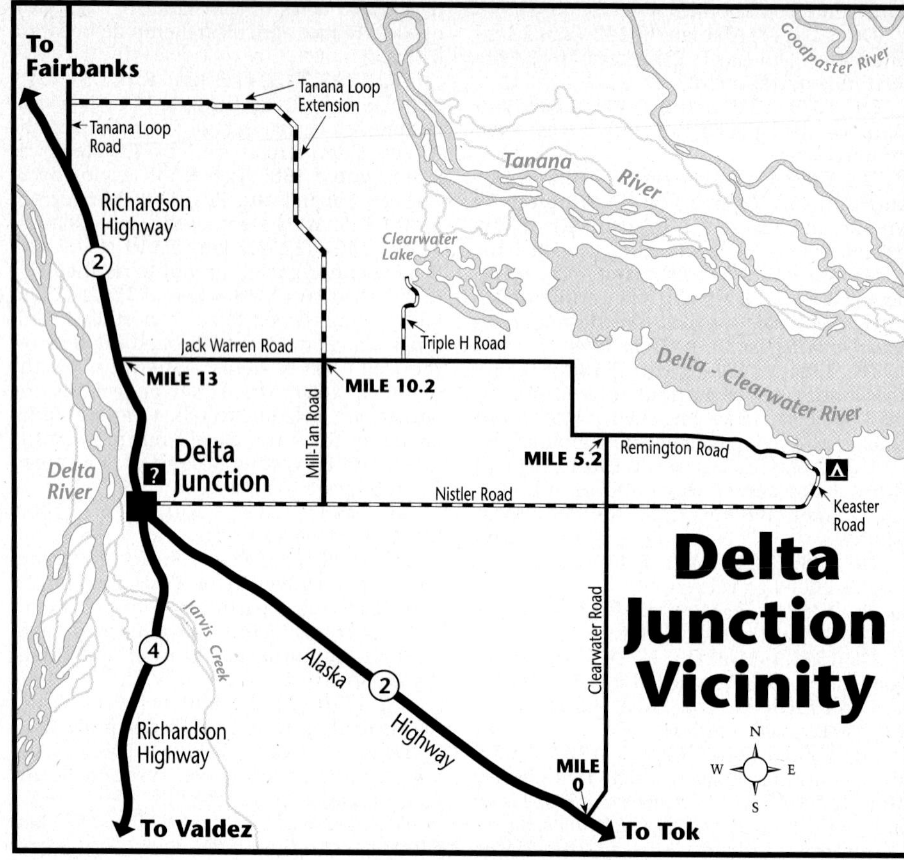

Delta Junction

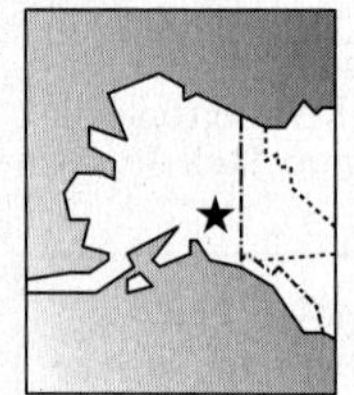

DC 1422 (2288.4 km) **F 98** (157.7 km) **V 266** (428.1 km). Located at the junction of the Alaska and Richardson highways. **Population:** 736. **Emergency Services:** Emergencies only phone 911. **Alaska State Troopers,** in the Jarvis Office Center at **Milepost DC 1420.5,** phone 895-4800. **Fire Department** and **Ambulance Service,** emergency only phone 911. **Clinics.** One doctor in private practice.

Visitor Information: Junction of Alaska and Richardson highways. Open daily 8:30 A.M. to 7:30 P.M., mid-May to mid-September, phone 895-9941 for information. Visitor center garden with local grains, flowers and vegetables. Pay phone located here. Highway information, phone 451-2207. Dept. of Fish and Game at north edge of town, **Milepost DC 1422.8;** phone 895-4632.

Elevation: 1,180 feet/360m. **Climate:** Mean monthly temperature in January, -15°F/-26°C; in July 58°F/14°C. Record low was -66°F/-54°C in January 1989; record high was 88°F/31°C in August 1990. Mean monthly precipitation in July, 2.57 inches/6.5cm. **Radio:** KUAC-FM 91.7 broadcasts from University of Alaska Fairbanks; Fort Greely broadcasts on 90.5 FM. **Television:** Three channels from Fairbanks.

Private Aircraft: Delta Junction airstrip, 1 mile/1.6 km north; elev. 1,150 feet/350m; length 2,400 feet/731m; gravel. Allen Army Airfield, 3 miles/4.8 km south; elev. 1,277 feet/389m; three asphalt-surfaced runways available, length to 7,500 feet/2,286m; fuel J4; joint-use military/civil airport (prior permission required).

Delta Junction is at the actual end of the Alaska Highway. From here, the Richardson Highway leads to Fairbanks. (*The MILEPOST®*

DELTA JUNCTION ADVERTISERS

Alaska Mechanical Fuel.....Ph. (907) 895-4067
Alaska 7 Motel.....Mile 270.3 Richardson Hwy.
Alaskan Designer Parkas...At the visitor center
Bed & Breakfast at the Home of Alys.........Ph. (907) 895-4128
Buffalo Center Auto Parts..........................Ph. (907) 895-4251
City Park Carwash...............Behind post office
Delta Self Service Laundry and Cleaners..........Mile 267.5 Richardson Hwy.
Delta Shop-Rite.....0.5 mile N. of visitor center
Delta Visitor Information Center.....................Mile 1422 Alaska Hwy.
Delta Windshield Repair..1202 Clearwater Rd.
Diehl's Shopping Center.............0.5 mile N. of visitor center
Granite View Sports.................Across from visitor center
Jack's Chevron and Jack's Liquor Store...............Mile 265.8 Richardson Hwy.
Kelly's Country Inn Motel.....................Ph. (907) 895-4667
Miner's House and Hide-a-way...........2 blks. S. of visitor center
OK Fuel Company........Across from post office
Pizza Bella Family Restaurant...........Across from visitor center
Riverside Trading Post......Ph. (907) 895-4674
Smith's Green Acres RV Park...................Mile 268 Richardson Hwy.

logs this stretch of highway as a continuation of the Alaska Highway.) Have your picture taken with the monument in front of the visitor center that marks the highway's end. The chamber of commerce visitor center also has free brochures and displays of Alaska wildflowers, mounted animals, and furs to touch. Travelers may also purchase certificates here, certifying that they have reached the end of the Alaska Highway.

Delta Junction is also the first view of the trans-Alaska pipeline for travelers coming up the Alaska Highway from Canada. A good spot to see and photograph the pipeline is at **Milepost V 275.4**, 9.5 miles/15.3 km north of town, where the pipeline crosses the Tanana River. Pump station No. 9, accessible from **Milepost V 258.3** Richardson Highway, offers free daily tours in summer; stop by or phone 869-3270. There is also an interesting display of pipe used in three Alaska pipeline projects outside the visitor center in Delta Junction.

Named after the nearby Delta River, Delta Junction began as a construction camp on the Richardson Highway in 1919. (It was first known as Buffalo Center because of the American bison that were transplanted here in the 1920s.)

The Richardson Highway, connecting Valdez at tidewater with Fairbanks in the Interior, predates the Alaska Highway by 20 years. The Richardson was already a wagon road in 1910, and was updated to automobile standards in the 1920s by the Alaska Road Commission (ARC).

In the last decade, the state has encouraged development of the agricultural industry in the Delta area. In 1978, the state began Delta Agricultural Project I, disposing of 60,000 acres and creating 22 farms averaging approximately 2,700 acres each. In 1982, the Delta II project disposed of 25,000 acres, creating 15 farms averaging more than 1,600 acres each.

In 1993, nearly 40,000 acres were in some form of agricultural use (including production of barley, oats, wheat, forage, pasture, grass seed, canola, potatoes, field peas, forage brassicas) and conservation use. Barley is the major feed grain grown in Delta. It is an excellent energy feed for

cattle, hogs and sheep. Production acreages are determined by the in-state demand for barley.

Delta barley is stored on farms or in a local co-op elevator, sold on the open market, or used to feed livestock. Small-scale farming of vegetables, two commercial potato farms, five active dairies, a dairy processing center, six beef producers, two beef feedlots, three swine producers, a bison ranch and two commercial greenhouses all contribute to Delta Junction's agriculture.

ACCOMMODATIONS

Delta Junction has motels, restaurants, gas stations, a laundromat and dry cleaners, a coin-operated car wash, a shopping center, post office, bank and other businesses. There are several churches. Delta Community Park, on Kimball Street one block off the highway, has softball and soccer fields.

Delta international hostel north of town: turn at **Milepost V 271.7** (Tanana Loop Road), drive 1 mile/1.6 km and turn right on Tanana Loop Extension then left on a gravel road named Main Street, USA (follow signs). Sleeping bags are required. Fee: $7 per night. Hostel open Memorial Day through Labor Day; phone 895-5074.

There are private RV parks just south and just north of town. Two public campgrounds are located nearby: Delta state campground at **Milepost V 267.1**, and Clearwater state campground on Remington Road (see **Milepost DC 1414.9** and **V 268.3**). ▲

Alaska 7 Motel, 16 large, clean, comfortable rooms with full bath and showers. Color TV and courtesy coffee in each room. Kitchenettes and phone available. Comfort at a comfortable price. Open year-round. Major credit cards accepted. Milepost 270.3 Richardson–Alaska Highway. (907) 895-4848. See display ad this section. [ADVERTISEMENT]

TRANSPORTATION

Air: Scheduled service via 40-Mile Air from Tok to Fairbanks; Delta stop on request. Local air service available. **Bus:** See Bus Lines in the GENERAL INFORMATION section for scheduled service to other communities.

ATTRACTIONS

Buffalo Herd: American bison were transplanted into the Delta Junction area in the 1920s. Because the bison have become costly pests to many farmers in the Delta area, the 70,000-acre Delta Bison Range was created south of the Alaska Highway in 1980. However, keeping the bison on their refuge and out of the barley fields is a continuing problem. Summer visitors who wish to look at the bison are advised to visit the viewpoint at **Milepost V 241.3** on the Richardson Highway; use binoculars. The herd contained 482 bison in 1992 when the last census was taken by the ADF&G.

Special Events: Delta Junction celebrates a traditional Fourth of July with a Buffalo Barbecue, sponsored by the Pioneers. Buffalo Wallow, a 4-day square dance festival hosted by Buffalo Squares, is held every Memorial Day weekend. The Buffalo Squares also sponsor a campout and dance at Delta state campground the second Saturday in July.

The Deltana Fair is held the first Friday, Saturday and Sunday in August. The fair includes a barbecue, Lions' pancake breakfast, local handicrafts, horse show, livestock display and show, games, concessions, contests and a parade. A highlight of the fair is the Great Alaska Outhouse Race, held on Sunday, in which four pushers and one sitter compete for the coveted "Golden Throne" award.

Tour the agriculture of the area by driving Sawmill Creek Road (turn off at **Milepost DC 1403.6** Alaska Highway) and Clearwater Road (see **Milepost DC 1414.9**). Sawmill Creek Road goes through the heart of the grain-producing Delta Ag Project and local farmers welcome visiting farmers' questions in between planting and harvesting. Along Clearwater and Remington roads you may view the older farms, which produce forage crops and livestock. Tanana Loop Road (**Milepost V 271.7**), Tanana Loop Extension and Mill–Tan Road also go past many farms. The visitor information center in downtown Delta Junction can answer many questions on local agriculture.

AREA FISHING: Delta–Clearwater River, grayling and whitefish; silver salmon spawn here in October. Access via Clearwater Road or Jack Warren Road (see Delta Vicinity map). (Although USGS topographic maps show this tributary of the Tanana River as Clearwater Creek, local residents refer to the stream as the Delta–Clearwater River.) **Goodpaster River,** accessible by boat via Delta–Clearwater and Tanana rivers; excellent grayling fishing.

There are 43 lakes in the Delta-Tok area that are stocked by the Alaska Dept. of Fish and Game. Lakes are stocked primarily with rainbow trout, and also with arctic grayling, lake trout, arctic char and king salmon. Most of these lakes are located close to the road system, but there are walk-in lakes available as well. **Quartz Lake**, at **Milepost V 277.7** north of Delta Junction, is the largest and most easily accessed of area lakes; angler success is excellent. Consult ADF&G offices in Delta or Tok for other locations.

Richardson–Alaska Highway Log

Although logged as a natural extension of the Alaska Highway, the highway between Delta Junction and Fairbanks is designated as part of the Richardson Highway, with existing mileposts showing distance from Valdez.

Distance from Valdez (V) is followed by distance from Dawson Creek (DC) and distance from Fairbanks (F).

V 266 (428 km) **DC 1422** (2288.5 km) **F 98** (157.7 km) Delta Junction visitor information center sits at the junction of the Alaska and Richardson highways. Turn south for Valdez (see RICHARDSON HIGHWAY section). Continue north for Fairbanks.

V 266.3 (428.6 km) **DC 1422.3** (2289 km) **F 97.7** (157.2 km) Delta Junction post office.

V 266.4 (428.7 km) **DC 1422.4** (2289.1 km) **F 97.6** (157.1 km) **City Park Carwash.** New high-pressure coin-operated car wash with seven special wash selections. Extra-tall RV bay. Change machine and vendors. Our bubble brush is famous for removing that Alcan Highway mud. Open 24 hours, seven days. Turn on Kimball Street. We're two blocks off Richardson–Alaska Highway behind post office. Watch for our sign. (907) 895-4306. [ADVERTISEMENT]

V 266.5 (428.9 km) **DC 1422.5** (2289.2 km) **F 97.5** (156.9 km) Delta Junction library and city hall.

V 266.8 (429.4 km) **DC 1422.8** (2289.7 km) **F 97.2** (156.4 km) Alaska Dept. of Fish and Game office.

V 267 (429.7 km) **DC 1423** (2290 km) **F 97** (156.1 km) BLM airstrip; current status unknown.

V 267.1 (429.8 km) **DC 1423.1** (2290.2 km) **F 96.9** (155.9 km) Delta state campground to east; 24 sites, water, tables, shelter with covered tables, toilets, $8 nightly fee or annual pass. Large turnout at campground entrance. Turnout on west side of highway on bank of the Delta River offers excellent views of the Alaska Range. ▲

V 267.2 (430 km) **DC 1423.2** (2290.4 km) **F 96.8** (155.7 km) Alaska Division of Forestry office.

V 267.5 (430.5 km) **DC 1423.5** (2290.9 km) **F 96.5** (155.3 km) Laundromat with showers.

V 267.9 (431.1 km) **DC 1423.9** (2291.5 km) **F 96.1** (154.7 km) Private RV park. ▲

V 268.3 (431.7 km) **DC 1424.3** (2292.1 km) **F 95.7** (154 km) **Junction** with Jack Warren Road (see Delta Vicinity map this section). Turn here for access to Clearwater state campground (10.5 miles/16.9 km). Clearwater campground has toilets, tables, water and boat launch; pleasant campsites on bank of river. Camping fee $6/night or annual pass. ▲

Driving this loop is a good opportunity to see local homesteads. Gas station on Clearwater Road near Mile 5.2; grocery and lodge on Remington Road near campground. Note that mileposts on these paved side roads run backward from Mile 13 at this junction to Mile 0 at the junction of Clearwater Road and the Alaska Highway.

V 270.3 (435 km) **DC 1426.3** (2295.3 km) **F 93.7** (150.8 km) Motel.

V 271 (436.1 km) **DC 1427** (2296.5 km) **F 93** (149.7 km) Medical clinic.

V 271.7 (437.2 km) **DC 1427.7** (2297.6 km) **F 92.3** (148.5 km) Tanana Loop Road. Turn here for Delta Junction youth hostel. To make a loop drive through farmlands, follow Tanana Loop Road approximately 1 mile/1.6 km, turn right on Tanana Loop

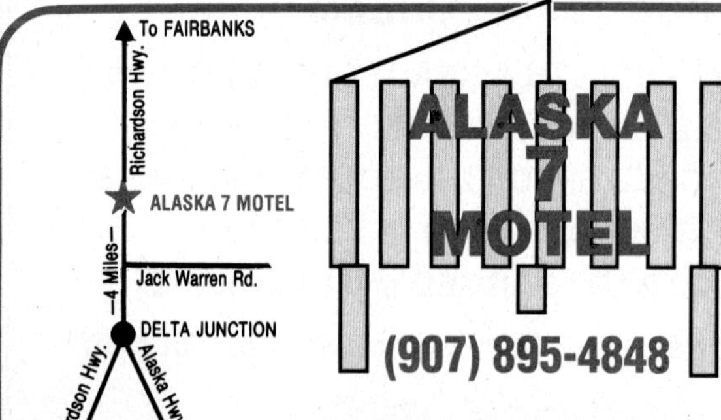

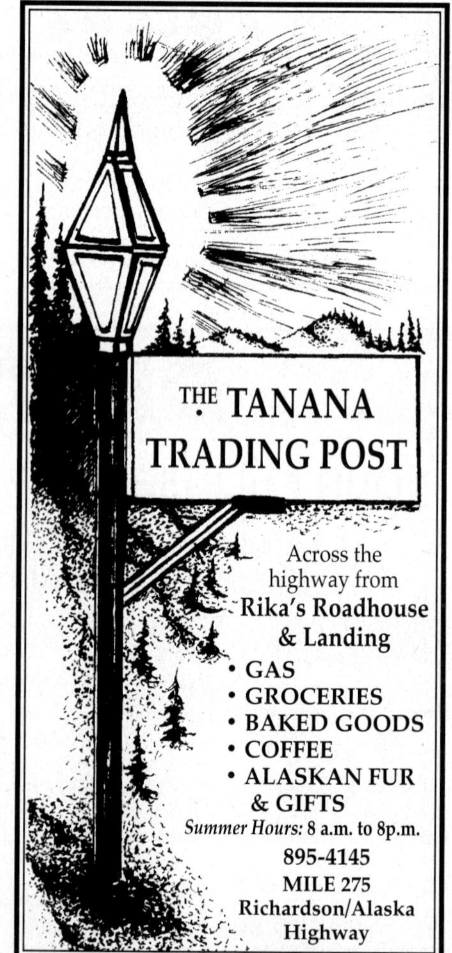

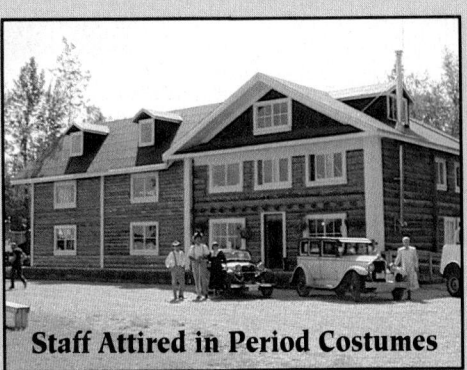

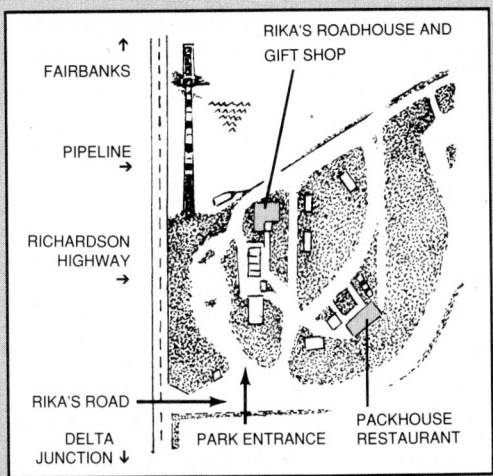

U.S. Army troops train on the Tanana River at the pipeline bridge at Milepost V 275.4 Alaska Highway. (Jerrianne Lowther, staff)

Extension, which connects with Jack Warren Road. Turn west on Jack Warren Road to return to highway.

V 272.1 (437.9 km) **DC 1428** (2298 km) **F 92** (148 km) Fire station.

V 275 (442.6 km) **DC 1431** (2303.9 km) **F 89** (143.2 km) **The Tanana Trading Post.** See display ad this section.

V 275 (442.6 km) **DC 1431** (2303.9 km) **F 89** (143.2 km) **Rika's Roadhouse at Big Delta State Historical Park.** Turn northeast at Rika's Road for Rika's Roadhouse and Landing on the banks of the Tanana River. Tour buses welcome. Parking areas with restrooms at both park entrances. The newly renovated Rika's Roadhouse offers worldwide postal service and gift shop specializing in fox furs, gold and diamond willow. Visit the sod-roofed museum, barn, Signal Corp

station and other historic structures. Local artisans at work. Live farm animals. Guides in period costumes are available to walk with you through the history of this important crossroads on the Valdez–Fairbanks trail. Meals served 9 A.M. to 5 P.M. in our Packhouse Restaurant, home of the Alaska Baking Co. Try our famous bear claws and homemade muffins. The Packhouse Restaurant also offers homemade soups, fresh salads and sandwiches. Guests rave about our homemade pies, featuring strawberry–rhubarb, pecan, chocolate truffle and coconut cream. Overnight RV parking and dump station. After the dust of the highway, the green gardens of the 10-acre park are a welcome haven. Brochure available. P.O. Box 1229, Delta Junction, AK 99737. Phone (907) 895-4201 or 895-4938 anytime. Free admission. Handicapped access. See display ad this section. [ADVERTISEMENT] ♿

Rika's Roadhouse, which reopened in 1986 after extensive restoration, was built in 1910 by John Hajdukovich. In 1923, Hajdukovich sold it to Rika Wallen, a Swedish immigrant who had managed the roadhouse since 1917. Rika ran the roadhouse into the late 1940s and lived there until her death in 1969. Big Delta State Historical Park campground; camping fee $6/vehicle, dump station ($3). ▲

V 275.4 (443.2 km) **DC 1431.4** (2303.6 km) **F 88.6** (142.6 km) Big Delta Bridge across the Tanana River; spectacular view of pipeline suspended across river. Slow down for parking area at south end of bridge with litter barrels and interpretive sign about pipeline.

From here to Fairbanks there are views of the Tanana River and the Alaska Range to the south. Farming community of **BIG DELTA** (pop. 400); gas, store, two bars, a church, Kenner Sawmill and Tanana River boat landing.

V 277.7 (446.9 km) **DC 1433.7** (2307.2 km) **F 86.3** (138.9 km) Turnoff to east for Quartz Lake Recreation Area. Drive in 2.5 miles/4 km on gravel road to intersection: turn left for Lost Lake, continue straight ahead for Quartz Lake (another 0.3 mile/0.5 km). Lost Lake, 0.2 mile/0.3 km from intersection, has eight campsites with picnic tables, toilet and a large parking area with tables and litter barrels. A shallow, picturesque lake with no fish. Quartz Lake has more developed campsites on good loop road, firepits, water, tables, toilet and two boat launches. Boat launch fee $3 or annual boat launch pass. Camping fees at both campgrounds: $6/night or annual pass. A trail connects Lost Lake and Quartz Lake camping areas. Excellent fishing for rainbow and silver salmon in **Quartz Lake.** Boat and motor rentals available from Black Spruce Lodge. ▲

V 277.9 (447.2 km) **DC 1433.9** (2307.5 km) **F 86.1** (138.6 km) Former U.S. Army petroleum station, now closed. Pay phone beside highway.

V 278.2 (447.7 km) **DC 1434.2** (2308 km) **F 85.8** (138.1 km) South end of long double-ended turnout to west. Several of these long turnouts northbound are old sections of the Alaska Highway.

V 280.3 (451.1 km) **DC 1436.3** (2311.4 km) **F 83.7** (134.7 km) Gravel turnout to east.

V 284 (457 km) **DC 1440** (2317.4 km) **F 80** (128.7 km) Watch for moose.

V 286.6 (461.2 km) **DC 1442.6** (2321.6 km) **F 77.4** (124.6 km) Shaw Creek bridge.

V 286.7 (461.4 km) **DC 1442.7** (2321.7 km) **F 77.3** (124.4 km) **Shaw Creek** road. Good to excellent early spring and fall grayling fishing; subject to closure (check locally). Good view northbound of Tanana River which parallels the highway. Fireweed and pale oxytrope along roadsides in summer.

V 287.2 (462.2 km) **DC 1443.2** (2322.5 km) **F 76.8** (123.6 km) Turnout and road to slough to east. Birch trees are thick along this stretch of highway.

V 288 (463.5 km) **DC 1444** (2323.8 km) **F 76** (122.3 km) Panoramic view to the south with vistas of three great peaks of the Alaska Range: Mount Hayes, elev. 13,832 feet/4,216m, almost due south; Hess Mountain, elev. 11,940 feet/3,639m, to the west (right) of Mount Hayes; and Mount Deborah, elev. 12,339 feet/3,761m, to the west (right) of Hess Mountain. Mount Hayes is named for Charles Hayes, an early member of the U.S. Geological Survey. Mount Deborah was named in 1907 by the famous Alaskan Judge Wickersham for his wife.

V 289.8 (466.4 km) **DC 1445.8** (2326.7 km) **F 74.2** (119.4 km) Paved double-ended turnout to east.

V 291.8 (469.6 km) **DC 1447.8** (2329.9 km) **F 72.2** (116.2 km) Northbound truck lane begins.

V 292.8 (471.2 km) **DC 1448.8** (2331.5 km) **F 71.2** (114.6 km) Truck lane ends. View of Tanana River valley.

V 294 (473.1 km) **DC 1450** (2333.5 km) **F 70** (112.7 km) Paved double-ended turnout.

V 294.2 (473.5 km) **DC 1450.2** (2333.8 km) **F 69.8** (112.3 km) Southbound truck lane begins.

V 294.9 (474.6 km) **DC 1450.9** (2334.9 km) **F 69.1** (111.2 km) Game Management Unit boundary between 20B and 20D. Entering Fairbanks North Star borough northbound.

V 295 (474.7 km) **DC 1451** (2335.1 km) **F 69** (111 km) Site of the original old Richardson Roadhouse, which burned down in December 1982.

V 295.4 (475.4 km) **DC 1451.4** (2335.7

km) **F 68.6** (110.4 km) Banner Creek bridge; historic placer gold stream.

V 296.4 (477 km) **DC 1452.4** (2337.3 km) **F 67.6** (108.8 km) Paved turnout to west; view of Alaska Range and Tanana River to south.

V 297.7 (479.1 km) **DC 1453.7** (2339.4 km) **F 66.3** (106.7 km) Large gravel parking area to west below highway; good scenic viewpoint. Paved access road to Tanana River.

V 298.2 (479.9 km) **DC 1454.2** (2340.2 km) **F 65.8** (105.9 km) Scenic viewpoint; paved double-ended turnout to west.

V 301.7 (485.5 km) **DC 1457.7** (2345.9 km) **F 62.3** (100.3 km) South end of long double-ended turnout to west.

V 304.3 (489.7 km) **DC 1460.3** (2350 km) **F 59.7** (96.1 km) Small paved turnout to east.

V 305.2 (491.2 km) **DC 1461.2** (2351.5 km) **F 58.8** (94.6 km) Birch Lake Road to east; access to military recreation area (restricted).

Birch Lake Military Recreation Area: access road, 0.5 mile to entrance; area restricted to United States military and government employees, active or retired; open Memorial Day to Labor Day; beach, lodge, boat rental, 22 cabins, 40 camper slots (electricity only), 14 tent sites. Reservations recommended; address 354 Services Squadron/SSRO, 3112 Broadway, Eielson AFB, AK 99702; telephone, (907) 377-1839/(907) 488-6161. [ADVERTISEMENT]

V 306 (492.4 km) **DC 1462** (2352.8 km) **F 58** (93.3 km) Large parking area with toilet to east overlooking **Birch Lake**; unimproved gravel boat launch and beach; fish from shore in spring, from boat in summer, for rainbow and silver salmon. Birch Lake is the site of summer homes of many Fairbanks residents.

V 306.1 (492.6 km) **DC 1462.1** (2352.9 km) **F 57.9** (93.2 km) Turnoff to west for **Lost Lake**. Drive in 0.7 mile/1.1 km on dirt road; silver salmon fishing.

V 307.2 (494.3 km) **DC 1463.2** (2354.7 km) **F 56.8** (91.4 km) Birch Lake highway maintenance station.

V 308.4 (496.3 km) **DC 1464.4** (2356.6 km) **F 55.6** (89.5 km) South end of long double-ended turnout to east.

V 310 (498.9 km) **DC 1466** (2359.2 km) **F 54** (86.9 km) Double-ended paved parking area to west.

V 313 (503.7 km) **DC 1469** (2364 km) **F 51** (82.1 km) Paved double-ended turnout to west. Access to **Silver Fox Pond**; stocked with arctic char.

V 314.8 (506.6 km) **DC 1470.8** (2366.9 km) **F 49.2** (79.2 km) **Midway Lodge** is open 7 A.M. to midnight daily. Bar open till midnight daily. Breakfast anytime, famous homemade chili, royal ½-pound hamburgers, fresh pies. Clean rooms starting at $35.

Showers. Gifts. We are a family-oriented stop on the Alaska Highway and welcome your visit. 11191 Richardson Highway, Salcha, AK 99714. Phone (907) 488-2939. [ADVERTISEMENT]

V 317.9 (511.6 km) **DC 1473.9** (2371.9 km) **F 45.4** (73.1 km) Double-ended gravel turnout to west.

V 319.3 (513.8 km) **DC 1475.3** (2374.2 km) **F 44.7** (71.9 km) Access road leads east to Harding Lake summer homes.

V 319.8 (514.7 km) **DC 1475.8** (2375 km) **F 44.2** (71.1 km) Second access road northbound leads east to Harding Lake summer homes. Access to **Little Harding Lake**, king salmon fishing.

V 321.5 (517.4 km) **DC 1477.5** (2377.8 km) **F 42.5** (68.4 km) **Harding Lake** State Recreation Area turnoff; drive east 1.5 miles/2.4 km on paved road to campground. Park headquarters, drinking water fill-up and dump station ($3 charge) at campground entrance. Picnic grounds on lakeshore, swimming, boat ramp ($3 launch fee or annual boat launch pass), ball fields and about 80 campsites. Camping fee $6/night or annual pass. Fishing for lake trout, arctic char, burbot, northern pike, salmon and trout. Lake is reported to be "hard to fish." Worth the drive! *Bring your insect repellent. You may need it!*

V 322.2 (518.5 km) **DC 1478.2** (2378.9 km) **F 41.8** (67.3 km) Salcha post office and lodge with food, gas and camping.

Salcha River Lodge. Alaskan hospitality. Gas, diesel, propane, RV parking, clean showers, modern motel, groceries, restaurant, gift shop, post office. Ice cream cones, shakes, sundaes, homemade pie. Mounted Alaska trophies on display. Close to rivers and lakes; excellent fishing. 9162 Richardson Highway, Salcha, AK 99714. Phone (907) 488-2233. [ADVERTISEMENT]

V 323.1 (520 km) **DC 1479.1** (2380.3 km) **F 40.9** (65.8 km) **Salcha River** State Recreation Site; large parking area with 75 sites, boat ramp ($3 launch fee or annual boat launch pass), picnic area, toilets and water. Camping fee $6/night per vehicle or annual pass. Fishing for king and chum salmon, grayling, sheefish, northern pike and burbot.

V 323.4 (520.4 km) **DC 1479.4** (2380.8 km) **F 40.6** (65.3 km) Salcha River bridge.

V 324 (521.4 km) **DC 1480** (2381.7 km) **F 40** (64.4 km) Clear Creek bridge.

V 324.6 (522.4 km) **DC 1480.6** (2382.7 km) **F 39.4** (63.4 km) Double-ended gravel turnout to east.

V 324.8 (522.7 km) **DC 1480.8** (2383 km) **F 39.2** (63.1 km) Munsons Slough bridge.

V 325.5 (523.8 km) **DC 1481.5** (2384.2 km) **F 38.5** (62 km) The community of **SALCHA** (pop. 354) stretches along the highway in both directions. The elementary school is located here. The post office (Zip 99714) is at **Milepost V 322.2.**

V 326.4 (525.3 km) **DC 1482.4** (2385.6 km) **F 37.6** (60.5 km) Salcha Baptist church to west.

V 327 (526.2 km) **DC 1483** (2386.6 km) **F 37** (59.5 km) Picturesque log home to west.

V 327.7 (527.4 km) **DC 1483.7** (2387.7 km) **F 36.3** (58.4 km) Little Salcha River bridge.

V 328.3 (528.3 km) **DC 1484.3** (2388.7 km) **F 35.7** (57.4 km) **Salcha Store and Service.** See display ad this section.

V 332.2 (534.6 km) **DC 1488.2** (2395 km) **F 31.8** (51.2 km) Access east to **31-Mile Pond**; stocked with arctic char.

V 332.3 (534.8 km) **DC 1488.3** (2395.1 km) **F 31.7** (51 km) **The Knotty Shop.** Stop and be impressed by a truly unique Alaskan gift shop and wildlife museum. Jim and Paula have attempted to maintain a genuine Alaskan flavor — from the unusual burl construction to the Alaskan wildlife displayed in a natural setting to the handcrafted Alaskan gifts. Don't miss the opportunity to stop and browse. See display ad this section. Show us *The MILEPOST®* advertisement for a free small ice cream cone. [ADVERTISEMENT]

V 334.5 (538.3 km) **DC 1490.5** (2398.7 km) **F 29.5** (47.5 km) Public dumpster at gravel pit.

V 334.7 (538.6 km) **DC 1490.7** (2399 km) **F 29.3** (47.2 km) South boundary of Eielson AFB. Watch for various military aircraft taking off and landing to the east. Aircraft include Air Force F-16s, F-15s, KC-135s, C-130s, C-141s, OA-10s, Navy A-6s, F-14s and others.

V 335.1 (539.3 km) **DC 1491.1** (2399.6 km) **F 28.9** (46.5 km) Access east to **28-Mile Pond;** stocked with rainbow and silver salmon.

V 340.7 (548.3 km) **DC 1496.7** (2408.6 km) **F 23.3** (37.5 km) Divided highway begins for northbound traffic. *CAUTION: Watch for heavy traffic southbound turning east into the base, 7-8 A.M., and merging northbound traffic, 3:45-5:30 P.M., weekdays.*

V 341 (548.8 km) **DC 1497** (2409.1 km) **F 23** (37 km) Entrance to **EIELSON AIR FORCE BASE**, constructed in 1943 and named for Carl Ben Eielson, a famous Alaskan bush pilot. A weekly tour is offered. Phone the Public Affairs office at (907) 377-1410 for reservations and more information.

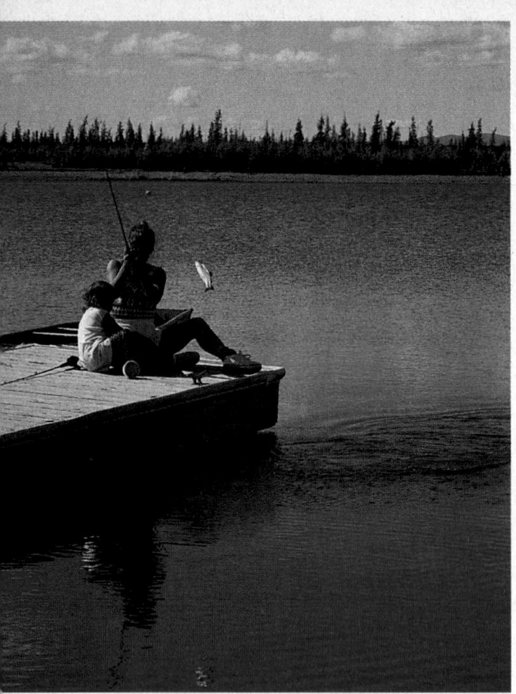

A mother and daughter land a fish at Chena Lakes Recreation Area. The lake is stocked with silver salmon, arctic char, grayling and rainbow trout.

(Jerrianne Lowther, staff)

V 343.7 (553.1 km) **DC 1499.7** (2413.5 km) **F 20.3** (32.7 km) Moose Creek Road and general store; diesel, gas, wrecker service.

Piledriver Slough parallels the highway from here north, flowing into the Tanana River. It is stocked with rainbow trout. Check with general store for access and fishing information. **Bathing Beauty Pond,** stocked with rainbow, arctic char and grayling, is accessible via Eielson Farm Road off Moose Creek Road.

V 344.7 (554.7 km) **DC 1500.7** (2415 km) **F 19.3** (31.1 km) Moose Creek bridge.

V 345.5 (556 km) **DC 1501.5** (2416.4 km) **F 18.5** (29.8 km) *CAUTION: Highway crosses Alaska Railroad tracks.*

V 346 (556.8 km) **DC 1502** (2417.2 km) **F 17.9** (28.8 km) Chena Flood Channel bridge. Upstream dam is part of flood control project initiated after the Chena River left its banks and flooded Fairbanks in 1967.

V 346.7 (558 km) **DC 1502.7** (2418.4 km) **F 17.3** (27.8 km) Laurance Road. Turn right northbound for Chena Lakes Recreation Area (follow signs, 2.2 miles/3.5 km to entrance). Constructed by the Army Corps of Engineers and run by Fairbanks North Star Borough, the recreation area has 80 campsites, 92 picnic sites (some with handicap access), pump water, volleyball courts, and a 250-acre lake with swimming beach. **Chena Lake** is stocked with silver salmon, arctic char, grayling and rainbow trout. Nonmotorized boats may be rented from a concessionaire. The **Chena River** flows through part of the recreation area and offers good grayling fishing and also northern pike, whitefish and burbot. Hiking and self-guiding nature trails. Open year-round. Fee charged Memorial Day to Labor Day; day use $3 per vehicle, camping $6 per day.

V 347.1 (558.6 km) **DC 1503.1** (2419 km) **F 16.9** (27.2 km) Newby Road.

V 347.7 (559.6 km) **DC 1503.7** (2419.9 km) **F 16.3** (26.2 km) Exit west for St. Nicholas Lane, east for Dawson Road.

V 348.7 (561.2 km) **DC 1504.7** (2421.5 km) **F 15.3** (24.6 km) North Pole Visitor Information Center. Turn right on Mission Road for radio station KJNP, turn left northbound for 5th Avenue businesses.

Santaland RV Park. Good Sampark. New 1992. Center of North Pole, next to Santa Claus House. 39 water and electric, 41 pull-throughs, 51 full hookups and limited dry. Private bathrooms, laundry, pay phones, facilities for handicapped. Malls and churches within walking distance. Daily shuttle bus to Fairbanks points of interest. Tour sales and reservations for your convenience. See display ad or call (907) 488-9123. [ADVERTISEMENT]

V 349 (561.6 km) **DC 1505** (2422 km) **F 15** (24.1 km) **Santa Claus House.** In 1949, Con Miller began wearing a Santa Claus suit on business trips throughout the territory, bringing the spirit of St. Nicholas to hundreds of children for the first time. Here the Miller family continues this tradition. Ask about Santa's Christmas letter. Enjoy the unique gift shop and exhibits. See display ad this section. [ADVERTISEMENT]

V 349.5 (562.3 km) **DC 1505.5** (2422.8 km) **F 14.5** (23.3 km) North Pole and North Pole Plaza to the left northbound via Santa Claus Lane; Badger Road to the right. Truck stop with diesel, two small shopping malls, motel and other businesses are located on Badger Road. Santa Claus Lane has several businesses along it, and connects with 5th Avenue, which loops back to the highway at **Milepost V 348.6.** Badger Road is a loop road leading 12 miles/19.3 km along Badger Slough. It reenters the Alaska Highway 7 miles/11.3 km outside of Fairbanks at **Milepost V 357.1.**

North Pole

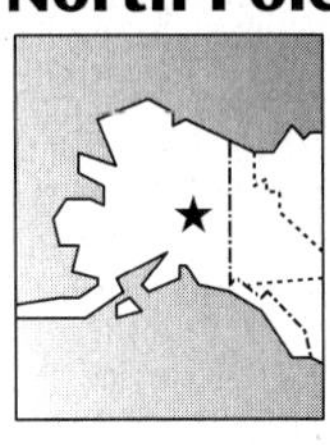

V 349.5 (562.3 km) DC 1505.5 (2422.8 km) F 14.5 (23.3 km) West of the Alaska Highway. **Population:** 1,456. **Emergency Services:** Emergencies only phone 911. **Police,** phone 488-6902. **Alaska State Troopers,** phone 452-2114. **Fire Department,** phone 488-2232.

Visitor Information: At **Milepost V 348.7.** Open June through August.

Elevation: 500 feet/152m. **Radio:** KJNP-AM 1170, KJNP-FM 100.3; also Fairbanks stations.

Private Aircraft: Bradley Sky Ranch, 0.9 mile/1.4 km northwest; elev. 483 feet/147m; length 4,100 feet/1,250m; gravel; fuel 100.

North Pole has most visitor facilities including restaurants, a motel, bed and breakfasts, campgrounds, laundromats, car wash, grocery and gas stops, gift stores, library, churches, a public park, pharmacy and supermarket. The post office is on Santa Claus Lane.

North Pole has an annual Winter Carnival with sled dog races, carnival games, food booths and other activities. In summer

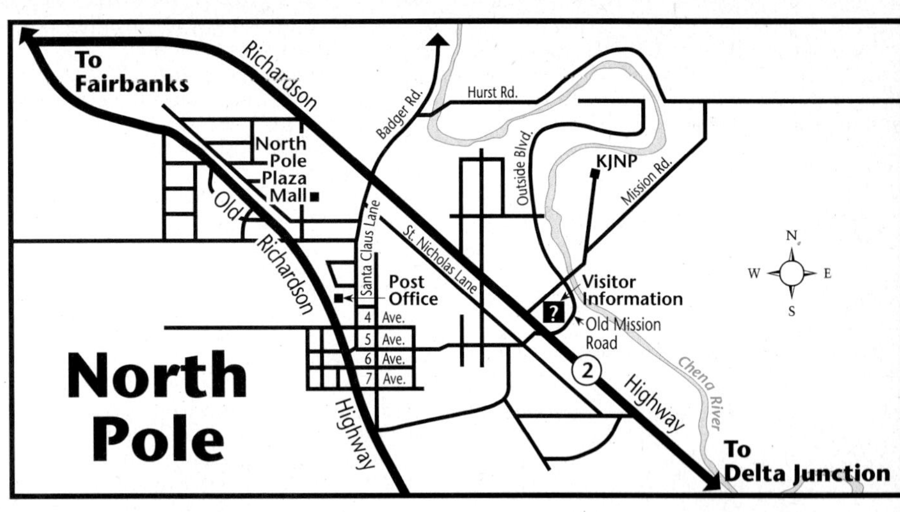

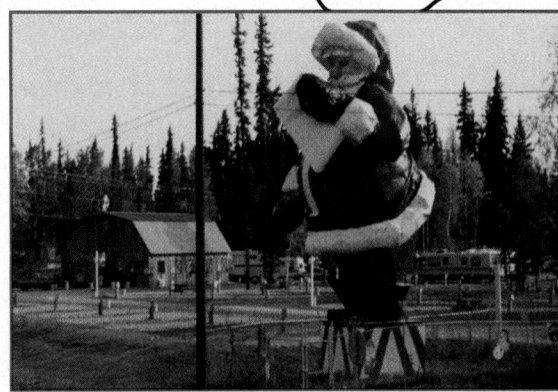

there's a big Fourth of July celebration.

In 1944 Bon V. Davis homesteaded this area. Dahl and Gaske Development Co. bought the Davis homestead, subdivided it, and named it North Pole, hoping to attract a toy manufacturer who could advertise products as being made in North Pole.

North Pole is the home of many Fairbanks commuters. It has an oil refinery that produces heating fuel, jet fuel and other products. Eielson and Wainwright military bases are nearby.

Radio station KJNP, operated by Calvary's Northern Lights Mission, broadcasts music and religious programs on 1170 AM and 100.3 FM. They also operate television station KJNP Channel 4. Visitors are welcome between 8 A.M. and 10 P.M.; tours may be arranged. KJNP is located on Mission Road about 0.6 mile/1 km northeast of the Alaska Highway. The missionary project includes a dozen hand-hewn, sod-roofed homes and other buildings constructed of spruce logs.

Full-service campgrounds downtown at Santaland RV Park and Campground and at Riverview RV Park on Badger Road. North Pole Public Park, on 5th Avenue, has tent sites in the trees along a narrow dirt road; no camping fee. Dump station available at North Pole Plaza. ▲

North Pole Coffee Roasting Company offers coffee beans from around the world roasted right here in North Pole. Coffee shop, espresso bar, pastries, light lunches. Gifts and T-shirts. From exit, turn south on Santa Claus Lane. We're at 220 Parkway, on your right, just beyond North Pole Plaza Mall. (907) 488-7190. [ADVERTISEMENT]

Richardson–Alaska Highway Log

(continued)

V 350.6 (564.2 km) **DC 1506.6** (2424.6 km) **F 13.4** (21.6 km) *CAUTION: Highway crosses Alaska Railroad tracks.*

V 351 (564.9 km) **DC 1507** (2425.3 km) **F 13** (20.9 km) Twelvemile Village exit.

NORTH POLE ADVERTISERS

Greenhouse with floral displays.

V 354.4 (570.3 km) **DC 1510.4** (2430.7 km) **F 9.6** (15.4 km) Old Richardson Highway exit.

V 356 (572.9 km) **DC 1512** (2433.3 km) **F 8** (12.9 km) Private RV park.

V 357.1 (574.7 km) **DC 1513.1** (2435 km) **F 6.9** (11.1 km) Badger Road. This loop road connects with the Alaska Highway again at North Pole. Motel, RV park, salmon bake and other businesses are located on Badger Road.

V 357.6 (575.5 km) **DC 1513.6** (2435.8 km) **F 6.4** (10.3 km) Weigh stations both sides of highway.

V 358.6 (577.1 km) **DC 1514.6** (2437.4 km) **F 5.4** (8.7 km) Entrance to Fort Wainwright.

V 359.2 (578.1 km) **DC 1515.2** (2438.4 km) **F 4.8** (7.7 km) *CAUTION: Highway crosses Alaska Railroad tracks.*

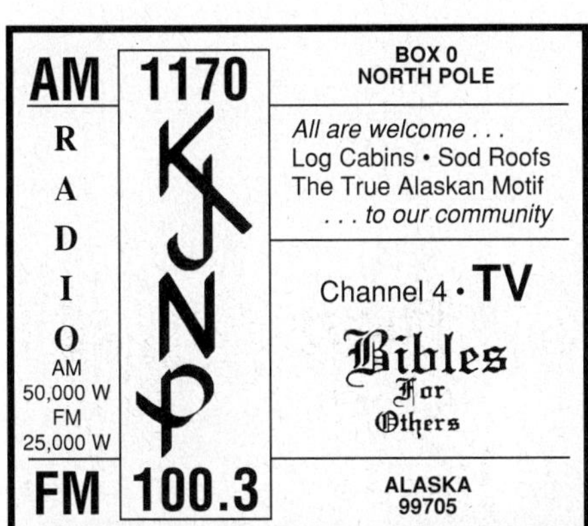

V 359.6 (578.7 km) **DC 1515.6** (2439.1 km) **F 4.4** (7.1 km) West truck route (Old Richardson Highway) exit for westbound traffic only. Access to motels, restaurants and Cushman Street business area.

V 360.6 (580.3 km) **DC 1516.6** (2440.7 km) **F 3.4** (5.5 km) Denali Park/Parks Highway (Alaska Route 3) exit northbound to bypass Fairbanks via the Robert J. Mitchell expressway. Hospital this exit.

V 361 (581 km) **DC 1517** (2441.4 km) **F 3** (4.8 km) Exit via 30th Avenue to Big Bend business area for east and westbound traffic. Access to motels, restaurants, Old Richardson Highway, Van Horn Road, Cushman Street and downtown Fairbanks.

V 361.3 (581.4 km) **DC 1517.3** (2441.8 km) **F 2.7** (4.3 km) 30th Avenue overpass; exits both sides of highway.

V 363 (584.2 km) **DC 1519** (2444.6 km) **F 1** (1.6 km) Turn right on Gaffney Road for Fort Wainwright; left on Airport Way for downtown Fairbanks, University of Alaska, Alaskaland and George Parks Highway (Alaska Route 3). Follow city center signs to downtown Fairbanks and visitor information center. Go straight ahead on the Steese Expressway for Gavora Mall, Bentley Mall, Fox, Steese and Elliott highways and Chena Hot Springs Road.

V 363.3 (584.7 km) **DC 1519.3** (2445 km) **F 0.7** (1.1 km) 10th Avenue exit to Fairbanks.

V 363.6 (585.1 km) **DC 1519.6** (2445.6 km) **F 0.4** (0.6 km) Steese Expressway crosses Chena River.

V 363.9 (585.6 km) **DC 1519.9** (2446 km) **F 0.1** (0.2 km) 3rd Street exit. Gavora Mall.

Mr. and Mrs. Claus welcome visitors to their home in North Pole. (Jerrianne Lowther, staff)

V 364 (585.8 km) **DC 1520** (2446.2 km) **F 0 FAIRBANKS.** College Road exit route to University of Alaska, Bentley Mall and city center (turn left). For details see FAIRBANKS section.

YELLOWHEAD HIGHWAY 16

Edmonton, Alberta, to Prince Rupert, British Columbia
(See maps, pages 179-181)

Yellowhead Highway 16 is a paved trans-Canada highway extending from Winnipeg, MB, through Saskatchewan, Alberta, and British Columbia to the coastal city of Prince Rupert. (The highway connecting Masset and Queen Charlotte on Graham Island has also been designated as part of Yellowhead Highway 16.) *The MILEPOST®* logs Yellowhead Highway 16 from Edmonton, AB, to Prince Rupert, BC, a distance of 906 miles/ 1,458 km.

Yellowhead Highway 16 terminates at Prince Rupert, BC, where you may connect with the Alaska Marine Highway System to southeastern Alaska cities, and the British Columbia ferry system to Port Hardy on Vancouver Island (see MARINE ACCESS ROUTES section).

This is a major east–west route, providing access to a number of attractions in Alberta and British Columbia. Yellowhead Highway 16 is also a very scenic highway, passing through both forest and farmland. Visitor services are readily available in towns along the way, and campsites may be found in town and along the highway at both private and provincial park campgrounds. (It is unsafe and illegal to overnight in rest areas.)

Watch for elk grazing in Jasper National Park. (Gerry Deiter)

Yellowhead Highway 16 Log

The Yellowhead Highway log is divided into two sections: Edmonton to Prince George, and Prince George to Prince Rupert.
This section of the log shows distance from Edmonton (E) followed by distance from Prince George (PG).

E 0 **PG 450** (724.2 km) **EDMONTON** city limit. See EAST ACCESS ROUTE section for description of city.

E 4 (6.4 km) **PG 446** (717.7 km) **Junction** of Highways 16 West and 60 (Devon Overpass); access to private campground. ▲

E 12 (19.3 km) **PG 438** (704.9 km) **SPRUCE GROVE** (pop. 11,861). All visitor facilities including a motel, restaurants, grocery stores and gas stations.

E 16 (25.7 km) **PG 434** (698.4 km) **STONY PLAIN** (pop. 7,223). All visitor facilities including hotels, restaurants, supermarket, shopping mall and gas stations with major repair service; RCMP and hospital; swimming pool and golf course. Housed in a historic site, the Multicultural Heritage

YELLOWHEAD HIGHWAY 16 *Edmonton, AB, to Prince George, BC*

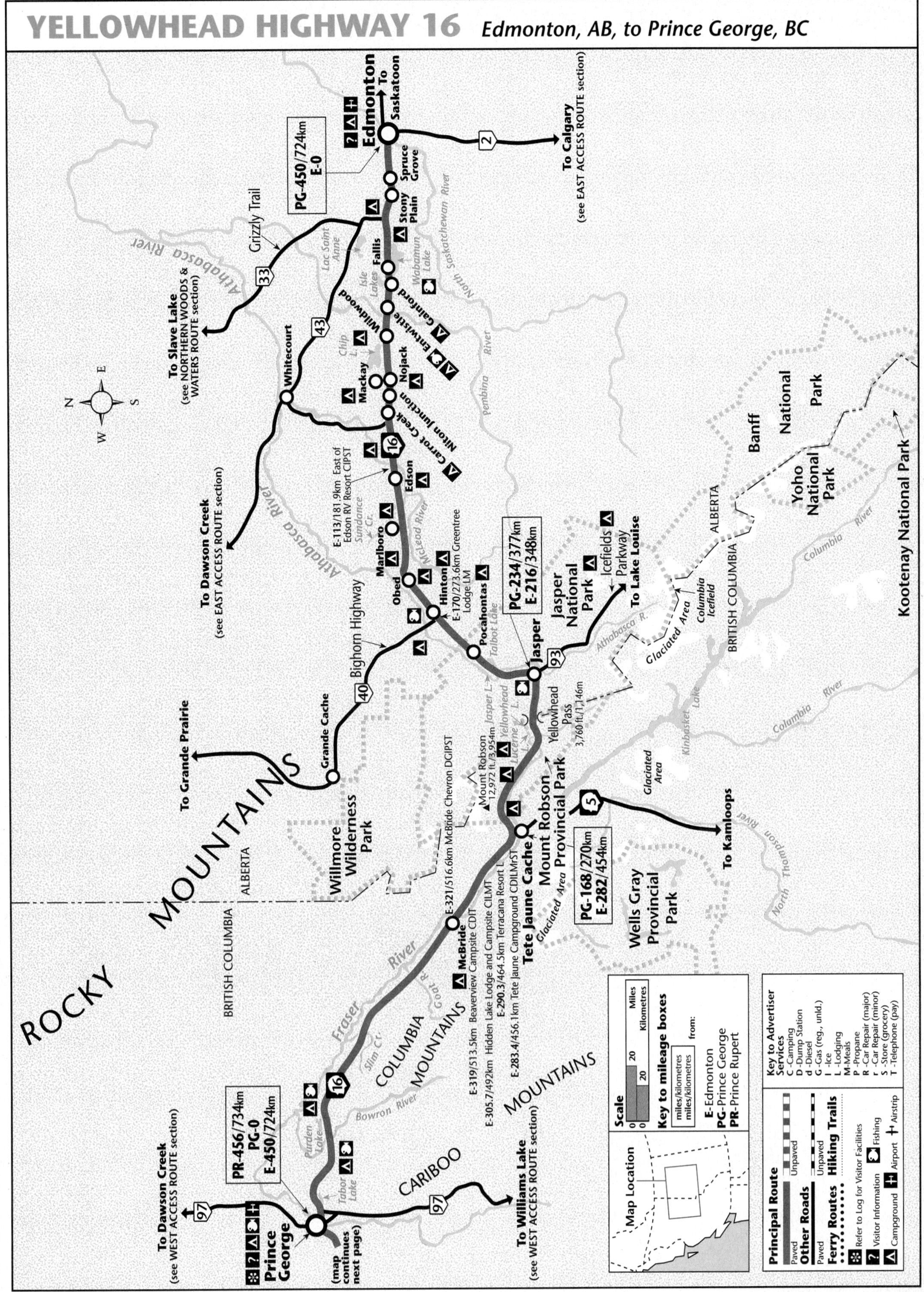

YELLOWHEAD HIGHWAY 16 *Prince George, BC, to Topley, BC*

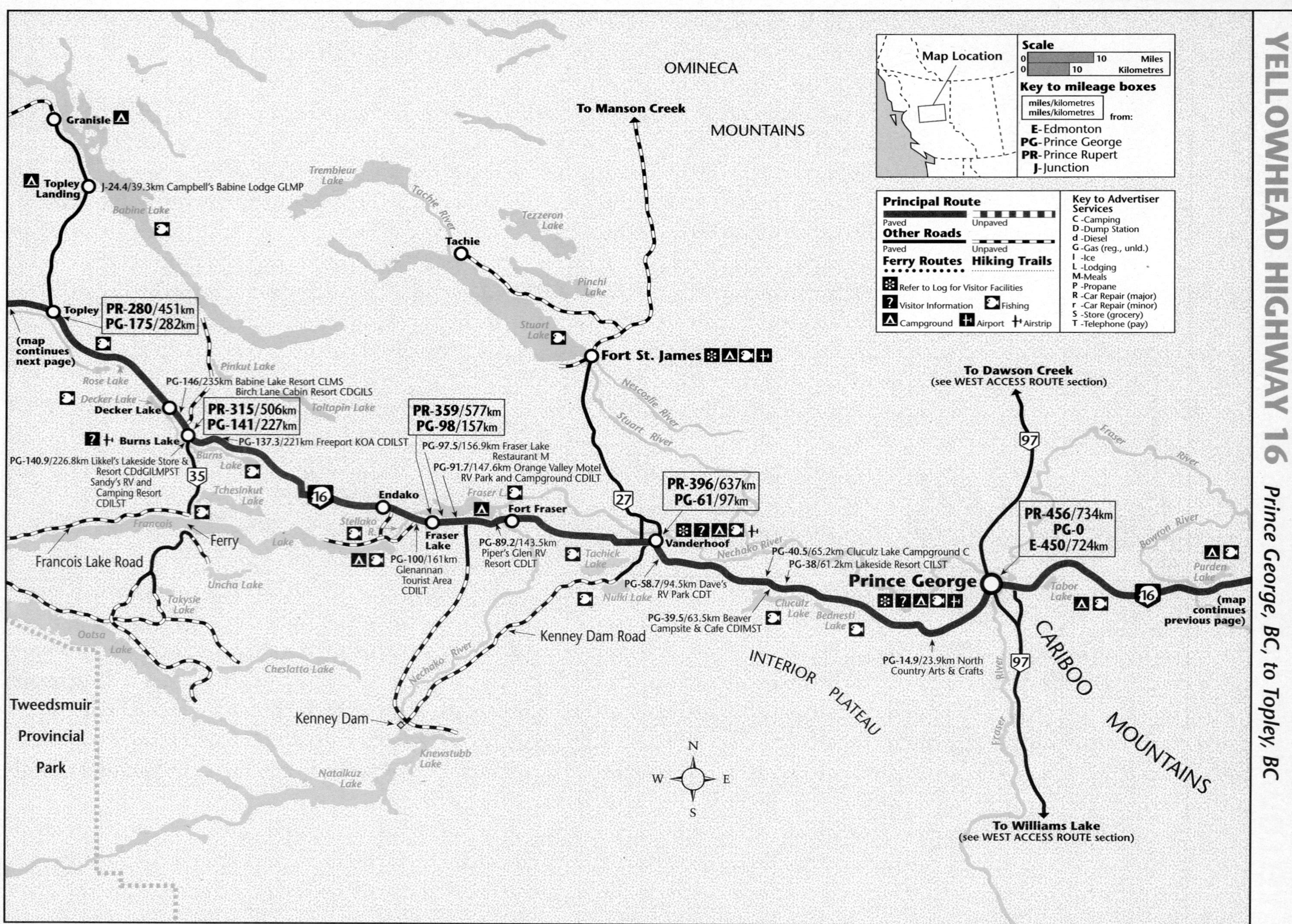

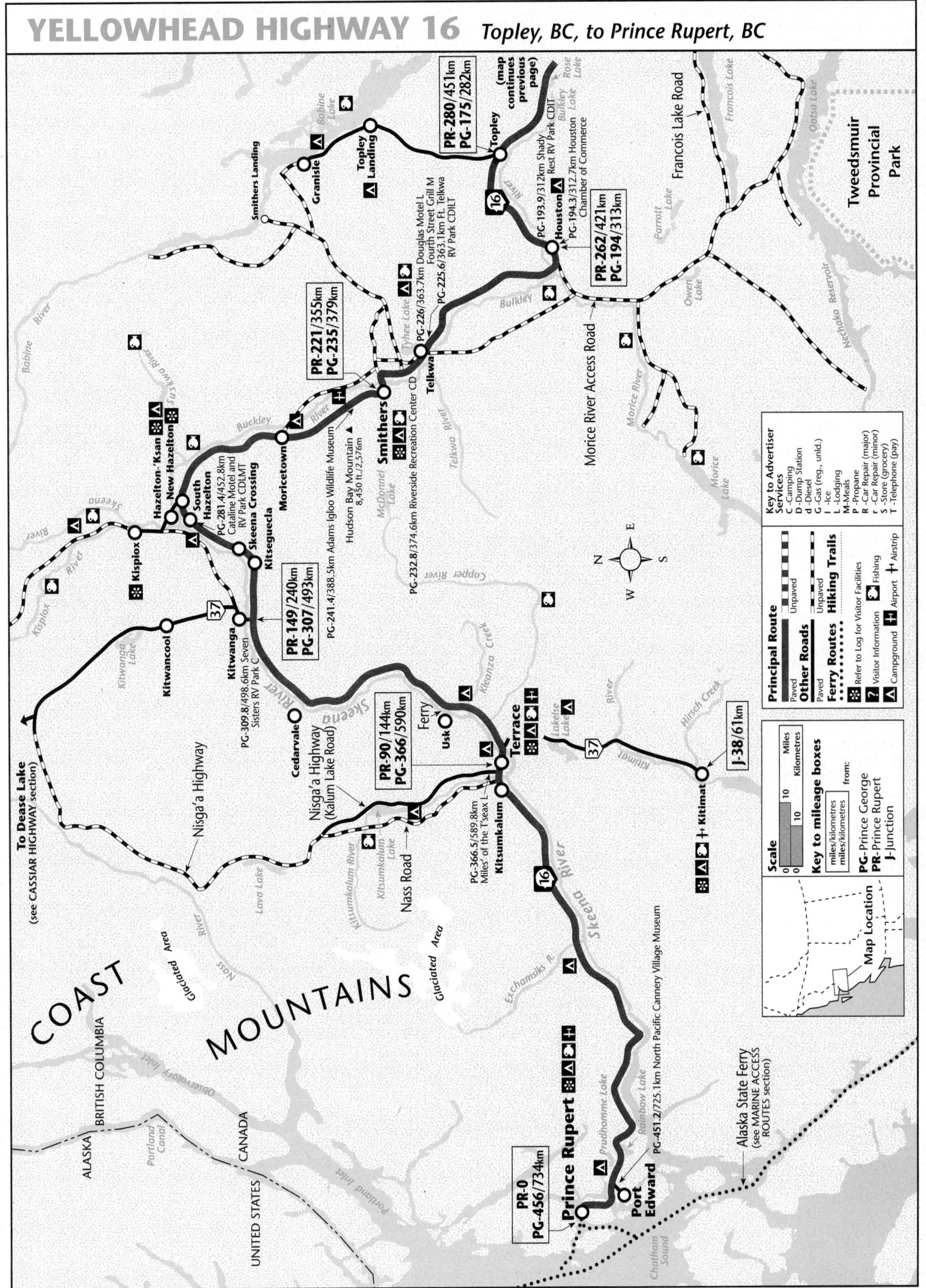
(map continues previous page)
PR-280/451km
PG-175/282km
Topley
Topley Landing
Granisle
Babine Lake
Smithers Landing
PG-193.9/312km Shady Rest RV Park CDIT
PG-194.3/312.7km Houston Chamber of Commerce
Houston
PR-262/421km
PG-194/313km
Francois Lake Road
Francois Lake
Ootsa Lake
Tweedsmuir Provincial Park
Parrott Lake
Owen Lake
Nechako Reservoir
Bulkley River
Morice River Access Road
Morice River
Morice Lake
PG-226/363.7km Douglas Motel L
Fourth Street Grill M
PG-225.6/363.1km Ft. Telkwa RV Park CDILT
Tyhee Lake
Telkwa
Telkwa River
PR-221/355km
PG-235/379km
Smithers
PG-232.8/374.6km Riverside Recreation Center CD
PG-241.4/388.5km Adams Igloo Wildlife Museum
Hudson Bay Mountain 8,450 ft./2,576m
McDonnel Lake
Copper River
Moricetown
Buckley River
Babine River
Suskwa River
Hazelton-'Ksan
New Hazelton
South Hazelton
PG-281.4/452.8km Cataline Motel and RV Park CDLMT
Skeena Crossing
Kitseguecla
Kispiox
Kispiox River
Skeena River
PR-149/240km
PG-307/493km
Kitwanga
PG-309.8/498.6km Seven Sisters RV Park C
Kitwancool
Kitwanga Lake
37
To Dease Lake (see CASSIAR HIGHWAY section)
Nisga'a Highway
Nisga'a Highway (Kalum Lake Road)
Cedarvale
Kleanza Creek
Usk
Ferry
PR-90/144km
PG-366/590km
Terrace
Lakelse Lake
Kitimat
J-38/61km
Hirsch Creek
Kitsumkalum
PG-366.5/589.8km Miles' of the T'seax L
Kitsumkalum Lake
Kitsumkalum River
Nass Road
Lava Lake
Nass River
Glaciated Area
COAST MOUNTAINS
Exchamsiks R.
Skeena River
16
Observatory Inlet
ALASKA
BRITISH COLUMBIA
UNITED STATES
CANADA
Portland Canal
Portland Inlet
Prince Rupert
PR-0
PG-456/734km
Prudhomme Lake
Rainbow Lake
PG-451.2/725.1km North Pacific Cannery Village Museum
Port Edward
Chatham Sound
Alaska State Ferry (see MARINE ACCESS ROUTES section)
Key to Advertiser Services
C -Camping
D -Dump Station
d -Diesel
G -Gas (reg., unld.)
I -Ice
L -Lodging
M -Meals
P -Propane
R -Car Repair (major)
r -Car Repair (minor)
S -Store (grocery)
T -Telephone (pay)
Principal Route
Paved
Other Roads
Paved
Unpaved
Ferry Routes
Hiking Trails
Refer to Log for Visitor Facilities
Visitor Information
Fishing
Campground
Airport
Airstrip
Scale
0 10 Miles
0 10 Kilometres
Key to mileage boxes
miles/kilometres
miles/kilometres
from:
PG-Prince George
PR-Prince Rupert
J-Junction
Map Location
N
E
S
W

Centre here has a candy store, a handicraft store, two art galleries, a library, archives, a museum and serves pioneer food. Open daily, 10 A.M. to 6 P.M. June through August and 10 A.M. to 4 P.M. the rest of the year. Visitor information at the Old Caboose by the railroad.

E 19 (30.6 km) **PG 431** (693.6 km) Private campground, 1.9 miles/3 km north. Day-use area, boat rental, playground and swimming. Fee for using facilities. Security gate controlled. ▲

E 19.6 (31.5 km) **PG 430.4** (692.6 km) Turnoff to south for Edmonton Beach and campground. ▲

E 20.1 (32.3 km) **PG 429.9** (691.8 km) Hubbles Lake turnoff to north.

E 21.2 (34.1 km) **PG 428.8** (690.1 km) Restaurant, gas station and store to north.

E 25 (40.2 km) **PG 425** (684 km) **Junction** with Highway 43. Turn north for access to Alaska Highway (see EAST ACCESS ROUTE section) and Northwest Territories (see MACKENZIE ROUTE section). Continue west for Prince George.

E 33 (53.1 km) **PG 417** (671.1 km) **Wabamun Lake** Provincial Park, 1 mile/1.6 km south on access road; 288 campsites, fishing, boating and swimming. ▲

E 34.8 (56.1 km) **PG 415.1** (668.1 km) Village of **WABAMUN** with gas, convenience store, car wash, laundromat, dump station, hotel and post office. Park with shelter, tables, litter barrels, washroom and flush toilets. Also located here is Transalta Utilities generating station, which generates electricity from coal.

E 43 (69.2 km) **PG 407** (655 km) **FALLIS** (pop. 190); no services. Strip mining of coal on north side of highway.

E 49 (78.9 km) **PG 401** (645.3 km) **GAINFORD** (pop. 205). Cafe, hotel and post office. Free public campground at west end of town with eight sites, firewood, tables, pit toilets and water. ▲

E 58 (93.3 km) **PG 392** (630.8 km) **ENTWISTLE** (pop. 477). Restaurants, gas station, two motels, post office, swimming pool and grocery store. **Pembina River** Provincial Park, 1.9 miles/3 km north; 129 campsites, firewood, tables, pit toilets, water and dump station. Camping fee $11. Fishing, swimming, playground and phone. ▲

E 68 (109.4 km) **PG 382** (614.8 km) **WILDWOOD** (pop. 375), the "Bingo Capital of Canada." Village with post office, hotel, gas station, restaurants and shops. Campground at **Chip Lake** with 14 sites, tables, firewood, pit toilets, water, fishing, swimming and boat launch. ▲

E 82 (131.9 km) **PG 368** (592.2 km) **NOJACK** and **MACKAY** (pop. 250). Grocery, post office, restaurant and gas station with towing, diesel and major repair service. Mackay is 1.9 miles/3 km north of Nojack on a gravel road. Campgrounds 1 mile/1.6 km and 3 miles/4.8 km west of town on Highway 16. ▲

E 90 (144.8 km) **PG 360** (579.3 km) **NITON JUNCTION.** Hamlet has two gas stations with tires and parts, diesel, propane, car wash, pay phone, groceries, post office, two restaurants, lounge, motel. Private campground with full hookups. ▲

E 94 (151.3 km) **PG 356** (572.9 km) **CARROT CREEK,** post office, grocery store, gas station and car wash. Campground 1.9 miles/3 km north with eight sites, tables, pit toilets, water, propane and phone. ▲

E 99 (159.3 km) **PG 351** (564.9 km) **Junction** with Highway 32 which leads to Whitecourt and Highway 43, 42 miles/68 km north on paved road. (See **Milepost E 112.7** in the EAST ACCESS ROUTE section.)

E 102.3 (164.6 km) **PG 347.7** (559.5 km) Wolf Creek public campground; 14 sites, pit toilets, tables, litter barrels. ▲

E 106.6 (171.6 km) **PG 343.4** (552.6 km) Edson rest area to south with flush toilets, water, tables, shelter and pay phone.

E 113 (181.9 km) **PG 337** (542.3 km) **East of Edson RV Resort.** 8 km (5 miles) east of Edson on Highway 16. Open May to October. Full services in the wilderness. Rustic drive-through sites with 30/15-amp service. Coin-op hot showers. Laundromat. Small store. Public phone. Walkways. Recreation activities. Security gate. Pets welcome. Reservations (403) 723-2287. Box 7378, Edson, AB T7E 1V6. [ADVERTISEMENT] ▲

E 116.1 (186.9 km) **PG 333.9** (537.4 km) McLeod River bridge.

E 118 (189.9 km) **PG 332** (534.4 km) **EDSON** (pop. 7,323). Large highway community with 14 motels, many restaurants and gas stations; 18-hole golf course, indoor pool; hospital and RCMP post. There is camping at Lions Club Campground east of town (42 sites), and at Willmore Recreation Park, 3.7 miles/6 km south of town on the McLeod River. Campground resort, 5 miles/8 km east of Edson, with full hookups; open May to October. Edson's economy is based on coal mining, forestry, oil and natural gas, and manufacturing (Weyerhaeuser oriented strand board plant). ▲

E 124 (199.6 km) **PG 326** (524.6 km) Food, gas, lodging.

E 130 (209.2 km) **PG 320** (515 km) Hornbeck Creek public campground to north; 35 sites. Camping fee $5.50. ▲

E 134.7 (216.8 km) **PG 315.3** (507.4 km) Small community of Marlboro to north.

E 140 (225.3 km) **PG 310** (498.9 km) First glimpse of Canadian Rockies westbound.

E 145.1 (233.5 km) **PG 304.9** (490.7 km) Turnout with litter barrel.

E 150.6 (242.4 km) **PG 299.4** (481.8 km) Obed Lake public campground to north; 13 sites, firewood, tables, pit toilets and water. ▲

E 152 (244.6 km) **PG 298** (479.6 km) **OBED.** Phone, gas and groceries.

E 158.7 (255.4 km) **PG 291.3** (468.8 km) Obed Summit, highest elevation on the Yellowhead Highway at 3,819 feet/1,164m.

E 159.5 (256.7 km) **PG 290.5** (467.5 km) Roundcroft public campground to south; nine sites, firewood, tables, pit toilets and water. ▲

E 170 (273.6 km) **PG 280** (450.6 km) **HINTON** (pop. 8,537). All visitor facilities including hotels and motels, golf course, hospital, dentist, RCMP and recreation complex with indoor pool. Campground with 50 sites, hookups and dump station. Site of St. Regis (Alberta) Ltd. pulp mill; tours of mill complex may be arranged. ▲

Greentree Lodge. See display ad this section.

E 175.7 (282.8 km) **PG 274.3** (441.4 km) South **junction** with Highway 40.

E 177 (284.8 km) **PG 273.2** (439.4 km) **Junction** with Bighorn Highway 40, which leads north 90 miles/145 km (paved) to Grande Cache then another 117 miles/188 km (gravel) to Grande Prairie.

E 179.2 (288.4 km) **PG 270.8** (435.8 km) Wildlife sanctuary to west with trails and information signs.

E 181.3 (291.8 km) **PG 268.7** (432.4 km) Maskuta Creek picnic area with tables, shelter, toilets and litter barrels.

E 182.4 (293.5 km) **PG 267.6** (430.6 km) Weigh scales and pay phone.

E 183.7 (295.6 km) **PG 266.3** (428.6 km) Public campground 3.1 miles/5 km north. ▲

E 186.2 (299.6 km) **PG 263.8** (424.5 km) Private campground, pay phone. ▲

E 187 (300.8 km) **PG 263** (423.3 km) Point of interest sign about Athabasca River to north.

E 187.5 (301.7 km) **PG 262.5** (422.4 km) Resort with lodging to north.

E 190 (305.8 km) **PG 260** (418.4 km) East entrance to Jasper National Park. Motor vehicle license sticker required for all visitors using facilities in Rocky Mountain national parks. Permit fees: one day, $5; four days, $10; annual permit, $30.

E 193 (310.6 km) **PG 257** (413.6 km) **POCAHONTAS.** Grocery, motel, cafe and gas station with minor repair service. **Junction** with Miette Hot Springs Road, which leads 0.6 mile/1 km south to Park Service campground (140 sites) and 11 miles/18 km south to Miette Hot Springs and resort. There are two thermal pools; towels and bathing suits for rent; admission fee $3 adult. Beautiful setting, look for mountain goats. ▲

E 196.1 (315.6 km) **PG 253.9** (408.6 km) Turnout to south with historical marker.

E 196.5 (316.2 km) **PG 253.5** (408 km) Turnout to north.

E 198.1 (318.8 km) **PG 251.9** (405.4 km) Turnout to north with litter barrels and picnic tables.

E 198.3 (319.1 km) **PG 251.7** (405.1 km) Rocky River bridge.

E 198.5 (319.4 km) **PG 251.5** (404.7 km) Turnout to north with historical marker.

E 200.7 (323 km) **PG 249.3** (401.2 km) Talbot Lake to south; picnic tables.

E 202.2 (325.4 km) **PG 247.8** (398.8 km) Turnout to south.

E 203 (326.7 km) **PG 247** (397.5 km) Jasper Lake to north.

E 204.6 (329.3 km) **PG 245.4** (394.9 km) Turnout with litter barrels to south.

E 206.3 (332 km) **PG 243.7** (392.2 km) Turnout to south; trailhead.

E 206.6 (332.5 km) **PG 243.4** (391.7 km) Athabasca River bridge. Watch for elk.

E 208.7 (335.9 km) **PG 241.3** (388.3 km) Snaring River bridge.

E 210.2 (338.3 km) **PG 239.8** (385.9 km) Jasper airfield to south.

E 211.3 (340 km) **PG 238.7** (384.1 km) Snaring rest area to south.

E 212.1 (341.3 km) **PG 237.9** (382.9 km) Pallsades rest area to south.

E 213.4 (343.4 km) **PG 236.6** (380.8 km) Turnout to south with litter barrels and view of Mount Edith Cavell.

E 214.5 (345.2 km) **PG 235.5** (379 km) Turnout with litter barrel to south.

E 215 (346 km) **PG 235** (378.2 km) Access road to Jasper Park Lodge.

E 216 (347.6 km) **PG 234** (376.6 km) Access to Jasper and **junction** with Highway 93, the scenic Icefields Parkway, south to Banff past Columbia Icefield.

Many residents in this area maintain hummingbird feeders. The two species of hummingbirds found in the Canadian Rockies are the Rufous and the Calliope.

E 216.5 (348.4 km) **PG 233.5** (375.8 km) Miette River.

E 218.3 (351.4 km) **PG 231.7** (372.9 km) Turnout with litter barrels to north.

E 220.7 (355.2 km) **PG 229.3** (369 km) Paved turnout to south with litter barrels and picnic table.

E 221.6 (356.7 km) **PG 228.4** (367.5 km) Paved turnout to north with outhouses, litter barrels and interpretive sign about Yellowhead Pass.

E 222.3 (357.7 km) **PG 227.7** (366.4 km) Meadow Creek.

E 222.7 (358.4 km) **PG 227.3** (365.8 km) Trailhead for Virl Lake, Dorothy Lake and Christine Lake.

E 225.5 (363 km) **PG 224.5** (361.3 km) Clairvaux Creek.

E 235 (378.2 km) **PG 215** (346 km) West entrance to Jasper National Park; motor vehicle license required for all visitors using facilities in Rocky Mountain national parks. Permit fees: one day, $5; four days, $10; annual permit, $30.

E 235.5 (379 km) **PG 214.5** (345.2 km) Yellowhead Pass (elev. 3,760 feet/1,146m), Alberta-British Columbia border. Named for an Iroquois trapper and guide who worked for the Hudson's Bay Co. in the early 1800s. His light-colored hair earned him the name Tete Jaune ("yellow head") from the French voyageurs.

East entrance to Mount Robson Provincial Park. Portal Lake picnic area with tables, toilets, information board and hiking trail.

TIME ZONE CHANGE: Alberta observes Mountain standard time. Most of British Columbia observes Pacific standard time. Both observe daylight saving time. See Time Zones in the GENERAL INFORMATION section for details.

E 237 (381.4 km) **PG 213** (342.8 km) **Yellowhead Lake**; picnic tables, viewpoint, boat launch and fishing.

E 240 (386.2 km) **PG 210** (338 km) Lucerne Campground; 32 sites, picnic tables, drinking water and swimming. Camping fee $9.50. ▲

E 241.4 (388.5 km) **PG 208.6** (335.7 km) Fraser Crossing rest area to south; tables, litter barrels and toilets.

E 241.5 (388.6 km) **PG 208.5** (335.6 km) Fraser River bridge No. 1.

E 244.5 (393.5 km) **PG 205.5** (330.7 km) Fraser River bridge No. 2.

E 248.2 (399.4 km) **PG 201.8** (324.8 km) Grant Brook.

E 250.9 (403.8 km) **PG 199.1** (320.4 km) Moose Creek bridge.

E 254 (408.2 km) **PG 196** (316 km) Turnout at east end of Moose Lake; tables, litter barrels, toilet and boat launch.

E 258.4 (415.8 km) **PG 191.6** (308.3 km) Information sign on avalanches and wildlife.

E 262.5 (422.4 km) **PG 187.5** (301.7 km) Turnout with litter barrels. Avalanche gates.

E 266.7 (429.2 km) **PG 183.9** (296 km) Turnout with litter barrels to south.

E 271.1 (436.3 km) **PG 178.9** (287.9 km) Overland Falls rest area to south; pit toilets, litter barrels. Hiking trail to Overlander Falls, about 30 minutes round-trip.

E 272 (437.7 km) **PG 178** (286.5 km) Viewpoint of Mount Robson (elev. 12,972 feet/3,954m), highest peak in the Canadian Rockies, and visitor information centre. Parking, picnic tables, restrooms, litter barrels, gas and restaurant. Berg Lake trailhead; hike-in campgrounds. Private campground north of highway. Robson Meadows government campground south of highway with 125 sites, dump station, pay phone, interpretive programs, tables, firewood, pit toilets, water and horseshoe pits. Camping fee is $14.50. ▲

E 272.5 (438.5 km) **PG 177.5** (285.6 km) Robson River government campground to north with 19 sites, tables, firewood, pit toilets, showers, water and horseshoe pits. Camping fee is $14.50. ▲

E 272.9 (439.2 km) **PG 177.1** (285 km) Robson River bridge. Look for Indian paintbrush June through August. The bracts are orange-red while the petals are green.

E 273.4 (440 km) **PG 176.6** (284.2 km) West entrance to Mount Robson Provincial Park. Turnout with litter barrels and statue.

E 273.5 (440.2 km) **PG 176.5** (284 km) Gravel turnout with litter barrels.

E 274.4 (441.6 km) **PG 175.6** (282.6 km) Swift Current Creek.

E 274.7 (442.1 km) **PG 175.3** (282.1 km) Turnout with litter barrels.

E 277.6 (446.7 km) **PG 172.4** (277.4 km) Mount Terry Fox Provincial Park picnic area with tables, restrooms and viewing telescope. The information board here points out the location of Mount Terry Fox in the Selwyn Range of the Rocky Mountains. The peak was named in 1981 to honour cancer victim Terry Fox, who before his death from the disease, raised some $25 million for cancer research during his attempt to run across Canada.

E 279.4 (449.7 km) **PG 170.6** (274.5 km) Gravel turnout to north with Yellowhead Highway information sign.

E 279.5 (449.8 km) **PG 170.5** (274.4 km) Rearguard Falls Provincial Park picnic area. Easy half-hour round-trip to falls viewpoint. Upper limit of 800-mile migration of Pacific salmon; look for chinook in late summer.

E 280.8 (451.9 km) **PG 169.2** (272.3 km) Gravel turnout. Avalanche gates.

E 281.3 (452.7 km) **PG 168.7** (271.5 km) Weigh scales.

E 281.7 (453.3 km) **PG 168.3** (270.8 km) Tete Jaune Cache rest area with tables, litter barrels and toilets.

E 282 (453.8 km) **PG 168** (270.4 km) **Junction** with Yellowhead Highway 5 to the small community of Tete Jaune Cache (0.5 mile/0.8 km south of junction) and Kamloops (208 miles/355 km south), British Columbia's fourth largest settlement. Food, gas and lodging just west of the junction. Yellowhead Highway 5 opened in 1969. A year earlier, construction of the section of the highway east from Prince George to Tete Jaune Cache had connected Highway 16 with a rough road east to Jasper National Park. The final link in Northern Trans-provincial Highway 16 (now Yellowhead Highway 16) — between Prince George and Edmonton — officially opened in 1969.

E 282.7 (454.9 km) **PG 167.3** (269.2 km) Turnoff for gas and lodging.

E 283.4 (456.1 km) **PG 166.6** (268.1 km) **Tete Jaune Campground**. See display ad this section. ▲

E 286.4 (461 km) **PG 163.6** (263.3 km) Spittal Creek Interpretive Forest; hiking trails.

West entrance to Mount Robson Provincial Park. Mount Robson, seen in the background, is the highest peak in the Canadian Rockies. (Gerry Deiter)

E 290.3 (467.2 km) **PG 159.7** (257 km) **Terracana Resort.** Modern spacious log chalets with private bathrooms by the Fraser River with a spectacular view. Some kitchenettes. Restaurant, lounge, fitness, games and TV rooms, BBQ patio. Canoe, mountain bike and jeep rentals. Jet boat tours on the Fraser River for all ages — try it and bring your camera! Phone (604) 968-4304, fax (604) 968-4445. Box 909 MP, Valemount, BC V0E 2Z0. [ADVERTISEMENT]

E 291.2 (468.6 km) **PG 158.8** (255.6 km) Small River rest area by stream with tables, toilets and litter barrels.

E 295.5 (475.5 km) **PG 154.5** (248.6 km) Horsey Creek.

E 301.9 (485.8 km) **PG 148.1** (238.3 km) Turnoff to south for settlement of Dunster; gas and general store.

E 305.6 (491.8 km) **PG 144.4** (232.4 km) Holiday Creek rest area with toilets, picnic tables, litter barrel and hiking trails.

E 305.7 (492 km) **PG 144.3** (232.2 km) **Hidden Lake Lodge.** Enjoy our quiet place between the Rocky and Cariboo Mountains. Stay in our cozy cabins and cottages with private bathrooms, some with kitchenettes.

Or park your RV at the campground (six sites). While you canoe the lake and observe wildlife, let us prepare your breakfast. Self-contained RVs only. Electric hookups. General Delivery, Dunster, BC V0J 1J0. Phone and fax (604) 968-4327. [ADVERTISEMENT] ▲

E 306.1 (492.6 km) **PG 143.9** (231.6 km) Baker Creek rest area with tables, litter barrels and toilets.

E 310 (498.9 km) **PG 140** (225.3 km) Neven Creek.

E 313 (503.7 km) **PG 137** (220.5 km) Turnouts at both ends of Holmes River bridge.

E 319 (513.5 km) **PG 131** (210.8 km) **Beaverview Campsite.** See display ad this section. ▲

E 319.6 (514.3 km) **PG 130.4** (209.9 km) Fraser River bridge. A forest fire swept through the Robson Valley in 1912. As you look at the sides of the mountain to the north of the highway it is possible to distinguish the new growth which has taken place in the last 81 years.

E 320.3 (515.4 km) **PG 129.7** (208.7 km) Turnout to north with litter barrels.

E 321 (516.6 km) **PG 129** (207.6 km) **McBRIDE** (pop. 620; elev. 2,369 feet/722m), located in the Robson Valley by the Fraser River. The Park Ranges of the Rocky Mountains are to the northeast and the Cariboo Mountains are to the southeast. A road leads to Teare Mountain lookout for a spectacular view of countryside. The village of McBride was established in 1913 as a divisional point on the railroad and was named for Richard McBride, then premier of British Columbia. Forest products are a major industry here today.

Visitor Information: Travel Infocentre located in railcar adjacent south side of Highway 16. Look for the carved grizzly bear family in front. When the Infocentre isn't open, try the McBride Village Office. Located beside the railcar in the same parking lot, it is open 9 A.M. to 5 P.M.

McBride has all visitor facilities, including four hotels/motels, a bed and breakfast, two supermarkets, clothing stores, restaurants, pharmacy, hospital and gas stations. There is a private campground just east of town. Dump station located at the gas station.

McBride Chevron. See display ad this section.

NOTE: Next gas stop westbound is 91 miles/146.4 km from here (Purden Lake).

E 324.1 (521.6 km) **PG 125.9** (202.6 km) Dore River bridge.

E 329.4 (530.1 km) **PG 120.6** (194.1 km) Macintosh Creek.

E 330.9 (532.5 km) **PG 119.1** (191.7 km) Clyde Creek.

E 339.6 (546.5 km) **PG 110.4** (177.7 km) West Twin Creek bridge.

E 348 (560 km) **PG 102** (164.1 km) Goat River bridge. Rest area to north with tables, toilets and litter barrels.

E 354.3 (570.2 km) **PG 95.7** (154 km) Snowshoe Creek.

E 359.3 (578.2 km) **PG 90.7** (146 km) Catfish Creek.

E 365.1 (587.6 km) **PG 84.9** (136.6 km) Ptarmigan Creek bridge.

E 368.2 (592.6 km) **PG 81.8** (131.6 km) Turnout with litter barrel to north.

E 371.5 (597.9 km) **PG 78.5** (126.3 km) Slate quarry to north.

E 373.4 (600.9 km) **PG 76.6** (123.3 km) Dome Creek bridge. Diner.

E 375.7 (604.6 km) **PG 74.3** (119.6 km) Ministry of Highways camp.

E 376.8 (606.4 km) **PG 73.2** (117.8 km) Slim Creek paved rest area to south with tables, playground, litter barrels and toilets. Watch for bears.

E 377.5 (607.5 km) **PG 72.5** (116.7 km) Slim Creek bridge.

E 388.7 (625.5 km) **PG 61.3** (98.6 km) Driscol Creek.

E 390.8 (628.9 km) **PG 59.2** (95.3 km) Gravel turnout with litter barrel to north.

E 392 (630.8 km) **PG 58** (93.3 km) Lunate Creek.

E 395 (635.7 km) **PG 55** (88.5 km) Hungary Creek. Watch for Ministry of Forests signs indicating the year in which a logged area was replanted. Wildflowers include fireweed, mid-July through August.

E 398.7 (641.6 km) **PG 51.3** (82.6 km) Sugarbowl Creek.

E 403.7 (649.7 km) **PG 46.3** (74.5 km) Paved turnout with litter barrel to north.

E 405 (651.8 km) **PG 45** (72.4 km) Kenneth Creek.

E 411.5 (662.2 km) **PG 38.5** (62 km) Purden Mountain ski resort.

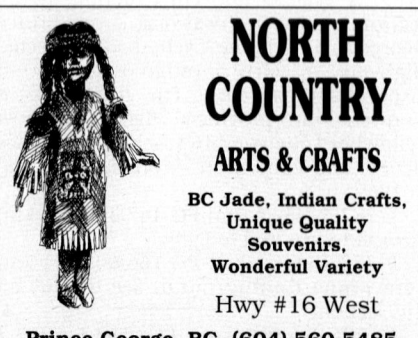

E 412 (663 km) **PG 38** (61.2 km) Resort with gas, lodging and camping. ▲

NOTE: Next gas stop eastbound is 91 miles/146.4 km from here (McBride).

E 414 (666.3 km) **PG 36** (57.9 km) **Purden Lake** Provincial Park; 78 campsites, 48 picnic sites, tables, water, dump station, firewood, playground and horseshoe pits. This recreation area offers a sandy beach, change houses, swimming, hiking trails, waterskiing and boat launch. Good rainbow fishing to 4 lbs., trolling.

E 415.5 (668.6 km) **PG 34.5** (55.5 km) Bowron River bridge. Paved rest area to north on river with toilets, tables and litter barrels.

E 422 (679.2 km) **PG 28** (45.1 km) Vama Vama Creek.

E 425 (684 km) **PG 25** (40.2 km) Wansa Creek.

E 428 (688.8 km) **PG 22** (35.4 km) Willow River bridge. Rest area at west end of bridge beside river; tables, litter barrels, toilets and nature trail. The 1.2-mile-/1.9-km-long Willow River Forest Interpretation Trail is an easy 45-minute walk.

E 430.4 (692.7 km) **PG 19.6** (31.5 km) Bowes Creek.

E 430.5 (692.8 km) **PG 19.5** (31.4 km) Turnout to north with litter barrels and information board on 1961 forest fire and moose habitat. Hiking trails to moose observation site.

E 436 (701.7 km) **PG 14** (22.5 km) Tabor Mountain ski hill.

E 436.2 (702 km) **PG 13.8** (22.2 km) Gravel turnout to north with litter barrels.

E 438.5 (705.7 km) **PG 11.5** (18.5 km) Turnoff for Log House Restaurant and RV Park. Access to **Tabor Lake**; good fishing for rainbow in spring.

E 444 (714.5 km) **PG 6** (9.7 km) **Junction,** Highway 16B with Highway 97 south bypass.

E 450 (724.2 km) **PG 0 PRINCE GEORGE, Junction** with Highway 97, north to Dawson Creek and the beginning of the Alaska Highway.

See WEST ACCESS ROUTE section for details on Prince George and the log of Highway 97 north. Continue west for Prince Rupert (log follows).

Yellowhead Highway 16 Log

(continued)

This section of the log shows distance from Prince George (PG) followed by distance from Prince Rupert (PR).

PG 0 PR 456 (733.8 km) From Prince George to Prince Rupert, Highway 16 is a two-lane highway with three-lane passing stretches. Fairly straight, with no high summits, the highway follows the valleys of the

Nechako, Bulkley and Skeena rivers, paralleling the Canadian National Railway route. There are few services between towns. *NOTE: There are few passing lanes between Prince George and Vanderhoof. Pass with caution.*

PG 3 (4.8 km) **PR 453** (729 km) KOA campground. ▲

PG 4.8 (7.8 km) **PR 451.2** (726.1 km) West Lake Provincial Park 8 miles/13 km south; day-use area with swimming, fishing and boat launch.

PG 14.9 (23.9 km) **PR 441.1** (709.9 km) **North Country Arts & Crafts.** See display ad this section.

PG 32.1 (51.7 km) **PR 423.9** (682.2 km) Rest area to north with picnic tables, toilets and litter barrels.

PG 38 (61.2 km) **PR 418** (672.7 km) Access to lakeside resort and fishing at **Cluculz Lake** (not visible from highway). Rainbow to 3 3/4 lbs. by trolling, use snell hook and worms; kokanee to 1 1/2 lbs., troll with snell hook and worms, in spring; arctic char to 57 lbs., use large flatfish, spoons, plugs and weights, early spring and late fall; whitefish to 5 lbs., anytime. Very good fishing in spring; ice goes out about the first week of May. Good ice fishing December to March. In September kokanee are at their peak. *Lake gets rough when windy.* ▲

Lakeside Resort. See display ad this section.

PG 39.1 (62.9 km) **PR 416.9** (670.9 km) Cluculz rest area to south with flush toilets (summer only), picnic tables and litter barrels.

PG 39.5 (63.5 km) **PR 416.5** (670.3 km) **Beaver Campsite & Cafe,** 45 restful sites in quiet pine forest. Eight pull-throughs. Electric hookups, laundromat, hot coin-op showers, sani-station. Ice. Store. Cafe with delicious home cooking. Laundromat. Playground. Water. Your hosts, Ed and Jean Sokoloski. RR 1, Site 17, Comp. 14, Vanderhoof, BC V0J 3A0. (604) 441-3385. [ADVERTISEMENT] ▲

PG 40.5 (65.2 km) **PR 415.5** (668.7 km) **Cluculz Lake Campground.** 5 km from Highway 16. Easy in and out. Pull-throughs, shaded campsites with shower, firepits and free wood. Lake and hiking trails nearby. Take Meier Road to West Meier. 5665 Meier Road W., Site 14, Comp. 24, RR 1, Vanderhoof, BC V0J 3A0. (604) 441-3564. [ADVERTISEMENT] ▲

PG 58.7 (94.5 km) **PR 397.3** (639.4 km) **Dave's RV Park.** Quiet rural setting 1/2 mile off highway; 2 miles east of downtown Vanderhoof. Level grassed and gravel sites, pull-throughs, full and partial hookups, firepits, picnic tables and sani-station. TV hookup available. New facilities include washrooms with flush toilets, free hot showers for guests, laundromat and pay phone. 1048 Derkson Road, Box 1512, Vanderhoof, BC V0J 3A0. (604) 567-3161. [ADVERTISEMENT] ▲

Vanderhoof

PG 60.5 (97.4 km) **PR 395.5** (636.5 km). **Population:** 4,025; area 12,000. **Emergency Services: Police,** phone 567-2222. **Fire Department,** phone 567-2345. **Ambulance,** phone 112-562-7241. **Hospital,** St. John's, Northside District, phone 567-2211.

Visitor Information: Travel Infocentre downtown on Burrard Street, one block off Highway 16. Write Vanderhoof & District Chamber of Commerce, Box 126-MP, Vanderhoof, BC V0J 3A0; phone (604) 567-2124.

Elevation: 2,086 feet/636m. **Radio:** CJCI 620, CFPR-FM 96.7, CKPG 550, CIVH 1340, CIRX-FM 95.9. **Television:** Channels 2, 4, 5, 6, 8. **Newspapers:** *Omineca Express–Bugle* (weekly). **Transportation: Air** — Vanderhoof airport, 2 miles/3.2 km from intersection of Highways 16 and 27; 5,000-foot/1,524-m paved runway. Seaplane landings on Nechako River at corner of View Street and Boundary Avenue. **Railroad** — VIA Rail, station at 2222 Church Ave. **Bus** — Greyhound.

Vanderhoof was named for Chicago publisher Herbert Vanderhoof, who founded the village in 1914 when he was associated with the Grand Trunk Development Co. Today, Vanderhoof is the supply and distribution centre for a large agricultural, lumbering and mining area.

The community's history is preserved at Vanderhoof Heritage Village Museum, just off Highway 16. Relocated pioneer structures furnished with period artifacts recall the early days of the Nechako Valley.

Located on the Nechako River, Vanderhoof is a stopping place in April and September for thousands of migrating waterfowl. The river flats upstream of the bridge are a bird sanctuary. Pelicans have been spotted feeding at Tachick Lake south of town.

Vanderhoof is also home to the second largest international air show in British Columbia, held in July or August (check with chamber of commerce).

There are seven hotels and motels and 16 restaurants in the town. All shopping facilities and several gas stations. Dump station at Dave's RV Park. Municipal campground is west of town on Highway 16. Nine-hole, par 35 golf course located 1.9 miles/3 km north of town. ▲

Area attractions include Fort St. James (see page 186), Tachick Lake and Kenney Dam. Follow the gravel road southwest from Vanderhoof 60 miles/96 km to Kenney Dam. At the time of its construction in 1951, it was North America's largest earth-filled dam. Near the dam site are Cheslatta Falls and Nechako River canyon (good area for rockhounding). Beautiful Tachick Lake (18 miles/29 km south) has a modern log building fishing resort and a lodge that serves European food. Also access to Nulki Lake; see fishing information following. Kenney Dam Road turnoff is at the Shell service station on Highway 16.

Nulki Lake, 12 miles/19.3 km south on Kenney Dam Road, rainbow to 6 or 7 lbs., average 2 lbs., use worms, year-round. **Tachick Lake,** 18 miles/29 km south on Kenney Dam Road, rainbow 2 to 7 lbs. year-round, largest fish in the area were taken from this lake; several small lakes in the area abound with rainbow and kokanee. Fishing charters available at Vanderhoof airport.

VANDERHOOF ADVERTISERS

Coach Light Motel & RV Park ....Ph. (604) 567-2296
O.K. Cafe ....Heritage Village Museum Park
Siesta Motel ....Ph. (604) 567-2365

Yellowhead Highway 16 Log

(continued)

PG 60.5 (97.4 km) **PR 395.5** (636.5 km) First **junction** westbound with Highway 27, which extends north from Vanderhoof several hundred miles. The 37 miles/59.6 km to Fort St. James are fully paved (see page 186).

PG 61.1 (98.3 km) **PR 394.9** (635.5 km) Vanderhoof Municipal Campground, pleasantly situated on a creek. ▲

PG 64.7 (104.2 km) **PR 391.3** (629.7 km) Second **junction** westbound with Highway 27 (see description at **Milepost PG 60.5**). This route skirts Vanderhoof. Truck weigh scales to north.

PG 70.8 (113.9 km) **PR 385.2** (619.9 km) Lone Willow Game Farm and Petting Zoo.

PG 72.8 (117.2 km) **PR 383.2** (616.7 km) Restaurant with pay phone and RV parking.

PG 73.7 (118.6 km) **PR 382.3** (615.2 km) Westar sawmill to south.

PG 83.8 (134.9 km) **PR 372.2** (599 km) Turnout to south with view of Nechako River. The Grand Trunk Pacific Railroad was completed near this site in 1914. The railroad (later the Canadian National) linked Prince Rupert, a deep-water port, with interior British Columbia.

PG 84.3 (135.7 km) **PR 371.7** (598.2 km) **FORT FRASER** (pop. 600). **Radio:** CBC-FM 102.9. Small community with food, gas,

Fort St. James

Fort St. James

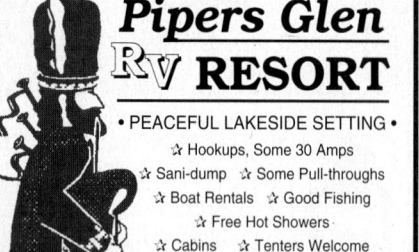

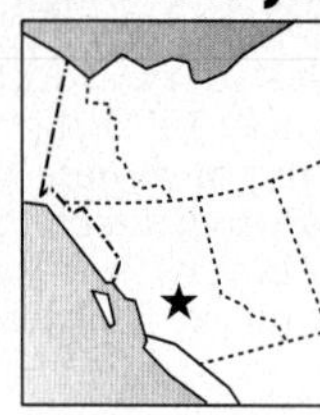

Located 37 miles/59.6 km north of Vanderhoof on Highway 27. **Population:** 1,983. **Emergency Services: Police,** phone 996-8269. **Ambulance:** phone 1-562-7241. **Elevation:** 2,208 feet/673m. **Radio:** CKPG 550, CBC-FM 1070, CJCI 1480.

Fort St. James is the site of **FORT ST. JAMES NATIONAL HISTORIC PARK.** Established in 1806 by Simon Fraser as a fur trading post for the Northwest Co., Fort St. James served throughout the 19th century as headquarters for the Hudson's Bay Co.'s New Caledonia fur trade district. The fur warehouse, fish cache, men's house, officers' dwelling and trade shop have been restored to the year 1896 and are open to the public. Check with the visitor centre regarding tours and interpretive programs.

From mid-May through June and in September, visitors may take guided tours from 10 A.M. to 5 P.M. daily. In July and August, visitors may explore the grounds on their own. Staff members are dressed in period costumes as part of a living history program; hours are 9:30 A.M. to 5:30 P.M. daily. For the remainder of the year, the site is closed.

The historic site and village are located on Stuart Lake. Named for John Stuart, the man who succeeded Simon Fraser as head of the New Caledonia district, the 59-mile-long lake is the southernmost in a three-lake chain that provides hundreds of miles of boating and fishing. Fort St. James also boasts the Nation Lakes, a chain of four lakes (Tsayta, Indata, Tchentlo and Chuchi) connected by the Nation River.

Attractions include the Our Lady of Good Hope Catholic Church and the Chief Kwah burial site. The recently renovated church is one of the oldest in British Columbia. Open for summer evening services only, check schedule. Chief Kwah was one of the first Carrier Indian chiefs to confront early white explorers. His burial site is located on the Nak'azdli Indian Reserve at the mouth of the Stuart River. At Cottonwood Park on the shore of Lake Stuart, look for a model of a Junkers airplane, which depicts the Fort's major role in early bush flying in Northern British Columbia.

Fort St. James has a hotel, lodge, resort, four motels, a bed and breakfast, two private campgrounds and a number of surrounding lodges and settlements, such as Tachie, Manson Creek and Germansen Landing in the Omineca Mountains. Other services in Fort St. James include four gas stations, four dump stations, two government marinas, two private marinas and several restaurants. The village also has a theatre and two shopping centres. Picnicking and swimming at Cottonwood Park on Stuart Lake. Murray Ridge ski area, a 20-minute drive from town, has 21 downhill-ski runs and 18.5 miles/30 km of cross-country ski trails.

FORT ST. JAMES ADVERTISERS

Stuart Lodge................Ph. (604) 996-7917
Stuart River Campgrounds........Ph. (604) 996-8690

Stuart Lodge, Stones Bay, Fort St. James. On Stuart Lake below the Mount Pope rock. Comfortable, fully supplied cabins, spectacular view, boat rental, sundecks, barbecue. Sorry, no pets. The friendly, quiet and clean place for vacationists, fishermen and business people. $35 (U.S.) and up per night. Phone (604) 996-7917. Enjoy Super, Natural North by Northwest. [ADVERTISEMENT]

Stuart River Campgrounds. Treed sites, tenting to full hookups, showers and laundry, firepits and firewood, pay phone. Playgrounds, horseshoe pits; marina with launching ramp and moorage space. Great fishing! Boat rentals, fishing licenses and tackle. Your hosts, George and Heather Malbeuf, Box 306, Fort St. James, BC V0J 1P0. (604) 996-8690. Enjoy Super, Natural North by Northwest. [ADVERTISEMENT] ▲

Camping is also available at Paarens Beach Provincial Park, located 6.8 miles/11 km off Highway 27 on Sowchea Bay Road; 36 campsites, picnic shelter, picnic tables, toilets, water, firepits, boat launch, swimming, camping fee. Sowchea Bay Provincial Park, located 10.6 miles/17 km off Highway 27 on Sowchea Bay Road, has 30 campsites, camping fee, picnic tables, toilets, water, firepits, boat launch and swimming. ▲

Good fishing in **Stuart Lake** for rainbow and char (to trophy size), kokanee and Dolly Varden.

Return to Milepost PG 60.5 or PG 64.7 Yellowhead Highway 16

propane, lodging and first-aid station. Gas station with hot showers, convenience store and restaurant. Named for Simon Fraser, who established a trading post here in 1806. Now a supply centre for surrounding farms and sawmills. The last spike of the Grand Trunk Railway was driven here on April 7, 1914.

PG 85.1 (137 km) **PR 370.9** (596.9 km) Nechako River bridge. Turnout to south with parking, litter barrels and access to **Nechako River;** fishing for rainbow and Dolly Varden, June to fall. At the east end of Fraser Lake, the Nautley River — less than a mile long — drains into the Nechako River.

PG 87 (140 km) **PR 369** (593.8 km) Beaumont Provincial Park, on beautiful Fraser Lake, north side of highway; site of original Fort Fraser. Boat launch, swimming, hiking, fishing, 49 campsites, picnic tables, firewood, restrooms, water, playground, horseshoe pits, dump station, $9.50 camping fee. Park gates closed from 10 P.M. to 7 A.M. ▲

Fishing in **Fraser Lake** for rainbow and lake trout, burbot, sturgeon and Dolly Varden.

PG 89.2 (143.5 km) **PR 366.8** (590.3 km) **Pipers Glen RV Resort.** See display ad this section. ▲

PG 90.7 (146 km) **PR 365.3** (587.9 km) Dry William Lake rest area to south with picnic tables, toilets and litter barrels.

PG 91.7 (147.6 km) **PR 364.3** (586.3 km) **Orange Valley Motel, RV Park and Campground.** Easy access featuring level sites, large pull-throughs, electricity, water, some with sewer. Free showers, flush toilets, sanidump, treed shaded sites with picnic tables. Firepits, firewood; freezer space available. Quiet relaxed setting. Pay phone, golf driving range, hiking trails, beaver dam. Phone (604) 699-6350. [ADVERTISEMENT] ▲

PG 93.8 (151 km) **PR 362.2** (582.9 km) Fraser Lake sawmill to north.

PG 95.5 (153.7 km) **PR 360.5** (580.2 km) Rest area to north. Trail to Fraser Lake.

PG 97.5 (156.9 km) **PR 358.5** (576.9 km) **FRASER LAKE** (pop. 1,400; elev. 2,580 feet/786m). **Visitor Information:** Travel Infocentre and museum in log building at east edge of town. **Radio:** CJCI 1450. Small community with all facilities. Created by Endako Mines Ltd. in 1964 on an older townsite; named after the explorer Simon Fraser. Endako Mines Ltd. began operating in 1965 and was Canada's largest molybdenum mine until production slowed in 1982. Mining resumed in 1986. Mine tours are available on Wednesdays; check with the Travel Infocentre for reservations. Also located here is Fraser Lake Sawmills, the town's largest employer.

Fraser Lake Restaurant. See display ad this section.

PG 100 (161 km) **PR 356** (572.9 km) **Junction** with main access road south to scenic Francois Lake; also accessible via roads from Burns Lake to Houston. Francois Lake Road (gravel) leads south 7 miles/11.2 km to the east end of Francois Lake (where the Stellako River flows from the lake) and back to Highway 16 at Endako. Molyhills golf course and several resorts with camping, cabins and boats are located on this scenic rural road through the Glenannan area. ▲

Glenannan Tourist Area. See display ad this section.

Francois Lake, good fishing for rainbow to 5 lbs., May to October; kokanee to 3/4 lb., use flashers, willow leaf, flashers with worms, flatfish or spinners, August and September; char to 30 lbs., use large flatfish or spoon, June and July. **Stellako River** is considered one of British Columbia's better fly-fishing streams with rainbow over 2 lbs., all summer; whitefish averaging 1 lb., year-round.

PG 100.1 (161.1 km) **PR 355.9** (572.7 km) Bridge over Stellako River. Highway passes through the Stellako Indian Reserve.

PG 105.9 (170.4 km) **PR 350.1** (563.4 km) **ENDAKO.** A small highway community with grocery (closed Sunday), post office, pub and gas station with minor repair service. Turnoff for molybdenum mine just east of town. Several private campgrounds are located along Francois Lake Road to the south in the Glenannan area.

PG 107 (172.2 km) **PR 349** (561.6 km) Endako River bridge.

PG 110.5 (177.8 km) **PR 345.5** (556 km) Savory rest area to north beside Watskin Creek.

PG 113.3 (182.3 km) **PR 342.7** (551.5 km) Ross Creek.

PG 122.1 (196.5 km) **PR 333.9** (537.3 km) Paved turnout to south.

PG 126.1 (202.9 km) **PR 329.9** (530.9 km) Babine Forest Products sawmill to south.

PG 128.7 (207.1 km) **PR 327.3** (526.7 km) Food and pay phone to south.

PG 133.7 (215.2 km) **PR 322.3** (518.7 km) Rest area to south with toilet, tables, litter barrels and Tintagel Cairn point of interest.

PG 137.3 (221 km) **PR 318.7** (512.9 km) **Freeport K.O.A.**, a day's drive from Prince Rupert ferry. Cabins, tenting to full hookups, store, heated showers, laundromat, game room, playground. Mini-golf, canoe and boat rentals, lake swimming and horseshoes. Open May 1 to Sept. 30. Pay phone. Your host, Ed Brown, Box 491, Burns Lake, BC V0J 1E0. (604) 692-3105. [ADVERTISEMENT] ▲

Free ferry crosses Francois Lake 18 miles/29 km south of Burns Lake. (Gerry Deiter)

PG 139.9 (225.1 km) **PR 316.1** (508.7 km) Welcome to Burns Lake sign.

PG 140.9 (226.8 km) **PR 315.1** (507.1 km) **Junction** with scenic Highway 35 (paved) south to Tchesinkut, Francois, Takysie and Ootsa lakes; lodging, camping and fishing. Another of the Yellowhead's popular fishing areas with a variety of family-owned camping and cabin resorts. ▲

Likkel's Lakeside Store and Resort. See display ad this section. ▲

Sandy's RV and Camping Resort. Comfortable, casual atmosphere where you'll be welcomed with northern hospitality. Located on a true fishing lake: catch rainbow and lake trout, kokanee and freshwater ling cod. Over 50 full-service sites; partial hookups available. Every site has a water view. Camping area with picnic shelter and barbecue pit, running water and pit toilets. Fully equipped cabins with heat, electricity, running water, linens and utensils. Hot showers, laundromat, playground, recreation centre. Boat and fishing equipment rentals. Sheltered marina with boat launch, fuel and moorage. On Highway 35, 18 paved miles south of Burns Lake on Francois Lake. Pets welcome. May 15 – Oct. 15. Phone/fax (604) 695-6321. Your hosts Chris and Sheila. Box 42, Burns Lake, BC V0J 1E0. Super Natural North by Northwest. [ADVERTISEMENT] ▲

Burns Lake

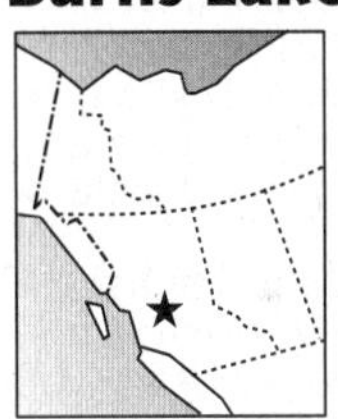

PG 141.3 (227.4 km) **PR 314.7** (506 km) **Population:** 2,300; area 10,000. **Visitor Information:** Government Travel Infocentre at the flashing light (the only one in town) on the west side of the village. The infocentre also houses a museum, art gallery and the chamber of commerce.

Elevation: 2,320 feet/707m. **Radio:** CBC-FM 99.1, CJCI 760. **Transportation:** Greyhound Bus, VIA Rail.

Burns Lake began about 1911 as a con-

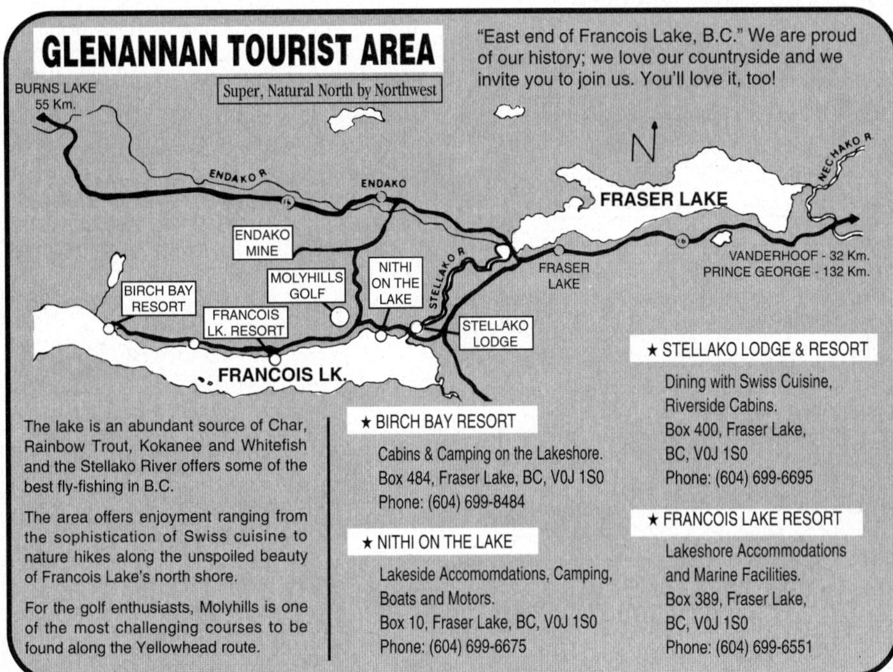

struction camp for the Grand Trunk Pacific Railway. Forestry is the economic mainstay of the area today, with ranching and tourism also important.

Located in the heart of the Lakes District, Burns Lake boasts "3,000 miles of fishing." Species include rainbow trout, char and salmon. Small family-owned fishing resorts offering lodging and camping are tucked along these lakes offering quality vacation experiences.

Burns Lake is also the gateway to Tweedsmuir Provincial Park, 50 miles/80 km south. This huge wilderness park is accessible by boat, trail and air.

Rock hounds can visit Eagle Creek opal deposits, a short drive south of Burns Lake (not recommended for motorhomes).

There are six gas stations (one with a dump station), five hotels/motels, seven restaurants, several gift shops — many of which feature local crafts and artists — and shopping malls.

The Burns Lake Municipal Park, located next to the civic centre, offers a pleasant setting for a picnic. On the north shore of the lake, the park has picnic tables and a small pier.

From Burns Lake, Highway 35 (paved) extends south 18 miles/29 km past **Tchesinkut Lake** to **Francois Lake** ferry landing. A free 36-car ferry departs from the south shore on the hour, from the north shore on the half-hour. From the south shore of Francois Lake, Highway 35 continues to **Takysie Lake** and **Ootsa Lake**, with access to a number of other fishing lakes. There are several resorts along Highway 35 offering camping and lodging. Gas stations, stores and food service are also available.

Yellowhead Highway 16 Log

(continued)

PG 146 (235 km) **PR 310** (498.9 km) Side road leads north to Babine Lake, the longest natural lake in the province. One of British Columbia's most important salmon producing lakes, Babine Lake drains into the Skeena River. At Mile 15/24 km on this road is Ethel F. Wilson Provincial Park on Pinkut Lake; 10 campsites, fishing, swimming, picnic tables, boat launch. Tours of nearby Pinkut Fish Hatchery available. Look for pictographs on cliffs across from hatchery. Pendleton Bay Provincial Park on Babine Lake offers 12 campsites, picnic tables, fishing, swimming and boat launch. Resorts with cabins and camping on Babine Lake. ▲

Birch Lane Cabin Resort. See display ad this section. ▲

Babine Lake Resort, 48 km from Burns Lake. British Columbia's largest natural body of water. Good fishing. Photographer's dream. Self-contained cabins, power, water hookups, showers, tenting, boats, smokehouses, store, licensed dining by reservation only. Ausserdem sprechen wir deutsch. Accepting VISA. Bill and Traude Hoff welcome you. Box 528, Burns Lake. JK-H-496674. [ADVERTISEMENT] ▲

PG 150 (241.4 km) **PR 306** (492.4 km) Small community of **DECKER LAKE.**

Decker Lake, good char and trout fishing; fly-fishing in **Endako River,** which joins Decker and Burns lakes.

PG 153.3 (246.7 km) **PR 302.7** (487.1 km) Palling rest area with picnic tables, toilets and litter barrels.

PG 157.1 (252.8 km) **PR 298.9** (481 km) Baker Lake airstrip to south is used by fire-fighting tankers. Weather station.

PG 160.2 (257.8 km) **PR 295.8** (476 km) Rose Lake to south.

PG 165.2 (265.9 km) **PR 290.8** (468 km) **Broman Lake,** rainbow and char to 4 lbs., use white-winged flies, spring and summer.

PG 169.1 (272.1 km) **PR 286.9** (461.7 km) China Nose Mountain Summit (elev. 4,669 feet/1,423m) to west.

PG 175.5 (282.4 km) **PR 280.5** (451.4 km) **TOPLEY** (pop. 300). Grocery, post office, cafe, motel and gas station. Turn north here for Babine Lake Recreation Area. This paved side road leads north to Topley Landing and Granisle on Babine Lake (descriptions follow). From its junction with the highway at Topley, mileages are as follows: Mile 4.3/7 km, Findlay Fall rest area; Mile 23.6/38 km, private lodge; Mile 24.4/39.3 km, turnoff to village of Topley Landing; Mile 28.8/46.3 km, Fulton River spawning channel; Mile 28/45 km, Red Bluff Provincial Park; Mile 31.4/50.5 km, Granisle; Mile 33.4/53.8 km, begin 16-mile/26-km gravel road to Smithers Landing Road, which connects Smithers Landing and Smithers. *CAUTION: Watch for moose along road.*

TOPLEY LANDING has several resorts and a provincial park for picnicking, swimming and fishing. The government-operated Fulton River spawning channel has two major spawning channels on the river, which connects Fulton Lake and Babine Lake. Babine Lake, which flows into the Skeena River, is one of the largest freshwater habitats for sockeye salmon. The salmon enhancement project at Fulton River produces about 95 million sockeye fry annually. The sockeye run takes place in August and September. Tours available at hatchery office. ▲

Campbell's Babine Lodge. See display ad this section.

GRANISLE (pop. 600) was established in 1966 as a company town for the Granisle Copper Mine. In 1972, Noranda Bell Mines Copper Division went into operation. Granisle Copper was closed in 1982 and the Noranda mine was closed in 1992. Granisle remains a resort area for fishing, boating, waterskiing and wilderness camping at Babine Lake. Facilities at Granisle include a gas station, grocery store, liquor outlet and hotel. Dump station and fresh water available at the Travel Infocentre. Red Bluff Provincial Park, south of Granisle at Babine Lake, has 64 campsites, 20 picnic tables, boat launch and swimming beach. ▲

Babine Lake, rainbow 6 to 8 lbs.; lake trout to 40 lbs., use spoons, flashers, and red-and-white spoons, May through November. When fishing for either early in the year, use a short troll.

PG 175.8 (282.9 km) **PR 280.2** (450.9 km) Rest area to south with view of coastal mountains.

PG 193.9 (312 km) **PR 262.1** (421.8 km) **Shady Rest RV Park.** See display ad this section. ▲

Houston

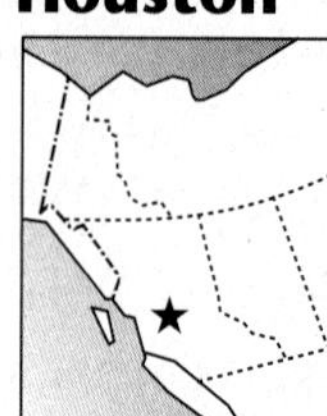

PG 194.3 (312.7 km) **PR 261.7** (421.2 km) **Population:** 3,960. **Emergency Services: Police,** phone 845-2204. **Ambulance,** phone 112-562-7241. **Visitor Information:** Travel Infocentre in log building on Highway 16 across from the mall; open year-round. Write Houston Travel Infocentre, Box 396, Houston, BC V0J 1Z0, or phone (604) 845-7640.

Elevation: 1,949 feet/594m. **Radio:** CJFW 105.5, CFBV 1450, CFPR-FM 102.1. **Transportation:** Greyhound bus, VIA Rail.

Established in the early 1900s, Houston was a tie-cutting centre during construction of the Grand Trunk Pacific Railway in 1912. It was named for Prince Rupert newspaperman John Houston, the former mayor of Nelson, BC. Logging continued to support the local economy with the rapid growth of mills and planer mills in the 1940s and 1950s. Houston was incorporated as a village in 1957.

The Equity Silver Mine began production in 1980. Although the mine recently closed down its pit, it continues to do underground mining.

Today, the main industry in Houston is

forest products. The two large sawmills here, Houston Forest Products and Northwood Pulp and Timber, offer forestry awareness tours. The chamber of commerce and Travel Infocentre arrange tours of the sawmills and also offer a day-long tour through the area's forests to provide a first-hand look at the forest industry.

Hunting, canoeing, cross-country skiing and especially sportfishing are major attractions here with the Bulkley River, nearby Morice River and several lakes. Look for the World's Largest Fly Fishing Rod on display at the Travel Infocentre. The 60-foot-long anodized aluminum fly rod was designed by a local avid fly fisherman and built by local volunteers. (The 21-inch fly is a fluorescent "Skykomish Sunrise.")

Houston has all visitor facilities, including motels, campgrounds, restaurants, gas stations, a shopping centre and golf courses. ▲

Houston Chamber of Commerce. See display ad this section.

Yellowhead Highway 16 Log

(continued)

PG 197.4 (317.7 km) **PR 258.6** (416.1 km) **Junction** with the Morice River access road which extends 52 miles/84 km south to Morice Lake. Approximately 20 miles/32 km along the Morice River Road you can turn east on a gravel road which leads past Owen Lake and Nadina River Road to Francois Lake. From Francois Lake ferry landing Highway 35 leads north to Burns Lake.

The two famous salmon and steelhead streams, **Morice** and **Bulkley**, unite near Houston and it is possible to fish scores of pools all along the Morice River. *NOTE: Special requirements apply to fishing these streams; check with Fish and Game office.*

PG 198.5 (319.4 km) **PR 257.5** (414.4 km) Bulkley River bridge; picnic spot with tables, litter barrel and toilets.

PG 202.5 (325.9 km) **PR 253.5** (407.9 km) View of Morice River valley eastbound. Westbound travelers are in the Bulkley River valley.

PG 205.3 (330.4 km) **PR 250.7** (403.5 km) Hungry Hill Summit (elev. 2,769 feet/844m). To the north are the snow-capped peaks of the Babine Mountains, to the west is the Hudson Bay Range.

PG 222.8 (358.6 km) **PR 233.2** (375.3 km) Bulkley View paved rest area with picnic tables, toilets and litter barrels.

PG 225.6 (363.1 km) **PR 230.4** (370.8 km) **Ft. Telkwa R.V. Park.** See display ad this section. ▲

PG 226 (363.7 km) **PR 230** (370.1 km) **TELKWA** (pop. 959). A pleasant village on the Bulkley River (you can fish the river from Main Street). Travel Infocentre at the village office. Facilities include a grocery, post office and a gas station with auto repair. Lodging at Douglas Motel, dining at Fourth Street Grill. A unique shop found here is Horsfield Harness and Leather, which specializes in handmade fishing rod cases, leather water bottles and other leather goods. Fishing and hunting information, licenses and supplies available at the general store. Kinsmen Barbecue is held over Labour Day weekend; games, contests and demolition derby. Eddy Park, on the western edge of town beside the Bulkley River, is a good spot for picnicking (look for the wishing well). St. Stephen's Anglican Church here was built in 1911 and the bell and English gate added in 1921. Other Heritage Buildings here date back to 1908.

Fourth Street Grill. Good, wholesome food prepared fresh daily. Wherever possible, we use local produce. Lunch or dine on our licensed patio or in our dining room. We pride ourselves in quality of our food and service. On Highway 16, 1/2 block north of stoplight. Spacious lot for RV parking at rear. (604) 846-9268. [ADVERTISEMENT]

PG 226.5 (364.5 km) **PR 229.5** (369.3 km) Turnoff to north for Tyhee Lake Provincial Park; 55 campsites, 20 picnic tables, dump station, hiking trails, fishing, swimming, boat launch. Seaplane base at lake; charter fly-in fishing. ▲

Also turnoff here on the Telkwa High Road, which intersects with Babine Lake access road (gravel) which leads 46 miles/74 km north to Smithers Landing on Babine Lake and 56 miles/90 km to Granisle.

Tyhee Lake, rainbow and lake trout to 2 lbs., use tee-spinners, spoons, worms, June through August; Kamloops trout to 2 lbs. Boat launching facilities available. **Babine River**, steelhead to 40 lbs., use winged bobbers, Kitamats and weighted spoons in late fall; can be reached by road or water. **Telkwa River**, spring and coho salmon to 24 lbs., summer to fall.

PG 231.5 (372.6 km) **PR 224.5** (361.3 km) Second turnoff westbound for Babine Lake.

PG 232.8 (374.6 km) **PR 223.2** (359.2 km) **Riverside Recreation Centre.** See display ad this section. ▲

PG 233.1 (375.1 km) **PR 222.9** (358.7 km) Turnoff to north on gravel road for Driftwood Canyon Provincial Park; picnic area and fossil beds in shale outcroppings along creekbank. This gravel side road continues north to Smithers Landing.

PG 233.7 (376.1 km) **PR 222.3** (357.7 km) Bridge over Bulkley River.

Smithers

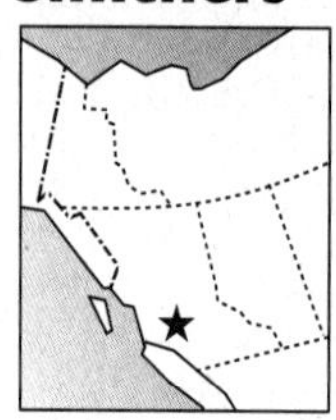

PG 235.4 (378.8 km) **PR 220.6** (355 km). **Population:** 5,000; area 30,000. **Emergency Services: Police**, phone 847-3233. **Hospital and Poison Centre**, 3950 8th Ave., phone 847-2611. **Ambulance**, phone 1-562-7241.

Visitor Information: Travel Infocentre at the intersection of Highway 16 and Main Street, east side of highway, in the rail car adjacent to the museum; open daily June through August. The chamber of commerce, located above the museum in the Central Park Building, provides information September through May.

Elevation: 1,621 feet/494m. **Climate:** Relatively warmer and drier than mountainous areas to the west, average temperature in July is 58°F/15°C, in January 14°F/-10°C; annual precipitation, 13 inches. **Radio:** CFBV 1230, CFPR-FM 97.5. **Television:** Channels 5, 13 and cable. **Newspaper:** *Interior News* (weekly).

Transportation: Air — Scheduled service to Vancouver and Terrace via Canadian Airlines International. Daily flights to Prince George, Terrace and Burns Lake via Central Mountain Air. **Railroad** — VIA Rail. **Bus** — Greyhound. **Car Rentals** — Available.

Sitting amidst rugged mountains, the alpine flavour of the town has been enhanced by Swiss-style storefronts that have been added to many of the buildings. Reconstructed in 1979, Main Street offers many shops and restaurants. Incorporated as a village in 1921, Smithers officially became a town in Canada's centennial year, 1967. The original site was chosen in 1913 by construction crews working on the Grand Trunk Pacific Railroad (the town was named for one-time chairman of the railway A.W. Smithers). Today it is a distribution and supply centre for farms, mills and mines in the area.

Smithers is the largest town in the Bulkley Valley and the site of Hudson Bay Mountain, a popular ski area (skiing from November to mid-April).

ACCOMMODATIONS

Smithers has several motels, gas stations, restaurants and good shopping. Government liquor store located on Queen Street at Broadway Avenue. There are two 18-hole golf courses, both with rentals and clubhouses.

There is a municipal campground with security and firewood (no hookups) at Riverside Park on the Bulkley River; turn north at the museum across from Main Street and drive up the hill about a mile and watch for sign. There are private campgrounds located east and west of town; see highway log. A dump station is located beside the railcar Infocentre on the corner of Highway 16 and Main Street. ▲

SMITHERS ADVERTISERS

Aspen Motor Inn ....Ph. (604) 847-4551
Capri Motor Inn................Ph. (604) 847-4226
Florence Motel..................Ph. (604) 847-2678
Jasmine's Restaurant.........Ph. (604) 847-4703
Smithers Chamber of Commerce..................Central Park Bldg.
Smitty's Family Restaurant ....Ph. (604) 847-3357
Trail's End RV Park............Ph. (604) 847-5457
Wash The Works...................On the access rd.

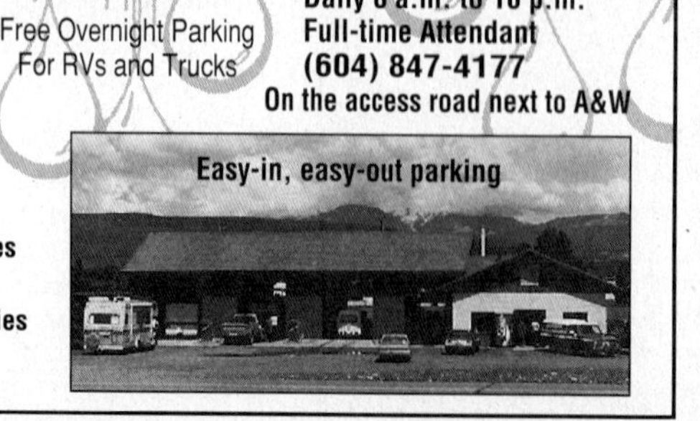

ATTRACTIONS

The Art Gallery and Museum, in the Central Park Bldg. at the corner of Main Street and Highway 16, displays both local and traveling art shows in addition to artifacts from the early days of the Bulkley Valley.

Bulkley Valley Fall Fair is held on the last weekend in August each year, and is one of the largest agricultural exhibitions in the province.

Area Attractions. Smithers offers a number of scenic drives. Hudson Bay Mountain (elev. 8,700 feet/2,652m) is a 14-mile/22-km drive from Highway 16; the plateau above timberline at the ski area is a good spot for summer hikes. In the winter months, Smithers boasts one of the largest ski hills in Northern BC. A 6,000-foot triple chair and two T-bars climb the 1,750-foot vertical, offering skiers 18 different runs.

Fossil hunters should drive to Driftwood Canyon Provincial Park; turn off Highway 16 just east of the Bulkley River bridge (travelers are advised to stop first at the visitor information centre in town for a map and directions). A display at the park illustrates the fossils, such as metasequoia, a type of redwood that occurs in the shale formation.

Adams Igloo Wildlife Museum, just west of town on Highway 16, has an excellent display of mammals found in British Columbia.

A beautiful spot not to be missed is Twin Falls and Glacier Gulch. Take the 4-mile-/6.4-km-long gravel road (steep in places) from Highway 16 on the western edge of town.

A 2.2-mile-/3.5-km-long interpretive nature trail with native wildlife and plant species is 10 miles/16 km west of Smithers on the Hudson Bay Mountain Ski Hill road in Smithers Community Forest. This trail can also be used in winter for cross-country skiing, and connects to other cross-country ski trails. Detailed maps of the area showing all hiking trails are available at the information centre.

Fishing: An extensive list of lakes in the area with information on boat launches, boat rentals, fishing and angling regulations is available from the Smithers District Chamber of Commerce, Box 2379, Smithers, BC V0J 2N0, phone 847-9854, or ask at the Travel Infocentre.

Hunting: Moose, mule deer, grizzly, black bear, mountain goat and caribou are found in the area, and guides and outfitters are available locally. All species of grouse can be hunted in the Bulkley Valley during the fall. Information is available from the Fish and Wildlife Branch office in Smithers.

Traditional Indian fishing spot at Moricetown Canyon and Falls. (Gerry Deiter)

Yellowhead Highway 16 Log

(continued)

PG 237.8 (382.7 km) **PR 218.2** (351.1 km) Paved access road to Lake Kathlyn. There is a municipal park with small beach and boat launch located here. Powerboats not permitted. Closed to waterfowl hunting. Side road continues 4 miles/6.4 km (gravel) to Twin Falls and Glacier Gulch.

PG 238.9 (384.5 km) **PR 217.1** (349.4 km) Road to north leads to Smithers airport.

PG 241.4 (388.5 km) **PR 214.6** (345.3 km) **Adams Igloo Wildlife Museum.** The finest collection of big game animals, furbearers and birds native to British Columbia. Mounted life-size and displayed in their natural habitat. The inside mural, painted by leading wildlife artist Tom Sander, gives a three-dimensional impression for realism. Stop at the White Dome 6 miles west of Smithers beside one of the highway's most beautiful viewpoints. Fur rugs and souvenirs for sale. Jack Adams, Curator. [ADVERTISEMENT]

PG 241.5 (388.6 km) **PR 214.5** (345.2 km) Hudson Bay rest area to west with picnic tables, toilets and litter barrels. Beautiful view of Hudson Bay Mountain.

PG 249.5 (401.6 km) **PR 206.5** (332.3 km) Trout Creek bridge. Store with groceries, post office and phone; fishing licenses available.

PG 255.5 (411.2 km) **PR 200.5** (322.7 km) Turnout to north with picnic tables and view of Bulkley River and Moricetown Canyon; good photo stop.

PG 255.7 (411.4 km) **PR 200.3** (322.3 km) Short side road on the north side of the highway leads to Moricetown Canyon and Falls on the Bulkley River and Moricetown campground. For centuries a famous Indian fishing spot, Indians may still be seen here gaffing, jigging and netting salmon in July and August. A worthwhile stop. ▲

PG 257.9 (415 km) **PR 198.1** (318.8 km) **MORICETOWN** (pop. 680; elev. 1,341 feet/408m). **Radio:** CBC-FM 96.5. Moricetown has a gas station with minor repair service and diesel fuel. There is a handicraft store. A campground is located in Moricetown Canyon (turnoff at **Milepost PG 255.7**). Moricetown is an Indian reserve and village, the oldest settlement in the Bulkley Valley. Traditionally, the Native people (Wet'su-wet'en) took advantage of the narrow canyon to trap salmon. The centuries-old Indian settlement ('Kyah Wiget) is named after Father A.G. Morice, a Roman Catholic missionary. Born in France, Father Morice came to British Columbia in 1880 and worked with the Indians of northern British Columbia from 1885 to 1904. He achieved world recognition for his authoritative writings in anthropology, ethnology and history.

PG 271.5 (436.9 km) **PR 184.5** (296.9 km) Turnoff to north for Forest Service campsite (7.5 miles/12 km) with pit toilets, tables and litter barrels. Fishing in **Suskwa River;** coho salmon to 10 lbs., use teespinners in July; steelhead to 20 lbs., use Kitamat #32 and soft bobbers in late fall.

PG 276.5 (445 km) **PR 179.5** (288.9 km) Turnoff to north for Ross Lake Provincial Park; 25 picnic sites, boat launch (no powerboats), swimming. Fishing at **Ross Lake** for rainbow to 4 lbs.

PG 278.5 (448.2 km) **PR 177.5** (285.6 km) Turnout with litter barrel and Hazelton area map.

PG 278.8 (448.6 km) **PR 177.2** (285.2 km) Entering New Hazelton, the first of three communities westbound sharing the name Hazelton; the others are Hazelton and South Hazelton.

New Hazelton

PG 279 (449 km) **PR 177** (284.8 km) **Junction** of Highway 16 and Highway 62 to Hazelton, 'Ksan and Kispiox. **Population:** area 1,300. **Emergency Services: Police,** phone 842-5244. **Visitor Information:** Travel Infocentre in two-story log building at the junction. Look for the three statues representing the gold rush packer Cataline, the Northwest miner, and the Upper Skeena logger. Museum located in Infocentre.

Elevation: 1,150 feet/350m. **Radio:** CBC 1170. **Transportation:** VIA Rail. Greyhound bus.

This small highway community has gas stations, major auto repair, restaurants, cafes, post office, general store, a hotel and motel. Laundromat, propane, sporting goods and hunting and fishing licenses available in town. Mount Rocher Deboule towers 8,000 feet/2,438m behind the town.

Attractions here include historic Hazelton, the Indian village of 'Ksan and sportfishing the Bulkley and Kispiox rivers. Descriptions follow.

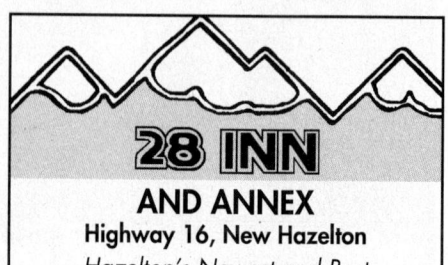

HAZELTON. Situated at the confluence of the Skeena and Bulkley rivers, Hazelton grew up at "The Forks" as a transshipping point at the head of navigation on the Skeena and a wintering place for miners and prospectors from the rigorous Interior. Thomas Hankin established a Hudson's Bay

Co. trading post in 1868. The name Hazelton comes from the numerous hazelnut bushes growing on the flats.

Cataline, famous pioneer packer and traveler, is buried near here. Jean Caux (his real name) was a Basque who, from 1852 to 1912, with loaded mules plodding 12 miles/19 km a day, supplied mining and construction camps from Yale and Ashcroft northward through Hazelton, where he often wintered. His mule trails became roads, his exploits legends.

For some years, before the arrival of railroad and highways, supplies for trading posts at Bear and Babine lakes and the Omineca goldfields moved by riverboat from the coast to Hazelton and from there over trails to the backcountry. Some of the Yukon gold rushers passed through Hazelton on their way to the Klondike, pack trains having made the trip from Hazelton to Telegraph Creek over the old Telegraph Trail as early as 1874.

This community has reconstructed much of what the town was like in the 1890s. Look for the antique machinery downtown. The history of the Hazelton area can be traced by car on the Hand of History tour. Pick up a brochure from the Travel Infocentre showing the location of the 19 historic sites on the driving tour.

'KSAN, a replica Gitksan Indian village, is 4.5 miles/7.2 km from Highway 16. It was constructed at the junction of the Bulkley and Skeena rivers by the 'Ksan Assoc. with the assistance of the governments of Canada and British Columbia. There are six communal houses, totem poles and dugout canoes. At the Carving House of All Times master carvers produce Indian arts and crafts that can be purchased in the Today House of the Arts.

For a nominal charge from May to September, you can join a guided tour of the communal houses. Performances of traditional dancing and singing are presented every Friday evening during July and August in the Wolf House.

A well-maintained full-service trailer park and campground on the banks of the Skeena and Bulkley rivers is operated by the Hazelton Band of Gitksan adjacent to 'Ksan village. ▲

KISPIOX (pop. 825) Indian village and three fishing resorts are 20 miles/32 km

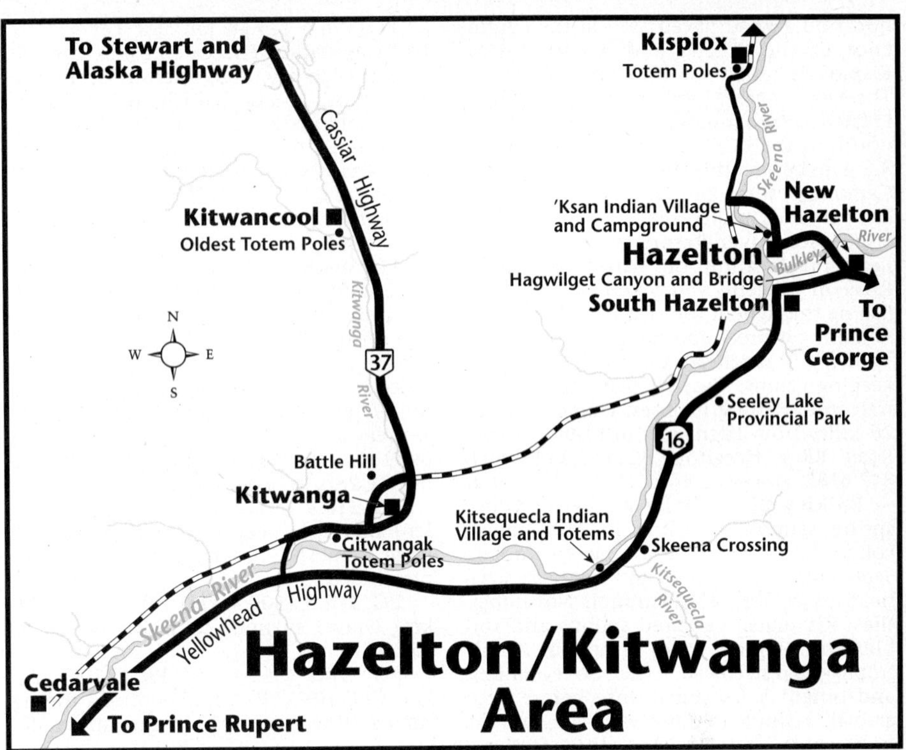

north on a good paved road at the confluence of the Skeena and Kispiox rivers. Kispiox is noted for its stand of totems. There is a market garden (fresh vegetables) located approximately 7 miles/11.3 km north on the Kispiox Road (about 2 miles/3.2 km before the Kispiox totem poles). Camping, cabins and fishing at lodges and campgrounds in the valley.

Kispiox River Resort & Campground. Beautiful location on banks of Kispiox River in peaceful valley setting. Excellent fishing throughout the year including spring salmon, cutthroat and rainbow trout, Dolly Varden and steelhead. Campground. Housekeeping cabins. Showers. Laundry. Tenters welcome. Fishing licenses. Guides. Tackle. 26 miles from Highway 16. Kispiox Valley Road. RR 1, Hazelton, BC V0J 1Y0. (604) 842-6182. [ADVERTISEMENT] ▲

Bulkley River, Dolly Varden to 5 lbs.; spring salmon, mid-July to mid-August; coho salmon 4 to 12 lbs., Aug. 15 through September, flies, spoons and spinners; steelhead to 20 lbs., July through November, flies, Kitamats, weighted spoons and soft bobbers. **Kispiox River** is famous for its trophy-sized steelhead. Check on regulations and obtain a fishing license before your arrival. Fishing is done with single-hook only, with catch-release for steelhead between Aug. 15 and Sept. 30. Season is July 1 to Nov. 30 for salmon, trout and steelhead. Excellent fly-fishing waters. Sizable Dolly Vardens and cutthroat. Steelhead average 20 lbs., with some catches over 30 lbs.

Yellowhead Highway 16 Log

(continued)

PG 281.4 (452.8 km) **PR 174.6** (281 km) Motel adjacent highway. Turnoff to north for 2-mile/3.2-km loop road through small community of **SOUTH HAZELTON;** restaurant, general store, gas station with minor repair, lodging.

Cataline Motel and RV Park. See display ad this section.

PG 285 (458.6 km) **PR 171** (275.2 km) **Seeley Lake** Provincial Park; 20 campsites, water pump, day-use area with picnic tables, swimming, fishing. Camping fee $9.50. ▲

PG 290.5 (467.5 km) **PR 165.5** (266.3 km) *CAUTION: Highway turns sharply to cross Canadian National Railway tracks.*

PG 294.7 (474.2 km) **PR 161.3** (259.6 km) Skeena Crossing. Historic CNR bridge (see plaque at Kitseguecla). *CAUTION: Blind sharp corner under bridge.*

PG 295.9 (476.2 km) **PR 160.1** (257.6 km) **KITSEGUECLA,** Indian village. Totem poles throughout village are classic examples, still in original locations. Historical plaque about Skeena Crossing.

PG 306.6 (493.4 km) **PR 149.4** (240.4 km) Gas station and cafe at **junction** with Cassiar Highway. Bridge across Skeena River to Kitwanga and Cassiar Highway to Stewart, Hyder and Alaska Highway. This is the principal access to the Cassiar Highway. Alternate access via Nass Road at **Milepost PG 379.9.** See CASSIAR HIGHWAY section.

Highway passes Seven Sisters peaks, the highest is 9,140 feet/2,786m.

PG 309.8 (498.6 km) **PR 146.2** (235.3 km) **Seven Sisters RV Park and Campground.** Outstanding Value. Beautiful parklike setting. Many treed sites. Fresh water, sani-dump, picnic tables at every site, flush toilets, shower, firepits with free firewood all for $7. Excellent salmon fishing close by. Tenters and cyclists welcome. (604) 849-5489 for reservations. Box 338, Kitwanga, BC V0J 2A0. [ADVERTISEMENT] ▲

PG 312.4 (502.8 km) **PR 143.6** (231.1 km) Boulder Creek rest area; parking for large vehicles; toilets, litter barrels and picnic tables.

PG 316.5 (509.4 km) **PR 139.5** (224.5 km) Gravel turnout to north with litter barrel.

PG 318.2 (512.1 km) **PR 137.8** (221.8 km) **CEDARVALE,** cafe. Loop road through rural setting. Historical plaque about Holy City.

PG 322.9 (519.6 km) **PR 133.1** (214.2 km) Gravel turnout to north on Skeena River.

PG 324.8 (522.7 km) **PR 131.2** (211.1 km) Paved turnout with historical plaque on Skeena riverboats. Watch for bears fishing the river for salmon in late July and early August.

PG 329.3 (530 km) **PR 126.7** (203.9 km) Gravel turnout to north with litter barrel.

PG 335.8 (540.4 km) **PR 120.2** (193.4 km) Watch for fallen rock on this stretch of highway.

PG 345.2 (555.6 km) **PR 110.8** (178.3 km) Paved rest area on riverbank with water pump, picnic tables, toilets and litter barrels. Historical plaque about Skeena River steamboats.

PG 345.5 (556.1 km) **PR 110.5** (177.8 km) Skeena Cellulose private bridge across Skeena River to access tree farms on north side.

PG 352.6 (567.4 km) **PR 103.4** (166.4 km) Tiny chapel to south serves small community of **USK;** the village is reached via the reaction ferry seen to north. The nondenominational chapel is a replica of the pioneer church that stood in Usk until 1936, when the Skeena River flooded, sweeping away the village and the church. The only item from the church to survive was the Bible, which was found floating atop a small pine table.

PG 354.9 (571.1 km) **PR 101.1** (162.7 km) Side road leads 0.5 mile/0.8 km south to **Kleanza Creek** Provincial Park; 23 campsites, 12 picnic sites, fishing. Short trail to remains from Cassiar Hydraulic Mining Co. gold sluicing operations here (1911–14). ▲

PG 360.7 (580.4 km) **PR 95.3** (153.4 km) Gas and lodging. **Copper (Zymoetz) River,** can be fished from Highway 16 or follow local maps. Coho salmon to 10 lbs., use teespinners in July; steelhead to 20 lbs., check locally for season and restrictions.

PG 362.4 (583.2 km) **PR 93.6** (150.6 km) Turnout to north with tourist information sign and area map.

PG 364.5 (586.6 km) **PR 91.5** (147.2 km) Northern Motor Inn.

PG 365.1 (587.6 km) **PR 90.9** (146.3 km) Four-way stop; east access to Terrace and **junction** with Highway 37 south to Kitimat. For access to downtown Terrace, turn north here and continue over one-lane bridge. For west access to Terrace and continuation of Yellowhead Highway 16 westbound, go straight at intersection. Turn south for Kitimat (see log of HIGHWAY 37 SOUTH on page 197).

PG 365.6 (588.3 km) **PR 90.4** (145.5 km) Bridge over Skeena River. Ferry Island municipal campground; 68 sites, some electrical hookups. Covered picnic shelters, barbecues, walking trails and a fishing bar are also available. ▲

Westbound, highway crosses railway overpass.

PG 366.2 (589.3 km) **PR 89.8** (144.5 km) Terrace Chamber of Commerce Travel Infocentre.

PG 366.3 (589.5 km) **PR 89.7** (144.4 km) Stoplight; west access to Terrace. Turn north at intersection for downtown (description of Terrace follows). Continue through intersection westbound for Prince Rupert, eastbound for Prince George.

CAUTION: No gas or services available between Terrace and Prince Rupert.

Terrace

Located on the Skeena River. City centre is located north of Highway 16: Exit at overpass (**PG 366.3**) or at Highway 37 junction (**PG 365.1**). **Population:** 12,000; area 17,000. **Emergency Services:** Police, fire and ambulance located at intersection of Eby Street and Highway 16. **Police,** phone 635-4911. **Fire Department,** phone 638-8121. **Ambulance,** phone 638-1102. **Hospital,** 2711 Tetrault St., phone 635-2211.

Visitor Information: Travel Infocentre located in the chamber of commerce log building at **Milepost PG 366.2.** Open in summer daily, 9 A.M. to 8 P.M.; in winter, Monday through Friday, 9 A.M. to 5 P.M. Write Box 107, Terrace, BC V8G 4A2; phone (604) 635-2063. Information also available from Municipal Hall, #5-3215 Eby St.; open weekdays, phone 635-6311.

Elevation: 220 feet/67m. **Climate:** Average summer temperature is 69°F/20°C; yearly rainfall 36 inches, snowfall 71.5 inches. **Radio:** CFPR-FM 95.3; CFTK 590, CJFW-FM 103.9. **Television:** Eight channels (cable). **Newspapers:** *Terrace Standard* (weekly).

Transportation: Air–Canadian Airlines International, Air BC and Central Mountain Air from Terrace–Kitimat airport on Highway 37 South. **Railroad**–VIA Rail, 4531 Railway Ave. **Bus**–Farwest Bus Lines and

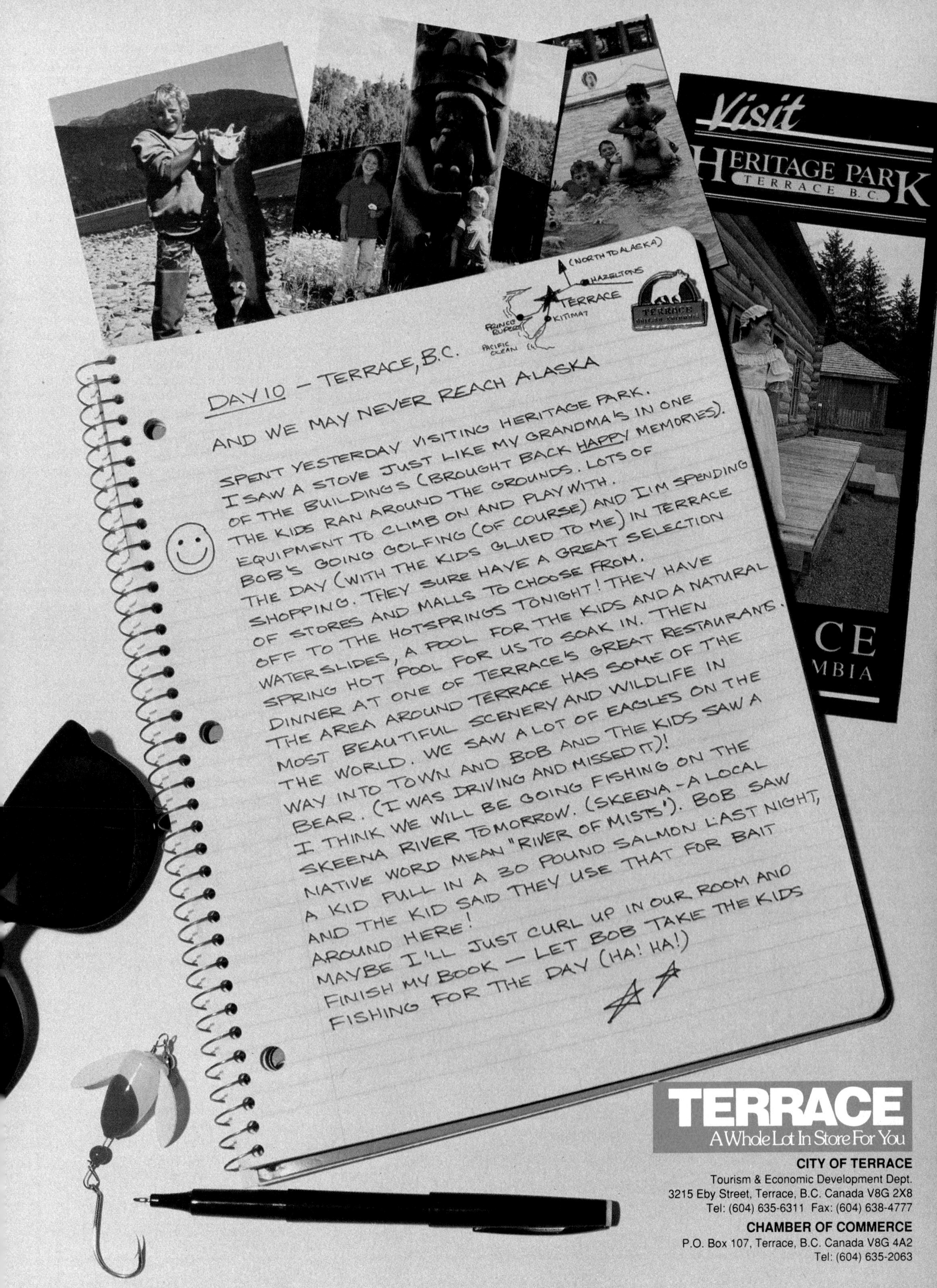

Visit
HERITAGE PARK
TERRACE B.C.
(NORTH TO ALASKA)
HAZELTONS
TERRACE
KITIMAT
PRINCE RUPERT
PACIFIC OCEAN
TERRACE
DAY 10 – TERRACE, B.C.
AND WE MAY NEVER REACH ALASKA
SPENT YESTERDAY VISITING HERITAGE PARK.
I SAW A STOVE JUST LIKE MY GRANDMA'S IN ONE
OF THE BUILDINGS (BROUGHT BACK HAPPY MEMORIES).
THE KIDS RAN AROUND THE GROUNDS. LOTS OF
EQUIPMENT TO CLIMB ON AND PLAY WITH.
BOB'S GOING GOLFING (OF COURSE) AND I'M SPENDING
THE DAY (WITH THE KIDS GLUED TO ME) IN TERRACE
SHOPPING. THEY SURE HAVE A GREAT SELECTION
OF STORES AND MALLS TO CHOOSE FROM.
OFF TO THE HOTSPRINGS TONIGHT! THEY HAVE
WATERSLIDES, A POOL FOR THE KIDS AND A NATURAL
SPRING HOT POOL FOR US TO SOAK IN. THEN
DINNER AT ONE OF TERRACE'S GREAT RESTAURANTS.
THE AREA AROUND TERRACE HAS SOME OF THE
MOST BEAUTIFUL SCENERY AND WILDLIFE IN
THE WORLD. WE SAW A LOT OF EAGLES ON THE
WAY INTO TOWN AND BOB AND THE KIDS SAW A
BEAR. (I WAS DRIVING AND MISSED IT)!
I THINK WE WILL BE GOING FISHING ON THE
SKEENA RIVER TOMORROW. (SKEENA - A LOCAL
NATIVE WORD MEAN "RIVER OF MISTS'). BOB SAW
A KID PULL IN A 30 POUND SALMON LAST NIGHT,
AND THE KID SAID THEY USE THAT FOR BAIT
AROUND HERE!
MAYBE I'LL JUST CURL UP IN OUR ROOM AND
FINISH MY BOOK — LET BOB TAKE THE KIDS
FISHING FOR THE DAY (HA! HA!)
TERRACE
A Whole Lot In Store For You
CITY OF TERRACE
Tourism & Economic Development Dept.
3215 Eby Street, Terrace, B.C. Canada V8G 2X8
Tel: (604) 635-6311 Fax: (604) 638-4777
CHAMBER OF COMMERCE
P.O. Box 107, Terrace, B.C. Canada V8G 4A2
Tel: (604) 635-2063

Greyhound. **Car Rentals**–Available.

Terrace has become an important service stop for motorists heading up the Cassiar Highway to the Alaska Highway. It is the last large retail-commercial centre for travelers until they reach the similar-sized community of Whitehorse, YT.

Tom Thornhill, the first white settler, found an Indian village just east of the present location of Terrace in 1892. When stern-wheelers were plying the Skeena, the first farmer in the area, George Little, gave land to the community that became a port of call and post office in 1905. Originally it was known as Little Town, and later was named Terrace because of the natural terraces cut by the river. The village site was laid out in 1910 and the Grand Trunk Pacific Railroad reached Terrace in 1914. The municipality was incorporated in 1927.

Terrace is a regional centre for trade, entertainment and government, with ties to the forestry industry.

ACCOMMODATIONS

There are 14 motels/hotels, 20 restaurants and two shopping centres. The government liquor store is at 4721 Lakelse Ave. There are four laundromats. The community has a library and art gallery, indoor swimming pool, tennis courts and a golf course.

Public campgrounds are located at Ferry Island, turn off at Skeena River bridge (**Milepost PG 365.6**); Kleanza Creek, 10 miles/16 km east of Terrace; and Lakelse Lake, 11.7 miles/18.8 km south. There are two private campgrounds, one on the Skeena River and the other at the east edge of the city (follow signs at junction of Highways 16 and 37). Fisherman's Park on the east side of the Kalum River, at its junction with the Skeena, provides picnic facilities. ▲

ATTRACTIONS

Heritage Park is a collection of original log buildings from this region. Chosen to represent both the different aspects of pioneer life, as well as different log building techniques, the structures include a trapper's cabin, miner's cabin and lineman's cabin. The nine structures also house artifacts from the period. Managed by the Terrace Regional Museum Society; guided tours available in summer, admission charged.

Lakelse Lake Provincial Park at Furlong Bay, 11 miles/18 km south of Terrace on Highway 37, offers a huge camping area, picnicking, washrooms and showers, sandy beaches, swimming, nature trails and interpretive programs.

Hiking trails in the Terrace area range from easy to moderate. Terrace Mountain Nature Trail is a 3.2-mile/5-km uphill hike which offers good views of the area; it begins at Halliwell and Anderson streets. Check with the Travel Infocentre for details on other area trails.

Special events in Terrace include the Skeena Valley Fall Fair, Labour Day weekend; and River Boat Days, B.C. Day weekend.

Nisga'a Memorial Lava Bed Provincial Park. The lava beds are 48 miles/77 km north of Terrace. Limited camping and picnic spots; interesting hikes. Much of the valley looks like the surface of the moon.

Sportfishing. Fish on the banks of the province's second largest river, the **Skeena.** Terrace is ideally situated for sportfishing, with easy access to the **Copper, Kalum, Kitimat** and **Lakelse rivers.** Cutthroat, Dolly Varden and rainbow are found in all lakes and streams; salmon (spring, king and coho) from May to late autumn. Chinooks average 40 to 70 lbs.; coho 14 to 20 lbs. Check locally for season and restrictions on steelhead. Information and fishing licenses are available from B.C. Government Access Centre, 3220 Eby St., Terrace (phone 638-3200), and at most sporting goods stores.

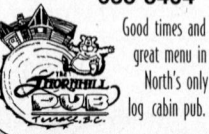

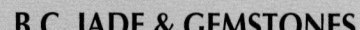

Yellowhead Highway 16 Log

(continued)

PG 366.3 (589.5 km) **PR 89.7** (144.4 km) Stoplight; west access to Terrace. Turn north at intersection for downtown. Continue through intersection eastbound for Prince George, westbound for Prince Rupert.

PG 366.5 (589.8 km) **PR 89.5** (144 km) **Junction** with Nisga'a Highway (Kalum Lake Road). Nisga'a Highway is paved until the junction with Nass Road. Beyond here the highway is a gravel road used by logging trucks as an alternate to Cassiar Highway. (The paved portion of Nisga'a Highway is recommended over the Nass Road, which is a gravel logging road.)

Miles of the T'Seax. 100K down Nisga'a Highway, overlooking the Nisga'a Memorial Lava Bed Park, Miles of the T'Seax Bed and Breakfast, other meals available on request. Variety of salmon in T'Seax River. Native art, groceries, gas available close by. Hike the local trails, crater of volcano, hot springs, trail rides, featuring Missouri Foxtrotters. (604) 633-2636; P.O. Box 230, New Aiyansh, BC V0J 1A0. VISA and MasterCard. Super, Natural North by Northwest. [ADVERTISEMENT]

PG 367.9 (592.1 km) **PR 88.1** (141.7 km) Access road to boat launch (fee charged) on the Kitsumkalum River downstream from Highway 16 bridge; RV parking.

Leaving Terrace, Highway 16 is in good condition westbound although the few straightaways are interrupted by some amazing 70-degree zigzags as the highway crosses the railroad tracks. The section of highway along the Skeena River is spectacular, with waterfalls cascading down the steep rock faces.

PG 369.3 (594.3 km) **PR 86.7** (139.5 km) **KITSUMKALUM.** Grocery store and craft center. This Native enterprise on reserve land handles only authentic arts and crafts such as totem poles, leather goods and local carvings. This is also the **junction** with Nass Road, a forest service road, which leads north 15 miles/24 km to Kitsumkalum Provincial Park with 20 campsites. This narrow gravel logging road joins the Nisga'a Highway, which turns into another forest service road that joins the Cassiar Highway. (Nisga'a Highway, also known as Kalum Lake Road from Terrace, past the community college is paved to the junction with Nass Road.)

Beyond the Nass Road junction Nisga'a Highway is a narrow gravel and pavement road used by logging trucks. The best route to the Cassiar Highway is from Kitwanga, **Milepost PG 306.6**. For details, see CASSIAR HIGHWAY section.

PG 373 (600.2 km) **PR 83** (133.6 km) Shames Mountain Ski Area.

PG 380.2 (611.9 km) **PR 75.8** (122 km) Paved turnout with litter barrels to south alongside the Skeena River; views of fishermen in salmon season.

PG 387.2 (623.1 km) **PR 68.8** (110.8 km) Rest area on left westbound with picnic tables and toilets.

PG 393.1 (632.6 km) **PR 62.9** (101.3 km) *CAUTION! Highway turns sharply across railroad tracks.*

PG 395.2 (636 km) **PR 60.8** (97.8 km) *CAUTION: Carwash Rock overhangs highway. Water cascades down mountain and onto highway during heavy rains.*

PG 395.5 (636.5 km) **PR 60.5** (97.4 km) Sharp curves and falling rocks approximately next mile westbound.

PG 397.2 (639.2 km) **PR 58.8** (94.6 km) *CAUTION: Slow down for sharp curve and steep grade.*

PG 400.6 (644.7 km) **PR 55.4** (89.2 km) Exchamsiks River Provincial Park; 18 campsites and 20 picnic sites among old-growth Sitka spruce. Open May to October, camping fee, water and pit toilets. Good salmon fishing in **Exchamsiks River.** Access to Gitnadoix River canoeing area across Skeena River. ▲

PG 401.1 (645.5 km) **PR 54.9** (88.4 km) Very pleasant rest area north side of road at west end of bridge; boat launch on Exchamsiks River.

Highway 37 South Log

Distance is measured from the junction with Yellowhead Highway 16 (J).

J 0.9 (1.5 km) Krumm Road. Turn east for golf course.

J 3.1 (5 km) Terrace–Kitimat airport access road. Daily jet flights to Vancouver.

J 7.9 (12.7 km) Lakelse Lake Provincial Park parking area and trail to Gruchy's Beach.

J 8.7 (14 km) Lakelse Lake Provincial Park parking areas and picnic area; tables, toilets, changehouses and beach. Park headquarters located here.

J 10.6 (17.1 km) Waterlily Bay; food, lodging, boat launch.

J 11.4 (18.3 km) Lakelse Lake Provincial Park Furlong Bay Campground and picnic area; 156 campsites, nature trail, swimming beach, flush toilets, dump station and boat launch. ▲

J 13.5 (21.8 km) Mount Layton Hot Springs; food, lodging, swimming.

J 13.8 (22.2 km) Onion Lake hiking and ski trails to west.

J 19.3 (31 km) Highway passes through forest of western hemlock planted in 1972.

J 20.6 (33.2 km) Access to Kitimat River.

J 27.4 (44.1 km) Kitimat Airpark landing strip for small planes.

J 34.8 (56 km) Hirsch Creek Park to west; picnic area, camping, fishing and hiking. ▲

J 35 (56.3 km) Hirsch Creek bridge.

J 35.8 (57.6 km) Kitimat Travel Infocentre to east.

J 36.2 (58.3 km) Minette Bay Road leads east to MK Bay Marina and salmon viewing area near Kitamaat Village.

J 36.6 (58.9 km) Viewpoint of Douglas Channel and city map. Picnic tables, garden.

Kitimat

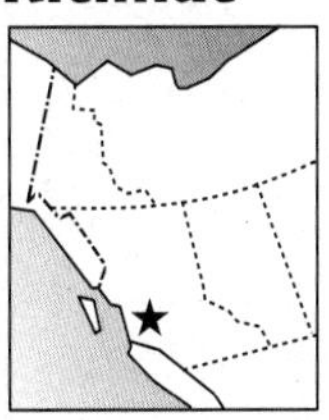

J 37.6 (60.5 km) Located at the head of Douglas Channel. **Population:** 12,000. **Emergency Services: RCMP,** phone 632-7111. **Fire Department,** phone 639-9111. **Ambulance,** phone 632-5433. **Hospital,** phone 632-2121. **Radio:** CBC-FM 101.1, CKTK 1230, CJFW-FM 103.1.

KITIMAT ADVERTISERS

Alcan Smelters and Chemicals Ltd. ....Ph. (604) 639-8259
City Centre Motel ......Ph. 1-800-663-3391
Kitimat Chamber of Commerce ....Ph. (604) 632-6294

PG 402.4 (647.6 km) **PR 53.6** (86.3 km) Conspicuous example of Sitka spruce on north side of highway. As you travel west, the vegetation becomes increasingly influenced by the maritime climate.

PG 406 (653.4 km) **PR 50** (80.5 km) Kasiks River; boat launch.

PG 416.4 (670.1 km) **PR 39.6** (63.8 km) Kwinitsa River bridge and boat launch. No public moorage.

PG 421.1 (677.7 km) **PR 34.9** (56.1 km) Telegraph Point rest area to south on bank of Skeena River; paved turnout with outhouses, picnic tables, litter barrels and water pump.

PG 427.8 (688.5 km) **PR 28.2** (45.4 km) Basalt Creek rest area to south with picnic tables and toilets.

PG 432.5 (696 km) **PR 23.5** (37.8 km) Turnout to south.

PG 435 (700 km) **PR 21** (33.8 km) Watch for pictograph, visible from the road for eastbound traffic only, which was discovered in the early 1950s by Dan Lippett of Prince Rupert.

PG 435.5 (700.9 km) **PR 20.5** (33 km) Scenic viewpoint to south with litter barrels and historical plaque about Skeena River. Highway leaves Skeena River westbound.

PG 440.5 (708.9 km) **PR 15.5** (24.9 km) Rainbow Summit, elev. 528 feet/161m.

PG 442.8 (712.6 km) **PR 13.2** (21.3 km) Side road south to Rainbow Lake Reservoir; boat launch. The reservoir water is used by the pulp mill on Watson Island.

PG 445.4 (716.8 km) **PR 10.6** (17.1 km) Prudhomme Lake Provincial Park; 24 campsites, well water. ▲

PG 446.3 (718.2 km) **PR 9.7** (15.6 km) Turnoff for Diana Lake Provincial Park, 1.5 miles/2.4 km south via single-lane gravel road (use turnouts). Very pleasant grassy picnic area on lakeshore with 50 picnic tables, kitchen shelter, firewood, grills, outhouses, water pump and garbage cans. Parking for 229 vehicles. The only freshwater swimming beach in the Prince Rupert area. Fish viewing at Diana Creek on the way into the lake.

PG 451.2 (725.1 km) **PR 4.8** (7.7 km) **Junction.** Turnoff for **PORT EDWARD,** pulp mill, historic canneries and Wolf Creek Hatchery (tour hours posted). The North Pacific Cannery Village and Fishing Museum at Port Edward is open daily in summer. Built in 1889, this is the oldest cannery village on the north coast. Phone (604) 628-3538 for more information.

North Pacific Cannery Village Museum. See display ad this section.

PG 451.3 (726.3 km) **PR 4.7** (7.6 km) Bridge. Prince Rupert is located on Kaien Island.

PG 451.5 (726.6 km) **PR 4.5** (7.2 km) Galloway Rapids rest area to south with litter barrels, picnic tables and visitor information sign. View of Watson Island pulp mill.

PG 453 (729 km) **PR 3** (4.8 km) Ridley Island access road. Ridley Island is the site of grain and coal terminals used for the transfer of coal from the North East Coal resource near Dawson Creek, and grain from Canada's prairies, to ships.

PG 453.4 (729.7 km) **PR 2.6** (4.2 km) Oliver Lake rest area to south just off highway; picnic tables, grills, firewood. Point of interest sign about bogs.

PG 454.1 (730.8 km) **PR 1.9** (3.1 km) Mount Oldfield and Butze Rapids hiking trails.

PG 455.4 (732.9 km) **PR 0.6** (0.9 km) Turnoff to north for viewpoint of Butze Rapids, a series of reversing rapids. The action of the tidal waters creates quantities of foam as the waters flow through the rapids. It is from these "foaming waters" that the island takes its Indian name *Kaien.*

PG 456 (733.8 km) **PR 0** Prince Rupert industrial park on the outskirts of Prince Rupert. Continue straight ahead 3 miles/4.8 km for the Travel Infocentre in downtown Prince Rupert. Yellowhead Highway 16 becomes McBride Street as you enter the city centre.

Newspaper: *The News Advertiser* (weekly); *Northern Sentinel* (weekly).

This community was planned and built in the early 1950s when the B.C. government attracted Alcan (Aluminum Co. of Canada) to establish a smelter here. Today, Kitimat is a major port and home to several industries. Free tours are available (reservations recommended) at Alcan, phone 639-8259; Eurocan Pulp and Paper, phone 632-6111; Methanex Corp., phone 639-9292; and Kitimat fish hatchery, phone 639-9616.

Kitimat's location at the head of Douglas Channel makes it a popular boating and fishing destination. There are several charter operators.

Kitimat has all visitor facilities, including a modern shopping mall, restaurants and motels; library, theatre, swimming pool and gym; and an 18-hole golf course. The Centennial Museum is located at city centre. For further information contact the Chamber of Commerce, Box 214, Kitimat, BC V8C 2G7; phone (604) 632-6294, fax 632-4685.

There is camping at Radley Park in town; electrical hookups, showers, toilets, playground and dump station. (Radley Park is also the site of a 165-foot/50-m Sitka spruce, largest of its kind in the province.) There is also camping at Hirsch Creek Park on the edge of town. ▲

Local fishermen line the banks of the **Kitimat River** in May for the steelhead run. Chinook salmon run in June and July. Coho run in August and into September.

Return to Milepost PG 365.1
Yellowhead Highway 16

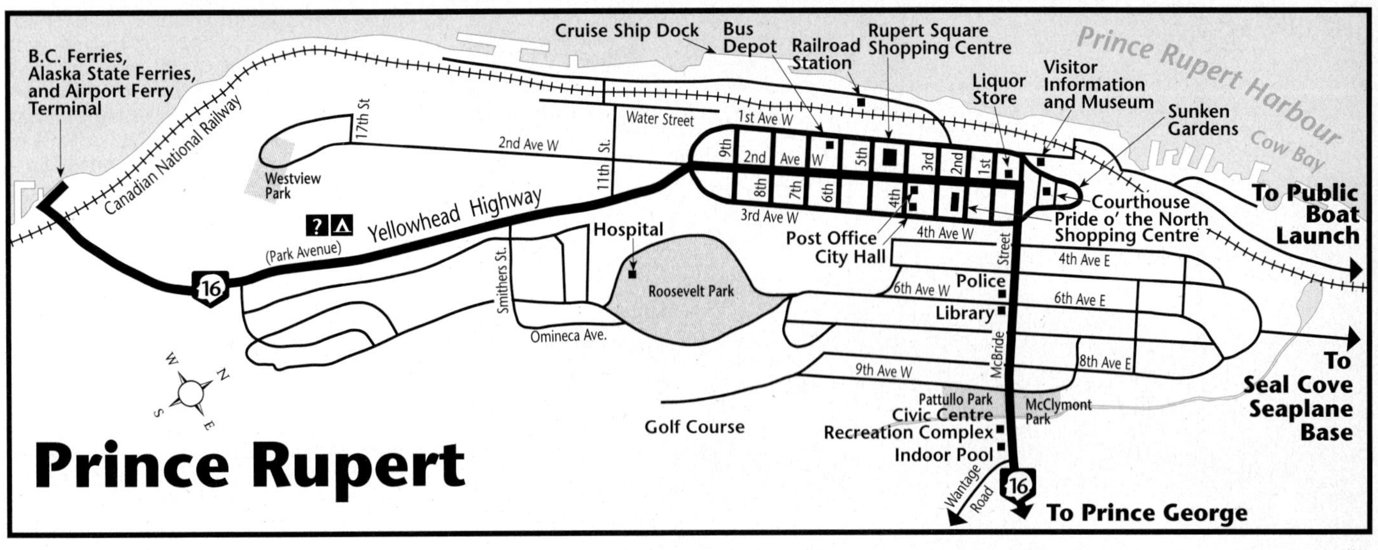

Prince Rupert

Located on Kaien Island near the mouth of the Skeena River, 90 miles/145 km by air or water south of Ketchikan, AK. **Population:** 17,500; area 25,000. **Emergency Services:** phone 911 for **Police, Ambulance** and **Fire Department. RCMP**, 6th Avenue and McBride Street, non-emergency phone 624-2136. **Hospital**, Prince Rupert Regional, phone 624-2171.

Visitor Information: Travel Infocentre at 1st Avenue and McBride Street. Open daily in summer, 9 A.M. to 9 P.M., Sunday 9 A.M. to 5 P.M. Open in winter Monday through Saturday, 10 A.M. to 5 P.M. Travel information is also available at the Park Avenue Campground; open daily in summer, 9 A.M. to 9 P.M., and until midnight for B.C. Ferry arrivals. Write Box 669-MP, Prince Rupert, BC V8J 3S1, phone (800) 667-1994 and (604) 624-5637, fax (604) 627-8009.

Elevation: Sea level. **Climate:** Temperate with mild winters. Annual precipitation 95.4 inches. **Radio:** CBC 860, CHTK 560, CJFW-FM 101.9. **Television:** 12 channels, cable. **Newspaper:** *The Prince Rupert Daily News, Prince Rupert This Week* (weekly).

Prince Rupert, "Gateway to Alaska," was surveyed prior to 1905 by the Grand Trunk Pacific Railway (later Canadian National Railway) as the terminus for Canada's second transcontinental railroad.

Twelve thousand miles/19,312 km of survey lines were studied before a final route along the Skeena River was chosen. Some 833 miles/1,340.6 km had to be blasted from solid rock, 50 men drowned, and costs went to $105,000 a mile (the final cost of $300 million comparable to Panama Canal construction) before the last spike was driven near Fraser Lake on April 7, 1914. Financial problems continued to plague the company, forcing it to amalgamate to become part of the Canadian National Railway system in 1923.

Charles M. Hays, president of the company, was an enthusiastic promoter of the new terminus, which was named by competition from 12,000 entries. While "Port Rupert" had been submitted by two contestants, "Prince Rupert" (from Miss Eleanor M. Macdonald of Winnipeg) called to mind the dashing soldier–explorer, cousin to Charles II of England and first governor of the Hudson's Bay Co., which had traded on the coast rivers for years. Three first prizes of $250 were awarded and Prince Rupert was officially named in 1906.

Prince Rupert's proposed port and adjacent waters were surveyed by G. Blanchard Dodge of the Hydrographic branch of the Marine Dept. in 1906, and in May the little steamer *Constance* carried settlers from the village of Metlakatla to clear the first ground on Kaien Island. Its post office opened Nov. 23, 1906, and Prince Rupert, with a tent-town population of 200, began an association with communities on the Queen Charlotte Islands, with Stewart served by Union steamships and CPR boats, and with Hazelton 200 miles/321.9 km up the Skeena River on which the stern-wheelers of the Grand Trunk Pacific and the Hudson's Bay Co. traveled.

Incorporated as a city March 10, 1910, Prince Rupert attracted settlers responding to the enthusiasm of Hays, with his dreams of a population of 50,000 and world markets supplied by his railroad. Both the city and the railway suffered a great loss with the death of Charles M. Hays when the *Titanic* went down in April 1912. Even so, work went ahead on the Grand Trunk Pacific and two years later the first train arrived at Prince Rupert, linking the western port with the rest of Canada. Since then, the city has progressed through two world wars and economic ups and downs to its present period of growth and expansion, not only as a busy port but as a visitor centre.

During WWII, more than a million tons of freight and 73,000 persons, both military and civilian, passed through Prince Rupert on their way to military operations in Alaska and the South Pacific.

Construction of the pulp operations on Watson Island in 1951 greatly increased the economic and industrial potential of the area. The operations include a pulp mill and a kraft mill.

Mariner's Park at the foot of McBride Street offers a good view of harbour traffic.
(Judy Parkin, staff)

With the start of the Alaska State Ferry System in 1963, and the British Columbia Ferry System in 1966, Prince Rupert's place as an important visitor centre and terminal point for highway, rail and marine transportation was assured.

Prince Rupert is the second major deep-sea port on Canada's west coast, exporting grain, pulp, lumber and other resources to Europe and the Orient. The port of Prince Rupert has also become a major coal and grain port with facilities on Ridley Island. Other industries include fishing and fish processing and the manufacture of forest products.

Prince Rupert is built on a layer of muskeg (unstable organic matter) on solid rock that makes a difficult foundation to build on. Many sites are economically unfeasible for development as they would require pilings 70 feet/21m or more into the muskeg to provide a firm foundation. Some of the older buildings have sagged slightly as a result of unstable foundations.

ACCOMMODATIONS

More than a dozen hotels and motels accommodate the influx of ferry passengers each summer. Many restaurants feature fresh local seafood in season.

Modern supermarkets, shopping centres and a hospital are available. Government liquor store is at the corner of 2nd Avenue and Highway 16. There are five main banks, the Civic Centre Recreation Complex, 18-hole golf course, racquet centre, bowling alley, a swimming pool and tennis courts.

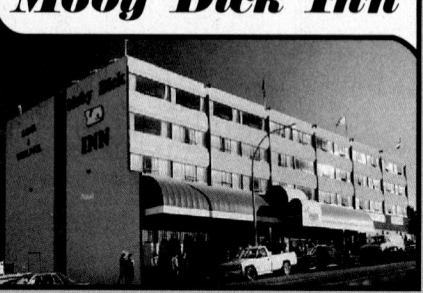

Park Avenue Campground on Highway 16 in the city has 87 campsites with hookups, unserviced sites, restrooms with hot showers, children's play area and picnic shelters. There are 24 campsites at Prudhomme Lake Park, 12.5 miles/20 km east on Highway 16. A private RV park on McBride Street offers camper and trailer parking. ▲

TRANSPORTATION

Air: Harbour Air, Wagair and North Coast Air Service to outlying villages and Queen Charlotte Islands; Canadian Airlines International daily jet service to Terrace and Vancouver; and Air BC to Vancouver and Victoria.

Prince Rupert airport is located on Digby Island, which is connected by city-operated ferry to Prince Rupert. There is a small terminal at the airport. The airport ferry leaves from the Fairview dock, next to the Alaska State ferry dock; cost is $10 one way for the 20-minute ferry ride. Check with the Canadian Airlines International office at the downtown Rupert Mall (office is open for passenger check-in only when planes are arriving or departing). Air BC check-in at corner of 6th Street and 1st Avenue West. Bus service to airport from airline check-in areas.

There is a seaplane base at Seal Cove with airline and helicopter charter services.

Ferries: British Columbia Ferry System, Fairview dock, phone 624-9627, provides automobile and passenger service from Prince Rupert to Port Hardy, and between Prince Rupert and Skidegate in the Queen Charlotte Islands. For details, see MARINE ACCESS ROUTES section.

Alaska Marine Highway System, Fairview dock, phone 627-1744, provides automobile and passenger service to southeastern Alaska. See MARINE ACCESS ROUTES section.

NOTE: Vehicle storage is available. See advertisements this section.

Car Rentals: Tilden (624-5318) and Budget.

Taxi: Available. Prince Rupert taxi cabs are powered by LNG (liquefied natural gas).

Railroad: VIA Rail, in British Columbia, phone 1-800-665-8630.

Bus: Greyhound, phone 624-5090. Farwest Bus Lines, phone 624-6400. Charter sightseeing tours available.

ATTRACTIONS

Take a Tour. Tour the city's historic and scenic points of interest. Maps are available at the Travel Infocentre. Scattered throughout the city are 18 large cedar totem poles, each with its own story. Most are reproductions by Native craftsmen of the original Tsimshian (SHIM shian) poles from the mainland and the Haida (HI duh) carvings from the Queen Charlotte Islands. The originals are now in the British Columbia Provincial Museum in Victoria. Several totem poles may be seen at Service Park, near 3rd Avenue W. and Fulton.

Check with the Museum of Northern British Columbia (1st and McBride) about tours of area archaeological sites. Included is a stop at "Old" Metlakatla in Prince Rupert harbour ("new" Metlakatla is located on Annette Island near Ketchikan, AK; see METLAKATLA section).

Prince Rupert Grain on Ridley Island (turn off Highway 16 at **Milepost PG 453**) offers a look at Canada's most advanced cleaning grain terminal. Tours may be arranged through the Travel Infocentre.

"Photographs and Memories" is a well done multimedia production on Prince Rupert's history. Plays daily in the Crest Motor Hotel. Admission charged.

Watch the Seaplanes. From McBride Street, head north on 6th Avenue East (watch for signs to seaplane base); drive a few miles to Solly's Pub, then turn right to Seal Cove seaplane base. Visitors can spend a fascinating hour here watching seaplanes loading, taking off and landing. Helicopter tours of the area are available at Seal Cove.

Swim at Diana Lake. This provincial park, about 13 miles/21 km from downtown on Highway 16, offers the only freshwater swimming in the Prince Rupert area. Picnic tables, kitchen shelter, parking and beach.

Swim at Earl Mah Aquatic Centre, located next to the Civic Centre Recreation Complex. There are an indoor swimming pool, weight room, saunas, showers and whirlpool, slides and diving boards. Access for handicapped. Phone 627-7946. An admission fee is charged. ♿

Museum of Northern British Columbia/Art Gallery displays an outstanding collection of artifacts depicting the settlement history of British Columbia's north coast. Traveling art collections are displayed in the gallery, and works by local artists are available for purchase. Centrally located at 1st Avenue and McBride Street, marked by several tall totem poles. Summer hours 9 A.M. to 9 P.M. Monday through Saturday, 9 A.M. to 5 P.M. Sunday; winter hours 10 A.M. to 5 P.M. Monday through Saturday. Phone 624-3207.

Kwinitsa Station Railway Museum. Built in 1911, Kwinitsa Station was one of nearly 400 identical stations along the Grand Trunk Pacific Railroad line. In 1985 the station was moved to the Prince Rupert waterfront. Restored rooms, exhibits and videos tell the story of early Prince Rupert and the role the railroad played in the city's development. Open daily in summer; contact the Museum of British Columbia for more information.

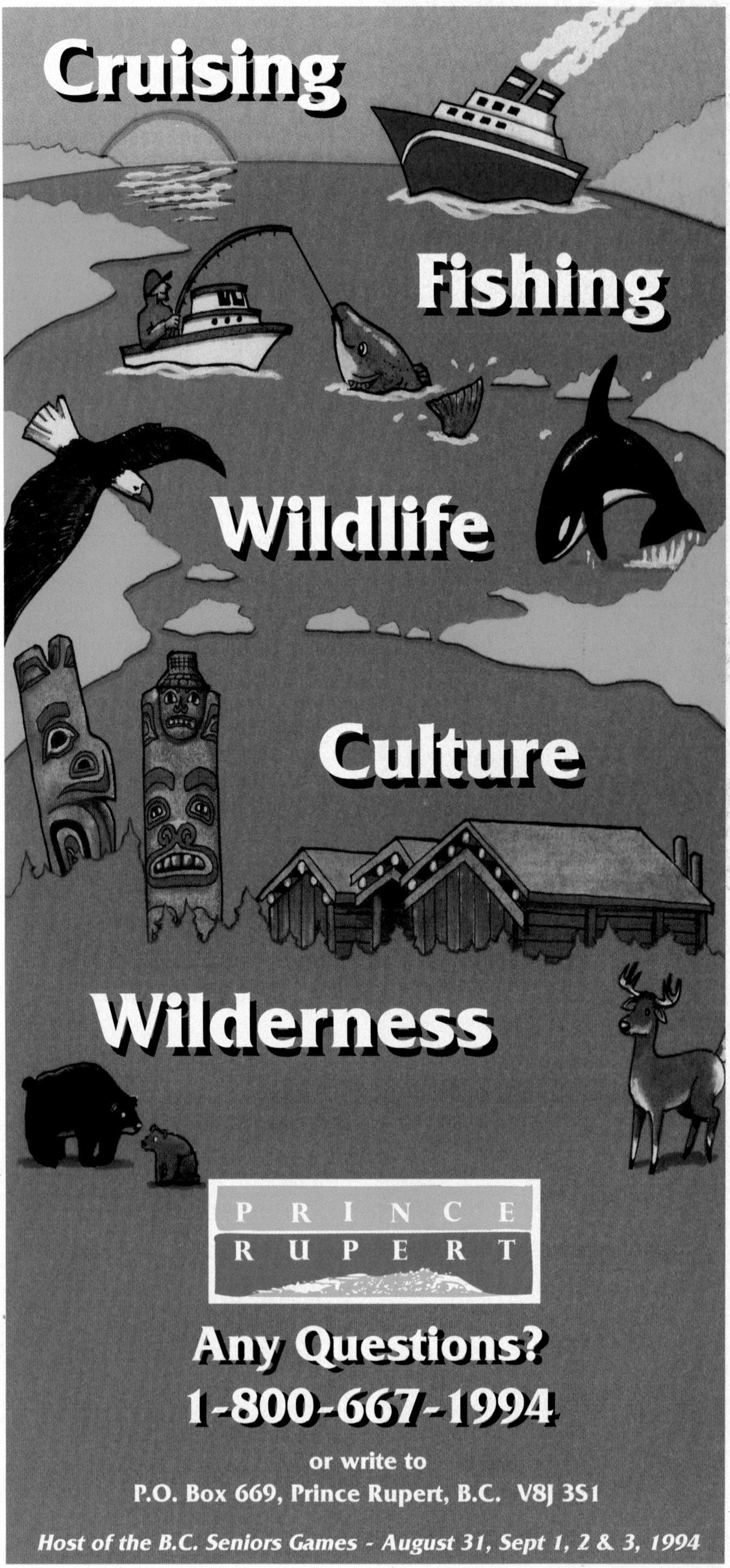

Cruising
Fishing
Wildlife
Culture
Wilderness
PRINCE RUPERT
Any Questions?
1-800-667-1994
or write to
P.O. Box 669, Prince Rupert, B.C. V8J 3S1
Host of the B.C. Seniors Games - August 31, Sept 1, 2 & 3, 1994

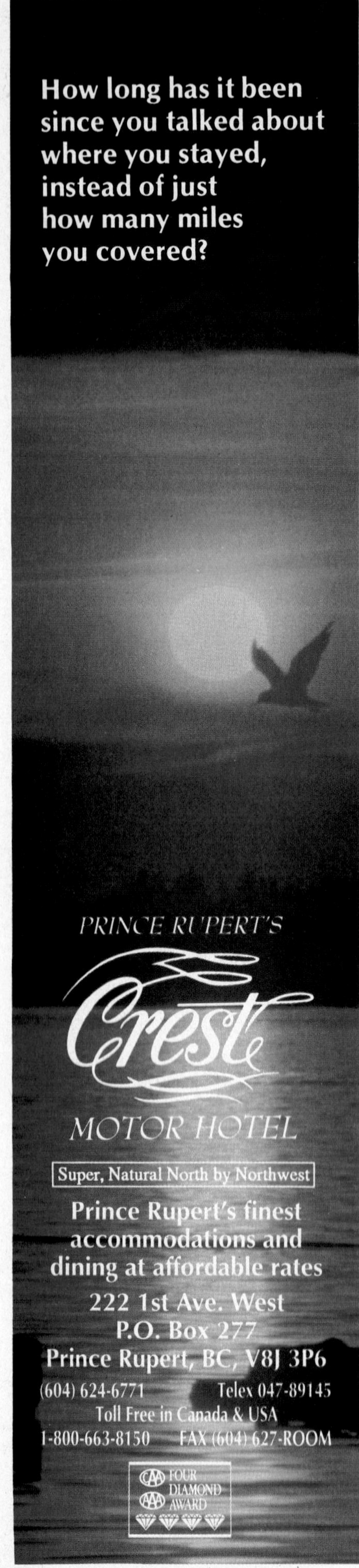

Archaeology Tours. Prince Rupert's inner harbour shelters more than 150 archaeological sites dating back 5,000 years. This fascinating harbour tour visits these sites and offers full descriptions of early inhabitants. The tour stops at the historic Indian village of Metlakatla for snacks and souvenirs. Guided by knowledgeable museum staff you'll travel in an enclosed ferry with ample window seating. Regular departures. Reserve with Museum of Northern British Columbia, Box 669, Prince Rupert, BC V8J 3S1. (604) 624-3207. [ADVERTISEMENT]

Cannery Tour. North Pacific Cannery Village Museum at Port Edward (turn off Highway 16 at **Milepost PG 451.2**). Built in 1889, this restored heritage site has dozens of displays on this once major industry of the region. A live performance highlights the history of the cannery. Open daily in summer, closed Mondays and Tuesdays October through April, admission charged.

Numerous freshwater fishing areas are available near Prince Rupert. For information on bait, locations, regulations and licensing, contact local sporting goods stores or the Travel Infocentre. This area abounds in all species of salmon, steelhead, crab, shrimp and abalone. Public boat launch facility is located at Rushbrook Public Floats at the north end of the waterfront. Public floats are also available at Fairview, past the Alaska state ferry terminal near the breakwater.

Harbour Tours and Fishing Charters are available. For information, contact the Prince Rupert charter operators, phone 624-5637.

The Civic Centre Recreation Complex located on McBride Street (Highway 16) welcomes visitors. Activities include fitness gym, squash, basketball and volleyball. Supervised children's activities during summer. Ice skating and roller skating rinks also located at the centre. Phone 624-6707 for more information.

Performing Arts Centre offers both professional and amateur theatre, with productions for children, and classical and contemporary plays presented. The 700-seat facility may be toured in summer; phone 627-8888.

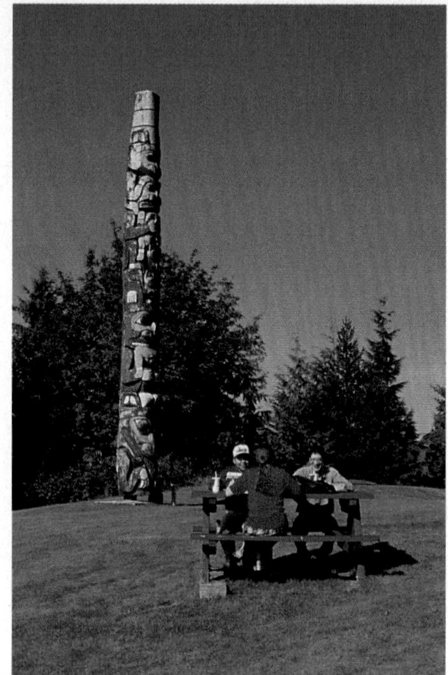

Roosevelt Park offers picnicking and viewpoints. (Judy Parkin, staff)

Golf Course includes 18-hole course, resident pro, equipment rental, clubhouse and restaurant. Entrance on 9th Avenue W.

Special Events. B.C. Seniors Games are scheduled for Aug. 31 through Sept. 3, 1994. Seafest is a four-day celebration held the second weekend in June that includes a parade and water-jousting competition. Indian Culture Days, a two-day event held during Seafest, features Native food, traditional dance, and arts and crafts. The All Native Basketball Tournament, held in February, is the largest event of its kind in Canada.

Visit the Queen Charlotte Islands. British Columbia ferry service is available between Prince Rupert and Skidegate on Graham Island, largest of the 150 islands and islets that form Queen Charlotte Islands. Located 100 miles/160 km west of Prince Rupert (an eight-hour ferry ride), Graham Island's paved road system connects Skidegate with Masset, largest town in the Queen Charlottes. Harbour Air has daily scheduled flights from Prince Rupert to Sandspit and Masset. Major attractions include the virgin forest, Indian culture and wildlife. *A Guide to Queen Charlotte Islands* by Neil Carey, and other books on the Queen Charlottes, are in local bookstores.

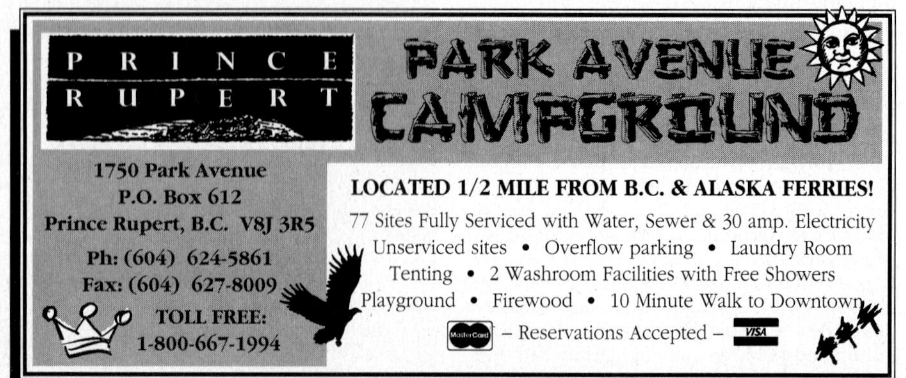

CASSIAR HIGHWAY

Junction with Yellowhead Highway 16, British Columbia, to Junction with the Alaska Highway
BC Highway 37
(See map, page 204)

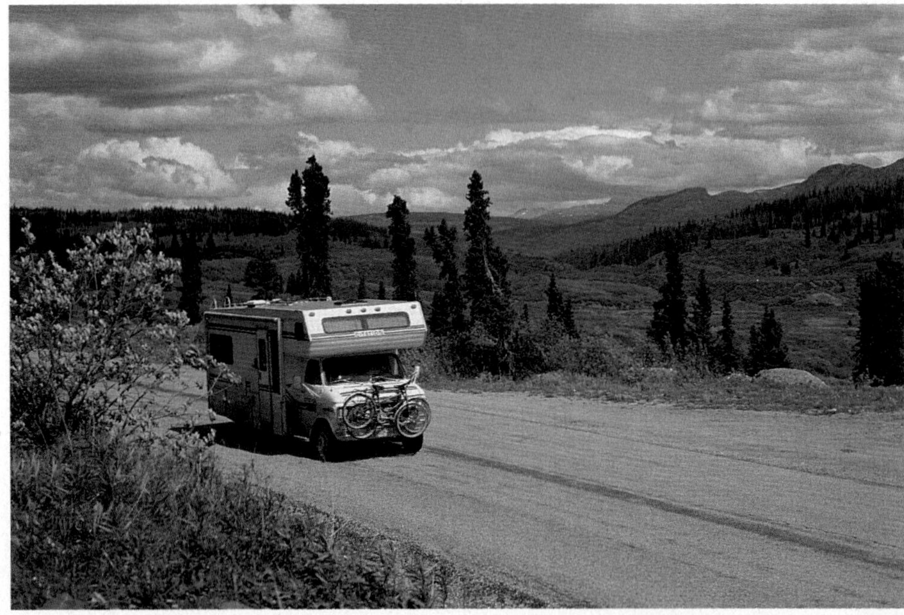

The Cassiar Highway offers outstanding and varied scenery. (Philip and Karen Smith)

The Cassiar Highway junctions with Yellowhead Highway 16 at the Skeena River bridge (**Milepost PG 306.6** in the YELLOWHEAD HIGHWAY 16 section) and travels north to the Stewart, BC–Hyder, AK, access road and Dease Lake, ending at the Alaska Highway about 14 miles/22 km west of Watson Lake, YT. Total driving distance is 455.6 miles/733.2 km. It offers a most enjoyable adventure drive with outstanding and varied scenery.

Completed in 1972, much of the Cassiar has been leveled, straightened and brought up to all-weather standards. The highway is paved from **Milepost J 0** to Meziadin junction. From Meziadin junction to the Alaska Highway, the highway is surfaced (pavement or seal coat) with the exception of three gravel sections. On gravel stretches watch for washboard and potholes. Gravel road may be dusty in dry weather and muddy in wet weather. Seal coat is subject to deterioration from weather and traffic. A few bridges are still single lane. Watch for potholes at bridge ends and slippery bridge decks. Resurfacing and other improvements may be expected in 1994. Drive with your headlights on. The Cassiar Highway is the route of commercial truckers headed north of 60°; it is several hours shorter than the alternative Alaska Highway route.

Watch for logging trucks on the lower Cassiar Highway and freight trucks anywhere on the highway. *WARNING: Exercise extreme caution when passing or being passed by these trucks; reduce speed and allow trucks adequate clearance.*

Increasingly popular with motorists in recent years, both because of its savings in travel time and its scenery, the Cassiar also provides access to Hyder and Stewart. These two communities are described in detail in this section beginning on page 206.

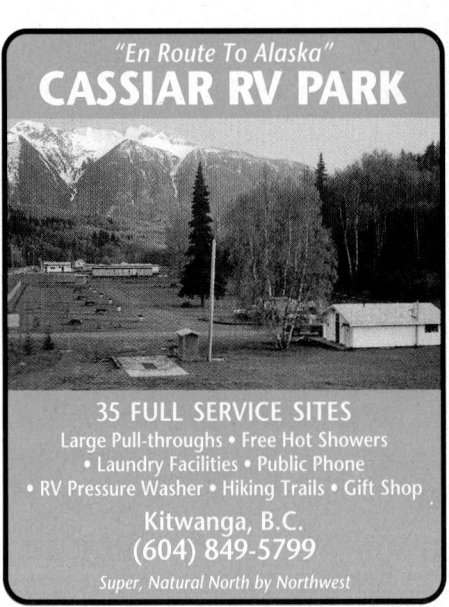

Food, gas and lodging are available along the Cassiar Highway, but check the highway log for distances between services. Be sure your vehicle is mechanically sound with good tires. It is a good idea to carry a spare tire and extra fuel, especially in the off season. In case of emergency, motorists are advised to flag down trucks to radio for help. It is unlawful to camp overnight in turnouts and rest areas unless otherwise posted. Camp at private campgrounds or in provincial park campgrounds.

Cassiar Highway Log

BC HIGHWAY 37

Kilometreposts are up along the Cassiar Highway about every 5 to 10 kms, but the posts do not always accurately reflect driving distance nor are they measured from a single starting point. *The MILEPOST®* log indicates the physical location of kilometreposts as they occurred in summer 1993.

Distance from junction with the Yellowhead Highway (J) is followed by distance from Alaska Highway (AH).

J 0 AH 455.6 (733.2 km) **Junction** with Yellowhead Highway 16 (see **Milepost PG 306.6** in the YELLOWHEAD HIGHWAY 16 section). Gas station. Bridge across Skeena River from Yellowhead Highway 16 to start of Cassiar Highway.

N&V Johnson Services Ltd. See display ad this section.

J 0.3 (0.5 km) **AH 455.3** (732.7 km) Turn on side road to view totem poles and church of **GITWANGAK.** The Native reserve of Gitwangak was renamed after sharing the name Kitwanga with the adjacent white settlement. Gitwangak has some of the finest authentic totem poles in the area. Also here is St. Paul's Anglican Church; the original old bell tower standing beside the church dates back to 1893.

CASSIAR HIGHWAY *Yellowhead Highway Junction to Alaska Highway Junction*

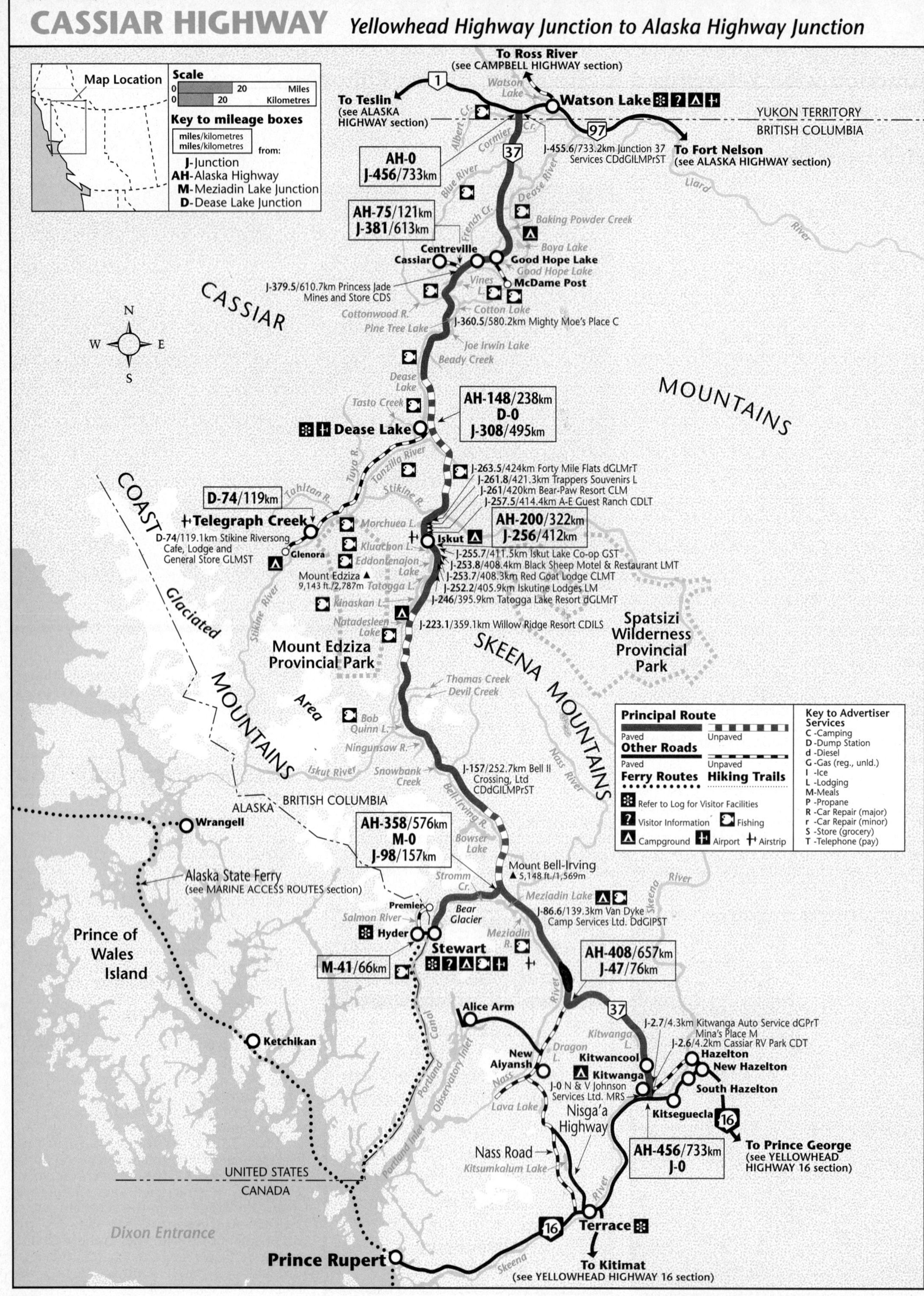

Map Location
Scale
Miles
Kilometres
Key to mileage boxes
miles/kilometres
miles/kilometres
from:
J-Junction
AH-Alaska Highway
M-Meziadin Lake Junction
D-Dease Lake Junction
To Ross River
(see CAMPBELL HIGHWAY section)
To Teslin
(see ALASKA HIGHWAY section)
Watson Lake
YUKON TERRITORY
BRITISH COLUMBIA
J-455.6/733.2km Junction 37 Services CDdGILMPrST
To Fort Nelson
(see ALASKA HIGHWAY section)
AH-0
J-456/733km
AH-75/121km
J-381/613km
Centreville
Cassiar
Good Hope Lake
McDame Post
Baking Powder Creek
Boya Lake
J-379.5/610.7km Princess Jade Mines and Store CDS
Cottonwood R.
Cotton Lake
Pine Tree Lake
J-360.5/580.2km Mighty Moe's Place C
Joe Irwin Lake
Beady Creek
CASSIAR
MOUNTAINS
Dease Lake
Tasto Creek
AH-148/238km
D-0
J-308/495km
J-263.5/424km Forty Mile Flats dGLMrT
J-261.8/421.3km Trappers Souvenirs L
J-261/420km Bear-Paw Resort CLM
J-257.5/414.4km A-E Guest Ranch CDLT
D-74/119km
Telegraph Creek
D-74/119.1km Stikine Riversong Cafe, Lodge and General Store GLMST
Glenora
AH-200/322km
J-256/412km
Iskut
J-255.7/411.5km Iskut Lake Co-op GST
J-253.8/408.4km Black Sheep Motel & Restaurant LMT
J-253.7/408.3km Red Goat Lodge CLMT
J-252.2/405.9km Iskutine Lodges LM
J-246/395.9km Tatogga Lake Resort dGLMrT
Mount Edziza ▲ 9,143 ft./2,787m
J-223.1/359.1km Willow Ridge Resort CDILS
Mount Edziza Provincial Park
Spatsizi Wilderness Provincial Park
COAST MOUNTAINS
Glaciated Area
SKEENA MOUNTAINS
Thomas Creek
Devil Creek
Bob Quinn L.
Ningunsaw R.
Snowbank Creek
J-157/252.7km Bell II Crossing, Ltd CDdGILMPrST
ALASKA
BRITISH COLUMBIA
Wrangell
AH-358/576km
M-0
J-98/157km
Bowser Lake
Mount Bell-Irving ▲ 5,148 ft./1,569m
Alaska State Ferry
(see MARINE ACCESS ROUTES section)
Meziadin Lake
J-86.6/139.3km Van Dyke Camp Services Ltd. DdGIPST
Premier
Bear Glacier
Hyder
Stewart
M-41/66km
AH-408/657km
J-47/76km
Prince of Wales Island
Alice Arm
J-2.7/4.3km Kitwanga Auto Service dGPrT
Mina's Place M
J-2.6/4.2km Cassiar RV Park CDT
Ketchikan
New Aiyansh
Kitwancool
Kitwanga
Hazelton
New Hazelton
South Hazelton
J-0 N & V Johnson Services Ltd. MRS
Kitseguecla
Lava Lake
Nisga'a Highway
Nass Road
Kitsumkalum Lake
AH-456/733km
J-0
To Prince George
(see YELLOWHEAD HIGHWAY 16 section)
UNITED STATES
CANADA
Dixon Entrance
Terrace
Prince Rupert
To Kitimat
(see YELLOWHEAD HIGHWAY 16 section)
Principal Route
Paved
Unpaved
Other Roads
Ferry Routes
Hiking Trails
Refer to Log for Visitor Facilities
Visitor Information
Fishing
Campground
Airport
Airstrip
Key to Advertiser Services
C -Camping
D -Dump Station
d -Diesel
G -Gas (reg., unld.)
I -Ice
L -Lodging
M -Meals
P -Propane
R -Car Repair (major)
r -Car Repair (minor)
S -Store (grocery)
T -Telephone (pay)

J 2.6 (4.2 km) **AH 453** (729 km) Kitwanga post office and a private RV park. ▲

Cassiar RV Park. See display ad on page 203. ▲

J 2.7 (4.3 km) **AH 452.9** (728.9 km) South end of 1.6-mile/2.5-km loop access road which leads to **KITWANGA** (pop. 1,200). **Radio:** CBC 630 AM. **Emergency Services:** Ambulance. The business area of Kitwanga has a visitor information booth (open June to August, local crafts for sale), gas station, car wash, a general store and small restaurant. There is a free public campground. ▲

Kitwanga is at the crossroads of the old upper Skeena "grease trail" trade. The "grease" was eulachon (candlefish) oil, which was a trading staple among tribes of the Coast and Interior. The grease trails are believed to have extended north to the Bering Sea.

A paved turnout with litter barrel and sign on the Kitwanga access road mark Kitwanga Fort National Historic Site, where a wooden fortress and palisade once crowned the large rounded hill here. Seven interpretive panels along the trail up Battle Hill explain the history of the site. Kitwanga Fort was the first major western Canadian native site commemorated by Parks Canada.

Kitwanga Auto Service. See display ad this section.

Mina's Place. See display ad this section.

J 4.2 (6.8 km) **AH 451.4** (726.4 km) North end of 1.6-mile/2.5-km loop access road (Kitwanga North Road) to Kitwanga; see description preceding milepost.

J 4.3 (6.9 km) **AH 451.3** (726.3 km) **Junction** with alternate access route (signed Hazelton–Kitwanga Road) from Hazelton to the Cassiar Highway via the north side of the Skeena River.

J 6.2 (10 km) **AH 449.4** (723.2 km) Between Kilometreposts 10 and 15, the mountain chain of Seven Sisters is visible to west (weather permitting).

J 13 (21 km) **AH 442.6** (712.3 km) Highway follows Kitwanga River and former grease trail route.

J 13.4 (21.6 km) **AH 442.2** (711.6 km) South access to **KITWANCOOL**, a small Indian village with many fine old recently restored totems, among them the famous Hole-in-the-Ice pole. A Native craft shop in the village sells local art. The village of Kitwancool was originally called Gitanyow, meaning place of many people, but was renamed Kitwancool, meaning place of reduced number, after many of its inhabitants were killed in raids.

J 16.5 (26.5 km) **AH 439.1** (706.6 km) North access to Kitwancool.

J 19.2 (30.9 km) **AH 436.4** (702.3 km) Bridge over Moon Lit Creek.

J 19.3 (31.1 km) **AH 436.3** (702.1 km) Road east to rest area by creek with tables, toilets and litter barrels. Road west is the old highway and access to Kitwanga Lake. Fishing, camping and boat launch spots on lake. Old highway may be in poor condition; drive carefully. It rejoins the main highway at Kilometrepost 40.3. Access to the lake is strictly from the old highway.

J 20.2 (32.5 km) **AH 435.4** (700.7 km) Access to Kitwanga Lake.

J 21.7 (34.9 km) **AH 433.9** (698.3 km) Good views of Kitwanga Lake to west; old highway visible, below west, winding along lakeshore.

J 26.3 (42.4 km) **AH 429.3** (690.9 km) Kitwancool Forest Road to west.

J 39.2 (63.1 km) **AH 416.4** (670.1 km) **Cranberry River** bridge No. 1. A favorite salmon stream in summer; consult fishing regulations.

J 47 (75.6 km) **AH 408.6** (657.5 km) Paved turnout to west.

J 47.3 (76.1 km) **AH 408.3** (657.1 km) **Junction** with the Nass Forest Service Road from Terrace.

J 47.6 (76.6 km) **AH 408** (656.6 km) Cranberry River bridge No. 2. Turnout with toilets, tables and litter barrels.

J 53.6 (86.2 km) **AH 402** (646.9 km) BC Hydro power line crosses and parallels highway. Completed in 1990, this line links Stewart to the BC Hydro power grid. Previously, Stewart's power was generated by diesel fuel.

J 59.3 (95.4 km) **AH 396.3** (637.8 km) Small lake with rest area at north end. First view northbound of Nass River.

J 64.7 (104.1 km) **AH 390.9** (629.1 km) Paved turnout.

J 66.3 (106.7 km) **AH 389.3** (626.5 km) View of Nass River to west. The Nass River is one of the province's prime producers of sockeye salmon.

J 67.1 (108 km) **AH 388.5** (625.2 km) Views northbound (weather permitting) of the Coast Mountains to the west. Watch for Cambrian ice field to west.

J 70.8 (114 km) **AH 384.8** (619.2 km) Paved turnout with litter barrel to west.

J 76.7 (123.5 km) **AH 378.9** (609.8 km) Road widens and serves as emergency airstrip; pull over for any approaching aircraft.

J 85.7 (137.9 km) **AH 369.9** (595.3 km) Paved turnout with litter barrels to west.

J 86.6 (139.3 km) **AH 369** (593.8 km) Elsworth logging camp; open to public; fuel, groceries, dump station, hunting and fishing licenses, emergency phone. Private airstrip.

VanDyke Camp Services Ltd. See display ad this section.

J 88.7 (142.8 km) **AH 366.9** (590.4 km) Nass River one-lane bridge. Paved rest area with picnic tables, toilets and litter barrel to east at south end of bridge. A plaque at the north end commemorates bridge opening. The gorge is almost 400 feet/122m wide; main span of bridge is 186 feet/57m. Steel reinforcement supports loads up to 90 tons. Bridge decking is 130 feet/40m above the riverbed.

J 94.1 (151.5 km) **AH 361.5** (581.8 km) Tintina Creek. Along with Hanna Creek, this stream produces 40 percent of the sockeye salmon spawning in the Meziadin Lake watershed.

J 95.6 (153.8 km) **AH 360** (579.3 km) Sockeye salmon spawn here in autumn. It is illegal to fish for or harass these fish. *CAUTION: Watch for bears.*

J 95.9 (154.3 km) **AH 359.7** (578.8 km) Large gravel turnout to west with litter barrels.

J 96.7 (155.7 km) **AH 358.9** (577.6 km) **Meziadin Lake** Provincial Park; 42 campsites (many on lake), drinking water, firewood, garbage containers, boat launch. The lake has a significant fish population, including rainbow trout, mountain whitefish and Dolly Varden. Fishing is especially good at the mouths of small streams draining into Meziadin Lake. *CAUTION: Watch for bears. The hills around the lake are prime bear habitat.* ▲

J 97.5 (157 km) **AH 358.1** (576.3 km) **Meziadin Lake Junction** (Mezy-AD-in); Cassiar Highway junctions with the access road to Stewart, BC, and Hyder, AK. Motel, cafe and gas station at junction. *(NOTE: Status of gas availability unknown at press time.)* A visitor information cabin is located here, open daily in summer. See STEWART, BC–HYDER, AK, ACCESS ROAD on page 206.

NOTE: This junction can be confusing. Choose your route carefully.

J 100.3 (161.4 km) **AH 355.3** (571.8 km) Kilometrepost 160.

J 103.2 (166.1 km) **AH 352.4** (567.1 km) Hanna Creek river and bridge.

Northbound: Pavement ends, gravel begins. Watch for upgrading and paving in 1994.

Southbound: Pavement begins, gravel ends.

J 116.6 (187.6 km) **AH 339** (545.5 km) Pleasant view of Mount Bell-Irving across pond. Watch for bears along this stretch of highway.

Travelers will notice large areas of clearcut along the southern half of the Cassiar Highway. Bark beetle infestation necessitated the harvest of timber along this particular stretch of highway. After logging, it was

(continued on page 209)

Stewart, BC–Hyder, AK, Access Road Log

HIGHWAY 37A
Distance is measured from Meziadin Lake Junction (M).

M 0 Junction with Cassiar Highway at **Milepost J 97.5**. Visitor information cabin open daily in summer.

M 4.8 (7.7 km) Picnic area with tables, toilets, litter barrels and boat launch.

M 7.7 (12.4 km) Surprise Creek bridge.

M 10.1 (16.3 km) Turnout to south with view of hanging glaciers.

M 11.5 (18.5 km) Windy Point bridge.

M 13 (20.9 km) Cornice Creek bridge.

M 13.5 (21.7 km) Strohn Creek bridge.

M 14.7 (23.7 km) Rest area with litter barrels, view of Bear Glacier.

M 15.8 (25.4 km) Turnouts along lake into which Bear Glacier calves its icebergs. Watch for falling rock from slopes above road in spring. Morning light is best for photographing spectacular Bear Glacier. At one time the glacier reached this side of the valley; the old highway can be seen hundreds of feet above the present road.

M 18.4 (29.6 km) Cullen River bridge.

M 18.9 (30.4 km) Huge delta of accumulated avalanche snow. Narrow road with little shoulder; no stopping.

M 21.5 (34.6 km) Argyle Creek.

M 23.2 (37.3 km) Narrow, steep-walled Bear River canyon. Watch for rocks on road.

M 24.5 (39.4 km) Turnout with litter barrel to north.

M 24.8 (39.9 km) Bear River bridge.

M 30.1 (48.4 km) Bitter Creek bridge.

M 32.5 (52.3 km) Wards Pass cemetery. The straight stretch of road along here is the former railbed from Stewart.

M 36.9 (59.4 km) Bear River bridge and welcome portal to Stewart.

M 38.5 (62 km) Highway joins main street of Stewart (description follows).

M 40.9 (65.8 km) U.S.–Canada border. Hyder (description follows).

TIME ZONE CHANGE: Stewart observes Pacific time, Hyder observes Alaska time. See Time Zones in the GENERAL INFORMATION section.

Stewart, BC–Hyder, AK

Stewart is at the head of Portland Canal on the AK–BC border. **Hyder** is 2.3 miles/3.7 km beyond Stewart. **Population: Stewart** about 1,000; **Hyder** 85. **Emergency Services:** In Stewart, **RCMP**, phone 636-2233. EMS personnel and Medivac helicopter in Hyder. **Fire Department**, phone 636-2345. **Hospital** and **Ambulance**, Stewart Health Care Facility (10 beds), phone 636-2221.

Visitor Information: Stewart Infocentre (Box 585, Stewart, BC V0T 1W0), located in museum at 6th and Columbia; phone 636-2111. Hyder Information Centre and Museum is located on the right as you drive into town.

Elevation: Sea level. **Climate:** Maritime, with warm winters and cool rainy summers. Summer temperatures range from 41°F/5°C to 57°F/14°C; winter temperatures range from 25°F/-4°C to 43°F/6°C. Average temperature in January is 27°F/-3°C; in July, 67°F/19°C. Reported record high 89°F/32°C, record low -18°F/-28°C. Slightly less summer rain than other Northwest communities, but heavy snowfall in winter. **Radio:** CFPR 1450, CFMI-FM 101. **Television:** Four channels.

Private Aircraft: Stewart airport, on 5th Street; elev. 10 feet/3m; length 3,900 feet/1,189m; asphalt; fuel 80, 100.

Stewart and Hyder are on a spur of the Cassiar Highway, at the head of Portland Canal, a narrow saltwater fjord approximately 90 miles/145 km long. The fjord forms a natural boundary between Alaska and Canada. Stewart has a deep harbor and boasts of being Canada's most northerly ice-free port.

Historic stone storehouse on the international boundary at Eagle Point. (Judy Parkin, staff)

Prior to the coming of the white man, Nass River Indians knew the head of Portland Canal as *Skam-A-Kounst,* meaning safe place, probably referring to the place as a retreat from the harassment of the coastal Haidas. The Nass came here annually to hunt birds and pick berries. Little evidence of their presence remains.

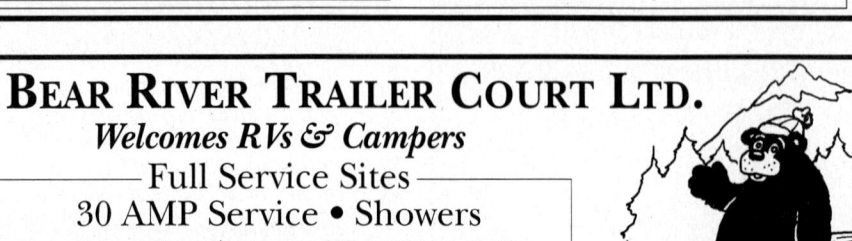

In 1896, Captain D.D. Gaillard (after whom the Gaillard Cut in the Panama Canal was later named) explored Portland Canal for the U.S. Army Corps of Engineers. Two years after Gaillard's visit, the first prospectors and settlers arrived. Among them was D.J. Raine, for whom a creek and mountain in the area were named. The Stewart brothers arrived in

1902 and in 1905 Robert M. Stewart, the first postmaster, named the town Stewart. Hyder was first called Portland City. It was then renamed Hyder, after Canadian mining engineer Frederick B. Hyder, when the U.S. Postal Authority told residents there were already too many cities named Portland.

Gold and silver mining dominated the early economy. Hyder boomed with the discovery of rich silver veins in the upper Salmon River basin in 1917–18. Hundreds of pilings, which supported structures during this boom period, are visible on the tidal flats at Hyder.

Hyder became an access and supply point for the mines, while Stewart served as the centre for Canadian mining activity. Mining ceased in 1956, with the exception of the Granduc copper mine, which operated until 1984. Currently, Westmin Resources Ltd. operates a gold and silver mine. Today the economy is driven by forestry, mining and tourism.

ACCOMMODATIONS

Stewart: Three hotels/motels, three restaurants, two grocery stores, two churches, service stations, dry cleaners with laundromat, pharmacy, post office, a bank (open 10 A.M. to 3 P.M. Monday through Thursday, Friday until 6 P.M.), liquor store and other shops. Camping at Stewart Lions Campground and RV Park; this park has washrooms with showers, 62 sites (35 with electrical hookups), a dump station and picnic tables. ▲

Hyder: a grocery, three gift shops, a post office, three cafes, a Baptist church, a motel and two bars. There is no bank in Hyder.

TRANSPORTATION

Air: Blue Ice Flightseeing air charter service available from Stewart. Ketchikan Air Service (charter) from Hyder to Ketchikan. **Bus:** Limousine service to

STEWART ADVERTISERS

Bear River Trailer Court Ltd. .Highway 37A
Brothers' Bakery............................5th Ave.
King Edward Motel/ Hotel............................5th & Columbia
Seaport Limousine.......Ph. (604) 636-2622
Shoreline Cleaners Ltd...........................Ph. (604) 636-2322
Stewart Lions Campground & RV Park...................Ph. (604) 636-2537
Stewart Tourist Information............Ph. (604) 636-2111

Terrace. **Ferry:** Once-a-week same day service between Ketchikan and Hyder. See the Alaska state ferry schedules (Southern Panhandle) in the MARINE ACCESS ROUTES section. *IMPORTANT: Check ferry departure times carefully!*

ATTRACTIONS

Historic Buildings: In Stewart, the former fire hall at 6th and Columbia streets built in 1910, which now houses the Historical Society Museum and visitor information centre; the Empress Hotel (now occupied by a hardware store) on 4th Street; and St. Mark's Church (built in 1910) on 9th Street at Columbia. On the border at Eagle Point is the stone storehouse built by Captain D.D. Gaillard of the U.S. Army Corps of Engineers in 1896. This is the oldest masonry building in Alaska. Originally four of these buildings were built to hold exploration supplies. This one was subsequently used as a cobbler shop and jail. Storehouses Nos. 3 and 4 are included on the (U.S.) National Register of Historic Places.

Stewart Historical Society Museum, in the fire hall, has a wildlife exhibit on the main floor and an exhibit of historical items on the top floor. Included is a display on movies filmed here: *Bear Island* (1978), John Carpenter's *The Thing* (1981), and *The Ice Man* (1982).

Hyder's night life is popular, and has helped Hyder earn the reputation and town motto of "The Friendliest Little Ghost Town in Alaska."

Recreation in Stewart includes winter sports at the indoor skating rink; swimming in the Paddy McNeil Memorial Swimming Pool (indoor); an outdoor tennis court; ball parks; and hiking trails.

Sightseeing tours of the area take in active and abandoned mine sites and glaciers, including the spectacular Salmon Glacier. Other sights include nearby Fish Creek and Summit Lake at the toe of Salmon Glacier. Once a year, usually in August, the ice dam holding back Summit Lake breaks, and the force of the meltwater results in a spectacular flooding of the Salmon River valley at Hyder. Multicolored chum and pink salmon are seen in their spawning colors in Fish Creek during August; they ascend the streams and rivers in great numbers to spawn. Visitors may photograph feeding bald eagles and black bears which are drawn to the streams by the salmon.

Visit the old mines. A 30-mile-long road leads to movie locations and former mine sites. *CAUTION: The road is narrow and winding.* Access to Premier Mine, Big Missouri Mine and Salmon Glacier. Inquire at the museum in Stewart for more information.

International Days. Fourth of July begins July 1 as Stewart and Hyder celebrate Canada Day and Independence Day. Parade and fireworks.

Charter trips by small boat on Portland Canal and vicinity available for sightseeing and fishing. Flightseeing air tours available.

AREA FISHING: Portland Canal, salmon to 50 lbs., use herring, spring and late fall; coho to 12 lbs. in fall, fly-fishing. *(NOTE: Alaska or British Columbia fishing license required, depending on whether you fish U.S. or Canadian waters in Portland Canal.)* **Fish Creek,** up the Salmon River road from Hyder, Dolly Varden 2 to 3 lbs. on salmon eggs and lures, best in summer. Fish Creek is a fall spawning ground for some of the world's largest chum salmon; it is illegal to kill chum in fresh water in British Columbia. It is legal to harvest chum at both salt and fresh water in Alaska.

Return to Milepost J 97.5 on the Cassiar Highway

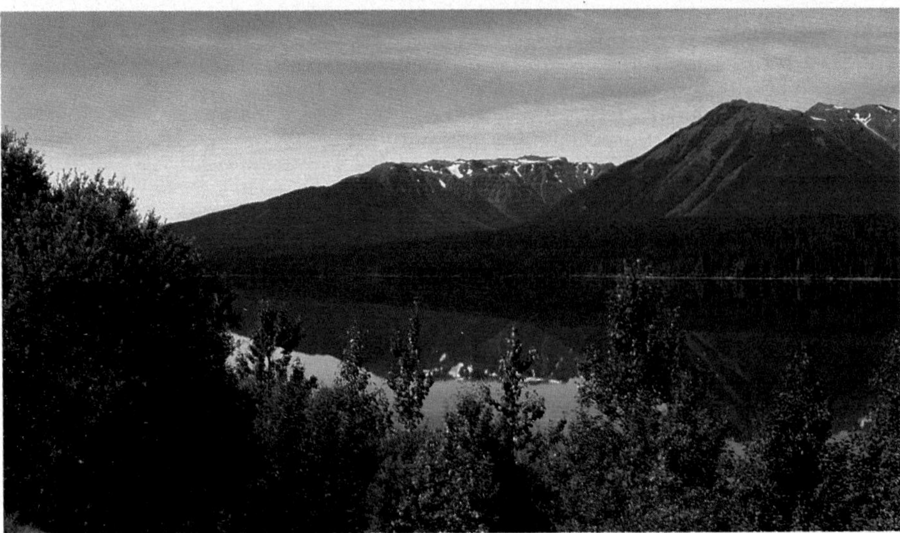

Beautiful Eddontenajon Lake, one of many picturesque lakes along the Cassiar.
(Judy Parkin, staff)

(continued from page 205)
burned off and reforested. *CAUTION: Watch for logging trucks.*

J 118.8 (191.2 km) **AH 336.8** (542 km) Bell I rest area at north end of Bell–Irving bridge; picnic tables, pit toilets, litter barrels.

J 121.1 (194.9 km) **AH 334.5** (538.3 km) Spruce Creek bridge.

J 125.6 (202.1 km) **AH 330** (531.1 km) Bell–Irving River parallels highway.

J 128 (206 km) **AH 327.6** (527.2 km) Cousins Creek.

J 129.7 (208.7 km) **AH 325.9** (524.5 km) Ritchie Creek bridge.

J 133.5 (214.8 km) **AH 322.1** (518.3 km) Taft Creek.

J 134.8 (216.9 km) **AH 320.8** (516.3 km) Kilometrepost 215.

J 139.2 (224 km) **AH 316.4** (509.2 km) Deltaic Creek. *NOTE: Watch for road construction next 16 miles/25.7 km northbound in 1994.*

J 144.7 (232.9 km) **AH 310.9** (500.3 km) Glacier Creek.

J 146.9 (236.4 km) **AH 308.7** (496.8 km) Large turnout with litter barrels. Skowill Creek bridge. The old one-lane bridge is visible to the east.

J 151.4 (243.6 km) **AH 304.2** (489.5 km) Oweegee Creek.

J 155.5 (250.2 km) **AH 300.1** (483 km) Provincial rest area by **Hodder Lake**; tables, litter barrels, pit toilets, boat launch. Fly or troll for small rainbows.

Northbound: Gravel ends, seal coat begins.

Southbound: Seal coat ends, gravel begins. Watch for road construction next 16 miles/25.7 km in 1994.

J 157 (252.7 km) **AH 298.6** (480.5 km) Food, gas (unleaded and diesel), propane and lodging.

Bell II Crossing Ltd. See display ad this section.

J 157.3 (253.1 km) **AH 298.3** (480 km) Second crossing northbound of Bell–Irving River.

J 162.9 (262.1 km) **AH 292.7** (471 km) Snowbank Creek.

J 163.3 (262.8 km) **AH 292.3** (470.4 km) Avalanche area: No stopping in winter or spring. Avalanche chutes are visible on slopes to west in summer.

J 165.2 (265.9 km) **AH 290.4** (467.3 km) Redflat Creek.

J 165.4 (266.2 km) **AH 290.2** (467 km) Highway serves as emergency airstrip. Watch for aircraft landing or taking off; keep to side of road! End avalanche area northbound.

J 167.9 (270.3 km) **AH 287.7** (463 km) Revision Creek.

J 170.6 (274.5 km) **AH 285** (458.6 km) Kilometrepost 115 reflects distance from Meziadin Lake junction.

J 173.7 (279.5 km) **AH 281.9** (453.7 km) Turnout with litter barrels to east overlooking large moose pasture, beaver ponds.

J 174 (280 km) **AH 281.6** (453.2 km) Liz Creek.

J 174.5 (281 km) **AH 281.1** (452.4 km) Ningunsaw Pass (elev. 1,530 feet/466m). Nass–Stikine water divide; turnout with litter barrels to west beside **Ningunsaw River**. Mountain whitefish and Dolly Varden. The highway parallels the Ningunsaw northbound. Watch for fallen rock on road through the canyon. The Ningunsaw is a tributary of the Stikine watershed.

J 176.5 (284 km) **AH 279.1** (449.2 km) Alger Creek. The massive piles of logs and debris in this creek are from a 1989 avalanche.

J 177.4 (285.5 km) **AH 278.2** (447.7 km) Ogilvie Creek.

J 181.8 (292.6 km) **AH 273.8** (440.6 km) Point of interest sign about Yukon Telegraph line. The 1,900-mile Dominion Telegraph line linked Dawson City with Vancouver. Built in 1899–1901, the line was a route for prospectors and trappers headed to Atlin; it was replaced by radio in the 1930s.

J 182.1 (293.1 km) **AH 273.5** (440.1 km) Echo Lake. Flooded telegraph cabins are visible in the lake below. Good view of Coast Mountains to west. Spectacular cliffs seen to the east are part of the Skeena Mountains (Bowser Basin).

J 185.1 (297.9 km) **AH 270.5** (435.3 km) Bob Quinn Forest Service Road, under construction as the Iskut Mining Road, will provide year-round access to goldfields west of Ningunsaw River. The road will follow the Iskut River Valley toward the Stikine River, with a side branch to Eskay Creek gold deposit.

J 185.7 (298.8 km) **AH 269.9** (434.3 km) **Little Bob Quinn Lake**, rainbow and Dolly Varden, summer and fall. Access to Bob Quinn Lake at **Milepost J 187.5**.

J 186 (299.3 km) **AH 269.6** (433.9 km) Bob Quinn flight airstrip. This is a staging site for supplies headed for the Stikine/Iskut goldfields. Paved rest area with litter barrels.

J 187.5 (301.7 km) **AH 268.1** (431.4 km) Bob Quinn highway maintenance camp; meals, lodging, helicopter base. Access to Bob Quinn Lake; toilet, picnic table, cartop boat launch.

J 189.4 (304.8 km) **AH 266.2** (428.4 km) Kilometrepost 145.

J 194.6 (313.2 km) **AH 261** (420 km) Devil Creek Canyon bridge.

J 198 (318.6 km) **AH 257.6** (414.6 km) Highway passes through Iskut burn, where fire destroyed 78,000 acres in 1958. This is also British Columbia's largest huckleberry patch.

Northbound, the vegetation begins to change from inland valley western hemlock forest to northern boreal white and black spruce.

J 204.3 (328.8 km) **AH 251.3** (404.4 km) Durham Creek.

Northbound: Gravel begins, pavement ends.

Southbound: Gravel ends, pavement begins.

J 209.7 (337.5 km) **AH 245.9** (395.7 km) Single-lane bridge crosses Burrage River. Note the rock pinnacle upstream.

J 210.5 (338.7 km) **AH 245.1** (394.4 km) Iskut River to west.

J 211.3 (340 km) **AH 244.3** (393.2 km) Kilometrepost 180.

J 212.5 (342 km) **AH 243.1** (391.2 km) Emergency airstrip crosses road; no stopping, watch for aircraft.

J 217.8 (350.5 km) **AH 237.8** (382.7 km) Rest area by Eastman Creek; picnic tables, outhouses, litter barrels and information sign with map and list of services in Iskut Lakes Recreation Area. The creek was named for George Eastman (of Eastman Kodak fame), who hunted big game in this area before the highway was built.

J 220.8 (355.3 km) **AH 234.8** (377.9 km) Slow down for one-lane bridge across Rescue Creek.

J 223.1 (359.1 km) **AH 232.5** (374.2 km) **Willow Ridge Resort.** See display ad this section. ▲

J 223.4 (359.6 km) **AH 232.2** (373.7 km) Slow down for one-lane bridge over Willow Creek.

J 226 (363.7 km) **AH 229.6** (369.5 km) Natadesleen Lake trailhead; toilets and litter barrel. Hike 0.6 mile/1 km west to lake.

J 227.4 (366 km) **AH 228.2** (367.2 km) Kilometrepost 205.

J 229.2 (368.9 km) **AH 226.4** (364.3 km) Snapper Creek.

J 230.5 (371 km) **AH 225.1** (362.2 km) Kilometrepost 210 reflects distance from Meziadin junction. Entrance to Kinaskan campground with 36 sites, outhouses, firewood, picnic area, drinking water and boat launch on **Kinaskan Lake;** rainbow fishing, July and August. Campground attendant on duty during summer. Start of 15-mile/24-km hiking trail to Mowdade Lake in Mount Edziza Provincial Park. ▲

Northbound: Seal coat surfacing begins, gravel ends.

Southbound: Gravel begins, seal coat surfacing ends.

J 235.2 (378.5 km) **AH 220.4** (354.7 km) Turnout with litter barrel and view of Kinaskan Lake.

J 236.1 (380 km) **AH 219.5** (353.2 km) Small lake to east.

J 236.3 (380.3 km) **AH 219.3** (352.9 km) Kilometrepost 220.

J 238.6 (384 km) **AH 217** (349.2 km) Todagin Creek one-lane bridge.

J 246 (395.9 km) **AH 209.6** (337.3 km) **Tatogga Lake Resort.** See display ad this section. ▲

J 246.6 (396.8 km) **AH 209** (336.3 km) Coyote Creek.

J 247.2 (397.8 km) **AH 208.4** (335.4 km) Ealue Lake (EE-lu-eh) turnoff.

J 247.3 (397.9 km) **AH 208.3** (335.2 km) Spatsizi trailhead to east.

J 248.9 (400.5 km) **AH 206.7** (332.6 km) Kilometrepost 240.

J 249.9 (402.2 km) **AH 205.7** (331 km) Turnout beside **Eddontenajon Lake** (Ed-don-TEN-ajon). It is unlawful to camp overnight at turnouts. People drink from the lake, be careful not to contaminate it. Use dump stations. Breakup in late May; freezeup early November. Rainbow fishing July and August.

J 250 (402.3 km) **AH 205.6** (330.9 km) Turnout with litter barrel.

J 252.2 (405.9 km) **AH 203.4** (327.3 km) **Iskutine Lodge.** A great destination adventure resort! Weekly packages start $399; includes full use facilities — rustic cabins, canoes, kayaks, bikes, fishing gear, sauna! Specializing 6–14 day guided wilderness tours (paddle/hike) start $699/person. No nightly camping or RVs! Please — support the other businesses in the area. Remember — it is illegal to camp (including RVs) overnight at all highway turnouts! Box 39, Iskut, BC V0J 1K0 (604) 234-3456. [ADVERTISEMENT]

J 253.7 (408.3 km) **AH 201.9** (324.9 km) **Red Goat Lodge** is a complete wilderness resort offering first-class lakeshore camping for RVs and tenters, an internationally rated hostel, and a bed and breakfast with an unparalleled reputation. The campsites have been landscaped to the same exacting standards used by B.C. Parks, with the addition of deluxe hot showers, washrooms and laundry. We have canoe rentals, and instruction is available. Fishing is great, and we sell licenses and tackle. Choose Red Goat if you are looking for real quality. Undoubtedly the best facility on Highway 37. May–Sept. Tony and Doreen Shaw, Iskut, BC. Preseason information available from Box 8749, Victoria, BC V8W 3S3. Phone (604) 383-1805. [ADVERTISEMENT] ▲

J 253.8 (408.4 km) **AH 201.8** (324.8 km) **Black Sheep Motel & Cafe.** See display ad this section.

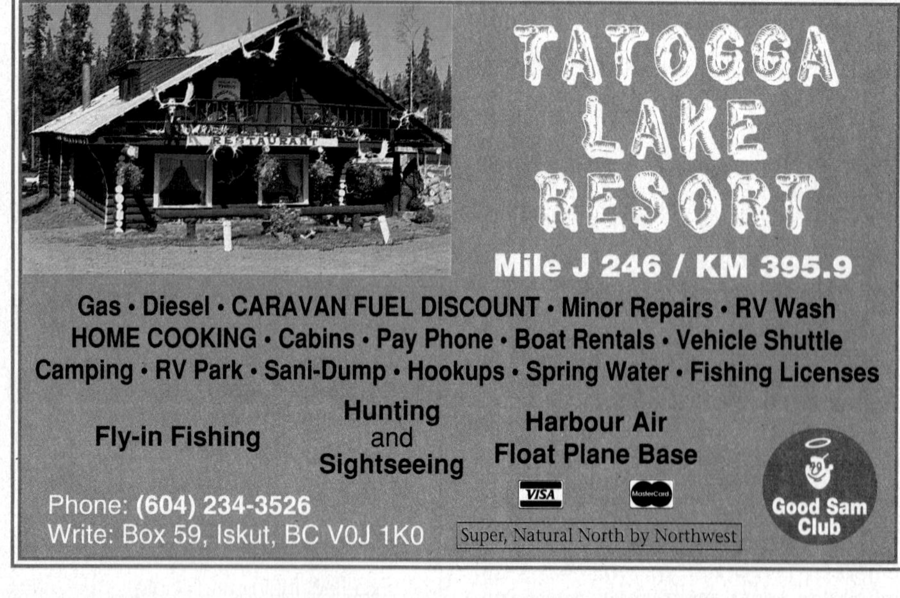

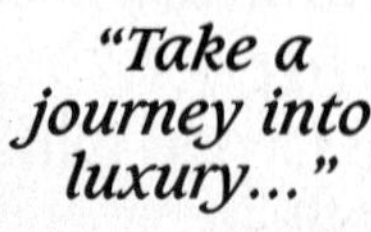

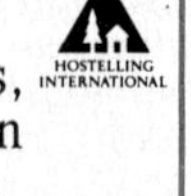

J 255.5 (411.2 km) **AH 200.1** (322 km) B.C. Hydro generating plant, supplies power for Iskut area.

J 255.7 (411.5 km) **AH 199.9** (321.7 km) **ISKUT** (pop. 300). Small Tahltan Indian community with post office, grocery store, motel and gas station. Quality beaded moccasins available locally. Camping and cabins available locally. Horse trips and river rafting may be available; inquire locally. Clinic open 1 to 3 P.M., five days a week. For a brochure on the area, write Northern Wilderness Travel Assoc., General Delivery, Iskut, BC V0J 1K0. ▲

Iskut Lake Co-op. See display ad this section.

Private Aircraft: Eddontenajon airstrip, 0.6 mile/1 km north of Iskut; elev. 3,100 feet/945m; length 3,000 feet/914m; gravel; fuel available at Trans-Provincial Airlines base south of here on Eddontenajon Lake.

J 257.5 (414.4 km) **AH 198.1** (318.8 km) **A-E Guest Ranch.** Campground and RV sites in secluded park-like setting within easy walking distance of Iskut Lake in the Cassiar Mountains with lovely glacier views. We have several streamside campsites and 70-foot pull-throughs with 15/30 amp service and water. All sites on crushed gravel pads. Sani-dump, water and power available. Nature walk to Iskut Lake and excellent lakeshore fishing. Day use area with boat launch. See display ad for contact information. [ADVERTISEMENT] ▲

J 258.2 (415.6 km) **AH 197.4** (317.7 km) Kilometrepost 255 reflects distance from Meziadin junction.

J 261 (420 km) **AH 194.6** (313.2 km) **Bear Paw Wilderness Resort.** Experience our 16-suite Alpine Hotel c/w hot tub, saunas, gourmet reserved dining, lounge and souvenir shop. Relax on our large picturesque sundeck. Join our outdoor BBQs, but plan on more than an overnight stay. We offer guided tours of Mount Edziza and the Spatsizi Plateau. You can pan for gold, jet boat on the Stikine River or fish for prize rainbow trout. Deluxe accommodations, guest cabins, licensed dining, campground, horseback riding and tours. Visa, MasterCard. Super Natural Scenic Adventure. [ADVERTISEMENT] ▲

J 261.6 (421 km) **AH 194** (312.2 km) Kilometrepost 260 reflects distance from Meziadin junction.

J 261.8 (421.3 km) **AH 193.8** (311.9 km) **Trappers Souvenirs.** See display ad this section.

J 263.5 (424 km) **AH 192.1** (309.1 km) **Forty Mile Flats.** See display ad this section. ▲

J 266.7 (429.2 km) **AH 188.9** (304 km) Turnout with litter barrels to west. From here the dormant volcano of Mount Edziza (elev. 9,143 feet/2,787m) and its adjunct cinder cone can be seen to the southwest. The park, not accessible by road, is a rugged wilderness with cinder cones, craters and lava flows. Panoramic view of Skeena and Cassiar mountains for next several miles northbound.

J 269 (433 km) **AH 186.6** (300.3 km) Northbound: Gravel begins, seal coat ends.

Southbound: Gravel ends, seal coat begins.

J 271.8 (438.4 km) **AH 183.8** (295.8 km) Turnout with litter barrel to west. Wild raspberry patch beside rest area.

J 273.8 (440.6 km) **AH 181.8** (292.6 km) Hairpin turn: Keep to right.

J 275.2 (442.9 km) **AH 180.4** (290.3 km) Turnout with litter barrels and toilets to west. Tourist map and services directory for Iskut Lakes Recreation Area located here.

J 275.6 (443.5 km) **AH 180** (289.7 km) Stikine River bridge.

J 277.2 (446.1 km) **AH 178.4** (287.1 km) Kilometrepost 285 reflects distance from Meziadin junction.

J 277.4 (446.4 km) **AH 178.2** (286.8 km) Turnout to east with litter barrel.

J 286.6 (461.2 km) **AH 169** (272 km) Kilometrepost 300 reflects distance from Meziadin junction.

J 290.1 (466.9 km) **AH 165.5** (266.3 km) Northbound: Seal coat begins, gravel ends.

Southbound: Gravel begins, seal coat ends.

J 290.7 (467.8 km) **AH 164.9** (265.4 km) Turnout on Upper Gnat Lake; tables, toilets, litter barrels. Long scar across Gnat Pass valley to the east is grading preparation for B.C. Railway's proposed Dease Lake extension from Prince George. Construction was halted in 1977. Railway grade is visible for several miles northbound.

J 292.3 (470.4 km) **AH 163.3** (262.8 km) Turnout overlooking **Lower Gnat Lake**, abundant rainbow.

J 292.8 (471.2 km) **AH 162.8** (262 km) Kilometrepost 310 reflects distance from Meziadin junction.

J 295.3 (475.2 km) **AH 160.3** (258 km) Gnat Pass Summit. *NOTE: Watch for road*

construction (widening and graveling).

J 296 (476.3 km) **AH 159.6** (256.8 km) Kilometrepost 315 reflects distances from Meziadin junction.

J 301.9 (485.8 km) **AH 153.7** (247.3 km) One-lane bridge across **Tanzilla River.** *NOTE: Watch for bridge construction in 1994.* Pleasant rest area with picnic tables and outhouses at south end of one-lane bridge beside river. Fishing for grayling to 16 inches, June and July; use flies.

J 303.2 (487.9 km) **AH 152.4** (245.3 km) Dalby Creek.

J 305.3 (491.3 km) **AH 150.3** (241.9 km) Kilometrepost 330 reflects distance from Meziadin junction.

J 306.9 (493.9 km) **AH 148.7** (239.3 km) Divide (elev. 2,690 feet/820m) between Pacific and Arctic ocean watersheds.

J 307.7 (495.2 km) **AH 147.9** (238 km) **Junction** with Telegraph Creek Road and access to Dease Lake (description follows). See TELEGRAPH CREEK ROAD log on opposite page.

Dease Lake

Located just west of the Cassiar Highway. **Emergency Services: RCMP** detachment. **Private Aircraft:** Dease Lake airstrip, 1.5 miles/2.4 km south; elev. 2,600 feet/793m; length 6,000 feet/1,829m; asphalt; fuel JP4, 100.

Dease Lake has motels, gas stations (with regular, unleaded, diesel, propane and minor repairs), food stores, restaurant, a post office, highway maintenance centre and government offices. Charter flights and regular air service to Terrace and Smithers.

A Hudson's Bay Co. post was established by Robert Campbell at Dease Lake in 1838, but abandoned a year later. The lake was named in 1834 by John McLeod of the Hudson's Bay Co. for Chief Factor Peter Warren Dease. Laketon, on the west side of the lake (see **Milepost J 334.6**), was a centre for boat building during the Cassiar gold rush of 1872–80. In 1874, William Moore, following an old Indian trail, cut a trail from Telegraph Creek on the Stikine River to the gold rush settlement on Dease Lake. This trail became Telegraph Creek Road, which was used in 1941 to haul supplies for Alaska Highway construction to Dease Lake. The supplies were then ferried down the Dease River to U.S. troops working on the highway.

Today, Dease Lake is a government centre and supply point for the district. The community has dubbed itself the "jade capital of the province." Jade is available locally. It is a popular point from which to fly in to Mount Edziza and Spatsizi wilderness parks or pack in by horse.

DEASE LAKE ADVERTISERS

Bonnie and Clyde's Hideout........................Ph. (604) 771-4242
Dease Lake Esso................Ph. (604) 771-3175
Foodmaster Store.............Ph. (604) 771-4381
Northway Motor Inn........Ph. (604) 771-5341
South Dease Service, Ltd..Ph. (604) 771-4381
Trapper's Den Gift Shoppe.......................Ph. (604) 771-3224

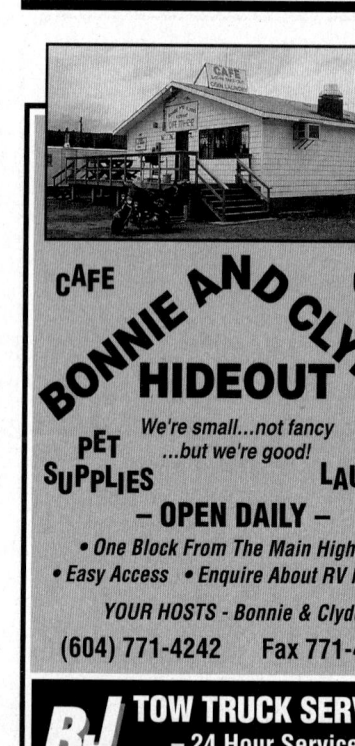

Telegraph Creek Road Log

Built in 1922, this was the first road in the vast Cassiar area of northern British Columbia. The scenery is remarkable and the town of Telegraph Creek is a picture from the turn of the century. *CAUTION: Telegraph Creek Road has some steep narrow sections and several sets of steep switchbacks; it is not recommended for trailers or large RVs. Car and camper drivers who are familiar with mountain driving should have no difficulty, although some motorists consider it a challenging drive even for the experienced. DRIVE CAREFULLY! Use caution when road is wet or icy. Very slippery when wet. Watch for rocks and mud.* There are no visitor facilities en route. Allow a minimum of two hours driving time with good conditions. Check road conditions at highway maintenance camp or RCMP office in Dease Lake before starting the 74 miles/119 km to Telegraph Creek. According to a Telegraph Creek resident, weather varies considerably: It may be raining in Dease Lake, but clear and sunny in Telegraph Creek. You may phone the Riversong Cafe (235-3196) for weather and road conditions.

Distance from Dease Lake junction (D) on the Cassiar Highway is shown.

D 0 **Dease Lake junction, Milepost J 307.7** Cassiar Highway.

D 0.9 (1.4 km) **Junction** with road to Dease Lake. Turn left for Telegraph Creek.

D 1.1 (1.7 km) Entrance to airport.

D 3.4 (5.4 km) Pavement ends, gravel begins westbound.

D 5 (8 km) Entering Tanzilla Plateau.

D 8 (12.9 km) Tatsho Creek (Eightmile).

D 17.4 (28 km) Augustchilde Creek, one-lane bridge.

D 19.1 (30.7 km) 19 Mile Creek.

D 19.7 (31.7 km) 22 Mile Creek.

D 36 (57.9 km) Cariboo Meadows. Entering old burn area for 12 miles/19.3 km.

D 37 (59.5 km) Halfway point to Telegraph Creek from Dease Lake. Turnaround with litter barrel. Old road diverges left to follow Tanzilla River and rejoins at **Milepost D 48.**

D 39 (62.8 km) To the southwest the cone of Mount Edziza is visible. Begin Stikine River Recreation Area.

D 48 (77.2 km) End of burn. Old road joins from left.

D 49 (78.9 km) Road enters small canyon.

D 52 (83.7 km) Tuya River bridge.

D 55 (88.5 km) Day's Ranch on left.

D 58 (93.3 km) Road runs through lava beds, on narrow promontory about 50 feet/15m wide, dropping 400 feet/122m on each side to Tahltan and Stikine rivers. Sudden 180-degree right turn begins steep descent to Tahltan River and Indian fishing camps. Excellent views of Grand Canyon of the Stikine and Tahltan Canyon can be seen by walking a short distance across lava beds to promontory point. Best views of the river canyon are by flightseeing trip. The Stikine River canyon is only 8 feet/2.5m wide at its narrowest point.

D 60 (96.6 km) Tahltan River bridge. Traditional communal Indian smokehouses adjacent road at bridge. Smokehouse on north side of bridge is operated by a commercial fisherman; fresh and smoked salmon sold. There is a commercial inland fishery on the Stikine River, one of only a few such licensed operations in Canada.

D 61 (98.2 km) Start of very narrow road on ledge rising steeply up the wall of the Stikine Canyon for 3 miles/4.8 km, rising to 400 feet/122m above the river.

D 64 (102 km) Old Tahltan Indian community above road. Private property: No trespassing! Former home of Tahltan bear dogs. The Tahltan bear dog, believed to be extinct, was only about a foot high and weighed about 15 pounds. Short-haired, with oversize ears and shaving-brush tail, the breed was recognized by the Canadian Kennel Club. First seen by explorer Samuel Black in 1824, the dogs were used to hunt bears.

D 65 (104.6 km) Ninemile homestead cabins.

D 66 (106.2 km) Eightmile Creek bridge. Spectacular falls into canyon on left below. Opposite the gravel pit at the top of the hill there is a trailhead and parking on the west side of the creek.

D 73 (117.5 km) Indian community. Road follows steep winding descent into old town, crossing a deep narrow canyon via a short bridge. Excellent picture spot 0.2 mile/0.3 km from bridge. Glenora Road **junction** on right.

D 74 (119.1 km) **TELEGRAPH CREEK** (pop. 300; elev. 1,100 feet/335m). Former head of navigation on the Stikine and once a telegraph communication terminal. An important centre during the gold rush days on the Telegraph trail to the Atlin and Klondike goldfields, and also during construction of the Alaska Highway.

There are a cafe, lodge, general store, post office, and a public school and nursing station here. Gas, minor auto and tire repair are available. Stikine River trips and charter flights are available.

Stikine River canyon near Telegraph Creek. (Gerry Deiter)

Residents here make their living fishing commercially for salmon, doing local construction work and guiding visitors on hunting, fishing and river trips. Telegraph Creek is becoming a jumping-off point for wilderness hikers headed for Mount Edziza Provincial Park.

The scenic view along the main street bordering the river has scarcely changed since gold rush days. The turn-of-the-century Hudson's Bay post, which now houses the Riversong Cafe, is a designated Heritage building. Historic St. Aidan's Church (Anglican) is also located here.

A 12-mile/19-km road continues west to Glenora, site of attempted railroad route to the Yukon and limit of larger riverboat navigation. There are two primitive B.C. Forest Service campsites on the road to Glenora. Several spur roads lead to the Stikine River and to Native fish camps. ▲

Stikine Riversong Cafe, Lodge & General Store. See display ad this section.

Return to Milepost J 307.7 Cassiar Highway

Placer mining on North Fork Creek off the Cassiar Highway. (Gerry Deiter)

Cassiar Highway Log

(continued)

J 307.7 (495.2 km) **AH 147.9** (238 km) **Dease Lake Junction.** Junction with access road to Dease Lake and Telegraph Creek Road (see log page 213).

J 308.2 (496 km) **AH 147.4** (237.2 km) Turnout with interpretive signs on Telegraph Creek and Stikine River Recreation Area.

J 310.9 (500.3 km) **AH 144.7** (232.9 km) Kilometrepost 5 reflects distance from Dease Lake junction.

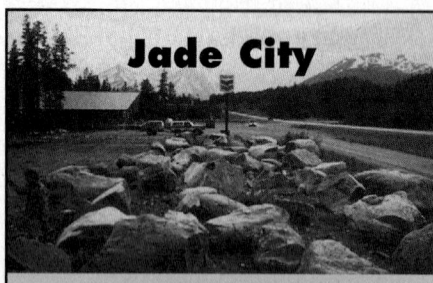

J 314 (505.3 km) **AH 141.6** (227.9 km) Kilometrepost 10 reflects distance from Dease Lake junction.

J 315.8 (508.2 km) **AH 139.8** (225 km) Turnout with litter barrel.

J 316.6 (509.5 km) **AH 139** (223.7 km) Serpentine Creek.

J 317.1 (510.3 km) **AH 138.5** (222.9 km) Seal coat ends northbound, gravel begins and extends 16.4 miles/26.4 km. Seal coat begins southbound and extends to Iskut.

J 323.4 (520.4 km) **AH 132.2** (212.7 km) Halfmoon Creek. Kilometrepost 25 reflects distance from Dease Lake junction.

J 326 (524.6 km) **AH 129.6** (208.6 km) Rest area with picnic tables, litter barrels and outhouses. View of Dease Lake.

J 326.5 (525.4 km) **AH 129.1** (207.8 km) Kilometrepost 30 reflects distance from Dease Lake junction.

J 329.6 (530.4 km) **AH 126** (202.8 km) Kilometrepost 35 reflects distance from Dease Lake junction.

J 330.2 (531.4 km) **AH 125.4** (201.8 km) Turnout with litter barrels to west.

J 331.4 (533.4 km) **AH 124.2** (199.9 km) Black Creek.

J 332.7 (535.4 km) **AH 122.9** (197.8 km) Kilometrepost 40 reflects distance from Dease Lake junction.

J 333.5 (536.7 km) **AH 122.1** (196.5 km) *NOTE: Pavement begins northbound and extends to end of highway at Alaska Highway junction; watch for resurfacing project. Pavement ends southbound, gravel begins and extends 16.4 miles/26.4 km.*

J 333.6 (536.9 km) **AH 122** (196.3 km) Side road leads west to **Dease Lake** for fishing. Lake trout to 30 lbs., use spoons, plugs, spinners, June to October, deep trolling in summer, spin casting in fall.

J 334.6 (538.5 km) **AH 121** (194.7 km) The site of the ghost town Laketon lies across the lake at the mouth of Dease Creek. Laketon was the administrative centre for the district during the Cassiar gold rush (1872–80). Boat building was a major activity along the lake during the gold rush years, with miners heading up various creeks and rivers off the lake in search of gold.

J 335.3 (539.6 km) **AH 120.3** (193.6 km) Dorothy Creek.

J 336.5 (541.5 km) **AH 119.1** (191.7 km) Kilometrepost 45 reflects distance from Dease Lake junction.

J 337.6 (543.3 km) **AH 118** (189.9 km) Beady Creek. Entering the Cassiar Mountains northbound.

J 339 (545.5 km) **AH 116.6** (187.6 km) Kilometrepost 50 reflects distance from Dease Lake junction.

J 339.2 (545.8 km) **AH 116.4** (187.3 km) Turnout to west with litter barrels.

J 340.9 (548.6 km) **AH 114.7** (184.6 km) Turnout with litter barrel to west. **Dease River** parallels the highway. Grayling to 17 inches; Dolly Varden and lake trout to 15 lbs.; northern pike 8 to 10 lbs., May through September.

J 341.9 (550.2 km) **AH 113.7** (183 km) Packer Tom Creek, named for a well-known Indian who lived in this area.

J 342.1 (550.5 km) **AH 113.5** (182.7 km) Kilometrepost 55 reflects distance from Dease Lake junction.

J 343.6 (552.9 km) **AH 112** (180.2 km) Elbow Lake.

J 345.2 (555.6 km) **AH 110.4** (177.7 km) Kilometrepost 60 reflects distance from Dease Lake junction.

J 349.4 (562.3 km) **AH 106.2** (170.9 km) Grassy turnout beside Pyramid Creek.

J 350 (563.3 km) **AH 105.6** (169.9 km) Dease River two-lane concrete bridge.

J 351.4 (565.5 km) **AH 104.2** (167.7 km) Beale Creek and Kilometrepost 70.

J 353.7 (569.2 km) **AH 101.9** (164 km) Look for an eagle's nest in a cottonwood tree to the east.

J 354.5 (570.5 km) **AH 101.1** (162.7 km) Turnout beside **Pine Tree Lake.** Good grayling and lake char fishing.

J 355 (571.3 km) **AH 100.6** (161.9 km) Turnout with litter barrels beside Pine Tree Lake.

J 357.8 (575.8 km) **AH 97.8** (157.4 km) Kilometrepost 80 reflects distance from Dease Lake junction.

J 359.1 (577.9 km) **AH 96.5** (155.3 km) Burn area. An abandoned campfire started the fire in July 1982.

J 360.5 (580.2 km) **AH 95.1** (153 km) **Mighty Moe's Place.** "Home of the world famous five-minute-one-hour show." Spend some time with this colourful outdoorsman and former trapper. Listen to the tall tales of Mighty Moe and stories of life in the North. Rustic campground in quiet natural wilderness. All sites for trailers, tenters and self-contained units $7. Bird watchers, rockhounds and groups welcome. Free showers and coffee for guests; boats, motors and canoes for rent. Some tackle, convenience foods, soft drinks for sale. Inquire about backpack and canoe trips on the historic Dease River. Fish Cotton Lake for lake trout, grayling, Dolly Varden, whitefish and freshwater ling cod. Come as a stranger, leave as a friend; home is where you hang your hat. Box 212, Dease Lake, BC V0C 1L0. [ADVERTISEMENT] ▲

J 366 (589 km) **AH 89.6** (144.2 km) **Cottonwood River** bridge; rest area 0.4 mile/0.6 km west on old highway on south side of river. Fishing for grayling and whitefish. Early summer runs of Dolly Varden.

J 366.2 (589.3 km) **AH 89.4** (143.9 km) Cottonwood River rest area No. 2 is 0.5 mile/0.9 km west on old highway on north side of river.

J 371.7 (598.2 km) **AH 83.9** (135 km) Turnout to west beside **Simmons Lake;** picnic tables, picnic shelter, toilets, small beach and dock. Fishing for lake trout.

J 373.4 (600.9 km) **AH 82.2** (132.3 km) Road runs on causeway between Twin Lakes.

J 375 (603.5 km) **AH 80.6** (129.7 km) Lang Lake and creek. Needlepoint Mountain visible straight ahead southbound.

J 375.6 (604.4 km) **AH 80** (128.7 km) **Vines Lake**, named for bush pilot Lionel Vines; fishing for lake trout.

J 376.6 (606 km) **AH 79** (127.1 km) Kilometrepost 110.

J 378.2 (608.6 km) **AH 77.4** (124.6 km) Erickson gold mine visible on slopes to east. The mine is closed and reclamation is under way.

J 378.7 (609.4 km) **AH 76.9** (123.8 km) Side road east leads down to McDame Lake.

J 379.1 (610.1 km) **AH 76.5** (123.1 km) Trout Line Creek.

J 379.3 (610.4 km) **AH 76.3** (122.8 km) **JADE CITY** (pop. 12), named for the jade deposits found to the east of the highway community. The huge jade boulders visitors can see being cut here are from the Princess Jade Mine, 82 miles/132 km east, one of the largest jade claims in the world.

J 379.5 (610.7 km) **AH 76.1** (122.5 km) **Princess Jade Mines and Store**. See display ad this section.

J 380.6 (612.5 km) **AH 75** (120.7 km) **Cassiar junction.** Service station with gas, propane and minor repairs. Take a sharp turn to west for the Cassiar Road which leads 9.7 miles/15.7 km to the former Cassiar townsite and Cassiar Asbestos Mine. Continue straight ahead for Alaska Highway.

NOTE: Watch for road construction next 75 miles/120.7 km northbound in 1994.

CASSIAR (pop. 25) was the company town of Cassiar Mining Corp. Much of the world's high-grade chrysotile asbestos came from Cassiar. It was shipped by container truck south to Stewart and from there to Vancouver. The mine closed in March 1992, and the site is not open to visitors. No services available.

J 380.8 (612.8 km) **AH 74.8** (120.4 km) Snow Creek. Gravel turnout with litter barrel to east.

J 381.6 (614.1 km) **AH 74** (119.1 km) Deep Creek.

J 382.8 (616.1 km) **AH 72.8** (117.2 km) Kilometrepost 120 reflects distance from Dease Lake junction.

J 385 (619.6 km) **AH 70.6** (113.6 km) No. 3 North Fork Creek. Placer gold mining operation visible east of highway.

J 386.4 (621.9 km) **AH 69.2** (111.4 km) No. 2 North Fork Creek.

J 388.9 (625.9 km) **AH 66.7** (107.3 km) Settling ponds from placer operation visible on east side of highway.

J 389.3 (626.5 km) **AH 66.3** (106.7 km) Historic plaque about Cassiar gold.

J 389.5 (626.8 km) **AH 66.1** (106.4 km) **CENTREVILLE** (pop. 2; elev. 2,600 feet/792m), a former gold rush town of 3,000, was founded and named by miners for its central location between Sylvester's Landing (later McDame Post) at the junction of McDame Creek with the Dease River, and Quartzrock Creek, the upstream limit of pay gravel on McDame Creek. A miner named Alfred Freeman washed out the biggest all gold (no quartz) nugget ever found in British Columbia on a claim near Centreville in 1877; it weighed 72 ounces. Active mining in area.

J 393.9 (633.9 km) **AH 61.7** (99.3 km) **GOOD HOPE LAKE** (pop. 100), Indian village with limited services; groceries and fuel may be available.

Turn east on Bush Road and drive 9 miles/14.5 km for **McDAME POST**, an early Hudson's Bay post, at the **confluence of Dease River and McDame Creek.** Good fishing and hunting here.

J 395.4 (636.3 km) **AH 60.2** (96.9 km) Turnout to east alongside Aeroplane Lake.

J 396.3 (637.7 km) **AH 59.3** (95.4 km) Dry Creek.

J 398 (640.5 km) **AH 57.6** (92.7 km) Mud Lake to east.

J 402.2 (647.3 km) **AH 53.4** (85.9 km) Turnout with litter barrels at entrance to **Boya Lake** Provincial Park. The park is 1.6 miles/2.5 km east of highway; 45 campsites, picnic area on lakeshore, boat launch, drinking water, firewood and swimming. Fishing for lake char, whitefish, grayling and burbot. Attendant on duty during summer. ▲

J 402.3 (647.4 km) **AH 53.3** (85.8 km) Turnout. Horseranch Range may be seen on the eastern horizon northbound. These mountains date back to the Cambrian period, or earlier, and are the oldest in northern British Columbia. According to the Canadian Geological Survey, this area contains numerous permatites with crystals of tourmaline, garnet, feldspar, quartz and beryl. Road crosses Baking Powder Creek and then follows Dease River.

J 402.5 (647.7 km) **AH 53.1** (85.5 km) Kilometrepost 150.

J 408 (656.6 km) **AH 47.6** (76.6 km) Beaverdam Creek.

J 409 (658.2 km) **AH 46.6** (75 km) Beaver View rest area with visitor information sign to west.

J 410 (659.8 km) **AH 45.6** (73.4 km) Leaving Cassiar Mountains, entering Yukon Plateau, northbound.

J 411.7 (662.5 km) **AH 43.9** (70.6 km) Baking Powder Creek. Kilometrepost 165.

J 414.8 (667.5 km) **AH 40.8** (65.6 km) Kilometrepost 170 reflects distance from Dease Lake junction.

J 419.7 (675.4 km) **AH 35.9** (57.8 km) Side road leads east down to lake.

J 420.1 (676 km) **AH 35.5** (57.1 km) French Creek two-lane concrete bridge.

J 426.4 (686.2 km) **AH 29.2** (47.1 km) Twentyeight Mile Creek. Cassiar Mountains rise to the south.

J 429.3 (690.9 km) **AH 26.3** (42.3 km) Wheeler Lake to west.

J 429.9 (691.9 km) **AH 25.7** (41.3 km) Kilometrepost 195 reflects distance from Dease Lake junction.

J 435.3 (700.5 km) **AH 20.3** (32.7 km) Blue River two-lane concrete bridge.

J 438.7 (706 km) **AH 16.9** (27.2 km) Turnout at **Blue Lakes;** litter barrels, picnic tables and fishing for pike and grayling.

J 449.6 (723.5 km) **AH 6.2** (10 km) Turnout with litter barrels beside Cormier Creek.

J 453.5 (729.8 km) **AH 2** (3.2 km) Informal turnout to west at BC–YT border, 60th parallel.

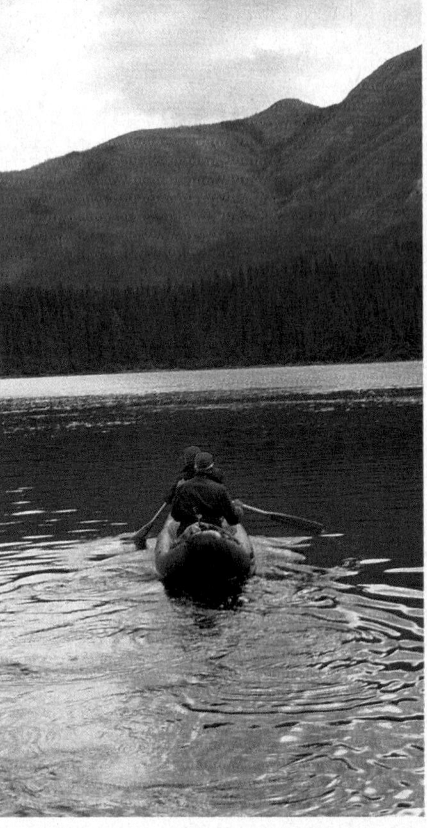

Paddling up the Dease River from Cotton Lake. *(Gerry Deiter)*

J 454.9 (732.1 km) **AH 0.7** (1.2 km) **Albert Creek.** Good grayling fishing. Yukon Territory fishing license required.

J 455 (732.3 km) **AH 0.6** (1 km) High Lake to east.

J 455.6 (733.2 km) **AH 0 Junction** of Cassiar Highway with Alaska Highway. Gas, store, campground, propane, towing and car repair at junction. Turn left for Whitehorse, right for Watson Lake, 13.6 miles/21.9 km southeast. Watson Lake is the nearest major community. ▲

NOTE: Watch for road construction next 75 miles/120.7 km southbound in 1994.

Junction 37 Services. See display ad this section.

Turn to **Milepost DC 626.2** in the ALASKA HIGHWAY section (page 109) for log of Alaska Highway from this junction.

NOTE: Pavement extends southbound to Dease Lake junction, but watch for resurfacing project in 1994.

LIARD HIGHWAY

Junction with Alaska Highway to Mackenzie Highway Junction BC Highway 77, NWT Highway 7

Travelers take a break along the Petitot River. (Earl L. Brown, staff)

The Liard Highway, also called the Liard Trail or "Moose Highway" (after the road sign logo), is named for the Liard River Valley through which it runs for most of its length. The Liard Highway begins about 17 miles/27 km north of Fort Nelson on the Alaska Highway and leads northeast through British Columbia and Northwest Territories for 244.4 miles/393.4 km to junction with the Mackenzie Highway (NWT Highway 1).

The Liard is a relatively straight two-lane gravel road through boreal forest and muskeg. In French, Liard means "black poplar," and this wilderness highway (officially opened in June 1984) is a corridor through a forest of white and black spruce, trembling aspen and balsam poplar.

The road can be dusty when dry and very muddy when wet. Travelers should check current road conditions by phoning 1-800-661-0750 or (403) 873-0157. Or inquire locally at the visitor information centres in Fort Nelson, BC, or Fort Simpson, NWT. Travel information for the Northwest Territories is also available from the Arctic Hotline; phone toll-free weekdays 1-800-661-0788. Food, gas and lodging are available at Fort Liard. Gas is also available at the Mackenzie Highway junction. It is a good idea to fill up in Fort Nelson.

Although the Northwest Territories portion of the Liard Highway parallels the Liard River, there is little access to the river. Travelers may enhance their trip by visiting Blackstone Territorial Park and exploring Nahanni National Park by air charter out of Fort Liard, Fort Simpson or Fort Nelson. Blackstone Territorial Park is accessible by road. Along the highway, travelers may walk the cut lines, drive to abandoned construction camps, swim in the borrow pits and bird watch at the barge landings. Remember to bring along lots of insect repellent! (Black flies are worst in September.)

Fishing the highway streams is only fair, but watch for wildlife such as moose, black bear, wood bison, grouse and red-tailed hawks.

Liard Highway Log

Physical kilometreposts are up on the British Columbia portion of the highway about every 5 kilometres, starting with Km 0 at the Alaska Highway junction and ending at the BC–NWT border. Kilometreposts are up about every 2 kilometres on the Northwest Territories portion of the highway, starting with Km 0 at the BC–NWT border and ending at the junction with the Mackenzie Highway.

Distance from the junction with the Alaska Highway (A) is followed by distance from the Mackenzie Highway junction (M).

A 0 M 244.4 (393.4 km) **Junction** with the Alaska Highway.

A 6.2 (10.1 km) **M 238.2** (383.3 km) Beaver Creek.

A 6.4 (10.3 km) **M 238** (383.1 km) Short side road east to Beaver Lake recreation site; two picnic tables, litter barrels, pit toilets, firewood, turnaround space. Short hike downhill through brush to floating dock; limited lake access.

A 14.3 (23.1 km) **M 230.1** (370.3 km) Stanolind Creek. Beaver dams to west.

A 15.6 (25.2 km) **M 228.8** (368.2 km) Gravel pit to west.

A 17.5 (28.2 km) **M 226.9** (365.2 km) Pond to west and cut line through trees shows Cat access in summer, ice road in winter.

A 21.1 (34 km) **M 223.3** (359.4 km) Westcoast Transmission Pipeline crossing. Pipeline transports natural gas from Pointed Mountain near Fort Liard to the company's gas plant on the Alaska Highway just south of Fort Nelson.

A 23.9 (38.4 km) **M 220.5** (355 km) Gravel pit to west.

A 24.2 (38.9 km) **M 220.2** (354.5 km) Road begins descent northbound to Fort Nelson River.

A 26.4 (42.5 km) **M 218** (350.9 km) Fort Nelson River bridge, single lane, reduce speed. The Nelson bridge is the longest Acrow bridge in the world at 1,410 feet/430m. It is 14 feet/4m wide, with a span of 230 feet/70m from pier to pier. The Acrow bridge, formerly called the Bailey bridge after its designer Sir Donald Bailey, is designed of interchangeable steel panels coupled with pins for rapid construction.

A 26.6 (42.9 km) **M 217.8** (350.5 km) Turnout at north end of bridge with pit toilet, table and garbage container.

A 39.7 (63.9 km) **M 204.7** (329.5 km) **Tsinhia Creek**, grayling run for about two weeks in spring.

A 43.4 (69.8 km) **M 201** (323.5 km) Trapper's cabin to east.

A 51.8 (83.3 km) **M 192.6** (310.1 km) Side road leads west 1.9 miles/3 km to Tsinhia Lake and dead-ends in soft sandy track. A recreation site is planned at Tsinhia Lake.

A 59.2 (95.3 km) **M 185.2** (298.1 km) Concrete beams on west side of highway were dropped from a truck during construction of the Petitot River bridge, setting completion of the bridge back a year. Known locally as the "million-dollar garbage heap."

There are several winter roads in this area used by the forest, oil and gas industries. To most summer travelers these roads look like long cut lines or corridors through the Bush.

The Liard Highway replaced the old Fort Simpson winter road which joined Fort

Nelson and Fort Simpson. The original Simpson Trail was first located in November 1942 by Alaska Highway engineers, including the 648th, Company A detachment.

A 69.4 (111.7 km) **M 175** (281.7 km) Bridge over d'Easum Creek. Good bird-watching area.

A 71.4 (115 km) **M 173** (278.4 km) Access to Maxhamish Lake via 8-mile/13-km winter road accessible in summer by all-terrain vehicles only. A recreation site is planned for Maxhamish Lake.

A 74 (119.1 km) **M 170.4** (274.3 km) Wide unnamed creek flows into Emile Creek to east. Good bird-watching area, beaver pond.

A 75.4 (121.4 km) **M 169** (272 km) Highway emerges from trees northbound; view west of Mount Martin (elev. 4,460 feet/1,360m) and the Kotaneelee Range.

A 80.6 (129.7 km) **M 163.8** (263.7 km) View northwest of mountain ranges in Northwest Territories.

A 81.2 (130.7 km) **M 163.2** (262.6 km) Highway begins descent (7 percent grade) northbound to Petitot River.

A 82.8 (133.2 km) **M 161.6** (260.2 km) Petitot River bridge. The **Petitot River** is reputed to have the warmest swimming water in British Columbia (70°F/21°C). A nine-hour canoe trip to Fort Liard is possible from here (some sheer rock canyons and rapids en route). Good bird-watching area. Also freshwater clams, pike and pickerel; short grayling run in spring.

The Petitot River was named for Father Petitot, an Oblate missionary who came to this area from France in the 1860s.

The Petitot River bridge was the site of the official opening of the Liard Highway on June 23, 1984. The ceremony was marked by an unusual ribbon-cutting: A 1926 Model T Ford, carrying dignitaries, was driven through the ribbon (which stretched for about 20 feet before snapping) while a guard of kilted pipers from Yellowknife played. The Model T, driven by Marl Brown of Fort Nelson, had been across this route in March 1975 just weeks after the bush road had been punched through by Cats and seismic equipment. This earlier trip, in which Mr. Brown was accompanied by Mickey Hempler, took 44 hours from Fort Nelson to Fort Simpson.

A 84.1 (135.4 km) **M 160.3** (258 km) Crest of Petitot River hill (10 percent grade).

A 85 (136.8 km) **M 159.4** (256.6 km) BC–NWT border. TIME ZONE CHANGE: British Columbia observes Pacific time, Northwest Territories observes Mountain time.

Northwest Territories restricts liquor importation as follows: one 40-oz. hard liquor or one 40-oz. wine or one dozen bottles of beer per person.

A 85.2 (137.1 km) **M 159.2** (256.2 km) Turnout to east with litter barrels.

A 107 (172.2 km) **M 137.4** (221.1 km) Vehicle inspection station and weigh scales to east.

A 108.6 (174.8 km) **M 135.8** (218.5 km) **Junction** with side road which leads 4 miles/6.4 km to Fort Liard (description follows). Gas and diesel available at junction. Current status of proposed tourist centre here unknown.

Views from road into Fort Liard across the Liard River of Mount Coty (elev. 2,715 feet/830m) and Pointed Mountain (elev. 4,610 feet/1,405m) at the southern tip of the Liard Range.

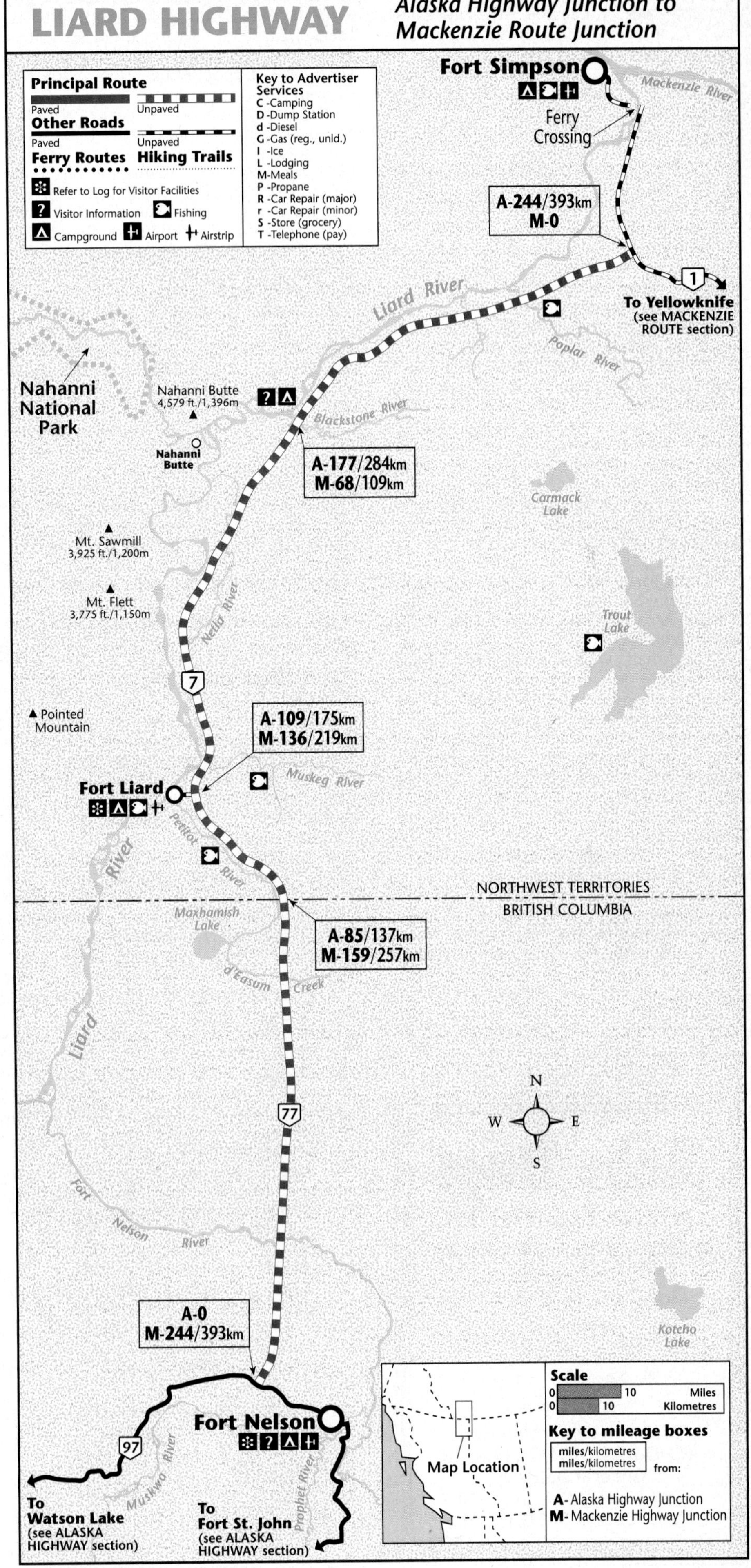

Fort Liard

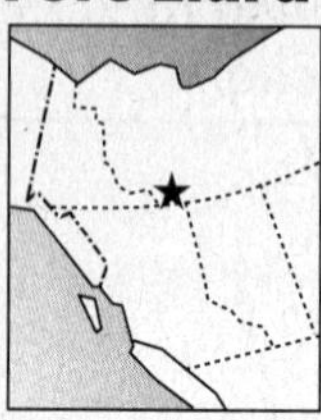

Located on the south bank of the Liard River near its confluence with the Petitot River (known locally as Black River because of its colour), about 50 miles/80 km south of Nahanni Butte. **Population:** 428. **Emergency Services: RCMP**, phone 770-4221. **Fire Department**, phone 770-4241. **Nursing Station**, phone 770-4301.

Elevation: 700 feet/213m. **Climate:** There is no permafrost here. Good soil and water, a long summer season with long hours of daylight, and comparatively mild climate considering Fort Liard's geographical location. Several luxuriant local gardens. The Liard River here is approximately 1,500 feet/450m wide, fairly swift, and subject to occasional flooding. **Radio** and **Television:** CBC radio (microwave), a Native language station from Yellowknife and a community radio station; four channels plus CBC Television (Anik) and private satellite receivers.

Private Aircraft: Fort Liard airstrip; elev. 700 feet/213m; length 2,950 feet/899m; gravel; fuel 100/130 (obtain from Deh Cho Air Ltd.).

Transportation: Air–Charter service year-round via Deh Cho Air. **Barge**–Non-scheduled barge service in summer from Fort Nelson and Hay River.

This small, well-laid-out settlement of traditional log homes and new modern housing, is located among tall poplar, spruce and birch trees on the south bank of the Liard River. The residents live a comparatively traditional life of hunting, trapping, fishing and making handicrafts, although there are more people taking jobs in construction and highway maintenance. Fort Liard residents are well known for the high quality of their birch-bark baskets and porcupine quill workmanship.

Recreation and sightseeing in the area include swimming and fishing (for pike, pickerel, goldeye and spring grayling) at the confluence of the Liard and Petitot rivers; air charter or canoe trip to Trout Lake, Bovie Lake, Fisherman's Lake, 300-foot-/91-m-high Virginia Falls in Nahanni National Park, Tlogotsho Plateau, or scenic Liard and Kotaneelee mountain ranges. Good viewing for Dall sheep, grizzly bear and caribou. Canoe rentals available from Deh Cho Air Ltd. Also check with Deh Cho Air about adventure tours. The traditional Dene settlement of **TROUT LAKE** (pop. 60) is also accessible by air from Fort Liard.

The North West Co. established a trading post near here at the confluence of the Liard and Petitot rivers called Riviere aux Liards in 1805. The post was abandoned after the massacre of more than a dozen residents by Indians. It was reestablished in 1820, then taken over by the Hudson's Bay Co. in 1821 when the two companies merged. The well-known geologist Charles Camsell was born at Fort Liard in 1876.

Facilities here include a motel with eight rooms, six with kitchenettes (reservations suggested), two general stores, playground, outdoor rink, curling rink, craft shop (open 1-5 P.M. weekdays), the modern Acho Dene School, and a Roman Catholic mission. There is no bank in Fort Liard. The community centre has a snack bar. Gas and diesel available at highway junction.

Community-run Hay Lake Campground located just off the access road into Fort Liard; campsites, picnic tables, toilets and floating dock. Campground road may be slippery when wet. ▲

Acho-Dene Native Crafts. See display ad this section.

Deh Cho Air Ltd. See display ad this section.

Liard Highway Log

(continued)

A 113.3 (182.4 km) **M 131.1** (211 km) **Muskeg River** bridge; turnout at north end. Gravel bars on the river make a good rest stop. Trapper's cabin on left. Fishing for pike, pickerel and freshwater clams. The Muskeg River is the local swimming hole for Fort Liard residents.

A 124.9 (201 km) **M 119.5** (192.4 km) Rabbit Creek bridge. Highway now runs close to the Liard River with good views of Liard Range to the west and northwest for the next 13 miles/21 km northbound.

A 128 (206 km) **M 116.4** (187.4 km) Kilometrepost 70.

A 131.1 (211 km) **M 113.3** (182.4 km) Good view of Mount Flett (elev. 3,775 feet/1,150m) ahead northbound.

A 136.7 (220 km) **M 107.7** (173.4 km) Access to Liard River (15-minute hike) via Paramount Mine winter road, an abandoned exploration road across the Liard River into the Liard Range.

A 146.9 (236.4 km) **M 97.5** (157 km) Short road west to locally named Whissel Landing on the Liard River, where road construction materials were brought in by barge during construction of the Liard Highway.

A 147.3 (237 km) **M 97.1** (156.4 km) Road widens for an emergency airstrip.

A 157.8 (253.9 km) **M 86.6** (139.5 km) Netla River bridge. The Netla River Delta is an important waterfowl breeding habitat and Indian fishing and hunting area.

A 163.7 (263.4 km) **M 80.7** (130 km) Road widens for an emergency airstrip.

A 165.9 (267 km) **M 78.5** (126.4 km) Turnoff to west for winter ice road which leads 13.8 miles/22.3 km to the Dene settlement of **NAHANNI BUTTE** (pop. 87), at the confluence of the South Nahanni and Liard rivers. Summer access by boat or floatplane.

A 171.8 (276.5 km) **M 72.6** (116.8 km) Creek Bridge, once called Scotty's Creek after an old trapper who had a cabin upstream. There are many such cabins in this area that once belonged (and still do) to prospectors and trappers, but they are not visible to the motorist. Stands of white spruce, white birch and balsam poplar along highway.

A 176.3 (283.7 km) **M 68.1** (109.7 km) Bridge over Upper Blackstone River. Picnic area on riverbank with tables, firewood, firepits and garbage containers.

A 176.6 (284.2 km) **M 67.8** (109.2 km) Blackstone River bridge.

A 179.1 (288.3 km) **M 65.3** (105.1 km) Entrance to Blackstone Territorial Park; 19 campsites with tables and firepits; firewood, water and garbage containers and boat dock. State-of-the-art restroom, designed by Gino Pin, referred to locally as the "half-million-dollar toilet and shower." The boat launch here is usable only in high water early in the season; use boat launch at Cadillac Landing, **Milepost A 182.9,** during low water. The visitor information building, built with local logs, is located on the bank of the Liard River with superb views of Nahanni Butte (elev. 4,579 feet/1,396m). The centre is open mid-May to mid-September. ▲

A 180.9 (291.2 km) **M 63.5** (102.2 km) Entrance to Lindberg Landing, the homestead of Liard River pioneers Edwin and Sue Lindberg. The Lindbergs offer overnight accommodations in self-contained units, canoe and ATV rentals, boat launch and river tours.

Air charter service operates floatplane flightseeing trips of Nahanni National Park.

A 182.9 (294.3 km) **M 61.5** (99.1 km) Barge landing once used to service Cadillac Mine and bring in construction materials. Access to river via 0.6-mile/0.9-km road (muddy when wet).

A 192.8 (310.3 km) **M 51.6** (83.1 km) Road widens for emergency airstrip.

A 197.8 (318.4 km) **M 46.6** (75 km) Kilometrepost 180.

A 211.3 (340.1 km) **M 33.1** (53.3 km) Bridge over Birch River.

A 216.7 (348.8 km) **M 27.7** (44.6 km) Kilometrepost 210.

A 222.8 (358.5 km) **M 21.6** (34.9 km) Good grayling and pike fishing in **Poplar River** culverts.

A 223 (358.8 km) **M 21.4** (34.6 km) Dirt road on left northbound leads 4 miles/6.4 km to Liard River; four-wheel drive recommended. Wide beach, good spot for viewing wildlife.

A 228.1 (367.1 km) **M 16.3** (26.3 km) Microwave tower to east. Vegetation changes northbound to muskeg with black spruce, tamarack and jackpine.

A 235.6 (379.2 km) **M 8.8** (14.2 km) Kilometrepost 240.

A 244.2 (393 km) **M 0.2** (0.4 km) Road maintenance camp.

A 244.4 (393.4 km) **M 0 Junction** with the Mackenzie Highway (NWT 1). Gas is available at Checkpoint Services. Turn right (south) for Hay River and Yellowknife; turn left (north) for Fort Simpson. See **Milepost G 550.6** on the Mackenzie Highway in the MACKENZIE ROUTE section for log.

MACKENZIE ROUTE

Edmonton, Alberta, to Yellowknife, Northwest Territories
Alberta Highway 35, NWT Highways 1, 2, 3, 4, 5 and 6
(See maps, pages 220-221)

Traditional Dene homestead at Willowlake River, now accessible via the Mackenzie Highway extension to Wrigley. (Lyn Hancock)

Named for explorer Alexander Mackenzie, who in 1779 navigated Great Slave Lake and sailed to the mouth of the Mackenzie River seeking a trade route for the Hudson's Bay Co., the Mackenzie Route is an adventure for modern explorers. It is not a trip for the impulsive. While there are accommodations, gas stations and other services in cities and settlements along the highways, long distances and some rough roads require motorists to plan in advance.

The Mackenzie Route covers the following highways: Alberta Highway 35 and NWT Highway 1 to Fort Simpson (Mackenzie Highway) and the extension to Wrigley; Highway 2 to Hay River; Highway 3 to Yellowknife; Highway 4 (Ingraham Trail); Highway 5 to Fort Smith; and Highway 6 to Fort Resolution. NWT Highway 7, the Liard Highway, connecting the Mackenzie Highway with the Alaska Highway north of Fort Nelson, is covered in the LIARD HIGHWAY section. The Dempster Highway (NWT Highway 8) to Inuvik is covered in the DEMPSTER HIGHWAY section.

Allow at least two weeks to travel the entire route. For general information on travel in the Northwest Territories, phone the Arctic Hotline toll free 1-800-661-0788 during business hours on weekdays.

Most Northwest Territories highways are gravel. Asphalt chip seal surfacing is under way on Highways 1 and 3. Gravel road is treated with calcium chloride to control the dust; wash your vehicle when possible. For road conditions phone 1-800-661-0750.

In summer, the Northwest Territories government provides free ferry service for cars and passengers across the Mackenzie River to Fort Providence and across the Liard River to Fort Simpson. In winter, traffic crosses on the ice. For current ferry information call (403) 873-7799 in Yellowknife, or 1-800-661-0751.

The Mackenzie Highway begins at Grimshaw, AB. There are several routes to Grimshaw to choose from. *The MILEPOST®* logs both the Valleyview–Peace River route from Edmonton to Grimshaw via Highways 16, 43 and 2, and the Highway 2 route north from Grande Prairie through Dunvegan and Fairview to Grimshaw (logs follow). You may also reach Grimshaw via Highway 2 or 33 north from Edmonton through Slave Lake and via Highways 2 and 49 (see NORTHERN WOODS & WATERS ROUTE section).

Log of the Valleyview–Peace River Route to the Mackenzie Highway

Distance from Edmonton (E) is shown.

E 0 **EDMONTON.** Head west on Yellowhead Highway 16. For details on facilities along the highway to Valleyview, turn to the EAST ACCESS ROUTE section.

E 31 (49.9 km) **Junction** of Yellowhead Highway 16 and Highway 43. Turn north on Highway 43.

E 216 (347.6 km) **VALLEYVIEW**; all visitor facilities. Continue north on Highway 43.

E 245 (393.6 km) **Junction** of Highways 43 and 2A; continue north on Highway 43. Little Smoky River Campground, just west of junction, has 50 sites. ▲

E 263 (422.6 km) **Junction** of Highways 43, 2 and 49 at Donnelly Corner. **DONNELLY** (pop. 362), just east of the junction, has a motel and 24-hour service station. Continue north on Highway 2.

Peace River

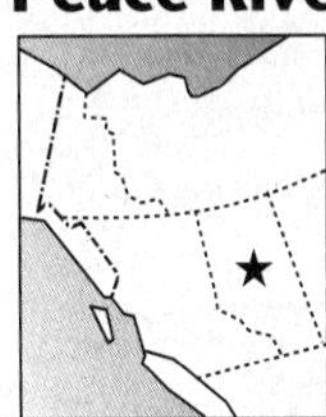

E 302 (486 km) Located on the banks of the Peace River, 15 miles/24 km northeast of Grimshaw (Mile 0 of the Mackenzie Highway). Population: 6,700. **Emergency Services: RCMP**, phone 624-6611. **Hospital**, phone 624-7500. **Ambulance**, phone 624-7511. **Fire Department**, phone 624-3911.

Visitor Information: Tourist Information Booth housed in log cabin next to the trestle at the east end of town; phone 624-2044. Open mid-May to mid-September, 9 A.M. to 9 P.M. The Mighty Peace Tourist Assoc., at the north end of Main Street in the restored railway station, also has information on northern Alberta destinations; phone 624-4042.

Elevation: 1,066 feet/325m. **Private Aircraft:** Peace River airport, 7 miles/11.2 km west; elev. 1,873 feet/571m; length 5,000 feet/1,524m; asphalt; fuel 80, 100, Jet B.

An important transportation centre on the Peace River, the town of Peace River was

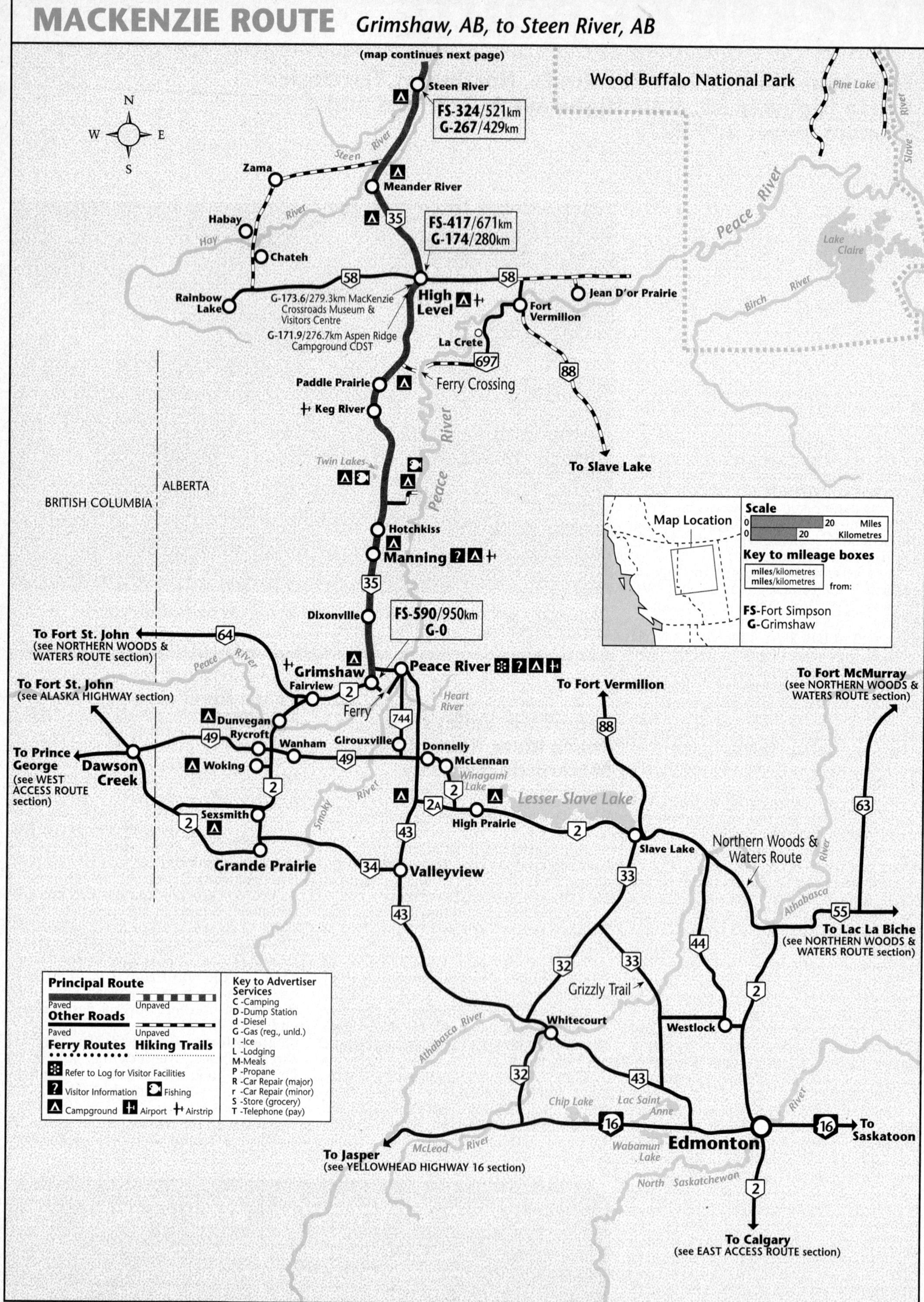
MACKENZIE ROUTE Grimshaw, AB, to Steen River, AB
(map continues next page)
Wood Buffalo National Park
Steen River
FS-324/521km
G-267/429km
Zama
Meander River
Habay
Chateh
Rainbow Lake
FS-417/671km
G-174/280km
High Level
G-173.6/279.3km MacKenzie Crossroads Museum & Visitors Centre
G-171.9/276.7km Aspen Ridge Campground CDST
Jean D'or Prairie
Fort Vermilion
La Crete
Ferry Crossing
Paddle Prairie
Keg River
Twin Lakes
To Slave Lake
BRITISH COLUMBIA
ALBERTA
Hotchkiss
Manning
Dixonville
FS-590/950km
G-0
To Fort St. John
(see NORTHERN WOODS & WATERS ROUTE section)
To Fort St. John
(see ALASKA HIGHWAY section)
Grimshaw
Peace River
Fairview
Ferry
Dunvegan
Rycroft
Wanham
Girouxville
Donnelly
McLennan
Woking
To Prince George
(see WEST ACCESS ROUTE section)
Dawson Creek
Sexsmith
Grande Prairie
High Prairie
Valleyview
Lesser Slave Lake
Winagami Lake
Slave Lake
To Fort Vermilion
To Fort McMurray
(see NORTHERN WOODS & WATERS ROUTE section)
Northern Woods & Waters Route
To Lac La Biche
(see NORTHERN WOODS & WATERS ROUTE section)
Grizzly Trail
Whitecourt
Westlock
Chip Lake
Lac Saint Anne
Wabamun Lake
Edmonton
To Saskatoon
To Jasper
(see YELLOWHEAD HIGHWAY 16 section)
To Calgary
(see EAST ACCESS ROUTE section)
Peace River
Hay River
Birch River
Slave River
Lake Claire
Pine Lake
Heart River
Smoky River
Athabasca River
McLeod River
North Saskatchewan River
Map Location
Scale
0 20 Miles
0 20 Kilometres
Key to mileage boxes
miles/kilometres
miles/kilometres
from:
FS-Fort Simpson
G-Grimshaw
Principal Route
Paved
Unpaved
Other Roads
Paved
Unpaved
Ferry Routes
Hiking Trails
Refer to Log for Visitor Facilities
Visitor Information
Fishing
Campground
Airport
Airstrip
Key to Advertiser Services
C -Camping
D -Dump Station
d -Diesel
G -Gas (reg., unld.)
I -Ice
L -Lodging
M -Meals
P -Propane
R -Car Repair (major)
r -Car Repair (minor)
S -Store (grocery)
T -Telephone (pay)

MACKENZIE ROUTE *Steen River, AB, to Yellowknife, NWT*

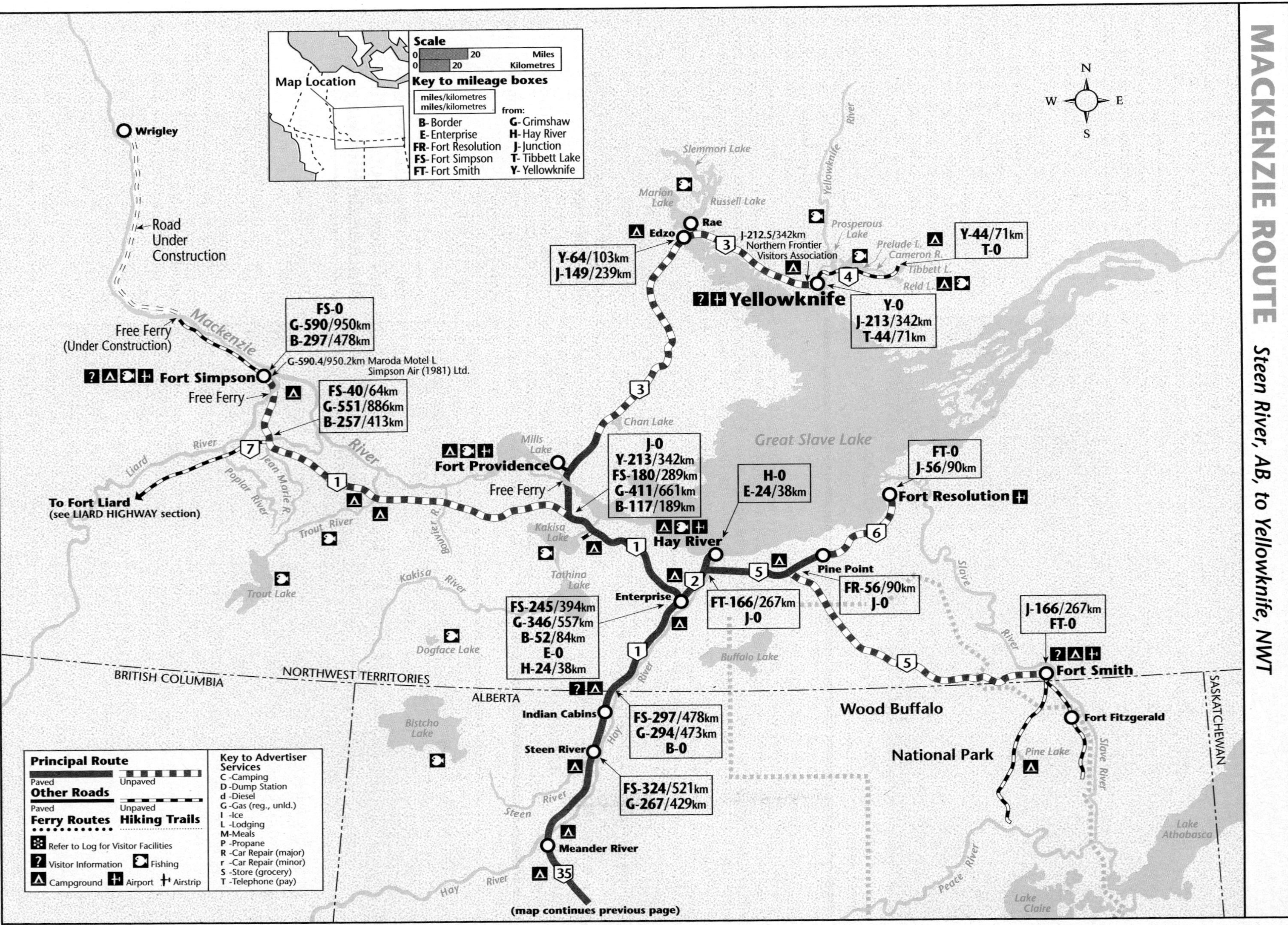

Peace River bridge. The Peace, Smoky and Heart rivers meet near the town of Peace River. (Earl L. Brown, staff)

incorporated in 1919, three years after the railroad reached Peace River Crossing. Today, Peace River is a centre for government services in the region. Area industry includes Peace River Pulp, Shell Canada and farming.

1994 is the 75th anniversary of the incorporation of the town of Peace River. Numerous activities are planned in celebration. For details, contact the Peace River Board of Trade, 624-4166.

Visitor facilities include three hotels, a motel and many restaurants. Camping at Lions Club Campground on the west side of the river; 85 sites, hookups, restrooms, dump station and laundry. ▲

There are nine campgrounds along the Peace River. For details, contact the Peace Valley Conservation, Recreation and Tourism Society, phone 835-2616; fax 835-3131.

The Centennial Museum (on the south side of town along the river) houses archives and exhibits on Sir Alexander Mackenzie, the fur trade and local history. Historical reenactments in summer. Open 9 A.M. to 5 P.M. Monday to Wednesday, noon to 8 P.M. Thursday to Saturday (May 1 to Aug. 31); 9 A.M. to 5 P.M. weekdays Sept. 1 to April 31. Rail transportation exhibit at restored NAR railway station. Museum phone 624-4261.

Visitors can take the Historic Mackenzie Moose Walking Trail by following the moose tracks from the Centennial Museum to various points of interest around town. The tour includes the statue of Twelve-Foot Davis, a gold miner who struck it rich on a 12-foot strip of land between two larger claims in the Cariboo gold fields. He invested his $15,000 in gold in a string of trading posts along the Peace. He is buried on Grouard Hill overlooking the Peace River Valley.

Log of Valleyview–Peace River Route

(continued)

E 309.5 (498 km) **Junction** with Highway 2 to Grimshaw.

E 314.4 (506 km) **Junction** with Highway 35 (Mackenzie Highway) at **Milepost G 3** (log follows). Grimshaw (description on opposite page) is 3 miles/4.8 km south of this junction.

Log of the Dunvegan–Fairview Route to the Mackenzie Highway

Distance from Grande Prairie (GP) is shown.

GP 0 GRANDE PRAIRIE; turn to the EAST ACCESS ROUTE section for details on Grande Prairie.

GP 3.7 (6 km) **Junction** of Highways 2 and 34. Continue north on Highway 2 for Fairview and Grimshaw.

GP 5.9 (9.5 km) Town of Clairmont to east.

GP 12.2 (19.7 km) **SEXSMITH,** sometimes called the "Grain Capital of Alberta," has a hotel, restaurants, banks, gas station and golf course. The municipal Heritage Park Campground has 13 RV sites, restrooms, showers, dump station, fishing and miniature golf. ▲

Sexsmith's economy is based on agriculture, petroleum and the Northern Alberta

Rapeseed Processing Plant. Attractions include historic blacksmith shop and Northern Alberta Railway station.

GP 14.3 (23 km) **Junction** with Highway 59 west.

GP 35.3 (56.8 km) **WOKING** (pop. 150), an agricultural community. Free provincial park campground with 20 sites, picnic shelter, firewood, fireplaces, tables, pit toilets and pump water. ▲

GP 43.2 (69.5 km) **Junction** with Highway 49 to Dawson Creek (see NORTHERN WOODS & WATERS ROUTE section). Town of **RYCROFT** (pop. 734) to west; food, gas and lodging. Rycroft municipal campground with 15 RV sites, tenting area, kitchen shelter, firewood and playground. Old Mission site located 1.5 miles/2.4 km west. ▲

GP 43.5 (70.1 km) Paved turnout with litter barrels.

GP 46.1 (74.3 km) Spirit River bridge.

GP 56.2 (90.5 km) Dunvegan Bridge, Alberta's longest suspension bridge, and the agricultural community of **DUNVEGAN.** Site of Fort Dunvegan, a Hudson's Bay Co. post, and St. Charles Mission, the first permanent Roman Catholic mission established in the Peace River district. Historic Dunvegan Provincial Park at the north end of the bridge includes a visitor centre and three restored buildings. There are several market gardens in the Dunvegan area.

Provincial campground at north end of Dunvegan Bridge has 67 campstalls, 29 with power hookups; dump station, pit toilets; firewood, fireplaces, and picnic shelters with stoves; playground; tap water; and public phone. Wheelchair accessible. ♿▲

GP 59.4 (95.7 km) Turnout to east with litter barrels and historical marker about the Peace River.

GP 64.3 (103.5 km) **Junction** with Highway 64 north.

Highway 64 leads west 118 miles/190 km to Fort St. John on the Alaska Highway. (See NORTHERN WOODS & WATERS ROUTE section for details.)

Fairview

GP 71.2 (114.7 km) Junction with Highway 64 west. Population: 2,500. **Emergency Services: RCMP**, phone 835-2211. **Hospital** and **Ambulance**, phone 835-4941. **Visitor Information**: Visitor centre located at south end of town, phone 835-5177.

An agricultural centre for the northwest Peace River region, Fairview has hotels, motels and restaurants. Recreational facilities include a municipal swimming pool and nine-hole golf course. Camping at Cummings Lake recreation area at north end of town; 28 sites, electric hookups, restrooms, firewood and water. Attractions here include the RCMP Centennial Museum downtown and Fairview College (phone 835-6600 for tours). ▲

Log of Dunvegan–Fairview Route

(continued)

GP 78.9 (127 km) Settlement of Bluesky; grain elevators.

GP 101.3 (163 km) Settlement of Berwyn; Bissell Memorial United Church located here.

GP 108.7 (175 km) Grimshaw; see description at Mile 0 of the Mackenzie Highway log following.

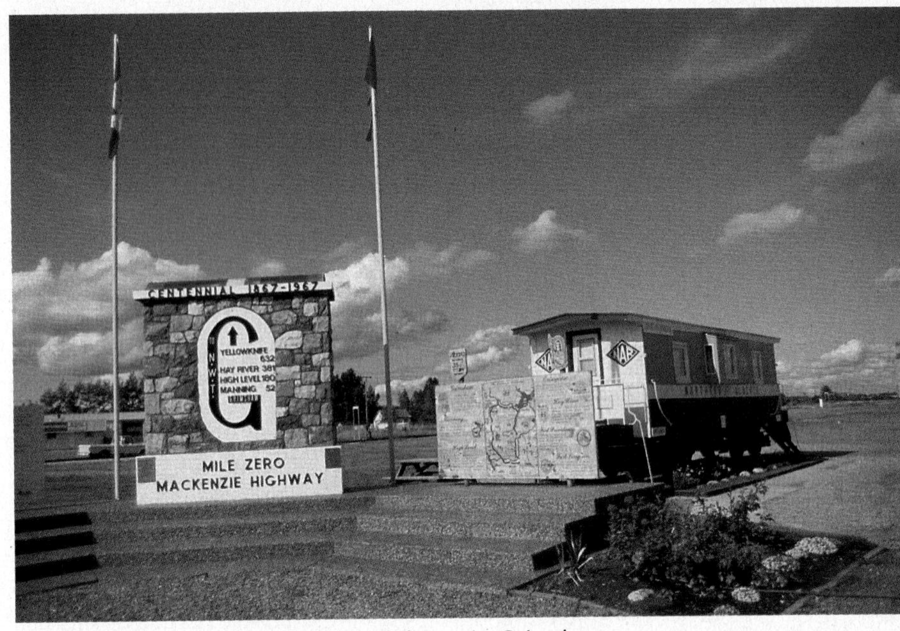

Mile 0 marker of the Mackenzie Highway in Grimshaw. (Earl L. Brown, staff)

Mackenzie Highway Log

ALBERTA HIGHWAY 35
Distance from Grimshaw (G) is followed by distance from Fort Simpson (FS).

Grimshaw

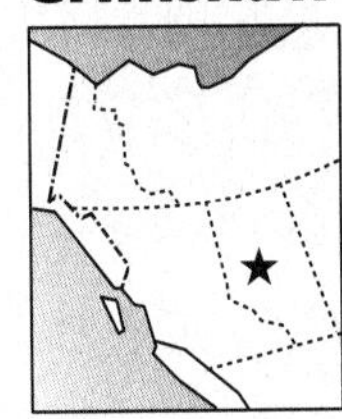

G 0 FS 590.4 (950.2 km) Mile 0 of the Mackenzie Highway. **Population:** 2,812. **Emergency Services: RCMP**, phone 332-4666. **Hospital and Ambulance**, phone 332-1155. **Fire Department**, phone 332-4430. **Visitor Information:** In the NAR railway car located adjacent the centennial monument marking Mile 0 of the Mackenzie Highway.

Named for pioneer doctor M.E. Grimshaw, who established a practice at Peace River Crossing in 1914, Grimshaw developed as a community centre for area farmers and as a shipping point with the arrival of the railroad in 1921. Scheduled air service from Edmonton and High Level to Peace River airport, 8 miles/12.8 km east.

Grimshaw became a town in February 1953. Local resources are wheat and grains, livestock, gravel, lumber, gas and oil.

Grimshaw has one motel, two hotels, six service stations, two car washes, a laundromat and all other visitor facilities. RV dump station and drinking water located south of the Mile 0 marker and two blocks east. Camping just north of town (see **Milepost G 1.9**). There are also an outdoor swimming pool, tennis courts, golf course and seasonal market garden located here.

Mackenzie Highway Log

(continued)

G 0.2 (0.4 km) **FS 590.2** (949.8 km) **Private Aircraft:** Airstrip to west; elev. 2,050 feet/625m; length, 3,000 feet/914m; turf; fuel 80, 100.

G 1.9 (3 km) **FS 588.5** (947.2 km) Grimshaw provincial campsite and Queen Elizabeth Provincial Park to west. Grimshaw campsite has 20 sites, picnic shelter, firepits, firewood, tables, outhouses, water pump and no camping fee. Queen Elizabeth park (located 3 miles/5 km west) on Lac Cardinal has 56 campsites, picnic shelter, firewood, firepits, toilets, playground and swimming. ▲

G 2.8 (4.6 km) **FS 587.6** (945.6 km) **Junction** of Highways 35 and 2 (east).

G 3.4 (5.5 km) **FS 587** (944.7 km) Sign about construction of the Mackenzie Highway.

G 4.1 (6.6 km) **FS 586.3** (943.6 km) Turnout to east with litter barrels.

G 5 (8 km) **FS 585.4** (942.1 km) **Junction** with Chinook Valley Road to east.

G 6.9 (11.1 km) **FS 583.5** (939.1 km) Truck scales to west.

G 7.8 (12.5 km) **FS 582.6** (937.6 km) Bear Creek Drive and golf course to west.

G 8.6 (13.8 km) **FS 581.8** (936.3 km) **Junction** with Secondary Road 737 (Warrensville) to west.

G 12.3 (19.8 km) **FS 578.1** (930.3 km) Road widens to four lanes northbound.

G 12.6 (20.3 km) **FS 577.8** (929.8 km) **Junction** with Secondary Road 686 to east.

G 13 (20.9 km) **FS 577.4** (929.2 km) Road narrows to two lanes northbound.

G 15.4 (24.8 km) **FS 575** (925.3 km) Logging road and landfill to west.

G 19 (30.6 km) **FS 571.4** (919.5 km) Entering Manning Ranger District northbound.

G 20.8 (33.5 km) **FS 569.6** (916.7 km) Chinook Valley to east; cafe, pay phone and 24-hour gas station with tire repair.

G 23 (37 km) **FS 567.4** (913.1 km) Whitemud River.

G 25.1 (40.4 km) **FS 565.3** (909.8 km) **DIXONVILLE** (pop. 200) has a post office, gas station and souvenir shop. Sulphur Lake provincial campground is located 34 miles/55 km west via Highway 689 (the first 14 miles/22.5 km are paved, the remainder is gravel to the campground).

G 26.9 (43.3 km) **FS 563.5** (906.8 km) Sulphur Lake Road leads west to junction with Highway 689 from Dixonville.

G 36 (57.9 km) **FS 554.4** (892.3 km) Microwave tower and radio tower to west.

G 36.9 (59.4 km) **FS 553.5** (890.7 km) Radio tower to east.

G 38.4 (61.8 km) **FS 552** (888.4 km) **Junction** with Secondary Road 690 east to Deadwood (6.8 miles/11 km). There is a private exotic bird farm located 2 miles east then 1 mile south. The Bradshaws have geese, peacocks, turkeys, pheasants and other birds; visitors welcome.

G 44.4 (71.5 km) **FS 546** (878.7 km) Buchanan Creek.

G 46.8 (75.4 km) **FS 543.6** (874.8 km) Community of **NORTH STAR** (pop. 52) to east.

Manning

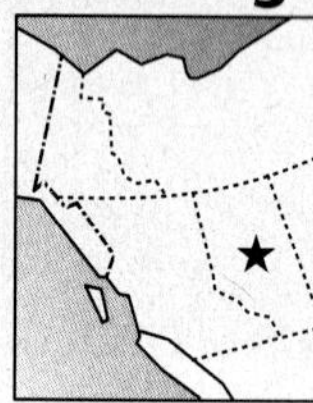

G 50.6 (81.4 km) **FS 539.8** (868.8 km) Located on the Notikewin River at the junction of Highways 35 and 691. **Population:** 1,260. **Emergency Services: RCMP**, phone 836-3007. **Hospital** and **Ambulance**, phone 836-3391. **Fire Department**, phone 836-3000.

Visitor Information: In the information centre. There is a playground adjacent the centre and a dump station across the street.

Named for an Alberta premier, Manning was established in 1947. The railway from Roma, AB, to Pine Point, NWT, reached Manning in September 1962. Today, Manning is a service centre and jumping-off point for hunters and fishermen.

Manning has five restaurants, three hotel/motels, a pharmacy, food market, golf course, swimming pool and ice rink. Attractions here include the Battle River Pioneer Museum, located on the grounds of the Battle River Agricultural Society, 0.6 mile/1 km east via Highway 691. The museum, which features tools and machinery from the pioneer days, is open daily 1-5 P.M., from June 1 to mid-September. A small ski hill is located 12.5 miles/20 km northeast of town via Highways 691 and 741; one T-lift and three runs.

Turn east at the information centre for Manning municipal campground; 14 sites on the banks of the Notikewin River, fireplaces, tables, water and flush toilets.

NOTE: Last sizable community with all facilities for the next 123 miles/198 km northbound.

Mackenzie Highway Log

(continued)

G 50.7 (81.6 km) **FS 539.7** (868.5 km) Downtown Manning; bridge over the Notikewin River.

G 52.9 (85.1 km) **FS 537.5** (865.1 km) **Private Aircraft**: Manning airstrip to west; elev. 1,611 feet/491m; length 5,577 feet/1,700m; asphalt; fuel 100/130, Jet B.

G 53.2 (85.6 km) **FS 537.2** (864.5 km) Hotel, restaurant and service station to west.

G 54.6 (87.8 km) **FS 535.8** (862.4 km) Community of Notikewin to west.

G 59 (94.9 km) **FS 531.4** (855.2 km) Railroad crossing.

G 60.6 (97.6 km) **FS 529.8** (852.6 km) Hotchkiss River bridge.

G 60.8 (97.8 km) **FS 529.6** (852.4 km) Hotchkiss Provincial Park to east; 10 tent and trailer sites, picnic shelter, tables, firepits, fishing, outhouses and water pump. No camping fee.

G 61.1 (98.3 km) **FS 529.3** (851.9 km) Microwave tower to east.

G 61.3 (98.6 km) **FS 529.1** (851.6 km) Community of Hotchkiss to east, golf course to west. Hotchkiss has a post office, service station, pay phone, coffee bar, grocery, and fuel and propane available. The Condy Meadow Golf Course (0.7 mile/1.2 km east) has nine holes, sand greens and clubhouse.

G 65.4 (105.3 km) **FS 525** (844.9 km) Chinchaga Forestry Road to west.

G 66.9 (107.6 km) **FS 523.5** (842.6 km) Meikle River bridge.

G 68 (109.4 km) **FS 522.4** (840.7 km) Railroad crossing.

G 68.1 (109.6 km) **FS 522.3** (840.5 km) Hawk Hills to east.

G 71.2 (114.6 km) **FS 519.2** (835.5 km) Turnout with litter barrel to west.

G 74.3 (119.5 km) **FS 516.1** (830.7 km) **Junction** with Highway 692 and access to Notikewin Provincial Park (18.6 miles/30 km) on the Notikewin and Peace rivers. Highway 692 is fairly straight with pavement for the first 8 miles/13 km followed by good gravel surface to the park, although the road narrows and the surfacing may be muddy in wet weather as you approach the park. Just past the entrance to the park is the Top of Hill trailer drop-off site; 10 campsites with tables, toilets, water pump and garbage container. The park road then winds down the hill for 1.4 miles/2.2 km (not recommended for trailers, slippery when wet) to the riverside campground and day-use area; 19 campsites on the **Notikewin River** and six picnic sites on the **Peace River**; facilities include tables, water pump, pit toilets, garbage containers, firepits, boat launch and fishing. *CAUTION: Bears in area.*

G 78.5 (126.3 km) **FS 511.9** (823.8 km) Stockpiles and highway equipment to east.

G 88.4 (142.3 km) **FS 502** (807.9 km) Twin Lakes Lodge to east; gas, food, lodging, pay phone and fishing supplies.

G 88.9 (143 km) **FS 501.5** (807.2 km) Twin Lakes Campground to west; 30 shaded sites, picnic shelter, fireplaces, firewood, tables, outhouses, water; beach, boat launch (no gas motors). No camping fee. **Twin Lakes** is stocked with rainbow; good fishing June to September.

G 89.3 (143.7 km) **FS 501.1** (806.5 km) Microwave tower to west.

G 95.8 (154.1 km) **FS 494.6** (796.1 km) Turnout to west.

G 96 (154.5 km) **FS 494.4** (795.7 km) Railroad crossing.

G 102.9 (165.6 km) **FS 487.5** (784.6 km) Kemp Creek.

G 111.2 (179 km) **FS 479.2** (771.2 km) **Junction** with Highway 695 East which leads 24 miles/38 km to community of **CARCAJOU** (pop. 50). Access to Keg River airstrip 0.4 mile/0.6 km east. **Private Aircraft**: Keg River airstrip; elev. 1,350 feet/410m; approximate length 2,700 feet/832m; turf; emergency only.

G 112.3 (180.8 km) **FS 478.1** (769.4 km) Keg River bridge. The community of **KEG RIVER** (area pop. 400) just north of the bridge has a gas station, post office, grocery, cafe, motel, pay phone and airstrip.

G 115.6 (186 km) **FS 474.8** (764 km) **Junction** with Secondary Road 695 West. This paved road leads 9 miles/14.5 km to Keg River Post.

G 123.8 (199.3 km) **FS 466.6** (750.9 km) Microwave tower to east.

G 124 (199.6 km) **FS 466.4** (750.6 km) Boyer River bridge.

G 129.5 (208.4 km) **FS 460.9** (741.8 km) **PADDLE PRAIRIE** (pop. 164), a Metis settlement. The Metis culture, a combination of French and Amerindian, played a key role in the fur trade and development of northwestern Canada.

G 134.2 (216 km) **FS 456.2** (734.2 km) Turnout to west with litter barrels.

G 135.1 (217.4 km) **FS 455.3** (732.7 km) Boyer River Campground to east; eight sites, tables, firewood, firepits, picnic shelter, toilets and water pump.

G 136.2 (219.2 km) **FS 454.2** (731 km) **Junction** with Highway 697, which leads east approximately 53 miles/85 km to the community of LaCrete, then 25 miles/40 km north to Fort Vermilion. Major access to Fort Vermilion is via Highway 58 east from High Level (junction at **Milepost G 174**). See side road log of HIGHWAY 58 EAST on page 226.

G 141 (226.9 km) **FS 449.4** (723.2 km) Entering High Level Ranger District northbound.

G 146.3 (235.4 km) **FS 444.1** (714.7 km) Chuckegg Creek.

G 151.3 (243.5 km) **FS 439.1** (706.7 km) Microwave tower to west.

G 153.5 (247 km) **FS 436.9** (703.2 km) Turnout with litter barrel to west. Watch for waterfowl in small lakes along highway.

G 161.2 (259.4 km) **FS 429.2** (690.7 km) Bede Creek.

G 161.9 (260.5 km) **FS 428.5** (689.6 km) Parma Creek.

G 165.5 (266.3 km) **FS 424.9** (683.9 km) Melito Creek.

G 167.5 (269.6 km) **FS 422.9** (680.6 km) Railroad crossing.

G 170.6 (274.6 km) **FS 419.8** (675.6 km) Turnout with litter barrel to west.

G 171.9 (276.7 km) **FS 418.5** (673.5 km) Private campground with hot showers and electrical hookups.

Aspen Ridge Campground. See display ad this section.

G 173.3 (278.9 km) **FS 417.1** (671.3 km)

Junction with Highway 58 West, which leads 84.5 miles/136 km to Rainbow Lake. See side road log of HIGHWAY 58 WEST this page.

High Level

G 173.6 (279.3 km) **FS 416.8** (670.9 km) Located at the junction of Highways 35 and 58. **Population:** 3,004. **Emergency Services: RCMP**, phone 926-2226. **Hospital,** 25 beds, six doctors, phone 926-3791. **Ambulance,** phone 926-2545. **Fire Department**, phone 926-3141.

Visitor Information: The visitors centre and Mackenzie Crossroads Museum are located at the south end of town. Open year-round. Summer hours 9 A.M. to 9 P.M. daily. Includes displays, souvenirs, rest area with dump station. **Radio:** 530 AM, 89.9, 104.1-FM.

Begun as a small settlement on the Mackenzie Highway after WWII, High Level grew with the oil boom of the 1960s and completion of the railroad to Pine Point. High Level has a strong agricultural economy and boasts the most northerly grain elevators in Canada. The community is also supported by a sawmill complex and serves as a transportation centre for the northwestern Peace River region. There is scheduled air service to Edmonton daily.

Visitor facilities include a hotel, six motels, restaurants and service stations with major repair. There are also an ice arena and curling rink, golf course, swimming pool, playgrounds, banks, schools and churches. Recreation includes hunting (moose, caribou, deer) and fishing for northern pike, perch, walleye, whitefish, goldeye and grayling.

There is a private campground at the south edge of town. A municipal campground is located just east of town on Highway 58. ▲

Highway 58 West Log

Distance is measured from junction with the Mackenzie Highway (J).

J 0 Junction with Mackenzie Highway at High Level.

J 6.1 (9.8 km) High Level Sporting Assoc. and Gun Club to north.

J 27.2 (43.8 km) Paved turnout with litter barrels to south.

J 31.2 (50.2 km) Entering Rainbow Lake Ranger District westbound.

J 39.7 (63.9 km) Microwave tower to south.

J 44.1 (71 km) Sand and gravel stockpiles to north.

J 44.2 (71.1 km) Bridge over Chinchaga River.

J 46.3 (74.5 km) Large turnout and gravel stockpiles to south.

J 50 (80.5 km) Bridge over East Sousa Creek.

J 56.5 (90.9 km) Bridge over West Sousa Creek.

J 56.9 (91.6 km) **Junction** with secondary road north to communities of Chateh, Habay and Zama.

J 59.7 (96.1 km) North Canadian Oils Ltd. wells and equipment to north.

J 60.7 (97.7 km) Oil pumping station to north.

J 63.3 (101.8 km) Paved turnout with litter barrel to north.

J 65.3 (105.1 km) Power station to north.

J 70.3 (113.1 km) Side road leads north to the Zama Tower.

J 70.4 (113.3 km) Sand stockpiles to south.

J 70.7 (113.8 km) Esso Resources Canada oil production plant to north.

J 71.5 (115 km) Rainbow Lake Field Office to north.

J 76.8 (123.6 km) Side road leads north to Rainbow Lake gas plant.

J 80.1 (128.9 km) Microwave tower to south.

J 80.5 (129.5 km) Oil station to south. Side road leads south to Rainbow Processing Plant.

J 82.5 (132.8 km) Turnout with picnic table to south.

J 83.3 (134 km) Rainbow Lake city limits.

J 88.5 (136 km) **RAINBOW LAKE** (pop. 1,146). **Emergency Services: RCMP**, phone 321-3753. **Nursing Station**, phone 356-3646. **Fire Department,** phone 956-3934. **Radio:** 103.7-FM.

Private Aircraft: Rainbow Lake airport 0.8 mile/1.3 km west, 0.5 mile/0.8 km south on Frontage Road; elev. 1,100 feet/335m; length 4,550 feet/1,390m; asphalt; fuel 80, 100, Jet B.

A service community for oil and natural gas development in the region. The first oil well was brought in by Banff Oil and Gas in 1965 at the Rainbow field. (The Zama field was discovered in 1967.)

Visitor facilities include a hotel, motel with licensed restaurant, three gas stations and a bank. The community also supports a school, three churches, two car washes, a grocery store, gift shop, laundromat and a nine-hole golf course. Rainbow Lake Campground is located 14 miles/24 km south of town via a secondary road.

Return to Milepost G 174 Mackenzie Highway

Mackenzie Highway Log

(continued)

G 173.6 (279.3 km) **FS 416.8** (670.9 km) Downtown High Level.

G 174 (280 km) **FS 416.4** (670.2 km) **Junction** with Highway 58 East to Jean D'or Prairie and Highway 88 to Fort Vermilion. See side road log of HIGHWAY 58 EAST on page 226.

G 176.2 (283.5 km) **FS 414.2** (666.7 km) High Level golf and country club to east. Open daily, May 1 to first snow, until midnight. Clubhouse, grass greens and nine holes.

G 176.6 (284.2 km) **FS 413.8** (665.9 km) Radio towers to west.

G 181.1 (291.5 km) **FS 409.3** (658.7 km) **Private Aircraft**: High Level airport; elev. 1,110 feet/338m; length 5,000 feet/1,524m; asphalt; fuel 80, 100, Jet B. Floatplane base at Footner Lake, 0.6 mile/1 km west.

G 193.4 (311.2 km) **FS 397** (639 km) Turnoff to west for Hutch Lake Recreation Area; parking, eight picnic sites with tables and firepits, toilets. Short path leads down to lake. Bring mosquito repellent.

G 196 (315.5 km) **FS 394.4** (634.7 km) Hutch Lake provincial campground, 2.9 miles/4.6 km west; 12 sites, firepits, firewood, tables, toilets. Beach and boat launch on Hutch Lake. Hiking trails. Good spot for bird watchers. Camping fee $7.50. ▲

G 196.8 (316.7 km) **FS 393.6** (633.5 km) Turnouts with litter barrels both sides of highway.

G 207.3 (333.6 km) **FS 383.1** (616.6 km) Wooden railway bridge to east.

G 219.3 (352.9 km) **FS 371.1** (597.3 km) **MEANDER RIVER** (pop. 340) has a post office, grocery store and confectionary with pay phone.

G 221.5 (356.4 km) **FS 368.9** (593.7 km) Mission Creek.

G 223.8 (360.1 km) **FS 366.6** (590.1 km) Meander River Campground to east; seven sites, camping fee $5.50, tables, firepits and firewood. ▲

The Mackenzie Highway crosses the Hay River here and follows it north into Northwest Territories.

G 227 (365.3 km) **FS 363.4** (584.9 km) Microwave tower to east.

G 227.5 (366.2 km) **FS 362.9** (584 km) Railway bridge over Hay River to east. Construction of the Great Slave Lake Railway (now part of Canadian National Railway's Peace River Division) was one of the largest railway construction projects since the boom of the first transcontinental railway lines in the late 1800s and early 1900s in Canada. The line extends 377 miles/607 km from Roma Junction near Peace River, AB, to Hay River, NWT, on the shore of Great Slave Lake. (A 54-mile/87-km branch line extended the line to the now-defunct lead–zinc mine at Pine Point, NWT.) Opened for traffic in 1964, the line carries mining shipments south and supplies north to Hay River.

G 228.1 (367.1 km) **FS 362.3** (583.1 km) Gravel road leads west 39 miles/63 km to **ZAMA** (pop. 200), an oil field community. Drilling and related operations take place at Zama in winter. Zama is the southern terminal of the interprovincial pipeline, carrying Norman Wells crude to Edmonton refineries.

G 231.5 (372.5 km) **FS 358.9** (577.6 km) Slavey Creek.

G 241.2 (388.2 km) **FS 349.3** (562 km) Rough patch in pavement. Watch for frost heaves north to NWT border.

G 241.8 (389.1 km) **FS 348.6** (561.1 km) Railroad crossing.

G 243.5 (391.9 km) **FS 346.9** (558.3 km)

Highway 58 East Log

Distance is measured from junction with the Mackenzie Highway (J).

J 0 Junction with Mackenzie Highway at High Level.

J 0.1 (0.2 km) Railroad crossing.

J 0.2 (0.4 km) High Level Lions Club Campground to south; 33 sites, no camping fee, picnic shelter, stoves, firewood, tables, toilets, water pump. ▲

J 0.4 (0.6 km) High Level rodeo grounds to north.

J 1.5 (2.5 km) Bushe River bridge.

J 15.3 (24.7 km) Turnoff to south for Machesis Lake Campground, 16 miles/27 km via gravel road; 21 sites, picnic shelter, firepits, firewood, tables, toilets, water. Fishing for rainbows in **Machesis Lake.** ▲

J 20.3 (32.7 km) Turn south for Eleskie Shrine (5 miles/8 km), Native church and burial grounds.

J 22.3 (35.9 km) Entering Fort Vermilion Ranger District eastbound.

J 27 (43.5 km) Turnout with litter barrels to north.

J 27.4 (44.1 km) Side road leads south 3.7 miles/6 km to Rocky Lane; museum located in school.

J 28 (45 km) Ponton River bridge.

J 35.4 (57 km) **Junction** of Highways 58 and 88. From this junction, Highway 58 turns to gravel road and continues 37 miles/59 km east to junction with a 5-mile/8-km side road to Jean D'or Prairie (no services). Highway 88 (renumbered and renamed the Bicentennial Highway to commemorate the 200th anniversary of Fort Vermilion in 1988) leads south to Fort Vermilion (log follows), then continues 255 miles/410 km to Slave Lake. Highway 88 is paved to Fort Vermilion; the 150-mile/242-km section to Red Earth Creek is gravel; the remaining 105 miles/168 km to Slave Lake are paved. There are no services along the road south of Fort Vermilion, and travel is not recommended on the gravel portion in wet weather.

HIGHWAY 88

J 40 (64.3 km) Boyer River bridge.

J 42.6 (68.5 km) Side road leads west 8.5 miles/14 km to Rocky Lane.

J 43.1 (69.3 km) Historical sign about Fort Vermilion and access to Fort Vermilion provincial campground (0.1 mile/0.2 km east); 16 sites, picnic shelter, fireplace, firewood, tables, toilets, water, no camping fee. ▲

J 43.4 (69.8 km) Fort Vermilion Bridge over the Peace River.

J 45.2 (72.7 km) **Junction** with Highway 697, which leads south 25 miles/40 km to **LA CRETE** (pop. 900), an agricultural community settled by Mennonites. Services there include a motel, restaurant, cafe, laundromat, service stations, bank, grocery, clothing and hardware stores. Highway 697 continues south and west 53 miles/85 km, returning to the Mackenzie Highway at **Milepost G 136.2.**

J 48 (77.2 km) **Junction** with Highway 88 south to Red Earth and Slave Lake (255miles/410 km). Continue straight ahead for Fort Vermilion (description follows).

J 48.5 (78 km) **FORT VERMILION** (pop. 800), located on the Peace River. **Emergency Services: RCMP** and **Hospital**, phone 927-3741. A trading post was established near here by the North West Co. in 1786. By 1831, the Hudson's Bay Co. had established a prosperous trading enterprise at Fort Vermilion. The area's farming potential gained attention when Fort Vermilion's wheat took top prize at the 1893 Chicago World's Fair. Transportation to the community was by riverboat until the Mackenzie Highway was built.

Visitor facilities include a motel, restaurants, service stations, bank and liquor store. The airport is located just east of town. Attractions include good hunting and fishing nearby and some historic buildings dating back to the 1800s.

Return to Milepost G 174 Mackenzie Highway

Paved turnout with litter barrels to west.

G 250.2 (402.6 km) **FS 340.2** (547.5 km) Lutose Creek.

G 256.6 (413 km) **FS 333.8** (537.2 km) Microwave tower to west.

G 263.1 (423.4 km) **FS 327.3** (526.8 km) Steen River Campground to west; six sites, $5.50 camping fee, picnic shelter, fireplaces, firewood, tables, outhouses, water. ▲

G 263.3 (423.7 km) **FS 327.1** (526.5 km) Steen River bridge.

G 266.7 (429.2 km) **FS 323.7** (521 km) **STEEN RIVER** (pop. 25) to east; current status of services unknown.

G 266.9 (429.5 km) **FS 323.5** (520.7 km) Steen River Forestry Tanker Base to west. Grass airstrip.

G 268.1 (431.5 km) **FS 322.3** (518.7 km) Sams' Creek.

G 270.1 (434.7 km) **FS 320.3** (515.4 km) Jackpot Creek.

G 276.2 (444.5 km) **FS 314.2** (505.6 km) Bannock Creek.

G 283.3 (455.9 km) **FS 307.1** (494.2 km) Indian Cabins Creek.

G 284 (457 km) **FS 306.4** (493.2 km) **INDIAN CABINS** (pop. 10) to east has a gas station, cafe, grocery, pay phone and historic log church. The old Indian cabins that gave this settlement its name are gone, but nearby is an Indian cemetery with spirit houses.

NOTE: No services next 61 miles/98 km northbound.

G 285.3 (459.1 km) **FS 305.1** (491 km) Delphin Creek.

G 287.5 (462.7 km) **FS 302.9** (487.5 km) Microwave tower to east.

G 293.7 (472.7 km) **FS 296.7** (477.5 km) 60th parallel. Border between Alberta and Northwest Territories. The Mackenzie Highway now changes from Alberta Highway 35 to NWT Highway 1.

NWT HIGHWAY 1

Highway 1 begins its own series of kilometre markers, starting with Kilometre 0 at the border, which appear about every 2 kilometres.

Distance from Grimshaw (G) is followed by distance from Fort Simpson (FS) and distance from the AB–NWT border (B).

G 293.7 (472.7 km) **FS 296.7** (477.5 km) **B 0** AB–NWT border, 60th Parallel. A government visitor information centre here has brochures, maps, fishing licenses, camping permits, a dump station and emergency radiophone. Déne (Indian) arts and crafts are on display. Also check here on road and ferry conditions before proceeding. The visitor centre is open May 15 to Sept. 15 from 8 A.M. to 10 P.M.

60th Parallel Campground and picnic area adjacent visitor centre. Facilities include 12 campsites, five picnic sites, kitchen shelter and drinking water. The park overlooks the Hay River and canoeists may launch here. ▲

Driving distance from the border to destinations in Northwest Territories are as follows (see individual highway logs this section for details): Hay River 76 miles/122 km; Fort Simpson 297 miles/478 km; Fort Providence 140 miles/225 km; Yellowknife 330 miles/531 km; Fort Smith 238 miles/383 km.

G 295.5 (475.6 km) **FS 294.9** (474.6 km) **B 1.8** (2.9 km) Reindeer Creek.

G 317.2 (510.5 km) **FS 273.2** (439.6 km) **B 23.5** (37.8 km) Microwave tower to east.

G 318.5 (512.6 km) **FS 271.9** (437.6 km) **B 24.8** (39.9 km) Grumbler Rapids, just off highway, is audible during low water periods in late summer.

G 319.1 (513.5 km) **FS 271.3** (436.6 km) **B 25.4** (40.8 km) Swede Creek.

G 319.8 (514.6 km) **FS 270.6** (435.5 km) **B 26.1** (42 km) Large turnout and gravel stockpile to west.

G 334.2 (537.8 km) **FS 256.2** (412.4 km) **B 40.5** (65.1 km) Mink Creek.

G 335.5 (539.9 km) **FS 254.9** (410.2 km) **B 41.8** (67.3 km) Large turnout and gravel stockpile to west.

G 338.8 (545.3 km) **FS 251.6** (404.9 km) **B 45.1** (72.6 km) Alexandra Falls picnic area to east. Paved parking area and gravel walkway to falls viewpoint, overlooking the Hay River, which plunges 109 feet/33m to form Alexandra Falls. Excellent photo opportunities; easy hike down to top of falls. A walking trail connects with Louise Falls.

G 340.3 (547.6 km) **FS 250.1** (402.6 km) **B 46.6** (74.9 km) Turnoff to east for Louise Falls picnic area and territorial campground; 18 campsites, six picnic sites, kitchen shelters, tables, toilets, firepits, firewood, water. Hiking trails to viewpoint overlooking three-tiered Louise Falls, which drops 50 feet/15m. (It is not advisable to walk down to the water.) Hike along bluff 3 miles/5 km for Alexandra Falls. ▲

G 341.9 (550.2 km) **FS 248.5** (400 km) **B 48.2** (77.5 km) Escarpment Creek picnic area; tables, shelter, toilets, firepits, garbage container, water pump. Spectacular series of waterfalls downstream.

G 342.1 (550.5 km) **FS 248.3** (399.7 km) **B 48.4** (77.8 km) Highway crosses Escarpment Creek.

G 345.4 (555.9 km) **FS 245** (394.3 km) **B 51.7** (83.2 km) Truck weigh scales to east, service station to west. Entering Enterprise northbound.

G 345.8 (556.5 km) **FS 244.6** (393.7 km) **B 52.1** (83.8 km) **Junction** of Highway 1 and Highway 2. Highway 2 leads 23.6 miles/38 km from here to **HAY RIVER** (pop. 2,891), the hub for transportation on Great Slave Lake and a major service centre with all visitor facilities (see HIGHWAY 2 log on page 229 for details on Hay River). Continue on Highway 1 for Enterprise (description follows) and Fort Simpson.

ENTERPRISE (pop. 56), a highway community with food, grocery store, gas, diesel and lodging. Pay phone. It is a good idea to fill up gas tanks here. View of Hay River Gorge just east of the highway.

G 346 (556.8 km) **FS 244.4** (393.3 km) **B 52.3** (84.1 km) Railroad crossing.

G 348.3 (560.5 km) **FS 242.1** (389.6 km) **B 54.6** (87.8 km) Gravel stockpile and highway equipment to east.

G 350.3 (563.7 km) **FS 240.1** (386.4 km) **B 56.6** (91.1 km) Microwave tower to east.

G 350.5 (564 km) **FS 239.9** (386.1 km) **B 56.8** (91.4 km) Microwave tower to east.

G 365.8 (588.7 km) **FS 224.6** (361.4 km) **B 72.1** (116 km) Microwave tower to east.

G 369.3 (594.3 km) **FS 221.1** (355.8 km) **B 75.6** (121.6 km) Turnout to east with view of McNally Creek Falls.

G 370.5 (596.2 km) **FS 219.9** (353.9 km) **B 76.8** (123.6 km) Large paved turnout to east.

G 374.7 (603 km) **FS 215.7** (347.2 km) **B 81** (130.3 km) Easy-to-miss Hart Lake Fire Tower access road turnoff to east, 0.5 mile/0.8 km to picnic area and forest fire lookout tower. Panoramic view over more than 100 square miles/259 square km of forest to Great Slave Lake and Mackenzie River. Path to ancient coral reef. *CAUTION: Keep the fly repellent handy and stay away from the edge of escarpment.*

G 379.4 (610.5 km) **FS 211** (339.7 km) **B 85.7** (137.8 km) Trapper's cabin to east.

G 382.4 (615.4 km) **FS 208** (334.7 km) **B 88.7** (142.7 km) Small lake to west beside highway.

G 385.6 (620.5 km) **FS 204.8** (329.6 km) **B 91.9** (147.9 km) Side road east to highway maintenance camp.

G 391.7 (630.3 km) **FS 198.7** (319.9 km) **B 98** (157.6 km) Turnout with litter barrels.

G 398.2 (640.8 km) **FS 192.2** (309.3 km) **B 104.5** (168.2 km) Highway maintenance camp and stockpiles to east.

G 398.7 (641.7 km) **FS 191.7** (308.5 km) **B 105** (169 km) Access road leads south 4.5 miles/7.2 km to Lady Evelyn Falls where the Kakisa River drops 49 feet/15m over an escarpment. Staircase down to viewing platform. Hiking trail to base of falls; swimming and wading. Ample parking, interpretive display, territorial campground with 10 tent sites, 18 RV sites and five picnic sites; tables, firepits, firewood, garbage containers, water pump, kitchen shelters. At end of road, 4 miles/6.4 km past campground, is Slavey Indian village and **Kakisa Lake**; fair fishing for walleye, pike and grayling.

G 399.6 (643.1 km) **FS 190.8** (307.1 km) **B 105.9** (170.4 km) Kakisa River bridge.

View of the Trout River at Whittaker Falls. A trail leads along the river to Coral Falls. (Lyn Hancock)

G 399.8 (643.4 km) **FS 190.6** (306.8 km) **B 106.1** (170.7 km) Kakisa River bridge picnic area with 10 sites, tables, fireplaces and firewood. Hiking trails along river lead upstream to Lady Evelyn Falls. Fair fishing in **Kakisa River** for grayling.

G 408.1 (656.7 km) **FS 182.3** (293.4 km) **B 114.4** (184.1 km) Restaurant and gas station to west (current status unknown).

G 410.5 (660.6 km) **FS 179.9** (289.5 km) **B 116.8** (187.9 km) Turnout with litter barrels, log cabin, outhouse, picnic tables and map display on Highways 1 and 3.

G 410.9 (661.2 km) **FS 179.5** (289 km) **B 117.2** (188.5 km) **Junction** of Highway 1 and Highway 3. Highway 3 (paved and gravel) leads 212.5 miles/342 km north to Yellowknife, capital of Northwest Territories (see YELLOWKNIFE HIGHWAY log this section). Highway 1 (gravel) leads west 179.5 miles/289 km to Fort Simpson. Continue with this log for Fort Simpson.

G 438.4 (705.5 km) **FS 152** (244.7 km) **B 144.7** (232.8 km) Emergency survival cabin and turnout with litter barrels and outhouse to south.

G 455.4 (732.8 km) **FS 135** (217.2 km) **B 161.7** (260.2 km) Microwave tower.

G 456.3 (734.3 km) **FS 134.1** (215.8 km) **B 162.6** (261.6 km) Dust-free passing zone.

G 466.2 (750.3 km) **FS 124.2** (199.9 km) **B 172.5** (277.6 km) Bouvier River.

G 467.2 (751.9 km) **FS 123.2** (198.3 km) **B 173.5** (279.2 km) Emergency survival cabin and turnout with litter barrels to south.

G 473.9 (762.6 km) **FS 116.5** (187.6 km) **B 180.2** (289.9 km) Wallace Creek. Scenic canyon to north.

G 477 (767.6 km) **FS 113.4** (182.6 km) **B 183.3** (294.9 km) Highway maintenance camp to south.

G 477.6 (768.6 km) **FS 112.8** (181.6 km) **B 183.9** (295.9 km) Redknife River.

G 488.7 (786.4 km) **FS 101.7** (163.8 km) **B 195** (313.7 km) Morrissey Creek.

G 495.7 (797.8 km) **FS 94.7** (152.4 km) **B 202** (325 km) Whittaker Falls (Saanba Deh) Territorial Park, located on a bluff overlooking the **Trout River.** There are three picnic sites, nine campsites, tables, litter barrels, showers, kitchen shelter, firepits and firewood. Walk along the river to view large deposits of shale and limestone. Grayling fishing, use dry flies in deep pools. Hike to Coral Falls.

G 523.7 (842.8 km) **FS 66.7** (107.3 km) **B 229.9** (370 km) **Ekali Lake** access; pike and pickerel fishing.

G 527.4 (848.7 km) **FS 63** (101.4 km) **B 233.6** (376 km) Winter ice road leads 17 miles/27 km to **JEAN MARIE RIVER** (pop. 67), a traditional Slavey community known for its hand-crafted moose hide clothing decorated with moose tufting, porcupine quilling and embroidery. Accessible in summer by plane or boat from Fort Simpson.

G 530.5 (853.7 km) **FS 59.9** (96.5 km) **B 236.8** (381 km) Emergency survival cabin and turnout to north with outhouse and litter barrels.

G 534.8 (860.7 km) **FS 55.6** (89.5 km) **B 241.1** (388 km) I.P.L. pipeline camp and pump station to north. Highway crosses pipeline.

G 536.3 (863 km) **FS 54.1** (87 km) **B 242.6** (390.4 km) Microwave tower to south.

G 550.4 (885.8 km) **FS 40** (64.4 km) **B 256.7** (413.1 km) Jean Marie Creek bridge.

G 550.5 (885.9 km) **FS 39.9** (64.3 km) **B 256.8** (413.2 km) Service station, referred to locally as "Checkpoint"; gas and food service available, open 24 hours a day.

G 550.6 (886.1 km) **FS 39.8** (64.1 km) **B 256.9** (413.4 km) **Junction** with the Liard Highway (NWT Highway 7), which leads south to Fort Liard and junctions with the Alaska Highway near Fort Nelson. See the LIARD HIGHWAY section for details.

G 552 (888.4 km) **FS 38.4** (61.8 km) **B 258.3** (415.7 km) Turnout to east.

G 563.7 (907.1 km) **FS 26.7** (43.1 km) **B 270** (434.4 km) Emergency survival cabin and turnout with litter barrels and outhouse to west.

G 577.8 (929.8 km) **FS 12.6** (20.4 km) **B 284.1** (457.1 km) Highway crests hill; view of Liard River ahead. Ferry landing 3,280 feet/1,000m.

G 578.2 (930.5 km) **FS 12.2** (19.7 km) **B 284.5** (457.8 km) Liard River Campground to accommodate travelers who miss the last ferry at night, has five sites, tables, firepits, outhouse and garbage container. ▲

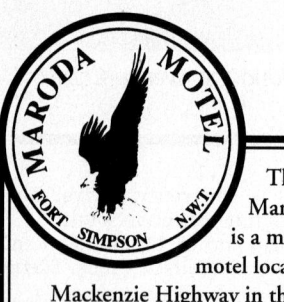

The Lafferty *crosses the Liard River. A ferry crossing at Camsell Bend on the Mackenzie River is planned for 1994.* (Lyn Hancock)

G 578.5 (930.9 km) **FS 11.9** (19.3 km) **B 284.8** (458.2 km) Free government-operated Liard River ferry operates daily May through October from 8 A.M. to 11:40 P.M., seven days a week. Crossing time is six minutes. Capacity is eight cars or two trucks, with a maximum total weight of 130,000 lbs./59,090kg. An ice bridge opens for light vehicles in late November and heavier vehicles as ice thickens. *NOTE: No crossing possible during breakup (about mid-April to mid-May) and freezeup (mid-October to mid-November).*

G 580.7 (934.6 km) **FS 9.7** (15.6 km) **B 287** (461.9 km) Fort Simpson airport. See Private Aircraft information in Fort Simpson.

G 588.1 (946.4 km) **FS 2.3** (3.8 km) **B 294.4** (473.7 km) **Junction** with Fort Simpson access road. The Mackenzie Highway extends beyond this junction approximately 52 miles/84 km to Camsell Bend on the Mackenzie River, then a rough summer trail (ice road in winter) proceeds north to Wrigley. The trail to Wrigley is currently being improved to all-weather road standards and is scheduled for completion in 1994. Ferry service across the Mackenzie River is also planned for 1994. Road mileages are as follows: Fort Simpson to Wrigley, 143 miles/230 km; Wrigley to Fort Norman, 148 miles/238 km; Fort Norman to Norman Wells, 50 miles/80 km; and Fort Norman to Fort Franklin, 68 miles/110 km.

G 589.7 (949 km) **FS 0.7** (1.2 km) **B 296** (476.3 km) Causeway to Fort Simpson Island.

G 590.1 (949.6 km) **FS 0.3** (0.6 km) **B 296.4** (476.9 km) Turnoff for village campground. ▲

Fort Simpson

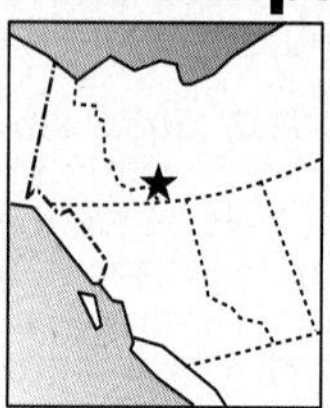

G 590.4 (950.2 km) **FS 0 B 296.7** (477.5 km) Located on an island at the confluence of the Mackenzie and Liard rivers. **Population:** 1,001. **Emergency Services: RCMP**, phone 695-3111. **Hospital** (12 beds), for medical emergency phone 695-2291. **Fire Department** (volunteer), phone 695-2222.

Visitor Information: Village office operates a visitor booth June through August. The visitor information centre is open till 8 P.M., seven days a week in summer; closed Sundays in winter. Nahanni National Park information centre on Main Street has a photo exhibit and films. For information on the park you may also write Superintendent, Postal Bag 300, Fort Simpson, NT X0E 0N0.

Television: Channels 2, 4, 6, 7, 9, 11. **Transportation:** Scheduled service to Yellowknife via NWT Airways and Ptarmigan Air. Fixed wing and helicopter charters available. **Rental cars**–Available. **Taxi service**–Available.

Private Aircraft: Fort Simpson airport; elev. 554 feet/169m; length 6,000 feet/1,829m; asphalt; fuel 100, Jet B. Fort Simpson Island; elev. 405 feet/123m; length 3,000 feet/914m; gravel; fuel 100, Jet B.

Fort Simpson is a full-service community. There is a motel with kitchenettes and a hotel; dining at the hotel (licensed premises) and three restaurants in town; gas stations with repair service (unleaded, diesel and propane available); two grocery stores, department store, hardware store, a bank, laundromat, post office, crafts shop and sports shop. Small engine repair shop and mechanics available. Fort Simpson has grade schools, churches (Anglican, Catholic and Pentecostal), the Stanley Isaiah Senior Citizen's Centre (designed by Gino Pin), and various territorial and federal offices. Recreational facilities include an arena, curling rink, gym, ball diamond, tennis, small indoor pool and a boat launch at government wharf. A number of community activities are held at the Papal Site, a large field with a cross, log tepee and stone monument commemorating Pope John Paul II's visit here in 1987.

Public campground at edge of town in wooded area has 30 campsites and four picnic sites. ▲

Fort Simpson is the oldest continuously occupied site on the Mackenzie River, dating from 1804 when the North West Co. established its Fort of the Forks. There is a historical marker on the bank of the Mackenzie. The Hudson's Bay Co. began its post here in 1821. At that time the fort was renamed after Sir George Simpson, one of the first governors of the combined North West Co. and Hudson's Bay Co. Fort Simpson served as the Mackenzie District headquarters for the Hudson's Bay Co. fur-trading operation. Its key location on the Mackenzie River also made Fort Simpson an important transportation centre. Anglican and Catholic missions were established here in 1858 and 1894.

Fort Simpson continues to be an important centre for the Northwest Territories water transport system. Visitors may walk along the high banks of the Mackenzie River and watch the boat traffic and floatplanes. According to resident Lyn Hancock, one of the easiest places to get down to the water is by Alfred Faille's cabin on Mackenzie Drive. Faille was a well-known Fort Simpson pioneer river runner.

For visitors, Fort Simpson has Slavey crafts, such as birch-bark baskets and beadwork. Fort Simpson is also the jumping-off point for the Mackenzie River and Nahanni National Park.

The 4,766-square-km **NAHANNI NATIONAL PARK,** listed as a unique geological area on the UNESCO world heritage site list, is accessible only by nonpowered boat or aircraft. Located southwest of Fort Simpson near the Yukon border, day trip flightseeing tours of the park may be arranged in Fort Simpson, Fort Liard and Yellowknife, and from Fort Nelson, BC, and Watson Lake, YT. Highlights include the spectacular Ram Plateau and Virginia Falls (300 feet/90m, twice as high as Niagara Falls). One of the most popular attractions in the park is running the South Nahanni River or its tributary, the Flat River. The South Nahanni River route stretches about 186 miles/300 km from Rabbitkettle Lake to the eastern park boundary. Rabbitkettle Hot Springs, a major feature on the upper section of the river, is reached by trail (restricted access, hikers must be guided by park staff). Near the east park boundary is Kraus Hot Springs, on the remains of the old Kraus homestead. The Flat River route stretches 80 miles/128 km from Seaplane Lake to the confluence with the South Nahanni. Charter air service for canoe drop-offs is available in Fort Simpson. For more information, contact the Park Superintendent by mail or check with the Parks Canada information centre on Main Street. The centre is open 8:30 A.M. to 5 P.M., seven days a week in July and August, weekdays the rest of the year.

AREA FISHING: Willow, Dogface and **Trout lakes** accessible by air. Good fishing for trout and grayling. Inquire locally for details.

Maroda Motel. See display ad this section.

Simpson Air (1981) Ltd. See display ad this section.

This Hay River school was designed by Douglas Cardinal; students chose the colour. (Lyn Hancock)

Hay River Highway Log

NWT HIGHWAY 2

Highway 2 is paved from Enterprise to Hay River; watch for rough spots in the surfacing. Kilometreposts along the highway reflect distance from Enterprise.

Distance from Enterprise (E) is followed by distance from Hay River (H).

E 0 H 23.6 (38 km) **Junction** of Highways 1 and 2.

E 8.7 (14 km) **H 14.9** (24 km) Private campground 0.7 mile/1.1 km east. Market garden in season. ▲

E 11.6 (18.6 km) **H 12** (19.4 km) Sawmill Road to east.

E 16 (25.7 km) **H 7.6** (12.3 km) Gravel road leads east 0.6 mile/1 km to Hay River Golf and Country Club; large log clubhouse, driving range, nine holes (par 36), sand greens. Site of the NWT Open every second year in late August.

E 20 (32.3 km) **H 3.6** (5.7 km) **Junction** with Highway 5 to Fort Smith (see Fort Smith Highway Log this section).

E 22.4 (36 km) **H 1.2** (2 km) Chamber of commerce Welcome to Hay River sign. Parking area to east, where the riverboat *Liard River* is on display.

Hay River

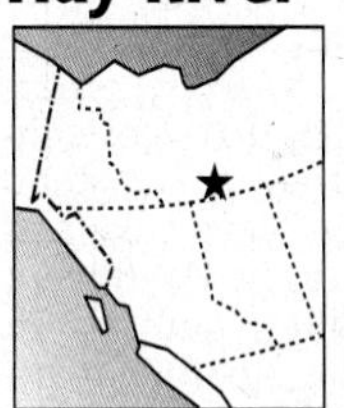

E 23.6 (38 km) **H 0** Located on the south shore of Great Slave Lake at the mouth of the Hay River, on both the mainland and Vale Island. **Population:** 2,891. **Emergency Services: Police,** phone 874-6555. **Fire Department,** phone 874-2222. **Hospital,** phone 874-2565.

Visitor Information: Visitor information centre, just east of the highway, is housed in a two-story brown structure. The centre is open mid-June to early September; 10 A.M. to 8 P.M., Monday through Saturday, noon to 8 P.M. on Sunday. There is a dump station located here. Write Chamber of Commerce, Box 1278, Hay River, NT X0E 0R0; phone 874-3277.

Radio: CKHR-FM 107.3, 93.7, 100.1-FM. **Television:** Channels 2, 6, 7, 10 and 12 via satellite. **Newspaper:** *The Hub* (weekly). **Transportation: Air**–Canadian Airlines International, Ptarmigan Airways, Landa Aviation, Carter Air and Buffalo Airways. **Bus**–Coachways. **Rental cars**–Available.

Private Aircraft: Hay River airport; elev. 543 feet/165m; length 6,000 feet/1,830m, paved; 4,000 feet/1,219m, gravel; fuel 100, Jet B.

Hay River was established in 1868 with the building of a Hudson's Bay Co. post. Today's economy combines transportation, communications, commercial fishing and service industries.

The community is the transfer point from highway and rail to barges on Great Slave Lake bound for arctic and subarctic communities. Hay River harbour is also home port of the Mackenzie River barge fleet that plies the river in summer. World-class jet boat racing takes place on the Mackenzie

Gift shop manager in Fort Providence displays moosetufting pictures, a craft common to this area. (Lyn Hancock)

River in July each year. The turnaround point is Hay River Gorge.

The airstrip was built in 1942 on Vale Island by the U.S. Army Corps of Engineers. Vale Island was the townsite until floods in 1951 and 1963 forced evacuation of the population to the mainland townsite, where most of the community is now concentrated. Vale Island, referred to as "Old Town," is bounded by Great Slave Lake and the west and east channels of the Hay River.

The town boasts the tallest building in the Northwest Territories; the 17-story apartment building is a landmark that can be seen for miles around. The ground floor houses some shops and the offices of *The Hub,* Hay River's weekly newspaper. Another unique structure in town is the high school, which was painted purple (the colour was chosen by the students).

There are 10 restaurants, gas stations with unleaded gas, propane and repair service, and grocery stores. Reservations are a must at the town's five hotels/motels; lodgings are booked solid in the busy summer season by construction and transportation workers. There is also a bed and breakfast. Other facilities include two banks, a laundromat and a variety of shops.

Hay River has schools, churches, a civic centre with a swimming pool (one of only two year-round swimming pools in Northwest Territories), curling sheets, hockey arena and dance hall. Northwest Territories Centennial Library headquarters is located here. There is a public boat launch at Porritt Landing on Vale Island.

There is a public campground on Vale Island (follow the signs; it is about 6 miles/10 km past the information centre). There are 21 sites (four with electrical hookups), showers, firewood and firepits, picnic area, playground and horseshoe pit. Rates are $5 for tents, $6 for RVs. Open mid-May to mid-September. ▲

Great sportfishing area with fly-in fishing camps (check with the chamber of commerce). Boat rentals on nearby **Great Slave Lake**, where northern pike up to 40 lbs. are not unusual. Inconnu (sheefish), pickerel and grayling also found here.

Yellowknife Highway Log

NWT HIGHWAY 3
Distance from the junction of Highways 1 and 3 (J) is followed by distance from Yellowknife (Y).

J 0 Y 212.5 (342 km) **Junction** of Highways 1 and 3. Turn right northbound for Fort Providence, Rae–Edzo and Yellowknife.

The first 40.4 miles/65 km of Highway 3 are paved. The remainder of the highway is gravel to Yellowknife, with the exception of a short stretch of pavement around Rae–Edzo. Plans call for extending the paved portion of this highway in the coming years.

J 4.8 (7.7 km) **Y 207.7** (334.3 km) Chikilee Creek.

J 4.9 (7.9 km) **Y 207.6** (334.1 km) Wolf Skull Creek.

J 9.1 (14.7 km) **Y 203.4** (327.3 km) Dory Point maintenance camp to west.

J 10.6 (17 km) **Y 201.9** (324.9 km) Turnoff for winter ice crossing to east.

J 13.2 (21.2 km) **Y 199.3** (320.8 km) Dory Point picnic area to east with five sites and kitchen shelter, no drinking water; overlooking Mackenzie River with view of passing riverboats.

J 13.9 (22.4 km) **Y 198.6** (319.6 km) Campground with hookups, service station with regular, unleaded and diesel, and restaurant. ▲

J 14.5 (23.3 km) **Y 198** (318.6 km) Dory Point marine access camp to west.

J 15.1 (24.3 km) **Y 197.4** (317.7 km) Free government-operated Mackenzie River ferry operates daily May through October or November from 6 A.M. to midnight. Crossing time is eight minutes. Capacity is 10 cars or four trucks, with a maximum total weight of 220,000 lbs./100,000kg. An ice bridge opens for light vehicles in December and heavier vehicles as ice thickens. *NOTE: No crossing possible during breakup (about April to mid-May).* Ice breaking procedures now keep the channel open for the ferry during freezeup while an ice bridge is being constructed. For ferry information phone 873-7799 or 1-800-661-0751.

J 15.9 (25.6 km) **Y 196.6** (316.4 km) Sign indicates Mackenzie Wood Bison Sanctuary. The wood bison are not often seen along the highway; however, sandhill cranes, squirrels, spruce grouse and ptarmigan may be seen in season.

J 19.4 (31.2 km) **Y 193.1** (310.8 km) Motel, restaurant and service station with unleaded, diesel and propane. Pay phone.

J 19.6 (31.6 km) **Y 192.9** (310.4 km) **Junction** with access road which leads 2.8 miles/4.5 km west to Fort Providence (description follows). There is an airstrip located 0.4 mile/0.6 km west on the access road.

NOTE: It is a good idea to fill gas tanks here if you are bound for Yellowknife. Next gas available is in Rae–Edzo.

Fort Providence territorial campground is located 0.7 mile/1.1 km west of the highway on the access road; 30 sites, tables, firewood, kitchen shelter, garbage container, pump water and dump station. Situated on the banks of the Mackenzie River. Rental boats, boat launch and fishing nearby. ▲

Entering Mackenzie Bison Sanctuary northbound.

Fort Providence

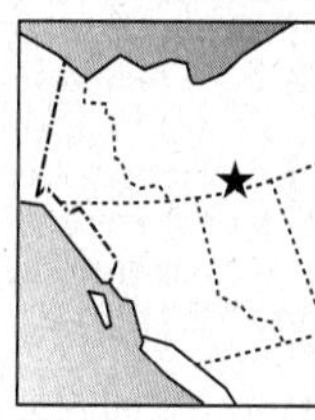

Located on the Mackenzie River, 2.8 miles/4.5 km northwest of Highway 3. **Population:** 688. **Emergency Services: Police,** phone 699-3291. **Fire Department,** phone 699-4222. **Nursing station,** phone 699-4311.

Elevation: 550 feet/168m. **Radio:** 1230. **Television:** Channels 6 and 13 (CBC). **Transportation: Air**–Air Providence and charter service. **Bus**–Coachways.

Private Aircraft: Fort Providence airstrip; elev. 530 feet/162m; length 3,000 feet/915m; gravel; fuel emergency only.

Facilities include two motels, two restaurants, gas stations with minor repair service, grocery and general stores.

A Roman Catholic mission was established here in 1861. Although noted for its early agricultural endeavors, Fort Providence is traditionally a trapping community. Three historical markers in the community commemorate the roles of the church and explorer Alexander Mackenzie in settling the area.

Unique and popular with northern collectors is the moose hair embroidery found in local gift shops. Local craftswomen are also noted for their porcupine quill work. Along with seeing the crafts, visitors may cruise the Mackenzie River. Spectacular photo opportunities here for sunsets on the Mackenzie.

Good to excellent fishing in **Mackenzie River;** guides and cabins available, also boats and air charter trips. Northern pike to 30 lbs., May 30 to September, use large Red Devils; grayling and pickerel from 1 to 6 lbs., June to September, use anything (small Red Devils will do).

Yellowknife Highway Log

(continued)

J 26.4 (42.5 km) **Y 186.1** (299.5 km) Side road west to highway maintenance camp and stockpiles.

J 27.5 (44.3 km) **Y 185** (297.7 km) Bluefish River.

J 29.8 (48 km) **Y 182.7** (294 km) Section of older road loops off to east and rejoins the highway at **Milepost J 30.7**.

J 37 (59.5 km) **Y 175.5** (282.4 km) Large turnout to east at sand and gravel stockpiles.

J 38.7 (62.3 km) **Y 173.8** (279.7 km) Small gravel turnout to east.

J 40.4 (65 km) **Y 172.1** (277 km) Pavement ends, gravel begins, northbound.

J 42.3 (68.1 km) **Y 170.2** (273.9 km) Turnout to east with litter barrels and sign about Mackenzie Bison Sanctuary.

J 54.6 (87.9 km) **Y 157.9** (254.1 km) Microwave tower to west.

J 59.2 (95.3 km) **Y 153.3** (246.7 km) Telecommunications building to east.

J 62.6 (100.8 km) **Y 149.9** (241.2 km) Begin dust-free passing zone northbound.

J 66.6 (107.2 km) **Y 145.9** (234.8 km) End dust-free passing zone northbound.

J 75.6 (121.6 km) **Y 136.9** (220.4 km) Chan Lake picnic area to east with kitchen shelter, tables, firepits and firewood. No drinking water. Watch for waterfowl.

J 76.1 (122.5 km) **Y 136.4** (219.5 km) Turnout with litter barrels to east.

J 79.8 (128.4 km) **Y 132.7** (213.5 km) Microwave tower to west.

J 96.1 (154.7 km) **Y 116.4** (187.3 km) Dust-free passing zone.

J 100 (160.9 km) **Y 112.5** (181.1 km) Turnout with litter barrels, outhouse and highway map sign to east. Watch for buffalo.

J 104.4 (168 km) **Y 108.1** (174 km) Telecommunications building to east.

J 108.4 (174.4 km) **Y 104.1** (167.5 km) Microwave tower to east.

J 109.8 (176.7 km) **Y 102.7** (165.3 km) Dust-free passing zone.

J 114.1 (183.6 km) **Y 98.4** (158.4 km) Gravel stockpiles to west.

J 124.7 (200.7 km) **Y 87.8** (141.3 km) Entering Yellowknife District northbound.

J 129.5 (208.4 km) **Y 83** (133.6 km) Gravel stockpiles to east.

J 129.7 (208.8 km) **Y 82.8** (133.2 km) Turnout with litter barrels to east. Northbound travelers may notice the trees are getting shorter as you move farther north.

J 140.2 (225.7 km) **Y 72.3** (116.3 km) Turnout to east. Steep downgrade northbound as highway approaches Mosquito Creek.

J 141.2 (227.3 km) **Y 71.3** (114.7 km) Highway crosses **Mosquito Creek**. Fishing for pickerel and whitefish, May and June.

J 142.9 (230 km) **Y 69.6** (112 km) Gravel stockpile to east.

J 144.2 (232 km) **Y 68.3** (110 km) North Arm Territorial Park on the shores of Great Slave Lake. Campground with kitchen shelter, tables, toilets, firewood, firepits and boat launch *(CAUTION: Reefs)*. Lowbush cranberries and other berries in area. *Beware of bears.* ▲

J 147.2 (236.9 km) **Y 65.3** (105.1 km) Pavement begins, gravel ends, northbound.

J 147.5 (237.4 km) **Y 65** (104.6 km) Radio tower to west.

J 148.3 (238.6 km) **Y 64.2** (103.3 km) **Junction** with winter ice road north to communities of Lac La Marte and Rae Lakes.

J 148.5 (239 km) **Y 64** (103 km) **Junction** with access road west to community of Edzo (see description at **Milepost J 152.2**).

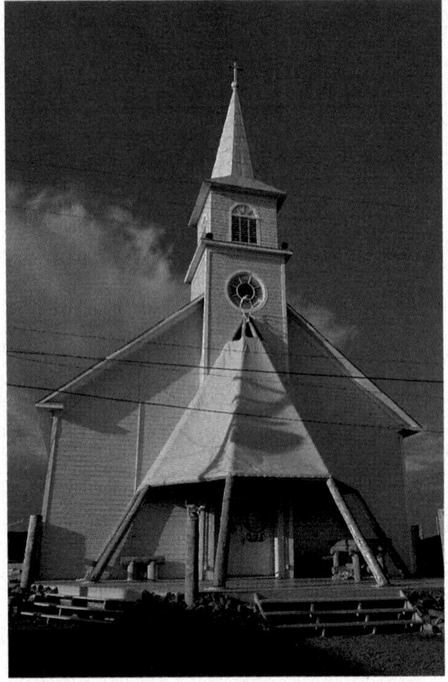

Picturesque Roman Catholic church in Rae. (Lyn Hancock)

J 148.8 (239.5 km) **Y 63.7** (102.5 km) Picnic area to west. Pickerel fishing in **West Channel** in spring.

J 149.3 (240.2 km) **Y 63.2** (101.8 km) West Channel.

J 151.5 (243.8 km) **Y 61** (98.2 km) Bridge over Frank Channel, which extends from the head of the North Arm of Great Slave Lake to the Indian village of Rae. Watch for turnoff to Rabesca's Bear Healing Rock; lodging, mud baths, boating and fishing for whitefish.

J 152.2 (245 km) **Y 60.3** (97 km) **Junction** with road which leads west 7 miles/11.2 km to community of Rae (description follows).

RAE–EDZO (pop. about 2,000). **Emergency Services: RCMP**, in Rae, phone 392-6181. **Nursing station** in Edzo, phone 371-3551. **Radio:** 105.9-FM. The two hamlets of Rae and Edzo contain the territories' largest Déne (Indian) community. The Rae area, where most of the community resides, is an old Indian hunting spot and was the site of two early trading posts. The Edzo site was developed in 1965 by the government to provide schools and an adequate sanitation system. Rae has grocery stores, a post office, Native crafts shop, two hotels, food service and gas stations with regular, unleaded and diesel. Pay phones are located at the community sports centre and at the cafe.

J 152.3 (245.1 km) **Y 60.2** (96.9 km) Pavement ends, gravel begins, eastbound.

J 159.8 (257.2 km) **Y 52.7** (84.8 km) Stagg River bridge. After crossing the North Arm of Great Slave Lake, the highway swings southeast toward Yellowknife. Winding road to Yellowknife, good opportunities to see waterfowl in the many small lakes.

J 160.4 (258.1 km) **Y 52.1** (83.9 km) Turnout with litter barrels to south.

J 171.8 (276.5 km) **Y 40.7** (65.5 km) Microwave tower to north.

J 189.2 (304.5 km) **Y 23.3** (37.5 km) Turnout with litter barrels to north.

J 189.5 (304.9 km) **Y 23** (37.1 km) Boundary Creek.

J 192.2 (309.3 km) **Y 20.3** (32.7 km) Microwave tower to south.

J 205.2 (330.2 km) **Y 7.3** (11.7 km) Yellowknife landfill to south.

J 208.5 (335.5 km) **Y 4** (6.5 km) Gravel ends, pavement begins.

J 208.7 (335.8 km) **Y 3.8** (6.2 km) Yellowknife Golf Club to north; nine holes, sand greens and course, licensed clubhouse. Site of the June 21 Midnight Tournament. Some modified rules have been adopted by this Far North golf course, among them: "No penalty assessed when ball carried off by raven."

J 209.8 (337.7 km) **Y 2.7** (4.3 km) Yellowknife airport to south.

J 210 (338 km) **Y 2.5** (4 km) Fred Henne Recreational Park on Long Lake. Attractive public campground with 82 sites, water, firewood, firepits, picnic area, boat launch, snack bar, showers and pay phone. Daily and seasonal rates available; open from mid-May to mid-September. Sandy beach and swimming in Long Lake. Interpretive trail. ▲

J 210.5 (338.7 km) **Y 2** (3.3 km) Old Airport Road access to Yellowknife. Just past the turnoff is the Welcome to Yellowknife sign and the hard-to-miss Wardair Bristol freighter to the south. A historical plaque commemorates the Bristol freighter, which was the first wheel-equipped aircraft to land at the North Pole. Picnic sites nearby.

J 211.4 (340.2 km) **Y 1.1** (1.8 km) Stock Lake to south.

J 211.7 (340.7 km) **Y 0.8** (1.3 km) **Junction** of Highway 3 and Highway 4 (Ingraham Trail); see log this section.

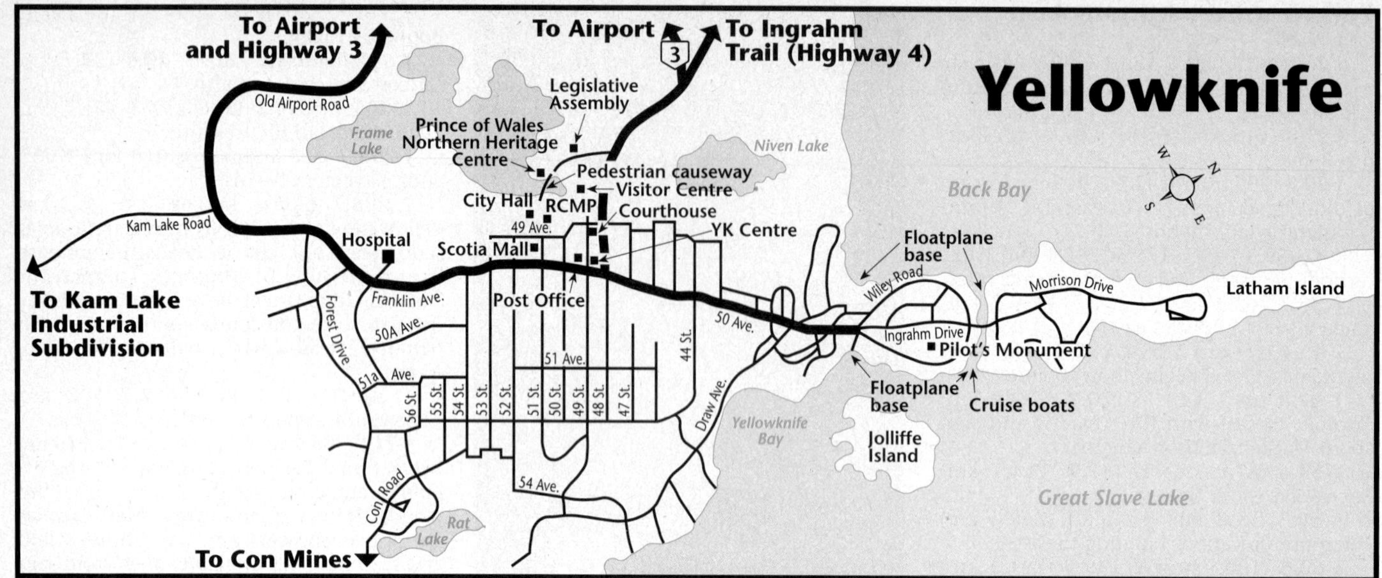

Yellowknife

J 212.5 (342 km) **Y 0** On the north shore of Great Slave Lake, approximately 940 miles/1513 km from Edmonton, AB. **Population:** 13,698. **Emergency Services: Police,** phone 920-8311. **Fire Department** and **Ambulance,** phone 873-3434 or 873-2222. **Hospital,** Stanton Yellowknife, phone 920-4111.

Visitor Information: Northern Frontier Regional Visitors Centre, showcasing the culture and crafts of the area, is located at 4807 49th St. Reservation desk for booking tours. Open daily year-round; summer hours 8 A.M. to 8 P.M. Phone (403) 873-4262. Information also available from Travel–Arctic, Dept. of Economic Development & Tourism, Yellowknife, NT X1A 2L9. Or write the Chamber of Commerce, Box 906, Yellowknife, NT X1A 2N7; phone 920-4944.

Radio: 1240, 1340, 101.1-FM. **Television:** Channel 8; 15 cable channels. **Newspapers:** *News/North* (weekly); *Yellowknifer* (twice weekly); *The Northern Star* (weekly).

Private Aircraft: Yellowknife airport; elev. 674 feet/205m; length 7,500 feet/ 2,286m; asphalt; fuel 100/130, Jet B. Floatplane bases located at East Bay and West Bay of Latham Island.

Yellowknife, capital of Northwest Territories and considered the only "city" in Northwest Territories, is a relatively new community. White settlers arrived in 1934 with the discovery of gold in the area. Cominco poured its first gold brick in 1938. WWII intervened and gold mining was halted until Giant Yellowknife Mines began milling May 12, 1948. It was not until 1960 that the road was completed connecting the city with the provinces. Yellowknife became capital of the Northwest Territories in 1967. The most recent mining boom in Yellowknife was the discovery of diamonds north of the community in 1992. The find set off a rush of claim stakers.

For two to six weeks each spring, vehicle traffic to Yellowknife is cut off during breakup on the Mackenzie River crossing near Fort Providence. All fresh meat, produce and urgent supplies must be airlifted during this period, resulting in higher prices.

Yellowknife has continued to develop as a mining, transportation and government administrative centre for the territories.

ACCOMMODATIONS

Accommodations at six hotels, three motels, seven bed and breakfasts, and the YWCA (co-ed). There are 14 restaurants, three dining lounges (no minors), eight cocktail lounges and several shopping malls. Northern handicraft shops for fur parkas and other Native crafts are a specialty here, and there are shops specializing in Northern art.

TRANSPORTATION

Air: Scheduled air service to Edmonton via NWT Airways and Canadian Airlines International; Winnipeg via NWT Airways. Carriers serving Yellowknife and arctic communities are NWT Airways, Canadian Airlines International, Ptarmigan Airways, Simpson Air, Air Providence and First Air. Charter service available. **Bus:** Greyhound from Edmonton with connections at Enterprise. **Rentals:** Several major car rental agencies; boat and canoe rentals.

ATTRACTIONS

Prince of Wales Northern Heritage Centre. Opened in 1979, this large museum complex was built to collect, preserve, document, exhibit, study and interpret the North's natural and cultural history. For visitors there are a variety of temporary exhibits ranging from Inuit stone sculpture to historical photographs, and permanent exhibits in the galleries. The orientation gallery gives general background on the Northwest Territories; the south gallery tells the story of the land and the Déne and Inuit people; the north gallery shows the arrival of the Euro–Canadians. The centre is located on Frame Lake, accessible via 48th Street or by way of a pedestrian causeway behind City Hall.

Tours. There are a variety of local tours offered. Public tours of the new Legislative Assembly are available by calling the Coordinator of Public Information at (403) 669-2230. Visitors may take a two- or three-hour tour of the city or a two-hour cruise on Great Slave Lake. Local tour operators also offer tours out Ingraham Trail (NWT Highway 4).

Explore Yellowknife. Walk along the popular Frame Lake Trail with its views of Yellowknife's skyline, including the new Armed Forces Northern Headquarters and Legislative Assembly buildings. The trail is a favourite with dog walkers, bicyclists, birdwatchers and commuters. Drive or walk down the hill and around the "Rock" where the original town sprang up on Yellowknife Bay and where there are now barges, fishing boats and a large floatplane base; climb steps to the cairn on top of the rock, a tribute to early-day bush pilots who opened up this country in the 1930s and 1940s. The log Wildcat Cafe at the bottom of the rock is open May to September. Drive out to Old Town on Latham Island to see some of the creative solutions builders have found to the problem of building on solid rock.

Ingraham Trail Log

NWT HIGHWAY 4

NWT Highway 4 begins in Yellowknife and extends 44 miles/71 km along an almost continuous chain of lakes and streams, ending at Tibbett Lake. It was named for pioneer prospector and hotelman Vic Ingraham.

Distance from Yellowknife (Y) is followed by distance from Tibbett Lake (T).

Y 0 T 44.1 (70.9 km) **Junction** of Highways 3 and 4. The first 12 miles/19.2 km of

Interpretive markers highlight sights along Yellowknife's Frame Lake Trail. (Lyn Hancock)

Highway 4 are paved, the remainder of the road is good gravel.

Y 1.9 (3.1 km) **T 42.2** (67.9 km) Giant Yellowknife Mines main office. The mine has been operating since 1947.

Y 4.7 (7.5 km) **T 39.4** (63.4 km) Single-lane bridge across the **Yellowknife River.** Historical sign at north end of bridge about the Ingraham Trail. Picnic area with tables and boat launch. Good fishing for northern pike, lake trout and grayling.

Y 6.1 (9.8 km) **T 38** (61.2 km) Turnoff to south by two transmission towers for 7-mile/11-km road to Detah Indian village; no services.

Y 11.9 (19.2 km) **T 32.2** (51.7 km) **Prosperous Lake** picnic area and boat launch to north. Fishing for northern pike, whitefish and lake trout.

Y 14.9 (24 km) **T 29.2** (46.9 km) **Madeline Lake** picnic area and boat launch to north. Fishing for northern pike, whitefish, cisco and yellow perch.

Y 16.4 (26.4 km) **T 27.7** (44.5 km) **Pontoon Lake** picnic area and boat launch to south. Fishing for northern pike, whitefish, cisco and suckers.

Y 17.5 (28.2 km) **T 26.6** (42.7 km) Side road leads north 1 mile/1.6 km to Prelude Lake territorial campground with 28 campsites, 20 picnic sites, boat launch and swimming. Prelude Wildlife Trail, which starts from and ends at the campground, is a one-and-a-half-hour walk. The trail has 15 interpretive stations showing the adaptations and relationships of wildlife in the North. Boat rentals, cabins and a restaurant located here. Fishing in **Prelude Lake** for lake trout, grayling, whitefish, cisco, burbot, suckers and northern pike.

Good views of Prelude Lake from the highway next 10 miles/16 km eastbound.

Y 28.6 (46 km) **T 15.5** (24.9 km) Powder Point on Prelude Lake to north; parking area. Boat launch for canoeists doing the route into Hidden Lake, Lower Cameron River, or four-day trip to Yellowknife River bridge.

Y 30.1 (48.4 km) **T 14** (22.5 km) Cameron River Falls trailhead to north; parking. This 0.6-mile/1-km trail leads to cliffs overlooking Cameron River Falls.

Y 35.4 (57 km) **T 8.7** (13.9 km) Single-lane Bailey bridge across Cameron River; parking area, picnicking, canoeing and swimming.

Y 37.9 (61 km) **T 6.2** (9.9 km) **Reid Lake** territorial campground with 27 campsites, 10 picnic sites, kitchen shelter, swimming, hiking trail, boat launch and fishing. Canoe launch point for Upper Cameron River and Jennejohn Lake routes. *CAUTION: Watch for bears.*

Y 44.1 (70.9 km) **T 0** Tibbett Lake. End of road. Launch point for Pensive Lakes canoe route (advanced canoeists only).

Fort Smith Highway Log

NWT HIGHWAY 5
Distance from Highway 2 junction (J) followed by distance from Fort Smith (FT).

J 0 FT 166 (267.2 km) Highway 5 begins its own series of markers giving distances in kilometres.

J 1.3 (2.2 km) **FT 164.7** (265 km) Railroad and auto bridge crosses Hay River.

J 1.5 (2.5 km) **FT 164.5** (264.7 km) Access road leads north 3.7 miles/5.9 km to Hay River reserve.

The first 37.7 miles/60.8 km of Highway 5 are paved. Watch for construction and rough spots in surfacing. There are no services or gas available until Fort Smith.

J 5.4 (8.8 km) **FT 160.6** (258.4 km) Highway crosses Sandy Creek.

J 11 (17.7 km) **FT 155** (249.5 km) Highway maintenance yard to south.

J 17.3 (27.9 km) **FT 148.7** (239.3 km) Birch Creek bridge.

J 23.7 (38.2 km) **FT 142.3** (229 km) Highway crosses Twin Creek.

J 30.3 (48.8 km) **FT 135.7** (218.4 km) Good gravel road leads 1 mile/1.6 km north to **Polar Lake.** Lake is stocked with rainbow; no motorboats allowed. Good bird watching.

J 33.8 (54.4 km) **FT 132.2** (212.7 km) Buffalo River bridge.

J 34.1 (55 km) **FT 131.9** (212.2 km) Turnout to north with litter barrel.

J 37.3 (60 km) **FT 128.7** (207.1 km) **Junction** with Highway 6 east to Pine Point and Fort Resolution (see log this section). Highway 5 turns south for Fort Smith (continue with this log). Highway maintenance camp.

J 37.6 (60.6 km) **FT 128.4** (206.6 km) Microwave tower to south.

J 54 (87 km) **FT 112** (180.2 km) Turnoff for **Sandy Lake,** 8 miles/13 km south; swimming, sandy beach, fishing for northern pike.

J 54.2 (87.2 km) **FT 111.8** (180 km) Pavement ends, gravel begins, southbound. Dust-free zone to Fort Smith.

J 59.6 (96 km) **FT 106.4** (171.2 km) Entrance to Wood Buffalo National Park. Established in 1922 to protect Canada's only remaining herd of wood bison, **WOOD BUFFALO NATIONAL PARK** (a UNESCO world heritage site) is a vast wilderness area of 44,800 square kilometres with the greater portion located in the northeast corner of Alberta. Park headquarters and Visitor Reception Centre are located in Fort Smith and Fort Chipewyan; excellent audio-video presentations, exhibits and visitor information are available. Or write the Superintendent, Wood Buffalo National Park, Box 750, Fort Smith, NT X0E 0P0; or phone (403) 872-2349 Fort Smith or (403) 697-3662 Fort Chipewyan.

The wood bison, a slightly larger and darker northern relative of the Plains bison, numbered about 1,500 in the area, representing the largest free-roaming herd in Canada at the time the park was established. Soon after this more than 6,600 Plains bison were moved from southern Alberta to the park. Today's herd of about 3,500 bison is considered to be mostly hybrids.

Also found within the park are many species of waterfowl and the world's only remaining natural nesting grounds of the endangered whooping crane.

The park is open year-round, with an interpretive program offered from June to September. Check the schedule of events at the park office.

J 63.8 (102.7 km) **FT 102.2** (164.4 km) Paralleling most of the highway to Fort Smith are hydro transmission power lines carrying power to Fort Smith, Pine Point and Fort Resolution that is generated at the Taltson Dam in the Canadian Shield north of the Slave River.

Much of the flora along this stretch of highway is new growth following the devastating forest fires of 1981. *NOTE: To report a forest fire, call the operator toll free and ask for Zenith 5555.*

J 66 (106.2 km) **FT 100** (160.9 km) Picnic area with tables to north at Angus Fire

Fine view of Salt Plains overlook on Highway 5. *(Earl L. Brown, staff)*

Tower. The sinkhole seen here is an example of karst topography. Sinkholes are formed when the roofs of caves (formed by underground water dissolving bedrock) collapse.

Buffalo wallow beside highway from here to approximately **Milepost J 98.9.**

J 70.6 (113.6 km) **FT 95.4** (153.5 km) Gravel stockpile to south.

J 74 (119.2 km) **FT 92** (148 km) Highway crosses Nyarling River, which runs under the dry creekbed.

J 74.2 (119.4 km) **FT 91.8** (147.7 km) Turnout to south with litter barrel.

J 84.7 (136.4 km) **FT 81.3** (130.8 km) Gravel stockpile to south.

J 98.9 (159.2 km) **FT 67.1** (108 km) Highway maintenance building to north.

J 110.8 (178.4 km) **FT 55.2** (88.8 km) Highway crosses Sass River. Shallow lakes from here south to Preble Creek provide nesting areas for whooping cranes.

J 116.2 (187 km) **FT 49.8** (80.1 km) Highway crosses Preble Creek.

J 130.5 (210 km) **FT 35.5** (57.1 km) The highway leaves and reenters Wood Buffalo National Park several times southbound.

J 131 (211 km) **FT 34.9** (56.1 km) Little Buffalo River bridge. Camping and picnic area. ▲

J 142.5 (229.4 km) **FT 23.5** (37.8 km) Turnoff for Parsons Lake Road (narrow gravel) which leads south 8 miles/13 km to Salt Plains overlook. Interpretive exhibit and viewing telescope. Springs at the edge of a high escarpment are bringing salt to the surface and spreading it across the huge flat plain; only plants adapted to high salinity can grow here. Fine view of a unique environment. Gravel parking area with tables, firepits and toilets at overlook; hiking trail down to Salt Plains (bring boots). *CAUTION: Parsons Lake Road beyond the overlook may be impassable in wet weather.*

J 144.7 (232.8 km) **FT 21.4** (34.4 km) Turnout to south and gravel stockpile.

J 147.9 (238 km) **FT 18.1** (29.1 km) Salt River bridge.

J 151.6 (244 km) **FT 14.4** (23.2 km) Thebacha (Salt River) private campground and picnic area 10 miles/16 km north via good gravel road. Located on the **Salt River;** eight sites, toilets, parking, small-boat launch (cruise down to Slave River), and fishing for pike, walleye, inconnu and goldeye. ▲

J 156.8 (252.4 km) **FT 9.2** (14.8 km) Pavement begins eastbound into Fort Smith.

J 163.4 (263 km) **FT 2.6** (4.2 km) Turnoff to north for Fort Smith airport and Queen Elizabeth Park campground with 19 campsites, 15 picnic sites, water, kitchen shelter, showers and dump station. Short hike from campground to bluff overlooking Rapids of the Drowned on the Slave River; look for pelicans feeding here. ▲

Fort Smith

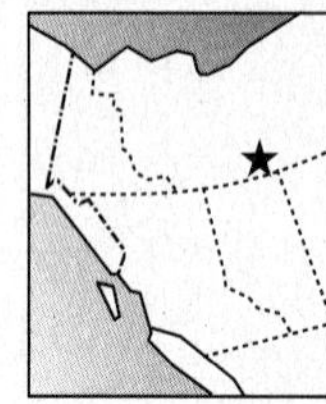

J 166 (267.2 km) **FT 0 Population:** 2,460. **Emergency Services: Police,** phone 872-2107. **Fire Department,** phone 872-6111. **Hospital,** phone 872-3111. **Visitor Information:** Chamber of commerce information centre in Conibear Park, open June to September. For general information on the area, contact the Economic Development and Tourism Office, Box 390, Fort Smith, NT X0E 0P0.

Climate: Mean high temperature in July 75°F/24°C; mean low 48°F/9°C. **Radio:** 860, 101.9-FM. **Television:** Channels 12 (local) and 5 (CBC) plus six cable channels. **Newspaper:** *Slave River Journal.*

Transportation: Air — Canadian Airlines International provides scheduled service; there are also three charter air services here. **Bus** — Available. **Rental cars** — Available.

Private Aircraft: Fort Smith airport; elev. 666 feet/203m; length, 6,000 feet/1,829m; asphalt; fuel 80, 100.

Fort Smith began as a trading post at a favorite campsite of the portagers traveling the 1,600-mile/2575-km water passage from Fort McMurray to the Arctic Ocean. The four sets of rapids, named (south to north) Cassette, Pelican, Mountain and the Rapids of the Drowned, separate the Northwest Territories from Alberta. In 1874 Hudson's Bay Co. established a permanent post, and the Roman Catholic mission was transferred here in 1876. By 1911 the settlement had become a major trading post for the area.

There are a hotel, a motel, two groceries, a takeout outlet, three bars, three convenience stores, and gas stations with unleaded gas and repair service.

Wood Buffalo National Park headquarters is located in the Federal Bldg. on McDougal Road, which also houses the post office. The multi-image presentation here is highly recommended. Exhibit area and trip planning assistance available at the visitor reception area. You can drive from Fort Smith to Peace Point via an all-weather gravel road. There are several hiking trails off the road, a picnic area at the Salt River, and a 36-site campground at Pine Lake, 38 miles/61 km south of Fort Smith. There is also a good opportunity for seeing bison on the road between Pine Lake and Peace Point. Contact the park office, phone 872-2349.

Other attractions in Fort Smith include Northern Life Museum, which features a comprehensive view of the area's Indian culture and life of the white settlers since the mid-19th century.

Fort Resolution Highway Log

NWT HIGHWAY 6

Distance from junction with Highway 5 (J) is followed by distance from Fort Resolution (FR).

J 0 FR 55.9 (90 km) **Junction** of Highways 5 and 6. The first 14.7 miles/23.7 km of the highway is paved; the rest is gravel to Fort Resolution. Narrow shoulders.

J 13.2 (21.3 km) **FR 42.7** (68.7 km) Main access road north to **PINE POINT;** no services. A mining town, Pine Point was built in the 1960s by Cominco Ltd. The open-pit lead–zinc mine shut down in 1987. Once a community of almost 2,000 residents, most people moved out in 1988 and houses and structures have been moved or destroyed. The Great Slave Lake Railway (now CNR) was constructed in 1961 from Roma, AB, to Pine Point to transport the lead–zinc ore to market.

J 14.1 (22.7 km) **FR 41.8** (67.3 km) Microwave tower to north.

J 14.6 (23.6 km) **FR 41.3** (66.4 km) Secondary access road to Pine Point.

J 14.7 (23.7 km) **FR 41.2** (66.3 km) Pavement ends, gravel begins, eastbound. Dust-free zone to Fort Resolution.

J 15.8 (25.5 km) **FR 40.1** (64.5 km) Pine Point airport to north, microwave and satellite dish to south.

J 24.6 (39.6 km) **FR 31.3** (50.3 km) Tailing piles from open-pit mining to south.

J 32.3 (52 km) **FR 23.6** (38 km) Turnoff to north for Dawson Landing viewpoint on Great Slave Lake, accessible via a 25-mile/40-km bush road (not recommended in wet weather).

J 36.5 (58.8 km) **FR 19.4** (31.2 km) Turnout to north with litter barrel.

J 37.8 (60.8 km) **FR 18.1** (29.1 km) Glimpse of Great Slave Lake to north.

J 38.4 (61.8 km) **FR 17.5** (28.1 km) Gravel stockpile to south.

J 41.4 (66.7 km) **FR 14.5** (23.3 km) Bridge over **Little Buffalo River.** Good fishing for northern pike and walleye.

J 42.4 (68.3 km) **FR 13.5** (21.7 km) Access road leads to Little Buffalo River Indian village.

J 54.5 (87.7 km) **FR 1.4** (2.2 km) Campground to west; five gravel sites, outhouses, tables and firepits. ▲

J 55.9 (90 km) **FR 0 FORT RESOLUTION** (pop. 447), located on the south shore of Great Slave Lake on Resolution Bay. **Emergency Services: RCMP,** phone 394-4111. This historic community grew up around a Hudson's Bay Co. post established in 1786, and was named Fort Resolution in 1821 when the Hudson's Bay Co. and North West Co. united. Missionaries settled in the area in 1852, establishing a school and hospital to serve the largely Chipewyan population. Walking tours through the village to visit the many old log buildings and sites may be arranged. The road connecting Fort Resolution with Pine Point was built in the 1960s.

Today's economy is based on trapping and a logging and sawmill operation. There are a small motel, two general stores, a gas station with minor repair service, a post office and cafe. Meals are also available at the community hall.

KLONDIKE LOOP

Alaska Highway Junction to Taylor Highway Junction via Dawson City, Yukon Territory Yukon Highways 2 and 9

(See maps, pages 236–237)

The Klondike Loop refers to the 327-mile-/526-km-long stretch of the Klondike Highway (Yukon Highway 2) from its junction with the Alaska Highway north of Whitehorse to Dawson City; the 65-mile/105-km Top of the World Highway; and 109 miles/175 km of the Taylor Highway (Alaska Route 5).

All of the Klondike Highway between the Alaska Highway junction and Dawson City is asphalt-surfaced. Watch for road construction on the Top of the World Highway.

Yukon Alaska Transport trucks, each carrying up to 50 tons of lead–zinc concentrates, routinely operate between Faro on the Campbell Highway and the port of Skagway on the south Klondike Highway. At press time, the mine was closed, but if it reopens watch for ore trucks on the highway south from Carmacks. The trucks are 8½ feet wide and 85 feet long. Drive with your headlights on at all times.

The Top of the World Highway (Yukon Highway 9) is a gravel road with some hills; a truly scenic route, but slippery in wet weather with some steep grades and winding sections. Drive with your headlights on. The Taylor Highway (Alaska Route 5) is a narrow, gravel road with some steep, winding sections and washboard. (For a detailed log of the Taylor Highway, see the TAYLOR HIGHWAY section.) Both the Taylor and Top of the World highways are closed in winter. Klondike Highway 2 is open year-round.

Alaska-bound motorists may turn off the Alaska Highway north of Whitehorse; follow the Klondike Highway to Dawson City; ferry across the Yukon River at Dawson; drive west via the Top of the World Highway into Alaska; then take the Taylor Highway south back to the Alaska Highway near Tok. Total driving distance is 502 miles/807 km. (Driving distance from Whitehorse to Tok via the Alaska Highway is approximately 396 miles/637 km.)

Travelers planning to make this loop should be aware that the Top of the World Highway (reached by ferry from Dawson City) may not open until late spring. In heavy traffic, there may be a wait for the ferry. Customs stations are open in summer only, 12 hours a day: 8 A.M. to 8 P.M. Alaska time, and 9 A.M. to 9 P.M. Pacific time. Travelers should anticipate the currency change when they cross the border and exchange their money at a bank.

The highway between Skagway and the Alaska Highway, sometimes referred to as the South Klondike, is also designated Klondike Highway 2 (see KLONDIKE HIGHWAY 2 section for log of that road).

Kilometreposts along the highway to Dawson City reflect distance from Skagway. Driving distance was measured in miles from the junction of the Alaska Highway to Dawson City by our field editor. These mileages were converted into kilometres with the exception of the kilometre distance following Skagway (S). That figure reflects the physical location of the kilometrepost and is not necessarily an accurate conversion of the mileage figure.

The route from Whitehorse to Dawson City began as a trail used by miners and trappers at the turn of the century. Steamships also provided passenger service between Whitehorse and Dawson City. A road was built connecting the Alaska Highway with the United Keno Hill Mine at Mayo in 1950. By 1955, the Mayo Road had been upgraded for automobile traffic and extended to Dawson City. In 1960, the last of three steel bridges was completed, crossing the Yukon, Pelly and Stewart rivers. The only ferry crossing remaining is the Yukon River crossing at Dawson City. Mayo Road (Yukon Highway 11) from Stewart Crossing to Mayo, Elsa and Keno was redesignated the Silver Trail in 1985 (see SILVER TRAIL section for road log).

Emergency medical services: Available at Whitehorse, Carmacks, Mayo and Dawson City on the Yukon portion of the highway.

View from Dome Mountain of Dawson City and the Yukon and Klondike rivers.
(Earl L. Brown, staff)

Klondike Loop Log

YUKON HIGHWAY 2

This section of the log shows distance from junction with the Alaska Highway (J) followed by distance from Dawson City (D) and distance from Skagway (S). Physical kilometreposts show distance from Skagway.

J 0 D 327.2 (526.5 km) **S 119.2** (191.8 km) **Junction** with the Alaska Highway.

J 0.6 (1 km) **D 326.6** (525.5 km) **S 119.8** (192.8 km) Road west leads to McPherson subdivision.

J 1 (1.6 km) **D 326.2** (525 km) **S 120.2** (193.4 km) Ranches, farms and livestock next 20 miles/32 km northbound.

J 2.3 (3.7 km) **D 324.9** (522.9 km) **S 121.5** (195.5 km) Takhini River bridge. The Takhini flows into the Yukon River.

J 3.8 (6.1 km) **D 323.4** (520.4 km) **S 123** (197.9 km) Takhini Hot Springs Road. Drive west 6 miles/10 km via paved road for Takhini Hot Springs; lodging, camping, cafe, trail rides, ski trails in winter. The source of the springs is a constant 117°F/47°C temper-

KLONDIKE LOOP *Milepost J 0 to Milepost J 296*

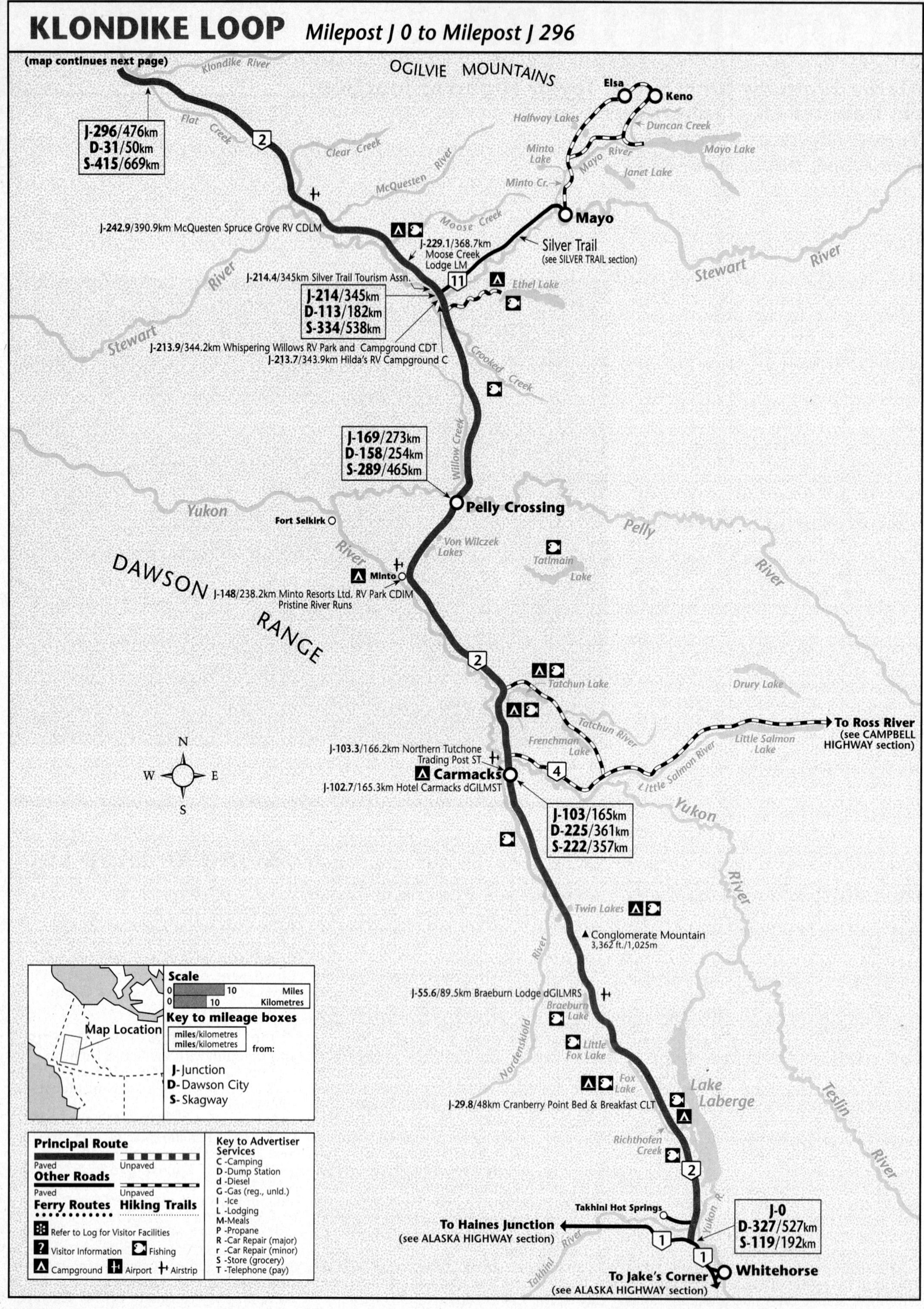

KLONDIKE LOOP

Milepost J 296 to Tetlin Junction, Alaska Highway (includes Taylor Highway)

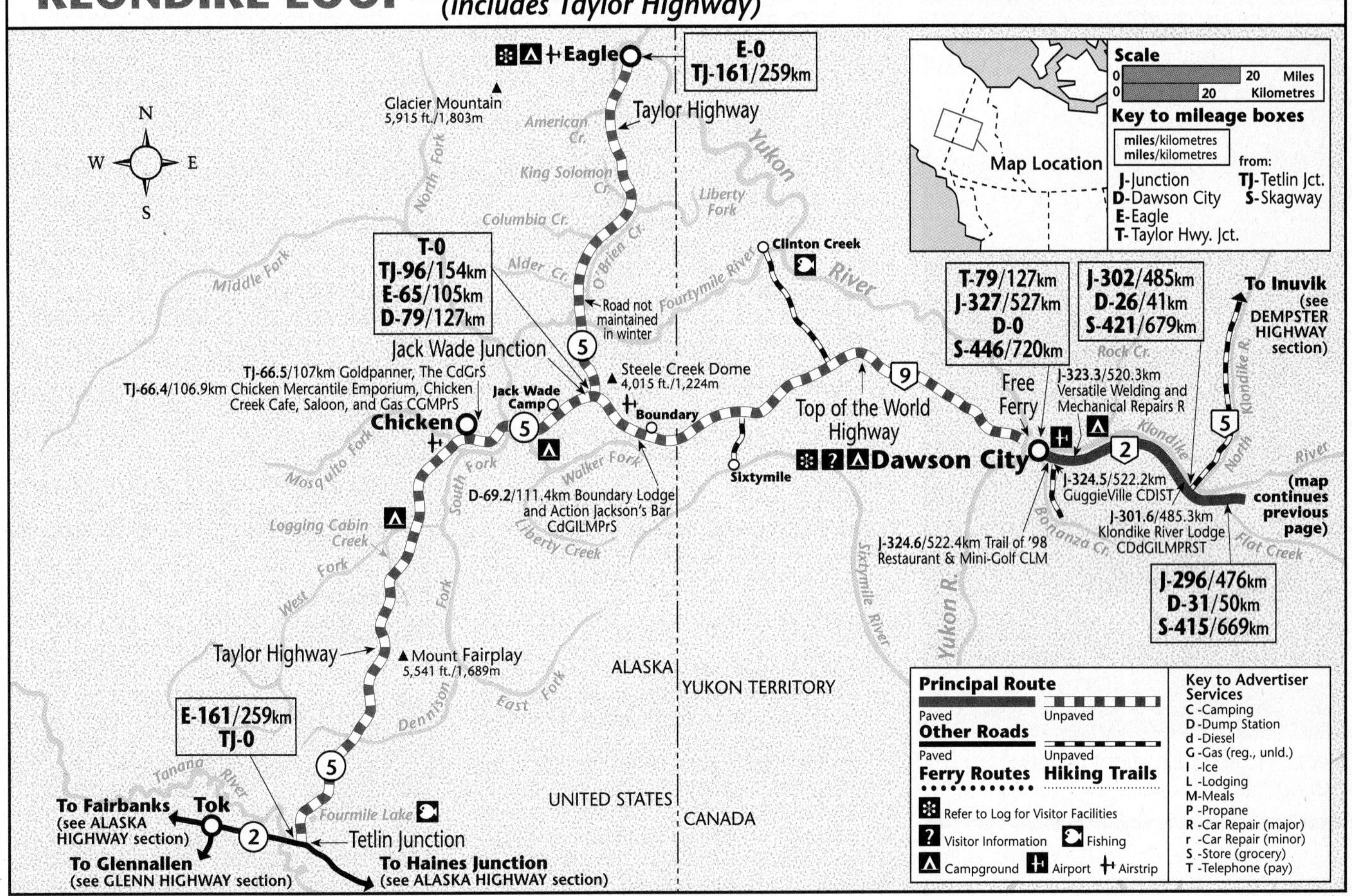

ature and flows at 86 gallons a minute. The hot springs pool averages 100°F/38°C year-round. The water contains no sulfur. The chief minerals present are calcium, magnesium and iron. ▲

Trappers and Indians used these springs around the turn of the century, arriving by way of the Takhini River or the old Dawson Trail. During construction of the Alaska Highway in the early 1940s, the U.S. Army maintained greenhouses in the area and reported remarkable growth regardless of the season.

J 9.4 (15.1 km) **D 317.8** (511.4 km) **S 128.6** (207 km) Sawmill to west.

J 10.7 (17.2 km) **D 316.5** (509.3 km) **S 129.9** (209 km) Shallow Bay Road. Access to Northern Splendor Reindeer Farm. This commercial reindeer farm is 0.8 mile/1.3 km east. Reindeer antlers from the farm are sold for export. The farm is open to visitors in summer; there is an admission charge.

J 12.7 (20.4 km) **D 314.5** (506.1 km) **S 131.9** (212.2 km) Horse Creek Road leads east to Lower Laberge Indian village and lakeshore cottages. **Horse Creek**; good grayling fishing from road.

J 15.8 (25.4 km) **D 311.4** (501.5 km) **S 135** (217.2 km) Microwave site near road.

J 16.8 (27 km) **D 310.4** (499.5 km) **S 136.1** (219.1 km) Large turnout to west.

J 17.4 (27.9 km) **D 309.8** (498.6 km) **S 136.7** (220 km) Lake Laberge to east. The Yukon River widens to form this 40-mile-/64-km-long lake. Lake Laberge was made famous by Robert W. Service with the lines: "The Northern Lights have seen queer sights, but the queerest they ever did see, was that night on the marge of Lake Lebarge I cremated Sam McGee," (from his poem *The Cremation of Sam McGee*).

J 18.2 (29.3 km) **D 309** (497.3 km) **S 137.4** (221.1 km) Gravel pit turnout to east.

J 20.3 (32.7 km) **D 306.9** (493.9 km) **S 139.5** (224.5 km) Deep Creek.

J 20.4 (32.8 km) **D 306.8** (493.7 km) **S 139.6** (224.6 km) Historical marker at turnoff for **Lake Laberge** Yukon government campground. The campground is situated 1.8 miles/2.9 km east on Lake Laberge next to Deep Creek; 28 sites, $8 camping fee, resident campground host, group camping area, kitchen shelter, water, boat launch, and fishing for lake trout, grayling and northern pike. ▲

CAUTION: Storms can blow up quickly and without warning on Lake Laberge as on other northern lakes. Canoeists and other small craft should stay to the west side of the lake, where the shoreline affords safe refuges should a storm come up. The east side of the lake is lined with high, rocky bluffs, and there are few places to pull out. Small craft should not navigate the middle of the lake.

J 20.9 (33.6 km) **D 306.3** (492.9 km) **S 140.1** (225.5 km) View of Lake Laberge for southbound travelers.

J 21.2 (34.1 km) **D 306** (492.4 km) **S 140.4** (225.9 km) Northbound the highway now enters the Miners Range, plateau country of the Yukon, an immense wilderness of forested dome-shaped mountains and high ridges, dotted with lakes and traversed by tributaries of the Yukon River. To the west, Pilot Mountain in the Miners Range (elev. 6,739 feet/2,054m) is visible.

J 22.8 (36.7 km) **D 304.4** (489.9 km) **S 142** (228.5 km) **Fox Creek**; grayling, excellent in June and July.

J 23.5 (37.8 km) **D 303.7** (488.7 km) **S 142.7** (229.8 km) Marker shows distance to Dawson City 486 km.

J 26.9 (43.3 km) **D 300.3** (483.3 km) **S 146.1** (235.1 km) Gravel pit turnout to east.

J 28.8 (46.3 km) **D 298.4** (480.2 km) **S 148** (238.2 km) Highway now follows the east shoreline of Fox Lake northbound.

J 29.4 (47.3 km) **D 297.8** (479.2 km) **S 148.6** (239.1 km) Turnout to west on Fox Lake. Historic sign here reads: "In 1883, U.S. Army Lt. Frederick Schwatka completed a survey of the entire length of the Yukon River. One of many geographical features that he named was Fox Lake, which he called Richthofen Lake, after geographer Freiherr Von Richthofen. Known locally as Fox Lake, the name was adopted in 1957. The Miners Range to the west was named by geologist/explorer George Mercer Dawson in 1887 'for the miners met by us along the river.' "

J 34.8 (56 km) **D 292.4** (470.5 km) **S 154** (247.8 km) Turnoff west for **Fox Lake** Yukon government campground; 30 sites, kitchen

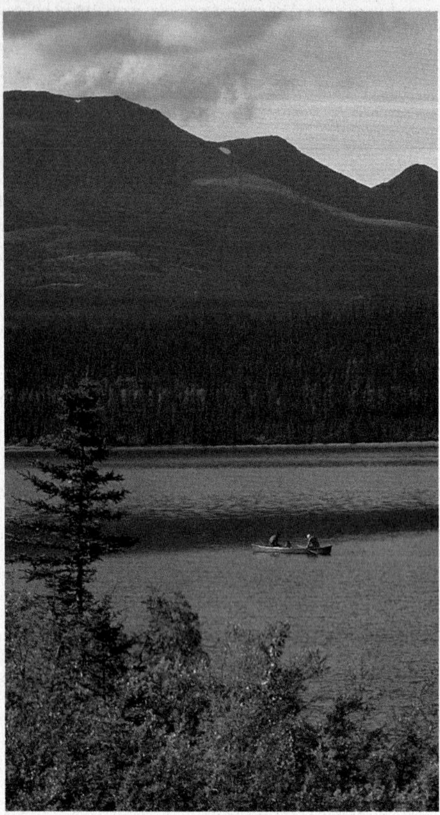

Fox Lake offers excellent grayling fishing. (Earl L. Brown, staff)

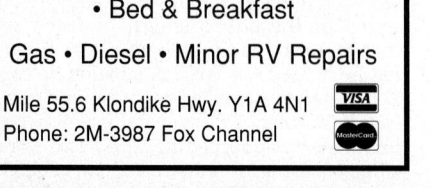

shelter, drinking water and boat launch. Good fishing for lake trout and burbot from the shore at the campground; excellent grayling year-round.

J **35.2** (56.6 km) **D 292** (469.9 km) **S 154.4** (248.5 km) Turnout with view of Fox Lake.

J **39.8** (64 km) **D 287.4** (462.5 km) **S 159** (255.8 km) North end of Fox Lake.

J **42** (67.6 km) **D 285.2** (459 km) **S 161.2** (259.4 km) **Little Fox Lake** to west; lake trout 3 to 8 lbs., fish the islands.

J **43.8** (70.5 km) **D 283.4** (456 km) **S 163** (262.1 km) Turnout with litter barrel to west beside Little Fox Lake. Small boat launch.

J **49.5** (79.7 km) **D 277.7** (446.9 km) **S 168.7** (271.5 km) Large turnout to west.

J **50.1** (80.6 km) **D 277.1** (445.9 km) **S 169.3** (272.4 km) First glimpse of Braeburn Lake for northbound travelers.

J **52.5** (84.5 km) **D 274.7** (442.1 km) **S 171.7** (276.3 km) Gravel pit turnout to east.

J **55.6** (89.5 km) **D 271.6** (437.1 km) **S 174.9** (281.5 km) Braeburn Lodge to west; food, gas, lodging and minor car repairs. One Braeburn Lodge cinnamon bun will feed four.

Braeburn Lodge. See display ad this section.

Private Aircraft: Braeburn airstrip to east, dubbed Cinnamon Bun Strip; elev. 2,350 feet/716m; length 3,000 feet/914m; dirt strip; wind sock.

J **66.3** (106.7 km) **D 260.9** (419.8 km) **S 185.5** (298.5 km) Photo stop; pull-through turnout on east side of highway with information sign about Conglomerate Mountain (elev. 3,361 feet/1,024m). Sign reads: "The Laberge Series was formed at the leading edge of volcanic mud flows some 185 million years ago (Early Jurassic). These flows solidified into sheets several kilometres long and about 1 km wide and 100m thick. This particular series of sheets stretches from Atlin, BC, to north of Carmacks, a distance of about 350 km. Other conglomerates of this series form Five Finger Rapids."

Rock hounds can find pieces of conglomerate in almost any borrow pit along this stretch of highway.

J **71.6** (115.2 km) **D 255.6** (411.3 km) **S 190.8** (307 km) Turnouts on both sides of highway between Twin Lakes. These two small lakes, one on either side of the road, are known for their beauty and colour.

J **72.3** (116.3 km) **D 254.9** (410.2 km) **S 191.5** (308.2 km) Turnoff to west for **Twin Lakes** Yukon government campground; 18 sites, $8 camping fee, drinking water, boat launch. Lake is stocked. Enjoyable fishing for lake trout, grayling and pike. Good swimming for the *hardy!*

J **81.4** (131 km) **D 245.8** (395.5 km) **S 200.6** (323 km) Large turnout with litter barrel to east at remains of Montague House, a typical early-day roadhouse which offered lodging and meals on the stagecoach route between Whitehorse and Dawson City. A total of 52 stopping places along this route were listed in the Jan. 16, 1901, edition of the *Whitehorse Star* under "On the Winter Trail between White Horse and Dawson Good Accommodations for Travellers." Montague House was listed at Mile 99.

J **87.4** (140.6 km) **D 239.8** (385.9 km) **S 206.6** (332.5 km) Small lake to west.

J **101.3** (163 km) **D 225.9** (363.5 km) **S 220.5** (354.8 km) **Nordenskiold River** to west was named by Lt. Frederick Schwatka, U.S. Army, for Swedish arctic explorer Erik Nordenskiold. Good grayling and pike fishing all summer. This river, which parallels the highway for several miles, flows into the Yukon River at Carmacks.

J **101.5** (163.3 km) **D 225.7** (363.2 km) **S 220.7** (355.2 km) Pull-through rest area to east with large mural of *Moment at Tantalus Butte.*

Carmacks

J **102.7** (165.3 km) **D 224.5** (361.3 km) **S 221.9** (357.1 km). Located on the banks of the Yukon River, Carmacks is the only highway crossing of the Yukon River between Whitehorse and Dawson City. **Population:** 424. **Emergency Services: RCMP,** phone 863-5555. **Fire Department,** phone 863-2222. **Nurse,** phone 863-4444. **Ambulance,** phone 1-667-3333.

Private Aircraft: Carmacks airstrip; elev. 1,770 feet/539m; length 5,200 feet/1,585m; gravel; no fuel.

Carmacks was once an important stop for Yukon River steamers traveling between Dawson City and Whitehorse, and it continues as a supply point today for modern river travelers, although Carmacks has survived — while other river ports have not — as a service centre for highway traffic and mining interests. Carmacks was also a main stopping point on the old Whitehorse to Dawson Trail. It was named for George Carmack, whose gold discovery started the Klondike gold rush, and whose roadhouse and coal mining interests here helped establish this settlement. (For more on George Carmack read *Carmack of the Klondike* by James Albert Johnson.)

Traveler facilities include a hotel, motel, restaurant, groceries, gas stations, bakery, and general store and laundromat in Hotel Carmacks. Post office, bank (open three hours a week in summer) and general store are located at the trading post at the north end of the bridge. A visitor information tent at the trading post has some Native crafts for sale. There are churches, a school and community library.

Carmacks Yukon government campground is situated on the banks of the Yukon River; 16 sites, $8 camping fee, resident campground host, kitchen shelter, drinking water and boat launch. Put in and takeout point for Yukon River travelers.

For guided wilderness tours, call 863-5905; boat tours of Five Fingers and Rink Rapids, 863-5001.

Hotel Carmacks. See display ad this section.

Klondike Loop Log
(continued)

J 103.2 (166.1 km) **D 224** (360.5 km) **S 222.4** (357.9 km) Yukon River bridge. Turnout and parking area at south end of bridge; 2.3-mile-/3.7-km-long trail to Coal Mine Lake.

J 103.3 (166.2 km) **D 223.9** (360.3 km) **S 222.5** (358.1 km) Trading post with store and post office at north end of Yukon River bridge. Fishing tackle and licenses available.

Northern Tutchone Trading Post. See display ad this section.

J 104.4 (168 km) **D 222.8** (358.5 km) **S 223.6** (359.8 km) **Junction** with Campbell Highway (Yukon Highway 4), also known as Watson Lake–Carmacks Road, which leads east and south to Faro, Ross River and Watson Lake. See CAMPBELL HIGHWAY section.

J 105.1 (169.1 km) **D 222.1** (357.4 km) **S 224.3** (361 km) Side road east to Tantalus Butte Coal Mine; the coal was used in Cyprus Anvil Mine's mill near Faro for drying concentrates. The butte was named by Lt. Frederick Schwatka because it is seen many times before it is actually reached.

J 105.4 (169.6 km) **D 221.8** (356.9 km) **S 224.6** (361.4 km) Turnout to west with view of Yukon River Valley.

J 108 (173.8 km) **D 219.2** (352.7 km) **S 227.2** (365.3 km) Side road west to agate site for rock hounds.

J 110 (177 km) **D 217.2** (349.5 km) **S 229.2** (368.8 km) Small lake to west.

J 117.5 (189.1 km) **D 209.7** (337.5 km) **S 236.7** (378.5 km) Pull-through rest area to west with toilets, litter barrels and view of Five Finger Rapids. Information sign here reads: "Five Finger Rapids named by early miners for the five channels, or fingers, formed by the rock pillars. They are a navigational hazard. The safest passage is through the nearest, or east, passage." Stairs (219 steps) lead down to a closer view of the rapids.

J 118.9 (191.3 km) **D 208.3** (335.2 km) **S 238.1** (380.6 km) Tatchun Creek. Side road to Five Finger Rapids boat tour operator.

J 119 (191.5 km) **D 208.2** (335 km) **S 238.2** (380.8 km) First turnoff (northbound) to east for **Tatchun Creek** Yukon government campground; 13 sites, $8 camping fee, kitchen shelter and drinking water. Good fishing for grayling, June through September; salmon, July through August. ▲

J 119.1 (191.6 km) **D 208.1** (334.9 km) **S 238.3** (380.9 km) Second turnoff (northbound) east for Tatchun Creek Yukon government campground.

J 119.6 (192.5 km) **D 207.6** (334.1 km) **S 238.8** (381.8 km) Side road leads east to **Tatchun Lake.** Follow side road 4.3 miles/7 km east to boat launch and pit toilets. Continue past boat launch 1.1 miles/1.8 km for Tatchun Lake Yukon government campground with 20 sites, $8 camping fee, pit toilets, firewood, litter barrels and picnic tables. Fishing for northern pike, best in spring or fall. ▲

This maintained side road continues east past Tatchun Lake to Frenchman Lake, then loops south to the Campbell Highway, approximately 25 miles/40 km distance. The main access to Frenchman Lake is from the Campbell Highway.

J 121.8 (196 km) **D 205.4** (330.6 km) **S 241** (388 km) Tatchun Hill.

J 126.6 (203.7 km) **D 200.6** (322.8 km) **S 245.8** (395.8 km) Large turnout overlooking Yukon River.

J 126.9 (204.2 km) **D 200.3** (322.3 km) **S 246.1** (396.3 km) Highway descends hill, northbound. Watch for falling rocks.

J 132 (212.4 km) **D 195.2** (314.1 km) **S 251.2** (404.5 km) McGregor Creek.

J 136.6 (219.8 km) **D 190.6** (306.7 km) **S 255.8** (411.9 km) Good representation of White River ash layer for approximately next mile northbound. Some 1,250 years ago a layer of white volcanic ash coated a third of the southern Yukon, or some 125,000 square miles, and it is easily visible along many roadcuts. This distinct line conveniently provides a division used by archaeologists for dating artifacts: materials found below this major stratigraphic marker are considered to have been deposited before A.D. 700, while those found above the ash layer are postdated A.D. 700. The small amount of data available does not support volcanic activity in the White River area during the same period. One theory is that the ash could have spewn forth from one violent volcanic eruption. The source may be buried under the Klutlan Glacier in the St. Elias Mountains in eastern Alaska.

J 144 (231.7 km) **D 183.2** (294.8 km) **S 263.2** (423.8 km) McCabe Creek.

J 144.1 (231.9 km) **D 183.1** (294.7 km) **S 263.4** (424 km) Midway Lodge (closed in 1993; current status unknown).

J 148 (238.2 km) **D 179.2** (288.4 km) **S 267.2** (430.4 km) **Minto Resorts Ltd. R.V. Park.** 1,400-foot Yukon River frontage. Halfway between Whitehorse and Dawson City on the Old Stage Road, Minto was once a steamboat landing and trading post. 27 sites, wide easy access, picnic tables, firepits, souvenirs, fishing licenses, ice, snacks, pop. Coin-op showers and laundry, clean restrooms, dump station, and water. Bus tour buffet, reservation only. Caravans welcome. Wildlife viewing opportunities. Try fishing the river. Owned and operated by Yukoners. Come and visit us! See display ad this section. [ADVERTISEMENT] ▲

J 148 (238.2 km) **D 179.2** (288.4 km) **S 267.2** (430.4 km) **Pristine River Runs.** See display ad this section.

J 148.6 (239.1 km) **D 178.6** (287.4 km) **S 267.8** (431.4 km) Minto Road, a short loop road, leads west to location of the former riverboat landing and trading post of **MINTO.** Drive in 1.2 miles/2 km for Minto Landing Yukon government campground situated on the scenic, grassy banks of the Yukon River; 10 sites, kitchen shelter and drinking water. Camping fee $8. Large flat grassy area may be used for parking. This campground is used as a put in and takeout site by river travelers. Check with Pristine River Runs about river tours to Sheep Mountain and Fort Selkirk leaving daily from Minto Resorts. ▲

Fort Selkirk, 22 river miles/35 km from here, was established by Robert Campbell in 1848 for the Hudson's Bay Co. In 1852, the fort was destroyed by Chilkat Indians, who had dominated the fur trade of central Yukon until the arrival of the Hudson's Bay Co. The site was occupied sporadically by traders and missionaries until 1950.

Private Aircraft: Minto airstrip; elev. 1,550 feet/472m; length 5,000 feet/1,524m; gravel.

J 160.3 (258 km) **D 166.9** (268.6 km) **S 279.5** (450.5 km) Side road east to Von Wilczek Lakes.

J 163.4 (262.9 km) **D 163.8** (263.6 km) **S 282.6** (455.5 km) Rock Island Lake to east.

J 164.2 (264.2 km) **D 163** (262.3 km) **S 283.4** (456.8 km) Turnout. Small lake to west.

J 168.7 (271.5 km) **D 158.5** (255.1 km) **S 287.9** (464 km) Road west to garbage dump.

J 169.4 (272.6 km) **D 157.8** (253.9 km) **S 288.6** (465 km) Side road to **PELLY CROSSING** (pop. about 230). RCMP, phone 537-5555. There are a nursing station, post office and trading post here, general store with phone, and gas station with unleaded, diesel and tire repair.

This Selkirk Indian community attracted residents from Minto when the highway to Dawson City was built. School, mission and sawmill located near the big bridge. The local economy is based on hunting, trapping, fishing and guiding. The Selkirk

Indian Band has erected signs near the bridge on the history and culture of the Selkirk people.

J 169.7 (273.1 km) **D 157.5** (253.5 km) **S 288.9** (465.5 km) Pelly River bridge.

J 170.4 (274.2 km) **D 156.8** (252.3 km) **S 289.6** (467 km) Turnout with litter barrel to east. View of Pelly Crossing and river valley. A historical marker here honours the Canadian Centennial (1867–1967). The Pelly River was named in 1840 by explorer Robert Campbell for Sir John Henry Pelly, governor of the Hudson's Bay Co. The Pelly heads near the Northwest Territories border and flows approximately 375 miles/600 km to the Yukon River.

J 171.5 (276 km) **D 155.7** (250.5 km) **S 290.7** (468.6 km) **Private Aircraft:** Airstrip to east; elev. 1,870 feet/570m; length 3,000 feet/914m; gravel. No services.

J 179.6 (289 km) **D 147.6** (237.5 km) **S 298.8** (481.7 km) Pull-through turnout to east.

J 180.9 (291.1 km) **D 146.3** (235.4 km) **S 300.1** (483.8 km) Small lake to west.

J 183.8 (295.8 km) **D 143.4** (230.8 km) **S 303** (488.6 km) Large turnout to west. Bridge over Willow Creek.

J 185.5 (298.5 km) **D 141.7** (228 km) **S 304.7** (491.3 km) Side road west to Jackfish Lake.

J 195.6 (314.8 km) **D 131.6** (211.8 km) **S 314.8** (506.6 km) Access road west to **Wrong Lake** (stocked); fishing.

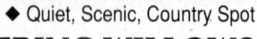

J 197.4 (317.7 km) **D 129.8** (208.9 km) **S 316.6** (511 km) Turnout with litter barrel to west. Winding descent begins for northbound traffic.

J 203.6 (327.6 km) **D 123.6** (198.9 km) **S 322.8** (521 km) Pull-through turnout to east.

J 205.9 (331.3 km) **D 121.3** (195.2 km) **S 325.1** (524.6 km) **Crooked Creek**; pike; grayling, use flies, summer best.

J 207.2 (333.4 km) **D 120** (193.1 km) **S 326.4** (526.7 km) Pull-through turnout with litter barrel to east at turnoff for **Ethel Lake** Yukon government campground. Drive in 16.6 miles/26.7 km on narrow and winding side road (not recommended for large RVs) for campground; 15 sites, boat launch, fishing. Camping fee $8.

J 213.7 (343.9 km) **D 113.5** (182.7 km) **S 332.9** (535.7 km) **Hilda's R.V. Campground** — new for 1994. Level, shaded campsites, pull-through sites, picnic tables and concession. (Sorry — no hookups.) Proposed for 1994 — washrooms and showers. A good spot to take a break on your northern adventure. Reasonable rates. Your host: Hilda Popadynec, phone (403) 996-2714. Mailing address: Box 22, Mayo, Yukon Y0B 1M0. [ADVERTISEMENT]

J 213.8 (344 km) **D 113.4** (182.5 km) **S 333** (537.3 km) Stewart Crossing government maintenance camp to east.

J 213.9 (344.2 km) **D 113.3** (182.3 km) **S 333.1** (537.5 km) Stewart Crossing Lodge (camping, food, lodging) and auto repair/gas station east side of highway, turnout with information sign west side of highway. Silver Trail information booth.

Whispering Willows RV Park and Campground. See display ad this section.

In 1886 Stewart Crossing was the site of a trading post established by Arthur Harper, Alfred Mayo and Jack McQuesten to support gold mining in the area. Later a roadhouse was built here as part of the Whitehorse to Dawson overland stage route. Stewart Crossing also functioned as a fuel stop for the riverboats and during the 1930s was a transfer point for the silver ore barges from Mayo.

Harper, Mayo and McQuesten are three prominent names in Yukon history. Harper, an Irish immigrant, was one of the first white men to prospect in the Yukon, although he never struck it rich. He died in 1898 in Arizona. (His son, Walter Harper, was on the first complete ascent of Mount McKinley in 1913. Walter died in 1918 in the SS *Princess Sophia* disaster off Juneau.)

Mayo, a native of Maine, explored, prospected and traded in the Yukon until his death in 1924. McQuesten, like Harper, worked his way north from the California goldfields. Often referred to as the "Father of the Yukon," Jack Leroy Napoleon McQuesten ended his trading and prospecting days in 1898 when he moved to California. He died in 1909 while in Seattle for the Alaska–Yukon–Pacific Exposition.

J 214.3 (344.9 km) **D 112.9** (181.7 km) **S 333.5** (538 km) Stewart River bridge. The Stewart River flows into the Yukon River upstream from Dawson City.

J 214.4 (345 km) **D 112.8** (181.5 km) **S 333.6** (538.2 km) **Silver Trail (Stewart Crossing) Junction** at north end of Stewart River bridge. Marker shows distance to Dawson 182 km. The Silver Trail information centre is located in the restored Binet House in Mayo; phone 996-2926 in summer. The Silver Trail (Yukon Highway 11) leads northeast to Mayo, Elsa and Keno; see SILVER TRAIL section.

Yukon Gold Explorer's Passports are stamped at the Keno City Mining Museum, one of 13 passport stamp locations.

Silver Trail Tourism Association. See display ad this section.

J 214.8 (345.6 km) **D 112.4** (180.9 km) **S 334** (538.8 km) View to west of Stewart River and mountains as highway climbs northbound.

J 220.8 (355.3 km) **D 106.4** (171.2 km) **S 340** (545.1 km) Dry Creek.

J 224.4 (361.1 km) **D 102.8** (165.4 km) **S 343.6** (556.2 km) Access to Stewart River to west. Historical information sign about Stewart River. A major tributary of the Yukon River, the Stewart River was named for James G. Stewart, who discovered it in 1849. Stewart was at the time assistant to Robert Campbell of the Hudson's Bay Co.

J 229.1 (368.7 km) **D 98.1** (157.8 km) **S 348.3** (561.9 km) **Moose Creek Lodge.** A must for Yukon travelers! An authentic trapper's cabin featuring a large selection of Northern books and gifts. Scrumptious snacks. Meet Max the Mosquito and Murray the Moose! Native tepee. Smokehouse. Cozy log cabins starting at $39. For reservations, dial 1311 and ask for JL3-9570 on Stewart Channel or write, Box 304, Dawson City, Yukon Y0B 1G0. Moose Creek is also serving group tours in their beautiful open-air gazebo, reservations suggested. VISA and MasterCard. [ADVERTISEMENT]

J 229.2 (368.8 km) **D 98** (157.7 km) **S 348.4** (562 km) Moose Creek bridge.

J 229.5 (369.3 km) **D 97.7** (157.2 km) **S 348.7** (562.4 km) Turnout to west at turnoff for Moose Creek Yukon government campground adjacent **Moose Creek** and Stewart River; good picnic spot. There are 30 campsites, six tent sites, kitchen shelter, playground and playfield. Camping fee $8.

Short trail to Stewart River. Good fishing for grayling, 1 to 1¹/₄ lbs.

J 242.7 (390.5 km) D 84.5 (136 km) S 361.9 (583.7 km) McQuesten River, a tributary of the Stewart River, named for Jack (Leroy Napoleon) McQuesten.

J 242.9 (390.9 km) D 84.3 (135.6 km) S 362.1 (584 km) McQuesten, a lodge with cafe, cabins and RV sites. Site of Old McQuesten River Lodge to east.

McQuesten Spruce Grove R.V. See display ad this section.

J 249.3 (401.2 km) D 77.9 (125.4 km) S 368.5 (594 km) **Private Aircraft:** McQuesten airstrip 1.2 miles/1.9 km west; elev. 1,500 feet/457m; length 5,000 feet/1,524m; gravel and turf. No services.

J 251.3 (404.4 km) D 75.9 (122.1 km) S 370.5 (596.5 km) Clear Creek, access via side road west.

J 260.4 (419.1 km) D 66.8 (107.5 km) S 379.6 (612 km) Barlow Lake, access via 0.6-mile-/1-km-long side road west.

J 263.7 (424.4 km) D 63.5 (102.2 km) S 382.9 (617.2 km) Beaver Dam Creek.

J 266 (428 km) D 61.2 (98.5 km) S 385.2 (621 km) Willow Creek.

J 268.5 (432.1 km) D 58.7 (94.5 km) S 387.7 (625 km) Flat Hill.

J 268.8 (432.5 km) D 58.4 (94 km) S 388 (625.5 km) Gravel Lake to east.

J 272.1 (437.9 km) D 55.1 (88.6 km) S 391.3 (630.8 km) Meadow Creek.

J 272.5 (438.5 km) D 54.7 (88 km) S 391.7 (631.4 km) Rest area with litter barrel to south.

J 276.5 (445 km) D 50.7 (81.6 km) S 395.7 (637.9 km) French Creek.

J 279.7 (450.1 km) D 47.5 (76.4 km) S 398.9 (643.1 km) Stone Boat Swamp.

J 288.9 (464.9 km) D 38.3 (61.6 km) S 408.1 (657.9 km) Rest area.

J 289.3 (465.5 km) D 37.9 (61 km) S 408.5 (658.5 km) Geologic point of interest turnout to east overlooking Tintina Trench. This geologic feature, which extends hundreds of miles across Yukon and Alaska, provides visible proof of plate tectonics.

J 295.1 (474.9 km) D 32.1 (51.6 km) S 414.3 (667.8 km) Flat Creek.

J 295.9 (476.2 km) D 31.3 (50.4 km) S 415.1 (669 km) Klondike River to east.

J 297.6 (478.9 km) D 29.6 (47.6 km) S 416.8 (671.9 km) Large turnout to east with historic sign about Klondike River and information sign on Dempster Highway.

J 298 (479.5 km) D 29.2 (47 km) S 417.2 (672.5 km) Watch for livestock.

J 301.6 (485.3 km) D 25.6 (41.2 km) S 420.8 (678.5 km) **Junction** of Klondike Highway and the Dempster Highway (Dempster Corner). Klondike River Lodge east side of highway just north of the junction; open year-round, food, lodging, gas, diesel and propane. The Dempster Highway leads northeast to Inuvik, NWT. See DEMPSTER HIGHWAY section for log of that road. (Details on the Dempster are also available from the Western Arctic Information Centre in Dawson City.)

Klondike River Lodge. See display ad this section.

J 307.3 (494.5 km) D 19.9 (32 km) S 426.5 (687.4 km) Goring Creek.

J 308.4 (496.3 km) D 18.8 (30.2 km) S 427.6 (689.2 km) Turnout to north with access to the Klondike River.

J 312.1 (502.2 km) D 15.1 (24.3 km) S 431.3 (695.1 km) Rock Creek Store.

J 315.2 (507.2 km) D 12 (19.3 km) S 434 (700 km) Turnoff to north for Klondike River Yukon government campground, located on Rock Creek near the Klondike River; 38 sites, kitchen shelter, drinking water, playground. Camping fee $8.

J 315.7 (508 km) D 11.5 (18.5 km) S 434.9 (700.8 km) Dawson City airport to south. **Private Aircraft:** Runway 02-20; elev. 1,211 feet/369m; length 5,000 feet/1,524m; gravel; fuel 80 (in drums at Dawson City), 100, JP4. Flightseeing trips and air charters available.

J 317.1 (510.3 km) D 10.1 (16.3 km) S 436.3 (703.4 km) Hunker Creek Road to south.

J 318.4 (512.4 km) D 8.8 (14.2 km) S 437.6 (705.4 km) Turnout to south with point of interest sign about Hunker Creek. Albert Hunker staked the first claim on Hunker Creek Sept. 11, 1896. George Carmack made the big discovery on Bonanza Creek on Aug. 17, 1896. Hunker Creek is 16 miles/26 km long, of which 13 miles/21 km was dredged between 1906 and 1966.

J 318.9 (513.2 km) D 8.3 (13.4 km) S 438.1 (706.1 km) Bear Creek Road to south.

J 319.6 (514.3 km) D 7.6 (12.2 km) S 438.8 (707.2 km) Turnout with historic sign about the Yukon Ditch and tailings to north. To the south is Bear Creek historical site, operated by Parks Canada. Open 9:30 A.M. to 5 P.M. daily in summer. This 62-acre compound of the Yukon Consolidated Gold Corp. features a complete blacksmith shop, machinery shop and gold room.

J 323.3 (520.3 km) D 3.9 (6.3 km) S 442.5 (712 km) Callison industrial area; charter helicopter service, bulk fuel plant and heavy equipment repairs.

Versatile Welding and Mechanical Repairs. See display ad this section.

J 324.5 (522.2 km) D 2.7 (4.3 km) S 443.7 (714 km) Bonanza Creek Road to Discovery Claim and historic Dredge No. 4, largest wooden hull dredge in North America. Restoration of the dredge is under way. Interpretive centre on site; tours 9 A.M. to 5 P.M. daily June through August. Bonanza Creek Road is maintained for 10 miles/16 km. Commercial RV park and gold panning at junction.

GuggieVille. Good Sam. This clean, attractive campground is built on dredge tailings at the former site of the Guggenheim's mining camp. 72 RV sites with water and electricity ($13.75), 28 unserviced sites ($8.75), public showers ($2 each). Rates include tax. Car wash, dump station and

laundromat are available. A mining display features gas diggers, a hand-built bulldozer, wagons and ore cars are open to the public free of charge. Gold panning discount for those staying at GuggieVille. Owners sell gold from their placer mine. Phone (403) 993-5008. Fax (403) 993-5006. [ADVERTISEMENT]

J 324.6 (522.4 km) D 2.6 (4.2 km) S 443.8 (714.2 km) **Trail of '98 Restaurant and Mini-Golf.** Home-style cafe features local dishes, homemade bread, daily spe-

cials, friendly service and economical prices. Cabins, RV parking, tent sites, gift shop, cafe and ice cream. Rustic log cabins, quiet and

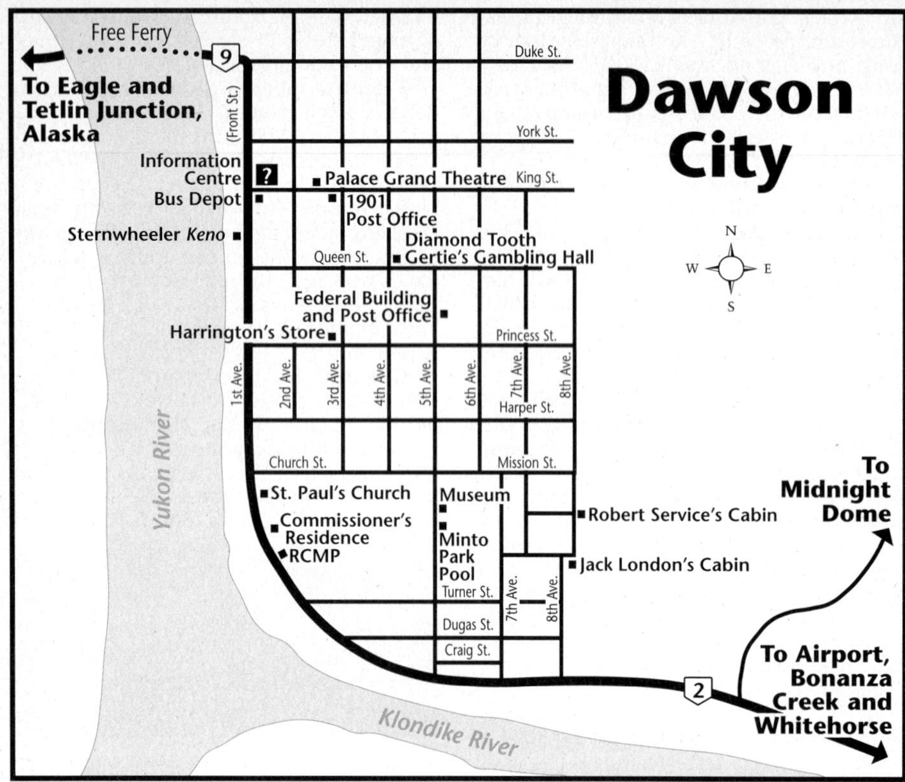

Dawson City has lost more than 50 historic buildings to fires, flood and demolition in past years. A dike protects downtown from flooding.

J 324.7 (522.5 km) **D 2.5** (4 km) **S 443.9** (715.3 km) Campground, gas station and store. ▲

Dawson City R.V. Park & Campground and **Bonanza Shell.** See display ad on page 241. ▲

J 324.8 (522.7 km) **D 2.4** (3.9 km) **S 444** (715.5 km) Klondike River bridge.

J 325.3 (523.5 km) **D 1.9** (3.1 km) **S 444.5** (716.4 km) Large turnout with information sign and map.

J 325.8 (524.3 km) **D 1.4** (2.3 km) **S 445** (717.2 km) Dome Road to north leads 5.7 miles/9.2 km to Dome Mountain (elev. 2,592 feet/790m), which offers views of Dawson City, the Yukon and Klondike rivers, Bonanza Creek and the Ogilvie Mountains.

J 326.1 (524.8 km) **D 1.1** (1.8 km) **S 445.3** (717.7 km) Fifth Avenue. Turnout with sign about the Klondike River to south: "With headwaters in the Ogilvie Mountains, the Klondike River and its tributaries gave birth to the world's greatest gold rush — the Klondike Gold Rush of '98."

J 327.2 (526.5 km) **D 0 S 446.4** (719.5 km) Dawson City, ferry at Yukon River. *Description of Dawson City follows.* *Log of Klondike Loop continues page 249.*

Dawson City

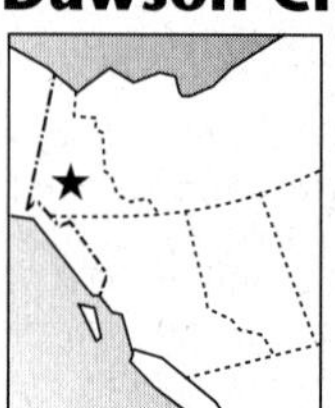

J 327.2 (526.5 km) **D 0 S 446.4** (719.5 km) Located 165 miles/266 km south of the Arctic Circle on the Yukon River at its junction with the Klondike River. **Population:** 1,852. **Emergency Services: RCMP,** 1st Avenue S., phone 993-5555. **Fire Department**, phone 993-2222. **Nursing station**, phone 993-4444. **Ambulance**, phone 1-667-3333.

Visitor Information: At Front and King streets, in a replica of the 1897 Alaska Commercial Co. store. Yukon information and a Dawson City street map are available. Video disks on a variety of subjects. Walking tours are part of the daily schedule. Open 9 A.M. to 9 P.M. daily, mid-May to mid-September, phone 993-5566, fax 993-6449.

The Dempster Highway and Northwest Territories Information Centre is located in the B.Y.N. (British Yukon Navigation) Bldg. on Front Street, across from the Yukon visitor centre; open 9 A.M. to 9 P.M., June to September. Information on Northwest Territories and the Dempster Highway. Phone (403) 993-6167.

Elevation: 1,050 feet/320m. **Climate:** There are 20.9 hours of daylight June 21, 3.8 hours of daylight on Dec. 21. Mean high in July, 72°F/22.2°C. Mean low in January, -30.5°F/-31.1°C. First fall frost end of August, last spring frost end of May. Annual snowfall 59.8 inches/151.8 cm. **Radio:** CBC 560; CFYT-FM 106, CKYN-FM 96.1 (summer visitor station). **Television:** CBC Anik Channel 7 and four other channels. **Newspaper:** *Klondike Sun* (monthly).

Private Aircraft: Dawson City airport located 11.5 miles/18.5 km southeast (see

Milepost J 315.7). Customs available.

Originally laid out to serve 30,000 people, Dawson City today still occupies much of the original townsite but with only a fraction of the buildings and people, although in the summer the city is crowded with visitors and with miners headed for the goldfields.

Historically, Dawson City dates from the discovery of gold on a Klondike River tributary (Rabbit Creek, renamed Bonanza Creek) in 1896. According to the Klondike Centennial Society, this was the richest gold strike ever in North America; gold is still being mined here. There were several hundred prospectors in the region before the big strike, and most of them swarmed over the creeks staking claims long before the stampeders began trickling into the country the following year.

Of the several routes followed by the hordes of gold seekers, most famous was the Trail of '98: by ship from Seattle to Skagway, AK, then over the ice and snow of Chilkoot Pass or White Pass to Lakes Lindeman and Bennett, then down the Yukon River to Dawson City by boat.

There were other routes as difficult. The longest was the all-water route by ocean steamer around Alaska's west coast to the port of St. Michael at the mouth of the 2,000-mile-/3,219-km-long Yukon River, followed by the long voyage upriver by stern-wheeler to Dawson.

The townsite was prepared by Joe Ladue, a trader and sawmill operator, and surveyed by William Ogilvie. The town was named for George Mercer Dawson of the Geological Survey of Canada. Trading companies moved to Dawson City from Forty Mile and Circle City and established warehouses along the waterfront. Food and mining supplies sufficient for their normal trade with Indian trappers and the 200 white men in the watershed at the time were not enough for the masses of people who had arrived by winter 1897. While additional steamers did start for Dawson City from St. Michael with extra cargo, at least three were frozen into the ice 200 miles/322 km before reaching their goal and forced to remain until the ice went out in May 1898. Men who said that gold would buy anything had not reckoned with Dawson City in 1897 — which had nothing to sell.

The next summer, when the great rush to the Klondike got into full swing, there was sufficient shipping to move the freight required to create a city in a wilderness where every stick, nail and scrap of paper had to be brought in. By 1900 Dawson City was the largest city west of Winnipeg and north of San Francisco.

These were the conditions and the days that built Dawson City. They prevailed until 1903, when stampedes to Nome and other Alaska points drew off the froth from

Dawson society, leaving a sturdy government-cum-mining fraternity that maintained an aura of big city worldliness until WWI.

In later years, Dawson City nearly became a ghost town. Each year a few more buildings were abandoned by owners. They did, however, keep possession by paying their taxes. With the tenacity of Yukoners "keen to find the gold," some still maintain their ownership today, allowing the buildings to deteriorate to shabbiness. Since they were privately owned, no one could use, repair or maintain them. Until recently the city of Dawson could not protect them. Fire and vandals destroyed many; neglect and permafrost have caused others to topple.

By 1953, Whitehorse — on the railway and the highway, and with a large airport — was so much the hub of activity that the federal government moved the capital from Dawson City, along with 800 civil servants, and years of tradition and pride. Some recompense was offered in the form of a road linking Whitehorse with the mining at Mayo and Dawson City. With its completion, White Pass trucks replaced White Pass steamers and that great highway, the Yukon River.

New government buildings were built in Dawson, including a fire hall. In 1962 the federal government reconstructed the Palace Grand Theatre for a gold rush festival that featured the Broadway musical, *Foxy,* with Bert Lahr. A museum was established in the Administration Bldg. and tours and entertainments were begun, which continue today.

Dawson City was declared a national historic site in the early 1960s. Parks Canada is currently involved with 35 properties in Dawson City. Many buildings will be restored, some reconstructed and others stabilized. Parks Canada offers a full interpretive program each summer for visitors to this historic city.

From 1993 to 2002, Dawson City is hosting a "Decade of Centennials." Highlights will include the centennials of the Northwest Mounted Police in 1995, the discovery of gold in 1996, and the great Klondike gold rush in 1998. For further information, contact the Klondike Centennial Society, Bag 1996, Dawson City, Yukon Y0B 1G0.

ACCOMMODATIONS

Accustomed to a summer influx of visitors, Dawson has modern hotels and motels (rates average $75 and up) and several bed and breakfasts. The community has a bank, restaurants, five laundromats (four with showers), two grocery stores (with bakeries), general stores, souvenir shops, churches, post office, government offices, government liquor store, information centre, swimming pool and plenty of entertainment. Dawson City's hotels and motels fill up early, especially at times of special events. Reservations are a must from June through August.

Dawson City Bed & Breakfast. AAA-approved. Located in a quiet setting at the junction of the Klondike and Yukon rivers. Northern hospitality with an Oriental theme. Walking distance to downtown attractions. Complimentary airport, bus and waterfront transportation provided. Open year-round. Reservations recommended. Single $59, double $69, queen with private bathroom $79. (10 percent discount for seniors with reservations). VISA and MasterCard. Includes full continental breakfast. Member, Northern Network of B&B. Send for free brochure package. Box 954, 451 Craig St., Dawson City, YT Y0B 1G0. Phone (403) 993-5649, Fax (403) 993-5648. [ADVERTISEMENT]

5th Avenue Bed and Breakfast. Located adjacent to the museum overlooking Victory Gardens. A modern home with a historic finish, serving a hearty, healthy, all-you-can-eat breakfast. We guarantee comfort, cleanliness and courteous service along with the most convenient location in town. VISA. Call or write Larry and Pat Vezina, Box 722, Dawson City, YT Y0B 1G0. Phone (403) 993-5941. [ADVERTISEMENT]

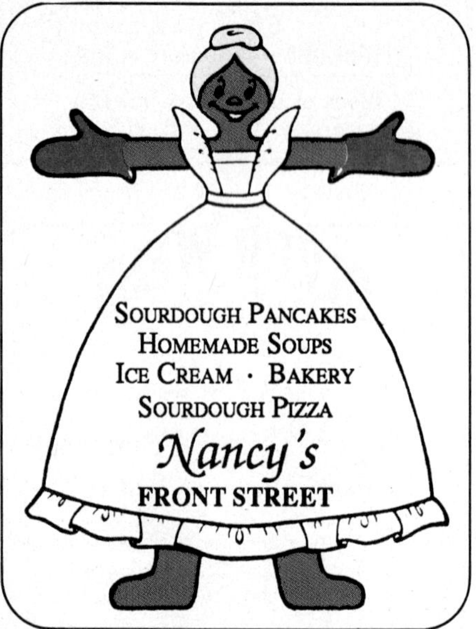

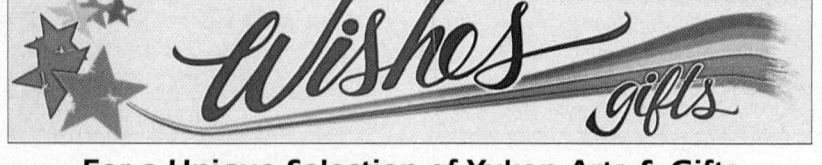

Northern Comfort Bed & Breakfast. Enjoy Northern comfort and hospitality within easy walking distance of all major Dawson City attractions. The Hunston family welcomes you. We have a separate three-room suite, complete with private bathroom, for your convenience. Reservations recommended. Families welcome. Babysitting service is available at reasonable rates. Box 135, Dawson City, YT Y0B 1G0. Phone (403) 993-5271. [ADVERTISEMENT]

White Ram Manor Bed & Breakfast, at 7th and Harper. (Look for the "pink" house.) Come stay with us while you take in Dawson's many attractions. Meet other guests and share your Northern experiences. Hot tub and barbecue area. Canoe rentals available from Up North. Reservations recommended. VISA, MasterCard. Call or write John/Gail Hendley, Box 302, Dawson City, YT Y0B 1G0. (403) 993-5772. Fax (403) 993-6509. [ADVERTISEMENT]

Arctic Cotton. Known throughout the Yukon for being the "best T-shirt shop" and offering the most unusual gifts. Exclusive designs by local artist Merlin M. Grade silkscreened on superior quality shirts. Located in a beautiful turn-of-the-century building on 2nd Avenue, between Queen and King streets, adjacent Madame Zoom's Ice Cream Parlour. Open seven days a week. 10 A.M. to 6 P.M. Phone (403) 993-5549, fax (403) 993-6620. [ADVERTISEMENT]

Madame Zoom's Ice Cream Parlour, featuring fine gourmet ice cream, and natural yogurt ice cream made with real fruit. Come in, sit down and enjoy the best coffee and cake in town. We're next to Arctic Cotton, the "best T-shirt shop" in the Yukon. Open every day from 11 A.M. to 11 P.M. Come see us after visiting the famous Palace Grand Theatre across the street. [ADVERTISEMENT]

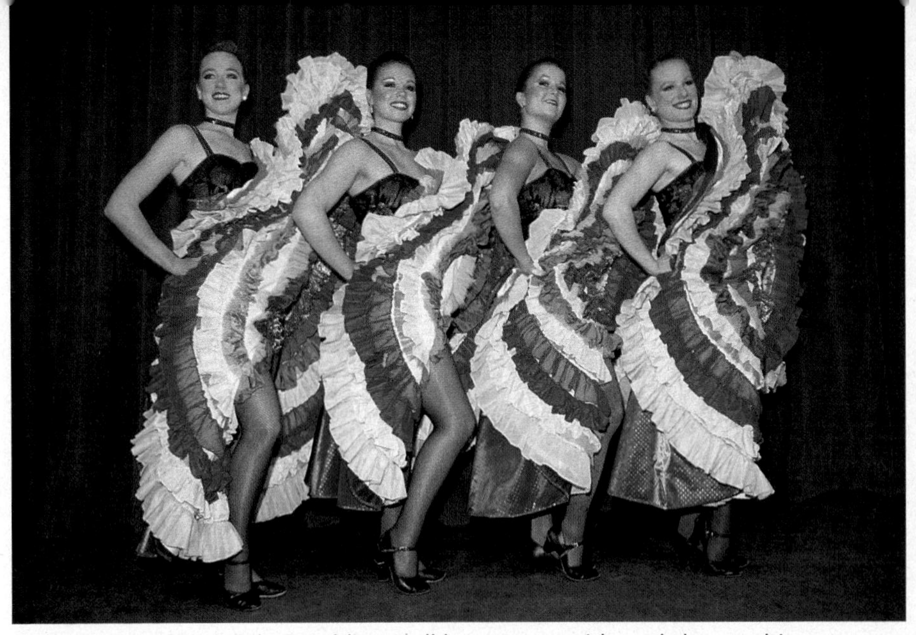

Diamond Tooth Gertie's Gambling Hall has cancan girls and slot machines.
(Philip and Karen Smith)

Blattler Services. Located in the Callison Industrial Subdivision. The public is served by certified mechanics for automotive, heavy equipment and recreational vehicle repairs, along with tire repair and 24-hour towing services. National Auto League–approved roadside service. Phone (403) 993-6232, fax (403) 993-6744. VISA accepted. Open year-round for your convenience. [ADVERTISEMENT]

There are two Yukon government (YTG) campgrounds in the Dawson area. Yukon River YTG campground is across the Yukon River (by ferry) from town, adjacent the west side ferry approach. Klondike River YTG campground is southeast of town near the airport (see **Milepost J 315.2**). Private RV parks in the Dawson area include Gold Rush Campground, downtown at 5th and York; GuggieVille, east of town at **Milepost**

J 324.5; Trail of '98 Mini-Golf at **Milepost J 324.6**; and Dawson City R.V. Park and Campground at **Milepost J 324.7.** ▲

TRANSPORTATION

Air: Dawson City airport is 11.5 miles/ 18.5 km southeast of the city. Alkan Air provides scheduled service to Inuvik, NWT, Old Crow, Mayo and Whitehorse. Air North connects Dawson City with Whitehorse (daily service in summer); with Old Crow and Juneau (three times weekly in summer); and Fairbanks (four times weekly in summer). Charter and flightseeing tours available from Bonanza Aviation. Helicopter tours from Trans North Air, Fireweed and Capital Helicopters.

Ferry: The Yukon government operates a free 24-hour ferry, the *George Black,* across the Yukon River from about the third week in May to mid-October (depending upon breakup and freezeup); ferry departs Dawson City on demand. The ferry carries vehicles and passengers across to the public campground and is the only connection to the Top of the World Highway (Yukon Highway 9).

Taxi: Airport taxi service available from downtown hotels. Scheduled and charter limo service available from Gold City Tours.

Bus: Service between Whitehorse and Dawson City, and to Inuvik, NWT (check with Gold City Tours).

Boat: Service to Eagle, AK, on the *Yukon Queen.* Canoe rentals available from Dawson Trading Post and White Ram Manor Bed & Breakfast.

ATTRACTIONS

Take a Walking Tour. Town core tours leave the visitor reception centre several times daily in summer. The Fort Herchmer walking tour starts at the Commissioner's Residence on Front Street. This handsome building was once the residence of Hon. George Black, M.P., Speaker of the House of Commons, and his famous wife, Martha Louise, who walked in over the Trail of '98 and stayed to become the First Lady of the Yukon. (For the complete and fascinating story of Martha Louise Black, read *Martha Black*; available in bookstores.) Pick up a schedule of daily events at the visitor reception centre.

Take a Bus Tour. Motorcoach and van tours of Klondike creeks, goldfields and Dawson City are available; inquire at Gold City Tours. For a panoramic view of Dawson City, the Klondike, Bonanza Creek and Yukon River, take the bus or drive your vehicle the 5 miles/8 km up to Midnight Dome mountain (elev. 3,050 feet/930m).

Take a River Tour: Tours aboard the miniature stern-wheeler launch *Yukon Lou* leave the dock below SS *Keno* at 1 P.M. daily in summer, and travel to Pleasure Island and the stern-wheeler graveyard. Cruise takes one and one-half hours. Westours operates the *Yukon Queen* between Dawson and Eagle; check with the Westmark about tickets. One-way and round-trip passage is sold on a space-available basis. The trip takes four hours downstream to Eagle, six hours back to Dawson.

Two- to seven-day cruises from Dawson to Eagle or Dawson to Circle are offered beginning in 1994 by Alaska Yukon Sternwheeler Co. The adventurous are invited to travel as deck passengers and pitch tents on the shore in the evening.

Cruise the Yukon River. Cruise from Dawson City down the famous Yukon River to Eagle, Alaska. Retrace the old sternwheeler route of this historic Gold Rush area as you cruise past abandoned settlements among the forested hills. A hearty prospector's meal is included. Daily departures. Roundtrip fare is $130 per person. Call (403) 993-5599. [ADVERTISEMENT]

Protect our environment. Don't litter.

Dawson City still occupies much of the original townsite.

Pleasure Island Restaurant and Yukon River Cruises. Don't miss this relaxing dinner and riverboat cruise. Travel aboard the MV *Yukon Lou* past the stern-wheeler graveyard and ancient village of Moosehide, to an island lodge. Experience a home-cooked all-you-can-eat king salmon dinner, caught fresh and delicately smoked, then barbecued to perfection. Dinner includes slow-baked potatoes, fresh biscuits, and garden fresh salad, topped off by mouthwatering chocolate cake and fresh-ground coffee! Grilled steak is available on request. Returns in time for the Palace Grand. For reservations: (403) 993-5482 (May–Sept.) or (907) 488-4602 (Sept.–May). Group rates. [ADVERTISEMENT]

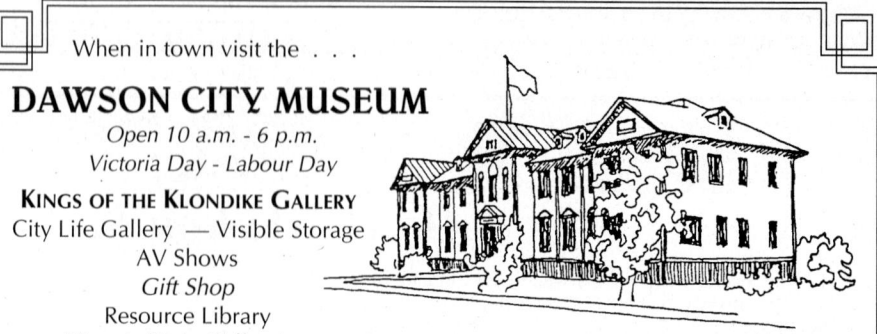

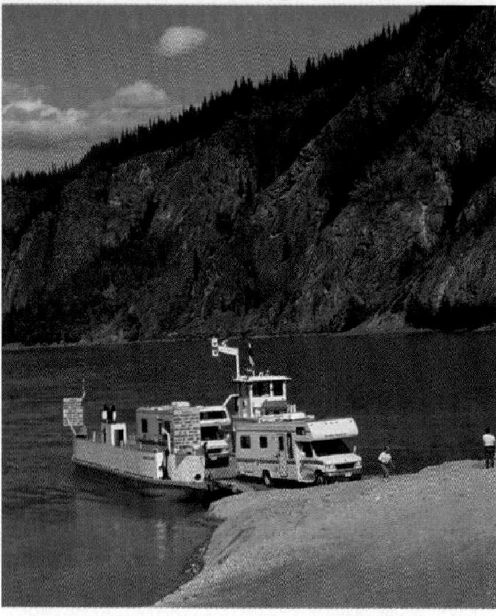

A free ferry crosses the Yukon River to Highway 9. (Earl L. Brown, staff)

Visit the Palace Grand Theatre. This magnificently reconstructed theatre, now a national historic site, is home to the "Gaslight Follies," a turn-of-the-century entertainment. Performances nightly except Tuesday, from late May to early September.

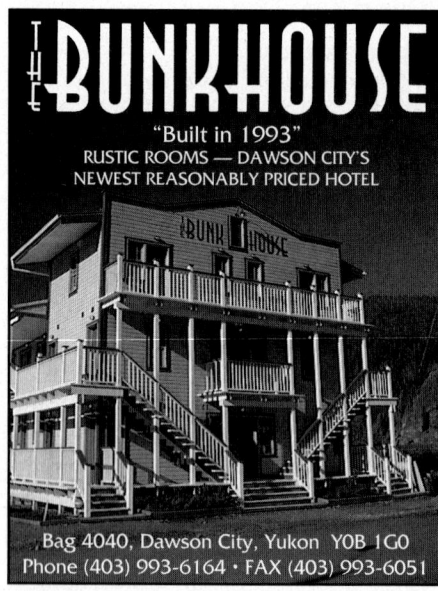

Arizona Charlie Meadows opened the Palace Grand in 1899, and today's visitors, sitting in the curtained boxes around the balcony, will succumb to the charm of this beautiful theatre. Tours of the building are conducted daily by Parks Canada, June through September. Films and presentations daily in summer.

Gamble. Klondike Visitors Assoc. (a non-profit community organization) operates Diamond Tooth Gertie's Gambling Hall, open May 14 to Sept. 24, 1994. There are Klondike gambling tables (specially licensed in Yukon), 52 "Vegas-style" slot machines, bar service and floor shows nightly. You may have a soft drink if you prefer, and still see the cancan girls present their floor show. Persons under 19 not admitted. Gertie's hosts Yukon Talent Night Aug. 28, 1994.

Visit the Dawson City Museum. Housed in the renovated Territorial Administration Bldg. on 5th Avenue, the museum is open daily from 10 A.M. to 6 P.M., June through Labour Day; by appointment the rest of the year. Featured are the Kings of the Klondike and City Life Galleries, daily audiovisual shows and the museum's collection of narrow-gauge locomotives, including a Vauclain-type Baldwin engine, the last one in existence. Weekly lecture series during summer; check for schedule. The slide show *Dawson City at -40°* is shown daily. A selection of silent film serials, news and documentary reels from 1903 to 1929, is also shown.

The museum has a gift shop, resource library, genealogy service and an extensive photography collection. A nominal admission fee is charged. For more information write the museum at P.O. Box 303, Dawson City, YT Y0B 1G0; phone (403) 993-5291, fax (403) 993-5839.

SS *Keno* National Historic Site. The SS *Keno* was the last steamer to run the Yukon River when she sailed from Whitehorse in 1960 to her present berth on the riverbank next to the bank. Although she is closed to the public while under stabilization, an interpretive display is set up beside the site.

Historic Harrington's Store, 3rd Avenue and Princess Street, houses a photographic exhibit entitled *Dawson As They Saw It.* Open daily; no admission charged.

Visit Robert Service's Cabin: On the hillside on 8th Avenue, the author–bank clerk's cabin has been restored by Parks Canada. Stories and poetry recitals (by actor Tom Byrne) are offered daily in summer at 10 A.M. and 3 P.M. Visitors come from every part of the world to sign the guest book on the rickety desk where Service wrote his famous poems, including *The Shooting of Dan McGrew* and *The Cremation of Sam McGee*. Open 9 A.M. to noon and 1-5 P.M. daily. No admission charged.

Visit the Historic Post Office, where you may buy stamps; all first-class mail sent from here receives the old hand cancellation stamp. Open daily.

Fire Fighters Museum, located at the fire hall at 5th Avenue and King Street, is open Monday through Saturday, 11 A.M. to 5 P.M.

Visit Jack London's Cabin: Along 8th Avenue and past Service's home is Jack London's cabin, built from half of the logs saved from the original cabin in the Bush where the writer stayed on his way to the Klondike. (The rest of the logs were used to build an identical cabin in Jack London Square in Oakland, CA.) Interpretation daily at 1 P.M. No admission charged. Dick North, author of *The Lost Patrol* and *The Mad Trapper of Rat River,* is curator and consultant at Jack London's cabin.

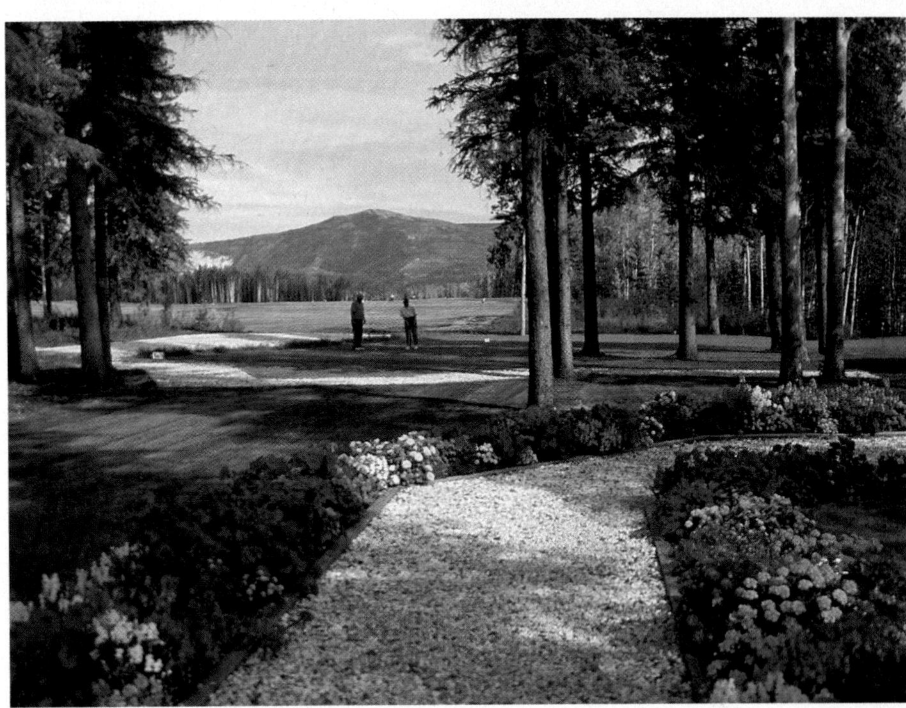

New nine-hole golf course near Dawson City. (Earl L. Brown, staff)

Special Events. Dawson City hosts a number of unique and unusual celebrations during the year. The Commissioner's Ball is held June 4, 1994. This gala event, commemorating Yukon becoming a territory in 1898, features turn-of-the-century fashion. The Yukon Gold Panning Championship is held July 1 each year in Dawson City. (For long-range planners, the World Gold Panning competition is scheduled to return to Dawson City in 1996.) Then on July 23, 1994, it's the international Midnight Dome Race, which attracts over 200 runners each year from all over the world. The 4.6-mile/7.4-km course rises a total elevation of 1,850 feet/564m.

The 15th Annual Dawson City Music Festival, scheduled for July 22–24, 1994, features entertainers and artists from Canada and the United States, free workshops, dances and dinners. Tickets and information in advance from the Music Festival Assoc., Box 456, Dawson City, YT Y0B 1G0. Phone (403) 993-5584.

If you are near Dawson Aug. 12–15, 1994, be sure to join the Discovery Days fun when Yukon Order of Pioneers stage their annual parade, and the town is packed with Yukoners for ball games and dances and a rare old time. This event is a Yukon holiday commemorating the Klondike gold discovery of Aug. 17, 1896.

The Great Klondike International Outhouse Race, held the Sunday of Labour Day weekend (Sept. 4, 1994), is a race of outhouses (on wheels) over a 3-km course through the streets of Dawson City. The International Dart Tournament is held the second weekend of September.

See the Midnight Sun: If you are in Dawson on June 21, be sure to make it to the top of the Dome by midnight, when the sun barely dips behind the 6,000-foot/1,829-m Ogilvie Mountains to the north — the picture of a lifetime. There's quite a local celebration up on the Dome June 21, so for those who don't like crowds, a visit before or after summer solstice will also afford fine views and photos. Turnoff for Midnight Dome mountain is at **Milepost J 325.8**; it's about a 5-mile/8-km drive.

Pan for Gold: The chief attraction for most visitors is panning for gold. There are several mining operations set up to permit you to actually pan for your own "colours" under friendly guidance. Take Bonanza Creek Road from **Milepost J 324.5** up famous Bonanza Creek, past No. 4 Dredge, Discovery Claim and miles of gravel tailings worked over two and three times in the continuing search for gold. The Klondike Visitors Assoc. sponsors a public panning area at No. 6 above Discovery, 13 miles/21 km from Dawson City on Bonanza Creek Road.

Bear Creek Camp, about 7 miles/11 km southeast of the city on the Klondike Highway, was operated by Yukon Consolidated Gold Corp. until 1966. Tours are conducted by Parks Canada interpreters; check with the information centre for current tour schedule. The compound features the Gold Room, where the gold was melted and poured into bricks, complete blacksmith and machinery shops, and other well-preserved structures. Open 9:30 A.M. to 5 P.M. from mid-June to late August. No admission charged.

Klondike Loop Log

(continued)

YUKON HIGHWAY 9

The Top of the World Highway (Yukon Highway 9) connects Dawson City with the Taylor Highway in Alaska. A free ferry carries

Remote Top of the World Highway winds along above tree line. (Philip and Karen Smith)

passengers and vehicles from Dawson City across the Yukon River to the beginning of the Top of the World Highway. The Alaska Highway is 176.6 miles/284.2 km from here; Eagle, AK, is 146.2 miles/235.3 km from here. Allow plenty of time for this drive; average speed for this road is 25 to 40 mph/ 40 to 64 kmph. DRIVE WITH YOUR HEADLIGHTS ON! Yukon Highway 9 and the Taylor Highway (Alaska Route 5) in Alaska are closed from fall freezeup to spring breakup.

IMPORTANT: U.S. and Canada customs are open from about May 15 to Sept. 15 for 12 hours a day. (1993 hours were 9 A.M. to 9 P.M. Pacific time on the Canadian side; 8 A.M. to 8 P.M. Alaska time.) Check with the RCMP or visitor information centre in Dawson City to make certain the border crossing at Milepost D 67 will be open. Serious fines are levied for crossing the border without clearing customs!

This section of the log shows distance from Dawson City (D) followed by distance from junction with the Taylor Highway (T) at Jack Wade Junction. Physical kilometreposts show distance from Dawson City.

D 0 T 78.8 (126.9 km) **DAWSON CITY.** Free ferry crosses the Yukon River daily in summer.

D 0.2 (0.3 km) T 78.6 (126.5 km) Yukon River government campground on riverbank opposite Dawson City; 76 sites, 20 tent sites, two kitchen shelters, playground and drinking water. Camping fee $8. Within walking distance of stern-wheeler graveyard. Put in and takeout spot for Yukon River travelers.▲

D 2.7 (4.4 km) T 76.1 (122.5 km) Access to nine-hole golf course via 3.2-mile/5.2-km gravel road; rentals.

D 2.9 (4.6 km) T 75.9 (122.1 km) Turnout for viewpoint overlooking Dawson City and the Yukon and Klondike rivers.

D 3.2 (5 km) T 75.6 (121.7 km) Turnout with good view of Yukon River and river valley farms.

D 9 (12.4 km) T 69.8 (112.3 km) Rest area with pit toilets, picnic tables, litter barrels and information sign.

D 11 (15.6 km) **T 67.8** (109.1 km) "Top of the World" view as highway climbs above tree line.

D 16.4 (26.2 km) **T 62.4** (100.4 km) Snow fence along highway next 8 miles/13 km westbound.

D 18.4 (29.4 km) **T 60.4** (97.2 km) Large turnout on left.

D 29.2 (47 km) **T 49.6** (79.8 km) Evidence of 1989 burn.

D 32.1 (51.2 km) **T 46.7** (75.1 km) First outcropping (westbound) of Castle Rock. Turnout to south with panoramic view of countryside.

D 33.1 (52.8 km) **T 45.7** (73.5 km) Distance marker shows customs 52 km, Dawson City 53 km.

D 35.2 (56 km) **T 43.6** (70.2 km) Main outcropping of Castle Rock; lesser formations are also found along this stretch. Centuries of erosion have created these formations. Turnout on left westbound.

D 37.4 (59 km) **T 41.8** (67.3 km) Unmaintained road leads 25 miles/40.2 km to the former settlement of Clinton Creek, which served the Cassiar Asbestos Mine from 1967–79. There are no facilities or services available there. Distance marker shows U.S. border 43 km.

The confluence of the Yukon and Fortymile rivers is 3 miles/4.8 km below the former townsite of Clinton Creek. Clinton Creek bridge is an access point on the Fortymile National Wild and Scenic River system, managed by the Bureau of Land Management. The Fortymile River offers intermediate and advanced canoeists over 100 miles/160 km of challenging water.

Yukon River, near Clinton Creek, grayling to 3 lbs. in April; chum salmon to 12 lbs. in August; king salmon to 40 lbs., July and August. **Fortymile River**, near Clinton Creek, grayling to 3 lbs. during ice breakup and fall freezeup; inconnu (sheefish) to 10 lbs. in July and August.

D 41 (66 km) **T 37.8** (60.9 km) *NOTE: Road construction scheduled westbound for 5 miles/8 km in 1994.*

D 54 (85.6 km) **T 24.8** (39.9 km) Old sod-roofed cabin on right westbound, originally a supply and stopping place for the McCormick Transportation Co.

D 54.3 (86.1 km) **T 24.5** (39.4 km) Road forks left westbound to old mine workings at Sixtymile, which have been reactivated by Cogasa Mining Co. Keep to right for Alaska. The road winds above timberline for many miles. The lack of fuel for warmth and shelter made this a perilous trip for the early sourdoughs.

D 65.2 (103.7 km) **T 13.6** (21.9 km) Pull-through rest stop with toilet and litter barrels. Good viewpoint. Just across the highway, short hike to cairn, excellent viewpoint.

D 66.1 (105.1 km) **T 13.2** (21.2 km) U.S.–Canada border (elev. 4,127 feet/ 1,258m). Canada Customs and Immigration Little Gold Creek office is open 9 A.M. to 9 P.M. (Pacific time) from about May 15 to Sept. 15. All traffic entering Canada must stop here. The U.S. border station Poker Creek office, just past the Canadian station, is open 8 A.M. to 8 P.M. (Alaska time) from about May 15 to Sept. 15. All traffic entering the United States must stop here. Both stations are closed in winter.

TIME ZONE CHANGE: Alaska observes Alaska time; Yukon Territory observes Pacific time. See Time Zones in GENERAL INFORMATION section for details.

D 67.1 (108 km) **T 12** (19.3 km) Turnout to north with view of mountains.

D 69.2 (111.4 km) **T 9.4** (15.1 km) **BOUNDARY.** Boundary Lodge was one of the first roadhouses in Alaska; food, gas and lodging.

Watch your gas supply. Between here and Tetlin Junction on the Alaska Highway, gas is available again only at Chicken, **Milepost TJ 66.6.** From here to Eagle, gas may be available at O'Brien Creek Lodge, **Milepost TJ 126.** Gas is available in Eagle. Emergency phone at roadhouse for contacting Alaska State Troopers.

Private Aircraft: Boundary airstrip; elev. 2,940 feet/896m; length 2,100 feet/640m; earth and gravel; fuel 80; unattended.

D 78 (125.6 km) **T 0.8** (1.3 km) Viewpoint.

D 78.8 (126.9 km) **T 0 Jack Wade Junction, Milepost TJ 95.7** on the Taylor Highway. The Taylor Highway (Alaska Route 5), also known as the Eagle Road or Eagle Cutoff, leads north 65.3 miles/105 km to Eagle, AK, or south 95.7 miles/154 km to Tetlin Junction, just east of Tok, on the Alaska Highway. *CAUTION: The Taylor Highway is a narrow, winding, mountain road, not well-maintained. Drive carefully!*

*NOTE: Eagle-bound and Alaska Highway-bound travelers turn to **Milepost TJ 95.7** on page 253 in the TAYLOR HIGHWAY section to continue log. Eagle-bound travelers continue with log forward from **Milepost TJ 95.7.** Alaska Highway-bound travelers read log backward from **Milepost TJ 95.7.***

TAYLOR HIGHWAY

Tetlin Junction to Eagle, Alaska
Alaska Route 5
(See map, page 237)

The 161-mile/259-km Taylor Highway (Alaska Route 5) begins at Tetlin Junction on the Alaska Highway and ends at the small town of Eagle on the Yukon River. This is a beautiful "top of the world" drive, and Eagle is well worth a visit. Construction of the Taylor Highway began in 1946, and was completed to Eagle in late 1953, providing access to the historic Fortymile Mining District.

The highway also provides river runners with access to the Fortymile River National Wild and Scenic River system. A brochure on access points and float times is available from the Bureau of Land Management, 1150 University Ave., Fairbanks, AK 99709-3844; phone 474-2350.

The Taylor Highway is a narrow, winding, dusty mountain road with many steep hills and some hairpin curves. Allow plenty of time to drive its length. The road surface is gravel, with sporadic soft spots during breakup or after heavy rains. Road surface ranges from very poor to good depending on maintenance. Large RVs and trailers especially should use caution in driving this road. The highway is not maintained in winter (from about Oct. 10 to April).

NOTE: Watch for road construction between TJ 0 and TJ 23 in 1994.

The Taylor is the shortest route to Dawson City, YT, from Alaska. Drive 95.7 miles/154 km north on the Taylor Highway to Jack Wade Junction, and turn east on the Top of the World Highway (Yukon Highway 9) for Dawson City. (See end of KLONDIKE LOOP section for log of Yukon Highway 9, which begins on page 249.) Dawson-bound travelers keep in mind that gas is available only at Chicken and at Boundary Lodge. Also, the U.S. and Canada customs offices at the border are open 12 hours a day from about mid-May to mid-September. In summer 1993, customs hours were 8 A.M. to 8 P.M. Alaska time, 9 A.M. to 9 P.M. Pacific time on the Canadian side. There are no restrooms available at the border.

IMPORTANT: You cannot cross the border unless the customs office for the country you are entering is open. Severe fines are levied for crossing without clearing customs. Officials at Canadian customs are concerned about child abductions. If you are traveling with children, remember to bring identification for them.

NOTE: All gold-bearing ground in area is claimed. Do not pan in streams.

Emergency medical services: Between Tetlin Junction and O'Brien Creek bridge at **Milepost TJ 113.2**, phone the Tok ambulance, 911 or 883-2300. Between O'Brien Creek bridge and Eagle, phone the Eagle EMS, 547-2300 or 547-2211. Use CB channel 21.

Taylor Highway Log

Distance from Tetlin Junction (TJ) is followed by distance from Eagle (E).

TJ 0 E 161 (259 km) **Tetlin Junction. Junction** with the Alaska Highway at **Milepost DC 1301.7.** 40-Mile Roadhouse; food, gas and lodging.

NOTE: Watch for road construction next 23 miles/37 km northbound in 1994.

Begin 9 miles/14.5 km of winding road up out of the Tanana River valley. Highway traverses stabilized sand dunes first 5 miles/8 km.

TJ **4.5** (7.2 km) E **156.5** (251.9 km) Gravel turnout to east. A 0.7-mile/1.1-km trail leads to **Four Mile Lake;** rainbow trout and sheefish.

TJ **5.4** (8.7 km) E **155.6** (250.4 km) Evidence of 1990 forest fire known as the Porcupine burn.

TJ **5.9** (9.5 km) E **155.1** (249.6 km) Entering Tok Management Area, Tanana Valley State Forest, northbound.

TJ **6** (9.7 km) E **155** (249.4 km) Double-ended turnout to east, easy for trailers but can be soft or bumpy.

Wildflowers along the highway include arnica, chiming bells, wild roses and Labrador tea. As the name suggests, Labrador tea leaves (and flowers) may be steeped in boiling water to make tea. However, according to Janice Scofield, author of *Discovering Wild Plants*, Labrador tea contains a narcotic toxin that can cause ill effects if used too frequently or in high concentrations.

NOTE: Winding road northbound. Watch for ruts and soft spots, and for loose gravel on curves.

TJ **9.4** (15.1 km) E **151.6** (244 km) Entering Game Management Unit 20E northbound; entering GMU 12 southbound. Road begins gradual climb of Mount Fairplay for northbound travelers.

TJ **12.1** (19.5 km) E **148.9** (239.6 km) Entering Tok Management Area, Tanana State Forest, southbound.

TJ **14.6** (23.5 km) E **146.4** (235.6 km) Small turnout to west. Blueberries in season.

TJ **16** (25.6 km) E **145** (232 km) Parking at one of Mount Fairplay's several summits.

TJ **18** (28.8 km) E **143** (228.8 km) *NOTE: Watch for soft spots after rain.*

TJ **21.2** (34.1 km) E **139.8** (225 km) Long descent northbound.

TJ **23** (37 km) E **138** (222.1 km) *NOTE: Watch for road construction next 23 miles/37 km southbound in 1994.*

TJ **27** (43.4 km) E **134** (215.6 km) Small turnout to west.

TJ **28.3** (45.5 km) E **132.7** (213.6 km) Turnout with view to west.

TJ **32.8** (52.8 km) E **128.2** (206.3 km) Turnout to west.

TJ **34.4** (55.4 km) E **126.6** (203.7 km) Double-ended turnout with view to west. Nine-percent downgrade northbound.

TJ **35.1** (56.5 km) E **125.9** (202.6 km) Entering Fortymile Mining District northbound. Double-ended turnout near summit of Mount Fairplay (elev. 5,541 feet/1,689m). Interpretive sign here.

Highway descends a 9-percent grade northbound. Southbound, the road descends for the next 25 miles/40 km from Mount Fairplay's summit, winding down through heavily forested terrain. Panoramic views of valleys of the forks of the Fortymile River. Views of the Alaska Range to the southwest.

TJ **39.1** (62.9 km) E **121.9** (196.2 km) Large turnout to west.

TJ **43** (69.2 km) E **118** (189.9 km) Logging Cabin Creek bridge; small turnout to west at south end of bridge. Side road to creek. This is the south end of the Fortymile River National Wild and Scenic River system managed by BLM.

TJ **49** (78.8 km) E **112** (180.2 km) Loop roads through BLM West Fork recreation site; 25 sites (seven pull-through sites), tables, firepits, no water, covered tables, toilets, dumpsters. Access point of Fortymile River canoe trail. Improved campground. ▲

TJ **49.3** (79.3 km) E **111.7** (179.7 km) Bridge over West Fork of the Dennison Fork of the Fortymile River. Access point for Fortymile River National Wild and Scenic River system.

TJ **50.5** (81.3 km) E **110.5** (177.8 km) Taylor Creek bridge. Watch for potholes and rough road at bridge approaches. All-terrain vehicle trail to Taylor and Kechumstuk mountains; heavily used in hunting season.

TJ **57** (91.7 km) E **104** (167.4 km) Scenic viewpoint turnout to east; no easy turnaround.

TJ **58.9** (94.8 km) E **102.1** (164.3 km) Scenic viewpoint turnout with litter barrels to east.

TJ **62.5** (100.6 km) E **98.5** (158.5 km) Turnout to west. Drive in, no easy turnaround.

TJ **63.2** (101.7 km) E **97.8** (157.4 km) View of Chicken.

TJ **63.3** (101.9 km) E **97.7** (157.2 km) Turnout to west. Drive in, no easy turnaround.

TJ **63.7** (102.5 km) E **97.3** (156.6 km) Steep descent northbound to Mosquito Fork.

TJ **64.1** (103.1 km) E **96.9** (155.9 km) Well-traveled road leads to private buildings, not into Chicken.

TJ **64.3** (103.5 km) E **96.7** (155.6 km)

Bridge over Mosquito Fork of the Fortymile River; day-use area with table, toilet and litter barrel at north end of bridge. The Mosquito Fork is a favorite access point for the Fortymile National Wild and Scenic River system, according to the BLM.

TJ 65.2 (104.3 km) E 95.8 (153.3 km) Turnout with pit toilets. Last public facilities available to those traveling to Canada — none available at border.

TJ 66 (106.2 km) E 95 (152.9 km) Entering **CHICKEN** (pop. 37), northbound. *(NOTE: Driving distance between* ***Mileposts 66*** *and 67 is 0.7 mile.)* This is the newer commercial settlement of Chicken. The original mining camp (abandoned, private property) is north of Chicken Creek (see **Milepost TJ 67**). Chicken is a common name in the North for ptarmigan. One story has it that the early miners wanted to name their camp ptarmigan, but were unable to spell it and settled for Chicken. Access point for the Fortymile River canoe trail is below Chicken airstrip.

TJ 66.3 (106.7 km) E 94.7 (152.4 km) Chicken post office (Zip code 99732) located on hill beside the road. The late Ann Purdy lived in this area. The book *Tisha* is based on her experiences as a young schoolteacher in the Alaska Bush.

TJ 66.4 (106.9 km) E 94.6 (152.2 km) Airport Road. Access to Chicken airstrip. Combination grocery store, restaurant, bar and gas station located here.

Private Aircraft: Chicken airstrip, adjacent southwest; elev. 1,640 feet/500m; length 2,500 feet/762m; gravel; maintained year-round.

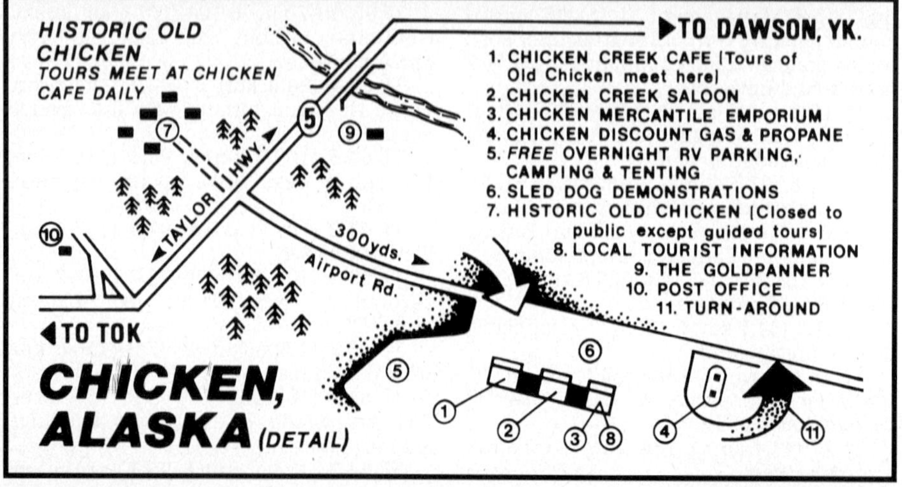

Chicken Mercantile Emporium, Chicken Creek Cafe, Saloon and Gas. Unfortunately, as too often happens, the main road bypasses the most interesting part of Chicken. If it's modern facilities you are looking for, original Chicken is not for you. The Chicken Creek Saloon and Cafe are some of the last remnants of the old frontier Alaska. It is a trading post where local miners (some straight out of Jack London) trade gold for supplies and drink. Tisha's schoolhouse and other historic buildings may be seen on the walking tour of old Chicken, meeting daily at the Chicken Creek Cafe at 1 P.M. It's also possible to purchase an autographed copy of *Tisha* at the Chicken Mercantile Emporium. Hunting and fishing licenses for sale at the Emporium. A wealth of gifts abound in the Chicken Mercantile Emporium and the cafe is famous throughout Alaska for its excellent food, homemade pies, pastries and cinnamon buns. For a bird's-eye view of this spectacular country and fantastic photo opportunities, check out the local flightseeing service. Chicken Creek Saloon, Cafe and Mercantile Emporium are a rare treat for those with the courage to stray just a few hundred yards from the beaten path. Major credit cards accepted. [ADVERTISEMENT]

TJ 66.5 (107 km) E 94.5 (152.1 km) **The Goldpanner.** Owners Bill, Mary, Grant and Dana Morris welcome you to Chicken. We have lots of parking and turnaround space. Our station has gas, diesel, tire repair and minor repairs. The store carries some groceries, staples, snacks, cold pop, canned meats and souvenirs. Chicken souvenirs include T-shirts, sweatshirts, hats, spoons, cups, patches, magnets, bumper stickers, postcards and hatpins. We also carry many other articles including the book *Tisha.* Try your hand at our FREE gold panning or get your local gold already in vials, nuggets or jewelry. For the sportsman, hunting and fishing licenses are available. For those interested in local history, old bones, rocks and mining artifacts are on display on the porch and throughout the store. There is no charge for our dry RV overnight parking. Buses and caravans are always welcome. [ADVERTISEMENT] ▲

TJ 66.6 (107.2 km) E 94.4 (151.9 km) Chicken Creek bridge.

TJ 67 (107.8 km) E 94 (151.3 km) View of abandoned old townsite of Chicken. The road in is blocked off, and the dozen or so old buildings are owned by a mining company. Private property, do not trespass. Guided walking tours available; inquire at Chicken Creek Cafe. Look upstream (northwest) on Chicken Creek to see the old gold dredge, which was shut down in the 1960s.

TJ 68.2 (109.8 km) E 92.8 (149.3 km) BLM Chicken field station; information and emergency communications. Trailhead for Mosquito Fork Dredge trail (3 miles roundtrip). *NOTE: Watch for potholes and soft spots.*

TJ 68.9 (110.9 km) E 92.1 (148.2 km) Lost Chicken Creek. Site of Lost Chicken Hill Mine, established in 1895. Mining was under way in this area several years before

the Klondike gold rush of 1897–98. The first major placer gold strike was in 1886 at Franklin Gulch, a tributary of the Fortymile. Watch for hydraulic mining operations in the creek.

TJ 70 (112.7 km) **E 91** (146.4 km) Turnouts at gravel pits on both sides of road.

TJ 71.7 (115.4 km) **E 89.3** (143.7 km) Steep descent northbound as road winds down to South Fork.

TJ 74.4 (119.7 km) **E 86.6** (139.4 km) South Fork River access road.

TJ 74.5 (119.9 km) **E 86.5** (139.2 km) South Fork DOT/PF state highway maintenance station.

TJ 75.3 (121.2 km) **E 85.7** (137.9 km) South Fork bridge. Day-use area with toilet and litter barrels at south end of bridge, west side of road. Access point for the Fortymile River National Wild and Scenic River system. The muddy, bumpy road leading into the brush is used by miners.

TJ 76.8 (123.6 km) **E 84.2** (135.5 km) Turnout with litter barrels to west. View of Oxbow lakes in South Fork valley.

TJ 78.5 (126.3 km) **E 82.5** (132.8 km) Views of Fortymile River valley northbound to **Milepost TJ 82.**

TJ 78.8 (126.8 km) **E 82.2** (132.3 km) Steep descent northbound.

TJ 81.9 (131.8 km) **E 79.1** (127.3 km) Walker Fork bridge.

TJ 82.1 (132.1 km) **E 78.9** (127 km) Walker Fork BLM campground with 16 sites; two picnic sites with covered tables. Improved campground. Access point for Fortymile River National Wild and Scenic River system. An old Alaska Road Commission road grader is on display here. ▲

CAUTION: Rough road next 5 miles/8 km northbound; roadbed has been mined. Slow down!

TJ 86.1 (138.5 km) **E 74.9** (120.5 km) Old Jack Wade No. 1 dredge in creek next to road. Turnout to east. This is actually the Butte Creek Dredge, installed in 1934 below the mouth of Butte Creek and eventually moved to Wade Creek. This was one of the first bucketline dredges used in the area, according to the BLM.

TJ 90 (144.8 km) **E 71** (114.2 km) Jack Wade, an old mining camp that operated until 1940. Active mining is under way in this area. *Do not trespass on mining claims.*

TJ 91.9 (147.9 km) **E 69.1** (111.2 km) Turnout to east. Primitive campsite by stream.

TJ 93.5 (150.5 km) **E 67.5** (108.6 km) *Slow down for hairpin curve.* Road climbs northbound. *NOTE: Large vehicles use turnouts when meeting oncoming vehicles.*

TJ 95.7 (154 km) **E 65.3** (105.1 km) **Jack Wade Junction.** Continue north on the Taylor Highway for Eagle. Turn east for Boundary Lodge and Alaska–Canada border. Dawson City is 78.8 miles/126.9 km east via the Top of the World Highway. The Top of the World Highway (Yukon Highway 9) is a winding gravel road with some steep grades. Slippery in wet weather. Drive carefully.

Dawson City-bound travelers turn to the end of the KLONDIKE LOOP section and read the Top of the World Highway log back to front. Eagle-bound travelers continue with this log.

TJ 96 (154.5 km) **E 65** (104.6 km) Turnout. View to the north-northeast of Canada's Ogilvie Mountains in the distance.

TJ 99.5 (160.1 km) **E 61.5** (99 km) Road winds around the summit of Steele Creek Dome (elev. 4,015 feet/1,224m) visible directly above the road to the east. *CAUTION: Road is slippery when wet.*

TJ 99.6 (160.3 km) **E 61.4** (98.8 km) *CAUTION: Slow down for hairpin curve.*

TJ 105.5 (169.8 km) **E 55.5** (89.3 km) Scenic viewpoint with litter barrel to east. The road descends next 7 miles/11.3 km northbound to the valley of the Fortymile River, so named because its mouth was 40 miles below Fort Reliance, an old trading post near the confluence of the Yukon and Klondike. Along the road are abandoned cabins, tailings and dredges.

TJ 109.2 (175.7 km) **E 51.8** (83.4 km) *Slow down for hairpin curve!*

TJ 109.7 (176.5 km) **E 51.3** (82.5 km) *CAUTION: Steep, narrow, winding road northbound. Slow down!* Frequent small turnouts and breathtaking views to north and west.

TJ 113 (181.8 km) **E 48** (77.2 km) Fortymile River bridge; parking area, toilet. No camping. Active mining in area. Nearly vertical beds of white marble can be seen on the northeast side of the river. Access to the Fortymile River National Wild and Scenic River system.

TJ 113.2 (182.2 km) **E 47.8** (76.9 km) Private home and mining camp.

TJ 113.6 (182.8 km) **E 47.4** (76.3 km) Highway maintenance camp located here.

TJ 113.7 (183 km) **E 47.3** (76.1 km) O'Brien Creek bridge. Access to creek.

TJ 114.2 (183.8 km) **E 46.8** (75.3 km) Winding road northbound with rock slide areas to **Milepost TJ 116.6**, highway parallels O'Brien Creek to Liberty Fork; several turnouts. *CAUTION: Watch for small aircraft using road as runway.*

TJ 117.6 (189.2 km) **E 43.4** (69.8 km) Alder Creek bridge.

TJ 118.3 (190.4 km) **E 42.7** (68.7 km) Road narrows northbound: Watch for falling rock next 1.5 miles/2.4 km northbound.

TJ 119.7 (192.6 km) **E 41.3** (66.5 km) Slide area, watch for rocks.

TJ 125.2 (201.5 km) **E 35.8** (57.6 km) Columbia Creek bridge.

TJ 126 (202.8 km) **E 35** (56.3 km) Lodge with gas.

TJ 132.6 (213.4 km) **E 28.4** (45.7 km) King Solomon Creek bridge. Primitive camping (no facilities) at south end of bridge, east side of road, at site of former BLM campground. Highway follows King Solomon Creek next 0.5 mile/0.8 km northbound.

TJ 135.7 (218.4 km) **E 25.3** (40.1 km) *CAUTION: Slow down for hairpin curve.*

TJ 136.7 (220 km) **E 24.3** (39.1 km) North Fork Solomon Creek bridge.

TJ 141 (227 km) **E 20** (32.2 km) Glacier Mountain management area; walk-in hunting only.

TJ 141.5 (227.7 km) **E 19.5** (31.4 km) Turnout to west. Primitive campsite.

TJ 144.2 (232.1 km) **E 16.8** (27 km) Turnout on summit. Top of the world views. Road begins winding descent northbound to Yukon River.

TJ 150.1 (241.5 km) **E 10.9** (17.5 km) Bridge over Discovery Fork.

TJ 151.8 (244.3 km) **E 9.2** (14.8 km) Old cabin by creek to west is a local landmark. Private property.

TJ 152.7 (245.7 km) **E 8.3** (13.4 km) American Creek bridge No. 1. Outcroppings of asbestos, greenish or gray with white, and serpentine along creekbank. Doyon, Limited, claims ownership of surface and mineral estates on these lands; do not trespass.

TJ 153.3 (246.7 km) **E 7.7** (12.4 km) Bridge No. 2 over American Creek.

TJ 154.1 (248 km) **E 6.9** (11.1 km) Small turnout. Springwater piped to road.

TJ 154.6 (248.8 km) **E 6.4** (10.3 km) Small turnout. Springwater piped to road.

TJ 160.6 (258.5 km) **E 0.4** (0.6 km) Turnout with historical sign about the settlement of Eagle.

TJ 161 (259 km) **E 0** Fourth Avenue, Eagle (description follows). Eagle school to east. Side road to west leads 1 mile/1.6 km to Fort Egbert mule barn, officers' quarters and parade ground. The U.S. Army established Eagle City Camp in 1899. Fort Egbert was built the following year, then abandoned in 1911. From here a road leads 0.8 mile/1.3 km to Eagle Campground; 13 sites. ▲

Eagle

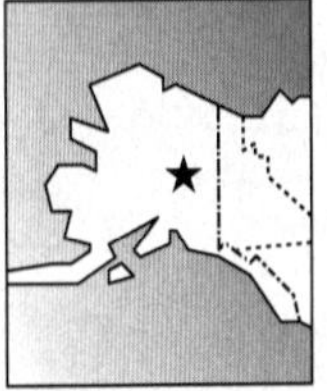

Population: 150. **Emergency Services:** Eagle health clinic. **Visitor Information:** According to Elva Scott, president of the Eagle Historical Society, Eagle is "a total history lesson," with perhaps more square feet of museum space than anywhere else in the state. "The only way to see it is on the two- to three-hour walking tour offered by the historical society." Tours are at 10 A.M. daily Memorial Day through Labor Day; meet at the courthouse. The tour includes the Wickersham courthouse, Waterfront Customs House and the mule barn, water wagon shed and NCO quarters at Fort Egbert; cost is $3 per person, members of Eagle Historical Society and children under 12 years free (annual society membership, $5). Special tours may be arranged. Books, maps and gifts available at the museum store in the courthouse. For more information contact the Eagle Historical Society, Box 23, Eagle City, AK 99738. Fort Egbert, renovated and restored by the BLM, has an interpretive exhibit and a photo display showing the stages of reconstruction.

Videos of the area are shown every Monday at 8 P.M. in the public library. Local craft demonstrations are given at 7 P.M. on Saturdays in July and August at the Improved Order of Redmends Hall.

The National Park Service office, headquarters for Yukon–Charley Rivers National Preserve, is located on the banks of the Yukon River at the base of Fort Egbert. Reference library available to the public. Office hours are 8 A.M. to 5 P.M. weekdays. The National Park Service Visitor Center offers maps and books for sale. Also a video on the preserve is shown on request. Informal talks and interpretive programs available. Visitor center hours are 8 A.M. to 5 P.M. daily in summer (Memorial Day weekend through Labor Day weekend). Check at the visitor center for information on the Yukon River, Yukon–Charley Rivers National Preserve and other parklands in Alaska. (Write them at Box 167, Eagle 99738, or phone 547-2233.)

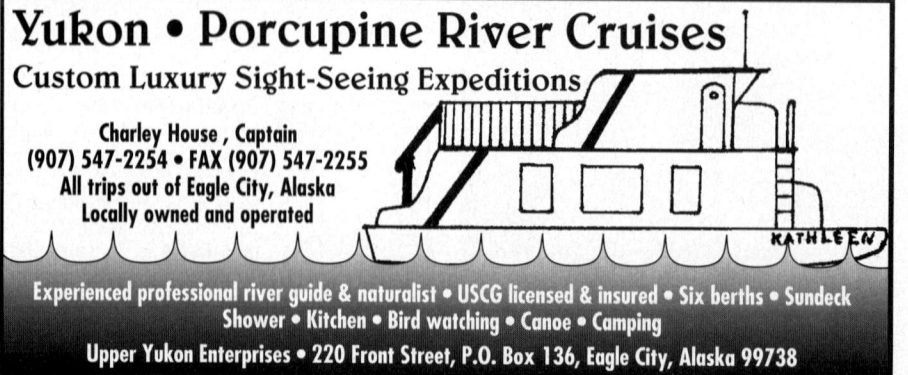

Elevation: 820 feet/250m. **Climate:** Mean monthly temperature in July 59°F/15°C; in January -13°F/-25°C. Record low -71°F/-57°C in January 1952; record high 95°F/35°C in July 1925. July also has the greatest mean number of days (21) with temperatures above 70°F/21°C. Mean precipitation in July 1.94 inches; in December 10.1 inches. Record snow depth 42 inches in April 1948.

Transportation: By road via the Taylor Highway (closed by snow October to April); air taxi, scheduled air service; dog team and snow machine in winter. Eagle is also accessible via the Yukon River. U.S. customs available at post office for persons entering Alaska via the Yukon River or by air.

Private Aircraft: Eagle airstrip, 2 miles/3.2 km east; elev. 880 feet/268m; length 3,500 feet/1,067m; gravel; unattended.

This small community was once the supply and transportation center for miners working the upper Yukon and its tributaries. Francois Mercier established his Belle Isle trading post here in the 1880s. By 1898, Eagle's population was 1,700. Gold strikes in Fairbanks and Nome lured away many, and by 1910, the population had dwindled to 178.

In the center of town stands a windmill and wellhouse (built in 1909); both still provide water for over half the town's population. There are gas stations, restaurants, gift shops, museum store, post office, showers, laundromat, hardware store and mechanic shop with tire repair. Groceries and sundries are available. Fax service is available at the village store. Overnight accommodations at motels and rental cabins. RV parking with hookups is available or stay at Eagle BLM campground just outside town (turn left on 4th Avenue and left again along airstrip at Fort Egbert). Eagle Village, an Athabascan settlement, is 3 miles/4.8 km from Eagle.

Historically an important riverboat landing, Eagle is still a popular jumping-off point for Yukon River travelers. Most popular is a summer float trip from Eagle downriver through the **YUKON–CHARLEY RIVERS NATIONAL PRESERVE** to Circle. Length of the Eagle–Circle trip is 154 river miles, with most trips averaging five to 10 days. Float trips may also be made from Dawson City, YT, to Circle (252 miles, seven to 10 days) with a halfway stop at Eagle. Boaters also often float the Fortymile to the Yukon River, then continue to the boat landing at Eagle to take out. Commercial boat trips are also available. Breakup on the Yukon is in May; freezeup in October. For details on weather, clothing, gear and precautions, contact the National Park Service, Box 167, Eagle 99738; phone 547-2233.

Westours (Gray Line of Alaska) operates the *Yukon Queen* boat service between Eagle and Dawson City, YT; Upper Yukon Enterprises offers Yukon and Porcupine river cruises aboard the MV *Kathleen*.

GLENN HIGHWAY/TOK CUTOFF

Tok to Anchorage, Alaska
Alaska Route 1
(See maps, pages 256–257)

*View of magnificent Matanuska Glacier from **Milepost A 102.8** on the Glenn Highway.* (Hugh B. White)

The Glenn Highway/Tok Cutoff (Alaska Route 1) is the principal access route from the Alaska Highway west to Anchorage, a distance of 328 miles/527.8 km. This route includes the 125-mile/201-km Tok Cutoff, between Tok and the Richardson Highway junction; a 14-mile/22.5-km link via the Richardson Highway; and the 189-mile/304-km Glenn Highway, between the Richardson Highway and Anchorage.

It is a full day's drive between Tok and Anchorage on this paved all-weather highway. The highway between Tok and Glennallen has some very narrow sections with no shoulders. Watch for road construction. Also watch for frost heaves and pavement breaks along the entire highway. Slow down at signs saying Bump — they mean it!

Four side roads are logged in this section: the Nabesna Road to the old Nabesna Mine, which also provides access to Wrangell-St. Elias National Park and Preserve; Lake Louise Road, which leads to Lake Louise Recreation Area; the Hatcher Pass Road, connecting the Glenn and George Parks highways to Independence Mine State Historical Park; and the Old Glenn Highway, an alternate route between Palmer and Anchorage.

Emergency medical services: Between Tok and Duffy's Roadhouse at **Milepost GJ 63**, phone the Tok ambulance at 883-2300 or 911. Between Duffy's and Gakona Junction, phone the Glennallen EMS at 822-3203 or 911. From Gakona Junction to Anchorage phone 911. CB channel 9 between **Milepost A 30.8** and Anchorage.

Tok Cutoff Log

Physical mileposts read from **Milepost 125** at Tok to **Milepost 0** at Gakona Junction, the north junction with the Richardson Highway.

Distance from Gakona Junction (GJ) is followed by distance from Anchorage (A) and distance from Tok (T).

GJ 125 (201.2 km) **A 328** (527.8 km) **T 0** Tok (see description in the ALASKA HIGHWAY section).

GJ 124.2 (199.9 km) **A 327.2** (526.6 km) **T 0.8** (1.3 km) Tok Community Center.

GJ 124.1 (199.7 km) **A 327.1** (526.4 km) **T 0.9** (1.4 km) Tok Community Clinic, Tok Fire Station.

GJ 124 (199.6 km) **A 327** (526.2 km) **T 1** (1.6 km) Dept. of Natural Resources.

GJ 123.9 (199.4 km) **A 326.9** (526.1 km) **T 1.1** (1.8 km) Dept. of Transportation and Public Facilities, Tok Station.

GJ 123.7 (199.1 km) **A 326.7** (525.8 km) **T 1.3** (2.1 km) Borealis Avenue.

GJ 123.3 (198.4 km) **A 326.3** (525.1 km) **T 1.7** (2.7 km) **Hayner's Trading Post.** Alaskan handmade jewelry and gifts, beads and supplies, greeting and note cards. Sporting goods and black powder supplies. Custom leather work and repairs. Free coffee and tea. Open year-round. Summer hours 10 A.M. to 8 P.M. Rocky and Sue Hayner, owners. (907) 883-5536. See display ad in Tok in the ALASKA HIGHWAY section. [ADVERTISEMENT]

GJ 122.8 (197.6 km) **A 325.8** (524.3 km) **T 2.2** (3.5 km) **Sourdough Campground's Pancake Breakfast** served 7-11 A.M. Genuine "Sourdoughs." Full and partial RV hookups. Dry campsites. Showers included. High-pressure car wash with brush. Evening video program. Located 1.7 miles from the junction toward Anchorage on Tok Cutoff (Glenn Highway). See display ad in Tok in the ALASKA HIGHWAY section. [ADVERTISEMENT] ▲

GJ 122.6 (197.3 km) **A 325.6** (524 km) **T 2.4** (3.9 km) Bayless and Roberts Airport. Paved bike trail from Tok ends here.

GJ 116.7 (187.8 km) **A 319.7** (514.5 km) **T 8.3** (13.4 km) Entering Tok Management Area, Tanana Valley State Forest, westbound.

GJ 113 (181.9 km) **A 316** (508.5 km) **T 12** (19.3 km) Beautiful mountain views westbound.

GJ 110 (177 km) **A 313** (503.7 km) **T 15** (24.1 km) Flashing lights are from U.S. Coast Guard loran station at **Milepost DC 1308.5** on the Alaska Highway. Watch for frost heaves westbound.

GJ 109.3 (175.9 km) **A 312.3** (502.6 km) **T 15.7** (25.3 km) Eagle Trail State Recreation Site; 40 campsites, 15-day limit, four picnic sites, water, toilets, firepits, rain shelter, hiking trail, Clearwater Creek. Camping fee $8/night or annual pass. The access road is designed with several loops to aid larger vehicles. A 0.9-mile/1.4-km section of the pioneer trail to Eagle is signed for hikers; trailhead near covered picnic tables. The historic Tok–Slana Cutoff road goes through this campground. ▲

GJ 106 (170.6 km) **A 309** (497.3 km) **T 19** (30.6 km) Mountain views westbound.

GJ 104.5 (168.2 km) **A 307.5** (494.9 km) **T 20.5** (33 km) Small paved turnout to north. Stream runs under highway in culvert.

GJ 104.1 (167.5 km) **A 307.1** (494.2 km) **T 20.9** (33.6 km) Bridge over Tok River, side road north to riverbank and boat launch.

Wildlife is abundant from here west to Mentasta Summit. Watch for moose in roadside ponds, bears on gravel bars, and Dall sheep on mountainsides. For best wildlife viewing, stop at turnouts and use good binoculars. Wildflowers include sweet peas, chiming bells, arnica, oxytrope and lupine.

GJ 103.5 (166.6 km) **A 306.5** (493.3 km) **T 21.5** (34.6 km) Paved turnout to north.

GJ 102.4 (164.8 km) **A 305.4** (491.5 km) **T 22.6** (36.4 km) Entering Tok Management Area, Tanana Valley State Forest, eastbound.

GJ 99.3 (159.8 km) **A 302.3** (486.5 km) **T 25.7** (41.4 km) Rest area; paved double-

GLENN HIGHWAY *Tok Cutoff (GJ-125 to GJ-0) to Milepost A 160*

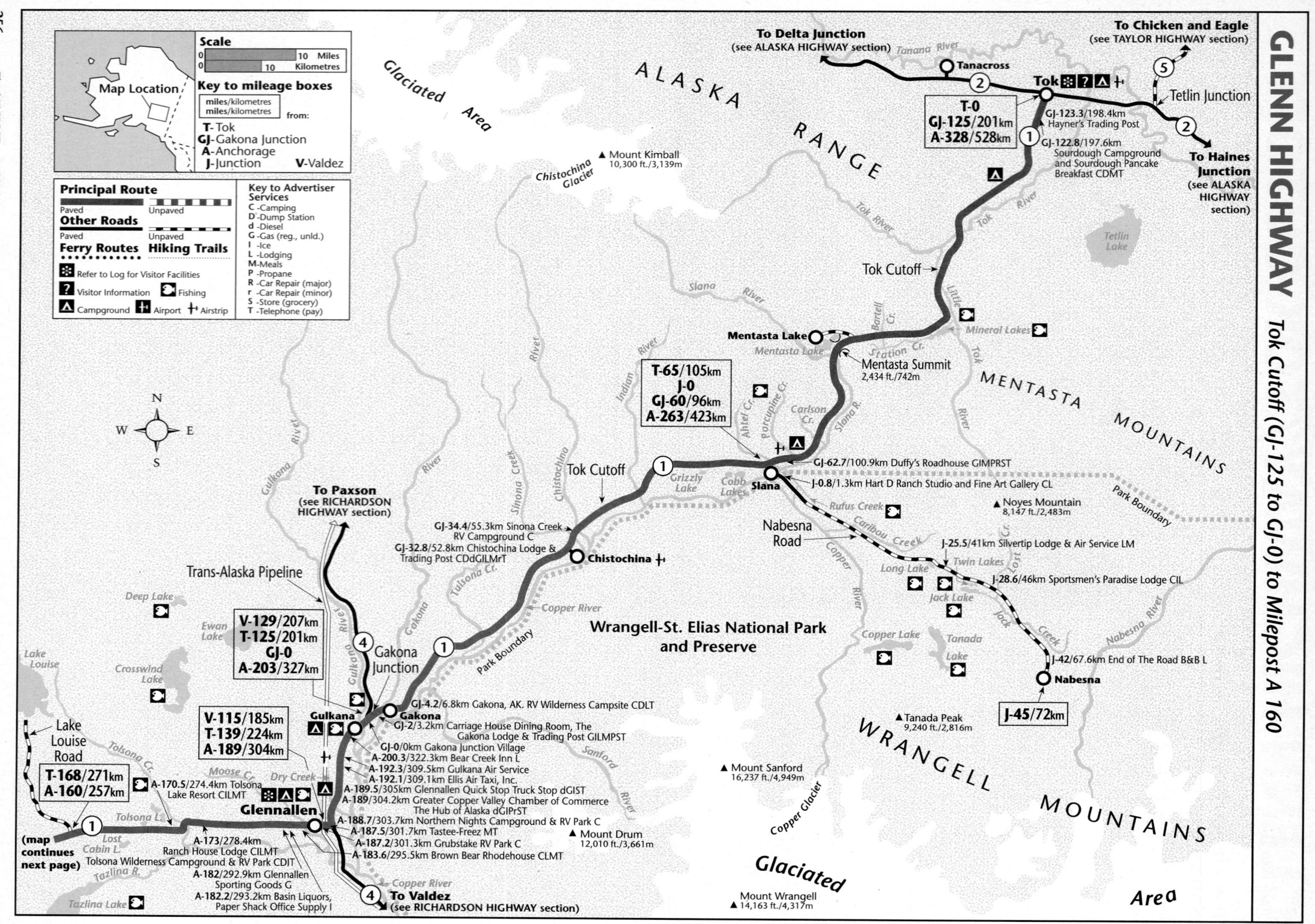

GLENN HIGHWAY *Milepost A 160 to Anchorage, AK*

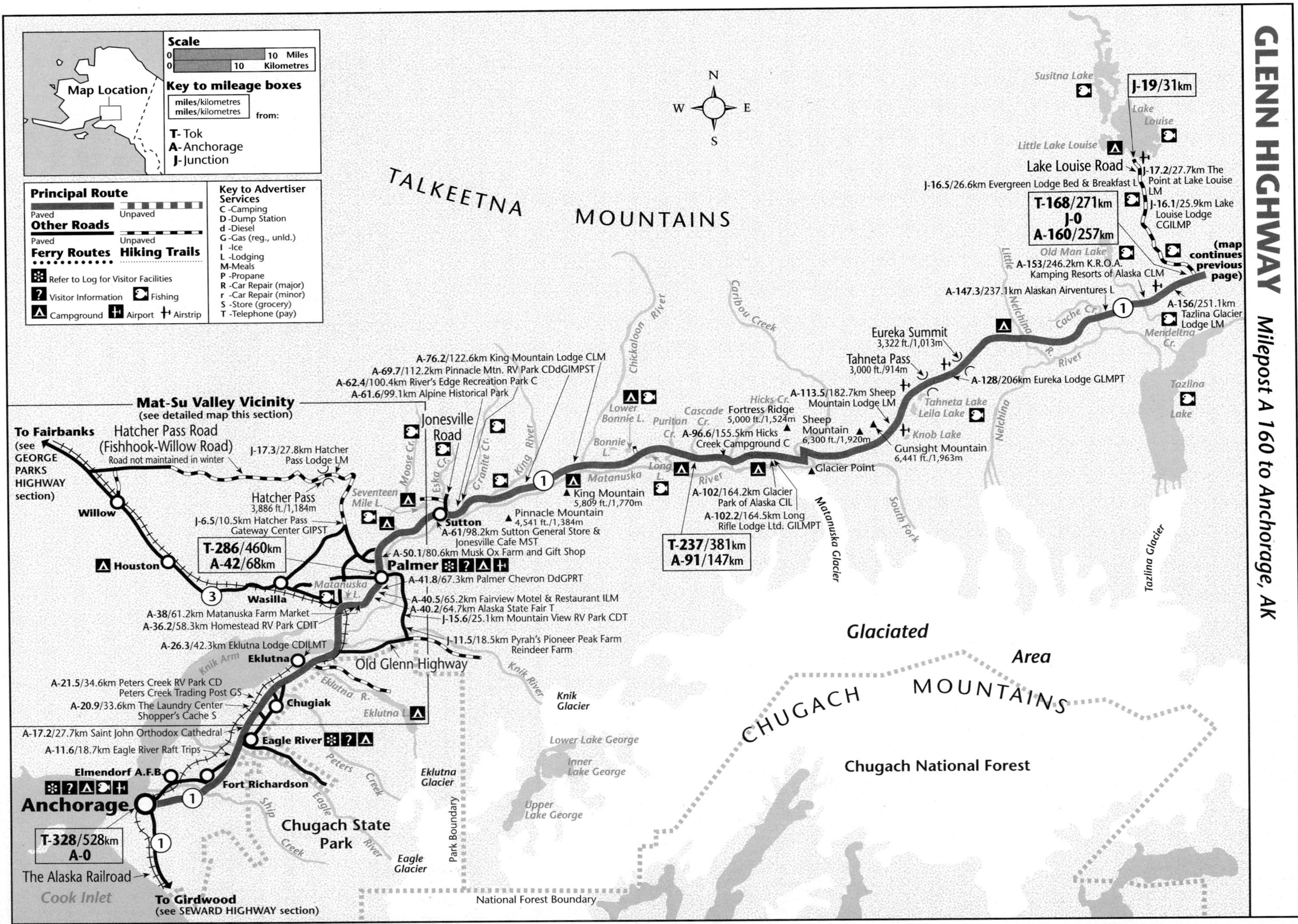

ended turnout to north. Cranberries may be found in late summer.

GJ 98 (157.7 km) **A 301** (484.4 km) **T 27** (43.5 km) Bridge over Little Tok River, which parallels highway. Parking at end of bridge.

GJ 97.7 (157.2 km) **A 300.7** (483.9 km) **T 27.3** (43.9 km) *NOTE: Westbound travelers watch for sections of narrow highway (no shoulders); some gravel patches, bumps, dips and pavement breaks; and frost heaves.*

GJ 95.2 (153.2 km) **A 298.2** (479.9 km) **T 29.8** (48 km) Rest area; paved turnout to south.

GJ 91 (146.4 km) **A 294** (473.1 km) **T 34** (54.7 km) Gravel turnout with dumpster to north. Side road with bridge (weight limit 20 tons) across **Little Tok River;** good fishing for grayling, 12 to 14 inches, use small spinner.

GJ 90 (144.8 km) **A 293** (471.5 km) **T 35** (56.3 km) Small paved turnout to south.

GJ 89.5 (144 km) **A 292.5** (470.7 km) **T 35.5** (57.1 km) **Mineral Lakes.** These are sloughs of the Little Tok River and provide both moose habitat and a breeding place for waterfowl. Good fishing for northern pike and grayling.

GJ 89 (143.2 km) **A 292** (469.9 km) **T 36** (57.9 km) Small paved turnout to south.

GJ 86.7 (139.5 km) **A 289.7** (466.2 km) **T 38.3** (61.6 km) Good place to spot moose.

GJ 85.7 (137.9 km) **A 288.7** (464.6 km) **T 39.3** (63.2 km) Turnout to north.

GJ 83.2 (133.9 km) **A 286.2** (460.6 km) **T 41.8** (67.3 km) Bridge over Bartell Creek. Just beyond is the divide between the drainage of the Tanana River, tributary of the Yukon River system flowing into the Bering Sea, and the Copper River system, emptying into the North Pacific near Cordova.

GJ 81 (130.4 km) **A 284** (457 km) **T 44** (70.8 km) Access road to **MENTASTA LAKE** (pop. 72), a Native village.

GJ 79.4 (127.8 km) **A 282.4** (454.5 km) **T 45.6** (73.4 km) Mentasta Summit (elev. 2,434 feet/742m). Watch for Dall sheep on mountainsides. Boundary between Game Management Units 12 and 13C and Sportfish Management Units 8 and 2. Mountain views westbound.

GJ 78.1 (125.7 km) **A 281.1** (452.4 km) **T 46.9** (75.5 km) Mentasta Lodge.

GJ 78 (125.5 km) **A 281** (452.2 km) **T 47** (75.6 km) View for westbound traffic of snow-covered Mount Sanford (elev. 16,237 feet/4,949m).

GJ 77.9 (125.4 km) **A 280.9** (452.1 km) **T 47.1** (75.8 km) Paved turnout to north by Slana Slough; salmon spawning area in August. Watch for beavers.

GJ 76.3 (122.8 km) **A 279.3** (449.5 km) **T 48.7** (78.4 km) Bridge over Mabel Creek. Mastodon flowers (marsh fleabane) in late July; very large (to 4 feet) with showy seed heads.

GJ 76 (122.3 km) **A 279** (449 km) **T 49** (78.8 km) Bridge over Slana Slough.

GJ 75.6 (121.7 km) **A 278.6** (448.3 km) **T 49.4** (79.5 km) Bridge over Slana River. Rest area to south with large paved parking area, dumpsters, toilets and picnic tables along the river. This river flows from its source glaciers some 55 miles/88.5 km to the Copper River.

GJ 74 (119.1 km) **A 277** (445.8 km) **T 51** (82.1 km) Large paved turnout to south overlooking Slana River.

GJ 69 (111 km) **A 272** (437.7 km) **T 56** (90.1 km) Paved turnout to north.

GJ 68 (109.4 km) **A 271** (436.1 km) **T 57** (91.7 km) Carlson Creek bridge. Paved turnout to south at west end of bridge.

GJ 65.5 (105.4 km) **A 268.5** (432.1 km) **T 59.5** (95.8 km) Paved turnout to south; viewpoint.

NOTE: Watch for major road construction westbound to ***Milepost GJ 52*** *in 1994.*

GJ 64.2 (103.3 km) **A 267.2** (430 km) **T 60.8** (97.8 km) Bridge over Porcupine Creek. State Recreation Site 0.2 mile/0.3 km from highway; 12 campsites, 15-day limit, $6 nightly fee or annual pass, drinking water, firepits, toilets, picnic tables and dumpster. Lowbush cranberries in fall. *CAUTION: Watch for bears.*

GJ 63 (101.4 km) **A 266** (428 km) **T 62** (99.8 km) Scenic viewpoint with view of Wrangell Mountains. The dominant peak to the southwest is Mount Sanford, a dormant volcano; the pinnacles of Capital Mountain can be seen against its lower slopes. Mount Jarvis (elev. 13,421 feet/4,091m) is visible to the south behind Mount Sanford; Tanada Peak (elev. 9,240 feet/2,816m) is more to the south. (Tanada Peak is sometimes mistaken for Noyes Mountain.)

Walk up the gravel hill behind the sign to view Noyes Mountain (elev. 8,147 feet/2,483m), named for U.S. Army Brig. Gen. John Rutherford Noyes, a one-time commissioner of roads in the territory of Alaska. Appointed adjutant general of the Alaska National Guard in 1953, he died in 1956 from injuries and frostbite after his plane crashed near Nome.

GJ 62.7 (100.9 km) **A 265.7** (427.6 km) **T 62.3** (100.3 km) **Duffy's Roadhouse**. See display ad this section.

Private Aircraft: Duffy's Tavern airstrip; elev. 2,420 feet/737m; length 900 feet/274m; gravel; fuel 100LL; unmaintained.

GJ 60.8 (97.8 km) **A 263.8** (424.6 km) **T 64.2** (103.3 km) Bridge over **Ahtell Creek;** grayling. Parking area to north at east end of bridge. This stream drains a mountain area of igneous rock, where several gold and silver-lead claims are located.

GJ 59.8 (96.2 km) **A 262.8** (422.9 km) **T 65.2** (104.9 km) **Junction** with Nabesna Road. See NABESNA ROAD log page 260.

GJ 59.7 (96.1 km) **A 262.7** (422.8 km) **T 65.3** (105.1 km) Gravel turnout to south. View of Tanada Peak, Mount Sanford, Mount Blackburn and Mount Drum to the south and southwest. The Mentasta Mountains are to the east.

GJ 59.2 (95.3 km) **A 262.2** (422 km) **T 65.8** (105.9 km) Gravel turnout to south with view of Tanada Peak and Mount Sanford.

GJ 57 (91.7 km) **A 260** (418.4 km) **T 68** (109.4 km) Cobb Lakes.

GJ 55.2 (88.8 km) **A 258.2** (415.5 km) **T 69.8** (112.3 km) Tanada Peak viewpoint; gravel turnout to south.

GJ 53 (85.3 km) **A 256** (412 km) **T 72**

(115.9 km) Grizzly Lake. Watch for horses on road.

*NOTE: Watch for major road construction eastbound to **Milepost GJ 65** in 1994.*

GJ 44.6 (71.8 km) **A 247.6** (398.5 km) **T 80.4** (129.4 km) Turnout to north. Eagle Trail access (not marked).

GJ 43.8 (70.5 km) **A 246.8** (397.1 km) **T 81.2** (130.6 km) Bridge over Indian River. This is a salmon spawning stream, usually late June through July. Picnic site to south at west end of bridge with tables, two firepits, litter barrels, toilets.

GJ 43.4 (69.8 km) **A 246.4** (396.5 km) **T 81.6** (131.3 km) Double-ended gravel turnout to south.

GJ 41.2 (66.3 km) **A 244.2** (393 km) **T 83.8** (134.8 km) Long, double-ended turnout overlooking pond.

GJ 40.1 (64.5 km) **A 243.1** (391.2 km) **T 84.9** (136.6 km) Small paved turnout to south.

GJ 39 (62.8 km) **A 242** (389.5 km) **T 86** (138.4 km) Views of the Copper River valley and Wrangell Mountains. Looking south, peak on left is Mount Sanford and on right is Mount Drum (elev. 12,010 feet/3,661m).

Look for cottongrass and mastodon flowers in late July and August.

GJ 38.7 (62.2 km) **A 241.7** (389 km) **T 86.3** (138.8 km) Paved turnout to north. Mankoman Lake trail.

GJ 35.5 (57.1 km) **A 238.5** (383.8 km) **T 89.5** (144 km) Chistochina River bridge No. 2. Mount Sanford is first large mountain to the southeast, then Mount Drum.

GJ 35.4 (57 km) **A 238.4** (383.7 km) **T 89.6** (144.2 km) Chistochina River bridge No. 1; parking at west end. Chistochina River trailhead. This river heads in the Chistochina Glacier on Mount Kimball (elev. 10,300 feet/3,139m). Chistochina is thought to mean marmot creek.

GJ 34.7 (55.8 km) **A 237.7** (382.5 km) **T 90.3** (145.3 km) Posty's Sinona Creek Trading Post (current status unknown).

GJ 34.6 (55.7 km) **A 237.6** (382.4 km) **T 90.4** (145.5 km) Bridge over Sinona Creek. Sinona is said to mean place of the many burls, and there are indeed many burls on area spruce trees.

GJ 34.4 (55.4 km) **A 237.4** (382 km) **T 90.6** (145.8 km) **Sinona Creek RV Campground.** See display ad this section. ▲

GJ 34.1 (54.9 km) **A 237.1** (381.6 km) **T 90.9** (146.3 km) Chistochina ball fields.

GJ 32.9 (52.9 km) **A 235.9** (379.6 km) **T 92.1** (148.2 km) Road access to Native village of **CHISTOCHINA** (pop. 43) .

Private Aircraft: Barnhart airstrip, 3 miles/4.8 km north; elev. 1,930 feet/588m; length 2,500 feet/762m; earth; unattended. Chistochina airstrip, adjacent southwest; elev. 1,850 feet/564m; length 2,000 feet/610m; turf and gravel.

GJ 32.8 (52.8 km) **A 235.8** (379.5 km) **T 92.2** (148.4 km) **Chistochina Lodge.** See display ad this section. ▲

GJ 30.1 (48.4 km) **A 233.1** (375.1 km) **T 94.9** (152.7 km) Paved turnout to south. Road narrows eastbound; no shoulders. Watch for frost heaves.

GJ 28.1 (45.2 km) **A 231.1** (371.9 km) **T 96.9** (155.9 km) Double-ended paved parking area to south with a marker on the Alaska Road Commission. The ARC was established in 1905, the same year the first automobile arrived in Alaska at Skagway. The ARC operated for 51 years, building roads, airfields, trails and other transportation facilities. It was replaced by the Bureau of Public Roads (referred to by some Alaskans at the time as the Bureau of Parallel Ruts) in 1956. In 1960 the Bureau of Public Roads was replaced by the Dept. of Public Works.

GJ 24 (38.6 km) **A 227** (365.3 km) **T 101** (162.5 km) Large rest area to south with paved double-ended parking area, toilets, picnic tables and firepits on grass under trees; paths lead to Copper River. Mount Sanford is to the southeast, Mount Drum to the south.

GJ 21.3 (34.3 km) **A 224.3** (361 km) **T 103.7** (166.9 km) Buster Gene trailhead to south.

GJ 20.9 (33.6 km) **A 223.9** (360.3 km) **T 104.1** (167.5 km) Turnout to south.

GJ 17.8 (28.6 km) **A 220.8** (355.3 km) **T 107.2** (172.5 km) **Tulsona Creek** bridge. Good grayling fishing.

GJ 11.6 (18.7 km) **A 214.6** (345.4 km) **T 113.4** (182.5 km) Yellow pond lily *(Nuphar polysepalum)* in ponds along highway.

GJ 9.4 (15.1 km) **A 212.4** (341.8 km) **T 115.6** (186 km) Paved turnout to north by lake.

GJ 8.8 (14.2 km) **A 211.8** (340.8 km) **T 116.2** (187 km) Paved turnout to north. BLM trailhead.

GJ 6.3 (10.1 km) **A 209.3** (336.8 km) **T 118.7** (191 km) Paved turnout to southeast.

GJ 4.2 (6.8 km) **A 207.2** (333.4 km) **T 120.8** (194.4 km) **Gakona, AK. R.V. Wilderness Campsite.** See display ad this section. ▲

GJ 2.7 (4.3 km) **A 205.7** (331 km) **T 122.3** (196.8 km) **GAKONA** (area pop. 200). The village of Gakona lies between the Gakona and Copper rivers (Gakona is Athabascan for "rabbit"). Originally Gakona was a Native wood and fish camp, and fish wheels are still common. The post office is located on the highway here.

GJ 2 (3.2 km) **A 205** (330 km) **T 123** (198 km) Gakona Lodge, entered on the National Register of Historic Places in 1977. Originally one of several roadhouses providing essential food and lodging for travelers, it opened in 1905 and was first called Doyle's Ranch. The original carriage house is now a restaurant.

Gakona Lodge & Trading Post and **The Carriage House Dining Room.** See display ad this section.

GJ 1.8 (2.9 km) **A 204.8** (329.6 km) **T 123.2** (198.3 km) Bridge over Gakona River. Entering Game Management Unit 13B westbound and 13C eastbound. The high-

(Continued on page 261)

Nabesna Road Log

The Nabesna Road leads 45 miles/72.4 km southeast from **Milepost GJ 59.8** Glenn Highway (Tok Cutoff) to the mining community of Nabesna. The first 4 miles/6.4 km of road is chip seal surface, the remainder is gravel. Beyond **Milepost J 28.6** the road becomes rough and crosses several creeks which may be difficult to ford. This side trip can be enjoyable for campers; there are no formal campgrounds but there are plenty of beautiful spots to camp. The area also offers good fishing. The Nabesna Road provides access to Wrangell–St. Elias National Park and Preserve. The National Park Service ranger station at Slana has information on current road conditions and on backcountry travel in the park. **Distance is measured from the junction with the Glenn Highway (J).**

J 0.1 (0.2 km) Highway maintenance station.

J 0.2 (0.3 km) Slana NPS ranger station; information on road conditions and on Wrangell–St. Elias National Park and Preserve. Open 8 A.M. to 5 P.M. daily, June 1 through September. Pay phone, USGS maps and bookstore. For more information contact: Superintendent, Wrangell–St. Elias National Park and Preserve, P.O. Box 29, Glennallen, AK 99588.

J 0.8 (1.3 km) The Slana post office is located at the picturesque Hart D Ranch, home of artist Mary Frances DeHart.

Hart D Ranch Studio and Fine Art Gallery. See display ad this section.

J 1 (1.6 km) **SLANA** (pop. 39), once an Indian village on the north bank of the Slana River, now refers to this general area. Besides the Indian settlement, Slana boasted a popular roadhouse, now a private home. Slana elementary school is located here.

J 1.5 (2.4 km) Slana River bridge; undeveloped camping area. Boundary between Game Management Units 11 and 13C.

J 2 (3.2 km) BLM homestead area next 2 miles/3.2 km southbound. Blueberries in the fall; grouse are seen in this area.

J 3.9 (6.2 km) Entering Wrangell–St. Elias National Park and Preserve. The Glenn Highway follows the northern boundary of the preserve between Slana and Gakona Junction; Nabesna Road provides access to the park.

J 4 (6.4 km) Turnouts. Hard surface ends, gravel begins, southbound.

J 7 (11.3 km) Road crosses **Rufus Creek** culvert. Dolly Varden to 8 inches, June to October. Watch out for bears, especially during berry season.

J 8.9 (14.3 km) Rough turnout.

J 11 (17.7 km) Suslota Lake trailhead No. 1 to north.

J 11.4 (18.3 km) Gravel pit, room to park or camp.

J 12.2 (19.6 km) Road crosses Caribou Creek culvert.

J 12.5 (20.1 km) Turnout to southeast; Copper Lake trailhead.

J 13 (20.9 km) Suslota Lake trailhead No. 2 to north.

J 15 (24.1 km) Turnout.

J 15.4 (24.8 km) Beautiful views of Mount Sanford and Tanada Peak in the Wrangell Mountains, across the great plain of the Copper River.

J 16 (25.7 km) Turnout to northeast.

J 16.6 (26.7 km) Turnout to southwest.

J 16.9 (27.2 km) Turnout by large lake which reflects Mount Sanford.

J 18 (29 km) Pond to northeast. The highly mineralized Mentasta Mountains are visible to the north. This is sparsely timbered high country.

J 18.8 (30.3 km) Caribou Creek culvert.

J 19.3 (31.1 km) Turnout at gravel pit to northwest. Look for poppies, lupine, arnica and chiming bells in season.

J 21.2 (34.1 km) Turnout at gravel pit to northwest.

J 21.8 (35.1 km) Rock Creek culvert.

J 22.3 (35.9 km) Rock Lake; turnouts both sides of road.

J 22.9 (36.8 km) Long Lake; no turnouts. Good place for floatplane landings.

J 23.4 (37.7 km) Turnout. Floatplane landing.

J 24.4 (39.3 km) Turnout to southwest with view of Wrangell Mountains. Tanada Lake trail.

J 25.2 (40.6 km) Boundary between Sportfish Areas C and K, and Game Management Areas 11 and 12.

J 25.5 (41 km) Glimpse of Tanada Lake beneath Tanada Peak to the south.

Silvertip Lodge & Air Service. See display ad this section.

J 25.9 (41.7 km) Little Jack Creek.

J 26.1 (42 km) Access road to private property; no turnaround.

J 27 (43.5 km) Turnout to north.

J 28.2 (45.4 km) Turnouts at Twin Lakes; primitive campsite, good place to observe waterfowl. Wildflowers in June include Lapland rosebay, lupine and 8-petalled avens.

AREA FISHING: Twin Lakes, grayling 10 to 18 inches, mid-May to October, flies or small spinner; also burbot. **Copper Lake** (fly in from Jack Lake), lake trout 10 to 12 lbs., mid-June to September, use red-and-white spoon; kokanee 10 to 12 inches, mid-June to July, use small spinner; grayling 12 to 20 inches, July through September; also burbot. **Long** and **Jack lakes,** grayling fishing. **Tanada Lake** (fly in from Long Lake), grayling and lake trout.

J 28.6 (46 km) The road deteriorates beyond this point and you may have to ford several creeks. If you are going on, inquire at lodge here about road conditions.

J 29.6 (47.6 km) Trail Creek crosses road; no culvert but road has gravel base here. Easy to drive through creek, especially in fall. Overnight hikers may hike up Lost Creek gravel bed and return via Trail Creek.

J 31.4 (50.5 km) Road crosses Lost Creek, a very wide expanse of water in spring and may remain difficult to cross well into summer. Loose gravel makes it easy to get stuck in creek if you spin your wheels. Scout it out first. If you hesitate once in the creek, wheels may dig in. The road crosses several more creeks beyond here; these may also be difficult to ford.

J 31.6 (50.9 km) Boyden Creek (may have to ford after rain or during spring melt).

Mentasta Mountains from Nabesna Road. *(George Wuerthner)*

J 32.4 (52.1 km) Chalk Creek culvert.

J 33 (53.1 km) Big Grayling Lake hiking trail. Horses allowed.

J 34.1 (54.9 km) Radiator Creek culvert.

J 35 (56.3 km) Creek (must ford).

J 36 (57.9 km) Jack Creek bridge.

J 36.1 (58.1 km) Informal campsite. The road crosses 5 creeks the next 4.3 miles/6.9 km southbound. Watch for loose gravel in creekbeds.

J 41 (66 km) A marked trail, approximately 5 miles/8 km long, leads to Nabesna River and old Reeves Field airstrip, once used to fly gold out and supplies in to mining camps. Devils Mountain is to the left of the trail. The trail on the river also leads to the old Indian village of Khiltat.

J 41.4 (66.6 km) Skookum Creek (may have to ford after rain or during spring melt).

J 42 (67.6 km) Devil's Mountain Lodge (private property). Four-wheel-drive vehicles only beyond this point.

End of the Road B&B. See display ad this section.

J 45 (72.4 km) **NABESNA** (area pop. less than 25; elev. 3,000 feet/914m). No facilities. This region has copper reserves, as well as gold in the streams and rivers, silver, molybdenum and iron ore deposits. Nabesna gold mine is located here. Area residents subsist on caribou, Dall sheep, moose, bear, fish and small game. Fire fighting and trapping also provide some income. Big game hunting is popular in this area and several outfitters have headquarters along Nabesna Road.

Return to Milepost GJ 59.8
Glenn Highway (Tok Cutoff)

(Continued from page 259)
way climbs a short hill and joins the Richardson Highway 1.8 miles/2.9 km from this bridge. From the hill there is a fine view of the many channels where the Gakona and Copper rivers join.

GJ 1 (1.6 km) **A 204** (328.3 km) **T 124** (200 km) Rest area to south has paved turnout overlooking the valley of the Gakona and Copper rivers; picnic tables and litter barrels. View of Mount Drum and Mount Sanford. Good photo stop.

GJ 0 A 203 (326.7 km) **T 125** (201.2 km) **Gakona Junction.** Junction of Tok Cutoff (Alaska Route 1) with the Richardson Highway (Alaska Route 4); the two roads share a common alignment for the next 14 miles/22.5 km westbound. Turn north here for Delta Junction via the Richardson Highway (see **Milepost V 128.6** in the RICHARDSON HIGHWAY SECTION). Turn south for Anchorage or Valdez. *NOTE: This junction can be confusing. Choose your route carefully.*

Gakona Junction Village. See display ad this section.

Glenn Highway Junction

To Delta Junction
4
Richardson Highway
Tok Cutoff
1
To Tok
Gakona Junction
N
W
E
S
Glennallen
To Anchorage
1
Glenn Highway
4
To Valdez

Richardson Highway Log

ALASKA ROUTE 4
Physical mileposts for the next 14 miles/22.5 km southbound give distance from Valdez. **Distance from Anchorage (A) is followed by distance from Tok (T) and distance from Valdez (V).**

A 203 (326.7 km) **T 125** (201.2 km) **V 128.6** (207 km) **Junction** of the Tok Cutoff with the Richardson Highway at Gakona Junction. Watch for frost heaves between here and **Milepost V 124.**

A 201 (323.5 km) **T 127** (204.4 km) **V 126.9** (204.2 km) Access road to **GULKANA** (pop. 82) on the bank of the Gulkana River. Camping is permitted along the river by the bridge. Grayling fishing and good king and sockeye salmon fishing (June and July) in the **Gulkana River.** Most of the Gulkana River frontage in this area is owned by Gulkana village and managed by Ahtna, Inc. Ahtna lands are closed to the public for hunting, fishing and trapping.

A **200.9** (323.3 km) T **127.1** (204.5 km) V **126.8** (204 km) Gulkana River bridge. Entering Game Management Unit 13B eastbound, 13A westbound.

A **200.3** (322.3 km) T **127.7** (205.5 km) **V 126.2** (203.1 km) **Bear Creek Inn.** See display ad this section.

A **200.1** (322 km) **T 127.9** (205.8 km) V **126** (202.8 km) Paved double-ended turnout to north.

A **197.3** (317.5 km) **T 130.7** (210.3 km) V **123.2** (198.3 km) Large paved turnout to south.

A **192.1** (309.1 km) **T 135.9** (218.7 km) **V 118.1** (190 km) **Private Aircraft:** Gulkana airstrip; elev. 1,578 feet/481m; length 5,000 feet/1,524m; asphalt; fuel 100. Flying service located here.

Ellis Air Taxi, Inc. See display ad on page 261.

Gulkana Air Service. See display ad this section.

A **192** (309 km) **T 136** (218.9 km) **V 118** (189.9 km) Dry Creek State Recreation Site; 58 campsites, 15-day limit, $6 nightly fee or annual pass, four picnic sites, toilets, picnic shelter. *Bring mosquito repellent!* ▲

A **189.5** (305 km) **T 138.5** (222.9 km) **V 115.5** (185.9 km) **Glennallen Quick Stop Truck Stop.** Stop for friendly family service and gas and diesel prices that are hard to beat. A well-stocked convenience

store contains ice, pop, snacks, postcards, ice cream, specialty items, a phone and free coffee. Several interesting items are on display, including an authentic Native Alaskan fish wheel. [ADVERTISEMENT]

A **189** (304.2 km) **T 139** (223.7 km) **V 115** (185.1 km) **Junction** of the Richardson Highway (Alaska Route 4) with the Glenn Highway (Alaska Route 1). Turn south here on the Richardson Highway for Valdez (see **Milepost V 115** in the RICHARDSON HIGHWAY section). Continue west on the Glenn Highway for Anchorage. *NOTE: This junction can be confusing. Choose your route carefully. See map, page 261.*

Greater Copper Valley Chamber of Commerce visitor information center and gas station. Alaska State Troopers, Dept. of Motor Vehicles, Fish and Wildlife Protection and courthouse located on east side of highway.

Greater Copper River Valley Visitor Information Center in log cabin; open 8 A.M. to 7 P.M. daily in summer. There's also a convenience grocery and a gas station (with diesel) at junction.

Greater Copper Valley Chamber of Commerce. See display ad this section.

The Hub of Alaska. See display ad this section.

Glenn Highway Log

ALASKA ROUTE 1

Physical mileposts between Glennallen and Anchorage show distance from Anchorage. **Distance from Anchorage (A) is followed by distance from Tok (T).**

A **188.7** (303.7 km) **T 139.3** (224.2 km) **Northern Nights Campground & RV Park.** See display ad this section. ▲

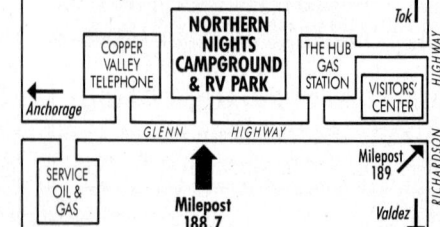

A 188.3 (303 km) **T 139.7** (224.8 km) Trans-Alaska pipeline passes under the highway.

A 187.5 (301.7 km) **T 140.5** (226.1 km) **Tastee–Freez.** This popular spot features an excellent menu of fast food, including breakfast, with some of the lowest prices on the highway. We satisfy appetites of all sizes, from a quick taco to double cheeseburgers, cooked fresh and fast. Our comfortable dining room displays a selection of the finest original drawings and paintings available in Alaska's "bush." Plan to stop! See display ad in Glennallen section. [ADVERTISEMENT]

A 187.2 (301.3 km) **T 140.8** (226.6 km) **Grubstake RV Park** offers secluded overnight camping in the heart of Glennallen. Take advantage of water and electric hookups at low rates and enjoy a variety of local gift shops, restaurants and services within walking distance of the Grubstake RV Park! Located between Last Frontier Pizza and Tastee–Freez. [ADVERTISEMENT] ▲

A 187.2 (301.3 km) **T 140.8** (226.6 km) Post office a block north of highway. Description of Glennallen follows.

Glennallen

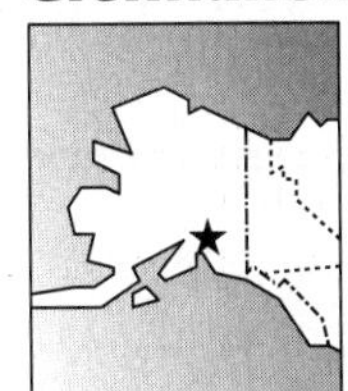

A 187 (300.9 km) **T 141** (226.9 km) Near the south junction of Glenn and Richardson highways. **Population:** 928. Emergency Services: **Alaska State Troopers, Milepost A 189**, phone 822-3263. **Fire Department**, phone 911. **Ambulance**, Copper River EMS, phone 911. **Clinic, Milepost A 186.6**, phone 822-3203. **Road Conditions**, phone 822-5511.

Visitor Information: Greater Copper River Valley Visitor Information Center is located in the log cabin at the junction of the Glenn and Richardson highways. **Milepost A 189**; open 8 A.M. to 7 P.M. daily in summer. The Alaska Dept. of Fish and Game office is located at **Milepost A 186.2** on the Glenn Highway; phone 822-3309.

Elevation: 1,460 feet/445m. **Climate:** Mean monthly temperature in January -10°F/-23°C; in July, 56°F/13°C. Record low was -61°F/-52°C in January 1975; record high, 90°F/32°C in June 1969. Mean precipitation in July, 1.53 inches/3.9cm. Mean precipitation (snow/sleet) in December, 11.4 inches/29cm. **Radio:** KCAM 790, KUAC-FM 92.1. **Television:** Rural Alaska Television Network and Wrangell Mountain TV Club via satellite; Public Broadcasting System.

Private Aircraft: Gulkana airstrip, 4.3 miles/6.9 km northeast of Glennallen at **Milepost A 192.1**; elev. 1,578 feet/481m; length 5,000 feet/1,524m; asphalt; fuel 100. Flight service station open 16 hours daily. Parking with tie downs. Mechanic available.

The name Glennallen is derived from the combined last names of Capt. Edwin F. Glenn and Lt. Henry T. Allen, both leaders in the early exploration of the Copper River region.

Glennallen lies at the western edge of the huge Wrangell–St. Elias National Park and Preserve. It is a gateway to the Wrangell

Mountains and the service center for the Copper River basin. Glennallen is also a fly-in base for several guides and outfitters.

Four prominent peaks of the majestic Wrangell Mountains are to the east; from left they are Mounts Sanford, Drum, Wrangell and Blackburn. The best views are on crisp winter days at sunset. The rest of the countryside is relatively flat with small lakes and streams.

The main business district is 1.5 miles/2.4 km west of the south junction of the Glenn and Richardson highways. There are also several businesses located at the south junction. About two-thirds of the area's residents are employed by trade/service firms; the balance hold various government positions. Offices for the Bureau of Land Management, the Alaska State Troopers and Dept. of Fish and Game are located here. There are several small farms in the area. There is a substantial Native population in the area and the Native-owned Ahtna Corp. has its headquarters near Glennallen at **Milepost V 104** Richardson Highway.

Also headquartered here is KCAM radio, which broadcasts on station 790. KCAM broadcasts area road condition reports daily and also airs the popular "Caribou Clatter,"

GLENNALLEN ADVERTISERS

Bishop's RV Park & Car Wash ....Downtown
Brown Bear Rhodehouse ....Mile 183.6 Glenn Hwy.
Caribou Cafe Family Restaurant ....Downtown
Glennallen Chevron..........Ph. (907) 822-3303
Greater Copper Valley Chamber of Commerce .....Mile 189 Richardson Hwy.
KCAM Radio......................Ph. (907) 822-3434
Last Frontier Pizza ....Ph. (907) 822-3030
Mechanix Warehouse Auto Parts....................Ph. (907) 822-3444
New Caribou Hotel, Gift Shop and Restaurant ....Ph. (907) 822-3302
Old Post Office Gallery ..Adjacent Tastee-Freez
Pardner's Crackerbarrel Store ....Mile 186.9 Glenn Hwy.
Park's Place Supermarket................Ph. (907) 822-3334
Tastee-Freez..................................Downtown
Tolsona Wilderness Campground ....Mile 173 Glenn Hwy.

Fishermen show off king salmon caught in the Gulkana River. (Jerrianne Lowther, staff)

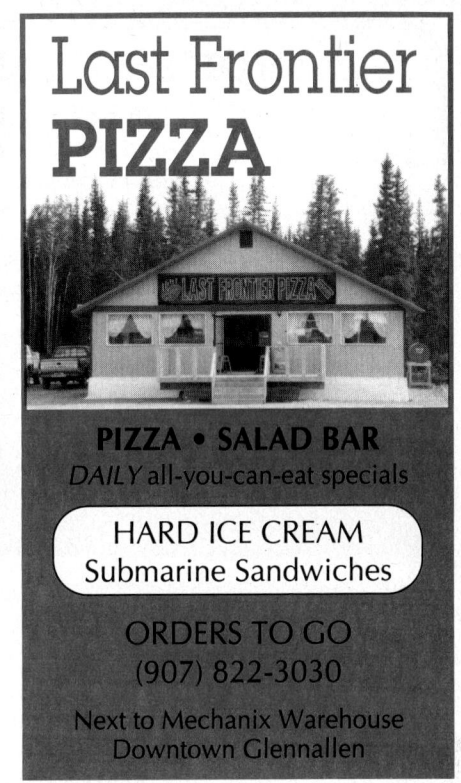

which will broadcast personal messages. Radio messages are still a popular form of communication in Alaska and a necessary one in the Bush. Similar programs throughout the state are KJNP's "Trapline Chatter"; KYAK's "Bush Pipeline"; KHAR's "Northwinds"; and KIAK's "Pipeline of the North." KFAR in Fairbanks broadcast "Tundra Topics" for 37 years; it was taken off the air in 1980.

ACCOMMODATIONS

Because of its strategic location, most traveler services are available. During summer months reservations are advised for visitor accommodations. Glennallen has several lodges and motels and a variety of restaurants. Auto parts, groceries, gifts, clothing, propane, sporting goods and other supplies are available at local stores. Services include a bank, a dentist, several churches, a chiropractic center, a laundromat, gas sta-

ALASKA STATE SYMBOLS:
Willow ptarmigan (bird), forget-me-not (flower), jade (gem), gold (mineral), dog mushing (sport), Sitka spruce (tree).

tions and major auto repair.

New Caribou Hotel, Gift Shop and Restaurant. The New Caribou Hotel in downtown Glennallen, on the edge of the largest national park in America, was completed fall of 1990. This 45-unit modern facility features custom built furniture, state-of-the-art color coordinated Alaskan decor, six rooms with two-person whirlpool baths, two-bedroom fully furnished suites with kitchens and cooking facilities. Alaskan art, handicap facilities, conference rooms, phones and fax lines, remote control color TVs. Large full menu restaurant with banquet room, unique Alaskan gift shop (a must stop in your travels). All major credit cards accepted. Tour buses welcome. Airport transportation. Ask us for travel and visitor information. Open year-round. Phone (907) 822-3302. Toll free in Alaska (800) 478-3302, fax (907) 822-3711. [ADVERTISEMENT]

There are private campgrounds west of town on the Glenn Highway (see **Milepost A 173** and **A 170.5**) and east of town at **Milepost A 188.7**. There are two private RV parks in Glennallen and at **Milepost V 110.5** Richardson Highway (4.5 m/7.2 km south of the junction). Northeast of Glennallen 5 miles/8 km is Dry Creek state campground (see **Milepost A 192**). ▲

TRANSPORTATION

Bus: Scheduled service between Valdez and Anchorage; Valdez and Fairbanks via Tok (summer only); and Anchorage and Whitehorse. Bus service between Glennallen and McCarthy via Copper Center and Chitina in summer.

ATTRACTIONS

The "Glenn and Allen Show," a locally produced historical comedy, can be seen three days a week during the summer months.

Recreational opportunities in the Glennallen area include hunting, rafting, bird watching and fishing. According to the ADF&G, approximately 50 lakes in the Glennallen area are stocked with grayling, rainbow trout and coho salmon. (A complete list of lakes, locations and species is available at the Copper River Valley Visitor Center.) Locally, there's good grayling fishing in **Moose Creek, Tulsona Creek** to the east at **Milepost GJ 17.5**, and west on the Glenn Highway at **Tolsona Creek, Milepost A 173**, and **Mendeltna Creek, Milepost A 152.8. Lake Louise**, approximately 27 miles/43 km west and 19 miles/30.5 km north from Glennallen, offers excellent grayling and lake trout fishing.

Many fly-in lakes are located in the Copper River basin and Chugach Mountains near Glennallen. **Crosswind Lake**, large lake trout, whitefish and grayling, early June to early July. **Deep Lake**, all summer for lake trout to 30 inches. **High Lake**, lake trout to 22 inches, June and early July with small spoons; some rainbow, fly-fishing; cabin, boats and motors rental. **Tebay Lakes**, excellent rainbow fishing, 12 to 15 inches, all summer, small spinners; cabin, boats and motors rental. **Jans Lake**, 12- to 14-inch silver salmon, June, spinners; also rainbow. **Hanagita Lake**, excellent grayling fishing all summer; also lake trout and steelhead in September. **Minnesota Lake**, lake trout to 30 inches, all summer; boat only, no cabins.

The Alaska Dept. of Fish and Game is located at **Milepost A 186.2**; phone 822-3309.

Glenn Highway Log

(continued)

A 186.6 (300.3 km) T 141.4 (227.6 km) Cross Road Medical Center clinic. Alaska Bible College, the state's only accredited resident four-year bible college, is located behind the clinic.

A 186.4 (300 km) T 141.6 (227.9 km) Bureau of Land Management district office.

A 186.2 (299.7 km) T 141.8 (228.2 km) Alaska State Dept. of Fish and Game.

A 186.1 (299.5 km) T 141.9 (228.4 km) Copper Valley library.

A 186 (299.3 km) T 142 (228.5 km) **Moose Creek** culvert; good grayling fishing in spring. From here westbound, the highway knifes across the southern rim of a vast tableland that reaches from the Alaska Range, 80 miles/129 km north, to the Chugach Mountains, 15 miles/24 km south. Watch for wildlife.

A 183.6 (295.5 km) T 144.4 (232.4 km) **Brown Bear Rhodehouse.** Because of the excellent food, reasonable prices and Alaskan hospitality, this famous old lodge is a favorite eating and gathering place for local people and travelers alike. If eating in the Glennallen area, we recommend stopping here, and if coming from south it is well worth the extra few minutes wait. Superb steaks and seafood are the specialties, along with broasted chicken and the widest sandwich selection in the area. Your hosts, Doug and Cindy Rhodes, have managed to take one of the largest grizzly-brown bear photograph collections anywhere. So, if not dining, you will enjoy just stopping and looking at the many photographs that cover the walls or listening to a few bear tales in the lounge. This is also the only place on the highway to get a bucket of golden brown broasted chicken to go. Phone (907) 822-3663. [ADVERTISEMENT]

A 183.5 (295.3 km) T 144.5 (232.5 km) Museum (private; fee charged).

A 182.2 (293.2 km) T 145.8 (234.6 km) **Basin Liquors, Paper Shack Office Supply.** Liquor store opens 8 A.M., seven days a week, 365 days a year. Liquor, snacks, ice, cigarettes. We invite you to take a break; walk around in one of the most beautiful yards on the Glenn Highway, longtime home of pioneer resident "Gramma Ole" Hanson. [ADVERTISEMENT]

A 182 (292.9 km) T 146 (235 km) **Glennallen Sporting Goods.** See display ad this section.

A 176.6 (284.2 km) T 151.4 (243.6 km) Paved turnout to south with interpretive sign about the Wrangell Mountains and view east across the Copper River valley to Mount Drum. Northeast of Mount Drum is Mount Sanford and southeast is Mount Wrangell (elev. 14,163 feet/4,317m), a semi-active volcano. Mount Wrangell last erupted in 1912 when lava flowed to its base and ash fell as far west as this point.

Wildflowers growing along the roadside include cinquefoil, oxytrope, Jacob's ladder and sweet pea.

A 174.7 (281.1 km) T 153.3 (246.7 km) Double-ended paved turnout to south.

A 173 (278.4 km) T 155 (249.4 km) **Tolsona Wilderness Campground & RV Park.** AAA approved, Good Sam Park. This beautiful campground, located three-quarter mile north of the highway, is surrounded on three sides by untouched wilderness. Each shady campsite is situated beside sparkling Tolsona Creek and is complete with table, litter barrel and fireplace. It is a full-service campground with tent sites, restrooms, dump station, coin-op showers, laundromat, water and electric hookups for RVs. Public phone. Open from May 20 through Sept. 10. $8 to $15 per night. Phone (907) 822-3865. [ADVERTISEMENT] ▲

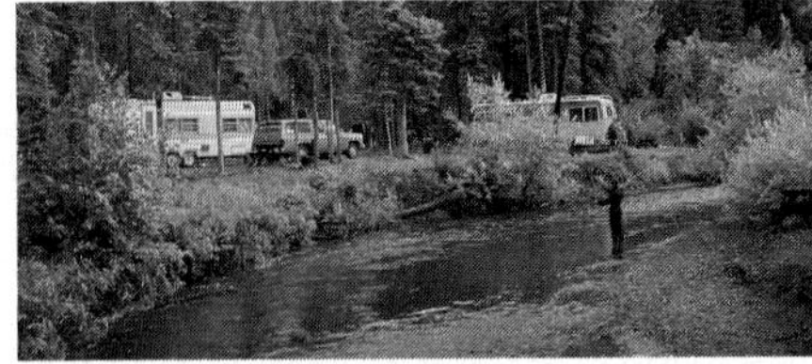

Tolsona Creek, grayling to 16 inches, use mosquito flies in still, clear pools behind obstructions, June, July and August. Best fishing 1.5 miles/2.4 km upstream from highway. **Tolsona** and **Moose lakes**, rainbow trout, burbot, grayling to 16 inches, all summer; good ice fishing for burbot in winter; boats, food and lodging.

A 173 (278.4 km) T 155 (249.4 km) **Ranch House Lodge**, established 1958. Enjoy friendly hospitality in an authentic rustic atmosphere in Alaska's most beautiful log lodge. Superb steaks and seafood. Our Ranchburgers are built on custom-made buns and are famous statewide. Cocktails over solid log bar. Large selection of tanned Alaska furs. Rustic log cabins. Liquor store. Ice. Alaskan gifts. Camping available. Located on beautiful Tolsona Creek. Your hosts: Burt and Dottie Ward. Phone (907) 822-3882 or write HC-01 Box 1980, Glennallen, AK 99588. [ADVERTISEMENT]

A 172.9 (278.2 km) T 155.1 (249.6 km)

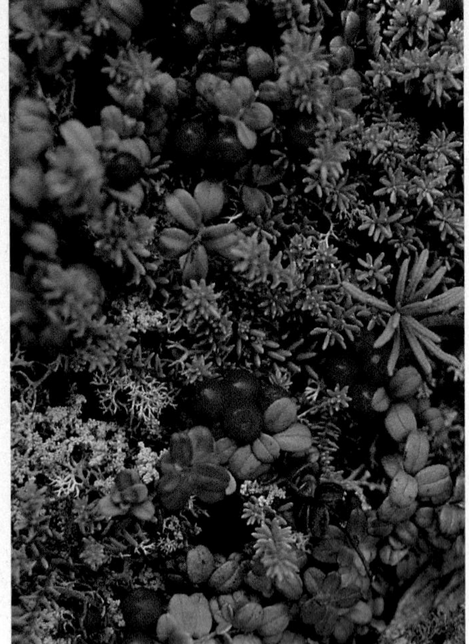

A creeping evergreen shrub, lowbush cranberries are edible. (Jennifer Beecroft)

Tolsona Creek day-use area; picnic tables.

A 170.5 (274.4 km) **T 157.5** (253.5 km) **Tolsona Lake Resort.** See display ad on page 267. ▲

Tolsona Lake, grayling to 16 inches, burbot, rainbow. **Crosswind Lake,** 18 miles/29 km north by floatplane, excellent fishing for lake trout, grayling and whitefish.

A 169.3 (272.3 km) **T 158.7** (255.4 km) Mae West Lake trail. Paved double-ended turnout to south. The long narrow lake, fed by Little Woods Creek, is a little less than 1 mile/1.6 km away.

Watch for bad frost heaves next 0.3 mile/0.5 km westbound.

A 168 (270.4 km) **T 160** (257.5 km) Rough road, patched pavement and frost heaves westbound. Soup Lake to north. Trumpeter swans can sometimes be seen in lakes and ponds along this section of highway. In June and July look for wildflowers such as sweet pea, fireweed, lupine, cinquefoil, oxytrope, Jacob's ladder and milk vetch.

A 166.1 (267.3 km) **T 161.9** (260.5 km) Atlasta House, a local landmark, was named by the homesteader who was happy to have a real house at last.

A 166 (267.2 km) **T 162** (260.7 km) Tolsona Mountain (elev. 2,974 feet/906m), a prominent ridge just north of highway, is a landmark for miles in both directions. This area is popular with berry-pickers in late summer and early fall. Varieties of wild berries include blueberries, lowbush cranberries and raspberries.

A 165.9 (267 km) **T 162.1** (260.9 km) Paved double-ended turnout to south and 2-mile/3.2-km trail to Lost Cabin Lake.

A 162.3 (261.2 km) **T 165.7** (266.7 km) Paved turnout to south.

A 162 (260.7 km) **T 166** (267.1 km) Tex Smith Lake to north.

A 161 (259 km) **T 167** (268.7 km) Bad frost heaves next 0.4 mile/0.6 km eastbound.

A 159.8 (257.2 km) **T 168.2** (270.7 km) **Little Junction Lake,** 0.3-mile/0.4-km hike south; grayling.

A 159.8 (257.2 km) **T 168.2** (270.7 km) **Junction** with Lake Louise Road to Lake Louise Recreation Area. See LAKE LOUISE ROAD log on opposite page.

A 159.6 (256.8 km) **T 168.4** (271 km) Little Junction Lake trailhead.

A 159 (255.8 km) **T 169** (272 km) Watch for bumps in pavement and frost heaves westbound to **Milepost A 133.**

A 156 (251.1 km) **T 172** (276.8 km) Tazlina Glacier, seen to the east, feeds into 20-mile-/32-km-long Tazlina Lake situated at its foot.

Tazlina Glacier Lodge and Crosswind Lake Resort. Inquire about the facilities and services available at historic Tazlina Glacier Lodge and Tazlina's new remote fly-in fishing resort on Crosswind Lake. We are now fully open to accommodate your stay with us and take great pride in providing a warm, friendly atmosphere and service. We have a state-maintained airstrip across the road and a floatplane lake in our backyard. Our services include groceries, hunting and fishing licenses, fishing trips and equipment, remote cabins with kitchenettes, boats and

motors, hunting, aerial sightseeing and photography, shopping at "The Tourist Trap and Guilt Shop," dog sled trips and cross-country skiing in winter. Relax over a fine meal, our espresso bar has no equal, our cabins are cozy and warm and we have group rates, too! We will be happy to help you plan an unforgettable Alaska trip, whether winter or summer. So, come ahead and take a step back in time. Phone (907) 822-3061. Art and Bonny Wikle, HC 01, Box 1862, Glennallen, AK 99588. [ADVERTISEMENT]

A 155.8 (250.7 km) **T 172.2** (277.1 km) **Private Aircraft:** Tazlina airstrip; elev. 2,450 feet/747m; length 1,200 feet/366m; gravel; unattended.

A 155.7 (250.6 km) **T 172.3** (277.3 km) **Arizona Lake** to south; fishing for grayling.

A 155.5 (250.2 km) **T 172.5** (277.6 km) Paved turnout to south.

A 155.2 (249.8 km) **T 172.8** (278.1 km) **Gergie Lake** to south; fishing for grayling and rainbow.

A 154.4 (248.5 km) **T 173.6** (279.4 km) Turnout at old road alignment.

A 153 (246.2 km) **T 175** (281.6 km) **K.R.O.A. Kamping Resorts of Alaska** on the Little Mendeltna, a natural spring-fed stream. Excellent fishing for grayling, whitefish and others. Many lakes nearby. Fishing, hunting guides available. Gateway to Tazlina Lake and Glacier. Ski, hiking, snow machine trails. Modern hookups. Pull-throughs. Laundromat. Hot showers. Can handle any size caravan. Rustic cabins. Brick oven fresh dough pizza. Homemade cinnamon rolls. Museum of Alaska's Drunken Forest, a large collection of unusual and artistic natural designs of trees. Minerals. Artifacts of Alaska's drunken forest. Free. [ADVERTISEMENT] ▲

A 152.8 (245.9 km) **T 175.2** (282 km) Mendeltna Creek bridge.

Lake Louise Road Log

This 19.3-mile-/31-km-long scenic gravel road from the Glenn Highway north to Lake Louise Recreation Area is open year-round. Lake Louise is known for its good lake trout fishing; ice fishing in winter. Excellent cross-country skiing. Many turnouts and parking areas along the road; views of Tazlina Glacier and Lake; berry picking for wild strawberries and blueberries (July and August), and cranberries (September).

Distance is measured from the junction with the Glenn Highway (J).

J 0.2 (0.3 km) **Junction Lake** to east; grayling fishing.

J 1.1 (1.8 km) Turnout with view of Tazlina Glacier and Crater Lake.

J 1.2 (1.9 km) Double-ended turnout to west. Just north is the road west to **Crater Lake.** There are a number of small lakes along the road with good fishing for grayling, rainbow and silver salmon.

J 9.4 (15.1 km) Beautiful pothole lakes. First view of Lake Louise northbound.

J 11 (17.7 km) Good view on clear days of the Alaska Range and Susitna River valley.

J 11.5 (18.5 km) Road west to **Caribou Lake;** silver salmon, rainbow and grayling fishing. Turnout to east by Elbow Lake.

J 14 (22.5 km) Boundary of Matanuska–Susitna Borough.

J 15.5 (24.9 km) Gas station, public dumpster.

J 16.1 (25.9 km) **Lake Louise Lodge.** Truly Alaskan. Rich in wildlife, scenic beauty and hospitality. Our lodge within a lodge blends the Alaska of yesterday and today. Enjoy good home-cooking as you

overlook beautiful Lake Louise. Experience real Alaska by visiting Lake Louise Lodge, HC 01 Box 1716, Glennallen, AK 99588. Phone (907) 822-3311. [ADVERTISEMENT]

J 16.5 (26.6 km) **Evergreen Lodge Bed & Breakfast.** See display ad this section.

J 16.8 (27 km) **Conner Lake,** grayling fishing.

J 17.2 (27.7 km) Side road to lodge and Lake Louise State Recreation Area's Army Point and Lake Louise campgrounds; 52 campsites on two loop roads, firepits, toilets (handicap accessible), covered picnic tables at lakeshore and a boat launch. Well water. Camping fee $6/night or annual pass. Swimming in Lake Louise. Winter ski trail access. ▲

J 17.2 (27.7 km) **The Point at Lake Louise.** See display ad this section.

J 17.6 (28.3 km) Turnout to west. Winter ski trail access.

Lake Louise, 8.5 miles/13.7 km long, offers excellent fishing. (Jerrianne Lowther, staff)

J 18.8 (30.3 km) Airport road to west. **Private Aircraft:** Lake Louise airstrip; elev. 2,450 feet/747m; length 2,000 feet/610m; gravel. Seaplane base adjacent.

J 19.3 (31 km) Road ends at Lake Louise rest area; picnic tables, fireplaces, toilets, parking, boat launch.

Lake Louise, excellent grayling and lake trout fishing; lake trout 20 to 30 lbs., average 10 lbs., good year-round, best spring through July, then again in late September; early season use herring or whitefish bait, cast from boat; later (warmer water) troll with #16 red-and-white spoon, silver Alaskan plug or large silver flatfish; grayling 10 to 12 inches, casting flies or small spinners, June, July and August; in winter jig for lake trout.

Susitna Lake can be reached by boat across Lake Louise; burbot, excellent lake trout and grayling fishing. Both lakes can be rough; underpowered boats not recommended.

Return to Milepost A 159.8 Glenn Highway

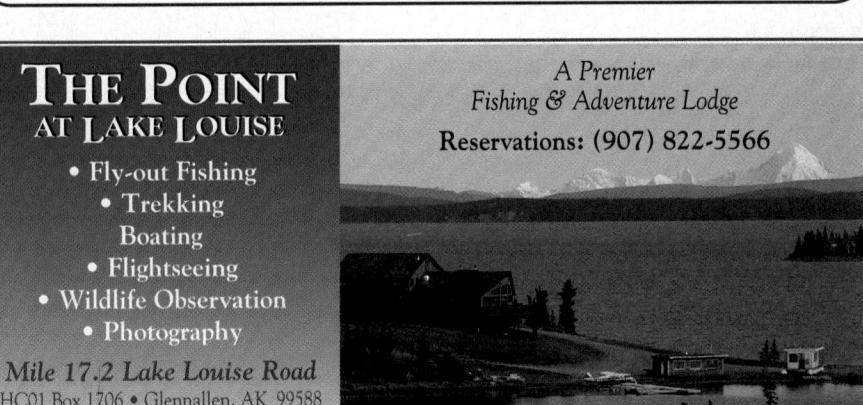

AREA FISHING: Mendeltna Creek, good fishing north to Old Man Lake; watch for bears. (The Mendeltna Creek drainage is closed to the taking of salmon.) Excellent fishing for grayling to 17½ inches, May to November, use spinners and flies; whitefish to 16 inches; burbot to 30 inches, May to November, use spinners or flies; rainbow, from May to November, use spinners or flies. Walk or boat away from the bridge.

A 152.7 (245.7 km) **T 175.3** (282.1 km) Paved double-ended rest area to north with picnic tables, dumpster and toilets. Rough road.

A 149 (239.8 km) **T 179** (288.1 km) **Mirror Lake**; fishing for grayling, whitefish and rainbow.

A 147.3 (237.1 km) **T 180.7** (290.8 km) **Alaskan Airventures.** See display ad on page 268.

A 147.3 (237.1 km) **T 180.7** (290.8 km) **Cache Creek** culvert. Grayling in late May and June. Trail leading from parking area to lake, approximately 0.5 mile/0.8 km. Small picnic area on east side of highway. Steep approach.

A 147 (236.6 km) **T 181** (291.3 km) Very bad frost heaves next 0.7 mile/1.1 km westbound.

A 144.9 (233.2 km) **T 183.1** (294.7 km) Lottie Sparks (Nelchina) Elementary School.

A 141.2 (227.2 km) **T 186.8** (300.6 km) Nelchina state highway maintenance station. Slide Mountain trailhead located behind station.

A 137.6 (221.4 km) **T 190.4** (306.4 km) Little Nelchina State Recreation Site 0.3 mile/0.5 km from highway; 11 campsites, 15-day limit, no camping fee, no drinking water, tables, firepits, toilet, boat launch. Watch for moose and bear. ▲

A 137.5 (221.3 km) **T 190.5** (306.6 km) Little Nelchina River bridge.

A 137 (220.5 km) **T 191** (307.4 km) Boundary of Matanuska–Susitna Borough.

A 135.7 (218.4 km) **T 192.3** (309.5 km) Small paved turnout. Highway widens eastbound.

NOTE: Watch for major road construction to ***Milepost A 118*** *in 1994.*

A 134.8 (216.9 km) **T 193.2** (310.9 km) Watch for loose livestock on highway.

A 132.1 (212.6 km) **T 195.9** (315.2 km) Caribou crossing. Gravel turnout to north. View of Mount Sanford eastbound. Caribou and moose seen in this area in winter. The Nelchina caribou herd passes through here in October–November. Watch for caribou westbound.

A 131 (210.8 km) **T 197** (317 km) View west to the notch of Gunsight Mountain. From here to Eureka Summit there are views of the Wrangell and Chugach mountains.

A 130.3 (209.7 km) **T 197.7** (318.2 km) Old Man Creek trailhead parking to north. Old Man Creek 2 miles/3 km; Crooked Creek 9 miles/14.5 km; Nelchina Town 14.5 miles/23 km. Established trails west from here to Palmer are part of the Chickaloon–Knik–Nelchina trail system.

A 129.3 (208.1 km) **T 198.7** (319.8 km) Eureka Summit (elev. 3,322 feet/1,013m). Highest point on the Glenn Highway, near timberline, with unobstructed views south toward the Chugach Mountains. The Nelchina Glacier winds downward through a cleft in the mountains. To the northwest are the peaks of the Talkeetnas, and to the west the highway descends through river valleys which separate these two mountain ranges. This is the divide of three big river systems: Susitna, Matanuska and Copper.

A 128 (206 km) **T 200** (321.9 km) Site of the first lodge on the Glenn Highway, the Eureka Roadhouse, which was opened in 1937 by Paul Waverly and has operated continuously ever since. The original log building is next to Eureka Lodge.

Eureka Lodge. See display ad this section.

Private Aircraft: Skelton airstrip; elev. 3,289 feet/1,002m; length 2,400 feet/732m; gravel; fuel mogas; unattended.

A 127 (204.4 km) **T 201** (323.4 km) Gravel turnout to south.

A 126.4 (203.4 km) **T 201.6** (324.4 km) Watch closely for turnout to Belanger Creek–Nelchina River trailhead parking to south. Eureka Creek 1.5 miles/2.4 km; Goober Lake 8 miles/13 km; Nelchina River 9 miles/14.5 km.

A 125 (201.2 km) **T 203** (326.7 km) Gunsight Mountain (elev. 6,441 feet/1,963m) is visible for the next few miles to those approaching from Glennallen. The notch or "gunsight" is plain if one looks closely.

A 123.3 (198.4 km) **T 204.7** (329.4 km) Belanger Pass trailhead: Belanger Pass 3 miles/5 km; Alfred Creek 6.5 miles/10.5 km; Albert Creek 8 miles/13 km.

A 123.1 (198.1 km) **T 204.9** (329.8 km) Old Tahneta Inn (closed).

Private Aircraft: Tahneta Pass airstrip; elev. 2,960 feet/902m; length 1,100 feet/335m; gravel/dirt. Floatplanes land on Tahneta Lake.

A 122.9 (197.8 km) **T 205.1** (330 km) Gunsight Mountain Lodge (closed 1993, current status unknown).

A 122 (196.3 km) **T 206** (333.5 km) Tahneta Pass (elev. 3,000 feet/914m). Double-ended paved turnout to north. **Leila Lake** trailhead (unsigned) on old alignment to north; grayling 8 to 14 inches abundant through summer, best fishing June and July. Burbot, success spotty for 12 to 18 inches in fall and winter.

A 120.8 (194.4 km) **T 207.2** (333.4 km) Boundary of Sportfish Management Area 2 and Sheep Mountain Closed Area.

A 120.3 (193.6 km) **T 207.7** (334.3 km) View eastbound overlooks Tahneta Pass. The largest lake is Leila Lake; in the distance is Tahneta Lake. Drive carefully along the southern part of Tahneta Pass. The road is narrow with frost heaves and little shoulder space.

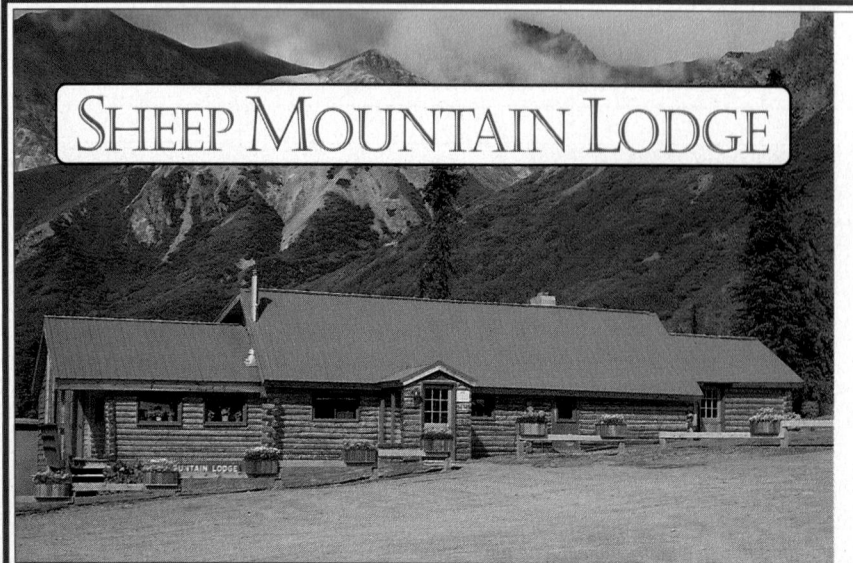

A 118.6 (190.9 km) **T 209.4** (337 km) Gravel turnout to south.

A 118.5 (190.7 km) **T 209.5** (337.1 km) FAA road south to communication towers.

A 118.3 (190.4 km) **T 209.7** (337.5 km) Large gravel turnout to south.

NOTE: Watch for major road construction eastbound to ***Milepost A 135*** *in 1994.*

A 117.8 (189.5 km) **T 210.2** (338.2 km) Turnout with viewpoint. Looking southeast of the highway, a tip of a glacier can be seen coming down South Fork Canyon. Knob Lake and the "knob" (elev. 3,000 feet/914m) can be seen to the northeast.

A 117.6 (189.3 km) **T 210.4** (338.6 km) Squaw Creek trailhead: Squaw Creek 3.5 miles/5.6 km; Caribou Creek 9.5 miles/ 15 km; Alfred Creek 13 miles/21 km; Sheep Creek 15 miles/24 km.

A 115 (185 km) **T 213** (342.8 km) Between **Mileposts A 115** and **116** there are three turnouts with views of mineralized Sheep Mountain and Matanuska Glacier area.

A 114.5 (184.3 km) **T 213.5** (343.6 km) In season, on slopes adjacent the highway and along old creek beds back from the road, are many kinds of flowers, including lupine, Labrador tea, bluebells, fireweed, chiming bells and large patches of forget-me-nots, Alaska's state flower.

A 114.3 (183.9 km) **T 213.7** (343.9 km) For Anchorage-bound travelers a vista of incomparable beauty as the road descends in a long straightaway toward Glacier Point, also known as the Lion Head, an oddly formed rocky dome. No turnouts for 1 mile/1.6 km.

A 114 (183.5 km) **T 214** (344.4 km) Winding road, long stretches without shoulders, watch for rocks and frost heaves westbound between here and Palmer.

A 113.5 (182.7 km) **T 214.5** (345.2 km) **Sheep Mountain Lodge.** Operated since 1946. Home-cooked meals and desserts, bar, liquor store, Alaskan gifts and souvenirs. Comfortable log cabins, RV hookups. Hot tub, sauna, telescope to view Dall sheep. Excellent hiking and cross-country ski trails. Open year-round. HCO3 Box 8490, Palmer, AK 99645. Phone and fax (907) 745-5121. [ADVERTISEMENT] ▲

Private Aircraft: Sheep Mountain airstrip; elev. 2,750 feet/838m; length 2,300 feet/701m; gravel/dirt; unattended.

A 113.5 (182.7 km) **T 214.5** (345.2 km) As the highway descends westbound into the valley of the Matanuska River, there is a view of the great glacier which is the main headwater source and gives the water its milky color.

A 113 (181.9 km) **T 215** (346 km) Gravel turnout.

A 112.5 (181.1 km) **T 215.5** (346.8 km) View to north of Sheep Mountain (elev. 6,300 feet/1,920m) for 11 miles/17.7 km between Tahneta Pass and Caribou Creek. Sheep are often seen high up these slopes. The area surrounding Sheep Mountain is closed to the taking of mountain sheep.

A 112 (180.2 km) **T 216** (347.6 km) Gravel turnout by creek. View westbound of Lion Head and first view of Matanuska Glacier.

A 111 (178.6 km) **T 217** (349.2 km) Sharp curves and falling rocks for the next mile westbound.

A 110.3 (177.5 km) **T 217.7** (350.3 km) Watch for mountain sheep.

A 109.7 (176.5 km) **T 218.3** (351.3 km) Paved turnout to south.

A 109.5 (176.2 km) **T 218.5** (351.6 km) Paved turnout to south.

View of Amulet Peak from a section of old highway near Milepost 92. (Hugh B. White)

A 108.4 (174.4 km) **T 219.6** (353.4 km) Large gravel turnout to south.

A 107.8 (173.5 km) **T 220.2** (354.4 km) Turnout with view of Glacier Point (Lion Head) and Matanuska Glacier. Exceptional picture stop.

A 107.1 (172.4 km) **T 220.9** (355.5 km) Large gravel turnouts to south, viewpoint.

A 106.8 (171.9 km) **T 221.2** (356 km) Caribou Creek bridge and Caribou Creek trailhead. Hiking distances: Squaw Creek 9 miles/14.5 km; Alfred Creek 13 miles/21 km; Sheep Creek 15 miles/24 km; and Squaw Creek trailhead 18.5 miles/30 km. Caribou Creek trail zigzags up the mountainside between the highway and the creek and leads back behind Sheep Mountain. A pleasant hike for good walkers.

Highway makes a steep descent (from both directions) down to Caribou Creek. The banks of this stream provide good rockhounding, particularly after mountain storms. There are turnouts on both sides of the highway here. Fortress Ridge (elev. 5,000 feet/1,524m) above the highway to the north. Sheep Mountain reserve boundary.

A 106 (170.6 km) **T 222** (357.3 km) Large gravel turnout overlooking Caribou Creek canyon. Steep descent eastbound.

A 105.8 (170.3 km) **T 222.2** (357.6 km) Road (closed to public) to FAA station on flank of Glacier Point. Mountain sheep occasionally are seen on the upper slopes.

A 105.5 (169.8 km) **T 222.5** (358.1 km) Gravel turnout to south.

A 105.3 (169.4 km) **T 222.7** (358.4 km) Turnout with views of Matanuska Glacier and the FAA station on Glacier Point.

A 104.1 (167.5 km) **T 223.9** (360.3 km) Access to Glacier View School, which overlooks Matanuska Glacier.

A 104 (167.4 km) **T 224** (360.5 km) From here to **Milepost A 98** several kinds of wild orchids and other wildflowers may be found along the trails into the roadside brush.

A 102.8 (165.4 km) **T 225.2** (362.4 km) Gravel turnout to south with view of Matanuska Glacier.

A 102.5 (165 km) **T 225.5** (362.9 km) Glacier Pass Overlook; campground overlooking Matanuska Glacier. ▲

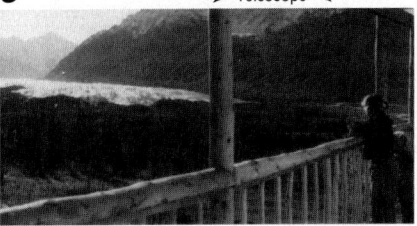

A **102.2** (164.5 km) T **225.8** (363.4 km) **Long Rifle Lodge**. Welcome to Alaska's most fabulous dining view of the Matanuska Glacier. We offer a complete breakfast, lunch and dinner menu, specializing in home-cooked meals. Twenty-five wildlife mounts and 500 gallons of tropical fish make our lodge a "must see" for all ages. Numerous hiking, cross-country skiing and snowmobile trails surround the area. In addition, we have motel rooms, gasoline, 24-hour wrecker service, laundry, showers, gift shop and a full-service lounge. Phone 1-800-770-5151. See display ad on page 271. [ADVERTISEMENT]

A **102** (164.2 km) T **226** (363.7 km) Access to foot of Matanuska Glacier via Glacier Park resort. Admission fee charged.

Glacier Park of Alaska. We would like to invite you to experience the Matanuska Glacier, at Glacier Park of Alaska. A 540-acre private resort located at the terminus of the Matanuska Glacier, in the heart of the Chugach Mountains. This is a great addition to your vacation. We offer glacier tours, hiking, flightseeing, backcountry adventures, recreation camping, tent camping, gift shop, rooms, laundry, showers, liquor store, film, snack foods, picnic area, snow-machining, cross-country skiing. Motorcoaches and tours welcome. Open all year. Access at Milepost 102 Glenn Highway. HC03 Box 8449, Palmer, AK 99645. Phone (907) 745-2534. [ADVERTISEMENT] ▲

A **101.7** (163.7 km) T **226.3** (364.2 km) Paved turnout with good view of Matanuska Glacier, which heads in the Chugach Mountains and trends northwest 27 miles/43.5 km. Some 18,000 years ago the glacier reached all the way to the Palmer area. The glacier's average width is 2 miles/3.2 km; at its terminus it is 4 miles/6.4 km wide. The glacier has remained fairly stable the past 400 years. At the glacier terminus meltwater drains into a stream which flows into the Matanuska River.

A **101** (162.5 km) T **227** (365.3 km) Matanuska Glacier State Recreation Site; 12 campsites on loop drive, three-day limit, $6 nightly fee or annual pass, water and toilets. Excellent views of the glacier from hiking trails along the bluff. (Use caution when walking near edge of bluff.) Wildflowers here in late July include fireweed, yarrow and sweet peas. ▲

A **100.8** (162.2 km) T **227.2** (365.6 km) Large gravel turnout to south.

NOTE: Watch for survey crews to ***Milepost A 56*** *in 1994.*

A **99.2** (159.6 km) T **228.8** (368.2 km) Gravel turnout to south, viewpoint. Pinochle–Hicks Creek trail.

A **97.8** (157.4 km) T **230.2** (370.5 km) Gravel turnout to west, viewpoint.

Winding road with steep grades westbound.

A **97** (156 km) T **231** (371.7 km) Gravel turnout to north.

A **96.6** (155.5 km) T **231.4** (372.4 km) Hicks Creek, named by Captain Glenn in 1898 for H.H. Hicks, the guide of his expedition. Private campground. Ridges back from here, right side Anchorage-bound, are good rockhound areas. Anthracite Ridge has jasper, rosy-banded agate, petrified wood and rock crystal. Difficult to reach on foot.

Hicks Creek Campground. See display ad this section. ▲

A **96.4** (155.1 km) T **231.6** (372.7 km) Small gravel turnout to south.

A **94.9** (152.7 km) T **233.1** (375.1 km) Victory Road. Slide area. Look for lupine and wild sweet pea.

A **93.4** (150.3 km) T **234.6** (377.5 km) Cascade state highway maintenance camp.

A **93** (149.7 km) T **235** (378.2 km) Gravel turnouts both sides of highway. Views of Amulet Peak and Monument Glacier and Valley.

A **91.3** (146.9 km) T **236.7** (380.9 km) Cascade Creek culvert.

A **91** (146.4 km) T **237** (381.4 km) First view eastbound of Matanuska Glacier.

A **90.6** (145.8 km) T **237.4** (382 km) Paved turnout to south.

A **90.1** (145 km) T **237.9** (382.9 km) Turnout to south.

A **89** (143.2 km) T **239** (384.6 km) Puritan Creek trailhead. Bridge over Puritan Creek. (Although signed Puritan, the stream is officially named Purinton Creek.) Good blueberry patches in season if you can beat the bears to them. The stream heads on Anthracite Ridge and flows into the Matanuska River. Westbound, watch for coal seams along the highway.

A **87.8** (141.3 km) T **240.2** (386.5 km) Two small gravel turnouts to south.

A **87.6** (141 km) T **240.4** (386.9 km) Large gravel turnout above Weiner Lake.

A **87.4** (140.6 km) T **240.6** (387.2 km) Weiner Lake access.

A **87.3** (140.5 km) T **240.7** (387.4 km) Turnout. Highway descends eastbound.

A **86.8** (139.7 km) T **241.2** (388.2 km) Slide area: Watch for falling rock.

A **86.5** (139.2 km) T **241.5** (388.6 km) Good gravel turnout overlooking Long Lake to south.

A **85.3** (137.3 km) T **242.7** (390.6 km) **Long Lake**, in a narrow canyon below the highway, is a favorite fishing spot for Anchorage residents. Fair for grayling to 18 inches, spring through fall; fish deeper as the water warms in summer. Good ice fishing in winter for burbot, average 12 inches. Long Lake State Recreation Site has nine campsites, 15-day limit, no camping fee tables, water pump, firepits and toilets. Wildflowers include roses, sweet pea, paintbrush and lupine. Long upgrade begins eastbound. ▲

A **84.6** (136.1 km) T **243.4** (391.7 km) There are several gravel turnouts westbound.

A **84.3** (135.7 km) T **243.7** (392.2 km) Large double-ended turnout. View of Matanuska River and unnamed mountains.

A **84.1** (135.3 km) T **243.9** (392.5 km) Large double-ended gravel turnout.

CAUTION: Watch for road equipment in slide areas next 4 miles/6.4 km eastbound.

A **83.2** (133.9 km) T **244.8** (394 km) Narrow gravel road to Ravine and Lower Bonnie lakes. (Side road not signed.) Drive in 0.8 mile/1.3 km on side road to reach **Ravine Lake**; fishing from shore for rainbows. **Lower Bonnie Lake** is a 2-mile/3.2-km drive from the highway; Bonnie Lake State Recreation Site has eight campsites, 15-day limit, no camping fee, toilets and boat launch. Fishing for grayling and rainbow. Steep and winding road beyond Ravine Lake is not recommended for large vehicles or trailers; during rainy season this side road is not recommended for any vehicle. ▲

A **82** (132 km) T **246** (395.9 km) Pyramid-shaped King Mountain is to the right (westbound) of the milepost as you look across the canyon. Several small gravel turnouts westbound.

A **80.8** (130 km) T **247.2** (397.8 km) Entering Matanuska Valley Moose Range westbound. Large gravel turnout to south.

A **79.5** (127.9 km) T **248.5** (399.9 km) Views of King Mountain (elev. 5,809 feet/1,770m).

A **79.1** (127.3 km) T **248.9** (400.6 km) Gravel turnout to south.

A **78.2** (125.8 km) T **249.8** (402 km) Gravel turnout with view of King Mountain and Matanuska River.

A **77.7** (125 km) T **250.3** (402.8 km) Chickaloon River bridge. Gravel turnout. Boundary between Game Management Units 13 and 14. The old Chickaloon Road winds upstream. In 1993, travelers reported seeing no trespassing and private property signs a short distance up this road, indicating Native land claims along the road and river. Inquire locally about public access to the Chickaloon River via this side road before driving in.

A **77.5** (124.7 km) T **250.5** (403.1 km) Gravel turnout to south. Steep ascent eastbound. Highway parallels Matanuska River.

A **76.5** (123.1 km) T **251.5** (404.7 km) Gravel turnout by river.

A **76.3** (122.8 km) T **251.7** (405.1 km) **CHICKALOON** (pop. 145); general store, gas station and river runner.

A **76.2** (122.6 km) T **251.8** (405.2 km) **King Mountain Lodge.** See display ad this section.

A **76.1** (122.5 km) T **251.9** (405.4 km) King Mountain State Recreation Site. Pleasant campground on the banks of the Matanuska River with 22 campsites, two picnic sites, fireplaces, picnic tables, water, toilets. Camping fee $6/night or annual pass; 15-day limit. King Mountain to the southeast. ▲

CAUTION: Watch for road equipment in slide areas westbound to ***Milepost A 60.***

A **73** (117.5 km) T **255** (410.4 km) Ida Lake/Fish Lake subdivision. Chickaloon

River loop road.

A 72.3 (116.4 km) **T 255.7** (411.5 km) Ida Lake is visible to the west.

A 71.2 (114.6 km) **T 256.8** (413.3 km) End slide area. Beaver pond to north.

A 71 (114.3 km) **T 257** (413.6 km) Turnouts to south by Matanuska River.

A 70.6 (113.6 km) **T 257.4** (414.2 km) Access to Matanuska River to south.

A 70 (112.7 km) **T 258** (415.2 km) Double-ended gravel turnout.

A 69.7 (112.2 km) **T 258.3** (415.7 km) Chickaloon post office (Zip code 99674), two private campgrounds.

Pinnacle Mtn. RV Park and Recreation Center. 42 wooded sites, picnic tables, full and partial hookups, large private showers, dump station, laundry, good water. Cafe with large dining area, gas, propane, country store, ice, video rentals, gift shop, post office. Low cost daily fishing trips, fishing hints and instruction for visitors or new arrivals. Maps to favorite fishing spots. Three-day and five-day family camp programs including your choice of side trips; river rafting, dog mushing, horseback riding, sightseeing, fishing, canoeing and other special activities. Full facilities for tour buses and groups. Snowmachine and hiking trail ties to 70-mile trail system. Year-round fun. For brochure write P.O. Box 1241, Chickaloon, AK 99674; phone (907) 745-0296. [ADVERTISEMENT] ▲

A 68.6 (110.4 km) **T 259.4** (417.5 km) Slide areas. Several gravel turnouts; watch for soft shoulders along highway.

A 68 (109.4 km) **T 260** (418.4 km) Pinnacle Mountain (elev. 4,541 feet/1384m) rises directly southeast of the highway — easy to identify by its unusual top. Cottonwoods and aspen along the highway. Talkeetna Mountains to the north.

A 66.5 (107 km) **T 261.5** (420.8 km) King River bridge. Turnouts both sides of road.

AREA FISHING: King River (Milepost A 66.5), trout, early summer best, use eggs. **Granite Creek (Milepost A 62.4)**, small Dolly Varden and trout, spring or early summer, use flies or single eggs. **Seventeenmile Lake (Milepost A 57.9 or 60.9)**, small grayling, early spring, use flies or spinners; trout, early spring, use eggs. **Eska Creek (Milepost A 60.8)**, small Dolly Varden, spring, use flies or single eggs; silver salmon, August or September, use eggs. **Moose Creek (Milepost A 54.6)**, trout and Dolly Varden, summer, use eggs.

A 66.4 (106.8 km) **T 261.6** (421 km) King River trailhead (unsigned in 1993); King River Crossing 5 miles/8 km.

A 62.7 (100.9 km) **T 265.3** (426.9 km) Large gravel turnout to south along Matanuska River. Dwarf fireweed and sweet pea in June.

A 62.4 (100.4 km) **T 265.6** (427.4 km) Granite Creek bridge and access to private campground. ▲

River's Edge Recreation Park. Our park offers secluded campsites for RVs and tents. We have fresh well water, restrooms and electric hookups. While camping or visiting for the day, play volleyball or horseshoes and enjoy the beauty of the Sutton area. Spawning salmon, bald eagles, wildflowers and plenty of firewood. (907) 746-CAMP. [ADVERTISEMENT] ▲

A 62.2 (100.1 km) **T 265.8** (427.7 km) Sutton post office. Sign in at their guest book.

A 61.6 (99.1 km) **T 267.6** (430.6 km) Alpine Historical Park. An open-air museum features the concrete ruins of the Sutton Coal Washery, built between 1920 and 1922. Indoor display of historical photographs. The park also has the Chickaloon Bunkhouse (circa 1917) and the first Sutton post office (1948). Access via Elementary School Road. The museum is still under development. Donations accepted.

Alpine Historical Park. See display ad this section.

A 61 (98.2 km) **T 267** (429.7 km) **SUTTON** (pop. 340) was established as a railroad siding about 1918 for the once-flourishing coal industry and is now a small highway community. Sutton has a fire department, general store, post office and gas station. Fossilized shells and leaves can be found in this area 1.7 miles/2.7 km up the Jonesville Road. Inquire locally for directions.

Sutton General Store and Jonesville Cafe. Full line menu, good food, homemade pies, orders to go. We supply all your camping, fishing and cooking needs. Clean restrooms, shower, washers and dryers, phone (but the people are a little strange). Tour buses welcome. Stop by and see us! (907) 746-7461 and (907) 746-7561. [ADVERTISEMENT]

A 60.9 (98 km) **T 267.1** (429.8 km) Jonesville Road. Access to Coyote Lake Recreation Area (3 miles/4.8 km); day-use area with pavilion, covered picnic tables, toilets, fireplaces, trails and swimming. Also access to Seventeenmile Lake (for recommended access see **Milepost A 57.9**). Drive north 1.7 miles/2.7 km to end of pavement; continue straight ahead for residential area and old Jonesville and Eska coal mines; turn left where pavement ends for Seventeenmile Lake. From the turnoff on Jonesville Road it is 3.1 miles/5 km via a rough dirt road (may be muddy) to **Seventeenmile Lake;** undeveloped parking area on lakeshore, boat launch, good grayling fishing. Inquire at local businesses about road conditions. ▲

A 60.8 (97.8 km) **T 267.2** (430 km) Eska Creek bridge.

A 60.7 (97.7 km) **T 267.3** (430.2 km) Paved double-ended turnout to south; pavement break.

A 60 (96.6 km) **T 268** (431.3 km) Long winding descent eastbound. *CAUTION: Watch for road equipment in slide areas eastbound to **Milepost A 76.***

A 59.5 (95.7 km) **T 268.5** (430.5 km)

A 58.6 (94.3 km) **T 269.4** (433.5 km) Small gravel turnout to south. View of Matanuska River.

A 57.9 (93.2 km) **T 270.1** (434.7 km) 58 Mile Road. Access to Palmer Correctional Center. Alternate access (see also **A 60.9**) to Seventeenmile Lake. Drive north 0.5 mile/0.8 km; turn right and drive 1.7 miles/2.7 km; turn left, drive 0.3 mile/0.5 km; turn right, drive 0.2 mile/0.3 km; turn right again and drive 0.2 mile/0.3 km to lake. Undeveloped camping on lakeshore.

The old Independence Mine is accessible via Hatcher Pass Road. (Sue Rheaume)

A 56.7 (91.2 km) **T 271.3** (436.6 km) Entering Matanuska Valley Moose Range eastbound.

A 56 (90.1 km) **T 272** (437.7 km) *NOTE: Watch for survey crews eastbound to* ***Milepost A 100*** *in 1994.*

A 54.6 (87.9 km) **T 273.4** (440 km) Bridge over Moose Creek. Highway ascends steeply from creek in both directions. Moose Creek State Recreation Site; 12 campsites, seven-day limit, $6 nightly fee or annual pass, four picnic sites, water, covered tables, firepits and toilets (wheelchair accessible). Look for fossils in the road bank on the west side of the highway. ♿▲

A 54 (86.9 km) **T 274** (440.9 km) Truck lane starts westbound.

A 53.6 (86.3 km) **T 274.4** (441.6 km) Truck lane ends westbound.

A 53 (85.3 km) **T 275** (442.6 km) Side road to Buffalo Coal Mine. Wild rose, geranium and chiming bells bloom along this section of highway.

A 52.3 (84.2 km) **T 275.7** (443.7 km) Soapstone Road.

A 51.2 (82.4 km) **T 276.8** (445.5 km) Fire station.

A 50.9 (81.9 km) **T 277.1** (445.9 km) Farm Loop Road, a 3-mile/4.8-km loop road connecting with Fishhook–Willow Road.

A 50.1 (80.6 km) **T 277.9** (447.2 km) Turn here for the Musk Ox Farm.

A 49.5 (79.7 km) **T 278.5** (448.2 km) **Junction** with Hatcher Pass (Fishhook–Willow) Road which leads west and north over Hatcher Pass to connect with the George Parks Highway at **Milepost A 71.2** north of Willow. See HATCHER PASS ROAD log this page.

A 49 (78.9 km) **T 279** (449 km) Entering Palmer, which extends to **Milepost A 41.** Actual driving distance between **Milepost 49** and 42 is 1 mile/1.6 km. Just beyond here the highway emerges on a hill overlooking the Matanuska Valley, a view of the farms and homes of one of Alaska's agricultural areas, and the business center of Palmer.

Hatcher Pass Road Log

The 49-mile-/79-km-long Hatcher Pass (Fishhook–Willow) Road leads north and west from **Milepost A 49.5** on the Glenn Highway to **Milepost A 71.2** on the George Parks Highway, providing access to Independence Mine State Historical Park (see Mat-Su Valley Vicinity map on page 280). It is a mostly gravel road, not recommended for large RVs or trailers beyond **Milepost J 14.** The road usually does not open until late June and snow may close the pass in September. The road stays open to the historical park and to Hatcher Pass Lodge in winter, a popular winter sports area for snowmobiling and cross-country skiing.

Distance from junction with the Glenn Highway (J) is followed by distance from junction with the George Parks Highway (GP).

J 0 GP 49.1 (79 km) **Junction** with the Glenn Highway at **Milepost A 49.5.** Fishhook–Willow Road heads west through farm country.

J 1.4 (2.3 km) **GP 47.7** (76.8 km) **Junction** with Farm Loop Road.

J 2.4 (3.9 km) **GP 46.7** (75.2 km) **Junction** with Trunk Road.

J 6.5 (10.5 km) **GP 42.5** (68.4 km) **Hatcher Pass Gateway Center.** See display ad this section.

J 6.8 (10.9 km) **GP 42.3** (68.1 km) **Junction** with Wasilla–Fishhook Road. This road leads south to connect with the George Parks Highway at Wasilla.

J 7.2 (11.6 km) **GP 41.9** (67.4 km) Pavement ends, gravel begins, northbound. Edgerton Parks Road to Wasilla.

J 8.1 (13 km) **GP 41** (66 km) Hatcher Pass Management Area boundary.

J 8.5 (13.7 km) **GP 40.6** (65.3 km) Little Susitna River bridge. Road parallels river. Several turnouts westbound.

J 9 (14.5 km) **GP 40.1** (64.5 km) Entering Hatcher Pass public-use area westbound. No flower picking or plant removal without a permit in public-use area.

J 14 (22.5 km) **GP 35.1** (56.5 km) Lodge. Side "road" (four-wheel-drive vehicle recommended) to mine and trails parallels Little Susitna River. Trailhead parking for Gold Mint trail and Arkose Ridge trail. Snowmobile trail. Hatcher Pass Road begins climb to Hatcher Pass via a series of switchbacks. There are several turnouts the next 2.4 miles/3.9 km westbound.

Motherlode Lodge. See display ad this section.

J 14.6 (23.5 km) **GP 34.5** (55.5 km) Archangel Valley Road to Mabel and Fern mines and Reed Lakes. Road crosses private property (do not trespass). Winter trails (snowmobiles prohibited east of Archangel Road).

J 16.4 (26.4 km) **GP 32.7** (52.6 km) Parking lot to east, snowmobile trail to west.

J 17.3 (27.8 km) **GP 31.8** (51.2 km) Gold Cord Road provides year-round access to lodge and Independence Mine State Historical Park (1.5 miles/2.4 km). The 271-acre **INDEPENDENCE MINE STATE HISTORICAL PARK** includes several buildings and old mining machinery. Park visitor center is housed in the red-roofed building, which was built in 1939 to house the mine manager. The visitor center and assay office are open 11 A.M. to 7 P.M. daily from June through Labor Day; weekends the rest of the year. (Hours and days may vary.) Guided tours of the bunkhouse, mess hall and warehouse are given from June to Labor Day (weather permitting) for a nominal fee; phone visitor center at 745-2827 or phone 745-3975 in Palmer for current information. Groups of 20 or more call ahead for tours. Office hours and tour times may vary, but visitors are always welcome to explore on their own.

Alaska Pacific Consolidated Mine Co., one of the largest gold producers in the Willow Creek mining district, operated here from 1938 through 1941. The Gold Cord Mine buildings (private property) are visible on the hill above and to the north of Independence Mine.

Recreational gold panning is permitted in the park. Some pans are available for loan at the visitor center.

Snowmobiling is prohibited in the park.

J **17.5** (28.2 km) **GP 31.6** (50.8 km) **Hatcher Pass Lodge.** See display ad this section.

J **18.7** (30.1 km) **GP 30.4** (48.9 km) Entering Summit Lake State Recreation Site; no ground fires permitted.

J **18.9** (30.4 km) **GP 30.1** (48.4 km) Hatcher Pass Summit (elev. 3,886 feet/ 1,184m). Several turnouts westbound.

J **19.2** (30.9 km) **GP 29.8** (48 km) Summit Lake, headwaters of Willow Creek. Summit Lake State Recreation Site under development. The road follows Willow Creek from here to the George Parks Highway. There are several old and new mines in the area.

J **20.4** (32.8 km) **GP 28.6** (46 km) Upper Willow Creek Valley Road to mine.

J **23.8** (38.3 km) **GP 25.3** (40.7 km) Craigie Creek Road (very rough) leads to mine sites. Remains of historic Lucky Shot and War Baby mines on hillside are visible on hillside ahead westbound.

J **24.3** (39.1 km) **GP 24.8** (39.9 km) Beaver lodges and dams.

J **25.6** (41.2 km) **GP 23.5** (37.8 km) View of Beaver Ponds to west; mine site visible to south below road. Road begins descent westbound into Little Willow Creek valley; numerous turnouts.

J **30.3** (48.8 km) **GP 18.7** (30.1 km) Leaving Hatcher Pass public-use area westbound.

J **34.2** (55 km) **GP 14.9** (24 km) Little Willow Creek bridge; large parking area.

J **38.9** (62.6 km) **GP 10.2** (16.4 km) Gravel ends, pavement begins, westbound.

J **47.9** (77.1 km) **GP 1.2** (1.9 km) Willow Creek State Recreation Area Deception Creek Campground; seven campsites, 15-day limit, $10 nightly fee per vehicle or annual pass, covered picnic tables, water, toilets (handicap accessible). ♿▲

J **48** (77.2 km) **GP 1.1** (1.8 km) Deception Creek bridge.

J **48.2** (77.5 km) **GP 0.9** (1.4 km) Deception Creek picnic area. Back road into Willow from here.

J **48.5** (78.1 km) **GP 0.6** (1 km) Road crosses Alaska Railroad tracks.

J **49.1** (79 km) **GP 0 Junction** with George Parks Highway at **Milepost A 71.2.** (Turn to the GEORGE PARKS HIGHWAY section.)

Return to Milepost A 49.5 Glenn Highway

A **42.1** (67.8 km) T **285.9** (460.1 km) Arctic Avenue leads east through Palmer to the Old Glenn Highway, a scenic alternate route to Anchorage that rejoins the highway at **Milepost A 29.6.** A recommended route if road construction is under way between Palmer and Anchorage. Highlights of this route include the original Matanuska Colony Farms, commercial reindeer farm, U-pick vegetable farms, camping and salmon spawning viewing areas. See OLD GLENN HIGHWAY log on page 281 (Anchorage-bound travelers read log back to front).

Access to Palmer High School west at this junction.

Palmer

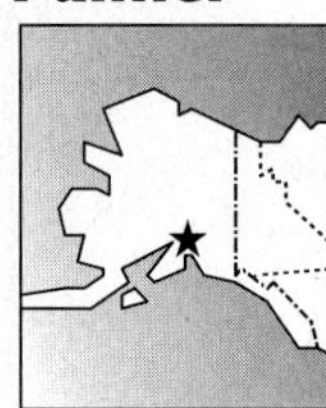

A **42** (67.6 km) T **286** (460.3 km) In the Matanuska Valley northeast of Anchorage. The city extends from about **Milepost A 49** to **A 41,** an actual driving distance of 2.1 miles/3.4 km. **Population:** 3,039. **Emergency Services:** Phone 911. **Alaska State Troopers,** phone 745-2131. **City Police,** phone 745-4811. **Fire Department** and **Ambulance,** phone 745-3271. **Valley Hospital,** 515 E. Dahlia, phone 745-4813.

Visitor Information: Visitor center in log cabin across the railroad tracks on South Valley Way at East Fireweed Avenue. Pick up a brochure and map of downtown Palmer's historic buildings. Open daily 9 A.M. to 6 P.M. May to October 1; weekdays 8:30 A.M. to 5:30 P.M. October to May. Pay phone. Small museum in basement; local crafts may be for sale on main floor. Mailing address: Chamber of Commerce, P.O. Box 45, Palmer, AK 99645. Matanuska Valley Agricultural Showcase adjacent visitor center features flower and vegetable gardens.

Excellent local library, located at 655 S. Valley Way; open noon to 6 P.M. Monday through Friday. Paperback and magazine exchange. Wheelchair accessible.

Elevation: 240 feet/74m. **Climate:** Temperatures range from 4° to 21°F/-16° to -6°C in January and December, with a mean monthly snowfall of 8 to 10 inches. Record low was -40°F/-40°C in January 1975. Temperatures range from 44° to 68°F/7° to 20°C in June and July, with a mean monthly precipitation of 2 inches. Record high was 89°F/32°C in June 1969. Mean annual rainfall is 15.5 inches, with 50.7 inches of snow. **Radio:** Anchorage stations; KMBQ (Wasilla). **Television:** Anchorage channels and cable. **Newspaper:** *The Frontiersman* (twice weekly).

Private Aircraft: Palmer Municipal Airport, adjacent southeast; elev. 232 feet/71m; length 6,000 feet/1,829m; asphalt; fuel 100LL, Jet A1, B. Butte Municipal, 6 miles/9.7 km southeast; elev. 64 feet/19m; length 1,800 feet/549m; gravel; unattended. Seaplane base on Finger Lake.

Palmer is a commercial center for the Matanuska and Susitna valleys (collectively referred to as the Mat–Su valleys). The town was established about 1916 as a railway station on the Matanuska branch of the Alaska Railroad.

In 1935, Palmer became the site of one of the most unusual experiments in American history: the Matanuska Valley Colony. The Federal Emergency Relief Administration, one of the many New Deal relief agencies created during Franklin Roosevelt's first year in office, planned an agricultural colony in Alaska to utilize the great agricultural potential in the Matanuska–Susitna valleys, and to get some American farm families — struck by first the dust bowl then the Great Depression — off the dole. Social workers picked 203 families, mostly from the northern counties of Michigan, Wisconsin and Minnesota, to join the colony, because it was thought that the many hardy farmers of Scandinavian descent in those three states would have a natural advantage over other ethnic groups. The colonists arrived in Palmer in the early summer of 1935, and though the failure rate was high, many of their descendants still live in the Matanuska Valley. Palmer gradually became the unofficial capital of the Matanuska Valley, acting as headquarters for a farmers cooperative marketing organization and as the business and social center for the state's most productive farming region.

Palmer is Alaska's only community that developed primarily from an agricultural economy. (Real estate now takes a close second to agriculture.) The growing season averages 80 to 110 days a year, with long

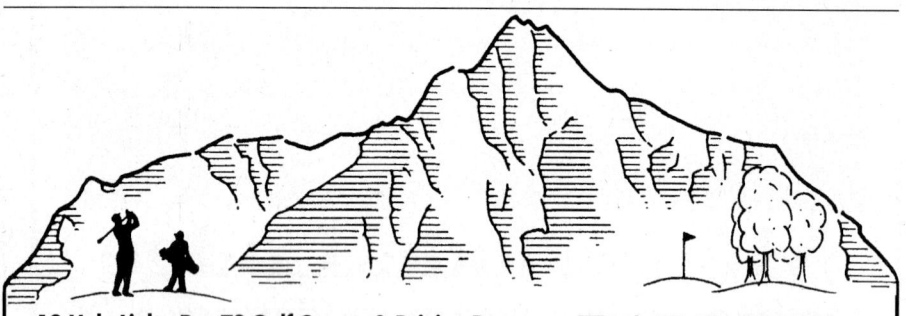

PALMER ADVERTISERS

Bushes Bunches Stand ... Across from Visitors Center
City of Palmer ... 231 W. Evergreen Ave.
Colony Inn ... 325 Elmwood St.
Glacier Airflight ... Palmer Municipal Airport
Gold Miner's Hotel ... Ph. 1-800-725-2752
Grasshopper Adventures ... Palmer Municipal Airport
Jean's B & B ... Ph. (907) 746-4373
Matanuska Valley Bed & Breakfast & Valley Tours ... Ph. (907) 745-2341
Mountain View RV Park ... Off Old Glenn Hwy.
Musk Ox Farm & Gift Shop ... Mile 50.1 Glenn Hwy.
Pioneer Motel & Apt. ... Ph. (907) 745-3425
Pollen's B & B ... Ph. (907) 745-8920
Reindeer Farm ... Mile J 11.5 Old Glenn Hwy.
Tara Dells Bed & Breakfast ... Ph. (907) 745-0407
Valley Hotel ... 606 S. Alaska St.
Wash Day Too ... 127 S. Alaska St.

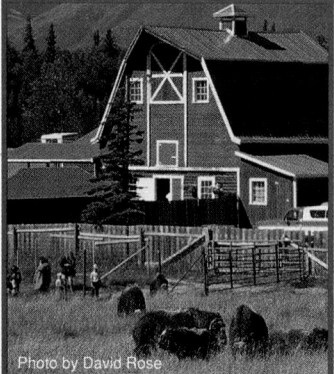

hours of sunshine. The University of Alaska–Fairbanks has an Agricultural and Forestry Experiment Station Office and a district Cooperative Extension Service Office here. The university also operates its Matanuska Research Farm, located on Trunk Road off the George Parks Highway, about a 7-mile/11.3-km drive from Palmer. The university farm conducts research in agronomy, horticulture and animal science.

The community has a hospital, the Mat-Su Community College (University of Alaska), a library, banks and several state and federal agency offices. Palmer has churches representing most denominations. The United Protestant Church in Palmer, the "church of a thousand logs," dates from Matanuska Colony days and is one of the oldest churches in Alaska still holding services. It is included in the National Register of Historic Places.

ACCOMMODATIONS

Palmer has all visitor facilities including two hotels, two motels, gas stations, grocery stores, laundromat, auto repair and parts, and shopping. The Matanuska Valley region has several lake resorts offering boat rentals, golf, fly-in fishing, hunting and horseback riding.

Jean's Bed & Breakfast. One story home, queen beds, shared bath. One mile off the Glenn Highway in Palmer. Open year-round. $50 for 2 persons. Write 317 Independence, Palmer, AK 99645. Phone (907) 746-4373. [ADVERTISEMENT]

There is a private RV park on Smith Road off the Old Glenn Highway. There are also private campgrounds on the Glenn Highway a few miles west of Palmer. The Mat-Su Borough operates Matanuska River Park, located 1.1 miles/1.8 km south of town at Mile 17.5 Old Glenn Highway; 51 campsites, picnic area, some pull-through sites, water, dump station (fee charged), firewood for sale, flush toilets, hot showers, camping fee. Finger Lake State Recreation Site, about 6 miles/9.7 km northwest of Palmer just off Bogard Road, has 69 campsites, seven-day limit, toilets, water, trails, boating and fishing. Camping fee $6/night or annual pass. To reach Finger Lake, take Palmer–Wasilla Highway north 4 miles/6.4 km from **Milepost A 41.8** to Trunk Road, then follow Trunk Road to Bogard Road. ▲

Mountain View RV Park offers breathtaking views of the Matanuska mountains. Watch wildlife from your door. Full hookups, hot showers included. New bathrooms and laundromat, dump station. Good Sam Park. Call (907) 745-5747 for reservations. Mail forwarding. Write P.O. Box 2521, Palmer, AK 99745. From Mile A 42.1 Glenn

Highway (Arctic), follow Old Glenn Highway 2.8 miles. Turn east on Smith Road, drive 0.6 mile, turn right (0.3 mile). We're 3.7 miles from the Glenn Highway. See display ad this section. [ADVERTISEMENT] ♿▲

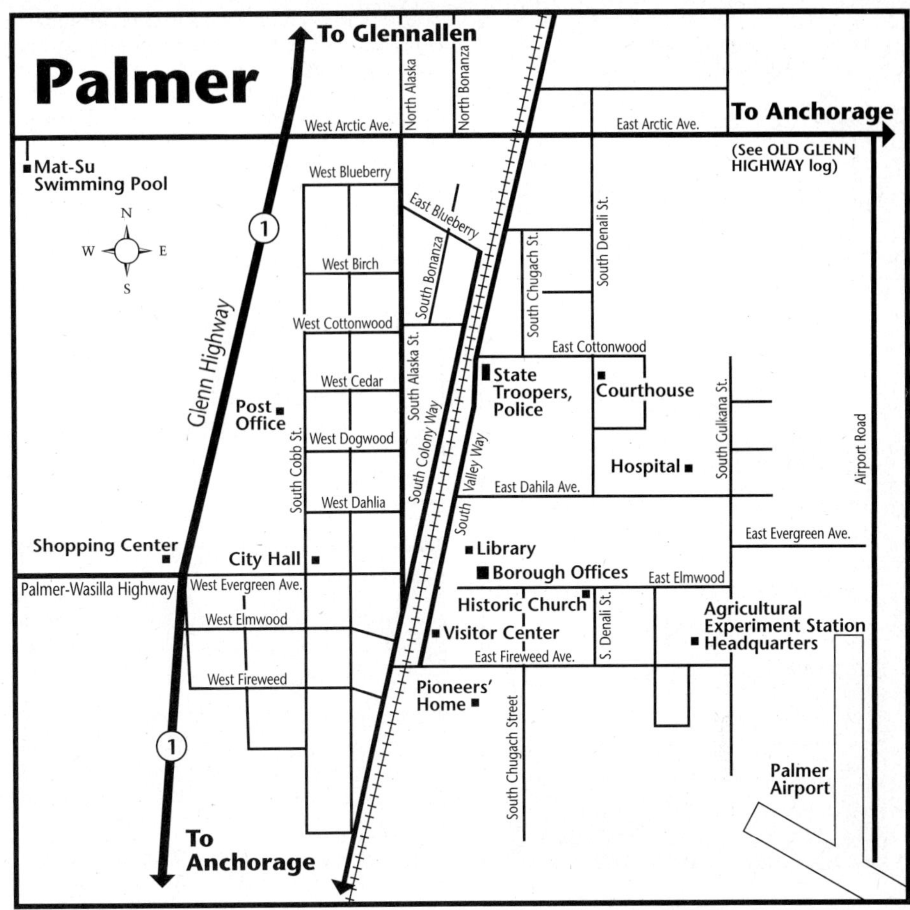

TRANSPORTATION

Air: No scheduled service, but the local airport has a number of charter operators. **Bus:** Scheduled and charter service.

ATTRACTIONS

Go Swimming: The 25-m Mat-Su swimming pool is open to the public seven days a week — $2 for adults and showers are available. The pool is located at Palmer High School; phone 745-5091.

Get Acquainted: Stop at the visitor information center, a log building just off the "main drag" (across the railroad tracks near the intersection of East Fireweed Avenue and

South Valley Way). The center includes a museum, artifacts, a gift shop and agricultural showcase.

Visit the Musk Ox Farm. Located east of Palmer on the Glenn Highway at **Milepost 50.1,** the Musk Ox Farm is the only place in the world these exotic animals are raised domestically. Hunted to near extinction in Alaska in 1865, the species was reintroduced in the 1930s. The farm is open May to September; admission is charged.

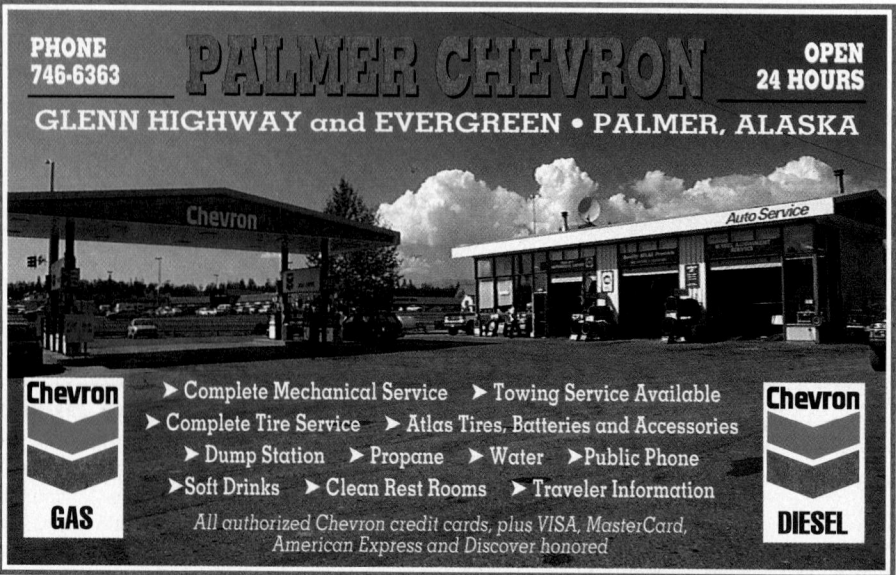

Visit a Reindeer Farm, located 8.1 miles/ 11.5 km south of Palmer via the Old Glenn Highway to Bodenburg Butte Loop Road. This commercial reindeer farm is open daily in summer; admission is charged.

Play Golf. Palmer links golf course has 18 holes (par 72, USGA rated), rental carts and clubs, driving range and clubhouse. Phone 745-4653.

Enjoy Water Sports. Fishing, boating, waterskiing and other water sports are popular in summer at Finger Lake west of Palmer. Kepler–Bradley Lakes State Recreation Area on Matanuska Lake has canoe rentals; turn off the Glenn Highway at **Milepost A 36.4.**

Colony Village, located at the state fairgrounds at **Milepost A 40.2** Glenn Highway, preserves some of the buildings from Palmer's early days. Included are two houses, a barn and a church from the

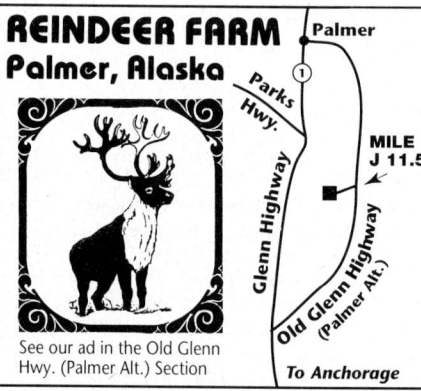

Matanuska Valley Colony of 1935. The Hesse House is used as a post office during the Alaska State Fair.

The Alaska State Fair, a 12-day annual event ending on Labor Day, has agricultural exhibits from farms throughout Alaska. There are also food booths, games and rides. This is a very popular event, and fairgoers from Anchorage can tie up traffic. But it's worth the drive just to see the vegetables: the winning cabbage in 1990 weighed 98 pounds.

Visit Scenic Hatcher Pass: A six- to eight-hour drive from **Milepost A 49.5** near Palmer that climbs through the beautiful Hatcher Pass Recreation Area and connects with the George Parks Highway at **Milepost A 71.2.** Access to Independence Mine State Historical Park. See HATCHER PASS ROAD log this section.

Grasshopper Adventures. Accessible guided and outfitted fly-in camping. Base camp located adjacent to the Knik Glacier. Glacier camp on Marcus Baker Glacier (5,000 ft.) at base of Mount Marcus Baker (13,000 ft.). Packages to fit your needs — overnighters welcome! Flightseeing, wildlife viewing, photographers' dream. Contact Dave Glenn, P.O. Box 3223, Palmer, AK 99645. Phone and fax: (907) 746-6923. [ADVERTISEMENT] ♿

See the Matanuska Glacier: Drive 50 miles/80 km east on the Glenn Highway from Palmer to visit this spectacular 27-mile-/43.5-km-long glacier, one of the few you can drive to and explore on foot. Access to the foot of the glacier is through a private campground at **Milepost A 102**; admission charged. If you're not interested in getting close, there are several vantage points along the highway and from trails at Matanuska Glacier Campground, **Milepost A 101.**

Glenn Highway Log

(continued)

A **41.8** (67.3 km) T **286.2** (460.6 km) **Junction** with Palmer–Wasilla Highway. Gas station and shopping mall. West Evergreen Avenue access to downtown Palmer.

Palmer–Wasilla Highway leads northwest 10 miles/16 km to the George Parks Highway. It provides access to a car wash, several other businesses, Mat–Su Community College, Finger Lake State Recreation Site (via Trunk and Bogard roads) and Wolf Lake State Recreation Site. At Mile 1.9 on the Palmer–Wasilla Highway is the Crevasse Moraine trailhead; parking, picnic tables, fireplaces and access to five loop hiking trails.

Carrs Pioneer Square shopping mall, located at this junction, is the site of a bronze sculpture by Jacques and Mary Regat dedicated to the Matanuska Valley pioneers.

A **41.6** (66.9 km) T **286.4** (460.9 km) **Palmer Chevron.** See display ad this section.

A **41.2** (66.3 km) T **286.8** (461.5 km) First access road to Palmer business district for eastbound travelers.

A **40.5** (65.2 km) T **287.5** (462.7 km) **Fairview Motel & Restaurant.** See display ad this section.

A **40.2** (64.7 km) T **287.8** (463.2 km) Main entrance to fairgrounds (site of Alaska State Fair), Herman Field (home of the Mat–Su Miners baseball team) and Colony Village. Colony Village preserves some of Palmer's buildings from the days of the Matanuska Valley Colony, and houses a collection of historic photographs and artifacts. Colony Days is held in June. Alaska State Fair is held the end of August to Labor Day.

Alaska State Fair. See display ad this section.

A **39.2** (63.1 km) T **288.8** (464.8 km) Outer Springer Loop. Short trail to Meiers Lake.

A **38** (61.2 km) T **290** (466.7 km) **Matanuska Farm Market.** See display ad this section.

A **37.4** (60.2 km) T **290.6** (467.7 km) Kepler Drive; access to private campground and lake. ▲

A **37** (59.5 km) T **291** (468.3 km) Echo

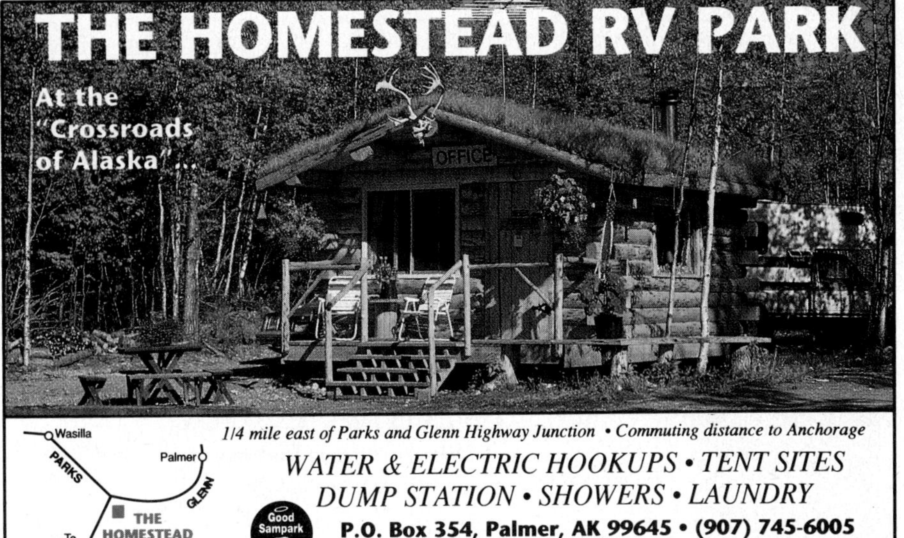

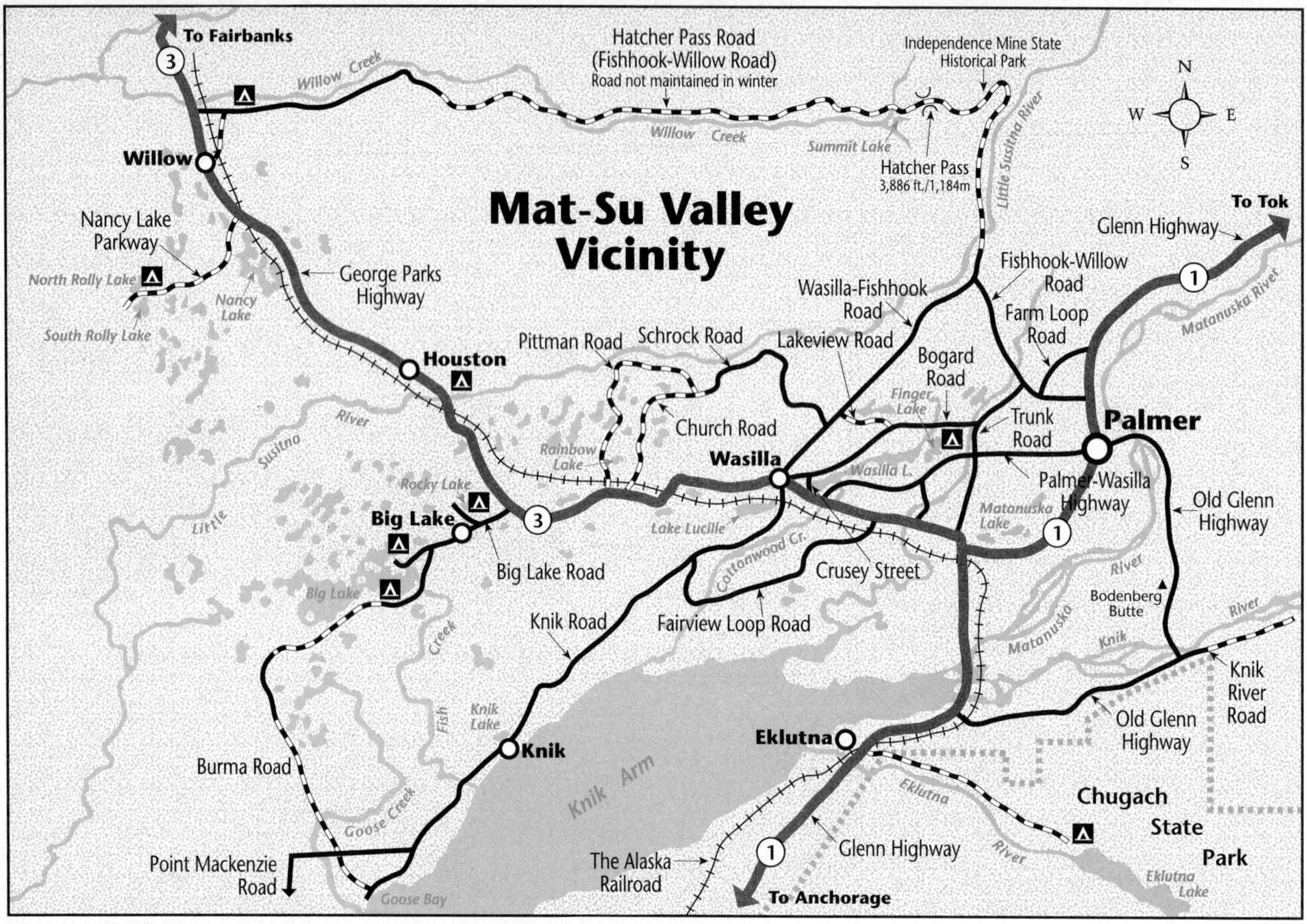

Mat-Su Valley Vicinity

Lake Road.

A 36.4 (58.6 km) **T 291.6** (469.3 km) Kepler–Bradley Lakes State Recreation Area on Matanuska Lake; day-use area with water, toilets, parking, picnic tables, canoe rentals, fishing and hiking. The lakes are **Matanuska Lake, Canoe Lake, Irene Lake** and **Long Lake.**

A 36.2 (58.3 km) **T 291.8** (469.6 km) **The Homestead RV Park.** Wooded pull-throughs to 70 feet, tent sites. Very clean restrooms and showers. Electric and water hookups; dump station; also, on-site portable dumping. Laundry. Picnic tables, pay phone. Area tours, evening entertainment. Heated, enclosed pavilion. Walking and jogging trails, trout fishing nearby. Good Sam park. 60 sites. Handicap access. Beautiful view. Commuting distance to Anchorage. Caravans welcome. Phone (907) 745-6005. Toll free in Alaska 1-800-478-3570. See display ad this section. [ADVERTISEMENT]

A 35.3 (56.8 km) **T 292.7** (471.1 km) *CAUTION: Traffic signal at busy **junction** of the Glenn Highway and George Parks Highway (Alaska Route 3), which form a common highway into Anchorage.* If headed for Fairbanks or Mount McKinley turn north on the George Parks Highway. See **Milepost A 35** GEORGE PARKS HIGHWAY section for details.

A 34.9 (56.2 km) **T 293.1** (471.7 km) *CAUTION: Highway crosses the Alaska Railroad tracks.*

A 34 (54.7 km) **T 294** (473.1 km) Paved double-ended turnout west side of highway. Rabbit Slough.

A 32.4 (52.1 km) **T 295.6** (475.7 km) Palmer Hay Flats state game refuge. According to the ADF&G, this is the most heavily utilized waterfowl hunting area in Alaska. Access to the refuge is via Fairview Loop Road off the George Parks Highway.

A 31.5 (50.7 km) **T 296.5** (477.2 km) Bridge over the Matanuska River, which is fed by the Matanuska Glacier.

A 30.8 (49.6 km) **T 297.5** (478.8 km) There are three Knik River bridges; parking areas below highway at south end of the two most southern bridges. The Knik River comes down from the Knik Glacier to the east and splits into several branches as it approaches Knik Arm. Game Management Unit 14C boundary. Also boundary of Matanuska–Susitna Borough.

Moose winter in this area and the cows and calves may be seen early in the morning and in the evening as late as early July. In winter, watch for moose on the road between here and Anchorage.

A 29.6 (47.6 km) **T 298.4** (480.2 km) **Junction** with the Old Glenn Highway (Palmer Alternate). See OLD GLENN HIGHWAY log opposite page. A recommended alternate route if major road construction is under way between Anchorage and Palmer.

A 27.6 (44.4 km) **T 300.4** (483.4 km) Divided highway from here to Anchorage.

A 27.3 (43.9 km) **T 300.7** (483.9 km) The highway crosses a swampy area known locally as Eklutna Flats. These flats are a protected wildflower area (picking flowers is strictly prohibited). Look for wild iris, shooting star, chocolate lily and wild rose in early June.

A 26.8 (43.1 km) **T 301.2** (484.7 km) Highway crosses Alaska Railroad via overpass.

A 26.3 (42.3 km) **T 301.7** (485.5 km) Eklutna overpass, exits both sides of highway. Access to Eklutna Road (description follows), the village of Eklutna and also access to Thunderbird Falls (see **Milepost A 25.3**) for Anchorage-bound travelers. West of the highway is the Indian village of **EKLUTNA** (pop. 25), site of Eklutna Village Historical Park, which preserves the heritage and traditions of the Athabascan Alaska Natives. Attractions include the historic St. Nicholas Russian Orthodox Church and a hand-built Siberian prayer chapel. Admission fee charged. Open daily mid-May to mid-September. The bright little grave houses or spirit houses in the cemetery are painted in the family's traditional colors.

Eklutna Lodge. See display ad this section.

Old Glenn Highway (Palmer Alternate) Log

This 18.6-mile/29.9-km paved road is a scenic alternate route between Palmer and Anchorage, intersecting the Glenn Highway near Anchorage at **Milepost A 29.6** and rejoining the Glenn Highway at **Milepost A 42.1** via Arctic Avenue in Palmer. The Old Glenn Highway gives access to Knik River Road and Bodenburg Butte Loop Road through the heart of the original Matanuska Colony agricultural lands.

Distance from south junction with the Glenn Highway (J) is followed by distance from Palmer (P).

J 0 P 18.6 (29.9 km) **Junction** with Glenn Highway at **Milepost A 29.6.** Paved parking area.

J 6.1 (9.8 km) **P 12.3** (19.8 km) Goat Creek bridge.

J 7.2 (11.6 km) **P 11.4** (18.3 km) View of Bodenburg Butte across Knik River.

J 8.6 (13.8 km) **P 10** (16.1 km) **Junction** with Knik River Road, a gravel side road which leads to view of Knik Glacier. Pioneer Ridge/Knik River trailhead 3.6 miles/5.8 km from bridge. Knik River Road dead ends 11.4 miles/18.3 km from here.

J 8.7 (14 km) **P 9.9** (15.9 km) Knik River bridge; parking at east end of bridge.

J 11.4 (18.3 km) **P 7.2** (11.6 km) Butte branch U.S. post office. Pioneer Peak dominates the skyline for southbound travelers.

J 11.5 (18.5 km) **P 7.1** (11.4 km) South **junction** with Bodenburg Butte Loop Road which leads west (see description following), and **junction** with Plumley Road to east. Plumley Road provides access to **Jim Creek** trail off Caudill Road; fishing for Dolly Varden, silver and red salmon.

The 5.8-mile/9.3-km Bodenburg Butte Road rejoins the Old Glenn Highway at Dack Acres Road (**Milepost J 12.6**). The **BODENBURG BUTTE** area (pop. 1,232) has original Matanuska Colony farms and a commercial reindeer farm (visitors welcome, fee charged).

Measuring mileages from the south junction, look for these attractions: Mile 0.6/1 km, Matanuska Colony log house and Bodenburg trailhead; Mile 0.8/1.3 km, reindeer farm; Mile 2.4/3.9 km, spur road to Alaska Division of Agriculture Plant Materials Center. The road circumnavigates Bodenburg Butte.

Reindeer Farm. Commercial reindeer farm on Bodenburg Butte Loop Road 0.8 mile off Old Glenn Highway (turn at Mile J 11.5 at the flashing light.) View tame reindeer and famous Pioneer Peak. Hand

feed reindeer. Bring camera. Hours 10 A.M.-6 P.M. daily. Families with children welcome. Large parties please phone ahead. (907) 745-4000. Fee charged. [ADVERTISEMENT]

Pyrah's Pioneer Peak Farm. See display ad this section.

J 12.6 (20.3 km) **P 6** (9.7 km) **Junction** with Dack Acres Road, north end of Bodenburg Butte Loop Road (see **Milepost J 11.5**).

J 13.3 (21.4 km) **P 5.3** (8.5 km) Turnout to west. Bodenburg Creek parallels highway next 0.7 mile/1.1 km northbound; red and pink salmon spawn here from late August through September. Eagles nest across the creek. *CAUTION: Use turnouts and watch for heavy traffic.*

J 14.5 (23.3 km) **P 4.1** (6.6 km) Maud Road. Access to **Mud Lake** (4 miles/6.4 km); fishing for Dolly Varden.

J 15.6 (25.1 km) **P 3** (4.8 km) **Junction** with Smith Road. Access to private campground. Trail rides available at a nearby ranch.

Mountain View RV Park. See display ad this section.

J 16.1 (25.9 km) **P 2.5** (4 km) Clark-Wolverine Road; access to Lazy Mountain recreation area hiking trails. Drive in 0.7 mile/1.1 km; turn right on Huntly Road at T; drive 1 mile/1.6 km on gravel road and take right fork to recreation area and overlook. Picnic tables, toilets, good berry picking.

J 16.8 (27 km) **P 1.8** (2.9 km) Matanuska River bridge. Access to river.

J 17.5 (28.2 km) **P 1.1** (1.8 km) Matanuska River Park; 51 campsites, picnic area, some pull-through sites, water, dump station, flush toilets, hot showers. Camping and dump station fees charged.

J 17.6 (28.3 km) **P 1** (1.6 km) Airport Road. View of Pioneer Peak southbound.

Pioneer Peak. (Jerrianne Lowther, staff)

J 18.6 (29.9 km) **P 0 Junction** of Old Glenn Highway (Arctic Avenue) at **Milepost A 42.1** Glenn Highway.

Return to Milepost A 42.1 or A 29.6 Glenn Highway

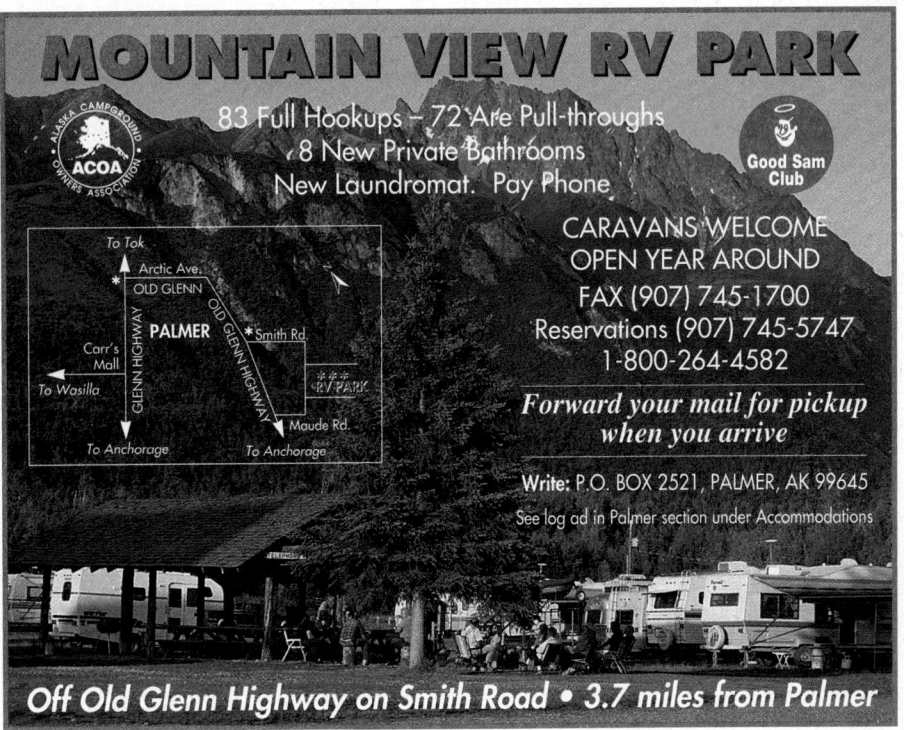

Eklutna Road leads east 10 miles/16.1 km to Eklutna Lake Recreation Area in Chugach State Park. General store at Mile 9. The recreation area has a campground, picnic area and hiking trails. The campground has 50 sites, drinking water, pit toilets and a 15-day limit. Camping fee $10/night or annual pass. The 32-unit picnic area is located at the trailhead parking lot, which will accommodate 80 cars and has a boat launch for hand-carried boats. Three trails branch off the trailhead: Twin Peaks, Lakeside and Bold Ridge. The Lakeside trail skirts Eklutna Lake and gives access to Eklutna Glacier (12.7 miles/20.4 km). **Eklutna Lake** is the largest lake in Chugach State Park, measuring approximately 7 miles long by a mile wide. Fed by Eklutna Glacier, it offers fair fishing for Dolly Varden. *CAUTION: Afternoon winds can make the lake dangerous for boaters.* Interpretive displays on wildlife and a telescope for viewing Dall sheep, eagles and other wildlife are located at the trailhead. ▲

A **25.7** (41.3 km) T **302.3** (486.5 km) Highway crosses Eklutna River.

A **25.3** (40.7 km) T **302.7** (487.1 km) Thunderbird Falls exit (northbound traffic only) and northbound access to Eklutna Road (see **Milepost** A **26.3** for description). Drive about 0.3 mile/0.5 km to parking area. Thunderbird Falls is about 1 mile/1.6 km from the highway. The scenic trail to the falls winds through private property on a 25-foot right-of-way and follows a hillside down to Thunderbird Creek. The falls are just upstream. *CAUTION: Do not climb the steep cliffs overhanging the falls!*

A **24.5** (39.4 km) T **303.5** (488.4 km) Southbound exit to Edmonds Lake residential area and Mirror Lake picnic wayside. The shallow, 73-acre Mirror Lake is located at the foot of Mount Eklutna.

A **23.6** (38 km) T **304.4** (489.9 km) Access to Mirror Lake picnic wayside for northbound traffic only.

A **23** (37 km) T **305** (490.8 km) North Peters Creek overpass, exits both sides of highway.

A **21.5** (34.6 km) T **306.5** (493.3 km) South Peters Creek underpass, exits both sides of highway. Access to Peters Creek and portion of the Old Glenn Highway, which parallels the newer highway south to Eagle River, and provides access to a number of local services. **PETERS CREEK** services include gas stations, grocery, car wash, body repair shop and restaurant.

Peters Creek RV Park. See display ad this section. ▲

Peters Creek Trading Post. See display ad this section.

A **21.2** (34.1 km) T **306.8** (493.7 km) Peters Creek bridge.

A **20.9** (33.6 km) T **306.9** (493.9 km) North Birchwood Loop Road underpass, exits both sides of highway; turn east for community of **CHUGIAK** and for portion of Old Glenn Highway, which leads south to Eagle River and north to Peters Creek. There are many services and attractions in the Peters Creek–Chugiak–Eagle River area.

NOTE: Watch for minor rut repair between North Birchwood and South Birchwood in 1994.

A **20.5** (33 km) T **307.3** (494.5 km) **The Laundry Center.** See display ad this section.

The Shopper's Cache. See display ad this section.

A **17.2** (27.7 km) T **310.8** (500.2 km) South Birchwood Loop Road underpass, exits both sides of highway. Access to St. John Orthodox Cathedral, Chugiak High School, Gruening Junior High School and Old Glenn Highway.

Saint John Orthodox Cathedral. Take a peaceful break from your travels. Visit this unique, geodesic-dome cathedral, with birch ceiling and beautiful icons. Discover how

this church connects to the early church and how Christianity came to Alaska 200 years ago. Bookstore. Monastery Drive off Old Glenn. (907) 696-2002. [ADVERTISEMENT]

A **15.3** (24.6 km) T **312.7** (503.2 km) Exits for Fire Lake residential area, Old Glenn Highway and Eagle River.

A **13.4** (21.6 km) T **314.6** (506.3 km) Eagle River overpass. Exit east for community of Eagle River (all visitor services), the North Anchorage Visitor Information Center (located at Valley River Mall in Eagle River) and Eagle River Road to Chugach State Park visitor center (a highly recommended stop); descriptions follow.

Eagle River

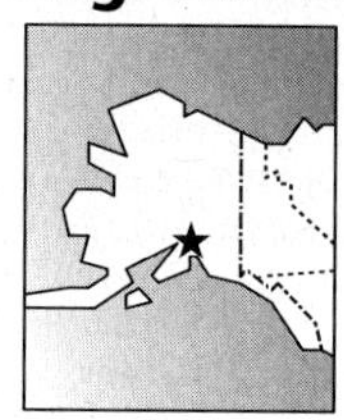

A **13.4** (21.6 km) T **314.6** (506.3 km) **Population:** Area 14,500. **Emergency Services: Clinic,** phone 694-2807. **Visitor Information:** The Anchorage Convention and Visitors Bureau North Anchorage Visitor Information Center is located at the Valley River Mall in Eagle River. Stop by for information on Anchorage events, parking maps and brochures. For information on Eagle River, contact the Chugiak–Eagle River Chamber of Commerce, P.O. Box 770353, Eagle River,

AK 99577; phone 694-4702. You can also visit the Chamber office at 11401 Old Glenn Highway, Ste. 110A, in the Eagle River Shopping Center.

The Chugiak–Eagle River area was homesteaded after WWII when the new Glenn Highway opened this rural area northeast of Anchorage. Today, the Eagle River community offers a full range of businesses, most located near or on Business Boulevard and the Old Glenn Highway east off the Glenn Highway. There are motels, restaurants, supermarkets, laundromat, post office, gas stations and shopping center. Eagle River also has 30 churches, eight public schools, a library and recreation center. Artist Jon Van Zyle's studio is located in Eagle River. Boondock Sporting Goods store here has an antique gun display and also rents fishing tackle.

From downtown Eagle River, follow scenic Eagle River Road (paved) 12.7 miles/20.4 km to reach the Chugach State Park Visitor Center. Beautiful views of the Chugach Mountains from the center's veranda; telescopes are set up for viewing Dall sheep and other wildlife. The center has a pay phone and restrooms, and is the trailhead for the Old Iditarod–Crow Pass trail. There are also short hiking trails from the center and scheduled ranger-led hikes and

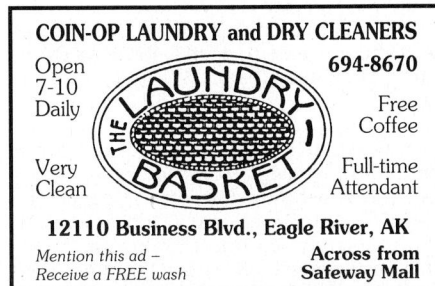

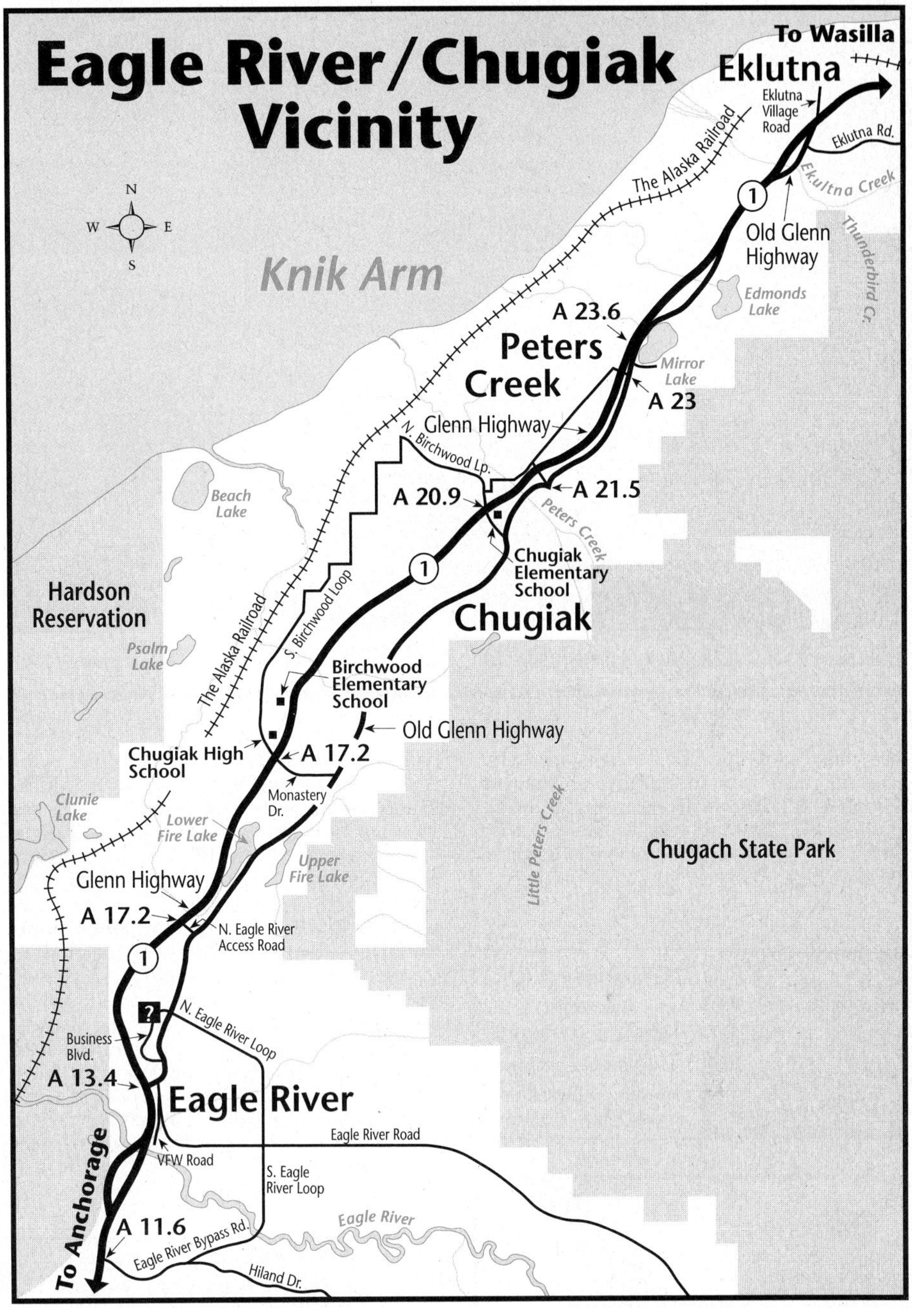

Eagle River/Chugiak Vicinity

To Wasilla
Eklutna
Eklutna Village Road
Eklutna Rd.
The Alaska Railroad
Eklutna Creek
Old Glenn Highway
Thunderbird Cr.
Knik Arm
Edmonds Lake
A 23.6
Peters Creek
Mirror Lake
A 23
Glenn Highway
N. Birchwood Lp.
A 20.9
A 21.5
Beach Lake
Peters Creek
Chugiak Elementary School
Hardson Reservation
Chugiak
S. Birchwood Loop
Psalm Lake
Birchwood Elementary School
Old Glenn Highway
Chugiak High School
A 17.2
Clunie Lake
Monastery Dr.
Lower Fire Lake
Upper Fire Lake
Little Peters Creek
Chugach State Park
Glenn Highway
A 17.2
N. Eagle River Access Road
N. Eagle River Loop
Business Blvd.
A 13.4
Eagle River
Eagle River Road
VFW Road
S. Eagle River Loop
Eagle River
A 11.6
Eagle River Bypass Rd.
Hiland Dr.
To Anchorage

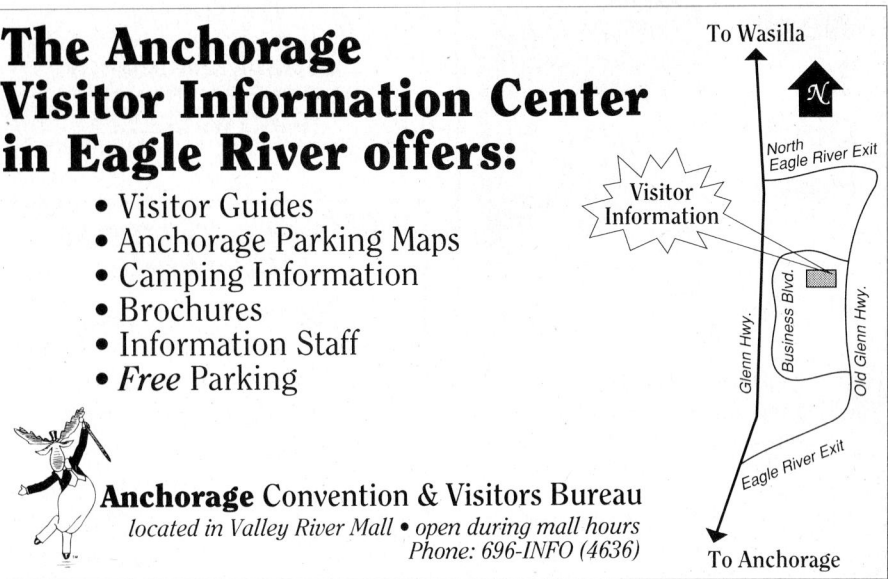

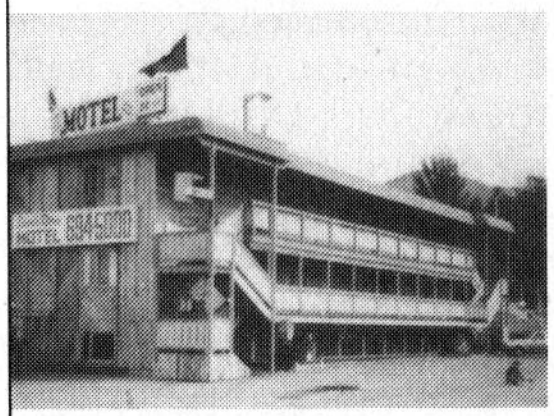

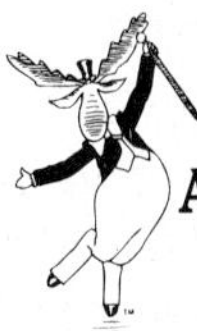

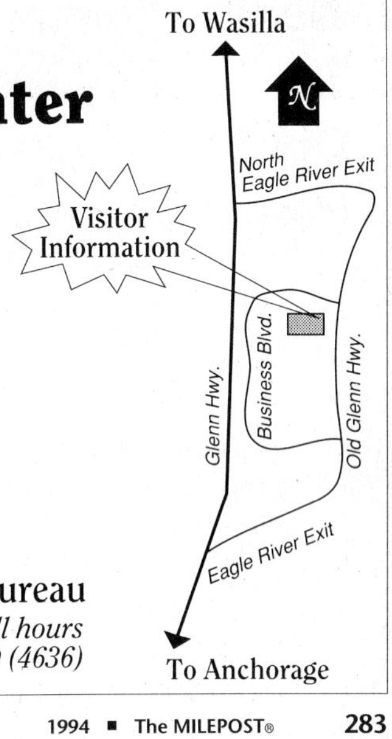

EAGLE RIVER ADVERTISERS

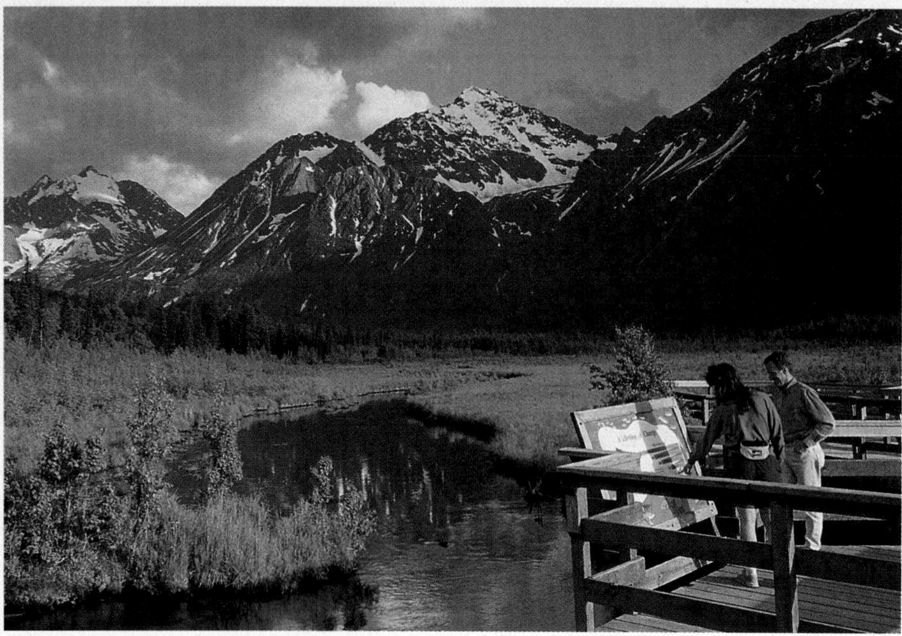

Visitors read interpretive sign along Gore Trail in Chugach State Park. (Michael DeYoung)

naturalist programs. The center is open year-round; hours vary in summer and winter. Phone 694-2108 for current information.

Kayaks, rafts and canoes can put in at Mile 7.5 Eagle River Road at the **North Fork Eagle River** access/day-use area with paved parking, toilets, fishing for rainbow trout, Dolly Varden and a limited king salmon fishery, along with cross-country skiing and snowmachining in winter. The Eagle River offers class II, III and IV float trips. Check with rangers at Chugach State Park for information on river conditions.

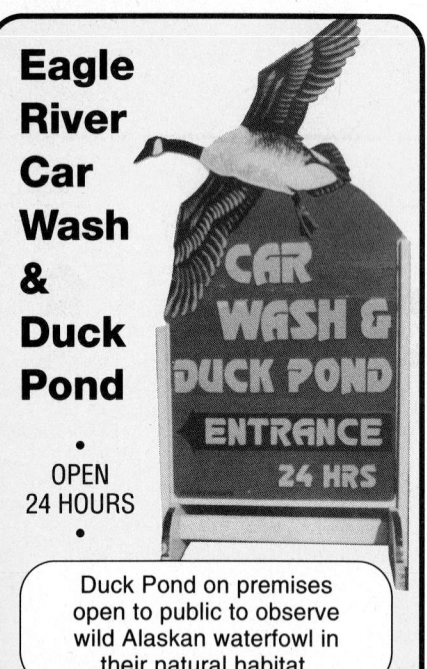

Eagle River Car Wash and Duck Pond. Facilities available for washing cars, campers, trucks, boats and travel homes. Vacuums available. A duck pond on the premises is open to the public and features cedar viewing decks for observing some of the natural wild Alaskan waterfowl in their natural habitat. Mile 15.5 Old Glenn Highway. Turn off at North Eagle River access for car wash. See display ad this section. [ADVERTISEMENT]

Glenn Highway Log

(continued)

A 12.8 (20.6 km) **T 315.2** (507.3 km) Eagle River bridge.

A 11.6 (18.7 km) **T 316.4** (509.2 km) Hiland Road exit. Access to Alaska State Forest Nursery and Eagle River Campground in Chugach State Park. The nursery welcomes visitors; phone 694-5880 for tours. Eagle River Campground, 1.4 miles/2.3 km from the highway, has 50 campsites, a four-day camping limit, 12 picnic sites, flush toilets and drinking water. Camping fee $12/night or annual pass. This is one of the most popular campgrounds in the state. The campground closed for improvements mid-1993 and will reopen in May 1994. Phone (907) 345-5014 for information. ▲

Eagle River Raft Trips, (907) 333-3001, P.O. Box 140141, Anchorage, AK 99514-0141. Fun whitewater raft trips 20 minutes from Anchorage ... a great trip for beginners as well as advanced paddlers! Also scenic floats with wildlife viewing. Free transportation as needed. Everything provided for a warm, comfortable trip. Trips daily. Call for reservations. [ADVERTISEMENT]

A 10.6 (17.1 km) **T 317.4** (510.8 km) Truck weigh stations on both sides of highway. Pay phones.

The last 9 miles/14.5 km of the Glenn Highway has been designated the Veterans' Memorial Parkway.

A 7.5 (12.1 km) **T 320.5** (515.8 km) Southbound exit to **FORT RICHARDSON** and Arctic Valley road. *CAUTION: Watch for moose.*

A 6.1 (9.8 km) **T 321.9** (518 km) Northbound exit to Fort Richardson and Arctic Valley Road. Road to Arctic Valley Ski Area is steep and winding but offers spectacular views of Anchorage and Cook Inlet. It is approximately 7.5 miles/12 km to the ski area. Good berry picking in summer. Not recommended for large vehicles.

A 6 (9.7 km) **T 322** (518.2 km) Ship Creek.

A 4.4 (7.1 km) **T 323.6** (520.8 km) Muldoon Road overpass. (Exit here to connect with Seward Highway via Muldoon and Tudor roads bypass.) U.S. Air Force Hospital and Bartlett High School to the north, Muldoon Road to the south. Exit south on Muldoon for Centennial Park municipal campground. To reach the campground, go south on Muldoon to first left (Boundary); go about 100 yards then make a second left; continue about quarter-mile to campground entrance. There is a bicycle trail from Muldoon Road to Mirror Lake, **Milepost** A 23.6. ▲

A 3 (4.8 km) **T 325** (523 km) Boniface Parkway; access to businesses. Russian Jack Springs city campground is located south of the Glenn Highway on Boniface Parkway just north of DeBarr. Turn north for Elmendorf AFB.

A 1.8 (2.9 km) **T 326.2** (525 km) Bragaw Street.

A 0.7 (1.1 km) **T 327.3** (526.7 km) Reeve Boulevard; access to **ELMENDORF AFB.**

A 0.3 (0.5 km) **T 327.7** (527.4 km) Concrete Street. Access to Elmendorf AFB.

A 0 T 328 (527.9 km) The Glenn Highway ends at Medfra Street. Continue straight ahead on 5th Avenue (one way westbound) to downtown Anchorage. Turn left at Gambell Street (one way southbound) for the Seward Highway and Kenai Peninsula. See ANCHORAGE section following for description of city.

ANCHORAGE

(See maps, pages 286, 289)

Anchorage and the Chugach range in summer. *(Ron Levy)*

And a winter view of Anchorage. *(Lee Foster)*

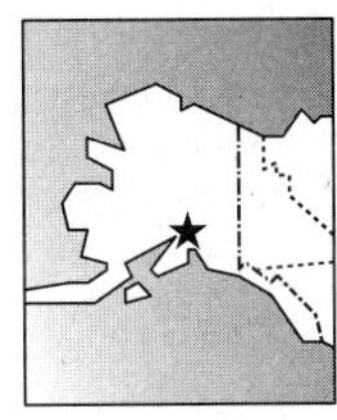

Located on the upper shores of Cook Inlet, at 61° north latitude and 150° west longitude, Anchorage is in the heart of Alaska's southcentral gulf coast. The townsite is on a low-lying alluvial plain bordered by mountains, dense forests of spruce, birch and aspen, and water. Cook Inlet's Turnagain Arm and Knik Arm define the broad peninsula on which the city lies. Anchorage is situated 358 miles/576 km south of Fairbanks via the George Parks Highway; 304 miles/489 km from Valdez, southern terminus of the trans-Alaska pipeline, via the Glenn and Richardson highways; 2,435 driving miles/3919 km, 1,644 nautical miles, and three hours flying time from Seattle. Anchorage has been called "Air Crossroads of the World." In terms of nonstop air mileages, Anchorage is the following distances from these cities: Amsterdam, 4,475/7202 km; Chicago, 2,839/4569 km; Copenhagen, 4,313/6941 km; Hamburg, 4,430/7129 km; Honolulu, 2,780/4474 km; London, 4,487/7221 km; Paris, 4,683/7536 km; San Francisco, 2,015/3243 km; Seattle, 1,445/2325 km; Tokyo, 3,460/5568 km.

Population: Anchorage Municipality 240,258. **Emergency Services: Police, Fire Department, Ambulance** and **Search & Rescue,** phone 911. **Police,** phone 786-8500. **Alaska State Troopers,** phone 269-5511. **Hospitals:** Humana Hospital, phone 276-1131; Alaska Native Medical Center, phone 279-6661; Providence, phone 562-2211; U.S. Air Force, phone 552-5555. **Dental Emergencies,** phone 279-9144 (24-hour service). **Civil Defense,** phone 786-8449. **Crisis Line,** phone 562-4048 or 563-3200 (24-hour service). **Rape & Assault,** phone 276-7273. **Battered Women,** phone 272-0100. **Pet Emergency,** phone 274-5636. **Poison Control,** phone 261-3193. **Road Conditions,** phone 243-7675.

Visitor Information: Log Cabin Visitor Information Center, operated by the Anchorage Convention and Visitors Bureau, is at 4th Avenue and F Street; open daily, year-round. Hours are 7:30 A.M. to 7 P.M. June through August; 8:30 A.M. to 6 P.M. in May and September; and 9 A.M. to 4 P.M. the remainder of the year. The cabin offers a wide assortment of free brochures and maps. Mailing address is 1600 A St., Suite 200, Anchorage 99501; phone 274-3531. The bureau also operates a year-round visitor information phone with a recorded message of the day's special events and attractions, including films, plays, sports events and gallery openings, and it produces several publications including two visitor guides, a restaurant directory, a fall/winter coupon book and a monthly calendar of events; phone 276-3200. Additional visitor information centers are open daily at Anchorage International Airport, one on the lower level for passengers arriving on domestic flights; another in the customs-secured area of the International concourse and a third in the lobby of the International terminal. The North Anchorage Visitor Information Center is located at Valley River Mall in Eagle River, just off the Glenn Highway. The Community Calendar Services of the Anchorage Convention and Visitors Bureau offers information on community events, phone 276-4118.

The Alaska Public Lands Information Center, 605 W. 4th, in the historic Federal Bldg., has extensive displays and information on outdoor recreation lands in Alaska; phone 271-2737. (See detailed description of the center under Attractions this section.)

Elevation: 38 to 120 feet/16 to 37m, with terrain nearly flat throughout the bowl area.

Climate: Anchorage has a climate closely resembling that of the Rocky Mountains area. Shielded from excess Pacific moisture by the Kenai Mountains to the south, the city has an annual average of only 15 inches of precipitation. Winter snowfall averages about 70 inches per year, with snow on the ground typically from October to April. Anchorage is in a transition zone, between the moderating influence of the Pacific Ocean and the extreme temperatures found in interior Alaska. The average temperature in January (coldest month) is 13°F/-11°C; in July (warmest month), 58°F/14°C. A record 40 days of 70°F/21°C temperatures or higher was set in 1936, according to the National Weather Service. The summer of 1993 ranked fifth with 27 "hot" days. Record high was 86°F/30°C in June 1953. Record low was -38°F/-39°C in February 1947. The growing season in the area is 100 to 120 days and typically extends from late May to early September. Anchorage has a daily maximum of 19 hours, 21 minutes of daylight in summer, and five hours, 28 minutes in winter. Prevailing wind direction is north at a mean speed of 6.6 mph/10.6 kmph.

Radio: KENI 550, KHAR 590, KYAK 650, KBYR 700, KFQD 750, KLEF 98.1, KFFR 1020, KKSD 1080, KRUA-FM 88.1, KATB-FM 89.3, KSKA-FM 91.1, KJMM-FM 94.5, KOOZ-FM 97.3, KYMG-FM 98.9, KBFX-FM 100.5, KGOT-FM 101.3, KPXR-FM 102.1, KKLV-FM 104.1, KNIK-FM 105.3, KWHL-FM 106.5, KASH-FM 107.5. **Television:** KTUU (NBC), Channel 2; KTBY (Fox), Channel 4; KYES (independent), Channel 5; KAKM (PBS), Channel 7; KTVA (CBS), Channel 11; KIMO (ABC), Channel 13; and UHF channels. Pay cable television is also available. **Newspapers:** *Anchorage Daily News* (daily); *Alaska Journal of Commerce and Pacific Rim Reporter*

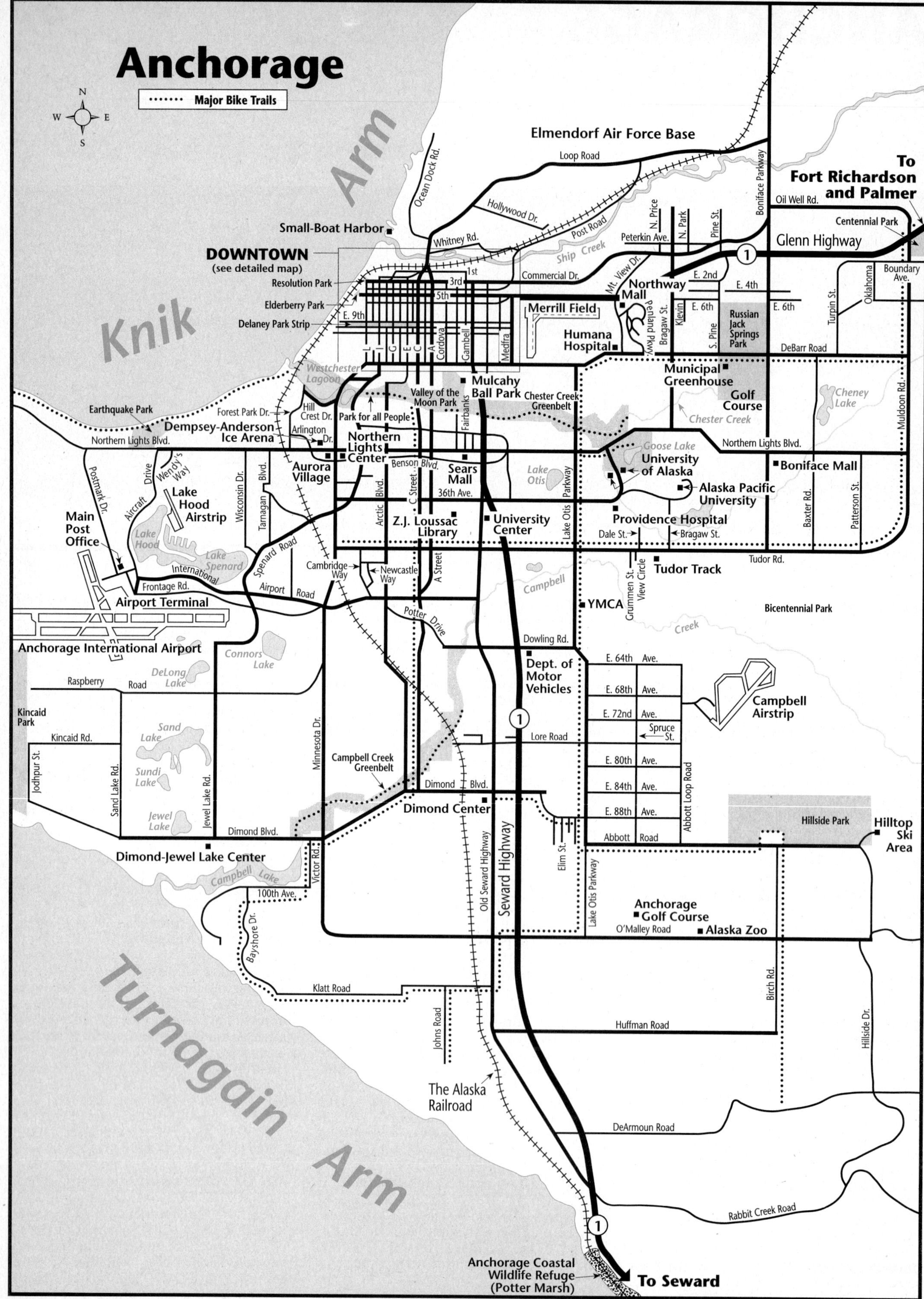

Anchorage
Major Bike Trails
N
S
E
W
Knik Arm
Turnagain Arm
Elmendorf Air Force Base
Loop Road
Ocean Dock Rd.
Hollywood Dr.
Whitney Rd.
Post Road
Ship Creek
Small-Boat Harbor
DOWNTOWN
(see detailed map)
Resolution Park
Elderberry Park
Delaney Park Strip
E. 9th
1st
3rd
5th
Commercial Dr.
Merrill Field
Humana Hospital
Mulcahy Ball Park
Westchester Lagoon
Valley of the Moon Park
Park for all People
Chester Creek Greenbelt
Earthquake Park
Forest Park Dr.
Hill Crest Dr.
Arlington Dr.
Dempsey-Anderson Ice Arena
Northern Lights Blvd.
Northern Lights Center
Aurora Village
Benson Blvd.
Sears Mall
36th Ave.
Z.J. Loussac Library
University Center
Lake Otis
Lake Otis Parkway
Postmark Dr.
Aircraft Drive
Wendy's Way
Lake Hood Airstrip
Lake Hood
Lake Spenard
Wisconsin Dr.
Tamagan Blvd.
Arctic Blvd.
C Street
A Street
Fairbanks
Spenard Road
International
Main Post Office
Frontage Rd.
Airport Terminal
Airport Road
Cambridge Way
Newcastle Way
Potter Drive
Anchorage International Airport
Connors Lake
DeLong Lake
Raspberry Road
Kincaid Park
Kincaid Rd.
Sand Lake
Sundi Lake
Jewel Lake
Jodhpur St.
Sand Lake Rd.
Jewel Lake Rd.
Minnesota Dr.
Campbell Creek Greenbelt
Dimond Blvd.
Dimond Center
Dimond-Jewel Lake Center
Campbell Lake
Victor Rd.
100th Ave.
Bayshore Dr.
Klatt Road
Johns Road
Old Seward Highway
Seward Highway
The Alaska Railroad
Anchorage Coastal Wildlife Refuge (Potter Marsh)
To Seward
Boniface Parkway
N. Price
N. Park
Pine St.
Peterkin Ave.
Mt. View Dr.
Northway Mall
E. 2nd
E. 4th
E. 6th
Penland Pkwy.
Bragaw St.
Klevin
S. Pine
Russian Jack Springs Park
Municipal Greenhouse
Golf Course
Chester Creek
Cheney Lake
Goose Lake
University of Alaska
Alaska Pacific University
Providence Hospital
Dale St.
Bragaw St.
Boniface Mall
Baxter Rd.
Patterson St.
Muldoon Rd.
Tudor Rd.
Tudor Track
Grummen St.
View Circle
YMCA
Bicentennial Park
Campbell Creek
Dowling Rd.
Dept. of Motor Vehicles
E. 64th Ave.
E. 68th Ave.
E. 72nd Ave.
Spruce St.
Lore Road
E. 80th Ave.
E. 84th Ave.
E. 88th Ave.
Abbott Road
Abbott Loop Road
Campbell Airstrip
Elim St.
Hillside Park
Hilltop Ski Area
Anchorage Golf Course
O'Malley Road
Alaska Zoo
Birch Rd.
Hillside Dr.
Huffman Road
DeArmoun Road
Rabbit Creek Road
Oil Well Rd.
To Fort Richardson and Palmer
Centennial Park
Glenn Highway
1
Oklahoma
Boundary Ave.
Turpin St.
DeBarr Road

(weekly); *Chugiak-Eagle River Star* (weekly).

Private Aircraft: Anchorage airports provide facilities and services to accommodate all types of aircraft. Consult the *Alaska Supplement*, the *Anchorage VFR Terminal Area Chart* and *Terminal Alaska Book* for the following airports: Anchorage International, Merrill Field, Campbell airstrip, and Lake Hood seaplane and strip.

HISTORY AND ECONOMY

In 1914 Congress authorized the building of a railroad linking an ocean port with the interior river shipping routes. The anchorage at the mouth of Ship Creek was chosen as the construction camp and headquarters for the Alaskan Engineering Commission. By the summer of 1915 the camp's population, housed mainly in tents, had grown to about 2,000.

The name Anchorage (earlier names included Woodrow, Ship Creek, Ship Creek Landing and Knik Anchorage) was chosen by the federal government when the first post office opened in May 1915. A few months later the bluff south of the creek was cleared and surveyed and 655 lots, on 347 acres, were auctioned off by the General Land Office for $148,000. The intersection of 4th Avenue and C Street was regarded as the center of the business district, and by late summer about 100 wooden structures had been built. Anchorage continued to prosper and was incorporated in 1920.

Anchorage's growth has been in spurts, propelled by: (1) construction of the Alaska Railroad and the transfer of its headquarters from Seward to Anchorage in 1917; (2) colonization of the Matanuska Valley, a farming region 45 miles/72 km to the north, in 1935; (3) construction of Fort Richardson and Elmendorf Field in 1940; (4) oil discoveries between 1957 and 1961 in Cook Inlet; and (5) the development of North Slope oil fields and the construction of the trans-Alaska pipeline — all since 1968.

The earthquake of March 27, 1964, which caused millions of dollars in damage, resulted in a flurry of new construction. Government relief funds (in the form of Small Business Administration loans) were offered to those who wished to rebuild. Most did, and a distinctly new Anchorage began to emerge.

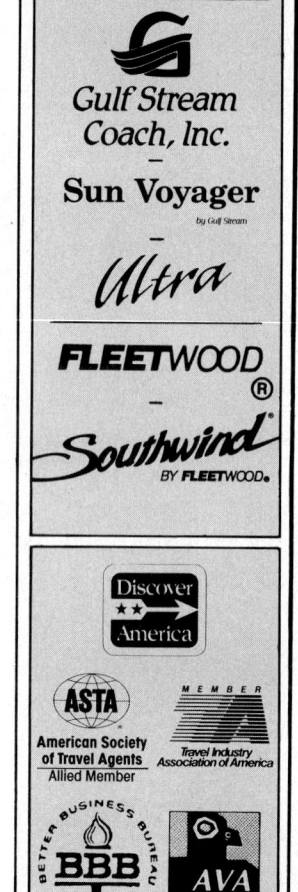

In the 1970s and '80s, Anchorage underwent a population and construction boom tied to oil production. The decline in oil prices in recent years has brought about a slower economy than was enjoyed in those

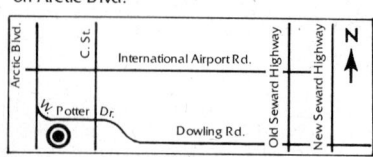

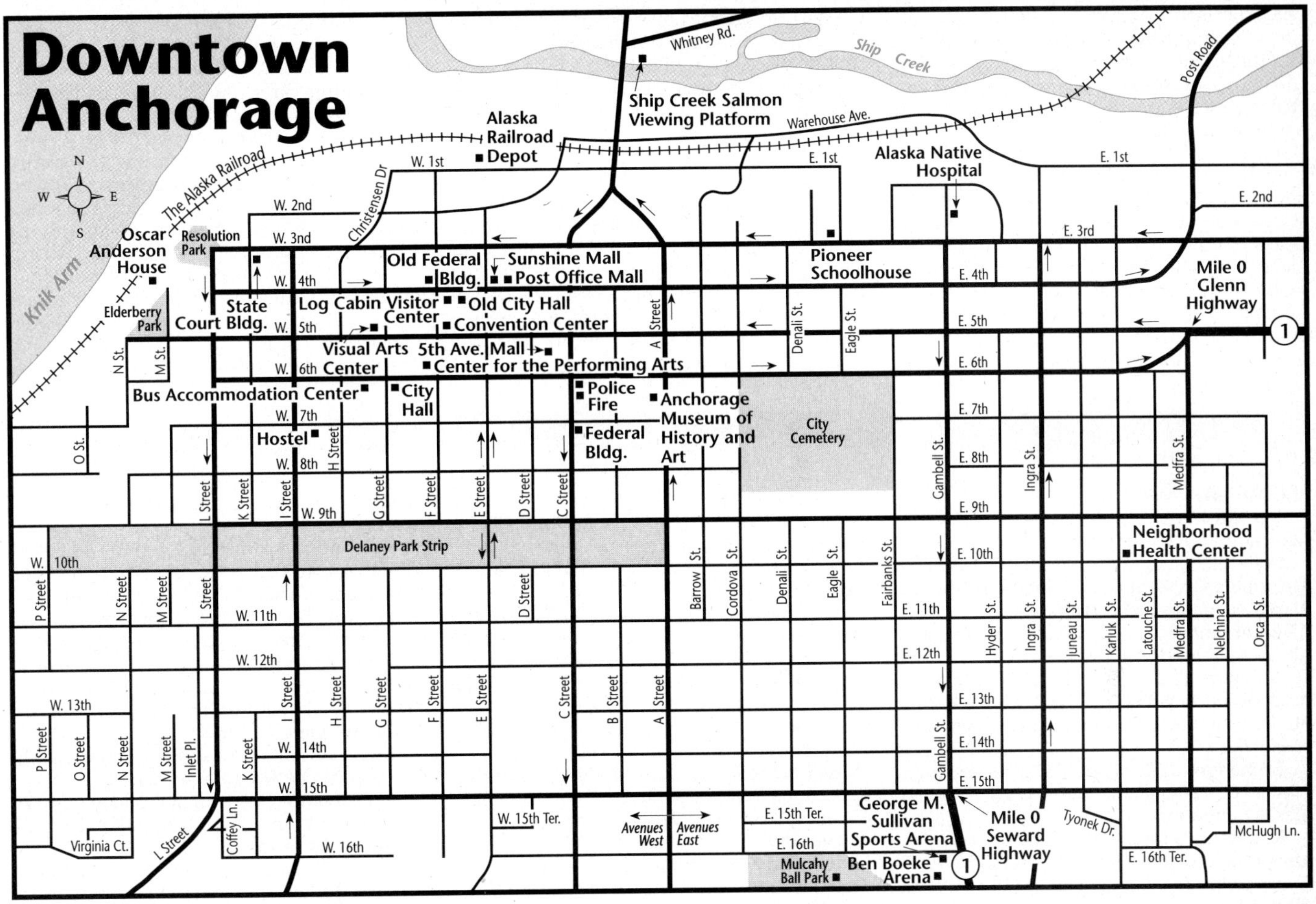

Downtown Anchorage

"boom" years.

Today, Anchorage is a center of commerce and distribution for the rest of Alaska. Mainstays of the economy are government agencies (federal and state), tourism, the oil industry, military bases and transportation facilities including an expanding port and international airport.

DESCRIPTION

Anchorage is a sprawling city, bordered on the east by the stunningly beautiful Chugach Mountain Range and on the west by Knik Arm of Cook Inlet. On a clear day, you can catch a tantalizing glimpse of Mount McKinley, 135 miles/217 km to the north.

Many new buildings dot the Anchorage skyline. Millions of dollars were allocated by the legislature for Project 80s, the largest construction program in Anchorage's history. Perhaps best known is the Alaska Center for the Performing Arts, located at the corner of 5th Avenue and F Street. Construction costs on the center grew from an original estimate of $22 million to more than $70 million. Visitors may notice the fences on the center's roof: these had to be added to prevent snow from sliding off the steep pitch of the roof and onto pedestrians below. Other completed projects include the George M. Sullivan Sports Arena, William A. Egan Civic and Convention Center, Z.J. Loussac Public Library, and a major expansion and renovation of the Anchorage Museum of History and Art.

With its curious mixture of the old frontier and the jet age, Anchorage is truly a unique place. In profile, the town has:

- About 80 schools, including special education and alternative public programs and a number of privately operated schools. University of Alaska, Alaska Pacific University and Alaska Business College.
- More than 200 churches and temples.
- Z.J. Loussac Public Library, plus four branch libraries, National Bank of Alaska Heritage Library Museum, Dept. of the Interior's Alaska Resource Library, the Oil Spill Public Information Center, Alaska State Library Services for the Blind and the University of Alaska Library.
- Municipal bus service: four taxi services.
- In the arts — **Dance:** Alaska Center for Performing Arts; Alaska Dance Theatre; Anchorage Concert Assoc.; Anchorage Opera; Ballet Alaska. **Music:** Alaska Airlines Autumn Classics; Anchorage Concert Chorus; Anchorage Community Concert Band; Anchorage Concert Assoc.; Anchorage Children's Choir; Anchorage Symphony Orchestra; Anchorage Festival of Music; Sweet Adelines (Cheechako and Sourdough chapters); University of Alaska–Anchorage Singers; Young People's Concerts. **Theater:** Out North Theater Company; Alaska Junior Theater; Alaska Theatre of Youth; Anchorage

Community Theatre; Alaska Stage Company; Valley Performing Arts; UAA Theatre; Alaska Festival Theatre; Cyrano's Off Center Playhouse. **Art:** About 20 art galleries.

ACCOMMODATIONS

There are more than 70 motels and hotels in the Anchorage area with prices for a double room ranging from $50 to $70 and up. Reservations are a must. Bed-and-breakfast accommodations are also available in more than 100 private residences.

Anchorage International Hostel is located at 700 H St., one block from the People Mover Transit Center in downtown Anchorage. The hostel is open 8 A.M.-noon and 5-12 P.M.; cost for members is $12 per night, nonmembers $15. American Youth Hostel cards available at the hostel or by mail. The hostel is open year-round and has kitchen facilities, common rooms, laundry room and TV room. For information phone 276-3635. Write for reservations (prepayment required): 700 H St., Anchorage 99501.

Restaurants number more than 600, with many major fast-food chains, formal dining rooms and specialty establishments including Cantonese, Italian, Japanese, Korean, Chinese, Mandarin, Mexican, Polynesian, Greek, German, Sicilian, Thai, soul food, seafood, smorgasbord and vegetarian.

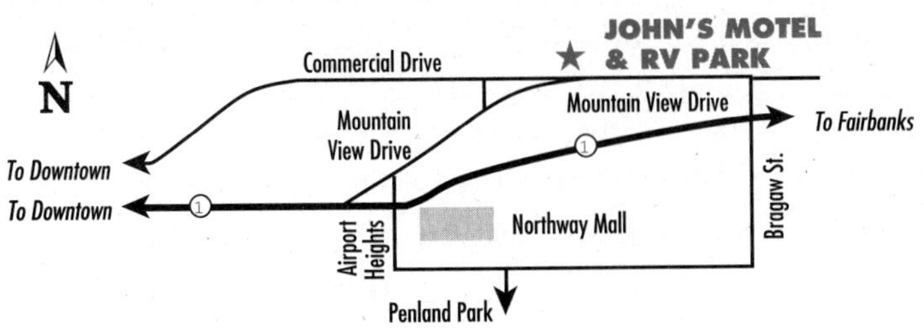

JOHN'S MOTEL
3543 Mountain View Drive
Anchorage, Alaska 99508
(907) 277-4332 • FAX (907) 272-0739
800-478-4332
Singles • Doubles • Kitchenettes
Individual Heat Control
Color TV with Radios • Direct Dial Phones
Combination Tub/ Shower
Off-Street Parking
DAILY & WEEKLY RATES

Alaskan Frontier Gardens Bed and Breakfast. Elegant accommodations on a scenic 3-acre wooded setting. Come enjoy our Alaskan hospitality with 30-year resident. Located in Anchorage's peaceful "hillside" area near the Chugach State Park, 20 minutes from downtown. Spacious rooms, luxury suite with Jacuzzi, sauna and fireplace. Great for honeymooners. Year-round. Gourmet breakfast. Laundry service. VISA and MasterCard accepted. 1011 Tudor Road, Suite 160, Anchorage, AK 99503. (907) 345-6556 or 345-6562, fax (907) 562-2923. [ADVERTISEMENT]

Arctic Fox Inn Bed & Breakfast. 326 E. 2nd Ct., Anchorage, AK 99501. Phone (907) 272-4818, fax (907) 272-4819. Quiet, convenient, downtown location with beautiful inlet view. Tastefully decorated rooms and corporate suites with moderate summer rates, low winter rates. Near all major downtown hotels, restaurants, museum, bike trail, train station and Ship Creek (salmon fishing). Laundry facilities, private baths, TV and phone in rooms. [ADVERTISEMENT]

Caribou Inn. 501 L Street, Anchorage, AK 99501. Clean, comfortable rooms in an excellent downtown Anchorage location. Shared or private bath, some with kitchenettes. Daily or weekly rates, major credit cards accepted. For reservations or information phone (907) 272-0444 or fax (907) 274-4828. [ADVERTISEMENT]

Lynn's Pine Point Bed and Breakfast. Quiet, comfortable lodging in our beautiful cedar retreat located near the Chugach Mountains. Enjoy a large room with private shower, TV , VCR, microwave and queen bed. Continental or traditional breakfast, many other extras. Business travelers welcome. VISA and MasterCard accepted. The comforts of home only minutes from all of Alaska. 3333 Creekside Dr., Anchorage, AK 99504. Phone (907) 333-2244. [ADVERTISEMENT]

Puffin Inn. Experience the comfort of our friendly Alaskan hospitality. The Puffin Inn provides quality accommodations and exceptional service at reasonable rates. Complimentary coffee, rolls and newspaper served daily. Cable TV. Nonsmoking rooms, freezer space, dry cleaning/laundry service, and courtesy airport shuttle available. Located near Lake Hood floatplane airport. Seasonal daily, weekly rates available. 4400 Spenard Road, Anchorage, AK 99517. Fax (907) 248-6853, phone (907) 243-4044, (800) 4-PUFFIN. [ADVERTISEMENT]

Puffin Place Studios & Suites. Discover Anchorage's hotel alternative. 37 tastefully decorated studios and one-bedroom suites, each with a fully equipped kitchen, including microwave. Free local calls, cable TV, laundry facility, dry cleaning/laundry service, nonsmoking rooms, courtesy airport shuttle. Located near Lake Hood floatplane airport. Only minutes from downtown. Short walking distance from restaurants and shopping. Seasonal daily, weekly, monthly rates. 1058 W. 27th Ave., Anchorage, AK 99503. Fax (907) 276-4922, phone (907) 279-1058. [ADVERTISEMENT]

Sixth & B Bed & Breakfast. Prime downtown location. Complimentary bicycles. Call, write or fax for brochure. (907) 279-5293. Fax (907) 279-8338. Seven blocks from railroad station. Across the street from museum. Summer rates range from $50 to $60 to $88 and $98, depending on what month you stay. Winter rates range from $38 to $58. All rooms have color TV. Flexible check in, check-out times. Guests also receive a 10 percent discount at Arctic Images T-shirt shop, which is also at 6th and B and 5th and C. [ADVERTISEMENT]

Sourdough Motel. 1 mile north of downtown Anchorage on A Street — go across the bridge to the top of the hill. Free parking, pets OK, laundromat, several parks and restaurants within walking distance. We have suites with fully equipped kitchens, full bath, and cable TV. Priced lower than a regular room downtown. (907) 279-4148 or (800) 777-3716 (Outside Alaska) or (800) 478-3030 (Alaska only). [ADVERTISEMENT]

Susie's Lake View Bed & Breakfast. Enjoy the quiet setting overlooking scenic Campbell Lake. Unwind with a leisure tour of our quaint garden setting. The large deck areas offer comfortable privacy for an individual or big enough for a family BBQ. Start or end your day with a steamy hot tub — available 24 hours a day and located where it should be ... outside. Continental or traditional breakfast. Business travelers welcome. Located only 11 minutes from the airport. VISA and MasterCard accepted. 9256 Campbell Terrace, Anchorage, AK 99515. Phone (907) 243-4624. [ADVERTISEMENT]

12th & L Bed & Breakfast. One of Anchorage's newest and nicest B&Bs. Downtown location on bus route, near coastal trail. King and queen beds. TVs, continental-plus breakfast. Beautiful solarium has cable TV w/HBO. VCR and Alaska vacation literature. Seasonal rates. 1134 L St., Anchorage, AK 99501. 274-3344. [ADVERTISEMENT]

Two Morrow's Place Bed & Breakfast. "Your home away from home." Casual elegance in quiet downtown area. Walk to shops, restaurants, sites, lagoon, bike and coastal trail. Enjoy our nonsmoking home with guest living room, fireplace, gourmet or continental breakfasts. Homemade specialties. Shared or private baths. Open all year. Ideal for the business or pleasure traveler. Credit cards welcome. 1325 "O" St., Anchorage, AK 99501-4274. (907) 277-9939. [ADVERTISEMENT]

Anchorage has one public campground, Centennial Park, open from May through September. Fees are $12 for non-Alaskans; $10 for Alaska residents. To reach Centennial Park, take the Muldoon Road exit south off the Glenn Highway and take the first left (Boundary); take the next first left and follow the signs. Centennial, recommended for large RVs, has 90 RV sites, 40 tent sites, barracks-type showers, flush toilets and a dump station. It does not offer hookups. Call 333-9711 for details.

Chugach State Park has campgrounds located near Anchorage at Bird Creek (Seward Highway), and at Eagle River and Eklutna Lake (Glenn Highway). Anchorage also has several private campgrounds. ▲

TRANSPORTATION

Air: More than a dozen international and domestic air carriers and numerous intrastate airlines serve Anchorage International Airport, located 6.5 miles/10.5 km from downtown. Limousine service to and from major downtown hotels is available. Bus service to downtown is via People Mover (follow signs for city bus from baggage claim area to bus stop).

Ferry: There is no ferry service to Anchorage. The nearest port is Whittier on Prince William Sound, served by Alaska state ferry from Cordova and Valdez. Whittier is accessible by train from either Anchorage or Portage on the Seward Highway. See the Southwestern Ferry Schedules in the MARINE ACCESS ROUTES section for details.

Cruise Ships: See Cruise Ships in the MARINE ACCESS ROUTES section for ships making Anchorage a port of call.

Railroad: The Alaska Railroad offers daily passenger service in summer from Anchorage to Seward, to Denali National Park (Mount McKinley) and to Fairbanks. In addition, a shuttle train for both foot passengers and vehicles operates daily between Portage and Whittier, connecting with the Alaska Marine Highway to Valdez and Cordova. *NOTE: Rail transportation is NOT available between Anchorage and Portage.*

See the ALASKA RAILROAD section for passenger schedules. For more information, write the railroad at P.O. Box 107500, Anchorage 99510; phone 1-800-544-0552 or (907) 265-2494, fax (907) 265-2323.

The Alaska Railroad depot is located on 1st Avenue, within easy walking distance of downtown.

Bus: Local service via People Mover, which serves most of the Anchorage bowl from Peters Creek to Oceanview. Fares are $1 for adults, 50¢ for youth 5-18, 25¢ for senior citizens and disabled citizens with transit identification. Monthly passes are sold at the Transit Center (6th and H Street), the Penney Mall Transit Center, the Dimond Transit Center, municipal libraries. Day passes also available for visitors at the Transit Center. For bus route information, phone Rideline 343-6543.

Taxi: There are four taxi companies.

Car and Camper Rentals: There are more than 29 car rental agencies located at the airport and downtown. There are also several RV rental agencies (see advertisements this section).

RV Parking: The Anchorage Parking Authority's long-range plan is to have in operation spaces for oversized vehicles (motorcoaches, campers, large trucks). The first of these lots is located at 3rd Avenue, north of the Holiday Inn, between A and C streets. Parking is $5 per space, per day. For more information, phone 276-8970.

Highway: Anchorage can be reached via the Glenn Highway and the Seward Highway. See GLENN HIGHWAY and SEWARD HIGHWAY sections for details.

ATTRACTIONS

Get Acquainted: Start at the Log Cabin Visitor Information Center at 4th Avenue and F Street, open 7:30 A.M. to 7 P.M. June through August; 8:30 A.M. to 6 P.M. in May and September; and 9 A.M. to 4 P.M. the remainder of the year; phone 274-3531. Free visitor guidebooks.

Take a Historic Walking Tour: Start at the Log Cabin Visitor Information Center at 4th Avenue and F Street. The Anchorage Convention and Visitors Bureau's *Anchorage Visitors Guide* has an excellent guide for a downtown walking tour.

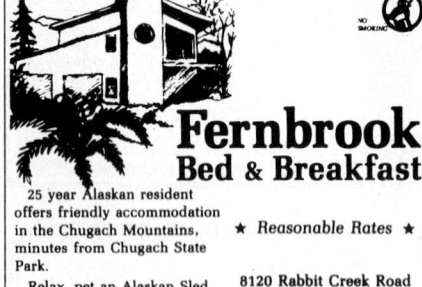

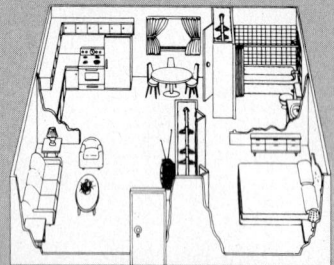

Take a Tour: Several tour operators offer local and area sightseeing tours. These range from a three-hour narrated motorcoach tour of Anchorage to full-day tours of area attractions such as Portage Glacier and Alyeska Resort. Two-day or longer excursions by motorcoach, rail, ferry and air travel to nearby attractions such as Prince William Sound or remote areas are also available. Inquire at your hotel, see ads this section or contact a travel agent.

The Alaska Public Lands Information Center, located in the historic Federal Bldg. on 4th Avenue and F Street, offers a wide variety of information on all of Alaska's state and federal parks, forests and wildlife refuges. Displays, video programs and computers permit self-help trip-planning. Expert staff provide additional assistance and supply maps, brochures and other aids. Federal passports (Golden Age, Eagle and Access) and state park passes are available. Reservations may be made here (in person or by mail only) for U.S. Forest Service cabins throughout the state. Most campground permits and shuttle bus coupons for Denali National Park are issued at the park's Visitor Access Center. A *limited* number of permits and coupons can be reserved in advance at the Anchorage Public Lands Information Center. Campground reservations can be made seven to 21 days in advance. Since these reservations generally are filled within a few hours of their becoming available, visitors are advised to be in line before the center opens at 9 A.M. exactly 21 days prior to their first night of stay in the park for the best chance of securing an advance campsite reservation. Shuttle bus coupons are available one to 21 days in advance. Those interested in shuttle bus coupons should come in no less than 18 days prior to visiting the park. All reservations must be made in person. Reservation requirements subject to change. Fees are collected when the reservation is made and are not refundable. Receive up-to-date public lands news by touch-tone phone by calling 258-PARK for recorded information. The center is open year-round. Summer hours are 9 A.M. to 6 P.M. daily;

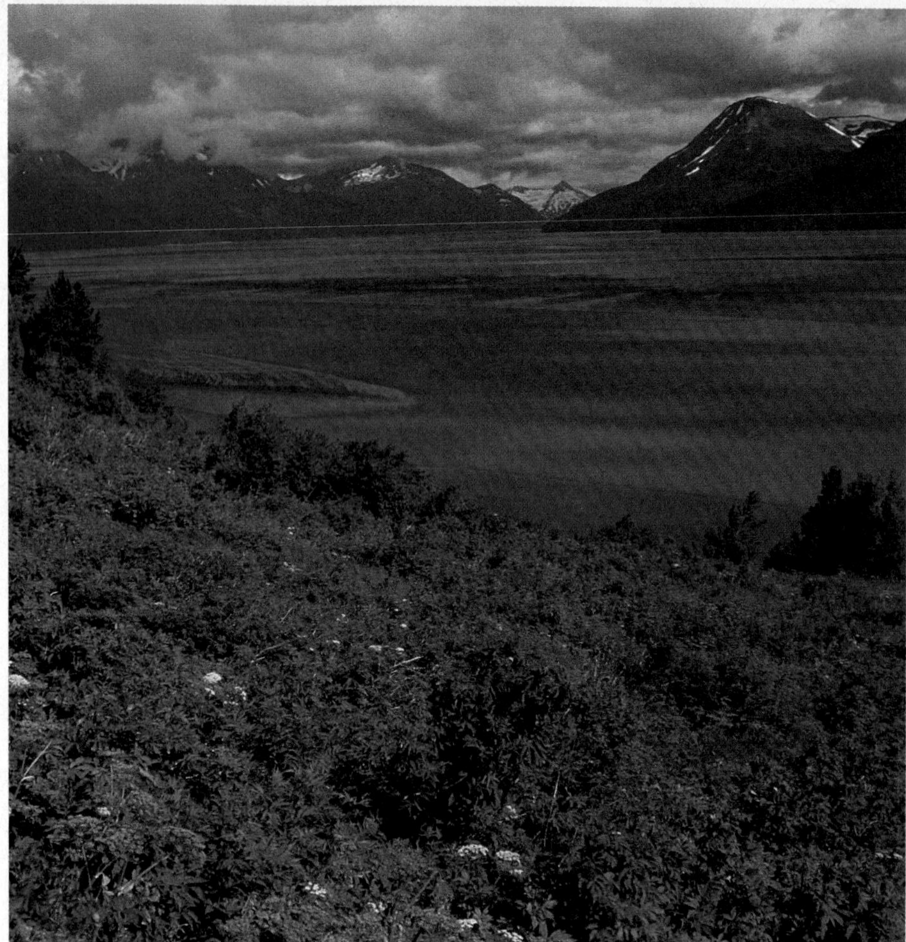

Scenic views of Turnagain Arm are found just a dozen miles south of Anchorage. (Sue Rheaume)

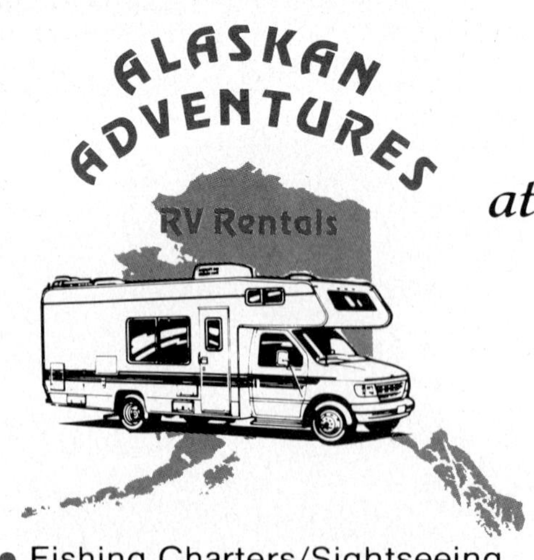

Chugach State Park

This 495,000-acre park flanking Anchorage to the north, east and south, offers wilderness opportunities for all seasons: hiking, wildlife viewing, camping, berry picking, skiing and snowmobiling. Information about the park is available from Chugach State Park, H.C. 52, Box 8999, Indian, AK 99540; phone 345-5014. The Chugach State Park office, located in Potter Section House on the Seward Highway, has maps showing access to the park's recreation areas.

Between June and September, park staff offer guided nature walks and more strenuous hikes on the weekends to various points of interest in the park. The nature walks, which last about two hours, focus on some aspect of natural history, such as wildflower identification or bird watching. The more strenuous hikes last approximately four hours. Phone 694-6391 for a recorded message.

There are several access points to Chugach State Park attractions from Anchorage. North from downtown on the Glenn Highway take the Eklutna Road exit (**Milepost A 26.3**) and drive in 10 miles/16 km to reach Eklutna Lake Recreation Area. Eklutna Lake is the largest lake in Chugach State Park. The recreation area has a campground, picnic area and hiking trails. Cross-country skiing and snowmobiling in winter.

You may also reach Eagle River Visitor Center for Chugach State Park by driving north on the Glenn Highway and taking the Eagle River exit (**Milepost A 13.4**). Follow Eagle River Road 12.7 miles/20.4 km to reach this beautifully situated visitor center, with its views of the Chugach Mountains. Excellent wildlife displays, a nature trail, Dall sheep viewing and other summer activities make this a worthwhile stop. Cross-country skiing and snowmobiling in winter. Phone 694-2108 for more information.

Another easily accessible park area from downtown is Arctic Valley. Turn off the Glenn Highway at Arctic Valley Road, **Milepost A 6.1**, and drive in 7.5 miles/12 km. Spectacular views of Anchorage and Cook Inlet. Good berry picking and hiking in summer; downhill and cross-country skiing in winter.

The park's hillside trailheads may be reached by driving south from downtown to the O'Malley Road exit at **Milepost S 120.8** on the Seward Highway. Follow O'Malley Road east for 4 miles/6.4 km until Hillside Drive enters from the right; turn on Hillside and proceed about 1.5 miles/2.4 km to the intersection of Upper Huffman Road and Hillside Drive. Turn left on Upper Huffman Road and continue 4 miles/6.4 km to the Glen Alps trailhead. Hiking in summer, cross-country skiing and snowmobiling in winter.

The Seward Highway south from Anchorage gives access to several Chugach State Park hiking trails.

open in winter 9 A.M. to 5:30 P.M. Monday through Friday, closed weekends and holidays. Phone 271-2737 or write the center at 605 W. 4th Ave., Suite 105, Anchorage, AK 99501, for more information.

The Anchorage Museum of History and Art, located at 121 W. 7th Ave., is a must stop. One of the most visited attractions in Anchorage, the museum features permanent displays of Alaska's cultural heritage and artifacts from its history. The 15,000-square-foot Alaska Gallery on the second floor is the Museum's showcase, presenting Alaska Native cultures — Aleut, Eskimo and Indian — and their encounters with the Russians, New England whalers and gold rush prospectors. Displays include full-scale dwellings and detailed miniature dioramas. The gallery contains some 300 photographs, more than 1,000 artifacts, 33 maps and specially made ship and aircraft models. The main floor of the museum consists of six connecting galleries displaying early Alaskan art through contemporary Alaskan artists, such as Sydney Laurence. The museum also has a reference library and archives, a free film series (daily in summer), the Museum Shop, and a cafe in the atrium. Admission is $4 for adults, $3.50 for seniors 65 and older, under 18 free. Open 9 A.M. to 6 P.M. daily, May 17 to Sept. 12; 10 A.M. to 6 P.M. Tuesday through Saturday, and 1-5 P.M. Sunday, in winter (closed Monday and holidays). Phone 343-6173 for recorded information about special shows, or 343-4326 during business hours for more information.

Visit the Oscar Anderson House: The city's first wood-frame house, built in 1915, was home to Oscar Anderson, a Swedish immigrant and early Anchorage pioneer and businessman. Now on the National Register of Historic Places, it has been beautifully restored and is well worth a visit. Located in the north corner of Elderberry Park, at the west end of 5th Avenue, 420 M St. Hours are noon to 4 P.M. daily, mid-May to mid-September. Swedish Christmas tour, weekends in December. Adults, $2; children 5 to 12 and seniors over 65, $1. Group tours may be arranged year-round by appointment. Phone 274-2336 or 274-3600.

Arctic Images. Waging war on the tacky tee since 1986. Original designs, quality shirts, reasonable prices. Located downtown at corner of 5th and C and also at 6th and B. Arctic Images is also home to Downtown Bicycle Rental, Sixth & B Bed & Breakfast and the Far From Fenway Fan Club. [ADVERTISEMENT]

Tour Elmendorf AFB. Free bus tours of the base are offered every Wednesday from June 1 to Aug. 30. Contact the Public Affairs office in advance by phoning (907) 552-5755. Groups of 10 or more persons call ahead for special arrangements. Elmendorf has a base population of approximately 7,000 military personnel.

Laura Wright Alaskan Parkys. Known worldwide for beautiful Eskimo-style summer and winter parkas. Off the rack or custom made. Started by Laura Wright in Fairbanks in 1947 and continuing the tradition is granddaughter Sheila Ezelle. Purchase "Wearable Alaskan Art" for the whole family at 343 W. 5th Ave., Anchorage, AK 99501. Phone (907) 274-4215. Bank cards welcome. Mail and phone orders accepted. We airmail worldwide. [ADVERTISEMENT]

Exercise Your Imagination: Visit the Imaginarium, 725 W. 5th Ave., a hands-on science discovery center offering unique insights into the wonders of nature, science and technology. Open daily year-round Monday–Saturday 10 A.M. to 6 P.M., Sunday noon to 5 P.M. Adults, $4; seniors, $3; children 2 to 12, $3. Handicapped accessible. Phone 276-3179. ♿

Major Marine Glacier Tours. Offering Anchorage's only cruise to awesome Blackstone Glacier. Tour includes an all-you-can-eat Alaska salmon dinner with dessert bar. The six-and-one-half-hour cruise through spectacular Prince William Sound is an easy day-trip from Anchorage and features abundant wildlife and up-close viewing of many glaciers. One of the trip's highlights is Blackstone Glacier, where you'll float among icebergs as you enjoy a salmon dinner and watch waterfalls and giant chunks of ice spill off the glacier. The large boat features reserved seating, indoor heated cabins and outdoor viewing decks. Complete tours cost only $89 and depart daily from Whittier's Boat Harbor mid-May to early September. Complete rail and bus packages are available from Anchorage. For reservations or free brochure, call: 800-764-7300 or (907) 274-7300. Major Marine Tours, 509 W. 3rd, Anchorage, AK 99501. [ADVERTISEMENT]

Tour a Campus: Two colleges are located in Anchorage: the University of Alaska-Anchorage at 3211 Providence Dr. and Alaska Pacific (formerly Alaska Methodist) University at 4101 University Dr.

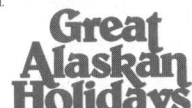

Alaska Pacific University was dedicated

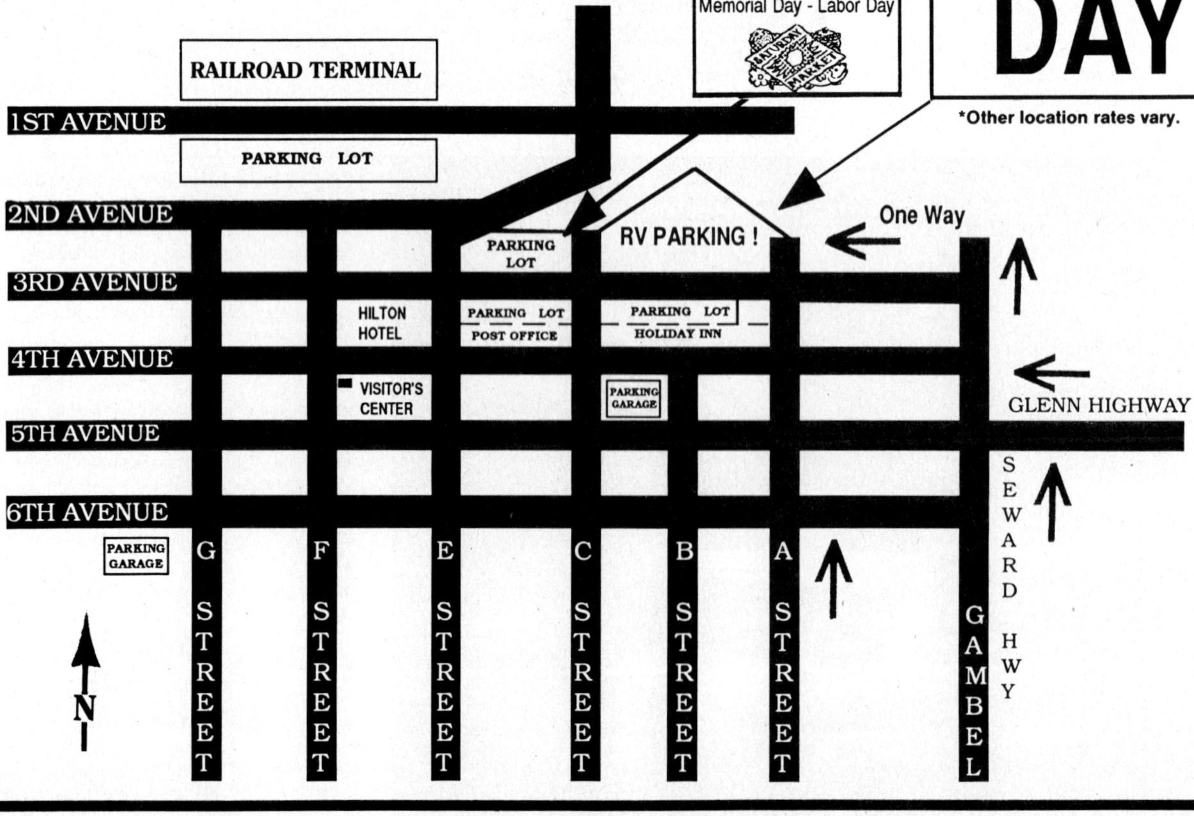

June 29, 1959, one day before Alaska was named the 49th state. It is Alaska's largest private university. APU hosts an Elderhostel and also offers other educational programs for all ages. The campus, located on 270 forested acres, features the three-tiered Atwood Fountain, Carillon Bell Tower and the Jim Mahaffey Trail system for skiers, runners, hikers and mountain bikers. Phone 561-1266 or toll free 1-800-ALASKA-U for information on tours and university programs.

The University of Alaska-Anchorage is one of three regional institutions in the state's university system (the others are in Fairbanks and Juneau). For information on tours of the UAF campus in Anchorage, phone 786-1525.

Go to the Zoo: The Alaska Zoo is located on 25 acres of wooded land and displays more than 85 species of Alaskan wildlife, including glacier bears, polar bears, brown and black bears, reindeer, moose, Dall sheep, otters, wolves, foxes, musk-oxen and marmots. Be sure to stop in at the gift shop, located on your right as you enter. The zoo is open 9 A.M. to 6 P.M. daily from May 1 to Oct. 1; 10 A.M. to 5 P.M. the remainder of the year (closed Tuesday from Oct. 1 to May 1). Drive south from the downtown area on the Seward Highway to **Milepost S 120.8.** Take O'Malley exit, turn left on O'Malley Road and proceed 2 miles/3.2 km to the zoo, which will be on your left. Admission $6 for adults, $5 for seniors, $4 students 13 to 18, and $3 for children 3 to 12. Free admission for children under 3. Handicap parking, wheelchair accessible. Phone 346-3242 for details. ♿

See Alaskan Wildlife: Fort Richardson Alaskan Fish and Wildlife Center, located in Bldg. 600 on Fort Richardson Military Reservation, has a display of approximately 250 mounts and trophies of Alaskan sport fish, birds and mammals, including a world-record Dall sheep. Open year-round, free admission. Phone 384-0431 for hours.

Portage Glacier and iceberg-filled Portage Lake are an hour-and-a-half drive from Anchorage. (Lee Foster)

Elmendorf Air Force Base Wildlife Museum is open weekdays year-round from noon to 5 P.M. Displays include more than 200 native Alaskan species from big game to small birds and fish. Handicap access; no handicap access to restroom. Enter the base from the intersection of Boniface Parkway and the Glenn Highway. Ask guards for directions to Bldg. 4-803. Phone 552-2282 for details. ♿

See an Old Schoolhouse: The Pioneer Schoolhouse at 3rd Avenue and Eagle Street is a two-story memorial to the late Ben Crawford, Anchorage banker. It was the first school in Anchorage.

Visit the Library, City Hall, Federal Building, Post Office: The city hall offices are at 6th Avenue and G Street. The Z.J. Loussac Public Library is located at 36th Avenue and Denali Street. The Federal Building, located at 7th Avenue and C Street, is one of the largest and most modern office buildings in Anchorage. The lobby features a multimedia collection of artwork, and the cafeteria is open to the public. In downtown Anchorage, the U.S. Post Office is located on the lower level of the Post Office Mall at 4th Avenue and D Street. The main post office, located near the airport, offers all services, 24 hours a day. Smaller postal stations are located throughout the city.

4th Avenue Theatre. Built in 1947 by Alaska millionaire "Cap" Lathrop, this Anchorage landmark has been refurbished and now operates as a gift shop, cafe and big screen entertainment center. Much of the original art-deco design has been preserved and the trademarks of the theater have been restored, including the ceiling lights marking the Big Dipper and the bas-relief gold leaf murals. There is no admission fee. The 4th Avenue Theatre is located a half block from the visitor center. For more information phone 257-5650.

Visit the Saturday Market. Located at the Lower Bowl parking lot, corner of Third and E Street, this open-air market is held Saturdays from Memorial Day weekend to Labor Day weekend. Hours are approximately 9 A.M. to 6 P.M. (subject to change). There is no admission fee. The market features made-in-Alaska products, fresh produce, fish, arts and crafts, antiques, food and entertainment. There are also garage sale and used car sale areas. For more information, contact the Anchorage Parking Authority at 276-7275 or the Downtown Anchorage Assoc. at 276-5015.

Visit the Port of Anchorage: The Anchorage waterfront, with its huge cargo cranes offloading supplies from container ships, makes an interesting stop, especially in winter when ice floes drift eerily past the dock on the fast-moving tide. Visitors may watch activity on the dock from a viewing platform on the 3rd floor of the port office building. To get there, drive north from the downtown area on A Street, take the Port off-ramp and follow Ocean Dock Road to the office; about 1.5 miles/2.4 km from downtown.

A good viewpoint of the port for downtown walkers is at the northeast corner of 3rd Avenue and Christensen Road.

Heritage Library Museum, in the National Bank of Alaska, Northern Lights Boulevard and C Street, has an excellent collection of historical artifacts, Native tools, costumes and weapons, paintings by Alaskan artists and a research library. Free admission. Open weekdays noon to 5 P.M.

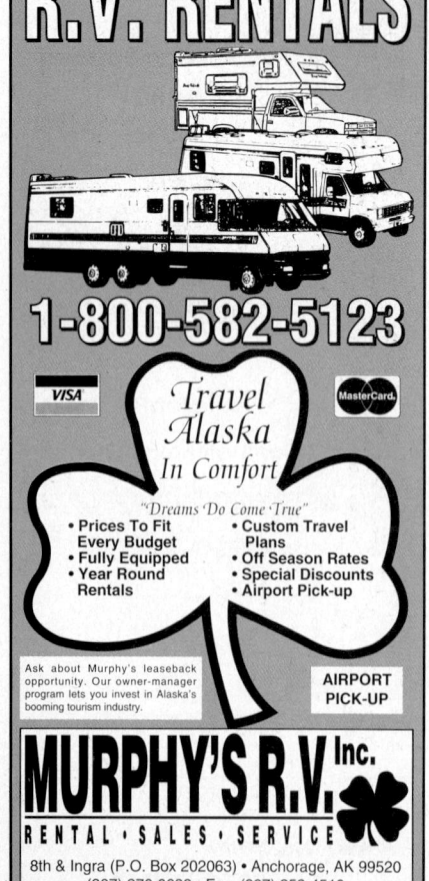

between Memorial Day and Labor Day, noon to 4 P.M. at other times of the year. Phone 265-2834.

Charter a Plane: Dozens of air taxi operators are based in Anchorage. Fixed-wheel (skis in winter) or floatplanes may be chartered for flightseeing trips to attractions such as Mount McKinley and Prince William Sound, for fly-in hunting and fishing, or just for transportation. Scheduled flightseeing trips by helicopter are also available.

Watch Small Planes: Drive out to Merrill Field, Lake Hood or Lake Spenard for an afternoon of plane watching. Lake Hood is the world's largest and busiest seaplane base, with more than 800 takeoffs and landings on a peak summer day. Merrill Field ranked 64th busiest airport in the nation in 1992, with more than 1,300 takeoffs and landings on a peak day.

Alaska Aviation Heritage Museum, located on the south shore of Lake Hood at 4721 Aircraft Dr., preserves the colorful history of Alaska's pioneer bush pilots. Included are rare historical films of Alaska's pioneer aviators as well as an extensive photo exhibit of pioneer pilot memorabilia. The museum features a rare collection of 25 Alaskan bush planes. RV parking. Open year-round, May 1 to Sept. 30, 9 A.M. to 6 P.M. daily; Oct. 1 to April 30, 11 A.M. to 4 P.M. Tuesday through Saturday, phone 248-5325. Adults $5, seniors and active military $3.75, children 12 and under $2. Handicapped accessible.

Era Helicopters. Experience a panoramic view of the Anchorage Bowl area and the unspoiled wilderness and wildlife of the Chugach Mountains. Soar through the picturesque mountains, valleys and glaciers, minutes away from Alaska's largest city. One- and two-hour tours. Phone (907) 248-4422 or outside Alaska 800-843-1947. Tours also available in Juneau, Denali and Valdez. [ADVERTISEMENT]

Train to Denali. Ride the luxurious private domed railcars of the *McKinley Explorer* to Denali National Park from either Anchorage or Fairbanks. Overnight packages in Denali with round-trip train service are available from only $210 ppdo. Call Gray Line of Alaska at (907) 277-5581 for train and package tour options. [ADVERTISEMENT]

Portage Glacier Cruise. See Alaska's most popular attraction, up close from the deck of the mv *Ptarmigan*. This Gray Line of Alaska cruise takes you right to the face of imposing 10-story-high Portage Glacier. An incredible experience. Tours depart Anchorage twice daily or you may drive to Portage Glacier and board the mv *Ptarmigan* for the cruise-only portion. Tour price is $54 per person; cruise-only price is $20 per person. Call (907) 277-5581. [ADVERTISEMENT]

Prince William Sound Cruise. Experience the spectacular beauty of Prince William Sound aboard the *Glacier Queen II*. This Gray Line of Alaska tour cruises past Columbia Glacier, the largest glacier in Prince William Sound. Watch for abundant marine life as you travel to picturesque Valdez. Return to Anchorage via the scenic Matanuska Valley. Two days, one night from $219 ppdo. Tour departs Anchorage daily. Call (907) 277-5581. [ADVERTISEMENT]

Fireweed Tours. See Alaska as you'd like it! Mini-van sightseeing excursions designed with your desires, needs and capabilities considered. Year-round; custom. Historical sites, parks, glaciers, flightseeing, rafting, trailhead transportation. Free pickup and delivery at RV parks, B&Bs, hotels. Reservations or information: Fireweed Tours, 705 Muldoon Rd., Ste. 116, Anchorage, AK 99504. [ADVERTISEMENT]

Take in an Alaska Film: Alaska films can be seen at the Anchorage Museum of History and Art, 121 W. 7th, at 3 P.M., seven days a week during summer. Alaska Experience Theatre, located at 6th and G Street, offers *Alaska the Great Land*, a 70mm film presented on a 180-degree domed screen, and a

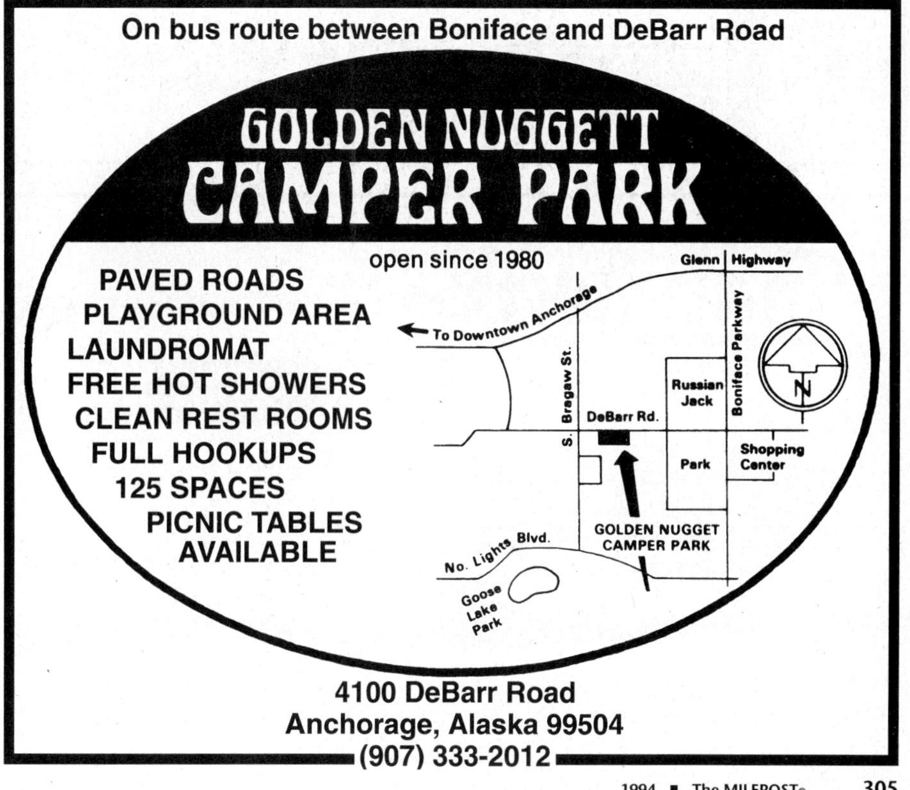

film on the 1964 earthquake. Admission fee charged; open year-round. Call 276-3730 for recorded information.

Watch the Tide Come In: With frequent tidal ranges of 30 feet/9m within six hours, and some approaching 40 feet/12m, one of Anchorage's best nature shows is the rise and fall of the tides in both the Knik and Turnagain arms of upper Cook Inlet. Among the better vantage points along Knik Arm are Earthquake Park, Elderberry Park (at the west end of 5th Avenue), Resolution Park (near the corner of 3rd Avenue and L Street) and the Anchorage small-boat harbor.

A good overlook for the tides in Turnagain Arm is Bird Creek state campground south of Anchorage at **Milepost S 101.2** on the Seward Highway. With good timing you just might see a tidal bore, an interesting phenomenon you probably won't see elsewhere. A bore tide is a foaming wall of tidal water, up to 6 feet/2m in height, formed by a flood tide surging into a constricted inlet, such as Knik and Turnagain arms.

CAUTION: In many places the mud flats of Turnagain and Knik arms are like quicksand. Don't go wading!

Play Golf: The municipality of Anchorage maintains two golf courses: Anchorage Golf Course, 3651 O'Malley Road, is an all-grass, 18-hole course which opened in 1987. The course is open from mid-May through mid-September; phone 522-3363 for more information. The nine-hole course at Russian Jack Springs, Debarr Road and Boniface Parkway features artificial turf greens and is open from mid-May through mid-September. Phone 333-8338 or 343-4474 for details. Two military courses are open to civilians. Eagle Glen Golf Course, an 18-hole, par 72 course, is located on Elmendorf Air Force Base, near the Post Road gate. Open mid-May through September. Call 552-2773 for tee times; rentals available. Fort Richardson's 18-hole Moose Run Golf Course is the oldest golf course in Alaska. The course is accessible from Arctic Valley Road (**Milepost A 6.1** Glenn Highway) and is open May through September. Rentals available. Call 428-0056 for tee times.

Play Tennis: The municipality of Anchorage maintains 54 tennis courts throughout the city. In addition, private clubs offer year-round indoor courts.

Picnic at a Park. Anchorage has several parks for picnicking. Chester Creek Green Belt, which stretches from Westchester Lagoon to Goose Lake, has a number of public parks along it and a paved bike trail (also popular with joggers) runs the length of the greenbelt. The greenbelt is accessible from several streets; Spenard Road leads to Westchester Lagoon and E Street to Valley of the Moon Park.

Elderberry Park, at the foot of 5th Avenue, overlooks Knik Arm. Nearby Resolution Park, at 3rd Avenue and L Street, where a statue of Capt. James Cook stands, has terraced decks overlooking Knik Arm. The Capt. James Cook statue was dedicated in 1976 as a Bicentennial project.

Tour Anchorage by Bicycle: The municipality has about 120 miles of paved bike trails (including trails in Eagle River and Girdwood) paralleling many major traffic arteries and also passing through some of the city's most beautiful greenbelt areas. Maps of the trail system are available at the Alaska Public Lands Information Center and the Anchorage Convention and Visitors Bureau Log Cabin Information Center. Offering an especially unique experience is the 11-mile/17.7-km Tony Knowles Coastal Trail, which begins at 3rd and Christensen avenues and follows the coast around Point Woronzof to Point Campbell and Kincaid Park. One of the most popular trails in the city, it is used by bicyclists, joggers and walkers who are treated to close-up views of Knik Arm (watch for beluga whales) and on clear days a beautiful view of the Alaska Range.

Another popular bike route for families is the Chester Creek Bike Trail from Westchester Lagoon, at 15th and U streets, to Russian Jack Springs Park. The 6.5-mile/10.5-km trail traverses the heart of Anchorage, following Chester Creek past Goose Lake, a favorite summer swimming beach.

Watch Birds: There are some surprisingly good bird-watching spots within the city

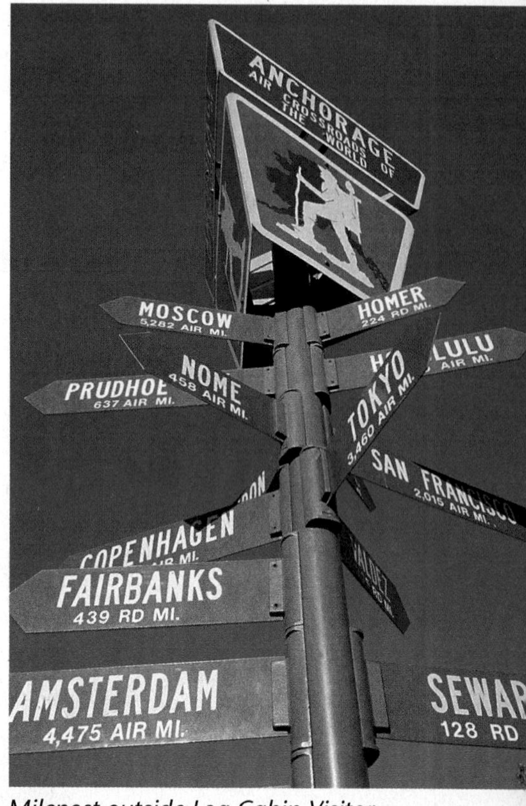

Milepost outside Log Cabin Visitor Information Center shows air and road mileages. (John W. Warden)

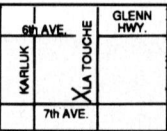

limits. Lakes Hood and Spenard, for instance, are teeming with seaplanes but also, during the summer, are nesting areas for grebes and arctic loons. Also seen are wigeons, arctic terns, mew gulls, green-winged teals, spotted and least sandpipers.

Another great spot is the Anchorage Coastal Wildlife Refuge, known locally as Potter Marsh, south of downtown on the Seward Highway at **Milepost S 117.4.** Early July evenings are best, according to local bird watchers. Forests surrounding Anchorage also are good for warblers, juncos, robins, white-crowned sparrows, varied thrushes and other species.

The Park for All People in the Chester Creek Green Belt on W. 19th Avenue near Spenard Road has a nature trail through a bird nesting area.

For a prerecorded message of local bird sightings and field trips, call the Anchorage Audubon Society's hot line at 248-2473.

Go for a Hike. Hiking trails in the Anchorage area are found in Chugach State Park and in Municipality of Anchorage parks. Three popular hikes in Chugach State Park's Hillside Trail System, accessed from the Glen Alps trailhead, are Flattop Mountain, Powerline Trail and Williwaw Lakes. To reach the trailhead, take the Seward Highway south to the O'Malley exit and go east to Hillside Drive; take a right on Hillside then a left at the trailhead sign and continue to Glen Alps parking lot. The hike up Flattop Mountain begins here; elevation gain is 1,550 feet in 3.5 miles/5.6 km, hiking time is three to five hours. Also accessible from Glen Alps is the Powerline Trail; total length

11 miles/18 km, elevation gain 1,300 feet. Williwaw Lakes trail branches off Powerline Trail to several small alpine lakes; round trip is 13 miles/21 km with a 742-foot elevation gain. For more information phone Chugach State Park at 345-5014.

Hilltop Ski Area, located off Abbott Road, acts as trailhead in summer for hiking trails in Bicentennial and Hillside municipal parks. The trails range in length from an easy mile walk to a strenuous 16-mile/26-km hike. From June until September, Hilltop provides free trail brochures, along with mountain bike rentals. For more information phone Hilltop Ski Area at 346-1446.

Other Anchorage parks offering hiking, jogging or biking include Kincaid Park, Russian Jack Springs Park and Arnold Muldoon Park. For more information phone Anchorage Parks and Recreation at 343-4474.

Summer Solstice. Alaskans celebrate the longest day of the year with a variety of special events. In Anchorage, there's the annual Mayor's Midnight Sun Marathon, a 26-mile, 385-yard run through the city. This event is usually scheduled on the Saturday nearest summer solstice (June 20 or 21).

See a Baseball Game: Some fine semi-pro baseball is played in Anchorage. Every summer some of the nation's top college players play for the Anchorage Glacier Pilots and Anchorage Bucs, the Peninsula Oilers, the Mat–su Miners and the Fairbanks Goldpanners. Anchorage games are played at Mulcahy Ball Park, Cordova and E. 16th Avenue. Check local newspapers for schedules or call the Anchorage Bucs, 277-2827 or the Glacier Pilots, 274-3627.

Watch a Salmon: King, coho, pink and a few chum salmon swim up Ship Creek and can be seen jumping a spillway in the dam just east of Ocean Dock Road. Watch for kings from early June until mid-July, and for other species from mid-August until September. A fine wooden viewing platform has been built to make salmon watching easy.

Watch an Equestrian Event. The

William Clark Chamberlin Equestrian Center in 530-acre Ruth Arcand Park hosts a variety of equestrian events every weekend from late May through August. This public facility is open from 9 A.M. to 9 P.M. Phone 522-1552.

Kayaking, Canoeing, Rafting: All are available in or near Anchorage. Guided tours from one to 14 days run on several rivers within 100 miles/160 km of Anchorage, including the Chulitna, Susitna, Little Susitna, Matanuska and Kenai rivers. Information on guided raft and canoe trips is available through travel agencies, local sporting goods stores and in the free *Visitors Guide* available from the Log Cabin Visitor Information Center.

Several flying services provide unguided float trips. The service flies customers to a remote river, then picks them up at a predetermined time and place downriver.

Several streams in the area make excellent canoeing and kayaking paths. Information on the Swanson River and Swan Lake canoe trails on the Kenai Peninsula is available from the Kenai National Wildlife Refuge Manager, P.O. Box 2139, Soldotna, AK 99669-2139; phone 262-7021. Nancy Lake State Recreation Area, 67 miles north of Anchorage, offers a popular canoe trail system. Contact the Division of Parks & Outdoor Recreation, Southcentral Division, P.O. Box 107001, Anchorage, AK 99510; phone 561-2020.

Sailing in the Anchorage area is limited to freshwater lakes and lagoons (usually ice free by May). A popular sailing area in the city is Jewel Lake *(CAUTION: low-flying aircraft)*.

Mirror Lake, 24.5 miles/39.4 km north of

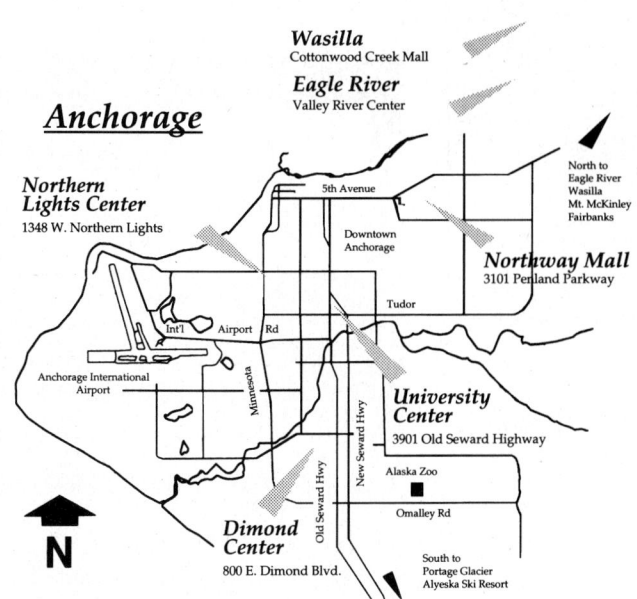

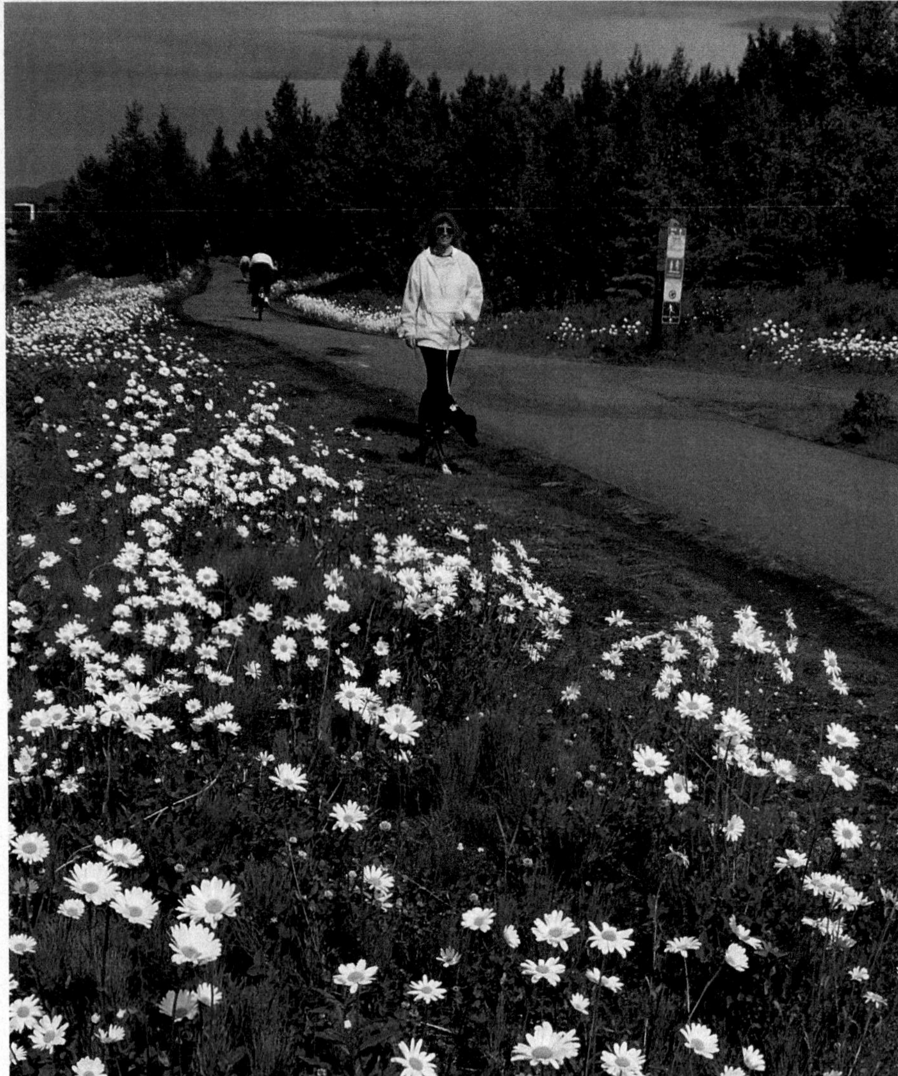

One of the most popular trails in the city, Tony Knowles Coastal Trail is used by bicyclists, joggers and walkers. (Bruce M. Herman)

Anchorage on the Glenn Highway, and Big Lake, 52 miles/84 km north of Anchorage on the George Parks Highway, are also popular spots for small sailboats.

Motorboating: Big Lake and Lake Lucille along the George Parks Highway offer motorboating. Several rivers, including the Susitna, offer riverboating, but the shallowness and shifting bottoms of most of Alaska's rivers mean a jet-equipped, flat-bottom boat is almost required.

Cruises on larger boats are available from Whittier into Prince William Sound, from Homer Spit into Kachemak Bay and Cook Inlet, and from Seward into Resurrection Bay and Kenai Fjords National Park. Venturing into those areas in small boats without a guide who has local knowledge of the area can be dangerous.

Cook Inlet waters around Anchorage are only for the experienced because of powerful bore tides, unpredictable weather, dangerous mud flats and icy, silty waters. Turnagain Arm is strictly off-limits for any boats and Knik Arm and most of the north end of Cook Inlet is the domain of large ships and experienced skiff and dory operators.

Swimming: Anchorage Parks and Recreation can answer questions about aquatics, phone 343-4474.

Goose Lake is open daily, June through Labor Day, from 10:30 A.M. to 5:30 P.M.; lifeguards, bathhouse and picnic area. Located 3 miles/4.8 km east from downtown Anchorage on UAA Drive.

Jewel Lake, 6.5 miles/10.4 km from downtown Anchorage on W. 88th off Jewel Lake Road, is open daily June through Labor Day, from 10:30 A.M. to 5:30 P.M.; lifeguards, restrooms and covered picnic area.

Spenard Lake is open daily, June through Labor Day, from 10:30 A.M. to 5:30 P.M.; lifeguards, restrooms, picnic area. Located 3 miles/4.8 km from downtown Anchorage on Spenard Road, then west on Wisconsin to Lakeshore Drive.

CAUTION: Do not even consider swimming in Cook Inlet! Soft mud, swift tides and icy water make this extremely dangerous!

The YMCA, 5353 Lake Otis Parkway, offers discounts to outside members with YMCA identification. Call 563-3211 for pool schedule and information on other facilities.

The following pools are also open to the

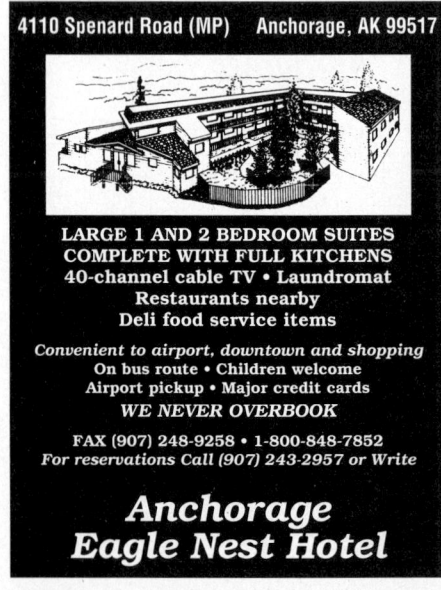

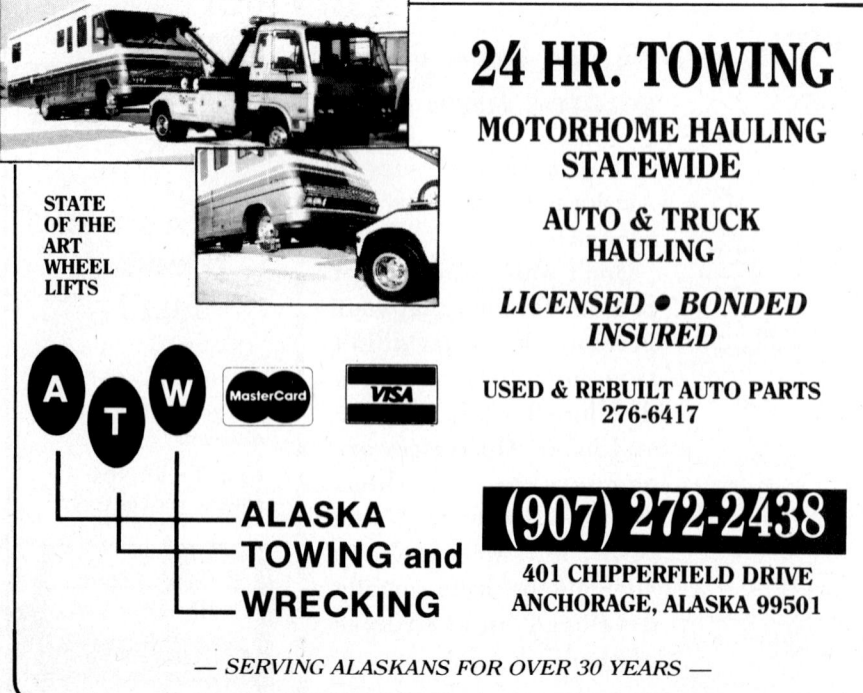

public: Service High School Pool, 5577 Abbott Road, phone 346-3040; Bartlett High School Pool, 2525 Muldoon Road, phone 337-6375; West High School Pool, 1700 Hillcrest Dr., phone 274-5161; East High School Pool, 4025 E. 24th Ave., phone 278-9761; Dimond High School Pool, 2909 W. 88th Ave., phone 249-0355; Chugiak High School Pool, Birchwood Loop Road, off the Glenn Highway north of Anchorage, phone 696-2010; and University of Alaska Pool, Providence Drive, phone 786-1233.

Charter Boats: Visitors must drive south to the Kenai Peninsula for charter boats. Sightseeing and fishing charters are available at Whittier, Seward and Homer.

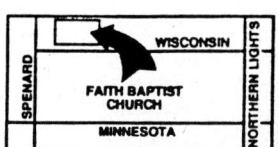

Fishing: The Alaska Dept. of Fish and Game annually stocks about 30 lakes in the Anchorage area with rainbow trout, landlocked chinook (king) salmon, grayling and

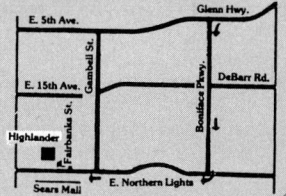

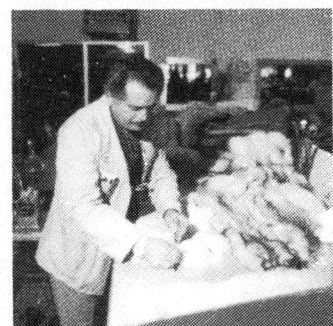

Day Trips From Anchorage

Several interesting and memorable sights may be taken in on a day's drive from Anchorage by heading either south of downtown on the Seward Highway or north on the Glenn or George Parks highways. Following are some of the points of interest along these roads. Follow the mile-by-mile logs given in the related highway sections in *The MILEPOST®*. Keep in mind that several companies offer motorcoach tours to many of these same attractions and that you can see a great many attractions in a short amount of time by taking a flightseeing trip out of Anchorage; there's even a one-day trip to Kotzebue from Anchorage.

South from Anchorage, the Seward Highway offers some spectacular views of Turnagain Arm less than 10 miles/16 km from downtown. Stop at one of the scenic viewpoints for photos. Other stops close-in to Anchorage include Potter Marsh for bird watching and the Potter Section House, which serves as the Chugach State Park Visitor Center and features displays of railroad history.

Continue south to **Milepost S 90** (37 miles/59.5 km from Anchorage) for the Girdwood/Alyeska Road turnoff. About 2 miles/3.2 km up this road a gravel road forks to the left and leads 3.1 miles/5 km to Crow Creek Mine, a historic 1898 mining camp where visitors can pan for gold and tour the camp's old buildings. Returning from the mine to the main road, continue about another mile for Alyeska Resort.

Back out on the Seward Highway, continue south 11 miles/17.7 km to **Milepost S 79.1** and the Portage Glacier Access Road. On the 5-mile/8-km drive to the glacier, watch for salmon spawning at Williwaw Creek and look for the hanging Explorer Glacier. The Begich, Boggs Visitor Center at Portage Glacier has interpretive displays on glaciers, regular showings of films of interest, and Forest Service naturalists are available to answer your questions. You can stand on the shore of Portage Lake for a close-up view of the fantastically shaped blue and white icebergs calved by Portage Glacier.

Return to the Seward Highway. Depending on your time, you may wish to head back up the highway to Anchorage (which would add up to about 114 miles/183.5 km total driving distance), or extend your trip farther south to take in the old gold mining town of Hope.

North from Anchorage, the Glenn and George Parks highways offer many attractions. Drive out the Glenn Highway from downtown Anchorage to Palmer, 42 miles/67.6 km. Heart of the Matanuska–Susitna Valley, the Palmer–Wasilla area has the Alaska State Fair, Colony Village, a musk-oxen farm, Knik Museum and Mushers' Hall of Fame, Wasilla Museum and Frontier Village, and the Iditarod Trail headquarters visitor center. Drive 59 miles/95 km east on the Glenn Highway from Palmer to see the spectacular Matanuska Glacier. Several lakes in the area offer picnicking and water sports. Largest is Big Lake, a year-round recreation area accessible from Big Lake Road off the George Parks Highway, 52 miles/84 km from Anchorage. Kepler–Bradley State Recreation Area on Matanuska Lake, at **Milepost A 36.4** Glenn Highway, has canoe rentals.

You may wish to stop off at Eklutna Lake or the Eagle River Visitor Center. Also, take the Eklutna Road exit for Eklutna Village Historical Park, which features 350 years of Athabascan culture. The park includes St. Nicholas Russian Orthodox Church and spirit houses. It is open daily, 9 A.M. to 9 P.M., from the end of May to mid-September; admission charged.

arctic char. Nearly 135,000 6- to 8-inch rainbow trout are released each year along with about 50,000 salmon. All lakes, except those on Elmendorf Air Force Base, are open to the public. In addition, salmon-viewing areas and limited salmon fishing are available in the immediate Anchorage area. For specific information, check the Alaska fishing regulations book, call the agency at 267-2218, or phone 349-4687 for a recorded message. Urban salmon fisheries have been developed recently by the Alaska Dept. of Fish and Game in several Anchorage-area streams. King salmon can be caught in Ship Creek in downtown Anchorage through July as well as in Eagle River just north of town. Coho salmon fisheries opened for the first time in 1993 in Campbell Creek in Anchorage and at Bird Creek just north of Girdwood on the Seward Highway.

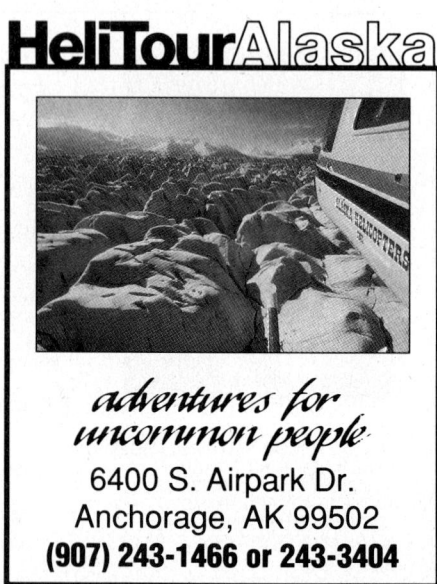

Within a day's drive of Anchorage are several excellent fishing spots. The Kenai Peninsula offers streams where king, red, silver, pink and chum salmon may be caught during the season. Dolly Varden and steelhead also run in peninsula streams. Several lakes contain trout and landlocked salmon. Saltwater fishing for halibut, rockfish and several species of salmon is excellent in season at many spots along the peninsula and out of Whittier, Homer and Seward. For specific fishing spots both north and south of Anchorage see the Seward, Sterling, Glenn and George Parks highways sections. Because of the importance of fishing to Alaska both commercially and for sport, regulations are strictly enforced. Regulations are updated yearly by the state, often after *The MILEPOST®* deadline, so it is wise to obtain a current regulations book.

WINTERTIME ATTRACTIONS

Alyeska Resort. Located in the community of Girdwood, Alyeska Resort is a 45-mile/65-km drive south from Anchorage along scenic Turnagain Arm via the Seward Highway. Judged by *Conde Nast Traveler* as having the "best view" of any U.S. ski resort, Alyeska Resort is Alaska's largest ski resort, with snow from early November to the end of April. Snow-making equipment at the base of the mountain guarantees snow throughout the season. Night skiing is available during holiday periods in November and December and from January through March. Ski facilities include a high-speed detachable bubble quad, two fixed grip quads, three double chair lifts and two pony tows. Chair 7, a fixed grip quad opened for the 1993-94 ski season, added 20 acres of beginner and intermediate ski terrain to the mountain's existing 450 acres of skiing. Also added for the 1993-94 season was a 60-passenger aerial tram — the first in Alaska — to take sightseers and skiers from the mountain's base at 250 feet/76m to a mountaintop facility at the 2,300-foot/701-m level. This new facility, open year-round and accessible by wheelchair, features a large viewing deck, a cafeteria-style restaurant and

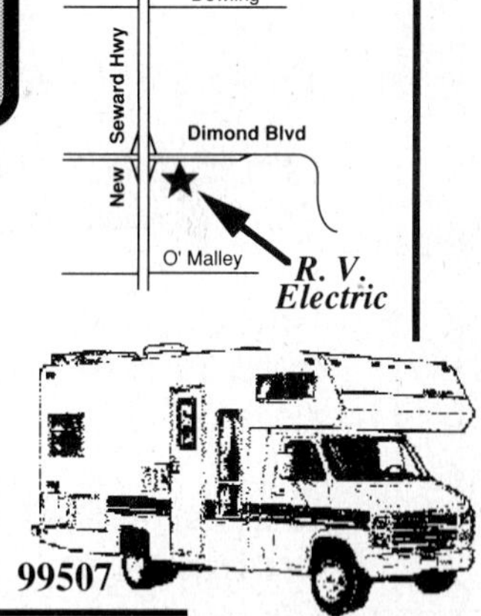

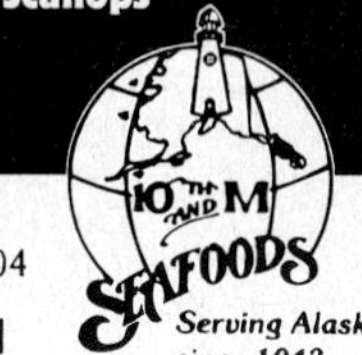

a fine dining restaurant and lounge. Centerpiece for the resort is the 307-room, chateau-style Alyeska Prince Hotel, scheduled to open in late summer 1994. The hotel features a fitness facility with indoor swimming pool and 12-person Jacuzzi, four restaurants and two lounges. Existing resort facilities include a 29-room inn, a day lodge, rental condos, a restaurant and lounge, ski rental shop, ski school and sport shop. During the ski season, shuttle service is available between Anchorage and the resort. For more information, phone 783-2222.

Alpenglow at Arctic Valley: East of downtown Anchorage in the Chugach Mountains, Alpenglow Ski Area has a 4,500-foot/1,372-m double chair lift, a 2,200-foot/671-m double chair lift, a 2,800-foot/873-m T-bar platter lift combination and a 700-foot/213-m rope tow for beginners. There is a day lodge with full cafeteria and ski shop. Cross-country skiing is available, but trails are not maintained. The ski area operates from about late October until early May. Hours are 3-9 P.M. Wednesday and Thursday, 10 A.M. to 9 P.M. Friday and Saturday, and noon to 6 P.M. Sunday. Drive northeast from downtown on the Glenn Highway. Just beyond Ship Creek, turn right on Arctic Valley Road and follow the main road 7.5 miles/12 km to the ski area. For more information, phone 428-1208.

Hilltop Ski Area: Located 15 minutes from downtown Anchorage off Abbott Road, Hilltop has 2 miles/3.2 km of lighted slopes classified as beginner to intermediate. Ski facilities include a double chair lift; a beginner rope tow; a 10m, 30m and 50m jump; and certified half-pipe. Ski rentals, ski school, gift shop and restaurant available. The area is open seven days a week with complete night lighting. Hours are 3-10 P.M. Monday through Thursday, noon to 10 P.M. Friday, and 9 A.M. to 10 P.M. weekends. There are also 9 miles/15 km of cross-country ski trails in adjoining Hillside and Bicentennial parks, with 5 miles/8 km offering night lighting. For more information, phone 346-1446.

Chugach State Park: Although the entire park is open to cross-country skiers, most maintained ski trails are found in the Hillside Trail System/Campbell Creek area, accessible via Upper Huffman Road and Upper O'Malley Road. Skiers are encouraged to use established trails as most of Chugach State Park is prime avalanche country.

Four major areas in the park are open to snowmobiling when snow levels are deep enough: Eklutna Valley, reached from the Glenn Highway via Eklutna Road; Eagle

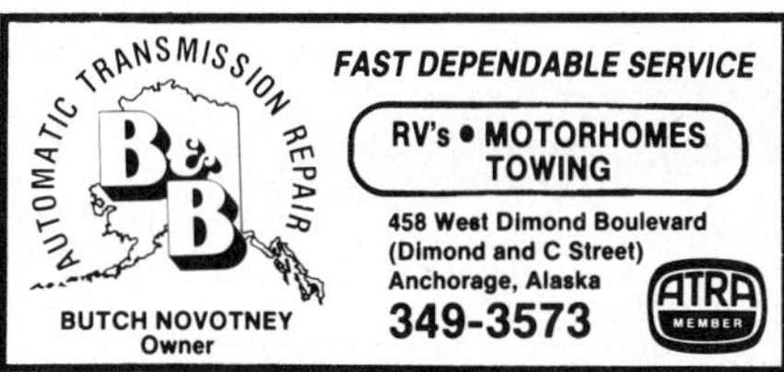

River valley, also accessible from the Glenn Highway; Bird Creek, **Milepost S 101.2** Seward Highway; and portions of the Hillside/Campbell Creek area, accessible from Upper Huffman Road.

Ski trail maps and snowmobiling information are available at the trailheads or from the park office, phone 345-5014.

Russian Jack Springs: Located at DeBarr Road and Boniface Parkway. This ski area has a chalet, a ski rope tow and almost 6.8 miles/11 km of cross-country ski trails, 3 miles/5 km of which are lighted. The ski area is maintained by the Municipality of Anchorage.

Far North Bicentennial Park (Campbell Creek Resource Land): Best access to this 5,000-acre tract in the eastern portion of the Anchorage bowl is via Hilltop Ski Area on Abbott Road. Cross-country skiing is allowed anywhere in the area except on dogsled trails. For further information, contact the Municipality of Anchorage, Division of Parks and Recreation, P.O. Box 196650, Anchorage 99519; phone 343-4474.

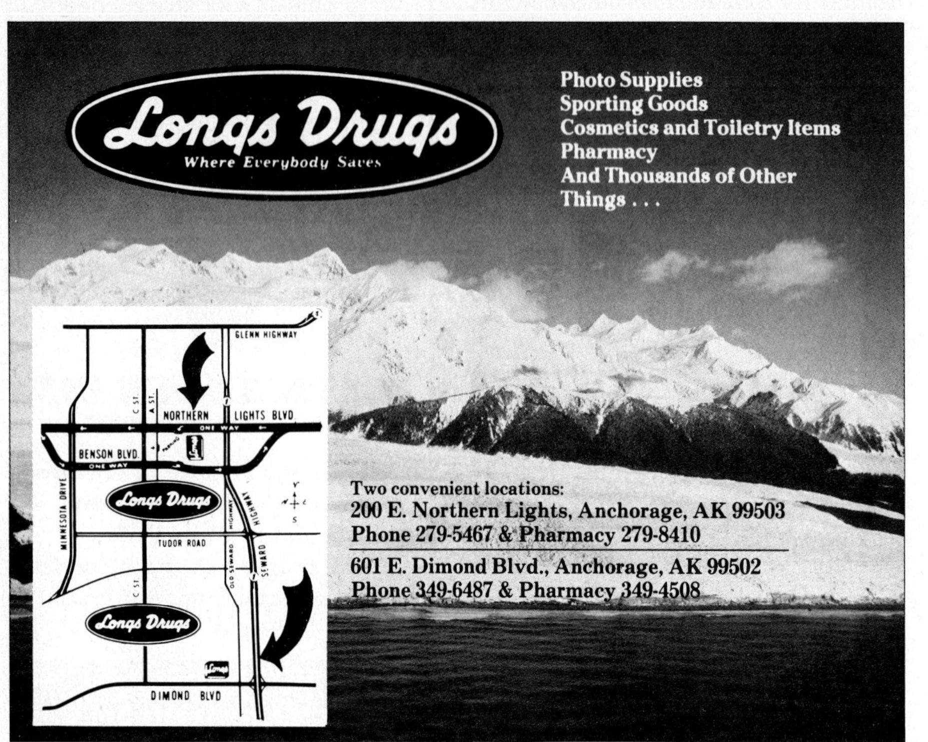

Beach Lake Park: 6 miles/10 km of groomed cross-country ski trails with 2 miles/3.5 km lighted. There are approximately 20 miles/32 km of dog mushing trail. Handicap-accessible lodge and cabins available for a minimal user fee. Outstanding views of lake and wildlife from lodge deck and cabins. Contact Anchorage Parks and Recreation, phone 343-4474.

Centennial Park: 3.1 miles/5 km of wooded cross-country ski trails over some hilly terrain. Maintained by the Municipality of Anchorage and located near Glenn Highway and Muldoon Road.

Chester Creek Green Belt: Located in the heart of Anchorage, the municipality maintains more than 6.2 miles/10 km of cross-country ski trails.

Hillside Park: The Municipality of Anchorage maintains more than 5 miles/8 km of cross-country ski trails located just off Abbott Road; 1.6 miles/2.5 km are lighted trails.

Kincaid Park: 15 miles/24 km of cross-country ski trails are marked and maintained for novice, intermediate and expert skiers by the municipality. There are 1.6 miles/2.5 km of lighted trails and a warm-up chalet. Access is from the west end of Raspberry Road.

Skiers at Alyeska Resort escape the overcast at lower elevations. (Michael DeYoung)

Turnagain Pass: On the Seward Highway, about 59 miles/95 km south of downtown Anchorage. Turnagain Pass (elev. 988 feet/301m) is a popular winter recreation area in the Chugach National Forest. The west side of the pass is open to snowmobiling as soon as snow cover permits; the east side is reserved for skiers. Snow depths in this pass often exceed 12 feet/4m.

Dog Mushing begins in December. Dog mushing organizations in the Montana Creek area, Knik, Chugiak, Palmer and Anchorage sponsor races every weekend. Anchorage races usually begin in January at the Tudor Track and continue through the end of February. In addition, some of the clubs offer instruction in the sport. Several of the races are considered preliminaries to the World Championship races held during the Anchorage Fur Rendezvous.

The annual Iditarod Trail Sled Dog Race, 1,049 miles/1688.2 km to Nome, takes place in March. The race begins on 4th Avenue in downtown Anchorage and mushers on the trail can be seen along the Glenn Highway, in the Knik Bridge area about 30 miles/ 48.2 km north of Anchorage and at Knik on the west side of Knik Arm.

To find a race, watch local newspapers for times, dates and places.

Anchorage Fur Rendezvous: Major

event of the winter season is the Anchorage Fur Rendezvous. Billed as the "Mardi Gras of the North," this elaborate winter festival, held in February, attracts thousands of celebrants annually.

The 10-day-long celebration dates from 1936 when it began primarily as a fur auction where trappers could bring their pelts to town and make a few extra dollars selling them to buyers from around the world. Trappers still bring their pelts to town, and the fur auction, held downtown, still attracts many buyers.

Alaskans shake off cabin fever during "Rondy" (the local term for the Fur Rendezvous). There are arts and crafts exhibits, a parade, the Miners' and Trappers' Ball, a blanket toss, a carnival and pet shows. Past Rondy competitions have been unique: a beard-growing contest, a waiter and waitress race, an ice and snow sculpturing contest and a home-brew competition, to name a few.

During the first weekend of the Fur Rendezvous, the Annual World Championship Dog Weight Pulling Contest attracts several thousand spectators at Mulcahy Park, located at E. 16th and Cordova streets.

The highlight of the Fur Rendezvous, however, is dog mushing. The World Championship Sled Dog Race, held during the last three days, attracts dozens of mushers from Alaska, Canada and the Lower 48. Thousands of spectators line the 25-mile/40-km race course, which begins and ends on 4th Avenue in downtown Anchorage. *(CAUTION: Leave pets and flashbulbs home, as they'll distract the dog teams.)* The musher with the best total elapsed time in three heats over three days is declared the winner. The women's and junior world championship sled dog races are held at Tudor Track the first weekend of Fur Rendezvous. For more information, phone 277-8615.

Ice Skating: Three municipal facilities, Ben Boeke Ice Arena (334 E. 16th Ave., phone 274-2767), Dempsey-Anderson Ice

Pony ride entertains youngster at Fur Rondy. (John W. Warden)

Arena (1741 W. Northern Lights, phone 277-7571) and Firelake Recreation Center (13701 Old Glenn Highway in Eagle River, phone 696-0051) offer a total of four indoor rinks for spectator as well as participatory uses. The University of Alaska also has one indoor rink as does the Dimond Center shopping mall. Outdoor ice-skating areas include Cheney Lake, DeLong Lake, Delaney Community Center, Goose Lake, Jewel Lake Park, Mountain View Community Center, Spenard Lake, Tikishla Park and Westchester Lagoon. In addition, about 40 Anchorage schools maintain outdoor hockey rinks.

Sledding: Popular sledding hills are at Centennial Park, Nunaka Valley Park, Sitka Street Park, Service High School and Alaska Pacific University.

Snowshoeing: Muldoon Park, Far North Bicentennial Park and Campbell Creek Green Belt are used for snowshoeing, as are backcountry areas of Chugach National Forest and Chugach State Park.

Winter Basketball. Anchorage hosts two major collegiate basketball events. The Great Alaska Shoot-Out, held every Thanksgiving weekend, features eight major college basketball teams in this well-known invitational tournament. The Northern Lights Invitational showcases women's collegiate basketball with eight teams in a three-day playoff the last weekend in February.

Ice Fishing: Countless lakes in the Anchorage and the Matanuska–Susitna Valley areas offer excellent ice fishing. Ice fishing is especially good in the early winter in Southcentral. Some Anchorage lakes are stocked each year with silver salmon or rainbow trout. Among them: **Jewel Lake, Little Campbell Lake** in Kincaid Park, **Beach Lake, Cheney Lake** and the lake on C Street in the Taku/Campbell Park. For more information contact the Alaska Dept. of Fish and Game at (907) 344-0541; for a recorded message on fishing and ice conditions, phone (907) 349-4687.

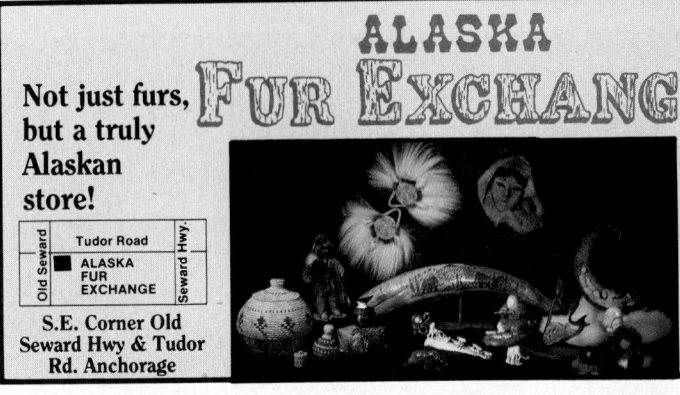

GEORGE PARKS HIGHWAY

Anchorage to Fairbanks, Alaska
Alaska Route 3
(See maps, pages 323–324)

Popular viewpoint of Mount McKinley is at ***Milepost A 135.2*** *on the Parks Highway.* *(Michael DeYoung)*

The George Parks Highway connects Anchorage and Fairbanks, Alaska's largest population centers. The route, called the Anchorage–Fairbanks Highway after its completion in 1971, was renamed in July 1975, in honor of George A. Parks (1883–1984), the territorial governor from 1925 to 1933.

The highway runs 358 miles/576.1 km through some of the grandest and most rugged land that Alaska has to offer. The road is a modern paved highway, maintained year-round. The highway is mostly in good condition with some pavement breaks and frost heaves.

Motorists who plan to drive the highway during the winter (roughly from Oct. 1 to June 1) should check highway conditions before proceeding. Severe winter storms and extremely low temperatures can create hazardous driving conditions. Contact the Alaska Dept. of Transportation or the Alaska State Troopers in Anchorage or Fairbanks.

Some facilities along the highway north of the Talkeetna turnoff (**Milepost A 98.7**) and south of Nenana (**Milepost A 304.5**) are open in summer only.

From approximately **Milepost A 70** north of Anchorage there are many places where Mount McKinley — also called Denali — (elev. 20,320 feet/6,194m) is visible from the highway, weather permitting.

The George Parks Highway provides the most direct highway access to Denali National Park and Preserve (formerly Mount McKinley National Park) from either Anchorage or Fairbanks. Driving distance to the park entrance is 237.3 miles/381.9 km from Anchorage and 120.7 miles/194.2 km from Fairbanks. See DENALI NATIONAL PARK section for details.

Emergency medical services: Between the Glenn Highway junction and **Milepost A 202.1**, phone 911. Between **Milepost A 174** at Hurricane Gulch bridge and **Milepost A 224** at Carlo Creek bridge, phone the Cantwell ambulance at 768-2982 or the state troopers at 768-2202. Between **Milepost A 224** and Fairbanks, phone 911.

George Parks Highway Log

ALASKA ROUTE 1
Distance from Anchorage (A) is followed by distance from Fairbanks (F).

A 0 F 358 (576.1 km) **ANCHORAGE.** Follow the Glenn Highway (Alaska Route 1) north 35 miles/56.3 km to junction with the George Parks Highway. (Turn to the end of the GLENN HIGHWAY section and read log back to front from Anchorage to junction with the George Parks Highway.)

ALASKA ROUTE 3

A 35 (56.3 km) **F 323** (519.8 km) Traffic light at **junction** of the George Parks Highway (Alaska Route 3) and the Glenn Highway (Alaska Route 1). Produce stand just north of junction.

Bushes Bunches Stand. See display ad this section.

A 35.4 (57 km) **F 322.6** (519.2 km) Trunk Road. Turn right, northbound, for Mat-Su Community College and the University of Alaska–Fairbanks' Matanuska Research Farm. The Matanuska Research Farm conducts research in agronomy, horticulture and animal science. No formal tours are conducted.

A 35.5 (57.1 km) **F 322.5** (519 km) Welcome Way; access to Mat–Su Visitors Center, operated by the Mat–Su Convention & Visitors Bureau. Open May 15 to Sept. 15, 8 A.M. to 6 P.M. daily. This large center offers a wide variety of displays and information on the Mat–Su Valley; pay phone. Write HC01, Box 6616J21, Palmer, AK 99645; or phone (907) 746-5002. The visitors bureau also operates a booking and reservation service; phone (907) 746-5003 or 1-800-770-5003.

Best View RV Park. See display ad on page 325. ▲

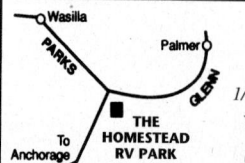

GEORGE PARKS HIGHWAY *Anchorage, AK, to Milepost A 169*

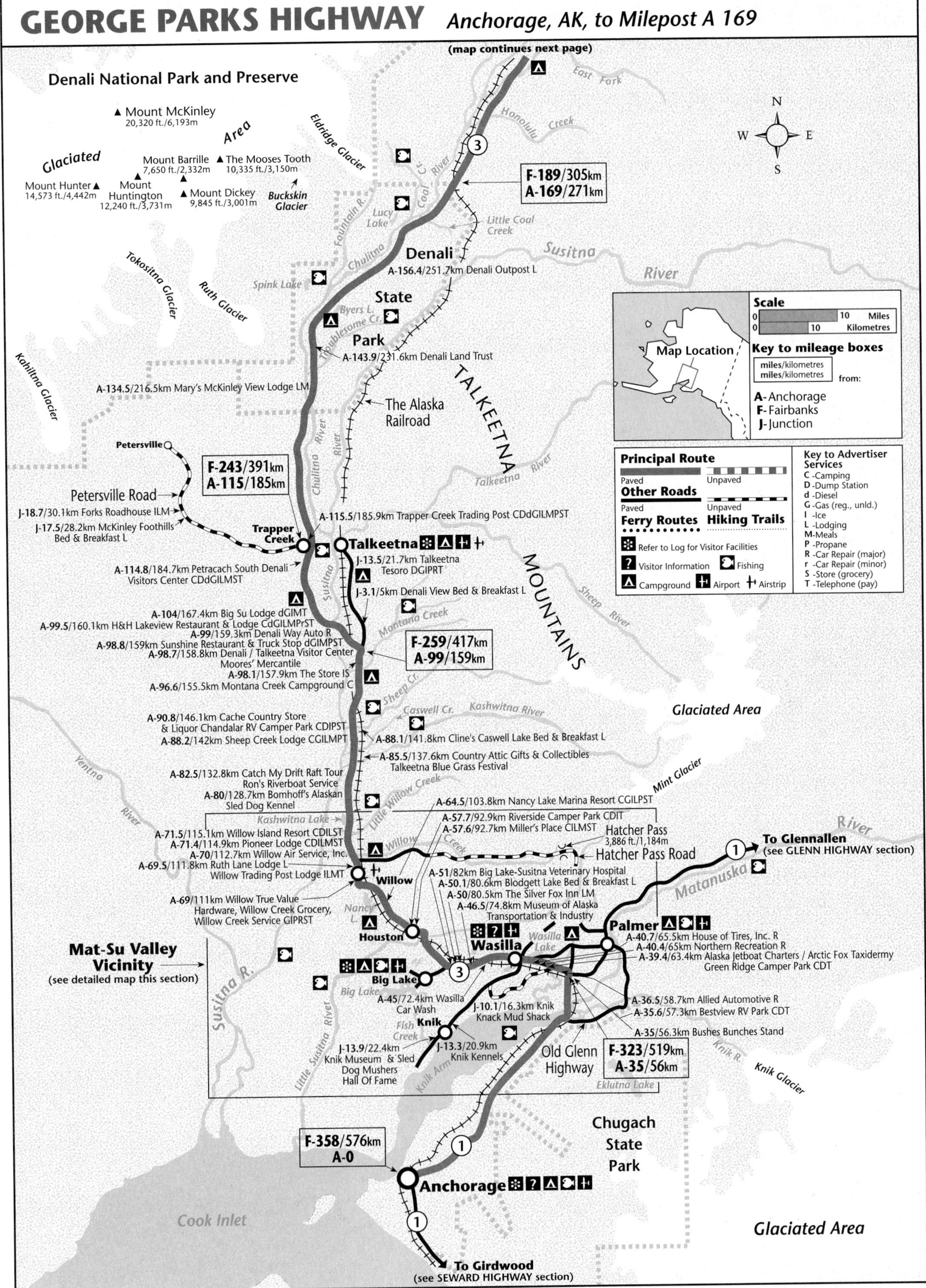

GEORGE PARKS HIGHWAY *Milepost A 169 to Fairbanks, AK*

Scale
0 10 Miles
0 10 Kilometres
Key to mileage boxes
miles/kilometres
miles/kilometres
from:
A-Anchorage
J-Junction
Map Location
Principal Route
Paved
Unpaved
Other Roads
Paved
Unpaved
Ferry Routes
Hiking Trails
Refer to Log for Visitor Facilities
Visitor Information
Fishing
Campground
Airport
Airstrip
Key to Advertiser Services
C -Camping
D -Dump Station
d -Diesel
G -Gas (reg., unld.)
I -Ice
L -Lodging
M-Meals
P -Propane
R -Car Repair (major)
r -Car Repair (minor)
S -Store (grocery)
T -Telephone (pay)
To Livengood
(see ELLIOTT HIGHWAY section)
To Circle
(see STEESE HIGHWAY section)
F-0
A-358/576km
Murphy Dome
2,930 ft./893m
A-355.2/571.6km Goldhill RV Park and Cabins CDLT
To Chena Hot Springs
Ester
A-351.7/566km Ester Gold Camp CDLM
Fairbanks
Chena R.
Tanana River
The Alaska Railroad
To Delta Junction
(see ALASKA HIGHWAY section)
Little Goldstream Cr.
A-309/497.3km Monderosa IM
Nenana
A-304.5/490km A Frame Service dGIPST
F-53/86km
A-305/490km
Wood River
A-302.1/486.2km Finnish Alaskan Bed and Breakfast L
Teklanika River
Fish Creek
Anderson
Clear
A-290.2/467km Alaska Panache' Bed and Breakfast L
A-289.8/466.4km Summer Shades Campground CDILS
Julius Creek
F-75/120km
A-284/456km
A-280.1/450.8km Rochester Lodge CLM
A-280/450.6km Clear Sky Lodge GIMPT
N
W
E
S
A-276/444.2km Tatlanika Trading Co. CD
Rex Dome
4,155 ft./1,266m
Bear Cr.
Nenana River
Jumbo Dome
4,493 ft./1,369m
Walker Dome
3,942 ft./1,202m
A-248.7/400.2km Dome Home Bed & Breakfast L
A-248.5/399.9km McKinley KOA Kampground CDIPST
A-247/397.5km Healy Heights Bed & Breakfast L
Homestead Bed & Breakfast L
Otto Lake R.V. Park
A-245.1/394.4km Denali RV Park & Motel CLT
A-251.1/404.1km Beaver View Bed & Breakfast L
Panguingue Cr.
A-249.6/401.7km Evans Industries, Inc. R
A-249.5/401.5km Motel Nord Haven L
A-249.3/401.2km Dry Creek Bed & Breakfast L
A-249.2/401km Larry's Healy Service dGIPST
Healy
Suntrana
Usibelli
Healy Cr.
Dora Peak
5,572 ft./1,698m
Sugarloaf Mountain
4,450 ft./1,356m
Otto Lake
Dry Cr.
A-240.4/386.9km Last Resort At Denali CD
Mount Healy
5,716 ft./1,742m
A-238.9/384.5km Alaska Cabin Nite Dinner Theatre M
McKinley Chalet Resort LM
Northern Lights Photosymphony IS
A-238.8/384.3km Sourdough Cabins L
A-238.7/384.1km Mt. McKinley Motor Lodge LT
A-238.5/383.8km Denali Crow's Nest Log Cabins and Overlook Bar & Grill LMT
Denali Wilderness Lodge LM
McKinley/Denali Cabins ILMT
McKinley/Denali Gift Shop
McKinley/Denali Steakhouse and Salmon Bake ILMT
A-238.1/383.2km Denali Raft Adventures
Park Road
(see DENALI NATIONAL PARK section)
Park Entrance
Mount Fellow
4,476 ft./1,364m
Yanert Fork
F-121/194km
A-237/382km
Denali National Park and Preserve
A-229/368.5km Denali Cabins L
Pyramid Peak
5,201 ft./1,585m
A-231.1/371.9km Denali Grizzly Bear Cabins & Campground CILPST
Denali River Cabins L
McKinley Village Lodge LM
Fang Mountain
6,736 ft./2,053m
Kantishna
A-224/360.5km The Perch LM
McKinley Wilderness Lodge LT
F-148/238km
A-210/338km
Carlo Cr.
RANGE
A-223.9/360.3km Carlo Creek Lodge CDILPST
A-210.2/338.3km Parkway Gift Shop
Cantwell
ALASKA
Nenana River
Broad Pass
2,300 ft./701m
A-209.9/337.8km Backwoods Lodge L
Cantwell Lodge CILMT
A-209.7/337.4km Reindeer Mtn. Lodge 1L
To Paxson
(see DENALI HIGHWAY section)
West Fork
Middle Fork
A-188.5/303.4km The Igloo dG
Glaciated Area
East Fork
Chulitna R.
Chulitna River
Mount McKinley
20,320 ft./6,194m
Eldridge Glacier
Honolulu Creek
Coal Cr.
Mount Huntington
12,240 ft./3,731m
The Mooses Tooth
10,335 ft./3,150m
Mount Barrille
7,650 ft./2,332m
Mount Dickey
9,845 ft./3,001m
Buckskin Glacier
F-189/305km
A-169/271km

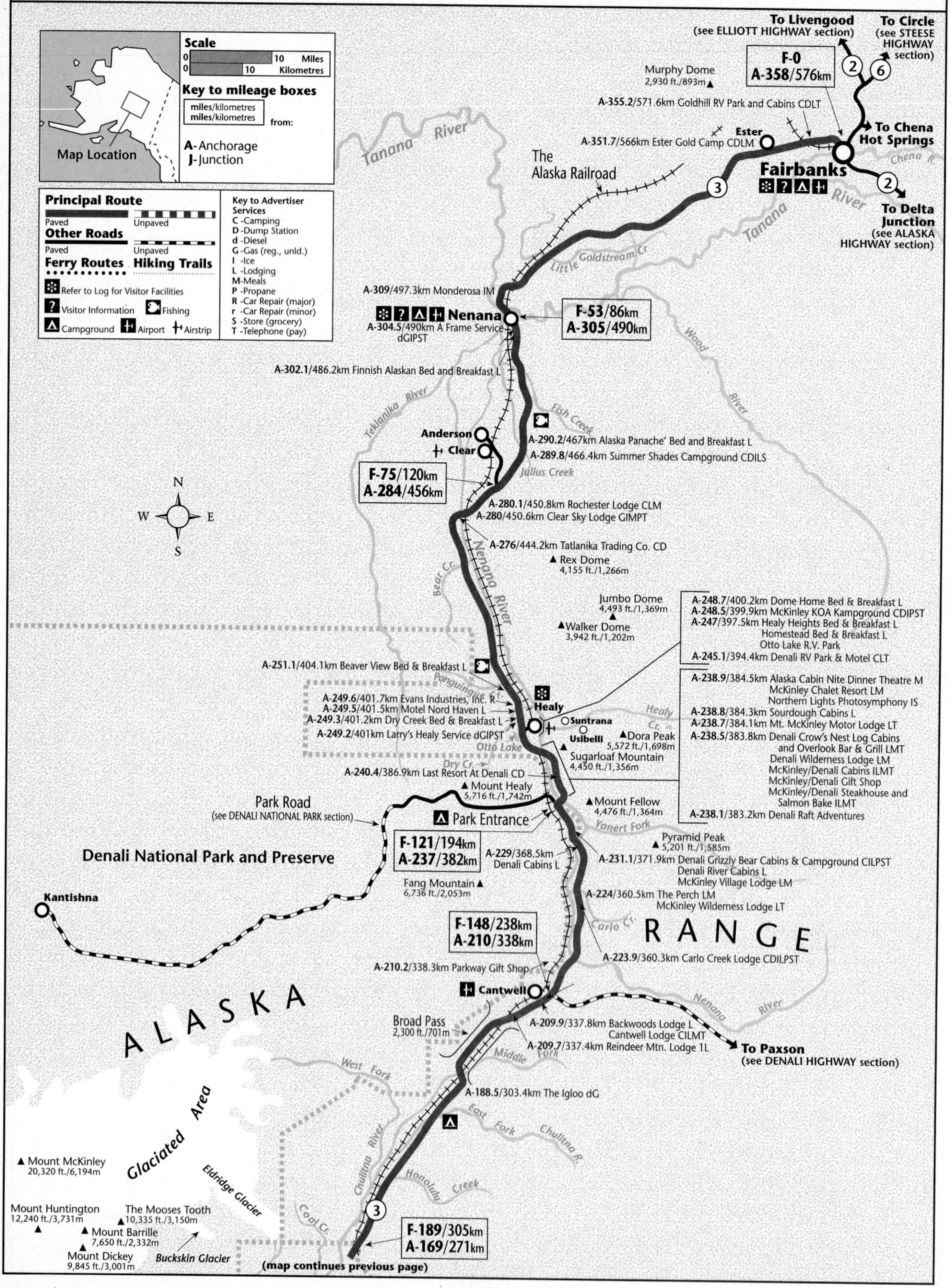

(map continues previous page)

A 36.2 (58.3 km) **F 321.8** (517.9 km) Highway narrows to two lanes northbound.

A 36.5 (58.7 km) **F 321.5** (517.4 km) **Allied Automotive.** See display ad this section.

A 37.4 (60.2 km) **F 320.6** (515.9 km) Updraft Road; road to airstrip.

A 37.8 (60.8 km) **F 320.2** (515.3 km) Hyer Road. Wasilla Creek bridge.

A 38 (61.2 km) **F 320** (515 km) Fairview Loop Road to west leads 11 miles/17.7 km to connect with Knik Road. Access to Palmer Hay Flats State Game Refuge.

A 38.4 (61.8 km) **F 319.6** (514.3 km) **Alaska Jetboat Charters, Arctic Fox Taxidermy.** Fishing charters, taxidermy shop, Alaska Jetboat Charters (907) 376-4776. Offers guided full day or half-day fishing trips for king salmon May 25 to July 14. Silver, red, pink and chum salmon July 15 to September. Arctic Fox Taxidermy, a full service taxidermy shop, specializes in Alaskan fish and big game mounts. (907) 376-4776.
[ADVERTISEMENT]

A 39.4 (63.4 km) **F 318.6** (512.7 km) **Green Ridge Camper Park.** See display ad this section. ▲

A 39.4 (63.4 km) **F 318.6** (512.7 km) Seward Meridian Road, which junctions with the Palmer–Wasilla Highway, which leads east to Palmer and provides access to Finger Lake state recreation site (see **Milepost A 41.1**). Shopping center.

A 39.5 (63.6 km) **F 318.5** (512.6 km) Wasilla city limits; medical clinic (376-1276). Wasilla shopping, services and attractions are located along the highway (from here north to **Milepost A 45**) and at Main Street in Wasilla city center.

A 40 (64.4 km) **F 318** (511.8 km) Veterinary clinic.

A 40.4 (65 km) **F 317.6** (511.1 km) **Northern Recreation.** Complete parts, accessories, service and repairs for campers, travel trailers, motorhomes and fifth-wheelers. We stock parts and do repair work on all major appliances, water systems, waste systems and running gear. Open Monday-Friday 8 A.M. to 6 P.M., Saturday 9 A.M. to 5 P.M. Phone (907) 376-8087.
[ADVERTISEMENT]

A **40.5** (65.2 km) F **317.5** (511 km) **House of Tires, Inc.** See display ad this section.

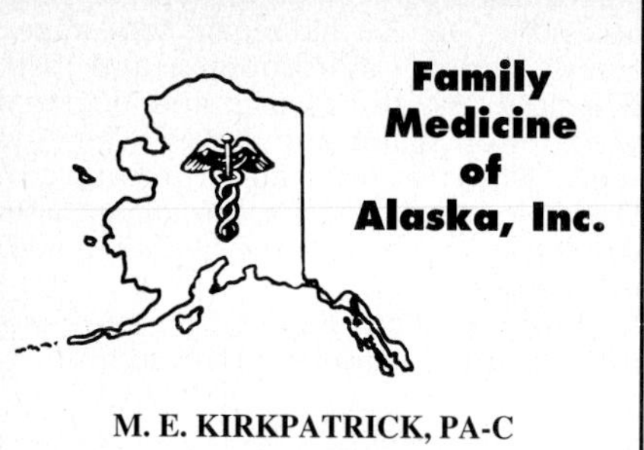

A 40.8 (65.7 km) **F 317.2** (510.5 km) Cottonwood Creek bridge.

A 41.1 (66.1 km) **F 316.9** (510 km) **Junction** with Palmer–Wasilla Highway, which leads east 10 miles/16 km to the Glenn Highway at Palmer. It provides access to several businesses, Finger Lake state recreation site and a day-use area with picnic sites and playground.

A 41.7 (67 km) **F 316.3** (509 km) Park with picnic shelter, restrooms, playground and swimming beach on Wasilla Lake; limited parking. Monument to George Parks.

A 41.8 (67.3 km) **F 316.2** (508.9 km) Crusey Street, access to Bogard Road, a resort with motel and dining, and Finger Lake state recreation site. Turn right (northbound) and drive 3.7 miles/6 km via Crusey Street and Bogard Road to reach Finger Lake. (The recreation site is also accessible from Palmer–Wasilla Highway, or turn east at **Milepost A 42.2** and drive 0.3 mile/0.5 km to intersection of Wasilla–Fishhook and Bogard roads, then follow Bogard Road 4.1 miles/6.6 km to Finger Lake.) Finger Lake has picnic tables, campsites, water, toilets and a boat launch. Also access to Wolf Lake state recreation site, off Bogard Road, which has picnic sites, toilets and hiking trail. ▲

A 42 (67.6 km) **F 316** (508.5 km) Art gallery and food market.

A 42.1 (67.8 km) **F 315.9** (508.4 km)

Knik Road Log

Distance is measured from the junction (J) with George Parks Highway.

J 0.1 (.2 km) *CAUTION: Road crosses railroad tracks.*

J 0.7 (1.1 km) Glenwood Avenue, Senior center.

J 1.5 (2.4 km) Gas station.

J 2.1 (3.4 km) Smith ball fields.

J 2.2 (3.5 km) Iditarod Trail Committee headquarters and visitor center; historical displays, souvenir shop. Open 8 A.M. to 5 P.M., daily in summer, weekdays the rest of the year.

J 2.3 (3.7 km) **Lake Lucille** Mat–Su Borough Park Campground and day-use area 0.6 mile/1 km north via gravel road; 64 campsites, pavilion with covered picnic tables, firepits, parking. Camping fee charged. Fishing for landlocked silver salmon. Non-motorized lake access. ▲

J 4.1 (6.6 km) **Junction** with Fairview Loop Road, which joins the Parks Highway at **Milepost A 38**; access to Palmer Hay Flats State Game Refuge. Shopping center with gas and groceries at this junction.

J 7 (11.3 km) Knik fire hall.

J 8 (12.9 km) Settlers Bay, a housing development built around a lodge; golf course and stables.

J 10.1 (16.3 km) Turnoff for Homestead Museum, with a large collection of early Alaskan memorabilia, and gift shop.

Knik Knack Mud Shack. See display ad this section.

J 11.1 (17.9 km) Laurence airport.

J 13 (20.9 km) **Knik Kennels.** See display ad this section.

J 13.3 (21.4 km) KNIK on **Knik Lake.** There is a bar here with a pay phone, also a liquor store, gas station and private campground. Lake fishing for rainbow; inquire at the Knik Bar. Knik is a checkpoint on the Iditarod Trail Sled Dog Race route and is often called the "Dog Mushing Center of the World"; many famous Alaskan dog mushers live in this area. ▲

J 13.9 (22.4 km) Knik Museum and Sled Dog Mushers' Hall of Fame, open noon to 6 P.M. Wednesday through Sunday, from June 1 through Aug. 31. The museum is housed in one of two buildings remaining from Knik's gold rush era (1898–1916). Regional memorabilia, artifacts, archives, dog mushing equipment, mushers' portraits and historical displays on the Iditarod Trail. Admission fee $2 for adults, $1.50 for seniors, free for children under 18. Phone (907) 376-7755, from Sept. through May call 376-2005.

Traditional Athabascan graveyard with fenced graves and spirit houses south; next to Knik Museum. The gravesite can be observed from the Iditarod Trail.

Knik Museum and Sled Dog Mushers' Hall of Fame. See display ad this section.

J 16.1 (25.9 km) **Fish Creek** bridge; parking, fishing for silver salmon.

J 17.2 (27.7 km) Goose Bay Point Road to Little Susitna River public-use facility at state game refuge (12 miles/19.3 km); 83 parking spaces, 65 campsites, boat ramps, dump station, water, tables, toilets. Also access to Point Mackenzie.

J 18.5 (29.8 km) Pavement ends at small bar beside road. Road continues into rural area.

Return to Milepost A 42.2 George Parks Highway

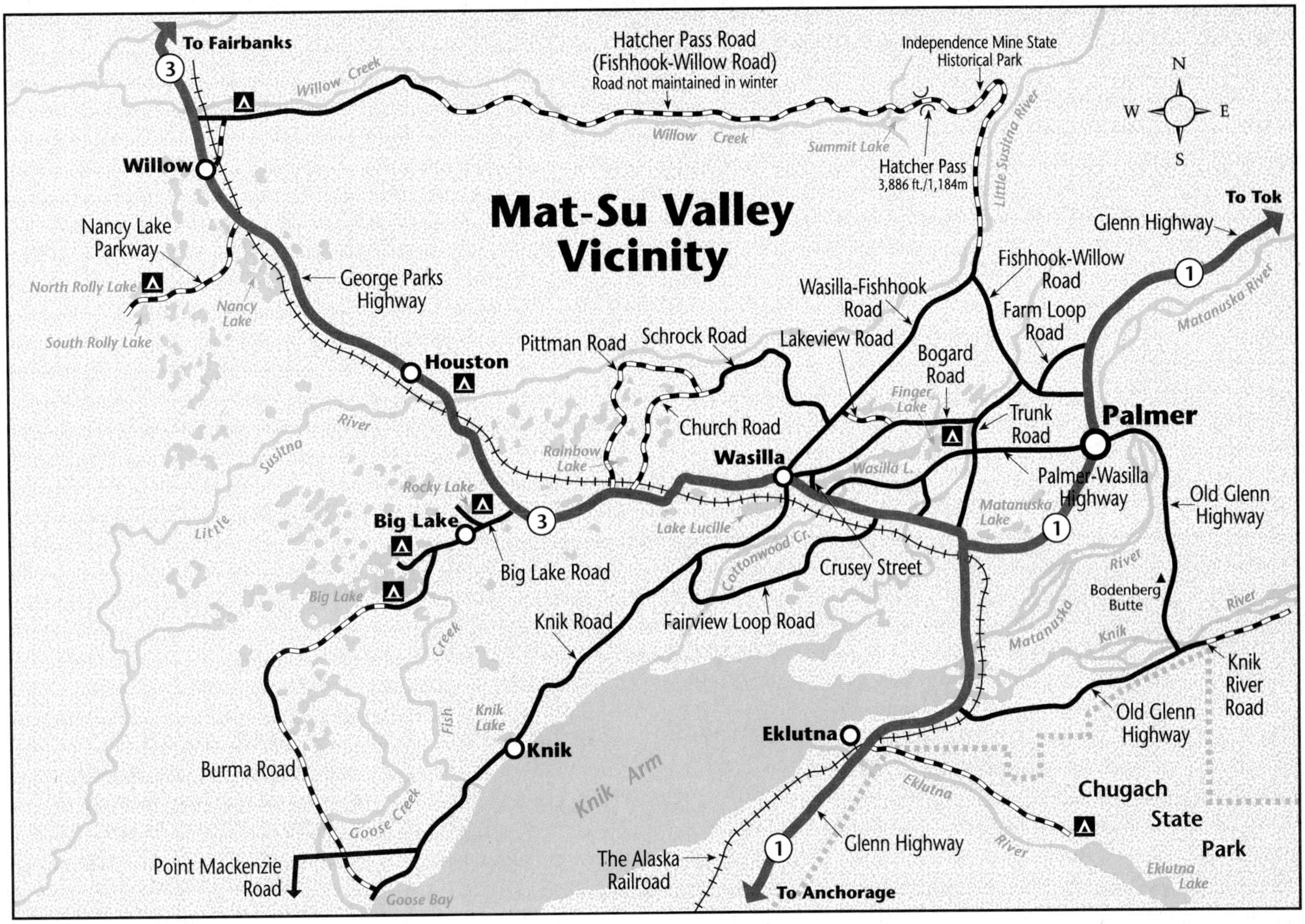

Mat-Su Valley Vicinity

To Fairbanks
Hatcher Pass Road (Fishhook-Willow Road) Road not maintained in winter
Independence Mine State Historical Park
Willow Creek
Willow
Summit Lake
Hatcher Pass 3,886 ft./1,184m
Little Susitna River
To Tok
Glenn Highway
Nancy Lake Parkway
North Rolly Lake
South Rolly Lake
Nancy Lake
George Parks Highway
Fishhook-Willow Road
Wasilla-Fishhook Road
Farm Loop Road
Matanuska River
Pittman Road
Schrock Road
Lakeview Road
Bogard Road
Houston
Finger Lake
Trunk Road
Palmer
Church Road
Susitna River
Rainbow Lake
Wasilla
Wasilla L.
Palmer-Wasilla Highway
Rocky Lake
Old Glenn Highway
Big Lake
Matanuska Lake
Little
Lake Lucille
Cottonwood Cr.
Crusey Street
Big Lake Road
Bodenberg Butte
Big Lake
Knik Road
Fairview Loop Road
Knik River
Creek
Knik
Knik River Road
Fish
Knik Lake
Old Glenn Highway
Knik
Eklutna
Burma Road
Knik Arm
Chugach State Park
Goose Creek
Eklutna
Point Mackenzie Road
The Alaska Railroad
Glenn Highway
Eklutna Lake
Goose Bay
To Anchorage

Boundary Street, Lake Lucille Park.

A 42.2 (67.9 km) **F 315.8** (508.2 km) Wasilla's Main Street; visitor center and museum one block north; post office two blocks north (Zip code 99687). Access to Hatcher Pass and Knik from this intersection. Turn south across railroad tracks for Knik Road to Knik, the "Dog Mushing Center of th World" (see KNIK ROAD log on opposite page). Turn north on Wasilla's Main Street for downtown Wasilla and Hatcher Pass. Description of Wasilla follows. ▲

Wasilla–Fishhook Road leads northeast about 10 miles/16 km to junction with the Hatcher Pass (Fishhook–Willow) Road to Independence Mine State Historical Park; turn to the Hatcher Pass side road log in the GLENN HIGHWAY section, page 274, for a description of the road to Hatcher Pass from this junction (**J 6.8** in that log). See also the Mat–Su Valley Vicinity map above. The 49-mile/79-km Hatcher Pass Road junctions with the George Parks Highway at **Milepost A 71.2.**

Wasilla

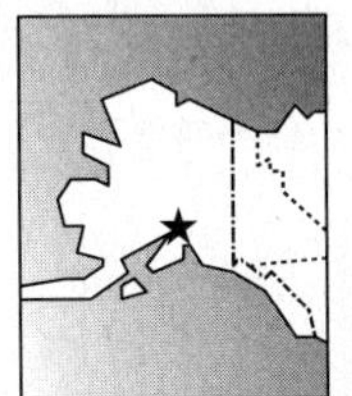

A 42.2 (67.9 km) **F 315.8** (508.2 km). Located between Wasilla and Lucille lakes in the Susitna Valley, about an hour's drive from Anchorage. **Population:** 3,666. **Emergency Services: State Police,** phone 745-2131, emergency only phone 911. **Fire Department**

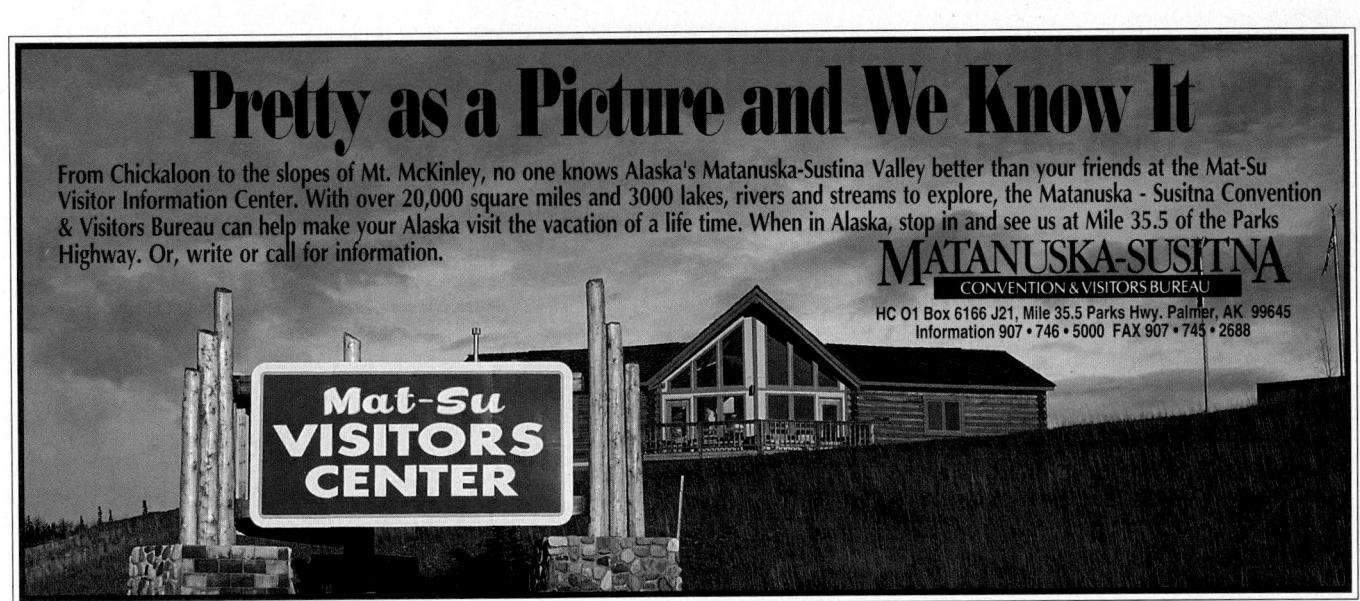

and **Ambulance**, phone 376-5320, emergency only phone 911. **Hospital,** in Palmer. **Doctor** on Seward Meridian Road, **Milepost A 39.5**, phone 376-1276, and at West Valley Medical Center, E. Bogard Road, phone 376-5028. Chiropractic clinics on Main Street.

Visitor Information: At the Dorothy G. Page Museum and Old Wasilla Town Site Park on Main Street just off the George Parks Highway, phone 373-9071, fax 373-9072. Or contact the chamber of commerce, P.O. Box 871826, Wasilla 99687, phone 376-1299.

Radio and Television via Anchorage stations; KNBZ-FM 99.7. **Newspaper:** *The Valley Sun* (weekly); *The Frontiersman* (semiweekly). **Transportation: Air**–Charter service available. **Railroad**–Alaska Railroad. **Bus**–Matanuska Valley commuter to Anchorage.

Private Aircraft: New Wasilla airstrip, 3 miles/4.8 km southeast; elev. 348 feet/106m; length 3,700 feet/1,128m; gravel; unattended. Wasilla Lake seaplane base, 0.9 mile/1.4 km east; elev. 330 feet/100m. Numerous private airstrips and lakes in vicinity.

Wasilla is one of the Matanuska–Susitna Valley's pioneer communities. Long before the George Parks Highway was built, local residents and visitors bound for Lake Lucille, Wasilla Lake, Big Lake and Knik, drove over the valley roads from Palmer to the village of Wasilla. Wasilla became a station on the Alaska Railroad about 1916.

Today, Wasilla is the largest community on the George Parks Highway between Anchorage and Fairbanks. Shopping malls and businesses here offer a wide assortment of services. *NOTE: There are no banks between Wasilla and Fairbanks.*

ACCOMMODATIONS

All visitor facilities are available here, including sporting goods stores, post office, gas stations, tire and RV repair, and other services. Mat–Su Ice Arena, at Bogard Road

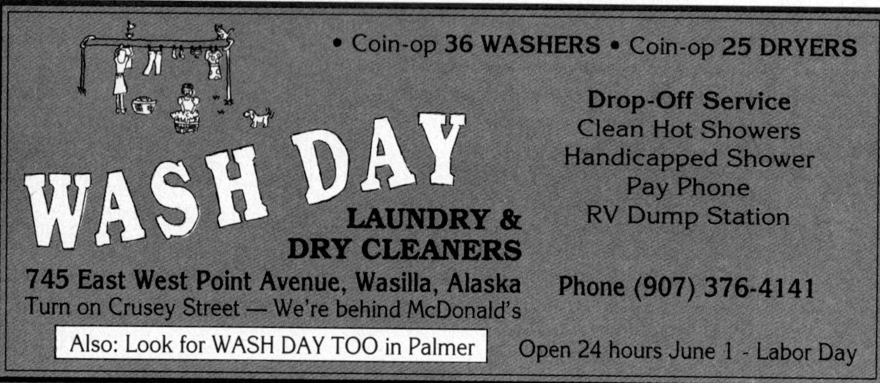

Photo by Jim Brown

and Crusey Street, has ice skating, picnic area and fitness court. Swimming and showers are available at Wasilla High School.

Valley Chiropractic Clinic Inc. (907) 373-2022. 24-hour emergency service. Complete modern facility, same day emergency care. Reasonable fees with VISA and MasterCard accepted. We're accustomed to treating travelers' needs. We're located at 400 N. Main St., in Wasilla. Turn north on to Main Street from the Parks Highway and go up two blocks on the left, directly across the street from the post office. [ADVERTISEMENT]

ATTRACTIONS

On the town's Main Street, north of the Parks Highway, are the Dorothy G. Page Museum and Visitors Center, the library and the post office. The museum is open daily year-round, 10 A.M. to 6 P.M. in summer, 8 A.M. to 5 P.M. in winter; admission fees are $3 adults, $2.50 senior citizens; under 18 years free. Included in the price of admission to the museum is entrance to the

*Transportation museum at **Milepost A 46.5** features historic aircraft, as well as old farm machinery and road-building equipment.* (Jerrianne Lowther, staff)

WASILLA ADVERTISERS

Bear Air....Ph. (907) 373-3373
Chimo Guns Sporting Goods...505 E. Herning
Curio Cabin....270 Main St.
Dorothy G. Page Museum and Old Wasilla Town Site.Ph. (907) 373-9071
Family Medicine of Alaska, Inc.....Ph. (907) 376-1276
Iditarod Trail Committee, Inc.....Mile 2.2 Knik Rd.
Kashim Inn....Ph. (907) 376-5800
Lake Lucille Inn....Ph. (907) 373-1776
Lakeshore Bed and Breakfast....Ph. (907) 376-1380
Larson Chiropractic....Ph. (907) 376-2225
Mat–Su Valley Tours....Ph. (800) 499-2608
Matanuska–Susitna Convention & Visitors Bureau....Ph. (907) 746-5000
Northern Recreation....Mile 40.4 Parks Hwy.
Save-U-More....Mile 36.5 Parks Hwy.
Snowbird Inn Bed & Breakfast....Ph. (907) 376-7048
Southshore Bed & Breakfast....S. Shore Lake Lucille
Town Square Art Gallery..Ph. (907) 376-0123
Valley Chiropractic Clinic.Ph. (907) 373-2022
Wash Day Laundry & Dry Cleaners......Crusey St., Behind McDonald's
Wasilla Home Style Laundry....Wasilla Shopping Center
Wasilla One-Hour Photo....Wasilla Shopping Center
Windbreak Hotel, Cafe and Lounge....Mile 40.5 Parks Hwy.

Alaska is one-fifth the size of the continental United States.

Old Wasilla Town Site Park, located behind the museum. This historical park has seven renovated buildings from before, during and after Wasilla's pioneer days, including Wasilla's first schoolhouse (built in 1917). Adjacent to the park is the Herning/Teeland Country Store, which is currently under restoration. The school, store and nearby railroad depot are on the National Register of Historic Sites.

Wasilla is home to the Iditarod Trail Committee, the organization which stages the famous 1,049-mile Iditarod Trail Sled Dog Race from Anchorage to Nome. The Iditarod headquarters and visitors center is located at Mile 2.2 Knik Road. The center has historical displays on the Iditarod, race videos, Iditarod puppies, and a gift shop with unique souvenirs. Open daily in summer, weekdays in winter, from 8 A.M. to 5 P.M. Historical displays on the Iditarod Trail and Alaskan mushers can be found at the Knik Museum at Mile 13.9 Knik Road (see Knik Road log this section).

The Wasilla Water Festival is held the Fourth of July weekend. Iditarod Days is held in conjunction with the Iditarod Race, usually the first week in March. Other area winter events include ice golf at Mat–Su Resort and ice bowling at Big Lake.

George Parks Highway Log

(continued)

A 42.7 (68.7 km) **F 315.3** (507.4 km) Airport Drive; food and shopping.

A 43.3 (69.7 km) **F 314.7** (506.4 km) Lucas Road; access to Lake Lucille.

A 43.5 (70 km) **F 314.5** (506.1 km) Divided highway ends northbound.

A 44.4 (71.4 km) **F 313.6** (504.7 km) Church Road.

A 45 (72.4 km) **F 313** (503.7 km) Wasilla city limits. Shopping and services are located along the highway to **Milepost A 39.5** and at Main Street in Wasilla city center.

Wasilla Car Wash. See display ad this section.

A 46.4 (74.7 km) **F 311.6** (501.5 km) *CAUTION: Railroad crossing.*

A 46.5 (74.8 km) **F 311.5** (501.3 km) Rocky Ridge Road. Turnoff for the Museum of Alaska Transportation and Industry, open 10 A.M. to 6 P.M. Monday–Saturday in summer, and 8 A.M. to 4 P.M. in winter. Admission fees are $3 adults, $2 children, $7 families. Group tours can be arranged.

Museum of Alaska Transportation & Industry. See display ad this section.

A 48.8 (78.5 km) **F 309.2** (497.6 km) Turnoff on Pittman Road to Rainbow Lake. Medical center, convenience store, gas station, cafe and Meadow Lakes post office.

A 50 (80.5 km) **F 308** (495.7 km) **The Silver Fox Inn.** See display ad this section.

A 50.1 (80.6 km) **F 307.9** (495.5 km) **Blodgett Lake Bed and Breakfast.** Turn on Sheele Road, 1,000 ft. off highway. Quiet lake, queen-size beds, lake views, full breakfasts and Alaskan hospitality. Write or call for brochure: P.O. Box 878025, Wasilla, AK 99687. (907) 892-6877 for reservations. [ADVERTISEMENT]

A 51 (82 km) **F 307** (494 km) **Big Lake–Susitna Veterinary Hospital.** See display ad this section.

A 52.3 (84.2 km) **F 305.7** (492 km) **Junction** with Big Lake Road. Meadowood shopping mall located here with a service station, hardware store, automatic teller cash machine, grocery and emergency phone (dial 911). See BIG LAKE ROAD log page 332.

A 53.3 (85.8 km) **F 304.7** (490.4 km) Houston High School and Wasilla Senior Center. Turnout to west with map and information sign.

A 56.1 (90.3 km) **F 301.9** (485.8 km) Miller's Reach Road.

A 56.4 (90.8 km) **F 301.6** (485.4 km) *CAUTION: Railroad crossing.*

A 57.1 (91.9 km) **F 300.9** (484.2 km) Bridge over the Little Susitna River; turnouts either side. This river heads at Mint Glacier in the Talkeetna Mountains to the northeast and flows 110 miles/177 km into Upper Cook Inlet.

A 57.4 (92.4 km) **F 300.6** (483.8 km) Turnoff to Houston city-operated Little Susitna River Campground. Large, well-maintained campground with 86 sites (many wide, level gravel sites); camping fee, water, restrooms, covered picnic area, 10-day limit. Off-road parking lot near river with boat launch and access to river. Follow signs to camping and river. Day-use area with water and toilets west side of highway. ▲

The **Little Susitna River** has a tremendous king salmon run and one of the largest silver salmon runs in southcentral Alaska. Kings to 30 lbs. enter the river in late May and June, use large red spinners or salmon eggs. Silvers to 15 lbs., come in late July and August, with the biggest run in August, use small weighted spoons or fresh salmon roe. No bait is allowed and artificials are required during the early weeks of the fishery in the first part of August. Also red salmon to 10 lbs., in mid-July, use coho flies or salmon eggs. Charter boats nearby.

A 57.5 (92.5 km) **F 300.5** (483.6 km) **HOUSTON** (pop. 878) has a grocery store, restaurant (open daily), laundromat, gift shop, inn with food, lodging and pay phone, a campground and gas station. Post office located in the grocery store. Fishing charter operators and marine service are located here. Emergency phone at Houston fire station. ▲

Homesteaded in the 1950s, incorporated as a city in 1966. Houston is a popular fishing center for anglers on the Little Susitna River.

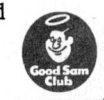

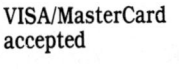

A 57.6 (92.7 km) F 300.4 (483.4 km) **Miller's Place.** Don't miss this stop! Groceries, post office, laundry, RV parking, cabin rentals, tenting on riverbank. Gift shop, fishing tackle and licenses, fresh salmon eggs. Ice, sporting goods sales and rental, pay phone. Fishing charters available; full day only $40. Probably the best soft ice cream and hamburgers in Alaska. Clean restrooms. Visitor information experts. Family-run Christian business. Gary and Debbie Miller. (907) 892-6129. [ADVERTISEMENT] ▲

A 57.7 (92.9 km) F 300.3 (483.3 km) **Riverside Camper Park.** See display ad on page 331. ▲

A 64.5 (103.8 km) F 293.5 (472.3 km) **Nancy Lake Marina, Resort.** See display ad on page 331.

A 66.5 (107 km) F 291.5 (469.1 km) Highway crosses Alaska Railroad tracks. Turnoff (not well marked) for Nancy Lake state recreation site; 30 campsites, 30 picnic sites, toilets, boat launch, horseshoe pits. Camping fee $6/night or annual pass. ▲

A 67.2 (108.1 km) F 290.8 (468 km) Wide gravel road into Nancy Lake Recreation Area in the mixed birch and spruce forest of the Susitna River valley (good mushroom hunting area). At Mile 2.5/4 km on the access road there is a well-marked nature trail, toilets and parking area. At Mile 4.7/7.6 km there is a canoe launch, toilet and parking area. At Mile 5.7/9.2 km a hiking trail leads 3 miles/4.8 km to Chicken Lake, 5.5 miles/8.9 km to Red Shirt Lake. At Mile 6.2/10 km is South Rolly Lake overlook (day use only) with barbecues, 11 picnic tables, litter barrels and toilets. There are 106

Big Lake Road Log

The 6.5-mile/10.5-km Big Lake Road leads south from the George Parks Highway junction at **Milepost A 52.3** to **BIG LAKE** (pop. 2,333), a recreation area with swimming, camping, boating, fishing, jet skiing and tour boat rides in summer. Wintersports include snowmachining. Businesses are found along Big Lake Road and along North Shore Drive, which forks off Big Lake Road at Mile J 3.6. **Distance is measured from the junction (J) with the George Parks Highway.**

J 0 Junction with George Parks Highway. Meadowood Mall and gas station.

J 3.4 (5.5 km) Beaver Lake Road turnoff. Lions Club dump station at gas station located at intersection. Turn right here for public and private campgrounds. Drive 0.5 mile/0.8 km on Beaver Lake Road (gravel) for Rocky Lake state recreation site; 10 campsites, $6 nightly fee or annual pass, toilets, firepits, water and boat launch. ▲

J 3.6 (5.8 km) Fisher's Y; gas station and Big Lake post office (Zip code 99652). Big Lake Road forks here: Go straight ahead for North Shore Drive (description follows); keep to left for south Big Lake Road businesses and Big Lake South state recreation site (continue with this log).

North Shore Drive provides access to Klondike Inn and restaurant (1.4 miles/2.3 km) and Big Lake North state recreation site (1.6 miles/2.6 km), which has parking for 120 vehicles, overnight RV parking, tent sites, $6 nightly fee per vehicle or annual pass, covered picnic tables, water, toilets, dumpsters, boat launch ($5 fee) and sandy beach. ▲

The Klondike Inn is nestled on the shore of beautiful Big Lake just 60 paved miles from Anchorage. At the Klondike Inn you will find a full-service resort complete with hotel, saunas, restaurant, lounge, marina and boat launch. Floatplane landing and mooring. 20- to 30-person party barge rental. Fly-in fishing or sightseeing trips available. An ideal location to headquarter your stay in Alaska. Phone (907) 892-6261, fax (907) 892-6445. P.O. Box 521020, Big Lake, AK 99652. [ADVERTISEMENT]

Big Lake Houseboat Rental. Relax in a secluded cove or cruise 53 miles of shoreline aboard one of our comfortable houseboats. Each vessel features a full galley, bath with shower and sleeping for

six. Limited number of jet skis available. Season May 15–Sept. 15. Located at Klondike Lodge on Big Lake. For reservations and rates: P.O. Box 520270, Big Lake, AK 99652. 1-800-770-9187, (907) 892-9187. [ADVERTISEMENT]

J 3.7 (6 km) Shopping mall.

J 3.9 (6.3 km) Big Lake fire station.

J 4 (6.4 km) East Lake Mall; visitor information center, restaurant and grocery.

J 4.1 (6.6 km) Turnoff for Islander paddlewheel tour boat dock, dining and picnic area on Long Island.

J 4.7 (7.6 km) Aero Drive and Big Lake airport. Big Lake is a 15-minute flight from Anchorage.

Private Aircraft: 1 mile/1.6 km southeast; elev. 150 feet/46m; length 2,400 feet/732m; gravel; fuel 100LL.

J 5 (8 km) Big Lake Motel. Bridge over Fish Creek. Fish Creek park picnic area; fish weir with salmon spawning view area. Fishing prohibited.

J 5.1 (8.2 km) Private RV park. ▲

J 5.2 (8.4 km) Big Lake South state recreation site; 13 campsites, six picnic sites, toilets, water, dumpsters, boat ramp ($5 fee). Camping fee $6/night per vehicle or annual pass. ▲

J 5.3 (8.5 km) Double-ended turnout with picnic tables and water.

J 5.7 (9.2 km) Gravel turnout, Echo Lake Road. Dog mushers' race track.

J 6.5 (10.5 km) Pavement ends. Burma Road continues into rural area, providing access to Point MacKenzie dairy project and Little Susitna River public-use facility at state game refuge (also accessible via Knik Road); parking, camping, boat ramps.

Big Lake is connected with smaller lakes by dredged waterways. It is possible to boat for several miles in the complex. Fish in Big Lake include lake trout, Dolly Varden, rainbow, red and coho salmon, and burbot.

Return to Milepost A 52.3
George Parks Highway

BIG LAKE ADVERTISERS

Big Lake Houseboat Rental .... Ph. (800) 770-9187
Big Lake Motel ...... Mile 5 S. & Big Lake Rd.
Islander & Talk of the Town Restaurants .. Ph. (907) 892-7144
Klondike Inn, The .... Ph. (907) 892-6261

Canoe rentals are available at Nancy Lake state recreation area. (Sue Rheaume)

campsites at South Rolly Lake Campground, at Mile 6.6/10.6 km, with firepits, toilets, water, canoe rentals and boat launch; firewood sometimes is provided. Camping fee $6/night or annual pass. ▲

South Rolly Lake, small population of rainbow, 12 to 14 inches.

A 68.7 (110.6 km) **F 289.3** (465.6 km) Newman's Hilltop Service and Miner's Last Stand; gas, diesel, gift shop.

A 69 (111 km) **F 289** (465.1 km) **WILLOW** (pop. 494). Visitor facilities include two gas stations, grocery, hardware and notions store, air taxi service, lodges, RV parks, video rental and restaurants. The Willow civic organization sponsors an annual Winter Carnival in January.

Willow extends about 2.5 miles/4 km north along the George Parks Highway. The community is also a stop on the Alaska Railroad. Willow had its start about 1897, when gold was discovered in the area. In the early 1940s, mining in the nearby Talkeetna Mountains slacked off, leaving Willow a virtual ghost town. The community made a comeback upon completion of the Parks Highway in 1972.

In 1976, Alaska voters selected the Willow area for their new capital site. However, funding for the capital move from Juneau to Willow was defeated in the November 1982 election.

Willow True Value Hardware, Willow Creek Grocery and Willow Creek Service. See display ad on page 333.

A 69.2 (111.4 km) **F 288.8** (464.8 km) Long Lake Road. Alternate access to Deshka Landing. Cafe, bed and breakfast.

A 69.4 (111.7 km) **F 288.6** (464.4 km) Willow library.

A 69.5 (111.8 km) **288.5** (464.3 km) Short road to Willow post office, lodge, trading post with cabins and camper spaces, and Alaska Railroad depot. ▲

Ruth Lake Lodge. See display ad on page 333.

Willow Trading Post Lodge. See display ad on page 333. ▲

A 69.6 (112 km) **F 288.4** (464.1 km) Willow elementary school.

A 69.7 (112.2 km) **F 288.3** (464 km) Willow Community Center, open daily; covered picnic pavilion, grills, ball court, boat launch and pay phone.

A 69.9 (112.5 km) **F 288.1** (463.6 km) Fire station.

A 70 (112.7 km) **F 288** (463.5 km) **Private Aircraft:** Willow airport; elev. 220 feet/67m; length 4,200 feet/1,280m; gravel; fuel 100LL.

A 70 (112.7 km) **F 288** (463.5 km) **Willow Air Service Inc.** See display ad on page 333.

A 70.8 (113.9 km) **F 287.2** (462.2 km) Willow Creek Parkway (**Susitna River** access road) to Willow Creek state recreation area (4 miles/6.4 km); parking, litter barrels, trail to mouth of creek. Access to Deshka Landing boat launch. Fishing for king and silver salmon, rainbow trout.

A 71 (114.3 km) **F 287** (461.9 km) Willow DOT/PF highway maintenance station.

A 71.2 (114.6 km) **F 286.8** (461.5 km) **Junction** with Hatcher Pass (Fishhook–Willow) Road. This road leads east and south across Hatcher Pass 49 miles/79 km to junction with the Glenn Highway. Independence Mine State Historical Park is 31.8 miles/51.2 km from here. Turn to the Hatcher Pass side road in the GLENN HIGHWAY section, page 274, for log of this road. (Parks Highway travelers should read that log back to front.) See also the Mat–Su Valley Vicinity map this section. Hatcher Pass Road is mostly gravel with some steep, narrow, winding sections.

Access to Willow Creek state recreation area via Hatcher Pass Road. Deception Creek main campground, with 17 campsites, is located 1.2 miles/1.9 km from this junction via Hatcher Pass Road. Additional campsites and a picnic area are located 0.8 mile/1.3 km east. Both sites have tables, firepits and toilets. Camping fee $10/ night or annual pass. ▲

A 71.4 (114.9 km) **F 286.6** (461.2 km) Lodge. Bridge over **Willow Creek.** This stream heads in Summit Lake, west of Hatcher Pass on the Hatcher Pass Road, and is a favorite launch site for airboat enthusiasts. Excellent king salmon fishing; also silvers, rainbows. Inquire at either lodge or resort for information. Entering Game Management Subunit 14B northbound, 14A southbound.

Pioneer Lodge. One of Alaska's oldest, original log lodges. Restaurant overlooking Willow Creek. Full RV hookups starting at $12, campground — tent sites $8, showers, laundromat, dump station. Rooms. Fishing,

hunting charters, drop offs, wilderness tours, fly-ins, bank fishing — four types of salmon, rainbows, grayling. Hiking trails. Boat launch. Bait, tackle, fishing rentals. Groceries, ice, gift shop. (907) 495-6883. See display ad. [ADVERTISEMENT] ▲

From here to Denali National Park and Preserve watch for views of the Alaska Range to the east of the highway.

A 71.5 (115.1 km) **F 286.5** (461.1 km) **Willow Island Resort.** Scenic riverside RV park, cabins and campground. Great salmon and trout fishing from the banks of crystal clear Willow Creek. Full hookups

on level riverbank sites. Hot showers, laundry, dump station, tackle, mini-grocery, good water. Excellent king and silver salmon fishing. Rainbows to 10 lbs. Fly-in, boat-in, scenic fishing and hunting charters. Guided fishing charters available. Gold panning. Open year-round. Winter cross-country skiing, snowmobiling, dogsledding. Close to Hatcher Pass; three hours from Denali National Park. Plan to stay awhile. Write: P.O. Box 85, Willow, AK 99688 or call (907) 495-6343. See display ad this section. By request of a majority of customers, RV park sites are priced without showers. [ADVERTISEMENT] ▲

A 74.7 (120.2 km) **F 283.3** (455.9 km) Bridge over Little Willow Creek. Large undeveloped parking areas below highway on either side of creek.

A 76.4 (122.9 km) **F 281.6** (453.2 km) Paved double-ended turnout to west by Kashwitna Lake. Small planes land on lake. Good camera viewpoints of lake and Mount McKinley (weather permitting).

A 80 (128.7 km) **F 278** (447.4 km) **Bomhoff's Alaskan Sled Dog Kennel.** See display ad this section.

A 81.3 (130.8 km) **F 276.7** (445.3 km) Grey's Creek, gravel turnouts both sides of highway.

A 82.5 (132.8 km) **F 275.5** (443.4 km) Susitna Landing boat launch on Susitna River, 1 mile/1.6 km on side road; operated by state park concessionaire. The Susitna River heads at Susitna Glacier in the Alaska Range to the northeast and flows west then south for 260 miles/418 km to Cook Inlet.

Ron's Riverboat Service. See display ad this section.

"Catch My Drift" Raft Tour. A leisurely and scenic four- to five-hour rafting tour, including an all-you-can-eat salmon bake and a live Alaskana show performed for you from the banks of the Big Su! For reservations call 373-6360 or 1-800-478-6360. A reasonably priced Alaskana experience. [ADVERTISEMENT]

A 83.2 (133.9 km) **F 274.8** (442.2 km) Bridge over the Kashwitna River; parking areas located at both ends of bridge. The river heads in a glacier in the Talkeetna Mountains and flows westward 60 miles/

96.5 km to enter the Susitna River 12 miles/19 km north of Willow.

A 84 (135.2 km) **F 274** (440.9 km) Large paved turnout to west.

A 84.3 (135.7 km) **F 273.7** (440.5 km) Gravel turnout to west. Walk-in for fishing at **Caswell Creek**; kings, silvers, pinks and rainbow.

A 85.1 (137 km) **F 272.9** (439.2 km) Caswell Creek, large gravel turnout.

A 85.5 (137.6 km) **F 272.5** (438.5 km) Gift shop and art gallery.

Country Attic Gifts & Collectibles. See display ad on page 335.

Talkeetna Blue Grass Festival, "dirty Ernie style," Aug. 5-6-7, 1994, is not in Talkeetna. Alaska's greatest musicians, handcrafts, food, best variety, good roads, outhouses, RV parking, no hookups. Great family weekend camping. Bring camping gear and cushions. $15 weekend, seniors and children 12 and under, free. No carry in alcohol please. Phone (907) 495-6718 to confirm location for 1994. [ADVERTISEMENT]

A 86 (138.4 km) **F 272** (437.7 km) Public access road leads 1.3 miles/2.1 km to mouth of Sheep Creek public boat launch and Bluffs on Susitna. **Sheep Creek** has parking, toilets, dumpster and wheelchair accessible trail to mouth of creek; fishing for kings, silvers, pinks and rainbow. Bluffs on Susitna is the site of an annual bluegrass festival.

A 88.1 (141.8 km) **F 269.9** (434.4 km) **Cline's Caswell Lake Bed & Breakfast.** See display on page 335.

A 88.2 (142 km) **F 269.8** (434.2 km) **Sheep Creek Lodge.** Beautiful log lodge, built with Alaskan white spruce logs, some over 200 years old. Fine dining, cocktail lounge, serving breakfast, lunch and dinner. Warm cozy cabins, creekside RV parking or camping. Excellent salmon and trout fishing within walking distance of lodge. Package liquor store, ice, fuel and propane. Gift shop featuring unique local Alaskan gifts, many Alaskan wildlife mounts and local tour information. Open year-round with winter activities including cross-country skiing, marked snow machine trails, ice fishing and dog mushing. Phone (907) 495-6227. See display ad on page 335. [ADVERTISEMENT] ▲

A 88.6 (142.6 km) **F 269.4** (433.5 km) Bridge over Sheep Creek. Unimproved picnic area on west side below bridge by creek.

A 90.8 (146.1 km) **F 267.2** (430 km) **Chandalar RV Park & Cache Country Store & Liquor.** See display ad this section. ▲

A 91.7 (147.6 km) **F 266.3** (428.5 km) *CAUTION: Railroad crossing.*

A 93 (149.7 km) **F 265** (426.5 km) Gravel turnout to west.

A 93.4 (150.3 km) **F 264.6** (425.8 km) Gravel turnouts both sides of highway.

A 93.5 (150.5 km) **F 264.5** (425.7 km) **Goose Creek** culvert; gravel turnout. Fishing.

A 93.6 (150.6 km) **F 264.4** (425.5 km) Goose Creek community center; park pavilion, picnic tables, grills, litter barrels.

A 95.1 (153 km) **F 262.9** (423.1 km) **Private Aircraft:** Montana Creek airstrip; elev. 250 feet/76m; length 2,400 feet/731m; gravel; fuel 80, 100.

A 96.5 (155.3 km) **F 261.5** (420.8 km) Montana Creek state recreation site with campsites, tables, firepits, toilets, water and trails (wheelchair accessible). Parking and access to Susitna River. Interpretive signs about salmon. Camping fee $6/night per vehicle or annual pass.

A 96.6 (155.5 km) **F 261.4** (420.7 km) **Montana Creek Campground.** Located on the north side of Montana Creek, all campsites in this private campground are scenic, with many overlooking one of Alaska's best salmon and trout fishing streams. Picnic tables, campfires, toilets. Only a short walk to the Susitna River. Conveniently located within 3 miles of grocery store, cafe, laundromat and showers. [ADVERTISEMENT]

A 96.6 (155.5 km) **F 261.4** (420.7 km) Bridge over Montana Creek. Homesteaders settled in the area surrounding this creek in the 1950s. Today, about 200 families live in the Montana Creek area. In winter, the Montana Creek Dog Mushers Club holds races and maintains trails. Camping and picnic areas on both sides of **Montana Creek**; excellent king salmon fishing, also silvers, pinks (even-numbered years), grayling, rainbow and Dolly Varden.

A 97.8 (157.4 km) **F 260.2** (418.7 km) Sunshine Community Health Center (medical clinic) and Alaska State Troopers post (phone 733-2556 or 911 for emergencies).

A 98 (157.7 km) **F 260** (418.4 km) For weather information, tune your radio to 830-AM (99.7-FM).

The Store. See display ad this section.

A 98.3 (158.2 km) **F 259.7** (417.9 km) Large gravel turnout to east.

A 98.4 (158.3 km) **F 259.6** (417.8 km) Susitna Valley High School. Five-kilometer trail for running in summer, cross-country skiing in winter.

A 98.7 (158.8 km) **F 259.3** (417.3 km) **Junction** with Talkeetna Spur Road; visitor information cabin. Access to hardware, lumber and feed store with cash machine. Turn right northbound on paved spur road that leads 14.5 miles/23.3 km to Talkeetna (description begins on page 338). See TALKEETNA SPUR ROAD log on page 338. Continue straight ahead on the George Parks Highway for Fairbanks.

Denali/Talkeetna Visitor Center. This quaint log cabin located at the junction of the Talkeetna Spur Road and the Parks Highway offers information on Denali National Park, Talkeetna-area attractions, fishing and flightseeing around Mount McKinley. Tackle shop and gift store. Large picnic area and public restrooms available. Phone (907) 733-2223 year-round. [ADVERTISEMENT]

Moores' Mercantile. See display ad this section.

A 98.8 (159 km) **F 259.2** (417.1 km) **Sunshine Restaurant & Tesoro Truck Stop.** See display ad this section.

A 99 (159.3 km) **F 259** (416.8 km) **Denali Way Auto.** See display ad this section.

A 99.3 (159.8 km) **F 258.7** (416.3 km) Lakes both sides of highway; watch for floatplanes.

A 99.5 (160.1 km) **F 258.5** (416 km) **H & H Lakeview Restaurant & Lodge.** See display ad this section.

A 99.8 (160.6 km) **F 258.2** (415.5 km) Access road to YMCA camp on Peggy Lake.

A 100.4 (161.6 km) **F 257.6** (414.6 km) *CAUTION: Railroad crossing.*

A 102.2 (164.5 km) **F 255.8** (411.7 km) Paved double-ended turnout to east.

A 102.4 (164.8 km) **F 255.6** (411.3 km) Turnout at Sunshine Road; access to **Sunshine Creek** for fishing via dirt road.

A 104 (167.4 km) **F 254** (408.8 km) **Big Su Lodge.** See display ad this section.

(Continues on page 342)

Talkeetna Spur Road

Distance from George Parks Highway junction (J) at Milepost A 98.7 is shown.

J 0 Junction with the George Parks Highway; visitor center.

J 3.1 (5 km) Turn west on Jubilee Road for bed and breakast. Turn east on Yoder Road (gravel) for **Benka Lake.** Drive in 0.6 mile/1 km on the gravel road, turn left and drive 0.7 mile/1.1 km to lake. Small turnaround space at lake and a steep boat launch; fishing for silvers and Dolly Varden. No camping.

Denali View B&B. This cozy cedar home, off Jubilee Road to west, offers hunting and fishing motif, antiques,

great homemade breakfasts. Located 12 miles south of Talkeetna and midway between Anchorage and Denali Park. View of Denali. Lush gardens. Wonderful, friendly atmosphere. A must for the discerning traveler. HC 89 Box 8360, Talkeetna, AK 99676. Phone/fax (907) 733-2778. [ADVERTISEMENT]

J 5.3 (8.5 km) Answer Creek.

J 7.1 (11.4 km) Question Lake.

J 7.8 (12.6 km) Paradise Lodge.

J 9.2 (14.8 km) Fish Lake private floatplane base.

J 11.5 (18.5 km) Bays Bed and Breakfast.

J 12 (19.3 km) Turn east on paved Comsat Road (unmarked) for **Christianson Lake;** drive in 0.7 mile/1.1 km on Comsat Road, turn left at Christianson Lake Road sign onto gravel road and drive 0.7 mile/1.1 km, turn right and follow signs to floatplane base. Fishing for silvers and rainbow. Good place to observe loons and waterfowl.

J 13 (20.9 km) Large gravel double-ended turnout with interpretive sign and viewpoint at crest of hill. Splendid views of Mount McKinley, Mount Foraker and the Alaska Range above the Susitna River. A must photo stop when the mountains are out. *CAUTION: Watch for traffic.*

J 13.3 (21.4 km) *CAUTION: Alaska Railroad crossing.*

J 13.5 (21.7 km) Talkeetna public library. Gas station

Talkeetna Tesoro. See display ad this section.

J 13.8 (22.2 km) Restaurant and motel.

J 13.9 (22.4 km) RV park.

J 14 (22.5 km) East Talkeetna Road leads to state airport, municipal campground, boat launch on Susitna River and businesses.

J 14.2 (22.9 km) Talkeetna post office (Zip code 99676).

J 14.3 (23 km) Welcome to Beautiful Downtown Talkeetna sign and Talkeetna Historical Society visitor center log cabin; walking tour brochures available. (Description of Talkeetna follows.)

J 14.5 (23.3 km) Talkeetna Spur Road ends at Talkeetna River Park Campground (no facilities).

Talkeetna

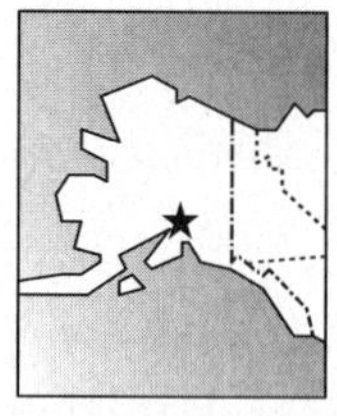

Located on a spur road, north of **Milepost A 98.7** George Parks Highway. **Population:** 441. **Emergency Services: Alaska State Troopers, Fire Department** and **Ambulance,** phone 911 or 733-2556. **Doctor,** phone 733-2708.

Visitor Information: Stop by the Talkeetna Historical Society Museum one block off Main Street opposite the Fairview Inn. Visitor information also available at log cabin at junction of Parks Highway and spur road. Or, write the Chamber of Commerce, P.O. Box 334, Talkeetna 99676.

The National Park Service maintains a ranger station that is staffed full time from mid-April through mid-September and intermittently during the winter. Mountaineering rangers provide information on Denali National Park and climbing within the Alaska Range. A reference library and video program are available to climbers. All climbers must register for climbs of Mount McKinley and Mount Foraker. Mountaineering information may be obtained from Talkeetna Ranger Station, P.O. Box 588, Talkeetna, AK 99676; phone (907) 733-2231.

Elevation: 346 feet/105m. **Radio:** KSKA-FM (PBS). **Television:** Channels 4, 6, 9.

Private Aircraft: Talkeetna airstrip (state airport), adjacent east; elev. 358 feet/109m; length 3,500 feet/1,067m; paved; fuel 100LL, Jet B. Talkeetna village airstrip on Main Street; elev. 346 feet/105m; length 1,200 feet/366m; gravel; village airstrip not recommended for transient aircraft or helicopters (watch for closures and poor conditions).

A Welcome to Beautiful Downtown Talkeetna sign is posted at the town park as you enter Talkeetna's old-fashioned Main Street, the only paved street in town. Log cabins and clapboard homes and businesses line Main Street, which dead ends at the Susitna River. Walk or drive down to the riverside park at the end of Main Street, where there is parking, picnicking and sometimes a volleyball game in progress. There are also fishing and picnicking on the gravel bars of the Susitna.

Talkeetna was one of the pioneer mining and trapping settlements in the upper Susitna River valley. The first settlers came via the Susitna River about 1901 and built roads into the coal, gold and silver mines to the east in the Talkeetna Mountains.

The town reportedly gets its name from an Indian word meaning "where the rivers meet"; the Talkeetna and Chulitna rivers join the Susitna River here. The upper Susitna and Talkeetna

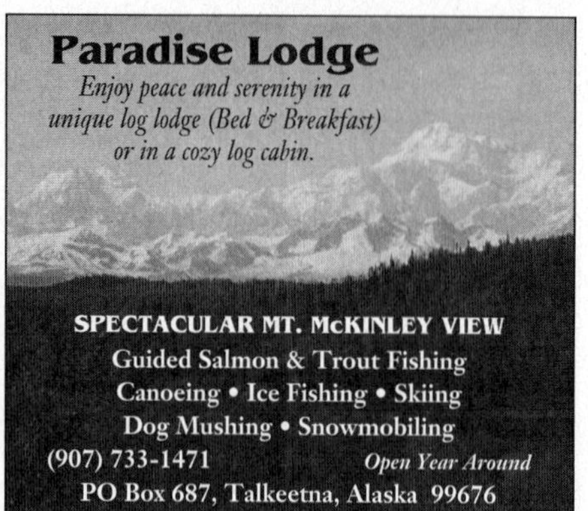

rivers are popular with big game hunters, guides and river runners.

Talkeetna is the jumping-off point for many climbing expeditions to Mount McKinley. Most climbing expeditions use the West Buttress route, pioneered by Bradford Washburn, flying in in specially equipped ski-wheel aircraft from Talkeetna to Kahiltna Glacier. The actual climb on Mount McKinley is made from about 7,000 feet/2,134m (where the planes land) to the summit of the South Peak (elev. 20,320 feet/6,194m). Talkeetna is also headquarters for a private guide service that guides climbing expeditions on Mount McKinley and other peaks in the Alaska Range.

ACCOMMODATIONS

Talkeetna has five motels/hotels, several bed and breakfasts, six restaurants, two gas stations, laundromats, gift and clothing shops, grocery and general stores. Dump station located at Three Rivers Tesoro.

There is a campground with toilets and shelters at the public boat launch (fee charged) just beyond the Swiss Alaska Inn; take East Talkeetna Road (a right turn at Mile 14 on the Spur Road as you approach Talkeetna). There is also camping at Talkeetna River Park located at the end of the Talkeetna Spur Road (Mile 14.5). ▲

Bays Bed and Breakfast. 11.5 miles on Talkeetna Spur Road. New modern log home, three large rooms (no smoking), shared baths, 1.5 miles from downtown Talkeetna. Enjoy flightseeing,

riverboating, fishing. View Mount McKinley. Call (907) 733-1342. Write P.O. Box 527, Talkeetna, AK 99676 for reservations. Open year-round. [ADVERTISEMENT]

Talkeetna Motel, Restaurant and Lounge. Built in 1964 by "Evil Alice" and Sherm Powell, the "Tee-Pee" (nicknamed by oldtimers) became known for its excellent food, fast service and sincere Alaskan hospitality. Today, we also offer private baths, color TV in rooms and lounge, full menu for casual and fine dining. MC/VISA welcome. See display ad this section. [ADVERTISEMENT]

Talkeetna Roadhouse. Authentic "Old Alaska" roadhouse providing comfortable lodging and delicious home-cooked meals since 1944. Full menu, breakfast, lunch and dinner. Home of Alaska's Homestead B-B-Q Sauce, available throughout the state. Family atmosphere. Reasonable rates. Open year-round. We can help you arrange your local tour plans. Summer: fishing, river rafting and jet boat tours. Winter: dog sled tours, northern lights viewing. Step out our front door to your adventure. (907) 733-1351. See display ad this section. [ADVERTISEMENT]

TRANSPORTATION

Air: There are four air taxi services in Talkeetna. Charter service, flightseeing

TALKEETNA ADVERTISERS

Alaska Log Cabin B & B ....Ph. (907) 733-2584
Bays Bed and Breakfast ....Ph. (907) 733-1342
Bikes, Flights, Etc. ....Main St.
Chase-on-the-Susitna Remote Bed & Breakfast .....Ph. (907) 733-3038
Denali Dry Goods ....Main St.
Denali Floats...............Ph. (907) 733-2384
Denali River Guides ....Main St.
Doug Geeting Aviation.................Ph. (907) 733-2366
Hudson Air Service, Inc. ....Main St.
K2 Aviation ....State Airport
Latitude 62° Lodge/ Motel..................................Mile J 13.8
Mahay's Riverboat Service...................Ph. (907) 733-2223
Mountain Gift Shop and Talkeetna Historical Society Visitor Information Center, The............................Main St.
Mt. McKinley Flight Tours ....Main St.
Museum of Northern Adventure ....Mile J 14.2
Paradise Lodge...........Ph. (907) 733-1471
River Beauty Bed & Breakfast ....Ph. (907) 733-2741
Swiss-Alaska Inn ....Ph. (907) 733-2424
Talkeetna Air Taxi ....Ph. (907) 733-2218
Talkeetna & Beyond Bed & Breakfast .....Ph. (907) 733-3050
Talkeetna Gifts and Collectables.........................Mile J 14.2
Talkeetna Motel, Restaurant and Lounge...........Ph. (907) 733-2323
Talkeetna Reflections...................Main St.
Talkeetna River RV Park ....G St. & Main
Talkeetna Riverboat Service.........Main St.
Talkeetna Roadhouse ....Main St.
Three Rivers Tesoro ....Main St.
Trapper John's Bed & Breakfast .....Ph. (907) 733-2354
Ultimate Alaska Experiences...........Ph. (907) 733-2584
Village Arts & Crafts ....Main St.

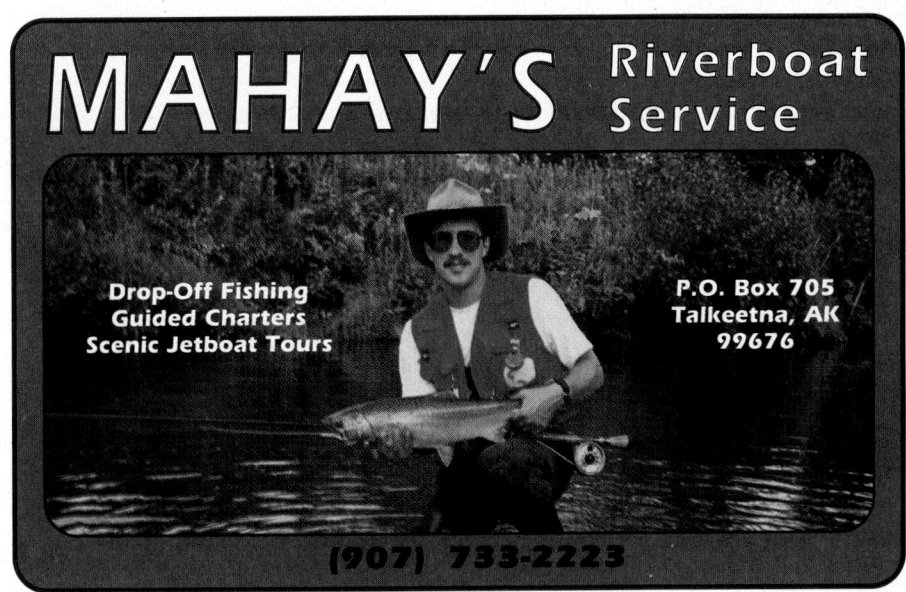

and glacier landings are available. **Railroad:** The Alaska Railroad. **Limousine:** From Anchorage airport and Denali National Park.

ATTRACTIONS

The Talkeetna Historical Society Museum is located one block off Main Street opposite the Fairview Inn. The original one-room schoolhouse, built in 1936, exhibits historical items, local art, a historical library and a display on the late Don Sheldon, famous Alaskan bush pilot. In the Railroad Section House see the impressive 12-foot-by-12-foot scale model of Mount McKinley (Denali) with photographs by Bradford Washburn. A mountaineering display features pioneer and recent climbs of Mount McKinley plus background on the late Ray Genet, who climbed Mount McKinley 25 times. The former railroad depot has a restored ticket office and transportation exhibit. The Ole Dahl cabin, an early trapper/miner's cabin located on the museum grounds, is furnished with period items. Admission: $1 adult, under 12 free. Pick up a walking tour map of Talkeetna's historic sites here. Picnic area adjacent museum. Museum buildings open 10 A.M. to 5 P.M. daily in summer. Reduced hours other seasons. Phone (907) 733-2487. Privately operated guided history tours.

Miners Day. Held the weekend before Memorial Day, this family-oriented event has a trade and craft fair, local cancan dancers, softball tournament, pie auction, a thrilling outhouse race, street dance and parade.

Annual Moose Dropping Festival is held second Saturday in July as a fund-raising project for the museum. Activities include a five-kilometer run and walk, a parade, entertainment, music, barbecue, food and game booths, and, of course, a moose dropping throwing contest.

Riverboat tours up Talkeetna Canyon, Devils Canyon, Chulitna River and Tokositna River are available. Several guides also offer riverboat fishing trips from Talkeetna. Inquire locally for details.

Mt. McKinley Flight Tours. Experience a flight with renowned glacier and flying expert Doug Geeting, who knows the climbers and all the lore and legend of Denali (the great one). You can experience a glacier landing and look up at 5,000-foot walls of ice and rock that will

astound the most world-weary traveler. This flight will definitely be the high point of all your Alaska adventures! Intercom-equipped. Group rates available. Guest house available, $65 per night. Fly-in fishing cabins. Open year-round. For reservations and prices write or call Doug Geeting Aviation, Box 42 MP, Talkeetna, AK 99676; (800) 770-2366 or (907) 733-2366. Fax (907) 733-1000. See display ad in the DENALI NATIONAL PARK section. [ADVERTISEMENT]

The braided Susitna River at Talkeetna. (Jerrianne Lowther, staff)

K2 Aviation. Always something to see — every day, every season. Let K2 help you discover hidden Alaska: mile-high rock walls, icy peaks, twisting glaciers, salmon-filled rivers, hillsides of bear, caribou and sheep, meadows of moose and wildflowers, clear winter days, sunny summer nights. All in the shadow of Mount McKinley. Jim Okonek's K2 Aviation offers: experienced McKinley pilots, glacier landings, fly-in fishing and hunting, remote cabins, climbing expedition

air support, scenic flights, headphones for every passenger, natural history and local lore. Denali Park Grand Tour, Summit Overflight, Wildlife Air Safari and Overnight Park Package. Office at Talkeetna airport. P.O. Box 545, Talkeetna, AK 99676. Phone (907) 733-2291, fax (907) 733-1221. Alaska 800-478-2291. [ADVERTISEMENT]

The Mountain Gift Shop and Talkeetna Historical Society Visitor Information Center. Located in historic log cabin by the famous Welcome to Beautiful Downtown Talkeetna sign. View of Mount McKinley from porch. A fun place to shop with mountain, railroad and moose theme items: books, maps, posters, T-shirts, flags and hand-painted gold pans. Moose nugget items our specialty! Open 10 A.M. to 5:30 P.M. — May 15 to Labor Day. Free town map with list of attractions. [ADVERTISEMENT]

Talkeetna Air Taxi. Fly Mount McKinley with Talkeetna Air Taxi. An awe-inspiring, memorable experience. Tour this vast glimmering world of towering peaks, glaciers and snow. Watch for animals — climbers — and take pictures. Satisfaction guaranteed. Glacier

landings available. Sportfishing and hunting flights, aerial photography. Climbing expedition support. Office at state airport coming into Talkeetna. Follow our signs. Write Box 73-MP, Talkeetna, AK 99676. (907) 733-2218. [ADVERTISEMENT]

Museum of Northern Adventure. Experience highlights of Alaska's exciting history in this colorful collection of 3-D exhibits, featuring life-sized figures. Entertaining, educational and exciting for all age groups. Meander through the historic railroad building, experiencing Alaskana at every turn. Two floors of exhibits. Gift shop, too! Open daily mid-May through Labor Day. Special winter openings by request. Admission charged. Groups welcome. Clean restrooms. Mention this ad and get a discount. Main Street, Box 101, Talkeetna, AK 99676. Phone (907) 733-3999. [ADVERTISEMENT]

Talkeetna Spur Road (continued)

Mahay's Riverboat Service. Fish clear-water streams for all five species of Pacific salmon and trout. Custom-designed jet boats allow access to over 200 miles of prime fishing territory. Guided fishing charters include all equipment needed. Fishing packages are also available that include accommodations, meals and all the "extras." Spend the afternoon exploring an authentic trapper's cabin, viewing nesting bald eagles and sightseeing on the McKinley View river cruise. Drop-off fishing also available at reasonable rates. Credit cards accepted. (907) 733-2223, fax (907) 733-2712. [ADVERTISEMENT]

Talkeetna Gifts and Collectables. "One of the nicest and most complete gift shops in Alaska." Located in a spacious log building with two floors of handmade keepsakes, souvenirs, jewelry, books, Alaskana, birch bowls, quilts and other treasures. Also sealskin slippers, fur accessories, beautiful sweatshirts and sweaters. For the kids, plush toys, puppets and huggable Eskimo dolls. Alaskan foods and sourdough mix. We carry Alaska counted cross-stitch patterns featuring Suzy's exclusive "Alaska Map Sampler." We strive for quality with friendly service. Pan for gold, too. Gold guaranteed. Open year-round. See display ad this section. [ADVERTISEMENT]

Fishing. A Calico (chum) Salmon Derby is held the first three weeks of August. The **Susitna River** basin offers many top fishing streams and lakes, either accessible by road, plane or riverboat.

Return to Milepost A 98.7 George Parks Highway

(Continued from page 337)

A 104.2 (167.7 km) **F 253.8** (408.4 km) Entering Game Management Unit 16A, northbound, Unit 14B southbound.

A 104.3 (167.8 km) **F 253.7** (408.3 km) Bridge over Big Susitna River. State rest area to west on south bank of river; loop road, parking area, tables, firepits, toilets, no drinking water. ▲

Some of the finest stands of white birch in Alaska may be seen for several miles on both sides of the river. This area is also noted for its fiddlehead ferns. The ferns (lady fern, ostrich fern and shield fern) are harvested in the spring, when their young shoots are tightly coiled, resembling a fiddle's head. The fiddleheads should be picked clean of the brown flakes which coat them. (Of the three ferns, ostrich fern is favored because it has the least amount of this coating.) Fiddleheads should be cooked before consumption.

A 104.6 (168.3 km) **F 253.4** (407.8 km) Rabideu Creek access; parking, 0.3 mile/0.5 km trail to mouth of creek. Watch for seasonal flooding.

A 104.8 (168.7 km) **F 253.2** (407.5 km) Double-ended turnout to west.

A 105.9 (170.4 km) **F 252.1** (405.7 km) Rabideaux Creek access and bridge.

A 107.6 (173.2 km) **F 250.4** (403 km) View of Mount McKinley for northbound travelers.

A 114.8 (184.7 km) **F 243.2** (391.4 km) Cluster of businesses (lodges with gift shops, gas and restaurant) serving highway travelers and Trapper Creek the next mile northbound. ▲

Petracach South Denali Visitors Center. Chevron gas, diesel, travelers' supplies, gift shop. Deluxe lodging. Large Good Sam RV park with full hookups and dump station, restrooms, laundry, pay phone. Caravan fuel discounts. Deli and mini-grocery, coffee, ice, etc. Flightseeing and fishing charters. Major credit cards accepted. Phone (907) 733-2302. See large display ad in this section. [ADVERTISEMENT]

A 114.9 (184.9 km) **F 243.1** (391.2 km) **TRAPPER CREEK** (area pop. about 700), at **junction** with Petersville Road. Trapper Creek post office (Zip code 99683). Miners built the Petersville Road in the 1920s and federal homesteading began here in 1948, with settlement continuing through the 1950s and 1960s. The George Parks Highway opened as far as Trapper Creek in 1967. Today it is the southern gateway to Denali park and the Alaska Range, with access via the Petersville Road (description follows). Trapper Creek businesses are located along the Parks Highway and up Petersville Road.

Petersville Road leads west and north from Trapper Creek approximately 40 miles/64 km (no winter maintenance beyond Mile 14). This scenic gravel road (with excellent views of Mount McKinley) goes through a homestead and gold mining area that also contains some new subdivisions. At Mile 17.2/27.7 km is a bed and breakfast. At Mile 18.7/30.1 km is The Forks Roadhouse. Turn down the right fork for the abandoned mining camp of Petersville (four-wheel drive recommended). The left fork leads 0.2 mile/0.3 km to Peters Creek stream. The bridge across Peters Creek is impassable. The road to Petersville is rough and used primarily by miners and trappers beyond The Forks Roadhouse. ▲

The Forks Roadhouse. See display ad this section.

A 115.2 (185.4 km) **F 242.8** (390.7 km) Trapper Creek community park.

A 115.5 (185.9 km) **F 242.5** (390.2 km) **Trapper Creek Trading Post.** See display ad on page 344. ▲

A 115.6 (186 km) **F 242.4** (390.1 km) Highway crosses Trapper Creek.

A 121.1 (194.9 km) **F 236.9** (381.2 km) Chulitna highway maintenance camp.

A 121.5 (195.5 km) **F 236.5** (380.6 km) Easy-to-miss large paved double-ended rest area to east with tables, firepits, drinking water, toilet and interpretive bulletin board. Shade trees; cow parsnip grows lush here.

A 123.4 (198.6 km) **F 234.6** (377.5 km) Wooded area with many dead trees covered with "conks" (a term applied to a type of bracket fungus).

A 126.6 (203.7 km) **F 231.4** (372.4 km) Large paved turnout to east.

A 128.4 (206.6 km) **F 229.6** (369.5 km) Undeveloped parking area below highway by creek.

A 132 (212.4 km) **F 226** (363.7 km) Boundary of Denali State Park (see description next milepost).

A 132.7 (213.6 km) **F 225.3** (362.6 km) Denali State Park entrance sign. This 324,240-acre park has 48 miles/77.2 km of hiking trails. Camping at Troublesome Creek (**Milepost A 137.3**) and at Byers Lake (**Milepost A 147**). Hunting is permitted in the park, but discharge of firearms is prohibited within 0.3 mile of highway or 0.5 mile of a developed facility.

A 132.8 (213.7 km) **F 225.2** (362.4 km) **Chulitna River** bridge. Fishing for grayling, rainbow. Game Management Unit 13E, leaving unit 16A, northbound.

A 134.5 (216.5 km) **F 223.5** (359.7 km) **Mary's McKinley View Lodge.** See display ad on page 344.

A 134.8 (216.9 km) **F 223.2** (359.2 km) Small turnout to east. Springwater piped to road.

A 135.2 (217.6 km) **F 222.8** (358.6 km) Large paved turnout with litter barrels and view of 20,320-foot/6,194-m Mount McKinley; a display board here points out peaks. From here northbound for many miles there are views of glaciers on the southern slopes of the Alaska Range to the west. Ruth, Buckskin and Eldridge glaciers are the most conspicuous.

Ruth Glacier trends southeast through the Great Gorge for 31 miles/50 km. The glacier was named in 1903 by F.A. Cook for his daughter. The Great Gorge was named by mountain climbers in the late 1940s. Nicknamed the Grand Canyon of Alaska, peaks on either side of the gorge tower up to 5,000 feet/1,500m above Ruth Glacier. The gorge opens into Don Sheldon Amphitheater, at the head of Ruth Glacier, where the Don Sheldon mountain house sits. Donald E. Sheldon (1921–75) was a well-known bush pilot who helped map, patrol and aid search and rescue efforts in this area.

Flightseeing trips can be arranged that take you close to Mount McKinley, into the Don Sheldon Amphitheater, through the Great Gorge and beneath the peak of The Mooses Tooth. Inquire at Petracach, **Mile-**

Fall colors along the shore at Byers Lake campground. (Bill Sherwonit)

post A 114.8, or with air taxi operators in Talkeetna and in the national park.

Peaks to be sighted, left to right, along the next 20 miles/32.2 km to the west are: Mount Hunter (elev. 14,573 feet/4,442m); Mount Huntington (elev. 12,240 feet/ 3,731m); Mount Barrille (elev. 7,650 feet/ 2,332m); and Mount Dickey (elev. 9,845 feet/3,001m).

A 137.3 (221 km) **F 220.7** (355.1 km) Troublesome Creek bridge. Lower Troublesome Creek state recreation site has 10 campsites, $6/night camping fee per vehicle or annual pass, day-use area with sheltered picnic sites, toilets, water and litter barrels. Lower Troublesome Creek trailhead. This is usually a clear runoff stream, not silted by glacial flour. The stream heads in a lake and flows 14 miles/22.5 km to the Chulitna River.

Troublesome Creek, rainbow, grayling and salmon (king salmon fishing prohibited); June, July, August and September.

A 137.6 (221.4 km) **F 220.4** (354.7 km) Upper Troublesome Creek trailhead and parking area. Trails to Byers Lake (15 miles/ 24 km) and Tarn Point, elev. 2,881 feet/ 878m (10.8 miles/17.3 km). *NOTE: Trailhead and trail to Mile 5.5 closed from mid-July through end of season due to the high concentration of bears feeding on spawning salmon.*

A 139.9 (225.1 km) **F 218.1** (351 km) Paved turnout with litter barrels to west.

A 143.2 (230.5 km) **F 214.8** (345.7 km) Large double-ended turnout to east.

A 143.9 (231.6 km) **F 214.1** (344.6 km) Bridge over Byers Creek.

A 145.7 (234.5 km) **F 212.3** (341.6 km) Paved turnout to west.

A 147 (236.6 km) **F 211** (339.6 km) **Byers Lake** state campground with 66 sites, $8/night camping fee or annual pass, picnic tables, firepits, water, toilets (wheelchair accessible) and access to Byers Lake (electric motors permitted). Fishing for grayling, burbot, rainbow, lake trout and whitefish. Remote campsite 1.8-mile/2.9-km hike from campground (see directions posted on bulletin board). Hiking trail to Curry Ridge and south to Troublesome Creek. *CAUTION: Black bears frequent campground. Keep a clean camp.*

A 147.2 (236.9 km) **F 210.8** (339.2 km) Alaska Veterans Memorial loop road to rest area with toilets (wheelchair accessible), picnic shelter, drinking water, picnic tables and firepits. There is a unique concrete memorial — five sculpted upright slabs, statue and flagpole — at this wayside honoring the armed forces.

A 155.6 (250.4 km) **F 202.4** (325.7 km) For the next mile northbound, there are views of Eldridge Glacier to the left. The snout of the glacier is 6 miles/9.7 km from the road. The Fountain River heads at the terminus of the glacier and flows into the Chulitna.

A 156.2 (251.4 km) **F 201.8** (324.8 km) Chulitna River Lodge.

NOTE: No gas available from here north to ***Milepost A 188.5.***

AREA FISHING (fly in): Lucy Lake, lake trout and grayling, use spinners and spoons, June and July, 10-minute flight. **Spink Lake**, rainbow, use spinners and spoons, July, August and September, 15-minute flight. **Portage Creek**, rainbow, grayling and salmon, use spoons, spinners, flies, July, August and September, 20-minute flight. **Chulitna Lake**, rainbow, July, August and September, 20-minute flight. **Donut Lake**, Dolly Varden, use spinners, spoons, flies, July and August, 20-minute flight. **Bull Lake**, lake trout and grayling, use spoons, spinners, July and August, 20-minute flight.

A 156.4 (251.7 km) **F 201.6** (324.4 km) **Denali Outpost**. New for 1994: Bed and breakfast cabins for rent in beautiful Denali State Park. We also plan on a late summer 1994 opening date for our new cafe and gas station with diesel and emergency road service. We'll be open year-round with hiking trails nearby in summer and lots of cross-country ski opportunities in winter. Call (907) 733-1321 (radio phone) or (907) 373-4609 for reservations and information. KM and Matol products available. Your hosts: Reinhard and Beverly Grenz, P.O. Box 13069, Trapper Creek, AK 99683. [ADVERTISEMENT]

A 157.7 (253.8 km) **F 200.3** (322.3 km) Small paved turnout to west.

A 159.4 (256.5 km) **F 198.6** (319.6 km) Double-ended paved turnout to west.

A 159.9 (257.3 km) **F 198.1** (318.8 km) Parking area by Horseshoe Creek.

A 160.8 (258.8 km) **F 197.2** (317.4 km) The highway makes a steep descent northbound with moderate S-curves to Little Coal Creek.

A 161 (259.1 km) **F 197** (317 km) Large gravel turnout to east.

A 162.4 (261.4 km) **F 195.6** (314.8 km) Large paved turnout to west; Denali viewpoint.

A 162.7 (261.8 km) **F 195.3** (314.3 km) Small paved turnout to east. Watch for beaver pond to west northbound.

A 163.1 (262.5 km) **F 194.9** (313.6 km) Large double-ended paved turnout to west.

A 163.2 (262.6 km) **F 194.8** (313.5 km) Bridge over Little Coal Creek.

Coal Creek, rainbow, grayling and salmon, July through September.

A 163.8 (263.6 km) **F 194.2** (312.5 km) Little Coal Creek trailhead and parking area. According to park rangers, this trail offers the easiest access (one-and-one-half-hour hike) to alpine area within Denali State Park.

A 165.6 (266.5 km) **F 192.4** (309.6 km) A small stream passes under the road; paved turnouts on both sides of highway. Good berry picking in the fall.

A 168.5 (271.2 km) **F 189.5** (305 km) Denali State Park boundary sign.

A 169 (272 km) **F 189** (304.2 km) *CAUTION: Railroad crossing.* A solar collector here helps power the warning signals.

Denali State Park boundary (leaving park northbound, entering park southbound).

A 170.3 (274 km) **F 187.7** (302.1 km) Paved viewpoint area to west.

A 171 (275.2 km) **F 187** (300.9 km) There are several small turnouts next 5 miles/8 km northbound.

A 174 (280 km) **F 184** (296.1 km) Bridge over Hurricane Gulch; rest area. From the south end of the bridge, scramble through alders up the east bank of the gulch to find photographers' trail (unmarked). A 0.3-mile/0.4-km trail along edge of Hurricane Gulch offers good views of the bridge span and gulch. A pleasant walk, good berry picking in the fall. *Do not go too near the edge.* Parking areas at both ends of bridge.

Construction costs for the bridge were approximately $1.2 million. The 550-foot/168-m deck of the bridge is 260 feet/79m above Hurricane Creek, not as high as the railroad bridge that spans the gulch near the Chulitna River. From this bridge the highway begins a gradual descent northbound to Honolulu Creek.

A 176 (283.2 km) **F 182** (292.9 km) Paved turnout to east. There are several small turnouts next 5 miles/8 km southbound.

A 176.5 (284 km) **F 181.5** (292.1 km) Double-ended gravel turnout to west with view of the Alaska Range. Highway descends long grade northbound.

A 177.8 (286.1 km) **F 180.2** (290 km) Paved turnout and view of eroded bluffs to west.

A 178.1 (286.6 km) **F 179.9** (289.5 km) Bridge over Honolulu Creek. The highway begins a gradual ascent northbound to Broad Pass, the gap in the Alaska Range crossed by both the railroad and highway. Undeveloped parking areas below highway on the creek.

A 179.5 (288.9 km) **F 178.5** (287.3 km) Paved turnout to west by small lake. In early September blueberries are plentiful for the next 25 miles/40 km.

A 180 (289.7 km) **F 178** (286.5 km) Small paved turnout to west by small lake.

A 183.2 (294.8 km) **F 174.8** (281.3 km) Large paved turnout to west of highway. Look to the west across the Chulitna River for dramatic view of the Alaska Range.

A 184.5 (296.9 km) **F 173.5** (279.2 km) Paved turnout to west.

Alaska Veterans Memorial at Milepost A 147.2. (Bruce M. Herman)

A 185 (297.7 km) **F 173** (278.4 km) East Fork DOT/PF highway maintenance station.

A 185.1 (297.9 km) **F 172.9** (278.3 km) Bridge over East Fork Chulitna River.

A 185.6 (298.7 km) **F 172.4** (277.4 km) East Fork rest area (no sign at turnoff) on right northbound. A 0.5-mile/0.8-km paved loop gives access to a gravel picnic area with overnight parking, 23 tables, concrete fireplaces, picnic shelter, pit toilets, water pump, dump station, restrooms with cold water and flush toilets. The rest area is in a bend of the East Fork Chulitna River amid a healthy growth of Alaskan spruce and birch. Cut wood is often available.

A 186.4 (300 km) **F 171.6** (276.2 km) Small paved turnout to east.

A 187.5 (301.8 km) **F 170.5** (274.4 km) Paved double-ended turnout to west; small paved turnout east side of highway.

A 188.5 (303.4 km) **F 169.5** (272.8 km) **The Igloo.** 50 miles south of entrance to Denali National Park. Unleaded, regular, diesel fuels. Ask for 5¢ discount for cash fill-up. Caravan discounts. Postcards, candy, soft drinks, snacks. Many quality Alaskan gifts and souvenirs. Specialty T-shirts and sweats. Open year-round. (907) 768-2622. Free camper parking with fill-up. [ADVERTISEMENT]

A 189.9 (305.6 km) **F 168.1** (270.5 km) Gravel double-ended turnout. Watch for beaver dam to east northbound.

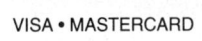

A 191.5 (308.2 km) **F 166.5** (267.9 km) Large paved turnout to west. Look for cotton grass.

A 194.3 (312.7 km) **F 163.7** (263.4 km) *CAUTION: Railroad crossing.*

A 194.5 (313 km) **F 163.5** (263.1 km) Bridge over Middle Fork Chulitna River. Undeveloped parking area southwest of bridge below the highway. *CAUTION: Windy area through Broad Pass.*

A 195 (313.8 km) **F 163** (262.3 km) Entering Broad Pass northbound. Good views of Broad Pass.

A 201.1 (323.6 km) **F 156.9** (252.5 km) Large paved parking area to east with mountain view.

A 201.3 (324 km) **F 156.7** (252.2 km) Summit of Broad Pass (not signed). Broad Pass is one of the most beautiful areas on the George Parks Highway. A mountain valley, bare in some places, dotted with scrub spruce in others, and surrounded by mountain peaks, there's a top-of-the-world feeling for the traveler, although it is one of the lowest summits along the North American mountain system. Named in 1898 by George Eldridge and Robert Muldrow, the 2,300-foot/701-m pass, sometimes called Caribou Pass, marks the divide between the drainage of rivers and streams that empty into Cook Inlet and those that empty into the Yukon River.

Orange towers of weather service station building west of highway.

A 202.1 (325.2 km) **F 155.9** (250.9 km) Boundary of Matanuska–Susitna Borough.

A 203.1 (326.9 km) **F 154.9** (249.3 km) *CAUTION: Railroad crossing.*

A 203.7 (327.8 km) **F 154.3** (248.3 km) Paved parking area with view to east.

A 206.5 (332.3 km) **F 151.5** (243.8 km) Watch for frost heaves next 3 miles/ 4.8 km southbound.

A 208 (334.7 km) **F 150** (241.4 km) Turnout to west at end of bridge over Pass Creek; blueberries in season.

A 209.4 (337 km) **F 148.6** (239.1 km) Large gravel parking area to east.

A 209.5 (337.1 km) **F 148.5** (239 km) Bridge over Jack River; paved turnout.

A 209.7 (337.4 km) **F 148.3** (238.7 km) **Reindeer Mtn. Lodge.** Lodging, towing, gifts, fishing licenses, snacks and furs. Beautiful view of Mount McKinley. Rooms have private baths and color TV. Beautiful log office has ornate wood carvings and two stuffed moose on porch. Open year-round. Wildlife, scenery, skiing, snowmobiling, fishing, hunting, hiking or relaxing. Call (907) 768-2420 or fax (907) 768-2942. Write Box 7, Cantwell, AK 99729. [ADVERTISEMENT]

A 209.9 (337.8 km) **F 148.1** (238.3 km) **Junction** of the George Parks Highway with the Denali Highway. **CANTWELL** post office and school, as well as a motel, lodge, restaurant, grocery and gas stations are located here. **Emergency Services: Alaska State Troopers**, phone 768-2202. **Ambulance**, phone 768-2982. The original town of Cantwell, 1.8 miles/2.9 km east of this junction, has a cafe, bar and liquor store. Turn west on the Denali Highway for Cantwell, turn east for Paxson (see DENALI HIGHWAY section for description of Cantwell and Denali Highway log).

Backwoods Lodge. See display ad this section.

Cantwell Lodge. See display ad this section.

A 210 (338 km) **F 148** (238.2 km) Cantwell post office (Zip code 99729).

A 210.2 (338.3 km) **F 147.8** (237.9 km) **Parkway Gift Shop.** See display ad this section.

A 211.5 (340.4 km) **F 146.5** (235.8 km) Paved parking area to west.

A 212.7 (342.3 km) **F 145.3** (233.8 km) Gravel turnout to west by Nenana River. Watch for large beaver dam to west southbound.

A 213.9 (344.2 km) **F 144.1** (231.9 km) Paved double-ended turnout to west among tall white spruce and fireweed.

A 215.3 (346.5 km) **F 142.7** (229.6 km) Access road to Nenana River, which parallels the highway northbound.

A 215.7 (347.1 km) **F 142.3** (229 km) First bridge northbound over the Nenana River. Highway narrows northbound.

A 216.2 (347.9 km) **F 141.8** (228.2 km) Entering Game Management Unit 20A and leaving unit 13E northbound.

A 216.3 (348.1 km) **F 141.7** (228 km) Paved double-ended turnout to west. Good spot for photos of Panorama Mountain (elev. 5,778 feet/1,761m), the prominent peak visible to the east.

A 217.6 (350.2 km) **F 140.4** (225.9 km) Small gravel turnout to west.

A 218.6 (351.8 km) **F 139.4** (224.3 km) Double-ended turnout to west with beautiful view of Nenana River.

A 219 (352.4 km) **F 139** (223.7 km) Slide area: Watch for rocks next 0.4 mile/0.6 km northbound.

A 219.8 (353.7 km) **F 138.2** (222.4 km) Paved double-ended turnout to west overlooking Nenana River.

A 220 (354 km) **F 138** (222.1 km) Slime Creek.

A 220.2 (354.4 km) **F 137.8** (221.8 km) Wide gravel turnout to east.

A 222.2 (357.6 km) **F 135.8** (218.5 km) Large, paved double-ended turnout to west beside Nenana River slough. Snow poles beside roadway guide snowplows in winter.

A 223.9 (360.3 km) **F 134.1** (215.8 km) **Carlo Creek Lodge.** (907) 683-2576, 683-2573. 12 miles south of Denali Park entrance. 32 wooded acres bordered by beautiful Carlo Creek, the Nenana River and Denali National Park. Cozy log cabins with own bathroom and shower on creek. RV park, dump station, tent sites, large barbecue pit with roof. Public bathrooms with showers. Small general store, propane, gift shop with Alaskan made gifts from fur to lace. Information and pay phone. Walking distance to The Perch Restaurant. See display ad this section. [ADVERTISEMENT] ▲

A 224 (360.5 km) **F 134** (215.7 km) **The Perch.** A beautiful new restaurant-bar perched on a private hill. Spectacular dining, specializes in freshly baked bread, seafood and steaks. Also, take-out giant cinnamon rolls. Breakfast 6 A.M. to 11 A.M. Open for dinner daily, Memorial Day weekend through September. Sleeping cabins with central bath, one with kitchenette, beside Carlo Creek. Owners/operators, Jerry and Elaine Pollock. (907) 683-2523. HC2 Box 1525, Healy, AK 99743. See display ad in the DENALI NATIONAL PARK section. [ADVERTISEMENT]

A 224 (360.5 km) **F 134** (215.7 km) Bridge over Carlo Creek.

McKinley Wilderness Lodge. Bed and breakfast on the banks of beautiful Carlo Creek, 13 miles south of park entrance. Large, private sleeping cabins, central bath and shower. Continental breakfast. Park information, tour assistance. Reservations: (907) 683-2277. P.O. Box 89, Denali Park, AK 99755. See display ad in DENALI NATIONAL PARK section. [ADVERTISEMENT]

A 226 (363.7 km) **F 132** (212.4 km) Fang Mountain (elev. 6,736 feet/2,053m) may be visible to the west through the slash in the mountains.

A 229 (368.5 km) **F 129** (207.6 km) **Denali Cabins.** Private cabins with bath, outdoor hot tubs, complimentary coffee and extensive information about Denali National Park. Seasonal service mid-May through mid-September. VISA, MasterCard accepted. Winter: (907) 258-0134 or summer: (907) 683-2643. See display ad in DENALI NATIONAL PARK section. [ADVERTISEMENT]

A 229.7 (369.7 km) **F 128.3** (206.5 km) Paved turnout to west.

A 231.1 (371.9 km) **F 126.9** (204.2 km) **Mt. McKinley Village Lodge.** McKinley Village Lodge is convenient to all Denali National Park activities. This comfortable lodge is located on a quiet stretch of the Nenana River. Lounge with light dining, coffee shop, gift shop, complete tour and raft arrangements and transfers. [ADVERTISEMENT]

Sunrise bathes Mount McKinley in pink. (Loren Taft)

A 231.1 (371.9 km) **F 126.9** (204.2 km) **Denali Grizzly Bear Cabins & Campground.** South boundary Denali National Park. AAA approved. Drive directly to your individual kitchen, sleeping, or tent cabin with its old-time Alaskan atmosphere overlooking scenic Nenana River. Two conveniently located buildings with toilets, sinks, coin-operated hot showers. Advance cabin reservations suggested. Tenting and RV campsites also available in peaceful lower wooded area. Hookups. Propane. Caravans welcome! Hot coffee and rolls, ice cream, snacks, groceries, ice, liquor store, Alaskan gifts. Specialty sweatshirts. VISA and MasterCard accepted. Owned and operated by a pioneer Alaskan family. Reservations (907) 683-2696 (summer); (907) 457-2924 (winter). See display ad in DENALI NATIONAL PARK section. [ADVERTISEMENT] ▲

A 231.1 (371.9 km) **F 126.9** (204.2 km) **Denali River Cabins & RV Park.** Located on the banks of the Nenana River, at the border of Denali National Park, our facilities offer the ideal base for your Denali Park experience. There are 30 cabins on the site with hot tubs for guest use. The cozy cedar cabins are fully furnished with private or centralized bath overlooking the river. New sun deck right on the river, looking into Denali Park. 1-800-230-PARK. See display ad in DENALI NATIONAL PARK section. [ADVERTISEMENT] ▲

A 231.3 (372.2 km) **F 126.7** (203.9 km) Crabb's Crossing, second bridge northbound over the Nenana River.

At the north end of this bridge is the boundary of Denali National Park and Preserve. From here north for 6.8 miles/10.9 km the George Parks Highway is within the boundaries of the park and travelers must abide by park rules. No discharge of firearms permitted.

A 233.1 (375.1 km) **F 124.9** (201 km) Gravel turnout to east.

A 234.1 (376.7 km) **F 123.9** (199.4 km) Double-ended turnout with litter barrels to east; scenic viewpoint. No overnight parking or camping. Mount Fellows (elev. 4,476 feet/1,364m) to the east. The constantly changing shadows make this an excellent camera subject. Exceptionally beautiful in the evening. To the southeast stands Pyramid Peak (elev. 5,201 feet/1,585m).

A 235.1 (378.4 km) **F 122.9** (197.8 km) *CAUTION: Railroad crossing.*

A 236.7 (380.9 km) **F 121.3** (195.2 km) Alaska Railroad crosses over highway. From this point the highway begins a steep descent northbound to Riley Creek.

A 237.2 (381.7 km) **F 120.8** (194.4 km) Riley Creek bridge.

A 237.3 (381.9 km) **F 120.7** (194.2 km) Entrance to Denali National Park and Preserve (formerly Mount McKinley National Park) to west. Fresh water fill-up hose and dump station 0.2 mile/0.3 km from junction on Park Road; Visitor Access Center is 0.5 mile/0.8 km from the highway junction. Campsites within the park are available on a first-come, first-served basis; sign up at the

Visitor Access Center. You may also pick up schedules for the shuttle bus service at the Visitor Access Center (private vehicle access to the park is restricted). See DENALI NATIONAL PARK section for details. Highway businesses (lodges, cabins, campground, restaurants) serving park visitors are located both south and north of the park entrance between Cantwell and Healy.

A 238 (383 km) **F 120** (193.4 km) Third bridge northbound over the Nenana River. The 4.8 miles/7.7 km of road and seven bridges in the rugged Nenana Canyon cost $7.7 million to build.

Sugarloaf Mountain (elev. 4,450 feet/ 1,356m), to the east, is closed to the hunting of Dall sheep, which are regularly sighted in the early and late summer months. Mount Healy (elev. 5,716 feet/1,742m) is to the west.

Southbound for 6.8 miles/10.9 km the George Parks Highway is within the boundaries of Denali National Park and Preserve and travelers must abide by park rules. No discharge of firearms.

A 238.1 (383.2 km) **F 119.9** (193 km) **Denali Raft Adventures.** Come with the original Nenana River rafters! Paddleboats, too! Age 5 or older welcome, seven departures daily. White water or scenic floats. Get away to untouched wilderness! two-hour,

four-hour and six-hour trips. See display ad in DENALI NATIONAL PARK section. Phone (907) 683-2234. VISA, MasterCard accepted. [ADVERTISEMENT]

A 238.3 (383.5 km) **F 119.7** (192.6 km) Kingfisher Creek.

A 238.5 (383.8 km) **F 119.5** (192.3 km) Alaska flag display features a 10-by-15-foot/ 3-by-5-m state flag and plaques detailing history of flag design and song.

A 238.5 (383.8 km) **F 119.5** (192.3 km) **McKinley/Denali Steakhouse and Salmon Bake.** Satisfy that hearty Alaskan appetite at a real home-style barbecue restaurant, featuring char-broiled burgers, steaks, sandwiches, fresh salmon and halibut, tender beef ribs, barbecued chicken with rice pilaf, baked beans, extensive salad bar, homemade soups and desserts. Rustic heated indoor seating with majestic view of mountains.

Free shuttle from all local hotels. Sourdough breakfasts. Large selection of postcards in our upstairs gift shop. T-shirts, sweatshirts and ice for sale. Pay phone. Open daily 5 A.M. to 11 P.M. in summer. Phone (907) 683-2733. See display ad in DENALI NATIONAL PARK section. [ADVERTISEMENT]

A 238.5 (383.8 km) **F 119.5** (192.3 km) **McKinley/Denali Gift Shop.** Largest gift shop in park area — upstairs at McKinley/ Denali Steakhouse and Salmon Bake. Largest selection of Mount McKinley and Denali National Park T-shirts and sweatshirts. Hundreds of souvenirs and gifts. Photo calendars and postcards. Open 5 A.M. to 11 P.M. Call for free shuttle service. [ADVERTISEMENT]

The George Parks Highway winds through the rugged Nenana River canyon. (Ruth Fairall)

A 238.5 (383.8 km) **F 119.5** (192.3 km) **McKinley/Denali Cabins.** Economy tent cabins with electric heat and lights from $60. Closest full-service facility to park entrance, wildlife shuttles. Close to raft trips, store, gift shop, gas. Beds, linens, blankets. Central showers. Pay phone. Some cabins with private baths. Shuttle to visitor center, railroad depot available. Free visitor information. Call us for reservations on many area activities. Reservations: (907) 683-2258 or 683-2733 or write: Box 90M, Denali Park, AK 99755. See display ad in DENALI NATIONAL PARK section. [ADVERTISEMENT]

A 238.5 (383.8 km) **F 119.5** (192.3 km) **Denali Crow's Nest Log Cabins and the Overlook Bar & Grill.** Open mid-May to mid-September, offering the finest view in

area. Close to park entrance. Authentic Alaska log cabins with hotel comforts; all rooms with private bath. Courtesy transportation. Hot tubs, tour bookings. Dine on steaks, seafood, burgers, salmon and halibut indoors or on the deck at The Overlook Bar & Grill. 64 varieties of beer, four draft beers; meals 11 A.M. to 11 P.M. Bar open till midnight. For restaurant courtesy shuttle from all local hotels, call (907) 683-2723, fax (907) 683-2323. See display ad in DENALI NATIONAL PARK section. [ADVERTISEMENT]

A 238.5 (383.8 km) **F 119.5** (192.3 km) **Denali Wilderness Lodge** is Alaska's historic fly-in wilderness lodge — an authentic bush homestead nestled in the pristine Wood River Valley just outside Denali Park. The bush plane flight to the lodge, over the mountains and glaciers of the Alaska Range,

is spectacular. Comfortable accommodations, gourmet meals, naturalist programs, horseback riding, nature/photo walks and hikes, bird-watching, wildlife museum. This is the Alaska of your dreams! Overnight packages and day trips available. Free brochure. 1-800-

541-9779. See display ad: DENALI NATIONAL PARK section. [ADVERTISEMENT]

A 238.6 (384 km) **F 119.4** (192.2 km) Denali Princess (formerly Harper) Lodge.

A 238.7 (384.1 km) **F 119.3** (192 km) **Mt. McKinley Motor Lodge.** We specialize in serving the highway traveler. Close to park entrance. Rooms with full bath, color TV, beautiful park view. Front door parking, out-

door barbecue area. Reasonable rates. Central booking for all park activities. Your hosts: Rick and Keri Zarcone. (907) 683-1240 (summer); (907) 683-2567 (anytime). See display ad in the DENALI NATIONAL PARK section. [ADVERTISEMENT]

A 238.8 (384.3 km) **F 119.2** (191.8 km) **Sourdough Cabins.** Office and front desk are located adjacent to the McKinley Raft Tours office. Sourdough offers brand new individual heated cabins, nestled in a spruce forest located below the office, away from the highway noise. Phone (907) 683-2773, fax (907) 683-2357. VISA, MasterCard accepted. See display ad in the DENALI NATIONAL PARK section. [ADVERTISEMENT] ▲

A 238.9 (384.5 km) **F 119.1** (191.7 km) **Northern Lights Photo Symphony Theatre/Northern Lights Gift Shop.** Come experience a Northern Lights or Denali Park Photo Symphony on a 34-foot-wide screen. These two multi-image presentations are one of a kind, entertaining and informative displays of the aurora borealis or Denali National Park. Stop by for show times and

tickets. Don't miss Denali's largest gift shop in a beautiful, natural log building next door, specializing in quality Alaskan gifts. Full mount, world-class polar bear on display. Groceries at Denali General Store. Located 1.5 miles north of park entrance. Large parking area, picnic tables. VISA/MasterCard. Dont miss this attraction! P.O. Box 65, Denali Park, AK 99755. Phone (907) 683-4000. [ADVERTISEMENT]

A 238.9 (384.5 km) **F 119.1** (191.7 km) **Alaska Cabin Nite Dinner Theatre.** Two locations: McKinley Chalet Resort and Mt. McKinley Village Lodge. Sourdough style salmon and ribs dinner served family style in beautiful handcrafted log cabin. Dinner is followed by a rousing 40-minute wilderness revue. Two seatings nightly. See display ad in DENALI NATIONAL PARK section. [ADVERTISEMENT]

A 238.9 (384.5 km) **F 119.1** (191.7 km) **McKinley Chalet Resort,** 288 two-room mini-suites in chalet-style cedar lodges overlooking the Nenana River. Dining room, deli, lounge, gift shop. Indoor swimming pool, hot tub. Sauna and exercise room. Home of Alaska Cabin Nite Theatre. Phone (907) 276-7234. See display ad in DENALI NATIONAL PARK section. [ADVERTISEMENT]

A 239 (384.6 km) **F 119** (191.5 km) Miniature golf.

A 240.1 (386.4 km) **F 117.9** (189.7 km) Bridge over Ice Worm Gulch. *CAUTION: Rock slide areas north- and southbound. Slow down.* High winds in the Nenana Canyon can make this stretch of road dangerous for campers and motorhomes.

WARNING: The highway has many sharp curves. Do not park along the highway. Use the many parking areas provided.

A 240.2 (386.6 km) **F 117.8** (189.6 km) Hornet Creek bridge. Paved double-ended turnout to west beside Nenana River.

A 240.4 (386.9 km) **F 117.6** (189.3 km) **The Last Resort at Denali.** See display ad this section.

A 240.5 (387 km) **F 117.5** (189.1 km) Large gravel parking area to west by river.

A 240.7 (387.4 km) **F 117.3** (188.8 km) Paved double-ended turnout to west beside river.

A 241 (387.7 km) **F 117** (188.3 km) Paved turnout to west.

A 241.2 (388.2 km) **F 116.8** (188 km) Bridge over Fox Creek; gravel road to creek. Large gravel turnout to west. Slide area next 0.4 mile/0.6 km northbound.

A 241.7 (389 km) **F 116.3** (187.2 km) Large gravel turnout to west.

A 242.3 (389.9 km) **F 115.7** (186.2 km) Paved double-ended turnout to west.

A 242.4 (390.1 km) **F 115.6** (186 km) Dragonfly Creek bridge; paved double-ended turnout to west.

A 242.8 (390.7 km) **F 115.2** (185.4 km) Paved double-ended turnout to west. *CAUTION: Windy area next mile northbound.*

A 242.9 (390.9 km) **F 115.1** (185.2 km) Moody Bridge. The fourth bridge northbound over the Nenana River. This bridge measures 174 feet/53m from its deck to the bottom of the canyon. Dall sheep can be spotted from the bridge. Entering Game Management Unit 20A northbound, 20C southbound.

A 243.6 (392 km) **F 114.4** (184.1 km) Bridge over Bison Gulch. Paved viewpoint to east. A steep grade follows northbound, end wind area.

A 244.1 (392.8 km) **F 113.9** (183.3 km) Paved turnout to east. Watch for frost heaves next 1 mile/1.6 km northbound.

A 244.6 (393.6 km) **F 113.4** (182.5 km) Bridge over Antler Creek.

A 245.1 (394.4 km) **F 112.9** (181.7 km) **Denali RV Park & Motel.** 14 newly remodeled, budget motel rooms. Full and partial RV hookups; 90 sites with 30-amp electric, most with water. Level sites, pull-throughs, easy access from highway. Dump station, good TV reception, pay phones. Individual restrooms with private showers. TV lounge, outdoor gathering area. Caravans welcome. Reasonable rates. VISA, MasterCard accepted. Located 8 miles north of park entrance. Close to all park facilities. Beautiful mountain views. Hiking trails. We'll be happy to book your reservations for national park wildlife tours, rafting, flightseeing, dinner theater, etc. Phone (907) 683-1500. 1-800-478-1501 in Alaska. Box 155, Denali Park, AK 99755. See display ad in DENALI NATIONAL PARK section. [ADVERTISEMENT] ▲

A 245.6 (395.2 km) **F 112.4** (180.9 km) Watch for rough road, frost heaves and dips 0.4 mile/0.6 km northbound.

A 246.9 (397.3 km) **F 111.1** (178.8 km) Paved turnout to east with litter barrels and beautiful view of Healy area.

A 247 (397.5 km) **F 111** (178.6 km) Side

road leads 1 mile/1.6 km to Otto Lake, 5 miles/8 km to Black Diamond Coal Mine. Primitive parking area on lakeshore (0.8-mile/1.3-km drive in) with toilet, litter barrels, shallow boat launch. Denali hostel. Access to bed and breakfasts.

Healy Heights Bed & Breakfast. 12 miles north of Denali National Park entrance. Beautiful rural setting on 12 private wooded acres overlooking the Alaska Range. Four secluded, tastefully furnished cedar cabins with decks and private baths. Two with kitchens. One large two-bedroom cabin. Hearty self-serve continental breakfast stocked in each cabin. Log/rock sauna. VISA/MasterCard. Brochure: Box 277, Healy, AK 99743. Phone/fax (907) 683-2639. [ADVERTISEMENT]

Otto Lake R.V. Park and Campground. Beautiful mountain views from primitive lakeside RV and tent sites, 0.5 mile west of Parks Highway on Otto Lake Road. Spacious and secluded sites with picnic tables, firepits, firewood, potable water, toilets and dump station. Located 9.7 miles north of Denali National Park entrance. [ADVERTISEMENT] ▲

Homestead Bed & Breakfast. See display ad this section.

A 248.5 (399.9 km) **F 109.5** (176.2 km) **McKinley KOA Kampground.** One of the nicest campgrounds around; 92 sites, 13 full hookups, 47 electrical. Only store building is seen from the highway. Laundromat, showers (private), pay phone, ice, groceries, Alaska gifts. Wooded landscape, picnic tables, grills, firewood and Alaska

movie. Caravans, groups welcome. Fax service available. Propane available. Reservations recommended. Write Box 340MP, Healy, AK 99743. Phone (907) 683-2379, fax (907) 683-2281. In Alaska call 1-800-478-2562. [ADVERTISEMENT] ▲

A 248.5 (399.9 km) **F 109.5** (176.2 km) Paved turnout with litter barrel to east. Looking south, Mount Healy is visible just west of the highway; first mountain east of the highway is Sugarloaf; to the northeast is Dora Peak (elev. 5,572 feet/1,698m).

A 248.7 (400.2 km) **F 109.3** (175.9 km) Healy Spur Road to community of Healy (description follows); food, gas and lodging. Homes and businesses of this growing Alaska community are widely dispersed along the highway, spur road and east of the highway toward the Nenana River. A hotel and several bed and breakfasts are located along the spur road.

Dome Home Bed, Breakfast and Hospitality is a 6,200-foot geodestic home run year-round by the Miller Family and located one turn and 15 minutes from Denali National Park. The Dome has eight bedrooms, six baths, two living rooms, sauna, fireplace, decks, and large off-street parking on 2.75 wooded acres. The Millers are happy to advise or arrange your Denali Park vacation. Very reasonable rates. MasterCard and VISA accepted. Call (907) 683-1239 or write Box 262, Healy, AK 99743 for free brochure. [ADVERTISEMENT]

Healy

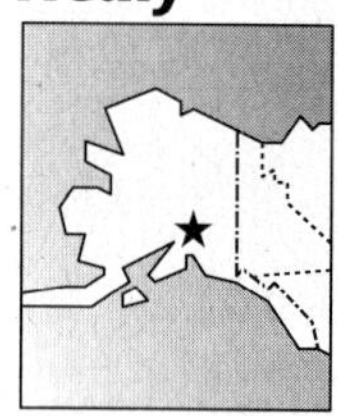

A **248.8** (400.4 km) **F 109.2** (175.7 km) Located on a spur road off the George Parks Highway. **Population:** 487. **Emergency Services: Alaska State Troopers,** phone 683-2232. **Fire Department,** Tri–Valley Volunteer Fire Dept., phone 911 or 683-2223. **Clinic,** Healy Clinic, located on 2nd floor of Tri–Valley Community Center at Mile 0.5 Usibelli Spur Road, phone 683-2211 or 911 (open 24 hours). **Radio:** KUAC-FM 101.7.

Visitor Information: Available at the Healy Senior Center, located on Healy Spur Road behind the grocery store. Open 11 A.M. to 7 P.M., year-round; phone 683-1317.

Private Aircraft: Healy River airstrip adjacent north; elev. 1,294 feet/394m; length 2,800 feet/853m; gravel; unattended.

Healy's power plant has the distinction of being the largest coal-fired steam plant in Alaska, as well as the only mine-mouth power plant. This plant is part of the Golden Valley Electric Assoc., which furnishes electric power for Fairbanks and vicinity. The Fairbanks–Tanana Valley area uses primarily coal and also oil to meet its electrical needs.

Across the Nenana River lie the mining settlements of Suntrana and Usibelli. Dry Creek, Healy and Nenana river valleys comprise the area referred to as Tri–Valley. Coal mining began here in 1918 and has grown to become Alaska's largest coal mining operation. Usibelli Coal Mine, the state's only commercial coal mine, mines about 800,000 tons of coal a year, supplying South Korea, the

HEALY ADVERTISERS

Denali Suites	Ph. (907) 683-2848
GrandView Bed & Breakfast	Ph. (907) 683-2468
Historical Healy Hotel and Restaurant	Mile 248.8 Parks Hwy.
Pat & Windell's Bed and Breakfast	Ph. (907) 683-2472
Totem Inn	Mile 248.7 Parks Hwy.

University of Alaska, the military and other Fairbanks-area utilities. The Usibelli Coal Mine began a successful reclamation program in 1971; Dall sheep now graze where there was once only evidence of strip mining.

From the highway, you may see a 33-cubic-yard walking dragline (named Ace in the Hole by local schoolchildren in a contest) removing the soil, or overburden, to expose the coal seams. This 4,275,000-pound machine, erected in 1978, moves an average of 24,000 cubic yards each 24 hours. Private vehicles are not allowed into the mining area and no tours are available.

Denali Suites. Located 15 minutes north of entrance to Denali National Park on Healy Spur Road. Units include two or three bedrooms, kitchen and dining area, living room with queen-sized hide-a-bed, TV and VCR, and private baths. Coin-operated laundry facilities. Clean, comfortable, affordable. Each unit accommodates up to six people, one accommodates eight, with two private baths; families welcome. VISA, MasterCard. Open all year. Call (907) 683-2848 or write Box 393, Healy, AK 99743. See display ad in the DENALI NATIONAL PARK section. [ADVERTISEMENT]

GrandView Bed & Breakfast. Located minutes from the entrance to Denali National Park. Relax and enjoy the spectacular view of the Alaska Range. Deck, barbecue, sitting area. Continental breakfast. Open year-round. VISA/MasterCard. Write GrandView Bed & Breakfast, Box 109, Healy, AK 99743 or call (907) 683-2468. See display ad in DENALI NATIONAL PARK section. [ADVERTISEMENT]

Historical Healy Hotel and Restaurant was moved and remodeled, with 29 private baths in rooms sleeping one to four people. Hot water heat. Reasonable rates. Family meals, short orders. Beautiful scenery. 12 miles north of Denali National Park entrance. Box 380, Healy, AK 99743. Phone (907) 683-2242, fax (907) 683-2243. [ADVERTISEMENT]

George Parks Highway Log

(continued)

A 249.1 (400.9 km) **F 108.9** (175.3 km) Suntrana Road, post office and Tri–Valley School.

A 249.2 (401 km) **F 108.8** (175.1 km) **Larry's Healy Service.** See display ad this section.

A 249.3 (401.2 km) **F 108.7** (174.9 km) Dry Creek bridge No. 1.

A 249.4 (401.4 km) **F 108.6** (174.8 km) **Dry Creek Bed & Breakfast** is also home to D-N-J Kennels. Open year-round. Dogsled trips, short rides and demonstrations also available by appointment. Complete breakfast, clean rooms, reasonable rates with Alaskan hospitality. For reservations call (907) 683-2386 or write Dry Creek Bed & Breakfast, D-N-J Kennels, P.O. Box 371, Healy, AK 99743. [ADVERTISEMENT]

A 249.5 (401.5 km) **F 108.5** (174.6 km) **Motel Nord Haven.** Opening in 1994. West side of highway in the trees. Peaceful and secluded. 12 miles to Denali National Park entrance. Moderately priced family motel run by Alaskan family. 16 large rooms with private baths. Handicapped access room. Open year-round. For reservations phone (907) 683-4500, or drop in. [ADVERTISEMENT]

A 249.6 (401.7 km) **F 108.4** (174.4 km) **Evans Industries, Inc.** See display ad this section.

A 249.8 (402 km) **F 108.2** (174.1 km) Dry Creek bridge No. 2. Good berry picking area first part of August.

A 251.1 (404.1 km) **F 106.9** (172 km) Stampede Road and lodge to west. Lignite Road and bed and breakfast to east.

Beaver View Bed and Breakfast. Located 2 miles east of Parks Highway on Lignite Road. Enjoy your stay in a private, clean, comfortable cabin beside the friendly beavers in their natural habitat. Continental breakfast and television is provided. Call (907) 683-2585 or write P.O. Box 18, Healy, AK 99743. [ADVERTISEMENT]

A 251.2 (404.3 km) **F 106.8** (171.9 km) Paved turnout to west. Coal seams visible in bluff to east. Cotton grass and lupine along roadside in June, fireweed in July.

A 252.4 (406.2 km) **F 105.6** (169.9 km) Gravel turnout to west.

A 252.5 (406.4 km) **F 105.5** (169.8 km) Bridge over **Panguingue Creek;** turnout at end. Moderate success fishing for grayling. This stream, which flows 8 miles/13 km to the Nenana River, was named for a Philippine card game.

Watch for frost heaves northbound.

A 259.4 (417.5 km) **F 98.6** (158.7 km) Large paved turnout to east. Views of Rex Dome to the northeast. Walker and Jumbo domes to the east. Liberty Bell mining area lies between the peaks and highway.

A 261.1 (420.2 km) **F 96.9** (155.9 km) Gravel turnout to east. Look for bank swallows, small brown birds that nest in clay and sand banks near streams and along highways.

A 262 (421.6 km) **F 96** (154.5 km) Watch for rough patches in pavement and gravel shoulders, northbound. Watch for frost heaves southbound.

A 263 (423.2 km) **F 95** (152.9 km) Small gravel turnout to east. Wildflowers include sweet pea and oxytrope.

A 264.5 (425.7 km) **F 93.5** (150.5 km) Paved turnout to west.

A 269 (432.9 km) **F 89** (143.2 km) June Creek rest area and picnic spot to east; large gravel parking area. Gravel road leads down to lower parking area on June Creek (trailers and large RVs check turnaround space before driving down). Wooden stairs lead up to the picnic spot and a view of the Nenana River. There are picnic tables, fireplaces, toilets, a litter bin and a sheltered table. Cut wood may be available.

A 269.3 (433.4 km) **F 88.7** (142.8 km) Bridge over Bear Creek. Gravel turnout to east.

A 271.4 (436.8 km) **F 86.6** (139.4 km) Paved turnout to west. Highway northbound leads through boggy area with few turnouts.

A 275.6 (443.5 km) **F 82.4** (132.6 km) Entering Game Management Unit 20A northbound, 20C southbound.

A 275.8 (443.9 km) **F 82.2** (132.3 km) Rex Bridge over Nenana River.

A 276 (444.2 km) **F 82** (132 km) **Tatlanika Trading Co.** Located in a beautiful pristine wilderness setting. Tent sites and RV parking with electricity, water, dump station, showers, TV. 39 miles from Denali National Park on the Nenana River. Our gift shop features a gathering of handmade art/crafts/artifacts from various villages. Excellent selection of furs at reasonable prices — see the rare Samson fox, along with relics and antiques from Alaska's colorful past in a museum atmosphere with a world-class polar bear. Many historical and educational displays. Nothing sold from overseas. Visitor information. Coffee, pop, juice, snacks. Clean restrooms. This is a must stop. See display ad on page 351. [ADVERTISEMENT] ▲

A 276.5 (445 km) **F 81.5** (131.2 km) *CAUTION: Railroad crossing.* Yellow arnica blooms along roadside.

A 280 (450.6 km) **F 78** (125.5 km) Lodge with dining and a cafe/grocery are located here.

Clear Sky Lodge. See display ad this section.

A 280.1 (450.8 km) **F 77.9** (125.4 km) **Rochester Lodge.** See display ad this section.

A 280.4 (451.2 km) **F 77.6** (124.9 km) Entering Clear Air Force Station northbound.

A 283.5 (456.2 km) **F 74.5** (119.9 km) Access road west to **ANDERSON** (pop. 628) and **CLEAR.** Clear is a military installation (ballistic missile early warning site), and a sign at turnoff states it is unlawful to enter without permission. However, you can drive into Anderson without permission. Located 6 miles/9.7 km northwest of Clear, Anderson has a city campground in an 80-acre park with 10 sites on the Tanana River. RV dump station, toilets, showers. The community also has churches, a restaurant, softball fields and shooting range. For more information call the city office at 582-2500. Emergency aid is available through the Clear Air Force Site Fire Department; phone 585-6321. ▲

Private Aircraft: Clear airstrip, 2.6 miles/4.2 km southeast; elev. 552 feet/168m; length 3,900 feet/1,189m; gravel; unattended. Clear Sky Lodge airstrip, 4.3 miles/6.9 km south; elev. 650 feet/198m; length 2,500 feet/762m; gravel, earth.

A 285.7 (459.8 km) **F 72.3** (116.3 km) Julius Creek bridge.

A 286.3 (460.7 km) **F 71.7** (115.4 km) View of Mount McKinley southbound.

A 286.8 (461.5 km) **F 71.2** (114.6 km) Double-ended paved parking area to east. Watch for frost heaves northbound.

A 288 (463.5 km) **F 70** (112.7 km) Entering Clear Military Reservation southbound.

Watch for frost heaves and dip in pavement.

A 289.8 (466.4 km) **F 68.2** (109.7 km) **Summer Shades Campground.** See display ad this section. ▲

A 290.2 (467 km) **F 67.8** (109.1 km) **Alaska Panaché Bed and Breakfast.** See display ad this section.

A 296.7 (477.5 km) **F 61.3** (98.7 km) Bridge over **Fish Creek.** Small gravel turnout with litter barrels by creek. Access to creek at south end of bridge; moderate success fishing for grayling.

A 302.1 (486.2 km) **F 55.9** (90 km) **Finnish Alaskan Bed and Breakfast.** See display ad this section.

A 302.9 (487.4 km) **F 55.1** (88.7 km) Nenana municipal rifle range.

A 303.7 (488.7 km) **F 54.3** (87.4 km) Nenana airport (see Private Aircraft information in Nenana).

A 304.5 (490 km) **F 53.5** (86.1 km) **A Frame Service.** See display ad this section.

Nenana

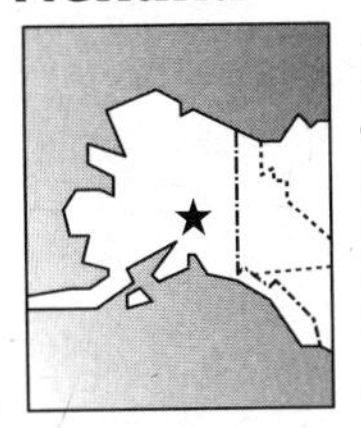

A 304.5 (490 km) **F 53.5** (86.1 km) Located at the confluence of the Tanana and Nenana rivers. **Population:** 393. **Emergency Services:** Emergency only (fire, police, ambulance), phone 911. **Alaska State Troopers,** phone 832-5554, at **Milepost A 310** George Parks Highway. **City Police,** phone 832-5632. **Fire Department,** phone 832-5632.

Visitor Information: In a picturesque log cabin with sod roof at junction of the highway and A Street, phone 832-9953. Open

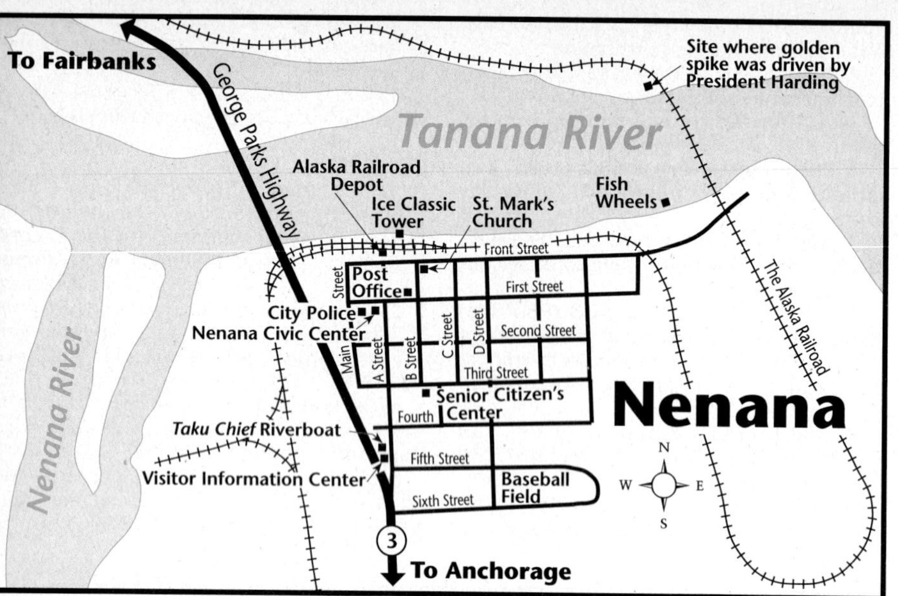

8 A.M. to 6 P.M., seven days a week, Memorial Day to Labor Day. Pay phone and ice for sale. Ice Classic tickets may be purchased here.

Marge Anderson Senior Citizen Center, located on 3rd Street between Market and B streets, also welcomes visitors.

Elevation: 400 feet/122m. **Radio:** KUAC-FM 91.1. **Transportation: Air**–Nenana maintains a FAA-approved airport. **Railroad**–The Alaska Railroad.

Private Aircraft: Nenana Municipal Airport, 0.9 mile/1.4 km south; elev. 362 feet/110m; length 5,000 feet/1,524m; asphalt; fuel 100, Jet B. Floatplane and skiplane strip.

The town got its name from the Indian word Nenana, which means "a good place to camp between the rivers." It was first known as Tortella, a white man's interpretation of the Athabascan word *Toghotthele.* In 1902 Jim Duke built a roadhouse and trading post here, trading with Indians and supplying river travelers with goods and lodging.

Nenana boomed as a construction base for the Alaska Railroad. Today, Nenana is home port of the tug and barge fleet that in summer carries tons of freight, fuel and supplies to villages along the Tanana and Yukon rivers. Because the Tanana is a wide, shallow, muddy river, the barges move about 12 mph downstream and 5 mph upstream. The dock area is to the right of the highway northbound. Behind the Nenana visitor information center is the *Taku Chief:* This old tug, which has been renovated, once pushed barges on the Tanana.

On July 15, 1923, Pres. Warren G. Harding drove the golden spike at Nenana, signifying completion of the Alaska Railroad. A monument to the event stands east of the depot here. The Nenana Railroad Depot, located at the end of Main Street, is on the National Register of Historic Places. Built in 1923 and renovated in 1988, the depot has a pressed metal ceiling and houses the state's Alaska Railroad Museum; open 9 A.M. to 6 P.M. daily.

One block from the depot is St. Mark's Mission Church. This Episcopal church was built in 1905 upriver from Nenana; it was moved to its present location in the 1930s when riverbank erosion threatened the structure. A school was located next door to the mission until the 1940s, and pupils were brought in by tug from villages along the river. The recently restored log church has pews with hand-carving and an altar covered with Native beadwork-decorated moosehide.

Nenana is perhaps best known for the Nenana Ice Classic, an annual event that offers cash prizes to the lucky winners who can guess the exact minute of the ice

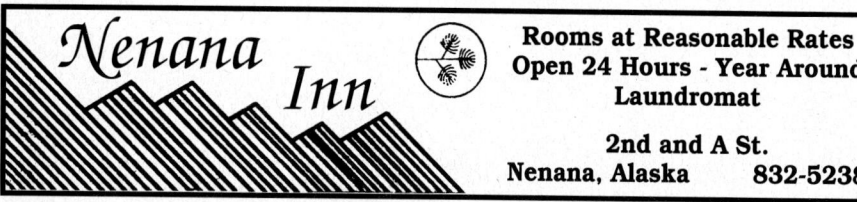

NENANA ADVERTISERS

Bed & Maybe Breakfast.................Above Depot Museum
Coghill's General Merchandise......Downtown
Corner Bar..Main St.
Crafter's Cabin..............................Downtown
Last Resort.......................Next to visitor center
Nenana Inn....................................2nd & A St.
Nenana Valley RV Park & Campground...............................4th St.
Nenana Visitor Center...................Downtown
Parks Highway Service & Towing......................Ph. 1-800-478-TOWS
Tolovana Lodge................Ph. (907) 832-5569
Tripod Gift Shop and Mini Mall............Across from visitor center
Tripod Motel.................Mile 304.4 Parks Hwy.

St. Mark's Mission Church was built in 1905. (Jerrianne Lowther, staff)

breakup on the Tanana River. Ice Classic festivities begin the last weekend in February with the Tripod Raising Festival and Nenana Ice Classic Dog Race, and culminate at breakup time (late April or May) when the surging ice on the Tanana River dislodges the tripod. A line attached to the tripod stops a clock, recording the official breakup time.

Nenana celebrates River Daze the first weekend in June. The main event is "The Annihilator," the toughest 10-kilometer foot race in Alaska, over Tortella Hill.

Nenana has an auto repair shop, radio station, several churches, restaurants, a laundromat, gift shops, a grocery and general store. Accommodations at local motel, inn and bed and breakfast; access to wilderness lodge. RV facilities include an RV park with electric hookups and camping. River charters and guide service available. Picnic tables and rest area beside the restored *Taku Chief* are behind the visitor information center. ▲

Bed & Maybe Breakfast. Step back in time and charm yourself in the atmosphere of the old railroad depot built for President Harding's historic visit in 1923. Oak or brass beds, hardwood floors and braided rugs enhance the decor of these rooms. Overlook the hustling loading dock area of the barge lines on the Tanana River. View the Native cemetery and the historic railroad bridge from your window. Credit cards accepted. Reservations: (907) 832-5272 or 582-2776. [ADVERTISEMENT]

Tripod Gift Shop and Mini Mall. "Take time to smell the flowers." Over 12,000 flowers are planted each year to enhance the

beauty of one of the loveliest gift shops in Alaska. A fun stop! Enjoy old-time concertina music played by Joanne Hawkins. Take the boardwalk to our Art Lovers' Gallery; Fur Shop stocked with fur products and a wide selection of local furs; king- and queen-size shirt shop; and Bargain Corner with special prices on T-shirts, products and mugs. Enjoy ice cream or snacks at our Sweets and Treats Shoppe and purchase our fine canned smoked salmon. Also available: ice, worldwide postcard stamps, assorted camera batteries and wildflower seeds. Complimentary gold panning with $5 purchase in any of these shops. These shops are a must, a highlight of any vacation. Interesting displays include record size moose antlers, Kodiak grizzly bear trap (largest ever manufactured), antique ice saw, working fish wheel, trapper's steam boiler, dog salmon drying rack and authentic 1977 Ice Classic tripod. Be sure to have your picture taken with Sourdough Pete and rub his head for luck. Tour operators may call ahead to reserve a guided tour of Nenana, compliments of Tripod Gift Shop. Joanne Hawkins has hosted tour groups for over 20 years at no charge. Allow 30-45 minutes if the tour is to be included with your rest stop. A little history, a little fact, a little music and a lot of fun are packed into this tour. Have a pic-

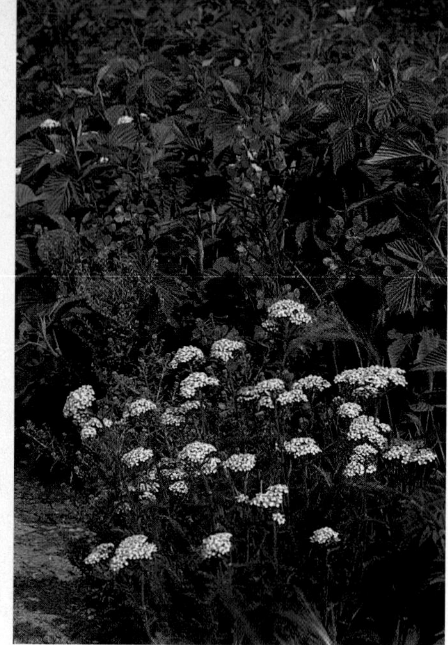

Colorful fireweed and white yarrow.
(Loren Taft)

ture taken of your coach, escort and driver for our display board. Over 15 years of tour operator photos are on display. This tour is a must! Remember, reservations are necessary. [ADVERTISEMENT]

George Parks Highway Log
(continued)

A 305.1 (491 km) **F 52.9** (85.1 km) Tanana River bridge. Large paved turnout to west at north end of bridge. The Tanana is formed by the joining of the Chisana and the Nabesna rivers near Northway and flows 440 miles/708 km westward to the Yukon River. From the bridge, watch for freight-laden river barges bound for the Yukon River. North of this bridge, fish wheels sometimes may be seen in action and occasionally fish may be purchased from the owners of the wheels. Entering Game Management Unit 20B northbound, 20A southbound.

A 305.5 (491.6 km) **F 52.5** (84.5 km) Paved turnout to west by Tanana River. There is a Native cemetery 0.6 mile/1 km to east on side road.

A 305.6 (491.8 km) **F 52.4** (84.3 km) Paved turnout to west overlooking Tanana River.

A 305.9 (492.3 km) **F 52.1** (83.8 km) Double-ended gravel turnout to east.

A 308.9 (497.1 km) **F 49.1** (79 km) *CAUTION: Alaska Railroad crossing.*

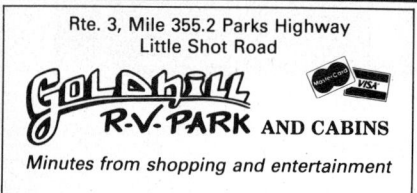

A 309 (497.3 km) **F 49** (78.9 km) **Monderosa.** See display ad on page 355.

A 314.6 (506.3 km) **F 43.4** (69.8 km) Paved double-ended turnout to west.

A 314.8 (506.6 km) **F 43.2** (69.5 km) Bridge over Little Goldstream Creek.

A 315.4 (507.6 km) **F 42.5** (68.6 km) Truck lane next 2.8 miles/4.5 km northbound.

A 318.8 (513 km) **F 39.2** (63.1 km) Paved double-ended turnout to west with scenic view. The view is mostly of bogs, small lakes and creeks, with names like Hard Luck Creek, Fortune Creek, All Hand Help Lake and Wooden Canoe Lake.

Southbound travelers will see the Tanana River on both sides of the highway. It follows a horseshoe-shaped course, the top of the closed end being the bridge at Nenana.

A 321 (516.6 km) **F 37** (59.5 km) Fairbanks-bound traffic: Highway climbs a steep grade with sweeping curves next 1 mile/1.6 km; truck lane next mile northbound. Mount McKinley is visible to the southwest on a clear day.

A 323 (519.8 km) **F 35** (56.3 km) Tanana River visible to east in valley below highway.

A 323.8 (521.1 km) **F 34.2** (55 km) Truck lane next 0.3 mile/0.5 km northbound.

A 324.5 (522.2 km) **F 33.5** (53.9 km) Paved double-ended turnout to east with scenic view to south.

A 325 (523 km) **F 33** (53.1 km) This stretch of highway is often called Skyline Drive; views to west. Downgrade northbound.

A 325.7 (524.1 km) **F 32.3** (52 km) Entering Fairbanks North Star Borough northbound.

A 328.3 (528.3 km) **F 29.7** (47.8 km) Truck lane next 3 miles/4.8 km southbound.

A 329.5 (530.3 km) **F 28.5** (45.9 km) There is a healthy population of black bears in this area. Occasionally a bear may be seen from the highway.

A 331.6 (533.6 km) **F 26.4** (42.5 km) Long paved double-ended turnout to east. Intermittent truck lanes northbound to Fairbanks.

A 338.2 (544.3 km) **F 19.8** (31.9 km) Wide view to east. Look for Murphy Dome (elev. 2,930 feet/893m) with white communication installations on summit to west.

A 339.3 (546 km) **F 19.7** (30.1 km) Viewpoint and sign to east. This is the south end of a 1-mile/1.6-km scenic loop road that rejoins the highway at **Milepost A 339.9.** Highway begins downgrade northbound.

A 339.9 (547 km) **F 18.1** (29.1 km) Turnoff (unmarked) for Bonanza Experimental Forest via 1-mile/1.6-km loop road east; scenic viewpoint. Established by the Alaska Division of Lands and U.S. Forest Service to study the Interior forest ecosystem. For information contact the Institute of Northern Forestry, U.S. Dept. of Agriculture, in Fairbanks.

A 342.2 (550.7 km) **F 15.8** (25.4 km) Rosie Creek Road.

A 342.4 (551 km) **F 15.6** (25.1 km) Old Nenana Highway.

A 344.2 (553.9 km) **F 13.8** (22.2 km) Monument in honor of George Alexander Parks, former governor of Alaska. Also here is a Blue Star Memorial highway plaque honoring the armed forces. Viewpoint and litter barrels to east. Tanana River can be seen below the Parks monument.

A 348 (560.1 km) **F 10** (16.1 km) Highway passes through forest of aspen.

A 349 (561.6 km) **F 9** (14.5 km) Cripple Creek Road to south (access to TIVI kennels), Park Ridge Road to north. Truck lane next 4.2 miles/6.8 km southbound.

A 350 (563.3 km) **F 8** (12.9 km) Alder Creek.

A 351.2 (565.2 km) **F 6.8** (10.9 km) Old dredges visible in the distance.

A 351.7 (566 km) **F 6.3** (10.1 km) Watch for turnoff to west for **ESTER** (pop. 166), a former gold mining camp and current visitor attraction; food, lodging, entertainment, gift shop and camping. Drive 0.4 mile/0.6 km in on road, turn right on a second road marked Ester, and drive 0.2 mile/0.3 km to an intersection: Turn left at intersection for Ester Gold Camp and Malemute Saloon (descriptions follows); turn right for Ester residential area and another saloon. Southbound access to Old Nenana Highway.

Ester Gold Camp. Since 1936. Historic District. P.O. Box 109MP, Ester, AK 99725. (907) 479-2500. 800-676-6925. Fax (907) 479-1780. Open May 27 through Sept. 3. Hotel: 20 modest rooms with semi-private baths. $46 – $64 plus tax. Continental breakfast included. Reservations accepted. RV parking: dry camping, no hookups, water, dump station, showers. $9. Restaurant: serving dinner daily from 5–9. Featuring all-you-care-to-eat buffet and Alaska Dungeness Crab. Reservations advised. Home to the World Famous Malemute Saloon. Open daily. Shows Monday through Saturday 9 P.M. featuring music, songs, dance, humor and the poetry of Robert Service. Reservations highly recommended. Northern Lights Show: Leroy Zimmerman's "The Crown of Light." Photography and music. A spectacular look at the northern lights. Nightly at 8 P.M. The Alaska Show: "Alaska From The Heart." Nightly at 7 P.M. Reservations recommended. Pick and Poke Gift Shop: Alaska gifts and souvenirs. See display ad in FAIRBANKS section. [ADVERTISEMENT] ▲

A 351.8 (566.2 km) **F 6.2** (10 km) Weigh stations.

A 353.5 (568.9 km) **F 4.5** (7.2 km) Gas station and store. Public dumpster.

A 355.2 (571.6 km) **F 2.8** (4.5 km) **Goldhill RV Park and Cabins.** See display ad this section. ▲

A 355.8 (572.6 km) **F 2.2** (3.5 km) Sheep Creek Road and Tanana Drive. Road to Murphy Dome (a restricted military site).

A 356.8 (574.2 km) **F 1.2** (1.9 km) Turnoff to University of Alaska, Geist Road, Chena Ridge Loop and Chena Pump Road.

Watch for construction of new interchange here in summer 1994.

A 357.6 (575.5 km) **F 0.4** (0.6 km) Bridge over Chena River.

NOTE: Watch for road construction from Chena River to Peger Road in 1994.

A 357.7 (575.6 km) **F 0.3** (0.5 km) Fairbanks airport exit.

A 358 (576.1 km) **F 0** Fairbanks exit; George Parks Highway (Robert J. Mitchell Expressway) continues to Richardson Highway, bypassing Fairbanks. Take Fairbanks exit to Airport Way for University Avenue (access to University of Alaska and Chena River state recreation site); Peger Road (access to private campground, flying service and Alaskaland); and Cushman Street turnoff to downtown and to connect with the Richardson Highway and Steese Expressway. (See Fairbanks Vicinity map in the FAIRBANKS section.)

NOTE: There are no banks between Fairbanks and Wasilla at ***Milepost A 42.2.***

FAIRBANKS

(See maps, page 361)

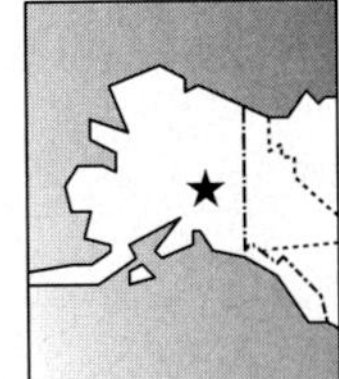

Located in the heart of Alaska's Great Interior country. By highway, Fairbanks is approximately 1,475 miles/2374 km north of Dawson Creek, BC, start of the Alaska Highway (traditional milepost distance is 1,523 miles); 98 miles/158 km from Delta Junction (official end of the Alaska Highway); 358 miles/576 km from Anchorage via the George Parks Highway; and 2,313 miles/3722 km from Seattle.

Population: Fairbanks–North Star Borough, 77,720. **Emergency Services: Alaska State Troopers**, 1979 Peger Road, phone 452-1313 or, for nonemergencies, 452-2114. **Fairbanks Police**, 656 7th Ave., phone 911 or, for nonemergencies, phone 459-6500. **Fire Department** and **Ambulance Service** (within city limits), phone 911. **Hospitals**, Fairbanks Memorial, 1650 Cowles St., phone 452-8181; Bassett Army Hospital, Fort Wainwright, phone 353-5143; Eielson Clinic, Eielson AFB, phone 377-2259. **Crisis Line**, phone 452-4403. **Civil Defense**, phone 459-6500. **Borough Information**, phone 459-1000.

Visitor Information: Fairbanks Visitor Information Center at 550 1st Ave. (1st and Cushman, where a riverside marker shows the distance of Fairbanks from some 75 cities); phone 456-5774 or 1-800-327-5774. Open 8 A.M. to 8 P.M. (subject to change), daily in summer; 8:30 A.M. to 5 P.M., weekdays in winter; 10 A.M. to 4 P.M. Saturdays and Sundays. Phone 456-INFO for their daily recorded information service.

Visitor information is also available at Fairbanks International Airport in the baggage claim area, at the Alaska Railroad depot and at Alaskaland.

For information on Alaska's state parks, national parks, national forests, wildlife refuges and other outdoor recreational sites, visit the Alaska Public Lands Information Center downstairs in historic Courthouse Square at 250 N. Cushman St. The center is a free museum featuring films on Alaska, interpretive programs, lectures, exhibits, artifacts, photographs and short video programs on each region in the state. The exhibit area and information desk are open seven days a week in summer; Tuesday through Saturday in winter. Phone 456-0527. For recorded information on Denali National Park, phone 456-0510. TDD (Telephone Device for the Deaf) information line is 456-0532.

Elevation: 434 feet/132m at Fairbanks International Airport. **Climate:** January temperatures range from -4°F/-20°C to -21°F/-29°C. The lowest temperature ever recorded was -66°F/-54°C in January 1934. July temperatures average 62°F/17°C, with a record high of 99°F/37°C in July 1919. The summer of 1993 was one of Fairbanks's hottest and driest. Temperatures averaged 78.4 degrees in July, which was the hottest summer month since June 1969, and the second-hottest month since 1905, when temperatures began to be tracked. July 15 set a record high for the day of 93 degrees. Measurable rain in July was only about one-third of an inch, a fraction of the usual 1.77-inch average for the month. In June and early July daylight lasts 21 hours — and the nights are really only twilight. Annual precipitation is 10.4 inches, with an annual average snowfall of 65 inches. The record for snowfall is 147.3 inches, set the winter of 1990–91. **Radio:** KSUA-FM, KFAR, KCBF, KAKQ, KWLF-FM, KIAK, KIAK-FM, KJNP-AM and FM (North Pole), KUAC-FM 104.7. **Television:** Channels 2, 4, 9, 11 and cable. **Newspapers:** *Fairbanks Daily News–Miner.*

Private Aircraft: Facilities for all types of aircraft. Consult the *Alaska Supplement* for information on the following airports: Eielson AFB, Fairbanks International, Fairbanks International Seaplane, Metro Field and Fort Wainwright. For more information phone the Fairbanks Flight Service Station at 474-0137.

Alaskaland's historic buildings now house shops. (Jerrianne Lowther, staff)

HISTORY

In 1901, Captain E.T. Barnette set out from St. Michael on the sternwheeler *Lavelle Young*, traveling up the Yukon River with supplies for his trading post, which he proposed to set up at Tanana Crossing (Tanacross), the halfway point on the Valdez to Eagle trail. But the sternwheeler could not navigate the fast-moving, shallow Tanana River beyond the mouth of the Chena River. The captain of the sternwheeler finally dropped off the protesting Barnette on the Chena River, near the present site of 1st Avenue and Cushman Street. A year later, Felix Pedro, an Italian prospector, discovered gold about 16 miles/26 km north of Barnette's temporary trading post. The opportunistic Barnette quickly abandoned his original plan to continue on to Tanana Crossing.

In September 1902, Barnette convinced the 25 or so miners in the area to use the name "Fairbanks" for the town he expected to grow up around his trading post. The name had been suggested that summer by Alaska Judge James Wickersham, who admired Charles W. Fairbanks, the senior senator from Indiana. The senator later became vice president of the United States under Theodore Roosevelt.

The town grew, largely due to Barnette's promotion of gold prospects and discoveries in the area, and in 1903 Judge Wickersham moved the headquarters of his Third Judicial District Court (a district which encompassed 300,000 square miles) from Eagle to Fairbanks.

Thanks to Wickersham, the town gained government offices and a jail. Thanks to Barnette, it also gained a post office and a branch of the Northern Commercial Com-

pany, a large Alaska trading firm based in San Francisco. In addition, after Barnette became the first mayor of Fairbanks in 1903, the town arranged telephone service, set up fire protection, passed sanitation ordinances and contracted for electric light and steam heat. In 1904, Barnette started a bank.

The name "Fairbanks" first appeared in the U.S. census in 1910 with a population of 3,541 listed. Miners living beside their claims on creeks north of town brought the area population figure to about 11,000.

Barnette stayed in Fairbanks until late 1910, when he resigned the presidency of the Washington-Alaska Bank and moved to California. When the bank collapsed early in 1911, the people of Fairbanks blamed Barnette. The tale of the "most hated man in Fairbanks" is told in *E.T. Barnette, The Strange Story of the Man Who Founded Fairbanks.*

RIVER'S EDGE

RV PARK & CAMPGROUND

F A I R B A N K S

- Full and partial hook-up pull-throughs
- 30-amp electric
- Dump station
- Dry sites
- Tent camping
- FREE showers
- Laundry
- Gift shop
- Pay phones
- Car/RV wash facility
- Over 150 sites
- Grocery items
- Tour information and ticket sales

"Word of mouth is our best advertising"

River's Edge RV Park & Campground is centrally located within walking distance to major shopping centers.

We also offer **free** shuttle service to Sternwheeler Discovery and Alaska Salmon Bake.

Ask about our **Denali Park** One-Day Wildlife Tour.

In the words of one of our visitors, Dr. Helen Stover of Richmond, VA,

"River's Edge is RV heaven!"

4140 Boat Street (off Airport Way) Fairbanks, Alaska • 1-800-770-3343

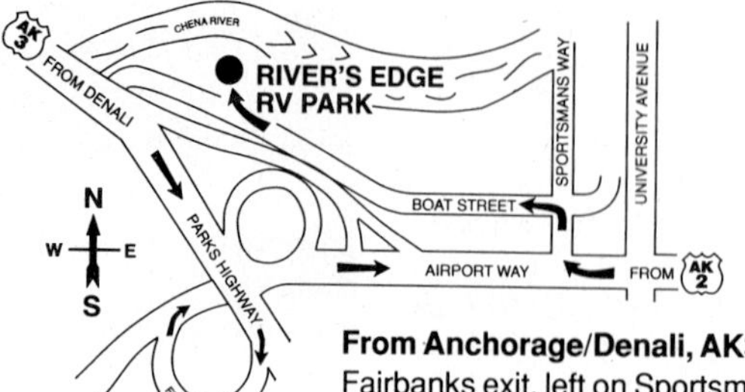

From Anchorage/Denali, AK3: take Fairbanks exit, left on Sportsmans Way, left on Boat Street.

From Tok/Richardson Hwy., AK2: left on Airport Way, cross University Avenue, right on Sportsmans Way, left on Boat Street.

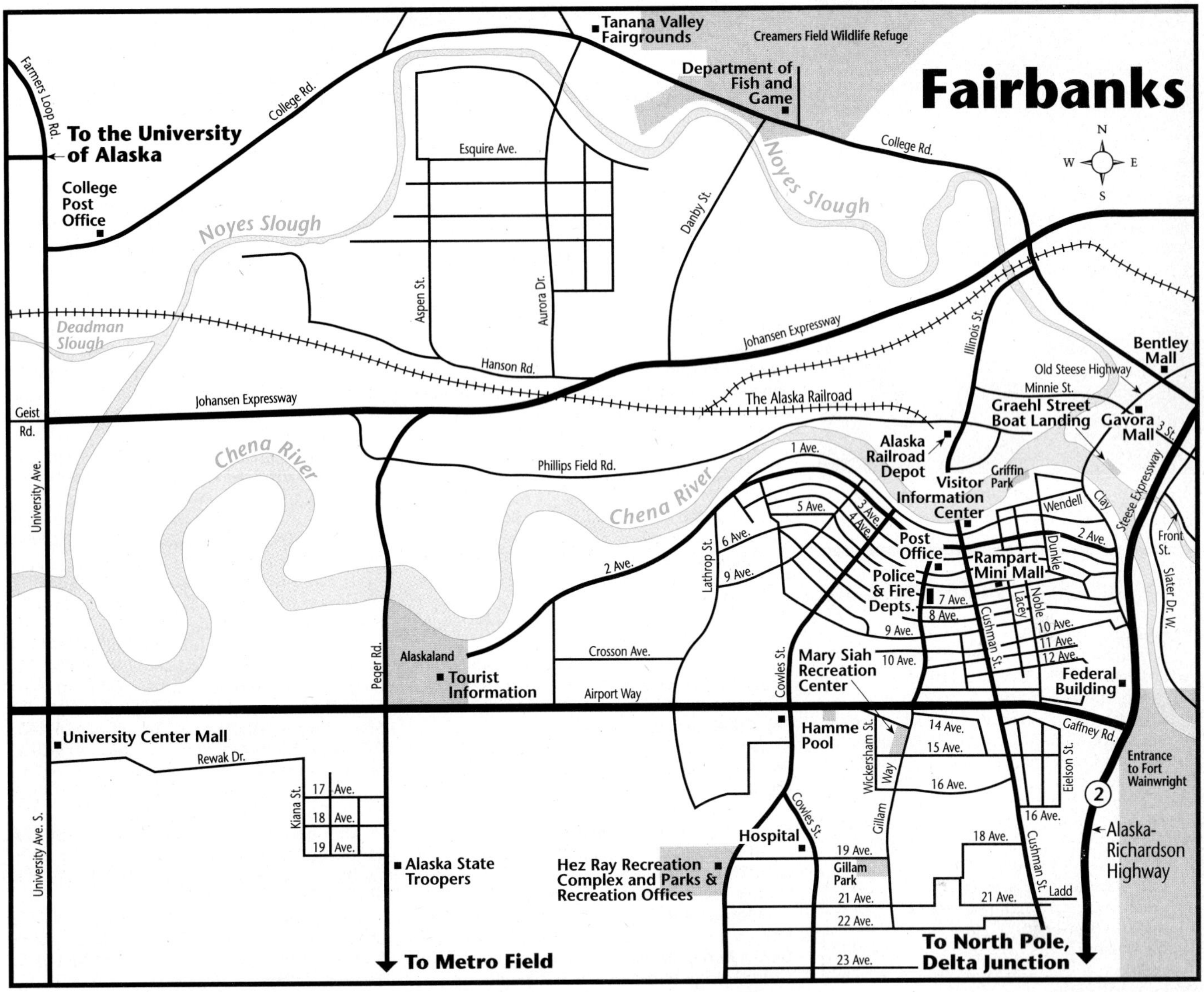

Fairbanks

N
W E
S

Tanana Valley Fairgrounds
Creamers Field Wildlife Refuge
Department of Fish and Game
College Rd.
Farmers Loop Rd.
To the University of Alaska
College Post Office
Esquire Ave.
Noyes Slough
Danby St.
Aspen St.
Aurora Dr.
Deadman Slough
Hanson Rd.
Johansen Expressway
Illinois St.
Bentley Mall
Old Steese Highway
Minnie St.
The Alaska Railroad
Geist Rd.
Graehl Street Boat Landing
Gavora Mall
3 St.
Chena River
Alaska Railroad Depot
1 Ave.
Phillips Field Rd.
Visitor Information Center
Griffin Park
Steese Expressway
University Ave.
5 Ave.
3 Ave.
4 Ave.
Wendell
Clay
Front St.
6 Ave.
Post Office
2 Ave.
2 Ave.
Lathrop St.
9 Ave.
Rampart Mini Mall
Dunkle
Police & Fire Depts.
7 Ave.
8 Ave.
Lacey
Noble
Slater Dr. W.
9 Ave.
Cushman St.
10 Ave.
11 Ave.
12 Ave.
Peger Rd.
Alaskaland
Crosson Ave.
Cowles St.
Mary Siah Recreation Center
10 Ave.
Federal Building
Tourist Information
Airport Way
Hamme Pool
Gaffney Rd.
University Center Mall
14 Ave.
15 Ave.
Entrance to Fort Wainwright
Rewak Dr.
Wickersham St.
Way
16 Ave.
Eielson St.
17 Ave.
18 Ave.
19 Ave.
Kiana St.
Cowles St.
16 Ave.
2
Alaska-Richardson Highway
Gillam
Hospital
18 Ave.
Cushman St.
University Ave. S.
Alaska State Troopers
Hez Ray Recreation Complex and Parks & Recreation Offices
19 Ave.
Gillam Park
21 Ave.
21 Ave.
Ladd
22 Ave.
To Metro Field
23 Ave.
To North Pole, Delta Junction

Fairbanks and Vicinity

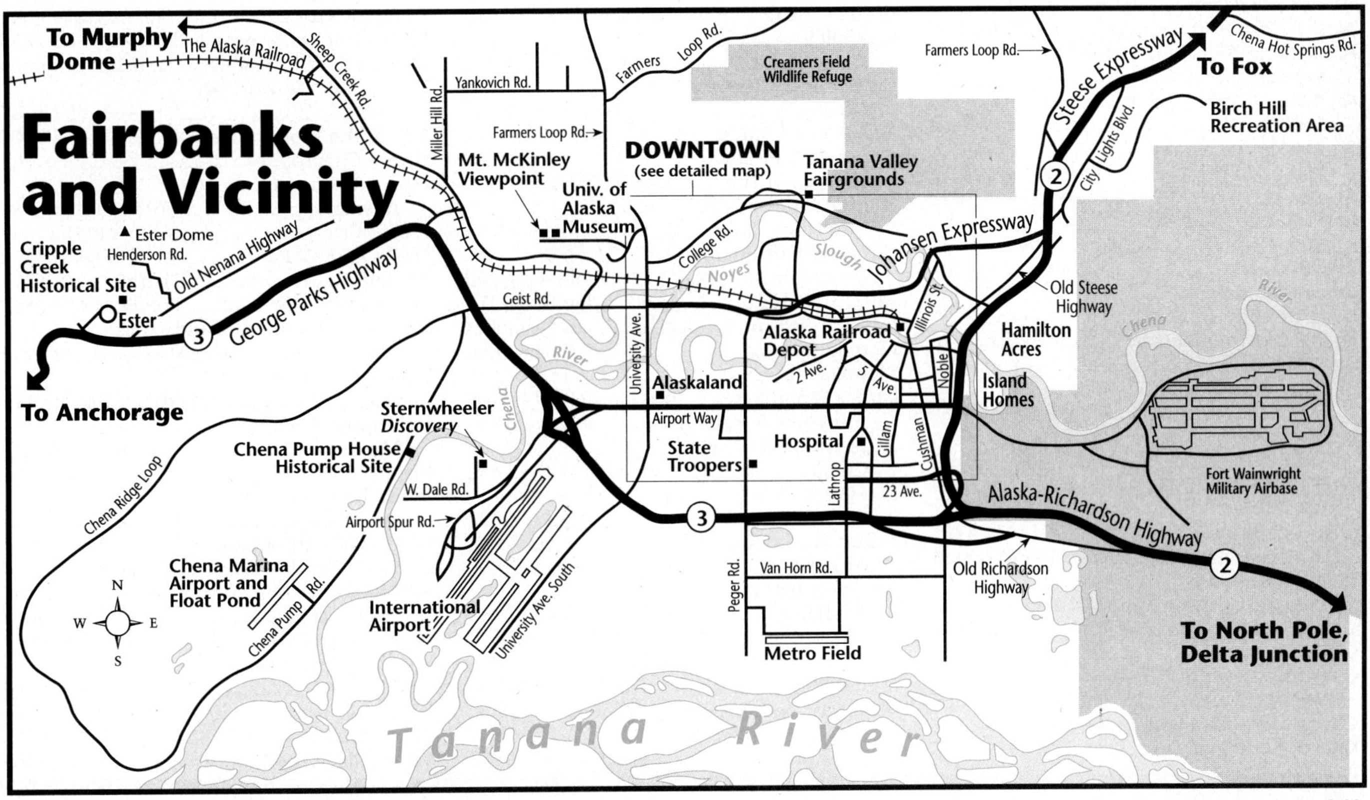

To Murphy Dome
The Alaska Railroad
Sheep Creek Rd.
Yankovich Rd.
Farmers Loop Rd.
Creamers Field Wildlife Refuge
Farmers Loop Rd.
Steese Expressway
To Fox
Chena Hot Springs Rd.
Miller Hill Rd.
Farmers Loop Rd.
Birch Hill Recreation Area
Mt. McKinley Viewpoint
DOWNTOWN (see detailed map)
Tanana Valley Fairgrounds
City Lights Blvd.
2
Univ. of Alaska Museum
Ester Dome
Cripple Creek Historical Site
Henderson Rd.
Old Nenana Highway
College Rd.
Slough
Noyes
Johansen Expressway
George Parks Highway
Geist Rd.
Old Steese Highway
River
Ester
3
Alaska Railroad Depot
Illinois St.
Hamilton Acres
Chena
River
University Ave.
2 Ave.
5 Ave.
Noble
To Anchorage
Alaskaland
Island Homes
Sternwheeler *Discovery*
Chena
Airport Way
Chena Pump House Historical Site
State Troopers
Hospital
Gillam
Cushman
Lathrop
Fort Wainwright Military Airbase
W. Dale Rd.
23 Ave.
Alaska-Richardson Highway
Chena Ridge Loop
Airport Spur Rd.
3
Chena Marina Airport and Float Pond
Peger Rd.
Van Horn Rd.
Old Richardson Highway
2
N
W E
S
Chena Pump Rd.
International Airport
University Ave. South
Metro Field
To North Pole, Delta Junction
Tanana River

A tour guide models Athabascan coat.
(Lee Foster)

FAIRBANKS ADVERTISERS

AAAA Care Bed & Breakfast.....Ph. 1-800-478-2705
Affordable Car Rental.....3101 S. Cushman
Ah, Rose Marie Bed and Breakfast.....302 Cowles St.
Alaska Motel.....1546 Cushman St.
Alaska Rag Co., The.....547 2nd Ave.
Alaska Raw Fur Co......Ph. (907) 479-2462
Alaska River Charters.....Ph. (907) 455-6827
Alaska Salmon Bake.....Alaskaland
Alaska Spring.....Ph. (907) 563-3802
Alaska Welcomes You Bed & Breakfast.....Ph. (907) 451-6378
Alaskaland.....Airport Way & Peger Rd.
Alaskaland Pioneer Air Museum.....Ph. (907) 451-0037
Alaskan Apparel.....Alaskaland
Alaskan Iris Bed and Breakfast.....Ph. 1-800-474-7262
Alaskan Motor Inn.....419 4th Ave.
Alaskan Photographic Repair Service.....551½ 2nd Ave.
Alaska's 7 Gables Bed & Breakfast.....4312 Birch Lane
An Alaskan Viewpoint Bed and Breakfast.....Ph. 1-800-479-7252
Applesauce Inn.....Ph. (907) 457-3392
Arctic Safari Tours & Auto Rentals.....Ph. 1-800-852-8424
Artworks, The.....3677 College Rd.
Aurora Animal Clinic.....Ph. (907) 452-6055
Beads & Things.....Ph. (907) 456-2323
Bean's Old Time Photos.....Alaskaland #28
Bear Paw B&B.....1101 Kodiak St.
Bed and Breakfast Reservation Service.....Ph. 1-800-770-8165
Big Ray's All Weather Outfitters.....507 2nd Ave.
Birch Grove Bed & Breakfast.....Ph. (907) 457-2981
Birch Grove Inn.....Ph. (907) 479-5781
Birch Haven Inn B&B.....Ph. (907) 457-2451
Blue Goose Bed & Breakfast, The.....Ph. 1-800-478-6973
Captain Bartlett Inn, The Ph. 1-800-544-7528
Cedar Creek Inn.....Ph. (907) 457-3392
Chena Hot Springs Resort.....Ph. (907) 452-7867
Chena Marina RV Park.....Ph. (907) 479-4653
Chena Pump Inn.....Ph. (907) 479-6313

FAIRBANKS ADVERTISERS (continued)

Chocolate Rush Bed & Breakfast, The.....Ph. (907) 474-8633
Chokecherry Inn.....Ph. (907) 474-9381
Circle Hot Springs Resort.....Mile 8.3 Circle Hot Springs Rd.
Cookie Jar's Garden Café, The.....Washington Plaza
Cushman Plaza Laundry.2301 S. Cushman St.
Denali Motorhome Rentals.....Ph. 1-800-722-6392
Eleanor's Northern Lights Bed & Breakfast.....Downtown
Elliott, Bob, Licensed Guide.....Ph. (907) 479-6323
Ester Gold Camp.....Ph. (907) 479-2500
Fairbanks Athletic Club.....Ph. (907) 452-6801
Fairbanks Convention and Visitors Bureau.....Ph. 1-800-327-5774
Fairbanks Educators' Bed & Breakfast Network.....5 locations—See ad
Fairbanks Fast Foto and Video.....2 locations—See ad
Fairbanks Golf and Country Club.....Ph. (907) 479-6555
Fairbanks Princess Hotel .Ph. 1-800-426-0500
Fairbanks RV Service Center.....2 locations—See ad
Fireweed Hideaway B&B, A.....Ph. (907) 457-2579
Fireweed R.V. Rentals.....Ph. (907) 474-3742
Forget Me Not Lodge.....Ph. (907) 474-0911
Fox Creek Bed & Breakfast.....Mile 1.1 Elliott Hwy.
Fox Roadhouse.....2195 Old Steese Hwy.
Frontier Flying Service, Inc......3820 University Ave.
G & J's Midnight Sun Bed & Breakfast.....Ph. 1-800-453-4017
G.O. Shuttle Service.....Ph. (907) 474-3847
Gabe's Peger Road Muffler & Motorhome Repair.....Ph. (907) 479-6162
Gene's.....1804 S. Cushman St.
Geni's Bed & Breakfast.....Ph. (907) 488-4136
Gold Dredge Number 8 Hotel & Bed & Breakfast.....Mile 9 Old Steese Hwy.
Golden North Motel.....Ph. 1-800-447-1910
Goldhill RV Park & Cabins.....Ph. (907) 474-8088
Goldpanner Chevron Service, Inc......809 Cushman St.
Gray Line of Alaska.....Ph. (907) 452-2843
Great Alaskan Bowl Company, The.....4630 Old Airport Rd.
Home "Suite" Home Bed & Breakfast.....Ph. (907) 474-9517
Hot Licks Homemade Ice Cream.....2 locations — see ad
Hotel Hotline.....Ph. 1-800-528-4916
Interior Custom Topper.....604 Hughes
Ivory Jacks.....Ph. (907) 455-6666
Klondike Inn.....1316 Bedrock St.
Larry's Flying Service, Inc. Ph. (907) 474-9169
Larson's Fine Jewelers.....405 Noble St.
Little El Dorado Gold Camp.....Ph. (907) 479-7613
Log Cabin Bed & Breakfast.....Ph. (907) 479-2332
Malemute Saloon, The.....Ester Gold Camp
Mapco Express.....3 locations—See ad
Marilyn's Bed and Breakfast.....Ph. (907) 456-1959
Marina Air, Inc......1219 Shypoke St.
McCauley's Reprographics.....721 Gaffney Rd.
Midnight Sun Aviation.....Ph. (907) 452-7039
Motor Inn Safety Lane.....2550 Cushman St.
Mountain View Bed & Breakfast.....Ph. (907) 474-9022
Native Village at Alaskaland.....Ph. (907) 456-3851
Noah's Rainbow Inn.....Ph. 1-800-770-2177
Norlite Campground, Inc......1660 Peger Rd.
Northern Alaska Tour Company.....Ph. (907) 474-8600
Novus Windshield Repair .229 Forty Mile Ave.
Palace Theatre & Saloon, The.....Alaskaland
Petroleum Sales.....Several locations—See ad
Phillips Recreation.....Ph. (907) 474-0444
Photo Express.....2 locations—See ad
Pick 'N Poke Gift Shop.....3175 College Rd.
Pioneer Bed & Breakfast, A.....1119 2nd Ave.
Pioneer RV & Trailer Court.....2201 S. Cushman St.
Plane Country Bed & Breakfast.....Ph. (907) 479-3710
Plaza Cleaners and Laundry.....3417 Airport Way
Regency Fairbanks, The.....95 10th Ave.
Ridgecrest Bed & Breakfast.....Ph. (907) 479-6833
Riverboat *Discovery III*.....Ph. (907) 479-6673
River's Edge RV Park & Campground.....4140 Boat St.
Riverview RV Park.....Ph. (907) 488-6281
Rose's Forget-Me-Not Bed & Breakfast.....Ph. (907) 456-5734
Santaland RV Park.....Ph. (907) 488-9123
Santa's Smokehouse.....2400 Davis Rd.
Save-U-More.....2800 Cushman Rd.
Sears Hairdesigners.....Ph. (907) 474-4455
7 Bridges Boats & Bikes...Ph. (907) 479-0751
Sleepy Moose Bed & Breakfast.....Ph. (907) 452-4814
Snow Goose Fibers & Quilting Company.....3550 Airport Way
Stonefrost Downtown Inn.....Ph. (907) 457-5337
Such A Deal Bed & Breakfast.....Ph. (907) 474-8159
Super 8 Motel.....Ph. 1-800-800-8000
Tamarac Inn Motel.....252 Minnie St.
Tanana Valley Campground.....Mile 2 College Rd.
Tanana Valley Farmers Market.....College Rd.
Taste of Alaska Lodge, A..Ph. (907) 488-7855
Taylor's Gold-n-Stones.....107 Cushman
Thompson's Downtown B&B.....Ph. (907) 452-5787
Top of the World Hotel....Ph. (907) 852-3900
Totem Chevron, Inc......768 Gaffney Rd.
Towne House Motel and Apartments.....1010 Cushman St.
Trailer Craft, Inc......2145 Van Horn Rd.
Trail's End RV Park.....Ph. (907) 456-8838
Trident Apartments.....Ph. (907) 479-6313
Turtle Club, The.....Ph. (907) 457-3883
University Avenue Car and Truck Wash.....University Ave. & Cameron
University Center Mall.....University & Airport Way
University of Alaska Museum.....907 Yukon Dr.
Vista Travel, Inc......Ph. 1-800-448-7181
Warbelow's Air Ventures, Inc......Ph. (907) 474-0518
Wet Willy's Automatic Car & Truck Wash.....2 locations—See ad
White Fox Inn Bed and Breakfast.....Ph. (907) 488-6811
Woolworth Alaska.....3rd Ave. & Cushman St.
World Eskimo–Indian Olympics.....Ph. (907) 452-6646
Wright Air Service Inc....Fairbanks Int. Airport
Yukon Quest.....Ph. (907) 451-8985
Yukon River Tours.....Ph. (907) 452-7162

ECONOMY

The city's economy is linked to its role as a service and supply point for Interior and Arctic industrial activities. Fairbanks played a key role during construction of the trans-Alaska pipeline in the 1970s. The Dalton Highway (formerly the North Slope Haul Road) to Prudhoe Bay begins about 75 miles/121 km north of town. Extractive industries such as oil and mining continue to play a major role in the economy.

Government employment — both civilian and military — contributes significantly to the Fairbanks economy. Fort Wainwright plays an important role in both the economy and also in emergency services by assisting with search and rescue operations. (Ladd Field — now Fort Wainwright — was the first Army airfield in Alaska, begun in 1938.) Eielson AFB, located 23 miles/37 km southeast of Fairbanks on the Alaska–Richardson Highway, also has a strong eco-

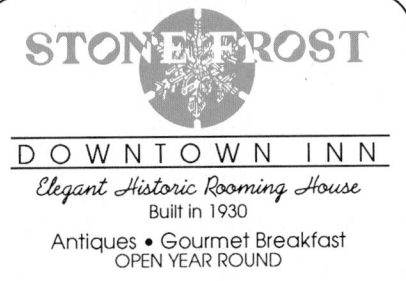

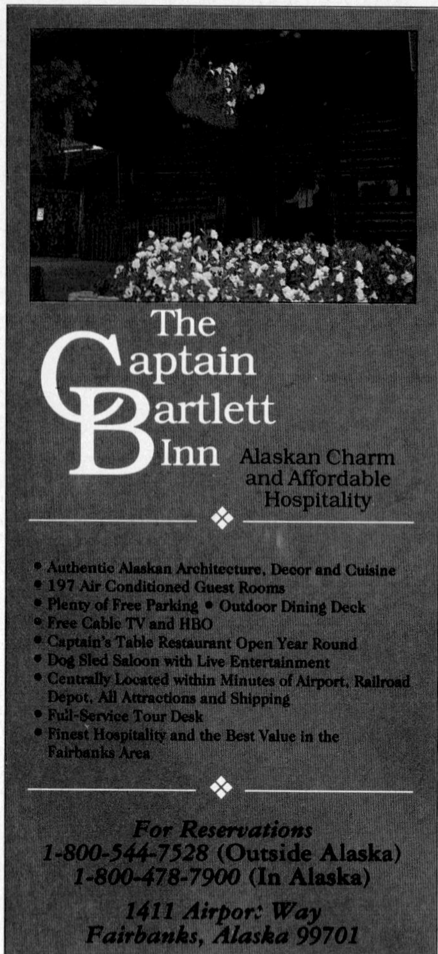

nomic impact on the city. Eielson has about 3,600 military personnel and approximately 5,100 dependents assigned, with about 1,700 military personnel and 1,700 family members living off base.

The University of Alaska Fairbanks and tourism are also primary economic factors.

DESCRIPTION

Alaska's second largest city and the administrative capital of the Interior, Fairbanks lies on the flat valley floor of the Tanana River on the banks of the Chena River. Good views of the valley are available from Chena Ridge Road to the west and Farmers Loop Road to the north. (Also on Farmers Loop Road, at Mile 5.5, is "the permafrost house." This contemporary home was built on permafrost, which occurs throughout the Interior, causing the foundation to sink and the house to buckle.)

The city is a blend of old and new: Modern hotels and shopping malls stand beside log cabins and historic wooden buildings.

Fairbanks is bounded to the north, east and west by low rolling hills of birch and white spruce. To the south is the Alaska

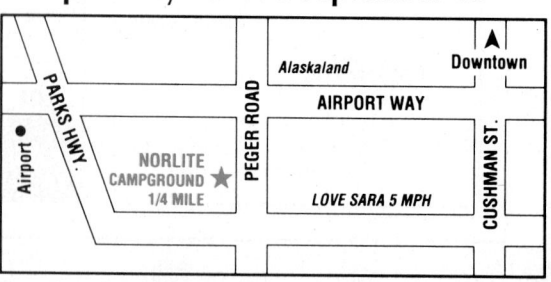

Range and Denali National Park, about a two-and-one-half-hour drive via the George Parks Highway. The Steese and Elliott highways lead north to the White Mountains.

ACCOMMODATIONS

Fairbanks has about two dozen hotels and motels and more than 100 bed and breakfasts during the summer. Rates vary widely, from a low of about $40 for a single to a high of $150 for a double. Reservations for accommodations are suggested during the busy summer months.

There are several private campgrounds in the Fairbanks area. Chena River recreation site, a state campground, is located on University Avenue by the Chena River bridge. The campground is closed until approximately July 4, 1994. When it reopens, it will have 57 sites, tables, firepits, toilets, water, dump station, $15/nightly camping fee or annual pass, $3 for use of dump station, $3 for use of boat launch.

There is overnight camping for self-contained RVs only at Alaskaland; four-night limit, $7 fee. City dump station on 2nd Avenue. ▲

The town has at least 100 restaurants ranging from deluxe to fast food.

Ah, Rose Marie Bed and Breakfast. Charming 1928 Fairbanks home. Very centrally located, downtown. Light/hearty breakfasts on enclosed front porch. Families welcomed. Friendly cat and dog. Outdoor smoking area. Year-round service. Extraordinary hospitality. Single $40 up, double $55 up. John E. Davis, 302 Cowles, Fairbanks, AK 99701. (907) 456-2040. [ADVERTISEMENT]

An Alaskan Viewpoint Bed and Breakfast. Lifetime Alaskans invite you to their gracious country home with breathtaking view of Alaska Range. Scrupulously clean, comfortable rooms, convenient location, reasonable rates. Laundry facilities, outdoor smoking deck. Lions (LCI) and educators welcome. 1244 Viewpoint, Fairbanks, AK 99709. Phone 1-800-479-7252. Member Fairbanks Visitors and Convention Bureau, Fairbanks Educators' Bed and Breakfast Network. VISA, MasterCard. [ADVERTISEMENT]

Alaska Welcomes You Bed & Breakfast. Enjoy real Alaskan native food while staying in a comfortable room with your own private bath. Convenient downtown location adjacent from the Chena River. Families welcome. Open year-round. Alaskan family owned and operated. Please contact us at (907) 451-6378 or 696 Slater Drive, Fairbanks, AK 99701-3445. Thanks and see you soon! [ADVERTISEMENT]

Applesauce Inn, on the wooded edge of town, offers full breakfast on a large screened gazebo for your mosquito-free dining. You may grill your own dinner. Good northern lights viewing when available! Private and shared baths. Elegant bedrooms decorated in Alaskan themes. A unique and friendly home hosted by Corbett and Christine Upton. For brochure and reservations: Applesauce Inn, P.O. Box 10355, Fairbanks, AK 99710. (907) 457-3392. [ADVERTISEMENT]

Bear Paw B&B. Share our warm and friendly family atmosphere and lovable cocker spaniel! Our private residence provides convenient in-town location, walking distance to Alaskaland, churches, restaurants and comfortable, clean quiet rooms. Complimentary airport/train depot transportation. Reasonable rates. Teachers and quilters are our specialty! Call/write Renée Kulikowski, 1101 Kodiak St., Fairbanks, AK 99709. Telephone (907) 474-4275. [ADVERTISEMENT]

Cedar Creek Inn. Ideal vacation or business home all your own! Beautiful, modern, impeccably clean. Available year-round. Privately nestled on 2 acres of spruce and birch, just 7 miles north of town. Excellent northern lights viewing when showing. Two bedrooms, one-and-one-half baths, phone, TV, laundry. Kitchen stocked for breakfast. For illustrated brochure and weekly rates: Cedar Creek Inn, P.O. Box 10355, Fairbanks, AK 99710. (907) 457-3392. [ADVERTISEMENT]

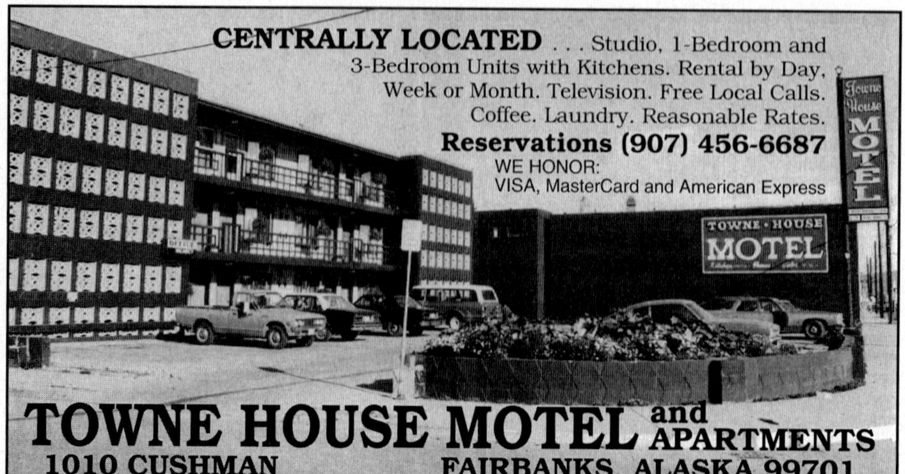

The Chocolate Rush Bed & Breakfast. Attractive, comfortable accommodations in remodeled 1940s home. Downtown Fairbanks location. Full or continental breakfast and our delicious Blue Ribbon Chocolate Truffles. Single $50, double $60, private bath unit $70. MC/VISA. For brochure and reservations, write P.O. Box 72296, Fairbanks, AK 99707. Or call (907) 474-8633. Open year-round. [ADVERTISEMENT]

Ester Gold Camp. RV parking. Historic district. Located 5 miles west of Fairbanks, Mile 351.7 George Parks Highway. P.O. Box 109MP, Ester, AK 99725. (907) 479-2500. 800-676-6925. Fax (907) 474-1780. Dry camping, no hookups, water, dump station, showers. $9. Reservations accepted. Dinner restaurant, home of the world famous Malemute Saloon. Shows Monday through Saturday. Leroy Zimmerman's Northern Lights and Alaska Shows nightly. Gift shop. See log ad **Milepost A 351.7** Parks Highway

and display ads in FAIRBANKS section.
[ADVERTISEMENT] ▲

Fairbanks Princess Hotel. Air-conditioned 200-room hotel located on the banks of the Chena River. Terraced deck area, gift shop, fine or casual dining, tour desk. Five minutes from downtown and Fairbanks International Airport. Meeting rooms to accommodate up to 200 guests. Open year-round. Write 2815 2nd Ave., Suite 400, Seattle, WA 98121-1299, or call (800) 426-0500.
[ADVERTISEMENT]

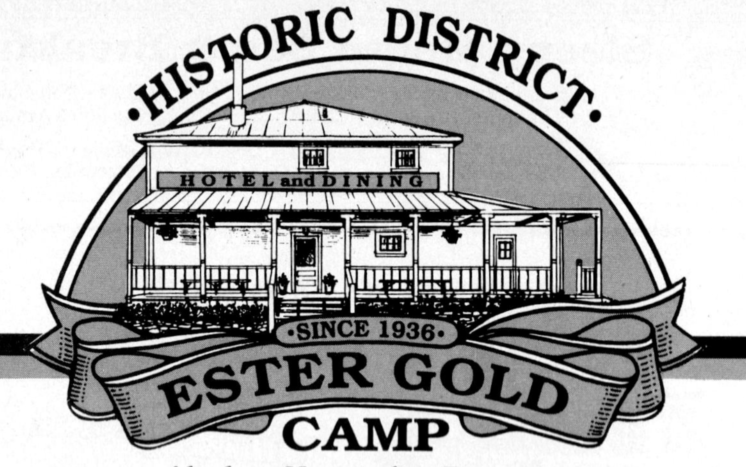

Alaskan Hospitality Featuring

ESTER CRAB HOUSE

Baked Halibut, Reindeer Stew, Country-style Chicken, Homemade Biscuits, Rice Pilaf, Garden Fresh Vegetables, Baked Beans, and Apple Crisp.

House Specialty

Alaska Dungeness Crab

5pm-9pm Nightly
Reservations Advised • Visa, MC, Discover

HOTEL & RV PARKING

Popular overnight for visitors traveling the Parks Hwy
Perfect setting for reliving the gold rush days.

HOTEL ... Clean, modest rooms with semi-private bathrooms & includes a continental breakfast. $46.00 - $64.00 plus tax

RV PARKING...Dry camping, water, dump station, showers • $9.00/ night

A peaceful gold camp just 5 miles from Fairbanks

NORTHERN LIGHTS SHOW

• The Crown of Lights •
Experience the majestic splendor of the Aurora Borealis.

• Alaska From The Heart •
Scenes of Alaskan Wildlife and Denali National Park.
Both shows available nightly

Home of The World Famous

MALEMUTE SALOON

Live Performances featuring ...

SONGS • MUSIC • DANCE • STORIES
ROBERT SERVICE POETRY

Mon- Sat 9pm • Reservations Advised

ESTER GOLD CAMP PO Box 109MP, Ester, Alaska 99725
907-479-2500 •800-676-6925 •Fax 474-1780

For more information see log ad. Mile 351.7 George Parks Hwy.

Geni's Bed & Breakfast. Country hospitality May to September. Two bedrooms with queen-sized beds, shared full bath. No pets, smoking on deck only. Continental or full country breakfast. Affordable accommodations in woodland setting 15 minutes

from Fairbanks at Mile 5.3 Chena Hot Springs Road. Handmade Alaska crafts available. George and Nila Lyle, P.O. Box 10352, Fairbanks, AK 99710; phone (907) 488-4136.
[ADVERTISEMENT]

ELEANOR'S Northern Lights
BED & BREAKFAST
SINGLE $50 • DOUBLE $55-$70
(907) 452-2598
360 STATE STREET, FAIRBANKS, ALASKA 99701
Near downtown • Credit cards accepted

BED & BREAKFAST
Stay with local teachers in their spacious home.
Bienvenue
Bienvenidos

- Continental breakfast
- Transportation (to and from airport and train)
- Telephone, T.V., VCR (Alaska videos)
- Excellent hospitality

1-800-453-4017
(907) 479-2564

Reservations made to other B&Bs in Alaska and Canada

It's not unusual to see a floatplane parked in front of Chena River homes. (Lee Foster)

Gold Dredge Number 8 Hotel & Bed & Breakfast. Nice accommodations reasonably priced. Acres of safe secure RV parking.

Plenty of things to do. Touring Dredge Number 8 gold panning is fun for everyone. Gold fever under every rock. See display ad in this section. [ADVERTISEMENT]

Goldhill RV Park & Cabins is proud to be Fairbanks's only park successfully combining nature with modern conveniences. Located on the northwest side of Fairbanks, Goldhill is convenient to all attractions, shopping and the University of Alaska. Nestled in a spruce forest on 12.5 acres of an old F.E. Co. mining claim, Goldhill is ideally situated for family fun and safety. Goldhill's policy of cleaning and disinfecting the private showers after each use and their sparkling clean laundry and restrooms are popular with all family members. Personal, friendly service is always first at Goldhill. See display ad this section. [ADVERTISEMENT] ▲

Marilyn's Bed and Breakfast. Enjoy true pioneer friendliness in a comfortable, homey atmosphere. Continental or full Alaskan breakfast with homemade jams. Perhaps you may persuade Marilyn to fix waffles made from her 1877 sourdough starter. Located downtown Fairbanks. No smoking. Off-street parking. For reservations, Marilyn Nigro, 651

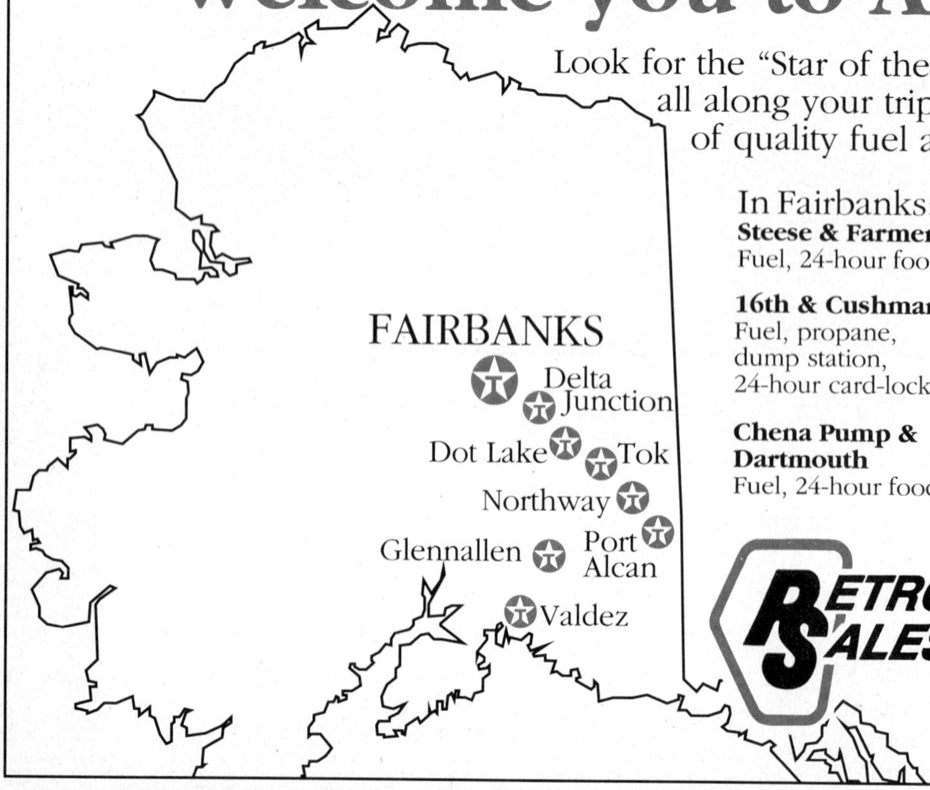

9th Ave., Fairbanks, AK 99701. (907) 456-1959. [ADVERTISEMENT]

Norlite Campground, Inc. Centrally located just 0.3 mile south off Airport Road on Peger Road, Norlite is the most complete of all Fairbanks's campgrounds. City water, sewer and electric hookups, showers, dump station, tour tickets, laundry, liquor store, truck/car wash, snack and ice cream bar and grocery store are all on the grounds. (907) 474-0206, fax (907) 474-0992. (See ad in this section.) [ADVERTISEMENT] ▲

River's Edge RV Park & Campground. Fairbanks's newest and most modern facility. Centrally located. Only full-service RV park on the Chena River. Pull-through sites, full and partial hookups, 30 amp, dump station, free showers, laundry. Daily free shuttle to stern-wheeler *Discovery* and Alaska Salmon Bake at Alaskaland. See map in ad. Phone (907) 474-0286. [ADVERTISEMENT] ▲

TRANSPORTATION

Scheduled Air Carriers: Several international, interstate and intra-Alaska air carriers serve Fairbanks; see Air Travel in the GENERAL INFORMATION section for details.

Charter Flights: A large number of air charter services are available for flightseeing, fly-in fishing and hunting trips and trips to bush villages; see ads in this section.

Warbelow's Air Ventures, Inc. Local scheduled and charter air service. Get off the beaten path and experience the ultimate in bush excursions! Available daily: bush mail flights, Arctic Circle tours, hot springs fly-in packages, flightseeing. Located at 3758 University Ave. S., Fairbanks, AK 99709; phone (907) 474-0518. In business for almost 40 years. [ADVERTISEMENT]

Alaska Railroad: Passenger depot at 280 N. Cushman St. in the downtown area. Daily passenger service in summer between Fairbanks and Anchorage with stopovers at Denali National Park; less frequent service in winter. For details see the ALASKA RAILROAD section, or phone 456-4155.

Bus: Scheduled motorcoach service to Anchorage and points south. Local daily bus service by Metropolitan Area Commuter Service (MACS), and regular MACS service is

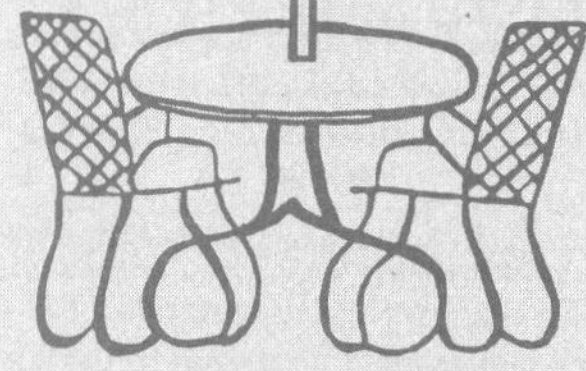

also now available to North Pole; no service on Sundays and some legal holidays. Drivers do not carry change, and exact change or tokens must be used. Fares are: $1.50 or one token. Tokens are available at Transit Park or the UAF Woodcenter. Information is available via the Transit Hotline, phone 459-1011, or from MACS offices at 3175 Peger Road, phone 459-1002.

Tours: Local and area sightseeing tours are available.

Arctic Safari Tours & Auto Rentals. Sheila Taranto introduces the world's most Northern Limousine! We'll make your trip to the Arctic unforgettable. Come for the famous Bowhead whaling, birdwatching, photo safaris and backpacking trips. Imagine touring the "last" frontier along the Arctic Ocean in a limousine! Arctic Safari has a special way of showing off Barrow. We do more than the others can offer you all year long. Limo on call to host you while in Barrow. "Go Native." Call 1-800-852-8424 or (907) 852-4444. P.O. Box 66, Barrow, AK 99723. [ADVERTISEMENT]

Train to Denali. Ride the luxurious private domed railcars of the McKinley Explorer to Denali National Park from either Anchorage or Fairbanks. Overnight packages in Denali with roundtrip train service are available from only $210 ppdo. Call Gray Line of Alaska at (907) 452-2843 for train and package tour options. [ADVERTISEMENT]

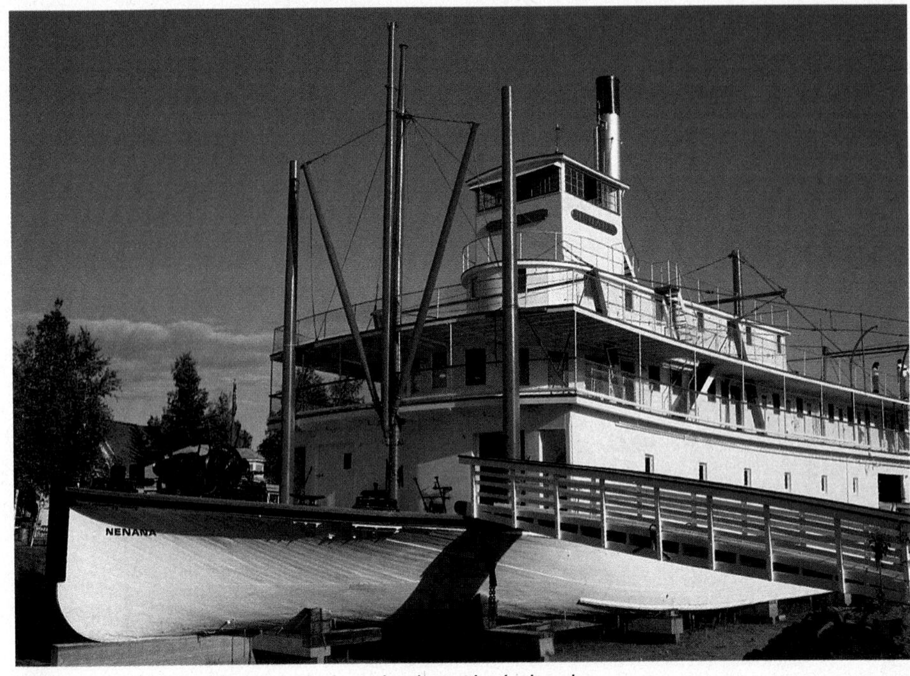

The sternwheeler Nenana *is beached at Alaskaland.* (Jerrianne Lowther, staff)

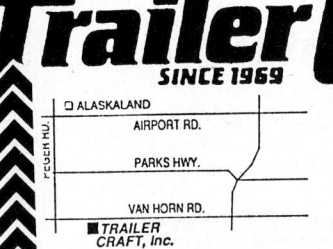

Taxi Service: Eight cab companies (see phone book).

Car, Camper and Trailer Rentals: Several companies rent cars, campers and trailers; see ads in this section.

ATTRACTIONS

Get Acquainted: A good place to start is at the visitor information center at 550 1st Ave., where you'll find free brochures, maps and tips on what to see and how to get there. Phone 456-5774, 456-INFO, or 1-800-327-5774 for a recording of current daily events.

Next to the log cabin visitor information center is Golden Heart Park, site of the 18-foot/5-m bronze monument, *Unknown First Family*. The statue, by sculptor Malcolm Alexander, and park were dedicated in July 1986 to celebrate Fairbanks's history and heritage.

The Alaska Public Lands Information Center, located in the lower level of historic Courthouse Square at 3rd Avenue and Cushman Street, is a free museum and information center featuring Alaska's natural history, cultural artifacts and recreational opportunities. In addition to detailed information on outdoor recreation in the state, the center offers films, interpretive programs, lectures and a book shop.

Tour the University of Alaska main campus, situated on a 2,250-acre ridge overlooking the city and Tanana River valley. The campus has all the features of a small town, including a fire station, post office, radio and TV station, medical clinic and a 1,000-seat concert hall.

UAF offers special tours and programs from June through August. These include tours of the Large Animal Research Station, Poker Flat Research Range and a slide show and tour at the Geophysical Institute, where research and study range from the center of the earth to the phenomena of the aurora.

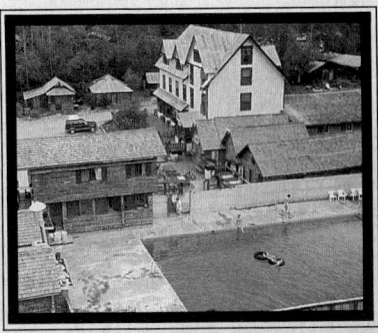

Films on mining in Alaska are also shown. Visitors can take a guided tour or tour on their own at the Agricultural and Forestry Experiment Station's Georgeson Botanical Garden, which is open to the public June through September. Free guided tours of the campus are provided Monday through Friday at 10 A.M.; tours begin at the UA Museum. Phone 474-7581 for information.

The University of Alaska Museum is a

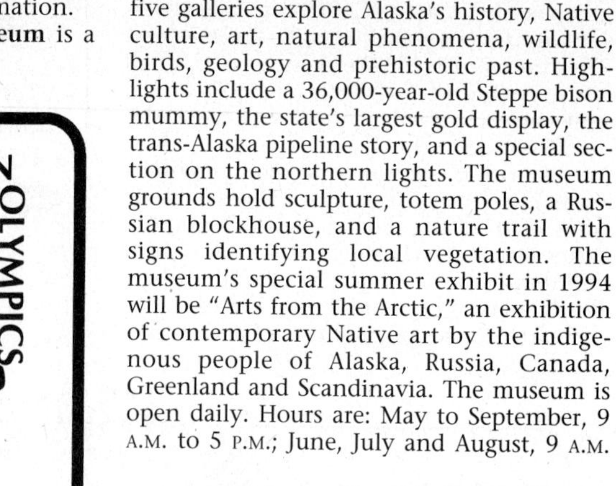

must stop for Fairbanks visitors. The museum features cultural and natural history displays from all the state's regions. The five galleries explore Alaska's history, Native culture, art, natural phenomena, wildlife, birds, geology and prehistoric past. Highlights include a 36,000-year-old Steppe bison mummy, the state's largest gold display, the trans-Alaska pipeline story, and a special section on the northern lights. The museum grounds hold sculpture, totem poles, a Russian blockhouse, and a nature trail with signs identifying local vegetation. The museum's special summer exhibit in 1994 will be "Arts from the Arctic," an exhibition of contemporary Native art by the indigenous people of Alaska, Russia, Canada, Greenland and Scandinavia. The museum is open daily. Hours are: May to September, 9 A.M. to 5 P.M.; June, July and August, 9 A.M.

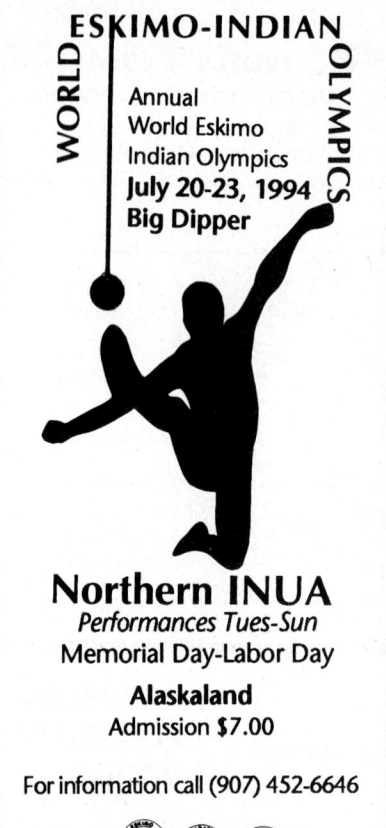

Summer Tourist Information
Phone 459-1095
Airport Way
and Peger Road
TRADING POST
MCCP
The frontier spirit of Alaska waits for you at Alaskaland. Enter a gold mine; you can almost hear the prospectors' shouts of discovery. Board a paddle wheel riverboat and imagine cruising the Yukon. Feel the spirit of a sourdough at your shoulder.
The Pioneer Museum. A scrumptious salmon bake. The recreated Native Village. A gold rush town. All this and more beckons you to Alaskaland, the only pioneer theme park in all of Alaska. To really understand today's Alaska you've got to visit the Alaska of yesterday.
Concessionaires, cabin curio shops and tourist information center are open 11 a.m. to 9 p.m. daily
Alaskaland

Gold Dredge Number 8, just north of Fairbanks, is open for tours. (Jerrianne Lowther, staff)

to 7 P.M.; October through April, noon to 5 P.M. Admission fees: $4 adults; $3 senior citizens and military; $12.50 for family with up to four adults; children under 12 are free. For 24-hour information, call 474-7505.

Take in Some Local Events: Fairbanks has some unique summer celebrations. Late June is a busy time as Fairbanks celebrates the longest day of the year (summer solstice is June 21). The Midnight Sun Baseball Game will be played at 10:45 P.M. on solstice weekend, when no artificial lights are used. The Yukon 800 also gets under way; a marathon outboard boat race of 800 miles/1287 km on the Chena, Tanana and Yukon rivers to Galena and back. A Midnight Sun 10K Fun Run begins at 10 P.M.

Golden Days, when Fairbanksans turn out in turn-of-the-century dress and celebrate the gold rush, is July 14–23, 1994. Golden Days starts off with a Felix Pedro look-alike taking his gold to the bank and includes a parade and rededication of the Pedro Monument honoring Felix Pedro, the man who started it all when he discovered gold in the Tanana hills. Other events include pancake breakfasts, a dance, canoe and raft races and free outdoor concerts.

The World Eskimo and Indian Olympics, with Native competition in such events as the high kick, greased pole walk, stick pull, fish cutting, parka contest and muktuk-eating contest will be held July 20–23, 1994.

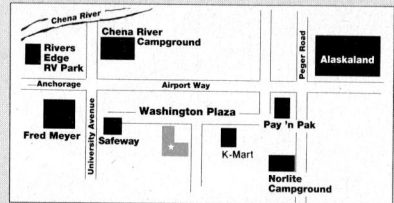

The annual Tanana Valley Fair will be held Aug. 13–20, 1994. Alaska's oldest state fair, the Tanana Valley Fair features agricultural exhibits, arts and crafts, food booths, a rodeo and other entertainments.

Fairbanks Summer Arts Festival, two weeks of workshops and concerts involving jazz to classics, dance, theater and the visual arts, will be held July 22 to Aug. 7, 1994.

Check with the Fairbanks visitor information center for more information on local events.

Besides these special events, summer visitors can take in a semi-pro baseball game at Growden Park where the Fairbanks Goldpanners take on other Alaska league teams.

Visit Creamer's Field. Follow the flocks of waterfowl to Creamer's Field Migratory Waterfowl Refuge. Located 1 mile/1.6 km from downtown Fairbanks, this 1,800-acre refuge managed by the Alaska Dept. of Fish and Game offers opportunities to observe large concentrations of ducks, geese, shorebirds and cranes in the spring and fall. Throughout the summer, sandhill cranes take advantage of the barley fields planted to provide them with food.

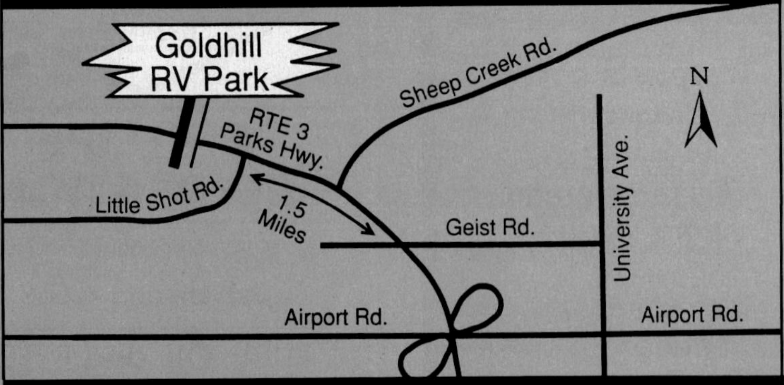

Explore the 2-mile/3.2-km self-guided nature trail and the renovated historic farmhouse that serves as a visitor center. Stop at 1300 College Road to find the trailhead, viewing areas and brochures on Creamer's Field. For more information, phone 452-1531.

Tanana Valley Farmers Market. Visit the Tanana Valley Farmers Market, College Road at the fairgrounds, the only farmers market in the Interior of Alaska. Open seasonally from July through September,

Wednesdays noon-5 P.M. and Saturdays 9 A.M. to 4 P.M. We have a great selection of locally grown vegetables and cut flowers. Handmade crafts, baked goods, Alaskan

meats and fish, and pottery are also available. Perennial flowers, shrubs and berry plants ready for transplanting into your garden. Meet you at the Market! [ADVERTISEMENT]

The Alaska Rag Co. A must-see for Fairbanks travelers. This unique Alaskan gift shop manufactures beautiful handwoven rag rugs from 100 percent recycled clothing, towels, afghans and scarves. The store also features works from many Alaskan artists. Items include pottery, paintings, stained glass, qiviut, dog hair hats, mittens and much more. Stop in, meet our weavers, and see their work. 547 2nd Ave., Fairbanks, AK 99701. (907) 451-4401. [ADVERTISEMENT]

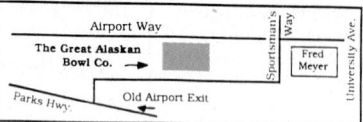

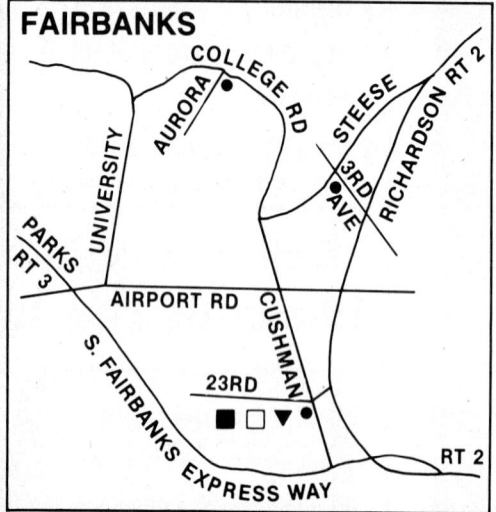

The Great Alaskan Bowl Company. A mile from the airport, the Great Alaskan Bowl Company is one of only two mills in the country still turning out one-piece wooden bowls. Watch demonstrations using 1800s ingenuity and 1990s technology from our large viewing area and learn about Alaska's forests. Ask for your free birch flowers! (907) 474-9663. 4630 Old Airport Road, Fairbanks, AK 99706. [ADVERTISEMENT]

Chena Pump House National Historic Site. Built between 1931 and 1933 by the Fairbanks Exploration Co. to pump water from the Chena River to dredging operations at Cripple Creek, the pump house was remodeled in 1978 and now houses a restaurant and saloon. The sheet metal cladding, interior roof and some equipment (such as the intake ditch) are from the original pump house, which shut down in 1958 when the F.E. Co. ceased its Cripple Creek dredging operations. The pump house is located at Mile 1.3 Chena Pump Road.

Sled Dog Racing. The Alaska Dog Mushers' Assoc. hosts a series of dog races beginning in mid-December with preliminary races, and ending in March with the Open North American Championship. The Open is a three-day event with three heats (of 20, 20, and 30 miles) with teams as large as 20 dogs; this race is considered by many to be the "granddaddy of dog races." Fairbanks also hosts the 1,000-mile Yukon Quest Sled Dog Race between Fairbanks and Whitehorse, YT. The Yukon Quest alternates start and finish between the two cities: the race will start in Fairbanks in 1994. For more information, contact the Alaska Dog Musher's Assoc. at 457-MUSH, or the Yukon Quest office at 451-8985.

See Bank Displays: The Key Bank, at 1st Avenue and Cushman Street, has a display of gold nuggets and several trophy animals. Mount McKinley Mutual Savings Bank features a display of McKinley prints and the original cannonball safe used when the bank first opened. The bank is at 531 3rd Ave.

Visit Historic Churches: St. Matthew's Episcopal, 1029 1st Ave., was originally built in 1905, but burned in 1947 and was rebuilt the following year. Of special inter-

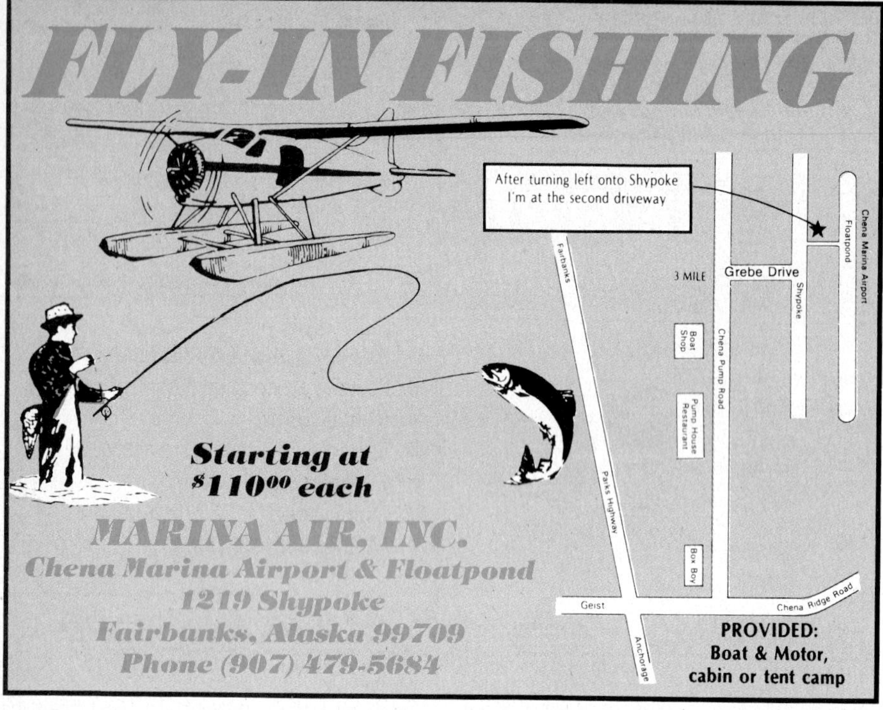

est is the church's intricately carved altar, made in 1906 of interior Alaska birch, saved from the fire.

Immaculate Conception Church, on the Chena River at Cushman Street bridge, was moved to its present location by horse in the winter of 1911 from its original site at 1st and Dunkel streets.

See the Pipeline: Drive about 10 miles/16 km north from downtown on the Steese Highway to see the trans-Alaska pipeline. Clearly visible are the thermal devices used to keep the permafrost frozen around the pipeline support columns.

View Mount McKinley: Best spot to see McKinley is from the University of Alaska Fairbanks campus (on Yukon Drive, between Talkeetna and Sheenjek streets) where a turnout and marker define the horizon view of Mount Hayes (elev. 13,832 feet/4,216m); Hess Mountain (elev. 11,940 feet/3,639m); Mount Deborah (elev. 12,339 feet/3,761m); and Mount McKinley (elev. 20,320 feet/6,194m). Distant foothills seen from the viewpoint are part of the Wood River Butte.

Cruise Aboard the Riverboat *Discovery*: Every day at 8:45 A.M. and 2 P.M. in summer, the riverboat *Discovery* departs for a half-day cruise on the Chena and Tanana rivers. Drive out Airport Road, turn south at Dale Road and continue 0.5 mile/0.8 km on Dale to Discovery Drive. Reservations are advised, as this is one of the most popular attractions in town. For the first leg of the trip, the *Discovery* winds its way down the meandering Chena River, its banks lined by

old homesteads, modern homes and bush planes. Passengers have the opportunity to see Susan Butcher's Iditarod dog team, and possibly four-time Iditarod winner Susan herself, or her husband, Dave. The Chena River also junctions with Cripple Creek, the Interior's richest gold rush stream. On the Tanana River, fishwheels turn in the swift glacial water, scooping up salmon to be dried and smoked for winter food. On the way back up the Chena River, the boat stops at Old Chena Indian Village, where Mary Shields, one of Alaska's premier dog mushers, puts on an informative and fun demonstration of how dogs are used for work and play. After the presentation, passengers disembark for a tour of the village. Guides from the *Discovery*, who are of Indian or Eskimo heritage, are on hand to explain past and present Native culture. For more information on the riverboat *Discovery*, contact Alaska Riverways, Inc., 1975 Discovery Dr., Fairbanks, AK 99709; phone 479-6673, fax 479-4613.

Visit Alaskaland Pioneer Park. Visitors will find a relaxed atmosphere at Alaskaland, a pleasant park with historic buildings, small shops, food, entertainment, playgrounds and four covered picnic shelters. The park — which has no admission fee — is open year-round.

The 44-acre historic park was created in 1967 as the Alaska Centennial Park to commemorate the 100th year of American sovereignty. Designed to provide a taste of interior Alaska history, visitors may begin their visit at the information center (inside the newly renovated stern-wheeler *Nenana*, a national landmark). Walk through Gold Rush Town, a narrow winding street of authentic old buildings that once graced downtown Fairbanks and now house gift shops. Here you will find: the Kitty Hensley and Judge Wickersham houses, furnished with turn-of-the-century items; the First Presbyterian Church, constructed in 1906; and the Pioneers of Alaska Museum, dedicated to those who braved frontier life to found Fairbanks. Free guided historical walking tours take place each afternoon.

The top level of the Civic Center houses an art gallery, featuring rotating contemporary exhibits and paintings; open year-round, 11 A.M. to 9 P.M. daily, Memorial Day through Labor Day; noon to 8 P.M. daily, except Monday, during the rest of the year. *Northern Inua*, a show celebrating Native culture, performed nightly, except Mondays, at 8 P.M. in summer in the Civic Center theater. Admission is $7, or $4 for children 5-12. Call 452-6646 for more information.

Behind the Civic Center, you'll find the Pioneer Air Museum, which features antique aircrafts and stories of their Alaskan pilots, with displays from 1913–1948. Call (907) 451-0037, May 15–Oct. 15, for information.

In the back of the park is the Native Village Museum and Kashims with Native wares, artifacts, crafts and exhibitions of Native dancing. Across from the Native Village is Mining Valley, with displays of gold-mining equipment. A covered picnic area and the Salmon Bake are also part of Mining Valley. A popular feature, the Salmon Bake is open daily for lunch from noon to 2 P.M. (June 10 to Aug. 15), and for dinner from 5-9 P.M. (end of May to mid-September). Salmon, barbecued ribs, halibut and 16-ounce porterhouse steaks are served, rain or shine. Heated indoor seating area available.

There's entertainment seven nights a

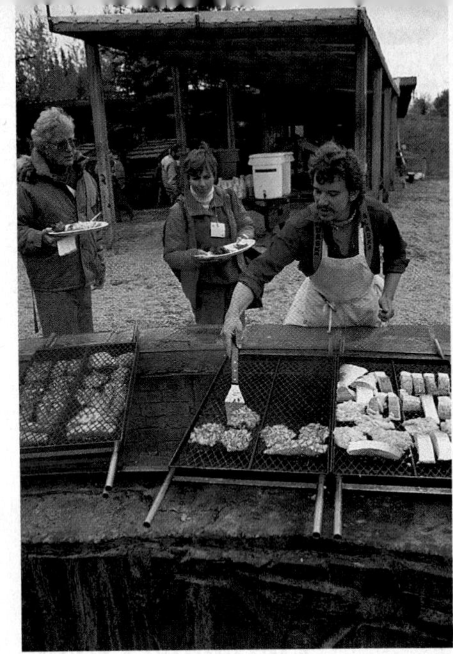

Alaskaland's popular salmon bake.
(Lee Foster)

week starting at 8 P.M. at the Palace Theatre & Saloon, featuring a musical comedy review about life in Fairbanks titled *Golden Heart Review*. The Big Stampede show in Gold Rush Town is a theatre in the round presenting the paintings of Rusty Heurlin depicting the trail of '98; narrative by Ruben Gaines.

A Pioneer Aviation Museum, opened in June 1992, features artifacts of Alaskan aviation. Historic aircraft engines and photos are displayed. $1 admission.

The Crooked Creek & Whiskey Island Railroad, a 30-gauge train, takes passengers for a 12-minute ride around the park. Other types of recreational activities available at Alaskaland include miniature golf and an antique carousel. A public dock is located on the Chena River at the rear of the park.

Visitors are welcome to take part in square and round dances year-round at the Alaskaland Dance Center. Square dances are Tuesday and Wednesday at 7:30 P.M., Friday and Saturday at 8 P.M. Round dances are at 7:30 P.M. Thursday. For more information about Alaskaland, call 459-1087.

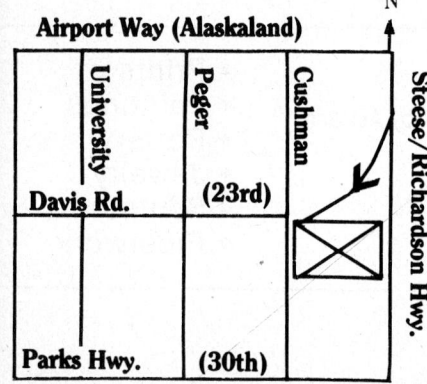

Area Attractions: Fairbanks is a good jumping-off point for many attractions in Alaska's Interior. Head out the Steese Highway for swimming at Chena Hot Springs or Circle Hot Springs. At Fox, 11.5 miles/18.5 km north of Fairbanks, the Steese Highway junctions with the Elliott Highway, which leads to the start of the Dalton Highway (formerly the North Slope Haul Road). Popular attractions in this area include Gold Dredge Number 8 (take Goldstream Road exit to Old Steese Highway), a historic five-deck, 250-foot dredge, and Little El Dorado Gold Camp at Mile 1.2 Elliott Highway, which offers gold mining demonstrations and gold panning. See highway sections for details.

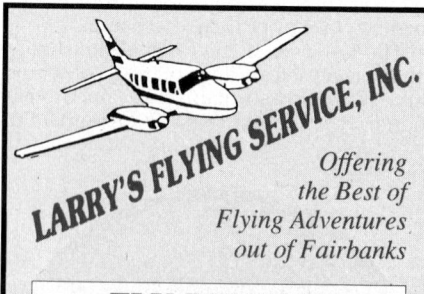

Denali National Park is a two-and-one-half-hour drive by bus or car, or a three-and-one-half-hour train trip via the Alaska

Railroad, from Fairbanks. Once there, take the shuttle bus or guided tour through the park. For area road conditions, phone the Dept. of Transportation at 451-2206.

Eielson AFB, 23 miles/37 km south of Fairbanks on the Richardson–Alaska Highway, was built in 1943. Originally a satellite base to Ladd Field (now Fort Wainwright) and called Mile 26, it served as a storage site for aircraft on their way to the Soviet Union under the WWII Lend–Lease program. Closed after WWII, the base was reactivated in 1948 and renamed Eielson AFB, after Carl Ben Eielson, the first man to fly from Alaska over the North Pole to Greenland. A weekly tour of the base is offered every Friday from 9–10:30 A.M.; phone the public affairs office at 377-2116 for reservations and more information.

There are one-day or longer sightseeing trips to Point Barrow, Prudhoe Bay, Fort Yukon and other bush destinations. See ads in this section or consult local travel services.

Play Tennis: There is one outdoor plexipave court at Hez Ray Recreation Complex, 19th Avenue and Lathrop Street. There are six outdoor asphalt courts at the Mary Siah Recreation Center, 1025 14th Ave. No fees or reservations. For more information phone 459-1070.

Play Golf: Maintaining a scenic nine-hole course with artificial greens, the Fairbanks Golf and Country Club (public invited) is west of the downtown area at Farmers Loop and Ballaine Road, phone 479-6555 for information and reservations. The nine-hole Chena Bend Golf Course is located on Fort Wainwright; phone 355-6749. North Star Golf Club, located 10 minutes north of downtown on the Old Steese Highway, also offers a regulation nine-hole course; phone 457-4653 or 452-2104.

Ride Bikes Around Fairbanks: There are many day-touring choices in Fairbanks. A round-trip tour of the city, the University of Alaska and the College area can be made by leaving town on Airport Way and returning on College Road. The Farmers Loop Road or a ride out the highway toward Fox are two more easy tours.

Go Skiing: Fairbanks has several downhill ski areas: Cleary Summit, **Milepost F 20.6** Steese Highway; Skiland, **Milepost F 20.9** Steese Highway; Eielson Air Force Base and Fort Wainwright ski hills; Moose Mountain Ski Resort, Spinach Creek Road on Murphy Dome; and an alpine ski hill at Chena Hot Springs Resort at **Milepost J 56.5** Chena Hot Springs Road.

Cross-country ski trails are at Birch Hill Recreation Area; drive 2.8 miles/4.5 km north of Fairbanks via Steese Expressway to a well-marked turnoff, then drive in 2.3 miles/3.7 km. University of Alaska Fairbanks has 26 miles/42 km of cross-country ski trails. The trail system is quite extensive; you may ski out to Ester Dome.

Go Ice Skating: Hez Ray Recreation Complex, 19th and Lathrop, offers both indoor and outdoor skating rinks; rental skates available. Phone 459-1070 for public skating hours.

Go Swimming. Fairbanks North Star Borough Parks and Recreation Dept. offers three pools: Mary Siah Recreation Center, 1025 14th Ave., phone 459-1467; Robert Hamme Memorial Pool, 901 Airport Way, phone 459-1468; and Robert Wescott Memorial Pool, 8th Avenue in North Pole, phone 488-9401. Call for swim hours and fees.

Chena Lakes Recreation Area. This 2,178-acre park, located 17 miles/27 km southeast of Fairbanks on the Richardson

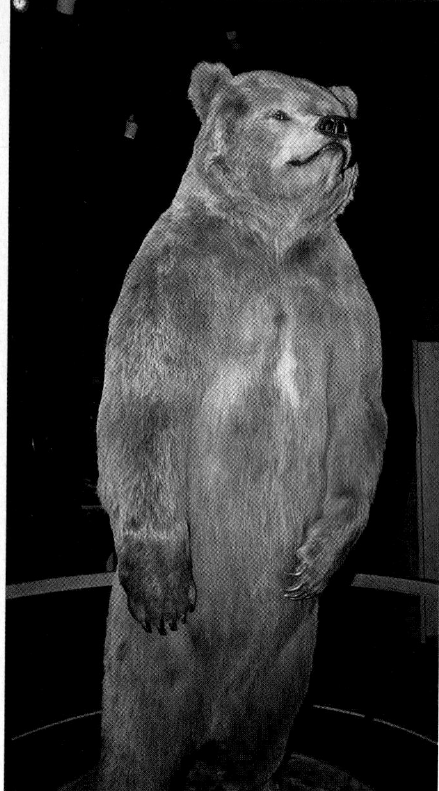

University of Alaska Museum's bear.
(Lee Foster)

Highway, offers a wide assortment of outdoor recreation. There are 80 campsites for both RV and tent camping, including campsites on an island; canoe, sailboat and rowboat rentals; bike paths and trails for nature hikes, skiing, ski-joring and dog mushing; and boat-ramp access to the nearby Chena River ($6 fee charged). Admission to the park, maintained by the Fairbanks North Star Borough, is $3 per vehicle between Memorial Day and Labor Day. No admission is charged the rest of the year.

Go Fishing: There are several streams and lakes within driving distance of Fairbanks, and local fishing guides are available. **Chena Lake**, about 20 miles/32 km southeast of the city via the Richardson–Alaska Highway at Chena Lakes Recreation Area, is stocked with rainbow trout, silver salmon and arctic char. The **Chena River** and its tributaries offer fishing for sheefish, whitefish, northern pike and burbot. The Chena River flows through Fairbanks. Chena Hot Springs Road off the Steese Highway provides access to fisheries in the Chena River Recreation Area (see the STEESE HIGHWAY section). The Steese Highway also offers access to the **Chatanika River** for northern pike and burbot fishing. Special regulations apply in these waters for grayling and salmon fishing. Phone the ADF&G office at (907) 456-4359.

Air taxi operators and guides in Fairbanks offer short trips from the city for rainbow trout, grayling, northern pike, lake trout and sheefish in lakes and streams of the Tanana and Yukon river drainages. Some operators have camps set up for overnight trips while others specialize in day trips. The air taxi operators usually provide a boat and motor for their angling visitors. Rates are reasonable, and vary according to the distance from town and type of facilities offered.

DENALI NATIONAL PARK

(Formerly Mount McKinley National Park) Includes log of Park Road

(See map, page 394)

Hikers cross the autumn tundra above the McKinley River. Clouds obscure the top of Mount McKinley. (Michael DeYoung)

Denali National Park and Preserve (formerly Mount McKinley National Park) lies on the north flank of the Alaska Range, 250 miles/402 km south of the Arctic Circle. The park entrance, accessible by highway, railroad and aircraft, is 237 highway miles/382 km north of Anchorage, and about half that distance from Fairbanks.

The park is open year-round to visitors, although the hotel, most campgrounds, gas, food and shuttle bus service within the park are available only from late May or early June to mid-September. (Opening dates for facilities and activities for the summer season are announced in the spring by the Park Service and depend mainly on snow conditions in May.)

When you arrive be sure to stop at the Visitor Access Center, near the park entrance. The center offers information on campgrounds in the park; maps, brochures and schedules of events; details on campfire talks, hikes, nature walks, sled dog demonstrations, wildlife tours; shuttle bus schedules; and other tips on what to see and do in the park. The center is open daily in summer, generally from early morning into the evening.

During the peak summer season, visitors should allow a minimum of two full days in order to obtain bus seats and campground sites within the park. Lodging and camping are available outside the park on the George Parks Highway, and there are a variety of activities — river rafting, hikes and ranger programs — to enjoy. The Denali experience is considered well worth the wait. Check with operators outside the park and with personnel at the Visitor Access Center about programs and activities.

Parking space is limited within the park at the Visitor Access Center. Overflow parking is available at Riley Creek Campground (walk or mini-shuttle to Visitor Access Center).

First-time visitors should be particularly aware of the controlled-access system for Park Road use. Private vehicle traffic on the 91-mile/146-km road into the park is restricted beyond Savage River check station (**Milepost J 14.8**). Campers must register for all campgrounds at the Visitor Access Center; see Accommodations this section. The free shuttle bus system and concession-operated tours are available to allow visitors a means of viewing the park without disturbing the wildlife; see Transportation this section for details on the shuttle service.

NOTE: The following announcement by the National Park Service pertains to the Park Road: "Since 1974, wildlife sightings along the Denali National Park Road corridor have declined significantly as a result of increased vehicle traffic and the activities associated with private vehicle use." In an effort to preserve the wildlife viewing opportunities for the public, the National Park Service has set road traffic limits. Traffic will be held to the 1984 averages. Consequently, there are limited bus seats available. When planning trips to the park, visitors should plan activities in the entrance area, such as attending naturalist programs, for the first one or two days, until bus seats can be obtained.

An admission fee of $4 per person ($8 per family) is charged to visitors traveling beyond the Savage River checkpoint at Mile 14.8 on the Park Road (see log this section). The fee is collected when visitors obtain shuttle bus tickets and campground permits at the Visitor Access Center. Persons 16 years of age or less, and U.S. citizens 62 years or older, are exempt from the admission fee. (A $15 annual park pass, and the $25 Golden Eagle Pass, are valid for admission.)

For information about the park, write Denali National Park and Preserve, P.O. Box 9, Denali Park, AK 99755; winter phone (907) 683-2294, summer phone (907) 683-1266 or 1267. Or contact the Alaska Public Lands Information centers in Anchorage at 605 W. 4th Ave., 99501, phone (907) 271-2737, and in Fairbanks at 250 Cushman St., Suite 1A, 99701, phone (907) 456-0527.

One of the park's best known attractions is Mount McKinley, North America's highest mountain at 20,320 feet/6,194m. On a clear day, Mount McKinley is visible from Anchorage. However, cloudy, rainy summer weather frequently obscures the mountain, and travelers have about a 20 percent chance of seeing it.

First mention of Mount McKinley was in 1794, when English explorer Capt. George Vancouver spotted a "stupendous snow mountain" from Cook Inlet. Early Russian explorers and traders called the peak *Bolshaia Gora,* or "Big Mountain." The Tanana Indian name for the mountain is Denali, said to mean the "high one." The mountain was named McKinley in 1896 by a Princeton-educated prospector named William A. Dickey for presidential nominee William McKinley of Ohio. Even today, the mountain has two names: Mount McKinley according to USGS maps, and Denali according to the state Geographic Names Board.

The history of climbs on McKinley is as intriguing as its many names. In 1903, Judge James Wickersham and party climbed to an estimated 8,000 feet, while Dr. Frederick A. Cook and party reached the 11,000-foot level. In 1906, Cook returned to the mountain and made two attempts at the summit — the first unsuccessful, and the second (according to Cook) successful. Cook's vague description of his ascent route and a questionable summit photo led many to doubt his claim. Tom Lloyd, of the 1910 Sourdough Party (which included Charles McGonagall, Pete Anderson and Billy Taylor), claimed they reached both summits (north and south peaks) but could not provide any photographic evidence. (Much later it was verified that the men had reached the summit of the lower north peak.) The first complete ascent of the true summit of Mount McKinley was made in 1913 by Hudson Stuck, Harry Karstens and Walter Harper.

Today, close to a thousand people attempt to climb Mount McKinley each year between April and June, most flying in to base camp at 7,000 feet. (The first airplane landing on the mountain was flown in 1932 by Joe Crosson.) Geographic features of McKinley and its sister peaks bear the names of many early explorers: Eldridge and Muldrow glaciers, after George Eldridge and Robert Muldrow of the USGS who determined the peak's altitude in 1898; Wickersham Wall; Karstens Ridge; and Mount Carpe and Mount Koven, named for Allen Carpe and Theodore Koven, both killed in a 1932 climb.

Timberline in the park is 2,700 feet/823m. The landscape below timberline in this subarctic wilderness is called taiga, a term of Russian origin that describes the scant growth of trees. Black and white spruce, willow, dwarf birch and aspen grow at lower elevations. The uplands of alpine tundra are carpeted with lichens, mosses, wildflowers and low-growing shrubs. Wildflowers bloom in spring along the steep banks of the passes and in alpine meadows, usually peaking by early July.

Denali National Park represents one of the last intact ecosystems in the world, according to the Park Service. Here, visitors have the opportunity to observe the natural behavior of wild animals. Grizzly bears, caribou, wolves and red fox freely wander over the tundra. Moose wade through streams and lake shallows. A few lynx pursue snow-

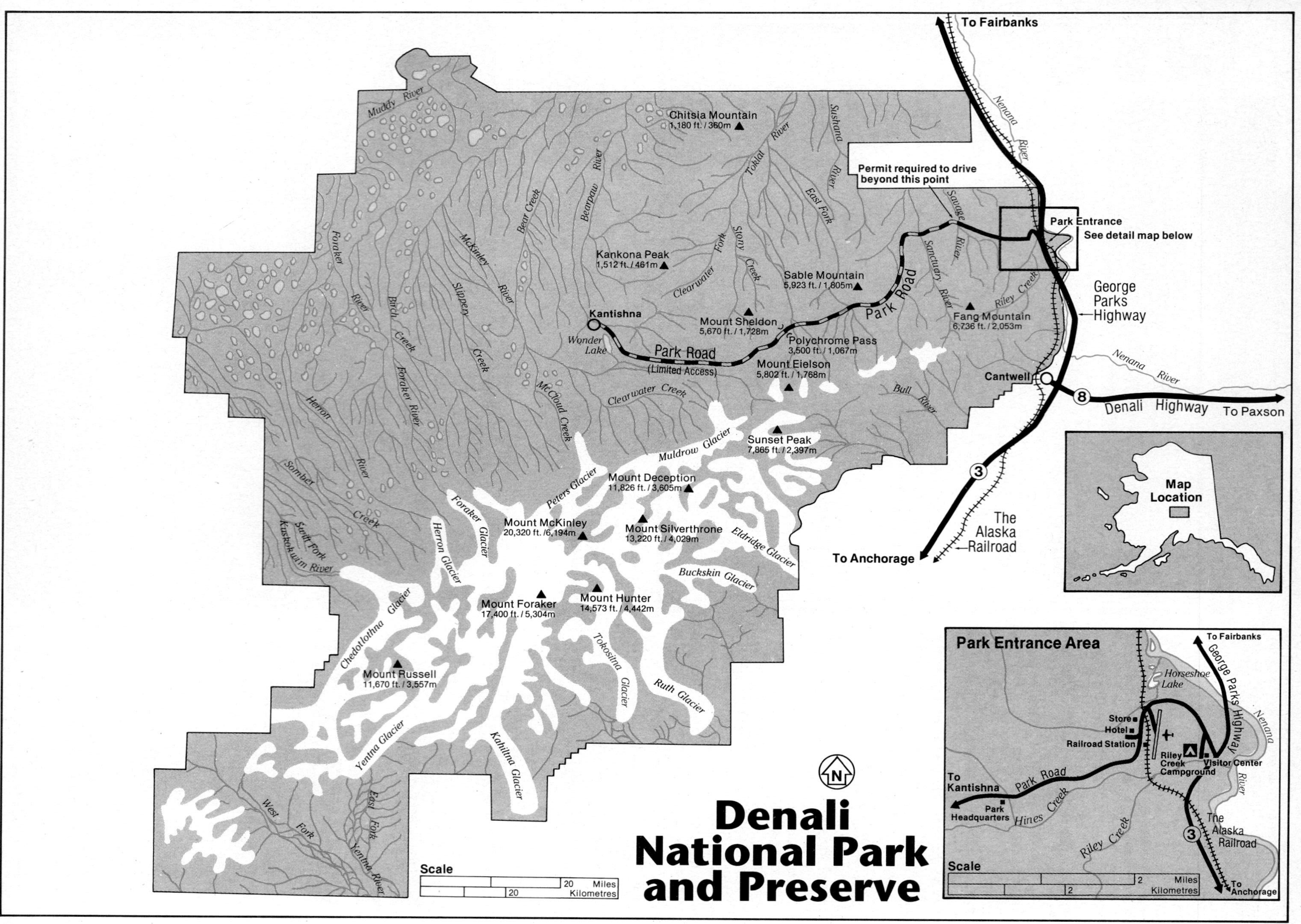
Denali National Park and Preserve
To Fairbanks
Nenana River
Park Entrance
See detail map below
George Parks Highway
Nenana River
Denali Highway
To Paxson
Cantwell
The Alaska Railroad
To Anchorage
Map Location
Permit required to drive beyond this point
Savage River
Sanctuary River
Riley Creek
Fang Mountain 6,736 ft. / 2,053m
Bull River
Park Road
Sable Mountain 5,923 ft. / 1,805m
Polychrome Pass 3,500 ft. / 1,067m
Mount Eielson 5,802 ft. / 1,768m
Sunset Peak 7,865 ft. / 2,397m
Sushana River
East Fork
Toklat River
Stony Creek
Mount Sheldon 5,670 ft. / 1,728m
Chitsia Mountain 1,180 ft. / 360m
Clearwater Fork
Kankona Peak 1,512 ft. / 461m
Park Road (Limited Access)
Clearwater Creek
Kantishna
Wonder Lake
Bearpaw River
McCloud Creek
Bear Creek
McKinley River
Slippery Creek
Muldrow Glacier
Eldridge Glacier
Buckskin Glacier
Mount Deception 11,826 ft. / 3,605m
Mount Silverthrone 13,220 ft. / 4,029m
Ruth Glacier
Mount Hunter 14,573 ft. / 4,442m
Tokositna Glacier
Peters Glacier
Mount McKinley 20,320 ft. /6,194m
Mount Foraker 17,400 ft. / 5,304m
Foraker Glacier
Kahiltna Glacier
Herron Glacier
Muddy River
Birch Creek
Foraker River
Mount Russell 11,670 ft. / 3,557m
Chedotlothna Glacier
Yentna Glacier
East Fork
Yentna River
West Fork
Herron River
Somber Creek
Swift Fork
Kuskokwim River
Scale
20 Miles
20 Kilometres
Park Entrance Area
To Fairbanks
George Parks Highway
Nenana River
Horseshoe Lake
Store
Hotel
Railroad Station
Riley Creek Campground
Visitor Center
To Kantishna
Park Road
Park Headquarters
Hines Creek
Riley Creek
The Alaska Railroad
To Anchorage
Scale
2 Miles
2 Kilometres

DENALI PARK ADVERTISERS

shoe hare in taiga forests. Marmots, pikas and Dall sheep inhabit high, rocky areas. The arctic ground squirrel's sharp warning call is heard throughout the park.

Migratory bird life encompasses species from six continents, including waterfowl, shorebirds, songbirds and birds of prey. Ptarmigan, gray jays and magpies are year-round residents.

The park's silty glacial rivers are not an angler's delight, but grayling, Dolly Varden and lake trout are occasionally caught in streams and small lakes.

ACCOMMODATIONS

There is only one hotel within the park, but several motels will be found outside the park along the George Parks Highway (turn to **Milepost A 237.3** in the GEORGE PARKS HIGHWAY section). Accommodations are also available in the Kantishna area. *NOTE: Visitors should make reservations for lodging far in advance.* The park hotel and area motels are often filled during the summer. Visitors must book their own accommodations.

Camp Denali, begun in 1951, is known as a premier national park wilderness vacation lodge and nature center. Its log cabins dot a hillside looking out onto an expansive view of Mount McKinley and the Alaska Range. Activities focus on guided hiking with experienced naturalists, photography, canoeing, biking, rafting, flightseeing, gold-panning, evening natural history programs and periodic summer seminars. Central dining; 35 to 40 guests; all-expense. See display ad. [ADVERTISEMENT]

Carlo Creek Lodge. (907) 683-2576, 683-2573. Located 12 miles south of Denali Park entrance. 32 wooded acres bordered by beautiful Carlo Creek, the Nenana River and Denali National Park. Cozy log cabins with

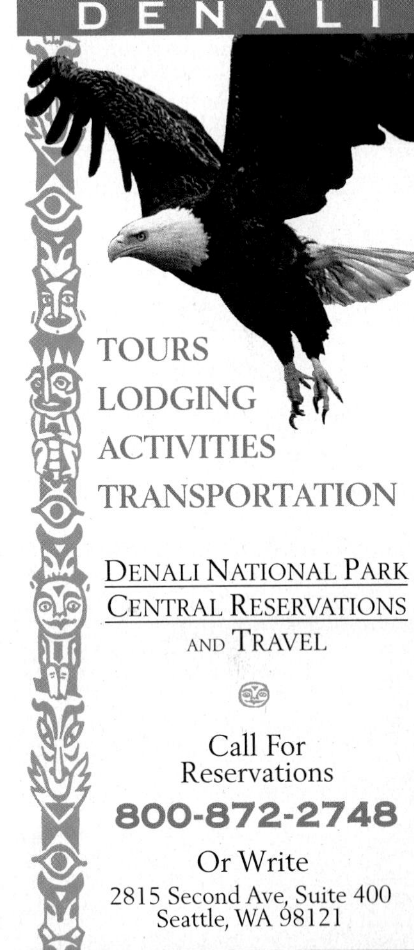

own bathroom and shower on creek. RV park, dump station, tent sites, large barbecue pit with roof. Public bathrooms with showers. Small general store, gift shop with Alaskan made gifts from fur to lace. Information and pay phone. Walking distance to The Perch Restaurant. See display ad at Mile 224 Parks Highway. [ADVERTISEMENT]

Denali Backcountry Lodge. Don't pass up a visit to this lodge if you want to escape the park's crowded east entrance and immerse yourself deep within the park for a few days. The lodge is located at the end of the 97-mile park road. Full-service accommodations feature a comfortable wilderness lodge, cozy cedar cabins, dining room and lounge. One- to four-night all-inclusive stays include round-trip transportation from the train depot, all meals and lodging, guided hikes, wildlife viewing, bicycling, photography, and natural history programs. Credit cards accepted. P.O. Box 189, Denali Park, AK 99755. Call (800) 841-0692. See display ad this section. [ADVERTISEMENT]

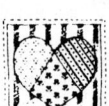

Denali National Park Central Reservations & Travel. Central booking agency for lodging, excursions, transportation and wilderness resorts in the Denali Park area. VISA, MasterCard. Call 1-800-872-2748, year-round. [ADVERTISEMENT]

Denali National Park Hotel and **McKinley Chalet Resort** offer the area's finest accommodations, dining and gift shops. Both offer tour desk services to help you reserve wildlife bus tours, rafting and flightseeing. The McKinley Chalet Resort at **Milepost A 238.9** Parks Highway features a health club complete with indoor heated swimming pool, sauna, hot tub and exercise room, and Alaska Cabin Nite dinner theater. The McKinley Village Lodge is convenient to all Denali National Park activities, located nearby at **Milepost 229** Parks Highway. Newly remodeled, it offers friendly service and comfortable accommodations including a lounge, coffee shop, gift shop and complete tour/activity desk. All accommodations, activities and transportation can be arranged with just one call! (907) 276-7234. See display ad this section. [ADVERTISEMENT]

Denali Princess Lodge. Offering 280 rooms and suites with phones and TVs. Free shuttle to rail depot and park activities. Spas, gift shop, fine dining and cafe. Handicap accommodations. Seasonal service mid-May to mid-September. Rates from $75. VISA, MasterCard and American Express. Write Princess Tours, 2815 2nd Ave., Suite 400, Seattle, WA 98121-1299, or call (800) 426-0500. [ADVERTISEMENT] ♿

Denali RV Park and Motel. 14 newly remodeled, budget motel rooms. Full and partial RV hookups; 90 sites with 30-amp electric, most with water. Level sites, pull-throughs, easy access from the highway. Dump station, good TV reception, pay phones. Individual restrooms with private showers. TV lounge, outdoor gathering area. Caravans welcome. Reasonable rates. VISA, MasterCard accepted. Located 8 miles north of park entrance, Mile 245.1 Parks Highway. Close to all park facilities. Beautiful mountain views. Hiking trails. We'll be happy to book your reservations for national park wildlife tours, rafting, flightseeing, dinner theatre, etc. Phone (907) 683-1500. 1-800-478-1501 in Alaska. Box 155, Denali Park, AK 99755. See display ad this section. [ADVERTISEMENT] ▲

Denali Wilderness Lodge is Alaska's historic fly-in wilderness lodge — an authentic bush homestead nestled in the pristine Wood River Valley. Comfortable accommodations, gourmet meals, naturalist programs, horseback riding, nature/photo walks and hikes, bird watching, wildlife museum. This is the Alaska so many hope to see but few ever experience! Overnight packages and day trips available. See display ad this section. [ADVERTISEMENT] ▲

Kantishna Roadhouse. Premier wilderness lodge located at the quiet west end of Denali National Park offers opportunities to view, photograph and explore the park. Packages include comfortable log cabins with private baths, guided hiking, gold panning, horses, fishing, fine meals and Alaskan hospitality. P.O. Box 130, Denali Park, AK 99755. Phone 1-800-942-7420. [ADVERTISEMENT]

Lynx Creek Pizza. "The Best Pizza in Alaska!" We also offer Mexican specialties, hand-dipped ice cream, espresso, extensive beer/wine selection. In addition, great campground and grocery store. Only 1 mile north of park entrance (Mile 238.6 Parks Highway). In Denali, call (907) 683-2547. [ADVERTISEMENT]▲

McKinley/Denali Cabins at McKinley/Denali Steakhouse and Salmon Bake. Economy tent cabins with electric heat and lights from $60. Some cabins with private baths. Closest full-service facility to park entrance, wildlife shuttles. Close to raft trips, store, gas. Largest T-shirt selection in park area on premises. Shuttle to visitor center, railroad depot available. Free visitor information. Reservations: (907) 683-2258 or (907) 683-2733 or write P.O. Box 90M, Denali Park, AK 99755. See display ad this section. [ADVERTISEMENT]

North Face Lodge is a small, well-appointed North Country inn in the heart of Denali National Park with a spectacular view of Mount McKinley. It features twin-bedded rooms with private baths, a central dining room and living room. Guest activities include guided hiking with experienced naturalists, canoeing, biking, flightseeing and evening natural history programs. All expense. See display ad. [ADVERTISEMENT]

White Moose Lodge. (907) 683-1233. This is a small Alaskan frontier-style motel with hanging baskets, wildflowers and a rustic deck, set in a quiet wooded environment. Each newly decorated room has two double beds, private bath and a mountain view. A central location to services and activities, and reasonable rates make this a good place to stay while visiting Denali. Mile 248.1 Parks Highway. [ADVERTISEMENT]

There are six campgrounds in the park along the 87-mile/140-km Park Road (see log of Park Road in this section for locations). Wonder Lake, Sanctuary River and Igloo Creek campgrounds are tent only and accessible only by shuttle bus. ▲

The campgrounds are open from about late May to early September, except for Riley Creek, which is open year-round (snow-covered and no facilities in winter). There is a fee and a 14-day limit at all campgrounds in summer. There is a three-night minimum stay requirement at Teklanika River Campground, and also a limit of one round-trip to this campground for registered campers with vehicles. Additional travel to and from Teklanika is by free shuttle bus. See chart below for facilities at each campground.

Campground	Spaces	Tent	Trailer	Pit toilets	Flush toilets	Tap water	Fee
Riley Creek	102	•	•		•	•	$12
Savage River	33	•	•		•	•	$12
Sanctuary River	7	•		•		•	$12
Teklanika River	50	•	•	•		•	$12
Igloo Creek	7	•		•		•	$12
Wonder Lake	28	•			•	•	$12

Several private campgrounds are located outside the park along the George Parks Highway. See display ads this section.

For area accommodations, also turn to pages 347-350 in the GEORGE PARKS HIGHWAY section.

Registration System: Register at the Visitor Access Center at **Milepost J 0.5** Park Road for a campsite. Registration for campsites is in person for same day (if space is available) or up to two days in advance. During peak season, campgrounds fill up midmorning for the following day and, on occasion, the day after.

The Alaska Public Lands Information centers in Fairbanks and Anchorage have a *limited* number of campground permits and shuttle-bus coupons that can be reserved in advance. Reservations must be made in person; reservations are not accepted by phone or by mail. Campground reservations can be made seven to 21 days in advance only, while shuttle-bus reservations can be made on a next-day basis or up to 21 days in advance, however *most reservations are completely filled within a few hours of becoming available.* All fees are collected in advance when making reservations. Reservation requirements are subject to change! For more current information, call the Anchorage center at 271-2737, or the Fairbanks center at 456-0527.

Visitor Services: Available from late May to mid-September, depending on weather. The Denali National Park Hotel has a gift shop, restaurant, snack bar and saloon. Gas

Visitors photograph bears from the park shuttle buses. (John W. Warden)

and propane *only* are available at the gas station near the hotel, no repair service. A public shower is located behind the gas station; groceries available at gas station. The post office is near the hotel. There is a dump station near Riley Creek Campground.

There are no vehicle or food services after you leave the headquarters entrance area.

Campers should bring a gasoline or propane stove or purchase firewood from concessionaire; a tent or waterproof shelter because of frequent rains; and rain gear for everyone. Camper mail should be addressed in care of General Delivery, Denali National Park, Denali Park, AK 99755.

Talkeetna Ranger Station: The National Park Service maintains a ranger station that is staffed full time from mid-April through mid-September and intermittently during the winter. Mountaineering rangers provide information on climbing within the Alaska Range. A reference library and slide/tape program are available for climbers. All climbers must register for climbs of Mount McKinley and Mount Foraker. Mountaineering information may be obtained from: Talkeetna Ranger Station, P.O. Box 588, Talkeetna, AK 99676; phone (907) 733-2231.

ATTRACTIONS

Organized activities put on by the Park Service include ranger-led nature hikes; sled dog demonstrations at park headquarters; campfire programs at Riley Creek, Savage River, Teklanika River and Wonder Lake campgrounds; and interpretive programs at the hotel auditorium.

Private operators in the park offer flightseeing tours, bus tours, raft tours and wintertime dogsled tours. Cross-country skiing and snowshoeing are also popular in winter.

There are few established trails in the park, but there is plenty of terrain for cross-country hiking. Free permits are required for any overnight hikes.

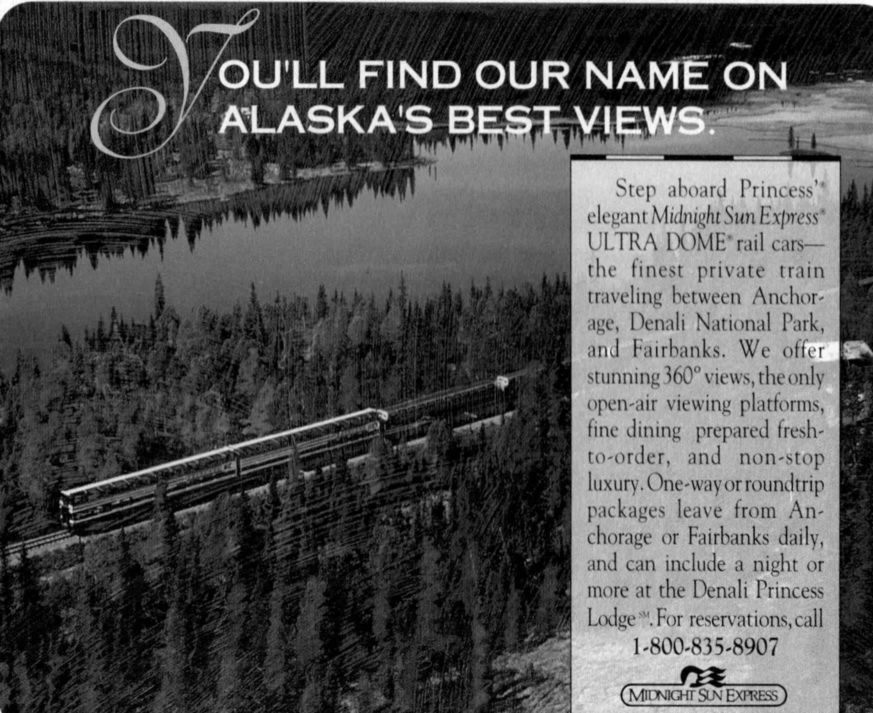

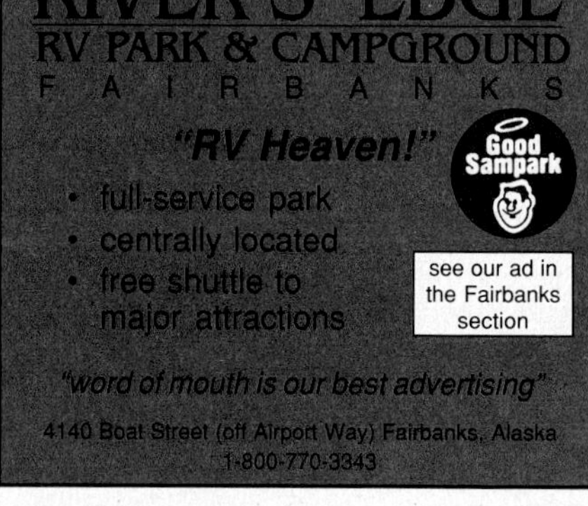

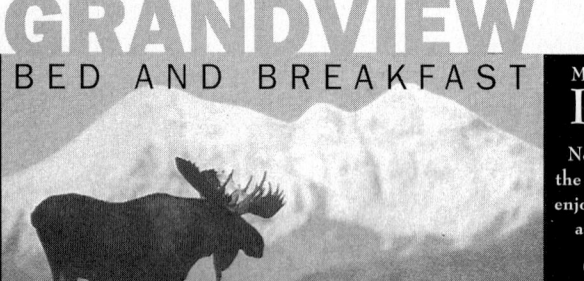

Permits and information on ranger-led hikes and other activities are available at the Visitor Access Center near the park entrance.

Tundra Mini-Golf. Eighteen holes of golf with an all-Alaskan theme. Driving practice net. Hours are 2-10 P.M. Turn toward the river on Quigley Trail at McKinley Chalets and left at Sourdough Cabins. Fun for the whole family, come on out and join us! (907) 683-GOLF (4653). [ADVERTISEMENT]

TRANSPORTATION

Highway: Access via the George Parks Highway and the Denali Highway.

The Park Road runs westward 91 miles/146.4 km from the park's east boundary to Kantishna. The road is paved only to Savage River (**Milepost J 14.7**). Private vehicle travel is restricted beyond the Savage River checkpoint at Mile 14.8. Mount McKinley is first visible at about **Milepost J 9** Park Road, but the best views begin at about **Milepost J 60** and continue with few interruptions to Wonder Lake. At the closest point, the summit of the mountain is 27 miles/43.5 km from the road. See log this section.

Shuttle bus: The National Park Service provides a free shuttle bus service from the Visitor Access Center to Eielson Visitor Center and Wonder Lake. Boarding coupons are available at the Visitor Access Center for the same day (if space is available) or up to two days in advance. During peak season, bus coupons for the next day's shuttles are generally gone by midmorning. Shuttle buses pick up and drop off passengers along the Park Road, stopping for scenic and wildlife viewing as schedules permit. A round-trip between the Visitor Access Center and Eielson Visitor Center takes about eight hours. The round-trip to Wonder Lake takes about 11 hours. Bring a lunch, camera, binoculars, extra film, warm clothes and rain gear. Buses run daily from about Memorial Day in May through Labor Day in September, weather permitting.

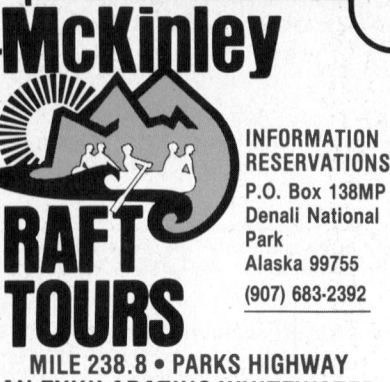

Air: Charter flights are available from most nearby towns with airfields, and flightseeing tours of the park are offered by operators from the park area or out of Talkeetna, Anchorage or Fairbanks. A round-trip air tour of the park from Anchorage takes three to four hours. See display ads this section.

Era Helicopters. Enjoy an eagle-eyed view of the grandeur of Denali National Park with Alaska's oldest and largest helicopter company. Look for moose, sheep and bear in the valleys and mountains below. Located 0.5 mile north of the park entrance, or phone (907) 683-2574 from mid-May to mid-September, or outside Alaska, 1-800-843-1947. [ADVERTISEMENT]

Railroad: The Alaska Railroad offers daily northbound and southbound trains between Anchorage and Fairbanks, with stops at Denali Park Station, during the summer season. For details on schedules and fares see the ALASKA RAILROAD section.

Midnight Sun Express®. Travel aboard the fully domed ULTRA DOME® rail cars between Anchorage, Denali National Park and Fairbanks. Enjoy on-board dining prepared fresh-to-order and the only outdoor viewing platform on the Alaska Railroad system. Overnight accommodations available at Denali Park. Seasonal service mid-May through mid-September. Write Princess Tours®, 2815 2nd Ave., Suite #400, Seattle, WA 98121-1299 or call 1-800-835-8907 year-round. [ADVERTISEMENT]

Bus: Daily bus service to the park is available from Anchorage and Fairbanks, and special sightseeing tours are offered throughout the summer months. A six- to eight-hour guided bus tour of the park is offered by the park concessionaire. Tickets and information are available in the hotel lobby at the front desk tour window.

A FEW SPECIAL NOTES FOR VISITORS

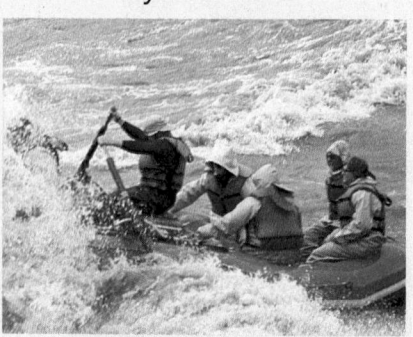

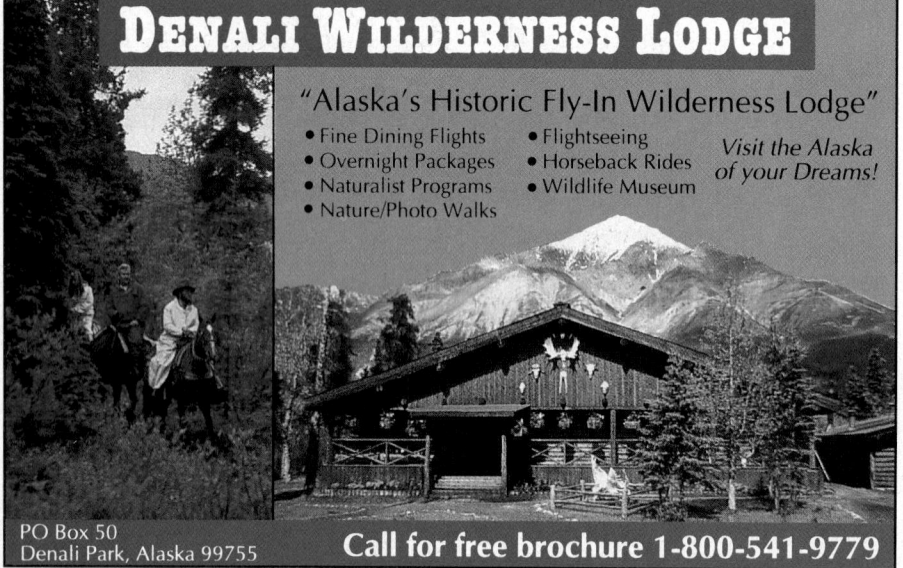

The 1980 federal legislation creating a much larger Denali National Park and Preserve also changed some rules and regulations normally followed in most parks. The following list of park rules and regulations apply in the Denali Wilderness Unit — the part of the park that most visitors come to. Contact the Superintendent at Denali (P.O. Box 9, Denali Park, AK 99755) for more information on regulations governing the use of aircraft, firearms, snow machines and motorboats, in the park additions and in the national preserve units.

For those driving: The Park Road was built for scenic enjoyment and not for high speed. Maximum speed is 35 mph except where lower limits are posted. Fast driving is dangerous to you and the wildlife you have come to see.

Your pets and wildlife don't mix. Pets are allowed only on roadways and in campgrounds and must be leashed or in a vehicle at all times. Pets are not allowed on shuttle buses, trails or in the backcountry.

Hikers who stay overnight *must obtain a free backcountry permit* and return it when the trip is completed. Permits available at the Visitor Access Center, **Milepost J 0.5** Park Road.

Mountaineering expeditions are required to register with the superintendent before climbing Mount McKinley or Mount Foraker. At least two months' prior notice is recommended. Contact the Talkeetna Ranger Station, P.O. Box 588, Talkeetna, AK 99676; phone (907) 733-2231.

Natural features: The park was established to protect a natural ecosystem.

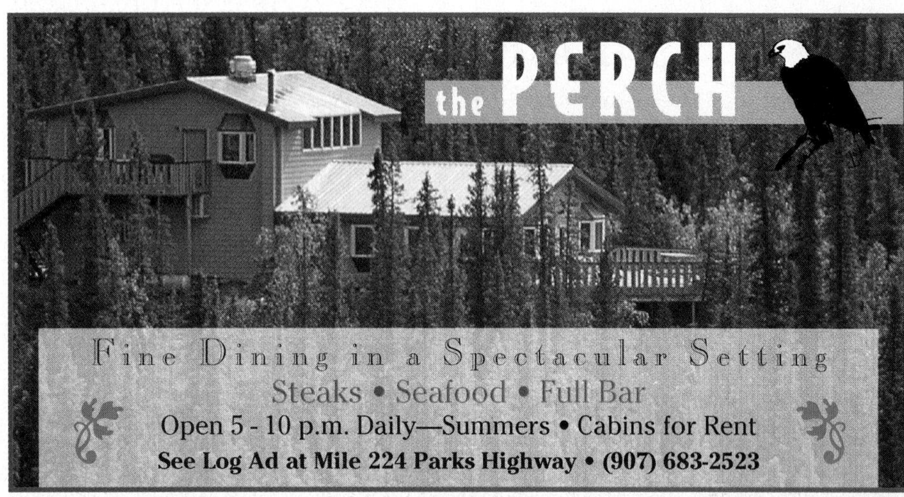

Destroying, defacing or collecting plants, rocks and other features is prohibited. Capturing, molesting, feeding or killing any animal is prohibited.

Firearms and hunting are not allowed in the wilderness area.

Fishing licenses are not required in the wilderness area; state law is applicable on all other lands. Limits for each person per day are: lake trout (two fish); grayling and other fish (10 fish or 10 lbs. and one fish). Fishing is poor because most rivers are silty and ponds are shallow.

Motor vehicles of any type, including trail bikes, motorcycles and mopeds, may not leave the Park Road.

Feeding wildlife is prohibited. Wild animals need wild food; your food will not help them.

Park Road Log

Distance from the junction (J) with George Parks Highway is shown.

J 0 (146.4 km) **Junction.** Turn west off the George Parks Highway (Alaska Route 3) at **Milepost A 237.3** onto the Park Road. The Park Road is paved to the Savage River bridge.

J 0.2 (0.3 km) Turnoff for Riley Creek Campground and overflow parking area. A dump station is also located here.

J 0.5 (0.8 km) Visitor Access Center has information on all visitor activities as well as camping and overnight hiking permits. A park orientation program is available in the theater. The center is open daily. This is also the shuttle bus departure point.

J 1.2 (1.9 km) Alaska Railroad crossing. Horseshoe Lake trailhead.

J 1.4 (2.3 km) Gas station, showers and

OPEN MAY - SEPTEMBER

DENALI

Discover Why We Say: "The Mountain Is Just The Beginning."

Three Distinct Hotels To Choose From.

McKinley Chalet Resort offers 288 mini-suites for your comfort. This chalet-style resort features a full-service dining room, dinner theatre, gift shop, lounge and deli, meeting facilities, indoor swimming pool, hot tub, sauna and exercise room.

After an adventurous day touring the Park, river rafting or hiking, unwind in our indoor swimming pool and hot tub.

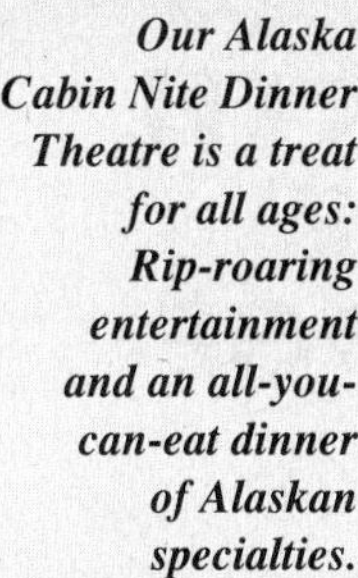

Our Alaska Cabin Nite Dinner Theatre is a treat for all ages: Rip-roaring entertainment and an all-you-can-eat dinner of Alaskan specialties.

Denali National Park Hotel is located 1.5 miles inside the entrance to Denali National Park. The 100-room hotel has a dining room, snack shop, gift shop and lounge as well as an auditorium where the National Park Service provides a variety of free programs.

Mt. McKinley Village Lodge rests quietly on the banks of the Nenana River. The 50-room lodge has a full-service cafe, gift shop, meeting facilities and a cozy lounge with pool tables and a river-rock fireplace for your relaxation.

A Wide Range Of Activities Awaits You.

You'll never be at a loss for something to do when you stay with us. Simply drop by the front desk at any of our hotels and we'll help you arrange: Park tours, river rafting, scenic river floats, flightseeing tours, helicopter tours, dinner theatre, ongoing Visitor Access Center Park programs and more!*

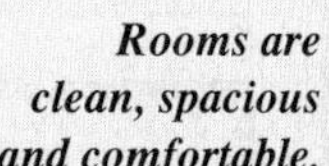

Rooms are clean, spacious and comfortable.

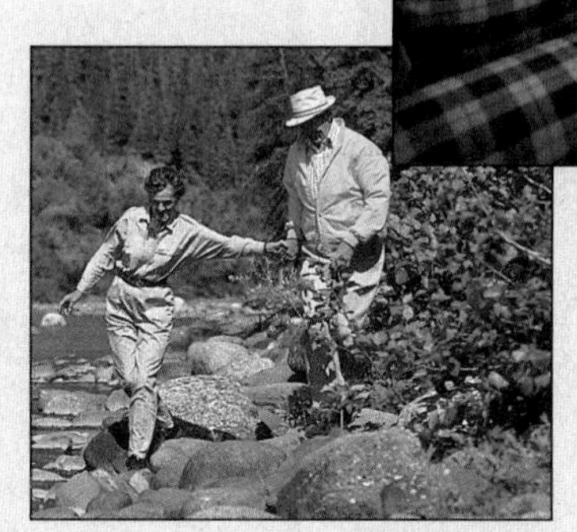

There are numerous hiking and scenic spots to explore in Denali and we can show them to you!

First In The Heart Of The Last Frontier.

At Denali Park Hotels, our goal is to make sure that your visit to Denali National Park is everything you want it to be. With our more than 20 years of experience you'll be assured of a complete and grand Alaska adventure.

DENALI PARK HOTELS
ARA LEISURE SERVICES

For Reservations:
907/276-7234

Or write us at:
825 W. 8th Ave #240, Anchorage, AK 99501

ARA Denali Park Hotels is an authorized concessioner of the National Park Service.
*Check front desk for departure times/dates.

grocery store. No gas available on Park Road beyond this point.

J 1.5 (2.4 km) **Denali National Park Hotel.** Located in Denali National Park, this hotel is the bustling center for visitor activities in the park. Facilities include dining room, snack shop, cocktail lounge, gift shop, grocery store and gas station. The hotel auditorium is the center for national park interpretive services. Wilderness activities include wildlife bus tours, rafting and flightseeing. All arrangements can be made with one call, including accommodations, activities and transportation to and from the park. Phone (907) 276-7234. See display ad this section. [ADVERTISEMENT]

J 1.6 (2.5 km) Denali Park Station (elev. 1,730 feet/527m), the Alaska Railroad station where visitors may make train connections to Anchorage and Fairbanks, daily service during the summer. Denali National Park Hotel is across from the depot. The post office and a flying service office are located in the hotel area.

Private Aircraft: McKinley Park airstrip, 1.7 miles/2.7 km northeast of park headquarters; elev. 1,720 feet/524m; length 3,000 feet/914m; gravel; unattended.

J 3.5 (5.6 km) Park headquarters. This is the administration area for Denali National Park and Preserve. In winter, information on all visitor activities can be obtained here. Report accidents and emergencies to the rangers; phone (907) 683-9100.

J 5.5 (8.9 km) Paved turnout with litter barrel. Sweeping view of countryside. There are numerous small turnouts along the Park Road.

J 12.8 (20.6 km) Savage River Campground (elev. 2,780 feet/847m). Wildlife in the area includes moose, grizzly bear and fox. ▲

J 14.7 (23.7 km) Bridge over the Savage

Wolves are common in the park.

(Bruce M. Herman)

River. Blacktop pavement ends. Access to river, toilet and picnic tables at east end of bridge.

J 14.8 (23.8 km) Savage River check station. PERMIT REQUIRED BEYOND THIS POINT.

NOTE: Road travel permits for access to the Kantishna area are issued at park headquarters only under special conditions.

J 17.3 (27.8 km) Viewpoint of the Alaska Range and tundra.

J 21.3 (34.3 km) Hogan Creek bridge.

J 22 (35.4 km) Sanctuary River bridge, ranger station and campground (tents only). Wildlife: moose, fox, grizzly bear, wolf. ▲

J 29.1 (46.8 km) Teklanika River Campground (elev. 2,580 feet/786m). Grizzly bears may sometimes be seen on the gravel bars nearby. ▲

J 30.7 (49.4 km) Rest stop with chemical toilets.

J 31.3 (50.4 km) Bridge over Teklanika River.

J 34.1 (54.8 km) Igloo Creek Campground (tents only); accessible by shuttle bus only. Wildlife in the area includes Dall sheep, grizzly bear, moose, fox and wolf. ▲

J 37 (59.5 km) Igloo Creek bridge.

J 39.1 (62.9 km) Sable Pass (elev. 3,900 feet/1,189m). *NOTE: The area within 1 mile/1.6 km of each side of the Park Road from **Milepost J 38.3** to **J 42.9** is closed to all off-road foot travel as a special wildlife protection area.* Toklat grizzlies are often seen in the area.

J 43.4 (69.8 km) Bridge over East Fork Toklat River. Views of Polychrome Mountain, the Alaska Range and several glaciers are visible along the East Fork, from open country south of the road. Wildlife includes Dall sheep and caribou.

J 45.9 (73.8 km) Summit of Polychrome Pass (elev. 3,700 feet/1,128m); rest stop with toilets. The broad valley of the Toklat River is visible below to the south. Good hiking in alpine tundra above the road. Wildlife: wolf, grizzly bear, Dall sheep, marmot, pika, eagle and caribou.

J 53.1 (85.4 km) Bridge over the Toklat River. The Toklat and all other streams crossed by the Park Road drain into the Tanana River, a tributary of the Yukon River.

J 53.7 (86.4 km) Ranger station.

J 58.3 (93.8 km) Summit of Highway Pass (elev. 3,980 feet/1,213m). This is the highest point on the Park Road.

J 61 (98.1 km) Stony Hill (elev. 4,508 feet/1,374m). A good view of Mount McKinley and the Alaska Range on clear days. Wildlife: grizzly bear, caribou, fox and birds.

J 62 (99.7 km) Viewpoint.

J 64.5 (103.8 km) Thorofare Pass (elev. 3,900 feet/1,189m).

J 66 (106.2 km) Eielson Visitor Center. Ranger-led hikes, nature programs, displays, restrooms and drinking water. Film, maps and natural history publications for sale. Report accidents and emergencies here.

Excellent Mount McKinley viewpoint. On clear days the north and south peaks of Mount McKinley are visible to the southwest. The impressive glacier, which drops from the mountain and spreads out over the valley floor at this point, is the Muldrow. Wildlife: grizzly bear, wolf, caribou.

For several miles beyond the visitor center the road cut drops about 300 feet/91m to the valley below, paralleling the McKinley River.

J 84.6 (136.1 km) Access road leads left, westbound, to Wonder Lake Campground (elev. 2,090 feet/637m). Tents only; campground access by shuttle bus only. An excellent Mount McKinley viewpoint. ▲

The road continues to Wonder Lake, where rafting and canoeing are permitted (no rental boats available). Wildlife: grizzly bear, caribou, moose, beaver, waterfowl.

J 85.6 (137.8 km) Reflection Pond, a kettle lake formed by a glacier.

J 86.6 (139.4 km) Wonder Lake ranger station.

J 87.7 (141.1 km) Bridge over Moose Creek.

J 88 (141.6 km) North Face Lodge.

J 88.2 (141.9 km) Camp Denali.

J 91 (146.4 km) **KANTISHNA** (pop. 2 in winter, 135 in summer; elev. 1,750 feet/533m). Established in 1905 as a mining camp at the junction of Eureka and Moose creeks. Most of the area around Kantishna is private property and there may be active mining on area creeks in summer. Kantishna Roadhouse, which consists of a dozen log guest cabins and a dining hall, comprises the townsite of Kantishna.

Private Aircraft: Kantishna airstrip, 1.3 miles/2.1 km northwest; elev. 1,575 feet/480m; length 1,850 feet/564m; gravel; unattended unscheduled maintenance.

J 92 (148 km) Denali Backcountry Lodge.

DENALI HIGHWAY

Paxson to Cantwell, Alaska
Alaska Route 8

View of Upper Nenana River valley from the Denali Highway. (Jerrianne Lowther, staff)

The Denali Highway extends 135.5 miles/218.1 km from Paxson at **Milepost V 185.5** on the Richardson Highway to Cantwell, about 2 miles/3.2 km west of **Milepost A 209.9** on the George Parks Highway. The first 21 miles/33.8 km from Paxson are paved and the rest is gravel. The highway is closed from October to mid-May.

The condition of the gravel portion of the highway varies, depending on highway maintenance, weather and the opinion of the driver. The road surface is rough and washboard can develop quickly. Much of the road is in need of gravel, but the roadbed is solid. This can be a dusty and bumpy drive in dry weather. Watch for potholes in wet weather.

There are dozens of primitive campsites and turnouts along the highway (heavily used by hunters in the fall). Excellent fishing in lakes and streams accessible on foot or via designated off-road vehicle trails. The Denali Highway is popular with mountain bikers. There are also many unmarked trails leading off into the Bush. Inquire locally and carry a good topographic map when hiking off the highway.

The Denali Highway has very beautiful scenery and some interesting geography. Glacier-formed features visible from the road include: moraines (drift deposited by glaciers); kames (conical hills or terraces of gravel and sand); kettle lakes (holes formed by blocks of ice melting); and eskers (ridges of gravel formed by streams flowing under glaciers).

More than 400 archaeological sites lie in the Tangle Lakes Archeological District between **Mileposts 15** and **45**. To protect this delicate area, the BLM has restricted summer ORV use to nine signed trails. (Winter use is unrestricted when adequate snow cover exists.) Information and maps are available from the BLM office in Glennallen; phone (907) 822-3219, or write Box 147, Glennallen 99588.

The Denali Highway was the only road link to Denali National Park and Preserve (formerly Mount McKinley National Park) prior to completion of the George Parks Highway in 1972. Before the Denali Highway opened in 1957, Denali National Park was accessible only via the Alaska Railroad.

Emergency medical services: Between Paxson and **Milepost P 77.5** (Susitna Lodge), phone 911 or the state troopers at 822-3263. Between **Milepost P 77.5** and Cantwell, phone the Cantwell ambulance at 768-2982 or the state troopers at 768-2202.

Denali Highway Log

Distance from Paxson (P) is followed by distance from Cantwell (C).

P 0 C 135.5 (218.1 km) **PAXSON** (pop. 33; elev. 2,650 feet/808m). A lodge with restaurant, gas station, post office and small grocery store is located here. Wildlife often seen near here: grizzly bear, moose and porcupine.

Private Aircraft: Paxson airstrip, adjacent south; elev. 2,653 feet/809m; length 2,800 feet/853m; gravel; emergency fuel; attended.

Paxson Lodge. See display ad this section.

P 0.2 (0.3 km) **C 135.3** (217.7 km) Gulkana River bridge; parking at west end. In season, spawning salmon may be seen here. This portion of the Gulkana River is off-limits to salmon fishing.

P 0.3 (0.5 km) **C 135.2** (217.6 km) Entering Paxson Closed Area westbound. This area is closed to the taking of all big game. Side road leads south to Mud Lake.

Westbound, there are many long steep upgrades and many turnouts the next 21 miles/33.8 km. Wildflowers carpet the tundra in the spring and summer.

P 1.1 (1.8 km) **C 134.4** (216.3 km) **Mud Lake** below highway; grayling fishing.

P 3.6 (5.8 km) **C 131.9** (212.3 km) Paved turnout to south. Several more turnouts next 2.5 miles/4 km with views of Summit Lake to the north. Gakona Glacier to the northeast and Icefall Peak to the west of the glacier. West of Icefall Peak is Gulkana Glacier.

P 6.1 (9.8 km) **C 129.4** (208.2 km) Paved turnout to north; views of Gulkana and Gakona glaciers.

P 6.7 (10.8 km) **C 128.8** (207.3 km) Paved turnout to south.

P 6.8 (10.9 km) **C 128.7** (207.1 km) Access to **Sevenmile Lake** 0.8 mile/1.3 km north; excellent fishing for lake trout in summer.

P 7.1 (11.4 km) **C 128.4** (206.6 km) Paved turnout to south.

P 7.3 (11.7 km) **C 128.2** (206.3 km) Gravel turnout overlooking Sevenmile Lake. Two Bit Lake is the large lake to the north; Summit Lake is to the northeast.

P 7.5 (12.1 km) **C 128** (206 km) Paved

DENALI HIGHWAY *Paxson, AK, to Cantwell, AK*

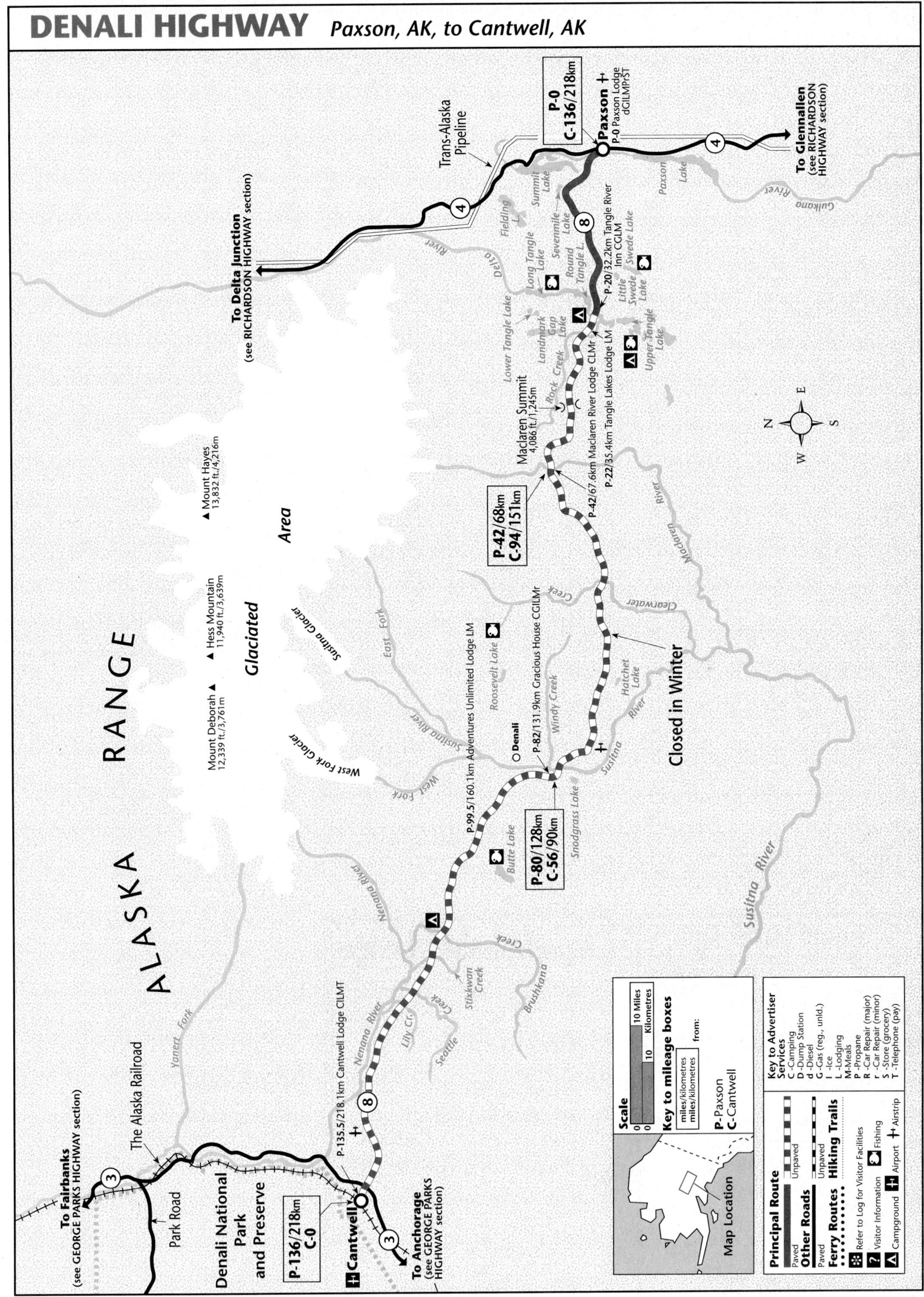

DENALI HIGHWAY
P-0
C-136/218km
Paxson
P-0 Paxson Lodge dGILMPrST
To Glennallen (see RICHARDSON HIGHWAY section)
Trans-Alaska Pipeline
To Delta Junction (see RICHARDSON HIGHWAY section)
Summit Lake
Paxson Lake
Gulkana River
Delta River
Fielding L.
Sevenmile Lake
Round Lake
Tangle L.
Long Tangle Lake
Lower Tangle Lake
Landmark Gap Lake
Little Swede Lake
Swede Lake
Upper Tangle Lake
P-20/32.2km Tangle River Inn CGLM
P-22/35.4km Tangle Lakes Lodge LM
P-42/67.6km Maclaren River Lodge CLMr
Rock Creek
Maclaren Summit 4,086 ft./1,245m
P-42/68km
C-94/151km
Maclaren River
Mount Hayes 13,832 ft./4,216m
Hess Mountain 11,940 ft./3,639m
Mount Deborah 12,339 ft./3,761m
Glaciated Area
ALASKA RANGE
Susitna Glacier
West Fork Glacier
East Fork
Susitna River
West Fork
Clearwater Creek
Roosevelt Lake
Windy Creek
Hatchet Lake
Closed in Winter
P-82/131.9km Gracious House CGILMr
P-99.5/160.1km Adventures Unlimited Lodge LM
Denali
Snodgrass Lake
Susitna River
P-80/128km
C-56/90km
Butte Lake
Nenana River
Brushkana Creek
Stixkwan Creek
Seattle Creek
Lily Cr.
P-135.5/218.1km Cantwell Lodge CILMT
Yanert Fork
The Alaska Railroad
To Fairbanks (see GEORGE PARKS HIGHWAY section)
Park Road
Denali National Park and Preserve
P-136/218km
C-0
Cantwell
To Anchorage (see GEORGE PARKS HIGHWAY section)
Scale
0 10 10 Miles
0 10 Kilometres
Key to mileage boxes
miles/kilometres
miles/kilometres
from:
P-Paxson
C-Cantwell
Map Location
Principal Route
Paved
Unpaved
Other Roads
Paved
Unpaved
Ferry Routes
Hiking Trails
Refer to Log for Visitor Facilities
Visitor Information
Fishing
Campground
Airport
Airstrip
Key to Advertiser Services
C -Camping
D -Dump Station
d -Diesel
G -Gas (reg., unld.)
I -Ice
L -Lodging
M -Meals
P -Propane
R -Car Repair (major)
r -Car Repair (minor)
S -Store (grocery)
T -Telephone (pay)
N E S W

turnout to north overlooking Sevenmile Lake.

P 8.2 (13.2 km) **C 127.3** (204.9 km) Paved turnout to north; small lakes (not visible from highway) in Hungry Hollow to the south.

P 9 (14.5 km) **C 126.5** (203.6 km) Gravel turnout. Entering BLM public lands westbound.

P 10.1 (16.3 km) **C 125.4** (201.7 km) Paved turnout to south overlooking **Ten Mile Lake**. Short hike downhill to outlet. Fishing for lake trout, grayling and burbot in summer.

P 10.6 (17.1 km) **C 124.9** (201 km) Paved turnout overlooking **Teardrop Lake** to south. Short hike down steep hill to lake; lake trout, grayling and burbot in summer.

For the next 4 miles/6.4 km westbound there are wide-open spaces with magnificent views of the great Denali country. Look for kettle lakes and kames.

P 11.1 (17.9 km) **C 124.4** (200.2 km) Paved turnout and trail to **Octopus Lake** 0.3 mile/0.5 km south; lake trout, grayling.

P 13.1 (21.1 km) **C 122.4** (197 km) Viewpoint at summit; interpretive plaque. In the spring from this spot a traveler can count at least 40 lakes and potholes. To the southeast are Mount Sanford, Mount Drum and Mount Wrangell in the Wrangell Mountain range.

Highway begins descent westbound to Tangle Lakes area. Lupine blooms alongside the road in late June.

P 15 (24.1 km) **C 120.5** (193.9 km) Fourteenmile Lake lies about 1.5 miles/2.4 km north of the highway, beyond eight smaller ponds.

P 16.8 (27 km) **C 118.7** (191 km) **16.8 Mile Lake** to north (walk up creek 200 yards); lake trout and grayling. **Rusty Lake**, 0.5 mile/0.8 km northwest of 16.8 Mile Lake; lake trout and grayling. Swede Lake trail, 3 miles/4.8 km long, to south; **Little Swede Lake**, 2 miles/3.2 km. This trail connects with the Middle Fork Gulkana River branch trail (access to Dickey Lake and Meier Lake trail) and the Alphabet Hills trail. **Big Swede Lake** has excellent fishing for lake trout, grayling and burbot. Little Swede Lake excellent for lake trout. Inquire at Tangle River Inn for directions.

P 17 (27.4 km) **C 118.5** (190.7 km) **17 Mile Lake** to north, turnout at west end of lake; lake trout and grayling fishing.

P 18.4 (29.6 km) **C 117.1** (188.4 km) Gravel turnout by **Denali–Clearwater Creek**; grayling fishing.

P 20 (32.2 km) **C 115.5** (185.9 km) **Tangle River Inn.** See display ad this section. ▲

P 20.1 (32.3 km) **C 115.4** (185.7 km) Large paved turnout to north overlooking lake.

P 20.6 (33.2 km) **C 114.9** (184.9 km) Paved parking area with toilets to north.

P 21 (33.8 km) **C 114.5** (184.3 km) The Nelchina caribou herd travels through this area, usually around the end of August or early in September.

P 21.3 (34.3 km) **C 114.2** (183.9 km) Pavement ends westbound. *NOTE: Highway from here to **Milepost P 42** being prepared for bituminous surface treatment in late 1994. Road and bridge construction to continue through 1995.*

P 21.4 (34.4 km) **C 114.1** (183.6 km) One-lane bridge over Tangle River.

P 21.5 (34.6 km) **C 114** (183.5 km) Tangle Lakes BLM campground and wayside, 0.7 mile/1.1 km north from highway on shore of Round Tangle Lake; 13 sites, toilets, boat launch, picnicking, hiking (no thick brush, good views). Blueberry picking in August. ▲

Easy access to boat launch for Delta River canoe trail, which goes north through Tangle Lakes to the Delta River. The two- to three-day float to the take-out point on the Richardson Highway requires one portage. The Delta National Wild, Scenic and Recreational River system is managed by the BLM. For details on the trail, contact the Bureau of Land Management, Box 147, Glennallen 99588; phone (907) 822-3217.

Watershed divide. The Gulkana River joins the Copper River, which flows into Prince William Sound. The Delta River joins the Tanana River, which flows into the Yukon River. The Yukon flows into the Bering Sea.

P 21.7 (34.9 km) **C 113.8** (183.1 km) Tangle River BLM campground; toilets, water pump, boat launch. Watch for caribou on surrounding hills. Watch for arctic warblers nesting along the Tangle River. ▲

The name Tangle is a descriptive term for the maze of lakes and feeder streams contained in this drainage system. Access to Upper Tangle Lakes canoe trail, which goes south through Tangle Lakes (portages required) to Dickey Lake, then follows the Middle Fork to the main Gulkana River.

AREA FISHING: Tangle Lakes system north and south of the highway (**Long Tangle, Round Tangle, Upper Tangle** and **Lower Tangle Lake**). Good grayling and lake trout fishing. Fishing begins as soon as the ice goes out, usually in early June, and continues into September. Good trolling, and some fish are taken from the banks. Early in season, trout are hungry and feed on snails in the shallows at the outlet. Inquire at Tangle Lakes Lodge or Tangle River Inn for information and assistance in getting to where the fish are.

P 22 (35.4 km) **C 113.5** (182.6 km) **Tangle Lakes Lodge**, originally known as Butcher's Hunting Camp, was built in 1952, the first lodge on the Denali Highway. Now owned by Rich and Linda Holmstrom, it still boasts some of the finest Arctic grayling fishing on the road system. It is also quickly becoming a premier birding destination. Arctic warblers, wandering tattlers, gyrfalcons, ptarmigan and many others are commonly sighted along the Tangle Lakes. An avid birder, Holmstrom has some of the most accurate birding information on the highway. A special this year is a log cabin, canoe, breakfast, lunch and dinner for two, all for $135. Fine dining, cocktails and a beautiful setting make the Tangle Lakes Lodge a must stop. See display ad this section. [ADVERTISEMENT]

P 24.8 (39.9 km) **C 110.7** (178.2 km) Landmark Gap BLM trail to north open to ORVs to **Landmark Gap Lake**. Grayling in stream at trail end; trout in main lake. Mountain biking is also popular on this trail.

P 24.9 (40 km) **C 110.6** (178 km) **Rock Creek** one-lane bridge; parking and informal campsites both ends of bridge. Fair grayling fishing. Landmark Gap Lake lies north of highway between the noticeable gap in the mountains (a caribou migration route).

P 28.1 (45.2 km) **C 107.4** (172.8 km) Downwind Lake north side of road.

P 30.6 (49.2 km) **C 104.9** (168.8 km) Cat trail leads 2 miles/3.2 km north to **Glacier Lake**; lake trout, grayling.

P 32 (51.5 km) **C 103.5** (166.6 km) Amphitheater Mountains rise above High Valley to the north. Glacier Lake is visible in the gap in these mountains.

P 35.2 (56.6 km) **C 100.3** (161.4 km) Turnout at Maclaren Summit (elev. 4,086 feet/1,245m). Highest highway pass in Alaska (not including 4,800-foot/1,463-m Atigun Pass on the Dalton Highway, formerly the North Slope Haul Road). A profusion of flowers — notably the various heaths and frigid shooting star.

P 36 (57.9 km) **C 99.5** (160.1 km) **36 Mile Lake** 0.5-mile/0.6-km hike north; lake trout and grayling.

P 36.4 (58.6 km) **C 99.1** (159.5 km) Entering Clearwater Creek controlled-use area westbound. Closed to motorized hunting.

P 36.6 (58.9 km) **C 98.9** (159.2 km) Osar Lake ORV trail south; 5 miles/8 km.

P 37 (59.5 km) **C 98.5** (158.5 km) Turnout with view of Susitna River valley, Mount Hayes and the Alaska Range. Osar Lake trail leads 5 miles/8 km south toward the Alphabet Hills; Maclaren Summit trail leads 3 miles/4.8 km north to good view of Alaska Range; mountain biking. Osar Lake was first named Asar Lake, the Scandinavian

Active mining site at Valdez Creek near the old Denali camp site. (Jerrianne Lowther, staff)

word for esker. (An esker is a ridge of sand and gravel marking the former stream channel of a glacier.)

P 39.8 (64.1 km) **C 95.7** (154 km) Sevenmile Lake ORV trail to north; 6.5 miles/10.5 km long, parallels Boulder Creek, crosses peat bog.

P 42 (67.6 km) **C 93.5** (150.5 km) Maclaren River and bridge, a 364-foot/111-m multiple span crossing this tributary of the Susitna River. Parking and litter barrels. Maclaren River Lodge west side. Look for cliff swallows nesting under bridge. *NOTE: Highway from here to* ***Milepost P 21.3*** *being prepared for bituminous surface treatment in late 1994. Road and bridge construction to continue through 1995.*

Maclaren River Lodge. Maclaren River Lodge, "where Alaska embraces you" with a sportsman's and nature lover's paradise. More than Denali Park could ever offer you, without the lines, buses and hassle. Open year-round, with winter transportation to the lodge available by warm, comfortable snow track vehicle. Ice fishing, cross-country skiing, snow machining. See display ad this section. [ADVERTISEMENT] ▲

P 43.3 (69.7 km) **C 92.2** (148.4 km) Maclaren River Road leads north 12 miles/17 km to Maclaren Glacier; mountain biking. Maclaren River trailhead to south. The Maclaren River rises in the glaciers surrounding Mount Hayes (elev. 13,832 feet/4,216m). For the next 60 miles/96.5 km westbound, the highest peaks of this portion of the mighty Alaska Range are visible, weather permitting, to the north. From east to west: Mount Hayes, Hess Mountain (elev. 11,940 feet/3,639m) and Mount Deborah (elev. 12,339 feet/3,761m). Mount Hayes, first climbed in August 1941, is named after Charles Hayes, an early member of the U.S. Geological Survey. Mount Deborah, first climbed in August 1954, was named in 1907 by Judge Wickersham after his wife.

P 44.1 (71 km) **C 91.4** (147.1 km) Small turnout to south. Beaver lodge and dam.

P 44.6 (71.8 km) **C 90.9** (146.3 km) Highway crosses Crazy Notch gap.

P 46.9 (75.5 km) **C 88.6** (142.6 km) Road north to **46.9 Mile Lake**; fishing for grayling in lake and outlet stream.

P 47 (75.6 km) **C 88.5** (142.4 km) Beaver dam. Excellent grayling fishing in **Crooked Creek** which parallels the highway.

P 48.6 (78.2 km) **C 86.9** (139.8 km) Informal campsite by small lake.

P 49 (78.8 km) **C 86.5** (139.2 km) The road follows an esker between four lakes. Parts of the highway are built on eskers. Watch for ptarmigan, swans, arctic terns, ducks and beaver.

P 51.8 (83.4 km) **C 83.7** (134.7 km) Private hunting camp to south. Trail to north.

P 56.1 (90.3 km) **C 79.4** (127.8 km) **Clearwater Creek** one-lane bridge and rest area with toilets and litter barrels. Informal camping. Cliff swallows nest under bridge. Grayling fishing in summer.

P 58.2 (93.6 km) **C 77.3** (124.4 km) Clearwater Creek walk-in (no motorized vehicles) hunting area north of highway.

P 58.8 (94.6 km) **C 76.7** (123.4 km) Road winds atop an esker flanked by kames and kettle lakes. Watch for moose.

P 64 (103 km) **C 71.5** (115 km) Road descends westbound into Susitna Valley. Highest elevation of mountains seen to north is 5,670 feet/1,728m.

P 65.7 (105.7 km) **C 69.8** (112.3 km) Waterfall Creek.

P 68.9 (110.9 km) **C 66.6** (107.2 km) Raft Creek. Hatchet Lake lies about 2 miles/3.2 km south of highway. Inquire at Gracious House, **Milepost P 82**, for directions.

P 71.5 (115 km) **C 64** (103 km) Moose often sighted in valley below road.

P 72.2 (116.2 km) **C 63.3** (101.9 km) Nowater Creek.

P 72.8 (117.2 km) **C 62.7** (100.9 km) Swampbuggy Lake.

P 75 (120.7 km) **C 60.5** (97.4 km) Clearwater Mountains to north; watch for bears on slopes. View of Susitna River in valley below.

P 77.5 (124.7 km) **C 58** (93.3 km) Susitna Lodge (status unknown).

Private Aircraft: Susitna Lodge airstrip (private), adjacent west; elev. 2,675 feet/815m; length 2,300 feet/701m; gravel, dirt.

P 78.8 (126.8 km) **C 56.7** (91.2 km) Valdez Creek Road. Former mining camp of Denali, about 6 miles/10 km north of the highway via a gravel road, was first established in 1907. Active mining area; watch for large trucks and equipment on road. Do not trespass on private mining claims. Fair fishing reported in **Roosevelt Lake** and area creeks. Watch for bears.

P 79.3 (127.6 km) **C 56.2** (90.4 km) Susitna River one-lane bridge, a combination multiple span and deck truss, 1,036

feet/316m long. The Susitna River heads at Susitna Glacier in the Alaska Range (between Mounts Hess and Hayes) and flows southwest 260 miles/418 km to Cook Inlet. Downstream through Devil's Canyon it is considered unfloatable. The river's Tanaina Indian name, said to mean "sandy river," first appeared in 1847 on a Russian chart.

Entering Game Management Unit 13E westbound, leaving unit 13B eastbound.

P 81 (130.3 km) **C 54.5** (87.7 km) Snodgrass Lake (elev. 2,493 feet/760m) is about 2 miles/3.2 km south of the highway. Check with Gracious House, **Milepost P 82**, for directions. *CAUTION: Watch for horses.*

P 82 (131.9 km) **C 53.5** (86.1 km) **Gracious House.** Centrally located on the shortest, most scenic route to Denali National Park. 16 modern cabins or motel units, most with private baths, bar, cafe featuring ice cream and home-baked pies. Tent sites, parking for self-contained RVs overlooking lake. Water available. Restrooms and showers at lodge. Chevron products, towing, welding, mechanical repairs, tire service. Air taxi, guide service available in a variety of combinations serving the sportsman, tourist, photographer, families with tours and outings to individual desires, from campouts to guided hunts. Same owners/operators for 36 years. Reasonable rates. Reservations not required. For brochure on hunting and fishing trips, write to the Gracious Family. Summer address: P.O. Box 88, Cantwell, AK 99729. Winter address: 859 Elaine Dr., Anchorage, AK 99504. Message phone (907) 333-3148. [ADVERTISEMENT]

P 83 (133.5 km) **C 52.5** (84.5 km) Visible across the Susitna River is Valdez Creek mining camp at the old Denali townsite. Valdez Creek Mine is operated by Cambior Alaska, Inc. *CAUTION: Watch for truck traffic.*

P 84 (135.2 km) **C 51.5** (82.9 km) **Stevenson's Lake** 0.5 mile/0.8 km south; grayling fishing.

P 88.7 (142.7 km) **C 46.8** (75.3 km) Large turnout by pond. Good stop for pictures of the Alaska Range (weather permitting).

P 90.5 (145.6 km) **C 45** (72.4 km) A major water drainage divide occurs near here. East of the divide, the tributary river system of the Susitna flows south to Cook Inlet. West of the divide, the Nenana River system flows north to the Yukon River, which empties into the Bering Sea.

P 91.2 (146.8 km) **C 44.3** (71.3 km) Turnout and access to small lake beside road.

P 93.8 (151 km) **C 41.7** (67.1 km) **Butte Lake,** 5 miles/8 km south of highway. Motorized access by tracked vehicle. Best fishing June through September. Lake trout to 30 lbs., troll with red-and-white spoons or grayling remains; grayling to 20 inches, small flies or spinners; burbot to 12 lbs., use bait on bottom.

P 94.3 (151.8 km) **C 41.2** (66.3 km) Short road leads to parking area above pond. View of Monahan Flat and Alaska Range to the north.

P 94.8 (152.5 km) **C 40.7** (65.5 km) Bridge over Canyon Creek.

P 96.1 (154.6 km) **C 39.4** (63.4 km) Good viewpoint of the West Fork Glacier. Looking north up the face of this glacier, Mount Deborah is to the left and Mount Hess is in the center.

P 97 (156.1 km) **C 38.5** (62 km) Looking at the Alaska Range to the north, Mount Deborah, Mount Hess and Mount Hayes are the highest peaks to your right; to the left are the lower peaks of the Alaska Range and Mount Nenana.

P 99.5 (160.1 km) **C 36** (57.9 km) **Adventures Unlimited Lodge.** See display ad this section.

P 100 (160.9 km) **C 35.5** (57.1 km) Residents of this area say it is a wonderful place for picking cranberries and blueberries in August.

P 103 (165.8 km) **C 32.5** (52.3 km) Highway is built on an esker between kettle lakes.

P 104.6 (168.3 km) **C 30.9** (49.7 km) **Brushkana River** bridge and BLM campground; 12 sites beside river, tables, firepits, toilets, litter barrels and water. Fishing for grayling and Dolly Varden. Watch for moose.

P 106.6 (171.6 km) **C 28.9** (46.5 km) **Canyon Creek,** grayling fishing.

P 107.2 (172.5 km) **C 28.3** (45.5 km) **Stixkwan Creek** flows under highway in culvert. Grayling.

P 111.2 (179 km) **C 24.3** (39.1 km) **Seattle Creek** one-lane bridge. Fishing for grayling and Dolly Varden.

P 112 (180.2 km) **C 23.5** (37.8 km) Lily Creek. Matanuska–Susitna Borough boundary.

P 113.2 (182.2 km) **C 22.3** (35.9 km) View to east of the Alaska Range and extensive rolling hills grazed by caribou.

P 115.7 (186.2 km) **C 19.8** (31.9 km) Large gravel turnout with beautiful view of the Nenana River area.

P 117.1 (188.4 km) **C 18.4** (29.6 km) Log cabin beside Nenana River.

P 117.5 (189.1 km) **C 18** (29 km) Leaving BLM public lands westbound.

P 117.7 (189.4 km) **C 17.8** (28.6 km) Highway parallels the Nenana River, which flows into the Tanana River at the town of Nenana.

P 120 (193 km) **C 15.5** (24.9 km) A variety of small water birds, including ducks, snipes and terns, can be observed in the marshy areas along both sides of the road for the next 1 mile/1.6 km westbound.

P 122.3 (196.8 km) **C 11.3** (18.2 km) View (westbound) of Mount McKinley.

P 125.7 (202.3 km) **C 9.8** (15.8 km) **Joe Lake,** about 0.5 mile/0.8 km long (large enough for floatplane), is south of highway. **Jerry Lake** is about 0.2 mile/0.3 km north of the highway. Two small turnouts provide room for campers and fishermen. Both lakes have grayling.

P 128.1 (206.2 km) **C 7.4** (11.9 km) Fish Creek bridge. Access to creek and informal campsite at east end of bridge.

P 128.2 (206.3 km) **C 7.3** (11.7 km) Beautiful view of Talkeetna Mountains to the south.

P 128.6 (206.9 km) **C 6.9** (11.1 km) Small pond just off highway. Good berry picking in the fall. Fishing for grayling in unnamed creek.

P 130.3 (209.7 km) **C 5.2** (8.3 km) The small town of Cantwell, nestled at the foot of the mountains, can be seen across a long, timbered valley dotted with lakes. Excellent view of Mount McKinley, weather permitting.

P 131.5 (211.6 km) **C 4** (6.4 km) Airstrip; current status unknown.

P 132 (212.4 km) **C 3.5** (5.6 km) Good grayling fishing in stream beside road.

P 133 (214 km) **C 2.5** (4 km) Cantwell Station highway maintenance camp.

P 133.1 (214.2 km) **C 2.4** (3.9 km) **Junction** with old Anchorage–Fairbanks Highway; turn right westbound for Alaska State Troopers complex located approximately 0.2 mile/0.3 km north on left side of road.

P 133.7 (215.2 km) **C 1.8** (2.9 km) **Junction** of Denali and George Parks highways. Cantwell post office and school, a lodge, two restaurants, mini-grocery, gas stations and gift shop are located here. Continue straight ahead 2 miles/3.2 km for the original town of Cantwell. Turn left (south) for Anchorage or right (north) for Denali National Park and Fairbanks. See **Milepost A 209.9** in the GEORGE PARKS HIGHWAY section for details.

Cantwell

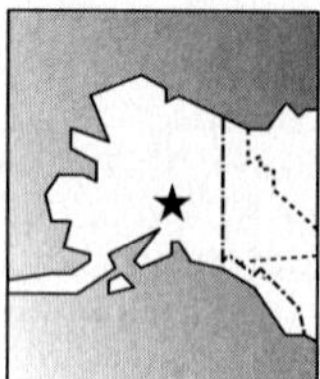

P 135.5 (218.1 km) **C 0** Western terminus of the Denali Highway. **Population:** 91. **Emergency Services: Alaska State Troopers,** phone 768-2202. **Ambulance,** phone 768-2982. **Elevation:** 2,190 feet/667m. **Television:** Channels 2 and 9.

Private Aircraft: Cantwell airport, adjacent north; elev. 2,190 feet/667m; length 2,100 feet/640m; gravel, dirt; fuel 100LL.

Cantwell began as a railroad flag stop between Seward on Prince William Sound and Fairbanks on the Chena River. The Alaska Railroad now serves Cantwell several times a week on its Anchorage to Fairbanks run during summer. The village was named for the Cantwell River, which is the former name of the Nenana River.

Cantwell's newer businesses are located at the intersection of the Denali and George Parks highways. Cantwell Lodge, with cafe, bar and laundry, is located in the older section of Cantwell, along the railroad tracks 2 miles/3.2 km west of intersection.

Cantwell Lodge. See display ad this section.

STEESE HIGHWAY

Fairbanks to Circle, Alaska
Alaska Routes 2 and 6
Includes logs of Chena Hot Springs Road and Circle Hot Springs Road
(See map, page 412)

The Steese Highway connects Fairbanks with Chena Hot Springs (61.5 miles/99 km) via Chena Hot Springs Road; the town of Central (127.5 miles/205.2 km); Circle Hot Springs (136.1 miles/219 km) via Circle Hot Springs Road; and with Circle, a small settlement 162 miles/260.7 km to the northeast on the Yukon River and 50 miles/80.5 km south of the Arctic Circle. The scenery alone makes this a worthwhile drive.

The first 44 miles/70.8 km of the Steese Highway are paved. Beyond this it is good wide gravel road into Central, where there is a stretch of paved road. From Central to Circle, the highway is a narrow, winding road with good gravel surface.

*NOTE: Watch for road construction from **Milepost F 11** to **F 22** in 1994.*

The highway is open year-round; check with the Dept. of Transportation in Fairbanks regarding winter road conditions.

The Steese Highway was completed in 1927 and named for Gen. James G. Steese, U.S. Army, a former president of the Alaska Road Commission.

Among the attractions along the Steese are the sites of old and new mining camps; Eagle Summit, highest pass on the highway, where there is an unobstructed view of the midnight sun at summer solstice (June 21) and great wildflower viewing in June and July; the Chatanika River and Chena River recreation areas; and Chena and Circle hot springs, where early prospectors bathed in comfort and modern visitors can do the same. There are also a number of fine picnic areas and campgrounds along the Steese.

Emergency medical services: Between Fairbanks and Circle, phone the state troopers at 911 or 452-1313. Use CB Channels 2, 19, 22.

Alyeska Pipeline visitor center at Milepost F 8.4 offers a close-up look at the pipeline and displays of equipment. (Jerrianne Lowther, staff)

Steese Highway Log

ALASKA ROUTE 2
Distance from Fairbanks (F) is followed by distance from Circle (C).

F 0 C 162 (260.7 km) **FAIRBANKS. Junction** of Airport Way, Richardson–Alaska Highway and the Steese Expressway. Follow the four-lane Steese Expressway north.

F 0.4 (0.6 km) **C 161.6** (260.1 km) Tenth Avenue exit.

F 0.6 (1 km) **C 161.4** (259.7 km) Expressway crosses Chena River.

F 0.9 (1.4 km) **C 161.1** (259.3 km) Third Street exit.

F 1 (1.6 km) **C 161** (259.1 km) College Road exit to west and access to Bentley Mall and University of Alaska.

F 1.4 (2.3 km) **C 160.6** (258.5 km) Trainer Gate Road; access to Fort Wainright.

F 2 (3.2 km) **C 160** (257.5 km) Johansen Expressway (Old Steese Highway) to west, City Lights Boulevard to east.

F 2.8 (4.5 km) **C 159.2** (256.2 km) Fairhill Road; access to Birch Hill Recreation Area, 2.3 miles/3.7 km from the highway via a paved road. Access to Farmers Loop Road to the west; residential areas of Birch Hill, Fairhill, Murray Highlands and View Crest to the east. Birch Hill Recreation Area is mainly for winter use as a ski area; open from 8 A.M. to 10 P.M. There are picnic areas, toilets, firepits and hiking trails. Day use only.

F 4.9 (7.9 km) **C 157.1** (252.8 km) Chena Hot Springs Road underpass, exits both sides of highway. Turn east at exit for Chena Hot Springs Road; see CHENA HOT SPRINGS ROAD log page 413. Turn west for grocery, gas and pay phone at Old Steese Highway.

F 6.4 (10.3 km) **C 155.6** (250.4 km) Steele Creek Road. Exit for Bennett Road, Hagelbarger Road, Old Steese Highway and Gilmore trail. Exit to left northbound for scenic view of Fairbanks.

F 7 (11.3 km) **C 155** (249.4 km) View of pipeline from top of hill.

F 7.6 (12.2 km) **C 154.4** (248.4 km) Watch for frost heaves.

F 8 (12.9 km) **C 154** (247.8 km) End four-lane divided highway, begin two lanes, northbound. *CAUTION: Watch for moose.*

F 8.4 (13.5 km) **C 153.6** (247.2 km) Trans–Alaska pipeline viewpoint with interpretive displays. Excellent opportunity for pipeline photos. Alyeska Pipeline Service Co. visitor center open May to Sept., seven days a week. Free literature and information; phone (907) 456-9391. Highway parallels pipeline.

F 9.5 (15.3 km) **C 152.5** (245.4 km) Goldstream Road exit to Old Steese Highway and Gold Dredge Number 8. The dredge, built in 1928, was added to the list of national historic sites in 1984 and designated a National Historical Mechanical Engineering Landmark in 1986. The five-deck, 250-foot-long dredge operated until 1959; it is now privately owned and open to the public for tours (admission fee).

Gold Dredge Number 8. Turn left on Goldstream Road, then left again on the Old

STEESE HIGHWAY *Fairbanks, AK to Circle, AK*

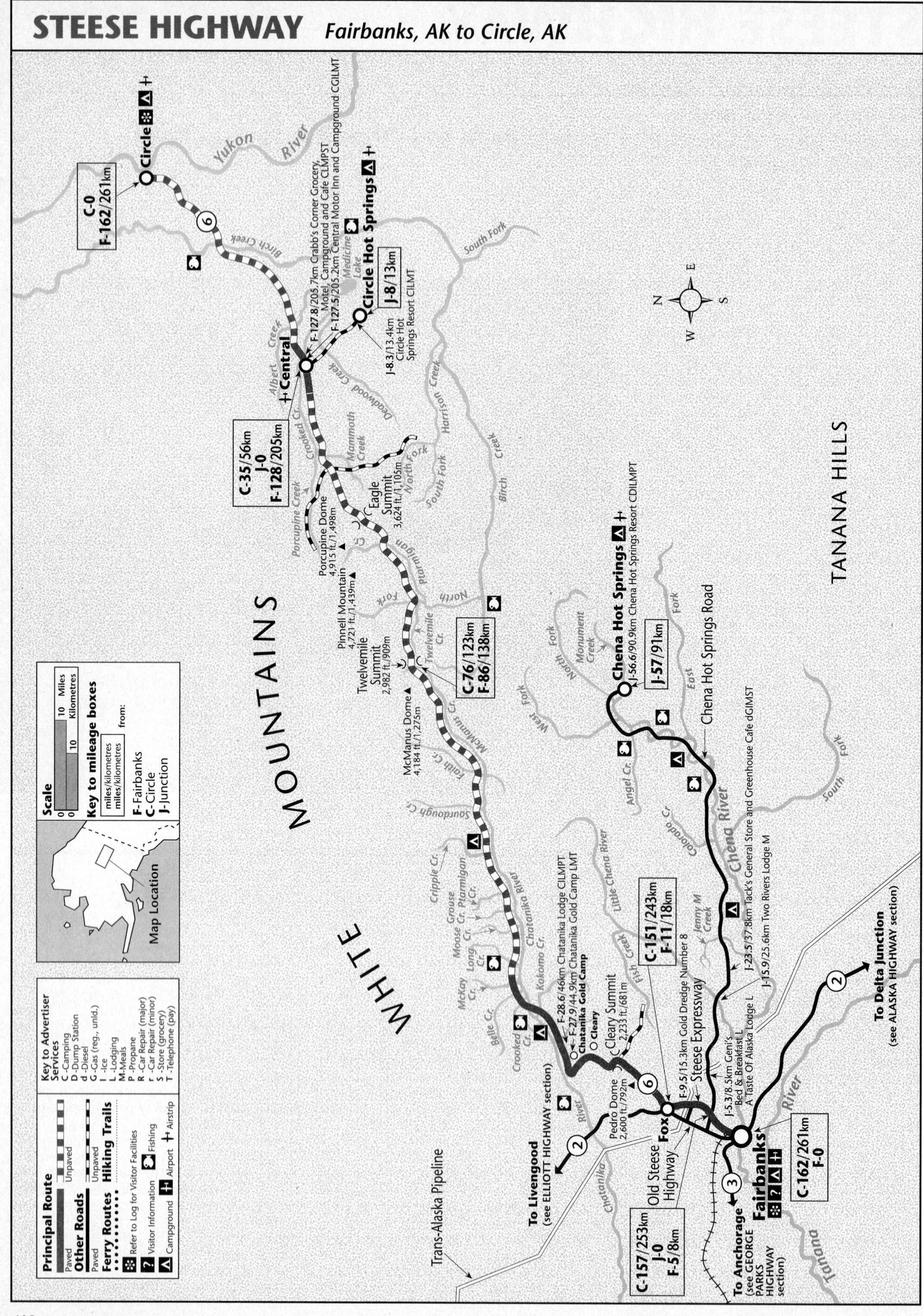

Steese Highway. Drive 0.3 mile to Gold Dredge Number 8 on your right. Tours of Dredge Number 8 and gold panning is one

of the Interior's top attractions. Visit Gold Dredge Number 8 early on while in Fairbanks. It's so interesting and so authentic that many people come back again and again. Families love it. See display ad in the FAIRBANKS section. [ADVERTISEMENT]

F 10.4 (16.7 km) **C 151.6** (244 km) Road to permafrost tunnel to east (research area, not open to public). Excavated in the early 1960s, the tunnel is maintained cooperatively by the University of Alaska–Fairbanks and the U.S. Army Cold Regions Research and Engineering Laboratory.

F 11 (17.7 km) **C 151** (243 km) End of Steese Expressway. Weigh station. Check here for current information on Dalton Highway conditions. Turn east at this junction for continuation of Steese Highway, which now becomes Alaska Route 6 (log follows). *NOTE: Watch for road construction to **Milepost F 22** in 1994.* Continue straight ahead (north) on Alaska Route 2, which now becomes the Elliott Highway, for access to Dalton Highway and Manley Hot Springs (see ELLIOTT HIGHWAY section for details).

Turn west for Old Steese Highway and for **FOX**, a once famous mining camp established before 1905 and named for nearby Fox Creek. Gas, food and lodging.

ALASKA ROUTE 6

F 13.6 (21.9 km) **C 148.4** (238.8 km) Eisele Road; turnoff on right northbound for NOAA/NESDIS Command and Data Acquisition Station at Gilmore Creek. This facility monitors two polar orbiting satellites. Tours of the satellite tracking station are available 9 A.M. to 4 P.M., Monday through Saturday, from June through August. Phone (907) 451-1200 for more information.

F 16.4 (26.4 km) **C 145.6** (234.3 km) Turnout by gold-bearing creek. Now privately claimed; no recreational gold panning permitted.

F 16.5 (26.6 km) **C 145.5** (234.2 km) Gravel turnout to west. Monument to Felix Pedro, the prospector who discovered gold on Pedro Creek in July 1902 and started the rush that resulted in the founding of Fairbanks.

F 17.4 (28 km) **C 144.6** (232.7 km) Gravel turnout to east. Winding ascent northbound to Cleary Summit area.

F 19.6 (31.5 km) **C 142.4** (229.2 km) Large gravel turnout to east.

F 20.3 (32.7 km) **C 141.7** (228 km) Cleary Summit (elev. 2,233 feet/681m) has a weekend ski area in winter. Named for early prospector Frank Cleary. On a clear day there are excellent views of the Tanana Valley and Mount McKinley to the south and the White Mountains to the north. Road north to Pedro Dome military site.

Fairbanks Creek Road to the south leads several miles along a ridge crest; access to Fish Creek Road and dirt roads leading to Solo Creek, Bear Creek and Fairbanks Creek.

Highway descends steep grade northbound. Watch for frost heaves.

(Continued on page 415)

Chena Hot Springs Road Log

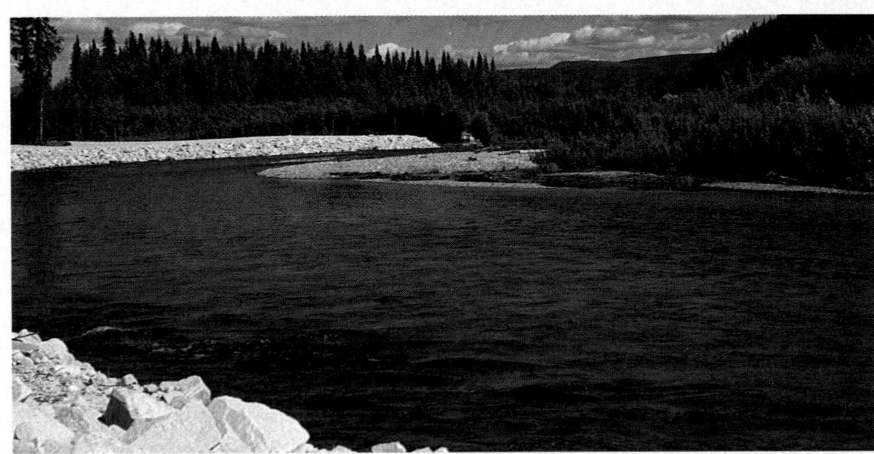

Riprap bank helps channel Chena River. (Jerrianne Lowther, staff)

This paved road, open year-round, leads 56.5 miles/90.9 km east to Chena Hot Springs, a private resort open daily year-round. Chena Hot Springs Road passes through the middle of Chena River Recreation Area, 254,000 acres of mostly undeveloped river bottom and alpine uplands. This is an exceptional recreation area with numerous picnic sites, campgrounds and easy access to the Chena River, one of the most popular grayling fisheries in the state. There's also a whitefish spear fishery (check season and limits). King and chum salmon migrate up the Chena River in July and August. *IMPORTANT: Check current ADF&G regulations regarding the taking of any fish.* Hiking trails include the Colorado Creek trail, Granite Tors trail, Angel Rocks trail and the Chena Dome trail. During winter this area is popular for snow machining, cross-country skiing and dog mushing. **Distance is measured from junction with the Steese Highway (J).**

J 0 Chena Hot Springs Road exit at **Milepost F 4.9** Steese Highway.

J 0.5 (0.8 km) Bad frost heaves.

J 1.8 (2.9 km) Bennett Road.

J 3.5 (5.6 km) Steele Creek Road.

J 4 (6.4 km) Frost heaves.

J 5.3 (8.5 km) **Geni's Bed & Breakfast.** See display ad this section.

A Taste of Alaska Lodge. 15 minutes from Fairbanks. Private, modern log house. Full panoramic view of Alaska Range mountains. Exceptional northern lights viewing and wildlife encounters. 160 sunny hillside acres. Jacuzzi. Year-round service. Rates $70 and up. Brochure. Write Dept. MP, 551 Eberhardt Rd., Fairbanks, AK 99712. (907) 488-7855, fax (907) 488-3772. [ADVERTISEMENT]

J 6.3 (10.1 km) Nordale Road.

J 8.3 (13.4 km) Paved double-ended turnout to south.

J 10.3 (16.6 km) Mini-mart, public dumpster.

J 11.9 (19.2 km) Bridge over Little

Chena River. Water gauging station in middle of bridge. The six rain gauges and three stream-flow meters in the upper Chena River basin help measure the water level in the Chena River. The stations send signals to a master control computer in Anchorage, which in turn sends instructions to the Moose Creek dam on the Richardson Highway. This Army Corps of Engineers flood control project, completed in 1979, was designed to prevent floods such as the one which devastated Fairbanks in 1967. The first high-water test of the project was in July 1981, when the floodgates at Moose Creek dam were lowered.

J **14** (22.5 km) Bumpy paved double-ended turnout to south.

J **15** (24.1 km) Rough road next 2 miles/3.2 km eastbound.

J **15.9** (25.6 km) **Two Rivers Lodge**. See display ad on page 413.

J **18** (29 km) Watch for moose.

J **18.6** (29.9 km) Two Rivers Road. Access to Two Rivers School and Two Rivers Recreation Area (maintained by Fairbanks North Star Borough) with cross-country ski and hiking trails. Public dumpster.

J **20.1** (32.3 km) Jenny M. Creek. Some 2,000 people reside along the road between here and its junction with the Steese Highway.

J **20.2** (32.5 km) Large, double-ended paved parking area to south.

J **23** (37 km) Double-ended gravel turnout.

J **23.4** (37.7 km) Grocery, public dumpster.

J **23.5** (37.8 km) **Tacks' General Store and Greenhouse Cafe.** See display ad this section.

Two Rivers post office is in store.

J **25.6** (41.2 km) HIPAS Observatory, UCLA Plasma Physics Lab (Geophysical Institute Chena Radio Facility).

J **25.7** (41.4 km) Road passes sloughs and ponds of the Chena River area. Fine place for berry pickers, furred and human.

J **26.1** (42 km) Entering **Chena River** Recreation Area. No shooting except at target range. Grayling fishing (check current regulations).

J **26.5** (42.6 km) Flat Creek culvert.

J **26.7** (43 km) Paved turnout to south for picnic area with tables and toilets.

J **27** (43.5 km) Rosehip state campground to south; 25 sites, picnic tables, firepits, toilets, water, $6 nightly fee or annual pass. Large, flat, gravel pads and an easy 0.7-mile/1.1-km loop road make this a good campground for large RVs and trailers. ▲

Canoe exit point. The Chena is popular with paddlers, but should not be underestimated: The river is cold and the current very strong. Watch for river-wide logjams and sweepers. Secure your gear in waterproof containers. Local paddlers suggest a float from **Milepost J 39.5** to **J 37.9** for easy paddling; **J 44** to **J 37.9** for a longer float; and **J 52.3** to **J 47.3** for paddlers with more skill. Allow about an hour on the river for each road mile traveled.

J **27.5** (44.2 km) Paved turnout to south.

J **27.9** (44.9 km) Toilets and access to river via road to south which leads 0.9 mile/1.4 km to large parking area with picnic tables, dumpster, loop turnaround. Canoe exit point.

J **28.8** (46.3 km) Access road to river, drive 0.7 mile/1.1 km south to canoe launch in brushy area along river; picnic table, toilet, dumpster, parking.

J **29.4** (47.3 km) Pleasant double-ended paved turnout to south on Chena River; picnic table.

J **30** (48.3 km) Outdoor education camp (available for rent by groups). Small lake stocked with grayling.

J **30.4** (48.9 km) River access and paved turnout with picnic table. Canoe exit point.

J **31.3** (50.4 km) Bridge over Colorado Creek. River access.

J **31.5** (50.7 km) River access.

J **31.8** (51.2 km) Colorado Creek ATV trail.

J **33.9** (54.6 km) Fourmile Creek flows under the road.

J **35.8** (57.6 km) Paved turnout to south.

J **36.5** (58.7 km) Target shooting range to north. ORV trails, toilets and picnic tables. Cathedral Bluffs view.

J **37.9** (61 km) First bridge over the **North Fork Chena River.** Water gauge in center of bridge (see **Milepost J 11.9**). Grayling fishing (check current special regulations).

Side road leaves highway to the south and forks. Left fork is a short road to the river and toilet; right fork leads 0.2 mile/0.3 km to picnic tables by the river. Canoe launch. This road is bordered by dense underbrush which may scratch wide vehicles.

J **39.2** (63.1 km) Paved turnout to south.

J **39.5** (63.5 km) Second bridge over North Fork Chena River. Loop road through Granite Tors trail state campground; 20 large sites among tall spruce trees, parking area, water, toilets, tables, firepits, $6 nightly fee or annual pass. Canoe launch. Picnic area on loop road along river. ▲

Trailhead for Granite Tors trail; follow dike (levee) on west side upstream 0.3 mile/0.4 km to trail sign. It is a 6-mile/9.7-km hike to the nearest tors, 8 miles/12.9 km to the main grouping. Tors are high, isolated pinnacles of jointed granite jutting up from the tundra.

J **39.7** (63.9 km) A 0.2-mile/0.3-km side road leads south to Chena River picnic area with tables, toilets and a riverbank of flat rocks ideal for sunbathing.

J **39.8** (64.1 km) Campground loop road exit; toilet beside road.

J **41.8** (67.3 km) Paved turnout to south by slough.

J **42.1** (67.8 km) Large turnout south of road. Watch for muskrats and beaver in ponds here.

J **42.8** (68.8 km) Mile 43 Red Squirrel picnic area to north, one of the nicest on this road, with covered tables, firepits, toilets and water. Located on edge of small lake stocked with grayling. Watch for moose.

J **42.9** (69 km) Gravel turnouts to south.

J **43.8** (70.5 km) Small lake to north stocked with grayling.

J **44.1** (71 km) Third bridge over North Fork Chena River. Picnic area with tables and toilets to north at east end of bridge. A favorite place to sunbathe and fish. Canoe launch.

J **45.7** (73.5 km) Fourth bridge over North Fork Chena River.

J **46** (74 km) Paved turnout to south.

J **46.8** (75.3 km) Chena River flows alongside the road; good access point for fishermen. Paved parking to south opposite river.

J **47.3** (76.1 km) Access to river north side of road.

J **47.9** (77.1 km) Side road leads 0.1 mile/0.2 km south to **48-Mile Pond.** Stocked with grayling; picnic tables, informal campsites.

J **48.8** (78.5 km) Watch for people and horses next mile eastbound.

J **48.9** (78.7 km) Angel Rocks trailhead; table, toilet, dumpster. Angel Rocks trail is a 3.5-mile/5.6-km loop trail to spectacular rock outcroppings; strenuous hike.

J **49** (78.9 km) Fifth bridge over **North Fork Chena River**; parking. Excellent fishing from here.

J 49.1 (79 km) Lower Chena Dome trailhead. Side road leads 0.2 mile/0.3 km north to trailhead, parking, water, dumpster and toilets.

J 49.3 (79.3 km) Cathedral Bluffs, an unusual rock formation to southeast.

J 49.9 (80.3 km) Paved turnout to north. **Angel Creek**, grayling 12 to 17 inches.

J 50.5 (81.2 km) Chena Dome trailhead; this 29-mile loop trail exits at **Milepost J 49.1.** Angel Creek Cabin ATV trailhead (6 miles/10 km). Parking, toilets. Bring mosquito repellent!

J 50.7 (81.6 km) Chena River Recreation Area boundary.

J 52.3 (84.2 km) Bridge over West Fork Chena River. Gravel side road leads south to parking area along the river. CAUTION: Abrupt approaches to bridge.

J 55.3 (89 km) North Fork Chena River bridge. Double-ended paved turnout to south.

J 56.5 (90.9 km) **CHENA HOT SPRINGS:** food, lodging, camping, bar and swimming. To phone ahead, call (907) 452-7867. These mineral hot springs were first reported in 1904 by the U.S. Geological Survey's field teams. The springs take their name from the nearby Chena River, which flows southwest. There is an airstrip at the lodge. ▲

Chena Hot Springs Resort. Open all year round, relax in our natural spring-fed pool, spas, hot tub and sunbathe on our 2,800-sq.-ft. redwood deck with a 10-person spa! Enjoy the cozy atmosphere of our fine dining rooms and take time to refresh yourself in the lounge. Rent a hotel room, rustic cabin or use

our spacious campground/RV parking (hookups and dump station available). Summer activities offer hiking, horseback riding, canoeing, rafting and mountain bike rentals, hay rides, helicopter rides, full body massage (year-round service), picnicking, volleyball, baseball, badminton areas. 2,200-foot airstrip. Nearby fishing. Winter activities feature cross-country ski and snowshoe rentals, dog sled rides, horse-drawn sleigh rides, flight sightseeing. Guided snow machine rides. Summer and winter activity packages available. Meeting facilities. P.O. Box 73440, Fairbanks, AK 99707, (907) 452-7867 or in-state (800) 478-4681. [ADVERTISEMENT] ▲

Return to Milepost F 4.9
Steese Highway

(Continued from page 413)

F 20.6 (33.2 km) **C 141.4** (227.6 km) Very rough turnout next to ski area buildings; view of current mining operation and old buildings from early mining and dredging on Cleary Creek below.

F 22 (35.4 km) **C 140** (225.3 km) Road construction ends northbound (1994). *NOTE: Road construction southbound to **Milepost F 11**.*

F 23.9 (38.4 km) **C 138.1** (222.2 km) Gravel turnout to east. Watch for frost heaves.

F 27.6 (44.4 km) **C 134.4** (216.3 km) Tailings (gravel and boulders of dredged streambeds) from early mining activity which yielded millions of dollars in gold. There is quite a bit of mining in the Chatanika area now.

F 27.9 (44.9 km) **C 134.1** (215.8 km) Sharp right turn up hill for historic Fairbanks Exploration Co. gold camp at **CHATANIKA,** built in 1925 to support gold dredging operations in the valley. Between 1926 and 1957 the F.E. Co. removed an estimated $70 million in gold.

Chatanika Gold Camp, on the National Register of Historic Places, is open year-round. Rates are very reasonable for the bunkhouse and cabins on the 48-acre site. The dining room features a 12-ft.-long antique wood stove. Sourdough breakfast buffet every Sunday, 10 A.M. – 2 P.M. Activities include breathtaking aurora viewing from late fall to early spring, dog sled rides (with Awl Alaskan Kennels, Beverly Rickels, musher), skiing, snowmachine rides, sledding, gold panning, three-wheeler rides, fishing available in nearby ponds and river. Transportation to/from Fairbanks available. Phone or fax (907) 389-2414 for more information. [ADVERTISEMENT]

F 28.6 (46 km) **C 133.4** (214.6 km) Old gold dredge behind tailing piles to west (private property, *DO NOT TRESPASS*). Lodge to east with meals, lodging and RV parking.

Chatanika Lodge. Cafe open 9 A.M. daily (year-round). Halibut/catfish fry Friday and Saturday, country-fried chicken on Sunday, served family-style, all you can eat. Diamond Willow Lounge. Rustic atmosphere, Alaska artifacts. Historic Alaska gold dredge and aurora borealis videos on big-screen TV. Good grayling fishing. Rooms $32 to $40. RV parking. No hookups. See display ad this section. [ADVERTISEMENT]

F 29.5 (47.5 km) **C 132.5** (213.2 km) Neal Brown Road to Poker Flat rocket facility; off-limits except to authorized personnel. The Poker Flat rocket range, operated by the Geophysical Institute, University of Alaska, is dedicated to unclassified auroral and upper atmospheric research. It is the only university-owned sounding rocket range in the world and the only high latitude and auroral zone launch facility on U.S. soil. Tours for interested groups may be arranged by calling (907) 474-7634.

Fishing at gravel pit ponds from here north to **Milepost F 39.5.** Ponds are stocked with grayling. (Watch for green signs at access points.)

F 32.3 (52 km) **C 129.7** (208.7 km) Captain Creek bridge.

F 32.5 (52.3 km) **C 129.5** (208.4 km) *CAUTION: Severe frost heaves and cracks in pavement next 0.2 mile/0.3 km northbound.*

F 35 (56.3 km) **C 127** (204.4 km) Access to Chatanika River. Double-ended paved turnout to west.

F 36.5 (58.7 km) **C 125.5** (202 km) Gravel turnout alongside ponds to west. Pond stocked with grayling.

F 37.1 (59.7 km) **C 124.9** (201 km) *CAUTION: Severe frost heaves and dips in pavement next 0.1 mile/0.2 km northbound.*

F 37.3 (60 km) **C 124.7** (200.7 km) Kokomo Creek bridge.

F 39 (62.8 km) **C 123** (197.9 km) Chatanika River bridge. Upper Chatanika River State Recreation Site, just north of the bridge, is a beautiful state campground on the riverbank. There are 25 sites with fireplaces, and a gravel parking area near the bridge. A water pump is at the entrance. Firewood is usually available during the summer. Camping fee $6/night or annual pass. Look for wild roses here in June. ▲

Boats can be launched on the gravel bars by the river. Bring your mosquito repellent. This is an access point to the Chatanika River canoe trail. See **Milepost F 60** for more information on canoeing this river.

Chatanika River, grayling 8 to 20 inches, use flies or spinners, May to September.

F 39.5 (63.5 km) **C 122.5** (197.1 km) Pond stocked with grayling.

F 40.2 (64.7 km) **C 121.8** (196 km) *CAUTION: Watch for severe dips in road surface.*

F 40.4 (65 km) **C 121.6** (195.7 km) Bridge over Crooked Creek.

F 41.5 (66.8 km) **C 120.5** (193.9 km) Bridge over Belle Creek. Most homes here are of permanent residents.

F 42.7 (68.7 km) **C 119.3** (192 km) Bridge over McKay Creek.

F 42.9 (69 km) **C 119.1** (191.7 km) Turnout to east.

View from Twelvemile Summit at Milepost F 85.5. (Jerrianne Lowther, staff)

F 43.8 (70.5 km) **C 118.2** (190.2 km) Pavement ends; it is good gravel road to Circle with the exception of a short stretch of blacktop at Central. Highway parallels the Chatanika River for the next 10 miles/16 km.

F 45.4 (73.1 km) **C 116.6** (187.6 km) **Long Creek** bridge. Grayling 8 to 14 inches, use spinners or flies, May to September. Beautiful view of Chatanika River.

F 49 (78.9 km) **C 113** (181.9 km) View down Chatanika River valley to east.

F 53.5 (86.1 km) **C 108.5** (174.6 km) Ptarmigan Creek in valley below highway.

F 57.1 (91.9 km) **C 104.9** (168.8 km) White Mountains National Recreation Area (BLM). Access to this area's trails and cabins is from the Elliott Highway.

F 57.3 (92.2 km) **C 104.7** (168.5 km) U.S. Creek to west. The large pipe near U.S. Creek was part of the Davidson Ditch, built in 1925 by the Fairbanks Exploration Co., to carry water to float gold dredges. The 83-mile-/133.6-km-long ditch, designed and engineered by J.B. Lippincott, begins near **Milepost F 64** on the Steese Highway and ends near Fox. A system of ditches and inverted siphons, the pipeline was capable of carrying 56,100 gallons per minute. After the dredges closed, the water was used for power until 1967, when a flood destroyed a bridge and flattened almost 1,000 feet/305m of pipe.

All-weather road leads 6 miles/9.6 km west to Nome Creek; recreational gold panning. There are some mining claims on Nome Creek. No dredges allowed. The road to Nome Creek is very steep and not recommended for large or underpowered vehicles. Nome Creek is a historic mining area; additional recreational facilities are under development by the BLM.

F 59 (94.9 km) **C 103** (165.8 km) Wide double-ended gravel parking area to east.

F 60 (96.6 km) **C 102** (164.2 km) Cripple Creek BLM campground (seven-day limit), six tent, 15 trailer sites; water pumps, fireplaces, toilets, tables, nature trail. Parking for walk-in campers. Firewood is usually available all summer. Recreational gold panning permitted. *Bring mosquito repellent!* ▲

Access to Cripple Creek BLM recreation cabin. Preregister and pay $10 fee at BLM office, 1150 University Ave., Fairbanks 99709; phone 474-2200.

Cripple Creek bridge is the uppermost access point to the Chatanika River canoe trail (follow side road near campground entrance to canoe launch site). *CAUTION: This canoe trail may not be navigable at low water.* The Chatanika River is a clear-water Class II stream. The Steese Highway parallels the river for approximately 28 miles/45 km and there are many access points to the highway downstream from the Cripple Creek bridge. No major obstacles on this canoe trail, but watch for overhanging trees. Downstream pullout points are Perhaps Creek, Long Creek and Chatanika Campground.

F 62.3 (100.2 km) **C 99.7** (160.4 km) Viewpoint to east overlooking Chatanika River.

F 63.4 (102 km) **C 98.6** (158.7 km) View of historic Davidson Ditch pipeline.

F 65 (104.6 km) **C 97** (156.1 km) Side road east to viewpoint.

F 65.6 (105.6 km) **C 96.4** (155.1 km) Sourdough Creek bridge.

F 65.7 (105.7 km) **C 96.3** (155 km) Mile 66. Hendrickson's Miracle Mile Lodge.

F 66 (106.2 km) **C 96** (154.5 km) Sourdough Creek Road to north.

F 69 (111 km) **C 93** (149.7 km) Faith Creek bridge and road. Creek access to east at north end of bridge. Large parking area to west.

F 72 (115.9 km) **C 90** (144.8 km) View ahead for northbound travelers of highway route along mountains, McManus Creek below.

F 73.8 (118.8 km) **C 88.2** (141.9 km) Faith Creek Road to west.

F 79.1 (127.3 km) **C 82.9** (133.4 km) Road widens for parking next 500 feet/152m.

F 80.1 (128.9 km) **C 81.9** (131.8 km) Montana Creek state highway maintenance station. Montana Creek runs under road and into McManus Creek to the east. McManus Dome (elev. 4,184 feet/1,275m) to west.

F 81.2 (130.7 km) **C 80.8** (130 km) Turnout to east. Spring water (untested) piped to roadside. Wide gravel highway begins final ascent to Twelvemile Summit.

F 83 (133.6 km) **C 79** (127.1 km) Sharp turn to right northbound. Watch for the hoary marmot and other small mammals.

F 85.5 (137.6 km) **C 76.5** (123.1 km) Large parking area and viewpoint to east at Twelvemile Summit (elev. 2,982 feet/909m) on the divide of the Yukon and Tanana river drainages. Dozens of species of wildflowers carpet the alpine tundra slopes. Entering Game Management Unit 25C, leaving unit 20B, northbound. Fairbanks North Star Borough limits. This is caribou country; from here to beyond Eagle Summit (**Milepost F 108**) migrating bands of caribou may be seen from late July through mid-September.

Access to Pinnell Mountain national recreation trail (Twelvemile Summit trailhead). The trail is also accessible from **Milepost F 107.1.** Named in honor of Robert Pinnell, who was fatally injured in 1952 while climbing nearby Porcupine Dome. This 27-mile-/43-km-long hiking trail winds through alpine terrain, along mountain ridges and through high passes. Highest elevation point reached is 4,721 feet/1,439m. The trail is marked by rock cairns. Shelter cabins at Mile 10.7 and Mile 17.7. Vantage points along the trail with views of the White Mountains, Tanana Hills, Brooks Range and Alaska Range. Watch for willow ptarmigan, hoary marmot, rock pika, moose, wolf and caribou. Mid-May through July is the prime time for wildflowers, with flowers peaking in mid-June. Carry drinking water and insect repellent at all times. Additional information on this trail is available from the Bureau of Land Management, 1150 University Ave., Fairbanks 99708-3844; phone 474-2350.

F 88 (141.6 km) **C 74** (119.1 km) Twelvemile Creek to east below road.

F 88.7 (142.7 km) **C 73.3** (118 km) Bridge over Reed Creek.

F 90.5 (145.6 km) **C 71.5** (115.1 km) Turnout to east.

F 93.4 (150.3 km) **C 68.6** (110.4 km) Bridge over the North Fork Twelvemile Creek. Nice picnic spot to west below bridge.

F 94 (151.3 km) **C 68** (109.4 km) Side road leads 0.2 mile/0.3 km down to north fork of Birch Creek; parking area and canoe launch for Birch Creek canoe trail. This is the main put in point for canoeing Birch Creek, a Wild and Scenic River. Undeveloped campsite by creek. Extensive mining in area. **Birch Creek**, grayling to 12 inches; use flies, June to October.

F 95.8 (154.2 km) **C 66.2** (106.5 km) Bridge over Willow Creek.

Much gold mining activity along this part of the highway. These are private mining claims. *Do not trespass. Do not approach mining equipment without permission.*

F 97.7 (157.2 km) **C 64.3** (103.5 km) Bridge over Bear Creek.

F 98 (157.7 km) **C 64** (103 km) Gold mine and settling ponds in creek valley to east.

F 99.8 (160.8 km) **C 62.2** (100.1 km) Bridge over Fish Creek. Privately owned cabins.

F 101.5 (163.3 km) **C 60.5** (97.4 km) Bridge over Ptarmigan Creek (elev. 2,398 feet/731m). Alpine meadows carpeted with

Watch for willow ptarmigan—Alaska's state bird—along the road. (Bill Sherwonit)

Circle Hot Springs Road Log

Distance is measured from junction with Steese Highway (J).

J 0 Pavement extends next 0.3 mile/0.5 km.

J 0.9 (1.4 km) Graveyard Road, 0.5 mile/0.8 km to cemetery.

J 1.9 (3.1 km) Deadwood Creek Road.

J 2.9 (4.7 km) Bridge over Deadwood Creek.

J 5.7 (9.2 km) Bridge over Ketchem Creek. Primitive camping at site of former Ketchem Creek BLM campground on right before bridge; no facilities.

J 8.3 (13.4 km) **CIRCLE HOT SPRINGS;** year-round swimming, lodging, food and RV parking. A popular spot with Alaskans.

According to research done by Patricia Oakes of Central, the hot springs were used as a gathering place by area Athabascans before the gold rush. Local prospectors probably used the springs as early as the 1890s. Cassius Monohan homesteaded the site in 1905, selling out to Frank Leach in 1909. Leach built the airstrip, on which Noel Wien landed in 1924.

Private Aircraft: Circle Hot Springs state-maintained airstrip; elev. 956 feet/291m; length 3,600 feet/1,097m; gravel; lighted, unattended.

Return to Milepost F 127.8 Steese Highway

wildflowers in spring and summer for next 9 miles/14.5 km.

F 102.3 (164.6 km) **C 59.7** (96.1 km) Ptarmigan Creek access to west.

F 103 (165.8 km) **C 59** (94.9 km) Good view of mining operation next mile northbound.

F 105 (169 km) **C 57** (91.7 km) Snowpoles guide snowplows in winter.

F 105.4 (169.6 km) **C 56.6** (91 km) Large gravel parking area to west.

F 107.1 (172.4 km) **C 54.9** (88.4 km) Parking area to west. Pinnell Mountain trail access (Eagle Summit trailhead); see description at **Milepost F 85.6.**

F 108 (173.8 km) **C 54** (86.9 km) Eagle Summit (elev. 3,624 feet/1,105m) to the east. Steep, narrow, rocky side road leads from the highway 0.8 mile/1.3 km to the summit. This is the third and highest of three summits (including Cleary and Twelvemile) along the Steese Highway. *NOTE: Gates across the highway may be closed in bad weather.* Favorite spot for local residents to observe summer solstice (weather permitting) on June 21. Best wildflower viewing on Alaska highway system.

Scalloped waves of soil on hillsides to west are called solifluction lobes. These are formed when meltwater saturates the thawed surface soil, which then flows slowly downhill.

Wildflowers found here include: dwarf forget-me-nots, alpine rhododendron or rosebay, rock jasmine, alpine azalea, arctic bell heather, mountain avens, Jacob's ladder, anemones, wallflowers, Labrador tea, lupine, oxytropes, gentians and louseworts. The museum in Central has a photographic display of Eagle Summit alpine flowers to help highway travelers identify the wildflowers of this area.

F 109.2 (175.7 km) **C 52.8** (85 km) Large parking area to east with view down into Miller Creek far below. Excellent wildflower display. Highway begins steep descent northbound.

F 114.2 (183.8 km) **C 47.8** (76.9 km) Parking area to east looking down onto the Mastodon and Mammoth creeks area.

F 114.4 (184.1 km) **C 47.6** (76.6 km) Side road to east leads to Mammoth and Mastodon creeks; active gold placer mining areas.

F 116.2 (187 km) **C 45.8** (73.7 km) Road east to creek.

F 116.4 (187.3 km) **C 45.6** (73.4 km) Bridge over Mammoth Creek. Near here fossil remains of many species of preglacial Alaskan mammals have been excavated and may be seen at the University of Alaska museum in Fairbanks and at the museum in Central.

F 117 (188.3 km) **C 45** (72.4 km) Highway crosses over Stack Pup. From here the highway gradually descends to Central.

F 117.6 (189.3 km) **C 44.4** (71.5 km) Parking area to west.

F 119.1 (191.7 km) **C 42.9** (69 km) Bedrock Creek.

F 119.2 (191.8 km) **C 42.8** (68.9 km) Narrow dirt road leads to site of former Bedrock Creek BLM campground; closed.

F 121 (194.7 km) **C 41** (66 km) Bridge over Sawpit Creek.

F 122.5 (197.1 km) **C 39.5** (63.6 km) Road west to parking space by pond.

F 125.4 (201.8 km) **C 36.6** (58.9 km) Bridge over Boulder Creek.

F 126.8 (204.1 km) **C 35.2** (56.6 km) Paved highway begins and continues through Central.

F 127.1 (204.5 km) **C 34.9** (56.2 km) Central elementary school.

F 127.5 (205.2 km) **C 34.5** (55.5 km) **CENTRAL** (pop. approximately 400 in summer, 150 in winter; elev. 965 feet/294m). **Radio:** KUAC-FM 91.7. This small community, formerly called Central House, is situated on Crooked Creek along the Steese Highway.

Central is the central point in the huge Circle Mining District, one of the oldest and still one of the most active districts in the state. The annual Circle Mining District Picnic for local miners and their families is held in August.

Central has many facilities for the visitor: state airstrip (see **Milepost F 128.3**), cafes and bars, motel cabins, laundromat, showers, groceries, gas, tire repair, welding, pay phone and post office (Zip code 99730). Check with Crabb's Corner for emergency medical services. Report fires to BLM field station at **Milepost F 127.8.** Picnic area at Central Park.

The Circle District Historical Society museum has displays covering the history of the Circle Mining District and its people. Also here are a photo display of wildflowers, fossilized remains of preglacial mammals, a minerals display, library and archives, gift shop and visitor information. Admission is $1 for adults, 50¢ for children under 12; members free. Open daily noon to 5 P.M., Memorial Day through Labor Day.

Central Motor Inn and Campground. See display ad this section. ▲

F 127.8 (205.7 km) **C 34.2** (55 km) **Crabb's Corner Grocery, Motel, Campground and Cafe.** Jim and Sandy Crabb offer propane, cafe, bar, package store. Fresh beef hamburgers. RV parking. Fresh water. Laundromat. Complete variety of grocery

items including mosquito repellents. Pay phone. Open daily. (907) 520-5115. The place to eat in Central! [ADVERTISEMENT] ▲

F 127.8 (205.7 km) **C 34.2** (55 km) **Junction** with Circle Hot Springs Road; see CIRCLE HOT SPRINGS ROAD log on page 417.

BLM Alaska Fire Services office.

F 127.9 (205.8 km) **C 34.1** (54.9 km) Bridge over Crooked Creek. Site of Central House roadhouse on south side of bridge.

F 128.1 (206.1 km) **C 33.9** (54.5 km) Central DOT/PF highway maintenance station.

F 128.3 (206.5 km) **C 33.7** (54.2 km) **Private Aircraft**: Central state-maintained airstrip, adjacent north; elev. 932 feet/284m; length 2,700 feet/823m; gravel; unattended.

Pavement ends northbound. Watch for soft spots, curves and little or no shoulder between here and Circle; otherwise, the road is in good shape. Wildlife is frequently sighted on the road between Central and Circle.

F 130.5 (210 km) **C 31.5** (50.7 km) Pond frequented by a variety of ducks.

F 131.2 (211.1 km) **C 30.8** (49.6 km) Albert Creek bridge. Small parking area with litter barrel at end of bridge.

F 133 (214 km) **C 29** (46.7 km) Repair shop.

F 147.1 (236.7 km) **C 14.9** (24 km) One-lane bridge over Birch Creek; clearance 13 feet, 11 inches. Turnouts, undeveloped campsites, both ends of bridge. Usual take-out point for the Birch Creek canoe trail.

F 147.6 (237.5 km) **C 14.4** (23.2 km) Turnout to east.

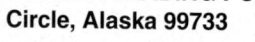

F 155.9 (250.9 km) **C 6.1** (9.8 km) Diamond (Bebb) willow along road. Diamond willow is used to make walking sticks.

F 156.7 (252.1 km) **C 5.3** (8.5 km) Large turnout opposite gravel pit. Look for bank swallow nests in cliffs.

F 159.6 (256.8 km) **C 2.4** (3.9 km) Old Indian cemetery to east.

Circle

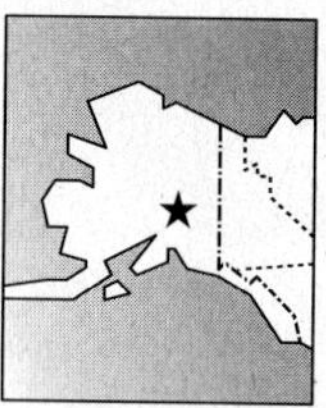

F 162 (260.7 km) **C 0** Located on the banks of the Yukon River, 50 miles/80.5 km south of the Arctic Circle. The Yukon is Alaska's largest river; the 2,000-mile/3,219-km river heads in Canada and flows west into Norton Sound on the Bering Sea. **Population:** 94. **Elevation:** 700 feet/213m. **Climate:** Mean monthly temperature in July 61.4°F/16.3°C, in January -10.6°F/-23.7°C. Record high 91°F/32.8°C July 1977, record low -60°F/-51.1°C in December 1961, February 1979 and January 1983. Snow from October (8 inches) through April (2 inches). Precipitation in the summer averages 1.45 inches a month.

Private Aircraft: Circle City state-maintained airstrip, adjacent west; elev. 610 feet/186m; length 3,000 feet/914m; gravel; fuel 100LL.

Before the Klondike gold rush of 1898, Circle City was the largest gold mining town on the Yukon River. Prospectors discovered gold on Birch Creek in 1893, and the town of Circle City (so named because the early miners thought it was located on the Arctic Circle) grew up as the nearest supply point to the new diggings on the Yukon River.

Today, Circle serves a small local population and visitors coming in by highway or by river. Gas, groceries, snacks and sundries are available at two local stores. The trading post houses the post office, cafe and liquor store. Hunting and fishing licenses are also available at the trading post. There's a lot of summer river traffic here: canoeists put in and take out; the tug *Brainstorm* docks here on its trip from Fort Yukon; Yutana Barge Lines docks here; and floatplanes land on the river.

Be sure to have your picture taken in front of the sign that welcomes you to Circle. From Dawson Creek, BC, you've driven approximately 1,685 miles/2,712 km along the Alaska Highway and the Steese Highway.

The old Pioneer Cemetery, with its markers dating back to the 1800s, is an interesting spot to visit. Walk a short way upriver (past the old machinery) on the gravel road to a barricade: You will have to cross through a private front yard (please be respectful of property) to get to the trail. Walk straight ahead on the short trail, which goes through dense underbrush (many mosquitoes), for about 10 minutes. Watch for a path on your left to the graves, which are scattered among the thick trees.

Camping on the banks of the Yukon at the end of the road; tables, toilets, parking area. In 1989, when the Yukon flooded, water covered the bottom of the welcome sign at the campground entrance. From the campground you are looking at one channel of the mighty Yukon. ▲

CIRCLE ADVERTISERS

Alaska Yukon Sternwheeler Co. ....Ph. (907) 455-4320
H.C. Company Store....................End of hwy.
Yukon Trading Post..........Ph. (907) 773-1217

ELLIOTT HIGHWAY

Fox to Manley Hot Springs, Alaska
Alaska Route 2
(See map, page 420)

View of the Elliott Highway from Grapefruit Rocks near Milepost F 38. (Steven Seiller)

The Elliott Highway leads 152 miles/244.6 km from its junction with the Steese Highway at Fox (11 miles/17.7 km north of Fairbanks) to Manley Hot Springs, a small settlement near the Tanana River with a natural hot springs. The highway was named for Malcolm Elliott, president of the Alaska Road Commission from 1927 to 1932.

The first 28 miles/45.1 km of the Elliott Highway are paved; the remaining 124 miles/200 km are gravel. The highway is wide, hard-based gravel to the Dalton Highway junction. (The road is treated with calcium chloride for dust control; wash your vehicle after travel to prevent corrosion.) From the junction into Manley, the road is narrower but fairly smooth with some soft spots and a roller-coaster section near Manley. Gas is available at **Milepost F 5.3, F 49.5** and at Manley.

Watch for heavy truck traffic. Drivers pulling trailers should be especially cautious when the road is wet. The highway is open year-round; check with the Dept. of Transportation in Fairbanks regarding winter road conditions.

The Elliott Highway also provides access to four trailheads in the White Mountains National Recreation Area. These hiking trails are managed by the BLM in Fairbanks.

Emergency medical services: Between Fox and Manley Hot Springs, phone the state troopers at 911 or 452-1313. Use CB channels 9, 14, 19.

Elliott Highway Log

Distance from Fox (F) is followed by distance from Manley Hot Springs (M).

F 0 M 152 (244.6 km) **FOX. Junction** of the Steese Highway with the Elliott Highway. Weigh station.

F 0.4 (0.6 km) **M 151.6** (244 km) Fox Spring picnic area; two tables, spring water.

F 1.2 (1.9 km) **M 150.8** (242.7 km) Turnoff for Little Eldorado Gold Mine, a commercial gold mine offering tours and gold panning to the public; admission charged.

F 3.4 (5.5 km) **M 148.6** (239.1 km) Rough side road leads west to Murphy Dome, 28 miles/45 km away. Road is signed "restricted military site."

F 5.3 (8.5 km) **M 146.7** (236.1 km) Gas station and cafe.

F 7.5 (12 km) **M 144.5** (232.5 km) Views to the east of Pedro Dome and Dome Creek. Buildings of Dome and Eldorado camps are in the valley below to the east (best view is southbound).

F 9.2 (14.8 km) **M 142.8** (229.8 km) Olnes, former railroad station of Tanana Valley Railroad and mining camp. Old tailings and abandoned cabins.

F 10.6 (17.1 km) **M 141.4** (227.6 km) Lower Chatanika River State Recreation Area Olnes Creek Campground, 1 mile/1.6 km west of highway on loop road; 50 campsites, toilets, water, tables, group area with campfire ring and benches. Camping fee $6/night or annual pass. ▲

F 11 (17.7 km) **M 141** (226.9 km) Chatanika River bridge. Lower Chatanika State Recreation Area Whitefish Campground at north end of bridge; picnic area (wheelchair accessible) with covered picnic tables, campsites, toilets, firepits, water, litter barrels, river access and boat launch. Camping fee $6/night or annual pass. ♿▲

F 11.5 (18.5 km) **M 140.5** (226.1 km) General store.

F 13.1 (21.1 km) **M 138.9** (223.5 km) Willow Creek bridge.

F 13.4 (21.6 km) **M 138.6** (223.1 km) Old log cabin to west is a landmark on the Elliott Highway.

F 18.3 (29.5 km) **M 133.7** (215.2 km) Double-ended paved turnout to west.

F 18.5 (29.8 km) **M 133.5** (214.8 km) Washington Creek. Parking area below bridge east of road; undeveloped campsite.

F 20.1 (32.3 km) **M 131.9** (212.3 km) Beaver pond with dam and lodge to east.

F 20.3 (32.7 km) **M 131.7** (212 km) Cushman Creek Road.

F 23.5 (37.8 km) **M 128.5** (206.8 km) Large double-ended turnout with view of forested valley to west.

F 24.2 (39 km) **M 127.8** (205.7 km) Double-ended gravel turnout to east at top of hill. Snowshoe Creek parallels the road.

F 24.7 (39.8 km) **M 127.3** (204.9 km) Long paved double-ended turnout to east.

F 27.7 (44.6 km) **M 124.3** (200 km) Large double-ended paved turnout to west. Highway winds around the base of Wickersham Dome (elev. 3,207 feet/977m). Views of the White Mountains, a range of white limestone mountains (elev. 5,000 feet/1,524m). Entering Livengood/Tolovana Mining District northbound, Fairbanks Mining District southbound.

Trailhead for White Mountains–Wickersham Creek trail and White Mountains–Summit trail to Borealis-LeFevre BLM cabin. The Wickersham Creek route is 20 miles/32 km in length; ATVs are permitted. The Summit route is 22 miles/35.4 km long and ATVs are prohibited. For more information and cabin registration, contact the BLM office in Fairbanks at 1150 University Ave.; phone 474-2350.

Pipeline access restricted to ensure public safety and security, and to protect the reseeding and restoration of construction areas.

F 28 (45.1 km) **M 124** (199.6 km) Pavement ends.

F 29.1 (46.8 km) **M 122.9** (197.8 km) Sled Dog Rocks ahead northbound.

F 29.5 (47.4 km) **M 122.5** (197.1 km) Double-ended gravel turnout to east.

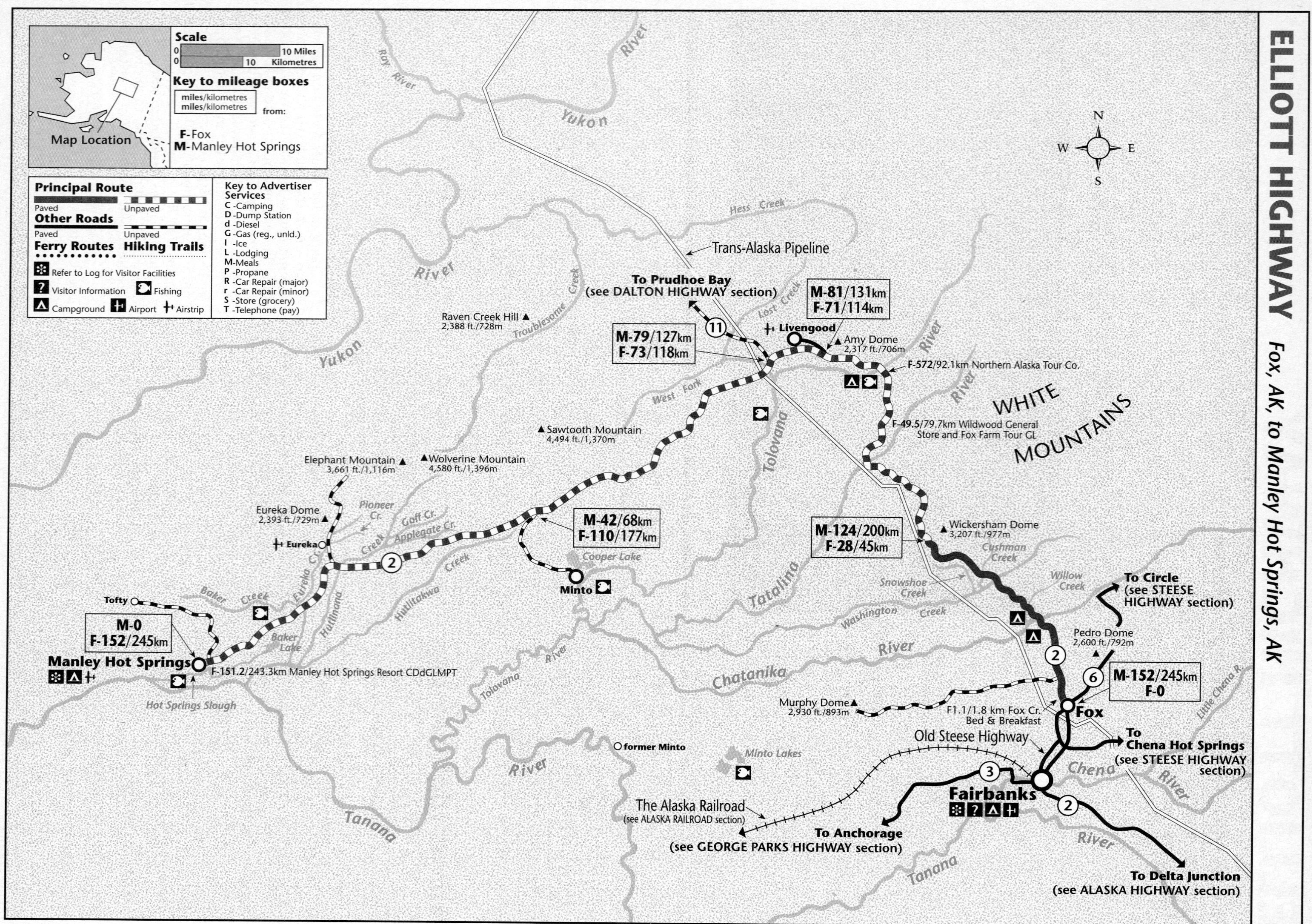
ELLIOTT HIGHWAY
Fox, AK, to Manley Hot Springs, AK
Scale
0 10 Miles
0 10 Kilometres
Key to mileage boxes
miles/kilometres
miles/kilometres
from:
F-Fox
M-Manley Hot Springs
Map Location
Principal Route
Paved Unpaved
Other Roads
Paved Unpaved
Ferry Routes Hiking Trails
Refer to Log for Visitor Facilities
Visitor Information
Fishing
Campground
Airport
Airstrip
Key to Advertiser Services
C -Camping
D -Dump Station
d -Diesel
G -Gas (reg., unld.)
I -Ice
L -Lodging
M -Meals
P -Propane
R -Car Repair (major)
r -Car Repair (minor)
S -Store (grocery)
T -Telephone (pay)
N E S W
Trans-Alaska Pipeline
To Prudhoe Bay (see DALTON HIGHWAY section)
M-81/131km F-71/114km
M-79/127km F-73/118km
Livengood
Amy Dome 2,317 ft./706m
F-572/92.1km Northern Alaska Tour Co.
F-49.5/79.7km Wildwood General Store and Fox Farm Tour GL
WHITE MOUNTAINS
Raven Creek Hill 2,388 ft./728m
Sawtooth Mountain 4,494 ft./1,370m
Elephant Mountain 3,661 ft./1,116m
Wolverine Mountain 4,580 ft./1,396m
Eureka Dome 2,393 ft./729m
Eureka
M-42/68km F-110/177km
Cooper Lake
Minto
Wickersham Dome 3,207 ft./977m
M-124/200km F-28/45km
To Circle (see STEESE HIGHWAY section)
Pedro Dome 2,600 ft./792m
M-152/245km F-0
Fox
Murphy Dome 2,930 ft./893m
F1.1/1.8 km Fox Cr. Bed & Breakfast
Old Steese Highway
To Chena Hot Springs (see STEESE HIGHWAY section)
Fairbanks
The Alaska Railroad (see ALASKA RAILROAD section)
To Anchorage (see GEORGE PARKS HIGHWAY section)
To Delta Junction (see ALASKA HIGHWAY section)
Tofty
M-0 F-152/245km
Manley Hot Springs
F-151.2/243.3km Manley Hot Springs Resort CDdGLMPT
Hot Springs Slough
former Minto
Minto Lakes
Ray River
Yukon River
Hess Creek
Troublesome Creek
Lost Creek
West Fork
Tolovana River
Tatalina River
Chatanika River
Washington Creek
Snowshoe Creek
Cushman Creek
Willow Creek
Little Chena R.
Chena River
Tanana River
Pioneer Cr.
Goff Cr.
Applegate Cr.
Eureka Cr.
Baker Creek
Baker Lake
Hutlinana Creek
Hutlitakwa Creek

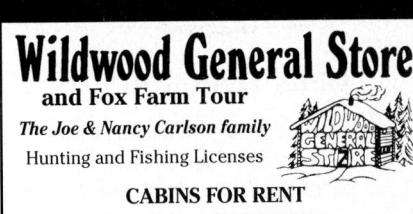

F 29.8 (48 km) **M 122.2** (196.7 km) Turnouts to west. Spring water piped to road.

F 30.4 (48.9 km) **M 121.6** (195.7 km) Rough double-ended turnout to west. Fairbanks/North Star Borough boundary.

F 31 (49.9 km) **M 121** (194.7 km) Long double-ended gravel turnout to east.

F 31.8 (51.2 km) **M 120.2** (193.4 km) Double-ended turnout to west.

F 34.7 (55.8 km) **M 117.3** (188.8 km) Good view of pipeline; creek.

F 36.4 (58.6 km) **M 115.6** (186 km) Large double-ended turnout to east.

F 37 (59.5 km) **M 115** (185.1 km) Globe Creek bridge. Steep access road to parking area next to bridge.

F 38 (61.1 km) **M 114** (183.5 km) Highway follows pipeline. View of Globe Creek canyon. Grapefruit Rocks to east.

F 39 (62.8 km) **M 113** (181.9 km) Double-ended turnout to east.

F 39.3 (63.2 km) **M 112.7** (181.4 km) Double-ended turnout with litter barrels to west.

F 40.6 (65.3 km) **M 111.4** (179.3 km) Scenic view from double-ended turnout to east at top of hill.

F 41.2 (66.3 km) **M 110.8** (178.3 km) Drive-in parking area to east; no easy turnaround.

F 42.8 (68.8 km) **M 109.2** (175.7 km) Pipeline pump station No. 7 to west.

F 44.8 (72.1 km) **M 107.2** (172.5 km) Tatalina Creek bridge; rest area to east at south end of bridge. The Tatalina is a tributary of the Chatanika.

F 47.1 (75.8 km) **M 104.9** (168.8 km) Turnout to east.

F 49.5 (79.7 km) **M 102.5** (165 km) Wildwood General Store. The store began as a lemonade stand run by some of the Carlsons' 16 adopted children.

Wildwood General Store. See display ad this section.

F 49.9 (80.3 km) **M 102.1** (164.3 km) Northern Lights School. This two-room public school has an enrollment of 22 students.

F 51.9 (83.5 km) **M 100.1** (161.1 km) Double-ended parking area, water. View of White Mountains to northeast and the Elliott Highway descending slopes of Bridge Creek valley ahead. Bridge Creek flows into the Tolovana River.

F 52 (83.7 km) **M 100** (160.9 km) Grizzly and black bear are sometimes seen in this area.

F 57.1 (91.9 km) **M 94.9** (152.7 km) **Tolovana River** bridge; parking. Recreational gold panning permitted. Grayling to 11 inches; whitefish 12 to 18 inches; northern pike.

Colorado Creek trail to Colorado Creek and Windy Gap BLM cabins. Check with BLM office in Fairbanks for details.

F 58 (93.3 km) **M 94** (151.3 km) Highway winds around Amy Dome (elev. 2,317 feet/706m) to east. The Tolovana River flows in the valley to the southwest, paralleling the road.

F 59.3 (95.4 km) **M 92.7** (149.2 km) Parking area to west by stream.

F 59.9 (96.4 km) **M 92.1** (148.2 km) Double-ended turnout to west.

F 62.3 (100.3 km) **M 89.7** (144.4 km) Access to Fred Blixt BLM cabin, east side of road. Preregister at BLM office in Fairbanks.

F 70.1 (112.8 km) **M 81.9** (131.8 km) Livengood Creek, two-lane bridge. Money Knob to northeast.

F 70.8 (113.9 km) **M 81.2** (130.7 km) Double-ended turnout at **junction** with Livengood access road. Drive 2 miles/3.2 km to **LIVENGOOD** (area pop. about 100); state highway maintenance station and EMT squad.

The settlement of Livengood began in July 1914 with the discovery of gold by Nathaniel R. Hudson and Jay Livengood. A lively mining camp until 1920, some $9.5 million in gold was sluiced out by miners. Large-scale mining was attempted in the late 1930s and again in the 1940s, but both operations were eventually shut down and Livengood became a ghost town.

With the building of the trans-Alaska pipeline and the North Slope Haul Road (now the Dalton Highway) in the 1970s, the town was revitalized as a construction camp. In 1977 a mining corporation acquired much of the gold-rich Livengood Bench. *NO TRESPASSING* on mining claims.

F 71.1 (114.4 km) **M 80.9** (130.2 km) Large double-ended turnout to south.

F 73.1 (117.6 km) **M 78.9** (127 km) **Junction** with the Dalton Highway (see DALTON HIGHWAY section); turn left (west) for Manley Hot Springs.

F 74.1 (119.2 km) **M 77.9** (125.4 km) Alyeska pipeline access road (restricted). Pipeline stretches for miles to the east.

F 74.3 (119.6 km) **M 77.7** (125 km) Site of old Livengood pipeline camp.

F 74.7 (120.2 km) **M 77.3** (124.4 km) Camping spot at west end of **Tolovana River** bridge; grayling to 15 inches, use spinners or flies.

F 76.3 (122.8 km) **M 75.7** (121.8 km) Cascaden Ridge (low hills to north).

F 79 (127.1 km) **M 73** (117.5 km) Travelers should appreciate the abundance of dragonflies seen along the Elliott Highway: their main food is mosquitoes.

F 85.5 (137.6 km) **M 66.5** (107 km) Looking south toward the Tolovana River valley, travelers should be able to see Tolovana Hot Springs Dome (elev. 2,386 feet/727m). (Hot springs are on the other side of dome; no road access.)

F 93.7 (150.8 km) **M 58.3** (93.8 km) Watch for foxes from here to top of hill. Wild rhubarb and fireweed border roadsides for miles.

F 94.5 (152.1 km) **M 57.5** (92.5 km) Long double-ended turnout to south. Good vantage point to view Minto Flats, Tanana River and foothills of the Alaska Range to the south.

F 97 (156.1 km) **M 55** (88.5 km) The mountains to the north are Sawtooth (elev. 4,494 feet/1,370m); Wolverine (elev. 4,580 feet/1,396m); and Elephant (elev. 3,661 feet/1,116m). To the south are Tolovana River flats and Cooper Lake. Wild rhubarb and fireweed grow in old burn area.

F 98.3 (158.2 km) **M 53.7** (86.4 km) Turnout to southwest with view of Minto Lakes.

F 100.4 (161.6 km) **M 51.6** (83 km) Turnout to east in former gravel pit.

F 106.8 (171.9 km) **M 45.2** (72.7 km) Turnout with view of Sawtooth Mountains to north.

F 110 (177 km) **M 42** (67.6 km) **Junction** with Minto Road which leads 11 miles/17.7 km to the Indian village of **MINTO** (pop. 233). The village was moved to its present location from the east bank of the Tanana River in 1971 because of flooding. Minto has a lodge with accommodations and meals and a general store. Most Minto residents make their living by hunting and fishing. Some local people also work in the arts and crafts center, making birch-bark baskets and beaded skin and fur items. Temperatures here range from 55°F to 90°F/13°C to 32°C in summer, and from 32°F to -50°F/0°C to -46°C in winter. Minto Flats is one of the most popular duck hunting spots in Alaska in terms of number of hunters, according to the ADF&G.

Private Aircraft: Minto airstrip 1 mile/1.6 km east; elev. 460 feet/140m; length 2,000 feet/610m; gravel; unattended.

Minto Lakes, pike to 36 inches, use wobblers, bait, red-and-white spoons, good all summer. Also grayling, sheefish and whitefish. Name refers to all lakes in this lowland area. Accessible only by plane or boat; best to fly in.

F 113 (181.9 km) **M 39** (62.8 km) Evidence of 1983 burn.

F 113.5 (182.7 km) **M 38.5** (62 km) West Fork Hutlitakwa Creek.

F 119 (191.5 km) **M 33** (53.1 km) The road travels the ridges and hills, providing a "top of the world" view of hundreds of square miles in all directions.

F 119.5 (192.3 km) **M 32.5** (52.3 km) Eureka Dome (elev. 2,393 feet/729m) to north.

F 121.1 (194.9 km) **M 30.9** (49.7 km) To the north, travelers look down into the draws of Applegate and Goff creeks.

F 123.2 (198.3 km) **M 28.8** (46.3 km) Small turnout to north. Road begins descent into the Eureka area.

F 123.7 (199.1 km) **M 28.3** (45.5 km) Dugan Hills visible to the south at this point.

F 129.3 (208.1 km) **M 22.7** (36.5 km) Hutlinana Creek bridge.

F 131.3 (211.3 km) **M 20.7** (33.3 km) Eureka Road turnoff; access to private ranch. Active mining is taking place in this area. *NO TRESPASSING* on private claims. A trail leads to the former mining camp of Eureka, at the junction of Pioneer and Eureka creeks, 3 miles/4.8 km south of Eureka Dome.

Private Aircraft: Eureka Creek airstrip; elev. 700 feet/213m; length 1,500 feet/457m; turf; unattended.

F 137.4 (221.1 km) **M 14.6** (23.5 km) One-lane bridge over **Baker Creek.** Grayling 5 to 20 inches, use flies, black gnats, mosquitoes, May 15 to Sept. 30.

Winding road with many ups and downs.

F 138.4 (222.7 km) **M 13.6** (21.9 km)

Fishing for pike at Manley Slough. (Jerrianne Lowther, staff)

Highway goes over Overland Bluff and through a 1968 burn area. Bracket fungus is growing on the dead birch trees.

F 150 (241.4 km) **M 2** (3.2 km) *NOTE: This part of the road can be extremely slick after heavy rains. Drive with caution.*

F 151.1 (243.2 km) **M 0.9** (1.4 km) Manley DOT/PF highway maintenance station.

F 151.2 (243.3 km) **M 0.8** (1.3 km) **Junction** with Tofty Road which leads 16 miles/25.7 km to former mining area of Tofty, founded in 1908 by pioneer prospector A.F. Tofty. Mining activity in area.

The hot springs is on a hillside on the right before entering the town. One spring runs 35 gallons a minute with a temperature of 136°F/58°C, another runs 110 gallons per minute at 135°F/57°C.

F 151.2 (243.3 km) **M 0.8** (1.3 km) **Manley Hot Springs Resort.** Open year-round. Swim in hot mineral spring-fed pool. Rooms with half baths, full baths or double Jacuzzis; log cabins, restaurant, bar, RV park, dump station, laundromat, showers, gift shop. Gas and diesel, boats available for grayling, northern pike, sheefish. Riverboat charters available. All our tours are to authentic operating fish camps, gold mines. See the real interior Alaska lifestyle. River tours include visits to fish camp (operating fish wheel). Dogsled rides cross-country in winter. Crystal clear winter nights for viewing aurora borealis. Cross-country skiing, snowshoeing, ice skating. We can accommodate up to 65 guests. Write Box 28, Manley Hot Springs Resort, Manley Hot Springs, AK 99756 or phone (907) 672-3611. Fax (907) 672-3461. [ADVERTISEMENT] ▲

Manley Hot Springs

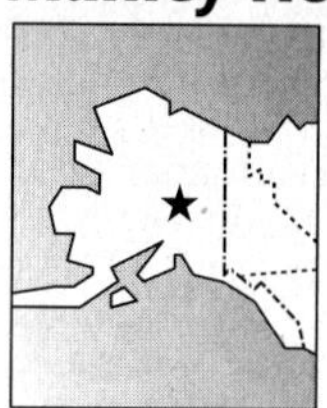

F 152 (244.6 km) **M 0** Located at the end of the Elliott Highway on Hot Springs Slough. **Population:** 88. **Elevation:** 330 feet/101m. **Climate:** Mean temperature in July is 59°F/15°C, in January -10.4°F/-23.6°C. Record high 93°F/33.9°C in June 1969, record low -70°F/-56.7°C in January 1934. Precipitation in summer averages 2.53 inches a month. Snow from October through April, with traces in September and May. Greatest mean monthly snowfall in January (11.1 inches). Record snowfall 49 inches in January 1937.

Private Aircraft: Manley Hot Springs civil airstrip (open year-round), adjacent southwest; elev. 270 feet/82m; length 2,900 feet/884m; gravel; fuel 100.

A pocket of "Pioneer Alaska." J.F. Karshner homesteaded here in 1902, about the same time the U.S. Army Signal Corps established a telegraph station nearby. The location soon became known as Baker Hot Springs, after nearby Baker Creek. Frank Manley built a four-story resort hotel here in 1907. The settlement's name was changed to Manley Hot Springs in 1957. Once a busy trading center during peak activity in the nearby Eureka and Tofty mining districts, Manley Hot Springs is now a quiet settlement with a trading post, roadhouse, airfield and hot springs resort. Many residents are enthusiastic gardeners, and visitors may see abundant displays of vegetables and berries growing around homes and businesses. Outstanding display of wild irises at the airstrip in June.

A restaurant, bar and overnight accommodations are at the roadhouse. The post office, gas station and grocery are at the trading post. There is an air taxi service here and scheduled service from Fairbanks.

The Manley Roadhouse. Come visit one of Alaska's oldest original roadhouses from the gold rush era. See the many prehistoric and Alaskana artifacts on display. The Manley Roadhouse is a great place to meet local miners, dog mushers, trappers or fishermen enjoying a cup of coffee. The Manley Roadhouse specializes in traditional Alaska home-style hospitality, fresh-baked pies, giant cinnamon rolls and good food. Largest liquor selection in Alaska. Stop by and see us. See display ad this section. [ADVERTISEMENT]

Manley Hot Springs Park Assoc. maintains a public campground near the bridge in town; fee $5 (pay at roadhouse). The hot springs are a short walk from the campground. There's a nice grassy picnic area on the slough near the campground. A boat launch is also nearby. ▲

Manley Boat Charters. Sightseeing, river tours, pike and sheefishing. Hourly rates for fishing or short scenic trips. Photography. Multi-day trips to Nowitna, Yukon rivers for three or more people. Reservations (907) 672-3271 or 672-3321, or write Frank or Dian Gurtler, Box 52, Manley Hot Springs, AK 99756. Fax (907) 672-3461. Frank's Tire Shop. Tire repair, used tires. [ADVERTISEMENT]

Manley Hot Springs Slough, pike 18 to 36 inches, use spinning and trolling lures, May through September. Follow the dirt road from the old Northern Commercial Co. store out of town for 2.5 miles/4 km to reach the Tanana River, king, silver and chum salmon from 7 to 40 lbs., June 15 to Sept. 30. Fish wheels and nets are used.

MANLEY HOT SPRINGS ADVERTISERS

Manley Boat Charters.......Ph. (907) 672-3271
Manley Hot Springs Resort.....................Mile 151.2 Elliott Hwy.
Manley Roadhouse...........Ph. (907) 672-3161
Manley Trading Post.....................Downtown

ALASKA RAILROAD

(See maps, pages 323–324 and 425)

The Alaska Railroad operates year-round passenger and freight service between Anchorage and Fairbanks, Portage and Whittier. In summer, passenger service is daily between Anchorage and Fairbanks via Denali Park; Portage and Whittier; and between Anchorage and Seward. Reduced service in winter. For additional information on the Alaska Railroad, write Passenger Services Dept., P.O. Box 107500, Anchorage, AK 99510.

Construction of the railroad began in 1915 under Pres. Woodrow Wilson. On July 15, 1923, Pres. Warren G. Harding drove the golden spike at Nenana, signifying completion of the railroad. The main line extends from Seward to Fairbanks, approximately 470 miles/756 km.

Following are services, schedules and fares available on Alaska Railroad routes. Keep in mind that schedules and fares are subject to change without notice.

ANCHORAGE–DENALI PARK–FAIRBANKS (Express Service)

Passenger service between Anchorage, Denali Park and Fairbanks is offered daily from May 20 to Sept. 18, 1994. The express service operates with a food service car, a vista-dome for all passengers to share, and coaches with comfortable reclining seats. Travel along the 350-mile route between Anchorage and Fairbanks is at a leisurely pace with comfortable window seats and good views of the countryside.

Luxury rail cars are available on the Anchorage–Denali Park–Fairbanks route through Gray Line of Alaska (Holland America Lines/Westours) and Princess Tours. These two tour companies operate (respectively) the *McKinley Explorer* and *Midnight Sun Express*. Both cars, which are coupled on to the end of the regular Alaska Railroad train, are glass-domed and offer gourmet cuisine along with other amenities. Higher priced than the regular Alaska Railroad cars, tickets are sold on a space-available basis. Packages with a Denali Park overnight are also available. Contact Princess (800-835-8907) or Gray Line (800-544-2206) for details.

The summer schedule is: Northbound express trains depart Anchorage at 8:30 A.M., arrive Denali Park at 3:45 P.M., and arrive Fairbanks at 8:30 P.M. Southbound express trains depart Fairbanks at 8:30 A.M., arrive Denali Park at 12:30 P.M., and arrive Anchorage at 8:30 P.M.

One-way fares are as follows: Anchorage–Denali Park, $88; Fairbanks–Denali Park, $47; Anchorage–Fairbanks, with a Denali Park stopover, $135. Children aged 2 through 11 ride for approximately half fare, under 2 ride free.

During fall, winter and spring, weekend-only rail service is provided between Anchorage and Fairbanks, with a self-propelled rail diesel car. The railcar travels from Anchorage to Fairbanks on Saturday and returns on Sunday.

Reservations: Reservations should be made 40 days prior to travel. Write the Alaska Railroad, Passenger Services Dept., P.O. Box 107500, Anchorage, AK 99510; or phone 1-800-544-0552 or (907) 265-2623, fax (907) 265-2323. Your letter should include the dates you plan to travel, point of departure and destination, the number of people in your party and your home phone number. Tickets may be purchased in advance by mail if you desire.

Baggage: Each adult is allowed three pieces of luggage to a maximum weight of 150 lbs. Children are allowed two pieces of baggage to a maximum weight of 75 lbs. Excess baggage may be checked for a nominal fee. Bicycles are accepted for a charge of $20 on a space-available basis on the day of travel. Keep in mind that baggage, including backpacks, must be checked before boarding and it is not accessible during the trip. Canoes, motors, motorcycles, items weighing over 150 lbs., etc., are not accepted for transportation on passenger trains. These items are shipped via freight train.

LOCAL SERVICE

Local rural service between Anchorage and Hurricane Gulch operates Wednesday, Saturday and Sunday each week between May 20 and Sept. 18, 1994. This one-day trip takes you past breathtaking views of Mount McKinley into some remote areas and provides an opportunity to meet local residents who use the train for access. Local service uses self-propelled rail diesel cars and has vending machine snacks available.

PORTAGE–WHITTIER

The Portage–Whittier shuttle train carries passengers and vehicles between Portage on the Seward Highway and Whittier on Prince William Sound. Portage, which has no facilities other than the railroad's vehicle loading ramp, is 47 miles/75 km south of Anchorage at **Milepost S 80.3** Seward Highway. Whittier, on Prince William Sound, is port to the Alaska Marine Highway's ferry MV *Bartlett*, which provides passenger and vehicle service to Cordova and Valdez. The Portage–Whittier railway line is 12.4 miles long, includes two tunnels (one 13,090 feet/3,990m long, the other 4,910 feet/1,497m long). Called the Whittier Cutoff, the line was constructed in 1942–43 as a safeguard for the flow of military supplies. It is a 35-minute train ride.

The shuttle makes several round-trips daily between Portage and Whittier, from mid-May through mid-September, connecting with Alaska Marine Highway ferry sailings and other vessels which operate between Whittier and Valdez. (Remember that ferry tickets are purchased separately from train tickets; see MARINE ACCESS ROUTES section, Southwest Ferry System.)

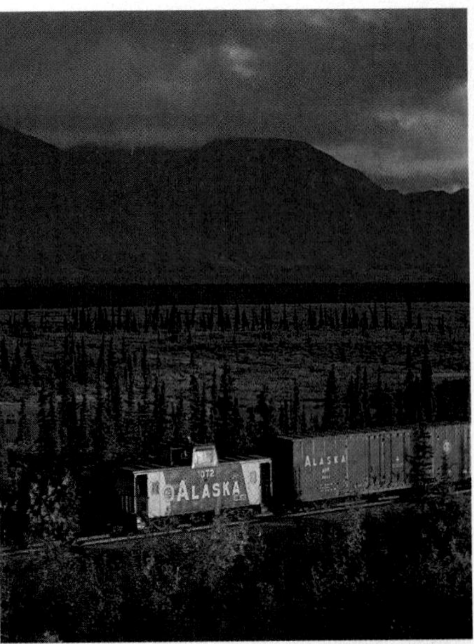

The Alaska Railroad near Denali Park.
(Ron Levy)

Train tickets for the Whittier shuttle may be purchased from ticket sellers at Portage. Reservations are not accepted for the shuttle train, although passengers with confirmed ferry connections are given priority boarding on the 1:20 P.M. shuttle between Portage and Whittier, if vehicles are at Portage by no later than 12:30 P.M. Standard vehicles under 24 feet in length are charged $70, round-trip between Portage and Whittier; includes driver fare. Other adult passengers in the vehicle are charged $16 round-trip; children (2 to 11 years of age) are $8 round-trip. Vehicle rates are based upon length. Some height and width restrictions apply.

During fall, winter and spring, service to Whittier is provided on Wednesday, Friday, Saturday and Sunday.

ANCHORAGE–SEWARD

Rail passenger service between Anchorage and Seward operates daily between May 21 and Sept. 5, 1994. (Weekend service to Seward is available throughout September.) The 230-mile excursion follows Turnagain Arm south from Anchorage and passes through some of the most beautiful scenery to be found on the railroad. Travel is aboard classic passenger coaches. Food service is available in the bar/deli car. Departs Anchorage at 6 A.M., arrives Seward at 11 A.M. The return trip departs Seward at 6 P.M., arriving Anchorage at 10 P.M. Reservations are required. The round-trip fare is $80 for adults; half fare for children 2 through 11. Overnight tours which include hotel and Resurrection Bay boat excursions are available from the railroad ticket office.

Kenai Peninsula
SEWARD HIGHWAY

Anchorage to Seward, Alaska
Alaska Routes 1 and 9

Rainbow over Twentymile River Valley, Chugach National Forest. (Michael DeYoung)

The 127-mile-/204-km-long Seward Highway connects Anchorage with the community of Seward on the east coast of the Kenai Peninsula. Leaving Anchorage, the Seward Highway follows the scenic north shore of Turnagain Arm through Chugach State Park and Chugach National Forest, permitting a panoramic view of the south shore and the Kenai Mountains.

The Seward Highway provides access to Alyeska ski resort, the Hope Highway, Portage Glacier and Kenai Fjords National Park. There is a bike trail between Anchorage and Girdwood. The bike route is marked by signs. Numerous hiking trails branch off the highway. The Seward Highway is a National Forest Scenic Byway.

The Seward Highway junctions with the other major Kenai Peninsula route, the Sterling Highway (see STERLING HIGHWAY section) at Tern Lake. Both these highways offer hiking, fishing and camping opportunities, and beautiful scenery.

Physical mileposts on the Seward Highway show distance from Seward. The Seward Highway is a paved, two-lane highway with passing lanes. It is open all year. Some sections of the highway are subject to avalanches in winter. Check Anchorage news sources for winter road conditions. In 1994–95, expect major road construction projects along the Seward Highway, with rock blasting and traffic delays.

CAUTION: The Seward Highway from Anchorage to just past Girdwood statistically has one of the highest number of traffic accidents in the state. DRIVE CAREFULLY!

Emergency medical services: Phone 911 or use CB channels 9, 11 or 19.

Seward Highway Log

ALASKA ROUTE 1
Distance from Seward (S) is followed by distance from Anchorage (A). Physical mileposts show distance from Seward.

S 127 (204.4 km) **A 0** Gambell Street and 10th Avenue in Anchorage. The Seward Highway (Gambell Street) connects with the Glenn Highway in Anchorage via 5th Avenue (westbound) and 6th Avenue (eastbound). (See area map in the ANCHORAGE section.) Follow Seward Highway signs south on Gambell.

S 126.7 (203.9 km) **A 0.3** (0.5 km) 15th Avenue (DeBarr Road).

S 126.6 (203.7 km) **A 0.4** (0.6 km) 16th Avenue; access to Sullivan sports arena, ice rinks and baseball stadium.

S 126 (202.8 km) **A 1** (1.6 km) Fireweed Lane.

S 125.8 (202.4 km) **A 1.2** (1.9 km) Northern Lights Boulevard (one-way westbound). Access to shopping centers.

S 125.7 (202.3 km) **A 1.3** (2.1 km) Benson Boulevard (one-way eastbound).

S 125.4 (201.8 km) **A 1.6** (2.6 km) Southbound access only to Old Seward Highway.

S 125.3 (201.6 km) **A 1.7** (2.7 km) 36th Avenue; hospital to east.

S 125.2 (201.5 km) **A 1.8** (2.9 km) Freeway begins southbound. There are no services or facilities along the new Seward Highway. However, there are several exits in the next 7.5 miles/12.1 km to the Old Seward Highway (which parallels the new Seward Highway) where traveler services are available.

S 124.7 (200.7 km) **A 2.3** (3.7 km) Tudor Road overpass; exits both sides of highway. (Tudor Road is used as a bypass route for northbound travelers, connecting them with the Glenn Highway via Muldoon Road.)

S 124.2 (199.8 km) **A 2.8** (4.5 km) Campbell Creek bridge.

S 123.7 (199.1 km) **A 3.3** (5.3 km) Dowling Road underpass; exits on both sides of highway.

S 122.7 (197.5 km) **A 4.3** (6.9 km) 76th Avenue exit, southbound traffic only.

S 122.2 (196.7 km) **A 4.8** (7.7 km) Dimond Boulevard underpass; exits on both sides of highway.

S 120.8 (194.4 km) **A 6.2** (10 km) O'Malley Road underpass; exits on both sides of highway. Turn east on O'Malley Road and drive 2 miles/3.2 km to reach the Alaska Zoo. Turn west for access to Old Seward Highway and major shopping area on Dimond Boulevard. Views of Chugach Mountains along this stretch.

S 119.7 (192.6 km) **A 7.3** (11.7 km) Huffman Road underpass; exits on both sides of highway.

S 118.5 (190.7 km) **A 8.5** (13.7 km) De Armoun Road overpass, exits both sides of highway.

S 117.8 (189.6 km) **A 9.2** (14.8 km) Overpass: Exits both sides of highway for Old Seward Highway (west); access to Rabbit Creek Road (east). The picturesque Chapel by the Sea overlooks Turnagain Arm. The church is often photographed because of its unique setting and its display of flowers.

S 117.6 (189.3 km) **A 9.4** (15.1 km) View of Turnagain Arm and Mount Spurr.

S 117.4 (188.9 km) **A 9.6** (15.4 km) Rabbit Creek Rifle Range to west. Boardwalk Wildlife Viewing exit leads east to Potter Point State Game Refuge. This is a very popular spot for bird watching. From the parking lot, an extensive boardwalk crosses Potter Marsh, a refuge and nesting area for waterfowl. The marsh was created when railroad construction dammed a small creek in the area. Today, the marsh is visited by arctic terns, Canadian geese, trumpeter swans, many species of ducks, and other water birds. Bring binoculars.

S 117.3 (188.8 km) **A 9.7** (15.6 km) Highway narrows to two lanes southbound.

S 117.2 (188.6 km) **A 9.8** (15.8 km) Small paved turnout at end of boardwalk.

SEWARD HIGHWAY *Anchorage, AK, to Seward, AK*

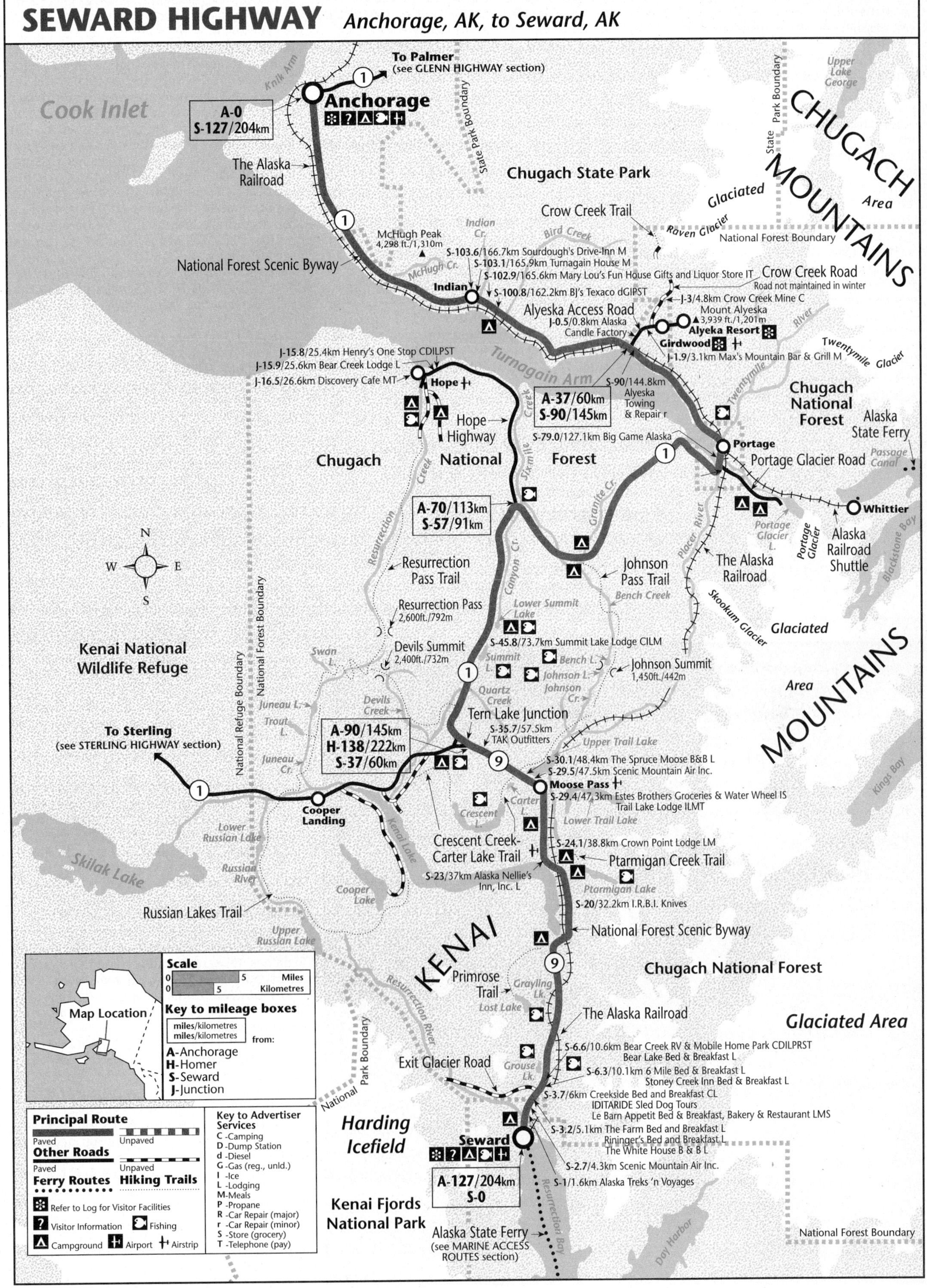
To Palmer
(see GLENN HIGHWAY section)
Knik Arm
Cook Inlet
Anchorage
A-0
S-127/204km
The Alaska Railroad
State Park Boundary
Chugach State Park
CHUGACH MOUNTAINS
Glaciated Area
Upper Lake George
Crow Creek Trail
Raven Glacier
National Forest Boundary
McHugh Peak
4,298 ft./1,310m
Indian Cr.
Bird Creek
National Forest Scenic Byway
McHugh Cr.
S-103.6/166.7km Sourdough's Drive-Inn M
S-103.1/165.9km Turnagain House M
S-102.9/165.6km Mary Lou's Fun House Gifts and Liquor Store IT
Crow Creek Road
Road not maintained in winter
Indian
S-100.8/162.2km BJ's Texaco dGIPST
J-3/4.8km Crow Creek Mine C
Mount Alyeska
3,939 ft./1,201m
Alyeska Access Road
J-0.5/0.8km Alaska Candle Factory
Alyeska Resort
Girdwood
J-1.9/3.1km Max's Mountain Bar & Grill M
Twentymile Glacier
Twentymile River
J-15.8/25.4km Henry's One Stop CDILPST
J-15.9/25.6km Bear Creek Lodge L
J-16.5/26.6km Discovery Cafe MT
Turnagain Arm
Hope
A-37/60km
S-90/145km
S-90/144.8km Alyeska Towing & Repair r
Chugach National Forest
Alaska State Ferry
Hope Highway
S-79.0/127.1km Big Game Alaska
Portage
Passage Canal
Chugach
National
Forest
Portage Glacier Road
Resurrection Creek
Sixmile Creek
Granite Cr.
A-70/113km
S-57/91km
Whittier
Portage Glacier L.
Portage Glacier
Alaska Railroad Shuttle
Blackstone Bay
Placer River
The Alaska Railroad
Resurrection Pass Trail
Canyon Cr.
Johnson Pass Trail
Bench Creek
Resurrection Pass
2,600ft./792m
Lower Summit Lake
Skookum Glacier
Glaciated
Kenai National Wildlife Refuge
National Refuge Boundary
National Forest Boundary
S-45.8/73.7km Summit Lake Lodge CILM
Devils Summit
2,400ft./732m
Swan L.
Summit L.
Bench L.
Johnson L.
Johnson Summit
1,450ft./442m
Johnson Cr.
Area
MOUNTAINS
Juneau L.
Trout L.
Devils Creek
Quartz Creek
Tern Lake Junction
S-35.7/57.5km TAK Outfitters
To Sterling
(see STERLING HIGHWAY section)
Juneau Cr.
A-90/145km
H-138/222km
S-37/60km
Upper Trail Lake
S-30.1/48.4km The Spruce Moose B&B L
S-29.5/47.5km Scenic Mountain Air Inc.
Moose Pass
S-29.4/47.3km Estes Brothers Groceries & Water Wheel IS
Trail Lake Lodge ILMT
Kings Bay
Cooper Landing
Carter L.
Crescent L.
Lower Trail Lake
Lower Russian Lake
Kenai Lake
Crescent Creek-Carter Lake Trail
S-24.1/38.8km Crown Point Lodge LM
Ptarmigan Creek Trail
Skilak Lake
Russian River
S-23/37km Alaska Nellie's Inn, Inc. L
Ptarmigan Lake
Cooper Lake
S-20/32.2km I.R.B.I. Knives
Russian Lakes Trail
National Forest Scenic Byway
Upper Russian Lake
KENAI
Chugach National Forest
Scale
0 5 Miles
0 5 Kilometres
Map Location
Key to mileage boxes
miles/kilometres
miles/kilometres
from:
A-Anchorage
H-Homer
S-Seward
J-Junction
Primrose Trail
Grayling Lk.
Lost Lake
Resurrection River
The Alaska Railroad
Glaciated Area
S-6.6/10.6km Bear Creek RV & Mobile Home Park CDILPRST
Bear Lake Bed & Breakfast L
S-6.3/10.1km 6 Mile Bed & Breakfast L
Stoney Creek Inn Bed & Breakfast L
National Park Boundary
Exit Glacier Road
Grouse Lk.
S-3.7/6km Creekside Bed and Breakfast CL
IDITARIDE Sled Dog Tours
Le Barn Appetit Bed & Breakfast, Bakery & Restaurant LMS
Principal Route
Paved
Unpaved
Other Roads
Paved
Unpaved
Ferry Routes
Hiking Trails
Refer to Log for Visitor Facilities
Visitor Information
Fishing
Campground
Airport
Airstrip
Key to Advertiser Services
C -Camping
D -Dump Station
d -Diesel
G -Gas (reg., unld.)
I -Ice
L -Lodging
M-Meals
P -Propane
R -Car Repair (major)
r -Car Repair (minor)
S -Store (grocery)
T -Telephone (pay)
Harding Icefield
Seward
S-3.2/5.1km The Farm Bed and Breakfast L
Rininger's Bed and Breakfast L
The White House B & B L
S-2.7/4.3km Scenic Mountain Air Inc.
A-127/204km
S-0
S-1/1.6km Alaska Treks 'n Voyages
Kenai Fjords National Park
Alaska State Ferry
(see MARINE ACCESS ROUTES section)
Resurrection Bay
Day Harbor
National Forest Boundary

S 116.1 (186.8 km) **A 10.9** (17.5 km) Paved double-ended turnout to east. Highway parallels Alaska Railroad southbound to **Milepost S 90.8.**

S 115.4 (185.7 km) **A 11.6** (18.7 km) **Junction** with Old Seward Highway; access to Potter Valley Road. Old Johnson trail begins 0.5 mile/0.6 km up Potter Valley Road; parking at trailhead. Only the first 10 miles/16 km of this state park trail are cleared. Moderate to difficult hike; watch for bears.

The natural gas pipeline from the Kenai Peninsula emerges from beneath Turnagain Arm here and follows the roadway to Anchorage.

WARNING: When the tide is out, the sand in Turnagain Arm might look inviting. DO NOT go out on it. Some of it is quicksand. You could become trapped in the mud and not be rescued before the tide comes in, as happened to a victim in 1989.

S 115.3 (185.6 km) **A 11.7** (18.8 km) Entering Chugach State Park southbound. Potter Section House, Chugach State Park Headquarters (phone 345-5014) to west; pay phone, snack and gift shop, large parking lot, wheelchair-accessible toilets. Open daily in summer, Monday to Friday 8 A.M. to 4:30 P.M. year-round. The renovated Potter Section House, dedicated in October 1986, was home to a small crew of railroad workers who maintained the Alaska Railroad tracks between Seward and Anchorage in the days of coal- and steam-powered locomotives. Displays here include photographs from the National Archives, a vintage snowblower and working model railroad. ♿

S 115.1 (185.2 km) **A 11.9** (19.2 km) Potter Creek trailhead to east.

S 115 (185 km) **A 12** (19.3 km) Watch for rockfalls. Avalanche area and hazardous driving conditions during winter for the next 25 miles/40.2 km.

From here to **Milepost S 90** there are many turnouts on both sides of the highway, some with scenic views of Turnagain Arm. An easterly extension of Cook Inlet, Turnagain Arm was called Return by the Russians. Captain Cook, seeking the fabled Northwest Passage in 1778, called it Turnagain River and Captain Vancouver, doing a better job of surveying in 1794, gave it the present name of Turnagain Arm.

Turnagain Arm is known for having one of the world's remarkably high tides, with a diurnal range of more than 33 feet/10m. A bore tide is an abrupt rise of tidal water just after low tide, moving rapidly landward, formed by a flood tide surging into a constricted inlet such as Turnagain Arm. This foaming wall of water may reach a height of 6 feet/2m and is very dangerous to small craft. To see a bore tide, check the Anchorage-area tide tables for low tide, then add approximately two hours and 15 minutes to the Anchorage low tide for the bore to reach points between Miles 32 and 37 on the Seward Highway. *CAUTION: The mud flats of Turnagain Arm are extremely dangerous. Bore tides sweep in at 10 to 15 miles per hour, and you cannot outrun them. DO NOT walk out on the mud flats.*

S 114.7 (184.6 km) **A 12.3** (19.8 km) Weigh station and pay phone to east.

S 114.5 (184.3 km) **A 12.5** (20.1 km) Double-ended gravel turnout to east. From here to **Milepost S 104**, patches of harebells (Bluebells of Scotland) can be seen in late July and early August.

S 113.3 (182.3 km) **A 13.7** (22.1 km) Large paved turnout for slow vehicles.

S 113.1 (182 km) **A 13.9** (22.4 km) Small gravel turnout to east at McHugh boulder area. Watch for rock climbers practicing on the steep cliffs alongside the highway. The cliffs are part of the base of McHugh Peak (elev. 4,298 feet/1,310m).

S 111.8 (179.9 km) **A 15.2** (24.5 km) McHugh Creek state wayside to east with 30 picnic sites. A stream and waterfall make this a very refreshing place to stop. *CAUTION: Steep but paved road into this picnic site. Be sure you have plenty of power and good brakes for descent, especially if you are towing a trailer.* There is also a parking area beside the highway. Good berry picking in season near the stream for wild currants, blueberries and watermelon berries. A 1-mile portion of the Old Johnson trail here is wheelchair accessible. ♿

S 111.6 (179.6 km) **A 15.4** (24.8 km) Double-ended gravel turnout to east. There are numerous turnouts southbound to Indian.

S 110.3 (177.5 km) **A 16.7** (26.9 km) Beluga Point scenic viewpoint and photo stop has a commanding view of Turnagain Arm. A good place to see bore tides and beluga whales. (The only all-white whale, belugas are easy to identify.) Large paved double-ended turnout to west with tables, benches, telescopes and interpretive signs on orcas, bore tides, mountain goats, etc.

WARNING: Do not go out on the mud flats at low tide. The glacial silt and water can create a dangerous quicksand.

S 109.2 (175.7 km) **A 17.8** (28.6 km) Paved turnout to west. Spring water is piped to the highway.

S 108.5 (174.6 km) **A 18.5** (29.8 km) Rainbow Road to Rainbow Valley.

S 108.4 (174.4 km) **A 18.6** (29.9 km) Rainbow trailhead and parking; access to Old Johnson trail.

S 107.3 (172.7 km) **A 19.7** (31.7 km) Gravel turnout to east. Rock climbers practice on the cliffs here.

S 107 (172.2 km) **A 20** (32.2 km) From here to Girdwood, in summer when snow is still on the peaks or after heavy rainfall, watch for many small waterfalls tumbling down the mountainsides to Turnagain Arm.

S 106.9 (172 km) **A 20.1** (32.3 km) Scenic viewpoint. Double-ended paved turnout to west; Old Johnson trail access. Watch for Dall sheep near road. *NOTE: DO NOT FEED WILDLIFE.*

S 106.7 (171.7 km) **A 20.3** (32.7 km) Paved turnout to east; Windy trailhead.

S 106.6 (171.5 km) **A 20.4** (32.8 km) Large paved turnout to west; watch for Dall sheep.

S 105.7 (170.1 km) **A 21.3** (34.3 km) Falls Creek trailhead and parking to east; Old Johnson trail access.

S 104 (167.4 km) **A 23** (37 km) Indian Valley Mine National Historic Site.

S 103.9 (167.2 km) **A 23.1** (37.2 km) Indian Road and Indian Valley businesses on east side of highway.

S 103.6 (166.7 km) **A 23.4** (37.7 km) **Sourdough's Drive-Inn**. Burgers, fish baskets, chili, shakes, cones and lots more. And under our huge tent next door, you'll find great Alaskan gifts, jams and jellies, smoked salmon and fresh Matanuska Valley vegetables in season. Watch Alaskan artists at work, and then try your hand at panning for gold. [ADVERTISEMENT]

S 103.5 (166.6 km) **A 23.5** (37.8 km) **INDIAN.** Restaurant at **Milepost S 103.1**, gifts and liquor store at **Milepost S 102.9**.

S 103.1 (165.9 km) **A 23.9** (38.5 km) Bore Tide Road, also called Ocean View Road. Turnagain House restaurant.

Turnagain House, Milepost 103.1 Seward Highway at Indian, AK. Fresh Alaskan seafood, fine steaks and baby back ribs. Located 16 miles south of Anchorage. Excellent view of Turnagain Arm and bore tides. Rustic and casual atmosphere. The Turnagain House is a year-round favorite of Anchorage residents and is considered one of the finest restaurants in the area. Major credit cards accepted. Reservations: (907) 653-7500. [ADVERTISEMENT]

S 103 (165.8 km) **A 24** (38.6 km) Bridge over Indian Creek.

Indian Creek, heavily fished! Pink salmon, sea-run Dolly Varden, few coho (silver) salmon and rainbow, June to September; pink salmon run from latter part of July to mid-August in even-numbered years. **Bird Creek**, same fishing as Indian Creek, except heavier run of pink salmon in July and August.

S 102.9 (165.6 km) **A 24.1** (38.8 km) Indian Creek rest area to west; wheelchair accessible toilets and parking. Bar and liquor store to east.

Mary Lou's Fun House Gifts and Liquor Store. See display ad this section.

S 102.1 (164.3 km) **A 24.9** (40.1 km) Bird Ridge trailhead and parking; Old Johnson trail access.

S 101.5 (163.3 km) **A 25.5** (41 km) Bridge over Bird Creek; parking. Watch for pedestrians next mile southbound.

S 101.2 (162.9 km) **A 25.8** (41.5 km) Bird Creek State Recreation Site with picnic sites and 19 campsites, firepits, pay phone, covered picnic tables, toilets and water. Firewood is sometimes available. Camping fee $8/night or annual pass. A pleasant campground densely wooded but cleared along the high banks of Turnagain Arm. Paved bike trail goes through campground (nice ride along Turnagain Arm). Great spot for sunbathing. This campground is full most weekends in the summer. ▲

WARNING: Do not go out on the mud flats at low tide. The glacial silt and water can create a dangerous quicksand.

S 100.8 (162.2 km) **A 26.2** (42.2 km) **BJ's Texaco.** See display ad this section.

S 100.5 (161.7 km) **A 26.5** (42.6 km) To the east is the Bird House Bar, a local landmark.

S 99.8 (160.6 km) **A 27.2** (43.8 km) Paved turnout to west. Southbound traffic entering avalanche area, northbound traffic leaving avalanche area.

S 99.3 (159.8 km) **A 27.7** (44.6 km) Large gravel turnout to west with view across Turnagain Arm to the cut in the mountains where Sixmile Creek drains into the arm; the old mining settlement of Sunrise was located here. The town of Hope is to the southwest. The peak visible across Turnagain Arm between here and Girdwood is Mount Alpenglow in the Kenai mountain range. Avalanche gates.

S 99.2 (159.6 km) **A 27.8** (44.7 km) Avalanche gun emplacement (motorists will notice several of these along the highway southbound).

S 97.2 (156.4 km) **A 29.8** (48 km) Southbound traffic leaving winter avalanche area, northbound traffic entering avalanche area.

S 96.8 (155.8 km) **A 30.2** (48.6 km) *CAUTION: Watch for road construction southbound in 1994 and 1995, next 7 miles/11.3 km, with traffic delays for rock blasting.* Winter avalanche area. There are many gravel turnouts the next 5 miles/8 km southbound.

S 95.5 (153.7 km) **A 31.5** (50.7 km) Turnout to west; avalanche gun emplacement.

S 94.4 (151.9 km) **A 32.6** (52.5 km) Gravel turnout to west. Avalanche safety zone.

S 90.8 (146.1 km) **A 36.2** (58.3 km) *CAUTION: Railroad crossing and very bad curve.*

S 90.6 (145.8 km) **A 36.4** (58.6 km) Bridge crosses Tidewater Slough. *NOTE: Bridge construction 1994.* Avalanche gun emplacement at south end of bridge.

S 90.4 (145.5 km) **A 36.6** (58.9 km) Leaving Chugach State Park southbound. The 1964 Good Friday earthquake caused land to sink in the Turnagain Arm area, particularly apparent from here to **Milepost S 74.** As a result, many trees had their root systems invaded by salt water, as seen by the stands of dead spruce trees along here. Good bird watching, including bald eagles, arctic terns, sandhill cranes.

S 90.2 (145.2 km) **A 36.8** (59.2 km) Girdwood highway maintenance station. End avalanche area southbound. *NOTE: Major construction northbound 1994–95, next 7 miles/11.3 km.*

S 90 (144.8 km) **A 37** (59.5 km) **Junction** with 3-mile/4.8-km Alyeska (pronounced al-ee-ES-ka) access road to Crow Creek road and mine, Girdwood and Alyeska Recreation Area. Worth the drive! ALYESKA ACCESS ROAD log starts on page 428. This intersection is "old" Girdwood; the railroad station, a school, gas station and shopping center are located here. After the 1964 earthquake, Girdwood moved up the access road 2.1 miles/3.4 km.

Alyeska Towing & Repair. See display ad this section.

S 89.8 (144.5 km) **A 37.2** (59.9 km) Glacier Creek bridge.

(Continues on page 431)

Alyeska Access Road Log

This 3-mile/4.8-km spur road provides access to Crow Creek Road, Girdwood and Alyeska Resort. There are numerous restaurants, gift shops, accommodations and attractions in the Girdwood/Alyeska area.

Distance is measured from junction with Seward Highway (J).

J 0.2 (0.3 km) Bridge over Alaska Railroad tracks. Paved bike trail to Alyeska Resort begins.

J 0.4 (0.6 km) Forest Station Road. Chugach National Forest Glacier Ranger District office (P.O. Box 129, Girdwood 99587; phone 783-3242). Open 8 A.M. to 5 P.M. Monday to Friday year-round; also 9 A.M. to 5 P.M. weekends Memorial Day through Labor Day. Maps and information on USFS cabins and campgrounds available here.

J 0.5 (0.8 km) **Alaska Candle Factory.** One-half mile off Seward Highway on Alyeska. Home of handcrafted candles made in the form of Alaska wild animals. Hand-dipped tapers and molded candles

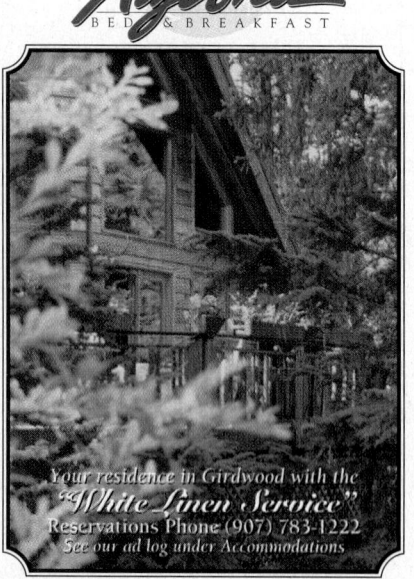

made daily. All candles have unique individual designs. Open seven days a week, 10 A.M. to 6 P.M. Visitors welcome. (907) 783-2354. P.O. Box 786, Girdwood, AK 99587. [ADVERTISEMENT]

J 1.6 (2.6 km) **Junction** with Brenner Road.

J 1.9 (3.1 km) **Junction** with Crow Creek Road. Two restaurants and Raven Glacier Lodge are located 0.2 mile/0.3 km up Crow Creek Road. This single-lane dirt road leads 3.1 miles/5 km to Crow Creek Mine, 7 miles/11.3 km to Crow Pass trailhead. In winter, the road is not maintained past Mile 0.6. Crow Creek Mine is a national historic site. The authentic gold mine and eight other buildings at the mine are open to the public (fee charged).

Max's Mountain Bar & Grill. See display ad this section.

Crow Creek Mine. Visit this historic 1898 mining camp located in the heart of Chugach National Forest. Drive 3 miles up Crow Creek Road (Old Iditarod trail). Eight original buildings. Pan for

gold. Visit our gift shop. Enjoy beautiful grounds, ponds, flowers. Animals and friendly people. Campground for tents and self-contained vehicles. Open May 15–Sept. 15, 9 A.M. to 6 P.M. daily. Phone (907) 278-8060 (messages). [ADVERTISEMENT]▲

Raven Glacier Lodge, on Crow Creek Road: central headquarters for Footloose Alaska Adventure Touring. Lifelong Alaskans John Spencer and Cathy Frost extend warm hospitality ranging from B&B overnights to full custom vacations. River rafting, fishing, mountain bike and horseback trips, flightseeing, hiking, remote out camps. "Let us make our Alaska yours." See display ad this section. [ADVERTISEMENT]

Crow Pass and Old Iditarod trailhead at Mile 7 Crow Creek Road. Crow Pass trail climbs steeply 3 miles/4.8 km to ruins of an old gold mine and a USFS public-use cabin at Crow Pass near Raven Glacier; hiking time approximately two and one-half hours. The Old Iditarod trail extends 22.5 miles/36.2 km north from Crow Pass down Raven Creek drainage to the Chugach State Park Visitor Center on Eagle River Road. All of the hiking trail, from Crow Creek Road trailhead to the state park visitor center, is part of the Iditarod National Historic Trail used in the early 1900s. Trail is usually free of snow by mid-June. Closed to motorized vehicles; horses prohibited during early spring due to soft trail conditions.

J 2 (3.2 km) California Creek bridge.

J 2.1 (3.4 km) **GIRDWOOD** (pop. 300), at the junction of Alyeska access road and Hightower Road. **Emergency Services: Alaska State Troopers, EMS** and **Fire Department,** phone 911 or 783-2704 (message only) or 269-5711. Located here are a post office, two restaurants, vacation rental offices, laundromat, grocery store, small shops and fire hall.

Private Aircraft: Girdwood landing strip; elev. 150 feet/46m; length 2,100 feet/640m; gravel; unattended.

Girdwood Community Center offers tennis courts, pay phone, Kinder Park day-care center and picnic area, and is the site of the Girdwood midsummer crafts fair. The town was named after Col. James Girdwood who established a mining operation near here in 1901.

Chair 5 Restaurant. Searching for that special place that's off the beaten path, is fun and relaxing to dine in? Nestled in the woods of downtown Girdwood is Chair 5 Restaurant. Quality food is served with true Alaskan hospitality. Highlights include fresh pasta, pizza, choice steak and Alaskan seafood dinners, priced from $8 to $15. Lunch features daily specials in the $5 to $8 range. MasterCard, VISA, American Express. Cocktails served. Hours 11 A.M. to midnight. Turn left Mile 2.1 Alyeska Access Road. [ADVERTISEMENT]

(Continues next page)

GIRDWOOD / ALYESKA ADVERTISERS

Alaska Candle Factory..............Mile 0.5 Alyeska Access Rd.
Alyeska Accommodations......................Mile 3 Alyeska Access Rd.
Alyeska Bed & Breakfast......................Ph. (907) 783-1222
Alyeska Resort..................Ph. (907) 754-1111
Alyeska View Bed & Breakfast ....Vail Dr.
Bake Shop, The..........................Alyeska Resort
Chair 5 Restaurant........................Linblad Ave.
Crow Creek Mine ....Crow Creek Rd.
Emmy's Hair Studio..............................Vail Dr.
Fireweed Inn Bed & Breakfast......................Ph. (907) 783-3153
Kobuk Valley Jade Co. ....Mile 3 Alyeska Access Rd.
Max's Mountain Bar & Grill...............Mile 1.9 Alyeska Access Rd.
Raven Glacier Lodge ....Crow Creek Rd.
Timberline Bed & Breakfast......................Ph. (907) 783-2917

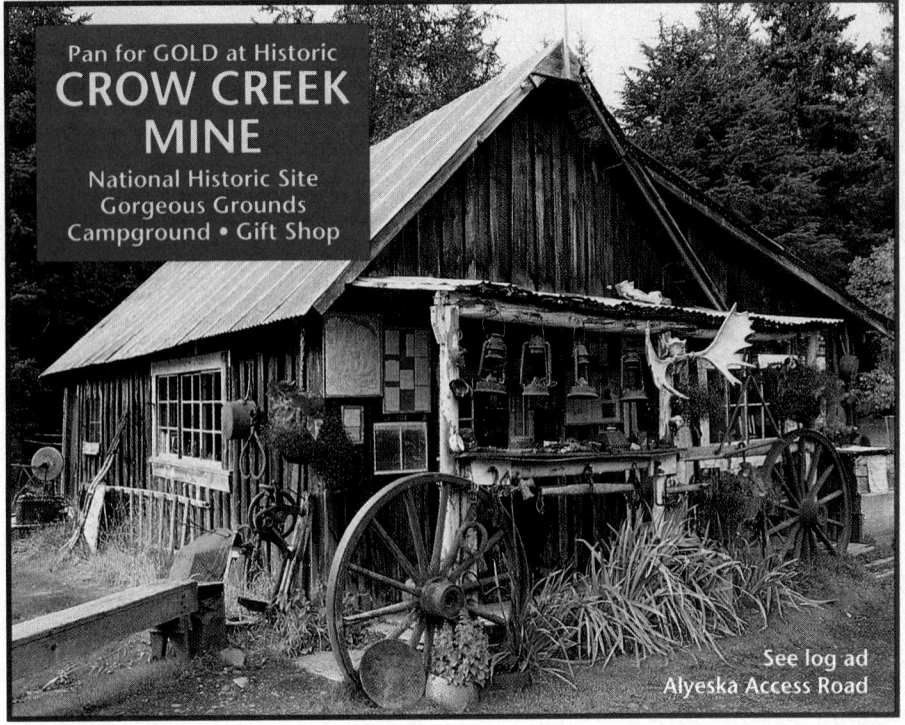

Alyeska Access Road Log (continued)

J 2.3 (3.7 km) Glacier Creek bridge.

J 2.6 (4.2 km) Donner access to Airport Road.

J 2.7 (4.3 km) Timberline Drive.

Alyeska Bed and Breakfast. Alpine Avenue. Cedar chalet offers a variety of luxurious accommodations with white linen service. One- or two-bedroom suites, private entry, bath, phone, kitchenette, cable TV, VCR. For the budget-minded, single with shared bath. Customized breakfast, in bed if you like, outdoor hot tub. Bird watching. View of Mount Alyeska. Call for more information and reservations. Mark and Laura Lyle, (907) 783-1222. [ADVERTISEMENT]

J 3 (4.8 km) **ALYESKA** Resort and recreation area at Mount Alyeska (elev. 3,939 feet/1,201m); jade shop, gift and crafts shops, restaurants, hotel and the ski resort.

Alyeska Resort is Alaska's largest ski area and a year-round resort. Owned and operated by Seibu Alaska Inc. since 1980. Latest improvements include a new wheelchair-accessible mountaintop cafeteria, restaurant and lounge (open year-round) accessed by a 60-passenger tram.

Ski season is generally from early November through April. Facilities include a high-speed detachable bubble quad, two fixed-grip quads, three double chair lifts and two pony tows. Night skiing available during holiday periods in November and December, and Wednesday through Saturday from January through March. Ski school, ski rental shop and sports shops.

Winter activities include cross-country skiing, dog sled rides, heli-skiing, ice fishing and snowmachining. Summer activities available are glacier skiing, hiking, mountain biking, flightseeing, canoeing, tennis, gold panning and river rafting.

Opening in late summer 1994 is a new 307-room chateau, the Alyeska Prince Hotel. It will include four restaurants, meeting facilities, fitness center, pool and Jacuzzi, and on-site parking for over 850 cars.

Gift shops and dining facilities are located at the base area. Accommodations available for 1993/94 ski season: local condominium rentals; 29-room Nugget Inn. For more information, call (907) 754-1111. ♿

Return to Milepost S 90 Seward Highway

(Continued from page 427)

S 89.1 (143.4 km) **A 37.9** (61 km) Virgin Creek bridge. View of three glaciers to east.

S 89 (143.2 km) **A 38** (61.2 km) Wide straight highway from here to Portage. The Alaska Railroad parallels the highway.

S 88.2 (141.9 km) **A 38.8** (62.4 km) Turnout to east.

S 87.5 (140.8 km) **A 39.5** (63.6 km) Avalanche gun emplacement.

S 86.1 (138.6 km) **A 40.9** (65.8 km) Small gravel turnout by ocean. Chugach National Forest boundary sign.

S 84.1 (135.3 km) **A 42.9** (69 km) Peterson Creek. View of Blueberry Mountain.

S 82.3 (132.4 km) **A 44.7** (71.9 km) Turnout to east.

S 81 (130.4 km) **A 46** (74 km) BLM observation platform with informative plaques on Twentymile River wetlands and wildlife. Watch for dipnetters in the spring fishing for hooligan (also known as eulachon or candlefish), a smelt. Road access east to Twentymile River.

Twentymile River, good hooligan fishing in May. These smelt are taken with long-handled dip nets. Pink, red and silver (coho) salmon 4 to 10 lbs., use attraction lures, best in August. Dolly Varden 4 to 10 lbs., eggs best, good all summer in clearwater tributaries.

S 80.7 (129.9 km) **A 46.3** (74.5 km) Bridge over Twentymile River, which flows out of the Twentymile Glacier and other glaciers through a long green valley at the edge of the highway. Twentymile Glacier can be seen at the end of the valley to the northeast. Twentymile River is a popular windsurfing area in summer. Gravel turnout west side of highway.

S 80.3 (129.2 km) **A 46.7** (75.2 km) Access to the Alaska Railroad motor vehicle loading area for ferry traffic taking the shuttle train to Whittier. Ticket office and pay phone. Small visitor information center and gift shop in station. Connections at Whittier with Alaska Marine Highway; regular ferry service is provided across Prince William Sound past the spectacular Columbia Glacier to Valdez. For details see the ALASKA RAILROAD and PRINCE WILLIAM SOUND sections.

S 80.1 (128.9 km) **A 46.9** (75.5 km) **PORTAGE.** No facilities here. The 1964 earthquake caused the land to drop between 6 and 12 feet along Turnagain Arm here. High tides then flooded the area, forcing the estimated 50 to 100 residents of Portage to move. Some old buildings are visible; more evidence of trees killed by the invading salt water. Leaving Game Management Unit 14C, entering unit 7, southbound.

S 80 (128.7 km) **A 47** (75.6 km) Second access to motor vehicle loading ramps and passenger parking for Alaska Railroad shuttle train from Portage to Whittier.

S 79.4 (127.8 km) **A 47.6** (76.6 km) Bridge No. 2 southbound over Portage Creek. Parking and interpretive sign to west at south end of bridge. This gray-colored creek carries the silt-laden glacial meltwater from Portage Glacier and Portage Lake to Turnagain Arm. Mud flats in Turnagain Arm are created by silt from the creek settling close to shore.

S 79 (127.1 km) **A 48** (77.2 km) Bridge No. 1 southbound over Portage Creek.

Big Game Alaska. See display ad this section.

Portage Glacier Road Log

Distance from the junction with the Seward Highway (J).

J 0 Junction with Seward Highway at **Milepost S 78.9.** *CAUTION: Alaska Railroad tracks, rough crossing.*

J 2 (3.2 km) Portage Glacier Work Center (USFS); no services available.

J 2.4 (3.8 km) Paved turnout. Explorer Glacier viewpoint on right.

J 3.1 (5 km) Bridge. Beaver dam visible from road.

J 3.7 (5.9 km) Black Bear USFS campground; 12 sites (two will accommodate medium-sized trailers), toilets, water, firepits, dumpsters, tables, $6 fee. Pleasant wooded area. ▲

J 4.1 (6.6 km) Bridge over Williwaw Creek. USFS campground, south of road below Middle Glacier; 38 campsites (under expansion for 1994), toilets, dumpsters, water, firepits, tables, $6 fee. Beautiful campground. Campfire programs in the amphitheater; check bulletin board for schedule. Spawning red salmon and dog salmon can be viewed (from late July to mid-September) from Williwaw Creek observation deck near campground entrance. Self-guided Williwaw nature trail off the campground loop road goes through moose and beaver habitat. ▲

J 5.2 (8.4 km) Paved road forks at Portage Glacier Lodge; left fork leads to visitor center (description follows). Take right fork 0.8 mile/1.3 km to parking lot; 1.2 miles/1.9 km to Byron Glacier overlook; and 1.5 miles/2.4 km to MV *Ptarmigan* sightseeing boat cruise dock and passenger waiting facility.

J 5.5 (8.8 km) Begich, Boggs Visitor Center at Portage Glacier and Portage Lake. Open daily in summer (9 A.M.-6 P.M.); weekends in winter (10 A.M.-4 P.M.). Phone the visitor center at 783-2326 or the U.S. Forest Service district office at 783-3242 for current schedule.

Forest Service naturalists are available to answer questions and provide information about Chugach National Forest resources. There are displays on glaciers and on the natural history of the area. The award-winning film *Voices from the Ice* is shown in the theater hourly. Schedules of hikes and programs led by naturalists are posted at the center. One of the most popular activities is the iceworm safari. (Often regarded as a hoax, iceworms actually exist; the small, black worms thrive at temperatures just above freezing.) A self-guided interpretive trail about glacial landforms begins just south of the visitor center.

Large paved parking area provides views of the glacier and icebergs in Portage Lake. There are several excellent spots in the area to observe salmon spawning (August and September) in Portage Creek and its tributaries.

Return to Milepost S 78.9 Seward Highway

S 78.9 (127 km) **A 48.1** (77.4 km) **Junction** with Portage Glacier access road. Portage Glacier is one of Alaska's most popular attractions. See PORTAGE GLACIER ROAD log this page. *NOTE: There is no gas or lodging available at the glacier.*

S 78.4 (126.1 km) **A 48.6** (78.2 km) Bridge over Placer River; boat launch. Second bridge over Placer River at **Milepost S 77.9.** Turnouts next to both bridges. Between Placer River and Ingram Creek, there is an excellent view on clear days of Skookum Glacier to the northeast. To the north across Turnagain Arm is Twentymile Glacier. Arctic terns and waterfowl are often seen in the slough here.

Placer River has good hooligan fishing in May. These smelt are taken with long-handled dip nets. Silver salmon may be taken in August and September.

S 77.9 (125.4 km) **A 49.1** (79 km) Bridge over Placer River overflow. Paved turnout to south.

S 77 (123.9 km) **A 50** (80.5 km) Boundary of Chugach National Forest.

S 75.5 (121.5 km) **A 51.5** (82.9 km) Paved double-ended scenic viewpoints both sides of highway.

S 75.2 (121 km) **A 51.8** (83.4 km) Bridge over **Ingram Creek**; pink salmon fishing (even years).

S 75 (120.7 km) **A 52** (83.7 km) Paved turnout to west. Highway begins ascent to Turnagain Pass southbound. Passing lane next 5 miles/8 km southbound.

S 74.5 (119.9 km) **A 52.5** (84.5 km) Double-ended paved turnout to east. Several kinds of blueberries, together with false azalea blossoms, are seen along here during summer months.

S 72.5 (116.7 km) **A 54.5** (87.7 km) Double-ended paved turnout to east.

S 71.5 (115.1 km) **A 55.5** (89.3 km) Double-ended paved turnout to west.

S 71.2 (114.6 km) **A 55.8** (89.8 km) Double-ended paved turnout to west.

S 71 (114.3 km) **A 56** (90.1 km) Paved turnout to east. The many flowers seen in surrounding alpine meadows here include yellow and purple violets, mountain heliotrope, lousewort and paintbrush.

S 69.9 (112.5 km) **A 57.1** (91.9 km) Scenic viewpoint with double-ended parking area to west. The highway traverses an area of mountain meadows and parklike stands of spruce, hemlock, birch and aspen, interlaced with glacier-fed streams. Lupine and wild geranium grow profusely here in the summer.

S 69.2 (111.4 km) **A 57.8** (93 km) Paved turnout to east.

S 69.1 (111.2 km) **A 57.9** (93.2 km) Passing lane ends southbound.

S 68.9 (110.9 km) **A 58.1** (93.5 km) Divided highway begins southbound, ends northbound.

S 68.5 (110.2 km) **A 58.5** (94.1 km) Turnagain Pass Recreation Area (elev. 988 feet/301m). Parking area, restrooms and dumpster (southbound lane); emergency call box. U-turn. Turnagain Pass Recreation Area is a favorite winter recreation area for snowmobilers (west side of highway) and cross-country skiers (east side of highway). Snow depths here frequently exceed 12 feet/4m.

S 68.1 (109.6 km) **A 58.9** (94.8 km) Parking area, restrooms and dumpster for northbound traffic. U-turn.

S 67.8 (109.1 km) **A 59.2** (95.3 km) Bridge over Lyon Creek.

S 67.6 (108.8 km) **A 59.4** (95.6 km) Divided highway ends southbound, begins northbound.

S 66.8 (107.5 km) **A 60.2** (96.9 km) Paved double-ended turnout with litter barrel to east.

S 65.3 (105.1 km) **A 61.7** (99.3 km) Bridge over Bertha Creek. Bertha Creek USFS campground; 12 sites, water, toilets, firepits, table, dumpsters and $6 fee. ▲

S 64.8 (104.3 km) **A 62.2** (100.1 km) Bridge over Spokane Creek.

S 64 (102.9 km) **A 63** (101.3 km) Granite Creek fireguard station.

S 63.7 (102.5 km) **A 63.3** (101.9 km) Johnson Pass north trailhead. This 23-mile-/37-km-long trail is a fairly level good family trail, which follows a portion of the Old Iditarod trail which went from Seward to Nome. See **Milepost S 32.6.**

Johnson Pass trail leads to **Bench Lake**, which has arctic grayling, and **Johnson Lake**, which has rainbow trout. Both lakes are about halfway in on trail.

S 63.3 (101.9 km) **A 63.7** (102.5 km) Bridge over Granite Creek. Traditional halfway point on highway between Anchorage and Seward.

S 63 (101.4 km) **A 64** (103 km) Granite Creek USFS campground, 0.8 mile/1.3 km from main highway; 19 sites (most beside creek), water, toilets, dumpsters, tables, firepits and $6 fee. **Granite Creek**, small Dolly Varden. ▲

S 62 (99.8 km) **A 65** (104.6 km) Bridge over East Fork Sixmile Creek.

S 61 (98.2 km) **A 66** (106.2 km) Bridge over Silvertip Creek.

S 59.7 (96.1 km) **A 67.3** (108.3 km) Gravel turnout next to Granite Creek. Excellent place to photograph this glacial stream. Beaver dam.

S 58.8 (94.6 km) **A 68.2** (109.8 km) Large gravel turnout to west. There are several turnouts along this stretch of highway.

S 57.6 (92.7 km) **A 69.4** (111.7 km) Bridge over Dry Gulch Creek.

S 57 (91.7 km) **A 70** (112.7 km) Bridge over Canyon Creek.

NOTE: Road construction next 7 miles/11.3 km southbound in 1994–95. Expect traffic delays for rock blasting.

S 56.8 (91.4 km) **A 70.2** (113 km) State wayside with picnic tables, toilets and litter barrels. Travelers sometimes confuse wayside entrance with Hope Highway turnoff.

S 56.7 (91.2 km) **A 70.3** (113.1 km) Southbound **junction** with Hope Highway to historic mining community of Hope. See HOPE HIGHWAY log opposite page.

NOTE: Southbound travelers may find this junction confusing. Hope Highway veers right; Seward Highway veers left.

S 56.6 (91.1 km) **A 70.4** (113.3 km) Northbound **junction** with Hope Highway. Numerous gravel turnouts next 6 miles/9.7 km southbound.

S 50.1 (80.6 km) **A 76.9** (123.8 km) Begin improved highway southbound with wide shoulders and passing lanes. Winter avalanche area next 1.5 miles/2.4 km southbound.

S 48 (77.2 km) **A 79** (127.1 km) Fresno Creek bridge; turnout to east at south end of bridge.

S 47.6 (76.6 km) **A 79.4** (127.8 km) Double-ended paved turnout to east on lake.

S 47.2 (76 km) **A 79.8** (128.4 km) Paved double-ended turnout to east next to Lower Summit Lake; a favorite photo stop. Extremely picturesque with lush growth of wildflowers in summer.

Upper and Lower Summit lakes, good spring and fall fishing for landlocked Dolly Varden (goldenfins), ranging in size from 6 to 11 inches, flies and single salmon eggs.

S 46.6 (74.7 km) **A 80.6** (129.7 km) Double-ended paved turnout to east on lake.

S 46 (74 km) **A 81** (130.4 km) Colorado Creek bridge. Tenderfoot Creek USFS campground 0.6 mile/0.9 km from highway; 28 sites, water, toilets (wheelchair accessible), dumpsters, tables, firepits, boat launch, $6 fee. ♿▲

S 45.8 (73.7 km) **A 81.2** (130.7 km) Lodge with restaurant and overnight accommodations; open year-round. Emergency radio. Winter avalanche area begins just south of lodge (avalanche gates).

S 45.5 (73.2 km) **A 81.5** (131.2 km) Upper Summit Lake. Paved turnout to east.

S 44.5 (71.6 km) **A 82.5** (132.7 km) Large paved double-ended turnout with interpretive sign to east at end of Upper Summit Lake.

S 44.3 (71.3 km) **A 82.7** (133.1 km) Beaver dams.

S 44 (70.8 km) **A 83** (133.6 km) Gravel turnout to east. Avalanche gun emplacement.

S 43.8 (70.5 km) **A 83.2** (133.9 km) Winter avalanche area begins northbound. Avalanche gates.

S 43.7 (70.3 km) **A 83.3** (134.1 km) Paved double-ended turnout to east.

S 42.6 (68.6 km) **A 84.4** (135.8 km) Summit Creek (not signed).

S 42.2 (67.9 km) **A 84.8** (136.5 km) Quartz Creek (not signed).

S 41.4 (66.6 km) **A 85.6** (137.8 km) Passing lane next 1 mile/1.6 km northbound.

S 39.6 (63.7 km) **A 87.4** (140.7 km) Avalanche gates.

S 39.4 (63.4 km) **A 87.6** (141 km) Devils Pass trailhead; parking area and toilets to west. This USFS trail starts at an elevation of 1,000 feet/305m and follows Devils Creek to Devils Pass (elev. 2,400 feet/732m), continuing on to Devils Pass Lake and Resurrection Pass trail. Hiking time to Devils Pass is about five and one-half hours.

S 39 (62.8 km) **A 88** (141.6 km) Truck lane extends northbound to **Milepost S 39.3.**

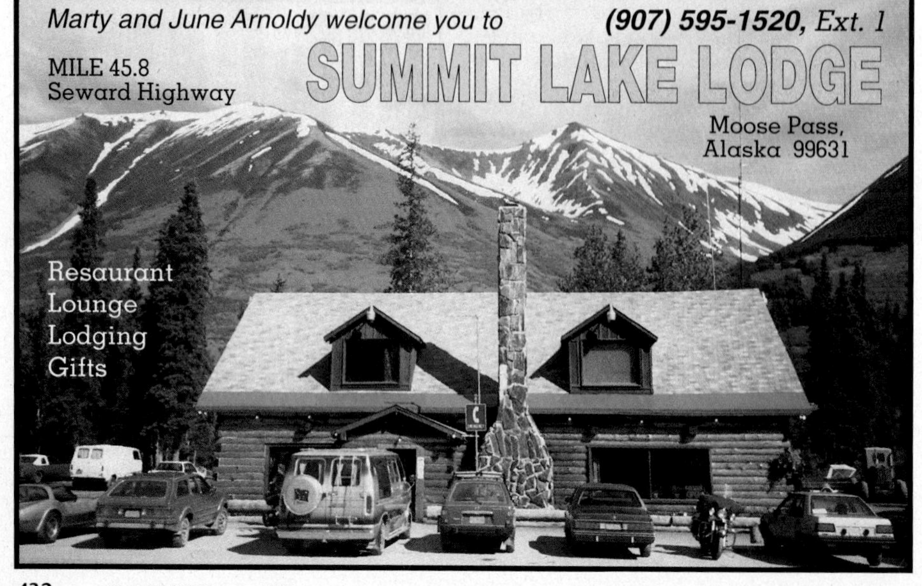

Hope Highway Log

The paved 17.7-mile/28.5-km Hope Highway leads northwest to the historic community of Hope on the south side of Turnagain Arm and provides access to the Resurrection Creek area.

Distance is measured from junction with the Seward Highway (J).

J 0 Junction with Seward Highway at **Milepost S 56.7.**

J 0.1 (0.2 km) Silvertip highway maintenance station.

J 0.6 (1 km) Double-ended paved turnout to east; road access to creek. Highway parallels Sixmile Creek, a glacial stream. There are many paved turnouts along the Hope Highway, some with views of Turnagain Arm.

J 1.4 (2.3 km) Beaver marsh to east.

J 2.3 (3.7 km) Large paved turnout to east. Moose may often be seen in Sixmile Creek valley below. The old gold mining town of Sunrise City, with a population of 5,000, was founded in 1895 at the mouth of Sixmile Creek. The present community of Sunrise has a population of about 20.

J 3.4 (5.5 km) Large paved turnout to east; trail access to creek.

J 3.9 (6.3 km) Large paved turnout to east; trail access to creek.

J 10 (16.1 km) Double-ended paved turnout to east overlooking Turnagain Arm.

J 11.1 (17.9 km) Large paved turnout to east overlooking Turnagain Arm.

J 11.8 (19 km) Double-ended paved turnout to east overlooking Turnagain Arm.

J 15.8 (25.4 km) **Henry's One Stop.** See display ad this section. ▲

J 15.9 (25.6 km) **Bear Creek Lodge.** See display ad this section.

J 16.2 (26 km) Turn left (south) for Hope airport; USFS Resurrection Pass trailhead, 4 miles/6.4 km south on Resurrection Creek Road; Paystreak, a privately owned gold mining town (burned down 1993), 4.6 miles/7.4 km; and Coeur d'Alene Campground on Palmer Creek Road, 7.6 miles/12.2 km. ▲

The 38-mile-/61-km-long Resurrection Pass USFS trail climbs from an elevation of 400 feet/122m at the trailhead to Resurrection Pass (elev. 2,600 feet/792m) and down to the south trailhead at **Milepost S 53.1** on the Sterling Highway. There are eight cabins on the trail. Parking area at the trailhead.

Coeur d'Alene, former USFS campground (semi-developed), has five sites (not recommended for large RVs or trailers); primitive camping only; no maintained facilities; no water, no camping fee. Palmer Creek Road continues past the campground to alpine country above 1,500 feet/457m elevation, and views of Turnagain Arm and Resurrection Creek valley. The road past the old campground is rough and narrow and not recommended for low-clearance vehicles.

J 16.5 (26.6 km) Turn on Hope Road for downtown **HOPE** (pop. 224). Hope Road leads past the post office down to the waterfront, a favorite fishing spot near the ocean; motel, cafe, grocery store and gift shop.

This historic mining community was founded in 1896 by gold seekers working Resurrection Creek and its tributary streams. Today, many Anchorage residents have vacation homes here.

Discovery Cafe. See display ad this section.

J 17 (27.3 km) Road to historic Hope townsite. Interpretive sign at intersection. The original townsite of Hope City was founded in 1896. Portions of the town destroyed by the 1964 earthquake are marked with dotted lines on the map sign.

J 17.1 (27.5 km) Resurrection Creek bridge.

J 17.7 (28.4 km) Gas station.

J 17.8 (28.6 km) Hope Highway ends at Porcupine USFS campground; 24 sites, tables, tent spaces, toilets, firepits, dumpster, drinking water and $6 fee. Gull Rock trailhead. ▲

Return to Milepost S 56.7 Seward Highway

Dall sheep. (Sue Rheaume)

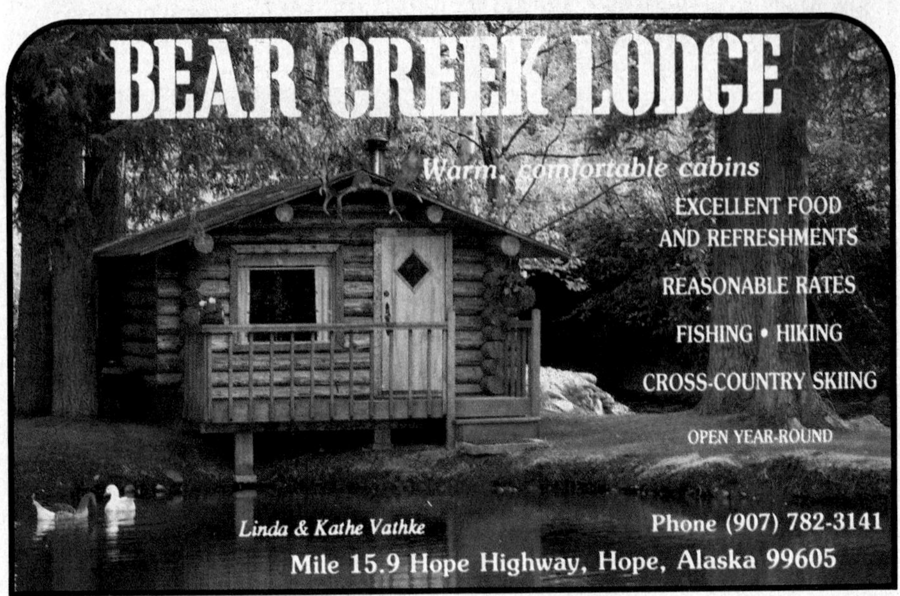

S 38.6 (62.1 km) **A 88.4** (142.3 km) Paved turnout to west adjacent **Jerome Lake,** rainbow and Dolly Varden to 22 inches, use salmon egg clusters, year-round, still fish. A sign here explains rainbow plant in lake.

S 38.3 (61.6 km) **A 88.7** (142.7 km) Paved double-ended turnout to west overlooking Jerome Lake. USFS interpretive sign about sticklebacks.

S 38.2 (61.5 km) **A 88.8** (142.9 km) Truck lane ends northbound.

S 37.7 (60.7 km) **A 89.3** (143.7 km) **Junction.** First southbound exit (one-way road) for Sterling Highway (Alaska Route 1) on right. Continue straight ahead on Alaska Route 9 for Seward.

If you are bound for Soldotna, Homer, or other Sterling Highway communities and attractions, turn to the STERLING HIGHWAY section and begin that log. Continue with this log if you are going to Seward.

Beautiful Kenai Lake. (© Alaskan Images/Loren Taft)

ALASKA ROUTE 9

S 37.2 (59.9 km) **A 89.8** (144.5 km) Paved turnout to west overlooking Tern Lake for Seward-bound travelers.

S 37 (59.5 km) **A 90** (144.8 km) **Tern Lake Junction.** Second southbound turnoff on right (two-way road) for Sterling Highway (Alaska Route 1) and access to Tern Lake USFS campground and salmon spawning channel. To reach campground, drive 0.4 mile/0.6 km around Tern Lake; 25 sites, water, toilets, picnic tables, firepits, canoe launch, $6 fee. Tern Lake is a good spot for bird watching in summer. See STERLING HIGHWAY section. ▲

Continue straight ahead on Alaska Route 9 for Seward.

S 36.7 (59.1 km) **A 90.3** (145.3 km) Truck lane begins northbound.

S 36.4 (58.6 km) **A 90.6** (145.8 km) Avalanche gates.

S 35.7 (57.5 km) **A 91.3** (146.9 km) **TAK Outfitters.** See display ad this section.

S 35.3 (56.8 km) **A 91.7** (147.6 km) End avalanche area southbound.

S 35 (56.3 km) **A 92** (148 km) For the next 3 miles/4.8 km many small waterfalls tumble down the brushy slopes. Winter avalanche area between **Milepost S 35.3** and **34.6.** You are driving through the Kenai mountain range.

S 33.1 (53.3 km) **A 93.9** (151.1 km) Carter Lake USFS trailhead No. 4 to west; parking and toilets. Trail starts at an elevation of 500 feet/152m and climbs 986 feet/300m to **Carter Lake** (stocked with rainbow trout). Trail is good, but steep; hiking time about one and one-half hours. Good access to sheep and mountain goat country. Excellent snowmobiling area in winter.

S 32.6 (52.5 km) **A 94.4** (151.9 km) Johnson Pass USFS south trailhead with parking area, toilet. North trailhead at **Milepost S 63.1.**

S 32.5 (52.3 km) **A 94.5** (152.1 km) Large paved double-ended turnout; USFS information sign on life cycle of salmon; short trail to observation deck on stream where spawning salmon may be seen in August.

S 32.4 (52.1 km) **A 94.6** (152.2 km) Cook Inlet Aquaculture Assoc. Trail Lake fish hatchery on Moose Creek. Display room and restrooms. Open 8 A.M. to 5 P.M. daily. Tours available daily at 10 A.M. June 1 to Sept. 15; phone 288-3688 for more information.

S 31.8 (51.1 km) **A 95.2** (153.2 km) Paved double-ended rest area to east on Upper Trail Lake; toilets, picnic tables.

S 30.1 (48.4 km) **A 96.9** (155.9 km) **The Spruce Moose B & B.** This three-story chalet is nestled among spruce trees on a 5-acre hillside with a spectacular view of Upper Trail Lake and Lark Mountain. The entire house is yours to enjoy. It will accommodate up to eight people comfortably and includes a fully equipped kitchen. Open June through August. MasterCard and VISA accepted. Roseann Hetrick, P.O. Box 7, Moose Pass, AK 99631. (907) 288-3667. [ADVERTISEMENT]

S 30 (48.3 km) **A 97** (156.1 km) Short side road to large undeveloped gravel parking area on Upper Trail Lake; boat launch.

S 29.9 (48.1 km) **A 97.1** (156.3 km) Gravel turnout by Trail Lake.

S 29.5 (47.5 km) **A 97.5** (156.9 km) **Scenic Mountain Air.** Soar with the eagles! Fly in our float plane over ice-blue glaciers, immense ice fields, turquoise mountain lakes, gushing waterfalls; see goats, sheep, bear. "It's like flying through a *National Geographic* special — better than McKinley!" Day fly-in fishing, guided and unguided, for rainbow, grayling, Dolly Varden and salmon. Air taxi service to Forest Service cabins. (907) 288-3646, P.O. Box 4, Moose Pass, AK 99631. [ADVERTISEMENT]

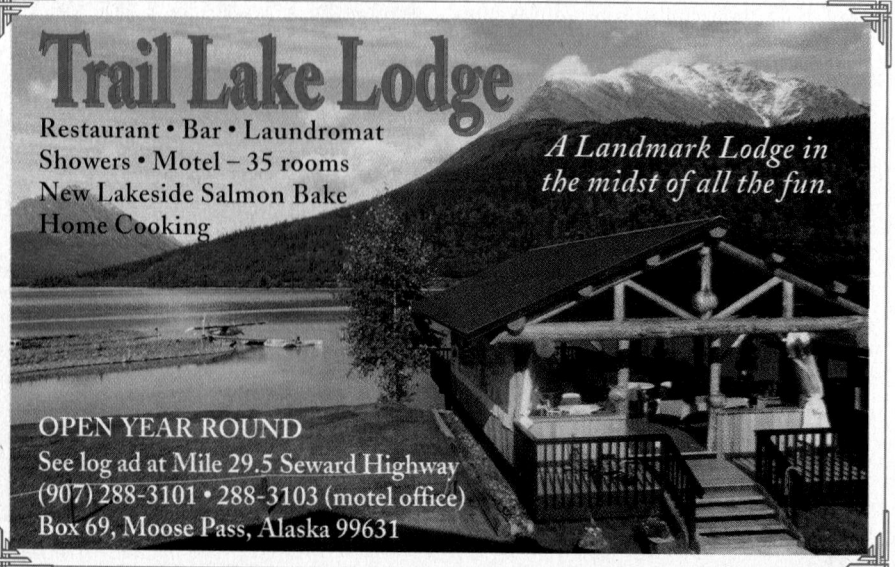

Creekside Bed & Breakfast. See display ad this section.

Le Barn Appétit. See display ad this section.

Iditaride Sled Dog Tours. See display ad this section.

S 3.2 (5.1 km) **A 123.8** (199.2 km) Nash Road; access to bed and breakfasts. It is a scenic 5-mile/8-km drive out Nash Road to Seward's Marine Industrial Center in the Fourth of July Creek valley. Fine views along the way and from Kertulla Point of Resurrection Bay and the city of Seward. At Mile 2.1 Nash Road is the trailhead for the Iditarod Trail, which begins at the ferry terminal in downtown Seward. Hike to Bear Lake; from north end of lake, trail continues to Mile 12 on the Seward Highway.

The White House B&B. See display ad this section.

The Farm Bed & Breakfast. Turn off Seward Highway on Nash Road, turn left immediately on Salmon Creek Road, and follow the signs to "The Farm." Tranquil country setting on acres of trees and green grass. Elegantly casual rooms, private baths, decks and entrances. Cable TV, barbecues.

Smoking restricted. Delightful continental breakfast. "We are not in the middle of everything." Reservations welcome. VISA and MasterCard accepted. Call (907) 224-5691, fax (907) 224-2300. Your host: Jack Hoogland. Open year-round. See display ad in Seward section. [ADVERTISEMENT]

Rininger's Bed & Breakfast (Mile 1.6 Nash Road) is located on Rabbit Run Road (left at fork). Open year-round. Large, sunny room with skylights and handcrafted furnishings. Private bath and kitchenette; sleeping loft, separate entrance. Breakfast in room at your leisure. Outdoor wood-heated sauna. Hiking and cross-country ski trails nearby. A perfect weekend getaway. Families welcome. Sleeps up to eight. Kent and Lisa Rininger, P.O. Box 548, Seward, AK 99664. (907) 224-5918. [ADVERTISEMENT]

S 3 (4.8 km) **A 124** (199.6 km) Resurrection River, three channels and three highway bridges. This river, formed by snowmelt from the Harding Icefield, empties into Resurrection Bay just northeast of Seward.

Seward city limits.

S 2.7 (4.3 km) **A 124.3** (200 km) Turnoff for Seward airport.

Scenic Mountain Air. Soar with the eagles! Take our scenic flights from Seward Airport over Harding Icefield and Kenai Fjords National Park, or to Mount McKinley or McCarthy. "It's like flying through a *National Geographic* special!" Charter flights to Homer and Anchorage. Our half-day photographic seminar includes a photo flight! (907) 288-3646, P.O. Box 4, Moose Pass, AK 99631. [ADVERTISEMENT]

S 2.4 (3.9 km) **A 124.6** (200.5 km) Forest Acres municipal campground; water, flush toilets, 14-day limit. No tables. ▲

S 2.1 (3.4 km) **A 124.9** (201 km) U.S. Air Force and U.S. Army Seward Recreation Area.

S 2 (3.2 km) **A 125** (201.1 km) Seward Chamber of Commerce visitor center. Seward High School.

S 1.2 (1.9 km) **A 125.8** (202.4 km) Large parking area to west with memorial to Benny Benson, who designed the Alaska state flag.

S 1 (1.6 km) **A 126** (202.8 km) Main entrance to boat harbor.

Alaska Treks 'n Voyages. See display ad this section.

S 0.3 (0.5 km) **A 126.7** (203.9 km) Intersection of 3rd Avenue (Seward Highway) and Jefferson. Post office one block east. Information Cache rail car at intersection.

Seward

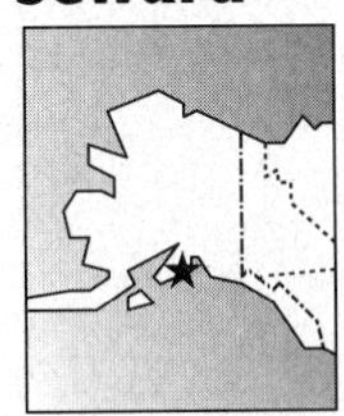

S 0 A 127 (204.4 km) Located on Resurrection Bay, east coast of Kenai Peninsula; 127 miles/204.4 km south of Anchorage by road, or 35 minutes by air. **Population:** 3,000. **Emergency Services: Police, Fire Department** and **Ambulance,** emergency only, phone 911. **State Troopers,** phone 224-3346. **Hospital,** Seward General, 1st Avenue and Jefferson Street, phone 224-5205. **Maritime Search and Rescue,** phone 1-800-478-5555.

Visitor Information: Available at two locations, operated by the Seward Chamber of Commerce. The visitor center at **Milepost S 2** Seward Highway (2001 Seward Highway) is open seven days a week from Memorial Day through Labor Day, weekdays the rest of the year; phone 224-8051. The Information Cache, located in the historic railroad car *Seward* at 3rd and Jefferson Street, is open daily from 11 A.M. to 5 P.M., June through August; phone 224-3094, or write Box 749, Seward 99664.

Kenai Fjords National Park Visitor Center, 1212 4th Ave. (in the Small Boat Harbor), is open 8 A.M. to 7 P.M. daily, Memorial Day to Labor Day; 8:30 A.M. to 5 P.M. weekdays the remainder of the year. Information on the park, slide show, interpretive programs and bookstore. Phone (907) 224-3175 or write P.O. Box 1727, Seward 99664.

Chugach National Forest, Seward Ranger District office, is located at 334 4th Ave. USFS personnel can provide information on hiking, camping and fishing opportunities on national forest lands. Open weekdays, 8 A.M. to 5 P.M. Mailing address: P.O. Box 390, Seward 99664. Phone 224-3374.

Elevation: Sea level. **Climate:** Average

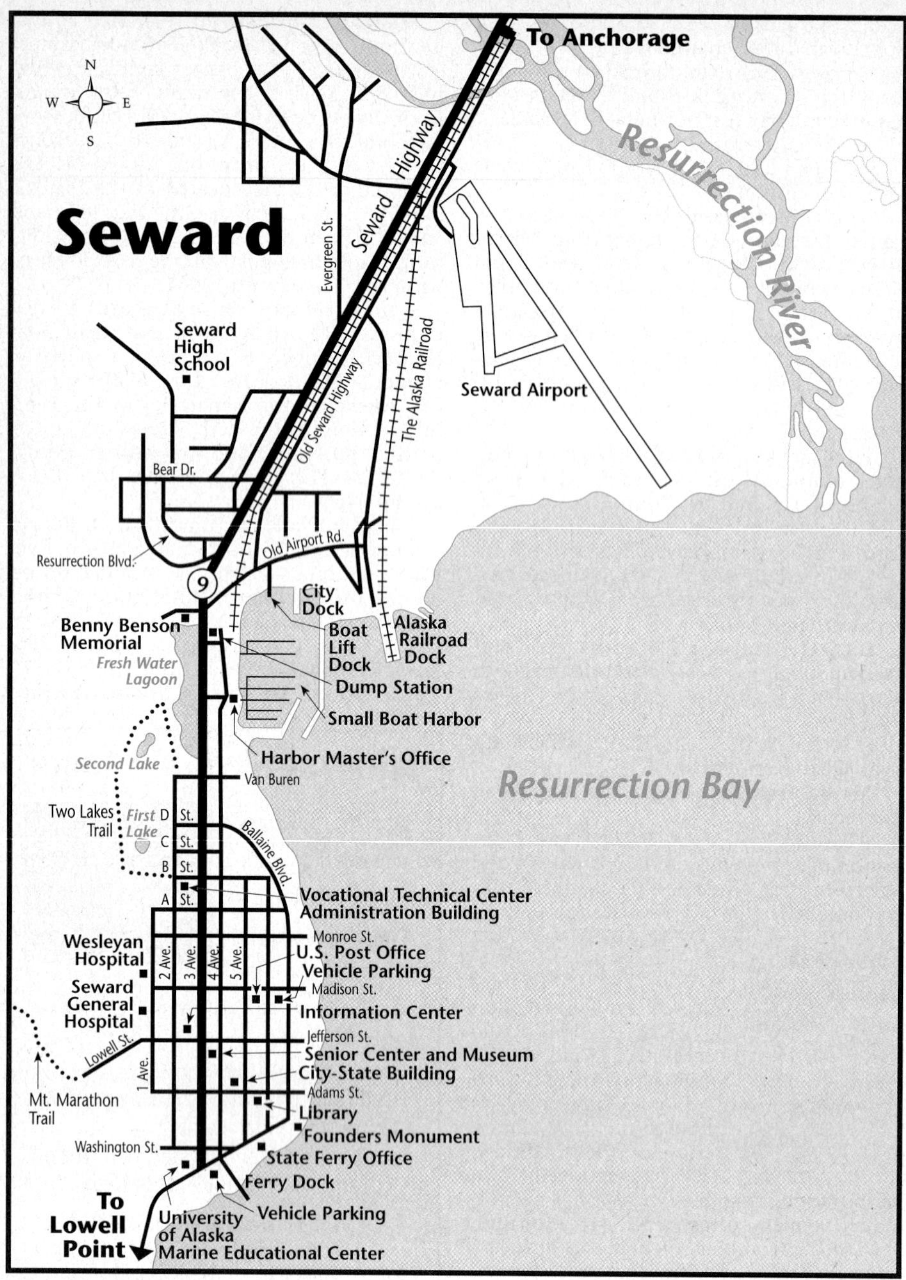

daily maximum temperature in July, 62°F/17°C; average daily minimum in January, 18°F/-7°C. Average annual precipitation, 67 inches; average snowfall, 80 inches. **Radio:** KSWD 950, KSKA-FM 92, KWAVE 104.9, KPEN 102.3. **Television:** Several channels by cable. **Newspaper:** *Seward Phoenix Log* (weekly).

Private Aircraft: Seward airport, 1.7 miles/2.7 km northeast; elev. 22 feet/7m; length 4,500 feet/1,371m; asphalt; fuel 80, 100, jet.

Seward — known as the "Gateway to Kenai Fjords National Park" — is a picturesque community nestled between high mountain ranges on a small rise stretching from Resurrection Bay to the foot of Mount Marathon. Thick groves of cottonwood and scattered spruce groves are found in the immediate vicinity of the city, with stands of spruce and alder growing on the surrounding mountainsides.

Downtown Seward (the main street is 4th Avenue) has a frontier-town atmosphere with some homes and buildings dating back to the early 1900s. The town was established in 1903 by railroad surveyors as an ocean terminal and supply center. The 470-mile/756-km railway connecting Fairbanks in the Interior with Seward, the railroad's southern terminus, was completed in 1923.

The city was named for U.S. Secretary of State William H. Seward, who was instrumental in arranging the purchase of Alaska from Russia in 1867. Resurrection Bay was named in 1791 by Russian fur trader and explorer Alexander Baranof. While sailing from Kodiak to Yakutat he found unexpected shelter in this bay from a storm and named the bay Resurrection because it was the Russian Sunday of the Resurrection.

Resurrection Bay is a year-round ice-free harbor and Seward is an important cargo port and fishing port. The Alaska state ferry MV *Tustumena* calls at Seward.

Seward's economic base includes tourism, a coal terminal, sawmill, fisheries and government offices. The Alaska Vocational Technical Center is located here.

ACCOMMODATIONS

All visitor facilities, including two hotels, three motels, several bed and breakfasts, many cafes and restaurants, post office, grocery stores, drugstore, travel agencies, gift shops, gas stations, bars, laundromats, churches, bowling alley and theater.

Benson Bed and Breakfast. Family atmosphere. Smoke-free room, queen bed, private bath. Full breakfast. Quiet neighborhood. Close to harbor, grocery store, bike path, bus, train, visitor center. Hosts: Rich and Sandy Houghton, long-time Alaskans with experience above the Arctic Circle. Open year-round. 209 Benson, P.O. Box 3506, Seward, AK 99664. (907) 224-5290. [ADVERTISEMENT]

Best Western Hotel Seward. Enjoy being in the center of activity, yet in a quiet setting overlooking Resurrection Bay. Our 1991 extensive expansion includes breathtaking view rooms with in-room coffee and your own refrigerator. And check this out! For your in-room entertainment, all rooms include (1) remote control TVs with cablevision, (2) remote control VCRs with videotape rental available and (3) two channels of free in-room movies featuring the latest hits! Complimentary scheduled shuttle bus service for our guests to boat harbor, train depot and airport. We accept all major credit cards. Reservations (907) 224-2378 or (800) 478-4050 inside Alaska. Fax (907) 224-3112. See display ad this section. [ADVERTISEMENT]

Bluefield Bed and Breakfast. Nestled at the foot of the mountains in a quiet neighborhood, surrounded by lovely gardens, trees and lawns. Walking distance to the boat harbor, fine restaurants and shops. Private entrance to your spacious room with king bed and double futon, sitting area, breakfast table and a Jacuzzi in your private bath. Serving a gourmet continental breakfast at your leisure. Liz, Duane and Darcy Harp, P.O. Box 2068, Seward, AK 99664. (907) 224-8732. [ADVERTISEMENT]

Creekside Bed and Breakfast. Clean, cozy cabins; tent sites. Heated restrooms with sauna and showers. Located on beautiful Clear Creek, surrounded by tall spruce. Peaceful country setting for a relaxing stay. Mile 0.5 on the road to Exit Glacier. Phone (907) 224-3834. See display ad Mile 3.7 Seward Highway. [ADVERTISEMENT] ▲

SEWARD ADVERTISERS

Adventures & Delights Eco Tours .... Small Boat Harbor
Alaska Railroad .... Ph. (800) 544-0552
Alaska Renown Charters ... Ph. (907) 224-3806
Alaska Treks 'n Voyages ...... Small Boat Harbor
All Alaskan Adventures .... Ph. (800) 898-TOUR
Aurora Charters .... Ph. (907) 224-3968
Bardarson Studio .... Ph. (907) 224-5448
Bay Vista B&B .... Ph. (907) 224-5880
Bear Lake Air and Guide Service .... Ph. (907) 224-5725
Benson Bed and Breakfast .... Ph. (907) 224-5290
Best Western Hotel Seward .... Ph. (907) 224-2378
Bluefield Bed and Breakfast .... Ph. (907) 224-8732
Breeze Inn .... Small Boat Harbor
Brown and Hawkins .... 4th Ave.
Charter Connection, The .... Ph. (907) 224-4446
Charter Option, The .... Ph. (907) 224-2026
Command Charters .... Ph. (800) 770-2833
Creekside Bed and Breakfast .... Ph. (907) 224-3834
Depot, The .... Opposite Marina Motel
Fantasea Charters .... Ph. (907) 345-0100
Farm Bed & Breakfast, The .... Ph. (907) 224-5691
Fifth Avenue Lodging .... Ph. (907) 224-3412
Fish House, The .... Small Boat Harbor
Harborview Bed and Breakfast .... Ph. (907) 224-3217
House of Diamond Willow .... 2 locations—See ad
J-Dock Vac N' Pac .... Ph. (907) 224-7272
Kenai Fjords RV Park .... Small Boat Harbor
Kenai Fjords Tours .... Ph. (907) 224-8068
Le Barn Appétit Restaurant, Bakery, Health Food Store and Bed and Breakfast .... Ph. (907) 224-8706
Mackinaw Charters .... Ph. (907) 224-3910
Major Marine Tours .... Ph. (907) 224-8030
Mariah Charters & Tours ..... Small Boat Harbor
Marina Motel .... Ph. (907) 224-5518
Miller's Landing .... Lowell Point Rd.
Mom Clock's Bed and Breakfast .... Ph. (907) 224-3195
Morning Calm Bed & Breakfast .... Ph. (907) 224-3049
Murphy's Motel .... 4th Ave. & D St.
New Seward Hotel & Saloon .... Ph. (907) 224-8001
Northern Nights Bed & Breakfast .... Ph. (907) 224-5688
Ray's Waterfront .... Small Boat Harbor
Resurrection Bay Galerie .... 4th & Madison
River Valley Cabins .... Ph. (907) 224-5740
Sablefish Charters .... Ph. (907) 224-3283
Select Charters .... Small Boat Harbor
Seward Chamber of Commerce .... Ph. (907) 224-8051
Seward Convention and Visitors Association ...... Ph. (907) 224-2026
Seward Drug Co. .... Downtown
Seward Laundry .... 806 4th Ave.
Seward Waterfront Lodging .... Ph. (907) 224-5563
Seward's Downtown Lodging .... Ph. (907) 224-3939
Sleep Inn .... Ph. (907) 224-8999
Taroka Inn .... Ph. (907) 224-8975
Trails North, Inc. .... Ph. (907) 224-3587
Treasure Chest, The .... Small Boat Harbor
Van Gilder Hotel .... 308 Adams St.
White House B&B, The .... Mile 1.7 Nash Rd.

Seward's busy Main Street. (Ron Levy)

Harborview Bed and Breakfast. 900 3rd and C Street. New rooms with private entrances, private baths, color cable television, telephone, Alaska Native fine art, fresh flowers. Just 10-minute walk to: tour boats, fishing charters, downtown and laundromat. Ask about "Seaview," our newly remodeled two-bedroom apartments on the beachfront, breathtaking view of snowcapped mountains and bay. All nonsmoking. $75. Early reservations advised. Alaska Native hostess. Phone/fax (907) 224-3217; P.O. Box 1305, Seward, AK 99664. [ADVERTISEMENT]

Le Barn Appétit Restaurant, Bakery, Health Food Store and Bed and Breakfast. Creekside setting in the trees; beautiful views. Nonsmoking, nonalcoholic. Families welcome. Petting park for small children. Giant teeter-totter. Breakfast, lunch and dinner. Continental cuisine. Omelettes, crêpes, quiches, seafood specialties. European-style coffees and teas. VISA, MasterCard accepted. Your hosts: Yvon and Janet Van Driessche, P.O. Box 601, Seward, AK 99664. Phone (907) 224-8706 or (907) 224-3462. Fax (907) 224-8461. Mile 3.7 Seward Highway, off Exit Glacier Road. [ADVERTISEMENT]

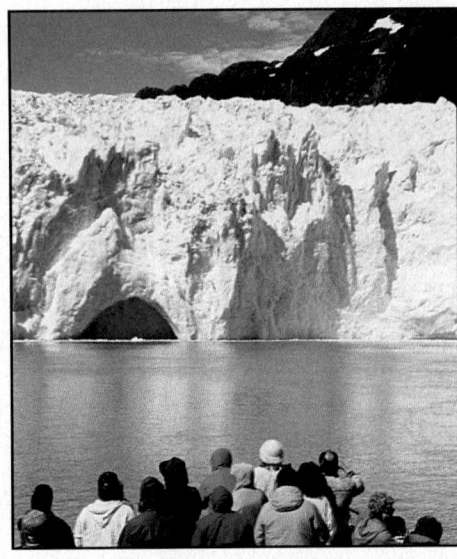

Morning Calm Bed & Breakfast. A touch of the Orient in Alaska. Located within walking distance of the Small Boat Harbor, railroad depot and information center. Smoke-free environment. Two rooms, queen and twin, with shared bath. In-room TV/VCR. Open year-round. Kerry and Kim Martin. (907) 224-3049. P.O. Box 816, Seward, AK 99664. [ADVERTISEMENT]

New Seward Hotel & Saloon. Centrally located in downtown Seward, within walking distance of shops, ferry, bus terminal, boat harbor; 35 rooms featuring TV, phones, free videos. Some kitchenettes. Salmon and halibut fishing charters or Kenai Fjords tours available. Year-round service. Brochure. All major credit cards accepted. Reservations (907) 224-8001. Fax (907) 224-3112. See display ad this section. [ADVERTISEMENT]

Sleep Inn. Best location in Seward — on the water's edge in the Small Boat Harbor. Closest to Alaska Railroad Depot. Departure point to the Kenai Fjords National Park, one of Alaska's "Big Three." Salmon, halibut and deep sea charters available. Opening spring 1994. Toll free in Alaska: 1-800-475-3376. Also (907) 224-8999. Fax (907) 224-2089. See display ad this section. [ADVERTISEMENT]

Taroka Inn. Originally built to house officers stationed in Seward during WWII

(Taroka is the local Indian name for the coastal brown bear). Taroka Inn has nine cozy units with private baths and kitchenettes. Walking distance to downtown attractions and Seward Trolley stop. Fishing charters and sightseeing tours arranged. (907) 224-8975. See display ad this section. [ADVERTISEMENT]

The White House B&B, (nonsmoking) bed and breakfast, is nestled in a mountain panorama. Country charm. Private or shared bath. Breakfast self-served in our guest kitchen. Families and groups welcome. Room rates $50 to $80. Open year-round, winter rates. (907) 224-3614. Mile 1.7 Nash Road. (See display ad at Mile 3.2 Seward Highway.) [ADVERTISEMENT]

The Harbormaster Building has public restrooms and pay showers, mailbox and pay phones. Weather information is available here during the summer. Public restrooms on Ballaine Boulevard along the ocean between the boat harbor and town. Dump station and drinking water fill-up at the Small Boat Harbor at the end of 4th Avenue (see city map). There are picnic areas with covered tables along Ballaine Blvd. just south of the harbor, and at Adams Street.

Seward has made a good effort to provide overnight parking for self-contained RVs. There are designated camping areas along the shore south of Van Buren; camping fee charged. RV parking is marked by signs. (Caravans: contact the City Parks and Recreation Dept. for reservations, phone 224-3331.) Forest Acres municipal campground is at **Milepost S 2.4** Seward Highway. Private RV parks at Small Boat Harbor, at **Milepost S 6.6** and on Lowell Point Road. Tent camping also available at Exit Glacier (turnoff at **Milepost S 3.7** Seward Highway). ▲

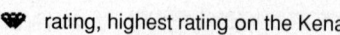

Miller's Landing. Alaskan family operated fishing and tent/RV campground located on family homestead. Boat and pole rentals, fishing/sightseeing charters (full and half day), water taxi service to remote fishing areas, boat launch, kayak dropoffs to Aialik Glacier, Holgate Arm, Fox Island. Catch king salmon, Dolly Varden, pink, silver, chum salmon from beach, catch halibut from boat rentals or charters. Scenic campground located on Resurrection Bay. See sea otters, eagles, seals from camp. Private beaches. Hiking trail to Caine's Head State Park. Cozy cabin rentals. Country store sells bait, tackle, ice, fishing licenses, T-shirts, hats, gifts. Pull-through electric RV sites; large tent sites. Beach sites or forested sites. Showers, RV dump expected nearby in 1994. Phone. Mike Miller homesteaded here. He's an expert on fishing advice and visitor information. Survived 1964 earthquake. Free coffee. Fishing advice 5¢. Guaranteed effective or your nickel back! Down-home Alaskan atmosphere. Reservations accepted/advisable for guaranteed arrivals only. Box 81, Seward, AK 99664. (907) 224-5739. [ADVERTISEMENT] ▲

TRANSPORTATION

Air: Seward airport is reached by turning east on Airport Road at **Milepost S 2.7** on the Seward Highway. Scheduled daily service to Anchorage; charters also available.

Highway: Seward is reached via the 127-mile/203.2-km Seward Highway from Anchorage.

Ferry: The offices of the Alaska Marine Highway system in Seward are in the former Alaska Railroad depot, now one of Seward's historic buildings, at the south end of 5th Avenue. The Alaska ferry MV *Tustumena* departs Seward for Kodiak and Valdez. For schedule information see the MARINE ACCESS ROUTES section.

Bus: Scheduled service to Anchorage.

Railroad: The Alaska Railroad connects Seward to Anchorage and Fairbanks. See the ALASKA RAILROAD section.

Taxi: Service available.

ATTRACTIONS

The Railcar *Seward* houses the chamber of commerce information center. Located at 3rd and Jefferson Street, this railcar was the Seward observation car on the Alaska Railroad from 1936 until the early 1960s. Information and detailed map of the city are available.

Walking Tour of Seward encompasses more than 30 attractions including homes and businesses that date back to the early 1900s; some are still being used, while others have been restored as historic sites. A brochure containing details on all the attractions of the tour is available at the railcar information center. The complete tour covers about 2 miles/3.2 km and takes about one to two hours, depending upon how much time you wish to spend browsing.

Marine Educational Center, maintained by the University of Alaska, has laboratories, aquaculture ponds and the vessel *Alpha Helix,* which carries on oceanographic research in Alaskan waters. There is a marine display here. Open 1-5 P.M. weekdays, 10 A.M. to noon and 1-5 P.M. on Saturday, June through August.

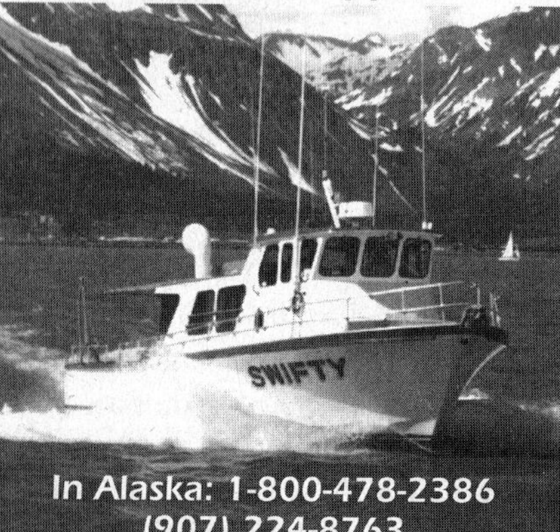

Visit the Small Boat Harbor. This municipal harbor, built after the 1964 earthquake, is home port to fishing boats, charter boats and sightseeing boats. The harbor is also home to sea otters; watch for them! Visitors may notice the great number of sailboats moored here: many are members of the William H. Seward Yacht Club, which sponsors an annual sailboat and yacht show.

Seward Museum, at Jefferson and 3rd Avenue, is operated by the Resurrection Bay Historical Society (Box 55, Seward 99664). The museum features artifacts and photographs from the 1964 earthquake, WWII, the founding days of Seward, and other highlights of Seward's history. Also on display is a collection of Native baskets and ivory carvings. The museum is open May 15 to Sept. 30, 11 A.M. to 5 P.M. weekdays, noon to 6 P.M. weekends; phone (907) 224-3902. A modest admission fee.

Seward Community Library, across from the City–State Bldg., presents (on request) short slide/sound shows on a variety of subjects and has some informative displays. A program on the 1964 earthquake is shown daily at 2 P.M. (except Sunday) from June 15 through the first Saturday in September. Library hours are 1-8 P.M. Monday through Friday, 1-6 P.M. Saturday.

St. Peter's Episcopal Church is three blocks west of the museum at the corner of 2nd Avenue and Adams Street. It was built in 1906 and is considered the oldest Protestant church on the Kenai Peninsula. A feature is the unique painting of the Resurrection, for which Alaskans were used as models and Resurrection Bay as the background. Well-known Dutch artist Jan Van Emple was commissioned to paint the picture in 1925 when he was living in Seward. Obtain key to church from the Information Cache in season.

Hiking Trails. Two Lakes trail is an easy mile-long loop trail along the base of Mount

Marathon. The trail passes through a wooded area and follows what used to be Hemlock Street. Beautiful view of marina below and north end of Resurrection Bay. Start at First Lake, behind the Alaska Vocational and Technical Center Administration Bldg. at 2nd Avenue and B Street.

The National Historic Iditarod Trail begins at the ferry terminal and follows a marked course through town, then north on the Seward Highway. At Mile 2.1 Nash Road (turn off at **Milepost S 3.2** Seward Highway), the trail continues from a gravel parking area on the east side of Sawmill Creek north to Bear Lake. The trail eventually rejoins the Seward Highway at **Milepost S 12.**

Caines Head State Recreation Area, 6 miles/9.6 km south of Seward, is accessible by boat or via a 4.5-mile/7.2-km beach trail (low tide only). The trailhead/parking is located about Mile 2 Lowell Point Road. The Caines Head area has bunkers and gun emplacements that were used to guard the entrance to Resurrection Bay during WWII.

Mount Marathon Race™, Seward's annual Fourth of July endurance race to the top and back of Mount Marathon (elev. 3,022 feet/921m), is a grueling test for athletes. The race is said to have begun in 1909 with a wager between two sourdoughs as to how long it would take to run up and down Mount Marathon. The first year of the official race is uncertain, but records indicate either 1912 or 1915. Fastest recorded time is 43 minutes, 23 seconds set in 1981 by Bill Spencer, who broke his own 1974 record. The descent is so steep that it's part run, part jump, and part slide. The race attracts competitors from all over, and thousands of spectators line the route each year.

Annual Seward Silver Salmon Derby™ in August is one of the largest sporting events in Alaska. It is held over nine days, starting the second Saturday in August through Sunday of the following weekend. 1994 will be the derby's 39th year. Record derby catch to date is a 19.87-lb. salmon caught off Caines Head by William Bixby of Soldotna.

There is more than $50,000 in prizes for the derby, including $10,000 in cash for the largest fish. Also part of the derby are the sought-after tagged silvers worth $7,500 and $10,000. Prizes are sponsored by various merchants and the chamber of commerce.

The town fills up fast during the derby: Make reservations! For more information contact the Seward Chamber of Commerce; phone (907) 224-8051.

Annual Seward Halibut Jackpot Tournament runs the entire month of July. First, second and third place prizes awarded for heaviest fish. In 1993 the winner weighed in at 248½ lbs. — but several hours later a 360-lb. halibut was reeled in — the largest halibut reported caught in southcentral Alaska in 1993. Sponsors include the chamber of commerce and Seward Charter Assoc.

Kenai Fjords National Park. Seward is the gateway to this popular 650,000-acre national park. Dominant feature of the park is the Harding Icefield, a 700-square-mile vestige of the last ice age. Harding Icefield can be reached by a strenuous all-day hike from the base of Exit Glacier or by a charter flightseeing trip out of Seward.

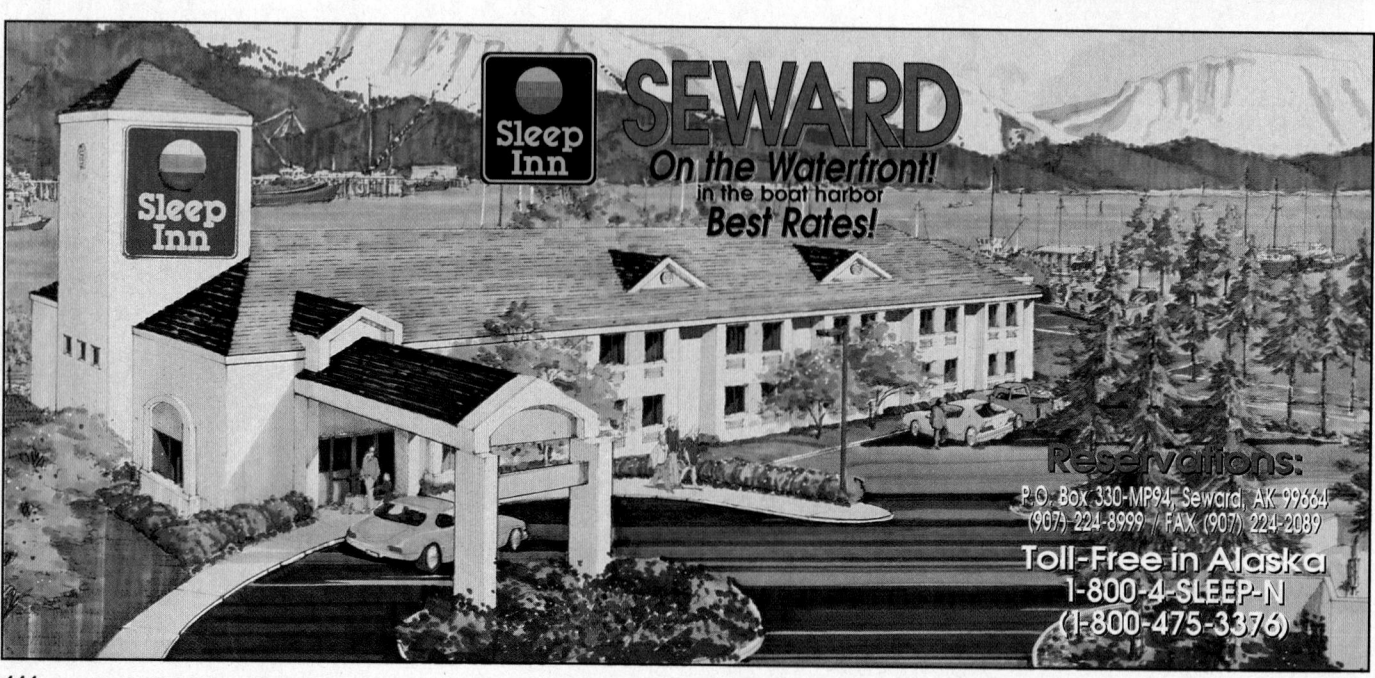

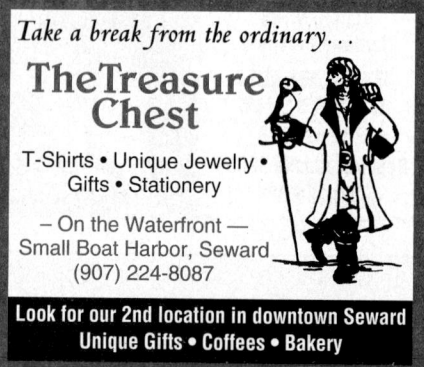

The fjords of the park were formed when glaciers flowed down to the sea from the ice field and then retreated, leaving behind the deep inlets that characterize the coastline here. Substantial populations of marine mammals inhabit or migrate through the park's coastal waters, including sea otters, Steller sea lions, dolphins and whales. Icebergs from calving glaciers provide ideal refuge for harbor seals, and the rugged coastline provides habitat for more than 100,000 nesting birds. The park's spectacular scenery and wildlife may be viewed by daily tour and charter boats or by charter planes. Four public-use cabins along the coast are available in summer by reservation; kayakers can also camp on beaches.

Exit Glacier is the most accessible of the park's glaciers. Turn at **Milepost S 3.7** on the Seward Highway and follow Exit Glacier Road to the visitor center parking area. The main trail to the glacier is 0.8 mile long, with the first 0.3 mile paved for wheelchair access. There are about 3 miles/4.8 km of nature trails that provide easy access to the glacier. Ranger-led hikes are available in summer at Exit Glacier, where there are a picnic area and walk-in campground. Visitor information is available at the Exit Glacier ranger station and visitor center; open summer only. Exit Glacier is accessible in winter by skis, dogsled or snow machine. Two public-use cabins are available in winter by reservation; phone 224-3175. *CAUTION: Active glacier with unstable ice. Do not walk past warning signs!* ♿

Slide programs, videos, exhibits and information on Kenai Fjords National Park and organized activities at the park are available at the park visitor center on 4th Avenue in the Small Boat Harbor area next to the Harbormaster's office. The center is open daily from Memorial Day to Labor Day; hours are 8 A.M. to 7 P.M. The remainder of the year hours are 8 A.M. to 5 P.M. weekdays. Phone (907) 224-3175 or write the park superintendent, Box 1727, Seward 99664.

CAUTION: The waters in this area can be extremely dangerous due to weather and violent storms that come out of the Gulf of Alaska, almost at a moment's notice. It is advisable to take a charter boat or flightseeing tour.

Alaska Treks 'n Voyages and Adventures & Delights Eco Tours. Enjoy sea kayaking, scenic beauty and marine wildlife on Resurrection Bay, Kenai Fjords National Park and Prince William Sound. Guided and

outfitted; no experience necessary. Day trips, extended tours, cabins or camping. Rentals, instruction and transportation. Our Seward location is in the harbor, across from the boat ramp, (907) 224-3960. To inquire call (800) 288-3134 or (907) 276-8282, or write 414 "K" St., Suite MP, Anchorage, AK 99501. [ADVERTISEMENT]

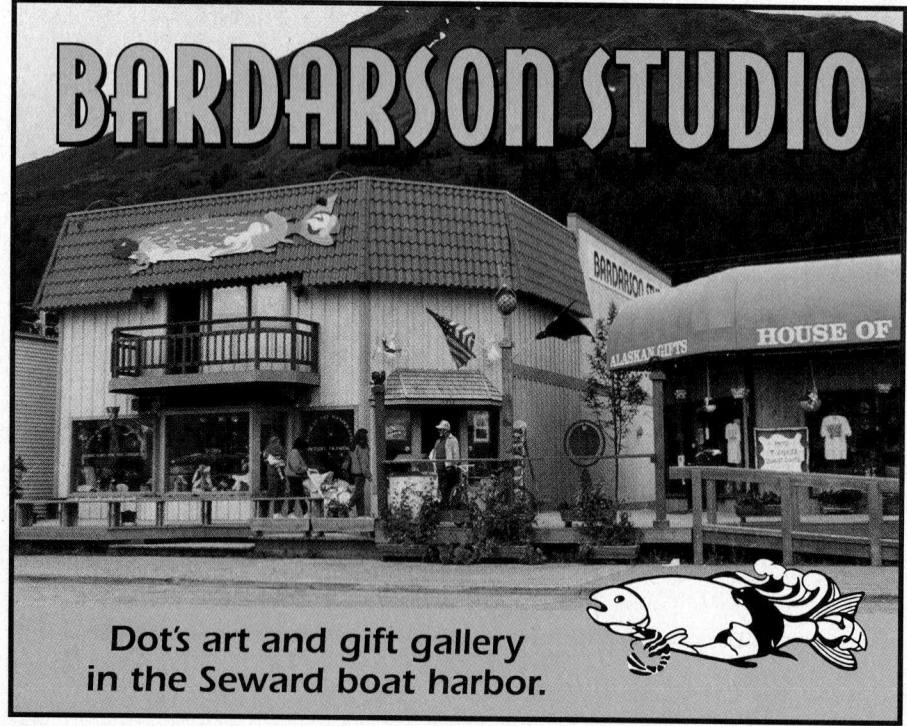

All Alaskan Adventures is a free reservation service offering customized itineraries for the independent traveler year-round. All areas of Alaska from Barrow to Ketchikan are unique. But, none are too remote for you to experience during your "once-in-a-lifetime adventure." Please don't go home thinking of the things you wish you had known before you came the first time. Our experienced staff are ready to advise and assist you. We arrange all types of accommodations, fishing and glacier sightseeing charters, flightseeing, and transportation to all areas of Alaska. Packages for every size budget are available. Telephone calls welcome from anywhere nationwide for information or to book accommodations, activities and transportation. Please call our toll-free number: 1-800-898-TOUR. Fax (907) 224-3689. See display ad this section. [ADVERTISEMENT]

Bardarson Studio and House of Diamond Willow. In the Seward boat harbor come sit on the boardwalk and listen to New Age music that is piped outdoors. Wander through two shops that complement each other with fine art and gifts that range from sophisticated to down home. Postal package wrap service, too. [ADVERTISEMENT]

Bear Lake Air and Guide Service. Exclusive floatplane service from beautiful Bear Lake. Flightseeing, air charters, fly-in day fishing. Guiding services for big game hunting. Bunkhouse for rent. Shuttle service available. Reservations welcome, (907) 224-5725. Bear Lake Air Service office located at Bear Creek RV Park, Mile 6.6 Seward Highway on Bear Lake Road. [ADVERTISEMENT]

Command Charters. Sportfishing for halibut, silver salmon, rockfish in beautiful Resurrection Bay/Kenai Fjords. Sightseeing and diving. USCG licensed. Individuals and small parties welcome. All gear provided. May to October. In Alaska phone (907) 694-2833 or 1-800-770-2833. [ADVERTISEMENT]

The Fish House. First and finest fishing charter service in Seward! Record class halibut and silver salmon fishing charters available now. While fishing, enjoy the scenic beauty of the Kenai Fjords National Park — glaciers, mountains, puffins, whales, sea otters and seals. The Fish House also supplies a complete line of fishing tackle, bait, ice and outboard motor repairs. Come, fish Alaska's biggest salmon derby with more than $50,000 in cash and prizes. Derby begins 2nd Saturday in August. Call now for reservations or information on fishing the scenic waters surrounding Seward, Alaska. 1-800-257-7760 or (907) 224-3674. Halibut charters: May 1–Oct. 1; Halibut Derby July 1–July 31. Salmon charters: July 1 – Sept. 20. P.O. Box 1209, Seward, AK 99664. See display ad this section. [ADVERTISEMENT]

J-Dock Vac N' Pac. Don't just catch the flavor of Alaska, take it home! Custom fish processing with the size portions you want, vacuum sealed to lock in fresh-caught taste. Packaged for overnight shipment via Federal Express anywhere in the U.S. or for acceptance as baggage on airlines. Plus: lots of free advice and totally unbelievable fish tales. Top of J-Dock, north ramp on the boardwalk. Small Boat Harbor. For more information call (907) 224-7272. [ADVERTISEMENT]

MACKINAW CHARTERS

Take fish home!

Halibut, Salmon, Bass, Lingcod

Glen Szymoniak, Capt.
USCG Licensed
Tackle furnished
Safe, seaworthy vessel

(907) 224-3910

P.O. Box 825, Seward, AK 99664

(907) 224-5880

BAY VISTA B&B

Spectacular View • Close to Harbor

New • Clean • Queen Beds • TV/VCR • Phone
Fridge • Private Entrance • Dining/Sitting Areas

P.O. Box 1232, Seward, AK 99664

Mariah Charters & Tours

EST. 1981 SEWARD, ALASKA

KENAI FJORDS & CHISWELL ISLANDS WILDLIFE & GLACIER TOURS!

SPECTACULAR NORTHWESTERN LAGOON AND GLACIER TOURS THROUGH GRANITE PASSAGE!

HALIBUT FISHING!

MARIAH CHARTERS & TOURS, based at Seward since 1981, operates in some of the most beautiful marine environment found in Alaska: Kenai Fjords National Park, the North Gulf Coast and Resurrection Bay.

MARIAH and MISTY are comfortable custom-built 43-foot ships.

Daily wildlife and glacier tours to Kenai Fjords National Park and the Chiswell Islands Wildlife Refuge. See them up close and in comfort aboard our 22-passenger vessels, for more personalized tours.
Also offering fishing charters for large Pacific Halibut.

See our log ad under Attractions

FOR PRICES and RESERVATIONS

Mariah Charters & Tours

MARIAH CHARTERS & TOURS
3812 Katmai Circle
Anchorage, AK 99517-1024
Office at Seward Boat Harbor

SEWARD OFFICE ---------------- April 20-Sept. 30
(907) 224-8623 FAX • (907) 224-8625
ANCHORAGE OFFICE ---------- Oct. 1-April 20
(907) 243-1238 FAX • (907) 243-1238

Seward Small Boat Harbor heads Resurrection Bay. (Jerrianne Lowther, staff)

Kenai Fjords Tours. The excitement begins the moment you pull away from the Seward boat harbor! You'll be greeted by playful sea otters, look for whales and porpoise, photograph colorful puffins, bald eagles, and watch a calving glacier. Kenai Fjords Tours is the original Kenai Fjords National Park tour, and continues to be the most popular. Our comfortable cruisers have walk-around decks, so you can easily watch and photograph the magnificent scenery. Our captains are experienced naturalists, so you'll learn all about this coastal wilderness from guides who really know the area. Bring warm clothing and your camera. Lunches and beverages are available on board, or you may bring your own. For reservations or more information about how you can enjoy Alaska's finest nature tour, call toll free 1-800-478-8068. Our office is located in The Landing at the Seward Small Boat Harbor. Look for our display ad in this section. [ADVERTISEMENT]

Major Marine Wildlife Tours. Offering Seward's only wildlife cruise of Resurrection Bay that includes an all-you-can-eat Alaska crab and shrimp buffet with dessert bar. The 4½-hour cruise through Kenai Fjords includes incredible scenery and glaciers, as well as otters, sea lions, puffins, eagles, porpoises and more. Features large boat with reserved seating and inside heated cabin with outside decks for close-up wildlife viewing and photography. The tour departs from Seward's boat harbor mid-May to early September — the 12:30 P.M. trip costs $74; the 6 P.M. trip costs $64. Complete rail and bus packages are available from Anchorage. For reservations or free brochure, call (800) 764-7300 or (907) 274-7300. Major Marine Tours, 509 West 3rd, Anchorage, AK 99501. Seward phone (May to mid-September) (907) 224-8030. [ADVERTISEMENT]

Mariah Charters & Tours. Established in 1981 at Seward, Mariah Charters & Tours takes pride in offering two custom-built 45-foot ships and personalized service. Daily wildlife and glacier tours to Kenai Fjords National Park and the Chiswell Islands Wildlife Refuge. Also offering weekly tours to spectacular Northwestern Lagoon and Glacier through Granite Passage, the most scenic area within the Kenai Fjords National Park. See it all up close and in comfort aboard our 22-passenger vessels for a more personalized, uncrowded tour. Also offering fishing charters for large Pacific halibut. All tackle and bait furnished; experienced crews. Popular exclusive tours for birding and naturalist groups and other interested parties. April 20–Sept. 30. For reservations April 20–Sept. 30 call (907) 224-8623; Oct. 1–April 20 call (907) 243-1238. Office located at Seward Boat Harbor. See display ad this section. [ADVERTISEMENT]

Resurrection Bay Galerie. A fine arts gallery representing the best of Alaska's painters and sculptors. Original paintings and artwork in various media depicting Alaskan settings, way of life and scenic beauty. Sculptures by leading Alaskan artists. Inquire after May 15th regarding schedules for presentations by Alaska's finest Eskimo and other prominent artists. Located on the corner of Fourth and Madison behind the Red Door. Open daily from 10 A.M. to 6 P.M. and by appointment. Phone (907) 224-3212, fax (907) 224-5990. [ADVERTISEMENT]

Trails North, Inc. Our homestead cabin tour has been so popular with cruise ship passengers we are offering it to the public this year. During this unique tour you will experience what it is really like to live in Alaska! A short drive takes you to our beautiful homestead, nestled among tall spruce trees — a storybook setting. Inside the rustic visitor center enjoy a photo display and listen closely as we entertain you with fascinating and humorous stories of our experiences while living in an old mining cabin in the rugged Chugach Mountains. Wander through our historic log cabin, meet friendly sled dogs, hold an adorable husky puppy! Don't forget your camera! May 28–Sept. 5. Departs 1:30 P.M. outside the National Park Building in the boat harbor. 1 hr. 45 min. Adults $25. Some dates not available due to cruise ship tours. Phone (907) 224-3587. [ADVERTISEMENT]

AREA FISHING: Resurrection Bay, coho (silver) salmon to 22 lbs., use herring, troll or cast, July to October; king salmon to 45 lbs., May to Aug.; also bottom fish, flounder, halibut to 300 lbs. and cod, use weighted spoons and large red spinners by jigging, year-round. Charter boats are available.

Kenai Peninsula
STERLING HIGHWAY

Junction with Seward Highway to Homer, Alaska
Includes Seldovia
Alaska Route 1
(See maps, pages 451–452)

Grizzly bear dines on Russian River salmon. *(Ron Levy)*

The Sterling Highway begins 90 miles/145 km south of Anchorage at its junction with the Seward Highway and travels 142.5 miles/229.3 km west and south to the community of Homer. The Sterling Highway junctions with several major Kenai Peninsula side roads: Skilak Lake Loop Road, Swanson River Road, Kenai Spur Highway, Kalifornsky Beach Road, Cohoe Loop Road and Anchor River Beach Road.

From its junction with the Seward Highway at Tern Lake (see SEWARD HIGHWAY section), the Sterling passes through Chugach National Forest and Kenai National Wildlife Refuge. The Kenai Mountains are home to Dall sheep, mountain goats, black and brown bears, and caribou. The many lakes, rivers and streams of the Kenai Peninsula are famous for their sportfishing. The highway also provides access to the Resurrection Pass Trail System.

From Soldotna south, the Sterling Highway follows the west coast of the peninsula along Cook Inlet. There are beautiful views on clear days of volcanic peaks on the Alaska Peninsula.

Physical mileposts on the Sterling Highway show distance from Seward. The Sterling Highway is a paved two-lane highway, open year-round. In summer 1994, watch for road construction along the highway at the community of Sterling.

Emergency medical services: phone 911 or use CB channels 9, 11 or 19.

Sterling Highway Log

Distance from Seward (S) is followed by distance from Anchorage (A) and distance from Homer (H). Physical mileposts show distance from Seward.

S 37.7 (60.7 km) **A 89.3** (143.7 km) **H 141.8** (228.2 km) **Junction** with Seward Highway. First exit southbound (one-way road) for Sterling Highway.

S 37 (59.5 km) **A 90** (144.8 km) **H 142.5** (229.3 km) **Tern Lake Junction.** Second southbound exit (two-way road) for Sterling Highway. This exit provides access to Tern Lake Campground (see description next milepost). Gravel turnout beside Tern Lake with interpretive sign on arctic terns.

S 37.4 (60.2 km) **A 90.4** (145.5 km) **H 142.1** (228.7 km) USFS Tern Lake Campground; 25 campsites, toilets, water, picnic tables, firepits, $6 camping fee. USFS spawning channel for king salmon on Daves Creek at outlet of Tern Lake. Short viewing trail with information signs illustrating use of log weirs and stream protection techniques. ▲

S 38 (61.1 km) **A 91** (146.4 km) **H 141.5** (227.7 km) Avalanche gates. Gravel turnouts.

S 38.3 (61.6 km) **A 91.3** (146.9 km) **H 141.2** (227.2 km) Gravel turnout. Emergency call box.

S 39 (62.8 km) **A 92** (148 km) **H 140.5** (226.1 km) **Daves Creek**, an unusually beautiful mountain stream which flows west into Quartz Creek. Dolly Varden and rainbow averaging 14 inches, June through September. A good place to view spawning salmon in late July and August.

S 40.5 (65.2 km) **A 93.5** (150.5 km) **H 139** (223.7 km) Double-ended gravel turnout to south.

S 40.9 (65.8 km) **A 93.9** (151.1 km) **H 138.6** (223 km) Bridge over Quartz Creek. This stream empties into Kenai Lake. You are now entering one of Alaska's best-known lake and river fishing regions, across the center of the Kenai Peninsula. The burn on the hillsides to the south was part of a Forest Service moose habitat improvement program.

S 41.1 (66.1 km) **A 94.1** (151.4 km) **H 138.4** (222.7 km) Cooper Landing Closed Area. This area is closed to the hunting of Dall sheep. The ridges to the north are a lambing ground for Dall sheep.

S 42.8 (68.9 km) **A 95.8** (154.2 km) **H 136.7** (220 km) Gravel turnouts on Quartz Creek.

S 43.1 (69.4 km) **A 96.1** (154.6 km) **H 136.4** (219.5 km) Double-ended gravel turnout to east on Quartz Creek.

S 43.5 (70 km) **A 96.5** (155.3 km) **H 136** (218.9 km) Double-ended gravel turnout to east.

S 44 (70.8 km) **A 97** (156.1 km) **H 135.5** (218.1 km) Gravel turnout on Quartz Creek.

S 44.3 (71.3 km) **A 97.3** (156.6) **H 135.2** (217.6 km) Solid waste transfer site to east; public dumpsters.

S 45 (72.4 km) **A 98** (157.7 km) **H 134.5** (216.5 km) Quartz Creek Road to Quartz Creek Recreation Area. Quartz Creek Campground, 0.3 mile/0.5 km from the highway, has 31 sites, boat launch, flush toilets, firepits and a $7 camping fee. Crescent Creek Campground, 3 miles/4.8 km from the highway, has nine sites, tables, water and pit toilets; $6 fee. Crescent Creek USFS trail leads 6.2 miles/10 km to the outlet of Crescent Lake. The trailhead is about 1 mile/1.6 km from Crescent Creek Campground. A public-use cabin is located at the lake; permit required for use; not accessible in winter or early spring due to extreme avalanche danger. ▲

The Sterling Highway from the junction with the Seward Highway west to Sterling takes the traveler through the heart of some

STERLING HIGHWAY *Tern Lake Junction to Soldotna, AK*

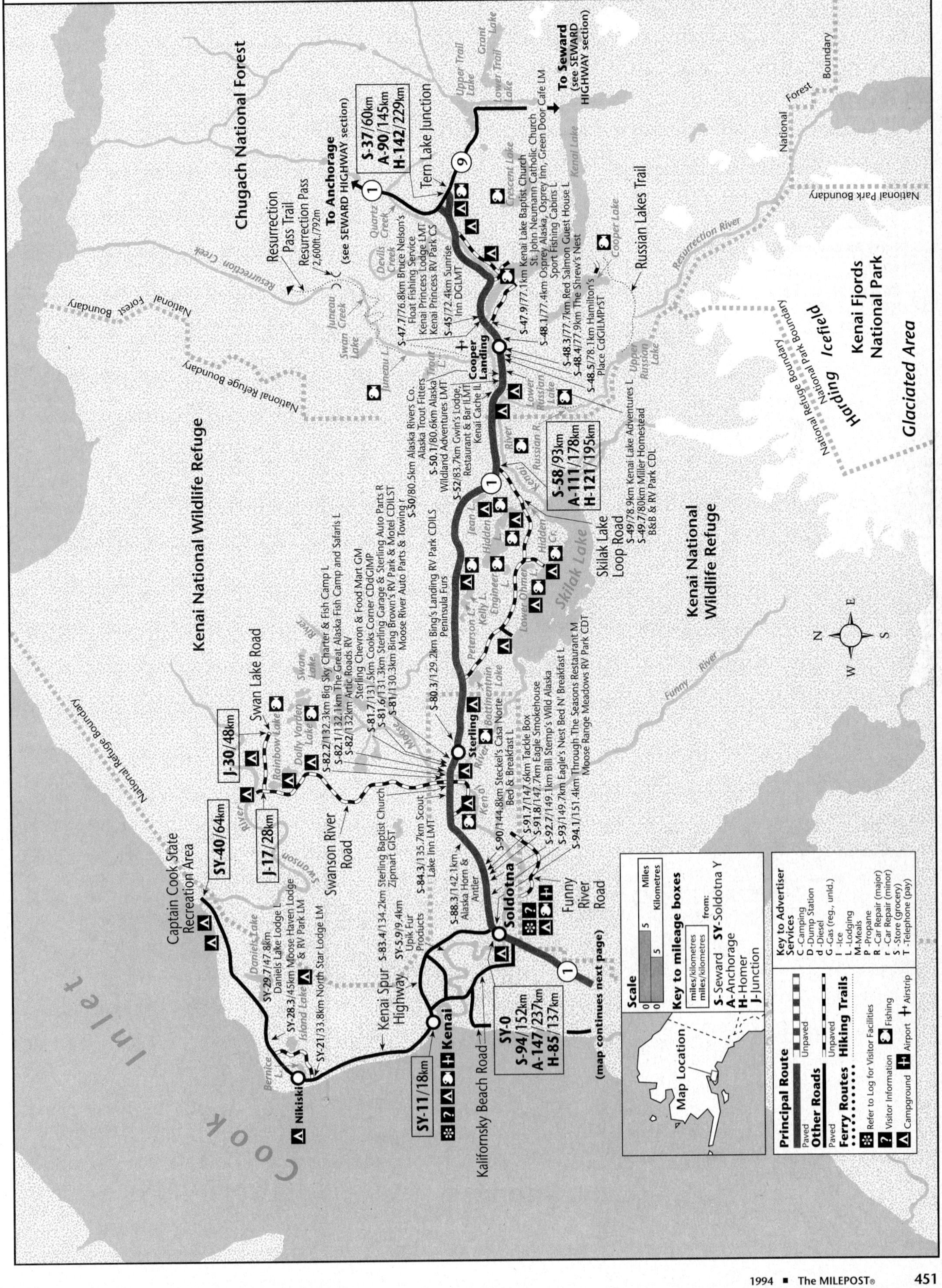

Cook Inlet

Captain Cook State Recreation Area

SY-40/64km

J-30/48km

J-17/28km

Swan Lake Road

Kenai National Wildlife Refuge

National Refuge Boundary

National Forest Boundary

Chugach National Forest

Resurrection Creek

Resurrection Pass Trail

Resurrection Pass 2,600ft./792m

To Anchorage (see SEWARD HIGHWAY section)

S-37/60km
A-90/145km
H-142/229km

Tern Lake Junction

Nikiski

Bernice L.

Daniels Lake

SY-29.7/47.8km Daniels Lake Lodge L

SY-28.3/45km Moose Haven Lodge & RV Park LM

Island Lake

SY-21/33.8km North Star Lodge LM

Swanson River

Rainbow Lake

Dolly Varden Lake

Swan Lake

Swanson River Road

S-82.2/132.3km Big Sky Charter & Fish Camp L

S-82.1/132.1km The Great Alaska Fish Camp and Safaris L

S-82/132km Artic Roads RV

Sterling Chevron & Food Mart GM

S-81.7/131.5km Cooks Corner CDdGIMP

S-81.6/131.3km Sterling Garage & Sterling Auto Parts R

S-81/130.3km Bing Brown's RV Park & Motel CDILST

Moose River Auto Parts & Towing r

Kenai Spur Highway

S-83.4/134.2km Sterling Baptist Church Zipmart GIST

SY-5.9/9.4km Upik Fur Products

S-84.3/135.7km Scout Lake Inn LMT

S-80.3/129.2km Bing's Landing RV Park CDILS Peninsula Furs

Moose River

Juneau L.

Swan Lake

Juneau Creek

Devils Creek

Quartz Creek

S-50/80.5km Alaska Rivers Co.

Alaska Trout Fitters

S-50.1/80.6km Alaska Wildland Adventures LMT

S-52/83.7km Gwin's Lodge, Restaurant & Bar ILMT

Kenai Cache IL

Trout L.

S-47.7/76.8km Bruce Nelson's Float Fishing Service

Kenai Princess Lodge LMT

Kenai Princess RV Park CS

S-45/72.4km Sunrise Inn DGLMT

Cooper Landing

SY-11/18km

Kenai

Kalifornsky Beach Road

S-88.3/142.1km Alaska Horn & Antler

Sterling

Kenai River

Bottinentnin Lake

Peterson L.

Kelly L.

Engineer L.

Jean L.

Hidden L.

Upper Trail Lake

Grant Lake

Lower Trail Lake

Crescent Lake

SY-0
S-94/152km
A-147/237km
H-85/137km

Soldotna

S-90/144.8km Steckel's Casa Norte Bed & Breakfast L

S-91.7/147.6km Tackle Box

S-91.8/147.7km Eagle Smokehouse

S-92.7/149.1km Bill Stemp's Wild Alaska

S-93/149.7km Eagle's Nest Bed N' Breakfast L

S-94.1/151.4km Through The Seasons Restaurant M

Moose Range Meadows RV Park CDT

Funny River Road

(map continues next page)

Lower Ohmer L.

Hidden Cr.

Skilak Lake

Kenai River

Russian R.

Lower Russian Lake

S-58/93km
A-111/178km
H-121/195km

Skilak Lake Loop Road

S-49/78.9km Kenai Lake Adventures L

S-49.7/80km Miller Homestead B&B & RV Park CDL

S-47.9/77.1km Kenai Lake Baptist Church

St. John Neumann Catholic Church

S-48.1/77.4km Osprey Alaska, Osprey Inn, Green Door Cafe LM

Sport Fishing Cabins L

S-48.3/77.7km Red Salmon Guest House L

S-48.4/77.9km The Shrew's Nest

S-48.5/78.1km Hamilton's Place CdGILMPrST

Kenai Lake

To Seward (see SEWARD HIGHWAY section)

Cooper Lake

Upper Russian Lake

Russian Lakes Trail

Funny River

Kenai National Wildlife Refuge

Resurrection River

National Refuge Boundary

National Park Boundary

Harding Icefield

Kenai Fjords National Park

Glaciated Area

National Park Boundary

National Forest Boundary

N E S W

Map Location

Scale

0 — 5 Miles

0 — 5 Kilometres

Key to mileage boxes

miles/kilometres
miles/kilometres

from:
S-Seward **SY**-Soldotna Y
A-Anchorage
H-Homer
J-Junction

Principal Route Paved / Unpaved

Other Roads Paved / Unpaved

Ferry Routes **Hiking Trails**

Refer to Log for Visitor Facilities

Visitor Information

Fishing

Campground

Airport

Airstrip

Key to Advertiser Services

C -Camping
D -Dump Station
d -Diesel
G -Gas (reg., unld.)
I -Ice
L -Lodging
M -Meals
P -Propane
R -Car Repair (major)
r -Car Repair (minor)
S -Store (grocery)
T -Telephone (pay)

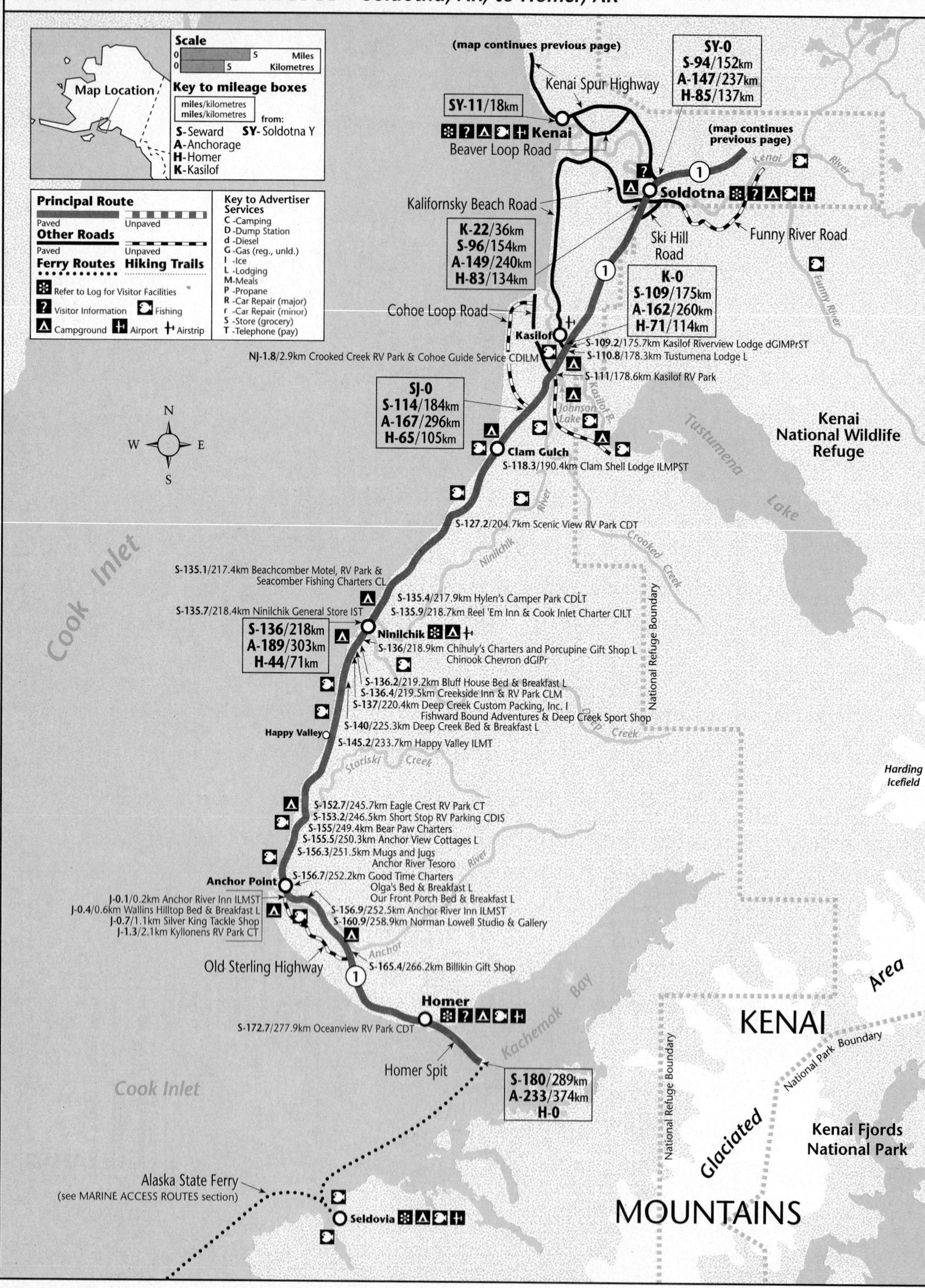
STERLING HIGHWAY Soldotna, AK, to Homer, AK
Map Location
Scale
0 5 Miles
0 5 Kilometres
Key to mileage boxes
miles/kilometres
miles/kilometres
from:
S-Seward
SY-Soldotna Y
A-Anchorage
H-Homer
K-Kasilof
Principal Route
Paved
Unpaved
Other Roads
Paved
Unpaved
Ferry Routes
Hiking Trails
Refer to Log for Visitor Facilities
Visitor Information
Fishing
Campground
Airport
Airstrip
Key to Advertiser Services
C -Camping
D -Dump Station
d -Diesel
G -Gas (reg., unld.)
I -Ice
L -Lodging
M -Meals
P -Propane
R -Car Repair (major)
r -Car Repair (minor)
S -Store (grocery)
T -Telephone (pay)
(map continues previous page)
Kenai Spur Highway
SY-0
S-94/152km
A-147/237km
H-85/137km
SY-11/18km
Kenai
Beaver Loop Road
(map continues previous page)
Soldotna
Kalifornsky Beach Road
K-22/36km
S-96/154km
A-149/240km
H-83/134km
Ski Hill Road
Funny River Road
Kenai River
Funny River
K-0
S-109/175km
A-162/260km
H-71/114km
Cohoe Loop Road
Kasilof
S-109.2/175.7km Kasilof Riverview Lodge dGIMPrST
NJ-1.8/2.9km Crooked Creek RV Park & Cohoe Guide Service CDILM
S-110.8/178.3km Tustumena Lodge L
S-111/178.6km Kasilof RV Park
SJ-0
S-114/184km
A-167/296km
H-65/105km
Johnson Lake
Kasilof R.
N
W
E
S
Clam Gulch
S-118.3/190.4km Clam Shell Lodge ILMPST
Tustumena Lake
Kenai National Wildlife Refuge
River
S-127.2/204.7km Scenic View RV Park CDT
Ninilchik
Crooked Creek
Cook Inlet
S-135.1/217.4km Beachcomber Motel, RV Park & Seacomber Fishing Charters CL
S-135.4/217.9km Hylen's Camper Park CDLT
S-135.7/218.4km Ninilchik General Store IST
S-135.9/218.7km Reel 'Em Inn & Cook Inlet Charter CILT
S-136/218km
A-189/303km
H-44/71km
Ninilchik
S-136/218.9km Chihuly's Charters and Porcupine Gift Shop L
Chinook Chevron dGIPr
National Refuge Boundary
S-136.2/219.2km Bluff House Bed & Breakfast L
S-136.4/219.5km Creekside Inn & RV Park CLM
S-137/220.4km Deep Creek Custom Packing, Inc. I
Fishward Bound Adventures & Deep Creek Sport Shop
S-140/225.3km Deep Creek Bed & Breakfast L
Deep Creek
Happy Valley
S-145.2/233.7km Happy Valley ILMT
Stariski Creek
Harding Icefield
S-152.7/245.7km Eagle Crest RV Park CT
S-153.2/246.5km Short Stop RV Parking CDIS
S-155/249.4km Bear Paw Charters
S-155.5/250.3km Anchor View Cottages L
S-156.3/251.5km Mugs and Jugs
Anchor River Tesoro
River
Anchor Point
S-156.7/252.2km Good Time Charters
Olga's Bed & Breakfast L
Our Front Porch Bed & Breakfast L
J-0.1/0.2km Anchor River Inn ILMST
J-0.4/0.6km Wallins Hilltop Bed & Breakfast L
J-0.7/1.1km Silver King Tackle Shop
J-1.3/2.1km Kyllonens RV Park CT
S-156.9/252.5km Anchor River Inn ILMST
S-160.9/258.9km Norman Lowell Studio & Gallery
Anchor
Old Sterling Highway
S-165.4/266.2km Billikin Gift Shop
Homer
S-172.7/277.9km Oceanview RV Park CDT
Kachemak Bay
Homer Spit
S-180/289km
A-233/374km
H-0
Cook Inlet
KENAI
Glaciated
Area
MOUNTAINS
National Park Boundary
National Refuge Boundary
Kenai Fjords National Park
Alaska State Ferry
(see MARINE ACCESS ROUTES section)
Seldovia

prime fishing country, and provides access to numerous fishing lakes and rivers. *NOTE: The diversity of fishing conditions and frequent regulation changes in all Kenai waters make it advisable to consult locally for fishing news and regulations.*

Beautiful views of Kenai Lake next 3 miles/4.8 km westbound. The lake's unusual color is caused by glacial silt.

Quartz Creek, rainbow, midsummer; Dolly Varden to 25 inches, late May through June. **Crescent Lake**, grayling, July 1 to April 14 (two grayling daily bag and possession limit). **Kenai Lake**, lake trout, May 15 to Sept. 30; trout, May to September; Dolly Varden, May to September. Kenai Lake and tributaries are closed to salmon fishing.

S 45 (72.4 km) **A 98** (157.7 km) **H 134.5** (216.5 km) **Sunrise Inn**. See display ad this section.

S 45.6 (73.4 km) **A 98.6** (158.7 km) **H 133.9** (215.5 km) Large turnout. This is an observation point for Dall sheep on near mountain and mountain goats on Cecil Rhode Mountain (directly across Kenai Lake); use binoculars.

S 46.2 (74.3 km) **A 99.2** (159.6 km) **H 133.3** (214.5 km) Small gravel turnout to east.

S 47 (75.6 km) **A 100** (160.9 km) **H 132.5** (213.2 km) Turnout to east.

S 47.1 (75.8 km) **A 100.1** (161.1 km) **H 132.4** (213.1 km) Kenai Lake Lodge (closed 1993; current status unknown).

S 47.3 (76.1 km) **A 100.3** (161.4 km) **H 132.2** (212.7 km) The Landing on Kenai Lake (current status unknown).

S 47.7 (76.8 km) **A 100.7** (162 km) **H 131.8** (212.1 km) Bean Creek Road, access to Bruce Nelson's guide service, and the Kenai Princess Lodge and RV Park, on the Kenai River. The lodge, which opened in 1990, has an interesting chandelier made from antlers in the lobby.

Bruce Nelson's Float Fishing Service. See display ad this section.

Kenai Princess Lodge at Cooper Landing. 50 deluxe rooms with sun porches, wood stoves, TVs and phones. Located on the Kenai River with outdoor deck, gift shop, dining room, lounge, hot tubs and tour office. River rafting, flightseeing, fishing and horseback riding. Seasonal service March to Jan. Meeting space available. Rates from $79. VISA, MasterCard, American Express. Write Princess Tours®, 2815 2nd Ave., Suite #400, Seattle, WA 98121-1299, or call (800) 426-0500 year-round. [ADVERTISEMENT]

Kenai Princess RV Park at Cooper Landing on the Kenai River. Water, power and septic at each site. General store, showers, laundry and hotel service. Hiking, fishing, river rafting. Seasonal service mid-May to late September. $15 per night; discount for three nights. VISA, MasterCard, American Express accepted. Write Princess Tours®, 2815 2nd Ave., Suite #400, Seattle, WA 98121-1299, or call (800) 426-0500 year-round. [ADVERTISEMENT]

S 47.8 (76.9 km) **A 100.8** (162.2 km) **H 131.7** (211.9 km) Kenai River bridge. Parking at west end of bridge, boat launch at both ends of bridge.

The Kenai River flows directly alongside the highway for the next 10 miles/16 km with several gravel turnouts offering good views.

Kenai River from Kenai Lake to Skilak Lake, including Skilak Lake within a half mile of the Kenai River inlet, closed to king salmon fishing; closed to all fishing April 15 through June 10. Silver salmon 5 to 15 lbs., August through October; pink salmon 3 to 7 lbs., July and August; red salmon 3 to 12 lbs., June 11 through mid-August (be familiar with regulations on closed areas); rainbow and Dolly Varden, June 11 through October.

S 47.9 (77.1 km) **A 100.9** (162.4 km) **H 131.6** (211.8 km) Snug Harbor Road. This side road leads 12 miles/19.3 km to Cooper Lake and trailhead for 23-mile/37-km USFS

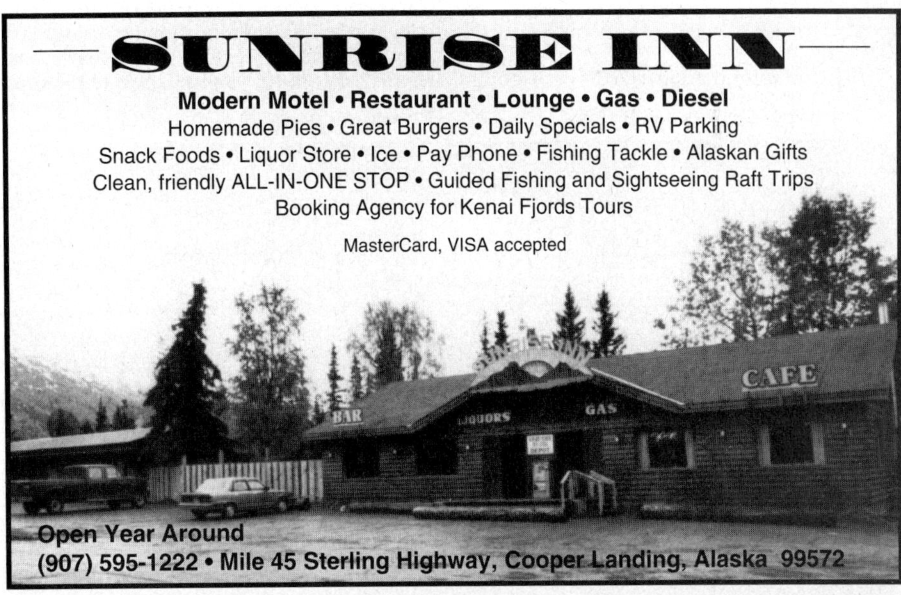

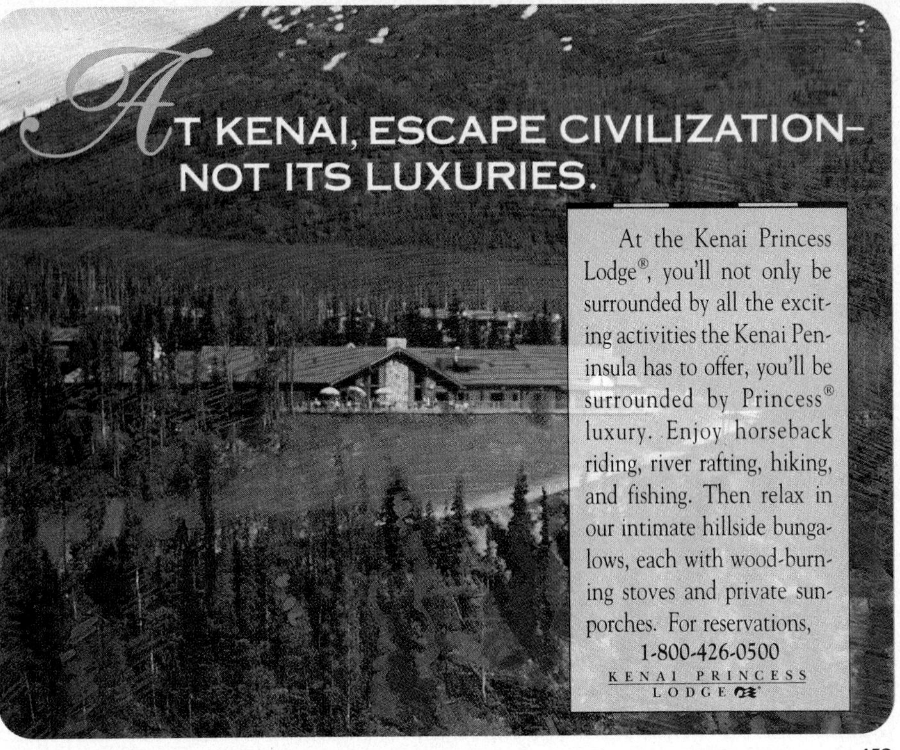

trail to Russian River Campground (see **Milepost S 52.6**). A Baptist church and the St. John Neumann Catholic Church, named after one of the first American saints, are on Snug Harbor Road.

Kenai Lake Baptist Church. See display ad this section.

St. John Neumann Catholic Church. See display ad this section.

S 48.1 (77.4 km) **A 101.1** (162.7 km) **H 131.4** (211.7 km) **Sport Fishing Cabins**. See display ad this section.

Osprey Alaska Inc. See display ad this section.

S 48.2 (77.6 km) **A 101.2** (162.9 km) **H 131.3** (211.3 km) Motel, grocery store and jewelry shop.

S 48.3 (77.7 km) **A 101.3** (163 km) **H 131.2** (211.1 km) **Red Salmon Guest House.** See display ad this section.

S 48.4 (77.9 km) **A 101.4** (163.2 km) **H 131.1** (211 km) **COOPER LANDING** (pop. 386) stretches along several miles of the highway. All visitor facilities. Cooper Landing ambulance, phone 595-1255.

The Shrew's Nest. See display ad this section.

Private Aircraft: Quartz Creek (Cooper Landing) airstrip, 4 miles/6.4 km west; elev. 450 feet/137m; length 2,200 feet/671m; gravel; unattended.

S 48.5 (78.1 km) **A 101.5** (163.3 km) **H 131** (210.8 km) **Hamilton's Place** river resort, only complete stop on the upper Kenai River. Information center for the famous Russian River and surrounding area. Centrally located for day trips to Seward, Soldotna/Kenai, Homer. Make us your Kenai Peninsula headquarters. Chevron services, 24-hour recovery and transport (flatbed) service, propane. (Good Sam road service

providers.) General store, groceries, licenses, tackle, ice, liquor store. Restaurant, lounge. Hair salon. RV hookups, modern cabins with cooking facilities, laundromat, phone. Fish freezing, storage, Federal Express shipping. Hamilton's Place, serving the public since 1952, hopes to make your stay enjoyable. Phone (907) 595-1260; fax (907) 595-1530. See display ad this section. [ADVERTISEMENT] ▲

S 49 (78.9 km) **A 102** (164.1 km) **H 130.5** (210 km) Cooper Landing post office, located in resort; open 9 A.M. to 5 P.M. weekdays and Saturday morning. Pay phone.

Kenai Lake Adventures. See display ad this section.

S 49.4 (79.5 km) **A 102.4** (164.8 km) **H 130.1** (209.4 km) Large paved turnout by Kenai River. The highway winds along the Kenai River. Many spruce trees in this area have died from a spruce bark beetle infestation and are being removed.

S 49.7 (80 km) **A 102.7** (165.3 km) **H 129.8** (208.9 km) **The Miller Homestead,** bed and breakfast and RV park on the Kenai River. Make us your headquarters for Kenai Peninsula guided fishing and float trips. Trophy rainbow, Russian River red salmon, Dolly Varden. Bank fishing available. Salmon charters for Kenai River kings and silvers. Halibut charters arranged. See display ad this section. [ADVERTISEMENT] ▲

S 49.8 (80.1 km) **A 102.8** (165.4 km) **H 129.7** (208.7 km) Haul road used by loggers removing dead spruce trees. Watch for trucks.

S 50 (80.5 km) **A 103** (165.8 km) **H 129.5** (208.4 km) **Alaska Rivers Co.**, right side westbound. Rafting daily on the beautiful Kenai River. Half-day scenic float, or full-day canyon trip with white water. Both trips include homemade picnic lunch, excellent viewing of wildlife, professional guides, all

equipment provided. All ages welcome. Personalized guided drift boat fishing for all species of fish. Overnight accommodations available. Family-owned and operated by

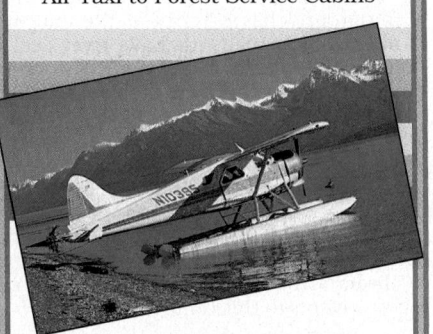

Cooper Landing residents. Gary Galbraith, owner. (907) 595-1226 for reservations or just stop by. [ADVERTISEMENT]

Alaska Troutfitters. See display ad this section.

S **50.1** (80.6 km) A **103.1** (165.9 km) H **129.4** (208.2 km) **Alaska Wildland Adventures.** Don't pass up taking a float or fishing trip with Alaska Wildland Adventures. You'll enjoy this facility's unique and scenic setting on the Kenai River. They offer daily guided float trips along with a delicious Alaskan picnic lunch. You can expect to see wildlife and enjoy the scenery of one of the world's most beautiful rivers. If you're seeking a quality fishing experience, ask about their guided fishing trips for salmon and rainbow trout. This company is well known for its professional guides and deluxe drift boats. All tackle, rods and reels are furnished. Operating since 1977. Within Alaska call toll free (800) 478-4100, or outside Alaska (800) 334-8730, for more information or reservations. See "Kenai River Trips" display ad. [ADVERTISEMENT]

S **50.4** (81.1 km) A **103.4** (166.4 km) H **129.1** (207.8 km) **Juneau Creek,** Dolly Varden and rainbow, mid-June through July.

S **50.5** (81.3 km) A **103.5** (166.6 km) H **129** (207.6 km) Bridge over Cooper Creek.

USFS Cooper Creek Campground. Camping area on the river side of highway (second entrance westbound) has 10 sites, several on the riverbank. Camping area on the other side of the highway has 16 sites. Both have tables, water and firepits. Fee is $6. ▲

S **52** (83.7 km) A **105** (169 km) H **127.5** (205.2 km) **Kenai Cache.** See display ad this section.

Gwin's Lodge, Restaurant and Bar, left side southbound. The best little eating house in Alaska. Where Alaskans always stop for the best food with the fastest service. Heart of the Kenai Peninsula fishing/hunting area. Package store, modern cabins, restaurant,

bar, ice, fishing tackle, shirts, caps, gifts. Your Russian River headquarters. Fishing trips available; local guides. Near Kenai and Russian rivers confluence, Russian Lakes and Resurrection Pass trailheads. Phone (907) 595-1266. [ADVERTISEMENT]

S **52.6** (84.6 km) A **105.6** (169.9 km) H **126.9** (204.2 km) USFS Russian River Campground has 84 sites at the end of a 2-mile/3.2-km road. All have river access, toilets, water, tables and firepits. Fish cleaning stations, covered picnic tables and dump station. The Russian River Campground is often full during the summer, particularly during the Russian River red salmon runs. Arrive early! Fees: $10 single RV occupancy, $16 double RV occupancy, $4 12-hour day-use parking, $5 dump station. Concessionaire-operated. ▲

Bears attracted by the salmon are frequent visitors to this campground.

Russian Lakes USFS trail, trailhead and parking at Mile 0.9/1.4 km on campground road. Lower Russian Lake at Mile 2.6/4.2 km (elev. 500 feet/152m; hiking time one and one-half hours). Good trail to Mile 3/4.8 km. Upper Russian Lake at Mile 12/19.3 km (elev. 690 feet/210m). Trail continues to Cooper Lake at end of Snug Harbor Road (see **Milepost S 47.9**). Public-use cabins along trail (see Cabins in the GENERAL INFORMATION section).

CAUTION: This is brown bear country. Winter use; good snowmobiling to lower lake only, avalanche danger beyond.

The **Russian River.** Closed to all fishing April 15 through June 10. Bait prohibited at all times in Russian River drainage. Check regulations for limits and other restrictions. Red (sockeye) salmon run starts mid-June. Second run begins July 20–25 and lasts about three weeks. Must use flies prior to Aug. 21. Silver (coho) salmon to 15 lbs., run begins mid-August. Catch-and-release only for rainbow trout in lower part of river at all times that season is open.

S 53 (85.3 km) **A 106** (170.6 km) **H 126.5** (203.6 km) Bridge over Kenai River.

S 53.2 (85.6 km) **A 106.2** (170.9 km) **H 126.3** (203.3 km) Well-marked entry point to Resurrection Pass USFS trail; parking at trailhead. This 38-mile-/61-km-long trail climbs to Resurrection Pass (elev. 2,600 feet/792m) and descends to north trailhead near Hope on Turnagain Arm.

S 54 (86.9 km) **A 107** (172.2 km) **H 125.5** (202 km) Kenaitze interpretive site.

S 54.7 (88 km) **A 107.7** (173.3 km) **H 124.8** (200.8 km) Leaving Chugach National Forest lands westbound. Gravel turnout to east. Many turnouts and access to the Kenai River between here and **Milepost S 58.**

S 55 (88.5 km) **A 108** (173.8 km) **H 124.5** (200.4 km) Kenai–Russian River recreation area, access to Russian River ferry. During salmon season this USF&WS campground, a favorite with fishermen, is heavily used; toilets, water, dumpsters, interpretive display, pay phone. Fee is $6 for camping or parking. Privately operated 28-person ferry crosses the Kenai River here offering access to good fishing on opposite bank and to the mouth of the Russian River. Ferry fee is $3 adults round-trip, $1.50 children.

Leaving Game Management Unit 7, entering Unit 15 westbound. Entering Kenai National Wildlife Refuge westbound, administered by the USF&WS; contains more than 1.97 million acres of land set aside to preserve the moose, bear, sheep and other wildlife found here.

S 57.1 (91.9 km) **A 110.1** (177.2 km) **H 122.4** (197 km) Fuller Lake trailhead (well marked), parking. **Lower Fuller Lake,** arctic grayling; **Upper Fuller Lake,** Dolly Varden.

S 58 (93.3 km) **A 111** (178.6 km) **H 121.5** (195.5 km) USF&WS visitor contact station opposite **junction** with Skilak Lake Loop Road. See SKILAK LAKE LOOP ROAD log this page. The information cabin is open Memorial Day through Labor Day; brochures and information on Kenai Peninsula attractions including federal, state and local recreation areas, such as Kenai National Wildlife Refuge.

S 59 (94.9 km) **A 112** (180.2 km) **H 120.5** (193.9 km) **Milepost S 59.** Actual driving distance between here and **Milepost S 61** is 2.6 miles/4.2 km or 0.6 mile/1 km more than the posts indicate.

Skilak Lake Loop Road Log

The 19.1-mile/30.7-km Skilak Lake Loop Road (good gravel) loops south through the Skilak Wildlife Recreation Area to campgrounds, trails and fishing spots.

Distance from east junction (EJ) with Sterling Highway at Milepost S 58 is followed by distance from west junction (WJ) with Sterling Highway at Milepost S 75.2.

EJ 0 WJ 19.1 (30.7 km) **Junction** with Sterling Highway at **Milepost S 58.**

EJ 0.1 (0.2 km) **WJ 19** (30.5 km) Jim's Landing Campground on Kenai River, 0.2 mile/0.3 km from road; five sites, toilets, dumpster, tables, firepits, water, boat launch, parking area.

EJ 0.6 (1 km) **WJ 18.5** (29.7 km) Kenai River trail (6.3-mile/10.1-km hike); parking area.

EJ 2 (3.2 km) **WJ 17.1** (27.5 km) Turnout overlooks scene of Pothole Lake forest fire of 1991; interpretive sign on fire.

EJ 2.4 (3.9 km) **WJ 16.7** (26.8 km) Kenai River trail (6.3-mile/10.1-km hike); parking area.

EJ 3.6 (5.8 km) **WJ 15.5** (24.9 km) Hidden Lake Campground is an exceptionally nice camping area with 44 sites on paved loop roads. Located 0.5 mile/0.8 km in from the road on the lakeshore, it has picnic pavilions, a dump station, wheelchair accessible toilets, tables, water, firepits and boat launch. There is an amphitheater for campfire programs and an observation deck for viewing wildlife. Campground hosts in residence. Camping fee $6; RV $10. Trailer parking area, interpretive exhibits and kitchen shelter with barbecue.

Hidden Lake, lake trout average 16 inches and kokanee 9 inches, year-round, best from May 15 to July 1, use spoon, red-and-white or weighted, by trolling, casting and jigging. This lake is a favorite among local ice fishermen from late December through March.

EJ 4.7 (7.6 km) **WJ 14.4** (23.1 km) Hidden Creek trail (1.5-mile/2.4-km hike); parking area.

EJ 5.5 (8.9 km) **WJ 13.6** (21.8 km) Skilak Lookout trail (2.6-mile/4.2-km hike); parking area.

EJ 6.2 (10 km) **WJ 12.9** (20.7 km) Bear Mountain trail (1-mile/1.6-km hike); parking area with firepit across from lily pond.

EJ 6.9 (11.1 km) **WJ 12.2** (19.6 km) Scenic viewpoint of Skilak Lake.

Skilak Lookout trail. (Ron Levy)

EJ 8.5 (13.6 km) **WJ 10.6** (17 km) Upper Skilak Lake Campground, drive 2 miles/3.2 km around Lower Ohmer Lake; 0.2-mile/0.3-km loop road through campground. There are 26 campsites (some sites on lakeshore), boat launch, toilets and tables; similar facilities to Hidden Lake Campground (**Milepost EJ 3.6**). Camping fee $6.

Lower Ohmer Lake, rainbow 14 to 16 inches, year-round. **Skilak Lake,** offers rainbow and Dolly Varden. Red (sockeye) salmon enter lake in mid-July.

EJ 8.6 (13.8 km) **WJ 10.5** (16.9 km) Lower Ohmer Lake, short side road to parking area on lakeshore; three campsites, toilet, boat launch, firepits and tables.

EJ 9.5 (15.2 km) **WJ 9.6** (15.4 km) Short side road to **Engineer Lake,** boat launch and Seven Lakes trail; turnaround and parking area with firepits. Stocked silver salmon to 15 inches, best in July.

EJ 9.6 (15.4 km) **WJ 9.5** (15.3 km) Engineer Lake wayside; gravel turnout.

EJ 13.8 (22.2 km) **WJ 6.3** (8.5 km) Well-marked 1-mile/1.6-km side road to Lower Skilak Lake Campground; 14 sites, tables, toilets, firepits, boat launch.

CAUTION: Skilak Lake is cold; winds are fierce and unpredictable. Wear life jackets!

EJ 14.2 (22.8 km) **WJ 4.9** (7.8 km) Fire guard station.

EJ 18.7 (30.1 km) **WJ 0.4** (0.6 km) Bottinentnin Lake; well-marked side road leads 0.3 mile/0.5 km to parking area on lakeshore. Shallow lake: No sportfish, but nice area for recreational canoeing.

EJ 19.1 (30.7 km) **WJ 0 Junction** with Sterling Highway at **Milepost S 75.2.**

Return to Milepost S 58 or S 75.2 Sterling Highway

S 60.6 (97.5 km) **A 113.6** (182.8 km) **H 118.9** (191.3 km) **Jean Lake,** small campground (three sites) and picnic area; boat launch, rainbow fishing.

S 61.4 (98.8 km) **A 114.4** (184.1 km) **H 118.1** (190.1 km) Skyline trail to north; double-ended gravel parking area to south.

S 62.3 (100.3 km) **A 115.3** (185.6 km) **H 117.2** (188.6 km) Large gravel turnout to north. Mystery Hills to the north and Hideout Hill to the south.

S 64.5 (103.8 km) **A 117.5** (189.1 km) **H 115** (185.1 km) Gravel turnout to north.

S 68.3 (109.9 km) **A 121.3** (195.2 km) **H 111.2** (179 km) Turnoff to south for Peterson Lake (0.5 mile/0.8 km) and Kelly Lake (1 mile/1.6 km) public campgrounds. Both have tables and firepits for three camping parties, water and boat launch, and parking space for self-contained RVs. **Kelly** and **Peterson lakes** have rainbow population. Access to Seven Lakes trail.

See the GENERAL INFORMATION section for details on Daylight Hours, Holidays and Mosquitoes.

S 70.4 (113.3 km) **A 123.4** (198.6 km) **H 109.1** (175.6 km) Egumen wayside with large parking area. East Fork Moose River and Seven Lakes trail. Half-mile marshy trail to **Egumen Lake** (lake not visible from highway); good rainbow population.

S 71.3 (114.7 km) **A 124.3** (200 km) **H 108.2** (174.1 km) Parking area at entrance to Watson Lake public campground; 0.4-mile/0.6-km drive from highway to small campground with three sites, toilets, picnic tables, fireplaces, water, dumpsters and steep boat launch (suitable for canoes or hand-carried boats). **Watson Lake**, rainbow. Views of Kenai Mountains next few miles westbound. ▲

S 72.8 (117.2 km) **A 125.8** (202.4 km) **H 106.7** (171.7 km) Paved double-ended turnout to south, lake to north.

S 75.2 (121 km) **A 128.2** (206.3 km) **H 104.3** (167.8 km) West **junction** with Skilak Lake Loop Road. See SKILAK LAKE LOOP ROAD log page 457.

Kenai River from Skilak Lake to Soldotna. Consult regulations for legal tackle, limits and seasons. King salmon 20 to 80 lbs., use spinners, excellent fishing June to August; red salmon 6 to 12 lbs., many, but hard to catch, use flies, best from July 15 to Aug. 10; pink salmon 4 to 8 lbs., abundant fish on even years Aug. 1 to Sept. 1, spoons; silver salmon 6 to 15 lbs., use spoons, Aug. 15 to Nov. 1; rainbow, Dolly Varden 15 to 20 inches, June through Sept., use spinners, winged bobber, small-weighted spoon.

S 79 (127.1 km) **A 132** (212.4 km) **H 100.5** (161.7 km) *NOTE: Watch for major road construction westbound to Moose River bridge in 1994.*

S 79.2 (127.4 km) **A 132.2** (212.7 km) **H 100.3** (161.4 km) Kenai Keys Road; access to private campground.

S 80.3 (129.2 km) **A 133.3** (214.5 km) **H 99.2** (159.6 km) Turnoff for Peninsula Furs, private RV park and Bing's Landing State Recreation Site with RV and tent camping, picnic area, water, boat launch, toilets (wheelchair accessible), dumpster and access to Kenai River. Camping fee $6/night or annual pass. Boat launch fee $5 or annual boat launch pass. ▲

Peninsula Furs. See display ad this section.

Swanson River and Swan Lake Roads Log

Swanson River Road leads north 17.2 miles/27.7 km, where it junctions with Swan Lake Road, which leads east 12.7 miles/20.4 km and dead ends at Paddle Lake. Both roads provide access to fishing, hiking trails and canoe trails. **Distance from junction with the Sterling Highway (J) is shown.**

J 0 **Junction** with Sterling Highway at **Milepost S 83.4.** Swanson River Road is a good gravel road but can be rough in spots; slow speeds are advised. There are numerous turnouts suitable for overnight camping in self-contained RVs.

J 0.7 (1.1 km) Robinson Loop Road; rejoins Sterling Highway at **Milepost S 87.5.**

J 1.3 (2.1 km) Airstrip.

J 4.4 (7.1 km) Entering Kenai National Wildlife Refuge.

J 7.9 (12.7 km) **Mosquito Lake,** turnout; 0.5-mile trail to lake. Rainbow trout.

J 9.1 (14.6 km) **Silver Lake** trailhead and parking: 1-mile/1.6-km hike to lake. Rainbow trout and arctic char.

J 9.8 (15.8 km) **Finger Lake** trailhead: 2.3-mile/3.7-km hike to lake. Good arctic char fishing.

J 10.6 (17.1 km) **Forest Lake** wayside, parking: 0.3-mile/0.5-km trail to lake. Rainbow trout; best fished from canoe or raft.

J 13 (20.9 km) **Weed Lake** wayside: small turnout by lake. Rainbow trout.

J 13.3 (21.4 km) **Drake** and **Skookum lakes** trailhead and parking; 2-mile/3.2-km trail. Rainbow trout and arctic char.

J 14 (22.5 km) Access to Breeze Lake.

J 14.2 (22.9 km) **Dolly Varden Lake** Campground; 15 sites, water, toilets, boat launch. Large RVs and trailers note: 0.5-mile/0.8-km access road to campground is narrow and bumpy; check turnaround space before driving in. Fishing for Dolly Varden and rainbow; best in late August and September. ▲

J 14.9 (24 km) Access road to canoe trails to east. Oil field road to west closed to private vehicles. The Swanson River Road was originally built as an access road to the Swanson River oil field. Chevron operated the field from 1958 to 1986; it is currently operated by Unocal.

J 15.7 (25.2 km) **Rainbow Lake** Campground; small three-unit camping area on lakeshore with toilets, water and boat launch. Fishing for Dolly Varden and rainbow trout. *CAUTION: Steep road; difficult turnaround. Large RVs: check visually before driving in.* ▲

J 17.2 (27.7 km) **Junction** with Swan Lake Road. Continue north 0.5 mile/0.8 km for Swanson River Landing at end of Swanson River Road; camping area with picnic tables, firepits, water, toilets, boat launch, large gravel parking area. This is the terminus of the Swanson River canoe route, which begins at Paddle Lake at the end of Swan Lake Road. Log now follows Swan Lake Road east. ▲

J 17.3 (27.8 km) Kenai National Wildlife Refuge Outdoor Environmental Education Center. Reservation required. Educational group use permits obtained at Refuge Visitor Center in Soldotna.

J 20.2 (32.5 km) **Fish Lake**; three sites, tables, firepits, toilets. Fishing for Dolly Varden.

J 21.2 (34 km) **Canoe Lake,** parking. West entrance to Swan Lake canoe route. Fishing for Dolly Varden.

J 21.8 (35.1 km) Sucker Creek wayside; campsite, table, fireplace. **Sucker Lake,** rainbow trout.

J 23.3 (37.5 km) **Merganser Lakes,** 0.5 mile/0.8 km south; rainbow trout.

J 25.4 (40.9 km) Nest Lakes trail, 0.5-mile/0.8-km hike north.

J 26.9 (43.3 km) Large turnout and toilet to west.

J 27 (43.5 km) **Portage Lake.** East entrance to Swan Lake canoe route. Lake is stocked with coho salmon.

J 27.3 (43.9 km) Informal pullout on lake.

J 29.4 (47.3 km) Y in road; bear left.

J 29.9 (48.1 km) End of road. **Paddle Lake** entrance to Swanson River canoe route; parking, picnic table, water and toilet. Fishing for rainbow and Dolly Varden.

Return to Milepost S 83.4 Sterling Highway

S 81 (130.3 km) A 134 (215.6 km) H 98.5 (158.5 km) **STERLING** (pop. 1,732; elev. 150 feet/45m). Traveler services include a gas station, a motel, several restaurants and cafes; gift, grocery, hardware, antique, fur and furniture stores, laundromat and a private camper park. Post office at **Milepost S 81.6.** (Businesses with a Sterling mailing address extend west to **Milepost S 85.**) Nearby recreational opportunities include fishing and the extensive canoe trail system (see description at **Milepost S 82**). Moose River Raft Race and Sterling Days held in July.

Bing Brown's RV Park & Motel. See display ad this section. ▲

Moose River Auto Parts & Towing. See display ad this section.

S 81.1 (130.5 km) A 134.1 (215.8 km) H 98.4 (158.4 km) Gift shop and grocery store.

S 81.6 (131.3 km) A 134.6 (216.6 km) H 97.9 (157.6 km) Sterling post office (Zip code 99672).

Sterling Garage & Sterling Auto Parts. See display ad this section.

S 81.7 (131.5 km) A 134.7 (216.8 km) H 97.8 (157.4 km) **Cook's Corner.** See display ad this section. ▲

S 82 (132 km) A 135 (217.3 km) H 97.5 (156.9 km) **Arctic Roads RV.** See display ad this section.

Sterling Chevron & Food Mart. See display ad this section.

S 82 (132 km) A 135 (217.3 km) H 97.5 (156.9 km) Pay phone on highway just before turnoff for Isaak Walton State Recreation Site, located at the confluence of the Kenai and Moose rivers. Paved access road, 25 campsites, parking, tables, toilets, water and dumpster. Camping fee $8/night or annual pass. Boat launch ($5 fee or annual boat launch pass) and good access to Kenai River. A small log cabin, totem pole and an information sign about Moose River archaeological site. ▲

Bridge over Moose River. *CAUTION: Drive carefully during fishing season when fishermen walk along bridge and highway.*

NOTE: Major construction eastbound to Kenai Keys Road in 1994.

Canoe rentals and shuttle bus service to the head of the canoe trail system are available by the Moose River bridge. This is the terminus of the Swan Lake canoe trail. There are two canoe routes in Kenai National Wildlife Refuge: Swan Lake route, a 60-mile/97-km route connecting 30 lakes; and the Swanson River route, an 80-mile/129-km route linking 40 lakes. Guided canoe tours and fishing charters are available. Portions of the canoe system may be traveled taking anywhere from one to four days. Contact Kenai National Wildlife Refuge, Box 2139, Soldotna 99669 for details. See SWANSON RIVER AND SWAN LAKE ROADS log this page.

Moose River, 0.3 mile/0.4 km of fishing down to confluence with Kenai River. Sockeyes here in June. Big summer run of reds follows into August; silvers into October.

Kenai and **Moose rivers** (confluence), Dolly Varden and rainbow trout, salmon (king, red, pink, silver). June 15 through October for trout; year-round for Dolly Varden. King salmon from May through July, pink salmon in August and silver salmon from August through October. This is a fly-fishing-only area from May 15 through Aug. 15; closed to fishing from boats, May 15 until the end of the king salmon season or July 31, whichever is later.

S 82.1 (132.1 km) **A 135.1** (217.4 km) **H 97.4** (156.7 km) **The Great Alaska Fish Camp and Safaris.** Kenai River charters for kings, reds and silvers, and canoe rentals for Swan Lake's Wilderness Canoe Trail. Most complete fishing and safari lodge in Alaska. Deluxe lodge packages and one-day fishing

trips out of Anchorage. Alaska's premier small group (six) safaris to Denali, glaciers and brown bear gatherings. Write HC 01 Box 218, Sterling, AK 99672. Phone (907) 262-4515 or (800) 544-2261. [ADVERTISEMENT]

S 82.2 (132.3 km) **A 135.2** (217.6 km) **H 97.3** (156.6 km) **Big Sky Charter & Fish Camp.** See display ad this section.

S 82.6 (132.9 km) **A 135.6** (218.2 km) **H 96.9** (155.9 km) Airstrip. Restaurant and bar.

S 83 (133.6 km) **A 136** (218.9 km) **H 96.5** (155.3 km) Truck weigh station and senior center.

S 83.4 (134.2 km) **A 136.4** (219.5 km) **H 96.1** (154.7 km) Convenience store with gas, church, laundromat and showers located here.

Sterling Baptist Church. See display ad this section.

ZIPMART. See display ad this section.

S 83.4 (134.2 km) **A 136.4** (219.5 km) **H 96.1** (154.7 km) Swanson River Road turnoff to north (see SWANSON RIVER AND SWAN LAKE ROADS log page 459). Scout Lake Loop Road turns off to south and rejoins the Sterling Highway at **Milepost S 85** (see that milepost for description). Sterling elementary school.

S 84.3 (135.7 km) **A 137.3** (221 km) **H 95.2** (153.2 km) **Scout Lake Inn,** a family-owned and operated restaurant and motel, is located in the heart of the Swanson River canoe system, Kenai and Moose River fishing area. Our restaurant is well known for fine food and has a large seating capacity. RV park, showers, laundry. Visit Bev's Alaskan Gift Shop. Fishing charters arranged. Tour buses welcome. See display ad this section. [ADVERTISEMENT]

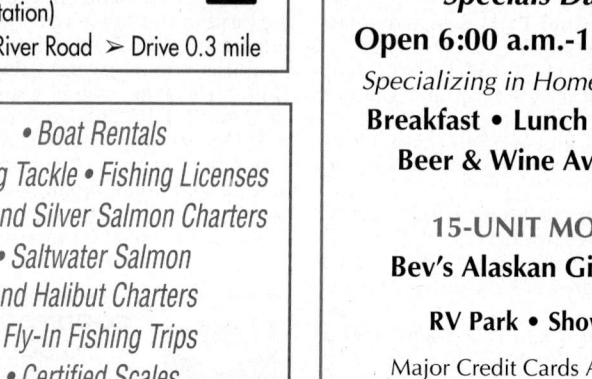

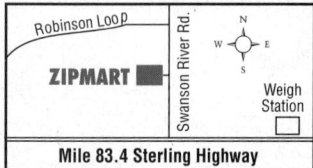

S 85 (136.8 km) **A 138** (222.1 km) **H 94.5** (152.1 km) Scout Lake State Recreation Site to south on Scout Lake Loop Road; 12 campsites, water, toilets, covered picnic shelter. Camping fee $6/night or annual pass. Scout Lake Loop Road loops south of the Sterling Highway for 7 miles/11.3 km and rejoins the Sterling Highway at **Milepost S 83.4.** Turn here and drive down Scout Lake Loop Road 1.6 miles/2.6 km to turnoff for Morgan's Landing: follow side road 2.4 miles/3.9 km to reach Morgan's Landing State Recreation Area; $8 nightly fee per vehicle or annual pass, 40 developed campsites with 10 pull-through sites and some double sites, toilets and water. The Alaska State Parks area headquarters is located here. (This campground was renovated in 1993.) Good access from here to the **Kenai River,** king salmon from mid-June through July, average 30 lbs. Red (sockeye) salmon average 8 lbs., use flies in July and August; silver (coho) salmon to 15 lbs., August and September, use lure; pink salmon average 4 lbs. with lure, best in July, even-numbered years only; rainbow and Dolly Varden, use lure, June through August.

S 87.5 (140.8 km) **A 140.5** (226.1 km) **H 92** (148.1 km) Robinson Loop Road.

S 88 (141.6 km) **A 141** (226.9 km) **H 91.5** (147.3 km) St. Theresa's Drive.

S 88.3 (142.1 km) **A 141.3** (227.4 km) **H 91.2** (146.8 km) **Alaska Horn & Antler.** See display ad this section.

S 90 (144.8 km) **A 143** (230.1 km) **H 89.5** (144 km) **Steckel's Casa Norte Bed and Breakfast and Sportfishing.** Welcome to the Kenai Peninsula, home of the famous Kenai River and its record-breaking king salmon. Come ... stay with us and settle into one of our private, comfortable rooms and enjoy our sincere hospitality. Licensed guide available. Sportfishing packages — salmon, halibut. Hosts: Capt. John and Marti Steckel (907) 262-1257 or write P.O. Box 2468, Soldotna, AK 99669. See display ad. [ADVERTISEMENT]

S 91.3 (146.9 km) **A 144.3** (232.2 km) **H 88.2** (141.9 km) Gas station and store.

S 91.7 (147.6 km) **A 144.7** (232.9 km) **H 87.8** (141.3 km) **The Tackle Box,** just 2 miles north of Soldotna, has one of the most complete selections of fishing tackle on the peninsula. The coffee is always on. Fishing information is free. Guided fishing trips, boat engine repair, and boat rentals available. Alaska-owned and operated. See display ad this section. [ADVERTISEMENT]

S 91.8 (147.7 km) **A 144.8** (233 km) **H 87.7** (141.1 km) **Eagle Smokehouse.** We will smoke (kipper) or pickle your salmon or halibut for you. We also vacuum pack and freeze your fresh fish. No luck fishing? We have all of the above for sale plus our smoked salmon/cream cheese spread in two flavors, pickled and fresh Alaskan shrimp and four flavors of smoked salmon jerky. All our products are all natural with no artificial colors, flavors or preservatives — no nitrites. We box and ship. Free samples. Box 4085, Soldotna, AK 99669. Phone and fax (907) 262-7007. [ADVERTISEMENT]

S 92.5 (148.9 km) **A 145.5** (234.2 km) **H 87** (140 km) State Division of Forest, Land and Water Management. Fire danger indicator sign.

S 92.7 (149.1 km) **A 145.7** (234.5 km) **H 86.8** (139.7 km) Mackey Lake Road. Private lodging is available on this side road.

Bill Slemp's Wild Alaska. See display ad this section.

S 93 (149.7 km) **A 146** (235 km) **H 86.5** (139.2 km) **Eagles' Nest Bed N' Breakfast.** See display ad this section.

S 93.1 (149.8 km) **A 146.1** (235.1 km) **H 86.4** (139 km) Loren Lake.

S 94 (151.2 km) **A 147** (236.6 km) **H 85.5** (137.6 km) Four-lane highway begins and leads through Soldotna.

S 94.1 (151.4 km) **A 147.1** (236.7 km) **H 85.4** (137.4 km) Turn on East Redoubt Street and follow the gravel road 0.5 mile/0.8 km for private RV park and Swiftwater Park municipal campground. The campground has 20 spaces on Kenai River (some pull-throughs), some tables, firepits, firewood, phone, dump station, two-week limit, litter barrels, toilets, boat landing, fee charged, good fishing. ▲

Moose Range Meadows RV Park, on the beautiful Kenai River, has 49 spaces (some pull-throughs) with picnic tables, firepits, firewood, dump station, clean toilet facilities, potable water, boat launch, pay phone. Tent campers welcome. Full-time attendant. Excellent fishing. Turn on East Redoubt Street. See display ad this section. [ADVERTISEMENT] ▲

Through the Seasons Restaurant specializes in fine dining in pleasant surroundings. Open daily for lunch and dinner. Sunday breakfast 9:30 A.M.-1 P.M. Lunch: homemade breads, gourmet soups, sandwiches made with freshly roasted meats. Dinner: seafoods, homemade pasta, steak and nightly specials. Through the Seasons cheesecakes. Fine wines and imported beers. See display ad in Soldotna section. [ADVERTISEMENT]

S 94.2 (151.6 km) **A 147.2** (236.9 km) **H 85.3** (137.3 km) **Junction** with Kenai Spur Highway. This junction is called the Soldotna Y.

There are two ways to reach the city of Kenai (see description of city on page 474): Turn right (westbound) at the Y, physical **Milepost S 94.2,** and continue 11 miles/17.7 km northwest to Kenai via the Kenai Spur Highway; or continue on the Sterling Highway to **Milepost S 96.1** and turn right (southbound) on the Kalifornsky Beach Road and continue 9.3 miles/14.9 km to Kenai via the Warren Ames Memorial Bridge. For details see KENAI SPUR HIGHWAY log on page 473 and KALIFORNSKY BEACH ROAD log on page 478. Description of Soldotna follows; description of Kenai begins on page 474.

S 94.4 (151.9 km) **A 147.4** (237.2 km) **H 85.1** (137 km) Soldotna DOT/PF highway maintenance station. Turn east here for

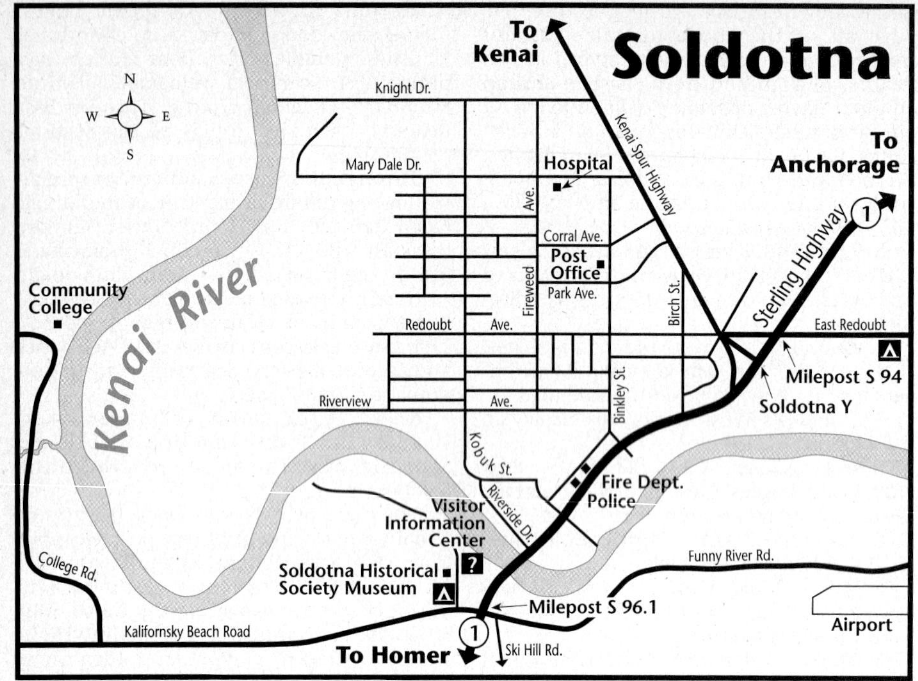

access to Soldotna Creek Park (day use only). Follow road behind restaurant.

S 95 (152.9 km) **A 148** (238.2 km) **H 84.5** (136 km) Soldotna city center; Peninsula Center shopping mall. Turn on Binkley Street for access to fire station, police station and post office. See description of city following. See city map this page.

Homer-bound travelers continue south across the Kenai River bridge past visitor center, then turn west on Kalifornsky Road for Soldotna city campground; turn east off the Sterling Highway on Funny River Road for airport. See descriptions at **Milepost S 96.1** on page 478.

Log of the Sterling Highway continues on page 478.

Soldotna

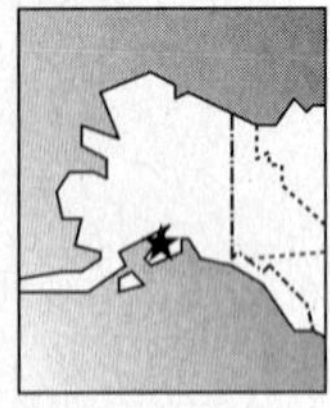

S 95.2 (153.2 km) **A 148.2** (238.5 km) **H 84.3** (135.7 km) On the western Kenai Peninsula, the city stretches over a mile southwest along the Sterling Highway and northwest along the Kenai Spur Highway. **Population:** 3,771; Kenai Peninsula Borough 40,802. **Emergency Services:** Phone 911 for all emergency services. **Alaska State Troopers** at Mile 22 Kalifornsky Beach Road just off Sterling Highway, phone 262-4453. **City Police**, phone 262-4455. **Fire Department**, phone 262-4792. **Ambulance**, phone 262-4500. **Hospital**, Central Peninsula General, 1 mile/1.6 km north of Public Safety Bldg. off Marydale Drive, phone 262-4404.

Visitor Information: The Kenai Peninsula Visitor Information Center is located in downtown Soldotna on the Sterling Highway south of the Kenai River bridge. The center is open seven days a week, mid-May through mid-September, 9 A.M. to 7 P.M. The remainder of the year the center is open weekdays from 9 A.M. to 5 P.M. Write: Greater Soldotna Chamber of Commerce, Box 236-MP, Soldotna 99669; phone 262-1337 or 262-9814.

Elevation: 115 feet/35m. **Climate:** Average daily temperature in July, 63°F to 68°F/17°C to 20°C; January, 19°F to 23°F/-7°C to -5°C. Annual precipitation, approximately 18 inches. **Radio:** KGTL 620, KFQD 750, KSRM 920, KGTL-FM 100.9/103.5, MBN-FM 95.3/97.7, KWHQ-FM 1001, KPEN-FM 101-7, KSLD 1140, KZXX 980. **Television:** Channels 2, 4, 9, 12 and 13 via booster line from Anchorage, cable and KANG public education channel. **Newspapers:** *Peninsula Clarion* (daily), *The Dispatch* (weekly).

Private Aircraft: Soldotna airstrip, 0.9 mile/1.4 km southeast; elev. 107 feet/32m; length 5,000 feet/1,524m; asphalt; fuel 100LL; unattended.

The town of Soldotna was established in the 1940s because of its strategic location at the Sterling–Kenai Spur Highway junction. Soldotna was named for a nearby stream (it is a Russian word meaning "soldier," although some believe the name came from an Indian word meaning the "stream fork").

Today, Soldotna is a business center, sportfishing capital of the Kenai Peninsula and a bedroom community for oil-related industry in Cook Inlet.

Soldotna was incorporated as a first-class city in 1967. It has a council–manager form of government. Kenai Peninsula Borough headquarters and state offices of the Depts. of Highways, Public Safety, Fish and Game, and Forest, Land and Water Management are located here. Soldotna is also headquarters for the Kenai Peninsula Borough school district. There are three elementary schools, a junior high school and two high schools. University of Alaska Kenai Peninsula College is also located in Soldotna.

Area terrain is level and forested, with many streams and lakes nearby. Large rivers of the area are the Swanson River, the Moose River, and the Kenai River, which empties into Cook Inlet just south of Kenai. The area affords a majestic view of volcanic mountains across Cook Inlet. Always snow-covered, they are Mount Spurr (elev. 11,100 feet/3,383m), which erupted in 1992; Mount Iliamna (elev. 10,016 feet/3,053m), which has three smaller peaks to the left of the larger one; and Mount Redoubt (elev. 10,197 feet/3,108m), which was identified by its very regular cone shape until it erupted in December 1989.

The Soldotna–Kenai area offers a wide variety of recreation and all goods and services. Many fishing guides operate out of Soldotna; write the chamber of commerce for more information.

ACCOMMODATIONS

All modern conveniences and facilities are available, including a 24-hour supermarket, banks, hotels/motels, restaurants and drive-ins, medical and dental clinics, bowling alley, golf course, veterinarians, churches and a library. Two shopping malls are located on the Sterling Highway near the center of town. Bed-and-breakfast accommodations are available.

Soldotna Creek Park (day use only), located behind Hutchings Chevrolet at the Y, has picnic facilities and offers river access for bank fishing.

The visitor information center is located in downtown Soldotna. (Jerrianne Lowther, staff)

Accommodations on the Kenai. One-call reservations service for bed & breakfast inns, lodges, cabins and condos. Hotels and motels, too. Personally inspected by AOK staff. Let us book your halibut, salmon and fly-in fishing charters. Deposit required to confirm reservations. Phone (907) 262-2139. P.O. Box 2956, Soldotna, AK 99669. [ADVERTISEMENT]

Alaska's Kenai Peninsula Lodging. Private fully furnished apartments. Downtown Soldotna. 162 S. Birch St. Walk to Kenai River — city parks — restaurants — shopping. Living room — equipped kitchenette. Private bathroom. Queen–twin beds. In-room telephone, cable TV. Affordable daily–weekly rates. Same location 16 yrs. Fax (907) 262-1902. Telephone (907) 262-1002. P.O. Box 343, Soldotna, AK 99669. [ADVERTISEMENT]

Best Western King Salmon Motel and Restaurant in Soldotna on Kenai Spur Highway. Large rooms, queen beds, some kitchenettes, cable TV, phones. Free in-room movies, coffee. Restaurant serves early fisherman's breakfast, lunch, dinner. Steaks, seafood, salad bar. Beer and wine available. Phone (907) 262-5857; fax (907) 262-9441. See display ad this section. [ADVERTISEMENT]

Cashman's Lodging. Finest lodging on the Kenai Peninsula. Spacious cabins on the Kenai River. Also, condos with one to three bedrooms, one or two baths, complete

kitchens. Laundry facilities available. Centrally located in Soldotna. Complete services for fishing or hunting. Groups and combination packages our specialty. (907) 262-4359. Write Box 3143, Soldotna, AK 99669. [ADVERTISEMENT]

SOLDOTNA ADVERTISERS

Accommodations on the Kenai ....Ph. (907) 262-2139
Alaska Recreational Rentals ....Ph. (907) 262-2700
Alaskan Game Fisher ....Ph. (907) 262-2980
Alaska's Kenai Peninsula Lodging .Downtown
Beemun's V & S Variety Store ....35277 Kenai Spur Hwy.
Best Western King Salmon Motel & Restaurant ....Kenai Spur Hwy.
Birch Tree Gallery......Mile 0.2 Funny River Rd.
Blazy's B & B....................Ph. (907) 262-4591
Bo's Fishing Guide Service ....Ph. (907) 262-5154
Cashman's Lodging..........Ph. (907) 262-4359
Ceramic Center..............Kalifornsky Beach Rd.
China Sea Restaurant .....Blazy's Soldotna Mall
Donna's Country & Victorian Gifts...........................Blazy's Soldotna Mall
Edgewater RV Park...........Ph. (907) 262-7733
Eighth Annual Soldotna Silver Salmon Derby ....Area guides and tackle shops
Fenton Bros. Guided Sportfishing................Ph. (907) 262-2502
First Baptist Church..................159 Binkley St.
Foto Quick.........................Ph. (907) 262-4279
Fun Fishin'.........................Ph. (907) 262-9655
Goodnight Inn Lodge.......Ph. (907) 262-4584
Greater Soldotna Chamber of Commerce ....Sterling Hwy. & Kenai River Bridge
Greatland Guide Service...Ph. (907) 567-3325
Harbor Terrace Inn...........Ph. (907) 262-9282
Harry Gaines Kenai River Fishing Guide..............Ph. (907) 262-5097
Irish Lord Charters............Ph. (907) 262-9512
Jim Rusk Fishing Guide.....Ph. (907) 262-4911
John Metcalf's Jughead Salmon Charters.......................Ph. (907) 277-1218
Johnson Bros. Guides & Outfitters ....Downtown
Kenai Custom Seafoods....Mile 14.4 Kalifornsky Beach Rd.
Kenai Peninsula Apts. ....Ph. (907) 262-1383
Kenai River Lodge Motor Inn.......................Kenai River Bridge
Ken's Alaskan Tackle ....Kenai River Bridge
King's Budget Charters ....Ph. (907) 262-4564
King's Kitchen Bed and Breakfast.................................309 Vine St.
Klondike City................................Downtown
Knight Manor Bed & Breakfast......................Ph. (907) 262-2438
Lakeside Bed & Breakfast .Ph. (907) 262-7110
Moose Range Meadows RV Park.....................Mile 94 Sterling Hwy.
Mykel's Restaurant...Mile 0.2 Kenai Spur Hwy.
Northcountry Fair............Ph. (907) 262-7715
Northstar ....Ph. (800) 869-9418
Oil Exchange, The ....Mile 1 Kenai Spur Hwy.
Orca Lodge ....Ph. (907) 262-5649
Peninsula Center Mall...................Downtown
Posey's Kenai River Hideaway....................Ph. (907) 262-7430
River Quest RV Park..........Ph. (907) 283-4991
River Terrace RV Park ....Ph. (907) 262-5593
Riverside Auto Supply Inc. ..Kenai River Bridge
RiverSide House, The........Ph. (907) 262-0500
Riverside Resort Bed and Breakfast...................355 Riverside Dr.
Rod 'N Real Charters ....Ph. (907) 262-6064
Sal's Klondike Diner......................Downtown
Slammin Salmon Charters.......................Ph. (907) 262-5661
Soldotna Bed & Breakfast......................Ph. (907) 262-4779
Soldotna Inn............Mile 0.2 Kenai Spur Hwy.
Soldotna Wash & Dry ....At the Y
Sports Den.........................Ph. (907) 262-7491
Spruce Avenue Bed & Breakfast.......................Ph. (907) 262-9833
Steckel's Casa Norte Bed & Breakfast ....Ph. (907) 262-1257
Through the Seasons Restaurant ....At the Y
Windwalkers Trading Post, Inc. .....Peninsula Center Mall

Orca Lodge. Beautiful, luxurious, handcrafted Kenai riverfront log cabins. Roomy cabins with loft and full bath accommodate up to four. Community picnic area for outdoor cooking. Great bank fishing or hire our

professional guides and catch the trophy of a lifetime. Ideal base camp for hunters. Hunter booking service. Open year-round. (907) 262-5649. [ADVERTISEMENT]

The RiverSide House. Hotel, restaurant and lounge, smack dab on the banks of the Kenai River. 26 rooms and a two-bedroom apartment, all completely renovated in 1993. Fine dining and lounge service overlooking the river. Fishing guides available May through October. 44611 Sterling Hwy., Soldotna, AK 99669. (907) 262-0500, 1-800-200-0504. [ADVERTISEMENT]

Riverside Resort Bed and Breakfast. Live the Alaskan dream. Stay in a beautiful log home overlooking famous Kenai River. Two rooms overlook river, third has private bath. Provisions: airport/guide service transportation, delicious home-cooked breakfasts (from menu) and/or sack lunches. Laundry facilities. Color cable TVs. Boat docking and excellent bank fishing. Walk-ins welcome. Phone/fax (907) 262-5371 or write 355 Riverside Dr., Soldotna, AK 99669. [ADVERTISEMENT]

Spruce Avenue Bed & Breakfast. Native Alaskan art decor in a large, conveniently located nonsmoking residence. Delicious breakfasts feature Finnish fare and a homey, friendly atmosphere. Hosts are long-time Alaskans. Information about fishing, sightseeing, available. Moderate rates from $50–$70. Sharon and Richard Waisanen, 35985 Pioneer Dr., Soldotna, AK 99669; (907) 262-9833. [ADVERTISEMENT]

For Swiftwater Campground, turn on East Redoubt Street at **Milepost S 94.1** Sterling Highway. Soldotna Alaska Purchase Centennial Park Campground is 0.1 mile/0.2 km from the Sterling Highway just south of the Kenai River bridge; turn west at **Milepost S 96.1**. Both campgrounds are operated by the city of Soldotna (fee charged); register for camping at either park at the Soldotna Alaska Purchase Centennial Park office. Dump stations at both campgrounds. These campgrounds are heavily used; good idea to

Albert W. Franzmann

D. Marshall Clark

D. Marshall Clark

check in early. There are several private campgrounds located in and near Soldotna; see ads this section. ▲

Edgewater RV Park is located on the banks of the Kenai River, across from the visitors center in downtown Soldotna. Full and partial hookups, laundry and shower facilities, grassy sites, picnic tables, guide service and fish cleaning facilities available. Complimentary weekly salmon/halibut barbecue. Call (907) 262-7733 or write P.O. Box 3456, Soldotna, AK 99669 for reservations and information. [ADVERTISEMENT] ▲

River Quest RV Park (formerly Porter's Campground) is located on the world-famous Kenai River with 2,000 feet of water frontage. 200-plus campsites, partial hookups, pull-throughs, tent sites, laundry, shower, phones, boat gas, propane, convenience store and snack bar all available on location. Full hookups planned for 1994. Boat launching, bank fishing, and guide service, fish weighing/cleaning facilities. Under new management. Your hosts: Jay and Debra Denney. For information or reservations call (907) 283-4991 or write P.O. Box 3457, Soldotna, AK 99669. [ADVERTISEMENT] ▲

River Terrace RV Park features 1,100 feet of Kenai River frontage in Soldotna at the bridge. Walking distance to Kenai Peninsula Visitor Center, restaurants, groceries and downtown shopping malls. Full and partial hookups, riverfront sites. Heated restrooms, showers with unlimited hot water, laundry. World-famous red salmon fishing from the riverbank. 800,000 salmon swam by our property in 1993, by sonar count. Boat rentals available. Tackle shop, ice, fish processing and taxidermy available on premises. Let our park resident master guides provide custom king and silver salmon charters on the Kenai and Kasilof rivers. Also available: saltwater halibut/salmon combination charters. Reserve early to avoid disappointment. Phone (907) 262-5593; fax (907) 262-9229; write P.O. Box 322, Soldotna, AK 99669. [ADVERTISEMENT] ▲

TRANSPORTATION

Air: Charters available. Soldotna airport is south of Soldotna 2 miles/3.2 km off the Sterling Highway; at **Milepost S 96.1**, just after crossing Kenai River bridge, turn left (east) on Funny River (Airport) Road 2 miles/3.2 km. **Local:** Taxi service, car rentals, vehicle leasing, boat rentals and charters.

ATTRACTIONS

Join in local celebrations. July's big event is the annual Soldotna Progress Days, held during the fourth weekend of the month. Activities include a parade, two days of rodeo, autocross competition, car show, community barbecue and dance, arts and crafts show, and other events.

During the month of August, the Cook Inlet Professional Sportfishing Assoc. (CIPSA) sponsors the annual Soldotna Silver Salmon Derby. 1994 marks the 8th year for this event. Daily prizes are awarded for the heaviest and smallest silver salmon caught, in addition to other categories. Several thousand dollars in cash and merchandise is awarded in this exciting event. The Peninsula Winter Games take place in February with a weekend in both Soldotna and Kenai. Activities include an ice sculpture contest, cross-country ski race, ice bowling and snow volleyball. Games, booths, concessions and demonstrations are held throughout both weekends. The Alaska State Championship Sled Dog Races and Dog Weight Pull Contest take place during the Winter Games.

Donna's Country & Victorian Gifts at Blazy's Soldotna Mall. A shopper's delight. The perfect place to spend an afternoon while your husband goes fishing. Roomfuls of wonderful things, constantly

changing, relaxing atmosphere. Don't miss our Santa room! You'll find things in our shoppe you never thought you'd find in Alaska! [ADVERTISEMENT]

Fish the Kenai River. Soldotna is one of Alaska's best-known sportfishing headquarters, and many claim that some of the world's best fishing is here at the Kenai River, which flows next to town. Many charter boats and fishing guides for Kenai River fishing are located in the Soldotna area. In May 1985, Les Anderson of Soldotna landed a 97-lb., 4-oz. king salmon, a new world's record. The mounted fish is on display at the Kenai Peninsula Visitor Information Center.

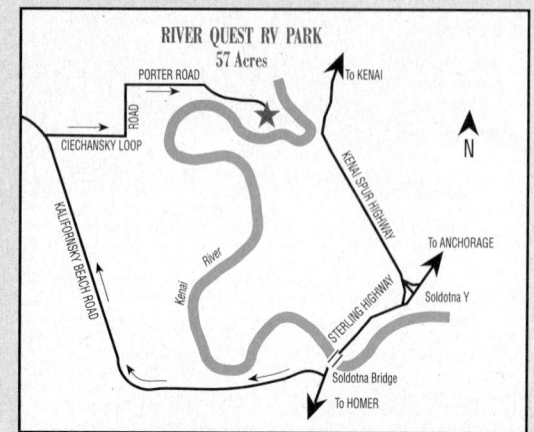

Soldotna gets very busy during fishing season, and for those fishermen who want a more remote fishing spot — or for visitors who want to see wildlife and glaciers — there are fly-in fishing trips for rainbow, grayling, salmon and Dolly Varden, and flightseeing trips to see Tustumena Glacier and wildlife, through local outfitters.

In Soldotna, the early run of kings begins about May 15, with the peak of the run occurring between June 12 and 20. The late run enters the river about July 1, peaking between July 23 and 31; season closes July 31. The first run of red salmon enters the river during early June and is present in small numbers through the month; the second run enters about July 15 and is present through early August. In even years pink

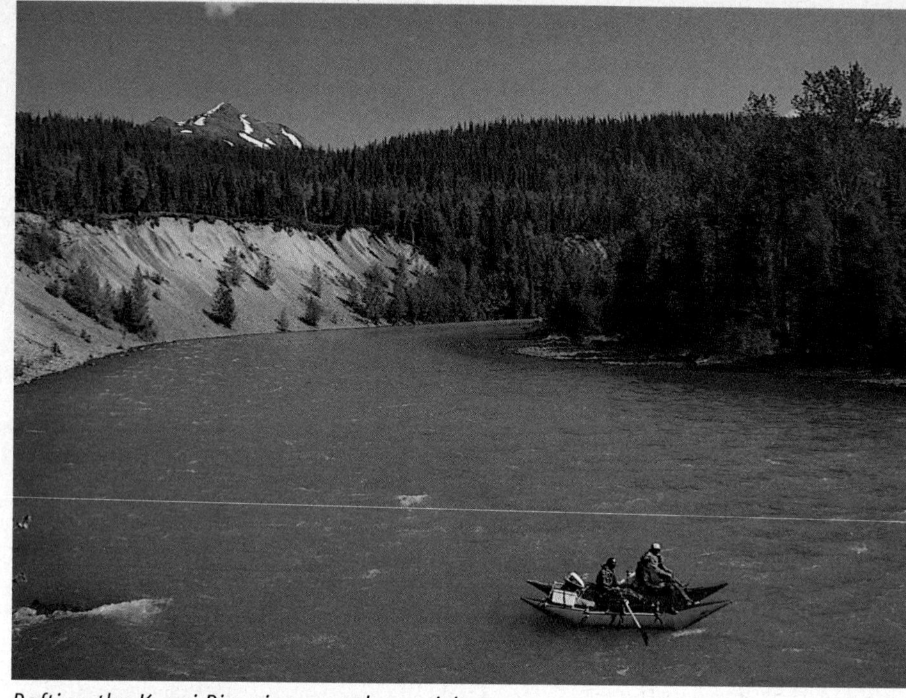

Rafting the Kenai River is a popular activity. (John W. Warden)

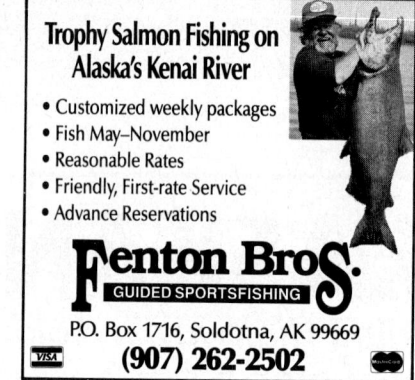

salmon are present from early through mid-August. The early silver salmon run arrives in early August, peaks in mid-August, and is over by the end of the month. Late run silver salmon enter the Kenai in early September, peak in mid- to late September, and continue to enter the river through October. Dolly Varden and rainbow trout can be caught all summer.

Eighth Annual Soldotna Silver Salmon Derby, Aug. 19–28, 1994, on the Kenai and Kasilof rivers. Over $12,000 cash in prize money, including $5,000 for largest silver salmon and $350 in day money. Derby tickets $15, good for entire derby, sold in many locations throughout Kenai and Soldotna. Sponsored by Trout Unlimited, CIPSA Chapter (Cook Inlet Professional Sportfishing Assoc.). [ADVERTISEMENT]

Ken's Alaskan Tackle, on the banks of the Kenai River, across the bridge in Soldotna, is one of the largest tackle shops on the Kenai Peninsula. We specialize in custom fishing trips for king and silver salmon, halibut, saltwater salmon and halibut combination charters, and steel-

head/rainbow. Call (907) 262-6870 for reservations or visitor fishing information, fax (907) 262-8300 or write P.O. Box 1168, Soldotna, AK 99669. See display ad this section.
[ADVERTISEMENT]

Soldotna Creek Park. This day-use park on the Kenai River has covered picnic tables, grills, playground and trails. Facilities include parking, wheelchair-accessible toilets and dumpsters. The park is located behind Hutchings Chevrolet at the Y. Turn at highway maintenance station and follow road behind restaurant. ♿

Central Peninsula Sports Center, adjacent Centennial Park on Kalifornsky Beach (K-Beach) Road, has an Olympic-sized hockey rink, a jogging track, two racquetball/volleyball courts, a weight and exercise room, dressing rooms and showers. The Sports Center also has convention facilities and meeting rooms. Phone 262-3150 for more information.

Play Golf. Birch Ridge Golf Course, located off the Sterling Highway in Soldotna, has nine holes, driving range, clubhouse, pro shop, lounge, and one-bedroom suites for rent. Open May through September. Phone 262-5270 for more information. Birch Ridge hosts several golf tournaments during the summer.

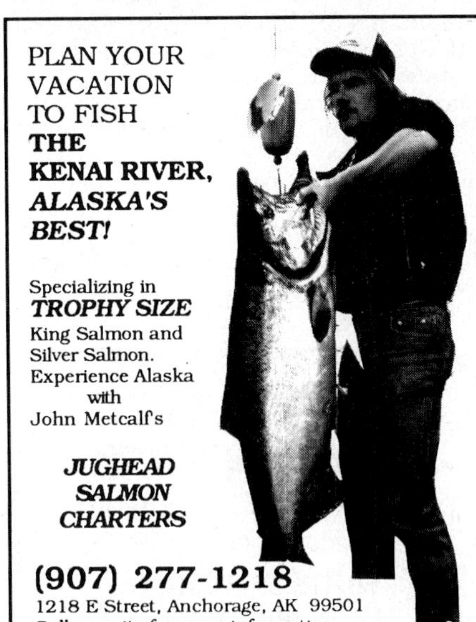

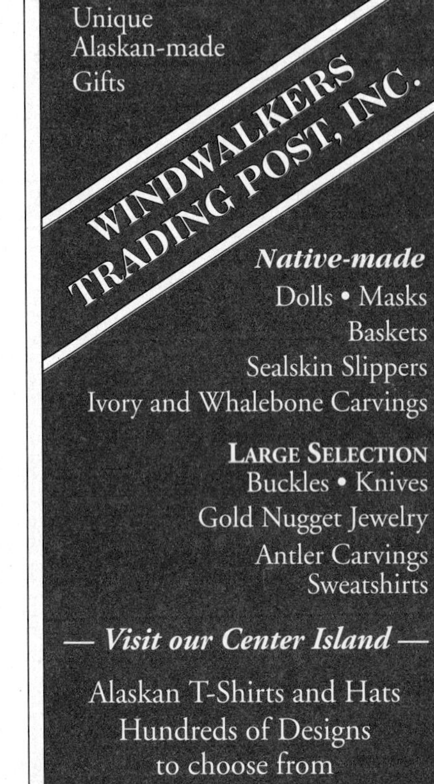

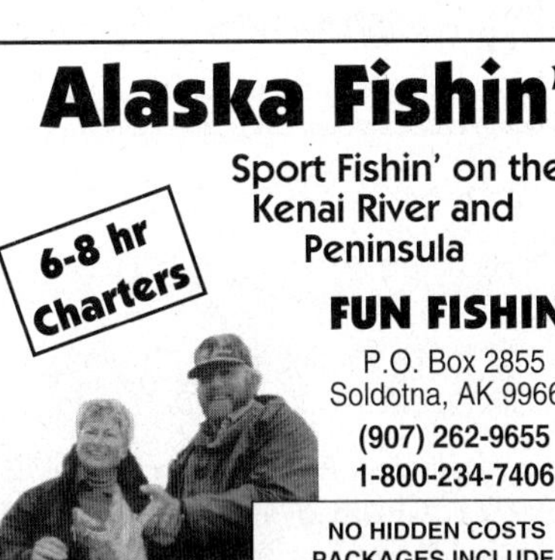

Soldotna Historical Society Museum, located on Centennial Park Road, features a wildlife museum and historic log village. Among the log buildings is the last territorial school built (in 1958). Soldotna's founding settlers arrived in 1947. The "habitable dwellings" that entitled two of these first homesteaders to 160 acres from what is now mid-town Soldotna are part of the village. How these latter-day pioneers lived is revealed in a collection of homestead artifacts and photos in the former Soldotna Chamber of Commerce log tourist center. Damon Hall, a large building constructed for the Alaska Centennial, features an outstanding display of wildlife mounts with a background mural of these species' natural habitat. Open 10 A.M. to 4 P.M., Tuesday through Friday and noon to 4 P.M. Saturday and Sunday in summer.

Joyce Carver Memorial Library offers temporary cards for visitors; large sun-lit reading areas for both adults and children; Alaska videos on summer Saturday afternoons at 2 P.M. Open 9 A.M. to 6 P.M. weekdays, noon to 6 P.M. Saturdays. 235 Binkley St., Soldotna, phone 262-4227.

Kenai National Wildlife Refuge Visitor Center, located at the top of Ski Hill Road (see **Milepost S 97.9**) and also accessible from Funny River Road (see **Milepost S 96.1**), hosts some 25,000 visitors annually. This modern center has dioramas containing lifelike mounts of area wildlife in simulated natural settings. There is a free video about the refuge shown on the hour, between noon and 4 P.M., weekdays in summer. Free wildlife films are shown on the hour every weekend from noon to 5 P.M. Information available here on canoeing, hiking and camping.

Keep a diary of your trip — pick up a copy of *The MILEPOST® Souvenir Log Book.* The log book includes historical photos and expense sheets. Available at your favorite bookstore.

There is a 1-mile-/1.6-km-long nature trail with an observation platform and spotting scope. The Alaska Natural History Assoc. has a sales outlet here with books, posters and slide sets. Pay phone located in center. Open weekdays, 8 A.M. to 4:30 P.M., and weekends 10 A.M. to 6 P.M. No admission fee.

The refuge was created in 1941 when Pres. Franklin D. Roosevelt set aside 1,730,000 acres of land (then designated the Kenai National Moose Range) to assure that the large numbers of moose, Dall sheep and other wild game would remain for people to

A moose grazes on the lawn at Kenai NWR visitor center. (Ron Levy)

enjoy. With the passage of the Alaska National Interest Lands Conservation Act in 1980, the acreage was increased to 1.97 million acres and redesignated Kenai National Wildlife Refuge. The area is managed by the U.S. Dept. of the Interior's Fish and Wildlife Service. Write: Refuge Manager, Kenai National Wildlife Refuge, P.O. Box 2139, Soldotna 99669-2139; phone 262-7021.

Take a canoe trip on one of several routes available in this part of the Kenai Peninsula. Enjoyment of wildlife in their natural habitat, true wilderness scenery, camping, and fishing for trout and salmon are a few highlights of a canoe trip.

Established canoe trails include the Swanson River route (80 miles/129 km) and Swan Lake route (60 miles/97 km). Complete information on Kenai Peninsula canoe trails is available at the USF&WS information cabin at Mile 58 Sterling Highway, the Kenai NWR information center in Soldotna and at chamber of commerce visitor centers in Kenai and Soldotna.

Kenai Spur Highway Log

Distance from Soldotna Y (SY). The Kenai Spur Highway branches off the Sterling Highway at the Soldotna Y. Milepost S 94.2.

SY 0 Junction with Sterling Highway at **Milepost S 94.2.**

SY 1.8 (2.8 km) Big Eddy Road to west. Access to Big Eddy state recreational site on Kenai River with wheelchair-accessible toilets, fishing guides, private camping, moorage, boat launches and rental facilities.

SY 2.2 (3.5 km) Big Eddy second access.

SY 2.5 (4 km) Sport Lake Road; access to bed and breakfast.

NOTE: Watch for road construction in 1994, possibly to Mile 10.6.

SY 4 (6.4 km) Kenai city limits.

SY 5.9 (9.4 km) Dogwood Street.

Upik Fur Products. See display ad this section.

SY 6.1 (9.8 km) Beaver Creek Park (day use only); parking, toilets, picnic tables, playground, basketball court, covered table, litter barrels.

SY 6.4 (10.3 km) Twin City Raceway. South **junction** with Beaver Loop Road: Drive 2.5 miles/4 km on Beaver Loop Road and turn south (left fork), crossing Warren Ames Memorial Bridge, to connect with Kalifornsky Beach Road. Turn north (right fork) for return to Kenai Spur Highway at Mile 10.9.

SY 9.3 (14.9 km) Tinker Lane. Access to Peninsula Oilers baseball park, municipal golf course and junior high school.

SY 10.2 (16.4 km) Airport Road (right), Walker Road (left). Begin divided four-lane highway, 35-mph/56-kmph zone, through Kenai business area.

SY 10.5 (16.9 km) Bridge Access Road; north **junction** with Beaver Loop Road. Access south to Bridge Access Road and Port of Kenai; public boat launch with parking and toilets available. Road crosses Warren Ames Bridge and junctions with Kalifornsky Beach Road. Kenai River Flats state recreation site south of bridge has toilets and dumpster. Good spot to see migrating waterfowl.

SY 11 (17.7 km) **KENAI** (description of city begins on page 474). Carr's/Kmart shopping complex. Willow Street access to Kenai Municipal Airport 1 mile northeast.

SY 12.1 (19.5 km) Forest Drive. Scenic viewpoint overlooking Cook Inlet.

SY 15 (24.1 km) Kenai city limits.

SY 21 (33.8 km) **North Star Lodge.** See display ad this section.

SY 21.3 (34.3 km) Miller Loop Road, connects with Island Lake Road. ▲

SY 22.1 (35.5 km) **NIKISKI** (pop. 5,000). **Emergency Services,** phone 911 for fire and paramedics. Also known as Port Nikiski and Nikishka, this area was homesteaded in the 1940s and grew with the discovery of oil on the Kenai Peninsula in 1957. By 1964, oil-related industries here included Unocal Chemical, Phillips LNG, Chevron and Tesoro. Oil docks servicing offshore drilling platforms today include Rigtenders, Standard Oil, Phillips 66 and Union Collier Chemical. Commercial fishing, hunting and trapping are still a source of income for some residents.

SY 22.5 (36.2 km) Access to Nikiski Rigtenders dock; tankers may be seen next to dock.

SY 23.5 (37.8 km) North Peninsula Recreation Area and Nikiski elementary school. Dome-shaped building in trees near highway is the modern Nikiski swimming pool; visitor observation area at pool. Other facilities include an ice rink, hiking and ski trails, a picnic area and ball fields. Phone 776-8472.

SY 25.8 (41.5 km) Island Lake Road.

SY 26.6 (42.8 km) Nikishka Mall shopping, restaurant, supermarket, gas station, laundromat with showers, and Nikiski branch Kenai post office.

SY 26.7 (43 km) Nikiski Beach Road; views of Nikishka Bay and Cook Inlet. Nikiski Fire Station No. 2.

SY 28.3 (45.5 km) **Moose Haven Lodge.** See display ad this section. ▲

SY 29.7 (47.8 km) Halbouty Road.

Daniels Lake Lodge Bed & Breakfast. See display ad this section.

SY 30 (48.2 km) Daniels Lake.

SY 32.5 (52.3 km) Turnout west opposite Twin Lakes.

SY 35.6 (57.3 km) Entering Captain Cook State Recreation Area.

SY 35.9 (57.8 km) Bishop Creek Campground; 15 sites, parking, toilets, water, picnic area and trail to beach. Camping fee $6/night or annual pass. Watch for spawning red salmon in creek in July and August, silvers August to September. Closed to salmon fishing. ▲

SY 36.5 (58.7 km) Access to **Stormy Lake** swimming area, changehouse, toilet, water, parking and rainbow and arctic char fishing.

SY 36.7 (59.1 km) Stormy Lake overlook; large paved turnout to east.

SY 36.9 (59.4 km) Stormy Lake picnic area; water, toilets, covered tables.

SY 37.8 (60.8 km) Stormy Lake boat launch; water, toilets, parking.

SY 38.6 (62.1 km) Swanson River canoe landing; drive 0.6 mile/1 km east to parking and toilets, river access.

SY 38.7 (62.3 km) Clint Starnes Memorial Bridge crosses **Swanson River;** parking next to bridge for fishing access, toilets, view of Mount Spurr. Fishing for silver and red salmon, and rainbow.

SY 39 (62.8 km) Pavement ends at T. Take left fork for Discovery Campground; 53 campsites, picnic area, hiking trail, water, beachcombing for agates, canoe landing area. Right fork leads to additional parking. Camping fee $8/night or annual pass. ▲

SY 39.6 (63.7 km) Picnic area with tables and toilets, on bluff overlooking ocean at end of Kenai Spur Highway.

Return to Milepost S 94.2 Sterling Highway

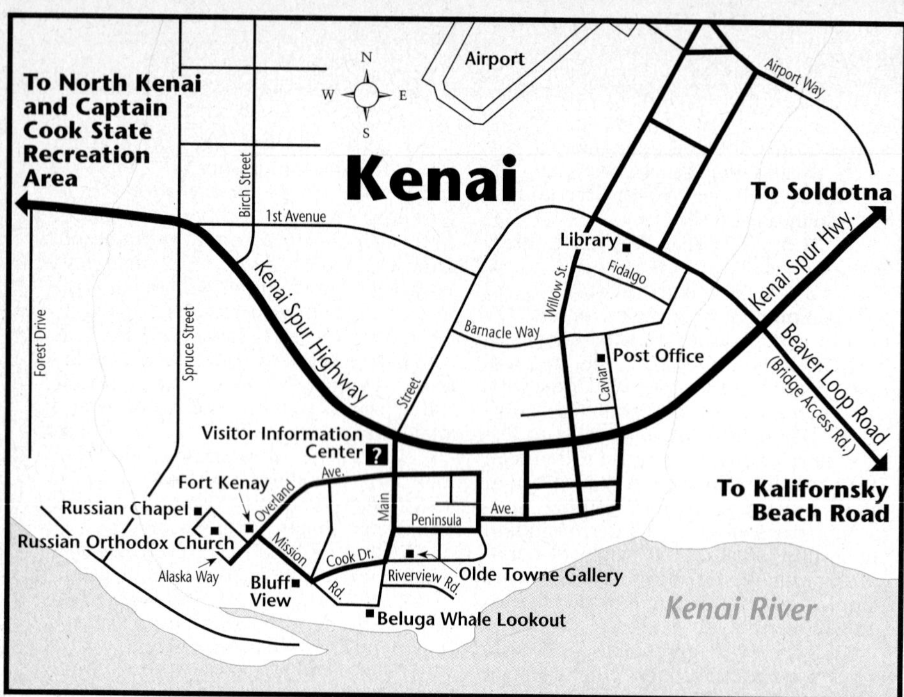

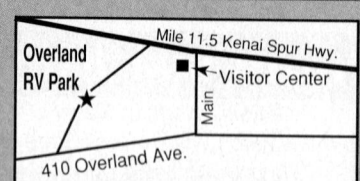

Kenai

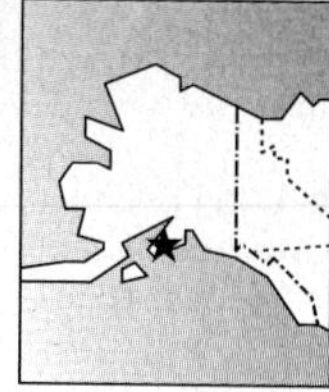

SY 11 (17.7 km). On the western Kenai Peninsula. Reached via the Kenai Spur Highway, or 9.3 miles/14.9 km from Sterling Highway via the Kalifornsky Beach Road, 158.5 miles/255 km from Anchorage, 89.3 miles/143.7 km from Homer. **Population:** 6,327.

Emergency Services: Phone 911 for all emergency services. **Alaska State Troopers** (in Soldotna), phone 262-4453. **Kenai City Police,** phone 283-7879. **Fire Department** and **Ambulance,** phone 911. **Hospital** (in Soldotna), phone 262-4404. **Maritime Search and Rescue,** dial 0 for Zenith 5555, toll free.

Visitor Information: The Kenai Bicentennial Visitors and Cultural Center, located in downtown Kenai, provides brochures and other visitor information. The center features a cultural museum, wildlife displays and movies (in summer). For a full list of visitor services available in Kenai, write the center care of the Kenai Visitors and Convention Bureau, 11471 Kenai Spur Highway, Kenai, AK 99611; phone (907) 283-1991.

Elevation: Sea level. **Climate:** Average daily maximum temperature in July, 61°F/16°C; January temperatures range from 11° to -19°F/-12° to -28°C. The lowest winter temperature ever recorded in Kenai was -48°F/-44°C. Average annual precipitation, 19.9 inches (68.7 inches of snowfall). **Radio:** KCSY 1140, KENI 550, KGTL 620, KSRM 920, KWVV 105, KGTL-FM 100.9/103.5, MBN-FM 95.3/97.7, KENY 980, KWHQ-FM 100.1, KPEN-FM 101.7. **Television:** Several channels and cable. **Newspaper:** *Peninsula Clarion* (daily).

Private Aircraft: Kenai Municipal Airport, adjacent north; elev. 92 feet/28m; length 7,575 feet/2,309m; asphalt; fuel 100LL; attended. Transient tie-down fees $2/day. Adjacent floatplane base offers 3,500-foot/1,067-m basin with 35 slips; transient fee $3/day.

Kenai, which celebrated its bicentennial in 1991, is situated on a low rise overlooking the mouth of the Kenai River where it empties into Cook Inlet. It is the largest city on the Kenai Peninsula. Prior to Russian Alaska,

KENAI ADVERTISERS

Beaver Creek Cabin Rentals..........................Ph. (907) 283-4262
Beluga Lookout RV Park...Ph. (907) 283-5999
Captain Bligh's "Beaver Creek Lodge" & Guide Services.........Ph. (907) 283-7550
Inlet Card & Craft..Mile 12.4 Kenai Spur Hwy.
Inlet Pharmacy.......Mile 12.4 Kenai Spur Hwy.
Katmai Hotel........Main St. & Kenai Spur Hwy.
Kenai Golf Course.................1420 Lawton Dr.
Kenai Kings Inn.............Kenai Spur Hwy. at Airport Way
Kenai Merit Inn.................Ph. (800) 227-6131
Kenai Visitors & Convention Bureau, Inc.............11471 Kenai Spur Hwy.
Kenai Wash & Dry..........................Downtown
Overland RV Park and Gift Shop...........Mile 11.5 Kenai Spur Hwy.
Save-U-More Discount Grocery...........35140 Kalifornsky Beach Rd.
Silver Pines Bed and Breakfast......................Ph. (907) 283-3352

Kenai was an Indian community. Indians fished, hunted, trapped, farmed and traded with neighboring tribes here. In 1791 it became the second permanent settlement established by the Russians in Alaska, when a fortified post called Fort St. Nicholas, or St. Nicholas Redoubt, was built near here by Russian traders. In 1869 the U.S. Army established Fort Kenai (Kenay); in 1899 a post office was authorized.

Oil exploration began in the mid-1950s, with the first major discovery in this area, the Swanson River oil reserves, 20 miles/32.2 km northeast of Kenai in 1957. Two years later, natural gas was discovered in the Kalifornsky Beach area 6 miles/9.6 km south of the city of Kenai. Extensive exploration offshore in upper Cook Inlet has established that Cook Inlet's middle-ground shoals contain one of the major oil and gas fields in the world.

The industrial complex on the North Kenai Road is the site of Unocal Chemicals, which produces ammonia and urea for fertilizer. Phillips Petroleum operates a liquid natural gas plant. Tesoro has a refinery here.

Offshore in Cook Inlet are 15 drilling platforms, all with underwater pipelines bringing the oil to the shipping docks on both sides of Cook Inlet for loading onto tankers.

Federal and state agencies based in and around Kenai contribute to the local economy. Next to oil, tourism, fishing and fish processing are the leading industries.

ACCOMMODATIONS

Kenai has all shopping facilities and conveniences. Medical and dental clinics, banks, laundromats, theaters, pharmacies, supermarkets and numerous gift and specialty shops are located on and off the highway and in the shopping malls. Several motels and hotels and about a dozen restaurants and drive-ins are located in Kenai. Local artists are featured at the Kenai Fine Arts Center on Cook Street. Showers, sauna, weight room, racquetball courts and gym at Kenai Recreation Center, on Caviar Street.

Fort Kenay, established in 1869, is now a museum operated by the City of Kenai.
(Jerrianne Lowther, staff)

Open 6 A.M. to 10 P.M. Monday through Saturday, Sunday 1-10 P.M. Phone 283-3855. For joggers there's the Bernie Huss Memorial Trail, a 0.5-mile jogging and exercise course located just off the Kenai Spur Highway on Main Street Loop. Dump stations located at several local service stations and city dock.

City of Kenai public boat ramp on Boat Launch Road off Bridge Access Road has 24-hour parking, restrooms with flush toilets, pay phone.

Kenai City Park has covered picnic tables and fireplaces. Arrangements for caravan camping may be made in advance through the Kenai Bicentennial Visitors and Cultural Center. Tent camping and private RV parks available in and near shopping areas. Ask at the Visitors Center for directions. ▲

Kenai Merit Inn. Located conveniently in downtown Kenai. Walk to see beluga and sometimes orca whales feeding at the mouth of the Kenai River. Also walk to view fishing activities, historic Russian Orthodox church, Visitor Center, shopping. Five minutes to 18-hole golf course. Very reasonable rates, 60 clean, quiet, comfortable rooms. 24-hour

desk, cable/color TV, phone, bath in each room. Free local calls. Full-service restaurant and lounge. Close to laundromat, cinema, recreation center. Conferences, groups welcome. Meeting spaces available. Book fly-in and Kenai River fishing, flightseeing, horseback riding, camping. Credit cards accepted. See display ad this section. [ADVERTISEMENT]

Overland RV Park and Gift Shop, next to Kenai Visitors Center, downtown Kenai, within a block of everything: Kenai River bluff view, Russian Orthodox church, restaurants, shopping. 50 full hookups, 30-amp power, level spaces, pull-throughs; picnic tables at each site. Dump station, clean restrooms, hot showers, laundry for guests only. Daily, weekly, monthly rates. Caravans

welcome. We can arrange fishing charters or tell you where to bank fish. Quality gifts and souvenirs at affordable prices. Alaska native handicrafts, T-shirts and postcards, too. VISA, MasterCard accepted. (907) 283-4512 (summer); (907) 283-4227 (winter). See display ad this section. [ADVERTISEMENT]

TRANSPORTATION

Air: Kenai is served by MarkAir and Era–Alaska. Several firms offer charter service out of Kenai. Kenai Municipal Airport (see description under Private Aircraft) is approximately two blocks west of the Carr's/Kmart complex on the Kenai Spur Highway. **Local:** Limousine and taxi service is available as well as car rentals, vehicle leasing, boat rentals and charters.

ATTRACTIONS

Get Acquainted. Pick up a brochure at the Kenai Bicentennial Visitors and Cultural Center. The center houses a cultural museum, which has wildlife displays and information on local activities. The center also shows films on Alaska daily in summer.

Kenai River Flats is a must stop for birdwatchers. Great numbers of Siberian snow geese and other waterfowl stop to feed on this saltwater marsh in the spring. The state recreation site on Bridge Access Road at Warren Ames Bridge has toilets, parking and interpretive signs. Boardwalk for wildlife-watchers. Also watch for caribou on the Kenai Flats.

Beluga Whale Lookout on the Kenai River at west end of Main Street is, as the name implies, a good place to watch for beluga whales, the only all-white whale. The Bluff Viewpoint offers a good view of Kenai's fish-processing industry.

Watch Baseball or Play Golf. Some fine semipro baseball is played at the Peninsula Oilers ball park on Tinker Lane. Golfers may try the 18-hole Kenai golf course on Lawton Drive.

Fort Kenay was the first American military installation in the area, established in 1869. More than 100 men were stationed here in the one and one-half years it officially served to protect American citizens in the area. A replica of the fort's barracks building was built as an Alaskan Purchase Centennial project by Kenai residents in 1967.

Holy Assumption Russian Orthodox Church is across from Fort Kenay. The original church was founded in 1846 by a Russian monk, Egumen Nicolai. The present church was built some 50 years after the original and with its three onion-shaped domes is considered one of the finest examples of a Russian Orthodox church built on a vessel or quadrilateral ground plan. It is one of the oldest Russian Orthodox churches in Alaska. In 1971 it was designated a national historic landmark. An 1847 edition of the book of the Holy Gospel of the four evangelists — Matthew, Mark, Luke and John — with five enameled icons on the cover, is awaiting restoration (not on display). Regular church services are held here, and tours are available; inquire at the Parish House near the church. Donations accepted.

Parish House, north across Mission Street from the Russian church, was built in 1886 and was used as a home for resident priests. The original Galanka fireplace may be seen here.

St. Nicholas Chapel, built in 1906, west of the Russian church, marks the burial location of Father Egumen Nicolai and other Russian Orthodox church workers.

Sterling Highway Log

(continued from page 462)

S 95.9 (154.3 km) **A 148.9** (239.6 km) **H 83.6** (134.5 km) Kenai River bridge.

Entering Soldotna northbound. Description of city begins on page 462.

S 96 (154.5 km) **A 149** (239.8 km) **H 83.5** (134.4 km) Soldotna visitor center at south end of Kenai River bridge.

S 96.1 (154.7 km) **A 149.1** (239.9 km) **H 83.4** (134.2 km) **Junction.** Funny River Road to east, Kalifornsky Beach Road to west. Kalifornsky Beach Road rejoins the Sterling Highway at **Milepost S 108.8.** (See KALIFORNSKY BEACH ROAD log this page.)

Soldotna Alaska Purchase Centennial Park campground, 0.1 mile/0.2 km west, on the banks of the Kenai River. There are 126 campsites (some on river), tables, firepits, firewood provided, water, restrooms, dump station, pay phone, two-week limit. Boat launch and favorite fishing site at far end of campground. Register at campground entrance (you may also register here for camping at Swiftwater Park in Soldotna). ▲

Funny River (Airport) Road leads east 2 miles/3.2 km to Soldotna airport and 11.5 miles/18.5 km to Funny River State Recreation Site; 12 campsites, $6 nightly fee per vehicle or annual pass, picnic tables, water, toilets, river access. Salmon and trout fishing at the confluence of the **Kenai** and **Funny rivers** at the recreation area. Turn on Funny River Road and take first right (Ski Hill Loop Road) for USF&WS visitor center. Funny River Road dead ends 17.2 miles/27.7 km from the highway. ▲

S 97.9 (157.6 km) **A 150.9** (242.8 km) **H 81.6** (131.3 km) Sky View High School. Easy-to-miss turnoff for Kenai National Wildlife Refuge headquarters and information center: Turn east off highway and drive 1 mile/1.6 km on Ski Hill Road, which loops back to Funny River Road (see preceding milepost). The center is open 8 A.M. to 4:30 P.M. on weekdays, 10 A.M. to 6 P.M. weekends.

S 99.9 (160.8 km) **A 152.9** (246.1 km) **H 79.6** (128.1 km) Echo Lake Road to west.

S 108.8 (175 km) **A 161.8** (260.4 km) **H 70.7** (113.8 km) South **junction** with Kalifornsky Beach Road. (See KALIFORNSKY BEACH ROAD log this page.) Drive west 3.6 miles/5.8 km to Beach Road for access to beach, Kasilof small-boat harbor and Kasilof River. This loop road rejoins Sterling Highway at **Milepost S 96.1.**

KASILOF (kuh-SEE-lawf; pop. 383; elev. 75 feet/23m) was originally a settlement established in 1786 by the Russians as St. George. An Indian fishing village grew up around the site, but no longer exists. Native inhabitants of the peninsula are mostly Kanai Indians, a branch of the great Athabascan family. The population is spread out over the general area which is called Kasilof. The area's income is derived from fishing and fish processing.

Kasilof River. The red salmon dip-net fishery here is open by special announcement for Alaska residents only. Check with the ADF&G for current regulations.

Private Aircraft: Kasilof airstrip, 1.7 miles/2.7 km north; elev. 125 feet/38m; length 2,300 feet/701m; gravel; unattended.

S 109.2 (175.7 km) **A 162.2** (261 km) **H 70.3** (113.1 km) **Kasilof Riverview Lodge.** See display ad this section.

S 109.4 (176.1 km) **A 162.4** (261.3 km) **H 70.1** (112.8 km) Bridge over Kasilof River, which drains Tustumena Lake, one of the largest lakes on the Kenai Peninsula. Kasilof River State Recreation Site; 16 campsites, $6 nightly fee or annual pass, five picnic sites on riverbank, picnic tables, toilets and water are on the south side of the bridge. Boat launch $5 fee or annual pass. Entering Game Management Subunit 15C southbound, 15B northbound. ▲

S 110 (177 km) **A 163** (262.3 km) **H 69.5** (111.8 km) Tustumena Elementary School and north end of Tustumena Lake Road. This is the first turnoff southbound for access to Johnson and Tustumena lakes. Also turn off here for picnic area with covered picnic tables, toilets (wheelchair accessible), firepits, water and dumpster. There is a huge metal T at Tustumena Lake Road, just beyond the picnic area: Turn east at the T for Johnson and Tustumena lakes. **Johnson Lake** is 0.3 mile/0.5 km from the highway. Johnson Lake state campground has 50 sites (some double and some pull-throughs), $8 nightly fee or annual pass, water, toilets, boat launch and firewood. Lake is stocked with rainbow. Watch for beaver, moose, and king salmon migrating up Crooked Creek. **Tustumena Lake** is 6.4 miles/10.3 km from the highway; a campground on the Kasilof River near the lake has 10 sites, toilets and boat launch. Fishing for lake trout and salmon. Tustumena Lake is closed to king and sockeye salmon fishing. ▲

CAUTION: This lake is 6 miles/10 km wide and 25 miles/40 km long and subject to severe winds.

S 110.5 (177.8 km) **A 163.5** (263.1 km) **H 69** (111 km) Double-ended paved parking by Crooked Creek.

Kalifornsky Beach Road Log

Also called K–Beach Road, Kalifornsky Beach Road leads west and south from the Sterling Highway at Soldotna, following the shore of Cook Inlet to Kasilof. **Distance from the Sterling Highway junction at Milepost S 96.1 at Soldotna (S) is followed by distance from Sterling Highway junction at Milepost S 108.8 at Kasilof (K). Mileposts run south to north.**

S 0 K 22.2 (35.7 km) **Junction** with Sterling Highway at **Milepost S 96.1.**

S 0.1 (0.2 km) **K 22.1** (35.6 km) Soldotna Alaska Purchase Centennial Park Campground, operated by the city of Soldotna. Kenai River access for bank fishing, boat launch (fee charged). ▲

S 0.2 (0.3 km) **K 22** (35.4 km) Alaska State Troopers.

S 0.4 (0.6 km) **K 21.8** (35.1 km) Rodeo grounds.

S 0.6 (1 km) **K 21.6** (34.8 km) Central Peninsula Sports Center; hockey, ice skating, jogging track and other sports available; phone 262-3150 for more information. Senior center.

S 1.7 (2.7 km) **K 20.5** (33 km) Kenai Peninsula Community College access road. Also access to Slikok Creek State Recreation Site, 0.7 mile/1.1 km north; day use only with 12-hour parking, wheelchair accessible toilets, picnic tables, information kiosk and trails. No fires or ATVs.

S 2.9 (4.7 km) **K 19.3** (31.1 km) K–Beach center. ADF&G office; stop in here for current sportfishing information.

S 3.5 (5.6 km) **K 18.7** (30.1 km) Red Diamond shopping center, Duck Inn Motel and restaurant.

S 4.6 (7.4 km) **K 17.6** (28.3 km) Firehouse.

S 4.7 (7.6 km) **K 17.5** (28.2 km) Ciechansky Road leads 2.2 miles/3.5 km to Ciechansky State Recreation Site, a day-use only picnic area with tables, toilets, dumpster and Kenai River access. Also access to private campgrounds with RV hookups on the Kenai River. ▲

S 6 (9.7 km) **K 16.2** (26.1 km) Turnoff for city of Kenai, 3.1 miles/5 km north via the Warren Ames Memorial Bridge.

S 6.8 (10.9 km) **K 15.4** (24.8 km) Magnificent beaver dam and lodge, lupine display in June.

S 7.6 (12.2 km) **K 14.6** (23.5 km) Robinsons mini-mall.

S 7.9 (12.7 km) **K 14.3** (23 km) Kenai Custom Seafoods.

S 8 (12.9 km) **K 14.2** (22.9 km) Cafe.

S 13 (20.9 km) **K 9.2** (14.8 km) Scenic viewpoint overlooking Cook Inlet.

S 17.4 (28 km) **K 4.8** (7.7 km) Kasilof Beach Road.

S 20.1 (32.3 km) **K 2.1** (3.4 km) Kasilof Airfield Road.

S 22.1 (35.6 km) **K 0.1** (0.2 km) Kasilof post office.

S 22.2 (35.7 km) **K 0 Junction** with Sterling Highway at **Milepost S 108.8** at Kasilof.

Return to Milepost S 96.1 or S 108.8 Sterling Highway

S 110.8 (178.3 km) **A 163.8** (263.6 km) **H 68.7** (110.6 km) **Tustumena Lodge.** Motel, cocktail lounge, fishing guides — (907) 262-4216. Clean, affordable rooms at half the price of town. Some kitchenettes. Friendly Alaskan atmosphere where a cold drink, light snack and good fish stories are always available. See the world's largest razor clam. Look for a hat from your hometown among the over 3,000 hats on display. [ADVERTISEMENT]

S 111 (178.6 km) **A 164** (263.9 km) **H 68.5** (110.2 km) Cohoe Loop Road north **junction** (turnoff to west). Crooked Creek State Recreation Site (camping and fishing) 1.8 miles/2.8 km west on Cohoe Loop Road. South end of Tustumena Lake Road (to east) for Johnson and Tustumena lakes (see description at **Milepost S 110**). Cohoe Loop Road rejoins the Sterling Highway at **Milepost S 114.3** (see COHOE LOOP ROAD log on page 480).

Just east of the highway on the Johnson and Tustumena lakes access road is Crooked Creek fish hatchery, open 8 A.M. to 5 P.M.; a sign explains the chinook and sockeye salmon operation here. For further information, contact Cook Inlet Aquaculture Assoc., phone (907) 283-5761. The hatchery-produced salmon create a popular fishery at the confluence of Crooked Creek and the Kasilof River, accessible via the Cohoe Loop Road. Just past the hatchery is Crooked Creek Road (private RV park and bed and breakfast) and just beyond is a huge metal T at Tustumena Lake Road. Continue past this monument for a picnic area, and return to Sterling Highway at **Milepost S 110**; turn at the T for lakes and camping.

Crooked Creek RV Park/Cohoe Lodge & Guide Service. See display ad this section.

Kasilof RV Park. 13 miles south of Soldotna, 0.5 mile off the Sterling Highway (Johnson Lake Road). View peaceful Johnson Lake to the east and scenic Mount Redoubt on the west. Centrally located for all your Kenai Peninsula vacation activities. Enjoy having fishing, canoeing, swimming and the fish hatchery all within walking distance. Electrical hookups, pull-throughs, dump station and sparkling fresh well-water are all available. [ADVERTISEMENT]

S 114.3 (183.9 km) **A 167.3** (269.2 km) **H 65.2** (104.9 km) Cohoe Loop Road south **junction** with the Sterling Highway. The 13-mile/21-km road loops north to **Milepost S 111**. See COHOE LOOP ROAD log page 480.

S 117.4 (188.9 km) **A 170.4** (274.2 km) **H 62.1** (99.9 km) Clam Gulch State Recreation Area (watch for easy-to-miss sign) is 0.5 mile/0.8 km from highway; picnic tables, picnic shelter, toilets, water, 116 campsites, $6 nightly fee or annual pass. *CAUTION: High ocean bluffs are dangerous.* Short access road to beach (recommended for four-wheel-drive vehicles only, limited turnaround space).

Clam digging for razor clams on most of the sandy beaches of the western Kenai Peninsula from Kasilof to Anchor Point can be rewarding. Many thousands of clams are dug each year at Clam Gulch. You must have a sportfishing license to dig, and these are available at most sporting goods stores. The bag limit is 60 clams regardless of size (always check current regulations). There is no legally closed season, but quality of the clams varies with month; check locally. Good clamming and fewer people in March and April, although there may still be ice on the beach. Any tide lower than a minus 1-foot tide is enough to dig clams; minus 4- to 5-foot tides are best. The panoramic view of Mount Redoubt, Mount Iliamna and Mount Spurr across Cook Inlet and the expanse of beach are well worth the short side trip even during the off-season.

S 118.2 (190.2 km) **A 171.2** (275.5 km) **H 61.3** (98.7 km) **CLAM GULCH** (pop. 79) post office, lodge and a sled dog racing outfitters shop.

S 118.3 (190.4 km) **A 171.3** (275.7 km) **H 61.2** (98.5 km) **Clam Shell Lodge.** See display ad this section.

S 122.8 (197.6 km) **A 175.8** (282.9 km) **H 56.7** (91.2 km) Paved, double-ended turnout oceanside (no view).

S 124.8 (200.8 km) **A 177.8** (286.1 km) **H 54.7** (88 km) Paved, double-ended turnout oceanside with view of Cook Inlet.

S 126.8 (204.1 km) **A 179.8** (289.4 km) **H 52.7** (84.8 km) Double-ended paved scenic wayside overlooking upper Cook Inlet. Polly Creek, due west across Cook Inlet, is a popular area for clam diggers (fly in). Across the inlet is Mount Iliamna; north of Iliamna is Mount Redoubt.

Mount Redoubt last erupted in December 1989. (Jerrianne Lowther, staff)

Cohoe Loop Road Log

The Cohoe Loop Road loops south 15.3 miles/24.7 km from **Milepost S 111** on the Sterling Highway. The popular Crooked Creek fishing and camping area is at the top or north end of the loop. The bottom (or south) 10 miles of the Cohoe Loop Road travels through mostly undeveloped parcels of land; no services, views or recreation. Motorists may wish to use the north junction approach.

Distance from north junction with the Sterling Highway (NJ) at Milepost S 111 is followed by distance from south junction (SJ) at Milepost S 114.3. Mileposts run south to north.

NJ 0 SJ 15.3 (24.6 km) **Junction** with Sterling Highway at **Milepost S 111.**

NJ 1.8 (2.9 km) **SJ 13.5** (21.7 km) **Crooked Creek RV Park, Cohoe Lodge & Guide Service.** Located at the confluence of Crooked Creek and Kasilof River. "The total number of adult king salmon which returned to Crooked Creek (last year) was 12,565. Of these 8,479 were hatchery-produced fish. Sportsmen harvested an estimated 8,146 fish. The total number of adult silver salmon which returned to Crooked Creek (last year) was 8,300. Of these 6,640 were hatchery-produced fish. The success rate of participating fishermen was the highest of all Peninsula salmon sport fisheries." (Excerpt from Alaska Dept. of Fish and Game, Division of Fisheries Rehabilitation, Enhancement and Development [FRED] Annual Report.) See display ad on page 479. [ADVERTISEMENT] ▲

NJ 1.8 (2.9 km) **SJ 13.5** (21.7 km) Crooked Creek/Rilinda Drive; access to private RV park and Crooked Creek State Recreation Site at the confluence of Crooked Creek and the Kasilof River. The recreation site has 83 campsites, 36 day-use sites, toilets and water trails to Kasilof River for fishermen. Camping fee $6/night or annual pass. ▲

Fishing in **Crooked Creek** for coho salmon from Aug. 1, peaks mid-August; steelhead from Aug. 1; closed to king salmon fishing and closed to all fishing near hatchery. Fishing access to confluence of Crooked Creek and Kasilof River is through the state recreation site. *NOTE: Fishing access to Crooked Creek frontage above confluence is through a private RV park; fee charged.* Fishing in the **Kasilof River** for king salmon, late May through July, best in mid-June; coho salmon, mid-August to September, use salmon egg clusters, wet flies, assorted spoons and spinners; steelhead in May and September.

NJ 2.4 (3.9 km) **SJ 12.9** (20.7 km) Webb–Ramsell Road. Kasilof River access across private property, fee charged.

NJ 5.3 (8.5 km) **SJ 10** (16 km) Cohoe Spur Road **junction.** A post office was established in 1950 at **COHOE** (area pop. 508), originally an agricultural settlement.

NJ 5.6 (9 km) **SJ 9.7** (15.6 km) T intersection; go west 0.8 mile/1.3 km for beach and boat launch. Cohoe Loop Road continues north. Pavement begins northbound.

NJ 6.6 (10.6 km) **SJ 8.7** (14 km) **Lape Fish Camp B&B.** Primitive, oceanside cabins at salmon set-net operation. Located on the east shore of Cook Inlet with sunset view of the unspoiled Alaska Range. Watch commercial fishermen at work, beachcomb, sport fish, enjoy our wood-heated sauna, dig razor clams or just relax around the campfire. P.O. Box 294, Kasilof, AK 99610. (907) 262-6016. [ADVERTISEMENT]

NJ 15.3 (24.6 km) **SJ 0 Junction** with Sterling Highway at **Milepost S 114.3.**

Return to Milepost S 114.3 or S 111 Sterling Highway

S 127.1 (204.5 km) **A 180.1** (289.8 km) **H 52.4** (84.3 km) Double-ended paved scenic viewpoint to west with interpretive display on Mount Redoubt and Mount Spurr volcanoes. Private RV park. ▲

Scenic View RV Park. See display ad this section. ▲

S 132.2 (212.7 km) **A 185.2** (298 km) **H 47.3** (76.1 km) Pay phone at bar.

S 134.5 (216.4 km) **A 187.5** (301.7 km) **H 45** (72.4 km) Ninilchik Beach Campground/Ninilchik State Recreation Area. $6 per site, 50 campsites, toilets, water. Popular beach for razor clamming. Access to the clamming beds adjacent to the campgrounds during minus tides. Use caution when working this area during incoming tides. Trail to **Ninilchik River;** fishing for king and silver salmon, steelhead and Dolly Varden. Camping fee $8/night or annual pass. ▲

S 134.7 (216.8 km) **A 187.7** (302 km) **H 44.8** (72.1 km) Coal Street; access west to Ninilchik's historic Russian Orthodox church at top of hill; plenty of parking and turnaround space.

S 134.8 (216.9 km) **A 187.8** (302.2 km) **H 44.7** (71.9 km) Large double-ended gravel turnout with dumpster. Construction improvements scheduled at turnout for early summer 1994; campsites, day-use sites, viewing area, toilets and water are planned.

S 135.1 (217.4 km) **A 188.1** (302.7 km) **H 44.4** (71.4 km) Double-ended gravel turnout and dumpsters at north end of Ninilchik River bridge. Side road leads to **NINILCHIK VILLAGE,** the original village of Ninilchik, and to the beach. A short road branches off this side road and leads into the old village of Ninilchik. Continue straight on side road for motel, beach, overnight RV parking, camping and toilets (follow signs). Sea breezes here keep the beach free of mosquitoes. Historic signs near beach and at village entrance tell about Ninilchik Village, which includes several old dovetailed log buildings. A walking tour brochure is available from businesses in the village and along the highway. Present-day Ninilchik is located at **Milepost S 135.5.** A beautiful white Russian Orthodox church sits on a hill overlooking the sea above the historic old village. Trail leads up to it from the road into town (watch for sign just past the old village store). The church and cemetery are still in use. You are welcome to walk up to it but use the well-defined path behind the store (please do not walk through private property), or drive up using the Coal Street access at **Milepost S 134.7.** ▲

Beachcomber Beachfront Motel, RV Park/Seacomber Fishing Charters. See display ad this section. ▲

S 135.3 (217.7 km) **A 188.3** (303 km) **H 44.2** (71.1 km) Gravel turnout to west.

S 135.4 (217.9 km) **A 188.4** (303.2 km) **H 44.1** (71 km) Kingsley Road; access to Ninilchik post office and two private campgrounds. Ninilchik View state campground is across the highway. (Descriptions follow.)

S 135.4 (217.9 km) **A 188.4** (303.2 km) **H 44.1** (71 km) **Hylen's Camper Park.** Next to post office and Senior Center. Fish Deep Creek and Ninilchik River for kings, silvers; Cook Inlet for record halibut, king salmon, May–September. Great clamming. Fish cleaning tables. Smoker. Local businesses, fishing charter discounts. Full, partial or no hookups. No tents. Daily, weekly, plus 30 monthly/seasonal-rated sites. Housekeeping cottages, showers, laundry, storage, social room. Horseshoes. Pay phone. Clean, friendly, reasonable rates. [ADVERTISEMENT] ▲

S 135.4 (217.9 km) **A 188.4** (303.2 km) **H 44.1** (71 km) Ninilchik View state campground overlooking the village and sea; 12 campsites, water, toilets, litter disposal, two dump stations ($3 fee), drinking water fill-up. Camping fee $8/night or annual pass. Foot trail from campground down to beach and village. DOT/PF road maintenance station. ▲

Ninilchik

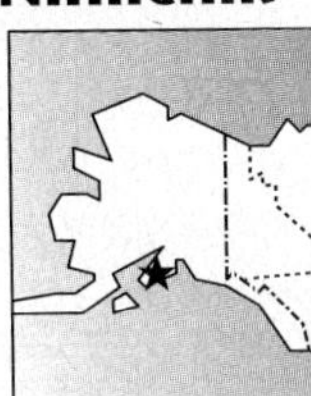

S 135.5 (218 km) **A 188.5** (303.4 km) **H 44** (70.8 km) Pronounced Nin-ILL-chick. **Population:** 456. **Emergency services:** Phone 911. **Clinic and ambulance,** phone 567-3412. **Visitor Information:** At Ninilchik Library, **Milepost S 135.6.** Local businesses are also very helpful. **Private Aircraft:** Ninilchik airstrip, 6.1 miles/9.8 km southeast; elev. 276 feet/84m; length 2,400 feet/732m; dirt; unattended.

Restaurant, lodging and charter service east side of road are part of the community of Ninilchik. Ninilchik extends roughly from Ninilchik State Recreation Area to the north to Deep Creek to the south, with services (grocery stores, gas stations, campgrounds, etc.) located at intervals along the highway. The original village of Ninilchik (signed Ninilchik Village) is reached by a side road from **Milepost S 135.1.**

On Memorial Day weekend, Ninilchik is referred to as the third biggest city in Alaska, as thousands of Alaskans arrive for the fishing (see Area Fishing following). The Kenai Peninsula State Fair is held at Ninilchik in late August. Dubbed the "biggest little fair in Alaska," it features a parade, horse show, livestock competition and exhibits ranging from produce to arts and crafts. Pancake breakfasts, bingo and other events, such as the derby fish fry, are held at the fairgrounds throughout the year. The king salmon derby is held from May to June 11. A halibut derby, sponsored by the Ninilchik Chamber of Commerce, runs from Father's Day through Labor Day. There is an active senior center offering meals and events. Swimming pool at the high school.

AREA FISHING: Well-known area for salt-

King salmon fishing on the Ninilchik River. (Jerrianne Lowther, staff)

water king salmon fishing and record halibut fishing. Charter services available. (Combination king salmon and halibut charters are available and popular.) Salt water south of the mouth of **Deep Creek** has produced top king salmon fishing in late May, June and July. Kings 50 lbs. and over are frequently caught. "Lunker" king salmon are available 1 mile/1.6 km south of Deep Creek in **Cook Inlet** from late May through July. Trolling a spinner or a spoon from a boat is the preferred method. Silver, red and pink salmon are available in salt water between Deep Creek and the Ninilchik River during July. A major halibut fishery off Ninilchik has produced some of the largest trophy halibut found in Cook Inlet, including a 466-lb. unofficial world record sport-caught halibut.

Sterling Highway Log

(continued)

S 135.6 (218.2 km) **A 188.6** (303.5 km) **H 43.9** (70.6 km) Ninilchik High School. Ninilchik Library and visitor information center. Open 10 A.M. to 4 P.M. daily in the summer.

S 135.9 (218.7 km) **A 188.9** (304 km) **H 43.6** (70.2 km) **Reel 'Em Inn & Cook Inlet Charters.** East one mile on Oilwell Rd. at the Chinook Chevron. Owned and operated by Alaskan family with the knowledge to show you how to experience the area's attractions. Full-service facility. We offer combination saltwater halibut/salmon charters in our large covered boat. Lodging with continental breakfast. RV hookups, full or partial. Showers, laundry and BBQ area. Fish-cleaning tables, freezing and storage for your catch. Equipment rental — fishing poles, raingear, boots, clam shovels. Reservations welcome. (907) 567-7335. See display ad. [ADVERTISEMENT]

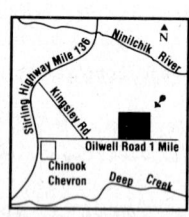

S 136 (218.9 km) **A 189** (304.1 km) **H 43.5** (70 km) **Chinook Chevron.** Between Ninilchik River and Deep Creek. Open year-round. Propane, filtered diesel. Self-serve gasoline. Light-duty mechanic, tire repair, ice, bait, cold pop, snacks. Water for RVs. Fishing, clamming and visitor information. Chevron, VISA, American Express, Discover, MasterCard and JCB cards welcome. See display ad this section. [ADVERTISEMENT]

S 136 (218.9 km) **A 189** (304.1 km) **H 43.5** (70 km) **Chihuly's Charters** and **Porcupine Shop.** See display ad this section.

S 136.2 (219.2 km) **A 189.2** (304.5 km) **H 43.3** (69.7 km) Peninsula Fairgrounds, access to bed and breakfast.

Bluff House Bed & Breakfast. See display ad this section.

S 136.4 (219.5 km) **A 189.4** (304.8 km) **H 43.1** (69.4 km) **Creekside Inn & RV Park.** See display ad this section. ▲

S 136.7 (219.9 km) **A 189.7** (305.3 km) **H 42.8** (68.9 km) Bridge over Deep Creek. Ample parking east side of highway both sides of creek; overnight camping for self-contained vehicles only (no facilities). Construction improvements scheduled for both pullouts in early summer 1994; campsites, water, toilets and viewing area planned.

Freshwater fishing in **Deep Creek** for king salmon up to 40 lbs., use spinners with red bead lures, Memorial Day weekend and the four weekends following; Dolly Varden in July and August; silver salmon to 15 lbs., August and September; steelhead to 15 lbs., late September through October. No bait fishing permitted after Aug. 31. Mouth of Deep Creek access from Deep Creek State Recreation Area turnoff at **Milepost S 137.3.**

S 137 (220.4 km) **A 190** (305.8 km) **H 42.5** (68.4 km) Cannery and sports shop with tackle and clam shovel rentals west side of road.

Deep Creek Custom Packing, Inc. See display ad this section.

Fishward Bound Adventures and Deep Creek Sport Shop. See display ad this section.

S 137.3 (220.9 km) **A 190.3** (306.2 km) **H 42.2** (67.9 km) Deep Creek State Recreation Area on the beach at the mouth of Deep Creek; parking for 300 vehicles, overnight camping, water, tables, dumpsters, toilets and fireplaces. Drive 0.5 mile/0.8 km down gravel road. Camping fee $6/night per vehicle or annual pass. Favorite area for surf fishing and to launch boats. Boat launch $5 fee or annual pass. (Seasonal checks by U.S. Coast Guard for personal flotation devices, boating safety.) Extensive rehabilitation in this area scheduled for completion in early summer 1994; toilets, road and parking area improvements planned. Good bird watching in wetlands behind beach; watch for eagles. Good clamming at low tide. The beaches here are lined with coal, which falls from the exposed seams of high cliffs. ▲

CAUTION: Rapidly changing tides and weather. Although the mouth of Deep Creek affords boaters good protection, low tides may prevent return; check tide tables.

S 140 (225.3 km) **A 193** (310.6 km) **H 39.5** (63.5 km) **Deep Creek Bed & Breakfast.** See display ad this section.

S 140.3 (225.8 km) **A 193.3** (311.1 km) **H 39.2** (63.1 km) Double-ended turnout with scenic view to west.

S 142.7 (229.6 km) **A 195.7** (314.9 km) **H 36.8** (59.2 km) Double-ended paved turnout with dumpster, view of Mount Iliamna across the inlet.

S 143.8 (231.4 km) **A 196.8** (316.7 km) **H 35.7** (57.4 km) Happy Valley Creek. The area surrounding this creek is known locally as the Happy Valley community.

S 145.2 (233.7 km) **A 198.2** (319 km) **H 34.3** (55.2 km) **Happy Valley.** See display ad this section.

S 148 (238.1 km) **A 201** (323.5 km) **H 31.5** (50.7 km) Scenic viewpoint. Sign here reads: "Looking westerly across Cook Inlet, Mt. Iliamna and Mt. Redoubt in the Chigmit Mountains of the Aleutian Range can be seen rising over 10,000 feet above sea level. This begins a chain of mountains and islands known as the Aleutian Chain extending west over 1,700 miles to Attu beyond the International Date Line to the Bering Sea, separating the Pacific and Arctic oceans. Mt. Redoubt on the right, and Iliamna on the left, were recorded as active volcanoes in the mid-18th century. Mt. Redoubt had a minor eruption in 1966."

Mount Redoubt had a major eruption in December 1989. The eruptions continued through April 1990, then subsided to steam plumes. Mount Redoubt is still considered to

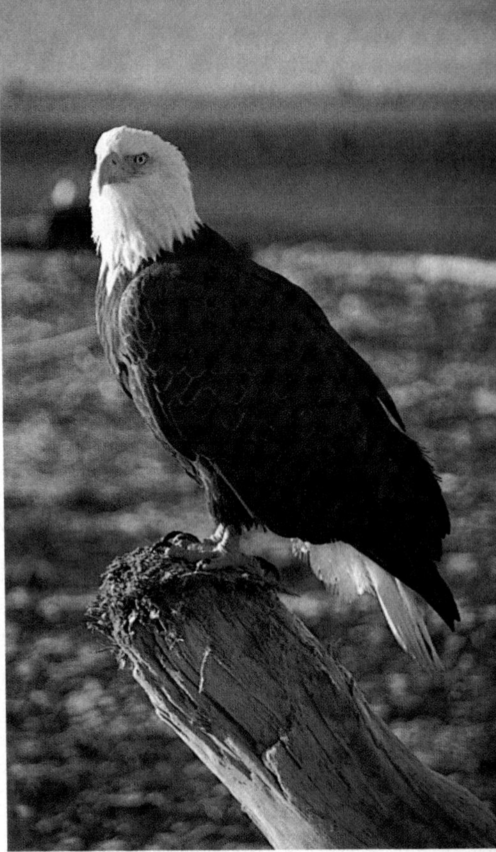

Watch for bald eagles. (Jennifer Beecroft)

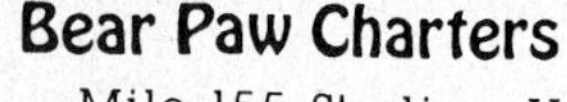

Cook Inlet has a popular halibut fishery. (John W. Warden)

be active.

S 150.9 (242.8 km) **A 203.9** (328.1 km) **H 28.6** (46 km) Bridge over Stariski Creek.

S 151.9 (244.4 km) **A 204.9** (329.7 km) **H 27.6** (44.4 km) Stariski Creek State Recreation Site on bluff overlooking Cook Inlet; 13 campsites, $8 nightly fee or annual pass, toilets (wheelchair accessible) and well water. ▲

S 152.7 (245.7 km) **A 205.7** (331 km) **H 26.8** (43.1 km) **Eagle Crest RV Park**. See display ad this section. ▲

S 153.2 (246.5 km) **A 206.2** (331.8 km) **H 26.3** (42.3 km) **Short Stop RV Parking**. See display ad this section. ▲

S 155 (249.4 km) **A 208** (334.7 km) **H 24.5** (39.4 km) **Bear Paw Charters.** This Anchor Point location is only minutes from trophy halibut and salmon fishing. All equipment provided plus free filleting. Small groups and personalized service are the focus of this family-owned and operated business. Water taxi for remote camping and hiking also available. You'll like the gift shop. Phone (907) 235-5399. See display ad this section. [ADVERTISEMENT]

S 155.5 (250.3 km) **A 208.5** (335.5 km) **H 24** (38.6 km) **Anchor View Cottages.** See display ad this section.

S 156.3 (251.5 km) **A 209.3** (336.8 km) **H 23.2** (37.3 km) **Anchor River Tesoro.** See display ad this section.

Mugs and Jugs. See display ad this section.

S 156.7 (252.2 km) **A 209.7** (337.5 km) **H 22.8** (36.7 km) Anchor Point post office at turnoff for Milo Fritz Road to west and North Fork Road to east, an 18-mile/29-km loop which rejoins the Sterling Highway at **Milepost S 164.3**. Post office is open 9 A.M. to 5 P.M. weekdays, 9 A.M. to noon on Saturday.

ANCHOR POINT (pop. 866) has groceries, gas stations with major repair service, motel, restaurant and fast-food stands, liquor store, clinic, sporting goods, gift shops and ceramic studio. Volunteer fire department and ambulance, phone 911. **Visitor Information:** Located in the log cabin just off the Sterling Highway on Old Sterling Highway. Open 10 A.M. to 4 P.M., Friday through Monday, from Memorial Day weekend through Labor Day. The center is manned by volunteers from Anchor Point Senior Citizens, Inc.

Good Time Charters. See display ad this section.

Olga's Bed and Breakfast. Have a quiet stay in the country, close to the main road. Our rooms are neat and clean. Help yourself, continental-style breakfast, available at your leisure. Walking distance to Anchor River and best fishing. Close to great clam beaches. Russian, Spanish and Denaki spoken. Turn west by Millie's Video on Milo Fritz Rd., right on Granross, left on Laida. (907) 235-6654. See display ad. [ADVERTISEMENT]

Our Front Porch Bed & Breakfast. See display ad this section.

S 156.9 (252.5 km) **A 209.9** (337.8 km) **H 22.6** (36.4 km) **Junction** with Old Sterling Highway; access to Anchor River businesses and Anchor River (Beach) Road. See ANCHOR RIVER (BEACH) ROAD log on page 486.

Anchor River Inn. See display ad this section.

S 157.1 (252.8 km) **A 210.1** (338.1 km) **H 22.4** (36 km) Anchor River bridge.

S 160.9 (258.9 km) **A 213.9** (344.2 km) **H 18.6** (29.9 km) Side road to artist Norman Lowell's studio and KWLS radio station.

Norman Lowell Studio & Gallery. See display ad this section.

S 161 (259.1 km) **A 214** (344.4 km) **H 18.5** (29.8 km) Anchor River bridge.

S 161.5 (259.9 km) **A 214.5** (345.2 km) **H 18** (29 km) Anchor River State Recreation Site; nine sites, $6 nightly fee or annual pass, toilets. Large RVs and trailers note: Do not take road to right as you turn in, limited turnaround space. ▲

S 164.3 (264.4 km) **A 217.3** (349.7 km) **H 15.2** (24.5 km) North Fork Loop Road to Anchor River.

S 164.8 (265.2 km) **A 217.8** (350.5 km) **H 14.7** (23.7 km) Old Sterling Highway leads 9.4 miles/15.1 km northwest in a loop to Anchor River (Beach) Road, which provides access to Cook Inlet, Anchor River recreation and Anchor Point businesses. See ANCHOR RIVER (BEACH) ROAD log this section and **Milepost S 156.9.**

S 165.4 (266.2 km) **A 218.4** (351.5 km) **H 14.1** (22.7 km) **Billikin Gift Shop (Rainbow's End).** See display ad this section.

S 167.1 (268.9 km) **A 220.1** (354.2 km) **H 12.4** (20 km) Diamond Ridge Road.

S 168.5 (271.2 km) **A 221.5** (356.5 km) **H 11** (17.7 km) Alaska State Parks' South District office is located on the bluff here. A small parking lot is adjacent to the log office where visitors may obtain information on Kachemak Bay state park, as well as other southern Kenai Peninsula state park lands.

S 169 (271.9 km) **A 222** (357.2 km) **H 10.5** (16.9 km) Homer DOT/PF highway maintenance station.

S 169.6 (272.9 km) **A 222.6** (358.2 km) **H 9.9** (15.9 km) Two viewpoints overlooking Kachemak Bay.

S 170 (273.6 km) **A 223** (358.9 km) **H 9.5** (15.3 km) Bay View Inn.

S 171.9 (276.6 km) **A 224.9** (361.9 km) **H 7.6** (12.2 km) West Hill Road; access to bed and breakfasts. Connects to Skyline Drive and East Hill Road for scenic drive along Homer Bluff.

S 172.5 (277.6 km) **A 225.5** (362.9 km) **H 7** (11.3 km) Bidarka Inn.

S 172.6 (277.8 km) **A 225.6** (363 km) **H 6.9** (11.1 km) Homer Junior High School.

S 172.7 (277.9 km) **A 225.7** (363.2 km) **H 6.8** (10.9 km) **Oceanview RV Park.** See display ad this section. ▲

Anchor River (Beach) Road Log

Turn off the Sterling Highway at **Milepost S 156.9** on to the Old Sterling Highway and continue past the Anchor River Inn to the Anchor River. Just beyond the bridge is the turnoff for Anchor River (Beach) Road, a 1.2-mile/1.9-km spur road providing access to Anchor River recreation area.

Distance from junction (J) is shown.

J 0 Junction of Old Sterling Highway and Sterling Highway at **Milepost S 156.9**.

J 0.1 (0.2 km) School Road. Anchor River visitor information center. A plaque across from the visitor center marks the westernmost point on the contiguous North American Highway system.

Anchor River Inn, overlooking beautiful Anchor River and in business for 20 years, has the finest family restaurant on the peninsula, serving breakfast, lunch and dinner. Smells of fresh-baked bread, cinnamon rolls, delicious pies, etc., fill the dining room from our bakery. Large cocktail lounge has a wide-screen TV, pool tables, dance floor and video games. 20 modern motel units with phones; 10 spacious units with color TV and two queen-sized beds, and 10 smaller units overlooking the river. Our new liquor and grocery store serves the Anchor Point area year-round. Both are fully stocked. Write: Box 154, Anchor Point, AK 99556; phone (907) 235-8531; fax (907) 235-2296. Your hosts: Bob and Simonne Clutts. [ADVERTISEMENT]

J 0.3 (0.5 km) Anchor River bridge, also known as "the erector set bridge."

Mount Iliamna. (Jerrianne Lowther, staff)

J 0.4 (0.6 km) Road forks: Old Sterling Highway continues south and rejoins Sterling Highway at **Milepost S 164.9**. Turn right for Anchor River (Beach) Road which follows the Anchor River west and dead ends at Cook Inlet. Viewing platform and plaque at end of road mark the westernmost point you can drive to on the contiguous North American road system.

Silver King state campground (Anchor River State Recreation Area); RV camping, toilets, dumpster, $6 nightly fee or annual pass. Public water source located at Mile 1.2, just beyond Slide Hole Campground. At west end of this campground is a special senior/handicapped campground. ♿▲

Wallin's Hilltop Bed & Breakfast. See display ad this section.

J 0.6 (1 km) Coho state campground (Anchor River SRA); camping, toilets, $6 nightly fee or annual pass. ▲

J 0.7 (1.1 km) Anchor Point Chamber of Commerce information center.

J 0.7 (1.1 km) **Silver King Tackle Shop.** See display ad this section.

J 0.8 (1.3 km) Steelhead state campground (Anchor River SRA); camping, toilets, $6 nightly fee or annual pass. ▲

J 1.1 (1.8 km) Slide Hole state campground (Anchor River SRA); newly developed, 30 units, $8 nightly fee or annual pass, shelter with tables, large day-use parking lot, trail access to river. ▲

J 1.2 (1.9 km) Public water source for campers.

J 1.3 (2.1 km) **Kyllonen's RV Park**, a few steps from famous Anchor River and picturesque Cook Inlet. Providing spring water, electricity and sewer. Additional amenities include fish cleaning station, BBQ pits, free firewood and picnic tables. Showers, restrooms. Gift shop. Fishing tackle and licenses. We book fishing charters and area sightseeing tours. May through September. Year-round area information center, phone (907) 235-7451, fax (907) 235-6435. See display ad this section [ADVERTISEMENT] ▲

J 1.5 (2.4 km) Halibut state campground (Anchor River SRA); camping, toilets, $6 nightly fee or annual pass. ▲

J 1.6 (2.6 km) Road ends on shore of Cook Inlet; beach access, 12-hour parking. Signs here mark the most westerly point on the North American continent accessible by continuous road system and depict outlines of Cook Inlet volcanoes.

The Anchor Point area is noted for seasonal king and silver salmon, steelhead and rainbow fishing. Saltwater trolling for king salmon to 80 lbs., halibut to 200 lbs., spring through fall. **Anchor River**, king salmon fishing permitted only on five consecutive weekends, beginning Memorial Day weekend; trout and steelhead from July to October; closed to all fishing Dec. 31 to June 30, except for king salmon weekends. Fishermen report excellent fishing for 12- to 24-inch sea-run Dollies in July and late summer. During the August silver runs, fishing with high tides is usually more productive, because the Anchor River's water level is lower at that time of year.

Anchor River King Salmon Derby is usually held the last weekend in May and the first four weekends in June. Prizes for first fish caught and heaviest fish, each weekend, plus a mystery fish special prize. A silver salmon derby is held in August.

Return to Milepost S 156.9 Sterling Highway

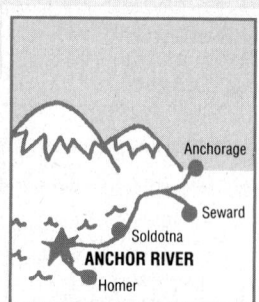

S 172.8 (278.1 km) **A 225.8** (363.4 km) **H 6.7** (10.8 km) Exit onto Pioneer Avenue for downtown **HOMER** (description follows). Drive 0.2 mile/0.3 km on Pioneer Avenue and turn left on Bartlett Avenue for the Pratt Museum (see Attractions in the Homer section) and Homer city campground (follow signs). Pioneer Avenue continues through downtown Homer to Lake Street and to East Hill Road. ▲

NOTE: Watch for road construction on Pioneer Avenue in 1994.

S 173.1 (278.6 km) **A 226.1** (363.9 km) **H 6.4** (10.3 km) Main Street, access to food, lodging and other services. Bishop's Beach Park.

S 173.5 (279.2 km) **A 226.5** (364.5 km) **H 6** (9.7 km) Eagle Quality Center; shopping, groceries.

S 173.7 (279.5 km) **A 226.7** (364.8 km) **H 5.8** (9.3 km) Heath Street. Post office (Zip code 99603).

S 173.9 (279.9 km) **A 226.9** (365.2 km) **H 5.6** (9 km) Lake Street. Access to downtown Homer and Lakeside Center.

S 174 (280 km) **A 227** (365.3 km) **H 5.5** (8.9 km) Beluga Lake floatplane base.

S 174.4 (280.7 km) **A 227.4** (366 km) **H 5.1** (8.2 km) Lambert Lane, access to floatplane base.

S 174.7 (281.1 km) **A 227.7** (366.4 km) **H 4.8** (7.7 km) Alaska Dept. of Fish and Game office.

S 175 (281.6 km) **A 228** (366.9 km) **H 4.5** (7.2 km) Airport Road. Sterling Highway crosses onto Homer Spit.

A series of boardwalks along the Spit house shops, charter services, food outlets, etc. Also on the Spit: a Chamber of Commerce Visitor Center, resort hotel, restaurants, seafood markets, general store, private campgrounds, and public camping areas (check in with camping registration office at visitor center); the harbormaster's office, small boat basin (shore fishing for salmon), Alaska Marine Highway ferry terminal and a boat ramp. ▲

S 179.5 (288.9 km) **A 232.5** (374.2 km) **H 0** Sterling Highway ends at Land's End Resort and Campground at the tip of Homer Spit.

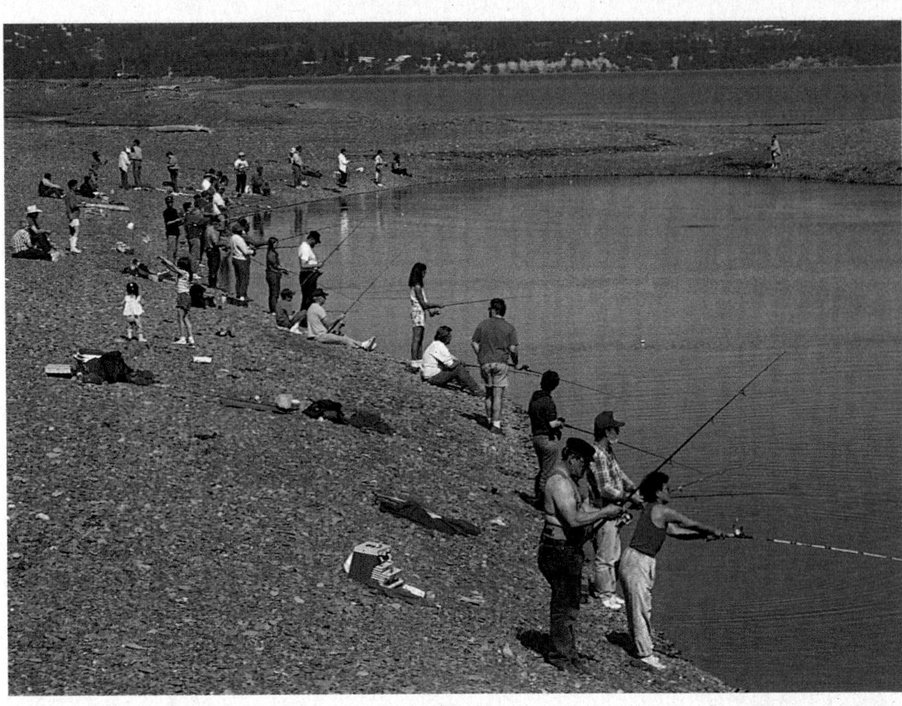

Fishermen try their luck at Homer boat basin. (Jerrianne Lowther, staff)

Homer

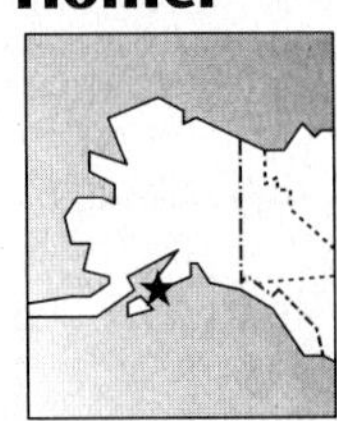

Located on the southwestern Kenai Peninsula on the north shore of Kachemak Bay at the easterly side of the mouth of Cook Inlet; 226 miles/364 km by highway or 40 minutes by jet aircraft from Anchorage. **Population:** 4,020. **Emergency Services:** Phone 911 for all emergency services. **City Police**, phone 235-3150. **Alaska State Troopers**, in the Public Safety Bldg., phone 235-8239. **Fire Department** and **Ambulance**, phone 235-3155. **Coast Guard**, phone Zenith 5555. (Coast Guard Auxiliary, phone 235-7277.) **Hospital**, South Peninsula, phone 235-8101. **Veterinary Clinic**, phone 235-8960.

Visitor Information: Chamber of Commerce Visitor Center is located on Homer Spit. Open from Memorial Day to Labor Day. Contact the Homer Chamber of Commerce, Box 541, Homer 99603; phone during business hours 235-7740 or 235-5300.

The Pratt Museum Visitor Information Center is open daily 10 A.M. to 6 P.M. from May through September; open noon to 5 P.M. Tuesday through Sunday from October through April; closed in January. Contact the Pratt Museum, 3779 Bartlett St., Homer 99603. Phone 235-8635.

Elevation: Sea level to 800 feet/244m. **Climate:** Winter temperatures occasionally fall below zero, but seldom colder. The Kenai Mountains north and east protect Homer from severe cold, and Cook Inlet provides warming air currents. The highest temperature recorded is 81°F/27°C. Average annual precipitation is 27.9 inches. Prevailing winds are from the northeast, averaging 6.5 mph/10.5 kmph. **Radio:** KGTL 620, KWAV 103.5/104.9/106.3, MBN-FM 107.1/96.7/95.3, KBBI 890, KPEN-FM 99.3/100.9/102.3, KWHQ-FM 98.3. **Television:** KENI Channel 2, KTVA Channel 4, KAKM

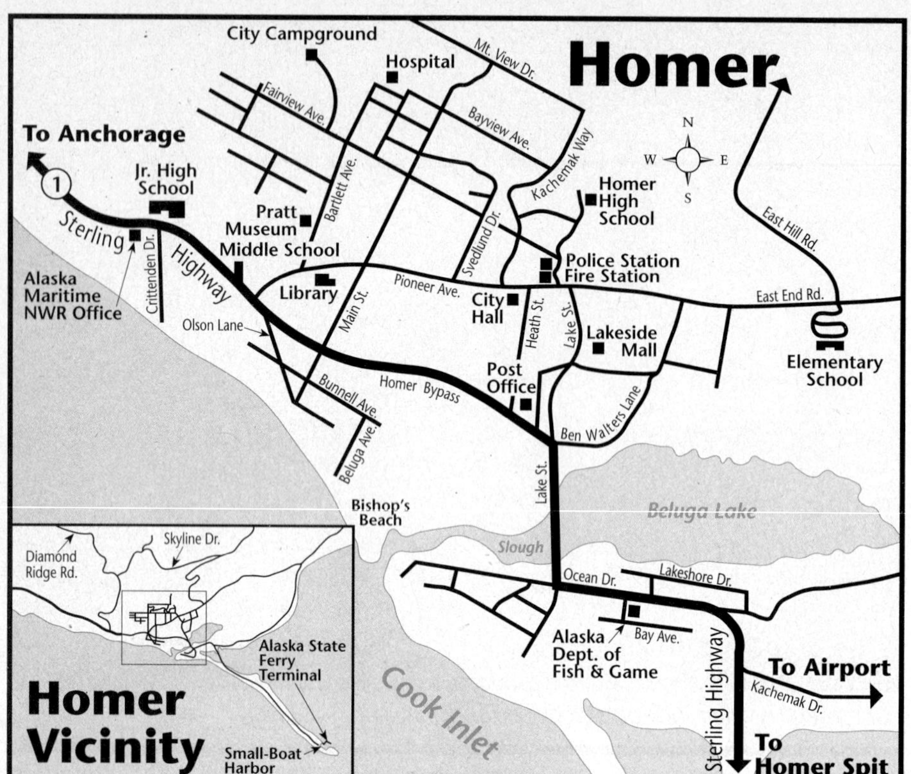

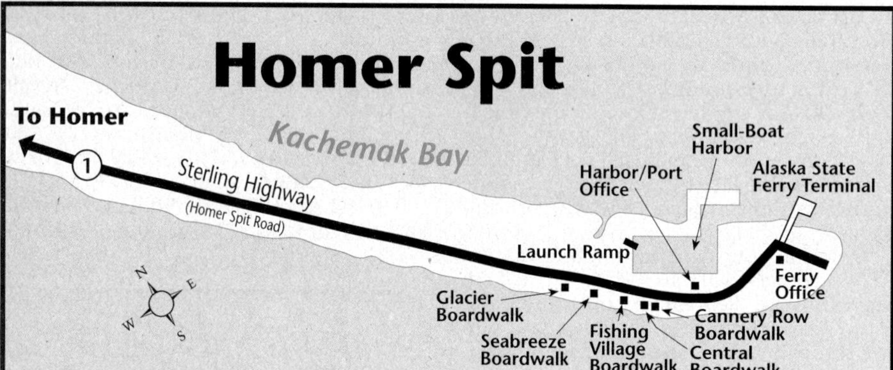

Channel 7, KIMO Channel 13. **Newspaper:** *Homer News* (weekly).

Private Aircraft: Homer airport, 1.7 miles/2.7 km east; elev. 78 feet/24m; length 7,400 feet/2,255m; asphalt; fuel 100LL, Jet A; attended.

In the late 1800s, a coal mine was operating at Homer's Bluff Point, and a railroad carried the coal out to the end of Homer Spit. (The railroad was abandoned in 1907.) Gold seekers debarked at Homer, bound for the goldfields at Hope and Sunrise. The community of Homer was established about 1896 and named for Homer Pennock.

Coal mining operations ceased about WWI, but settlers continued to trickle into the area, some to homestead, others to work in the canneries built to process Cook Inlet fish.

Today, Homer's picturesque setting, mild climate and great fishing (especially for halibut) attract thousands of visitors each year. In addition to its tourist industry and role as a trade center, Homer's commercial fishing industry is an important part of its economy. Homer calls itself the "Halibut Fishing Capital of the World." Manufacturing and seafood processing, government offices, trades and construction are other key industries.

Rising behind the townsite are the gently sloping bluffs which level off at about 1,200 feet/366m to form the southern rim of the western plateau of the Kenai. These green slopes are tinted in pastel shades by acres of wildflowers from June to September; fireweed predominates among scattered patches of geranium, paintbrush, lupine, rose and many other species. Two main roads (East Hill Road and West Hill Road) lead from the Homer business section to the "Skyline Drive" along the rim of the bluffs, and other roads connect with many homesteads on the "Hill."

The name *Kachemak* (in Aleut dialect said to mean "smoky bay") was supposedly derived from the smoke which once rose from the smoldering coal seams jutting from the clay bluffs of the upper north shore of Kachemak Bay and the cliffs near Anchor Point. In the early days many of the exposed coal seams were slowly burning from causes unknown. Today the erosion of these bluffs drops huge fragments of lignite and bituminous coal on the beaches, creating a plenti-

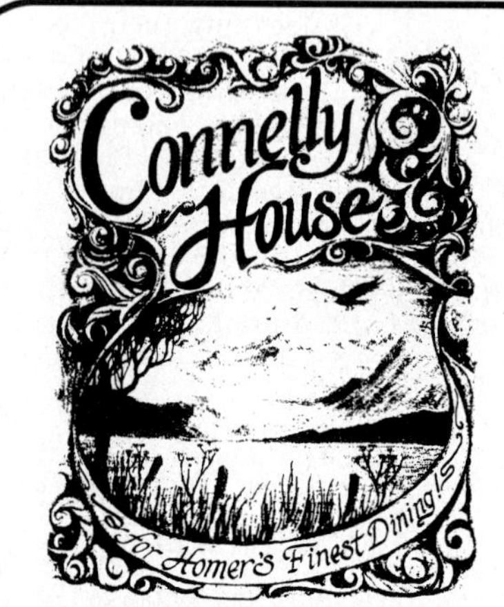

ful supply of winter fuel for the residents. There are an estimated 400,000,000 tons of coal deposit in the immediate vicinity of Homer.

Kachemak is a magnificent deep-water bay that reaches inland from Cook Inlet for 30 miles/48.3 km, with an average width of 7 miles/11.3 km. The bay is rich in marine life. The wild timbered coastline of the south shore, across from Homer, is indented with many fjords and inlets, reaching far into the rugged glacier-capped peaks of the Kenai Mountains.

Jutting out for nearly 5 miles/8 km from the Homer shore is the Homer Spit, a long, narrow bar of gravel. The road along the backbone of the Spit connects with the main road through Homer (all the Sterling Highway). The Spit has had quite a history, and it continues to be a center of activity for the town. In 1964, after the earthquake, the Spit sank 4 to 6 feet, requiring several buildings to be moved to higher ground. Today, the Spit is the site of a major dock facility for boat loading, unloading, servicing and refrigerating. The deep-water dock can accommodate up to two 340-foot vessels with 30-foot drafts at the same time, making it accessible to cruise and cargo ships. It is also home port to the Alaska Marine Highway ferry MV *Tustumena*. The small-boat harbor on the Spit has a five-lane load/launch ramp. Also in the small-boat harbor area are the harbormaster's office, canneries, parking/camping areas, charter services, small shops, restaurants and a motel.

In summer, the Homer Spit bustles with activity: people fish from its shores for salmon; fishermen come and go in their boats; cars, trucks and trailers line the road; tent camps are set up on the beach; and boat builders and repairers are busy at their craft. Fresh crab, shrimp and halibut, as well as smoked fish, can be purchased from seafood shops on the Spit or sometimes from the fishermen themselves. Seafood processors on Homer Spit offer custom smoking, freezing and air shipping for sport-caught fish. It is also possible to trade your sport-caught fish for similar fish already processed and ready to ship or take with you.

ACCOMMODATIONS

Homer has hundreds of small businesses offering a wide variety of goods and services. There are many hotels, motels and bed and breakfasts for lodging. Nearly 40 restaurants offer meals ranging from fast food to fine dining. Travelers are advised to book overnight accommodations well in advance during the busy summer months. Homer has a post office, library, museum, laundromats, gas stations with propane and dump stations, four banks and a hospital. There are many boat charters, boat repair and storage facilities, marine fuel at Homer marina, bait, tackle and sporting goods stores, and also art galleries, gift shops and groceries.

Homer Spit has both long-term parking

and camping. Camping and parking areas are well-marked. Camping fees are $7 per night for RVs and $3 per night for tents. Camping permits are available at the Chamber of Commerce Visitor Center on the Spit. There is a 14-day limit; restrooms, water and garbage available. Check with the harbormaster's office or the Chamber of Commerce Visitor Center on the Spit if you have questions on rules and regulations pertaining to camping, campfires, long-term parking, boat launching and moorage. Homer City Campground, on a hill overlooking town, is reached via Bartlett Avenue (follow signs). ▲

Following are paid advertisements for campgrounds, lodging, restaurants, and food, gift, clothing and equipment outlets. A number of other services and stores are listed under Attractions.

Homer Spit Campground. Beachfront campsites at the end of the Homer Spit. Shore fishing, crabbing, clamming, beachcombing within a minute's walk. Clean restrooms, plenty of hot water for showers. Electrical hookups, dump station and cheerful complete visitor information. Reservations advised. Headquarters for Kachemak Bay Adventures Boat Tours. Ask about puffin-viewing trips to Gull Island and Seldovia aboard our 60-foot MV *Endeavor*. Campground, boat tour packages. Box 1196, Homer, AK 99603; phone (907) 235-8206. [ADVERTISEMENT] ▲

Land's End RV Park. On the water's edge, at the tip of Homer Spit. Truly the most spectacular spot on the Kenai Peninsula. Gorgeous mountain views and sunsets. Minutes from the Spit's boardwalks and small-boat harbor. Electric hookups, laundry. Showers, ice, sundries. Open May through September. (907) 235-2525. P.O. Box 273, Homer, AK 99603. [ADVERTISEMENT] ▲

Oceanview RV Park just past Best Western Bidarka Inn on your right coming into Homer. Spectacular view of Kachemak Bay, beachfront setting. 85 large pull-through spaces in terraced park. Full/partial hookups, heated restrooms, showers, laundry, pay phone, free cable TV, picnic area. Walking distance to downtown Homer. Special halibut charter rates for park guests. Phone (907) 235-3951. See display ad at Mile 172.7 Sterling Highway. [ADVERTISEMENT] ▲

Addie's Porpoise Room Restaurant and Cocktail Lounge located on the world-famous Homer Spit. Overlooking the beautiful Homer boat harbor. On a clear day you can see the famous St. Augustine volcano across Cook Inlet. Fine dining; families welcome. Open all year. We cater to locals as well as tourists. Your hosts: Bob and Addie Klemke. (907) 235-8132. See display ad this section. [ADVERTISEMENT]

Alaska's Pioneer Inn/Bed & Breakfast, 243 Pioneer Ave., in downtown Homer. Comfortable one-bedroom suites with private baths and furnished kitchens. Sleeps up to four. Continental breakfast available or

prepare your own. Complimentary coffee. Single bedrooms available. Year-round. Homer's best value. Brochure: P.O. Box 1430, Homer, AK 99603. (907) 235-5670. In Alaska, 1-800-478-8765. [ADVERTISEMENT]

Almost Home B & B. Come and enjoy fantastic Alaskan hospitality with us! We have two bedrooms with mini-kitchen and shared bath. Continental breakfast includes homemade bread, fruit, cereal, gourmet coffees and teas. We also offer halibut charter packages and salmon driftboat charters. VISA, MasterCard accepted. Reservations recommended. (907) 235-2553. In Alaska, 1-800-478-2352; 1269 Upland Court, Homer, AK 99603. [ADVERTISEMENT]

Bay View Inn. Spectacular panoramic view from the top of the hill as you enter Homer. Every room overlooks Kachemak Bay and the Kenai Mountains. Clean, attractive rooms with firm, comfortable beds and private bathrooms. Options include kitchenettes, suite with fireplace, and secluded honeymoon cottage. Friendly, personal service with local tour information and activity recommendations. In a serene setting with a spacious lawn, picnic tables, and freshly brewed morning coffee. Mile 170 Sterling Highway. P.O. Box 804, Homer, AK 99603. Phone (907) 235-8485. In Alaska 1-800-478-8485. See display ad this section. [ADVERTISEMENT]

Brass Ring Bed and Breakfast. Beautiful custom log home nestled among towering spruce trees, walking distance to shops, restaurants. Six comfortable guest rooms, decorated with Norwegian stenciling, antiques and quilts. Large country kitchen, sumptuous breakfasts emphasizing Alaskan entrees and friendly atmosphere. Enjoy outdoor spa tub! Nonsmoking; children over 6 welcome (no pets, please). Open year-round, summer and winter rates. Hosts: longtime Alaskans Vince and Joyce Porte. 987 Hillfair Court, Homer, AK 99603. (907) 235-5450. [ADVERTISEMENT]

Driftwood Inn. Charming, historic beachfront hotel/motel, B&B, RV parking. Spectacular view overlooking beautiful Kachemak Bay, mountains, glaciers. Quiet downtown location. Completely renovated, color TVs, immaculately clean, unique rooms. Free coffee, tea, local pickup/delivery, local information. Comfortable common areas with TV, fireplace, library, microwave, refrigerator, barbecue, shellfish cooker, fish cleaning area, freezer, picnic and laundry facilities. Continental breakfast available. Friendly, knowledgeable staff, specializing in helping make your stay in Homer the best possible. Reasonable, seasonal rates. Open year-round. Write, call for brochure. 135 W. Bunnell Ave., MP, Homer, AK 99603. (907) 235-8019. In Alaska 1-800-478-8019. [ADVERTISEMENT]

Fresh Sourdough Express Bakery & Restaurant and Gift Shop. Enjoy our cozy restaurant on the way to Homer Spit. Warm, friendly atmosphere. We grind our flour fresh daily for highest quality. Sourdough breads. Gourmet full-line bakery. Healthy, hearty breakfast, lunch and dinners. Great local seafood. Fine beers and wine. Charter lunches and special orders. Fresh ground coffee and cappuccino. Credit cards accepted. (907) 235-7571. [ADVERTISEMENT]

Heritage Hotel-Lodge. One of Alaska's finest log hotels, conveniently located in the heart of Homer. Walking distance to beach, shops, museum. Accommodations: 36 rooms including suite with wet bar. Reasonable rates. Color TV, movie channels. Phones, free local calls. Courtesy coffee, airport shuttle. Restaurant on premises. Alaskan hospitality and decor greet you in our spacious lobby. Open year-round. 147 E. Pioneer Ave., phone (907) 235-7787. Reservations 1-800-478-7789 in Alaska. Fax (907) 235-2804. See display ad this section. [ADVERTISEMENT]

Homer B&B/Seekins: Located 2 miles up East Hill on Race Road. Spectacular view of Kachemak Bay, glacier, snow-covered mountains. Private bath, cable TV. Kitchen completely furnished, coffee, tea, popcorn and

Moonrise over Homer Spit. (Jerrianne Lowther, staff)

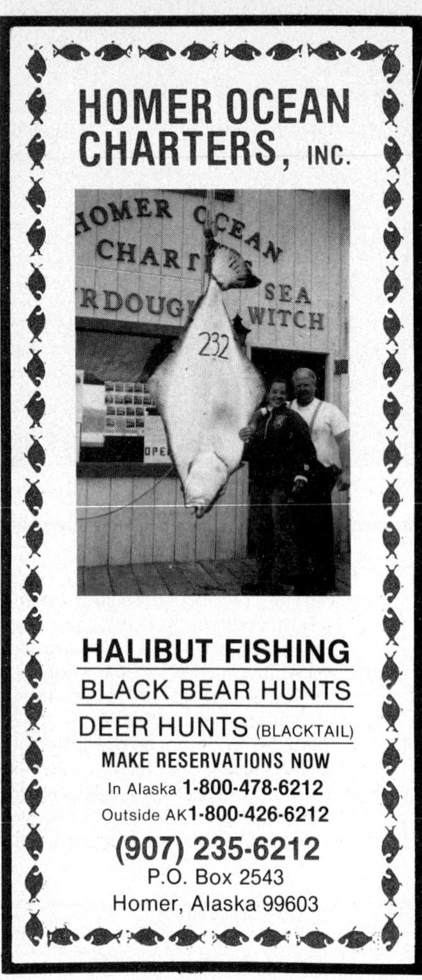

popper, dishes. Yummy breakfasts. Wildflowers, occasional moose, outdoor wood-heated sauna. Fishing charters, halibut, salmon, full/half days. Land tours. Reasonable rates, clean, fantastic view, Alaskan hospitality. Your hosts, Floyd and Gert, moved to Homer in 1969 from Wisconsin and Minnesota. Box 1264, Homer, AK 99603. (907) 235-8996 or 235-8998. Fax (907) 235-2625. [ADVERTISEMENT]

Journeymen's B & B. Join us — Ron, Gay and Peggy Pendleton — for some down-Homer hospitality in our spacious one-level home, Mile 3.8 East Road. Panoramic view of Kachemak Bay, Kenai Mountains, glaciers. Families welcome. Nonsmoking, no alcohol. Full breakfast, home-baked goodies. Winter rates September through April. Phone (907) 235-UBET (235-8238); P.O. Box 3106-MP, Homer, AK 99603. [ADVERTISEMENT]

Land's End Resort. Open year-round! Homer Spit's only hotel, on the water, at the tip of Homer Spit. Breathtaking views! Abundant sea life at your doorstep. Inside, one of Alaska's premier, full-service restaurants. Homer's favorite Sunday brunch! Wheelhouse lounge for lighter meals and live entertainment. Between Oct. 1 and April 30, rates 30 percent off. Truly an Alaskan landmark! (907) 235-2500. P.O. Box 273, Homer, AK 99603. [ADVERTISEMENT]

NOMAR (Northern Marine Canvas Products) began business the summer of 1978 in a yellow school bus. Today, visit our manufacturing facility and manufacturer's outlet store at 104 E. Pioneer Ave., downtown Homer. NOMAR manufactures a wide variety of products for our Alaskan lifestyles. Softsided 'Laska Luggage® that's stuffable and floatplane friendly. Watertight bags for kayak tours or whitewater expeditions. Warm polar fleece clothing to keep you warm, no matter what the adventure, and well-made, Homer-made, packable, mailable, useful gifts for everyone on the "list." Park in our spacious, paved parking lot and take a walk around our town. We'll gladly ship your purchases for you. See display ad this section. [ADVERTISEMENT]

Ocean Shores Motel. Beachfront property, two blocks to downtown. $40 to $90. Conventional motel rooms, kitchens, also available. Spectacular views, acres of grass,

flowers, picnic tables and fenced playground for children. Centrally located for fishing and sightseeing. (907) 235-7775 or 1-800-456-5593. Write: 3500-M Crittenden Dr., Homer, AK 99603. [ADVERTISEMENT]

Seaside Farm. Hostel bunkhouse, guest cottages, tent campground with picnic area, BBQ, beach trails. For budget-minded travelers, backpackers, nature lovers, families wanting a friendly, fun, informal atmosphere. Beautiful gardens, scenic horse pastures, raspberry patch, birds, ducks, farm pets. Drop-ins welcome. 58335 East End Rd., Homer, AK 99603; phone (907) 235-7850. [ADVERTISEMENT]

SunSpin Guest House. Affordable! Clean! Quiet! Private comfortable room or large bunkroom. Share spacious living room, TV/VCR. Heart of town on wooded acre, beautiful view mountains, glacier, bay. Full

Kachemak Bay boat traffic includes craft of all sizes. (Jerrianne Lowther, staff)

homemade breakfast. Warm hospitality. Close walk to everything except harbor or airport; courtesy shuttle from transportation terminals. Randi Somers, 358 E. Lee Dr., Homer, AK 99603. 1-800-391-6677 or (907) 235-6677. Fax (907) 235-1022. [ADVERTISEMENT]

Woodside Apartments and Bed & Breakfast. Your hosts, Merle and Billie Meisinger, welcome guests with hospitality, enthusiasm and a wealth of local information. Offering plush, spacious furnished apartments with really comfortable beds. Sparkling kitchens and bathrooms, dishes, pots, pans, linens, phones and cable TV, along with freezer space and laundry facilities, make for the most comfortable, convenient stay in Homer. Bed-and-breakfast rooms are also available. Quiet. Reasonable rates. Nightly/weekly. We can make all your reservations for halibut fishing — salmon fishing — lodging — sightseeing or wildlife tours. Everything organized for you when you arrive for your "Alaskan Adventure." From the Sterling Highway turn left onto Pioneer Ave., then turn left immediately on Woodside Ave. (behind the intermediate school, see Homer map). Phone (907) 235-8389; see display ad. [ADVERTISEMENT]

TRANSPORTATION

Air: Regularly scheduled air service to Anchorage. Several charter services also operate out of Homer.

Ferry: The Alaska State ferry *Tustumena* serves Seldovia, Kodiak, Seward, Port Lions, Valdez and Cordova from Homer with a limited schedule to Sand Point and King Cove. Natural history programs offered on ferry in summer by Alaska Maritime National Wildlife Refuge naturalists. See MARINE ACCESS ROUTES section for details, or contact the offices of the Alaska Marine Highway System at the City Dock, phone 235-8449. Tour boats offer passenger service to Seldovia and Halibut Cove.

Local: Two major rental car agencies and several taxi services.

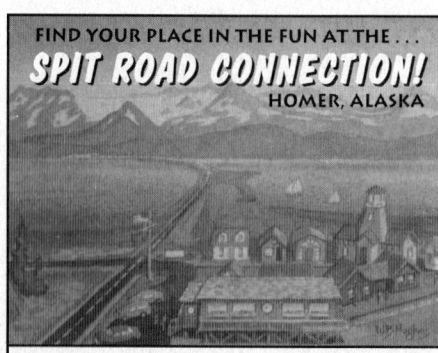

ATTRACTIONS

The **Pratt Museum**, focusing on the natural and cultural history of southcentral Alaska, is located at 3779 Bartlett St. Exhibits include artifacts from the area's first Native people, thousands of years ago, to homesteaders of the 1930s and 1940s. Excellent aquariums and a touch-tank feature live Kachemak Bay sea creatures. Also exhibited are Alaskan birds and land and sea mammals, including the complete skeletons of a Bering Sea beaked whale and a beluga whale.

Changing exhibits feature Alaskan artwork and other topics of special interest. Beautiful handmade quilts depict local natural history themes. Summer visitors may take a self-guided tour through the botanical garden for a look at local wild plants. The Museum Store features books and Alaskan collectibles.

The Pratt Museum is sponsored by the Homer Society of Natural History. All facili-

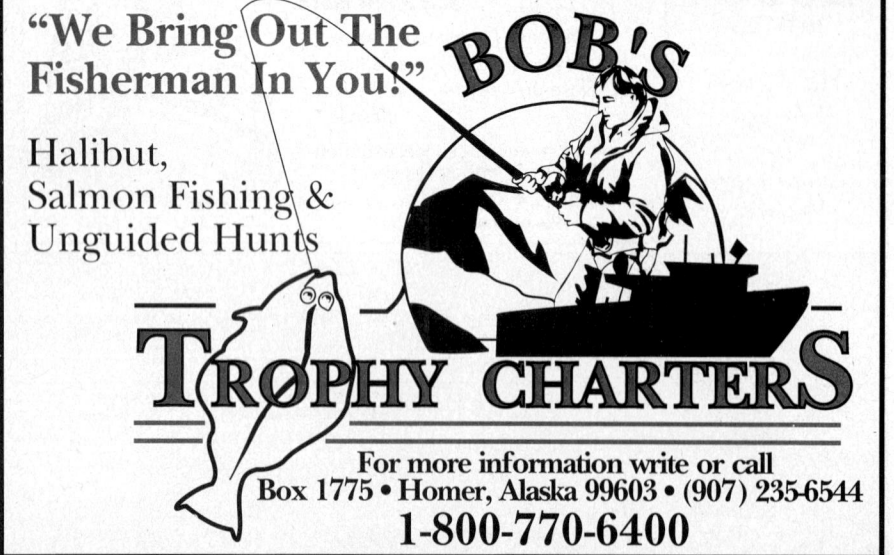

ties are handicap accessible. A 45-minute taped audiotour is available. Admission charged; children under 18 years free, members and their guests free. Summer hours (May through September), 10 A.M. to 6 P.M. daily. Winter hours (October through April), noon to 5 P.M., Tuesday through Sunday. Closed January. Phone (907) 235-8635. ♿

The U.S. Fish and Wildlife Alaska Maritime National Wildlife Refuge protects the habitats of seabirds and marine mammals on 3,500 islands and rocks along the coastline from Ketchikan to Barrow. The visitor center is open in summer from 9 A.M. to 6 P.M. daily. Winter hours are 10 A.M. to 5 P.M. weekdays only. The center has displays focusing on the marine environment, videos and a small shop selling books and pamphlets. Wildlife programs include guided bird walks and beach walks, special slide presentations and a children's nature hour. Join the naturalists at the visitor center for an informative day. Phone (907) 235-6961. It is located at 509 Sterling Hwy., Homer 99603.

The Kachemak Bay Shorebird Festival is usually held on the second weekend in May (sceduled for May 6–8, 1994) to celebrate the arrival of 100,000 migrating birds on the Homer Spit. The festival features dozens of activities, from guided bird walks to an art gallery "migration." Co-sponsored by the Wildlife Refuge and the Homer Chamber of Commerce; phone (907) 235-7740.

Fish the Homer Halibut Derby. The annual Jackpot Halibut Derby, sponsored by the Homer Chamber of Commerce, runs from May 1 through Labor Day. The state's largest cash halibut derby ($85,000) provides four monthly cash prizes, tagged fish and final jackpot prize. Tickets are $5 and available at the Jackpot Halibut Derby headquarters on Homer Spit, visitor center or local charter service offices. Phone (907) 235-7740. The 1992 winner was a 308½-lb. halibut (cash prize was $20,096).

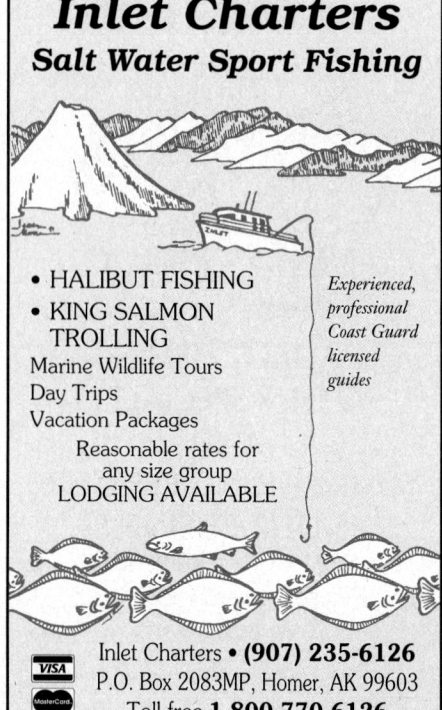

Charter boats, operating out of the boat harbor on Homer Spit, offer sightseeing and halibut fishing trips. (Charter salmon fishing trips, clamming, crabbing, and sightseeing charters are also available.) These charter operators provide gear, bait and expert knowledge of the area. Homer is one of Alaska's largest charter fishing areas (most charters are for halibut fishing). Charter boats for halibut fishermen cost about $120 to $155 a day. Several sightseeing boats operate off the Homer Spit, taking visitors to view the bird rookery on Gull Island, to Halibut Cove and to Seldovia. (Most sightseeing trips are available Memorial Day to Labor Day.)

AREA FISHING: The Kachemak Bay and Cook Inlet area is one of Alaska's most popular spots for halibut fishing, with catches often weighing 100 to 200 lbs. Guides and charters are available locally. Halibut up to 350 lbs. are fished from June through September, bottom fish with herring. Year-round trolling for king salmon is popular, use small herring; pink salmon 4 to 5 lbs., July and August, use winged bobbers, small weighted spoons and spinners; silver salmon 6 to 8 lbs., August and September. Dolly Varden and rainbow are pulled from nearby streams and Tutka Lagoon from April to October, try candlefish for bait.

Fishermen have had great success in recent years casting from the shore of Homer Spit for king salmon. The Fishin' Lagoon on the Homer Spit supports a large run of hatchery-produced kings and silvers beginning in late May and continuing to August. Kings range from 20 to 30 lbs. The fishery is open seven days a week in season; limit of two kings per day from lagoon up to season limit of five Cook Inlet kings. (Check current regulations.)

Pink and coho salmon are also released on Homer Spit. Pink salmon return in July, and coho provide the best fishing in August and September. The limit for both these species is six fish per day.

Take a scenic drive. East End Road, a 20-mile/32-km drive from downtown Homer, climbs through hills and forests toward the head of Kachemak Bay; pavement ends at Mile 10, beautiful views of the bay. Or turn off East End Road on to East Hill Road and drive up the bluffs to Skyline Drive; beautiful views of the bay and glaciers. Return to town via West Hill Road, which intersects the Sterling Highway at **Milepost S 167.1**.

The glaciers that spill down from the Harding Icefield straddling the Kenai Mountains across the bay create an ever-changing panorama visible from most points in Homer, particularly from the Skyline Drive. The most spectacular and largest of these glaciers is Grewingk Glacier in Kachemak Bay State Park, visible to the east directly across Kachemak Bay from Homer. The glacier was named by Alaska explorer William H. Dall in 1880 for Constantin Grewingk, a German geologist who had published a work on the geology and volcanism of Alaska. The Grewingk Glacier has a long gravel bar at its terminal moraine, behind which the water draining from the ice flows into the bay. This gravel bar, called Glacier Spit, is a popular excursion spot, and may be visited by charter plane or boat. (There are several charter plane operators and charter helicopter services in Homer.) Portlock and Dixon glaciers are also visible directly across from the spit.

Kachemak Bay State Park is located on the south shore of the bay and includes glaciers, alpine tundra, forests, fjords, bays and high-country lakes. Recently the state enlarged this park by the purchase of 23,802 additional acres of land with funds from the settlement of the Exxon Valdez oil spill. The trail system offers hiking from Glacier Spit to China Poot Peak. Crabs, clams, Dolly Varden and salmon abound. Campsites available on Glacier Spit, Halibut Cove Lagoon and China Poot Lake. Inquire locally about transportation to the park. Phone the district office at 235-7024 for more information or stop by the state park office at **Milepost S 168.5**.

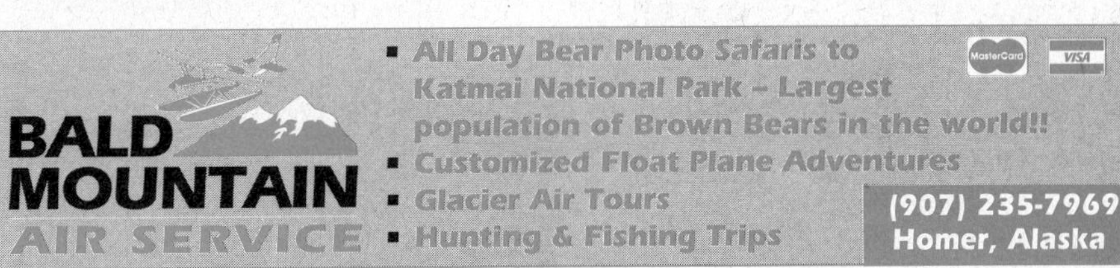

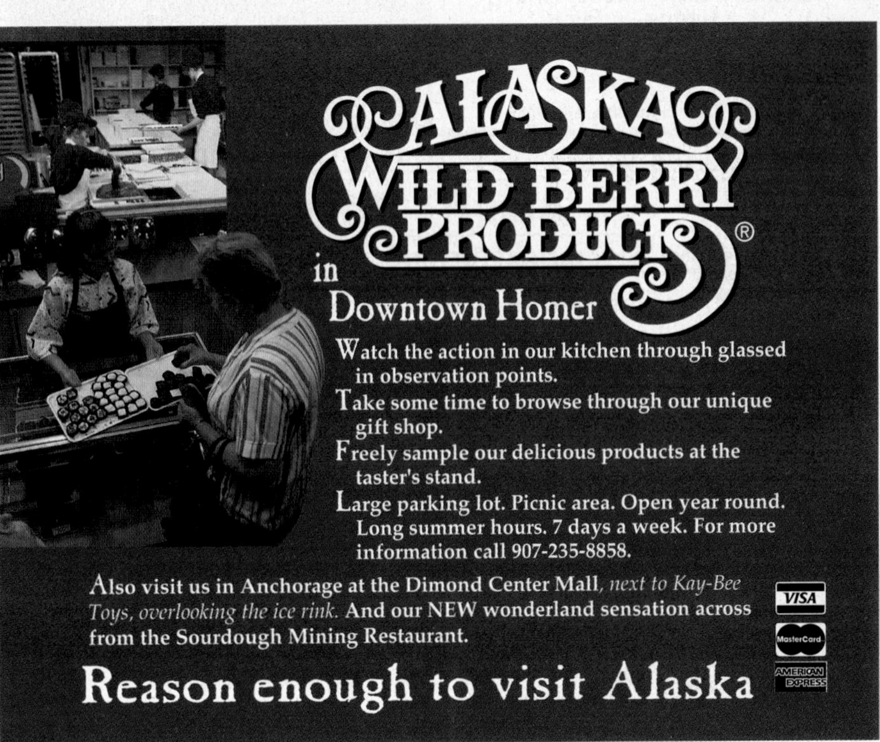

McNeil River State Game Sanctuary. Homer is the main base for visitors flying across Cook Inlet to the sanctuary, where the world's largest concentration of bears in a natural area this size is found. Brown bears congregate near the mouth of the river, where a falls slows down migrating salmon, making fishing easy for the bears. Visits to the game sanctuary are on a permit basis; a drawing for the limited number of permits is held in April each year. Permit applications are available from the Alaska Dept. of Fish and Game, Attn: McNeil River, 333 Raspberry Road, Anchorage 99518. Phone 267-2180.

Study Marine Environment. The Center for Alaskan Coastal Studies is located across Kachemak Bay from Homer. Volunteer naturalists lead a day tour which includes Gull Island bird rookery, coastal forest and intertidal areas. Write the Center for Alaskan Coastal Studies, P.O. Box 2225-MP, Homer 99603; phone 235-6667. Reservations, phone 235-7272.

AH!LASKA Connection Gift Shop and Espresso. Sip and shop. Great deals on all kinds of Alaskan-made products. Headquarters for AH!LASKA baking mixes, cocoas, books — products with a purpose. Free samples. We ship. Gift packs available. Visitor information. On Bartlett Street, near Pratt Museum. (907) 235-7770. Box 940, Homer, AK 99603. [ADVERTISEMENT]

Alaska Maritime Tours. Enjoy the only half-day wildlife tour from Homer to Seldovia which includes Gull Island bird rookery. Top quality, personal service is provided aboard the 50-foot MV *Denaina*. Two daily departures: 8 A.M. and 1:30 P.M. Weekly all-day birding trips to Barren Islands scheduled June–August. Bring camera, extra film, warm jacket, light rain gear to be prepared to spend time outside on deck for close-up views of puffins, sea otters and occasional whales. Located on Homer Spit in the Dockside Bldg., 4460 Homer Spit Rd., two doors beyond Salty Dawg. Call (907) 235-2490 or in Alaska 1-800-478-2490 for reservations or brochure. See display ad this section. [ADVERTISEMENT]

Bald Mountain Air. All-day bear photo safaris. Direct from Homer via floatplane to the heart of Katmai National Park. Let lifelong Alaskans Gary and Jeanne Porter take you on an adventure you'll never forget. Fly-in fishing supreme. All five species of salmon, rainbow and lake trout. Expect the best out of your Alaskan vacation — Call or write us for more information. (907) 235-7969. P.O. Box 3134, Homer, AK 99603. [ADVERTISEMENT]

The Bookstore, located in Eagle Quality Center, specializes in Alaskan, nature, cooking and children's books. It is acclaimed as one of the nicest bookstores in the state. Besides a great selection of paperback books, it features the most original card selection on the Peninsula (many by local artists) and a very special kids' corner. Browsers invited. Hours 10 A.M. to 7 P.M. 436 Sterling Highway. (907) 235-7496. [ADVERTISEMENT]

Brown Bear Viewing. Fly across Cook Inlet in a Kachemak Air Service, Inc. floatplane to see Alaskan brown bears as they walk along beaches and fish streams for salmon. Inquire about these flights; or about a five-day Bear Viewing Cruise; or about guided camping trips to view bears. Write or phone Kachemak Air Service, Inc., P.O. Box 1769, Homer, AK 99603, phone: (907) 235-8924. Brochures available. [ADVERTISEMENT]

Central Charters Booking Agency Inc. We offer full-service bookings for charter fishing, wildlife tours, lodging, ferries to Halibut Cove (*Danny-J*), Seldovia and Kachemak Bay State Park, and complete fishing and lodging packages. See our selection of T-shirts, sweatshirts, Alaskan gifts and postcards. Also available are bait, ice, fishing licenses, sundries, shipping boxes and derby tickets. Free information and maps. Saltwater aquarium. Located on the Homer Spit. See display ad this section. [ADVERTISEMENT]

Cié Jae Ocean Charters. Homer halibut fishing on USCG-licensed vessels. Single-day excursions, multi-day packages available. Tackle, bait and filleting included. Meals available. Seasonal service May 15–Sept 7. Brochure available. Major credit cards accepted. Sea Breeze Boardwalk, P.O. Box 380-MP, Homer, AK 99603. Phone 1-800-677-5587; (907) 235-5587. See display ad this section. [ADVERTISEMENT]

Discovery Adventures offers a day to warm your heart; all ages and ability levels. Hiking, beach walks, stream fishing, clamming, canoeing, helicopter glacier tours. Your enthusiasm is all that is needed. A guide/naturalist shares a love for the natural wonders, going at your pace, giving instruction whenever needed. Wildlife viewing/photography opportunities. Box 1278MP, Homer, AK 99603. (907) 235-6942. See display ad this section. [ADVERTISEMENT]

Kachemak Air Service, Inc. can fly you in one of their floatplanes over the glaciers that you see across Kachemak Bay. Fly over Halibut Cove, then maybe past a goat or black bear; return via Yukon Island and perhaps a seal or sea otter. P.O. Box 1769, Homer, AK 99603; phone (907) 235-8924. [ADVERTISEMENT]

Kachemak Bay Adventures Boat Tours. Join us on the 60-foot MV *Endeavor* for a memorable experience on beautiful Kachemak Bay. See puffins, murres, kittiwakes and other nesting birds at Gull Island seabird rookery. Sea otters, seabirds, porpoises, seals and even whales are commonly seen on our Seldovia excursions. Headquarters at Homer Spit Campground. Camping and boat tour packages. Scheduled departures daily. VISA, MasterCard accepted. Brochure available. P.O. Box 1196, Homer, AK 99603. Reservations and information (907) 235-8206 or (907) 235-6669. Senior citizen or group discounts available. [ADVERTISEMENT]

Maritime Helicopters, Inc. Our glacier tour invites you to share an eagle's eye view of nature's "River of Ice" with its blue crevasses and miles of snow fields. We also offer custom tours. Visit an oyster farm, or do a bit of fishing or hiking in an unspoiled Alaskan wilderness. (907) 235-7771, 3520 FAA Road, Homer, AK 99603. VISA, MasterCard, JCB. [ADVERTISEMENT]

North Country Charters, originally owned and operated by Sean and Gerri Martin since 1979, has brought in some of the largest halibut catches ever landed in Homer. Two 50-foot boats for large groups from 16 to 20 passengers. Three six-passenger boats. All twin-engine, Coast Guard-equipped, heated cabins, full restrooms. See display ad. [ADVERTISEMENT]

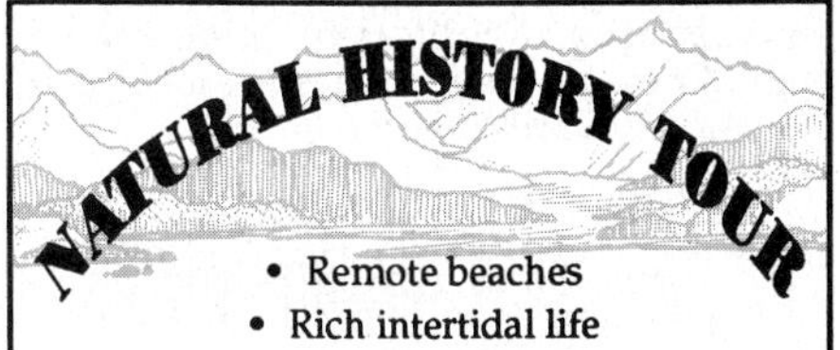

Pier One Theatre. Local talent lights up an intimate stage in an Alaskan-friendly waterfront atmosphere halfway out of Homer Spit. Plays, new productions, readings, dance theatre, musicals. Offered summer weekends with some midweek shows. Season information locally. Phone (907) 235-7333. [ADVERTISEMENT]

Quiet Sports, located on Pioneer Avenue, since 1972, offers quality outdoor equipment for the camper, backpacker or nordic skier. Rentals include packs and tents, skis, bikes. In addition, Quiet Sports is also an excellent source of information and maps for guided and nonguided outdoor activities in the surrounding backcountry. (907) 235-8620. [ADVERTISEMENT]

Trail's End Horse Adventures. Hourly trail rides, or longer. Overnight pack trips. Horseback ride along the shores of Kachemak Bay or in the Homer Hills. Gentle, Alaskan horses! Horses and Alaska are my life; enjoy them both with Mark Marette, Mile 11 East End Rd. Write: P.O. Box 1771, Homer, AK 99603, or call (907) 235-6393. [ADVERTISEMENT]

Tutka Bay Lodge (remote). Leave the crowds behind. Visit our beautiful nature lodge, across Kachemak Bay from Homer. Prime sea otter and eagle viewing. Peaceful forest and coastal trails. Secluded beaches. Mountain biking. Sea kayaking available. Fresh seafood. Deluxe accommodations, private restrooms. Two days/nights $550 per person. Box 960, Homer, AK 99603. (907) 235-3905. [ADVERTISEMENT]

Seldovia

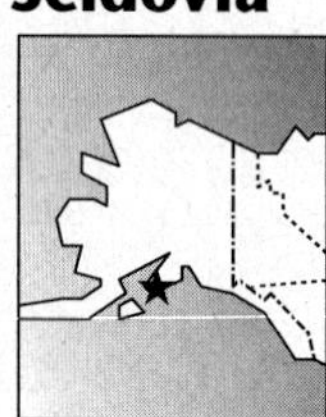

Reached by air, tour boat or ferry. Located on the southwestern Kenai Peninsula on Seldovia Bay, an arm of Kachemak Bay, 16 miles/25.7 km southwest of Homer. **Population:** 403. **Emergency Services: City Police, Ambulance, Fire** and **Rescue**, emergency only, phone 911, monitor CB Channel 9. **Seldovia Medical Clinic**, phone 234-7825. Seldovia has a resident doctor and dentists.

Visitor Information: Seldovia Chamber of Commerce, Drawer F, Seldovia, AK 99663. Information cache at Synergy Art Works on Main Street, across from the boat harbor. You may also stop by the Seldovia Native Assoc. office on Main Street. The office features a small museum with Native artifacts; open 8 A.M. to 5 P.M. weekdays.

Elevation: Sea level. **Climate:** Rather mild for Alaska, with a year-round average temperature of about 39°F/4°C. Annual precipitation, 28 inches. Wind is a small factor due to the protecting shield of the Kenai Mountains. **Radio:** Homer stations. **Television:** KENI Channel 2, KTVA Channel 4, KAKM Channel 7, KIMO Channel 13.

Private Aircraft: Seldovia airport, 0.6 mile/1 km east; elev. 29 feet/9m; length 2,000 feet/610m; gravel; unattended.

Seldovia is a small community connected to Homer by the Alaska Marine Highway Southwest ferry system. Because it is removed from Kenai Peninsula highways, Seldovia has retained much of its old Alaska charm and traditions (its historic boardwalk dates from 1931). There are some areas just outside town, accessible by car, that have been called "Alaska's hidden paradises." A good place to observe bald eagles, seabirds, and sea otters, Seldovia is included as a stop on some tour boat cruises out of Homer.

The name Seldovia is derived from Russian *Seldevoy,* meaning "herring bay." Between 1869 and 1882, a trading station was located here. A post office was established in November 1898.

The economy has long depended on commercial fishing and fish processing, and to a lesser degree on the lumber industry. Lower Cook Inlet oil exploration and tourism are expected to increase in economic importance.

ACCOMMODATIONS

Seldovia has most visitor facilities, including two hotels, seven bed and breakfasts, two lodges, general store, three restaurants, sports shop and gift shops. The post office is in the center of town. Public restrooms, showers, and pay phone in front of the boat harbor near town center. Pay phones are also located at the ferry dock outside ferry office, at the airport, and library.

Annie McKenzie's Boardwalk Hotel. Waterfront view. 14 lovely rooms with private baths. Large harbor view deck. Bicycles. Interior features local art, plants and library. Free airport or harbor pickup. Friendly service. Romantic getaway. Package prices from Homer. P.O. Box 72, Seldovia, AK 99663. (907) 234-7816. [ADVERTISEMENT]

Gerry's Place. Bed and breakfast one block from harbor. Convenient for fishermen and divers. Private entrance. Close to everything. Air fills available. Rates for families. Freshly baked continental breakfast. Accommodates six, share bathroom. Box 74, Seldovia, AK 99663. (907) 234-7471. [ADVERTISEMENT]

Harmony Point Wilderness Lodge. Easily reached by sea or air from Homer. We offer sea kayaking, boating, mountain biking, fishing, hiking, wildlife, sauna and fun. Private guest cabins and local seafood served in a new, handcrafted lodge. Come, explore or relax. Call (907) 234-7858 or write Box 110, Seldovia, AK 99663. [ADVERTISEMENT]

Undeveloped campground for tent camping only at Outside Beach; picnic tables, litter containers, pit toilet. RV camping at the city-owned Seldovia Wilderness Park located just outside the city. From downtown, drive 1 mile/1.6 km out via Anderson Way to fork in road; turn left and drive 0.9 mile/1.4 km to beach. ▲

TRANSPORTATION

Air: Scheduled and charter service. **Ferry:** Alaska's Southwestern Marine Highway system serves Seldovia, with connections to and from Homer, Port Lions, Kodiak, Valdez, Cordova and Seward. See MARINE ACCESS ROUTES section for schedules. **Charter and Tour Boats:** Available for passenger service; inquire locally and in Homer.

ATTRACTIONS

Special Events. Just about the whole town participates in Seldovia's old-fashioned Fourth of July celebration. The holiday includes a barbecue, parade, games and contests. Seldovia also holds a summer-long fishing derby. Check with the chamber of commerce for details.

Scenic drives. Outside Beach, a beautiful spot with undeveloped tent camping, beachcombing, surf fishing, rockhounding, and a view of Kachemak Bay, Mount Iliamna and Mount Redoubt, is 1.9 miles/3.1 km from town. Drive out Anderson Way from downtown 1 mile/1.6 km to a fork in the road by a gravel pit; turn left and drive 0.9 mile/1.4 km to beach.

Continue on Anderson Way (past the Outside Beach turnoff) to hilly and unpaved Jakolof Bay Road, which offers panoramic views of Kachemak Bay, McDonald Spit, Jakolof Bay and Kasitsna Bay. At Mile 7.5, steps lead down to 1.5-mile-long McDonald Spit, a favorite spot for seabirds and marine life. Spend an afternoon exploring the spit, or continue out to Jakolof Bay, where the road offers many opportunities to get onto the beach. The road becomes impassable to vehicles at Mile 13.

It is a pleasant drive out to Seldovia's refuse dump, with wonderful blueberry picking in the fall. From downtown, cross the bridge over Seldovia Slough; then turn right on North Augustine Avenue, then left on Rocky Street for the dump. This is a 1.4-mile/2.3-km drive.

Inquire locally about hiking trails (Red Mountain, city reservoir, Seldovia Otterbahn trail) and mountain biking opportunities in the area.

Fishing: Kachemak Bay, king salmon, January through August; halibut June through October; Dolly Varden, June through September; silver salmon in August; red salmon, July through August. **Seldovia Bay,** king, silver and red salmon, also halibut, June through September. Excellent bottom fishing.

St. Nicholas Orthodox Church, built in 1891, is open to visitors by prior arrangement. There are some interesting icons here. Donations are welcome.

SELDOVIA ADVERTISERS

Annie McKenzie's Boardwalk Hotel ....Seldovia Harbor
Dancing Eagles Lodge B&B ....Ph. (907) 234-7627
Gerry's Place ....One blk. from harbor
Harmony Point Wilderness Lodge ....Ph. (907) 234-7858

KODIAK

Fishing for pink salmon at the mouth of Myrtle Creek, Kalsin Bay. (Barb Michaels)

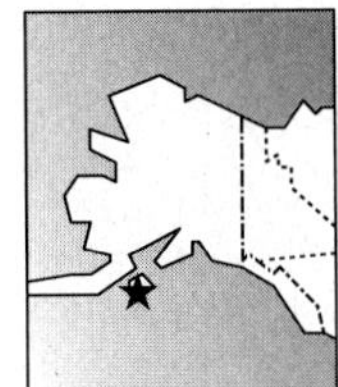

The Kodiak Island group lies in the Gulf of Alaska, south of Cook Inlet and the Kenai Peninsula. The city of Kodiak is located near the northeastern tip of Kodiak Island, at the north end of Chiniak Bay. By air it is 60 minutes from Anchorage. By ferry from Homer it is 12 hours.

Population: 15,535 Kodiak Island Borough. **Emergency Services in Kodiak:** Dial 911 for emergencies. **Alaska State Troopers,** phone 486-4121. **Police,** phone 486-8000. **Fire Department,** phone 486-8040. **Hospital,** Kodiak Island Hospital, Rezanof Drive, phone 486-3281. **Coast Guard,** Public Affairs Officer, phone 487-5542. **Crime Stoppers,** phone 486-3113.

Visitor Information: Located at Center Avenue and Marine Way; open weekdays, 8:30 A.M. to 5 P.M., year-round. Knowledgeable local staff will answer your questions and help arrange tours and charters. Free maps, brochures, hunting and fishing information. For information, contact the Kodiak Island Convention & Visitors Bureau, 100 Marine Way, Kodiak 99615; phone 486-4782 or 486-4070 or write the Kodiak Area Chamber of Commerce, Box 1485, Kodiak 99615; phone 486-5557.

Elevation: Sea level. **Climate:** Average daily temperature in July is 54°F/12°C; in January, 30°F/1°C. September, October and May are the wettest months in Kodiak, with each month averaging over 6 inches of rain. **Radio:** KVOK 560, KMXT-FM 100.1, MBN-FM 107.1, KJJZ-FM 101.1, KPEN-FM 102.3, KWVV-FM 105. **Television:** Via cable and satellite. **Newspapers:** *The Kodiak Daily Mirror* (daily except Saturday and Sunday).

Private Aircraft: Kodiak state airport, 3 miles/4.8 km southwest; elev. 73 feet/22m; length 7,500 feet/2,286m; asphalt; fuel 100LL, Jet A-1. Kodiak Municipal Airport, 2 miles/3.2 km northeast; elev. 139 feet/42m; length 2,500 feet/762m; paved; unattended. Kodiak (Lily Lake) seaplane base, 1 mile/1.6 km northeast; elev. 130 feet/40m. Inner Harbor seaplane base, adjacent north; unattended, docks; watch for boat traffic; no fuel. Seaplane landings also at Near Island Channel.

Gravel airstrips at Akhiok, length 3,000 feet/914m; Karluk, length 1,900 feet/579m; Larsen Bay, length 2,400 feet/732m; Old Harbor, length 2,000 feet/610m; Ouzinkie, length 2,500 feet/762m; and Port Lions, length 2,600 feet/792m.

Kodiak Island, home of the oldest permanent European settlement in Alaska, is about 100 miles/161 km long. Known as "the emerald isle," Kodiak is the largest island in Alaska and the second largest island in the U.S. (after Hawaii), with an area of 3,670 square miles and about 87 miles/140 km of road (see logs this section). The Kodiak Borough includes some 200 islands, the largest being Kodiak, followed in size by Afognak, Sitkalidak, Sitkinak, Raspberry, Tugidak, Shuyak, Uganik, Chirikof, Marmot and Spruce islands. The borough has only one unincorporated townsite: **KARLUK** (pop. 71), located on the west coast of Kodiak Island, 75 air miles/121 km from Kodiak.

The six incorporated cities in the Kodiak Island Borough are: **KODIAK** (pop. 7,581) on Chiniak Bay, with all visitor services (see Accommodations, Transportation and Attractions this section); **AKHIOK** (pop. 78) at Alitak Bay on the south side of Kodiak Island, 80 miles/129 km southwest of Kodiak; **LARSEN BAY** (pop. 144) on the northwest coast of Kodiak Island, 62 miles/100 km southwest of Kodiak; **OLD HARBOR** (pop. 307) on the southeast side of Kodiak Island, 54 miles/87 km from Kodiak; **OUZINKIE** (pop. 210) on the west coast of Spruce Island; and **PORT LIONS** (pop. 259) on Settler Cove on the northeast coast of Kodiak Island.

Kodiak Island was originally inhabited by the Alutiiq people, who were maritime hunters and fishermen. More than 7,000 years later, the Alutiiq' still call Kodiak home.

In 1763, the island was discovered by Stephen Glotov, a Russian explorer. The name Kodiak, of which there are several variations, was first used in English by Captain Cook in 1778. Kodiak was Russian Alaska's first capital city, until the capital was moved to Sitka in 1804.

Kodiak's turbulent past includes the 1912 eruption of Novarupta Volcano, on the nearby Alaska Peninsula, and the tidal wave of 1964. The Novarupta eruption covered the island with a black cloud of ash. When the cloud finally dissipated, Kodiak was buried under 18 inches of drifting pumice. On Good Friday in 1964 the greatest earthquake ever recorded in North America (9.2 on the Richter scale) shook the Kodiak area. The tidal wave that followed virtually leveled downtown Kodiak, destroying the fishing fleet, processing plants, canneries and 158 homes; in all about $30 million in damage.

Because of its strategic location for defense, military facilities were constructed on Kodiak in 1939. Fort Abercrombie, now a state park and a national historic landmark, was one of the first secret radar installations in Alaska. Cement bunkers still remain for exploration by the curious.

The Coast Guard occupies the old Kodiak Naval Station. Kodiak is the base for the Coast Guard's North Pacific operations; the Coast Guard cutters USCGC *Yocona, Storis, Ironwood* and *Firebush* patrol from Kodiak to seize foreign vessels illegally fishing U.S. waters. (The 200-mile/322-km fishing limit went into effect in March 1977.) A 12-foot star, situated halfway up the side of Old Woman Mountain overlooking the base, was

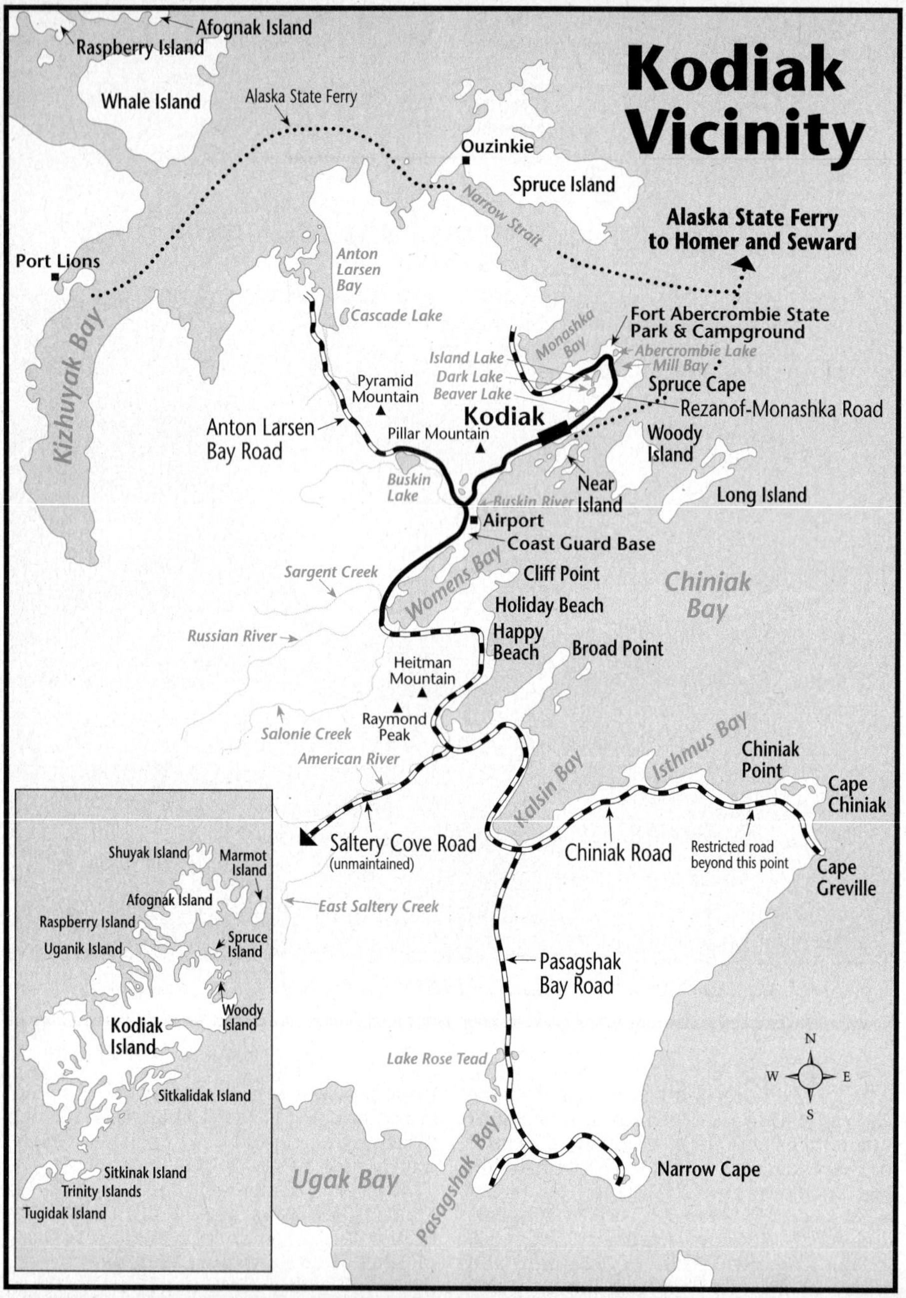

Kodiak Vicinity

Afognak Island
Raspberry Island
Whale Island
Alaska State Ferry
Ouzinkie
Spruce Island
Narrow Strait
Alaska State Ferry to Homer and Seward
Port Lions
Anton Larsen Bay
Cascade Lake
Kizhuyak Bay
Monashka Bay
Fort Abercrombie State Park & Campground
Abercrombie Lake
Mill Bay
Island Lake
Dark Lake
Beaver Lake
Pyramid Mountain
Spruce Cape
Rezanof-Monashka Road
Kodiak
Anton Larsen Bay Road
Pillar Mountain
Woody Island
Buskin Lake
Buskin River
Near Island
Long Island
Airport
Coast Guard Base
Sargent Creek
Womens Bay
Cliff Point
Chiniak Bay
Holiday Beach
Russian River
Happy Beach
Broad Point
Heitman Mountain
Raymond Peak
Salonie Creek
American River
Isthmus Bay
Kalsin Bay
Chiniak Point
Cape Chiniak
Saltery Cove Road (unmaintained)
Chiniak Road
Restricted road beyond this point
Cape Greville
East Saltery Creek
Pasagshak Bay Road
Lake Rose Tead
Pasagshak Bay
Ugak Bay
Narrow Cape
N
W
E
S

Shuyak Island
Marmot Island
Afognak Island
Raspberry Island
Uganik Island
Spruce Island
Woody Island
Kodiak Island
Sitkalidak Island
Sitkinak Island
Trinity Islands
Tugidak Island

rebuilt and rededicated in 1981 in memory of military personnel who have lost their lives while engaged in operations from Kodiak. Originally erected in the 1950s, the star is lit every year between Thanksgiving and Christmas.

Kodiak's St. Paul harbor is home to 800 local fishing boats and host to 4,500 outside vessels each year.

Commercial fishing is the backbone of Kodiak's economy. Kodiak is one of the largest commercial fishing ports in the U.S. Some 3,000 commercial fishing vessels use the harbor each year, delivering salmon, shrimp, herring, halibut and whitefish, plus king, tanner and Dungeness crab to the 15 seafood processing companies in Kodiak. Cannery tours are not available. Kodiak's famous seafood is premarketed, with almost all the commercially caught seafood exported. (Kodiak is the only city in Alaska with more tonnage exported than imported.) A trip through the boat harbor offers the opportunity to talk to local fishermen, see nets being mended, vessels repaired, and — if you're on hand when a fishing boat is unloaded — possibly sample the catch. You can celebrate Kodiak's main industry at the Kodiak Crab Festival, May 26–30, 1994.

Kodiak is also an important cargo port and transshipment center. Container ships stop here to transfer goods to smaller vessels bound for the Aleutians, the Alaska Peninsula and other destinations.

ACCOMMODATIONS

There are several hotels/motels in Kodiak. Bed-and-breakfast accommodations are also available. A variety of restaurants offer a wide range of menus and prices. Shopping is readily available for gifts, general merchan-

KODIAK ADVERTISERS

Kodiak Island Convention & Visitors Bureau ....100 Marine Way
Kodiak-Katmai Marketing Group.................................P.O. Box 8630
Kodiak Western Charters .Ph. (907) 486-2200
Uyak Air Service................Ph. (907) 486-3407

KODIAK ISLAND

Kodiak Island Convention & Visitors Bureau

1-800-789-4782

OCEANSIDE BED & BREAKFAST

Beautiful Spacious Oceanside Home

Hosts - Dick & Sue Rohrer, 23 year residents of Kodiak

907-486-5835

P.O. Box 2219.... Kodiak, AK 99615

CY'S SPORTING GOODS & OUTFITTERS

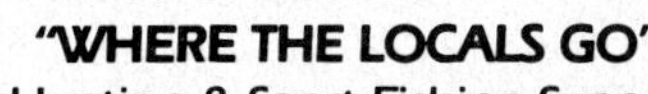

"WHERE THE LOCALS GO"

Complete Hunting & Sport Fishing Supplier, including Sport & Commercial Licenses

OPEN 7 DAYS A WEEK SERVING KODIAK FOR 25 YEARS

202 Shelikof, Kodiak, Alaska 486-3900

ELKAY BICYCLE SHOP

A Full Service-One Stop Bike Shop

Spring & Summer Bike Rentals

SALES • REPAIRS • PARTS

118 W. Rezanof Drive

Kodiak, AK 907-486-4219

Cameras & Photo Supplies

— 1-HOUR FILM PROCESSING —

A large selection of special ivory carving & gold nugget jewelry

Authentic Alaskan Gifts

NORMAN'S

"ON THE MALL"

Kodiak, Alaska

414 Marine Way

Phone (907) 486-3315

Established 1944

PRISTINE CHARTERS

OCEAN VOYAGES

GAME HUNTING	MARINE RESEARCH
SPORT FISHING	BUSINESS SEMINARS
PLEASURE CRUISES	FISHERIES STUDIES
NATURE VIEWING	COLD WATER DIVING

Chaco Pearman, Owner • 1281 Baranof • Kodiak, AK 99615

(907) 486-FISH • Fax: (907) 486-5275

Kodiak Bed and Breakfast

Comfortable, gracious hospitality in downtown Kodiak

1994 Rates: Single $60 - Double $72 + Tax

(907) 486-5367

Mary Monroe, Coordinator • Fax (907) 486-6567

308 Cope Street, Kodiak, Alaska 99615

King's Diner

Family Restaurant

1941 Mill Bay Rd.

Kodiak, Alaska

Phone: 486-4100

Hours:
Mon-Fri 5:30-7:30
Sat & Sun 6:30-7:00

YOU CAN VISIT THE BEARS WITHOUT SLEEPING WITH THEM.

BY STAYING IN ONE OF OUR FLOATING CABINS

1-800-478-6196

(In State 800 # Only)

ISLAND AIR SERVICE

907-486-6196 KODIAK, ALASKA

PORT OF KODIAK GIFTS

JEWELRY - ALASKANA GIFTS

T-SHIRTS - SWEATSHIRTS - HATS

486-8550

516 Marine Way — On The Mall

"Five Locations Statewide to Better Serve You"

MEXICAN-AMERICAN-ITALIAN FOOD

486-9477

1517 Mill Bay Road Kodiak, Alaska

Roads End

486-2885

Mile 42 CHINIAK RD

Box 5620

Chiniak, AK 99615

where the fun begins ROADS END

ROOMS • COCKTAILS • RESTAURANT

KODIAK ALUTIIQ DANCERS

Living History like you've never seen before!

Cost: $15.00 per person

CALL 486-4449

FOR RESERVATIONS

Monday thru Saturday

May 1 — September 30

713 Rezanof Drive-5 Minutes from Downtown

★ Kodiak Star Motel ★

Comfort and Convenience at Resonable Rates

- 11 Channel TV
- Kitchenettes
- Complimentary Coffee
- Private Entrance
- Laundry Facilities
- Private Telephones
- Downtown Location

119 YUKON, KODIAK, ALASKA 99615

Phone (907) 486-5657

Henry's Sports Restaurant & Lounge

FULL AMERICAN AND CHINESE MENU

Open 11 AM - 7 Days A Week

American & Chinese Food: Mon-Sat

American Only: Sunday

EAST MEETS WEST

512 Marine Way-On the Mall

486-2625

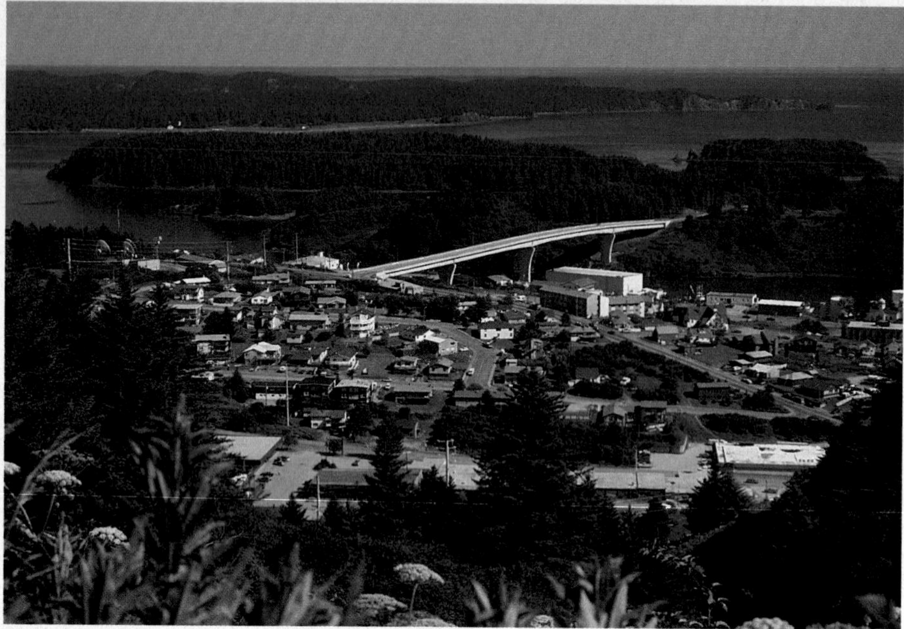

View from Pillar Mountain Road of Kodiak and Near Island. (Barb Michaels)

dise and sporting goods. There is a movie theater and 500-seat performing arts center.

There are three state campgrounds: Fort Abercrombie, north of town (see Rezanof–Monashka Road log); Buskin River state recreation site, south of town (see Chiniak Road log); and Pasagshak River state recreation site at the end of Pasagshak Bay Road (see log). City campground at Gibson Cove has showers and restrooms, $2 per person/per night camping fee. ▲

Dump stations are located at the Buggy Banya station on Mill Bay Road, at the Union 76 service station in downtown Kodiak, and at Buskin River state recreation site at Mile 4.4 Chiniak Road.

There are several remote fly-in hunting and fishing lodges in the Kodiak area, several roadhouses on the island road system, and recreation cabins available within Kodiak National Wildlife Refuge. Privately run remote fly-in cabins are available throughout the Kodiak area.

TRANSPORTATION

Air: Scheduled service via MarkAir, Era and Alaska Airlines (jet service, summer only).

Ferry: The Alaska state ferry MV *Tustumena* serves Kodiak from Homer and Seward. It also stops at Port Lions on the north side of Kodiak Island. Ferry terminal is downtown; phone 486-3800 or toll free in the U.S. 1-800-642-0066. See MARINE ACCESS ROUTES section for details.

Highways: There are four roads on Kodiak Island (see logs this section). The 11.4-mile/18.3-km Rezanof–Monashka Road leads from downtown Kodiak north to Fort Abercrombie and Monashka Bay. Chiniak Road leads 47.6 miles/76.6 km south from Kodiak along the island's eastern shore to Cape Greville (it is a beautiful drive!). Anton Larsen Bay Road leads 11.6 miles/18.7 km from junction with Chiniak Road near Kodiak airport to Anton Larsen Bay. Pasagshak Bay Road branches off Chiniak Road and leads 16.4 miles/26.4 km to Fossil Beach at Pasagshak Point.

Car Rental and Taxi: Available.

ATTRACTIONS

State fair and rodeo held Labor Day weekend, at the fairgrounds in Womens Bay, includes all-state competitions in crafts, gardening, 4-H livestock raising and home products. Stock car races are held at the fairgrounds on weekends during the summer.

St. Herman's Day, Aug. 9, is of particular significance to the Kodiak community as Father Herman, the first saint of the Russian Orthodox Church in North America, was canonized in Kodiak in 1970. Father Herman arrived in Kodiak in 1794.

Alutiiq Culture Center is a nonprofit institution dedicated to the preservation and study of the language and culture of Kodiak's native people. It is located at 214 West Rezanof Drive in Kodiak and is open 10 A.M. to 5 P.M. Monday through Friday. The center features exhibits of archaeological and ethnographic material pertaining to Eskimo, Aleut and Alutiiq cultures; an ethobotanical collection from Kodiak Island; photo archives of Kodiak natives and their villages; and Alutiiq language and culture audiotapes and videotapes.

Picnic on the beach. There are some outstandingly beautiful beaches along Chiniak Road (see log this section). These unpopulated beaches are also good for beachcombing. Watch for Sitka deer and foxes.

Kodiak Tribal Council's Barabara sod house is an authentic Alutiiq dwelling that features presentations of Alutiiq dancing. The Kodiak Alutiiq Dancers form the only Alutiiq dance group in Alaska. The group was created when Margaret Roberts and several other Alutiiqs took an interest in long-lost Alutiiq songs and dances, and went to work researching their people's past. In 1989 the dance group was formed with seven members, and by 1993 it had grown to include 35 members between the ages of 6 and 80. The traditional dress of the dancers was designed based on artifacts on display at the Smithsonian and Leningrad museums. Traditional garments of the Koniag Aleuts were made from the skins of sea otters, seals and birds. Waterproof clothing was made from carefully prepared gutskin. The dances were re-created from stories passed down through generations of the Alutiiq people, who have inhabited Kodiak Island for more than 7,000 years. Dance performances are held through the summer at the barabara, located at 713 Rezanof Drive; 486-4449.

City Parks and Recreation Department maintains a swimming pool year-round and the school gyms are available on a year-round basis for community use. The town has eight parks and playgrounds including the 7-acre Baranof Park with four tennis courts, baseball field, track, playgrounds and picnic areas.

Fort Abercrombie State Park. Site of a WWII coastal fortification, bunkers and other evidence of the Aleutian campaign. The park is located north of Kodiak on scenic Miller Point. Picnicking and camping in a setting of lush rain forest, wildflowers, seabirds and eagles.

The Frank Brink Amphitheater puts on productions of "*Cry of the Wild Ram*" every August.

The Baranov Museum (Erskine House), maintained by the Kodiak Historical Society (101 Marine Way, Kodiak 99615; phone 486-5920), is open in summer, 10 A.M. to 4 P.M. weekdays, and noon to 4 P.M. Saturday and Sunday. (Winter hours 11 A.M. to 3 P.M. weekdays, except Thursday, and noon to 3 P.M. Saturday. Closed in February.) The building was originally a warehouse built circa 1808 by Alexander Andreevich Baranov to store precious sea otter pelts. Purchased

KODIAK ISLAND

Kodiak Island Convention & Visitors Bureau
1-800-789-4782

Kodiak Islands Katmai National Park

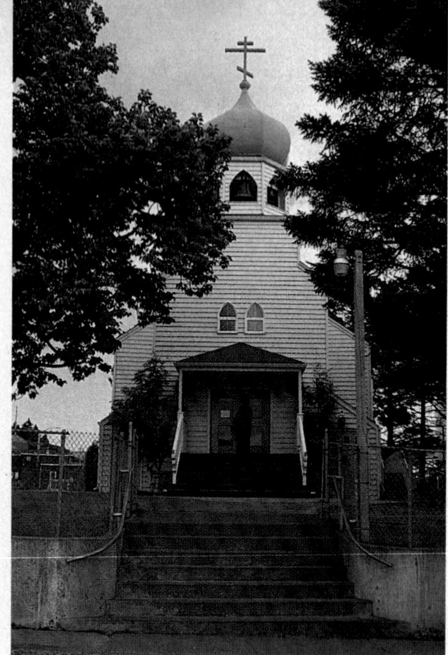

Kodiak's Russian Orthodox Church.

(Barb Michaels)

by the Alaska Commercial Co. around 1867, the building was sold to W.J. Erskine in 1911, who converted it into a residence; it was then referred to as the Erskine House. In 1962 it was declared a national historic landmark. Many items from the Koniag and Russian era are on display. In the gift shop, Russian samovars, Russian Easter eggs, Alaska Native baskets and other items are for sale. A walking tour map of Kodiak is available here. Donations accepted, $2 per adult, children under 12 free.

Shuyak Island State Park encompasses 11,000 acres and is located 54 air miles north of Kodiak. Access is by boat or by plane only. Hunting, fishing and kayaking are the major recreational activities. Four public-use cabins are available at $30 per night, December through May, and $50 per night, June through November. Cabins are 12 feet by 20 feet and sleep up to eight people. Reservations accepted up to six months in advance with a full nonrefundable payment.

Russian Orthodox Church. The oldest parish in Alaska was established when a group of 10 monks from the Valaam Monastery of Russian Finland arrived in Kodiak on Sept. 24, 1794. Within two years of their arrival, they built the first Russian Orthodox church in Alaska. While the church is on the National Register of Historic Places, the structure that stands in downtown Kodiak today only dates back to 1945. The original structure was rebuilt in 1874, and again in 1943 after it was destroyed by fire.

The newly arrived monks dedicated themselves to converting natives and blessing the Koniags who were forced by Russian leaders to conduct perilous, season-long group hunts. The monks were critical of Russian leaders' and fur traders' conduct, as well as their treatment of the native people. Several conflicts resulted, and in 1800 the colonizing company's manager, Alexander Baranov, prohibited the monks from having contact with the natives. The power struggle that ensued resulted in the monks' refusal to hold public services for more than a year.

Inquire at the visitor center about hours. Within the church are handmade brass works, rare paintings and several icons dating back to the Czarist period. The hand-rung church bells visitors may hear were a gift of Kodiak residents. St. Herman Theological Seminary, founded in 1973, is a degree-granting institution for the training of orthodox readers, deacons and priests. The seminary is located on Mission Road, north of the church.

The St. Innocent Veniaminov Research Institute Museum at St. Herman Theological Seminary has Native artifacts, icons and arts and crafts used by Orthodox missionaries on the Yukon River in the 1800s on display. Father Herman was one of the monks in the 1794 missioner party to Kodiak. In the early 1800s he went to Spruce Island, which he called New Valaam. Among other things, Father Herman educated the native people and cared for orphaned children, and was believed to have powers of healing and prophecy. He was canonized on Aug. 9, 1970. The institute has a bookstore and gift shop. Check with the visitor information center for hours.

Charter a boat for fishing and hunting trips, sightseeing and photography. There are several marine charter services in Kodiak.

Kodiak National Wildlife Refuge encompasses 2,491 square miles on Kodiak Island, Uganik Island and Afognak Island. The refuge was established in 1941 to preserve the natural habitat of the famed Kodiak bear and other wildlife. Biologists estimate that more than 2,700 bears inhabit Kodiak Island. Most bears enter dens by December and remain there until April. Bears are readily observable on the refuge in July and August when they congregate along streams to feed on salmon. At other times they feed on grasses or berries.

Native wildlife within the refuge includes the red fox, river otter, short-tailed weasel, little brown bat and tundra vole. Introduced mammals include the Sitka black-tailed deer, beaver, snowshoe hare and mountain goat. On Afognak Island, an introduced band of elk share the island with the bears. The coastline on the Kodiak refuge shelters a large population of waterfowl and marine mammals. Bald eagles are common nesting birds on the refuge, along with 215 other bird species that have been seen on the island.

Vegetation comprises fireweed, salmon berry, blueberry and roseberry bushes, stands of alder, willow and elderberry, and thorny patches of devil's club. This plant life is interspersed with wetlands — lakes, marshes, bogs, salt flats, etc.

Visitors to the refuge typically go to fish, observe/photograph wildlife, backpack, canoe, camp and hunt.

NOTE: The refuge is accessible only by floatplane or boat. There are public-use recreation cabins available for use; applications must be made in advance to the refuge manager. For more information contact the Kodiak National Wildlife Refuge Manager, 1390 Buskin River Road, Kodiak, AK 99615; phone 487-2600. You may also stop by the U.S. Fish and Wildlife Service Visitor Center at Mile 4.4 Chiniak Road. The center is open weekdays, 8 A.M. to 4:30 P.M., and weekends noon to 4:30 P.M., year-round. Besides fishing, the refuge is used for exhibits and films on Kodiak wildlife are featured.

Wildlife Watching. The best time to observe animals is when they are most active: at daybreak. Bald eagles can be seen near the city of Kodiak from January through March, and nesting near water in the summer. Peregrine falcons are spotted frequently from the road in October. In the summer, puffins can be seen at Miller Point on calm days. Narrow Cape, Spruce Cape and Miller Point are good stakeout points in the spring for those in search of gray whales. Womens Bay is home to a variety of migrating geese in April.

Other varieties of wildlife — including bears — can be seen in the backcountry throughout the summer.

AREA FISHING: Kodiak Island is in the center of a fine marine and freshwater fishery and possesses some excellent fishing for rainbow, halibut, Dolly Varden and five species of Pacific salmon. Visiting fishermen will have to charter a boat or aircraft to reach remote lakes, rivers and bays, but the island road system offers many good salmon streams in season.

Afognak Island and adjacent Raspberry Island, both approximately 30 air miles/48 km northeast of Kodiak, offer excellent remote hunting and fishing. There is a lodge on Afognak Island with accommodations for 12 people. Both islands are brown bear country. Hikers and fishermen should make noise as they travel and carry a .30-06 or larger rifle. Stay clear of bears. If you take a dog, make sure he is under control. Dogs can create dangerous situations with bears.

Rezanof–Monashka Road Log

Distance is measured from the junction of Rezanof Drive and Marine Way in downtown Kodiak (K).

K 0.1 (0.2 km) Mill Bay Road access to library, post office and Kodiak businesses.

K 0.4 (0.6 km) Entrance to Near Island bridge to St. Herman Harbor and Northend Park.

K 1.5 (2.4 km) Kodiak Island Hospital on left.

K 3.1 (5 km) Turnout with picnic tables by beach, good viewpoint.

K 3.6 (5.8 km) Road on right leads to Fort Abercrombie State Park. Drive in 0.2 mile/0.3 km to campground; 13 campsites with seven-night limit at $6 per night, water, toilets, trails, fishing, swimming and picnic shelter. View of bay and beach, WWII fortifications. Just beyond the campground entrance is the Alaska State Parks ranger station, open weekdays 9 A.M. to 2 P.M.; pay phone, public restrooms, park information.

K 6.9 (11.1 km) Road on right leads to VFW.

K 8.4 (13.5 km) Road to right leads to Pillar Creek Beach, a fishing and picnicking spot.

K 9.3 (15 km) Viewpoint with beautiful, panoramic view.

K 11.3 (18.2 km) Bridge over Monashka Creek.

K 11.4 (18.3 km) Road end. Paths lead

through woods to secluded Monashka beach.

Chiniak Road Log

Distance from Kodiak's U.S. post office building (K) is followed by distance from Cape Greville (CG).

K 0 CG 47.6 (76.6 km) Kodiak U.S. post office building.

K 2.3 (3.7 km) **CG 45.3** (72.9 km) Gibson Cove city campground with showers and restrooms. Fee $2 per person/per night. ▲

K 4.4 (7.1 km) **CG 43.2** (69.5 km) U.S. Fish and Wildlife Service Visitor Center and Kodiak National Wildlife Refuge headquarters; open weekdays year-round, 8 A.M. to 4:30 P.M., weekends, noon to 4:30 P.M. Exhibits and films on Kodiak wildlife. Road on left to Buskin River state recreation site; 15 RV campsites with a 14-night limit at $6 per night, picnic tables and shelter, water, pit toilets, trails, beach access and dump station. Fishing along **Buskin River** and on beach area at river's mouth for red, silver and pink salmon and trout. Parking for fishermen.

K 5 (8 km) **CG 42.6** (68.5 km) Turnoff on right for Anton Larsen Bay Road (see log this section).

K 5.1 (8.2 km) **CG 42.5** (68.4 km) Entrance to Kodiak airport.

K 5.6 (9 km) **CG 42** (67.6 km) *CAUTION: Jet blast area at end of runway. Stop here and wait if you see a jet preparing for takeoff.*

K 6.7 (10.8 km) **CG 40.9** (65.8 km) Entrance to U.S. Coast Guard station.

K 7.2 (11.6 km) **CG 40.4** (65 km) Road continues around Womens Bay. The drive out to Cape Greville affords excellent views of the extremely rugged coastline of the island.

K 9.5 (15.3 km) **CG 38.1** (61.3 km) Rodeo and fairgrounds.

K 10.1 (16.3 km) **CG 37.5** (60.3 km) Sargent Creek.

K 10.7 (17.2 km) **CG 36.9** (59.5 km) Russian River and Bells Flat Road.

K 11 (17.7 km) **CG 36.6** (58.9 km) Pavement ends, gravel begins.

K 11.1 (17.9 km) **CG 36.5** (58.7 km) Grocery and liquor store, diesel and unleaded gas.

K 11.2 (18 km) **CG 36.4** (58.6 km) View of Bells Flat.

K 11.3 (18.2 km) **CG 36.3** (58.4 km) Store and gas station (diesel and unleaded).

K 12.3 (19.8 km) **CG 35.3** (56.8 km) Saloni Creek.

K 14.1 (22.7 km) **CG 33.5** (53.9 km) Turnout with view of Mary Island and Womens Bay.

K 16.5 (26.6 km) **CG 31.1** (50 km) USCG Holiday Beach radio station. Watch for livestock on road from here on.

K 17.4 (28 km) **CG 30.2** (48.6 km) Road east to Holiday Beach.

K 17.7 (28.5 km) **CG 29.9** (48.1 km) USCG receiving station; emergency phone.

K 19.8 (31.9 km) **CG 27.8** (44.7 km) Undeveloped picnic area in grove of trees along beach of Middle Bay; access to beach. Watch for cattle.

K 20 (32.2 km) **CG 27.6** (44.4 km) Small Creek bridge.

K 20.2 (32.5 km) **CG 27.4** (44.1 km) Salt Creek bridge.

K 21.4 (34.4 km) **CG 26.2** (42.2 km) American River bridge. River empties into Middle Bay.

K 21.8 (35.1 km) **CG 25.8** (41.5 km) Unimproved road on right, suitable only for four-wheel-drive vehicles, leads toward Saltery Cove. Check road conditions in Kodiak before driving it.

K 24.5 (39.4 km) **CG 23.1** (37.2 km) Mayflower Beach; rock in distance resembling square-rigged vessel is Mayflower Rock.

K 25 (40.2 km) **CG 22.6** (36.4 km) View of Kalsin Bay.

K 26.2 (42.2 km) **CG 21.4** (34.4 km) Turnout.

K 28.3 (45.5 km) **CG 19.3** (31.1 km) Road drops down to head of Kalsin Bay.

K 28.6 (46 km) **CG 19** (30.6 km) Kalsin Inn Ranch; food, bar, gas (no unleaded), camping and lodging. ▲

K 29.6 (47.6 km) **CG 18** (29 km) Olds River.

K 30 (48.3 km) **CG 17.6** (28.3 km) Kalsin River (creek) bridge. Slow down for cattle guard in road just before bridge.

K 30.3 (48.8 km) **CG 17.3** (27.8 km) Road forks: Turn left for Chiniak, right for Pasagshak Bay. Northland Ranch Resort; food, lodging and horseback rides. See Pasagshak Bay Road log this section.

K 31.1 (50 km) **CG 16.5** (26.6 km) Highway maintenance station.

K 32 (51.5 km) **CG 15.6** (25.1 km) Picnic area with tables beside Kalsin Bay.

K 33.2 (53.4 km) **CG 14.4** (23.2 km) Myrtle Creek, picnic site.

K 36 (57.9 km) **CG 11.6** (18.7 km) Brookers Lagoon.

K 36.6 (58.9 km) **CG 11** (17.7 km) Roslyn River. Access to Isthmus Bay beach, a beautiful area with picnic tables.

K 39.2 (63.1 km) **CG 8.4** (13.5 km) Access to a beautiful point overlooking the sea; site of WWII installations. Good place for photos.

K 39.5 (63.6 km) **CG 8.1** (13 km) Beautiful beach on Chiniak Bay with rolling breakers.

K 40 (64.4 km) **CG 7.6** (12.2 km) Twin Creek.

K 40.3 (64.8 km) **CG 7.3** (11.7 km) **Pony Lake** (stocked).

K 41.1 (66.1 km) **CG 6.5** (10.5 km) Chiniak School and public library.

K 42.2 (67.9 km) **CG 5.4** (8.7 km) Road's End bar and restaurant; phone 486-2885.

K 42.3 (68.1 km) **CG 5.3** (8.5 km) Chiniak Point. State-maintained road ends. Unmaintained road continues as public easement across Leisnoi Native Corp. land.

K 42.4 (68.2 km) **CG 5.2** (8.4 km) Road to Chiniak Lake.

K 47.6 (76.6 km) **CG 0** Cape Greville. Named by Captain Cook in 1778.

Pasagshak Bay Road Log

Distance from junction with Chiniak Road (J) is followed by distance from road end (RE).

J 0 RE 16.4 (26.4 km) Turn right at **Milepost K 30.3** Chiniak Road for Pasagshak Bay. Road leads up the valley of Kalsin Creek past a private ranch.

J 6.6 (10.6 km) **RE 9.8** (15.8 km) Road crosses Lake Rose Tead on causeway. Good fishing in river from here to the ocean.

J 8.9 (17.5 km) **RE 7.5** (12.1 km) Pasagshak River state recreation site: seven campsites with a 14-night limit (no fee), toilets, water, picnic sites, fishing and beach access. ▲

J 16.4 (26.4 km) **RE 0** Rough road ends at Fossil Cliffs; Narrow Cape Trail.

WWII gun emplacement at Mile K 39.2 Chiniak Road. (Barb Michaels)

Anton Larsen Bay Road Log

Distance from the turnoff (T) is followed by distance from the end of the road (E).

T 0 E 11.6 (18.7 km) Turnoff for Anton Larsen Bay Road is on Chiniak Road immediately before crossing the Buskin River bridge; turnoff is unmarked.

T 1.2 (1.9 km) **E 10.4** (16.7 km) USCG communications site Buskin Lake. Road leads through this facility.

T 1.4 (2.2 km) **E 10.3** (16.4 km) Turn on unpaved road to Anton Larsen Bay.

T 2 (3.2 km) **E 9.6** (15.4 km) High hill on right is Pyramid Mountain (elev. 2,420 feet/738m).

T 7.3 (11.7 km) **E 4.3** (6.9 km) Red Cloud River bridge. A small, unimproved campsite is adjacent to river on right. ▲

T 8.7 (14 km) **E 2.9** (4.7 km) Cascade Lake trail leads off to the right.

T 9 (14.5 km) **E 2.6** (4.2 km) Head of Anton Larsen Bay. The bay is named for an early Scandinavian settler of this area. Bears are occasionally spotted in the Anton Larsen area.

T 10.1 (16.3 km) **E 1.5** (2.4 km) A public small-boat launch is adjacent to the road. Road continues on left side of bay for approximately 1.5 miles/2.4 km.

T 11.6 (18.7 km) **E 0** Road ends. A footpath continues beyond this point.

PRINCE WILLIAM SOUND

Includes Columbia Glacier, Whittier, Valdez and Cordova

(See map, page 568)

The Prince William Sound community of Cordova on Orca Inlet. (Lee Foster)

Southcentral Alaska's Prince William Sound lies at the north extent of the Gulf of Alaska. It is just as spectacular as southeastern Alaska's Inside Passage. The area is also rich in wildlife. Visitors may see Dall sheep, mountain goats, sea lions, sea otters, whales, harbor seals, bald eagles and other birds. The waters carry all species of Pacific salmon; king, Dungeness and tanner crab; halibut; and rockfish.

This section includes: Columbia Glacier; Whittier; Valdez, start of the Richardson Highway; and Cordova, start of the Copper River Highway.

There are several ways to explore Prince William Sound. From Anchorage, drive south on the Seward Highway 47 miles/75.6 km to Portage and board the Alaska Railroad shuttle train for a 30-minute ride to Whittier (there is no road connection to Whittier), or take the Alaska Railroad train from Anchorage to Whittier. (See the ALASKA RAILROAD section.) You may also start your trip across Prince William Sound from Valdez by driving 304 miles/498.2 km from Anchorage to Valdez via the Glenn and Richardson highways (see GLENN HIGHWAY and RICHARDSON HIGHWAY sections).

From Whittier or Valdez, board the ferry or one of the privately operated excursion boats to tour Prince William Sound. Flightseeing trips are also available. Depending on your itinerary and type of transportation, you may see the glacier and return to Anchorage in a day or have to stay overnight along the way. All-inclusive tours of Prince William Sound are available out of Anchorage.

Plan your trip in advance. Reservations for the ferry or cruise boats are necessary. The Alaska Railroad does not take reservations, although passengers with confirmed ferry reservations are given first priority when loading.

Columbia Glacier

Star attraction of Prince William Sound is Columbia Glacier, one of the largest and most magnificent of the tidewater glaciers along the Alaska coast. The Columbia Glacier has an area of about 440 square miles/1144 square km. The glacier is more than 40 miles/64 km long; its tidewater terminus, which visitors will see on their trip across Prince William Sound, is more than 6 miles/9.7 km across. Columbia Glacier has receded almost a mile in recent years, and scientists are currently studying the glacier's retreat and increased iceberg production, which could pose a hazard to oil tankers from Valdez.

The face of the glacier, which is visible from the bay, varies in height above sea level from 164 to 262 feet/50 to 80m. Columbia Bay teems with life at the face of the glacier. An abundance of plankton (microscopic water plants and animals) thrives here attracting great numbers of fish which in turn attract bald eagles, kittiwakes, gulls and harbor seals. Seals can usually be seen resting on ice floes or swimming about in the icy waters.

The glacier was named by the Harriman Alaska expedition in 1899 for Columbia University in New York City.

The present-day glacier is born in the perpetual snows of Mount Einstein (elev. 11,552 feet/3,521m) in the Chugach Mountains. Near the glacier's source is Mount Witherspoon (elev. 12,012 feet/3,661m). Both peaks are visible from the face of the glacier in clear weather.

By boat you can enjoy close-up views of the glacier face and watch giant icebergs calve (break off) from the ice wall. There are daily and weekly charters by yacht or sailboat. You might also try a flightseeing trip over the glacier. (See the ads in Whittier, Valdez and Cordova in this section for charter boats offering sightseeing trips and flying services offering flightseeing trips.) See the MARINE ACCESS ROUTES section for ferry schedule.

Whittier

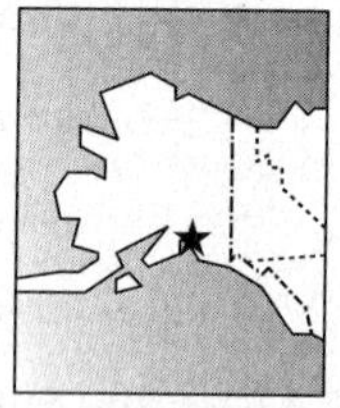

Located at the head of Passage Canal on Prince William Sound, 75 miles/121 km southeast of Anchorage. **Population:** 243. **Emergency Services: Police, Fire** and **Medical,** phone 472-2340. **Visitor Information:** Information kiosk at the Harbor Triangle.

Elevation: 30 feet/9m. **Climate:** Normal

daily temperature for July is 56°F/13°C; for January, 25°F/-4°C. Mean annual precipitation is 174 inches, including 264 inches of snow.

Private Aircraft: Airstrip adjacent northwest; elev. 30 feet/9m; length 1,500 feet/457m; gravel; no fuel; unattended.

Named after the poet John Greenleaf Whittier, Whittier is nestled at the base of mountains that line Passage Canal, a fjord that extends eastward into Prince William Sound. The community is connected to the Seward Highway by railroad and to other Prince William Sound communities by ferry. No roads lead to Whittier.

Whittier was created by the U.S. government during WWII as a port and petroleum delivery center tied to bases farther north by the Alaska Railroad and later a pipeline. The railroad spur from Portage was completed in 1943 and Whittier became the primary debarkation point for cargo, troops and dependents of the Alaska Command. Construction of the huge buildings that dominate Whittier began in 1948 and the Port of Whittier, strategically valuable for its ice-free deep-water port, remained activated until 1960, at which time the population was 1,200. The government tank farm is still located here.

The 14-story Begich Towers, formerly the Hodge Bldg., houses more than half of Whittier's population. Now a condominium, the building was used by the U.S. Army for family housing and civilian bachelor quarters. The building was renamed in honor of U.S. Rep. Nick Begich of Alaska, who, along with Rep. Hale Boggs of Louisiana, disappeared in a small plane near here in 1972 while on a campaign tour.

The Buckner Bldg., completed in 1953, was once the largest building in Alaska and was called the "city under one roof." It is now privately owned and is to be renovated.

Whittier Manor was built in the early 1950s by private developers as rental units for civilian employees and soldiers who were ineligible for family housing elsewhere. In early 1964, the building was bought by another group of developers and became a condominium, which now houses the remainder of Whittier's population.

Since military and government activities ceased, the economy of Whittier rests largely on the fishing industry, tourism and the port.

Whittier has two inns providing accommodations, several restaurants, two bars, gift shops, laundry facilities, two general stores, and a camper park for tents and self-contained RVs ($5 nightly fee). There is no bank in Whittier. ▲

Quiana Charters. Explore Prince William Sound aboard the comfortable 44-foot F/V *Quiana*. (Sleeps six, has a galley, oil stove, microwave, shower and head.) Customized tours available. Private scenic tours of the Sound's pristine remote wilderness, soaring peaks of the Chugach Mountains, glaciers and icebergs. Private wildlife tours to observe whales, porpoise, seals, sea otters, puffins and a kittiwake rookery. Hunt black bear, Sitka black-tailed deer, ducks and geese. Fish for halibut, salmon, red snapper, crab and shrimp. Design your own adventure ashore exploring bays, coves and go beachcombing. Interested? Call (907) 235-4368 or write P.O. Box 3733, Homer, AK 99603-3733. [ADVERTISEMENT]

WHITTIER ADVERTISERS

Anchor Inn........................Ph. (907) 472-2354
Honey Charters.................Ph. (907) 344-3340
Irma's Outpost..................Ph. (907) 472-2461
Quiana Charters................Ph. (907) 235-4368
Sportsman's Inn................Ph. (907) 472-2352

Valdez

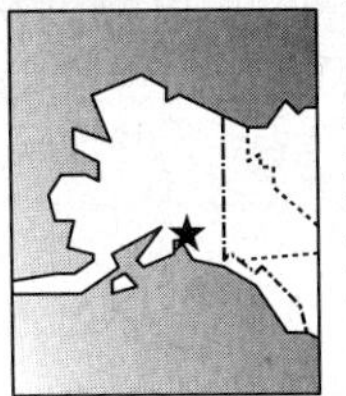

Located on Port Valdez (pronounced val-DEEZ), an estuary off Valdez Arm in Prince William Sound. Valdez is 115 air miles/185 km and 304 highway miles/489 km from Anchorage, 368 highway miles/592 km from Fairbanks. Valdez is the southern terminus of the Richardson Highway and the trans-Alaska pipeline. **Population:** 4,068.

Emergency Services: Alaska State Troopers, phone 835-4359 or 835-4350. **City Police, Fire Department** and **Ambulance**, emergency only phone 911. **Hospital**, Valdez Community, phone 835-2249. Report **oil spills** to Dept. of Environmental Conservation, dial 0 and ask for Zenith 9300. **Maritime Search and Rescue**, dial 0 for Zenith 5555, toll free.

Visitor Information: The visitor information center, located opposite city hall at 200 Chenega St., is open seven days a week from 8 A.M. to 8 P.M. The visitor center features daily films on the earthquake and offers a self-guided tour map of historic homes moved from old Valdez. Write: Valdez Convention and Visitors Bureau, Box

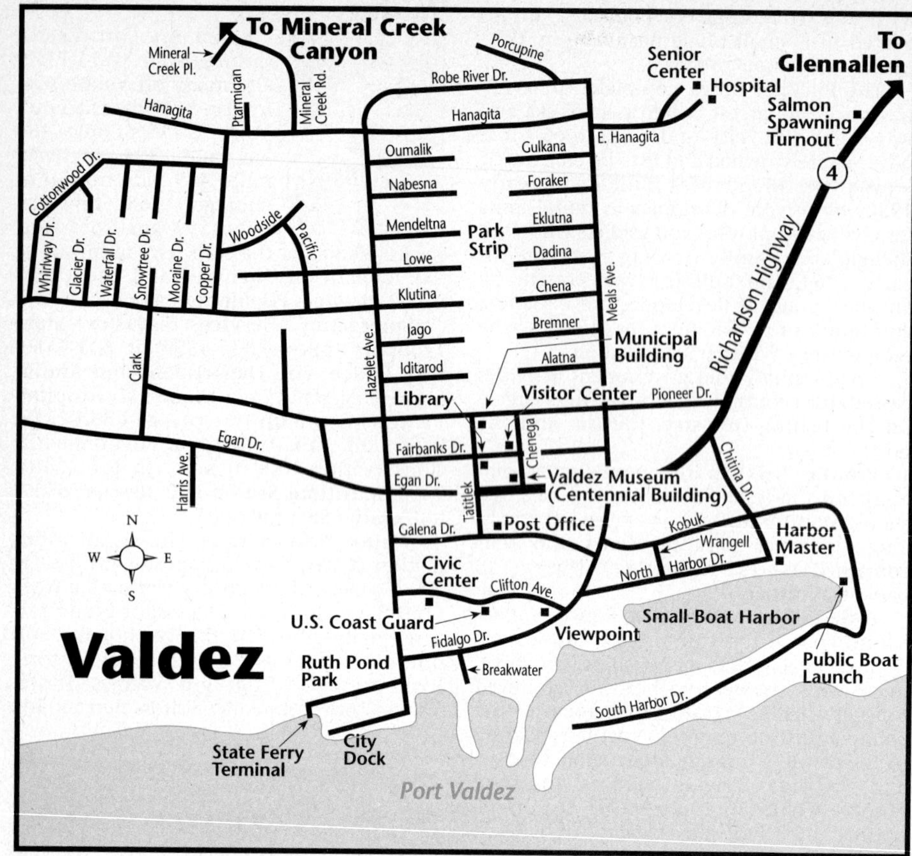

1603-MP, Valdez 99686; or phone 835-2984, fax 835-4845. Visitors may also check the community calendar at the Valdez Civic Center by phoning the hotline at 835-3200.

Elevation: Sea level. **Climate:** Record high was 81°F/27°C in August 1977; record low -20°F/-29°C in January 1972. Normal daily maximum in January, 30°F/-1°C; daily minimum 21°F/-6°C. Normal daily maximum in July, 61°F/16°C; daily minimum 46°F/8°C. Average snowfall in Valdez from October to May is 303 inches, or about 25 feet. (By comparison, Anchorage averages about 6 feet in that period.) New snowfall records were set in January 1990, with snowfall for one day at 47½ inches and snowfall for the month at 134 inches. Record monthly snowfall is 174.5 inches in February 1928. Windy (40 mph/64 kmph) in late fall. **Radio:** KCHU 770, KVAK 1230. **Television:** Seven channels via cable and satellite. **Newspaper:** *Valdez Vanguard* (weekly).

Private Aircraft: Valdez, 3 miles/4.8 km east; elev. 120 feet/37m; length 6,500 feet/1,981m; asphalt; fuel 100LL, Jet B; attended.

Flanked by the Alp-like Chugach Mountains, Valdez is often called Alaska's "Little Switzerland." The city lies on the north shore of Port Valdez, an estuary named in 1790 by Spanish explorer Don Salvador Fidalgo for Antonio Valdes y Basan, a Spanish naval officer.

Valdez was established in 1897–98 as a port of entry for gold seekers bound for the Klondike goldfields. Thousands of stampeders arrived in Valdez to follow the Valdez trail to the Eagle mining district in Alaska's Interior, and from there up the Yukon River to Dawson City and the Klondike. The Valdez trail was an especially deadly route, the first part of it leading over Valdez Glacier, where the early stampeders faced dangerous crevasses, snowblindness and exhaustion.

Copper discoveries in the Wrangell Mountains north of Valdez in the early 1900s brought more development to Valdez, and conflict. A proposed railroad from tidewater to the rich Kennicott copper mines at McCarthy began a bitter rivalry between Valdez and Cordova for the railway line. The Copper River & Northwestern Railway eventually went to Cordova, but not before Valdez had started its own railroad north. The Valdez railroad did not get very far: the only trace of its existence is an old hand-drilled railway tunnel at **Milepost V 14.9** on the Richardson Highway.

The old gold rush trail out of Valdez was developed into a sled and wagon road in the early 1900s. It was routed through Thompson Pass (rather than over the Valdez Glacier) by Captain Abercrombie of the U.S. Army, who was commissioned to connect Fort Liscum (a military post established in 1900 near the present-day location of the pipeline terminal) with Fort Egbert in Eagle. Colonel Wilds P. Richardson of the Alaska Road Commission further developed the wagon road, building an automobile road from Valdez to Fairbanks which was completed in the early 1920s.

Old photos of Valdez show Valdez Glacier directly behind the town. This is because until 1964 Valdez was located about 4 miles east of its present location, closer to the glacier. The 1964 Good Friday earthquake, the most destructive earthquake ever to hit southcentral Alaska, virtually destroyed Valdez. The quake measured

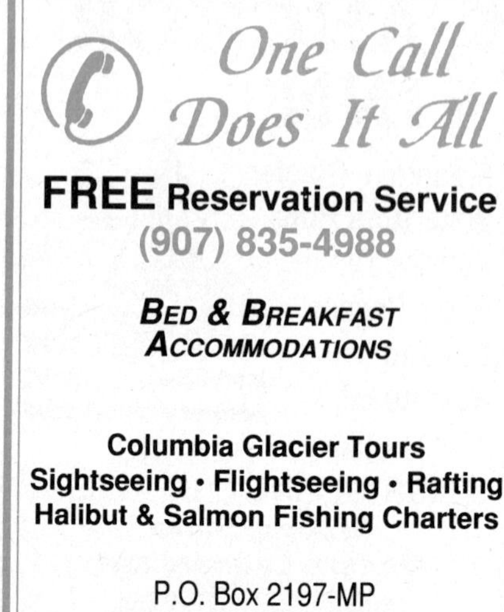

between 8.4 and 8.6 on the Richter scale (since revised to 9.2) and was centered in Prince William Sound. A series of local waves caused by massive underwater landslides swept over Valdez wharf and engulfed the downtown area. Afterward, it was decided that Valdez would be rebuilt at a new townsite. By late August 1964, reconstruction projects had been approved for Valdez and relocation was under way. The last residents remaining at "old" Valdez moved to the new town in 1968.

Since its days as a port of entry for gold seekers, Valdez has been an important gateway to interior Alaska. As the most northerly ice-free port in the Western Hemisphere, and connected by the Richardson Highway to the Alaska highway system, Valdez has evolved into a shipping center, offering the shortest link to much of interior Alaska for seaborne cargo.

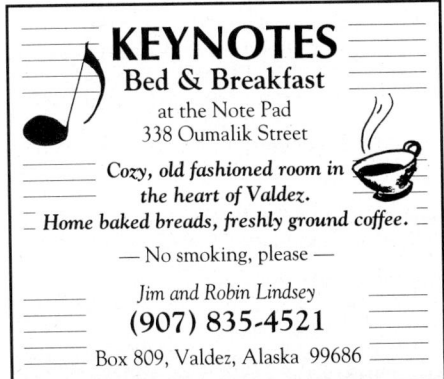

Construction of the trans-Alaska pipeline

was begun in 1974 and completed in 1977 (the first tanker load of oil shipped out of Valdez on Aug. 1, 1977). The 1,000-acre site at Port Valdez was chosen as the pipeline terminus; tours of the marine terminal are available (see Attractions).

From Prudhoe Bay on the Arctic Ocean, the 48-inch-diameter, 800-mile-/1287-km-long pipeline follows the Sagavanirktok River and Atigun Valley, crossing the Brooks Mountain Range at 4,747-foot/1,447-m Atigun Pass. South of the Brooks Range it passes through Dietrich and Koyukuk valleys and crosses the hills and muskeg of the Yukon–Tanana uplands to the Yukon River. South of the Yukon the line passes through more rolling hills 10 miles/16 km east of Fairbanks, then goes south from Delta Junction to the Alaska Range, where it reaches an elevation of 3,500 feet/1,067m at Isabel Pass before descending into the Copper River basin. It crests the Chugach Mountains at Thompson Pass (elev. 2,500 feet/762m) and descends through the Keystone Canyon to Valdez, where it is fed by gravity into tanks or directly into waiting oil tankers at the marine terminal.

Because of varying soil conditions along its route, the pipeline is both above and below ground. Where the warm oil would cause icy soil to thaw and erode, the pipeline goes above ground to avoid thawing. Where the frozen ground is mostly well-drained gravel or solid rock, and thawing not a problem, the line is underground.

The line has 10 pump stations and numerous large valves to control the flow of oil. The entire system is designed for central computer control from Valdez, or independent local control at each pump station.

National attention was focused on Valdez and the pipeline when the oil tanker *Exxon Valdez* ran aground in March 1989, causing an 11-million-gallon oil spill.

Valdez's economy depends on the oil industry, the Prince William Sound fishery and tourism. The city limits of Valdez comprise an area of 274 square miles/712 square km, including all surrounding mountains to timberline. Valdez has long been known for its beautiful setting, with the Chugach Mountains rising behind the city, and the small-boat harbor in front. The town has wide streets and open spaces, with the central residential district built around a park strip which runs from the business district almost to the base of the mountains behind town.

ACCOMMODATIONS

Services in Valdez include several restaurants and bars, grocery stores, sporting goods stores, two drugstores, gift shops, five service stations, hardware, hair stylists and numerous churches.

Valdez has seven motel/hotel facilities and numerous bed and breakfasts. You are advised to make reservations well in advance. Summer tourist season is also the peak work season, and accommodations fill up quickly. Expect to pay $100 and up for a double motel room with bath, $65 to $85 for a bed and breakfast.

Casa de LaBellezza Bed & Breakfast in beautiful Valdez. Elegant, first-class nonsmoking accommodations located within the city. Queen or twin beds. Private or shared bath. Family rates. Explore, go fish-

VALDEZ ADVERTISERS

Always Inn Bed & Breakfast.....Ph. (907) 835-4634
Anadyr Adventures.....Ph. (907) 835-2814
Angie's DownHome Bed & Breakfast.....Ph. (907) 835-2832
Anna's Bed & Breakfast.....Ph. (907) 835-2202
Bear Paw R.V. Park.....Small Boat Harbor
Bear Paw Trading Post.....Small Boat Harbor
Best of All Bed and Breakfast.....Ph. (907) 835-4524
Blueberry Mary's Bed and Breakfast.....Ph. (907) 835-5015
Boat House Bed and Breakfast, The.....Ph. (907) 835-4407
Capt. Jim's Great Alaska Charter Company.....Ph. (907) 835-2282
Casa de LaBellezza Bed & Breakfast.....Ph. (907) 835-4489
Chapel of the Sea.....Ph. (907) 835-5141
Cliff House Bed & Breakfast.....Ph. (907) 835-5244
Comfort and Joy Bed and Breakfast.....Ph. (907) 835-4605
Cooper's Cottage Bed & Breakfast.....Ph. (907) 835-4810
Downtown B & B Inn.....Ph. 1-800-478-2791
Eagle's Rest RV Park.....Richardson Hwy. & Pioneer Dr.
Eagle Roost Bed & Breakfast.....Ph. (907) 835-2757
Easy Living Bed & Breakfast.....Ph. (907) 835-4208
Edkath Charters.....Ph. (907) 835-4346
Eielson AFB Valdez Boat Operation.....Slip M39, Small Boat Harbor
Era Helicopters.....Ph. 1-800-843-1947
Glacier Charter Service.....Behind Totem Inn
Gussie's Lowe St. Inn.....Ph. (907) 835-4448
Harbor Landing General Store...Harbor Court
Headhunters Beauty Salon.....Ph. (907) 835-3818
Homeport Bed & Breakfast.....Ph. (907) 835-5545
Hook Line and Sinker.....Chitina & Kobuk sts.
Ketchum Air Service, Inc...Ph. 1-800-433-9114
Keynotes Bed & Breakfast.....Ph. (907) 835-4521
Keystone Raft & Kayak Adventures Inc......Ph. (907) 835-2606
L&L's B&B.....Ph. (907) 835-4447
Last Frontier Gallery.....Across from city museum
Lu-Lu Belle.....Behind Totem Inn
New Town Chevron.....Downtown
Northern Comfort B & B.....Ph. (907) 835-3042
Northern Comfort Charters.....Ph. (907) 835-2331
Old Edgerton Photography.....Ph. (907) 835-4868
One Call Does It All.....Ph. (907) 835-4988
Oscars.....143 N. Harbor Dr.
Prince William Sound Cruise.....Ph. (907) 835-2357
Prospector Apparel & Sporting Goods.....141 Galena St.
PWS Express.....Ph. (907) 835-5807
Raven Custom Sailing Charters.....Slip C21, Small Boat Harbor
Sea Otter R.V. Park.....2787 S. Harbor Dr.
Snowtree Inn Bed & Breakfast.....Ph. (907) 835-4399
Stan Stephens Cruises.....Westmark Dock
Starr's Country Inn Bed & Breakfast.....Ph. (907) 835-2917
Sugar & Spice.....Downtown
Totem Inn.....Richardson Hwy.
Valdez Christian Book & Coffee Shoppe.....126 Pioneer St.
Valdez Convention and Visitors Bureau.....Ph. (907) 835-2984
Valdez Drug & Photo.....321 Fairbanks Dr.
Valdez Harbor Boat & Tackle Rentals.....Ph. (907) 835-5002
Valdez Red Apple Market.....Egan Dr.
Valdez Village Inn.....Richardson Hwy. at Meals Ave.
Village Pharmacy.....Meals Ave. & Pioneer Dr.
Vintage B & B.....Ph. (907) 835-2092
Westmark Valdez.....Ph. 1-800-544-0970

ing, take tours to Columbia Glacier and Alyeska pipeline terminus. Evenings: Relax and enjoy Alaskan hospitality with coffee and pizzelles. Late night arrivals or early morning departures (ferry) okay. Hot breakfasts. See display ad. [ADVERTISEMENT]

Cliff House Bed & Breakfast offers a relaxing retreat on a 6-acre estate overlooking Valdez Bay. This lovely home features unique design and elegantly furnished smoke-free rooms, in a secluded setting only one-quarter mile from the Valdez Civic Center. Breathtaking, panoramic views of the Chugach Mountains and oceangoing vessel traffic in Valdez Arm. Gourmets will enjoy full breakfasts featuring homemade breads in our glassed-in dining room. Plan to make Cliff House your headquarters during your stay in Valdez and Prince William Sound. Let longtime Alaskan residents Christopher and Margie Lyon help make your stay a great one. By reservation only (907) 835-5244, P.O. Box 1995, Valdez, AK 99686. See display ad this section. [ADVERTISEMENT]

Downtown B & B Inn. Motel accommodations, 113 Galena Dr. Centrally located near small-boat harbor, museum, ferry terminal, downtown shopping. View rooms, private and shared baths, coin-op laundry, TV and phones in rooms. Wheelchair accessible. Complimentary breakfast. Reasonable rates. Single, double, family rooms. (800) 478-2791 or (907) 835-2791. See display ad this section. [ADVERTISEMENT] ♿

One Call Does It All. Free reservation service for bed-and-breakfast accommodations, Columbia Glacier tours, and rafting trips. Halibut and salmon fishing charters. We can find you a place to stay; accommodations at reasonable prices; some with wheelchair access. One call does it all! (907) 835-4988. See display ad this section. [ADVERTISEMENT]

Totem Inn, completely remodeled restaurant and lounge featuring an Old Town look with a New Town taste. Diners are surrounded by famous works of Alaska art. Restaurant opens at 5 A.M., serving breakfast, lunch and dinner. The lounge offers tall tales and a wide variety of libations. The motel provides deluxe rooms with private baths, satellite TV, phones, handicap

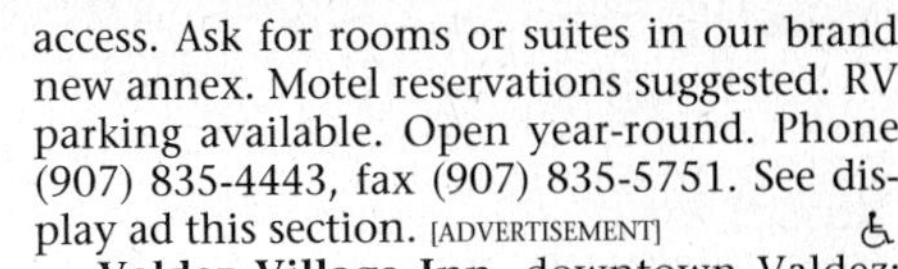

access. Ask for rooms or suites in our brand new annex. Motel reservations suggested. RV parking available. Open year-round. Phone (907) 835-4443, fax (907) 835-5751. See display ad this section. [ADVERTISEMENT] ♿

Valdez Village Inn, downtown Valdez: 100 modern rooms. Cable TV, private baths. Cottages with kitchenettes. Handicap access. Fitness center, sauna, Jacuzzi. Sugarloaf Restaurant & Saloon. Room/Glacier

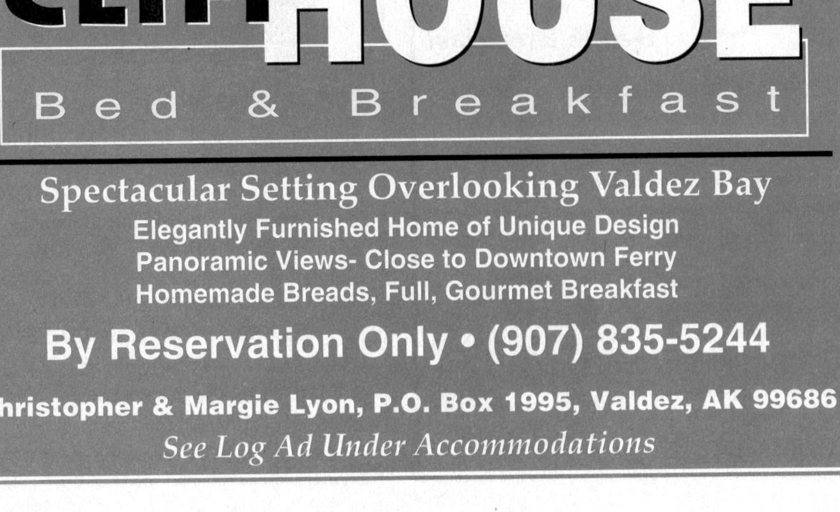

Sightseers get a close-up look at icebergs from Columbia Glacier. (Jerrianne Lowther, staff)

Cruise packages. Phone (907) 835-4445, fax (907) 835-2437. See display ad this section. [ADVERTISEMENT] 

There are three private RV parks with hookups near the small-boat harbor. The nearest public campground is Valdez Glacier campground, at the end of the airport road, about 6 miles/9.7 km from town; turn left at **Milepost NV 3.4** on the Richardson Highway. This city-operated campground has 101 sites, tent camping areas, picnic areas, firepits, tables, litter barrels, water and toilets; 15-day limit, $7 fee charged. ▲

Municipal dump station and freshwater fill-up on Chitina Drive in the small-boat docking area. Dump station and diesel at Valdez Tesoro. Dump station at Bear Paw R.V. Park for registered guests.

Bear Paw R.V. Park, centrally located on scenic North Harbor Drive overlooking the boat harbor, puts you within easy walking distance of museums, shops, restaurants, entertainment, charter boats — no need to unhook and drive to grocery stores or points of interest. Full, partial or no hookups;

immaculate private restrooms with hot showers. Dump station and coin-operated launderette for guests. Also available: waterfront full-hookup RV sites for adults only. Very nice, quiet, shaded tent sites, some platforms, among the salmonberries on Porcupine Hill. Fish-cleaning table and freezer available. Don't miss the Bear Paw Trading Post Gift Shop. Let us book your glacier tour at the reservations desk in our spacious office lounge, where the coffee pot is always on. Advance reservations recommended: (907) 835-2530. (Bear Paw does fill up!) Let us know if you're coming in on the evening ferry and we'll be there to help you get parked. See our large display ad this section. [ADVERTISEMENT] ▲

Eagle's Rest RV Park, the newest RV park in downtown Valdez, offers you service with a smile. Let Herb, Jeff or Laura take care of all your bookings on cruises, tours and charters. Enjoy the beautiful panoramic view of our mountains and glaciers right off our front porch! We also can let you know where the hottest fishing spots are or the

quietest walking trails! Fish-cleaning table and freezer available. Parking with us puts you within walking distance of our museum, gift shops, banks and even the largest grocery store on our same block! Shuttle service for glacier cruises. Call us for reservations, 1-800-553-7275 or (907) 835-2373. Fax (907) 835-KAMP (835-5267). Stay with us and leave feeling like family! See display ad this section. [ADVERTISEMENT] ▲

TRANSPORTATION

Air: Daily scheduled service to Anchorage via Alaska Airlines and Mark Air. Air taxi and helicopter services available.

Highway: The Richardson Highway extends north from Valdez to the Glenn Highway and the Alaska Highway. See the RICHARDSON HIGHWAY section.

Ferry: Scheduled state ferry service to Cordova, Whittier and Seward. Phone 835-4436. Reservations are a must! See MARINE ACCESS ROUTES section.

Bus: Regularly scheduled service to Anchorage and Fairbanks.

Taxi: One local taxi service.

Car Rental: Available at airport terminal.

ATTRACTIONS

See the Oil Painting: On display at the Church of the Epiphany is a famous artwork representation of the 15th century by Sr. Eugenio Cappilli of Florence, Italy.

Valdez Consortium Library, located on Fairbanks Street, has a magazine and paperback exchange for travelers. A trade is appreciated but not required. The library also has music listening booths, public computers, typewriters and a photocopier. Wheelchair accessible. Open Monday and Friday 10 A.M. to 6 P.M., Tuesday through Thursday, 10 A.M. to 8 P.M., and Saturday, noon to 6 P.M.

Celebrate Gold Rush Days: Held Aug. 3–7, 1994, this celebration includes a parade, contests and a casino night. During the celebration cancan girls meet the cruise ships and a jail is pulled through town by "deputies" who arrest citizens without beards and other suspects.

Bear Paw Trading Post Gift Shop, next to Bear Paw RV Park on Harbor Drive, features fine Alaska Native arts and crafts. Carved walrus ivory, scrimshaw, soapstone carvings, Native masks, fur items. Gold nugget jewelry, jade, hematite. Prints and books by Doug and Patti Lindstrand. Film, postcards, souvenirs, Alaska books. Phone (907) 835-2530. [ADVERTISEMENT]

Valdez Arm supports the largest sport fishery in Prince William Sound. Important species include pink salmon, coho (silver)

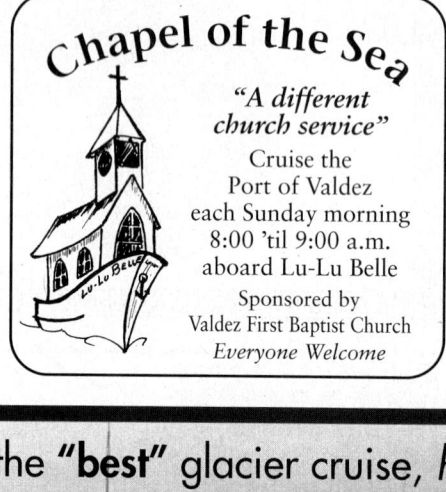

salmon, halibut, rockfish and Dolly Varden, with incidental catches of red, king and chum salmon. Charter boats are available in Valdez. A hot fishing spot near Valdez accessible by road is the **Allison Point** fishery (or "Winnebago Point" as it is known locally) created by the Solomon Gulch Hatchery, which produces major pink and silver salmon returns annually. Turn off the Richardson Highway at **Milepost V 2.9.** It is one of the largest pink salmon fisheries in the state. Pink salmon returns are best in odd years, but with hatchery production good pink runs are anticipated every year. Pinks average 3 to 5 lbs., from late June to early August. Silvers from 6 to 10 lbs., late July into September. Use light spinning gear or flies.

Fish a Derby. The Valdez Chamber of Commerce holds a halibut and silver salmon derby every year, with cash prizes awarded to the first through fifth place winners for both derbies. The Halibut Derby will be held May 7 through Sept. 4, 1994; the Silver Salmon Derby July 30 through Sept. 4, 1994. For further information contact the Valdez Chamber of Commerce at 835-2330.

Eielson AFB Valdez Boat Operation. Slip M 39 Valdez Small Boat Harbor; restricted to United States military and DOD government employees, active or retired; operational 2nd week of June to 1st week of

September; choice of craft with captain or operate your own rental craft. Reservations required. Address: 354 Services Squadron/ SSRO, 3112 Broadway, Eielson AFB, AK 99702. Telephone: (907) 377-1232/(907) 835-4681. [ADVERTISEMENT]

Prince William Sound Cruise. Experience the spectacular beauty of Prince William Sound aboard the *Glacier Queen II*. This Gray Line of Alaska tour cruises past Columbia Glacier, the largest glacier in Prince William Sound. Watch for abundant marine life as you travel round-trip between Valdez and Whittier. Two meals are included. This 12-hour tour departs daily from Valdez and costs $105 per person. Call (907) 835-2357. [ADVERTISEMENT]

Valdez Harbor Boat & Tackle Rentals. Enjoy the luxury of fishing and sightseeing at your leisure. View the many cascading waterfalls and the magnificent Shoup Glacier. We offer personalized boating and fishing instruction and will show you points

of interest and how and where to catch fish. We offer affordable, fully equipped boats, rental poles, bait, tackle. Floating office at boat harbor. (907) 835-5002. See display ad this section. [ADVERTISEMENT]

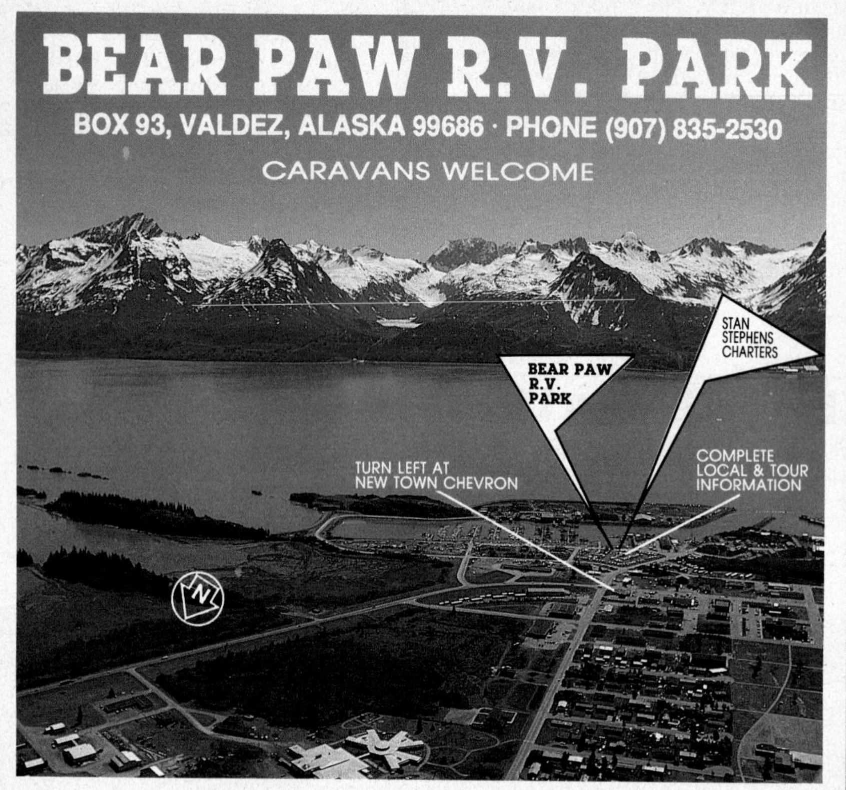
BEAR PAW R.V. PARK
BOX 93, VALDEZ, ALASKA 99686 · PHONE (907) 835-2530
CARAVANS WELCOME
STAN STEPHENS CHARTERS
BEAR PAW R.V. PARK
TURN LEFT AT NEW TOWN CHEVRON
COMPLETE LOCAL & TOUR INFORMATION
N

ON THE SMALL-BOAT HARBOR IN DOWNTOWN

VALDEZ

A BLOCK OR LESS TO MOST SHOPS AND STORES

- FULL AND PARTIAL HOOKUPS
- Level, crushed gravel pads
- Clean, private restrooms
- Hot unmetered showers
- Coin-operated launderette and dump station for registered guests only
- Two public telephones

Ticket Agent For

Stan Stephens Charters

SEE MAJESTIC COLUMBIA GLACIER

We can ticket:
- Major Columbia Glacier Cruises
- Pipeline Terminal Tours
- Halibut and Salmon Fishing Charters
- Flightseeing

You haven't seen glaciers until you've seen Columbia

BEAR PAW TRADING POST
Walrus Ivory
Furs Jade
Art Prints
Gold Nugget Jewelry
Film
Postcards
See log ad

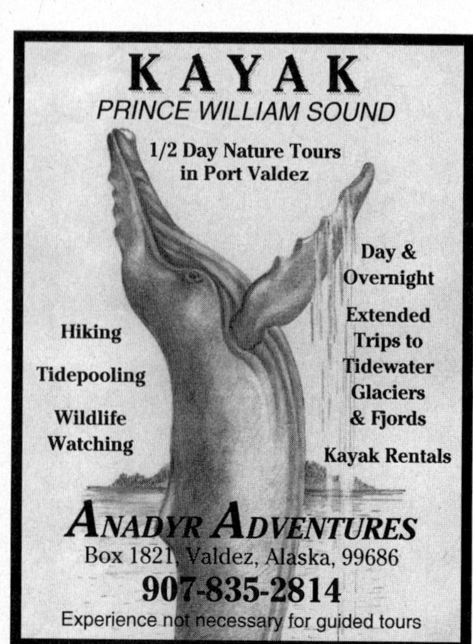
KAYAK
PRINCE WILLIAM SOUND
1/2 Day Nature Tours in Port Valdez
Day & Overnight
Extended Trips to Tidewater Glaciers & Fjords
Hiking
Tidepooling
Wildlife Watching
Kayak Rentals
ANADYR ADVENTURES
Box 1821, Valdez, Alaska, 99686
907-835-2814
Experience not necessary for guided tours

Take a boat tour to see Columbia Glacier, Shoup Glacier and other Prince William Sound attractions. Columbia Glacier, a tidewater glacier in Columbia Bay 28 miles/45 km southwest of Valdez, has become one of Alaska's best-known attractions. See ads in this section.

Raft and kayak trips of Prince William Sound, Keystone Canyon and surrounding rivers are available.

Go flightseeing and see Columbia Glacier, spectacular Prince William Sound and the surrounding Chugach Mountains from the air. There are several air charter services and two helicopter services in Valdez; see ads in this section.

Era Helicopters. Fly over Valdez and the Prince William Sound in the comfort and safety of Alaska's oldest and largest helicopter company. Soar over the breathtaking Columbia Glacier. Watch for otters, seals and bald eagles. Land at the face of Shoup Glacier. Phone (907) 835-2595 or outside Alaska (800) 843-1947. Tours also available in Anchorage, Juneau and Mount McKinley. [ADVERTISEMENT]

Ketchum Air Service, Inc. Alaska's outdoor specialists. Floatplane tours/charters into Prince William Sound, Wrangell–St. Elias park. Day fishing/fully equipped. Columbia Glacier tour. Drop-off cabins. Ken-

necott mine visit! Floatplane tour office located small-boat harbor Valdez. Call or write for brochure. VISA, MasterCard. Phone (907) 835-3789 or (800) 433-9114. Box 670, Valdez, AK 99686. [ADVERTISEMENT]

Visit Valdez Museum, located at 217 Egan Dr. Exhibits depict lifestyles and workplaces from 1898 to present. Displays include a beautifully restored 1907 Ahrens steam fire engine, the original Cape Hinchinbrook lighthouse lens, a Civil War-era field cannon, and an illuminated model of the Alyeska Marine Terminal. Interpretive exhibits explain the impact of the 1964 earthquake, the construction of the trans-Alaska oil pipeline, and the 1989 *Exxon Valdez* oil spill cleanup. Visitors can touch Columbia Glacier ice, play slot machines (for entertainment only!), sing along with the jukebox in the Pinzon Bar exhibit, and feel the luxurious softness of a sea otter pelt. The museum's William A. Egan Commons provides a showcase setting for the Ahrens steam fire engine, models of antique aircraft, and the lighthouse lens. Outside exhibits include displays of local wildflowers, an oil pipeline "pig" and a unique snow tractor. Valdez Museum is open year-round: daily during summer months (May to September); Tuesday through Saturday during off-season (October to April). Children free; $2 for adults (18 and older). Call (907) 835-2764 for more information.

Tour the oil pipeline terminus. The marine terminal of the Alyeska pipeline is across the bay from the city of Valdez. Free bus tours of the pipeline terminal are available daily from April to October from the Alyeska Pipeline Service Co. visitor center at

A fishing boat in Valdez Arm. (Jerrianne Lowther, staff)

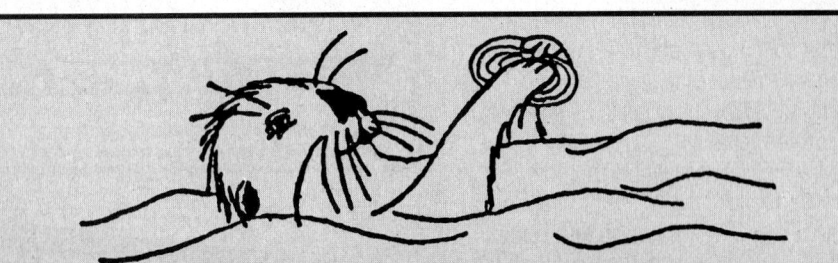

Prince William Sound tour boats take in scenery and wildlife, like this kittiwake rookery by a waterfall. (Jerrianne Lowther, staff)

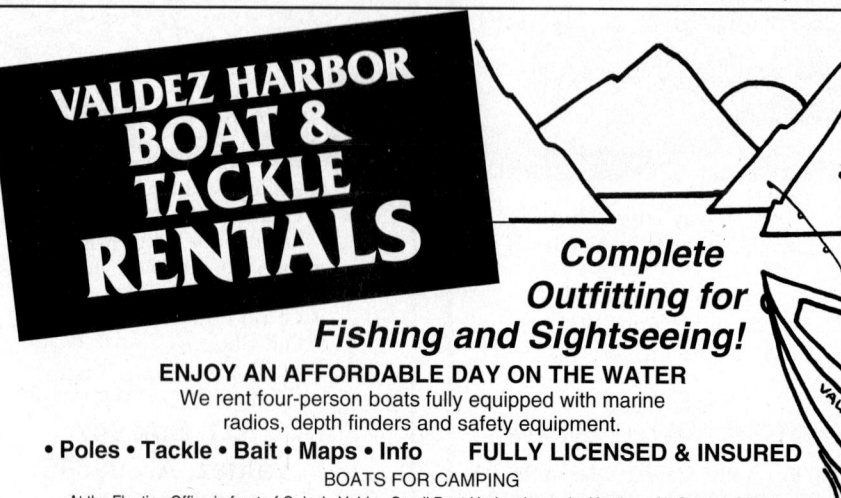

Valdez Airport. Reservations are suggested. Phone Alyeska for details on the tours: 835-2686 or 835-6983.

While entry to the terminal is restricted to authorized bus tours only, the drive out to the terminal is worthwhile. From Meals Avenue drive 6.8 miles/10.9 km out the Richardson Highway and turn right on the terminal access road (Dayville exit). The 5.4-mile/8.7-km road leading to the terminal passes Solomon Gulch dam and a spectacular view of Solomon Gulch Falls. There is also excellent fishing in season at Allison Point for pink and silver salmon. Entrance to the pipeline terminal is at the end of the road.

Outside the marine terminal gate is a bronze sculpture commemorating the efforts of men and women who built the trans-Alaska oil pipeline. Dedicated in September 1980, the sculpture was created by Californian Malcolm Alexander. It is composed of five figures representing various crafts and skills employed in the construction project. The work is the focal point of a small park from which visitors can watch tankers loading Alaska crude oil at the terminal. A small parking lot accommodates about 30 cars, and a series of signs explains the pipeline and terminal operations.

Stan Stephens Cruises. Let Alaskans show you Alaska. This family business, operated by year-round Alaskans, offers a variety of cruises to Columbia Glacier, designed to fit any budget. Economy tour departs Valdez daily, does not include stop on Growler Island. Extended cruises aboard the 80-foot *Glacier Spirit,* 75-foot *Nautilus* or our new 80-foot vessel, *Chugach,* include a stop at Growler Island where you will enjoy an Alaskan feast of salmon, halibut, chicken, salads, and all the trimmings. You can explore the beaches and intertidal zone. The longer excursions offer greater opportunity to view the wildlife of the Sound (sea otters, seal, sea lions, porpoise and the possibility of spotting orca,

humpback or minke whales). For those who wish to, you can stay overnight in heated tent/cabins at this wilderness camp, in view of the largest tidewater glacier in Prince William Sound. Now in '94, Stan Stephens Cruises will be offering a Whittier–Valdez schedule. All cruises will be stopping at Growler Island. Please see accompanying ad for our Photo Contest. Please call toll free for schedule information and a brochure. Westmark Dock, Box 1297-M, Valdez, AK 99686. Phone (907) 835-4731 or (800) 992-1297. Fax (907) 835-3765. [ADVERTISEMENT]

Our Point of View, an observation platform offering views of the original Valdez townsite, pipeline terminal and the town, is located by the Coast Guard office.

Visit Prince William Sound Community College, located at 303 Lowe St. Three huge wooden carvings on campus, by artist Peter Toth, are dedicated to the Indians of America. An Elderhostel is held at Prince William Sound Community College from mid-June through mid-August. This educational program (college credit given) is available for people over age 60. Subjects include Alaska history, wildlife and fisheries of

Prince William Sound, and Alaska literature. Contact Elderhostel, 80 Boylston St., Suite 400, Boston, MA 02116, for more information on its Alaska programs. A summer theater is also held at the college from June through August.

View salmon spawning at Crooked Creek. From Meals Avenue drive 0.9 mile/1.4 km out the Richardson Highway to the Crooked Creek salmon spawning area and hatchery. A U.S. Forest Service information station, open Memorial Day to Labor Day, has interpretive displays, and information on cultural history and recreation. An observation platform gives a close-up look at salmon spawning in midsummer and fall. This is also a waterfowl sanctuary and an excellent spot for watching various migrating birds.

Lu-Lu Belle. The motor yacht *Lu-Lu Belle* operates out of Glacier Charter Service. The *Lu-Lu Belle* is probably the cleanest and most plush tour vessel you will ever see. When you come aboard and see all the teak and mahogany, with hand-woven Oriental rugs, you will understand why Captain Rodolf asks you to wipe your feet. The *Lu-Lu Belle* has wide walk-around decks, thus assuring everyone ample opportunity for unobstructed outside viewing. She is equipped with several 110-volt current outlets for your battery chargers. Captain Fred Rodolf has logged over 2,000 Columbia Glacier cruises since 1979, and he will personally guide and narrate each and every cruise that the *Lu-Lu*

Belle makes. Come let Captain Rodolf show you why he refers to Switzerland as being the Valdez of Europe. The cruise leaves the tour dock at 2 P.M. each day from Memorial Day through Labor Day. During the busier part of the season, an 8 A.M. cruise may be added. The cost of our cruise is $60 per person. Up to June 15 we have an early-bird special of $55 each. Persons under 3 years of age and over 99 years of age are free. The cruise is approximately four and one-half hours long, depending on the wildlife and the amount of ice in Columbia Bay. There is a full service bar on board, with snacks. Friendliness and gracious hospitality on a beautiful yacht, no wonder people refer to the *Lu-Lu Belle* as being the limousine of Prince William Sound. There is also RV parking (full hookups only) available at the office lot. Our phone number in Valdez is (907) 835-5141, our winter phone is (206) 789-2204. For more information stop by our office on Kobuk Drive just off Chitina Drive behind the Totem Inn. [ADVERTISEMENT]

Marine terminal of Alyeska pipeline. (Jerrianne Lowther, staff)

Drive Mineral Creek Road. A 5.5-mile/8.9-km drive behind town leading northwest through the breathtaking alpine scenery along Mineral Creek. *Drive carefully!* This is a narrow road; conditions depend on weather and how recently the road has been graded. Bears are frequently sighted here. To reach Mineral Creek Road drive to the end of

Hazelet Street toward the mountains and turn left on Hanagita then right on Mineral Creek Road. Excellent view of the city from the water tower hill just to the right at the start of Mineral Creek Road.

Mineral Creek flows out of Mineral Creek Glacier. Mineral Creek Glacier is located approximately 2.5 miles/4 km beyond the end of the Mineral Creek Road. The old Hercules Mine, located at its base, is being mined again. Hike in about 30 minutes beyond the road end to the old stamp mill.

Cordova

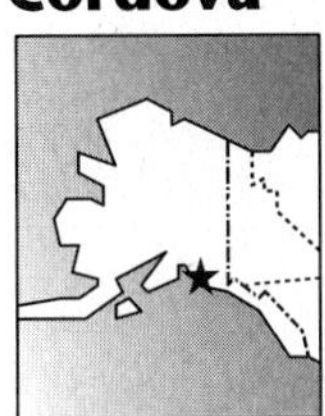

Located on the east side of Prince William Sound on Orca Inlet. **Population:** 2,585. **Emergency Services: Alaska State Troopers,** phone 424-7331, emergency phone 911. **Police, Fire Department, Ambulance,** phone 424-6100, emergency phone 911. **Hospital,** phone 424-8000.

Visitor Information: Information kiosk at the ferry office. Chamber of Commerce on 1st Street next to the National Bank of Alaska; phone 424-7260 or write Box 99, Cordova, AK 99574. There is also a visitor information center at the museum. A self-guided walking tour map of Cordova, prepared by the Cordova Historical Society, points out historic structures of the town.

Chugach National Forest Cordova Ranger District office is located at 612 2nd St. USFS personnel can provide information on trails, cabins and other activities on national forest lands. The office is open weekdays from 8 A.M. to 5 P.M. Write P.O. Box 280, Cordova 99574, or phone 424-7661.

Elevation: Sea level to 400 feet/122m. **Climate:** Average temperature in July is 54°F/12°C, in January 21°F/-6°C. Average annual precipitation is 167 inches. Prevailing winds are easterly at about 4 knots. **Radio:** KLAM-AM, KCHU-FM (National Public Radio). **Television:** Cable. **Newspaper:** *Cordova Times* (weekly).

Private Aircraft: Merle K. "Mudhole" Smith Airport, 11.3 miles/18.2 km southeast; elev. 42 feet/13m; length 7,500 feet/2,286m; asphalt; attended. Cordova Municipal (city air field), 0.9 mile/1.4 km east; elev. 12 feet/4m; length 1,900 feet/579m; gravel; fuel 100, 100LL; unattended. Eyak Lake seaplane base, 0.9 mile/1.4 km east.

Modern-day Cordova owes its origins to Michael J. Heney, builder of the Copper River & Northwestern Railway. A post office with this name was established in 1906. The town was chosen as the railroad terminus and ocean shipping port for copper ore shipped by rail from the Kennecott mines near Kennicott and McCarthy.

The railroad and town prospered until 1938 when the mine closed. Following the end of copper mining activity, fishing became the area's major economic base. One of the first producing oil fields in Alaska was located at Katalla, 47 miles/76 km southeast of Cordova on the Gulf of Alaska. The discovery was made in 1902 and the field produced until 1933.

Supporting the area's economy are the Prince William Sound fishery and fish processing plants. The fishing fleet can be seen at Cordova harbor, home port of the MV *Bartlett* and the USCG cutter *Sweetbrier*. Also at the harbor is the Cordova Fishermen's Memorial, *The Southeasterly*.

The fishing and canning season for salmon runs from about May to September, with red, king and silver (coho) salmon taken from the Copper River area, chum, red and pink salmon from Prince William Sound. Black cod, crab and shrimp season runs during winter. Dungeness crab season runs during the summer and early fall months. Razor clams, halibut and scallops are also processed.

ACCOMMODATIONS

Cordova has two motels and two hotels, five bed and breakfasts, eight restaurants, two laundromats and a variety of shopping facilities.

Cordova has one campground, Odiak

CORDOVA ADVERTISERS

Cordova Air Service, Inc. ..Ph. (907) 424-3289
Cordova Chamber of Commerce ....Ph. (907) 424-7260
Cordova Drug Co. ....First St.
Cordova Outboard, Inc. ..211 Breakwater Ave.
Cordova Rose Lodge ....Ph. (907) 424-ROSE
Ketchum Air Service, Inc. .Ph. (800) 433-9114
Oystercatcher Bed & Breakfast........................3rd & Council sts.
Powder House Bar and Restaurant ....Mile 2.1 Copper River Hwy.
Prince William Sound Adventures ....Ph. (907) 424-3350
Queen's Chair Bed and Breakfast, The..Mile 2.5 Copper River Hwy.
Reluctant Fisherman Inn, The ....Ph. (907) 424-3272

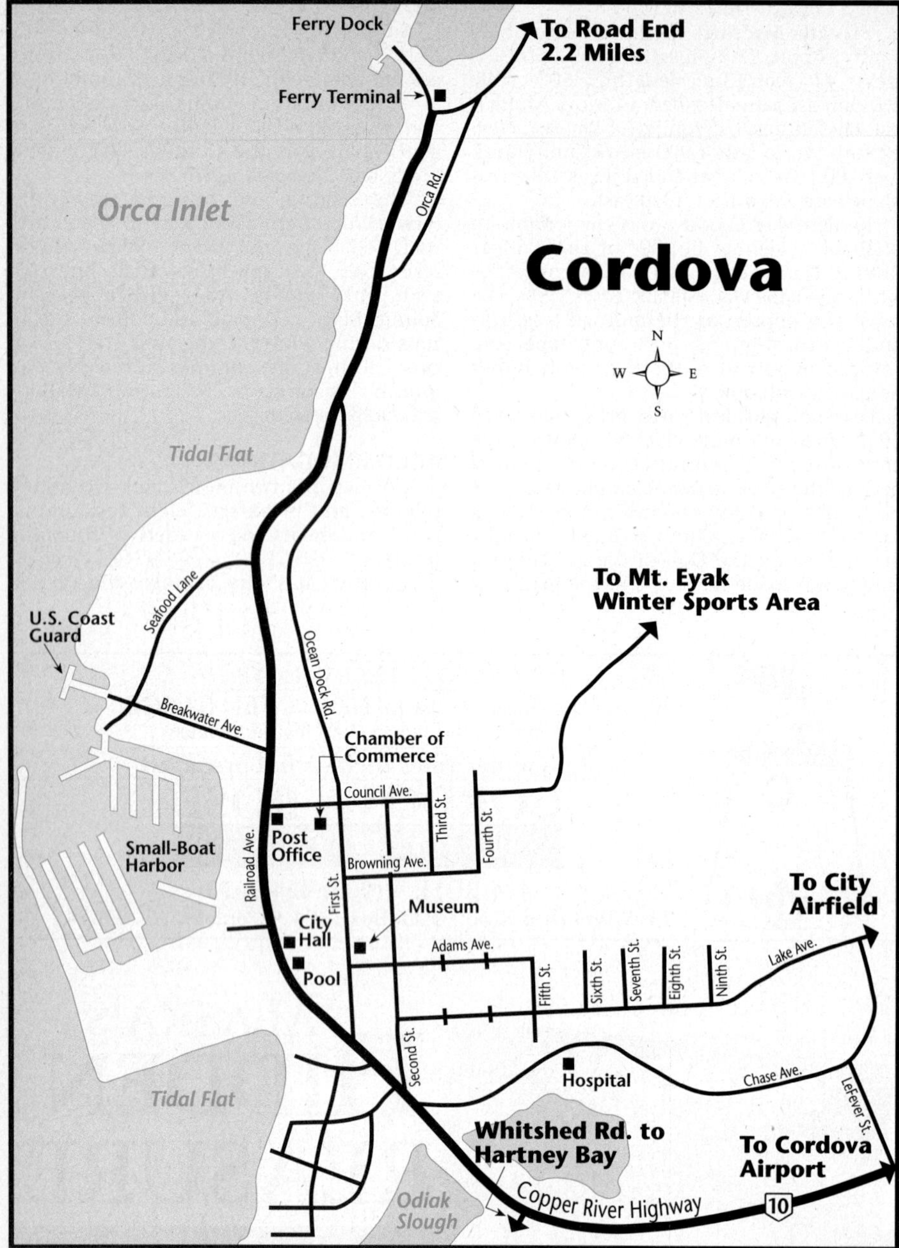

Camper Park, located on Whitshed Road and operated by the city. The camper park has 24 RV sites and a tenting area. Free shower tokens are available for paying campers. Contact Cordova's city hall at 424-6200. ▲

The U.S. Forest Service maintains 17 cabins in the Cordova district. Three are accessible by trail, the rest by boat or plane. Phone 424-7661 for current fees, reservations and information.

TRANSPORTATION

Air: Scheduled service via Alaska Airlines and Mark Air. Several air taxi services based at the municipal airport, Mile 13 airport and Eyak Lake offer charter and flightseeing service.

Ferry: The Alaska Marine Highway system ferries connect Cordova with Valdez, Whittier and Seward. Phone 424-7333. See the MARINE ACCESS ROUTES section for details.

Taxi: Local service available.

Car Rental: Available locally.

Highways: The Alaska state highway system does not connect to Cordova. The Copper River Highway leads 48 miles/77 km east and north of Cordova, ending at the Million Dollar Bridge and Childs Glacier. (See the COPPER RIVER HIGHWAY section.)

Private Boats: Cordova has an 850-slip boat harbor serving recreational boaters as well as the commercial fishing fleet. Berth arrangements may be made by contacting the Harbormaster's office at 424-6400 or on VHF Channel 16.

ATTRACTIONS

Silver Salmon Derby, held the last weekend in August and first weekend in September, offers cash and merchandise prizes. Contact the Chamber of Commerce, Box 99, Cordova 99574, for details. Tackle, licenses and supplies may be purchased locally. You can fish from the beach (the Fleming Creek area near the ferry terminal is especially popular).

Copper River Delta Shorebird Festival, May 4–8, 1994, offers five days of birding along the tidal mudflats and wetlands of the Copper River Delta and the rocky shoreline of Prince William Sound. The festival will include workshops, community activities and numerous field trip opportunities. Contact the Chamber of Commerce, Box 99, Cordova 99574, for details; phone (907) 424-7260.

Power Creek Road, from the corner of Lake and Chase avenues, leads out past the municipal airport to Crater Lake trailhead and Skaters Cabin picnic area (Mile 1.2), continues to Hatchery Creek salmon spawning channel (Mile 5.7), and ends at the Power Creek trailhead (Mile 6.9). The Crater Lake trailhead is directly northwest of the Eyak Lake Skaters Cabin. The 2.4-mile/3.8-km trail climbs to 1,500 feet/457m. Excellent views, alpine lake with fishing for cutthroat trout. Watch for bears. Visitors may view spawning salmon at the Hatchery Creek channel in July and August. Power Creek trail, 4.2 miles/6.7 km long, accesses both the USFS public-use cabin in Power Creek Basin and a ridge that connects with the Crater Lake trail creating a 12-mile/19.3-km loop. Power Creek trail offers spectacular scenery, with waterfalls, hanging glaciers and views of Power Creek Basin (called "surprise valley" by locals), the Chugach Range and Prince William Sound. Excellent berry picking. Watch for bears.

Drive the Copper River Highway to see the Million Dollar Bridge, Childs Glacier and the Copper River Delta. The 48-mile/77-km highway leads east from Cordova through the Delta to the historic Million Dollar

Bridge, built in 1909–10, and Childs Glacier. Viewing platform and picnic area at Childs Glacier. Wildlife seen along the highway includes brown and black bear, moose, beaver, mountain goats, trumpeter swans, and numerous other species of birds. See COPPER RIVER HIGHWAY section for log of road.

Cordova's Museum and Library, at 622 1st St., are connected by a central entryway. "Where Cultures Meet" is the theme of the museum. Native artifacts such as stone implements, a dugout canoe and skin bidarka (kayak-type boat) represent the rich Indian culture. One display tells of early explorers to the area, including Vitus Bering, who claimed Alaska for Russia in 1741. It was the Spanish explorer Don Salvador Fidalgo who named the adjacent water Puerto Cordoba in 1790. The town was named Cordova by railroad builder Michael J. Heney. By 1889, the town had grown into a fish camp and cannery site. Exhibits of the later mining and railroad era explain the development of the copper mines and of the town. Cordova was incorporated in 1909. Commercial fishing has now supplanted mining as the basis of the town's economy. Exhibits include a diorama of a vintage fishing vessel. The museum displays original work by Alaskan artists Sydney Lawrence, Eustace Ziegler and Jules Dahlager, who all worked in Cordova. The Cordova Historical Society operates a small gift shop at the museum, featuring books of local interest and Alaskan crafts.

Admission to the museum is free (donations are appreciated). Open 1-5 P.M. Tuesday through Saturday in summer; other times on request. Tours can be arranged. Write P.O. Box 391 or phone 424-6665 for more information. Library hours are 1-9 P.M. Monday, Tuesday, Thursday and Friday; 1-5 P.M. Saturday and Sunday; closed Wednesday.

Whitshed Road leads out past the lighthouse (Mile 0.4) to a large mudflat at Hartney Bay (Mile 5.5). The lighthouse is privately owned and maintained by the Gleins, who also operate a bed and breakfast in their home: a converted barge. Hartney Bay is part of the 300,000-acre Copper River Delta mudflats. The delta is one of the most important stopover places in the Western Hemisphere for the largest shorebird migration in the world. Birders can view up to 31 different species as millions of shorebirds pass through the delta each spring.

Attend the Iceworm Festival: Held the first full weekend in February, this festival offers a parade, art show, dances, craft show, ski events, survival suit race, beard judging and a King and Queen of Iceworm contest. Highlight is the 100-foot-/30-m-long "iceworm" that winds its way through the streets of Cordova.

Swim in the Bob Korn Memorial Swimming Pool, Cordova's Olympic-sized pool, located on Railroad Avenue below Main Street. Open year-round to the public. Check locally for hours.

Ski Hill, located at the end of 6th Street, operates between Dec. 15 and April 30, depending on the weather. Open Wednesday (adults only), Saturday, Sunday and holidays, 9 A.M. to dusk. The single chair lift rises 880 feet/268m up Eyak Peak.

Visit the USFS office on the third floor of the USFS Bldg. at 612 2nd St. Erected in 1925, it is the original federal building for the town of Cordova. Natural history display in second floor Interpretive Center. The USFS office is next to the old courtroom and jail. Open weekdays 8 A.M. to 5 P.M.

Area Fishing: Halibut year-round in Orca Inlet. Boat charters available locally. Winter king salmon fishing, January through March. Trolling for silver salmon mid-August through September. **Fleming Creek/lagoon,** near the ferry terminal off Orca Bay Road, is the site of an ADF&G coho and chinook enhancement project; excellent fishing for chinook (king) salmon in late May to early June, and for coho in late August. **Eyak Lake,** cutthroat and whitefish; salmon fishing within 200 yards of the weir (flies only). See also the COPPER RIVER HIGHWAY section for area fishing.

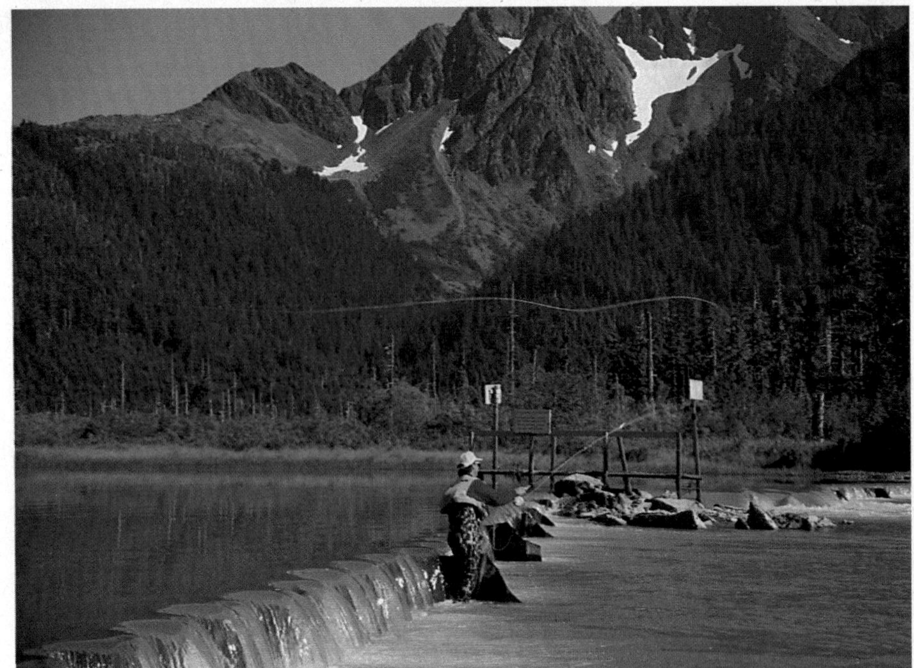

Cordova offers excellent fishing for salmon. (Ruth Fairall)

RICHARDSON HIGHWAY

Valdez to Delta Junction, Alaska
Alaska Route 4

Worthington Glacier is the most visited site in the Copper River Basin. (Lee Foster)

The Richardson Highway extends 368 miles/592 km from Valdez to Fairbanks. This section logs the first 270 miles/434.5 km of the Richardson Highway from Valdez to Delta Junction (the remaining 98 miles/ 157.7 km from Delta Junction to Fairbanks are logged in the ALASKA HIGHWAY section). Southbound travelers read log back to front.

The Richardson is a wide paved highway in good condition except for sporadic frost heaving. A new section of highway completed in 1989 bypasses the historic community of Copper Center. *The MILEPOST®* logs the old highway through town. The "new" Richardson Highway (bypass route) is of equal distance — 6.5 miles/10.5 km — with no notable features. You must exit the highway (watch for signs) to see Copper Center.

The Richardson Highway is a scenic route through the magnificent scenery of the Chugach Mountains and Alaska Range, leading past spectacular glaciers, through spruce forests and across tundra meadows. It also passes many fine king salmon streams including the Gulkana and Tonsina rivers.

The Richardson Highway was Alaska's first road, known to gold seekers in 1898 as the Valdez to Eagle trail. The gold rush trail led over the treacherous Valdez Glacier, then northeast to Eagle and the Yukon River route to the Klondike goldfields. Captain W.R. Abercrombie of the U.S. Army rerouted the trail in 1899 through Keystone Canyon and over Thompson Pass, thus avoiding the glacier. As the Klondike gold rush waned, the military kept the trail open to connect Fort Liscum in Valdez with Fort Egbert in Eagle. In 1903, the U.S. Army Signal Corps laid the trans-Alaska telegraph line along this route.

Gold stampeders started up the trail again in 1902, this time headed for Fairbanks, site of a big gold strike. The Valdez to Fairbanks trail became an important route to the Interior, and in 1910 the trail was upgraded to a wagon road under the direction of Gen. Wilds P. Richardson, first president of the Alaska Road Commission. The ARC updated the road to automobile standards in the 1920s. The Richardson Highway was hard-surfaced in 1957.

Emergency medical services: Phone 911 anywhere along the highway.

Richardson Highway Log

Mileposts on the Richardson Highway were erected before the 1964 Good Friday earthquake and therefore begin 4 miles/ 6.4 km from present-day downtown Valdez near the Old Valdez townsite (destroyed during the earthquake).

Distance from New Valdez (NV) is followed by distance from Old Valdez (OV).

NV 0 OV 4 (6.4 km) Intersection of Meals Avenue and the Richardson Highway.

NV 0.4 (0.6 km) **OV 3.6** (5.8 km) Paved double-ended turnout to north with Valdez information kiosk, maps, brochures, pay phones.

NV 0.5 (0.8 km) **OV 3.5** (5.6 km) DOT/PF district office.

NV 0.6 (1 km) **OV 3.4** (5.5 km) Valdez highway maintenance station.

NV 0.9 (1.4 km) **OV 3.1** (5 km) Double-ended turnout to north with litter barrels at Crooked Creek salmon spawning area and hatchery. Viewing platform on creek offers close-up look at salmon spawning in midsummer and fall. U.S. Forest Service information station is staffed Memorial Day through Labor Day. Interpretive displays, information on cultural history and recreational opportunities. Migrating birds such as Canada geese and various ducks are often here. It is a game sanctuary; no shooting is allowed. Good spot for pictures.

NV 1.3 (2.1 km) **OV 2.7** (4.3 km) Paved turnout to south.

NV 2 (3.2 km) **OV 2** (3.2 km) Paved turnout to south.

NV 2.1 (3.4 km) **OV 1.9** (3.1 km) Mineral Creek Loop Road through business and residential area on outskirts of Old Valdez comes out at **Milepost NV 3.4**. Access to Port of Valdez container terminal and grain elevators. The five grain elevators were built in 1982 in anticipation of the Port of Valdez receiving Delta barley for shipment.

NV 3.4 (5.5 km) **OV 0.6** (1 km) Road toward mountains leads 0.6 mile/1 km to Valdez Airport, 2 miles/3.2 km to Valdez Glacier campground, and 3.9 miles/6.3 km to a parking area next to the glacial moraine of Valdez Glacier. Good views of the glacier area are *not* available from this spot, nor is Valdez Glacier a very spectacular glacier. Valdez Glacier campground has 101 sites, tent camping, covered picnic area, litter barrels, water, toilets and fireplaces; 15-day limit, camping fee. *CAUTION: Beware of bears.* ▲

Mineral Creek Loop Road (turn toward ocean) leads to the original townsite of Valdez, destroyed during the Good Friday earthquake on March 27, 1964. A few homes and businesses are here now; there is little evidence of the earthquake's destruction.

NV 4 (6.4 km) **OV 0** Former access road to Old Valdez, now blocked off. Milepost 0 of the Richardson Highway is located here.

(Southbound travelers note: Physical mileposts end here, it is 4 miles/6.4 km to downtown Valdez.)

Distance from Old Valdez (V) is followed by distance from Fairbanks (F). Physical mileposts begin northbound showing distance from Old Valdez.

V 0 F 364 (585.8 km) **Milepost 0** of the Richardson Highway is located here at the former access road to Old Valdez.

RICHARDSON HIGHWAY *Valdez, AK, to Delta Junction, AK*

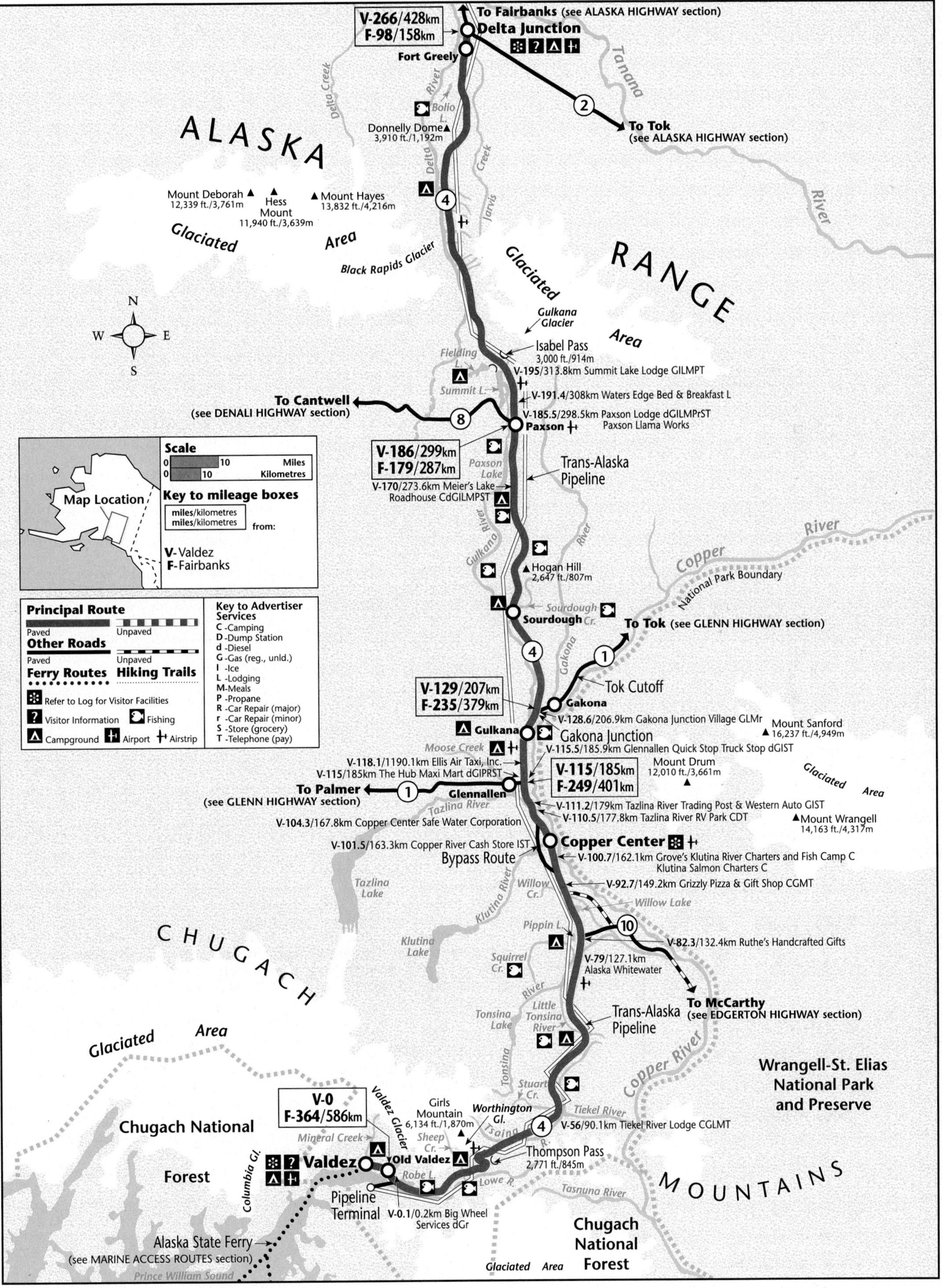

To Fairbanks (see ALASKA HIGHWAY section)
V-266/428km
F-98/158km
Delta Junction
Fort Greely
Tanana
2
To Tok
(see ALASKA HIGHWAY section)
River
Delta Creek
River
Bolio L.
Donnelly Dome 3,910 ft./1,192m
Delta
Creek
Jarvis
4
ALASKA
RANGE
Mount Deborah 12,339 ft./3,761m
Hess Mount 11,940 ft./3,639m
Mount Hayes 13,832 ft./4,216m
Glaciated Area
Black Rapids Glacier
Glaciated Area
Gulkana Glacier
Isabel Pass 3,000 ft./914m
Fielding L.
V-195/313.8km Summit Lake Lodge GILMPT
Summit L.
V-191.4/308km Waters Edge Bed & Breakfast L
To Cantwell
(see DENALI HIGHWAY section)
8
V-185.5/298.5km Paxson Lodge dGILMPrST
Paxson Llama Works
Paxson
V-186/299km
F-179/287km
Paxson Lake
Trans-Alaska Pipeline
V-170/273.6km Meier's Lake Roadhouse CdGILMPST
Gulkana River
River
Hogan Hill 2,647 ft./807m
Copper River
National Park Boundary
Sourdough Cr.
Sourdough
To Tok (see GLENN HIGHWAY section)
Gakona
1
Tok Cutoff
V-129/207km
F-235/379km
Gakona
V-128.6/206.9km Gakona Junction Village GLMr
Mount Sanford 16,237 ft./4,949m
Gulkana
Gakona Junction
Moose Creek
V-115.5/185.9km Glennallen Quick Stop Truck Stop dGIST
V-118.1/1190.1km Ellis Air Taxi, Inc.
V-115/185km The Hub Maxi Mart dGIPRST
V-115/185km
F-249/401km
Mount Drum 12,010 ft./3,661m
Glaciated Area
To Palmer
(see GLENN HIGHWAY section)
1
Glennallen
Tazlina River
V-111.2/179km Tazlina River Trading Post & Western Auto GIST
V-110.5/177.8km Tazlina River RV Park CDT
Mount Wrangell 14,163 ft./4,317m
V-104.3/167.8km Copper Center Safe Water Corporation
V-101.5/163.3km Copper River Cash Store IST
Copper Center
Bypass Route
V-100.7/162.1km Grove's Klutina River Charters and Fish Camp C
Klutina Salmon Charters C
Tazlina Lake
Klutina River
Willow Cr.
V-92.7/149.2km Grizzly Pizza & Gift Shop CGMT
Willow Lake
CHUGACH
Pippin L.
10
V-82.3/132.4km Ruthe's Handcrafted Gifts
Klutina Lake
Squirrel Cr.
V-79/127.1km Alaska Whitewater
River
To McCarthy
(see EDGERTON HIGHWAY section)
Little Tonsina River
Tonsina Lake
Trans-Alaska Pipeline
Glaciated Area
Tonsina
Copper River
Wrangell-St. Elias National Park and Preserve
Stuart Cr.
V-0
F-364/586km
Valdez Glacier
Girls Mountain 6,134 ft./1,870m
Worthington Gl.
Tiekel River
4
V-56/90.1km Tiekel River Lodge CGLMT
Chugach National Forest
Mineral Creek
Sheep Cr.
Tsaina R.
Thompson Pass 2,771 ft./845m
Valdez
Old Valdez
Columbia Gl.
Robe L.
Lowe R.
Tasnuna River
MOUNTAINS
Pipeline Terminal
V-0.1/0.2km Big Wheel Services dGr
Alaska State Ferry
(see MARINE ACCESS ROUTES section)
Prince William Sound
Chugach National Forest
Glaciated Area

N
W E
S

Map Location

Scale
0 10 Miles
0 10 Kilometres

Key to mileage boxes
miles/kilometres
miles/kilometres
from:
V-Valdez
F-Fairbanks

Principal Route
Paved Unpaved
Other Roads
Paved Unpaved
Ferry Routes **Hiking Trails**
Refer to Log for Visitor Facilities
Visitor Information
Fishing
Campground
Airport
Airstrip

Key to Advertiser Services
C -Camping
D -Dump Station
d -Diesel
G -Gas (reg., unld.)
I -Ice
L -Lodging
M -Meals
P -Propane
R -Car Repair (major)
r -Car Repair (minor)
S -Store (grocery)
T -Telephone (pay)

V 0.1 (0.2 km) **F 363.9** (585.6 km) **Big Wheel Services.** See display ad this section.

V 0.3 (0.5 km) **F 363.7** (585.3 km) Large turnout to east.

V 0.9 (1.4 km) **F 363.1** (584.4 km) The highway passes over the terminal moraine of the Valdez Glacier, bridging several channels and streams flowing from the melting ice.

V 1.4 (2.3 km) **F 362.6** (583.5 km) Valdez Trapshooting Range.

V 1.5 (2.4 km) **F 362.5** (583.4 km) City of Valdez Goldfields Recreation Area; trails, ponds, swimming, picnic sites and baseball field.

V 2.2 (3.5 km) **F 361.8** (582.2 km) Dylen Drive.

V 2.4 (3.9 km) **F 361.6** (581.9 km) Paved turnout to west.

V 2.5 (4 km) **F 361.5** (581.8 km) Valdez cemetery to east.

V 2.7 (4.3 km) **F 361.3** (581.5 km) Large paved double-ended turnout to west beside Robe River. During August and early September watch for pink and silver salmon spawning in roadside creeks and sloughs. Please *DO NOT* attempt to catch or otherwise disturb spawning salmon. *CAUTION: Beware of bears.*

V 2.9 (4.7 km) **F 361.1** (581.1 km) Turnoff for Old Dayville Road to Trans-Alaska Pipeline Valdez Marine Terminal and access to Allison Point fishery. This 5.4-mile/8.7-km paved road (open to the public) crosses the Lowe River four times. At Mile 2.4/3.9 km the road parallels the bay and there is excellent fishing in season at Allison Point, especially for pink and silver salmon; also watch for sea otters and bald eagles along here. At Mile 4.1/6.6 km is the Solomon Gulch water project and a spectacular view of Solomon Gulch Falls; a fish hatchery is located across from the water project. Entrance to the pipeline terminal is at the end of the road. Supertankers load oil pumped from the North Slope to this facility via the trans-Alaska pipeline. Bus tours of the terminal are available from the Alyeska Pipeline Service Co. visitor center at Valdez Airport. (For more information on the pipeline and terminal tours, see the VALDEZ section.)

V 3 (4.8 km) **F 361** (581 km) Weigh station.

V 3.4 (5.5 km) **F 360.6** (580.3 km) A 0.5-mile/0.8-km gravel road to Robe Lake and floatplane base. Watch for cow parsnip and river beauty (dwarf fireweed). Also watch for bears!

V 4.7 (7.5 km) **F 359.3** (578.2 km) Turnout to east. Access to **Robe River**; Dolly Varden, red salmon (fly-fishing only, mid-May to mid-June).

V 5.3 (8.5 km) **F 358.7** (577.3 km) Salmonberry Ridge ski area road to west.

V 7.3 (11.7 km) **F 356.7** (574 km) Lowe River parallels the highway next mile northbound.

V 9.6 (15.4 km) **F 354.4** (570.3 km) Fire station.

V 11.6 (18.7 km) **F 352.4** (567.1 km) Large paved turnout to east.

V 12.8 (20.6 km) **F 351.2** (565.2 km) Here the Lowe River emerges from Keystone Canyon. This is an area of special historic interest dating from the days of the great gold rush and the Copper River exploration of Abercrombie. Captain William Ralph Abercrombie was selected in 1884 to lead an expedition up the Copper River to the Yukon River. Although unsuccessful, he did survey the Copper River Delta and a route to Port Valdez. He returned in 1898 and again in 1899, carrying out further explorations of the area. The canyon was named by Abercrombie presumably for Pennsylvania, the Keystone State. He named the Lowe River for Lt. Percival Lowe, a member of his expedition. Glacier melt imparts the slate-gray color to the river.

V 13.5 (21.7 km) **F 350.5** (564.1 km) Horsetail Falls; large paved turnout to west.

CAUTION: Watch for pedestrians.

V 13.7 (22 km) **F 350.3** (563.7 km) Goat trail is visible on the west side of the highway; see description of this landmark at **Milepost V 15.2.**

V 13.8 (22.2 km) **F 350.2** (563.6 km) Bridal Veil Falls; large paved turnout to west.

V 14.9 (24 km) **F 349.1** (561.8 km) Lowe River bridge (first of three bridges northbound); view of Riddleston Falls. About 175 yards east of this bridge and adjacent to the highway is an abandoned hand-drilled tunnel. Large paved turnout with historical marker. Sign reads: "This tunnel was hand cut into the solid rock of Keystone Canyon and is all that is left of the railroad era when nine companies fought to take advantage of the short route from the coast to the copper country. However, a feud interrupted progress. A gun battle was fought and the tunnel was never finished."

V 15.2 (24.5 km) **F 348.8** (561.3 km) Small gravel turnout. On the far side just above the water are the remains of the old sled trail used in the early days. This trail was cut out of the rock just wide enough for two horses abreast. 200 feet above can be seen "the old goat trail." This road was used until 1945.

V 15.3 (24.6 km) **F 348.7** (561.2 km) Lowe River bridge No. 2, built in 1980, replaced previous highway route through the long tunnel visible beside highway. Turnout at south end of bridge. Traces of the old trail used by horse-drawn sleds can be seen about 200 feet/61m above the river.

V 15.9 (25.6 km) **F 348.1** (560.2 km) Leaving Keystone Canyon northbound, entering Keystone Canyon southbound. Raft trips of Keystone Canyon are available; check with outfitter in Valdez.

V 16.2 (26.1 km) **F 347.8** (559.7 km) Avalanche gun emplacement.

V 16.3 (26.2 km) **F 347.7** (559.6 km) Lowe River bridge No. 3.

V 18 (29 km) **F 346** (556.8 km) Large paved turnouts both sides of road.

V 18.6 (29.9 km) **F 345.4** (555.8 km) Sheep Creek bridge.

Truck lane begins northbound as highway ascends 7.5 miles/12 km to Thompson Pass. This was one of the most difficult sections of pipeline construction, requiring heavy blasting of solid rock for several miles. The pipeline runs under the cleared strip beside the road. Low-flying helicopters often seen along the Richardson Highway are usually monitoring the pipeline.

V 21.6 (34.8 km) **F 342.4** (551 km) Paved turnout to east.

V 23 (37 km) **F 341** (548.8 km) Large gravel turnout to east.

V 23.4 (37.7 km) **F 340.6** (548.1 km) Large paved turnout to east with view.

V 23.6 (38 km) **F 340.4** (547.8 km) Loop road past Thompson Lake to Blueberry Lake and state recreation site; see **Milepost V 24.1.**

V 23.8 (38.3 km) **F 340.2** (547.5 km) Small paved turnout to east.

V 24.1 (38.8 km) **F 339.9** (547 km) Loop road to Blueberry Lake State Recreation Site; drive in 1 mile/1.6 km. Tucked into an alpine setting between tall mountain peaks, this is one of Alaska's most beautifully situated campgrounds; 10 campsites, four covered picnic tables, toilets, firepits and water. Camping fee $6/night or annual pass. ▲

Blueberry Lake, and **Thompson Lake** (formerly Summit No. 1 Lake). Good grayling and rainbow fishing all summer.

V 24.4 (39.3 km) **F 339.6** (546.5 km) Large paved turnout to west. Bare bone peaks of the Chugach Mountains rise above the highway. Thompson Pass ahead; Marshall Pass is to the east.

During the winter of 1907, the A.J. Meals Co. freighted the 70-ton river steamer *Chitina* (or *Chittyna*) from Valdez over Marshall Pass and down the Tasnuna River to the Copper River. The ship was moved piece by piece on huge horse-drawn freight sleds and assembled at the mouth of the Tasnuna. The 110-foot-/34-m-long ship navigated 170 miles/274 km of the Copper and Chitina rivers above Abercrombie Rapids, moving supplies for construction crews of the Copper River & Northwestern Railway. Much of the equipment for the Kennicott mill and tram was moved by this vessel.

V 25.5 (41 km) **F 338.5** (544.7 km) Large paved turnout to west. Entering Game Management Unit 13D, leaving unit 6D, northbound.

V 25.7 (41.4 km) **F 338.3** (544.4 km) Large paved turnout to west with view; Keystone Glacier to the south.

V 26 (41.8 km) **F 338** (543.9 km) Thompson Pass (elev. 2,678 feet/816m) at head of Ptarmigan Creek. Truck lane ends northbound; begin 7.5-mile/12-km descent southbound.

Thompson Pass, named by Captain Abercrombie in 1899, is comparatively low elevation but above timberline. A wildflower lover will be well repaid if he rambles over the rocks in this area: tiny alpine plants may be in bloom, such as yellow heather (Aleutian heather) and bluebell (mountain harebell).

According to the National Climatic Center, snowfall extremes in Alaska are all credited to the Thompson Pass station, where record measurements are: 974.5 inches for season (1952-53); 298 inches for month (February 1953); and 62 inches for

Aurora borealis (northern lights) photographed near Copper Center. (Rick Ebrecht)

24-hour period (December 1955). Motorists may notice the snowpoles along the highway; these mark the road edge for snow plows.

Private Aircraft: Thompson Pass airstrip; elev. 2,080 feet/634m; length 2,500 feet/762m; turf, gravel; unattended.

V 27 (43.5 km) **F 337** (542.3 km) Thompson Pass highway maintenance station.

V 27.5 (44.3 km) **F 336.5** (541.5 km) Steep turnout to east by **Worthington Lake**; rainbow fishing.

V 27.7 (44.6 km) **F 336.3** (541.2 km) Good viewpoint of 27 Mile Glacier.

V 28 (45.1 km) **F 336** (540.7 km) Paved turnout to east.

V 28.6 (46 km) **F 335.4** (539.8 km) Paved turnout to west.

V 28.7 (46.2 km) **F 335.3** (539.6 km) Worthington Glacier State Recreation Site; glacier viewpoint with large viewing shelter, interpretive displays, toilets, picnic sites and parking. According to state park rangers, this is the most visited site in the Copper River Basin. The glacier, which heads on Girls Mountain (elev. 6,134 feet/1,870m), is accessible via a short road to the left. It is possible to drive almost to the face of the glacier. Care should be exercised when walking on ice because of numerous crevasses.

V 30.2 (48.6 km) **F 333.8** (537.2 km) Large paved turnout both sides of highway. Excellent spot for photos of Worthington Glacier.

V 31.1 (50 km) **F 332.9** (535.7 km) Small turnout to east. Avalanche gun emplacement.

V 32 (51.5 km) **F 332** (534.3 km) Highway parallels Tsaina River. Long climb up to Thompson Pass for southbound motorists.

V 33.6 (54.1 km) **F 330.4** (531.7 km) Tsaina River access to west.

V 34.7 (55.8 km) **F 329.3** (529.9 km) Tsaina Lodge.

V 36.5 (58.7 km) **F 327.5** (527 km) Pipeline runs under highway.

V 37 (59.5 km) **F 327** (526.2 km) Entering BLM public lands northbound.

V 37.3 (60 km) **F 326.7** (525.8 km) Tsaina River bridge at Devil's Elbow; turnout at south end of bridge.

V 40.5 (65.2 km) **F 323.5** (520.6 km) Pipeline passes under highway. Avalanche gun emplacement.

V 40.8 (65.7 km) **F 323.2** (520.1 km) Gravel turnout to west.

V 42 (67.6 km) **F 322** (518.2 km) Buried pipeline. View of waterbars (ridges on slope designed to slow runoff and control erosion).

V 43.3 (69.7 km) **F 320.7** (516.1 km) Long double-ended turnout.

V 43.5 (70 km) **F 320.5** (515.8 km) Small turnout to east.

V 45.6 (73.4 km) **F 318.4** (512.4 km) Large paved turnout to east at north end of Stuart Creek bridge.

V 45.8 (73.7 km) **F 318.2** (512.1 km) Watch for moose next 20 miles/32 km northbound.

V 46.9 (75.5 km) **F 317.1** (510.3 km) **Tiekel River** bridge; small Dolly Varden. Small turnout at north end of bridge.

V 47.9 (77.1 km) **F 316.1** (508.7 km) Large paved rest area by Tiekel River; covered picnic sites, toilets, no drinking water. Viewpoint and historical sign for Mount Billy Mitchell (straight ahead if you are headed south for Valdez). Lieutenant William "Billy" Mitchell was a member of the U.S. Army Signal Corps which in 1903 was completing the trans-Alaska telegraph line (Washington–Alaska Military Cable and Telegraph System) which was to connect all the military posts in Alaska. The 2,000 miles/3200 km of telegraph wire included the main line between Fort Egbert in Eagle and Fort Liscum at Valdez, and a branch line down the Tanana River to Fort Gibson and on to Fort St. Michael near the mouth of the Yukon and then to Nome. Mitchell was years later to become the "prophet of American military air power."

V 50.7 (81.6 km) **F 313.3** (504.1 km) Bridge over Tiekel River. Dead spruce trees in this area were killed by beetles.

V 53.8 (86.6 km) **F 310.2** (499.2 km) Squaw Creek culvert.

V 54.1 (87.1 km) **F 309.9** (498.7 km) Large paved turnout to east by Tiekel River. Look for lupine in June, dwarf fireweed along river bars in July.

V 54.3 (87.4 km) **F 309.7** (498.4 km) Old beaver lodge. Beaver may inhabit the same site for generations.

V 54.5 (87.7 km) **F 309.5** (498.1 km) Moose often seen here in the evenings.

V 55.1 (88.7 km) **F 308.9** (497.1 km) Large paved turnout to east by Tiekel River.

V 56 (90.1 km) **F 308** (495.7 km) **Tiekel River Lodge.** See display ad this section. ▲

Beavers eat a variety of vegetation.
(Bruce M. Herman)

V 56.3 (90.6 km) **F 307.7** (495.2 km) Large paved turnout to east by Tiekel River.

V 57 (91.7 km) **F 307** (494.1 km) Old beaver lodge and dams in pond to east. Tireless and skillful dam builders, beavers construct their houses in the pond created by the dam. Older beaver dams can reach 15 feet in height and may be hundreds of feet long. The largest rodent in North America, beaver range south from the Brooks Range. They eat a variety of vegetation, including aspen, willow, birch and poplar.

V 58.1 (93.5 km) **F 305.9** (492.3 km) Wagon Point Creek culvert.

V 60 (96.6 km) **F 304** (489.2 km) Large paved turnout to east. Highway parallels **Tiekel River**; fishing for small Dolly Varden.

V 62 (99.7 km) **F 302** (486 km) Ernestine Station highway maintenance camp.

V 62.4 (100.4 km) **F 301.6** (485.4 km) Boundary for Sport Fish Management areas. Entering Upper Susitna/Copper River Area N northbound, Prince William Sound southbound.

V 64.7 (104.1 km) **F 299.3** (481.7 km) Pump Station No. 12 to east. Interpretive viewpoint and parking to west. Short walk to viewpoint from parking area.

V 65 (104.6 km) **F 299** (481.2 km) Little Tonsina River.

V 65.1 (104.8 km) **F 298.9** (481 km) **Little Tonsina River** State Recreation Site with 10 campsites, firepits, water, litter barrels and toilets. Camping fee $6/night or annual pass. Dolly Varden fishing. Road to right as you enter wayside dead ends, road to left goes to the river (no turnaround space); follow loop road for easy access. Good berry picking in fall. *CAUTION: Beware of bears!*

Watch for moose next 20 miles/32 km southbound.

V 66.2 (106.5 km) **F 297.8** (479.2 km) Double-ended gravel turnout to west.

V 68.1 (109.6 km) **F 295.9** (476.2 km) Site of former Tonsina Camp (Alyeska Pipeline Service Co.) used during pipeline construction. These camps have been completely removed.

V 70.5 (113.5 km) **F 293.5** (472.3 km) Trans-Alaska pipeline follows base of mountains across valley.

V 71.2 (114.6 km) **F 292.8** (471.2 km) Long double-ended paved turnout to east.

V 72 (115.9 km) **F 292** (469.9 km) Double-ended paved turnout to west. Leaving BLM public lands northbound. View of trans-Alaska pipeline across the valley.

V 74.4 (119.7 km) **F 289.6** (466.1 km) Paved double-ended turnout to west. Vehicle access to Little Tonsina River.

V 78.9 (127 km) **F 285.1** (458.8 km) Bernard Creek trail. According to the BLM, this 15-mile loop road — which was originally part of the WAMCATS line (see **Milepost V 101.9**) — provides mountain bikers with an uphill ride on hard-pack dirt to near Kimball Pass.

V 79 (127.1 km) **F 285** (458.7 km) Tonsina Lodge. **Private Aircraft:** (Upper) Tonsina airstrip, adjacent south of lodge; elev. 1,500 feet/457m; length 1,400 feet/426m; turf; fuel 80; unattended.

Alaska Whitewater. Take a break from the road and travel by raft through a pristine valley where sightings of bald eagles, moose and bears are common occurrences. Whitewater or scenic, half-day and extended trips. Seasonal salmon fishing available. Direct ring down phone at Tonsina Lodge or call 1-800-337-RAFT. [ADVERTISEMENT]

V 79.2 (127.5 km) **F 284.8** (458.3 km) Bridge over Tonsina River, which rises in Tonsina Lake to the southwest.

V 79.6 (128.1 km) **F 284.4** (457.7 km) Bridge and Squirrel Creek state campground. Pleasant campsites on the bank of Squirrel Creek, some pull-through spaces; $6/night or annual pass; dumpster, boat launch, water, toilets and firepits. Rough access road through campground; low-clearance vehicles use caution. Large vehicles note: Limited turnaround on back loop road.

Mouth of **Squirrel Creek** at Tonsina River. Some grayling and salmon; grayling, small, use flies or eggs, all season; salmon, average size, egg clusters and spoons, all season. Also try the gravel pit beside the campground; according to state park rangers, some fishermen have good luck catching rainbow and grayling here using flies, eggs and spinners.

V 79.7 (128.3 km) **F 284.3** (457.5 km) Begin 1.3-mile/2.1-km truck lane northbound up Tonsina Hill. Hill can be slippery in winter. Watch for severe frost heaves.

V 82.3 (132.4 km) **F 281.7** (453.3 km) **Ruthe's Handcrafted Gifts.** Stop by our cabin for a visit and see quilts and critters, one-of-a-kind wearing apparel, and many

other functional and attractive gifts. I also do fun and practical things with recyclables. For a unique remembrance of Alaska, take home one of my handcrafted treasures. [ADVERTISEMENT]

V 82.6 (132.9 km) **F 281.4** (452.9 km) **Junction** with the Edgerton Highway. The Edgerton Highway leads east through the settlement of Kenny Lake to Chitina and connects with the McCarthy Road to McCarthy in Wrangell–St. Elias National Park and Preserve (see EDGERTON HIGHWAY section).

V 83 (133.6 km) **F 281** (452.2 km) Small paved turnout to west beside Pippin Lake.

V 87.7 (141.1 km) **F 276.3** (444.6 km) Paved double-ended turnout to east at Willow Lake. On a clear day this lake mirrors the Wrangell Mountains which lie within Wrangell–St. Elias National Park and Preserve. The park visitor center is at **Milepost V 105.1** and there is a good mountain viewpoint at **V 112.6.**

V 88.5 (142.4 km) **F 275.5** (443.4 km) Pipeline parallels road. Interpretive viewpoint to west on pipeline (one of three Alyeska pipeline displays along this highway). National Park Service plaque with schematic diagram of Wrangell Mountains.

V 90.8 (146.1 km) **F 273.2** (439.7 km) Large paved turnout to west by Willow Creek culvert; thick patches of diamond willow in woods off highway (and thick clouds of mosquitoes!).

V 91.1 (146.6 km) **F 272.9** (439.2 km) Turnoff to east is an 8-mile/12.9-km gravel cutoff that intersects Edgerton Highway at **Milepost J 7.3.** This is a drive through the rolling hills of homestead country and heavy thickets of birch and spruce.

V 92.7 (149.2 km) **F 271.3** (436.6 km) **Grizzly Pizza & Gift Shop.** See display ad this section.

V 98.1 (157.9 km) **F 265.9** (427.9 km) Microwave tower.

V 100.2 (161.2 km) **F 263.8** (424.5 km) IMPORTANT: South **junction** with Copper Center Bypass (New Richardson Highway). Northbound travelers TURN OFF on to Old Richardson Highway for scenic route through historic Copper Center (log and description follow). *The MILEPOST®* does not log the bypass route (New Richardson

Highway), which is the same distance as the old highway (6.5 miles/10.5 km) with no notable features. Although according to the BLM, there is an old four-wheel-drive road to Klutina Lake (25 miles/40 km) which is appropriate for mountain bikes. Turn west at Brenwick–Craig Road sign on the bypass and cross under pipeline. The old highway rejoins the bypass route at **Milepost V 106.**

V 100.7 (162.1 km) **F 263.3** (423.7 km) **Grove's Klutina River Charters and Fish Camp.** One of the friendliest places around. Great king and red salmon fishing. Also Dolly Varden, grayling and lake trout. Camping and RV parking on the south bank of the Klutina River. Electrical hookups and potable water. Dump station planned for 1994. Headquarters in historic log cabin on premises. Call 1-800-770-5822. See Klutina River Services ad in Copper Center. [ADVERTISEMENT] ▲

V 100.7 (162.1 km) **F 263.3** (423.7 km) **Klutina Salmon Charters.** See display ad this section. ▲

V 100.7 (162.1 km) **F 263.3** (423.7 km) Klutina River bridge. Excellent fishing in the **Klutina River** for king salmon (peaks in August); also grayling, Dolly Varden and red salmon (June through August). Campground and fishing charter services located here.

Copper Center

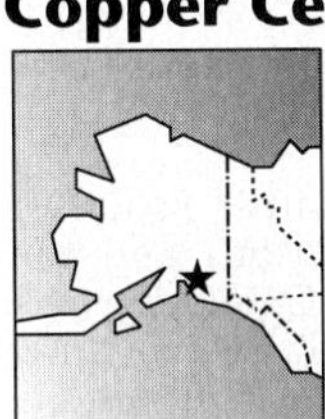

V 100.8 (162.2 km) **F 263.2** (423.6 km) The community of Copper Center extends down the road to the east then north through the trees and along the highway. An inner loop road leads through Copper Center and rejoins the Richardson Highway at **Milepost V 101.1. Population:** 449. **Emergency Services:** Phone 911. **Ambulance** in Glennallen, phone 911. **Elevation:** 1,000 feet/305m.

Private Aircraft: Copper Center NR 2 airstrip, 1 mile/1.6 km south; elev. 1,150 feet/351m; length 2,500 feet/762m; gravel; unattended.

Facilities include lodging, private campgrounds, meals, groceries, gas station, general store, post office and gift shops. Fishing charters, tackle, riverboat services and guides available.

A trading post was established in Copper Center in 1898. With the influx of gold seekers in 1898–99, following the trail from Valdez which joined the Eagle Trail to Forty Mile and Dawson country and later extended to Fairbanks, Copper Center became a mining camp. A telegraph station and post office were established in 1901 and Copper Center became the principal settlement and supply center in the Nelchina–Susitna region.

Copper Center Lodge on the inner loop road, selected by the Alaska Centennial Commission as a site of historic importance (a plaque is mounted to the right of the lodge's entrance), had its beginning as the Holman Hotel and was known as the Blix Roadhouse during the gold rush days of 1897–98. It was the first lodging place in the Copper River valley and was replaced by the Copper Center Lodge in 1932.

The George I. Ashby Memorial Museum, operated by the Copper Valley Historical Society, is housed in the bunkhouse annex at the Copper Center Lodge on the inner loop road. It contains early Russian religious articles, Athabascan baskets, telegraph and mineral displays, copper and gold mining memorabilia and trapping articles from early-day Copper Valley. Hours vary. Donations appreciated.

Historic buildings in Copper Center are located on private property. Please do not

COPPER CENTER ADVERTISERS

Copper Center Lodge.......Mile 101.1 Old Richardson Hwy.
Copper River Cash Store.........Mile 101.5 Old Richardson Hwy.
Grove's Klutina River Services....Mile 100.7 Old Richardson Hwy.
Klutina River Bed & Breakfast.....................Ph. (907) 822-5858

trespass.

The Copper River reportedly carries the highest sediment load of all Alaskan rivers. The river cuts through the Chugach Mountains and connects the interior of southcentral Alaska with the sea; it is the only corridor of its kind between Cook Inlet and the Canadian border.

The Richardson Highway offers good views of the trans-Alaska pipeline. (Nancy Faville)

Richardson Highway Log

(continued)

V 101 (162.5 km) **F 263** (423.3 km) A visitor attraction in Copper Center is the log Chapel on the Hill built in 1942 by Rev. Vince Joy with the assistance of U.S. Army volunteers stationed in the area. The chapel is open daily and there is no admission charge. A short slide show on the Copper River area is usually shown to visitors in the chapel during the summer. A highway-level parking lot is connected to the Chapel on the Hill by stairs.

V 101.1 (162.7 km) **F 262.9** (423 km) Turnoff on inner loop road to historic Copper Center Lodge and other businesses.

V 101.4 (163.2 km) **F 262.6** (422.6 km) Post office to east; outside mailbox.

V 101.5 (163.3 km) **F 262.5** (422.4 km) **Copper River Cash Store,** established in 1896, sits on part of the first farm started in Alaska. The center of the building is the original structure. Behind the store is the old jail, bars still on windows. Open six days a week, all year. Complete line of groceries, general merchandise, RV supplies, video rentals. [ADVERTISEMENT]

V 101.9 (164 km) **F 262.1** (421.8 km) Parking area. Historical marker about Copper Center reads: "Founded in 1896 as a government agriculture experiment station, Copper Center was the first white settlement in this area. The Trail of '98 from Valdez over the glaciers came down from the mountains and joined here with the Eagle Trail to Forty Mile and Dawson. 300 miners, destitute and lonely, spent the winter here. Many suffered with scurvy and died. Soon after the turn of the century, the Washington Alaska Military Cable and Telegraph System, known as WAMCATS, the forerunner of the Alaska communications system, operated telegraph service here between Valdez and Fairbanks."

V 102 (164.1 km) **F 262** (421.6 km) Brenwick–Craig Road. Access to Klutina River Bed & Breakfast.

V 102.2 (164.5 km) **F 261.8** (421.3 km) Copper Center Community Chapel and Indian graveyard.

V 102.5 (165 km) **F 261.5** (420.8 km) Fish wheel may sometimes be seen here operating in Copper River to east. The old school is a local landmark.

V 104 (167.4 km) **F 260** (418.4 km) Ahtna building houses Copper River Native Assoc.

V 104.3 (167.8 km) **F 259.7** (417.9 km) **Copper Center Safe Water Corporation.** See display ad this section.

V 104.5 (168.2 km) **F 259.5** (417.6 km) Silver Springs Road. Copper Center school.

V 104.8 (168.7 km) **F 259.2** (417.1 km) Paved turnout to east. Watch for horses.

V 105.1 (169.1 km) **F 258.9** (416.6 km) National Park Service headquarters and visitor center for Wrangell–St. Elias National Park and Preserve. Access to Wrangell–St. Elias National Park and Preserve is via the Edgerton Highway and McCarthy Road (see EDGERTON HIGHWAY section) and the Nabesna Road off the Tok Cutoff (see the GLENN HIGHWAY section). Ranger on duty, general information available. A 10-minute video is shown; additional video programs shown on request. Maps and publications are for sale. Open 9 A.M. to 6 P.M. daily, Memorial Day through Labor Day. Winter hours are 8 A.M. to 5 P.M. weekdays. For more information write P.O. Box 29, Glennallen, AK 99588; or phone 822-5234.

V 106 (170.6 km) **F 258** (415.2 km) IMPORTANT: North **junction** with Copper Center Bypass (New Richardson Highway). Southbound travelers TURN OFF on to Old Richardson Highway for scenic route through historic Copper Center (see description this section). *The MILEPOST®* does not log the bypass route (New Richardson Highway), which is the same distance as the old highway (6.5 miles/10.5 km) but without notable features. The old highway rejoins the bypass route at **Milepost V 100.2.**

V 110 (177 km) **F 254** (408.8 km) Dept. of Highways Tazlina station and Dept. of Natural Resources office. Report forest fires here or phone 822-5533.

V 110.5 (177.8 km) **F 253.5** (408 km) Pipeline storage area. Turn west on pipeline storage area road and take second right for private RV park.

V 110.5 (177.8 km) **F 253.5** (408 km) **Tazlina River RV Park.** See display ad this section. ▲

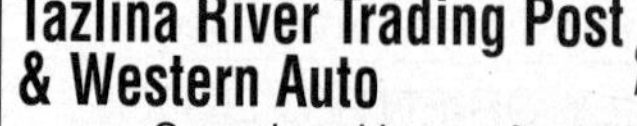

V 110.6 (178 km) **F 253.4** (407.8 km) Rest area to east on banks of Tazlina River; large paved surface, two covered picnic tables, water, toilets.

V 110.7 (178.2 km) **F 253.3** (407.6 km) Tazlina River bridge. *Tazlina* is Indian for "swift water." The river flows eastward from the glacier of the same name into the Copper River.

V 111.2 (179 km) **F 252.8** (406.8 km) Community college and trading post; groceries and gas.

Tazlina River Trading Post & Western Auto. See display ad this section.

V 111.7 (179.8 km) **F 252.3** (406 km) Copperville access road. Developed during pipeline construction, this area has a church and private homes. Glennallen fire station.

V 112.3 (180.7 km) **F 251.7** (405 km) Steep grade southbound from Tazlina River to the top of the Copper River bluffs.

V 112.6 (181.2 km) **F 251.4** (404.6 km) Paved parking area with historical information sign on the development of transportation in Alaska. Short (0.1 mile) walk to good viewpoint on bluff with schematic diagram of Wrangell Mountains: Mount Sanford (elev. 16,237 feet/4,949m); Mount Drum (elev. 12,010 feet/3,661m); Mount Wrangell (elev. 14,163 feet/4,317m); and Mount Blackburn (elev. 16,237 feet/4,949m).

Sign at viewpoint reads: "Across the Copper River rise the peaks of the Wrangell Mountains. The four major peaks of the range can be seen from this point, with Mount Drum directly in front of you. The Wrangell Mountains, along with the St. Elias Mountains to the east, contain the most spectacular array of glaciers and ice fields outside polar regions. The Wrangell Mountains are part of Wrangell–St. Elias National Park and Preserve, the nation's largest national park. Together with Kluane National Park of Canada, the park has been designated a World Heritage site by the United Nations."

Visitor information for Wrangell–St. Elias National Park is available at **Milepost V 105.1** Richardson Highway, or from ranger stations in Chitina and Slana.

V 115 (185 km) **F 249** (400.7 km) **South junction** of Richardson and Glenn highways at Glennallen. Greater Copper Valley Visitor Information Center at service center at junction, open daily in summer; pay phone, gas, groceries. The town of Glennallen extends west along the Glenn Highway from here, with businesses located at the junction and along the Glenn Highway. Anchorage is 189 miles/304 km, Tok 139 miles/224 km, from here.

Offices of the Alaska State Troopers (phone 822-3263), Dept. of Fish and Wildlife, Dept. of Motor Vehicles and Alaska Court located on east side of highway.

For the next 14 miles/22.5 km northbound the Richardson and Glenn highways share a common alignment. They separate at **Milepost V 128.6.**

*NOTE: Anchorage- or Tok-bound travelers turn to **Milepost A 189** in the GLENN HIGHWAY section. Valdez- or Fairbanks-bound travelers continue with this log.*

The Hub Maxi Mart. See display ad this section.

V 115.5 (185.9 km) **F 248.5** (399.9 km) **Glennallen Quick Stop Truck Stop.** Stop for friendly family service and gas and diesel prices that are hard to beat. A well-stocked convenience store contains ice, pop, snacks, postcards, ice cream, specialty items, a

phone and free coffee. Several interesting items are on display, including an authentic Native Alaskan fish wheel. [ADVERTISEMENT]

V 118 (189.9 km) **F 246** (395.9 km) Dry Creek State Recreation Site; 51 campsites, walk-in tent camping, water, tables, toilets, firepits, 15-day limit. Camping fee $6/night or annual pass. *Bring mosquito repellent!* Old ore car here was once used to haul gravel to Tonsina. ▲

V 118.1 (190.1 km) **F 245.9** (395.7 km) **Private Aircraft**: Gulkana airport; elev. 1,579 feet/481m; length 5,000 feet/1,524m; asphalt; fuel 100.

V 118.1 (190.1 km) **F 245.9** (395.7 km) **Ellis Air Taxi Inc.** The Ellis Family has been in Alaska for over 30 years with extensive experience flying in all of Alaska, scheduled air service Wednesday and Friday to Anchorage, Glennallen, McCarthy, Kennicott and May Creek. Single/multi engine aircraft charter service. More than just your Wrangell Mountains connection, we're the main line to all your Alaskan sightseeing and transportation needs. Phone (907) 822-3368. [ADVERTISEMENT]

V 123.2 (198.3 km) **F 240.8** (387.5 km) Large paved turnout to east and well-defined 1.5-mile/2.4-km trail east side of road to the mouth of the **Gulkana River** (see **Milepost V 126.9** for details on access and permits). Excellent fishing mid-June to mid-July for king salmon to 50 lbs. (average is 30 lbs.), and red salmon to 6 lbs. Use bright colored yarn or flies, half-inch hook. Heavy tackle with 25- to 30-lb.-test line recommended for kings. Check special regulations before fishing the Gulkana River.

V 126 (202.8 km) **F 238** (383 km) Paved double-ended turnout to west.

V 126.8 (204.1 km) **F 237.2** (381.7 km) Gulkana River bridge. Entering Game Management Unit 13B, leaving unit 13A, northbound.

V 126.9 (204.2 km) **F 237.1** (381.6 km) Access road to **GULKANA** (pop. 98) on the bank of the Gulkana River. Camping is permitted along the river by the bridge. ▲

NOTE: Gulkana River frontage from 2 miles/3.2 km downstream of Sourdough Roadhouse to the mouth of the Gulkana River is owned by Gulkana Village and managed by Ahtna, Inc. There are public easements along the Richardson Highway between Sourdough Roadhouse and the bridge.

V 128.6 (206.9 km) **F 235.4** (378.8 km) **North junction** (Gakona Junction) of the Richardson Highway and Tok Cutoff (Glenn Highway), known locally as Gulkana Junction. Gas, food and lodging. Here the Tok Cutoff branches off east to Tok on the Alaska Highway, 125 miles/201 km away. The Richardson Highway crosses the Gulkana River bridge and continues straight ahead north.

Gakona Junction Village offers high quality at great rates. Our modern hotel features standard and deluxe rooms with full bath and shower and color TV. Bunny's Cafe offers a full menu of great food from 6 A.M. to 9 P.M. daily. Buses welcome with reservations. Gakona Texaco always boasts the lowest gas prices in the area and a mechanic is on duty Monday through Saturday. Other services include: plug-ins, water, king salmon fishing guides, hunting and fishing licenses, Prince William Sound cruises and flightseeing. Call for reservations. 1-800-962-1933. See display ad at Gakona Junction in the GLENN HIGHWAY section. [ADVERTISEMENT]

*NOTE: Tok-bound travelers turn to **Milepost A 203** in the GLENN HIGHWAY section. Valdez- or Fairbanks-bound travelers continue* *with this log.*

V 129.2 (207.9 km) **F 234.8** (377.9 km) Pond with lily pads and occasionally a floatplane.

V 129.4 (208.2 km) **F 234.6** (377.5 km) Paved turnout to west. Sailor's Pit (gravel pit opposite lake to west); BLM trail across to **Gulkana River.** Fishing for rainbow trout, grayling, king and red salmon. Highway follows the Gulkana River.

V 132.1 (212.6 km) **F 231.9** (373.2 km) Paved turnout to west.

V 134.6 (216.6 km) **F 229.4** (369.2 km) Paved double-ended turnout with view of Gulkana River to west.

V 135.5 (218.1 km) **F 228.5** (367.7 km) Watch for caribou.

V 135.8 (218.5 km) **F 228.2** (367.2 km) Paved turnout to east.

V 136.4 (219.5 km) **F 227.6** (366.3 km) Coleman Creek bridge.

V 136.7 (220 km) **F 227.3** (365.8 km) Side road west to **Gulkana River** fishing access: Gulkana River Trail. Informal campsites along river.

V 138.1 (222.2 km) **F 225.9** (363.5 km) **Poplar Grove Creek** bridge; spring grayling fishing. Paved turnout to west at north end of bridge.

V 139 (223.7 km) **F 225** (362.1 km) Watch for frost heaves.

V 139.4 (224.3 km) **F 224.6** (361.4 km) Paved turnout to west with view of Gulkana River.

V 140.6 (226.3 km) **F 223.4** (359.5 km) Paved turnout to east.

V 141.2 (227.2 km) **F 222.8** (358.6 km) Side road west to Gulkana River fishing access. Informal campsites along river.

V 141.4 (227.6 km) **F 222.6** (358.2 km) Paved double-ended scenic viewpoint to west.

V 146 (234.9 km) **F 218** (350.8 km) Little lakes and potholes can be seen the next 9 miles/14.5 km northbound. Lily pads grow thickly. Watch for mallard ducks and other waterfowl. Views of Chugach Mountains for southbound travelers.

V 146.4 (235.6 km) **F 217.6** (350.2 km) Entering BLM public lands northbound.

V 147.1 (236.7 km) **F 216.9** (349.1 km) Double-ended paved scenic viewpoint.

V 147.6 (237.5 km) **F 216.4** (348.3 km) **SOURDOUGH.** BLM Sourdough Creek Campground; 60 sites, good king salmon fishing. Access to **Gulkana River,** marked trail to Sourdough Creek. Across the bridge (load limit 8 tons) and to the right a road leads to parking, toilets and boat launch on river. Watch for potholes in access roads. Native lands; check for restrictions.

The Sourdough Roadhouse next to the creek was established in 1903, approved as a historical site by the state of Alaska in the spring of 1974 and became a national historic landmark in 1979. A fire destroyed the roadhouse in December 1992. The old Valdez trail runs 150 yards/137m behind the few buildings left standing.

The Gulkana River is part of the National Wild and Scenic Rivers System managed by the BLM. A popular float trip for experienced canoeists begins at Paxson Lake and ends at Sourdough Campground. See description at **Milepost V 175.**

Gulkana River above Sourdough Creek, grayling 9 to 21 inches (same as Sourdough Creek below), rainbow 10 to 24 inches, spinners, June through September; red salmon 8 to 25 lbs. and king salmon up to 62 lbs., use streamer flies or spinners, mid-June through mid-July. **Sourdough Creek,** grayling 10 to 20 inches, use single yellow eggs or corn, fish deep early May through first week in June, use spinners or flies mid-June until freezeup.

V 150.7 (242.5 km) **F 213.3** (343.3 km) Large gravel turnout to east.

V 151 (243 km) **F 213** (342.8 km) Private gravel driveway to west by large pond; please do not trespass.

V 153.8 (247.5 km) **F 210.2** (338.3 km) Highway passes through boggy terrain; watch for caribou. *CAUTION: No turnouts, little shoulder. Watch for dips and rough patches in highway next 10 miles/16 km northbound.*

V 156.4 (251.7 km) **F 207.6** (334.1 km) As the highway winds through the foothills of the Alaska Range, over a crest called Hogan Hill (elev. 2,647 feet/807m), there are magnificent views of three mountain ranges: the Alaska Range through which the highway leads, the Wrangell Mountains to the southeast and the Chugach Mountains to the southwest. To the west is a vast wilderness plateau where the headwaters of the big Susitna River converge to flow west and south into Cook Inlet, west of Anchorage.

V 156.7 (252.2 km) **F 207.3** (333.6 km) Good view of pothole lakes to west.

V 157 (252.7 km) **F 207** (333.1 km) Good long-range viewpoints from highway. This is an area of lakes and ponds: Moose and other game may be spotted from here (use binoculars).

V 158.9 (255.7 km) **F 205.1** (330.1 km) Sweeping view of the Glennallen area to the south.

V 160.7 (258.6 km) **F 203.3** (327.2 km) **Haggard Creek** BLM trailhead; grayling fishing. Access to Gulkana River.

V 162.2 (261 km) **F 201.8** (324.8 km) Double-ended gravel turnout to east.

V 168.1 (270.5 km) **F 195.9** (315.3 km) **Gillespie Lake** trailhead and parking to west. Walk up creek 0.3 mile/0.5 km to lake; grayling fishing.

V 169.3 (272.5 km) **F 194.7**(313.3 km) Large gravel pit. Turnout to west.

V 169.4 (272.6 km) **F 194.6** (313.2 km) Middle Fork BLM trail to Meier's Lake and Middle Fork Gulkana River.

V 170 (273.6 km) **F 194** (312.2 km) Roadhouse with gas, food, lodging and camping. **Meier's Lake**; parking area, good grayling fishing.

Meier's Lake Roadhouse. See display ad this section.

V 171.6 (276.2 km) **F 192.4** (309.6 km) Gravel turnout by river to west. Long upgrade begins northbound.

V 172.7 (277.9 km) **F 191.3** (307.9 km) Small turnout to west, view of pipeline to east.

V 173.2 (278.7 km) **F 190.8** (307 km) **Dick Lake** to the east via narrow side road (easy to miss); no turnaround space. Good grayling fishing in summer. View of trans-Alaska oil pipeline across the lake. Good spot for photos.

V 175 (281.6 km) **F 189** (304.2 km) BLM Paxson Lake Campground turnoff. Wide gravel road (full of potholes if not recently graded) leads 1.5 miles/2.4 km to large camping area near lakeshore; 50 campsites, some pull-throughs, spaces for all sizes of vehicles but some sites on slope (RVs may need leveling boards); toilets, water, tables, firepits, dump station and concrete boat launch. Parking for 80 vehicles. Bring mosquito repellent. *CAUTION: Watch for bears.* Fishing in **Paxson Lake** for lake trout, grayling, red salmon and burbot.

This is the launch site for floating the Gulkana River to Sourdough Campground at **Milepost V 147.6.** Total distance is about 50 miles and four days travel, according to the BLM, which manages this national wild river. While portions of the river are placid, the Gulkana does have Class II and III rapids, with a gradient of 38 feet/mile in one section. Canyon Rapids may be Class IV depending on water levels (there is a portage). Recommended for experienced boaters only. For further information on floating the Gulkana, contact the BLM at Box 147, Glennallen 99588, or phone 822-3217.

V 177.1 (285 km) **F 186.9** (300.8 km) Small gravel turnout to west with view of Paxson Lake.

V 177.5 (285.7 km) **F 186.5** (300.1 km) Turnout to east. Trans-Alaska oil pipeline may be seen on the ridge northwest of the highway.

V 178.7 (287.6 km) **F 185.3** (298.2 km) Small gravel turnout to east.

V 179 (288.1 km) **F 185** (297.7 km) Gravel turnout overlooking Paxson Lake. The lake was named for the owner of the roadhouse (still Paxson Lodge) about 1906.

V 179.2 (288.4 km) **F 184.8** (297.4 km) Gravel turnout to west overlooking Paxson Lake.

V 182.1 (293 km) **F 181.9** (292.7 km) Large gravel turnout at head of Paxson Lake. Rough gravel trail to lake.

V 183.2 (294.8 km) **F 180.8** (291 km) Entering Paxson Closed Area northbound (closed to taking of all big game).

V 184.4 (296.8 km) **F 179.6** (289 km) Large gravel turnout to west.

V 184.7 (297.2 km) **F 179.3** (288.6 km) One Mile Creek bridge.

V 185.5 (298.5 km) **F 178.5** (287.3 km) **Junction** with Denali Highway to Denali National Park and George Parks Highway (see DENALI HIGHWAY section for details) at **PAXSON** (pop. 33), site of a lodge with gas station (open year-round), restaurant and small grocery store. Sled dog racing first weekend in April. Paxson Mountain (elev. 5,200 feet/1,585m) is 3 miles/4.8 km west-southwest.

V 185.5 (298.5 km) **F 178.5** (287.3 km) **Paxson Lodge.** See display ad this section.

Private Aircraft: Paxson airstrip (Hufman Field), adjacent south; elev. 2,653 feet/809m; length 2,800 feet/853m; gravel; emergency fuel; attended.

Paxson Llama Works lets you see Alaska as life-long Alaskans see it. Enjoy a two-hour gentle float trip over hundreds of spawning salmon. See nesting bald eagles, waterfowl and big game. Do what Alaskans do — enjoy the real Alaska. Guided llama trips for hiking, photography or fishing. Winter snowcat, snow machine or dogsled rides in season. Reservations recommended. Located Paxson Lodge, Box 2 Paxson, AK 99737; (907) 822-3330. [ADVERTISEMENT]

V 185.7 (298.9 km) **F 178.3** (286.9 km) Site of original Paxson Lodge.

V 185.8 (299 km) **F 178.2** (286.8 km) Paxson Station highway maintenance camp.

V 186.4 (300 km) **F 177.6** (285.8 km) Leaving BLM public lands northbound.

V 188.3 (303 km) **F 175.7** (282.8 km) Large paved double-ended rest area to east across from Gulkana River; tables, fireplaces, toilets, dumpster and water.

V 189.6 (305.1 km) **F 174.4** (280.7 km) Long paved double-ended turnout to west.

V 190.4 (306.4 km) **F 173.6** (279.4 km) Paved parking area by Gulkana River with picnic tables, dumpster and view of Summit Lake and pipeline. Access to Summit Lake. Interpretive sign about red salmon. Salmon spawning area; fishing for salmon prohibited. Access to **Fish Creek** at north end of turnout; grayling fishing. Access to Fish Lake is via trail paralleling creek for 2 miles/3.2 km, according to the ADF&G.

V 191 (307.4 km) **F 173** (278.4 km) Summit Lake to west; turnout at head of stream.

V 191.1 (307.5 km) **F 172.9** (278.2 km) Double-ended turnout to west.

V 191.4 (308 km) **172.6** (277.8 km) **The Water's Edge B&B.** Don't let our outside appearance fool you. Our accommodations offer continental breakfast, wonderfully cozy, decorated rooms. Cabin and duplex have cooking facilities, microwave, TV, VCR, stereo, private baths. Main house, king-size beds, cherrywood furniture, library, day bed, chaise lounge, handmade bedspreads. Owner was former decorator. We have guided fishing, boat rides, berry picking, information on area, tent and motorhome spaces, showers. Quiet setting, breathtaking view, wildflowers, lots of wildlife. For winter people, enjoy some of the best snowmobile country in the world, the ultimate adrenaline rush. We are 21-year Alaskans. For more information, write P.O. Box 3020, Paxson, AK 99737; message phone (907) 488-3619. [ADVERTISEMENT]

V 192.2 (309.3 km) **F 171.8** (276.5 km) Turnout with table and boat launch on **Summit Lake**; lake trout, grayling, burbot and red salmon.

V 192.6 (310 km) **F 171.4** (275.8 km) Large gravel turnout on Summit Lake.

V 193.3 (311.1 km) **F 170.7** (274.7 km) Gravel turnout to west by Summit Lake.

V 194.1 (312.4 km) **F 169.9** (273.4 km) Gravel turnout on Summit Lake.

V 195 (313.8 km) **F 169** (271.9 km) Large gravel turnout at **Summit Lake** (elev. 3,210 feet/978m). This lake, 7 miles/11.3 km long, is named for its location near the water divide between the Delta and Gulkana rivers. Fishing for lake trout, grayling, red salmon and burbot.

V 195 (313.8 km) **F 169** (272 km) Summit Lake Lodge; burned down in November 1993. Current status unknown.

Summit Lake Lodge. See display ad this section.

V 196.8 (316.7 km) **F 167.2** (269.1 km) Gunn Creek bridge. View of Gulkana Glacier to the northeast. This glacier, perched on 8,000-foot/2,438-m Icefall Peak, feeds through connecting streams and rivers into Prince William Sound.

V 197.6 (318 km) **F 166.4** (267.8 km) Large gravel turnout. Memorial monument honoring Gen. Wilds P. Richardson, for whom the highway is named, at summit of Isabel Pass (elev. 3,000 feet/914m). Sign here reads: "Captain Wilds P. Richardson presented the need for roads to Congress in 1903. His familiarity with Alaska impressed Congress with his knowledge of the country and his ability as an engineer. When the Act of 1905 became a law, he was placed at the head of the Alaska Road Commission in which position he served for more than a decade. The Richardson Highway, from Valdez to Fairbanks, is a fitting monument to the first great road builder of Alaska."

Entering Sport Fish Management Area C southbound.

V 198.5 (319.4 km) **F 165.5** (266.3 km) Gravel turnout to west.

V 200.4 (322.5 km) **F 163.6** (263.3 km) Gravel side road leads west 1.5 miles/2.4 km to **Fielding Lake** Campground. Pleasant area above tree line; seven campsites, picnic tables, pit toilets, large parking areas and boat ramp. Good fishing for lake trout, grayling and burbot.

Snow poles along highway guide snow-plows in winter.

V 201.5 (324.3 km) **F 162.5** (261.5 km) Phelan Creek bridge. Buried section of pipeline to west is a large animal crossing.

V 202 (325.1 km) **F 162** (260.7 km) Trans-Alaska oil pipeline parallels the highway above ground here. Entering BLM public lands northbound.

V 202.5 (325.9 km) **F 161.5** (259.9 km) McCallum Creek bridge, highway follows Phelan Creek northbound. This stream heads in Gulkana Glacier and flows northwest to the Delta River.

V 203.5 (327.5 km) **F 160.5** (258.3 km) Watch for beaver ponds (and beaver); lupine in June.

V 204 (328.3 km) **F 160** (257.5 km) Spring water piped to east side of highway; paved turnout.

V 204.7 (329.4 km) **F 159.3** (256.4 km) Large gravel turnouts both sides of highway.

V 205.3 (330.4 km) **F 158.7** (255.4 km) Small gravel turnout by stream. Good place for pictures of the pipeline up a very steep hill.

V 206.4 (332.2 km) **F 157.6** (253.6 km) Double-ended turnout with picnic tables, litter barrels and view of mineralized Rainbow Ridge to northeast. Wildflowers include yellow arnica and sweet pea.

V 207 (333.1 km) **F 157** (252.7 km) Good gravel turnout to west. There are frequent turnouts the next 6 miles/9.6 km northbound.

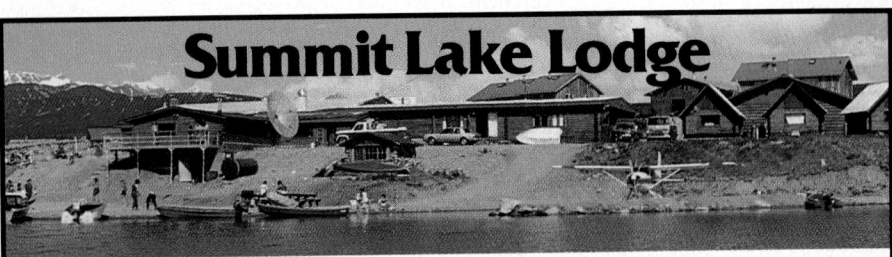

V 207.8 (334.4 km) **F 156.2** (251.4 km) Turnout. Rock slide and avalanche area next mile northbound; watch for rocks on road.

V 208.1 (334.9 km) **F 155.9** (250.9 km) Turnout to west by river. Look for wild, or Alaskan, rhubarb (*P. alaskanum*), a member of the buckwheat family. Grows to 6 feet with showy clusters of small yellowish-white flowers.

V 211.7 (340.7 km) **F 152.3** (245.1 km) Side roads signed APL are Alyeska pipeline access roads and closed to the public.

V 213.2 (343.1 km) **F 150.8** (242.7 km) Gravel turnout to west along Phelan Creek.

V 213.6 (343.7 km) **F 150.4** (242 km) Gravel turnout and road to gravel pit to east. Avalanche area ends northbound.

V 214 (344.4 km) **F 150** (241.4 km) Double-ended paved turnout with picnic tables and litter barrels. Highway follows Delta River northbound, Phelan Creek southbound.

V 215.1 (346.2 km) **F 148.9** (239.6 km) Pipeline crosses Miller Creek right next to bridge. Parking at both ends of bridge, access to creek.

V 215.9 (347.4 km) **F 148.1** (238.3 km) Pipeline interpretive viewpoint with information sign.

V 216.3 (348.1 km) **F 147.7** (237.7 km) Gravel turnout to east.

V 216.7 (348.7 km) **F 147.3** (237 km) Lower Miller Creek. Turnouts at both ends of bridge. This is a pipeline interpretive viewpoint and one of the best spots on the highway to photograph the pipeline.

V 217.2 (349.5 km) **F 146.8** (236.2 km) Castner Creek; parking at both ends of bridge, west side of road.

V 218.2 (351.1 km) **F 145.8** (234.6 km) Trims Station DOT/PF highway maintenance camp.

V 218.8 (352.1 km) **F 145.2** (233.7 km) Bridge over Trims Creek, parking. Wildflowers in the area include lupine, sweet pea and fireweed. Watch for caribou on slopes.

V 219.2 (352.8 km) **F 144.8** (233 km) Access to Pipeline Pump Station No. 10.

V 219.3 (352.9 km) **F 144.7** (232.9 km) Small gravel turnout. Note the flood control dikes (also called finger dikes) in stream to slow erosion.

V 219.9 (353.9 km) **F 144.1** (231.9 km) Michael Creek bridge; parking at both ends of bridge. Southbound drivers have a spectacular view of Pump Station No. 10 and the surrounding mountains.

V 220.9 (355.5 km) **F 143.1** (230.3 km) Flood Creek bridge; parking.

V 223 (358.9 km) **F 141** (226.9 km) Whistler Creek bridge; parking. Watch for frost heaves.

V 223.8 (360.2 km) **F 140.2** (225.6 km) Boulder Creek bridge; parking.

V 224.5 (361.3 km) **F 139.5** (224.5 km) Lower Suzy Q Creek bridge; parking.

V 224.8 (361.8 km) **F 139.2** (224 km) Suzy Q Creek bridge. Double-ended gravel turnout.

V 225.2 (362.4 km) **F 138.8** (223.4 km) Large gravel turnout to east.

V 225.4 (362.7 km) **F 138.6** (223.1 km) Double-ended paved turnout with picnic table and litter barrels. Historical marker here identifies the terminal moraine of Black Rapids Glacier to the west. This is a retreating glacier and little ice is visible. But this same glacier was nicknamed the Galloping Glacier when it advanced more than 3 miles/4.8 km during the winter of 1936–37, almost engulfing the Richardson Highway.

Black Rapids Lake trail begins across from historical sign (0.3 mile/0.4 km to the lake). Look for river beauty (dwarf fireweed), wild sweet pea and members of the saxifrage family blooming in June.

Private Aircraft: Black Rapids airstrip, adjacent north; elev. 2,125 feet/648m; length 2,200 feet/671m; gravel.

V 226 (363.7 km) **F 138** (222.1 km) Good gravel turnout by river to west.

V 226.3 (364.2 km) **F 137.7** (221.6 km) Falls Creek bridge.

V 226.7 (364.8 km) **F 137.3** (221 km) Black Rapids U.S. Army training site at Fall Creek. Boundary between Game Management Units 20D and 13.

V 227 (365.3 km) **F 137** (220.5 km) Gunnysack Creek. View of Black Rapids Glacier to west.

V 227.4 (366 km) **F 136.6** (219.8 km) Old Black Rapids Lodge. Dirt airstrip.

V 228.4 (367.6 km) **F 135.6** (218.2 km) Parking beside One Mile Creek bridge.

V 230.4 (370.8 km) **F 133.6** (215 km) Large paved turnout overlooks Delta River.

V 231 (371.7 km) **F 133** (214 km) Darling Creek. Gravel turnout to east.

V 233.3 (375.5 km) **F 130.7** (210.3 km) Bear Creek bridge; turnouts at either end, access to creek. Wildflowers include pale oxytrope, yellow arnica, fireweed, wild rhubarb and cow parsnip.

V 234.2 (376.9 km) **F 129.8** (208.9 km) Double-ended gravel turnout to east.

V 234.5 (377.4 km) **F 129.5** (208.4 km) Paved turnout with litter barrels to west. Pipeline access road. Pipeline comes up out of the ground here and goes through forest.

V 234.8 (377.9 km) **F 129.2** (207.9 km) Ruby Creek bridge; parking.

V 237.9 (382.9 km) **F 126.1** (202.9 km) Loop road (watch for potholes) through Donnelly Creek State Recreation Site; 12 campsites, tables, firepits, toilets and water. Camping fee $6/night or annual pass. ▲

V 238.7 (384.1 km) **F 125.3** (201.6 km) Watch for frost heaves northbound.

V 239.1 (384.8 km) **F 124.9** (201 km) Small gravel turnout to east.

V 241.3 (388.3 km) **F 122.7** (197.5 km) Large paved turnout to west with litter barrel.

V 242 (389.5 km) **F 122** (196.3 km) Pipeline parallels highway about 0.3 to 0.5 mile/0.4 to 0.6 km away. View of Donnelly Dome ahead northbound. Watch for dips in pavement.

V 242.1 (389.6 km) **F 121.9** (196.2 km) Coal Mine Road (four-wheel-drive vehicles only) leads east to fishing lakes; **Last Lake**, arctic char; **Coal Mine No. 5 Lake**, lake trout; **Brodie Lake** and **Pauls Pond**, grayling and lake trout. Check with the ADF&G for details.

V 243.4 (391.7 km) **F 120.6** (194.1 km) Pipeline viewpoint with interpretive signs. Good photo stop.

V 243.9 (392.5 km) **F 120.1** (193.3 km) Paved double-ended turnout with litter barrels to east. The trans-Alaska oil pipeline snakes along the ground and over the horizon. Zigzag design of pipeline converts pipe thermal expansion, as well as movement from other forces (like earthquakes), into a controlled sideways movement. A spectacular view to the southwest of three of the highest peaks of the Alaska Range about 40 miles/64.4 km in the distance. From west to south they are: Mount Deborah (elev. 12,339 feet/3,761m); Hess Mountain (elev. 11,940 feet/3,639m), center foreground; and Mount Hayes (elev. 13,832 feet/4,216m).

In spring look for wild sweet pea, chiming bells, lupine, lousewort (the bumblebee flower) and bluebell (mountain harebell) for the next 3 miles/4.8 km.

V 244.3 (393.2 km) **F 119.7** (192.6 km) Gravel turnout to east. Trail to **Donnelly Lake;** king and silver salmon, rainbow trout. View of Donnelly Dome ahead northbound.

V 245 (394.3 km) **F 119** (191.5 km) Gravel turnout to east overlooking lake.

V 245.2 (394.4 km) **F 118.9** (191.3 km) Large gravel turnout to east; ponds.

V 246 (395.9 km) **F 118** (189.9 km) Donnelly Dome immediately to the west (elev. 3,910 feet/1,192m), was first named Delta Dome. For years the mountain has been used to predict the weather: "The first snow on the top of the Donnelly Dome means snow in Delta Junction within two weeks."

V 246.9 (397.3 km) **F 117.1** (188.4 km) Gravel turnout to east.

V 247 (397.5 km) **F 117** (188.3 km) Cutoff to Old Richardson Highway loop to west; access to fishing lakes.

V 247.3 (398 km) **F 116.7** (187.8 km) From here northbound the road extends straight as an arrow for 4.8 miles/7.7 km.

V 249.3 (401.2 km) **F 114.7** (184.6 km) Bear Drop Zone. Military games area. Controlled access road: No trespassing.

V 252.8 (406.8 km) **F 111.2** (179 km) Scenic viewpoint to west with picnic tables and litter barrels.

V 253.9 (408.6 km) **F 110.1** (177.2 km) Good view of Pump Station No. 9 if southbound.

V 257.6 (414.6 km) **F 106.4** (171.2 km) Entrance to U.S. Army Cold Regions Test Center at Fort Greely.

Meadows Road (four-wheel-drive vehicles only) leads west to fishing lakes. Access to **Bolio Lake;** grayling, rainbow, lake trout. Rainbow-producing **Mark Lake** is 4.5 miles/7.2 km along this road. Meadows Road junctions with the Old Richardson Highway loop. Check with the ADF&G for details on fishing lakes.

V 258.3 (415.7 km) **F 105.7** (170.1 km) Pump Station No. 9 access road. Free tours of Pump Station 9 are offered daily from May to September. Phone (907) 869-3270 or 456-9391 for more information and tour reservations.

V 261.2 (420.3 km) **F 102.8** (165.4 km) **FORT GREELY** (restricted area) main gate. Fort Greely was named for A.W. Greely, arctic explorer and author of *Three Years of Arctic Service.*

V 262.6 (422.6 km) **F 101.4** (163.2 km) Double-ended paved turnout with scenic view. Watch for bison. Wind area next 2 miles/3.2 km northbound.

V 262.7 (422.8 km) **F 101.3** (163 km) FAA buildings. Big Delta.

V 264.9 (426.3 km) **F 99.1** (159.5 km) Jarvis Creek, rises near Butch Lake to the east and flows into the Delta River. Buffalo (bison) may be seen in this area.

V 266 (428 km) **F 98** (157.7 km) **Junction** of the Richardson Highway and the Alaska Highway, **Milepost DC 1422,** at Delta Junction. Visitor center is located at junction. Turn to page 166 for description of Delta Junction services and continuation of highway log to Fairbanks (the remaining 98 miles/157.7 km of the Richardson Highway leading into Fairbanks are logged in the ALASKA HIGHWAY section).

COPPER RIVER HIGHWAY

Cordova, Alaska, to the Million Dollar Bridge
Alaska Route 10
(See map, page 542)

The Copper River Highway leads 48.1 miles/77.4 km northeast from Cordova to the Million Dollar Bridge at the Copper River.

Construction of the Copper River Highway began in 1945. Built along the abandoned railbed of the Copper River & Northwestern Railway, the highway was to extend to Chitina (on the Edgerton Highway), thereby linking Cordova to the Richardson Highway.

Construction was halted by the 1964 Good Friday earthquake, which severely damaged the highway's roadbed and bridges. The quake also knocked the north span of the Million Dollar Bridge into the Copper River and distorted the remaining spans. The 48 miles of existing highway have been repaired and upgraded since the earthquake, but repairs to the Million Dollar Bridge remain temporary and travel across the bridge and beyond is not recommended. Road work along the abandoned railroad grade to Chitina has resumed periodically since 1991, pending approval of the highway extension.

Road rehabilitation work is scheduled in 1994 for the first 6.5 miles/10.5 km of highway out of Cordova.

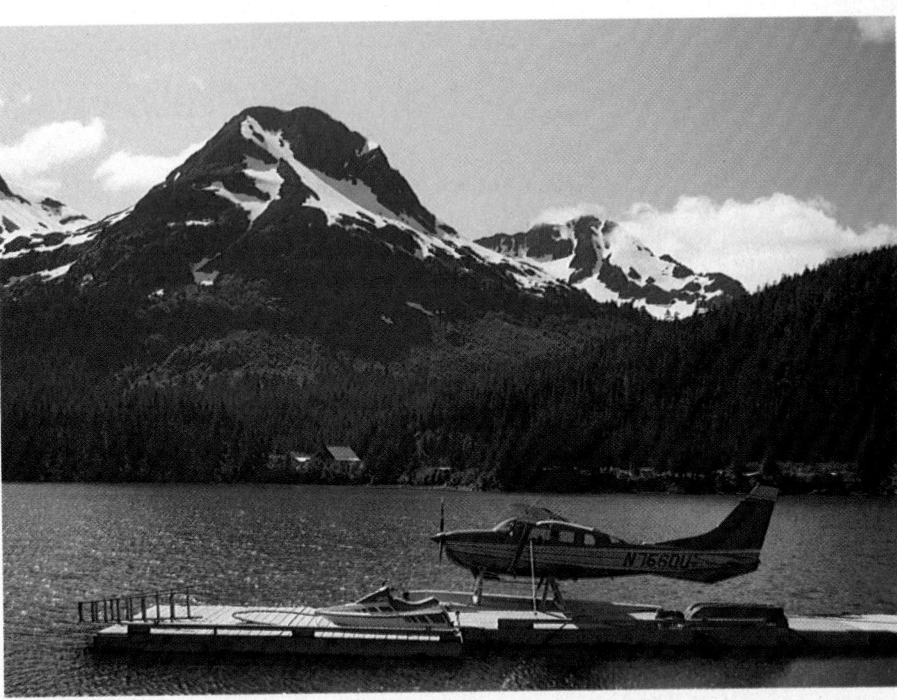

Floatplane at Eyak Lake, just east of Cordova. (Jerrianne Lowther, staff)

Copper River Highway Log

Distance is measured from Cordova (C).

C 0 **CORDOVA.** See description in PRINCE WILLIAM SOUND section. The Copper River Highway starts at the ferry terminal and leads east through town.

NOTE: Expect road construction next 6.5 miles/10.5 km in 1994.

C **1.4** (2.3 km) Whitshed Road on right leads 0.5 mile/0.8 km to Odiak municipal camper park (24 sites, tenting area, buy shower tokens at City Hall), 5.5 miles/8.9 km to **Hartney Bay.** Fishing from Hartney Bay bridge for Dolly Varden from May; pink and chum salmon, mid-July through August; closed for salmon upstream of bridge. Use small weighted spoons, spinners and eggs. Clam digging at low tide (license required). Shorebird migration in early spring.

C **2.1** (3.4 km) Powder House Bar and Liquor Store (restaurant) overlooking Eyak Lake. Site of CR&NW railway powder house.

C **2.3** (3.7 km) Paved turnout to north by Eyak Lake. View of the Heney Range to the south. Mount Eccles (elev. 2,357 feet/718m) is the first large peak. Pointed peak beyond is Heney Peak (elev. 3,151 feet/960m).

C **3.7** (5.9 km) Large paved turnout with litter barrels by Eyak Lake.

C **4.1** (6.6 km) Historical marker on left gives a brief history of the CR&NW railway. Also here is a monument erected by the railroad builder M.J. Heney in memory of those men who lost their lives during construction of the CR&NW. Begun in 1907 and completed in 1911, the CR&NW railway connected the port of Cordova with the Kennecott Copper Mines near Kennicott and McCarthy. The mine and railway ceased operation in 1938.

For the next 2 miles/3.2 km, watch for bears during early morning and late evening (most often seen in June).

C **5.3** (8.5 km) Paved turnout on lake to north.

C **5.6** (9 km) Paved turnout at lake to north.

C **5.7** (9.2 km) Bridge over Eyak River, access to Eyak River trail. This is a good spot to see waterfowl feeding near the outlet of Eyak Lake. An estimated 100 trumpeter swans overwinter on Eyak Lake.

Eyak River trailhead is on the west bank of the river. The 2.2-mile/3.5-km trail, much of which is boardwalk over muskeg, is popular with fishermen.

C **6** (9.7 km) **Eyak River**, outhouse and boat launch. Dolly Varden; red salmon, June–July; silvers, August–September. Also pinks and chums. Use Vibrax spoon, spinner or salmon eggs. Fly-fishing only for salmon within 200 yards of weir.

C **7.4** (11.9 km) Paved turnout. *CAUTION: High winds for next 4 miles/6.4 km.* In January and February, these winds sweep across this flat with such velocity it is safer to pull off and stop.

C **7.6** (12.2 km) Bridge over slough.

C **7.7** (12.4 km) First bridge across Scott River.

C **8.1** (13 km) Bridge over slough waters. Gravel turnout; access to slough.

C **8.4** (13.5 km) Scott River bridge.

C **9** (14.5 km) Between **Mileposts 9** and **10** there are four bridges across the Scott River and the slough. Sloughs along here are from the runoff of the Scott Glacier, visible at a distance to the northeast of the highway. Bear and moose are often seen in this area, especially in July and August. In May and August, thousands of dusky Canada geese, a subspecies of the Canada goose, nest here. This is the only known nesting area of the dusky geese, which winter in Oregon's Willamette Valley. Also watch for swans.

Moose feed in the willow groves on either side of the highway. Moose are not native to Cordova; the mountains and glaciers prevent them from entering the delta country. Today's herd stems from a transplant of 26 animals made between 1949 and 1959.

C **10.4** (16.7 km) Scott River bridge. Watch for old and new beaver dams and lodges beside the highway.

C **10.7** (17.2 km) U.S. Forest Service information pavilion (eight interpretive plaques) and large paved turnout with litter barrel to south. Game management area,

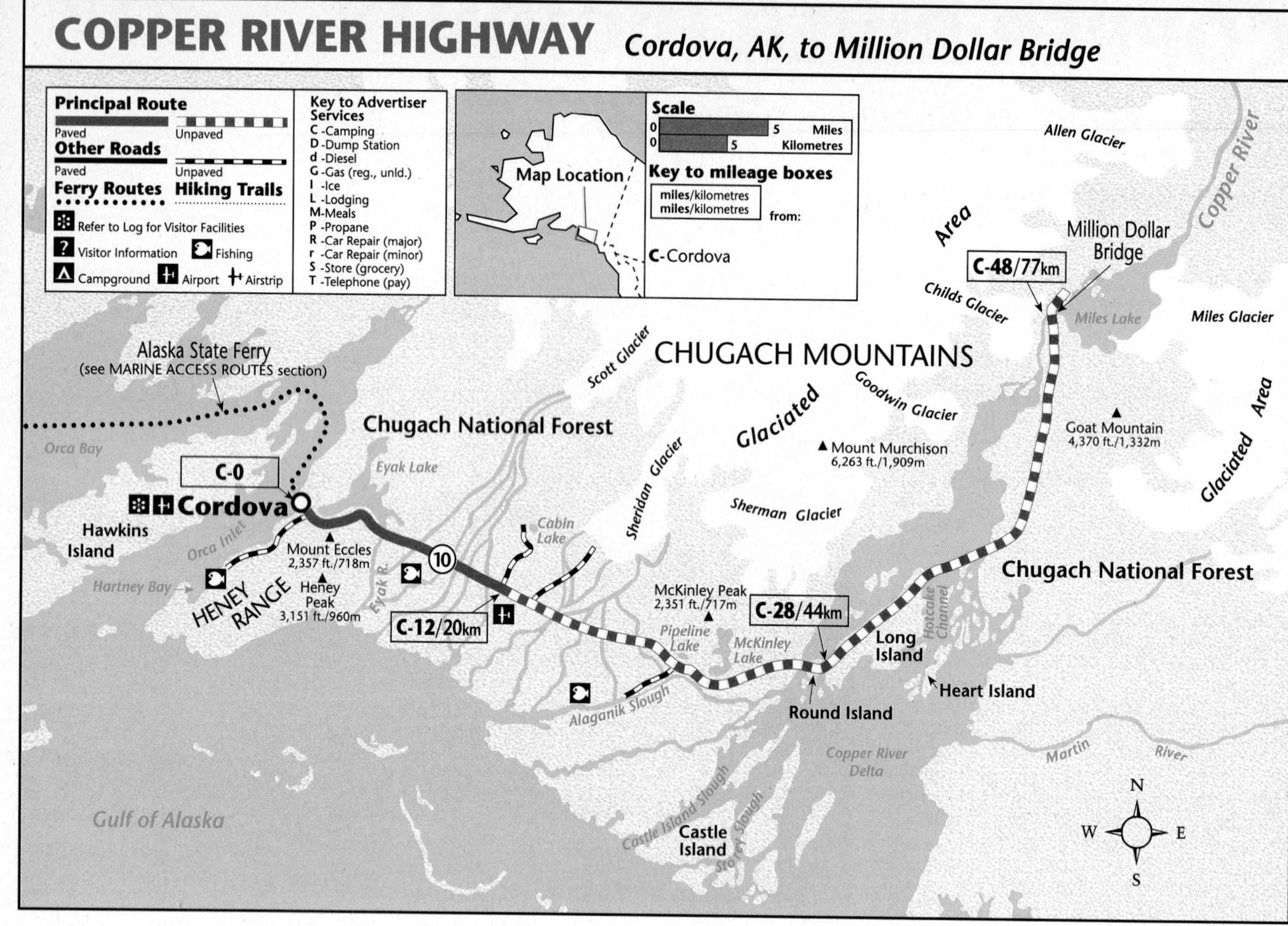

330,000 acres. Trumpeter swans and Canada geese. Look for arctic terns here.

C 10.8 (17.4 km) Bridge, beaver lodge.

C 11.1 (17.9 km) Elsner River bridge.

C 11.5 (18.5 km) Look for brown bears feeding in the outwash plains of Scott Glacier. Thousands of salmon swim up nearby rivers to spawn. There are numerous beaver lodges on both sides of the highway.

C 11.8 (19 km) State of Alaska Cordova highway maintenance station to northeast. U.S. Coast Guard station.

C 12.1 (19.5 km) Cordova airport and access to Cabin Lake Recreation Area. Drive north 2.8 miles/4.5 km for recreation area (gravel access road forks 0.3 mile/0.5 km in; right fork leads to gravel pit, continue straight ahead for recreation area). *CAUTION: Narrow road, no directional signs, active logging and logging trucks.* Picnic tables, toilet, litter barrel and firepits at **Cabin Lake**; cutthroat fishing.

C 12.4 (20 km) Pavement ends, gravel begins. Watch for potholes.

C 13 (20.9 km) Keep a lookout for snowshoe hare and birds of prey.

C 13.7 (22 km) Sheridan Glacier access road leads 4.3 miles/6.9 km to the terminus of Sheridan Glacier. *CAUTION: Narrow road, watch for logging trucks.* The glacier was named by U.S. Army explorer Captain Abercrombie for Gen. Philip H. Sheridan of Civil War fame. Sheridan Mountain trailhead, several picnic tables, litter barrels and a partial view of the glacier are available at the end of the access road. It is about a 0.5-mile/0.8-km hike to the dirt-covered glacial moraine.

C 14.8 (23.8 km) Bridge over Sheridan River. Raft take-out point. View of Sheridan Glacier. To the east of Sheridan Glacier is Sherman Glacier.

Winter moose range next 8 miles/13 km eastbound.

C 15 (24.1 km) Silver salmon spawn during September and October in the stream beside the highway.

C 16 (25.7 km) Beautiful view of Sheridan Glacier to the northeast.

C 16.3 (26.2 km) Second bridge over Sheridan River. Runoff from the Sheridan Glacier is joined upstream from this point by runoff from the Sherman Glacier (hidden from view).

C 16.9 (27.2 km) Turnoff for **Alaganik Slough,** Chugach National Forest Recreation Area. Drive south 3 miles/4.8 km via gravel road; picnic tables, firepits, wheelchair accessible toilets, litter barrel, information kiosk and boat launch. Wheelchair-accessible interpretive boardwalk for viewing birds and other Copper River Delta wildlife. The boardwalk is dedicated to the memory of ornithologist and conservationist Pete Isleib, who died in 1993. No water, informal camping. Interpretive plaque on side road reads: "Why are Delta moose the largest and healthiest? This moose herd, first introduced in 1949, maintains its vitality primarily due to its abundant willow supply. As part of a normal cycle, accelerated by the 1964 earthquake, much of the willow is becoming unavailable to moose. As the willow grows tall, the moose can no longer reach the tender new shoots. In the future this could cause a decrease in the numbers of moose on the delta. To slow the cycle down, the Forest Service is experimenting in this area, cutting back the shrubs. This should increase the amount of available willow browse. Biologists will evaluate the response of moose to new willow growth." Fishing in Alaganik Slough for Dolly Varden, sockeye (July) and silver salmon (August and September).

C 17.4 (28 km) Trumpeter swans often can be seen in the pond beside the highway. One of the largest of all North American waterfowl (with a wingspan of 6 to 8 feet), it faced extinction less than 40 years ago. Almost completely eliminated in the Lower 48 and Canada, Alaska harbors more than 80 percent of breeding trumpeters. More than 7 percent of the world population of trumpeter swans breeds in the Copper River Delta.

C 18 (29 km) For the next mile look for silver salmon spawning in the streams during September. To the left and on the slopes above timberline mountain goats may be seen.

The mountain to the left of the road ahead eastbound is McKinley Peak (elev. 2,351 feet/717m).

C 18.1 (29.1 km) Entering Chugach National Forest eastbound.

C 18.2 (29.3 km) Gravel road leads south to small picnic area with table, firepit, litter barrel and outhouse.

C 18.5 (29.8 km) Road narrows. *NOTE: Road not maintained in winter (after Nov. 1) beyond this point.*

C 18.8 (30.3 km) Turnout to north access

to Muskeg Meander cross-country ski trailhead; length 2.5 miles/4 km. According to the USFS district office, this trail offers a beautiful view of the Copper River Delta.

C **19.2** (30.9 km) Turnout to south leads to Haystack trailhead. Easy 0.8-mile/1.2-km trail leads to delta overlook with interpretive signs. Excellent place to see moose and bear according to the USFS district office in Cordova.

C **20.1** (32.3 km) Large gravel turnout to south; beaver dam, fishing.

C **21.4** (34.4 km) **Pipeline Lakes** trailhead to north, parking to south. The 1.8-mile/2.9-km trail was originally built as a water pipeline route to supply locomotives on the CR&NW railway. Segments of the pipeline are still visible. Fishing for grayling and cutthroat, fly or bait. Trail joins McKinley Lake trail. Rubber boots are necessary.

C **21.6** (34.8 km) Small turnout to north. **McKinley Lake** trail is an easy 2.1-mile/3.4-km hike with excellent fishing for sockeye, Dolly Varden and cutthroat. Access to USFS public-use cabins: McKinley Trail cabin (100 yards from highway) and McKinley Lake cabin (45-minute walk in from highway; also accessible by boat via Alaganik Slough).

C **22** (35.4 km) Double-ended turnout to north.

C **22.1** (35.5 km) **Alaganik Slough** boat ramp, picnic tables, firepits, toilets, litter barrel, wildflowers, interpretive signs on local cultural history and fishing access to south at west side of Alaganik Slough river bridge. Sockeye (red) and coho (silver) salmon, July to September. Also boat access to McKinley Lake.

C **23.7** (38.1 km) Salmon Creek bridge, parking. Beaver lodge.

C **24.5** (39.4 km) Turnout to north.

C **24.8** (39.9 km) Channel to beaver pond for spawning salmon. A plaque here reads: "Pathway to salmon rearing grounds. Channel provided access to beaver pond (north side of road) for coho fry. Beaver pond can support up to 25,400 young salmon. Fallen trees and brush provide cover from predators." One-mile/1.6-km access road north around pond leads to Saddlebag Glacier trailhead and parking area. According to the USFS office in Cordova, this is an easy 3-mile/4.8-km trail to Saddlebag Lake. View of Saddlebag Glacier and icebergs; look for goats on surrounding mountains. *CAUTION: Watch for bears.*

C **25.4** (40.9 km) Small gravel turnout by two spawning channels with weirs built in 1987 as part of a USFS stream enhancement project for resident sockeye and coho salmon. Interpretive signs along a short trail here explain the project: "Channel built by USDA Forest Service to provide high quality spawning habitat for coho and sockeye salmon. Before construction, the streambed was muddy and the stream dried up during low flow periods. Fish spawned in the streams but few eggs survived. Improved channel is deeper and ensures a consistent flow. Adjustable weirs control water depth. Clean gravels placed in the channel make better spawning conditions while large riprap on streambanks prevent erosion.

"Can you see small circles of gravel which appear to have been turned over? These are salmon 'redds,' or nests in which female salmon lay their eggs. Female salmon create the redds by digging with their tails. Environmental conditions and predators take a heavy toll on salmon eggs and small fry. Of the 2,800 eggs which the average female coho salmon lays, only about 14 will survive to adulthood. Most of these will then be caught by commercial, sport or subsistence fishermen. Only two salmon from each redd will actually return to spawn and complete their life cycle."

Near here was the cabin of Rex Beach, author of *The Iron Trail,* a classic novel about the building of the CR&NW railway.

C **26.4** (42.5 km) Flag Point. Turnout with view of the Copper River which empties into the Gulf of Alaska. Downriver to the southwest is Castle Island Slough. Storey Slough is visible a little more to the south. Castle Island and a number of small islands lie at the mouth of the Copper River. Monument on the riverbank is dedicated to the men who built these bridges and "especially to the crane crew who lost their lives on July 21, 1971."

CAUTION: Extreme high winds next 10 miles/16 km in fall and winter. Stay in your vehicle.

C **26.7** (43 km) Two bridges cross the Copper River to Round Island, a small island with sand dunes and a good place to picnic.

In midsummer the Copper River has half a million or more red (sockeye) and king salmon migrating 300 miles/483 km upstream to spawn in the river's clear tributaries. There is no sportfishing in this stretch of the Copper River because of glacial silt.

Candlefish (eulachon) also spawn in the Copper River. Candlefish oil was once a significant trade item of the Coastal Indians. These fish are so oily that when dried they can be burned like candles.

C **27.5** (44.3 km) Bridge from Round Island to Long Island. The 6.2 miles/10 km of road on Long Island pass through a sandy landscape dotted with dunes. Long Island is in the middle of the Copper River.

C **27.9** (44.9 km) Double-ended turnout to north; primitive campsite, beaver lodge.

C **28.5** (45.9 km) Lake to south is stocked with grayling.

C **30.8** (49.5 km) Watch for nesting swans, other birds and beaver in slough to south of road. *NOTE: Use extreme caution if you drive off road: sandy terrain.*

C **33** (53.1 km) View of two glaciers to the northwest; nearest is Goodwin, the other is Childs.

C **33.3** (53.6 km) First bridge leaving Long Island. View to south down Hotcake Channel to Heart Island. Road built on top of a long dike which stretches across the Copper River Delta. From here to **Milepost C 37.7** there are seven more bridges across the delta. The Copper River channels have changed in recent years, with many bridges now crossing almost dry gulches. The fifth bridge eastbound from here crosses what is now the main channel of the Copper River.

C **34.2** (55 km) Large gravel turnout to north.

C **34.3** (55.2 km) Copper River bridge.

C **35.7** (57.5 km) Large gravel turnout to north.

C **36.8** (59.2 km) Bridge crossing main flow of the Copper River (this is the fifth bridge after leaving Long Island eastbound). Access to river at east end of bridge. The Copper River constantly changes course: previously the main flow was at the two bridges at **Milepost C 26.7.** Currently, 40 percent of the river's flow is through this channel. Note the erosion and dying trees along the newer course, and the dry channels of the older course.

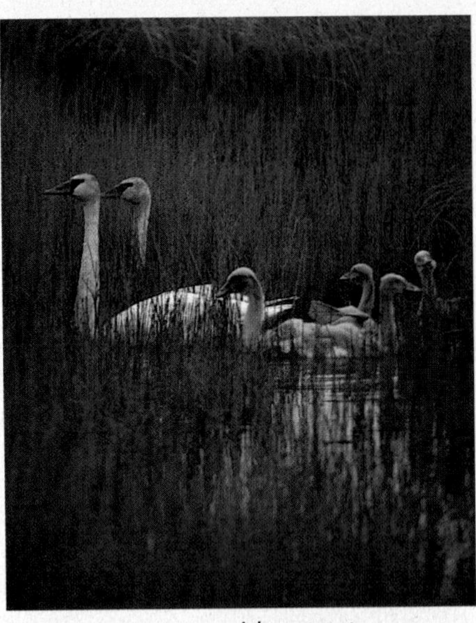

Trumpeter swans with cygnets may often be seen alongside the highway. (Ruth Fairall)

C **37.8** (60.8 km) Large gravel turnout to north.

C **38.8** (62.4 km) Childs Glacier directly ahead.

C **39.9** (64.2 km) Milky glacial waters of Sheep Creek pass through large culvert under road.

C **40.5** (65.2 km) **Clear Creek;** Dolly Varden, cutthroat, red salmon (July) and silvers (August–September). Use flies, lures, spinners or eggs. Watch for bears.

C **41.1** (66.1 km) Park on old railroad grade to south for access to Clear Creek.

C **41.7** (67.1 km) Goat Mountain (elev. 4,370 feet/1,332m) rises to the east of the highway. To the west parts of the Sherman and Goodwin glaciers flow down the sides of Mount Murchison (elev. 6,263 feet/1,909m).

C **42.1** (67.7 km) Side road to gravel pit, pond, informal camping and picnic site by Goat Mountain.

C **48** (77.2 km) Access to Childs Glacier Recreation Area with handicap-accessible covered viewing platform, picnic sites, covered tables, toilets and trails. No water. Limited RV parking. U.S. Forest Service hosts on site in summer. Childs Glacier was named by Capt. W.R. Abercrombie (1884 expedition) for George Washington Childs of Philadelphia. The glacier face is approximately 350 feet/107m high and very active. *CAUTION: Calving ice may cause waves to break over the beach and into the viewing area. Be prepared to run to higher ground!*

C **48.1** (77.4 km) The Million Dollar Bridge; viewing platform. The north span collapsed during the 1964 earthquake. Temporary repairs were made and people have been driving across it, but driving across the bridge and beyond is definitely a "drive at your own risk" venture. Primitive road extends only about 10 miles/16 km beyond the bridge to the Allen River. Heavy snow blocks road in winter; road may not be open until June. Proposed extension of the Copper River Highway to Chitina is currently under debate.

From here there is a view of Miles Glacier to the east. This glacier was named by Lieutenant Allen (1885 expedition) for Maj. Gen. Nelson A. Miles.

EDGERTON HIGHWAY

Richardson Highway Junction to Chitina, Alaska
Alaska Route 10
Includes log of McCarthy Road

The town of McCarthy lies at the end of the McCarthy Road. (Sue Rheaume)

Known locally as the Edgerton Cutoff, this scenic paved road leads 35.1 miles/56.5 km east through the settlement of Chitina, across the Copper River bridge to the start of the McCarthy Road. The Edgerton Highway is paved with some long, steep grades. From **Milepost 7.3**, the Edgerton Highway follows the approximate route of the old pack trail that once connected Chitina with Copper Center. The Edgerton Highway is named for U.S. Army Maj. Glenn Edgerton of the Alaska Territorial Road Commission.

Beyond Chitina, the gravel McCarthy Road leads 58.3 miles/93.8 km east and dead ends at the Kennicott River, about 1 mile/1.6 km west of the settlement of McCarthy, located within Wrangell–St. Elias National Park and Preserve. The McCarthy Road follows the right-of-way of the old Copper River & Northwestern Railway. Begun in 1907, the CR&NW (also referred to as the "can't run and never will") was built to carry copper ore from the Kennecott Mines to Cordova. It took four years to complete the railway. The railway and mine ceased operation in 1938.

Emergency medical services: Between the junction of the Richardson and Edgerton highways and McCarthy contact the Copper River EMS in Glennallen, phone 911 or 822-3203.

Edgerton Highway Log

Distance from junction with Richardson Highway (R) is followed by distance from junction with McCarthy Road (M).

R 0 M 35.1 (56.5 km) **Junction** at **Milepost V 82.6** Richardson Highway. Begin long downgrade eastbound. Watch for horses.

Excellent view of Mount Drum (to the left), a 12,010-foot/3,661-m peak of the Wrangell Mountains. Mount Wrangell (elev. 14,163 feet/4,317m) and Mount Blackburn (elev. 16,390 feet/4,996m) are visible straight ahead.

R 5.2 (8.4 km) **M 29.9** (48.1 km) Kenny Lake School.

R 5.3 (8.5 km) **M 29.8** (48 km) Paved turnout to north.

R 7.2 (11.6 km) **M 27.9** (44.9 km) **Kenny Lake Mercantile.** See display ad this section.

R 7.3 (11.7 km) **M 27.8** (44.7 km) Old Edgerton Loop Road (gravel) leads from here 8 miles/12.9 km through homestead and farm country to the Richardson Highway at **Milepost V 91.1.**

R 7.5 (12.1 km) **M 27.6** (44.4 km) Kenny Lake community hall, fairgrounds.

R 7.7 (12.4 km) **M 27.4** (44.1 km) Spacious double-ended paved rest area to south with picnic table on shore of Kenny Lake.

R 12.3 (19.8 km) **M 22.8** (36.7 km) Paved turnout to south.

R 12.5 (20.1 km) **M 22.6** (36.4 km) Paved turnout to north.

R 13 (20.9 km) **M 22.2** (35.7 km) **Tonsina Native Arts & Crafts.** See display ad this section.

R 18 (29 km) **M 17.1** (27.5 km) Steep downhill grade eastbound. Views of the Copper River and bluffs. A buffalo herd in the area can be seen occasionally on the bluffs across the river.

R 19.3 (31 km) **M 15.8** (25.4 km) Site of the settlement of Lower Tonsina, formerly a roadhouse for travelers using the Copper River. Tonsina and Copper rivers are visible here. Beyond are the Wrangell Mountains.

The road continues from here east up a steep bluff. Much of the highway has been hewn from solid rock, leaving great cuts on

EDGERTON HIGHWAY *Milepost V 82.6 Richardson Highway to McCarthy, AK*

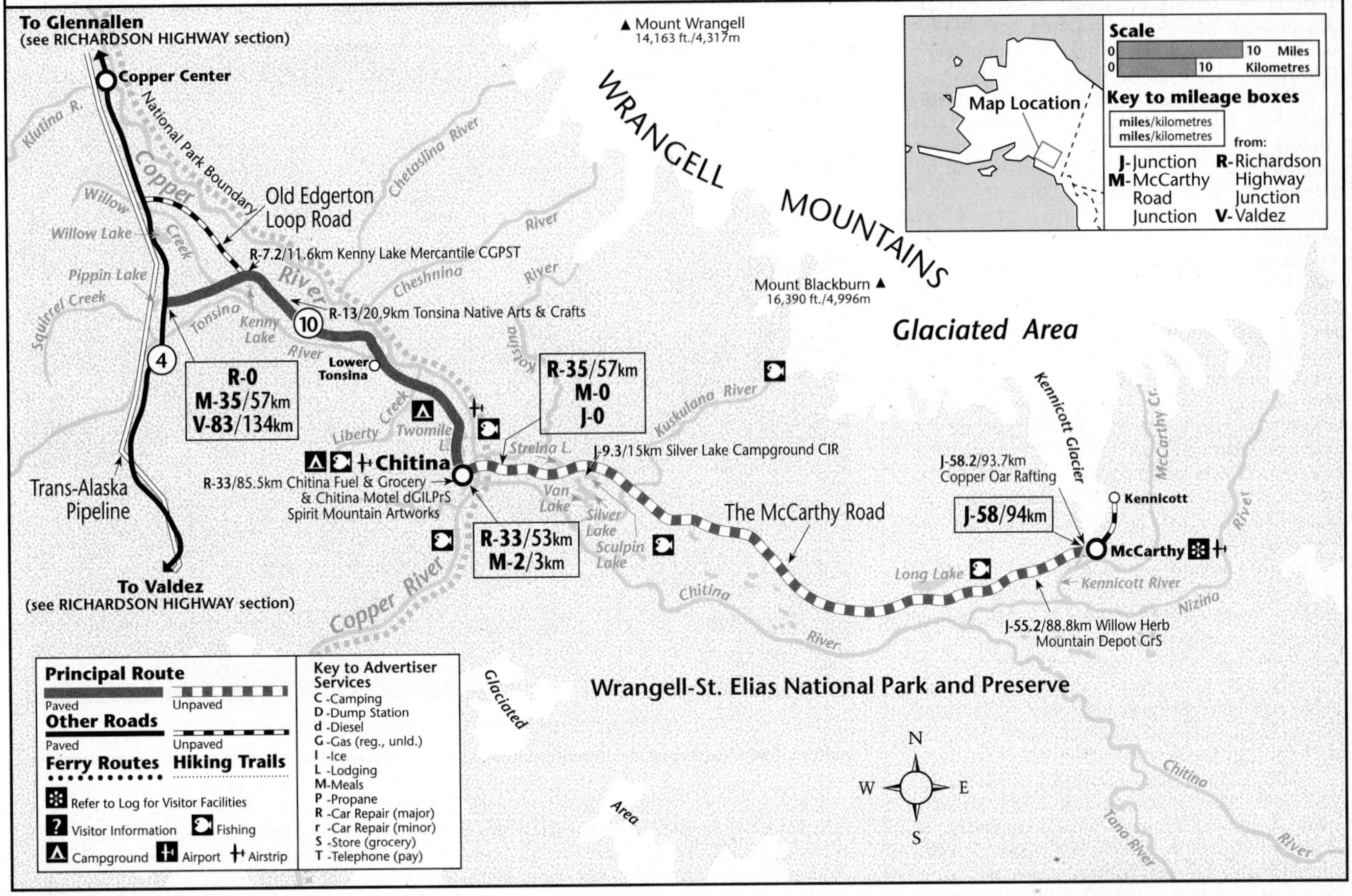

To Glennallen
(see RICHARDSON HIGHWAY section)
Copper Center
National Park Boundary
Old Edgerton Loop Road
R-7.2/11.6km Kenny Lake Mercantile CGPST
R-13/20.9km Tonsina Native Arts & Crafts
Mount Wrangell
14,163 ft./4,317m
WRANGELL MOUNTAINS
Mount Blackburn
16,390 ft./4,996m
Glaciated Area
Willow Lake
Pippin Lake
Squirrel Creek
Kenny Lake
Lower Tonsina
R-0
M-35/57km
V-83/134km
R-35/57km
M-0
J-0
Chitina
R-33/85.5km Chitina Fuel & Grocery & Chitina Motel dGILPrS
Spirit Mountain Artworks
J-9.3/15km Silver Lake Campground CIR
Trans-Alaska Pipeline
R-33/53km
M-2/3km
The McCarthy Road
J-58.2/93.7km
Copper Oar Rafting
Kennicott Glacier
Kennicott
J-58/94km
McCarthy
Long Lake
Kennicott River
J-55.2/88.8km Willow Herb Mountain Depot GrS
To Valdez
(see RICHARDSON HIGHWAY section)
Copper River
Wrangell-St. Elias National Park and Preserve
Scale
10 Miles
10 Kilometres
Map Location
Key to mileage boxes
miles/kilometres
miles/kilometres
from:
J-Junction
M-McCarthy Road Junction
R-Richardson Highway Junction
V-Valdez
Principal Route
Paved
Unpaved
Other Roads
Paved
Unpaved
Ferry Routes
Hiking Trails
Refer to Log for Visitor Facilities
Visitor Information
Fishing
Campground
Airport
Airstrip
Key to Advertiser Services
C -Camping
D -Dump Station
d -Diesel
G -Gas (reg., unld.)
I -Ice
L -Lodging
M -Meals
P -Propane
R -Car Repair (major)
r -Car Repair (minor)
S -Store (grocery)
T -Telephone (pay)

either side. Pockets of pure peat moss are evident in breaks in the rock walls along the road. *CAUTION: Peat fires can be a serious problem; be careful with campfires.*

R 19.4 (31.2 km) **M 15.7** (25.3 km) Tonsina River bridge. Former Lower Tonsina townsite to west of bridge.

R 19.5 (31.4 km) **M 15.6** (25.1 km) Turnout to south.

R 19.6 (31.5 km) **M 15.5** (24.9 km) Double-ended turnout at lake to north.

R 21 (33.8 km) **M 14.2** (22.9 km) Gravel turnout to north overlooking the Copper River.

R 21.6 (34.8 km) **M 13.5** (21.7 km) Paved viewpoint to north above Copper River.

R 21.9 (35.2 km) **M 13.3** (21.4 km) Small gravel turnout to north.

R 22 (35.4 km) **M 13.1** (21.1 km) Top of hill, steep descents both directions.

R 23.5 (37.8 km) **M 11.6** (18.7 km) Liberty Falls Creek trailhead to south.

R 23.7 (38.1 km) **M 11.4** (18.3 km) Liberty Creek bridge (8-ton load limit) and Liberty Falls State Recreation Site. The campground is just south of the highway on the banks of Liberty Creek, near the foot of the thundering falls. Loop road through campground (large RVs and trailers check road before driving in); five sites, no water, no camping fee. Berry picking; watch for bears. ▲

R 28.4 (45.7 km) **M 6.7** (10.8 km) Small gravel turnout to north overlooking river.

R 28.5 (45.9 km) **M 6.6** (10.6 km) Pavement break. Side road north to Chitina DOT/PF maintenance station and airstrip.

Private Aircraft: Chitina Municipal Airfield; elev. 556 feet/169m; length 2,800 feet/853m; gravel; unattended.

R 29.5 (47.5 km) **M 5.7** (9.2 km) Small gravel turnout by Threemile Lake.

R 29.7 (47.8 km) **M 5.4** (8.7 km) Paved turnout by **Threemile Lake**; good grayling and rainbow trout fishing.

R 30.1 (48.4 km) **M 5** (8 km) Small turnout to south by **Twomile Lake**; good grayling and rainbow trout fishing, canoe launch.

R 30.6 (49.2 km) **M 4.5** (7.2 km) Large paved turnout at end of Twomile Lake.

R 31.9 (51.3 km) **M 3.2** (5.1 km) Onemile Lake (also called First Lake). Access road to boat launch at east end of lake.

Chitina

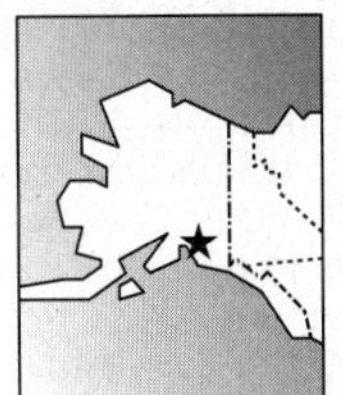

R 33 (53.1 km) **M 2.1** (3.4 km). Located about 120 miles/193 km northeast of Valdez, and about 66 miles/106 km southeast of Glennallen. **Population:** 49. **Emergency Services:** Copper River EMS, phone 822-3203.

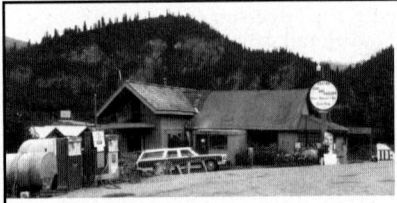

Visitor Information: National Park Service ranger station for Wrangell–St. Elias National Park and Preserve in Chitina is staffed by volunteers. Hours were 9 A.M. to 6 P.M., Friday to Monday, in 1993; hours may vary. Open Memorial Day to Labor Day. A slide show on the McCarthy Road is available. Write Box 29, Glennallen, AK 99588, or phone 822-5234 (park headquarters); Chitina ranger station, phone 823-2205.

Chitina has a post office, store, gas station, bar, restaurant, tire repair service and phone service. The National Park Service ranger station is housed in a historic cabin. One of the first buildings in Chitina, a hardware and sheet metal shop now on the National Register of Historic Places, houses an art gallery. A public pay phone is located beside Town Lake at the beginning of the McCarthy Road. There is also a pay phone at the Chitina Saloon.

Chitina (pronounced CHIT-na) was established about 1908 as a railroad stop on the Copper River & Northwestern Railway and as a supply town for the Kennecott Copper Mines at McCarthy. The mine and railroad were abandoned in 1938. The McCarthy Road east of town follows the old railroad bed, which is listed on the National Register of Historic Places.

Inquire locally about informal camping areas: Much of the land around Chitina is owned by the Chitina Native Corp. and is posted no trespassing. Primitive camping is available along the Edgerton Highway at Onemile and Twomile lakes. There is an eight-site state campground east of Chitina across the Copper River bridge, and two private campgrounds on the McCarthy Road. ▲

A big attraction in Chitina for fishermen and spectators is the seasonal salmon run (reds, kings or silvers), which draws hundreds of dip-netters to the **Copper River.** The dip-net fishery for salmon runs June through September (depending on harvest levels), and it's worth the trip to see fish wheels and dip nets in action. O'Brien Creek Road provides a state right-of-way access to popular fishing areas on large sandbars along the Copper River. This fishery is open only to Alaska residents with a personal-use or subsistence permit. Check with the ADF&G office in Chitina for details and current regulations.

Chitina Fuel & Grocery and Chitina Motel. See display ad this section.

Spirit Mountain Artworks. See display ad this section.

Edgerton Highway Log

(continued)

R 33.6 (54.1 km) **M 1.6** (2.6 km) Pavement ends eastbound. No road maintenance east of this point between Oct. 15 and May 15.

R 33.8 (54.4 km) **M 1.4** (2.3 km) Turnout overlooking the Copper River.

R 34.1 (54.9 km) **M 1.1** (1.8 km) Turnout overlooking the Copper River. Access to river.

R 34.7 (55.8 km) **M 0.5** (0.8 km) Copper River bridge. Completed in 1971, this 1,378-foot/420-m steel span was designed for year-round use. The $3.5 million bridge reestablished access across the river into the McCarthy–Kennicott area.

R 35.1 (56.5 km) **M 0 Junction** with McCarthy Road (see McCARTHY ROAD log this page). Dept. of Transportation campground on the **Copper River**; eight sites, picnic tables, fireplaces, toilets, boat launch, no water. Fishing for red and king salmon. Travelers are now within Wrangell–St. Elias National Park and Preserve. ▲

McCarthy Road Log

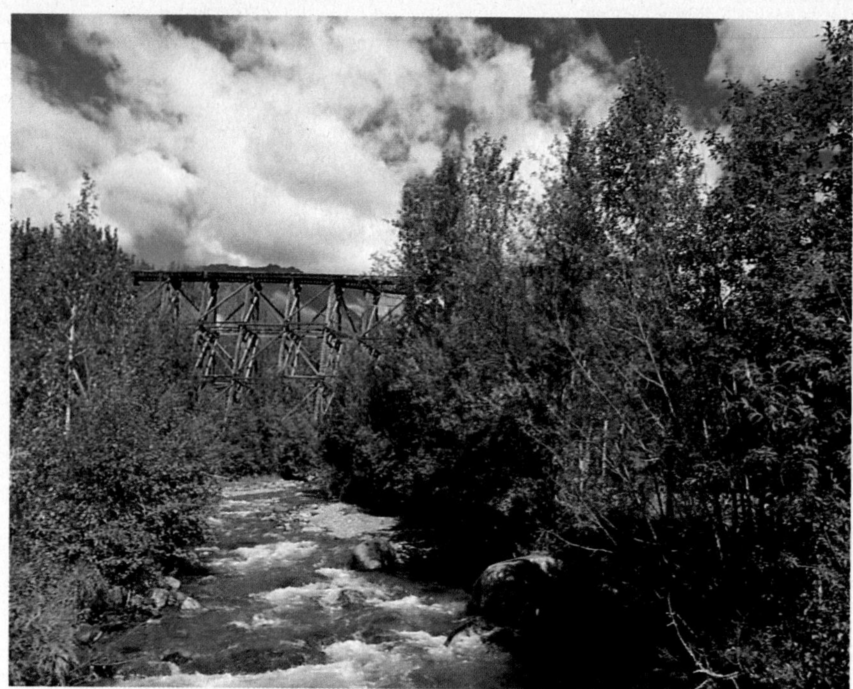

An old railroad trestle on the McCarthy Road. (Sue Rheaume)

The road to McCarthy is a 58.3-mile/93.8-km gravel road through virtually untouched Alaskan wilderness. (Although keep in mind that some of the wilderness might be privately owned land.) The road begins where the Edgerton Highway ends and dead ends on the west side of the Kennicott River. The McCarthy Road is recommended for the adventurous traveler and only in the summertime. Allow about three hours driving time. Maintained by the state Dept. of Transportation, the road is suitable for most vehicles to **Milepost 15** (Strelna Creek). The road is narrow and unpaved; it may be dusty in dry weather and muddy in wet weather. Beyond Strelna Creek there are turnouts for meeting oncoming vehicles. Motorists with large vehicles or trailers exercise caution, especially in wet weather. Watch for old railroad spikes in roadbed. Unless recently graded, watch for potholes, soft spots and severe washboard. Tire repair and mechanical light towing service are available at Silver Lake Campground, Mile 9.3. The National Park Service ranger station in Chitina has information on current road conditions and also on backcountry travel in Wrangell–St. Elias National Park and Preserve.

Distance is measured from junction with the Edgerton Highway (J). Traditional mileposts used by local residents are indicated in the log.

J 0 Junction with the Edgerton Highway.

J 3.7 (6 km) Turnout overlooking the Chitina River.

J 8.3 (13.4 km) **Milepost 10.** Physical mileposts indicate distance from Chitina. Trail opposite homestead leads 0.3 mile/0.5 km north to **Strelna Lake**; rainbow trout and silver salmon. (Private property adjacent trail.)

J 9.3 (15 km) **Milepost 11.** Private campground on **Silver Lake;** rainbow trout fishing, boat and canoe rentals, boat launch, tire repair. Trail access to **Van Lake,** located south of Silver Lake; good rainbow trout fishing. ▲

Silver Lake Campground. See display ad this section.

J 10.8 (17.4 km) **Milepost 12.** Private campground on **Sculpin Lake** (also known as Nelson Lake). Rainbow trout fishing. ▲

J 13 (20.9 km) Access road leads north 2.5 miles/4 km to trailheads for Dixie Pass, Kotsina and Nugget Creek trails. *NOTE: Access road crosses private homesteads. Please do not trespass.*

J 13.3 (21.4 km) **Milepost 15. Strelna Creek** (culvert); fair fishing for Dolly Varden.

J 16 (25.7 km) Kuskulana bridge. This old railroad bridge (built in 1910) is approximately 525 feet/160m long and 385 feet/117m above the river below. It is a narrow three-span steel railway bridge with wood decking. Before the bridge was rehabilitated in 1988 with new decking and guard rails, the Kuskulana crossing was called the "biggest thrill on the road to McCarthy."

Large gravel turnout at east end of bridge, small turnout at west end.

J 22.3 (35.9 km) Large gravel turnout to south with view of Wrangell Mountains.

There are several turnouts between here and the Kennicott River.

J 22.5 (36.2 km) Boundary between park and preserve lands (unmarked). Wrangell–St. Elias National Park and Preserve allows sport hunting with a valid Alaska state license.

J 23.5 (37.8 km) **Lou's Lake** to north; silver salmon and grayling fishing.

J 25.5 (41 km) Chokosna River bridge.

J 27.7 (44.6 km) One-lane bridge over Gilahina River. Old railroad trestle and parking.

J 40.3 (64.9 km) Crystal Lake. Trading post.

J 41.4 (66.6 km) Double-ended turnout with view to south.

J 42.9 (69 km) One-lane bridge over Lakina River, access to river at east end.

J 44.1 (71 km) Long Lake Wildlife Refuge next 2.6 miles/4.2 km eastbound.

J 44.2 (71.1 km) Watch for salmon spawning in Long Lake outlet (no fishing at outlet within 300 feet/91m of weir).

J 44.7 (71.9 km) Turnout on **Long Lake**; lake trout, silver salmon, grayling, Dolly Varden and burbot.

J 54.9 (88.4 km) Swift Creek culvert.

J 55.2 (88.8 km) **Willow Herb Mountain Depot.** Your gateway to McCarthy/Kennicott with all local information. Stop and chat about log building or winter life here. Our shop represents over 50 local, remote and other Alaska artisans. We also carry area maps, books, T-shirts, snacks and much more. Gas and tire repair available. Terry and Dee Frady, proprietors. [ADVERTISEMENT]

J 58.1 (93.5 km) Upper parking lot for visitors crossing Kennicott River to McCarthy (see description next milepost); toilets and dumpsters. Primitive camping. Park here when there is danger of glacial lake breaking out.

J 58.2 (93.7 km) Parking (subject to flooding). Here, two hand-pulled cable trams cross the Kennicott River. (There is a footbridge across the river's second channel.) The trams are small open platforms (built in 1982–83 by local residents and upgraded in 1988) and should be attempted only by travelers strong enough to pull themselves across several hundred feet (part of the distance uphill). It is easier if a friend pulls on the return cable from the riverbank. Wear gloves. *CAUTION: DO NOT attempt to wade across this glacial river; strong currents and cold water make it extremely treacherous.*

A CB radio at the tram has instructions for calling businesses in McCarthy and Kennicott (they monitor Channel 5).

Parking on the lower lot by the riverbank is not recommended in July or early August because of flooding when Hidden Lake breaks out from under Kennicott Glacier, usually in July, according to local residents. (The phenomenon is called a *jokulhaup,* an Icelandic term for "flooding that occurs when water bursts out of a glacier-dammed lake.") It is recommended you park just up the road at the upper parking lot.

After exiting the tram, follow the road for about a quarter of a mile to a fork; the right fork leads to McCarthy (less than a mile) and the left fork goes to Kennicott (about 5 miles).

Copper Oar Rafting. See display ad this section.

J 58.3 (93.8 km) McCarthy Road dead ends at Kennicott River.

McCarthy

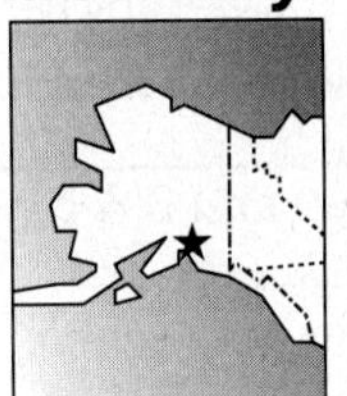

Located within the Wrangell–St. Elias National Park and Preserve 61 miles/98.1 km east of Chitina. **Population:** 25. There is a store in McCarthy and shuttle service between McCarthy and Kennicott. Lodging is available in McCarthy at the McCarthy Lodge, which also offers food service. The McCarthy area has a flightseeing service and an operating gold mine (tours available). Check with lodges about other activities in the area.

Private Aircraft: McCarthy airstrip, 1 mile/1.6 km south; elev. 1,494 feet/455m; length 1,400 feet/427m; turf, gravel; unattended. McCarthy Nr 2, 1 mile/1.6 km northeast; elev. 1,531 feet/467m; length 3,400 feet/1,036m; gravel; unattended.

The town of McCarthy is in a beautiful area of glaciers and mountains. The Kennicott River flows by the west side of town and joins the Nizina River which flows into the Chitina River. The local museum, located in the railway depot, has historical artifacts and photos from the early mining days.

It is 4.5 miles/7.2 km from McCarthy at the end of the CR&NW railroad bed to the old mining town of **KENNICOTT** (pop. 8 to 15). Perched on the side of a mountain next to Kennicott Glacier, the

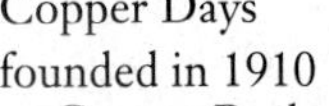

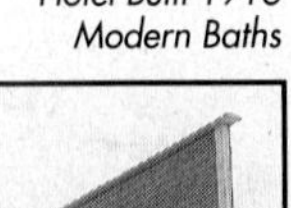

Kennicott Mine. *(Michael DeYoung)*

town was built by Kennecott Copper Corp. between 1910 and 1920. (An early-day misspelling made the mining company Kennecott, while the region and settlement are Kennicott.) The richest copper mine in the world until its closure in 1938, Kennicott's mill processed more than 591,535 tons of copper ore and employed some 800 workers in its heyday. Today, a lodge is located here. The mine buildings are on private land.

Kennicott Glacier Lodge, located in the ghost town of Kennicott, offers the area's finest accommodations and dining. Built in 1987, this new lodge has 25 clean, delightful guest rooms, two living rooms, a spacious dining room, and a 180-foot front porch with a spectacular panoramic view of the Wrangell Mountains, Chugach Mountains and Kennicott Glacier. The homemade food, served family-style, has been called "Wilderness Gourmet Dining." Guest activities at this destination resort include glacier trekking, flightseeing, photography, alpine hiking, historical and nature tours, rafting and horseback riding. May 15 to Sept. 20. (800) 582-5128. See display ad. [ADVERTISEMENT]

McCarthy lies within **WRANGELL–ST. ELIAS NATIONAL PARK AND PRESERVE.** This 12 million acre park encompasses the southeast corner of the Alaska mainland, stretching from the Gulf of Alaska to the Copper River basin. Access to the park is by way of the McCarthy Road, the Nabesna Road (off the Tok Cutoff) and out of Yakutat. This vast unspoiled wilderness offers backpacking, mountaineering, river running, hunting and sportfishing. For more information, contact: Superintendent, Wrangell–St. Elias National Park and Preserve, P.O. Box 29, Glennallen, AK 99588; phone (907) 822-5234.

Wrangell Mountain Air offers a convenient alternative to driving the McCarthy Road. Park your car in Chitina at the end of the paved highway. Fly direct to McCarthy/Kennicott through the spectacular Wrangell Mountains. Discover massive glaciers, towering mountain peaks and icefalls, the Kennecott mines, mountain goats and sheep. Fly with experienced Alaskan pilots. Reservations: (800) 478-1160 or (907) 345-1160 (radio phone). [ADVERTISEMENT]

McCARTHY/KENNICOTT ADVERTISERS

Kennicott Glacier Lodge.....................Ph. 1-800-582-5128
McCarthy Lodge..........Ph. (907) 333-5402
McCarthy Trail Rides and Bed & Breakfast..............................McCarthy
Nugget Gift Shop & Nugget Liquor Store............McCarthy
Wrangell Mountain Air.................Radioph. (907) 345-1160

MARINE ACCESS ROUTES

Alaska ports via BC Ferries, Alaska State Ferries and Cruise Ships
Includes: SOUTHEAST ferry system connecting Bellingham, WA, Port Hardy and Prince Rupert, BC, to Ketchikan and other southeastern Alaska ports
(See maps, pages 550–551)
SOUTHCENTRAL/SOUTHWEST ferry system connecting Kenai Peninsula, Kodiak and Prince William Sound ports
(See map, page 568)

Much of Alaska's southeastern region, with its thousands of islands, bays and steep, mountainous shorelines, prohibits building highways from city to city. The Alaska Marine Highway — which stretches almost 1,000 nautical miles from Bellingham, WA, to Skagway, AK — provides the vital link for people and their vehicles.

Many visitors to Alaska use the Alaska Marine Highway as an alternative route to driving to Alaska. Travelers often drive one direction and take the Marine Highway the other. This option not only eliminates the necessity of driving the road system twice, but affords the traveler the opportunity to take in the magnificent scenery and picturesque communities of Southeast Alaska and the Inside Passage.

The Alaska state ferries depart from Bellingham, WA (85 miles north of Seattle on Interstate 5, Exit 250), or Prince Rupert, BC, for southeastern Alaska communities. Alaska state ferries out of Bellingham do not stop in Canada. The cruise route goes up the famed Inside Passage through several hundred miles of forested islands and deep fjords in Canada and southeastern Alaska. Ferries out of Prince Rupert follow the same route as the ferries out of Bellingham from Chatham Sound north. Ketchikan (the first stop for both) is a 36-hour ferry ride from Bellingham and about six hours by ferry from Prince Rupert. There is also ferry service between Ketchikan, AK, and Stewart, BC/Hyder, AK, and feeder service between southern and northern panhandle communities. Descriptions of southeastern Alaska communities start on page 573. Details on the Alaska State Ferry System begin on page 554; schedules begin on page 556.

BC Ferries provides year-round service on 24 routes throughout coastal British Columbia, with a fleet of 40 passenger- and vehicle-carrying ferries. The longest route is the 15-hour Inside Passage cruise from Port Hardy (on Vancouver Island) to Prince Rupert. Many Alaska-bound travelers combine travel on BC Ferries and the Alaska Marine Highway to see all of the Inside Passage.

Cruise ships offer a variety of itineraries from West Coast ports through the Inside Passage and to Southcentral Alaska.

Kayakers stow their gear in preparation for boarding Alaska state ferry at Bellingham, WA. (Marion Stirrup)

BC Ferries

BC Ferries provides marine transportation for passengers and vehicles between Port Hardy, at the north end of Vancouver Island, and Prince Rupert, at the end of Yellowhead Highway 16, which is also the southern port for most Alaska state ferries.

BC Ferries also provides service on 23 other routes throughout coastal British Columbia. They include three major routes that link mainland British Columbia and Vancouver Island: Tsawwassen-Swartz Bay, Tsawwassen-Nanaimo and Horseshoe Bay-Nanaimo.

Service between Port Hardy and Prince Rupert is aboard the *Queen of the North,* which carries 750 passengers and 157 vehicles. The ferry has a cafeteria, buffet dining

(Continues on page 553)

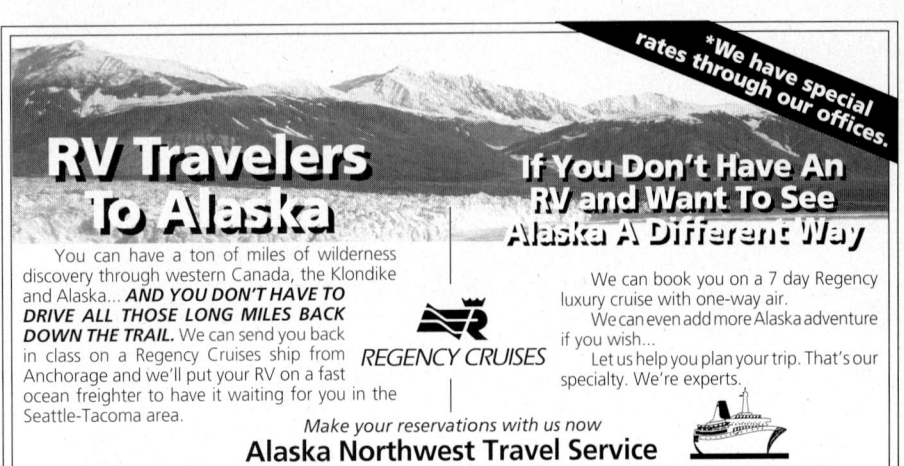

MARINE ACCESS ROUTES

Washington and British Columbia from Puget Sound to Hecate Strait

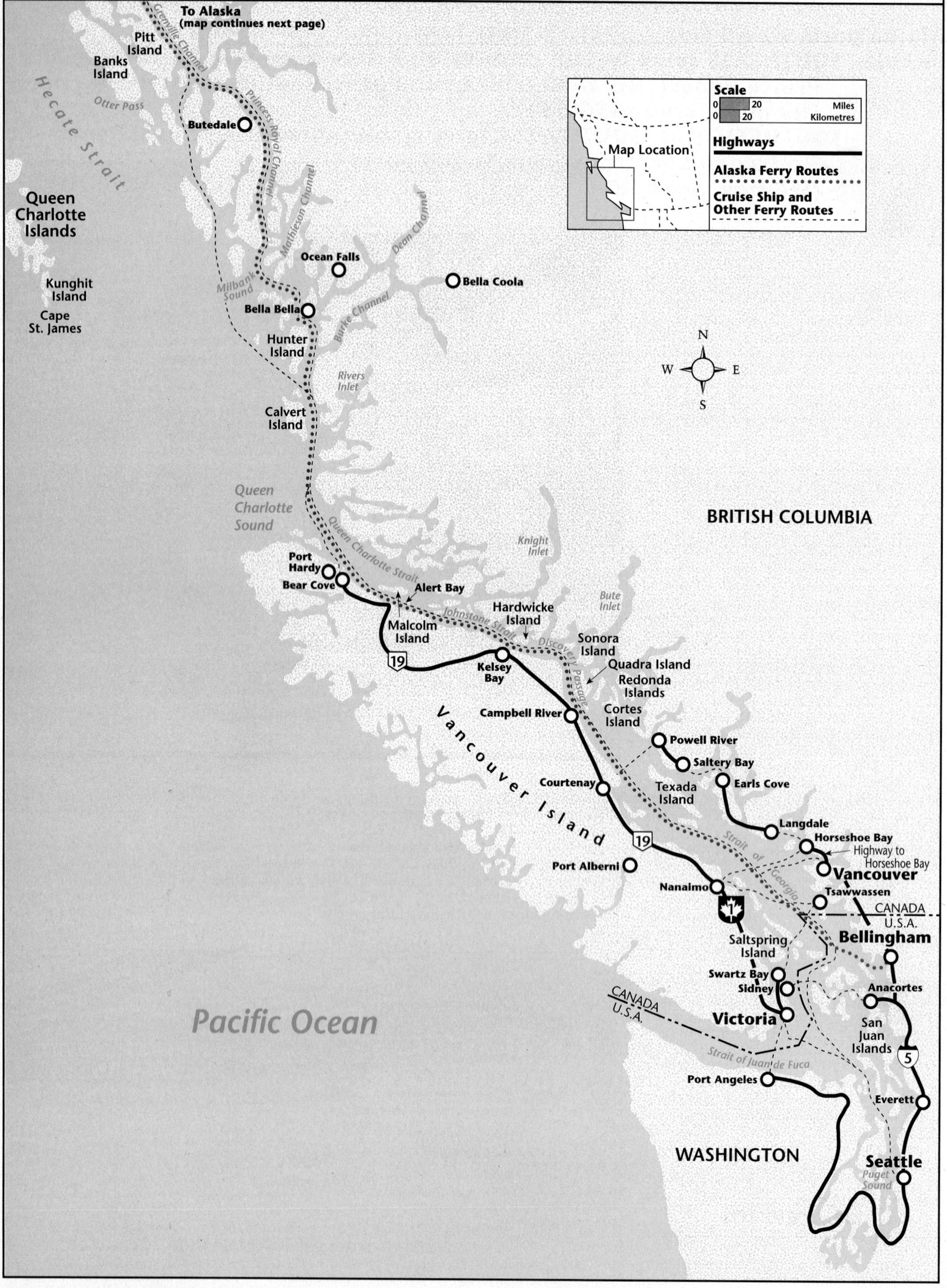

MARINE ACCESS ROUTES

British Columbia and Southeastern Alaska from Prince Rupert, BC, to Skagway, AK

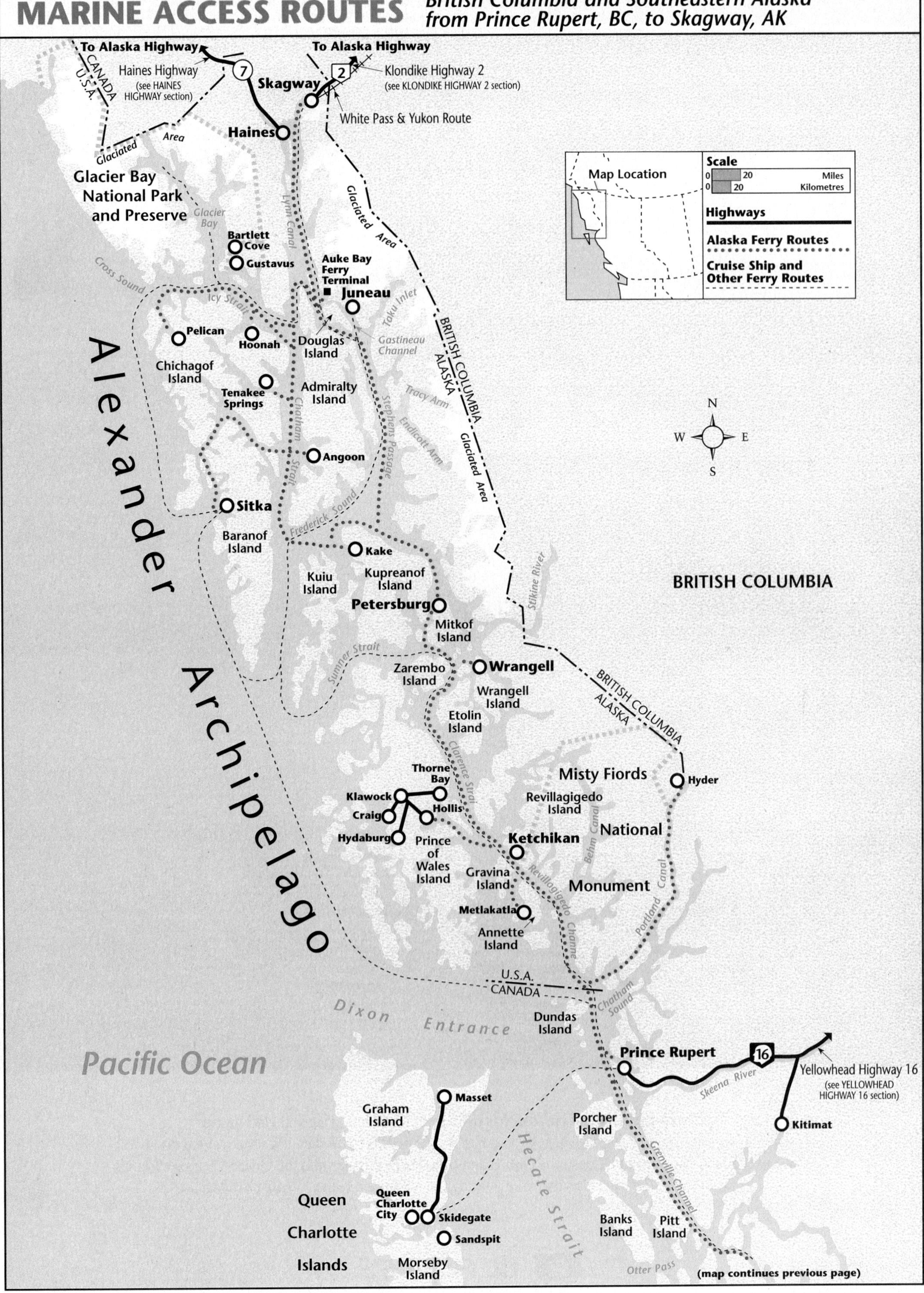

(Continued from page 549)
room, news/gift shop, licensed and view lounges, children's playroom, day cabins and staterooms (for round-trip use). Summer service on this route is during daylight hours to make the most of the scenery, so cabins are not necessary.

Reservations: Strongly recommended for passengers and vehicles on the Inside Passage route. Contact BC Ferries Reservations Centre, 1112 Fort St., Victoria, BC V8V 4V2, or phone the reservation office in Vancouver (604) 669-1211, in Victoria (604) 386-3431.

Fares and schedules: Following is the 1994 Inside Passage summer sailing schedule. Rates current at time of printing (subject to change) are as follows (one-way, in Canadian funds): Adult passenger, $90; child (5 to 11 years), $45; car, $185; camper/RV (up to 20 feet in length, over 7 feet in height), $318. Additional length, $15.90 per foot.

Check-in time is one and one-half hours before sailing. Cancellations made less than 30 days prior to departure are subject to a cancellation fee.

BC FERRIES SCHEDULE

PORT HARDY TO PRINCE RUPERT

May 23 to Sept. 29, 1994

*(*The summer season starts off with a once-a-year sailing of the* Queen of the North *from Tsawwassen to Port Hardy on May 23, 1994.)*

NORTHBOUND

Departs: Port Hardy 7:30 A.M.
Arrives: Prince Rupert 10:30 P.M.
Dates: May 24, 26, 28, 30
June, July, September (odd-numbered days, except Sept. 29)
August (even-numbered days)

SOUTHBOUND

Departs: Prince Rupert 7:30 A.M.
Arrives: Port Hardy 10:30 P.M.
Dates: May 25, 27, 29, 31
June, July, September (even-numbered days, except Sept. 30)
August (odd-numbered days)

View of residential area on Kaien Island from Prince Rupert harbour. (Judy Parkin, staff)

Prince Rupert is located 450 miles/724 km west of Prince George via the Yellowhead Highway (see YELLOWHEAD HIGHWAY 16 section). Port Hardy is approximately 307 miles/494 km north of Victoria via Trans-Canada Highway 1 and BC Highway 19. From Nanaimo it is 236 miles/380 km to Port Hardy. Allow at least eight hours driving time between Victoria and Port Hardy (the route is almost all two-lane highway between Victoria and Campbell River.) Or, take your time and spend several days exploring island communities along the way. Keep in mind that there are limited services between Campbell River and Port Hardy, a distance of 145 miles/233 km. The Port Hardy ferry terminal is located at Bear Cove, 4 miles/7 km from downtown Port Hardy.

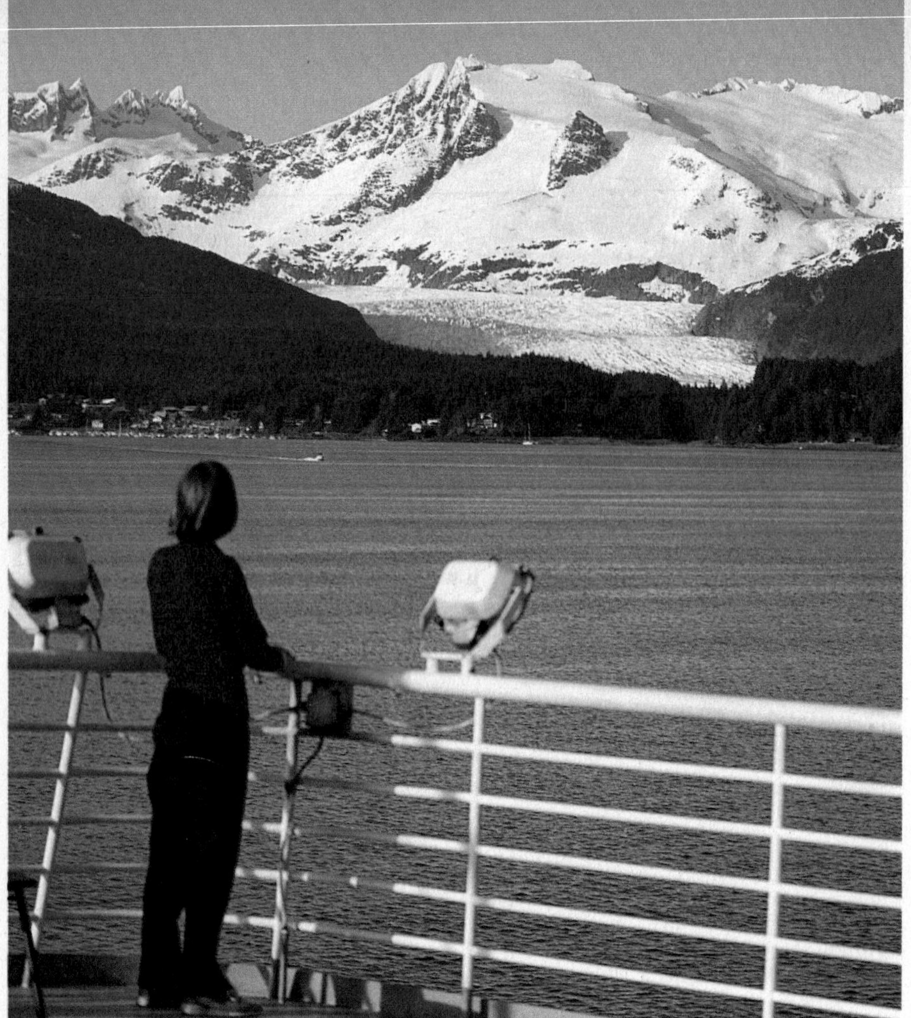
Ferry passenger takes in Mendenhall Glacier. (David Job)

To reach Vancouver Island from the lower British Columbia mainland, take BC Ferries from either Tsawwassen or Horseshoe Bay. Follow Highway 99 through Vancouver for the Horseshoe Bay terminal, 13 miles/21 km northwest of the city, and ferry service to Nanaimo. Or turn off Highway 99 approximately 17 miles/27 km north of the U.S. border for the Tsawwassen terminal and service to Swartz Bay near Victoria (one-and-one-half-hour crossing) and to Nanaimo (two-hour crossing). There are a minimum of 16 round-trips daily during summer between Tsawwassen and Swartz Bay, and eight round-trips daily year-round between Tsawwassen and Nanaimo. Reservations are not accepted for passengers or vehicles on these routes.

To reach Vancouver Island from Washington, you can take the Washington state ferry from Anacortes, WA, to Victoria (Sidney), cruising through the San Juan Islands or the MV *Coho* from Port Angeles, WA, to Victoria. Reservations are not accepted for either passengers or vehicles on the ferry out of Port Angeles. For information on Washington state ferries, phone (206) 464-6400 in Seattle or 1-800-542-0810 or 542-7052 toll free in Washington. For information on the MV *Coho* contact Black Ball Transport, 540 Belleville St., Victoria, BC V8V 1W0; phone (206) 822-2222 in Seattle, (206) 457-4491 in Port Angeles, or (604) 386-2202 in Victoria.

Bus service is available between Vancouver and Victoria, and between Victoria and Port Hardy from Pacific Coach Lines, 150 Dunsmuir St., Vancouver; phone (604) 662-8074. The bus depot in Victoria is located directly behind the Empress Hotel. Pacific Western Airlines and Air BC have scheduled air service to Port Hardy.

Alaska State Ferries

The main office of the Alaska Marine Highway is in Juneau. Write P.O. Box 25535, Juneau, AK 99802-5535; in the United States phone toll free 1-800-642-0066, fax (907) 277-4829; from Washington state, toll free 1-800-585-8445; from Canada, toll free 1-800-665-6414.

The Alaska State Ferry System is divided into two different systems serving two different areas: Southeast and Southcentral/Southwest. These two systems *DO NOT* connect.

If you are headed for Alaska from Bellingham, WA, or Prince Rupert, BC, via the Alaska Marine Highway, you'll take the Southeast system, which stops at southeastern Alaska cities from Ketchikan to Skagway. Keep in mind that only two Southeast communities are connected to the Alaska Highway: Haines, via the Haines Highway; and Skagway, via Klondike Highway 2. (See the HAINES HIGHWAY and KLONDIKE HIGHWAY 2 sections.) From June through August, the system also calls at Stewart/Hyder, located at the end of the Stewart–Cassiar Highway. Other Southeast communities are accessible only by ferry or by air.

The Southcentral/Southwest system serves coastal communities from Prince William Sound to the Aleutian Islands. With the exception of Cordova, Seldovia and Kodiak, Southcentral communities on the ferry system are also accessible by highway. These communities are Valdez, Seward and Homer. Whittier is accessible to vehicles only via shuttle train. Communities on the Southwest system are accessible only by ferry or air.

Travel on the Alaska state ferries is at a leisurely pace, with observation decks, food service and vehicle decks on all ferries. Cabins are available only on four Southeast ferries and one Southwest ferry.

Keep in mind that the state ferries are not cruise ships: They do not have beauty salons, gift shops, deck games and the like. The small stores on the larger ferries are open limited hours and sell a limited selection of items. Food service varies from vessel to vessel. There's dining room service on the *Columbia, Tustumena* and *Bartlett.* The *Columbia* also has a 24-hour snack bar. Cafeteria service is available on all other ferries. Cocktail lounges on board the larger vessels are open from late morning to midnight. It's a good idea to bring your own snacks, books, games and toiletries, since these are not always available on board.

Season: The Alaska Ferry System has two seasons — May 1 to Sept. 30 (summer), when sailings are most frequent, and Oct. 1 to April 30 (fall/winter), when departures are somewhat less frequent. Schedules and information appearing in this section are for the summer season only.

Contact the Alaska Marine Highway office for fall/winter schedules, fares and information. (Fares are normally reduced between Oct. 1 and April 30 and crowds are virtually nonexistent.)

Reservations: Required on all vessels. The Alaska state ferries are very popular in summer and we advise you make reservations as far in advance as possible to get the sailing dates you wish. Cabin space on summer sailings is often sold out by early December on the Bellingham sailings. Requests for space are accepted year-round and held until reservations open. For reservations, write the Alaska Marine Highway, P.O. Box 25535, Juneau, AK 99802-5535, or phone toll free in the U.S. 1-800-642-0066 (in Washington state 1-800-585-8445); in Canada 1-800-665-6414; fax (907) 277-4829.

Reservation requests must include departure dates and ports of embarkation/debarkation; full names of all members of the party, and the ages of those under 12 years; width, height and overall length (including hitch if with trailer) of vehicles; mailing address and phone number; alternate dates in the event cabin or vehicle space is not available on your first choice; and approximate date you will be leaving home.

If you are unable to obtain reservations at the time of advance booking, you may be wait listed. If a cancellation occurs you will be notified of confirmation of space. You may also choose to go standby, which is literally standing by in line until all reserved passengers and vehicles are on board; if there is space, standbys may board. Standbys

(Continues on page 558)

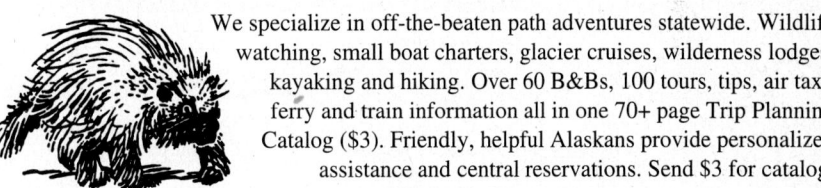

1994 Southeast Ferry Schedules

May 1994 Northbound Schedule

LEAVE BELLINGHAM	LEAVE PRINCE RUPERT	LEAVE STEWART/ HYDER	METLAKATLA	KETCHIKAN	HOLLIS	WRANGELL	PETERSBURG	KAKE	ARRIVE SITKA	ANGOON	TENAKEE	HOONAH	JUNEAU/ AUKE BAY	HAINES	ARRIVE SKAGWAY
								Lv. Sitka	S30 1:15P	S30 9:00P	SU1 12:15A	SU1 4:30A	SU1 7:45A		
	F29 12:30P			F29 6:30P	F29 10:15P	S30 5:15A	S30 12:30P		S30 11:30P				SU1 11:55A	SU1 5:30P	SU1 6:30P
F29 6:00P				SU1 7:15A		SU1 2:15P	SU1 8:00P						M2 6:00A	M2 11:30A	M2 12:30P
			T3 2:45P	T3 5:00P	T3 7:45P										
	T3 11:30A			T3 5:30P		W4 12:30A	W4 4:30A						W4 1:15P	W4 6:45P	W4 7:45P
			W4 2:30A	W4 4:45A	W4 7:30A										
				W4 1:15P	W4 5:30P		TH5 3:30A	TH5 8:30A	TH5 4:30P	F6 1:15A	F6 4:45A	F6 9:00A	F6 12:15P		
	F6 2:30P			F6 10:00P	S7 1:45A	S7 8:45A	S7 1:45P		S7 11:45P				SU8 12:45P	SU8 6:45P	SU8 7:45P
								Lv. Sitka	S7 8:00P	SU8 3:00A	SU8 6:30A	SU8 11:45A	SU8 3:00P		
F6 6:00P				SU8 10:15A		SU8 5:45P	SU8 10:45P						M9 9:15A	M9 3:45P	M9 4:45P
				T10 9:00A	T10 11:45A		T10 1:00P	T10 6:00P	W11 2:00A	W11 11:55A	W11 3:30P	W11 8:45P	TH12 11:55A	TH12 6:45P	TH12 7:45P
				T10 5:30P	T10 8:15P										
	T10 9:00A			T10 3:00P		T10 10:00P	W11 2:00A						W11 12:15P	W11 6:15P	W11 7:15P
			W11 8:15A	W11 10:30A	W11 1:15P										
			W11 8:45P	W11 11:00P	TH12 1:45A										
				TH12 5:30P	TH12 8:15P										
	F13 11:30A			F13 6:30P		S14 1:30A	S14 5:30A		S14 3:45P				SU15 7:00A	SU15 1:30P	SU15 2:30P
				F13 9:00A	F13 11:45A										
				F13 5:30P	F13 8:15P										
			S14 8:15A	S14 10:30A	S14 1:15P			Lv. Sitka	S14 4:15A	S14 12:45P	S14 4:15P	S14 8:30P	S14 11:45P		
			S14 8:45P	S14 11:00P	SU15 1:45A										
*F13 6:00P				SU15 9:30A		SU15 5:00P	SU15 10:00P						M16 8:30A	M16 2:30P	M16 3:30P
				SU15 9:00A	SU15 11:45A					**Lv. Pelican**	SU15 1:00P		SU15 7:15P		
				SU15 5:30P	SU15 8:15P										
	M16 10:30A			M16 5:30P	M16 8:15P										
	T17 8:30A			T17 2:30P		T17 9:15P	W18 1:00A						W18 12:15P	W18 6:15P	W18 7:15P
				T17 9:00A	T17 11:45A										
				T17 5:30P	T17 8:15P		T17 5:30P	T17 10:30P	W18 6:30A	W18 4:00P	W18 7:30P	W18 11:45P	TH19 1:00P	TH19 7:45P	TH19 8:45P
			W18 8:15A	W18 10:30A	W18 1:15P										
			W18 8:45P	W18 11:00P	TH19 1:45A										
				TH19 5:30P	TH19 8:15P										
	F20 10:15A			F20 4:15P		F20 11:15P	S21 3:00A		S21 4:30P				SU22 6:45A	SU22 1:15P	SU22 2:15P
				F20 9:00A	F20 11:45A										
				F20 5:30P	F20 8:15P										
			S21 8:15A	S21 10:30A	S21 1:15P			Lv. Sitka	S21 6:45P	SU22 1:45A	SU22 5:15A	SU22 10:30A	SU22 1:45P		
			S21 8:45P	S21 11:00P	SU22 1:45A										
F20 6:00P				SU22 10:15A		SU22 5:45P	SU22 10:45P						M23 9:15A	M23 3:15P	M23 4:15P
				SU22 9:00A	SU22 11:45A										
				SU22 5:30P	SU22 8:15P										
	M23 10:30A			M23 5:30P	M23 8:15P										
	T24 9:00A			T24 3:00P		T24 9:45P	W25 1:30A						W25 12:15P	W25 6:15P	W25 7:15P
				T24 9:00A	T24 11:45A										
				T24 5:30P	T24 8:15P		T24 12:45P	T24 5:45P	W25 1:45A	W25 12:15P	W25 3:45P	W25 9:00P	TH26 12:15P	TH26 7:00P	TH26 8:00P
			W25 8:15A	W25 10:30A	W25 1:15P										
			W25 8:45P	W25 11:00P	TH26 1:45A										
	TH26 8:30A			TH26 2:30P		TH26 9:30P	F27 1:30A						F27 10:45A	F27 4:45P	F27 5:45P
				TH26 5:30P	TH26 8:15P										
				F27 9:00A	F27 11:45A										
				F27 5:30P	F27 8:15P										
	F27 11:30A			F27 5:30P		S28 1:30A	S28 6:00A		S28 4:00P				SU29 5:45A	SU29 11:45A	SU29 12:45P
			S28 8:15A	S28 10:30A	S28 1:15P			Lv. Sitka	S28 11:00A	S28 7:00P	S28 10:30P	SU29 2:45A	SU29 6:00A		
			S28 8:45P	S28 11:00P	SU29 1:45A										
F27 6:30P				SU29 10:30A		SU29 6:30P	SU29 11:00P						M30 9:00A	M30 3:00P	M30 4:00P
				SU29 9:00A	SU29 11:45A					**Lv. Pelican**	SU29 3:30P		SU29 9:45P		
				SU29 5:30P	SU29 8:15P										
	SU29 11:30A			SU29 6:30P		M30 2:00A	M30 7:00A		M30 5:45P				T31 7:00A	T31 1:00P	T31 2:00P
	M30 10:30A			M30 5:30P	M30 8:15P										
	M30 3:30P			M30 11:15P		T31 6:45A	T31 11:45A						T31 10:45P	W1 4:15A	W1 5:15A
				T31 9:00A	T31 11:45A		T31 6:15P	T31 11:15P	W1 7:15A	W1 4:45P	W1 8:15P	TH2 12:30A	TH2 3:45A		
	T31 11:30A			T31 8:30P		W1 4:30A	W1 9:30A		W1 8:00P			Ar.	TH2 7:15A		
				T31 5:30P	T31 8:15P								TH2 1:45P	TH2 8:30P	TH2 9:30P

*THE FOLLOWING EVENT MAY AFFECT AVAILABILITY OF SPACE:
MAY 13-15 LITTLE NORWAY FESTIVAL - PETERSBURG

HOW TO READ YOUR SCHEDULE

1. Reading across the top of each page, find the month you wish to travel, and refer to either the Northbound or Southbound schedule. (Using the example on page 557 of traveling from Skagway to Juneau/Auke Bay, you would read the Southbound schedule on the right hand page.)
2. Reading across the top of the schedule, find the city from which you wish to depart. (e.g., Leave Skagway)
3. Read down the column to locate your desired departure date. For example: Leave Skagway SU30 (Sunday, the 30th) 4:45 P.M.
4. Beginning with departure date, read horizontally from left to right for dates and times of departure from various ports. For example: After departing Skagway, ferry will dock in Haines, and after a short time in port it will depart Haines on SU30, (Sunday, the 30th) at 8:00 P.M. for Juneau/Auke Bay. Refer to the Running Time Table on page 558 to calculate the time in port and approximate unlisted arrival time.)
5. The color of the horizontal bars indicates the ship on which you will travel.

VESSEL COLOR CODING

Aurora · Columbia · Le Conte · Malaspina · Matanuska · Taku

The state reserves the right to revise or cancel schedules and rates without prior notice and assumes no responsibility for delays and/or expenses due to such modifications.

Alaska state ferry schedules reprinted courtesy of Alaska Marine Highway

May 1994 Southbound Schedule

LEAVE SKAGWAY	HAINES	JUNEAU/ AUKE BAY	HOONAH	TENAKEE	ANGOON	ARRIVE SITKA	KAKE	PETERSBURG	WRANGELL	HOLLIS	KETCHIKAN	METLAKATLA	ARRIVE STEWART/ HYDER	ARRIVE PRINCE RUPERT	ARRIVE BELLINGHAM
		SU1 2:00P	SU1 6:15P	SU1 10:15P	M2 1:15A	M2 6:45A	M2 5:30P	M2 11:30P		T3 9:00A	T3 12:45P	T3 2:00P			
SU1 8:30P	SU1 10:30P	M2 4:00A						M2 2:30P	M2 6:30P		T3 1:30A			T3 8:30A	
M2 3:30P	M2 5:30P	M2 11:00P				T3 8:00A		T3 10:00P	W4 2:00A		W4 4:30P				F6 7:30A
										T3 8:45P	W4 12:30A	W4 1:45A			
W4 8:45P	W4 10:45P	TH5 4:15A						TH5 1:00P	TH5 5:00P	TH5 11:55P	F6 3:45A			F6 10:45A	
										W4 9:00A	W4 11:45A				
		F6 4:30P	F6 9:45P	S7 2:00A	S7 6:15A	S7 11:45A									
SU8 8:45P	SU8 10:45P	M9 4:15A						M9 12:45P	M9 4:30P		M9 11:30P			T10 6:30A	
		SU8 8:15P	M9 1:30A		M9 7:30A	M9 1:00P	T10 1:00A	T10 5:00A							
M9 7:45P	M9 10:15P	T10 4:45A				T10 1:30P		W11 3:30A	W11 7:45A		W11 4:30P				F13 7:30A
TH12 11:45P	F13 1:45A	F13 10:30A	F13 2:45P	F13 6:45P	F13 10:15P	S14 3:15A				T10 1:45P	T10 4:30P				
										T10 9:15P	W11 6:15A	W11 7:30A			
*W11 10:15P	TH12 12:15A	TH12 5:45A						TH12 2:30P	TH12 6:30P		F13 1:30A			F13 8:30A	
										W11 2:15P	W11 6:45P	W11 8:00P			
										TH12 6:15A	TH12 9:00A				
										F13 5:15A	F13 8:00A				
SU15 5:30P	SU15 8:30P	M16 2:00A						M16 10:45A	M16 2:45P		M16 10:45P			T17 5:45A	
										F13 1:45P	F13 4:30P				
										F13 9:15P	S14 6:15A	S14 7:30A			
		SU15 5:30A	**Ar. Pelican**	SU15 11:55A						S14 2:15P	S14 6:45P	S14 8:00P			
										SU15 5:15A	SU15 8:00A				
M16 6:30P	M16 8:30P	T17 3:00A				T17 11:45A		W18 2:00A	W18 6:45A		W18 4:30P				F20 7:30A
		M16 2:45A	M16 7:00A		M16 11:55A	M16 5:00P	T17 4:45A	T17 8:45A		SU15 1:45P	SU15 4:30P				
										SU15 9:15P	M16 1:00A			M16 8:30A	
										T17 5:15A	T17 8:00A				
W18 10:15P	TH19 12:15A	TH19 5:45A						TH19 2:30P	TH19 6:30P		F20 1:30A			F20 8:30A	
										T17 1:45P	T17 4:30P				
F20 12:45A	F20 2:45A	F20 2:00P	F20 7:15P	F20 11:30P	S21 3:45A	S21 10:15A				T17 9:15P	W18 6:15A	W18 7:30A			
										W18 2:15P	W18 6:45P	W18 8:00P			
										TH19 6:15A	TH19 9:00A				
										F20 5:15A	F20 8:00A				
SU22 5:15P	SU22 7:45P	M23 1:15A						M23 10:30A	M23 3:30P		M23 11:30P			T24 6:30A	
										F20 1:45P	F20 4:30P				
										F20 9:15P	S21 6:15A	S21 7:30A			
		SU22 7:00P	M23 12:15A		M23 6:15A	M23 12:15P	T24 12:15A	T24 4:15A		S21 2:15P	S21 6:45P	S21 8:00P			
										SU22 5:15A	SU22 8:00A				
M23 7:15P	M23 9:45P	T24 4:15A				T24 1:00P		W25 2:45A	W25 7:00A		W25 4:30P				F27 7:30A
										SU22 1:45P	SU22 4:30P				
										SU22 9:15P	M23 1:00A			M23 8:30A	
										T24 5:15A	T24 8:00A				
W25 10:15P	TH26 12:15A	TH26 5:45A						TH26 2:30P	TH26 6:30P		F27 1:30A			F27 8:30A	
										T24 1:45P	T24 4:30P				
TH26 11:55P	F27 2:00A	F27 5:00P	F27 9:15P	S28 1:15A	S28 4:30A	S28 10:00A				T24 9:15P	W25 6:15A	W25 7:30A			
										W25 2:15P	W25 6:45P	W25 8:00P			
										TH26 6:15A	TH26 9:00A				
F27 8:45P	F27 10:45P	S28 4:15A						S28 2:00P	S28 6:00P		SU29 1:30A			SU29 8:30A	
										F27 5:15A	F27 8:00A				
										F27 1:45P	F27 4:30P				
										F27 9:15P	S28 6:15A	S28 7:30A			
SU29 4:15P	SU29 6:15P	SU29 11:45P						M30 8:30A	M30 1:30P		M30 11:15P			T31 6:15A	
		SU29 7:00A	**Ar. Pelican**	SU29 1:30P						S28 2:15P	S28 6:45P	S28 8:00P			
										SU29 5:15A	SU29 8:00A				
M30 7:00P	M30 9:30P	T31 4:00A				T31 12:30P		W1 2:30A	W1 7:30A		W1 6:00P				F3 8:30A
		M30 3:15A	M30 7:45A		M30 12:45P	M30 5:45P	T31 5:30A	T31 9:30A		SU29 1:45P	SU29 4:30P				
										SU29 9:15P	M30 1:00A			M30 8:30A	
T31 5:00P	T31 7:00P	W1 12:30A						W1 10:00A	W1 2:00P		W1 9:15P			TH2 5:30A	
										T31 5:15A	T31 8:00A				
										T31 1:45P	T31 4:30P				

ALL TIMES SHOWN ARE LOCAL TIMES

EXAMPLE

LEAVE SKAGWAY	HAINES	JUNEAU/ AUKE BAY	HOONAH	TENAKEE	ANGOON	ARRIVE SITKA	KAKE	PETERSBURG	WRANGELL	HOLLIS	KETCHIKAN	ARRIVE METLAKATLA	PRINCE RUPERT	ARRIVE BELLINGHAM
SU30 4:45P	SU30 8:00P	M1 2:15A						M1 11:00A	M1 3:15P		M1 11:15P		T2 6:15A	
		SU30 9:30P	M1 1:30A	M1 5:15A	M1 8:15A	M1 5:30P	T2 5:00A	T2 9:00A						
										M1 8:30A	M1 12:30P	M1 1:45P		
M1 11:45P	T2 3:00A	T2 9:30A				T2 6:15P		W3 9:15A	W3 1:15P		W3 8:00P			F5 8:00A
										T2 6:15A	T2 9:00A			
W3 7:30P	W3 10:00P	TH4 3:45A						TH4 12:15P	TH4 4:15P		TH4 11:30P		F5 6:30A	

Day of week — Day of month — Time — AM or PM

June 1994 Northbound Schedule

LEAVE BELLINGHAM	LEAVE PRINCE RUPERT	LEAVE STEWART/ HYDER	METLAKATLA	KETCHIKAN	HOLLIS	WRANGELL	PETERSBURG	KAKE	ARRIVE SITKA	ANGOON	TENAKEE	HOONAH	JUNEAU/ AUKE BAY	HAINES	ARRIVE SKAGWAY
	M30 3:30P			M30 11:15P		T31 6:45A	T31 11:45A						T31 10:45P	W1 4:15A	W1 5:15A
							T31 6:15P	T31 11:15P	W1 7:15A	W1 4:45P	W1 8:15P	TH2 12:30A	TH2 3:45A		
	T31 11:30A			T31 8:30P		W1 4:30A	W1 9:30A		W1 8:00P			Ar.	TH2 7:15A		
													TH2 1:45P	TH2 8:30P	TH2 9:30P
	TH2 8:30A			TH2 2:30P		TH2 9:30P	F3 1:30A						F3 10:45A	F3 4:45P	F3 5:45P
	F3 6:45A			F3 1:30P		F3 8:30P	S4 1:30A						S4 1:00P	S4 7:30P	S4 8:30P
								Lv. Sitka	S4 6:45P	SU5 1:45A	SU5 5:15A	SU5 10:30A	SU5 1:45P		
	S4 8:30A			S4 3:30P		S4 10:30P	SU5 2:30A						SU5 11:45A	SU5 5:45P	SU5 6:45P
F3 6:30P				SU5 9:30A		SU5 5:00P	SU5 9:30P						M6 8:30A	M6 3:00P	M6 4:00P
	SU5 11:30A			SU5 6:30P		M6 2:00A	M6 7:00A		M6 6:00P				T7 6:30A	T7 12:30P	T7 1:30P
	M6 3:30P			M6 11:15P		T7 6:30A	T7 11:15A						T7 10:45P	W8 4:15A	W8 5:15A
							T7 11:55A	T7 4:45P	W8 12:45A	W8 11:00A	W8 2:30P	W8 7:45P	W8 11:00P		
	T7 11:30A			T7 7:30P		W8 2:30A	W8 9:30A		W8 7:30P			Ar.	TH9 6:30A		
													TH9 11:00A	TH9 5:45P	TH9 6:45P
	TH9 8:30A			TH9 2:30P		TH9 9:30P	F10 1:30A						F10 10:45A	F10 4:45P	F10 5:45P
	F10 6:45A			F10 1:30P		F10 8:30P	S11 1:30A						S11 1:00P	S11 7:30P	S11 8:30P
								Lv. Sitka	S11 9:45A	S11 6:00P	S11 9:30P	SU12 1:45A	SU12 5:00A		
	S11 8:30A			S11 2:30P		S11 9:30P	SU12 1:30A						SU12 11:15A	SU12 5:45P	SU12 6:45P
											Lv. Pelican	SU12 3:30P	SU12 9:45P		
F10 6:30P				SU12 10:30A		SU12 6:30P	SU12 11:30P						M13 11:30A	M13 6:00P	M13 7:00P
	SU12 11:30A			SU12 6:30P		M13 1:45A	M13 6:15A		M13 4:15P				T14 4:45A	T14 10:45A	T14 11:45A
	M13 3:30P			M13 9:45P		T14 4:30A	T14 9:15A						T14 8:15P	W15 2:45A	W15 3:45A
							T14 4:15P	T14 9:15P	W15 5:15A	W15 2:45P	W15 6:15P	W15 10:30P	TH16 1:45A		
	T14 11:30A			T14 7:30P		W15 3:30A	W15 7:45A		W15 5:45P			Ar.	TH16 5:30A		
													TH16 11:45A	TH16 6:30P	TH16 7:30P
	TH16 8:30A			TH16 2:30P		TH16 9:30P	F17 1:30A						F17 10:45A	F17 4:45P	F17 5:45P
	F17 6:45A			F17 1:30P		F17 8:30P	S18 1:30A						S18 1:00P	S18 7:30P	S18 8:30P
								Lv. Sitka	S18 5:00P	S18 11:55P	SU19 3:30A	SU19 8:45A	SU19 11:55A		
	S18 8:30A			S18 2:30P		S18 9:30P	SU19 1:30A						SU19 11:15A	SU19 5:15P	SU19 6:15P
F17 6:30P				SU19 9:30A		SU19 5:00P	SU19 9:30P						M20 8:15A	M20 2:45P	M20 3:45P
	SU19 11:30A			SU19 5:30P		M20 12:15A	M20 7:00A		M20 5:00P				T21 5:30A	T21 11:30A	T21 12:30P
	M20 3:30P			M20 10:45P		T21 6:00A	T21 10:45A						T21 10:15P	W22 4:15A	W22 5:15A
							T21 11:00A	T21 4:00P	T21 11:55P	W22 10:30A	W22 2:00P	W22 7:15P	W22 10:30P		
	T21 11:30A			T21 6:30P		W22 1:30A	W22 9:00A		W22 7:00P			Ar.	TH23 6:30A		
													TH23 10:30A	TH23 5:15P	TH23 6:15P
	TH23 8:30A			TH23 2:30P		TH23 9:30P	F24 1:30A						F24 10:45A	F24 4:45P	F24 5:45P
	F24 6:45A			F24 1:30P		F24 8:30P	S25 1:30A						S25 1:00P	S25 7:30P	S25 8:30P
								Lv. Sitka	S25 9:45A	S25 6:00P	S25 9:30P	SU26 1:45A	SU26 5:00A		
	S25 8:30A			S25 3:00P		S25 10:00P	SU26 2:00A						SU26 11:45A	SU26 5:45P	SU26 6:45P
											Lv. Pelican	SU26 3:30P	SU26 9:45P		
F24 6:30P				SU26 9:30A		SU26 5:30P	SU26 11:15P						M27 11:00A	M27 5:30P	M27 6:30P
	SU26 11:30A			SU26 6:30P		M27 2:00A	M27 6:30A		M27 4:30P				T28 5:00A	T28 11:00A	T28 11:55A
	M27 3:30P			M27 9:45P		T28 5:30A	T28 12:30P						T28 10:00P	W29 3:45A	W29 4:45A
							T28 4:45P	T28 9:45P	W29 5:45A	W29 3:00P	W29 6:30P	W29 10:45P	TH30 2:00A		
	T28 11:30A			T28 8:30P		W29 3:30A	W29 7:30A		W29 6:00P			Ar.	TH30 5:45A		
													TH30 11:55A	TH30 6:45P	TH30 7:45P
	TH30 8:30A			TH30 2:30P		TH30 9:30P	F1 1:30A						F1 10:45A	F1 4:45P	F1 5:45P

RUNNING TIME TABLE

INSIDE PASSAGE ROUTE:

Bellingham — Ketchikan	36 hrs.
Prince Rupert — Ketchikan	6 hrs.
Stewart/Hyder — Ketchikan	9 hrs. 45 min.
Ketchikan — Wrangell	6 hrs.
Wrangell — Petersburg	3 hrs.
Petersburg — Sitka	10 hrs.
Petersburg — Juneau	8 hrs.
Sitka — Juneau/Auke Bay	7 hrs. 45 min.
Juneau/Auke Bay — Haines	4hrs. 30 min.
Haines — Skagway	1 hr.

SOUTHCENTRAL ROUTE:

Whittier — Valdez	6 hrs. 45 min.
Valdez — Cordova	5 hrs. 30 min.
Cordova — Whittier	7 hrs.
Cordova — Seward	11 hrs.
Valdez — Seward	11 hrs.
Homer — Seldovia	1 hr. 30 min.

SOUTHCENTRAL/SOUTHWEST ROUTE CONNECTIONS:

Homer — Kodiak	10 hrs.
Homer — Port Lions	9 hrs. 45 min.
Seward — Kodiak	13 hrs. 30 min.

SOUTHWEST ROUTES:

Kodiak — Port Lions	2 hrs. 30 min.
Kodiak — Chignik	19 hrs.
Chignik — Sand Point	9 hrs. 15 min.
Sand Point — King Cove	6 hrs. 45 min.
King Cove — Cold Bay	1 hr. 45 min.
Cold Bay — Dutch Harbor	14 hrs. 15 min.

For more accurate arrival times, please contact the local Marine Highway office on the day of arrival.

(Continued from page 555)
are subject to off-loading at each port of call!

If cabin space is filled, you may go deck passage. This means you'll be sleeping on lounge chairs or on the deck itself. There is a limited number of recliner chairs and spaces to roll out sleeping bags. Pillows and blankets are available for rent on most sailings.

Fares and fare payment: See page 566 for Southeast passenger and vehicle, page 567 for cabin rates; see pages 569 and 571 for Southwest passenger, vehicle and cabin rates. Fares are charged for passengers, vehicles and cabins on a port to port basis. If you are traveling from Ketchikan to Skagway with a stopover at Juneau, you are charged from Ketchikan to Juneau and Juneau to Skagway, with the total ticket cost being slightly higher than if you were not stopping off in Juneau.

Full payment is required as follows: If you are booking 55 or more days in advance, payment is due 30 days after the date you book the reservation; if you are booking less than 55 days prior to departure, payment is

Columbia Le Conte Malaspina Matanuska Taku

June 1994 Southbound Schedule

LEAVE SKAGWAY	HAINES	JUNEAU/ AUKE BAY	HOONAH	TENAKEE	ANGOON	ARRIVE SITKA	KAKE	PETERSBURG	WRANGELL	HOLLIS	KETCHIKAN	METLAKATLA	ARRIVE STEWART/ HYDER	ARRIVE PRINCE RUPERT	ARRIVE BELLINGHAM
M30 7:00P	M30 9:30P	T31 4:00A				T31 12:30P		W1 2:30A	W1 7:30A		W1 6:00P				F3 8:30A
T31 5:00P	T31 7:00P	W1 12:30A						W1 10:00A	W1 2:00P		W1 9:15P			TH2 5:30A	
W1 8:15A	W1 10:15A	W1 4:15P						TH2 1:30A	TH2 5:45A		TH2 1:15P			TH2 8:45P	
		TH2 12:15P				TH2 9:00P		F3 11:30A	F3 3:30P		F3 10:30P			S4 5:30A	
F3 1:30A	F3 3:30A	F3 2:00P	F3 7:15P	F3 11:30P	S4 3:45A	S4 10:15A									
F3 8:45P	F3 10:45P	S4 4:15A						S4 1:00P	S4 5:30P		SU5 1:30A			SU5 8:30A	
S4 11:30P	SU5 1:30A	SU5 8:00A						SU5 5:15P	SU5 9:30P		M6 5:00A			M6 12:30P	
		SU5 7:00P	M6 12:15A		M6 6:00A	M6 11:55A	M6 11:55P	T7 4:00A							
SU5 9:45P	SU5 11:45P	M6 5:45A						M6 2:30P	M6 6:30P		T7 1:30A			T7 8:30A	
M6 7:00P	M6 9:30P	T7 4:00A				T7 12:30P		W8 2:15A	W8 7:15A		W8 5:00P				F10 7:30A
T7 4:30P	T7 7:00P	W8 2:00A						W8 10:45A	W8 2:45P		W8 10:30P			TH9 5:30A	
W8 8:15A	W8 10:15A	W8 4:15P						TH9 1:30A	TH9 5:45A		TH9 1:15P			TH9 8:45P	
		TH9 11:15A				TH9 8:00P		F10 11:30A	F10 3:30P		F10 10:30P			S11 5:30A	
TH9 10:45P	F10 12:45A	F10 3:45P	F10 8:00P	F10 11:55P	S11 3:15A	S11 8:45A									
F10 8:45P	F10 10:45P	S11 4:15A						S11 1:00P	S11 5:30P		SU12 1:30A			SU12 8:30A	
S11 11:30P	SU12 1:30A	SU12 8:00A						SU12 5:15P	SU12 9:30P		M13 5:00A			M13 12:30P	
		SU12 7:00A	**Ar. Pelican**	SU12 1:30P											
SU12 9:45P	SU12 11:45P	M13 5:45A						M13 2:30P	M13 6:30P		T14 1:30A			T14 8:30A	
		M13 1:45A	M13 6:00A		M13 11:00A	M13 4:15P	T14 3:45A	T14 7:45A							
M13 10:45P	T14 1:45A	T14 8:15A				T14 4:45P		W15 6:30A	W15 10:30A		W15 6:00P				F17 8:30A
T14 2:45P	T14 5:45P	W15 12:15A						W15 9:00A	W15 1:00P		W15 10:30P			TH16 5:30A	
W15 6:45A	W15 9:15A	W15 4:15P						TH16 1:30A	TH16 5:45A		TH16 1:15P			TH16 8:45P	
		TH16 10:00A				TH16 6:45P		F17 9:15A	F17 1:45P		F17 10:30P			S18 5:30A	
TH16 11:30P	F17 1:30A	F17 2:00P	F17 7:15P	F17 11:30P	S18 3:15A	S18 8:45A									
F17 8:45P	F17 10:45P	S18 4:15A						S18 1:00P	S18 5:30P		SU19 1:30A			SU19 8:30A	
S18 11:30P	SU19 1:30A	SU19 8:00A						SU19 5:15P	SU19 9:30P		M20 5:00A			M20 12:30P	
		SU19 5:15P	SU19 10:30P		M20 4:30A	M20 10:45A	M20 11:00P	T21 3:00A							
SU19 9:15P	SU19 11:15P	M20 5:15A						M20 2:00P	M20 6:00P		T21 1:30A			T21 8:30A	
M20 6:45P	M20 9:15P	T21 3:15A				T21 11:45A		W22 1:30A	W22 5:30A		W22 5:00P				F24 7:30A
T21 3:30P	T21 6:15P	W22 1:45A						W22 10:30A	W22 2:30P		W22 10:30P			TH23 5:30A	
W22 8:15A	W22 10:15A	W22 4:15P						TH23 1:30A	TH23 5:45A		TH23 1:15P			TH23 8:45P	
		TH23 11:00A				TH23 7:45P		F24 11:45A	F24 3:30P		F24 10:30P			S25 5:30A	
TH23 10:15P	F24 12:15A	F24 3:45P	F24 8:00P	F24 11:55P	S25 3:15A	S25 8:45A									
F24 8:45P	F24 10:45P	S25 4:15A						S25 1:00P	S25 5:30P		SU26 1:30A			SU26 8:30A	
S25 11:30P	SU26 1:30A	SU26 8:00A						SU26 5:15P	SU26 9:30P		M27 5:00A			M27 12:30P	
		SU26 7:00A	**Ar. Pelican**	SU26 1:30P											
SU26 9:45P	SU26 11:45P	M27 5:15A						M27 2:00P	M27 6:00P		T28 1:30A			T28 8:30A	
		M27 2:15A	M27 6:30A		M27 11:30A	M27 4:30P	T28 4:15A	T28 8:15A							
M27 10:45P	T28 1:15A	T28 8:15A				T28 4:45P		W29 7:00A	W29 11:00A		W29 6:30P				F1 9:00A
T28 3:00P	T28 5:30P	W29 12:30A						W29 9:15A	W29 1:15P		W29 10:30P			TH30 5:30A	
W29 7:45A	W29 9:45A	W29 4:15P						TH30 1:30A	TH30 5:45A		TH30 1:15P			TH30 8:45P	
		TH30 10:15A				TH30 7:00P		F1 9:30A	F1 2:00P		F1 10:30P			S2 5:30A	
TH30 11:45P	F1 1:45A	F1 2:00P	F1 7:15P	F1 11:30P	S2 3:15A	S2 8:45A									

ALL TIMES SHOWN ARE LOCAL TIMES

M/V AURORA SCHEDULE

How To Use This Schedule

The M/V AURORA operates a daily schedule between Ketchikan, Metlakatla and Hollis (Gateway to Prince of Wales Island). There are several sailings to and from these communities each day. To determine the best one for your trip, use this table. Please allow enough time to make appropriate connections with the mainline sailings from Ketchikan (see tables above).

Effective June 2-September 4, 1994

SUN	LV HOLLIS	5:15AM
	AR KETCHIKAN	8:00AM
	LV KETCHIKAN	9:00AM
	AR HOLLIS	11:45AM
	LV HOLLIS	1:45PM
	AR KETCHIKAN	4:30PM
	LV KETCHIKAN	5:30PM
	AR HOLLIS	8:15PM
	LV HOLLIS	9:15PM
	AR KETCHIKAN	11:57PM
MON	LV KETCHIKAN	6:15AM
	AR METLAKATLA	7:30AM
	LV METLAKATLA	8:15AM
	AR KETCHIKAN	9:30AM
	LV KETCHIKAN	10:30AM
	AR HOLLIS	1:15PM
	LV HOLLIS	3:00PM
	AR KETCHIKAN	5:45PM
	LV KETCHIKAN	6:45PM
	AR METLAKATLA	8:00PM
	LV METLAKATLA	8:45PM
	AR KETCHIKAN	10:00PM
	LV KETCHIKAN	11:00PM
TUE	AR HOLLIS	1:45AM
TUE	LV HOLLIS	5:15AM
	AR KETCHIKAN	8:00AM
	LV KETCHIKAN	9:00AM
	AR HOLLIS	11:45AM
	LV HOLLIS	1:45PM
	AR KETCHIKAN	4:30PM
	LV KETCHIKAN	5:30PM
	AR HOLLIS	8:15PM
WED	LV HOLLIS	6:15AM
	AR KETCHIKAN	9:00AM
	LV KETCHIKAN	5:30PM
	AR HOLLIS	8:15PM
	LV HOLLIS	9:15PM
	AR KETCHIKAN	11:57PM
THU	LV KETCHIKAN	1:00AM***
	AR HYDER	12:15PM
	LV HYDER	3:00PM
FRI	AR KETCHIKAN	12:45AM
	LV KETCHIKAN	2:00AM
	AR HOLLIS	4:45AM
FRI	LV HOLLIS	5:45AM
	AR KETCHIKAN	8:30AM
	LV KETCHIKAN	9:30AM
	AR HOLLIS	12:15PM
	LV HOLLIS	1:45PM
	AR KETCHIKAN	4:30PM
	LV KETCHIKAN	5:30PM
	AR HOLLIS	8:15PM
	LV HOLLIS	9:15PM
	AR KETCHIKAN	11:57PM
SAT	LV KETCHIKAN	6:15AM
	AR METLAKATLA	7:30AM
	LV METLAKATLA	8:15AM
	AR KETCHIKAN	9:30AM
	LV KETCHIKAN	10:30AM
	AR HOLLIS	1:15PM
	LV HOLLIS	2:15PM
	AR KETCHIKAN	5:00PM
	LV KETCHIKAN	6:45PM
	AR METLAKATLA	8:00PM
	LV METLAKATLA	8:45PM
	AR KETCHIKAN	10:00PM
	LV KETCHIKAN	11:00PM
SUN	AR HOLLIS	1:45AM

***BEGIN HYDER SERVICE JUNE 2

July 1994 Northbound Schedule

LEAVE BELLINGHAM	LEAVE PRINCE RUPERT	LEAVE STEWART/ HYDER	METLAKATLA	KETCHIKAN	HOLLIS	WRANGELL	PETERSBURG	KAKE	ARRIVE SITKA	ANGOON	TENAKEE	HOONAH	JUNEAU/ AUKE BAY	HAINES	ARRIVE SKAGWAY
	TH30 8:30A			TH30 2:30P		TH30 9:30P	F1 1:30A						F1 10:45A	F1 4:45P	F1 5:45P
	F1 6:45A			F1 1:30P		F1 8:30P	S2 1:30A						S2 11:00A	S2 5:00P	S2 6:00P
								Lv. Sitka	S2 5:00P	S2 11:55P	SU3 3:30A	SU3 8:45A	SU3 11:55A		
	S2 9:00A			S2 3:00P		S2 10:00P	SU3 2:00A						SU3 11:15A	SU3 5:15P	SU3 6:15P
F1 6:30P				SU3 9:30A		SU3 4:30P	SU3 8:30P						M4 6:00A	M4 11:30A	M4 12:30P
													M4 10:00P	T5 3:30A	T5 4:30A
	SU3 11:30A			SU3 6:30P		M4 1:30A	M4 6:30A		M4 4:30P				T5 5:00A	T5 11:00A	T5 11:55A
	M4 3:30P			M4 10:45P		T5 5:45A	T5 11:15A						T5 8:45P	W6 2:15A	W6 3:15A
							T5 4:45PA	T5 9:45P	W6 6:45A	W6 3:00P	W6 6:30P	W6 10:45P	TH7 2:00A		
	T5 11:30A			T5 6:30P		W6 1:30A	W6 8:00A		W6 6:00P			Ar.	TH7 5:15A		
													TH7 10:00A	TH7 4:45P	TH7 5:45P
	TH7 8:30A			TH7 2:30P		TH7 9:30P	F8 1:30A						F8 10:45A	F8 4:45P	F8 5:45P
	F8 6:45A			F8 1:30P		F8 8:30P	S9 1:30A						S9 11:00A	S9 5:00P	S9 6:00P
								Lv. Sitka	S9 9:00A	S9 5:00P	S9 8:30P	SU10 12:45A	SU10 4:00A		
	S9 9:00A			S9 3:00P		S9 10:00P	SU10 2:00A						SU10 11:15A	SU10 5:15P	SU10 6:15P
											Lv. Pelican	SU10 3:30P	SU10 9:45P		
F8 6:30P				SU10 9:30A		SU10 5:00P	SU10 9:45P						M11 9:30A	M11 4:00P	M11 5:00P
	SU10 11:30A			SU10 6:00P		M11 1:00A	M11 5:00A		M11 3:00P				T12 3:45A	T12 9:45A	T12 10:45A
	M11 1:30P			M11 8:15P		T12 4:00A	T12 8:45A						T12 5:45P	T12 11:45P	W13 12:45A
							T12 3:15P	T12 8:15P	W13 4:15A	W13 1:30P	W13 5:00P	W13 9:15P	W13 11:55P		
	T12 11:30A			T12 7:30P		W13 2:30A	W13 6:30A		W13 4:30P			Ar.	TH14 4:15A		
													TH14 10:30A	TH14 5:15P	TH14 6:15P
	TH14 8:30A			TH14 3:30P		TH14 11:00P	F15 3:00A						F15 12:15P	F15 5:45P	F15 6:45P
	F15 6:45A			F15 1:30P		F15 8:30P	S16 1:30A						S16 11:30A	S16 5:30P	S16 6:30P
								Lv. Sitka	S16 3:30P	S16 10:30P	SU17 2:00A	SU17 7:15A	SU17 10:30A		
	S16 8:30A			S16 2:30P		S16 9:30P	SU17 1:30A						SU17 10:45A	SU17 4:45P	SU17 5:45P
F15 6:30P				SU17 8:30A		SU17 3:30P	SU17 7:30P						M18 5:30A	M18 11:30A	M18 12:30P
													M18 10:00P	T19 3:30P	T19 4:30A
	SU17 1:00P			SU17 8:00P		M18 3:30A	M18 8:30A		M18 6:45P				T19 7:45A	T19 1:15P	T19 2:15P
	M18 3:30P			M18 10:15P		T19 5:15A	T19 10:15A						T19 7:45P	W20 1:45A	W20 2:45A
							T19 4:00P	T19 9:00P	W20 5:15A	W20 2:00P	W20 5:30P	W20 9:45P	TH21 1:00A		
	T19 11:30A			T19 5:30P		W20 12:30A	W20 7:45A		W20 5:45P			Ar.	TH21 5:00A		
													TH21 9:15A	TH21 4:00P	TH21 5:00P
	TH21 8:30A			TH21 3:00P		TH21 10:00P	F22 2:00A						F22 11:15A	F22 4:45P	F22 5:45P
	F22 6:45A			F22 1:30P		F22 8:30P	S23 1:30A						S23 10:30A	S23 4:00P	S23 5:00P
								Lv. Sitka	S23 9:00A	S23 5:00P	S23 8:30P	SU24 12:45A	SU24 4:00A		
	S23 9:00A			S23 3:00P		S23 10:00P	SU24 2:00A						SU24 11:15A	SU24 4:45P	SU24 5:45P
											Lv. Pelican	SU24 3:30P	SU24 9:45P		
F22 6:30P				SU24 9:30A		SU24 4:30P	SU24 10:30P						M25 8:00A	M25 1:30P	M25 2:30P
	SU24 11:30A			SU24 6:30P		M25 1:30A	M25 5:30A		M25 3:30P				T26 3:45A	T26 9:15A	T26 10:15A
	M25 1:30P			M25 8:15P		T26 3:15A	T26 8:00A						T26 5:45P	W27 12:15A	W27 1:15A
							T26 3:15P	T26 8:15P	W27 4:15A	W27 1:30P	W27 5:00P	W27 9:15P	W27 11:55P		
	T26 11:30A			T26 7:30P		W27 2:30A	W27 6:30A		W27 4:30P			Ar.	TH28 4:00A		
													TH28 10:30A	TH28 5:15P	TH28 6:15P
	TH28 8:30A			TH28 3:00P		TH28 10:00P	F29 2:00A						F29 11:15A	F29 4:45P	F29 5:45P
	F29 6:45A			F29 1:30P		F29 8:30P	S30 1:30A						S30 11:30A	S30 5:30P	S30 6:30P
								Lv. Sitka	S30 3:00P	S30 10:00P	SU31 1:30A	SU31 6:45A	SU31 10:00A		
	S30 9:00A			S30 3:00P		S30 10:00P	SU31 2:00A						SU31 11:15A	SU31 4:45P	SU31 5:45P
F29 6:30P				SU31 9:30A		SU31 4:30P	SU31 8:30P						M1 6:30A	M1 12:30P	M1 1:30P
	SU31 11:30A			SU31 6:15P		M1 1:15A	M1 5:15A		M1 3:15P				T2 3:30A	T2 9:00A	T2 10:00A

due within 10 days after the date you book the reservations; reservations booked 10 days or less prior to departure require payment at time of booking. Failure to meet this requirement may result in the cancellation of reservations. Payment may be made by mail with certified or cashier's check, or money order. Personal checks are not accepted unless written on an Alaska bank. Credit cards (VISA, MasterCard, American Express, Discover and Diners Club) are accepted at all terminals (some restrictions may apply) and by phone.

Cancellation fees are charged if a change or cancellation is made within 14 days of sailing.

Vehicle tariffs depend on the size of vehicle. You are charged by how much space you take up, so a car with trailer is measured from the front of the car to the end of the trailer, including hitch space. (In summer, drivers' fares are not included in the vehicle tariff.)

Bicycles, kayaks and inflatables are charged a surcharge. Check the Alternate Means of Conveyance charges in the tariff section.

Passenger tariffs are charged as follows: adults and children 12 and over, full fare; children 6 to 11, approximately half fare; children under 6, free. Passenger fares do not include cabins or meals. Special passes and travel rates are available to senior citizens (over 65) and persons with disabilities. Check with the Alaska Marine Highway or consult the official Marine Highway schedule for costs and restrictions.

Cabin rates depend on vessel, size of cabin and facilities. Only five vessels have cabins available.

Pick up cabin keys from the purser's office when you board. Cabins are sold as a unit, not on a per berth basis. In other words, the cost of the cabin is the same whether one person occupies it or 10 people share it.

All cabins on the Southeast system ferries have a toilet and shower. Linens (towels, sheets, blankets) are provided. Restrooms and shower facilities are available for deck-passage (walk-on) passengers.

Surcharges are assessed on pets ($10 to/from Bellingham, $5 to/from Prince Rupert and to/from Stewart/Hyder) and unattended vehicles ($30 to/from Bellingham, $10 to/from Prince Rupert and to/from Stewart/Hyder). The Marine Highway does not provide for loading and off-loading of unattended vehicles.

Check-in times: Summer check-in times for reserved vehicles prior to departure are: Bellingham and Prince Rupert, three hours; Ketchikan, Juneau, Haines, Skagway, Homer, Seward, Kodiak, two hours; Petersburg, one and one-half hours; all other ports, one hour. Call the Sitka terminal for check-in time

Columbia　Le Conte　Malaspina　Matanuska　Taku

July 1994 Southbound Schedule

LEAVE SKAGWAY	HAINES	JUNEAU/ AUKE BAY	HOONAH	TENAKEE	ANGOON	ARRIVE SITKA	KAKE	PETERSBURG	WRANGELL	HOLLIS	KETCHIKAN	METLAKATLA	ARRIVE STEWART/ HYDER	ARRIVE PRINCE RUPERT	ARRIVE BELLINGHAM
		TH30 10:15A				TH30 7:00P		F1 9:30A	F1 2:00P		F1 10:30P			S2 5:30A	
F1 8:45P	F1 10:45P	S2 4:15A						S2 1:00P	S2 5:30P		SU3 1:30A			SU3 8:30A	
TH30 11:45P	F1 1:45A	F1 2:00P	F1 7:15P	F1 11:30P	S2 3:15A	S2 8:45A									
S2 9:00P	S2 11:30P	SU3 6:00A						SU3 3:45P	SU3 8:30P		M4 5:00A			M4 12:30P	
		SU3 5:15P	SU3 10:30P		M4 4:30A	M4 10:30A	M4 10:45P	T5 2:45A							
SU3 9:15P	SU3 11:15P	M4 4:45A						M4 1:30P	M4 5:30P		T5 1:30A			T5 8:30A	
M4 2:00P	M4 4:30P	M4 9:00P													
T5 6:30A	T5 8:30A	T5 3:00P						W6 12:15A	W6 5:15A		W6 5:00P				F8 7:30A
T5 3:00P	T5 5:30P	W6 12:45A						W6 9:30A	W6 2:30P		W6 10:30P			TH7 5:30A	
W6 6:15A	W6 8:45A	W6 4:15P						TH7 1:30A	TH7 5:45A		TH7 1:15P			TH7 8:45P	
		TH7 10:15A				TH7 7:00P		F8 11:15A	F8 3:15P		F8 10:30P			S9 5:30A	
TH7 9:45P	TH7 11:45P	F8 3:00P	F8 7:15P	F8 11:15P	S9 2:30A	S9 8:00A									
F8 8:45P	F8 10:45P	S9 4:15A						S9 1:00P	S9 5:30P		SU10 1:30A			SU10 8:30A	
S9 9:00P	S9 11:30P	SU10 6:00A						SU10 3:15P	SU10 7:30P		M11 3:00A			M11 10:30A	
		SU10 7:00A	**Ar. Pelican**	SU10 1:30P											
SU10 9:15P	SU10 11:15P	M11 4:45A						M11 1:30P	M11 5:30P		T12 1:30A			T12 8:30A	
		M11 1:00A	M11 5:15A		M11 10:15A	M11 3:15P	T12 3:00A	T12 7:00A							
M11 9:00P	M11 11:55P	T12 7:00A				T12 3:30P		W13 5:30A	W13 9:30A		W13 6:00P				F15 8:30A
T12 1:45P	T12 4:15P	T12 10:45P						W13 7:30A	W13 12:30P		W13 10:30P			TH14 5:30A	
W13 3:45A	W13 6:45A	W13 3:15P						TH14 12:30A	TH14 4:45A		TH14 1:15P			TH14 8:45P	
		TH14 8:45A				TH14 5:30P		F15 8:00A	F15 1:00P		F15 10:30P			S16 5:30A	
TH14 10:15P	F15 12:15A	F15 1:30P	F15 6:15P	F15 10:30P	S16 1:45A	S16 7:15A									
F15 9:45P	S16 12:15A	S16 6:45A						S16 3:30P	S16 7:30P		SU17 3:00A			SU17 10:00A	
S16 9:30P	SU17 12:30A	SU17 8:00A						SU17 5:15P	SU17 9:30P		M18 5:00A			M18 12:30P	
		SU17 4:15P	SU17 9:30P		M18 3:30A	M18 9:30A	M18 11:15P	T19 3:15A							
SU17 8:45P	SU17 11:15P	M18 5:15A						M18 2:00P	M18 6:00P		T19 1:30A			T19 8:30A	
M18 2:00P	M18 4:30P	M18 9:00P													
T19 6:30A	T19 8:30A	T19 3:00P						W20 12:15A	W20 5:15A		W20 5:00P				F22 7:30A
T19 5:15P	T19 7:45P	W20 1:45A						W20 10:30A	W20 2:30P		W20 10:30P			TH21 5:30A	
W20 5:45A	W20 8:45A	W20 4:15P						TH21 1:30A	TH21 5:45A		TH21 1:15P			TH21 8:45P	
		TH21 10:00A				TH21 6:45P		F22 11:00A	F22 3:00P		F22 10:30P			S23 5:30A	
TH21 9:00P	TH21 11:00P	F22 3:00P	F22 7:15P	F22 11:15P	S23 2:30A	S23 8:00A									
F22 8:45P	F22 11:15P	S23 5:15A						S23 2:00P	S23 6:00P		SU24 1:30A			SU24 8:30A	
S23 8:00P	S23 11:00P	SU24 5:30A						SU24 2:45P	SU24 7:30P		M25 3:00A			M25 10:30A	
		SU24 7:00A	**Ar. Pelican**	SU24 1:30P											
SU24 8:45P	SU24 11:15P	M25 5:15A						M25 2:00P	M25 6:00P		T26 1:30A			T26 8:30A	
		M25 1:15A	M25 5:30A		M25 10:30A	M25 3:30P	T26 2:45A	T26 6:45A							
M25 5:30P	M25 7:30P	T26 1:15A				T26 9:45A		W27 1:45A	W27 6:45A		W27 5:00P				F29 7:30A
T26 1:15P	T26 3:45P	T26 10:15P						W27 7:00A	W27 11:55A		W27 10:30P			TH28 5:30A	
W27 4:15A	W27 7:45A	W27 4:15P						TH28 1:30A	TH28 5:45A		TH28 1:15P			TH28 8:45P	
		TH28 8:30A				TH28 5:15P		F29 7:30A	F29 11:55A		F29 10:30P			S30 5:30A	
TH28 10:15P	F29 12:15A	F29 1:30P	F29 5:45P	F29 10:00P	S30 1:15A	S30 6:45A									
F29 8:45P	F29 11:16P	S30 5:15A						S30 2:00P	S30 6:00P		SU31 1:30A			SU31 8:30A	
S30 9:30P	S30 11:55P	SU31 7:00A						SU31 4:45P	SU31 9:30P		M1 5:00A			M1 12:30P	
		SU31 3:45P	SU31 9:00P		M1 3:00A	M1 9:00A	M1 9:15P	T2 1:15A							
SU31 8:45P	SU31 11:15P	M1 5:15A						M1 2:00P	M1 6:00P		T2 1:30A			T2 8:30A	

ALL TIMES SHOWN ARE LOCAL TIMES

(747-3300). Passengers without vehicles must check in one hour prior to departure at all ports except Bellingham, where check-in is two hours prior to departure. For MV *Bartlett* departures from Whittier, check-in time at the Portage train loading ramp is noon.

Local times are shown on all Alaska Marine Highway schedules: That is Alaska time for Alaska ports on the Southeast and Southcentral/Southwest schedules, Pacific time for Prince Rupert, BC, Bellingham, WA, and Stewart/Hyder on the Southeast schedules.

Luggage: You are responsible for your own luggage! Foot passengers may bring hand luggage only (not to exceed 100 lbs.). There is no limit on luggage carried in a vehicle. Coin-operated storage lockers are available aboard most ships, and baggage carts are furnished on the car deck. Baggage handling is NOT provided by the Marine Highway. Bicycles, small boats and inflatables are not considered baggage and will be charged a fare.

Photographing a humpback whale in Frederick Sound. (Michael DeYoung)

August 1994 Northbound Schedule

LEAVE BELLINGHAM	LEAVE PRINCE RUPERT	LEAVE STEWART/ HYDER	METLAKATLA	KETCHIKAN	HOLLIS	WRANGELL	PETERSBURG	KAKE	ARRIVE SITKA	ANGOON	TENAKEE	HOONAH	JUNEAU/ AUKE BAY	HAINES	ARRIVE SKAGWAY
	SU31 11:30A			SU31 6:15P		M1 1:15A	M1 5:15A		M1 3:15P				T2 3:30A	T2 9:00A	T2 10:00A
	M1 3:30P			M1 10:15P		T2 5:45A	T2 10:45A						T2 8:15P	W3 2:15A	W3 3:15A
							T2 3:30P	T2 8:30P	W3 4:30A	W3 1:45P	W3 5:00P	W3 9:15P	TH4 12:30A		
	T2 11:30A			T2 6:00P		W3 1:00A	W3 7:00A		W3 5:00P			Ar.	TH4 4:15A		
													TH4 8:45A	TH4 3:30P	TH4 4:30P
	TH4 8:30A			TH4 3:00P		TH4 10:00P	F5 2:00A						F5 11:15A	F5 4:45P	F5 5:45P
	F5 6:45A			F5 1:30P		F5 8:30P	S6 1:30A						S6 10:30A	S6 4:00P	S6 5:00P
								Lv. Sitka	S6 8:00A	S6 4:30P	S6 8:00P	SU7 12:45A	SU7 4:00A		
	S6 9:00A			S6 3:00P		S6 10:00P	SU7 2:00A						SU7 11:15A	SU7 4:45P	SU7 5:45P
										Lv. Pelican	SU7 3:30P		SU7 9:45P		
F5 6:30P				SU7 9:30A		SU7 4:30P	SU7 8:30P						M8 6:00A	M8 11:30A	M8 12:30P
	SU7 11:30A			SU7 5:30P		M8 12:30A	M8 4:15A		M8 2:15P				T9 2:45A	T9 8:15A	T9 9:15A
	*M8 12:30P			M8 7:45P		T9 3:00A	T9 10:45A						T9 8:15P	W10 1:45A	W10 2:45A
							*T9 2:15P	T9 7:15P	W10 3:15A	W10 12:30P	W10 4:00P	W10 8:15P	TH11 12:30A	TH11 5:00A	
	*T9 11:30A			T9 6:30P		W10 1:30A	W10 5:30A		W10 3:30P			Ar.	TH11 2:45A		
													*TH11 11:30A	TH11 5:00P	TH11 6:00P
	*TH11 8:30A		TH11 3:30P			TH11 11:00P	F12 3:00A						F12 12:15P	F12 5:45P	F12 6:45P
	*F12 6:45A			F12 3:00P		F12 11:15P	S13 4:15A						S13 1:30P	S13 7:00P	S13 8:00P
								Lv. Sitka	S13 1:45P	S13 8:45P	SU14 12:15A	SU14 4:30A	SU14 9:00A	SU14 1:30P	
	S13 9:00A			S13 4:30P		SU14 12:30A	SU14 4:30A						SU14 1:15P	SU14 6:45P	SU14 7:45P
F12 6:30P				SU14 9:30A		SU14 4:30P	SU14 8:30P						M15 6:30A	M15 11:55A	M15 1:00P
													M15 10:30P	T16 4:00A	T16 5:00A
	SU14 11:30A			SU14 5:30P		M15 12:15A	M15 4:00A		M15 2:00P				T16 3:00A	T16 9:00A	T16 10:00A
	M15 3:30P			M15 10:15P		T16 5:45A	T16 10:30A						T16 8:30P	W17 2:30A	W17 3:30A
							T16 3:00P	T16 8:00P	W17 4:00A	W17 2:30P	W17 6:00P	W17 11:15P	TH18 2:30A		
	T16 11:30A			T16 5:30P		W17 12:30A	W17 6:30A		W17 4:30P			Ar.	TH18 3:45A		
													TH18 2:30P	TH18 9:15P	TH18 10:15P
	TH18 8:30A			TH18 3:00P		TH18 10:00P	F19 2:00A						F19 11:15A	F19 4:45P	F19 5:45P
	F19 6:45A			F19 1:30P		F19 8:30P	S20 1:30A						S20 11:30A	S20 5:30P	S20 6:30P
								Lv. Sitka	S20 7:45A	S20 4:30P	S20 8:00P	SU21 12:45A	SU21 4:00A		
	S20 9:00A			S20 3:00P		S20 10:00P	SU21 2:00A						SU21 11:15A	SU21 5:15P	SU21 6:15P
										Lv. Pelican	SU21 3:30P		SU21 9:45P		
F19 6:30P				SU21 8:15A		SU21 3:15P	SU21 9:30P						M22 7:30A	M22 2:00P	M22 3:00P
	SU21 11:30A			SU21 5:30P		M22 12:30A	M22 4:15A		M22 2:15P				T23 3:15A	T23 8:45A	T23 9:45A
	M22 3:30P			M22 10:15P		T23 5:45A	T23 10:45A						T23 8:15P	W24 2:15A	W24 3:15A
							T23 2:15P	T23 7:15P	W24 3:15A	W24 12:30P	W24 4:00P	W24 8:15P	W24 11:30P		
	T23 11:30A			T23 6:30P		W24 1:30A	W24 5:30A		W24 3:30P			Ar.	TH25 3:45A		
													TH25 9:30A	TH25 4:15P	TH25 5:15P
	TH25 8:30A			TH25 3:00P		TH25 10:00P	F26 2:00A						F26 11:15A	F26 4:45P	F26 5:45P
	F26 6:45A			F26 1:30P		F26 8:30P	S27 1:30A						S27 11:00A	S27 5:00P	S27 6:00P
								Lv. Sitka	S27 7:45P	SU28 2:45A	SU28 6:15A	SU28 11:30A	SU28 2:45P		
	S27 9:00A			S27 3:00P		S27 10:00P	SU28 2:00A						SU28 11:15A	SU28 5:15P	SU28 6:15P
F26 6:30P				SU28 9:30A		SU28 4:30P	SU28 8:30P						M29 7:30A	M29 2:00P	M29 3:00P
	SU28 10:30A			SU28 4:30P		SU28 11:15P	M29 3:00A		M29 1:00P				T30 1:15A	T30 7:15A	T30 8:15A
	M29 3:30P			M29 10:15P		T30 5:45A	T30 10:45A						T30 8:15P	W31 2:15A	W31 3:15A
							T30 2:00P	T30 7:00P	W31 3:00A	W31 1:30P	W31 5:00P	W31 10:15P	TH1 1:30A		
	T30 11:30A			T30 6:30P		W31 1:30A	W31 5:30A		W31 3:30P			Ar.	TH1 3:45A		
													TH1 1:30P	TH1 8:15P	TH1 9:15P

*THE FOLLOWING EVENT MAY AFFECT AVAILABILITY OF SPACE:
AUGUST 10-14 S.E. ALASKA STATE FAIR — HAINES

Stopovers: In-port time on all vessels is only long enough to unload and load. A stopover is getting off at any port between your point of origin and final destination and taking another vessel at a later time. For travelers with vehicles and/or cabins this can be done as long as reservations to do so have been made in advance. For example, travelers with a camper may wish to go from Prince Rupert to Haines but stop over at Petersburg for two days before continuing to Haines. As long as reservations for Prince Rupert to Petersburg and Petersburg to Haines are made before leaving Prince Rupert there will be no problems. But you cannot change your mind once you are loaded and under way. Passenger, vehicle and cabin fares are charged on a point-to-point basis, and stopovers will increase the total ticket cost.

NOTE: Check the schedules carefully. Ferries do *NOT* stop at all ports daily, and northbound and southbound routes vary. You may have to wait three to four days for the next ferry. Also keep in mind that ferries may be late; do not schedule connections too close together.

Vehicles: Reservations are required. Any vehicle that may be driven legally on the highway is acceptable for transport on the four larger vessels. Vessels on the Southeast system can load vehicles up to 70 feet/21m long with special arrangements. Maximum length on the *Tustumena* is 40 feet/12m. Vehicle fares are determined by the overall length and width of the vehicle. Vehicles from 8 to 9 feet wide are charged 125 percent of the fare listed for the vehicle length. Vehicles over 9 feet in width are charged 150 percent of the fare listed for vehicle length.

Motorcycles, motorscooters, bicycles and kayaks are charged.

Hazardous materials may not be transported on the ferries. Bottled gas containers must be turned off. Portable containers of fuel are permitted but must be stored with vessel personnel while en route.

The state assumes no responsibility for the loading and unloading of unattended vehicles. If you ship a vehicle on the ferry you must make your own arrangements for loading and unloading. Unaccompanied vehicles are assessed a surcharge of $30 to or from Bellingham, and $10 to or from Prince Rupert and to or from Stewart/Hyder.

Meals: The cost of meals is not included in passenger, cabin or vehicle fares. Food service varies from vessel to vessel, with dining room or cafeteria-style dining on all ferries.

Columbia   Le Conte   Malaspina   Matanuska   Taku

August 1994 Southbound Schedule

LEAVE SKAGWAY	HAINES	JUNEAU/ AUKE BAY	HOONAH	TENAKEE	ANGOON	ARRIVE SITKA	KAKE	PETERSBURG	WRANGELL	HOLLIS	KETCHIKAN	METLAKATLA	ARRIVE STEWART/ HYDER	ARRIVE PRINCE RUPERT	ARRIVE BELLINGHAM
SU31 8:45P	SU31 11:15P	M1 5:15A						M1 2:00P	M1 6:00P		T2 1:30A			T2 8:30A	
		SU31 3:45P	SU31 9:00P		M1 3:00A	M1 9:00A	M1 9:15P	T2 1:15A							
M1 4:30P	M1 7:30P	T2 1:30A				T2 10:00A		W3 12:45A	W3 5:15A		W3 5:00P				F5 7:30A
T2 1:00P	T2 4:00P	T2 10:30P						W3 7:45A	W3 12:15P		W3 10:30P			TH4 5:30A	
W3 6:15A	W3 8:45A	W3 4:15P						TH4 1:30A	TH4 5:45A		TH4 1:15P			TH4 8:45P	
		TH4 9:15A				TH4 6:00P		F5 10:15A	F5 2:15P		F5 10:30P			S6 5:30A	
TH4 8:30P	TH4 10:30P	F5 2:00P	F5 6:15P	F5 10:15P	S6 1:30A	S6 7:00A									
F5 8:45P	F5 11:15P	S6 5:15A						S6 2:00P	S6 6:00P		SU7 1:30A			SU7 8:30A	
S6 8:00P	S6 10:30P	SU7 5:00A						SU7 2:15P	SU7 6:30P		M8 2:00A			M8 9:30A	
		SU21 7:00A	**Ar. Pelican**	SU21 1:30P											
SU7 8:45P	SU7 11:15P	M8 5:15A						M8 2:00P	M8 6:00P		T9 1:30A			T9 8:30A	
		SU7 11:55P	M8 4:15A		M8 9:15A	M8 2:15P	T9 2:00A	T9 6:00A							
M8 3:30P	M8 6:00P	T9 12:15A				T9 8:45A		W10 12:45A	W10 5:45A		W10 5:00P				F12 7:30A
T9 12:15P	T9 2:45P	T9 8:45P						W10 6:00A	W10 11:00A		W10 10:30P			TH11 5:30A	
W10 5:45A	W10 8:45A	W10 3:15P						TH11 12:30A	TH11 4:45A		TH11 1:15P			TH11 8:45P	
	TH11 5:45A	TH11 10:15A													
		TH11 7:15A				TH11 4:00P		F12 8:00A	F12 1:00P		F12 10:30P			S13 5:30A	
TH11 9:15P	TH11 11:15P	F12 3:30P	F12 8:45P	S13 1:00A	S13 5:15A	S13 11:45A									
F12 9:45P	S13 12:15A	S13 5:45A						S13 2:30P	S13 6:30P		SU14 1:30A			SU14 8:30A	
*S13 11:00P	SU14 1:30A	SU14 8:00A						SU14 5:15P	SU14 9:30P		M15 5:00A			M15 12:30P	
	*SU14 3:00P	SU14 8:45P	M15 2:00A		M15 8:00A	M15 2:00P	T16 2:15A	T16 6:15A							
*SU14 10:45P	M15 12:45A	M15 6:15A						M15 2:45P	M15 6:30P		T16 1:30A			T16 8:30A	
*M15 2:00P	M15 5:00P	M15 9:30P													
T16 7:00A	T16 9:00A	T16 3:00P						W17 12:15A	W17 5:00A	W17 5:00P					F19 7:30A
T16 1:00P	T16 4:00P	T16 10:30P						W17 7:45A	W17 12:45P		W17 10:30P			TH18 5:30A	
W17 6:30A	W17 9:00A	W17 4:15P						TH18 1:30A	TH18 5:45A		TH18 1:15P			TH18 8:45P	
		TH18 8:45A				TH18 5:30P		F19 9:45A	F19 1:45P		F19 10:30P			S20 5:30A	
F19 2:15A	F19 4:15A	F19 1:30P	F19 5:45P	F19 10:00P	S20 1:15A	S20 6:45A									
F19 8:45P	F19 11:15P	S20 5:15A						S20 2:00P	S20 6:00P		SU21 1:30A			SU21 8:30A	
S20 9:30P	SU21 12:30A	SU21 8:00A						SU21 5:15P	SU21 9:30P		M22 5:00A			M22 12:30P	
		SU21 7:00A	**Ar. Pelican**	SU21 1:30P											
SU21 9:15P	SU21 11:15P	M22 5:15A						M22 2:00P	M22 6:00P		T23 1:30A			T23 8:30A	
		SU21 11:55P	M22 4:15A		M22 9:15A	M22 2:15P	T23 2:00A	T23 6:00A							
M22 7:00P	M22 11:00P	T23 6:15A				T23 2:45P		W24 4:30A	W24 9:30A		W24 5:30P				F26 8:00A
T23 12:45P	T23 3:15P	T23 9:30P						W24 6:15A	W24 11:15A		W24 10:30P			TH25 5:30A	
W24 6:15A	W24 8:45A	W24 3:45P						TH25 1:00A	TH25 5:15A		TH25 1:15P			TH25 8:45P	
		TH25 12:30P				TH25 10:15P		F26 11:45A	F26 3:30P		F26 11:00P			S27 6:00A	
TH25 9:15P	TH25 11:15P	F26 4:00P	F26 9:15P	S27 1:30A	S27 5:45A	S27 11:15A									
F26 8:45P	F26 11:15P	S27 4:45A						S27 1:30P	S27 5:30P		SU28 12:30A			SU28 7:30A	
S27 9:00P	S27 11:30P	SU28 6:00A						SU28 3:45P	SU28 8:30P		M29 5:00A			M29 12:30P	
		SU28 7:45P	M29 1:00A		M29 7:00A	M29 1:00P	T30 1:00A	T30 5:00A							
SU28 9:15P	SU28 11:15P	M29 5:15A						M29 2:00P	M29 6:00P		T30 1:30A			T30 8:30A	
M29 7:00P	M29 11:00P	T30 5:30A				T30 2:15P		W31 4:15A	W31 8:15A		W31 5:00P				F2 7:30A
T30 11:15A	T30 2:15P	T30 8:45P						W31 6:15A	W31 11:15A		W31 10:30P			TH1 5:30A	
W31 6:15A	W31 8:15A	W31 3:15P						TH1 12:30A	TH1 4:45A		TH1 1:15P			TH1 8:45P	

ALL TIMES SHOWN ARE LOCAL TIMES

Vehicle deck restrictions: U.S. Coast Guard regulations prohibit passenger access to the vehicle deck while under way, so plan on bringing up items you will need for the voyage soon after boarding the vessel. Passengers can gain access to their vehicle by applying to the purser's desk for an escort. Regulations prohibit sleeping in your vehicle while the vessel is under way.

Pet policy: Dogs and other pets are not allowed in cabins and must be transported on the vehicle deck only — *NO EXCEPTIONS.* Animals and pets are to be transported inside a vehicle or in suitable containers furnished by the passenger. Animals and pets must be cared for by the owner. Passengers who must visit pets or animals en route should apply to the purser's office for an escort to the vehicle deck. (On long sailings the purser periodically announces "cardeck calls.") You may walk your pet at port stops. Keep in mind that some port stops are very brief and that

(Continues on page 567)

Remains of A-J mine stamp mill along Gastineau Channel. (Lee Foster)

September 1994 Northbound Schedule

LEAVE BELLINGHAM	LEAVE PRINCE RUPERT	LEAVE STEWART/ HYDER	METLAKATLA	KETCHIKAN	HOLLIS	WRANGELL	PETERSBURG	KAKE	ARRIVE SITKA	ANGOON	TENAKEE	HOONAH	JUNEAU/ AUKE BAY	HAINES	ARRIVE SKAGWAY
							T30 2:00P	T30 7:00P	W31 3:00A	W31 1:30P	W31 5:00P	W31 10:15P	TH1 1:30A		
	T30 11:30A			T30 6:30P		W31 1:30A	W31 5:30A		W31 3:30P			Ar.	TH1 3:45A		
													TH1 1:30P	TH1 8:15P	TH1 9:15P
	TH1 8:30A			TH1 3:00P		TH1 10:00P	F2 2:00A						F2 11:15A	F2 4:45P	F2 5:45P
		TH1 3:00P		F2 2:00A	F2 4:45A										
				F2 9:30A	F2 12:15P										
				F2 5:30P	F2 8:15P										
	F2 6:45A			F2 1:30P		F2 8:30P	S3 1:30A						S3 11:00A	S3 5:00P	S3 6:00P
			S3 8:15A	S3 10:30A	S3 1:15P			Lv. Sitka	S3 1:00P	S3 9:00P	SU4 12:30A	SU4 4:45A	SU4 8:00A		
	S3 9:00A			S3 3:00P		S3 10:00P	SU4 2:00A						SU4 11:15A	SU4 4:45P	SU4 5:45P
			S3 8:45P	S3 11:00P	SU4 1:45A					**Lv. Pelican**	SU18 5:30P		SU18 11:45P		
F2 6:30P				SU4 11:00A		SU4 7:00P	SU4 11:00P						M5 9:00A	M5 3:00P	M5 4:00P
				SU4 9:00A	SU4 11:45A										
				SU4 5:30P	SU4 8:15P										
	SU4 10:30A			SU4 4:30P		SU4 11:30P	M5 3:15A		M5 1:15P				T6 1:45A	T6 7:45A	T6 8:45A
				M5 9:00A	M5 11:45A										
				M5 5:30P	M5 8:15P										
	M5 3:30P			T6 12:15A		T6 8:15A	T6 1:00P						T6 10:00P	W7 3:30A	W7 4:30A
				T6 9:00A	T6 11:45A										
				T6 5:30P	T6 8:15P		T6 6:15P	W7 12:15A	W7 8:30A	W7 5:30P	W7 9:00P	TH8 1:15A	TH8 4:30A		
	T6 11:30A			T6 5:30P		W7 12:45A	W7 4:30A		W7 2:30P			Ar.	TH8 2:45A		
			W7 8:15A	W7 10:30A	W7 1:15P								TH8 2:30P	TH8 9:15P	TH8 10:15P
			W7 8:45P	W7 11:00P	TH8 1:45A										
	*TH8 7:30A			TH8 1:30P		TH8 8:15P	F9 11:55P						F9 8:45A	F9 2:15P	F9 3:15P
				TH8 5:30P	TH8 8:15P										
				F9 9:00A	F9 11:45A										
				F9 5:30P	F9 8:15P										
	F9 6:45A			F9 2:30P		F9 10:15P	S10 3:15A						S10 12:15P	S10 6:00P	S10 7:00P
			S10 8:15A	S10 10:30A	S10 1:15P			Lv. Sitka	S10 7:00P	SU11 7:00P	SU11 5:30A	SU11 10:45A	SU11 2:00P		
	S10 9:00A			S10 4:00P		S10 11:30P	SU11 3:30A						SU11 12:15P	SU11 5:45P	SU11 6:45P
			S10 8:45P	S10 11:00P	SU11 1:45A										
F9 6:30P				SU11 9:30A		SU11 5:00P	SU11 9:30P						M12 8:30A	M12 3:00P	M12 4:00P
				SU11 9:00A	SU11 11:45A										
				SU11 5:30P	SU11 8:15P										
	SU11 12:30P			SU11 7:30P		M12 2:30A	M12 7:30A		M12 6:30P				T13 7:45A	T13 1:15P	T13 2:15P
				M12 9:00A	M12 11:45A										
				M12 5:30P	M12 8:15P										
	M12 3:30P			M12 10:15P		T13 5:45A	T13 10:45A						T13 8:15P	W14 1:45A	W14 2:45A
				T13 9:00A	T13 11:45A										
				T13 5:30P	T13 8:15P		T13 1:45P	T13 6:45P	W14 2:45A	W14 1:00P	W14 4:30P	W14 9:45P	TH15 1:00A		
	T13 11:30A			T13 8:30P		W14 4:30A	W14 11:15A		W14 9:15P			Ar.	TH15 8:30A		
			W14 8:15A	W14 10:30A	W14 1:15P								TH15 1:00P	TH15 7:45P	TH15 8:45P
			W14 8:45P	W14 11:00P	TH15 1:45A										
	TH15 8:30A			TH15 3:30P		TH15 10:30P	F16 2:30A						F16 11:45A	F16 5:15P	F16 6:15P
				TH15 5:30P	TH15 8:15P										
				F16 9:00A	F16 11:45A										
				F16 5:30P	F16 8:15P										
	F16 6:45A			F16 1:30P		F16 8:30P	S17 1:30A						S17 11:00A	S17 5:00P	S17 6:00P
			S17 8:15A	S17 10:30A	S17 1:15P			Lv. Sitka	S17 12:15P	S17 8:15P	S17 11:45P	SU18 4:00A	SU18 7:15A		
			S17 8:45P	S17 11:00P	SU18 1:45A					**Lv. Pelican**	SU18 5:30P		SU18 11:45P		
F16 6:30P				SU18 11:00A		SU18 7:30P	SU18 11:55P						M19 10:00A	M19 3:30P	M19 4:30P
				SU18 9:00A	SU18 11:45A										
				SU18 5:30P	SU18 8:15P										
	SU18 12:30P			SU18 7:30P		M19 2:30A	M19 8:45A		M19 7:30P				T20 7:45A	T20 1:15P	T20 2:15P
				M19 9:00A	M19 11:45A										
				M19 5:30P	M19 8:15P										
	M19 3:30P			M19 11:15P		T20 7:15A	T20 12:15P						T20 9:15P	W21 2:45A	W21 3:45A
				T20 9:00A	T20 11:45A										
				T20 5:30P	T20 8:15P		T20 6:45P	W21 12:15A	W21 8:15A	W21 5:30P	W21 9:00P	TH22 1:15A	TH22 2:30P	TH22 9:15P	TH22 10:15P
			W21 8:15A	W21 10:30A	W21 1:15P										
			W21 8:45P	W21 11:00P	TH22 1:45A										
	TH22 8:30A			TH22 3:00P		TH22 10:00P	F23 2:00A						F23 11:15A	F23 5:15P	F23 6:15P
				TH22 5:30P	TH22 8:15P										
				F23 9:00A	F23 11:45A										
				F23 5:30P	F23 8:15P										
	F23 6:45A			F23 2:00P		F23 9:15P	S24 2:15A						S24 11:55A	S24 6:00P	S24 7:00P
			S24 8:15A	S24 10:30A	S24 1:15P			Lv. Sitka	S24 6:15P	SU25 1:15A	SU25 4:45A	SU25 10:00A	SU25 1:15P		
			S24 8:45P	S24 11:00P	SU25 1:45A										
F23 6:30P				SU25 9:30A		SU25 5:00P	SU25 9:30P						M26 8:30A	M26 2:30P	M26 3:30P
				SU25 9:00A	SU25 11:45A										
				SU25 5:30P	SU25 8:15P										
	SU25 12:30P			SU25 7:30P		M26 2:45A	M26 7:00A		M26 5:00P				T27 6:30A	T27 11:55A	T27 1:30P
				M26 9:00A	M26 11:45A										
				M26 5:30P	M26 8:15P										
	M26 3:30P			M26 10:15P		T27 5:45A	T27 10:45A						T27 8:15P	W28 2:15A	W28 3:15A
				T27 9:00A	T27 11:45A		T27 11:55A	T27 5:00P	W28 1:00A	W28 11:15A	W28 2:45P	W28 8:00P	TH29 11:15A	TH29 6:00P	TH29 7:00P
				T27 5:30P	T27 8:15P										
			W28 8:15A	W28 10:30A	W28 1:15P										
			W28 8:45P	W28 11:00P	TH29 1:45A										
	TH29 8:30A			TH29 2:30P		TH29 9:30P	F30 1:30A						F30 10:45A	F30 4:45P	F30 5:45P
				TH29 5:30P	TH29 8:15P										
				F30 9:00A	F30 11:45A										
				F30 5:30P	F30 8:15P										

*THE FOLLOWING EVENT MAY AFFECT AVAILABILITY OF SPACE: SEPT. 9-10 KLONDIKE ROAD RELAY — SKAGWAY

September 1994 Southbound Schedule

LEAVE SKAGWAY	HAINES	JUNEAU/ AUKE BAY	HOONAH	TENAKEE	ANGOON	ARRIVE SITKA	KAKE	PETERSBURG	WRANGELL	HOLLIS	KETCHIKAN	METLAKATLA	ARRIVE STEWART/ HYDER	ARRIVE PRINCE RUPERT	ARRIVE BELLINGHAM
W31 6:15A	W31 8:15A	W31 3:15P						TH1 12:30A	TH1 4:45A		TH1 1:15P			TH1 8:45P	
										W31 9:15P	TH1 1:00A		TH1 12:15P		
		TH1 12:45P				TH1 10:30P		F2 11:45A	F2 3:30P		F2 11:00P			S3 6:00A	
F2 1:15A	F2 3:15A	F2 5:00P	F2 10:15P	S3 2:15A	S3 6:30A	S3 11:55A									
F2 8:45P	F2 11:15P	S3 4:45A						S3 1:30P	S3 5:30P		SU4 12:30A			SU4 7:30A	
										F2 5:45A	F2 8:30A				
										F2 1:45P	F2 4:30P				
										F2 9:15P	S3 6:15A	S3 7:30A			
S3 9:00P	S3 11:30P	SU4 7:00A						SU4 4:15P	SU4 8:30P		M5 5:00A			M5 12:30P	
		SU4 9:00A	**Ar. Pelican**	SU4 3:30P						S3 2:15P	S3 6:45P	S3 8:00P			
SU4 8:45P	SU4 11:15P	M5 5:15A						M5 2:00P	M5 6:00P		T6 1:30A			T6 8:30A	
		M5 4:45A	M5 9:30A		M5 2:30P	M5 7:30P	T6 7:00A	T6 11:00A		SU4 5:15A	SU4 8:00A				
M5 7:00P	M5 10:00P	T6 5:15A				T6 1:45P		W7 3:30A	W7 7:45A		W7 5:00P				F9 7:30A
										SU4 1:45P	SU4 4:30P				
										SU4 9:15P	SU4 11:57P				
T6 11:45A	T6 2:15P	T6 8:15P						W7 5:45A	W7 10:45A		W7 10:30P			TH8 5:30A	
										M5 1:45P	M5 4:30P				
										T6 5:15A	T6 8:00A				
W7 7:30A	W7 10:00A	W7 4:15P						TH8 1:30A	TH8 5:45A		TH8 1:15P			TH8 8:45P	
										T6 1:45P	T6 4:30P				
										T6 9:15P	W7 6:15A	W7 7:30A			
		TH8 11:45A				TH8 9:30P		F9 12:15P	F9 4:00P		F9 11:00P			S10 6:00A	
F9 2:15A	F9 4:15A	F9 3:15P	F9 8:30P	S10 12:45A	S10 5:00A	S10 10:30A				W7 2:15P	W7 6:45P	W7 8:00P			
										TH8 6:15A	TH8 9:00A				
F9 9:15P	F9 11:45P	S10 5:45A						S10 2:30P	S10 6:30P		SU11 2:30A			SU11 9:30A	
										F9 5:15A	F9 8:00A				
										F9 1:45P	F9 4:30P				
										F9 9:15P	S10 6:15A	S10 7:30A			
S10 10:00P	SU11 12:30A	SU11 8:00A						SU11 5:15P	SU11 9:30P		M12 5:00A			M12 12:30P	
		SU11 7:15P	M12 12:30A		M12 6:30A	M12 12:30P	T13 12:45A	T13 4:45A		S10 2:15P	S10 6:45P	S10 8:00P			
*SU11 9:45P	SU11 11:45P	M12 5:15A						M12 2:00P	M12 6:00P		T13 1:30A			T13 8:30A	
										SU11 5:15A	SU11 8:00A				
M12 8:00P	M12 11:00P	T13 5:00A				T13 1:45P		W14 6:15A	W14 10:15A		W14 5:45P				F16 8:15A
										SU11 1:45P	SU11 4:30P				
										SU11 9:15P	SU11 11:57P				
T13 5:15P	T13 7:45P	W14 1:45A						W14 10:30A	W14 2:30P		W14 10:30P			TH15 5:30A	
										M12 1:45P	M12 4:30P				
										T13 5:15A	T13 8:00A				
W14 5:45A	W14 8:15A	W14 3:45P						TH15 1:00A	TH15 5:15A		TH15 1:15P			TH15 8:45P	
										T13 1:45P	T13 4:30P				
										T13 9:15P	W14 6:15A	W14 7:30A			
		TH15 1:30P				TH15 10:15P		F16 11:45A	F16 3:30P		F16 11:00P			S17 6:00A	
F16 12:45A	F16 2:45A	F16 5:00P	F16 10:00P	S17 2:00A	S17 5:45A	S17 11:15A				W14 2:15P	W14 6:45P	W14 8:00P			
										TH15 6:15A	TH15 9:00A				
F16 9:15P	F16 11:45P	S17 5:45A						S17 2:30P	S17 6:30P		SU18 2:30A			SU18 9:30A	
										F16 5:15A	F16 8:00A				
										F16 1:45P	F16 4:30P				
										F16 9:15P	S17 6:15A	S17 7:30A			
S17 9:00P	SU18 12:30A	SU18 8:00A						SU18 5:15P	SU18 9:30P		M19 5:00A			M19 12:30P	
		SU18 9:00A	**Ar. Pelican**	SU18 3:30P						S17 2:15P	S17 6:45P	S17 8:00P			
		M19 5:00A	M19 9:15A		M19 2:15P	M19 7:15P	T20 7:00A	T20 11:00A		SU18 5:15A	SU18 8:00A				
M19 8:30P	M19 11:00P	T20 5:15A				T20 1:45P		W21 3:45A	W21 7:45A		W21 5:00P				F23 7:30A
										SU18 1:45P	SU18 4:30P				
										SU18 9:15P	SU18 11:57P				
T20 5:15P	T20 8:15P	W21 2:15A						W21 11:00A	W21 3:00P		W21 10:30P			TH22 5:30A	
										M19 1:45P	M19 4:30P				
										T20 5:15A	T20 8:00A				
W21 6:45A	W21 8:45A	W21 4:15P						TH22 1:30A	TH22 5:45A		TH22 1:15P			TH22 8:45P	
										T20 1:45P	T20 4:30P				
F23 2:15A	F23 4:15A	F23 2:00P	F23 7:15P	F23 11:30P	S24 3:45A	S24 10:00A				T20 9:15P	W21 6:15A	W21 7:30A			
										W21 2:15P	W21 6:45P	W21 8:00P			
										TH22 6:15A	TH22 9:00A				
F23 9:15P	F23 11:45P	S24 5:45A						S24 2:30P	S24 7:00P		SU25 2:30A			SU25 9:30A	
										F23 5:15A	F23 8:00A				
										F23 1:45P	F23 4:30P				
										F23 9:15P	S24 6:15A	S24 7:30A			
S24 10:00P	SU25 12:30A	SU25 8:00A						SU25 5:15P	SU25 9:30P		M26 5:00A			M26 12:30P	
		SU25 6:30P	SU25 11:45P		M26 5:45A	M26 11:00A	M26 11:00P	T27 3:00A		S24 2:15P	S24 6:45P	S24 8:00P			
										SU25 5:15A	SU25 8:00A				
M26 6:30P	M26 9:15P	T27 3:15A				T27 11:45A		W28 1:30A	W28 6:00A		W28 5:00P				F30 7:30A
										SU25 1:45P	SU25 4:30P				
										SU25 9:15P	SU25 11:57P				
T27 4:30P	T27 7:00P	W28 1:00A						W28 9:45A	W28 2:15P		W28 10:30P			TH29 5:30A	
										M26 1:45P	M26 4:30P				
										T27 5:15A	T27 8:00A				
W28 6:15A	W28 8:45A	W28 4:15P						TH29 1:30A	TH29 5:45A		TH29 1:15P			TH29 8:45P	
TH29 11:00P	F30 1:00A	F30 5:45A								T27 1:45P	T27 4:30P				
										T27 9:15P	W28 6:15A	W28 7:30A			
										W28 2:15P	W28 6:45P	W28 8:00P			
										TH29 6:15A	TH29 9:00A				
										F30 5:15A	F30 8:00A				
										F30 1:45P	F30 4:30P				
										F30 9:15P	F30 11:57P				

Southeast Alaska Passenger and Vehicle Tariffs

Effective May 1, 1994–September 30, 1994

ADULT 12 YEARS OR OVER (Meals and Berth NOT included) — ITEM ADT

BETWEEN AND	BELLINGHAM	PRINCE RUPERT	STEWART/HYDER	KETCHIKAN	METLAKATLA	HOLLIS	WRANGELL	PETERSBURG	KAKE	SITKA	ANGOON	HOONAH	JUNEAU	HAINES	SKAGWAY	PELICAN
KETCHIKAN	164	38	40													
METLAKATLA	168	42	44	14												
HOLLIS	178	52	54	20	22											
WRANGELL	180	56	58	24	28	24										
PETERSBURG	192	68	70	38	42	38	18									
KAKE	202	80	82	48	52	48	34	22								
SITKA	208	86	88	54	58	54	38	26	24							
ANGOON	222	100	102	68	72	68	52	40	28	22						
HOONAH	226	104	106	74	78	74	56	44	38	24	20					
JUNEAU	226	104	106	74	78	74	56	44	44	26	24	20				
HAINES	240	118	120	88	92	88	70	58	58	40	38	34	20			
SKAGWAY	246	124	126	92	96	92	76	64	64	44	42	40	26	14		
PELICAN	248	126	128	96	100	96	78	66	52	40	38	22	32	46	54	
TENAKEE	226	104	106	74	78	74	56	44	32	22	16	16	22	34	40	32

CHILD 6 THRU 11 YEARS (Under 6 Transported Free) — ITEM CHD

BETWEEN AND	BELLINGHAM	PRINCE RUPERT	STEWART/HYDER	KETCHIKAN	METLAKATLA	HOLLIS	WRANGELL	PETERSBURG	KAKE	SITKA	ANGOON	HOONAH	JUNEAU	HAINES	SKAGWAY	PELICAN
KETCHIKAN	82	18	20													
METLAKATLA	84	20	22	8												
HOLLIS	88	26	28	12	14											
WRANGELL	90	24	30	12	14	12										
PETERSBURG	96	34	36	20	22	20	10									
KAKE	102	40	42	24	26	24	18	12								
SITKA	104	42	44	26	28	26	20	14	12							
ANGOON	110	50	52	34	36	34	26	20	14	12						
HOONAH	114	52	54	38	40	38	28	22	20	12	10					
JUNEAU	114	52	54	38	40	38	28	22	22	12	12	10				
HAINES	120	60	62	44	46	44	36	30	30	20	20	18	10			
SKAGWAY	124	62	64	46	48	46	38	32	32	22	22	20	14	8		
PELICAN	126	64	66	48	50	48	40	34	26	20	20	12	16	24	28	
TENAKEE	114	52	54	38	40	38	28	22	16	12	8	8	12	18	20	16

ALTERNATE MEANS OF CONVEYANCE (Bicycles, Small Boats and Inflatables) — ITEM AMC

BETWEEN AND	BELLINGHAM	PRINCE RUPERT	STEWART/HYDER	KETCHIKAN	METLAKATLA	HOLLIS	WRANGELL	PETERSBURG	KAKE	SITKA	ANGOON	HOONAH	JUNEAU	HAINES	SKAGWAY	PELICAN
KETCHIKAN	28	10	11													
METLAKATLA	29	11	12	7												
HOLLIS	30	12	13	8	9											
WRANGELL	31	13	14	9	10	9										
PETERSBURG	32	14	15	11	12	11	8									
KAKE	34	16	17	12	13	12	10	8								
SITKA	35	17	18	13	14	13	11	9	8							
ANGOON	37	19	20	15	16	15	13	11	9	7						
HOONAH	38	20	21	16	17	16	14	12	11	8	8					
JUNEAU	38	20	21	16	17	16	14	12	12	9	9	8				
HAINES	39	22	23	18	19	18	16	14	14	11	10	10	8			
SKAGWAY	40	23	24	19	20	19	17	15	15	12	11	11	9	7		
PELICAN	41	23	24	19	20	19	17	15	13	11	10	8	10	12	13	
TENAKEE	38	20	21	16	17	16	14	12	10	8	7	7	9	10	11	10

TWO WHEELED MOTORCYCLES (Without Trailers - Driver NOT included) — ITEM 705

BETWEEN AND	BELLINGHAM	PRINCE RUPERT	STEWART/HYDER	KETCHIKAN	METLAKATLA	HOLLIS	WRANGELL	PETERSBURG	KAKE	SITKA	ANGOON	HOONAH	JUNEAU	HAINES	SKAGWAY	PELICAN
KETCHIKAN	116	24	27													
METLAKATLA	122	28	30	7												
HOLLIS	127	35	38	14	15											
WRANGELL	130	39	41	17	20	17										
PETERSBURG	139	47	50	26	29	26	12									
KAKE	147	57	59	35	38	35	23	15								
SITKA	151	61	63	39	42	39	26	17	16							
ANGOON	162	71	73	49	52	49	37	28	19	14						
HOONAH	166	75	77	53	56	53	40	31	26	16	13					
JUNEAU	166	75	77	53	56	53	40	31	31	17	16	13				
HAINES	177	85	87	63	66	63	50	41	41	27	26	23	13			
SKAGWAY	181	90	91	67	70	67	54	46	46	31	30	27	17	7		
PELICAN	183	92	93	69	72	69	56	46	36	28	26	15	23	33	38	
TENAKEE	166	75	77	53	56	53	40	31	22	15	11	11	15	24	28	23

VEHICLES UP TO 10 FEET (Driver NOT Included) — ITEM 710

BETWEEN AND	BELLINGHAM	PRINCE RUPERT	STEWART/HYDER	KETCHIKAN	METLAKATLA	HOLLIS	WRANGELL	PETERSBURG	KAKE	SITKA	ANGOON	HOONAH	JUNEAU	HAINES	SKAGWAY	PELICAN
KETCHIKAN	174	36	40													
METLAKATLA	178	42	45	11												
HOLLIS	190	53	57	21	23											
WRANGELL	194	58	61	25	30	25										
PETERSBURG	207	71	75	39	43	39	18									
KAKE	220	84	88	52	57	52	34	22								
SITKA	227	91	94	58	63	58	39	26	24							
ANGOON	242	106	109	73	78	73	55	42	29	21						
HOONAH	248	112	115	79	84	79	60	47	39	24	20					
JUNEAU	248	112	115	79	84	79	60	47	47	26	24	19				
HAINES	264	128	130	94	99	94	75	61	61	41	39	34	20			
SKAGWAY	270	134	136	100	105	100	81	68	68	47	45	41	26	11		
PELICAN	273	137	139	103	107	103	83	69	54	42	39	23	34	50	57	
TENAKEE	248	112	115	79	84	79	60	47	33	22	16	16	22	36	42	34

VEHICLES UP TO 15 FEET (Driver NOT Included) — ITEM 715

BETWEEN AND	BELLINGHAM	PRINCE RUPERT	STEWART/HYDER	KETCHIKAN	METLAKATLA	HOLLIS	WRANGELL	PETERSBURG	KAKE	SITKA	ANGOON	HOONAH	JUNEAU	HAINES	SKAGWAY
KETCHIKAN	374	75	83												
METLAKATLA	372	84	95	21											
HOLLIS	394	107	119	41	46										
WRANGELL	405	117	129	51	61	51									
PETERSBURG	433	145	158	80	90	80	35								
KAKE	460	174	187	109	119	109	70	44							
SITKA	473	187	200	122	132	122	80	52	49						
ANGOON	505	220	233	155	164	155	116	86	60	41					
HOONAH	534	240	246	168	177	168	126	98	82	49	39				
JUNEAU	534	240	246	168	177	168	126	98	98	52	47	38			
HAINES	568	273	278	200	210	200	158	129	129	85	80	71	39		
SKAGWAY	581	286	291	213	224	213	172	143	143	99	94	85	53	21	
PELICAN	570	285	298	220	228	220	176	147	114	86	80	47	70	104	119

VEHICLES UP TO 19 FEET (Driver NOT Included) — ITEM 719

BETWEEN AND	BELLINGHAM	PRINCE RUPERT	STEWART/HYDER	KETCHIKAN	METLAKATLA	HOLLIS	WRANGELL	PETERSBURG	KAKE	SITKA	ANGOON	HOONAH	JUNEAU	HAINES	SKAGWAY
KETCHIKAN	445	90	99												
METLAKATLA	443	100	113	25											
HOLLIS	470	128	141	49	55										
WRANGELL	482	139	153	61	73	61									
PETERSBURG	515	172	188	95	107	95	42								
KAKE	548	207	223	130	141	130	83	52							
SITKA	563	223	238	145	157	145	96	63	58						
ANGOON	602	261	277	184	196	184	138	103	71	49					
HOONAH	636	285	292	200	211	200	150	117	97	58	47				
JUNEAU	636	285	292	200	211	200	150	117	117	62	56	45			
HAINES	676	325	331	238	250	238	188	154	154	101	95	84	46		
SKAGWAY	692	341	347	254	267	254	205	171	171	117	112	101	63	25	
PELICAN	679	339	354	261	271	261	210	175	136	103	95	56	83	124	141

VEHICLES UP TO 21 FEET (Driver NOT Included) — ITEM 721

BETWEEN AND	BELLINGHAM	PRINCE RUPERT	STEWART/HYDER	KETCHIKAN	METLAKATLA	HOLLIS	WRANGELL	PETERSBURG	KAKE	SITKA	ANGOON	HOONAH	JUNEAU	HAINES	SKAGWAY
KETCHIKAN	557	112	127												
METLAKATLA	572	129	145	31											
HOLLIS	606	164	182	62	70										
WRANGELL	622	179	197	78	93	78									
PETERSBURG	665	222	242	122	137	122	53								
KAKE	707	267	287	167	182	167	107	67							
SITKA	727	287	307	187	202	187	123	80	74						
ANGOON	777	337	357	237	252	237	177	132	91	63					
HOONAH	821	368	377	257	272	257	193	150	125	74	60				
JUNEAU	821	368	377	257	272	257	193	150	150	79	72	57			
HAINES	872	419	427	307	322	307	242	198	198	130	122	108	59		
SKAGWAY	893	440	447	327	344	327	264	220	220	151	144	130	81	31	
PELICAN	877	437	457	337	350	337	270	225	175	132	122	71	107	159	182

VEHICLES UP TO 23 FEET (Driver NOT Included) — ITEM 723

BETWEEN AND	BELLINGHAM	PRINCE RUPERT	STEWART/HYDER	KETCHIKAN	METLAKATLA	HOLLIS	WRANGELL	PETERSBURG	KAKE	SITKA	ANGOON	HOONAH	JUNEAU	HAINES	SKAGWAY
KETCHIKAN	646	130	147												
METLAKATLA	663	150	168	36											
HOLLIS	703	190	211	72	81										
WRANGELL	721	208	228	90	108	90									
PETERSBURG	771	257	281	141	159	141	61								
KAKE	820	310	333	194	211	194	124	78							
SITKA	843	333	356	217	234	217	143	93	86						
ANGOON	901	391	414	275	292	275	205	153	105	73					
HOONAH	952	426	437	298	315	298	224	174	145	86	69				
JUNEAU	952	426	437	298	315	298	224	174	174	92	83	66			
HAINES	1011	486	495	356	373	356	281	230	230	151	141	125	68		
SKAGWAY	1036	510	518	379	399	379	306	255	255	175	167	151	94	36	
PELICAN	1017	507	530	391	406	391	313	261	203	153	141	82	124	184	211

*VEHICLES UP TO 25 FEET (Driver NOT Included) — ITEM 725

BETWEEN AND	BELLINGHAM	PRINCE RUPERT	STEWART/HYDER	KETCHIKAN	METLAKATLA	HOLLIS	WRANGELL	PETERSBURG	KAKE	SITKA	ANGOON	HOONAH	JUNEAU	HAINES	SKAGWAY
KETCHIKAN	768	154	175												
METLAKATLA	789	177	199	42											
HOLLIS	836	226	251	85	96										
WRANGELL	858	246	271	107	128	107									
PETERSBURG	917	306	333	168	188	168	72								
KAKE	975	368	395	230	251	207	147	92							
SITKA	1003	395	423	257	278	257	169	110	101						
ANGOON	1072	464	492	326	347	326	244	182	125	86					
HOONAH	1132	507	520	354	375	354	266	206	172	101	82				
JUNEAU	1132	507	520	354	375	354	266	206	206	108	99	78			
HAINES	1203	578	589	423	444	423	333	273	273	179	168	148	81		
SKAGWAY	1232	607	616	451	474	451	364	303	303	208	198	179	111	42	
PELICAN	1210	602	630	464	482	464	372	310	241	182	168	97	147	219	251

* For information on fares for vehicles longer than 25' please contact any Marine Highway office.

Southeast Alaska Cabin Tariffs

Effective May 1, 1994–September 30, 1994

FOUR BERTH CABIN/SITTINGROOM - OUTSIDE/COMPLETE FACILITIES ITEM 4BS
M/V COLUMBIA - M/V MALASPINA

BETWEEN AND	BELLINGHAM	PRINCE RUPERT	KETCHIKAN	WRANGELL	PETERSBURG	SITKA	JUNEAU	HAINES
KETCHIKAN	247	63						
WRANGELL	273	89	58					
PETERSBURG	289	103	71	47				
SITKA	319	128	91	71	60			
JUNEAU	337	145	107	91	78	54		
HAINES	356	164	129	108	97	74	51	
SKAGWAY	356	164	129	108	97	74	51	39

FOUR BERTH CABIN - OUTSIDE/COMPLETE FACILITIES ITEM 4BF
M/V COLUMBIA - M/V MALASPINA - M/V MATANUSKA - M/V TAKU

BETWEEN AND	BELLINGHAM	PRINCE RUPERT	KETCHIKAN	WRANGELL	PETERSBURG	SITKA	JUNEAU	HAINES
KETCHIKAN	225	58						
WRANGELL	249	80	53					
PETERSBURG	263	92	65	41				
SITKA	290	114	84	64	55			
JUNEAU	306	128	100	80	69	48		
HAINES	329	152	121	100	90	67	45	
SKAGWAY	329	152	121	100	90	67	45	35

FOUR BERTH CABIN - INSIDE/COMPLETE FACILITIES ITEM 4BI
M/V COLUMBIA - M/V MALASPINA - M/V MATANUSKA - M/V TAKU

BETWEEN AND	BELLINGHAM	PRINCE RUPERT	KETCHIKAN	WRANGELL	PETERSBURG	SITKA	JUNEAU	HAINES
KETCHIKAN	191	50						
WRANGELL	212	69	48					
PETERSBURG	227	80	57	39				
SITKA	250	100	75	56	48			
JUNEAU	265	112	88	69	60	42		
HAINES	283	131	106	88	79	59	39	
SKAGWAY	283	131	106	88	79	59	39	31

THREE BERTH CABIN - OUTSIDE/COMPLETE FACILITIES ITEM 3BF
M/V COLUMBIA - M/V MATANUSKA

BETWEEN AND	BELLINGHAM	PRINCE RUPERT	KETCHIKAN	WRANGELL	PETERSBURG	SITKA	JUNEAU	HAINES
KETCHIKAN	184	45						
WRANGELL	202	63	44					
PETERSBURG	211	72	52	35				
SITKA	231	90	67	52	45			
JUNEAU	246	102	77	62	55	40		
HAINES	267	119	91	74	67	53	37	
SKAGWAY	267	119	91	74	67	53	37	30

TWO BERTH - OUTSIDE/COMPLETE FACILITIES ITEM 2BF
M/V COLUMBIA - M/V MALASPINA - M/V MATANUSKA - M/V TAKU

BETWEEN AND	BELLINGHAM	PRINCE RUPERT	KETCHIKAN	WRANGELL	PETERSBURG	SITKA	JUNEAU	HAINES
KETCHIKAN	161	43						
WRANGELL	175	58	37					
PETERSBURG	185	67	46	33				
SITKA	206	84	61	47	40			
JUNEAU	221	97	72	58	50	37		
HAINES	239	113	84	69	62	48	34	
SKAGWAY	239	113	84	69	62	48	34	27

TWO BERTH CABIN - INSIDE/COMPLETE FACILITIES ITEM 2BI
M/V COLUMBIA - M/V MALASPINA - M/V MATANUSKA - M/V TAKU

BETWEEN AND	BELLINGHAM	PRINCE RUPERT	KETCHIKAN	WRANGELL	PETERSBURG	SITKA	JUNEAU	HAINES
KETCHIKAN	142	38						
WRANGELL	158	53	34					
PETERSBURG	164	60	41	29				
SITKA	181	74	53	41	35			
JUNEAU	192	83	63	51	44	33		
HAINES	206	98	76	63	57	44	31	
SKAGWAY	206	98	76	63	57	44	31	25

All tariffs and rates quoted are in U.S. dollars

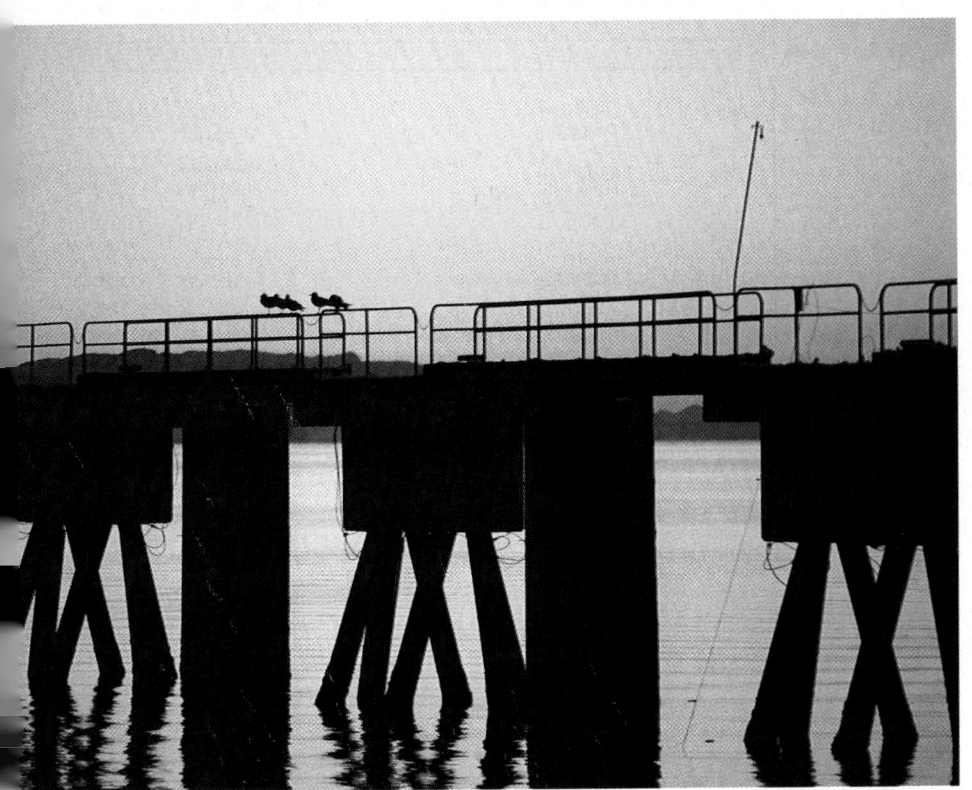

Sunset silhouettes Cordova ferry dock. *(Ruth Fairall)*

sailing time between some ports will be as long as 36 hours (Bellingham to Ketchikan).

Dogs, cats, or larger animals are assessed a charge of $10 to or from Bellingham and $5 to or from Prince Rupert and to or from Stewart/Hyder. This surcharge applies even if the animal is traveling inside the owner's vehicle.

Deck passage: Because access to the vehicle deck is not permitted and because of the limited number of cabins available, many people ride the ferries overnight without cabin accommodations. This is done by sleeping in one of the reclining lounge chairs or rolling out your sleeping bag in an empty corner or even out on deck. Public washrooms are available.

Crossing the U.S.–Canada border: If any part of your trip is to, from or through Canada, you must report to customs at the port of entry. No passport is required for citizens of either country, but you will be required to furnish proof of citizenship, financial responsibility, and vehicle registration, ownership and liability coverage. Special restrictions govern firearms and animals. See Customs Requirements in the GENERAL INFORMATION section.

Information aboard state ferries: There are U.S. Forest Service interpreters on duty in summer aboard most vessels. They provide information about points of interest, lectures, audiovisual presentations and answer questions concerning the area.

(Continues on page 571)

SOUTHCENTRAL/SOUTHWEST FERRY SYSTEM

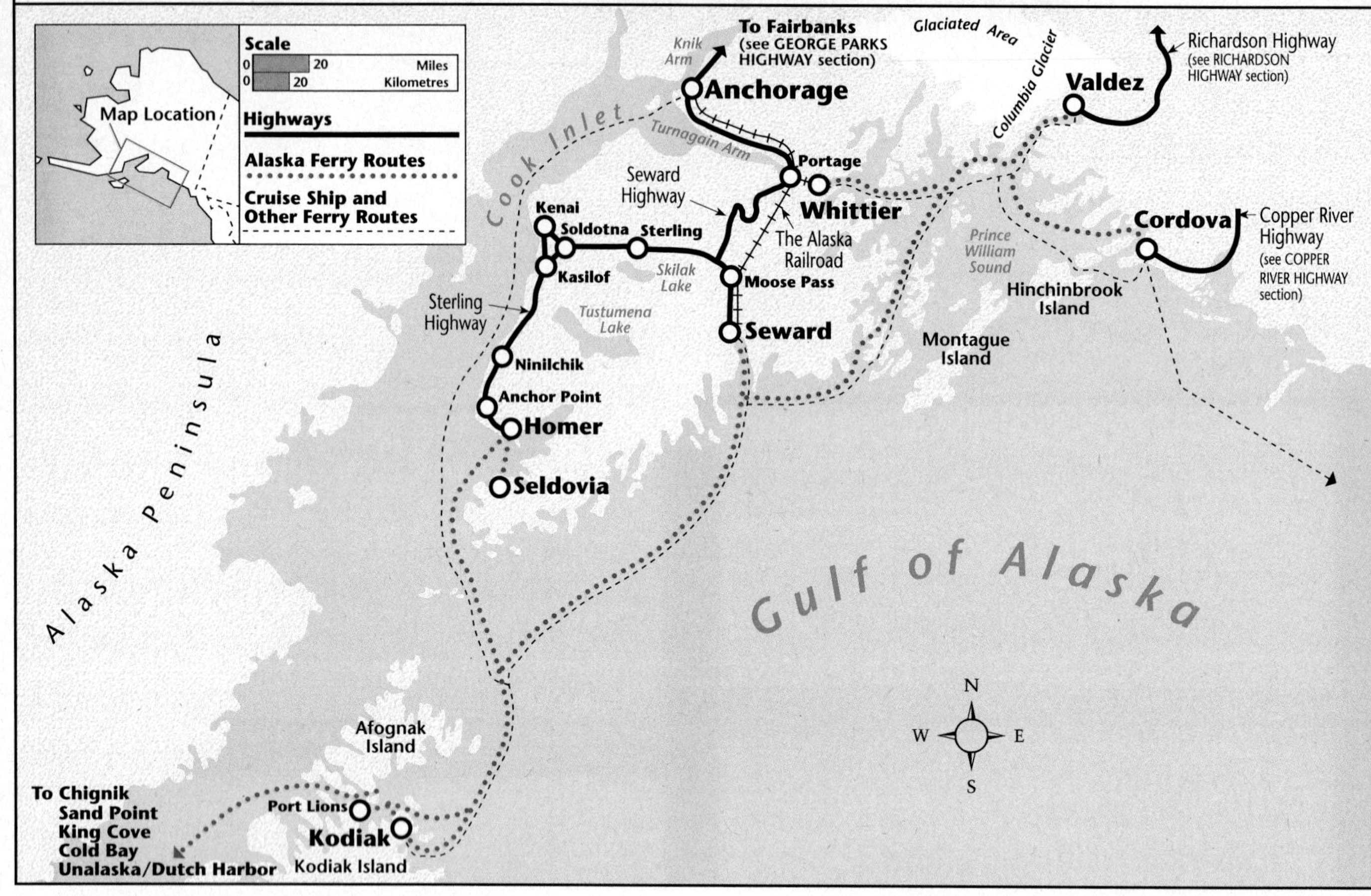

M/V BARTLETT–ALASKA RAILROAD Schedule

Effective May 1, 1994, through September 23, 1994

The M/V *BARTLETT* serves the port of Whittier using the Alaska Railroad shuttle between Portage and Whittier. In Portage, passengers and their vehicles load on an Alaska Railroad flatcar for a 40-minute sight-filled trip through mountain tunnels to Whittier, a former military town. Ferry service from Whittier is available to Cordova and Valdez.

PORTAGE TO WHITTIER*
Alaska Railroad Service

LV	PORTAGE	7:25 A.M.
AR	WHITTIER	8:05 A.M.
LV	PORTAGE	10:15 A.M.
AR	WHITTIER	10:55 A.M.
LV	PORTAGE	1:20 P.M.
AR	WHITTIER	2:00 P.M.

WHITTIER TO PORTAGE
Alaska Railroad Service

LV	WHITTIER	3:30 P.M.
AR	PORTAGE	4:10 P.M.
LV	WHITTIER	6:15 P.M.
AR	PORTAGE	2:00 P.M.

*Check-in time in Portage is one hour earlier than departure.

PORTAGE TO WHITTIER ALASKA RAILROAD SHUTTLE
PRICES (One-Way)

Adult Vehicle Occupants Other than Driver	13.00
Child 6-11 (under 6 free)	6.50
Motorcycles and Kayaks	19.00
Vehicles to 23 feet	56.00
Vehicles to 40 feet	75.00

Southwest System Schedule–M/V BARTLETT

Effective May 1, 1994 through September 23, 1994

MAY 1 SUN	LV VALDEZ	7:15AM		AR CORDOVA	1:00PM
MON	LV CORDOVA	6:30AM	FRI	LV CORDOVA	7:00AM
	AR WHITTIER	1:30PM		AR WHITTIER	2:00PM
MON	LV WHITTIER	2:45PM	FRI	LV WHITTIER	2:45PM
	AR CORDOVA	9:45PM		AR CORDOVA	9:45PM
TUE	LV CORDOVA	12:30AM	SAT	LV CORDOVA	12:30AM***
	AR VALDEZ	6:15AM		AR VALDEZ	6:15AM
	LV VALDEZ	7:15AM		LV VALDEZ	7:15AM
	AR WHITTIER	2:00PM		AR WHITTIER	2:00PM
TUE	LV WHITTIER	2:45PM	SAT	LV WHITTIER	2:45PM
	AR VALDEZ	9:30PM		AR VALDEZ	9:30PM
WED	LV VALDEZ	6:45AM	SUN	LV VALDEZ	7:15AM
	AR CORDOVA	12:30PM		AR WHITTIER	2:00PM
WED	LV CORDOVA	6:30PM	SUN	LV WHITTIER	2:45PM
	AR VALDEZ	11:55PM		AR VALDEZ	9:30PM
				LV VALDEZ	10:45PM
THU	LV VALDEZ	7:15AM	MON	AR CORDOVA	4:30AM
	AR WHITTIER	2:00PM			
THU	LV WHITTIER	2:45PM			
	AR VALDEZ	9:30PM			
FRI	LV VALDEZ	12:15AM			
FRI	AR CORDOVA	6:00AM			

***PRINCE WILLIAM SOUND ROYAL FLUSH REGATTA MAY 14, 1994

SAT	LV CORDOVA	12:30AM ***
	AR WHITTIER	7:30AM
SAT	LV WHITTIER	9:00AM
	AR VALDEZ	6:00PM

Effective September 24-30, 1994

SAT SEP 24	LV CORDOVA	1:00PM	WED SEP 28	LV VALDEZ	8:45AM
	AR VALDEZ	6:45PM		AR CORDOVA	2:30PM
SUN SEP 25	LV VALDEZ	8:45AM	THU SEP 29	LV CORDOVA	8:45AM
	AR CORDOVA	2:30PM		AR VALDEZ	2:30PM
TUE SEP 27	LV CORDOVA	8:45AM	FRI SEP 30	LV VALDEZ	8:45PM
	AR VALDEZ	2:30PM		AR CORDOVA	2:30PM

Southcentral/Southwest Passenger and Vehicle Tariffs — Effective May 1, 1994–September 30, 1994

PASSENGER 12 YEARS AND OVER (Meals and Berths NOT included) ITEM ADT

BETWEEN AND	UNALASKA	AKUTAN	FALSE PASS	COLD BAY	KING COVE	SAND POINT	CHIGNIK	KODIAK	PORT LIONS	SELDOVIA	HOMER	SEWARD	WHITTIER	VALDEZ
AKUTAN	16													
FALSE PASS	46	34												
COLD BAY	62	50	18											
KING COVE	74	66	34	18										
SAND POINT	98	90	58	42	32									
CHIGNIK	132	124	92	76	66	42								
KODIAK	202	194	162	146	136	112	76							
PORT LIONS	202	194	162	146	136	112	76	20						
SELDOVIA	246	240	208	192	180	156	122	52	52					
HOMER	242	236	204	188	176	152	118	48	48	18				
SEWARD	250	242	210	194	184	160	124	54	54	100	96			
WHITTIER	316	308	276	260	250	226	190	120	120	166	162			
VALDEZ	292	286	254	238	226	202	168	98	98	142	138	58	58	
CORDOVA	292	286	254	238	226	202	168	98	98	142	138	58	58	30

CHILDREN 6 THROUGH 11 YEARS OLD (Under 6 Transported Free) ITEM CHD

BETWEEN AND	UNALASKA	AKUTAN	FALSE PASS	COLD BAY	KING COVE	SAND POINT	CHIGNIK	KODIAK	PORT LIONS	SELDOVIA	HOMER	SEWARD	WHITTIER	VALDEZ
AKUTAN	8													
FALSE PASS	24	18												
COLD BAY	32	26	10											
KING COVE	38	34	18	10										
SAND POINT	50	46	30	22	16									
CHIGNIK	66	62	46	38	34	22								
KODIAK	102	98	82	74	68	56	38							
PORT LIONS	102	98	82	74	68	56	38	10						
SELDOVIA	124	120	104	96	90	78	62	26	26					
HOMER	122	118	102	94	88	76	60	24	24	10				
SEWARD	126	122	106	98	92	80	62	28	28	50	48			
WHITTIER	158	154	138	130	126	114	96	60	60	84	82			
VALDEZ	146	144	128	120	114	102	84	50	50	70	70	30	30	
CORDOVA	146	144	128	120	114	102	84	50	50	70	70	30	30	16

ALTERNATE MEANS OF CONVEYANCE (Bicycles-Small Boats-Inflatables) ITEM AMC

BETWEEN AND	UNALASKA	AKUTAN	FALSE PASS	COLD BAY	KING COVE	SAND POINT	CHIGNIK	KODIAK	PORT LIONS	SELDOVIA	HOMER	SEWARD	WHITTIER	VALDEZ
AKUTAN	6													
FALSE PASS	10	8												
COLD BAY	12	10	8											
KING COVE	14	12	10	6										
SAND POINT	18	16	12	9	8									
CHIGNIK	23	18	14	15	13	9								
KODIAK	33	23	18	25	23	20	15							
PORT LIONS	33	23	23	25	23	20	15	6						
SELDOVIA	40	33	23	32	30	26	21	11	11					
HOMER	39	40	33	31	29	26	21	10	10	5				
SEWARD	40	39	40	32	30	27	22	11	11	18	17			
WHITTIER	50	44	42	42	40	37	31	21	21	28	27			
VALDEZ	47	54	52	38	37	33	28	18	18	24	24	10	8	
CORDOVA	47	54	52	38	37	33	28	18	18	24	24	10	8	8

TWO-WHEELED MOTORCYCLES (Without trailers - Driver NOT included) ITEM 705

BETWEEN AND	UNALASKA	AKUTAN	FALSE PASS	COLD BAY	KING COVE	SAND POINT	CHIGNIK	KODIAK	PORT LIONS	SELDOVIA	HOMER	SEWARD	WHITTIER	VALDEZ
FALSE PASS	33	N												
COLD BAY	45	O	12											
KING COVE	53		24	12										
SAND POINT	171	V	42	30	22									
CHIGNIK	197	E	68	56	48	30								
KODIAK	149	H	121	109	100	182	56							
PORT LIONS	149	I	121	109	100	182	56	13						
SELDOVIA	183	C	153	141	133	115	89	37	37					
HOMER	180	L	151	139	131	113	86	34	34	10				
SEWARD	185	E	155	143	135	117	91	39	39	73	70			
WHITTIER	230	S	202	190	182	164	139	87	87	121	117			
VALDEZ	214		185	173	165	147	121	71	71	105	103	35	25	
CORDOVA	214		185	173	165	147	121	71	71	105	103	35	25	21

VEHICLES UP TO 10 FEET (Driver NOT included) ITEM 710

BETWEEN AND	UNALASKA	AKUTAN	FALSE PASS	COLD BAY	KING COVE	SAND POINT	CHIGNIK	KODIAK	PORT LIONS	SELDOVIA	HOMER	SEWARD	WHITTIER	VALDEZ
FALSE PASS	49	N												
COLD BAY	67	O	18											
KING COVE	79		36	18										
SAND POINT	106	V	63	45	33									
CHIGNIK	145	E	102	84	72	45								
KODIAK	223	H	180	162	150	123	84							
PORT LIONS	223	I	180	162	150	123	84	20						
SELDOVIA	273	C	229	211	199	172	133	55	55					
HOMER	268	L	225	207	195	168	129	51	51	15				
SEWARD	276	E	232	214	202	175	136	58	58	109	105			
WHITTIER	349	S	306	288	276	249	210	132	132	183	178			
VALDEZ	324		280	262	250	223	184	106	106	157	153	54	39	
CORDOVA	324		280	262	250	223	184	106	106	157	153	54	39	31

VEHICLES UP TO 15 FEET (Driver NOT included) ITEM 715

BETWEEN AND	UNALASKA	AKUTAN	FALSE PASS	COLD BAY	KING COVE	SAND POINT	CHIGNIK	KODIAK	PORT LIONS	SELDOVIA	HOMER	SEWARD	WHITTIER	VALDEZ
FALSE PASS	104	N												
COLD BAY	142	O	38											
KING COVE	168		72	34										
SAND POINT	226	V	131	93	67									
CHIGNIK	311	E	215	177	151	93								
KODIAK	480	H	384	346	320	262	177							
PORT LIONS	480	I	384	346	320	262	177	39						
SELDOVIA	587	C	492	454	428	369	285	116	116					
HOMER	577	L	482	444	418	359	275	106	106	29				
SEWARD	593	E	498	460	434	376	291	122	122	233	223			
WHITTIER	753	S	657	619	593	535	450	281	281	392	382			
VALDEZ	697		602	564	538	480	395	226	226	337	327	112	72	
CORDOVA	697		602	564	538	480	395	226	226	337	327	112	72	64

VEHICLES UP TO 19 FEET (Driver NOT included) ITEM 719

BETWEEN AND	UNALASKA	AKUTAN	FALSE PASS	COLD BAY	KING COVE	SAND POINT	CHIGNIK	KODIAK	PORT LIONS	SELDOVIA	HOMER	SEWARD	WHITTIER	VALDEZ
FALSE PASS	123	N												
COLD BAY	169	O	46											
KING COVE	200		87	41										
SAND POINT	269	V	156	110	80									
CHIGNIK	370	E	257	211	180	110								
KODIAK	571	H	458	412	381	312	211							
PORT LIONS	571	I	458	412	381	312	211	46						
SELDOVIA	699	C	586	540	509	439	339	138	138					
HOMER	687	L	574	528	497	428	327	126	126	35				
SEWARD	706	E	594	548	517	447	347	145	145	277	265			
WHITTIER	896	S	783	737	706	637	536	335	335	467	455			
VALDEZ	830		718	672	641	571	470	269	269	401	389	134	85	
CORDOVA	830		718	672	641	571	470	269	269	401	389	134	85	76

VEHICLES UP TO 21 FEET (Driver NOT included) ITEM 721

BETWEEN AND	UNALASKA	AKUTAN	FALSE PASS	COLD BAY	KING COVE	SAND POINT	CHIGNIK	KODIAK	PORT LIONS	SELDOVIA	HOMER	SEWARD	WHITTIER	VALDEZ
FALSE PASS	158	N												
COLD BAY	217	O	59											
KING COVE	257		111	52										
SAND POINT	347	V	201	142	102									
CHIGNIK	477	E	331	272	232	142								
KODIAK	737	H	591	532	492	402	272							
PORT LIONS	737	I	591	532	492	402	272	59						
SELDOVIA	902	C	756	697	657	567	437	177	177					
HOMER	887	L	741	682	642	552	422	162	162	44				
SEWARD	912	E	766	707	667	577	447	187	187	357	342			
WHITTIER	1157	S	1011	952	912	822	692	432	432	602	587			
VALDEZ	1072		926	867	827	737	607	347	347	517	502	172	110	
CORDOVA	1072		926	867	827	737	607	347	347	517	502	172	110	97

VEHICLES UP TO 23 FEET (Driver NOT included) ITEM 723

BETWEEN AND	UNALASKA	AKUTAN	FALSE PASS	COLD BAY	KING COVE	SAND POINT	CHIGNIK	KODIAK	PORT LIONS	SELDOVIA	HOMER	SEWARD	WHITTIER	VALDEZ
FALSE PASS	184	N												
COLD BAY	252	O	68											
KING COVE	298		128	60										
SAND POINT	402	V	233	165	118									
CHIGNIK	553	E	383	315	269	165								
KODIAK	855	H	685	617	571	466	315							
PORT LIONS	855	I	685	617	571	466	315	68						
SELDOVIA	1046	C	876	808	762	658	507	205	205					
HOMER	1029	L	859	791	745	640	489	188	188	51				
SEWARD	1058	E	888	820	774	669	518	217	217	414	397			
WHITTIER	1342	S	1172	1104	1058	953	803	501	501	698	681			
VALDEZ	1243		1074	1006	959	855	704	402	402	600	582	200	128	
CORDOVA	1243		1074	1006	959	855	704	402	402	600	582	200	128	112

*VEHICLES UP TO 25 FEET (Driver NOT included) ITEM 725

BETWEEN AND	UNALASKA	AKUTAN	FALSE PASS	COLD BAY	KING COVE	SAND POINT	CHIGNIK	KODIAK	PORT LIONS	SELDOVIA	HOMER	SEWARD	WHITTIER	VALDEZ
FALSE PASS	218	N												
COLD BAY	299	O	81											
KING COVE	354		152	71										
SAND POINT	478	V	276	195	140									
CHIGNIK	658	E	456	375	320	195								
KODIAK	1016	H	815	734	678	554	375							
PORT LIONS	1016	I	815	734	678	554	375	81						
SELDOVIA	1244	C	1042	961	906	782	602	244	244					
HOMER	1223	L	1022	941	885	761	582	223	223	60				
SEWARD	1258	E	1056	975	920	796	616	257	257	492	471			
WHITTIER	1596	S	1394	1313	1258	1134	954	596	596	830	809			
VALDEZ	1479		1277	1196	1141	1016	837	478	478	713	692	237	151	
CORDOVA	1479		1277	1196	1141	1016	837	478	478	713	692	237	151	133

* For information on fares for vehicles longer than 25' please contact any Marine HIghway office.

Southcentral/Southwest System Schedule

M/V TUSTUMENA SCHEDULE

Effective May 1, 1994 through September 30, 1994

MAY EASTBOUND

Leave SELDOVIA	Leave HOMER	PORT LIONS	Arrive KODIAK	Leave SEWARD	Arrive VALDEZ
M2 5:30P	M2 8:30P	T3 7:30A	T3 10:00A		
	W4 2:00A		W4 11:55A		
	*** FROM ALEUTIAN CHAIN TRIP ***		M9 7:30P		
T10 6:00P	T10 10:00P	W11 9:00A	Lv.W11 5:00P	TH12 11:45A	TH12 11:45P
SU15 5:00A	SU15 8:00A		SU15 6:00P		
	M16 9:30A		M16 7:30P		
T17 6:00P	T17 10:00P	W18 9:00A	Lv.W18 5:00P	TH19 11:45A	TH19 11:45P
SU22 5:00A	SU22 8:00A		SU22 6:00P		
	M23 9:30A		M23 7:30P		
	*T24 10:00P		Lv.W25 5:00P	TH26 11:45A	TH26 11:45P
SU29 5:00A	SU29 8:00A		SU29 6:00P		
	M30 12:30P		M30 10:30P		

* The following event may affect availability of space: Kodiak King Crab Festival May 24-31

MAY WESTBOUND

Leave VALDEZ	Leave SEWARD	Leave KODIAK	PORT LIONS	Leave HOMER	Arrive SELDOVIA
	SU1 8:00A	M2 12:30A	M2 3:00A	M2 2:30P	M2 4:00P
		T3 12:30P		Ar. T3 10:30P	
		W4 5:00P	***TO ALEUTIAN CHAIN TRIP***		
		T10 12:30A		T10 12:30P	T10 2:00P
F13 7:00A	F13 9:00P	S14 11:30A	S14 2:30P	SU15 2:30A	SU15 4:00A
		SU15 10:00P		Ar. M16 8:00A	
		T17 12:30A		T17 12:30P	T17 2:00P
F20 7:00A	F20 9:00P	S21 11:30A	S21 2:30P	SU22 2:30A	SU22 4:00A
		SU22 10:00P		Ar. M23 8:00A	
		T24 12:30A		Ar. T24 10:30A	
F27 7:00A	F27 9:00P	S28 11:30A	S28 2:30P	SU29 2:30A	SU29 4:00A
		SU29 10:00P		Ar. M30 8:00A	
		*T31 6:30A		Ar. T31 4:30P	

JUNE EASTBOUND

Leave SELDOVIA	Leave HOMER	PORT LIONS	Arrive KODIAK	Leave SEWARD	Arrive VALDEZ
	W1 2:00A		W1 11:55A		
*** FROM ALEUTIAN CHAIN TRIP ***			M6 7:30P		
T7 6:00P	T7 10:00P	W8 9:00A	Lv.W8 5:00P	TH9 11:45A	TH9 11:45P
SU12 5:00A	SU12 8:00A		SU12 6:00P		
	M13 9:30A		M13 7:30P		
T14 6:00P	W15 2:00A		W15 11:55A		
*** FROM ALEUTIAN CHAIN TRIP ***			M20 7:30P		
T21 6:00P	T21 10:00P	W22 9:00A	Lv.W22 5:00P	TH23 11:45A	TH23 11:45P
SU26 5:00A	SU26 8:00A		SU26 6:00P		
	M27 9:30A		M27 7:30P		
T28 6:00P	T28 10:00P	W29 9:00A	Lv.W29 5:00P	TH30 11:45A	TH30 11:45P

JUNE WESTBOUND

Leave VALDEZ	Leave SEWARD	Leave KODIAK	PORT LIONS	Leave HOMER	Arrive SELDOVIA
		W1 5:00P	*** TO ALEUTIAN CHAIN TRIP ***		
		T7 12:30A		T7 12:30P	T7 2:00P
F10 7:00A	F10 9:00P	S11 11:30A	S11 2:30P	SU12 2:30A	SU12 4:00A
		SU12 10:00P		Ar. M13 8:00A	
		T14 12:30A		T14 12:30P	T14 2:00P
		W15 5:00P	*** TO ALEUTIAN CHAIN TRIP ***		
		T21 12:30A		T21 12:30P	T21 2:00P
F24 7:00A	F24 9:00P	S25 11:30A	S25 2:30P	SU26 2:30A	SU26 4:00A
		SU26 10:00P		Ar. M27 8:00A	
		T28 12:30A		T28 12:30P	T28 2:00P

JULY EASTBOUND

Leave SELDOVIA	Leave HOMER	PORT LIONS	Arrive KODIAK	Leave SEWARD	Arrive VALDEZ
SU3 5:00A	SU3 8:00A		SU3 6:00P		
	M4 9:30A		M4 7:30P		
T5 6:00P	T5 10:00P	W6 9:00A	Lv.W6 5:00P	TH7 11:45A	TH7 11:45P
SU10 5:00A	SU10 8:00A		SU10 6:00P		
	M11 9:30A		M11 7:30P		
T12 6:00P	W13 2:00A		W13 11:55A		
*** FROM ALEUTIAN CHAIN TRIP ***			M18 7:30P		
T19 6:00P	T19 10:00P	W20 9:00A	Lv.W20 5:00P	TH21 11:45A	TH21 11:45P
SU24 5:00A	SU24 8:00A		SU24 6:00P		
	M25 9:30A		M25 7:30P		
T26 6:00P	T26 10:00P	W27 9:00A	Lv.W27 5:00P	TH28 11:45A	TH28 11:45P
SU31 5:00A	SU31 8:00A		SU31 6:00P		

JULY WESTBOUND

Leave VALDEZ	Leave SEWARD	Leave KODIAK	PORT LIONS	Leave HOMER	Arrive SELDOVIA
F1 7:00A	F1 9:00P	S2 11:30A	S2 2:30P	SU3 2:30A	SU3 4:00A
		SU3 10:00P		Ar. M4 8:00A	
		T5 12:30A		T5 12:30P	T5 2:00P
F8 7:00A	F8 9:00P	S9 11:30A	S9 2:30P	SU10 2:30A	SU10 4:00A
		SU10 10:00P		Ar. M11 8:00A	
		T12 12:30A		T12 12:30P	T12 2:00P
		W13 5:00P	*** TO ALEUTIAN CHAIN TRIP ***		
		T19 12:30A		T19 12:30P	T19 2:00P
F22 7:00A	F22 9:00P	S23 11:30A	S23 2:30P	SU24 2:30A	SU24 4:00A
		SU24 10:00P		Ar. M25 8:00A	
		T26 12:30A		T26 12:30P	T26 2:00P
F29 7:00A	F29 9:00P	S30 11:30A	S30 2:30P	SU31 2:30A	SU31 4:00A
		SU31 10:00P		Ar. M1 8:00A	

AUGUST EASTBOUND

Leave SELDOVIA	Leave HOMER	PORT LIONS	Arrive KODIAK	Leave SEWARD	Arrive VALDEZ
	M1 9:30A		M1 7:30P		
T2 6:00P	T2 10:00P	W3 9:00A	Lv. W3 5:00P	TH4 11:45A	TH4 11:45P
SU7 5:00A	SU7 8:00A		SU7 6:00P		
	M8 9:30A		M8 7:30P		
T9 6:00P	T9 10:00P	W10 9:00A	Lv. W10 5:00P	TH11 11:45A	TH11 11:45P
SU14 5:00A	SU14 8:00A		SU14 6:00P		
	M15 9:30A		M15 7:30P		
T16 6:00P	W17 2:00A		W17 11:55A		
*** FROM ALEUTIAN CHAIN TRIP ***			M22 7:30P		
T23 6:00P	T23 10:00P	W24 9:00A	Lv. W24 5:00P	TH25 11:45A	TH25 11:45P
SU28 5:00A	SU28 8:00A		SU28 6:00P		
	M29 9:30A		M29 7:30P		
T30 6:00P	T30 10:00P	W31 9:00A	Lv. W31 5:00P	TH1 11:45A	TH1 11:45P

AUGUST WESTBOUND

Leave VALDEZ	Leave SEWARD	Leave KODIAK	PORT LIONS	Leave HOMER	Arrive SELDOVIA
		T2 12:30A		T2 12:30P	T2 2:00P
F5 7:00A	F5 9:00P	S6 11:30A	S6 2:30P	SU7 2:30A	SU7 4:00A
		SU7 10:00P		Ar. M8 8:00A	
		T9 12:30A		T9 12:30P	T9 2:00P
F12 7:00A	F12 9:00P	S13 11:30A	S13 2:30P	SU14 2:30A	SU14 4:00A
		SU14 10:00P		Ar. M15 8:00A	
		T16 12:30A		T16 12:30P	T16 2:00P
		W17 5:00P	*** TO ALEUTIAN CHAIN TRIP ***		
		T23 12:30A		T23 12:30P	T23 2:00P
F26 7:00A	F26 9:00P	S27 11:30A	S27 2:30P	SU28 2:30A	SU28 4:00A
		SU28 10:00P		Ar. M29 8:00A	
		T30 12:30A		T30 12:30P	T30 2:00P

SEPTEMBER EASTBOUND

Leave SELDOVIA	Leave HOMER	PORT LIONS	Arrive KODIAK	Leave SEWARD	Arrive VALDEZ
SU4 5:00A	SU4 8:00A		SU4 6:00P		
	M5 9:30A		M5 7:30P		
T6 6:00P	T6 10:00P	W7 9:00A	Lv. W7 5:00P	TH8 11:45A	TH8 11:45P
SU11 5:00A	SU11 8:00A		SU11 6:00P		
	M12 9:30A		M12 7:30P		
T13 6:00P	W14 2:00A		W14 11:55A		
*** FROM ALEUTIAN CHAIN TRIP ***			M19 7:30P		
T20 6:00P	T20 10:00P	W21 9:00A	Lv. W21 5:00P	TH22 11:45A	TH22 11:45P
SU25 5:00A	SU25 8:00A		SU25 6:00P		
	M26 9:30A		M26 7:30P		
T27 6:00P	W28 2:00A		W28 11:55A		

SEPTEMBER WESTBOUND

Leave VALDEZ	Leave SEWARD	Leave KODIAK	PORT LIONS	Leave HOMER	Arrive SELDOVIA
F2 7:00A	F2 9:00P	S3 11:30A	S3 2:30P	SU4 2:30A	SU4 4:00A
		SU4 10:00P		Ar. M5 8:00A	
		T6 12:30A		T6 12:30P	T6 2:00P
F9 7:00A	F9 9:00P	S10 11:30A	S10 2:30P	SU11 2:30A	SU11 4:00A
		SU11 10:00P		Ar. M12 8:00A	
		T13 12:30A		T13 12:30P	T13 2:00P
		W14 5:00P	***TO ALEUTIAN CHAIN TRIP***		
		T20 12:30A		T20 12:30P	T20 2:00P
F23 7:00A	F23 9:00P	S24 11:30A	S24 2:30P	SU25 2:30A	SU25 4:00A
		SU25 10:00P		Ar. M26 8:00A	
		T27 12:30A		T27 12:30P	T27 2:00P
		W28 5:00P	*** TO ALEUTIAN CHAIN TRIP ***		

M/V TUSTUMENA ALEUTIAN CHAIN TRIPS

TUE	LV	SELDOVIA	6:00PM
WED	LV	HOMER	2:00AM
	LV	KODIAK	8:00PM
THU	LV	CHIGNIK	4:00PM
FRI	LV	SAND POINT	2:30AM
	LV	KING COVE	10:30AM
	LV	COLD BAY	1:30PM
	LV	FALSE PASS	7:00PM
SAT	LV	AKUTAN	6:00AM
	AR	UNALASKA	10:00AM
SAT	LV	UNALASKA	1:00PM
SUN	LV	COLD BAY	4:00AM
	LV	KING COVE	6:30AM
	LV	SAND POINT	2:15PM
MON	LV	CHIGNIK	1:00AM
TUE	LV	KODIAK	12:30AM
	LV	HOMER	12:30PM
	AR	SELDOVIA	2:00PM

M/V TUSTUMENA–Cabin Rates

Effective May 1, 1994–September 30, 1994

FOUR BERTH CABIN - OUTSIDE/COMPLETE FACILITIES — ITEM 4BF

BETWEEN / AND	UNALASKA	AKUTAN	FALSE PASS	COLD BAY	KING COVE	SAND POINT	CHIGNIK	KODIAK	PORT LIONS	SELDOVIA	HOMER	SEWARD	VALDEZ
AKUTAN	23												
FALSE PASS	80	57											
COLD BAY	109	86	29										
KING COVE	122	129	72	43									
SAND POINT	152	165	108	79	68								
CHIGNIK	194	210	153	124	113	80							
KODIAK	282	295	238	209	194	166	124						
PORT LIONS	282	295	238	209	194	166	124	43					
SELDOVIA	337	350	293	264	250	216	182	96	96				
HOMER	328	342	285	256	242	209	175	88	88	43			
SEWARD	349	362	305	276	262	228	194	98	98	163	155		
VALDEZ			(NO DIRECT SAILINGS)					164	164	216	209	91	
CORDOVA			(NO DIRECT SAILINGS)					164	164	216	209	91	59

FOUR BERTH CABIN - INSIDE/NO FACILITIES — ITEM 4NO

BETWEEN / AND	UNALASKA	AKUTAN	FALSE PASS	COLD BAY	KING COVE	SAND POINT	CHIGNIK	KODIAK	PORT LIONS	SELDOVIA	HOMER	SEWARD	VALDEZ
AKUTAN	19												
FALSE PASS	66	47											
COLD BAY	91	72	25										
KING COVE	102	108	61	36									
SAND POINT	127	138	91	66	57								
CHIGNIK	162	175	128	103	94	67							
KODIAK	235	246	199	174	162	138	103						
PORT LIONS	235	246	199	174	162	138	103	36					
SELDOVIA	281	292	245	220	208	180	152	80	80				
HOMER	274	285	238	213	202	174	146	73	73	36			
SEWARD	291	302	255	230	218	190	162	82	82	136	129		
VALDEZ			(NO DIRECT SAILINGS)					137	137	180	174	76	
CORDOVA			(NO DIRECT SAILINGS)					137	137	180	174	76	49

TWO BERTH CABIN - OUTSIDE/NO FACILITIES — ITEM 2NO

BETWEEN / AND	UNALASKA	AKUTAN	FALSE PASS	COLD BAY	KING COVE	SAND POINT	CHIGNIK	KODIAK	PORT LIONS	SELDOVIA	HOMER	SEWARD	VALDEZ
AKUTAN	13												
FALSE PASS	47	33											
COLD BAY	64	51	17										
KING COVE	75	79	45	28									
SAND POINT	100	97	63	46	40								
CHIGNIK	129	129	95	78	68	43							
KODIAK	179	192	158	141	130	110	76						
PORT LIONS	179	192	158	141	130	110	76	28					
SELDOVIA	213	226	192	175	164	140	115	56	56				
HOMER	208	221	187	170	159	136	111	52	52	28			
SEWARD	218	230	196	179	168	144	119	60	60	101	96		
VALDEZ			(NO DIRECT SAILINGS)					103	103	144	140	54	
CORDOVA			(NO DIRECT SAILINGS)					103	103	144	140	54	38

Cruise Ships

From May through September, large luxury cruise ships and small explorer-class ships carry visitors to Alaska via the Inside Passage. There are more than 30 ships to choose from and almost as many itineraries. There's also a bewildering array of travel options. Both round-trip and one-way cruises are available, or a cruise may be sold as part of a packaged tour that includes air, rail and/or motorcoach transportation. Various shore excursions may be included in the cruise price or offered to passengers for added cost. Ports of call may depend on length of cruise, which ship you choose, time of sailing or debarkation point. Because of the wide variety of cruise trips available, it is wise to work with your travel agent.

Following is a list of cruise ships serving Alaska in the 1994 season. See your travel agent for more details.

Alaska Sightseeing/Cruise West, Suite 700, 4th & Battery Bldg., Seattle, WA 98121; phone 1-800-426-7702 or (206) 441-8687, fax (206) 441-4757. *Spirit of Glacier Bay* (58 passengers); three days from Juneau cruising up Glacier Bay's East and West arms. *Sheltered Seas* (90 passengers); five- or six-day daylight cruises between Ketchikan and Juneau. Ports of call: Petersburg, LeConte Glacier, Frederick Sound and Tracy Arm with overnights in Ketchikan, Petersburg and Juneau. *Spirit of Alaska* (82 passengers), *Spirit of Discovery* (84 passengers) and *Spirit of '98* (101 passengers); offer seven-night one-way cruises between Seattle and Juneau. Ports of call: Ketchikan, Petersburg, Sitka, Glacier Bay.

Clipper Cruise Lines, 7711 Bonhomme Ave., St. Louis, MO 63105-1965; phone 1-800-325-0010 or (314) 727-2929, fax (314) 727-6576. Marketing the *World Discoverer* and the *Yorktown Clipper* (138 passengers). 14-night cruises (May 28 and Sept. 3) between Seattle and Juneau. Ports of call: San Juan Islands/Friday Harbor, Victoria, Hartley Bay, Prince Rupert/Ketchikan, Misty Fiords/Rudyerd Bay, Wrangell/The Brothers, Baranof Island, Sitka, Glacier Bay National Park, Haines/Skagway, Tracy Arm (Sawyer Glaciers). 11-night cruise (May 16) from Seattle to Vancouver. Ports of call: Saltspring Island/Belle Chain Islets, Hartley Bay, Misty Fiords National Monument, Tracy Arm (Sawyer Glacier), Taylor Bay, The Brothers. Queen Charlotte Islands, King Island, Telegraph Cove. 12-night cruise (May 27) between Vancouver and Ketchikan. Ports of call: Victoria, Hartley Bay, Queen Charlotte Islands, Misty Fiords/Rudyerd Bay, Wrangell, Sitka, Taylor Bay, Tracy Arm (Sawyer Glaciers). Seven-night cruises (June, July, August). Ports of call: Juneau, Tracy Arm (Sawyer Glaciers)/The Brothers, Baranof Island, Sitka, Glacier Bay National Park, Haines/Skagway. 10-night cruises (June and August) between Prince Rupert and Homer. Ports of call: Misty Fiords National Monument, Wrangell, Tracy Arm (Sawyer Glaciers), Taylor Bay, Hubbard Glacier, Icy Bay, Prince William Sound, Seward/Chiswell Islands, Katmai National Park. 12-night cruises between Homer and Nome (July 8 and Aug. 9). Ports of call: Katmai Peninsula, Semidi Islands, Shumagin Islands, Dutch Harbor/Aleutian Islands, Pribilof Islands, St. Matthew Island, St. Lawrence Island, Provideniya/Novoye Chaplino, Russian Far East,

Cruise ships at Ketchikan, first port of call in Alaska. (John W. Warden)

Arakamchechen Archipelago. 10-night cruises in July from Nome with calls at King Island/Little Diomede, St. Lawrence Island, Provideniya/Novoye Chaplino, Russian Far East, Arakamchechen Archipelago, Bering Strait/Inchoun, Arctic Circle, Chukchi Sea, Uelen.

Cunard Line Ltd., 555 5th Ave., New York, NY 10017-2453; phone 1-800-5-CUNARD or (212) 880-7500. *Sagafjord* (589 passengers); 10- and 11-day cruises between Vancouver, BC, and Anchorage. Ports of call: Ketchikan, Endicott Arm, Juneau, Skagway, Glacier Bay (northbound only), Sitka, Yakutat Bay/Hubbard Glacier, Valdez, Columbia Glacier/Harvard Glacier/College Fjords, Seward, Kenai Fjords, Homer. 14-day round-trip from San Francisco. Ports of call: Vancouver, Ketchikan, Glacier Bay, Juneau, Skagway, Hubbard Glacier, Sitka, Victoria. 14-day cruise from San Francisco to Vancouver. Ports of call: Victoria, Sitka, College Fjord/Harvard Glacier/ Columbia Glacier, Valdez, Yakutat Bay, Glacier Bay, Juneau, Skagway, Ketchikan. 14-day cruise from Vancouver to Los Angeles. Ports of call: Sitka, Valdez, Hubbard Glacier, Glacier Bay, Skagway, Juneau, Ketchikan, Victoria. *Cunard Crown Dynasty* (800 passengers); seven-day cruises between Seward and Vancouver. Ports of call: Hubbard Glacier, Sitka (northbound), Juneau, Wrangell and Skagway (southbound), Tracy Arm (northbound), Ketchikan, Misty Fiords (southbound). Nine-day cruise from Los Angeles to Vancouver. Ports of call: San Francisco, Victoria, Misty Fiords, Ketchikan. 12-day cruise from Vancouver to Los Angeles. Ports of call: Ketchikan, Tracy Arm, Skagway, Juneau, Misty Fiords, Victoria, San Francisco.

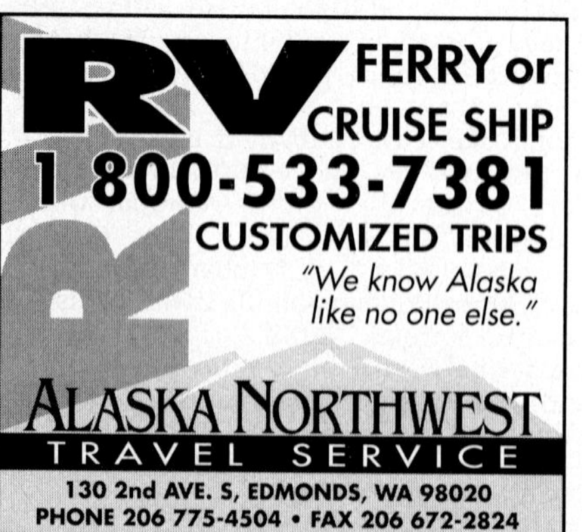

Glacier Bay Tours & Cruises, 520 Pike St., Suite 1610, Seattle, WA 98101; phone 1-800-451-5952 or (206) 623-2417, fax (206) 623-7809. *Executive Explorer* (49 passengers); seven-day cruises between Ketchikan and Juneau. Ports of call: Misty Fiords, Sitka, Baranof Island, Tracy Arm, Point Adolphus, Glacier Bay, Haines, Skagway. Also three-day cruises into Glacier Bay's East and West arms. *Spirit of Adventure* (225 passengers); one-day, fly/cruise up the West Arm of Glacier Bay from Juneau, Skagway and Haines. *Wilderness Explorer* (36 passengers); two-person cabins only, two-night cruises in Glacier Bay and three-night cruises to Admiralty Island, Tracy Arm, Point Adolphus and Inian Islands. Kayaking and canoeing are available on these wilderness cruises.

Holland America Line, 300 Elliott Ave. W., Seattle, WA 98119; phone (206) 281-3535. 96 cruise departures for 1994. Brand new MS *Maasdam* (1,266 passengers), MS *Westerdam* (1,494 passengers) and flagship SS *Rotterdam* (1,075 passengers) sail on seven-day round-trip cruises from Vancouver, BC; depending on availability some three-day northbound and four-day southbound one-way cruises may be offered. Ports of call: Ketchikan, Juneau, Glacier Bay National Park, Sitka. Sister ships MS *Nieuw Amsterdam* and MS *Noordam* (1,214 passengers) sail on seven-day one-way cruises between Vancouver and Seward. Ports of call: Ketchikan, Juneau, Sitka and Valdez, with visits to Hubbard Glacier, Columbia Glacier and College Fjord. Special children's rates available for all cruise departures. Also offered, 49 different cruisetours ranging in length from six to 23 days, including two special "Northern Exposure" escorted cruisetours. Selected cruise departures feature special themes, including photography, square dancing, personal finance, big band and country western music. All departures in May feature the Mayfest celebration.

Norwegian Cruise Line, 95 Merrick Way, Coral Gables, FL 33134; phone 1-800-327-7030 or (407) 445-0866. *Windward* (1,246 passengers); seven-day round-trip from Vancouver cruises Glacier Bay with ports of call at Ketchikan, Sitka and Juneau. Seven-day "Gold Rush" round-trip from Vancouver cruises Tracy Arm and Misty Fiords with ports of call at Skagway, Haines, Juneau and Ketchikan.

Princess Cruises, 10100 Santa Monica Blvd., Los Angeles, CA 90067; phone (310) 553-1770. *Regal Princess* and *Crown Princess* (1,590 passengers); seven-day sailings between Seward/Anchorage and Vancouver, BC. Ports of call: College Fjord, Glacier Bay, Skagway, Juneau and Ketchikan. *Sky Princess* (1,200 passengers); seven-day trips also cruise from Seward/Anchorage to Vancouver. Ports of call: Sitka, Yakutat Bay, College Fjord, Ketchikan and Juneau. *Star Princess* (1,490 passengers) and *Golden Princess* (830 passengers); seven-day round-trip from Vancouver. Ports of call: Juneau, Skagway and Ketchikan, plus Glacier Bay on most sailings, with a few cruising instead to Tracy Arm. *Fair Princess* (890 passengers); 10-day round-trip from San Francisco. Ports of call: Victoria, Vancouver, Juneau, Sitka and Ketchikan.

Regency Cruises, 260 Madison Ave., New York, NY 10016; phone (212) 972-4774. *Regent Sea* (729 passengers) and *Regent Star* (950 passengers); seven days between Vancouver, BC, and Anchorage (Seward). Ports of call: Ketchikan, Juneau, Skagway, Sitka and Endicott or Tracy Arm (northbound), Valdez and Hubbard (southbound), Columbia Glacier/College Fjord. May and September southbound cruises feature Glacier Bay.

Royal Caribbean Cruise Line, 1050 Caribbean Way, Miami, FL 33132. *Nordic Prince* (1,012 passengers); seven-night round-trip from Vancouver, BC. Ports of call: Tracy Arm, Skagway, Haines, Juneau, Ketchikan, Misty Fiords. *Sun Viking* (714 passengers); 10-night round-trip from Vancouver, BC. Ports of call: Victoria, Sitka, Hubbard Glacier, Skagway, Haines, Juneau, Tracy Arm, Ketchikan and Wrangell.

Royal Cruise Line, 1 Maritime Plaza, San Francisco, CA 94111; phone (415) 956-7200, fax (415) 956-1656. New *Star Odyssey* (750 passengers); seven-day cruises between Vancouver and Anchorage (Seward). Ports of call: Ketchikan, Juneau, Tracy Arm, Skagway, Hubbard Glacier, Columbia Glacier, Glacier Bay, Prince William Sound. On May 25, seven-day cruise from San Francisco to Vancouver. Ports of call: Victoria and Ketchikan. On Aug. 24, 10-day cruise between Vancouver and San Francisco. Ports of call: Ketchikan, Juneau, Tracy Arm, Glacier Bay, Skagway, Sitka and Victoria.

Special Expeditions, 720 5th Ave., New York, NY 10019; phone 1-800-762-0003 or (212) 765-7740. *Sea Bird* and *Sea Lion* (70 passengers); 10-day wilderness cruises between Ketchikan and Sitka. Ports of call: Glacier Bay, Misty Fiords, LeConte Glacier, Tracy Arm, Haines, Point Adolphus, Elfin Cove.

World Explorer Cruises, 555 Montgomery St., San Francisco, CA 94111-2544; phone 1-800-854-3835, fax (415) 391-1145. SS *Universe* (550 passengers); 14-day round-trip from Vancouver, BC. Ports of call: Wrangell, Juneau, Skagway, Haines, Glacier Bay, Hubbard Glacier/Yakutat Bay, Seward, Sitka, Ketchikan, Victoria.

SOUTHEASTERN ALASKA

(See map, page 551)

Ketchikan

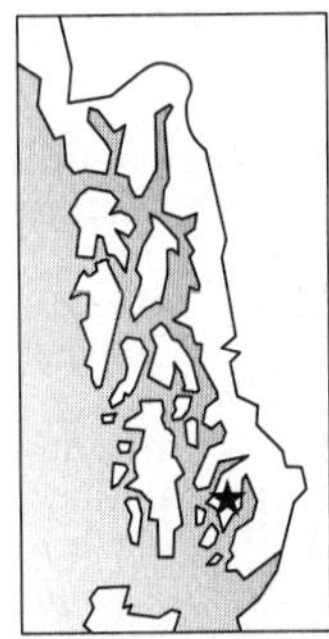

Located on Revillagigedo Island in southeastern Alaska, 235 miles/378 km south of Juneau, AK, 90 miles/145 km north of Prince Rupert, BC, and 600 miles/966 km north of Seattle, WA. **Population:** Ketchikan Gateway Borough and city, 13,828. **Emergency Services: Alaska State Troopers,** phone 225-5118. **City Police,** phone 225-6631, or 911 for all emergency services. **Fire Department,** phone 225-9616. **Ambulance,** phone 225-9616. **Hospital,** Ketchikan General at 3100 Tongass Ave., phone 225-5171. **Ketchikan Volunteer Rescue Squad,** phone 225-9616. **Maritime Search and Rescue,** call the Coast Guard at 225-5666.

Visitor Information: Ketchikan Visitors Bureau office is located on the downtown dock, open during daily business hours and weekends May through September. Write them at 131M Front St., Ketchikan 99901; or phone 225-6166 or 1-800-770-2200; fax (907) 225-4250. U.S. Forest Service office for Misty Fiords National Monument and Ketchikan Ranger District is located at 3031 Tongass Ave.; open 8 A.M. to 5 P.M. weekdays; phone 225-2148. Ketchikan Area Supervisor's office and visitor information center is located at the Federal Building; open 8 A.M. to 4:30 P.M., seven days a week, mid-May through mid-September, and weekdays the rest of the year; phone (907) 225-3101.

Elevation: Sea level. **Climate:** Rainy. Yearly average rainfall is 162 inches and snowfall is 32 inches. Average daily maximum temperature in July 65°F/18°C; daily minimum 51°F/11°C. Daily maximum in January 39°F/4°C; daily minimum 29°F/-2°C. **Radio:** KTKN 930, KRBD-FM 105.9, KGTW-FM 106.7. **Television:** CFTK (Prince Rupert, BC) and 27 cable channels. **Newspapers:** *Ketchikan Daily News* (daily); *Southeastern Log* (monthly); *New Alaskan* (monthly).

Private Aircraft: Ketchikan International Airport on Gravina Island; elev. 88 feet/27m; length 7,500 feet/2,286m; asphalt; fuel 100LL, A. Ketchikan Harbor seaplane base downtown; fuel 80, 100, A.

Ketchikan is located on the southwest side of Revillagigedo (ruh-vee-uh-guh-GAY-doh) Island, on Tongass Narrows opposite Gravina Island. The name Ketchikan is derived from a Tlingit name, Kitschk-Hin, meaning the creek of the "thundering wings of an eagle." The creek flows through the town, emptying into Tongass Narrows. Before Ketchikan was settled, the area at the mouth of Ketchikan Creek was a Tlingit Indian fish camp. Settlement began with interest in both mining and fishing. The first salmon cannery moved here in 1886, operating under the name of Tongass Packing Co. It burned down in August 1889. Gold was discovered nearby in 1898. This, plus residual effects of the gold, silver and copper mines, caused Ketchikan to become a booming little mining town. It was incorporated in 1901.

As mining waned, the fishing industry began to grow. By the 1930s more than a dozen salmon canneries had been built; during the peak years of the canned salmon industry, Ketchikan earned the title of "Salmon Capital of the World." Overfishing caused a drastic decline in salmon by the 1940s, and today only four canneries and a cold storage plant operate. Trident Seafoods Corp., owner of Ketchikan's oldest and largest cannery, provides lodging for 200-plus salmon processors in a floating bunkhouse. An industry under development is the commercial harvest of abalone near Ketchikan.

As fishing reached a low point, the timber industry expanded. The first sawmill was originally built in 1898 at Dolomi on Prince of Wales Island to cut timber for the Dolomi Mine. It was dismantled and moved to Ketchikan and rebuilt in 1903. A large pulp mill was constructed in 1953 at Ward Cove, a few miles northwest of town.

Tourism is a very important industry here; Ketchikan is Alaska's first port of call for cruise ships and Alaska Marine Highway vessels.

Ketchikan is Alaska's southernmost major city and the state's fourth largest (after Anchorage, Fairbanks and Juneau). The closest city in British Columbia is Prince Rupert. Ketchikan is a linear waterfront city, with much of its 3-mile-/4.8-km-long business district suspended above water on pilings driven into the bottom of Tongass Narrows. It clings to the steep wooded hillside and has many homes perched on cliffs that are reached by climbing long wooden staircases or narrow winding streets.

The area supports four public grade schools, four parochial grade schools, a junior high school, two high schools and a University of Alaska Southeast campus.

ACCOMMODATIONS

Ketchikan has nine hotels/motels. Bed-and-breakfast and dorm-style accommodations are also available. There are two major shopping districts, downtown and west end.

Ketchikan AYH hostel is located at the First United Methodist Church, Grant and Main streets; write Box 8515, Ketchikan, AK 99901, phone 225-3319 (summer only). Open Memorial Day to Labor Day, the hostel has showers, sleeping pads (bring sleeping bag) and kitchen facilities. Check-in time is 6-11 P.M. Reservations not necessary. Cost is $7 per night for members (AYH membership passes may be purchased at the hostel), $10 for nonmembers.

There are six campgrounds (four public campgrounds and a private resort) north of the city on North Tongass Highway and Ward Lake Road, and a private campground south of town. See highway logs in this section. Dump station located at Ketchikan Public Works office, two blocks north of state ferry terminal. Contact the visitors bureau for location of RV parking. ▲

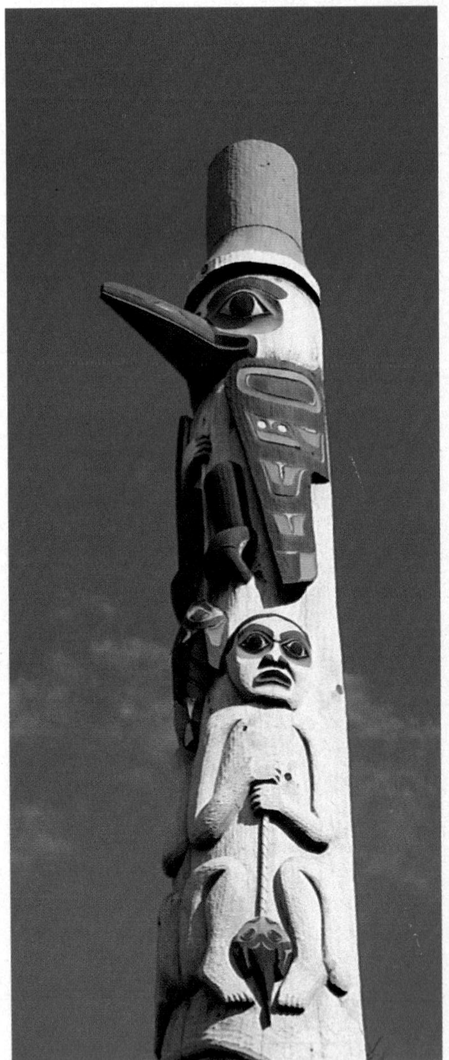

Ketchikan's totem poles are a popular attraction. (Lee Foster)

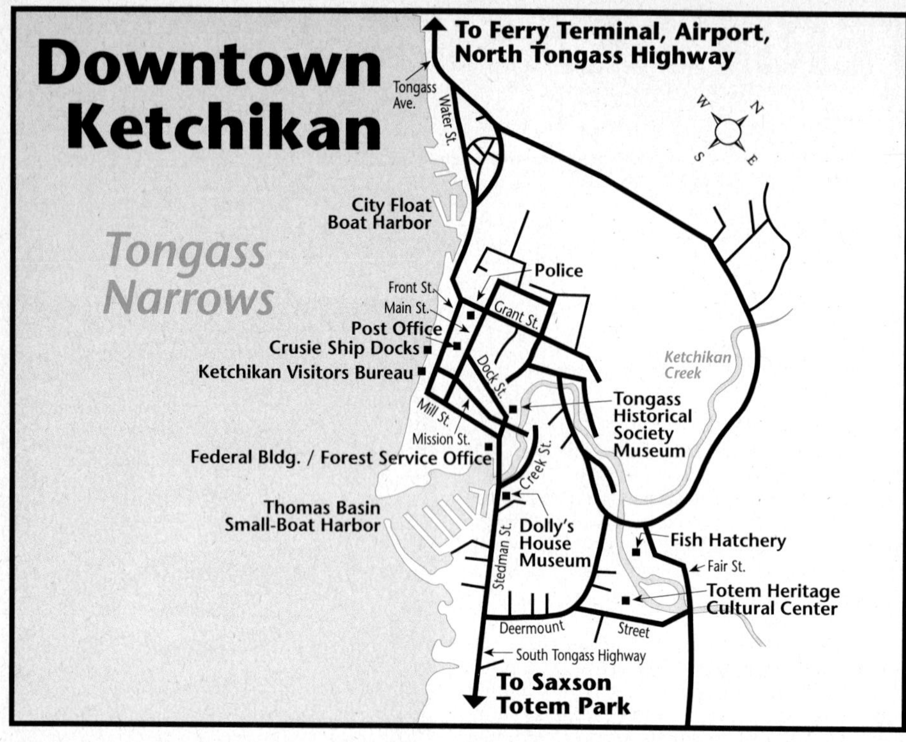

TRANSPORTATION

Air: Daily scheduled jet service is provided from the Ketchikan International Airport by Alaska Airlines to other Southeast cities, Anchorage and Seattle, WA. Trans Provincial has scheduled flights to Prince Rupert, BC. Commuter and charter service to other Southeast communities is available via Ketchikan Air and Taquan Air.

Airport terminal, across Tongass Narrows on Gravina Island, is reached via shuttle ferry (10-minute ride, $2.50 per person, $5 per vehicle, one way) departing from the ferry terminal on North Tongass Avenue at half-hour intervals. Airporter service between downtown and airport is $11 to $12 (includes ferry fare). Taxi service is also available for about $8 from downtown.

Ferry: Alaska Marine Highway vessels connect Ketchikan with all mainline southeastern Alaska port cities, Prince Rupert, BC, and Bellingham, WA. There are also state ferry connections from Ketchikan to Metlakatla on Annette Island; to Hollis on Prince of Wales Island; and once-weekly service to Hyder in summer. See MARINE ACCESS ROUTES section for schedules.

Terminal building with waiting room, ticket counter and loading area is on North Tongass Avenue (Highway), 2 miles north of downtown. Phone 225-6181. Foot passengers can walk from the ferry to a post office, restaurant and grocery store if stopover time permits. Taxi service available.

Rental Cars: Available at airport and downtown locations.

Taxi: Available at ferry terminal and airport.

Bus: Borough bus returns to every stop at half-hour intervals; operates to city limits only. Schedules available at visitors bureau. Fee charged.

Highways: North Tongass, South Tongass, Ward Lake Road and Harriet Hunt Lake Road. See logs this section.

Cruise Ships: Ketchikan is the first port of call for many cruise ships to Alaska. Cruises depart from U.S. West Coast ports and Vancouver, BC. Two cruise lines depart from Ketchikan.

Private Boats: Two public docks downtown, Thomas Basin and City Float, provide transient moorage. In the West End District, 1 mile from downtown, Bar Harbor has moorage, showers. No gas available. Permits required.

ATTRACTIONS

Ketchikan's waterfront is the center of the city. A narrow city on a mountainside, Ketchikan has a waterfront that runs for several miles and consists of docks, stores on pilings, seaplane floats, three picturesque boat harbors, a seaplane base and ferry terminals. There is constant activity here as seaplanes take off and vessels move in and out of the harbor. Walking tour maps are available at the visitors bureau and at the ferry terminal.

The Plaza. Southeast Alaska's premier shopping center. Thirty fine merchants on two comfort-controlled levels feature a variety of retail shops and services for complete one-stop shopping. Plenty of free parking. Less than a mile south of the ferry terminal. Open every day. [ADVERTISEMENT]

Fish Pirate's Daughter, a well-done local musical-comedy melodrama, portrays Ketchikan's early fishing days, with some of the

KETCHIKAN ADVERTISERS

Alaska Cruises	Ph. (907) 225-6044
Ingersoll Hotel, The	303 Mission St.
Ketchikan Visitors Bureau	131M Front St.
Landing, The	3434 Tongass Ave.
Plaza, The	214 Plaza Port W.
Race Avenue Drug	2300 Tongass Ave.
Salmon Busters Charters	Ph. (907) 225-2731
Super 8 Motel	Ph. 1-800-800-8000

city's spicier history added. Performed 7 P.M. and 8:45 P.M. Fridays July through August. Contact First City Players, 338 Main St., phone 225-4792 or 225-2211, for more information. Admission fee.

Tongass Historical Museum, in the Centennial Bldg., on Dock Street on Ketchikan Creek in central downtown area, featuring a re-created timber camp bunkhouse; a history of the commercial fishing industry; and an exhibit of Native life before the arrival of outsiders. Open in summer from 8:30 A.M. to 5 P.M. Monday through Saturday; and 1-5 P.M. Sunday. Winter (Oct. to mid-May) hours are 1-5 P.M. Wednesday through Friday, 1-4 P.M. Saturday and Sunday. The Raven Stealing the Sun totem stands just outside the entrance. Salmon viewing platforms. Admission fee is $1 for adults; free admission Sundays. Phone 225-5600 for more information.

Chief Kyan Totem at the top of Main Street is a favorite spot for visitors.

Creek Street is Ketchikan's famous "red-light district," where Black Mary, Dolly, Frenchie and others plied their trade for over half a century until 1954. Nearly 20 houses lined the far side of Ketchikan Creek; many have been restored. There are also several art and gift shops. Dolly's House, a former brothel, is open during the summer. Admission charged. Creek Street is a wooden street on pilings that begins just past the bridge on Stedman (South Tongass Highway). Watch for salmon in the creek below the bridge in late August.

Totem Heritage Center, at 601 Deermount St., houses 33 totem poles and fragments retrieved from deserted Tlingit and Haida Indian villages. This national landmark collection comprises the largest exhibit of original totems in the United States. Facilities include craft exhibits, craft shops for local artists and reference library. Gift shop, crafts demonstrations, videos and guided tours during summer months. Summer admission fee $2. No admission charged off-season. Summer hours are 8 A.M. to 5 P.M. Monday through Saturday, 9 A.M. to 5 P.M. Sunday. Winter hours are 1-5 P.M. Tuesday through Friday and 6-9 P.M. Tuesday.

Deer Mountain Hatchery is located in the city park within walking distance of downtown (take the bridge across Ketchikan Creek from the Totem Heritage Center). The hatchery produces about 150,000 king and 200,000 coho fingerlings annually. Observation platforms and information signs provide education on the life cycles of salmon. Open from 8 A.M. to 4:30 P.M. seven days a week in summer.

The Ketchikan Mural on Stedman Street was created by 21 Native artists in 1978. The 125-by-18-foot/38-by-4-m design is collectively entitled *The Return of the Eagle.*

Fourth of July is a major celebration in Ketchikan. The Timber Carnival takes place over the Fourth of July with events such as ax throwing and chopping, power saw bucking and a tug-of-war. There are also fireworks, the Calamity Race (by canoe and kayak, bicycle and on foot), a parade and other events.

The Blueberry Arts Festival, held the second Saturday in August, features arts and crafts, the performing arts and plenty of homemade blueberry pies, blueberry crêpes, blueberry cheesecakes and other culinary delights. Events include a slug race, international bed race, pie-eating contest, trivia contest and spelling bee. A juried art show, fun run and dance are also part of the festival. Sponsored and coordinated by the Ketchikan Area Arts and Humanities Council, Inc. (338 Main St., Ketchikan 99901; 225-2211).

AREA FISHING: Check with the Alaska Dept. of Fish and Game at 2030 Sea Level Dr., Suite 207, or phone 225-2859 for details on fishing in the Ketchikan area. Good fishing spots range from Mountain Point, a 5-mile/8-km drive from Ketchikan on South Tongass Highway, to lakes, bays and inlets 50 miles/80 km away by boat or by air. Half-day and longer charters available out of Ketchikan. There are fishing resorts at George Inlet, Yes Bay, Clover Pass and at the entrance to Behm Canal (Salmon Falls Resort); and eight fishing resorts on Prince of Wales Island. Fish include salmon, halibut, steelhead, Dolly Varden, cutthroat and rainbow, lingcod and rockfish. Ketchikan has two king salmon derbies, a silver salmon derby and a halibut derby in summer.

Saxman Totem Park, at Milepost 2.5 South Tongass Highway, is included in local sightseeing tours. Open year-round. There is no admission charge, but there is a fee for guided tours. The totem park has 26 totems. The tour includes demonstrations at the Carving Center and performances by the Cape Fox Dancers at the Beaver Tribal House. Guided tours are given from May to September. For more information on hours, tours and events phone the Saxman Visitor Center at 225-8687 or 225-2853, or Cape Fox Tours at 225-5163.

Totem Bight community house and totem park, Milepost 9.9 North Tongass Highway, contain an excellent model of a Tlingit community house and a park with 13 totems. Situated on a point overlooking Tongass Narrows, it is reached by a short trail through the forest from parking area.

Misty Fiords National Monument, 30 miles/48.3 km east of Ketchikan, encompasses more than 2 million acres of pristine coastal rain forest and glacially carved fjords. Rich in forests, marine wildlife, waterfalls and spectacular geologic features, the monument offers great scenic and scientific interest. The Forest Service maintains more than 20 miles of trails and several public-use cabins, located mostly on freshwater lakes and available for rent. Access to the monument is by boat or floatplane from Ketchikan. Sea kayaking is a popular means of exploring the coastlines and venturing into remote areas. A system of marine buoys is provided for saltwater

Creek Street has several art and gift shops. (Lee Foster)

boaters; fishing and photography are favorite pastimes in the monument. Cabin reservations, maps and natural history publications are available from the District Office, 3031 Tongass Ave., Ketchikan, AK 99901; phone 225-2148.

Charter boats: About 40 yachts operate out of Ketchikan for half-day, all-day or overnight sightseeing or fishing trips, transport to USFS public-use cabins and outlying communities. See advertisements this section and check with the visitors bureau or at the marinas.

Fishing resorts in the area are top quality. There are several; the most distant is an hour by floatplane. One resort is located at a renovated fish cannery.

Charter planes operate from the airport and from the waterfront on floats and are available for fly-in fishing, flightseeing or service to lodges and smaller communities.

Picnic areas include Settlers Cove by Settlers Cove Campground, **Milepost 18.2** North Tongass Highway; Refuge Cove, **Milepost 8.7** North Tongass Highway; Rotary Beach at **Milepost 3.5** South Tongass Highway; and Grassy Point and Ward Lake, **Milepost 1.1** Ward Lake Road.

Hiking trails include Deer Mountain trail, which begins at the corner of Fair and Deermount streets. The 3-mile/4.8-km, 3,001-foot/915-m ascent gives trekkers an excellent vantage of downtown Ketchikan and Tongass Narrows. Good but steep trail. Access to Deer Mountain cabin, the only USFS public-use cabin accessible by trail from Ketchikan. Perseverance Lake trail, 2.4 miles/3.8 km from Ward Lake to Perseverance Lake. Connell Lake trail, about 1.5 miles/2.4 km along north shore of Connell Lake, is in poor condition. An easy and informative 1-mile/1.6-km nature trail circles Ward Lake.

Forest Service Exhibition: The Tongass Visitor Center, in the Forest Service offices on Stedman Street, offers exhibits and films on Tongass National Forest. Open 8 A.M. to 4:30 P.M., seven days a week in summer.

USFS public-use cabins are available for $20 a night. There are 48 cabins in the Ketchikan management area of the Tongass National Forest. Most are accessible by floatplane, with some accessible by hiking or on salt water by boat. Reservations may be made at Ketchikan Ranger Station, 3031 Tongass Ave.; office hours are 8 A.M. to 5 P.M. five days a week. Phone 225-2148. For additional information see Cabins in the GENERAL INFORMATION section.

North Tongass Highway Log

The North Tongass Highway is 18.4 miles/29.6 km long with 15.2 miles/24.5 km paved. It begins at the corner of Mill Street and Stedman (at the Federal Bldg.) and proceeds north to Ward Lake Road, Totem Bight, Clover Pass and Settlers Cove Campground.

0 Federal Bldg. on left with area information display. Proceeding on Mill Street.

0.2 (0.3 km) Turning right onto Front Street, cruise ship dock on left where passengers disembark from major ships.

0.3 (0.5 km) Tunnel. North of this, Front Street becomes Water Street.

0.5 (0.8 km) City Float on left. Note older vessels, some dating back to the early 1900s.

0.7 (1.1 km) Highway turns left, then right, and becomes Tongass Avenue.

1.2 (1.9 km) West end shopping area begins.

1.7 (2.7 km) Bar Harbor boat basin on left.

2 (3.2 km) Ketchikan General Hospital on right, Ketchikan Ranger Station and Misty Fiords National Monument on left, northbound.

2.3 (3.7 km) Ferry terminals for Alaska Marine Highway.

2.4 (3.9 km) Main branch post office.

2.6 (4.2 km) Carlanna Creek and bridge.

2.7 (4.3 km) Airport shuttle ferry.

3.2 (5.1 km) Almer Wolfe Memorial viewpoint of Tongass Narrows. 24-hour RV parking. Airport terminal is visible across the narrows on Gravina Island.

4 (6.4 km) Hillside on right is a logged area, an example of clear-cut logging method and regrowth.

4.4 (7.1 km) Alaska State Troopers and Highway Dept.

5.5 (8.8 km) Small paved viewpoint overlooking Tongass Narrows and floatplane dock.

6 (9.6 km) Ward Cove Cannery next to road. Cannery Creek and bridge.

6.8 (10.9 km) **Junction** with Ward Lake Road (see log this section).

7 (11.3 km) Ward Creek and bridge, Ketchikan sawmill. Tours available, call for time.

7.3 (11.7 km) **WARD COVE**. Post office, gas station and grocery.

7.8 (12.5 km) Ketchikan Pulp Co. entrance. Pulp mill and high-speed compact sawmills (opened 1989). Tours available May through August. Call 225-2151 for times and information or write P.O. Box 6600, Ketchikan, AK 99901.

8.7 (14 km) Refuge Cove state recreation site with 14 picnic sites.

9.4 (15.1 km) Mud Bight; "float houses" rest on mud at low tide and float during high tide.

9.9 (15.9 km) Totem Bight state historical park; parking area, restrooms and phones. A short trail leads through the woods to Totem Bight community house and totem park. A striking setting. Don't miss this!

10.8 (17.4 km) Grocery store and gas station.

12.9 (20.8 km) Scenic viewpoint overlooking Guard Island lighthouse built in 1903 and manned until 1969 when finally automated.

14.2 (22.9 km) Clover Pass Resort turnoff. Left, North Point Higgins Road leads 0.6 mile/1 km to turnoff to resort; food, lodging, camping.

Left, then immediately right, is Knudson Cove Road, leading 0.4 mile/0.6 km to Knudson Cove Marina with public float, boat launch and boat rentals. Road rejoins North Tongass Highway at **Milepost 14.8.▲**

14.8 (23.8 km) Knudson Cove Marina to left 0.5 mile/0.8 km.

15.2 (24.5 km) Pavement ends.

16.6 (26.8 km) Salmon Falls Resort; private fishing lodge with restaurant and boat rentals.

18.2 (29.3 km) Settlers Cove state campground, parking area and picnic area; nine tent spaces and seven car and trailer pads. Camping fee $6 per night. Tables, water, pit toilets; 11 picnic units along beach to either side of campground. Parking area available for overnight. Good gravel beach for kids and boats. To right is **Lunch Creek** (pink salmon in August) and falls and trail to beach. ▲

18.4 (29.6 km) Road end.

Ward Lake Road Log

An 8.3-mile/13.4-km road leading to Ward Lake Recreation Area and Harriet Hunt Road. Motorists and hikers should be aware of private property boundaries,

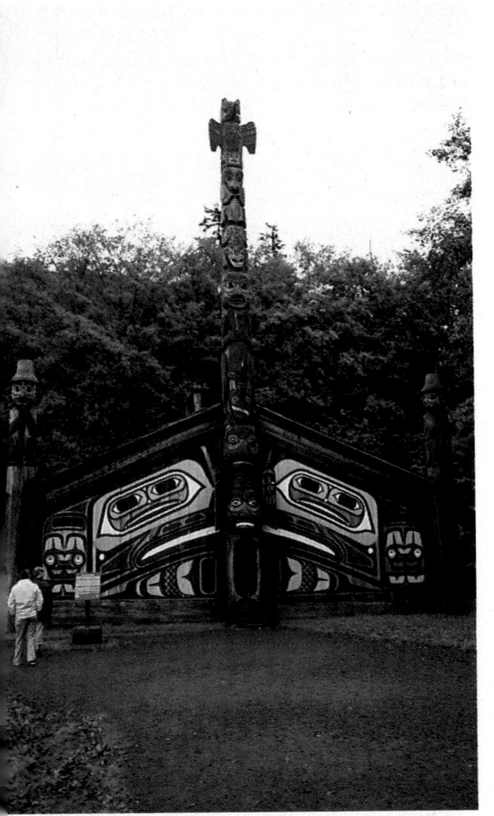

Totem Bight community house at Mile 9.9 North Tongass Highway. (Lee Foster)

posted by Cape Fox Corp. (CFC), and logging and trucking activities.

0 Right turn northbound from North Tongass Highway at **Milepost 6.8.**

0.1 (0.2 km) Tongass National Forest boundary.

0.4 (0.6 km) Small scenic turnout on right. Pond with lily pads surrounded by pine in muskeg.

0.7 (1.1 km) Signal Creek USFS campground on left; 24 sites with tables, water and pit toilets. Camping fee. Located among large trees on shore of Ward Lake. One end of nature trail around Ward Lake begins here and encircles lake; a 30- to 50-minute easy walk on well-graveled path. ▲

0.9 (1.4 km) Beginning of Perseverance Lake trail on right. Trailhead is within 100 feet of CCC Campground with parking across road. Site of WWII Aleut internment camp. A 2.4-mile/3.9-km boardwalk trail leads to **Perseverance Lake** (elev. 518 feet/158m); brook trout fishing.

1 (1.6 km) CCC (or Three C's) USFS campground entrance on right; four campsites, camping fee. ▲

1.1 (1.8 km) Ward Creek bridge. Grassy Point USFS picnic area. Several walk-in picnic sites with tables and shelters near road. Footbridge across Ward Creek leads to Ward Lake trail.

Ward Creek and **Ward Lake**, rainbow, cutthroat, Dolly Varden, March to June; steelhead to 16 lbs.; silver salmon to 18 lbs. and pink salmon to 5 lbs., August to October. (Hatchery-raised coho salmon and steelhead; bring head of tagged fish to ADF&G.)

1.3 (2.1 km) Ward Lake USFS picnic area; beach, parking area and picnic shelters. One end of nature trail around Ward Lake.

2.9 (4.7 km) Right, Last Chance USFS campground; 23 spaces, tables, pit toilets, water, camping fee. ▲

3 (4.8 km) Connell Lake Road, on right, a narrow gravel road extending 0.6 mile/1 km to Connell Lake Reservoir. At Mile 0.4 Connell Lake Road, a bridge passes over large pipe, which carries water from the reservoir to the pulp mill at Ward Cove. Connell Lake trail at reservoir.

3.3 (5.3 km) Turnout.

7.1 (11.4 km) **Junction** with Harriet Hunt Lake Road (log follows), turn left.

8.3 (13.4 km) End public road. Private logging road begins.

Harriet Hunt Lake Road Log

Harriet Hunt Lake Road leads 2.4 miles/3.9 km from **Milepost 7.1** Ward Lake Road to Harriet Hunt Lake; road is on CFC lands. Watch for logging trucks.

0 Turn left at **Milepost 7.1** Ward Lake Road.

2 (3.2 km) Turnout, alpine meadows.

2.2 (3.5 km) Left, small scenic waterfall.

2.4 (3.9 km) **Harriet Hunt Lake** Recreation Area; pit toilets. Rainbow to 20 inches, May to November. Road end and parking area.

South Tongass Highway Log

The South Tongass Highway is a 12.9-mile/20.8-km road (paved for 8.5 miles/13.7 km) leading from the corner of Mill Street and Stedman south to Saxman Totem Park and ending at the power plant.

0 Federal Bldg. on right.

0.1 (0.2 km) Ketchikan Creek and bridge. Beginning of Creek Street boardwalk on left next to bridge.

0.2 (0.3 km) Thomas Street begins on right, a boardwalk street where old-time businesses are located. Thomas Basin boat harbor.

0.5 (0.8 km) Cannery and cold storage plant.

0.9 (1.4 km) U.S Coast Guard base.

2.5 (4 km) **SAXMAN** (pop. 369) was founded in 1894 by Tlingit Indians and named after a Presbyterian missionary who served the Tlingit people. Saxman has a gas station and convenience store and is the site of Saxman Totem Park. Developed by Cape Fox Corp., this popular attraction includes a carving center and tribal house. Guided tours available.

2.7 (4.3 km) Gas station.

3.5 (5.6 km) Rotary Beach, public recreation area, contains a shelter and table.

5 (8.1 km) Mountain Point parking area. Good salmon fishing from shore in July and August.

5.6 (9 km) Boat ramp on right.

8.2 (13.2 km) Herring Cove bridge and sawmill. Private hatchery for chum, king and coho salmon on short road to left; no tours.

8.5 (13.7 km) Pavement ends.

8.8 (14.2 km) Whitman Creek and bridge.

9 (14.5 km) Scenic turnout on right. Note different shades of green on trees across the water. Light green are cedar; medium, hemlock; and the darker are spruce. Species grow intermixed.

10.3 (16.6 km) Left, scenic waterfall.

11 (17.7 km) Scenic turnout.

11.8 (19 km) Lodge.

12.9 (20.8 km) Road end, view of power plant, an experimental sockeye salmon hatchery (no tours) and an abandoned cannery.

Metlakatla

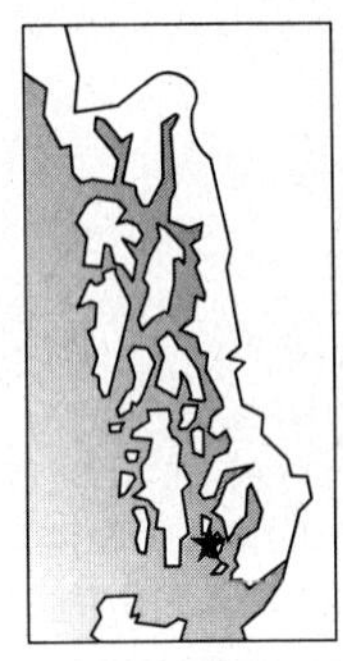

Located on the west coast of Annette Island, 15 miles/24 km south of Ketchikan, southeastern Alaska's southernmost community. **Population:** 1,386. **Emergency Services: Police, fire** and **ambulance,** emergency only phone 911. **Visitor Information:** Contact the city clerk, phone 886-4441. A permit from the Metlakatla Indian Community is required for long-term visits to Metlakatla.

Elevation: Sea level. **Climate:** Mild and moist. Summer temperatures range from 36°F/12°C to 65°F/18°C; winter temperatures from 28°F/-2°C to 44°F/7°C. Average annual precipitation is 115 inches: October is the wettest month with a maximum of 35 inches of rainfall. Annual snowfall averages 61 inches. **Radio:** KTKN (Ketchikan). **Television:** 20 channels via cable.

Private Aircraft: Floatplane services.

Transportation: Air–Charter and air service. **Ferry**–State ferry from Ketchikan.

Overnight accommodations, restaurant, groceries and banking services available.

Metlakatla was founded in 1887 by William Duncan, a Scottish-born lay minister, who moved here with several hundred Tsimshian Indians from a settlement in British Columbia after a falling-out with church authorities. Congress granted reservation status and title to the entire island in 1891, and the new settlement prospered under Duncan, who built a salmon cannery and sawmill. Today, fishing and lumber continue to be the main economic base of Metlakatla. The community and island also retain the status of a federal Indian reservation, which is why Metlakatla has the only salmon fish traps in Alaska. (Floating fish traps were outlawed by the state shortly after statehood.)

The well-planned community has a town hall, a recreation center with an Olympic-sized swimming pool, well-maintained wood-frame homes, a post office, the mill and cannery. The Metlakatla Indian Community is the largest employer in town, with retail and service trades the second largest. Many residents also are commercial fishermen. Subsistence activities remain an important source of food for residents, who harvest seaweed, salmon, halibut, cod, clams and waterfowl.

Attractions include the Duncan Museum, the original cottage occupied by Father William Duncan until his death in 1918. A replica of the turn-of-the-century William Duncan Memorial Church, built after the original was destroyed by fire in 1948, is also open to the public.

Red salmon spawn in island streams. (John W. Warden)

Prince of Wales Island

Includes Craig, Klawock, Hydaburg, Thorne Bay and Hollis

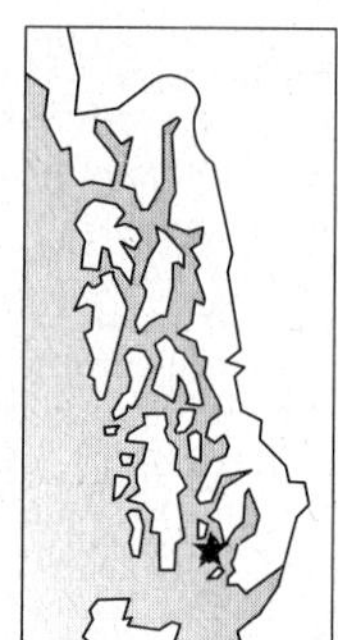

In southern southeastern Alaska, about 45 miles/72 km west of Ketchikan. **Population:** On the island, approximately 6,000. **Emergency Services: Alaska State Troopers,** in Klawock, phone 755-2918. **Police,** in Craig, phone 826-3330, emergencies only, phone 911; **Village Public Safety Officers** in Thorne Bay, phone 828-3905; in Hydaburg, phone 285-3321. **Ambulance,** Hydaburg emergency response team, phone 911. **Health Clinics,** in Craig, phone 826-3257; in Klawock, phone 755-2777, or emergencies, 911; in Thorne Bay, phone 828-3906; in Hydaburg, phone 285-3462 (911 for emergencies). **Maritime Search and Rescue,** call the Coast Guard at 1-800-478-5555.

Elevation: Sea level to 4,000 feet/1,219m. **Climate:** Mild and moist, but variable due to the island's size and topography. Rainfall in excess of 100 inches per year, with modest snowfall in winter at lower elevations. **Radio:** KRSA 580 (Petersburg), KTKN (Ketchikan), KRBD-FM 90.1 (Ketchikan). **Television:** Via satellite. **Newspaper:** *Island News* (Thorne Bay, weekly).

Private Aircraft: Klawock airstrip, 2 miles/3.2 km northeast; elev. 50 feet/15m; length 5,000 feet/1,524m; paved; fuel 100LL. Seaplane bases adjacent to all four communities and in several bays.

A heavily forested island with low mountains, Prince of Wales Island measures roughly 130 miles/209 km north–south by 30 miles/48 km east–west. The third largest island under the American flag (Kodiak is second, the big island of Hawaii is first), it is 2,731 square miles/7,101 square km. The four major communities on the island — Craig (the largest with 1,637 residents), Klawock, Thorne Bay, Hydaburg — and the smaller camps and communities of Coffman Cove, Whale Pass, Labouchere Bay and Naukati are connected by road. Among the small scattered villages not connected by road are **KASAAN**, a small Haida village at the head of Kasaan Bay, and **PORT PROTECTION** and **POINT BAKER**, both at the northwest tip of the island. (See *The ALASKA WILDERNESS GUIDE* for details on these communities.)

Prince of Wales Island has been the site of several lumbermills and mining camps since the 1800s. But it was salmon that led to permanent settlement on the island. Klawock was the site of one of Alaska's first canneries, built in 1878. In the following years, some 25 canneries were built on the island to process salmon. Today, logging is prevalent on the island.

Prince of Wales Island offers uncrowded backcountry, fishing for salmon and trout, good canoeing waters, good opportunities for viewing wildlife (black bear, Sitka black-tailed deer, bald eagles), adequate visitor facilities and some historical attractions. Most of the island is national forest land. The Forest Service manages five large, designated wilderness areas on Prince of Wales Island. There are also some Native corporation and private land holdings. Respect No Trespassing signs.

There is a city-run trailer park in Klawock for monthly rentals and a private campground at Mile 0.4 Big Salt Road. RV camping is also available at the Eagle's Nest Campground operated by the USFS just east of the Thorne Bay Road near Control Lake; water, chemical toilets, camping fee $5. Altogether, there are five USFS campsites on the island (see map this section). There are also more than 20 USFS cabins (accessible by plane, boat or on foot) available for public use; reservations and a fee are required. Contact the USFS office in Ketchikan or the local ranger districts at Craig and Thorne Bay (phone 828-3304). Also see Cabins in the GENERAL INFORMATION section. ▲

There are several good fishing spots along the roads on Prince of Wales Island. See the road logs in this section for details. Lakes and streams support red, pink and silver salmon; cutthroat and rainbow; and Dolly Varden.

TRANSPORTATION

Air: Craig, Klawock, Thorne Bay and Hydaburg are served by floatplane; wheel planes land at Klawock. Daily scheduled service from Ketchikan.

Ferry: Alaska Marine Highway ferry operates from Ketchikan to Hollis. See MARINE ACCESS ROUTES section for rates and schedule. Van taxi service meets ferry at Hollis and offers service to Craig and Klawock.

Car rental in Klawock at Prince of Wales Lodge.

Highways: The island's main roads are the Hollis–Klawock–Craig Highway, Big Salt Road, Thorne Bay Road, Hydaburg Road, Coffman Cove Road and North Island Road (USFS Road No. 20) to Labouchere Bay. See the map and road logs in this section for details.

DRIVER CAUTION: Watch for heavily loaded logging trucks while driving; they have the right-of-way. Carry a spare tire and spare gas. (Gas is available in Coffman Cove, Hydaburg, Craig, Klawock, Whale Pass and Thorne Bay.) Use turnouts and approach hills and corners on your side of the road. Spur roads are *NOT* recommended for large RVs or cars with trailers. Some side roads may be closed intermittently during logging operations or highway construction. Watch for signs posted when roads are closed and expect delays.

DESCRIPTION AND ACCOMMODATIONS

COFFMAN COVE (pop. approximately 300), 53 miles/85 km north of Klawock. Coffman Cove is a second-class city, one of the largest independent logging camps in Southeast. Housing is in mobile homes. Recreation includes hunting (deer and bear), good fishing in area lakes and streams, boating, hiking, and also TV and VCRs.

Coffman Cove has a general store, gift shop and gas pump. There is a dock and a small beach with access to salt water for canoes and cartop boats.

CRAIG (pop. 1,535), 31 miles/50 km from Hollis, is on a small island connected to Prince of Wales Island by a short causeway. Set on a hillside facing the waterfront, it has a boat harbor, seaplane float, fuel dock and an old cannery dock. There are two smaller harbors on either side of the causeway. Craig has sidewalks and a paved main street.

Visitor information is available from Craig City Hall, phone 826-3275; open weekdays 8 A.M. to 5 P.M. U.S. Forest Service office, open weekdays 8 A.M. to 4:30 P.M., phone 826-3271. Prince of Wales Chamber of Commerce, phone 826-3870.

Craig was once a temporary fish camp for the Tlingit and Haida people of this region. In 1907, with the help of local Haidas, Craig Millar established a saltery at Fish Egg Island. Between 1908 and 1911, a permanent saltery and cold storage facility, along with about two dozen homes, were built at the city's present location, and the settlement was named for its founder. In 1912, the year the post office was established, E.M. Streeter opened a sawmill and

Craig constructed a salmon cannery, both of which peaked during WWI. Craig was incorporated in 1922, and continued to grow throughout the 1930s, with some families from the Dust Bowl relocating to this Prince of Wales Island community. Although the salmon industry has both prospered and foundered over the years, fishing still accounts for about half of the employment in Craig today. In recent years, increased timber harvesting on the island has contributed jobs in logging and timber processing. There is also employment in government and construction.

In front of the old school gym is a totem that was found washed up on the beach, then restored and painted by local people. The town has a big Fourth of July celebration, and the annual Criag Salmon Derby is held April 15–June 30.

Craig has a motel and Haida Way Lodge, a post office, four restaurants, two grocery stores, clothing stores and general stores, a gas station, a laundromat, three gift shops, three liquor stores, three bars, beauty shops, a library and two banks. Propane available. Towing and auto repair service available. Charter boats are also available.

HOLLIS, 25 road miles/40 km from Klawock, 35 water miles/56 km west of Ketchikan. Hollis was a mining town with a population of 1,000 from about 1900 to 1915. In the 1950s, Hollis became the site of Ketchikan Pulp Co.'s logging camp, and served as the base for timber operations on Prince of Wales Island until 1962, when the camp was moved to Thorne Bay. Recent state land sales have spurred the growth of a small residential community here. The ferry terminal and a school are located here.

HYDABURG (pop. 457), 36 miles/58 km from Hollis, 45 miles/72 km from Craig. Hydaburg was founded in 1911 and combined the populations of three Haida villages: Sukkwan, Howkan and Klinkwan. President William Howard Taft established an Indian reservation on the surrounding land in 1912, but, at the residents' request, most of the land was restored to its former status as part of Tongass National Forest in 1926. Hydaburg was incorporated in 1927, three years after its people became citizens of the United States.

Most of the residents are commercial fishermen, although there are some jobs in construction and the timber industry. Subsistence is also a traditional and necessary part of life here. Hydaburg has an excellent collection of restored Haida totems. The totem park was developed in the 1930s by the Civilian Conservation Corps, who brought in poles from the three abandoned Haida villages. There is also good salmon fishing here in the fall.

Three boardinghouses provide rooms and meals for visitors. Groceries, hardware and sundry items available locally. There are a gift shop, gas station, video store and cafe. Cable television is available.

KLAWOCK (pop. 897), 24 miles/39 km from Hollis. Klawock originally was a Tlingit Indian summer fishing village; a trading post and salmon saltery were established here in 1868. Ten years later a salmon cannery was built — the first cannery in Alaska and the first of several cannery operations in the area. Over the years the population of Klawock, like other Southeast communities, grew and then declined with the salmon harvest. The local economy is still dependent on fishing and cannery operations, along with timber cutting and sawmilling. A state fish hatchery is located on Klawock

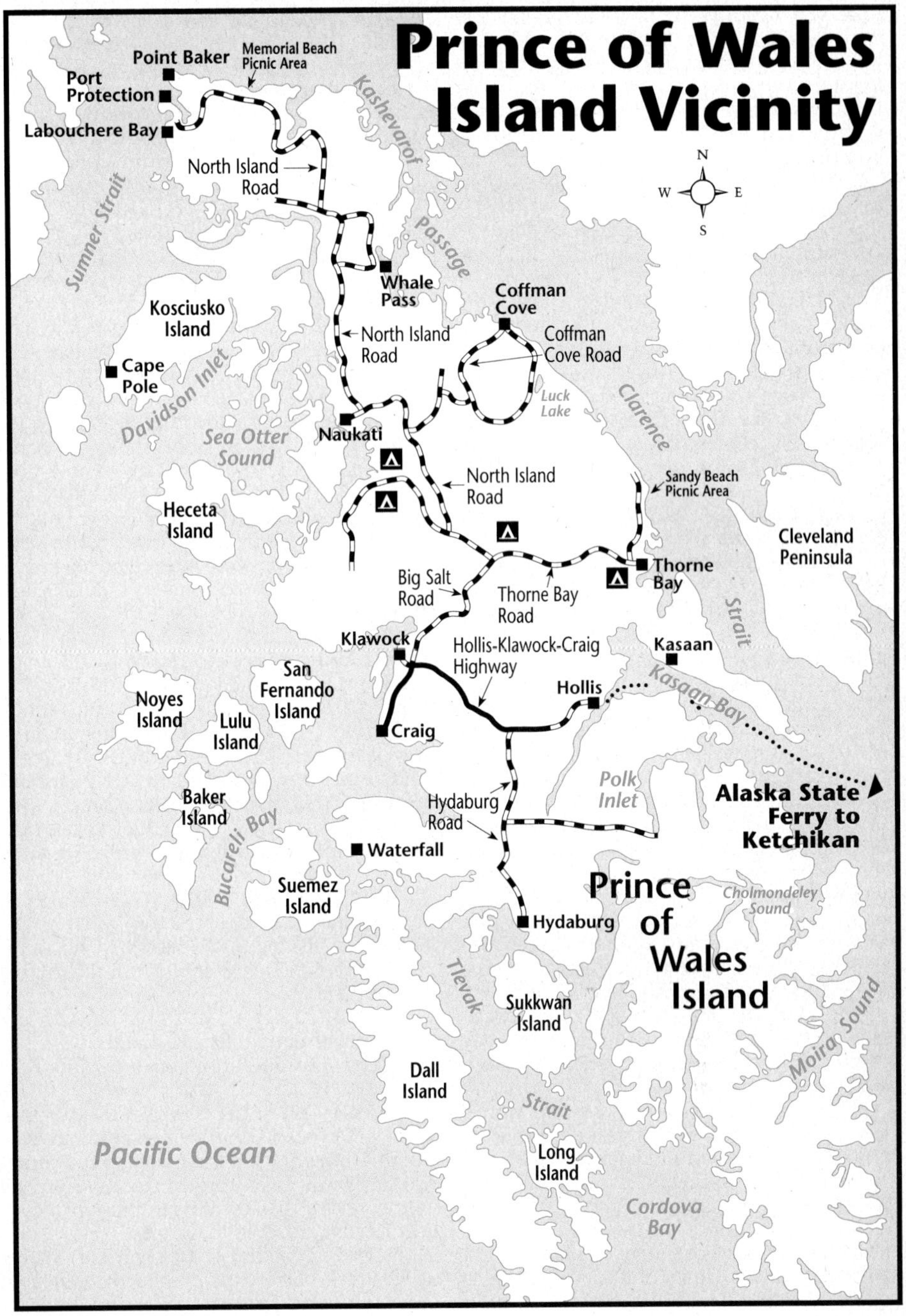

Prince of Wales Island Vicinity

Lake, very near the site of a salmon hatchery that operated from 1897 until 1917. Klawock Lake offers good canoeing and boating.

Recreation here includes good fishing for salmon and steelhead in Klawock River, salmon and halibut fishing, and deer and bear hunting. Klawock's totem park contains 21 totems — both replicas and originals — from the abandoned Indian village of Tuxekan.

Groceries and gas are available in Klawock. Laundromat at Black Bear Quick Stop. Banking service available. Accommodations and meals available at two lodges just outside town (Fireweed Lodge and Log Cabin Resort). Log Cabin Resort also offers RV sites. Towing service available. Boat charters and rentals are also available. ▲

Fireweed Lodge. See display ad this section.

Log Cabin R.V. Park & Resort. See display ad this section. ▲

THORNE BAY (pop. 637), 59 miles/95 km from Hollis. Thorne Bay was incorporated in 1982, making it one of Alaska's newest cities. The settlement began as a logging camp in 1962, when Ketchikan Pulp Co. (a subsidiary of Louisiana Pacific Corp.) moved its operations from Hollis. Thorne Bay was connected to the island road system in 1974. Camp residents created the community — and gained city status from the state — as private ownership of the land was made possible under the Alaska Statehood Act. Employment here depends mainly on the lumber company and the U.S. Forest Service, with assorted jobs in municipal government and in local trades and services. Thorne Bay is centrally located between two popular Forest Service recreation areas: Eagle's Nest Campground and Sandy Beach picnic area. The Thorne River offers excellent canoeing and kayaking, and the bay offers excellent sailing and waterskiing (wetsuit advised).

There are grocery and hardware stores, gas stations, small-boat repair, tackle shop and gift shop. Accommodations available at several bed and breakfasts, a lodge and rental cabins. Propane is available. Fuel oil is also available. Boat charters and rentals are available. Gas for boats may be purchased at the tackle shack float (unleaded fuel). It is open Monday and Wednesday through Friday from 1-7 P.M.; Saturday and Sunday 11 A.M. to 4 P.M. Aviation fuel available through Petro Alaska. City-operated dump station. Facilities include boat dock, cement boat launch ramp, helicopter landing pad, and floatplane float and parking facility. ▲

There is scheduled floatplane service to Thorne Bay from Ketchikan.

WHALE PASS (pop. approximately 100), accessible by loop road from the North Island Road, was the site of a floating logging camp. The camp moved out in the early 1980s, but new residents moved in with a state land sale. The community has a small grocery store and gas pump. Accommodations at Whale Pass Lodge and a bed and breakfast. Good fishing on the loop road into Whale Pass.

Hollis–Klawock–Craig Highway Log

This highway, 31.5 miles/50.7 km long, begins at the ferry landing at Hollis and heads west through Klawock then south to Craig. It is a wide paved road. Posted speed is 35 to 50 mph/56 to 80 kmph. *CAUTION: Watch for logging trucks.*

Distance from Hollis (H) is followed by distance from Craig (C). Physical mileposts show distance from Craig.

H 0 C 31.5 (50.7 km) **HOLLIS.** Alaska Marine Highway ferry terminal.

H 1.4 (2.3 km) **C 30.1** (48.4 km) Stop sign. Turn right for Craig and Klawock; turn left for boat ramp.

H 2 (3.2 km) **C 29.5** (47.5 km) **Maybeso Creek** bridge. Scenic viewpoint to left. Cutthroat; Dolly Varden; pink and silver salmon; steelhead run begins in mid-April. Pools offer the best fishing. Walking good along streambed but poor along the bank. Watch for bears.

H 3.2 (5.1 km) **C 28.3** (45.5 km) Hollis townsite area. Virtually no ruins of the original townsite remain. Large rotting tree stumps in woods are evidence of logging in the early 1900s. Road continues along Harris River valley.

H 5.2 (8.4 km) **C 26.3** (42.3 km) Left, **Harris River** bridge road extends 0.7 mile/1.1 km down into the valley to the bridge. Cutthroat; steelhead run mid-April; salmon and Dolly Varden run beginning in mid-July. Easy walking on the gravel bars in the middle of river. Bridge across river passable by foot or trail bike. Watch for bears.

H 7 (11.3 km) **C 24.5** (39.4 km) Upper Harris River Road (rough) extends 0.6 mile/1 km to Harris River.

H 11 (17.7 km) **C 20.5** (33 km) Road crosses Harris River. **Junction** with Hydaburg Road (see log this section).

H 11.8 (19 km) **C 19.7** (31.7 km) Harris River bridge.

H 12.4 (20 km) **C 19.1** (30.7 km) End of Harris River valley. Island divide is here at 500 feet/152m elevation; streams now flow west.

H 14.1 (22.7 km) **C 17.4** (28 km) East end of Klawock Lake on left. Klawock Lake is about 7 miles/11 km long and up to 1 mile/1.6 km wide. Lake borders the road on the left at several places. Private property; contact Heenya Corp. in Klawock.

H 19.5 (31.4 km) **C 12** (19.3 km) Threemile Creek passes under road through two large culverts. Private property; contact Heenya Corp. in Klawock.

H 22.3 (35.9 km) **C 9.2** (14.8 km) Turnout on left. Short trail leads to Klawock River and view of rapids and salmon run in season. Private property; contact Heenya Corp. in Klawock.

H 22.5 (36.2 km) **C 9** (14.5 km) Klawock Lake Hatchery, operated by the Division of Fisheries Rehabilitation, Enhancement and Development, Alaska Dept. of Fish and Game. The hatchery produces sockeye and coho salmon and steelhead. Visitors welcome Monday through Friday, 8 A.M. to 4:30 P.M.

H 24.1 (38.8 km) **C 7.4** (11.9 km) **Junction** with Big Salt Road (see log this section). A state highway maintenance station and a grocery store with gas station are located at this junction.

H 24.3 (39.1 km) **C 7.2** (11.6 km) Fireweed Lodge: food and lodging.

H 24.5 (39.4 km) **C 7** (11.3 km) Entering village of **KLAWOCK**. State troopers in building on right.

H 24.6 (39.6 km) **C 6.9** (11.1 km) **Klawock River** bridge spans tidal estuary where river meets salt water. Fishing from bridge.

Watch for black bear and other wildlife.
(Michael DeYoung)

H 25.2 (40.6 km) **C 6.3** (10.1 km) Alaska Timber Corp. mill (closed 1986).

H 27.3 (43.9 km) **C 4.2** (6.8 km) Scenic viewpoint on right overlooking bay.

H 28.3 (45.5 km) **C 3.2** (5.1 km) Left, short road to Craig sanitary fill. Bears can usually be seen here.

H 30.5 (49 km) **C 1** (1.6 km) Craig school.

H 31.5 (50.7 km) **C 0** Downtown **CRAIG.**

Big Salt Road Log

Big Salt Road begins at **Milepost C 7.5** on the Hollis–Klawock–Craig Highway and extends 17.1 miles/27.5 km, ending at its junction with Thorne Bay Road. It is a gravel road with much logging traffic. Top speed for much of the road is about 25 mph/40 kmph.

Distance is measured from Klawock.

0 Black Bear Quick Stop: grocery store, laundromat and gas station.

0.1 (0.2 km) Klawock city trailer park on right with some overnighter sites; obtain permits from the city clerk. A camping fee is charged. ▲

0.4 (0.6 km) Log Cabin R.V. Park & Resort: tackle store, skiff rentals, lodging and campground. ▲

0.5 (0.8 km) Lodge and restaurant.

2.3 (3.7 km) Road on left leads 0.7 mile/1.1 km to Klawock airport and highway maintenance station.

4 (6.4 km) View of Big Salt Lake and mountains.

8.7 (14 km) Big Salt Lake, actually a saltwater body protected by small islands but permitting tidal flow in and out, is visible to the left from several spots along road. Waterfowl and bald eagles are often observed here. Wreckage of a military aircraft can be seen across lake. The plane crashed in 1969 en route to Vietnam; all aboard survived the crash.

8.9 (14.3 km) Boat ramp and canoe launching area on Big Salt Lake. If boating on this tidal lake, be aware of strong currents.

9.7 (15.6 km) **Black Bear Creek**, cutthroat; Dolly Varden; red, pink, dog and silver salmon, run mid-July to mid-September. Except for the lower 2 miles/3.2 km, creek can be fished from the bank. Best at the mouth of stream, 200 yards/183m upstream from the bridge or in large meadow 1.5 miles/2.4 km from the mouth. Road on right leads to Black Lake. Watch for heavy equipment.

12.6 (20.3 km) **Steelhead Creek**, cutthroat; Dolly Varden; steelhead; pink, dog and silver salmon. Creek can be reached by boat through south entrance to Big Salt Lake. Lake should only be entered during high and low slack tides due to the strong tidal currents. High tide in lake is delayed two hours from outside waters. Bank fishing restricted by undergrowth.

16.6 (26.7 km) Short boardwalk on right leads to **Control Lake**, cutthroat; Dolly Varden; pink and silver salmon; good red salmon stream in August. USFS cabin on other side is available for public use. Skiff docked at end of boardwalk is for registered cabin users.

17.1 (27.5 km) End of Big Salt Road (SR 929), **junction** with Thorne Bay Road (USFS Road No. 30) and North Island Road (USFS Road No. 20). Road to Thorne Bay (log follows) is on the right. Road to Labouchere Bay, with access to Whale Pass and Coffman Cove, is on the left; see North Island Road log this section. Turn right for USFS RV park (no services). ▲

Thorne Bay Road Log

Thorne Bay Road extends 18 miles/29 km to Thorne Bay logging camp.
Physical mileposts show distance from Thorne Bay post office.

18 (29 km) **Junction** with Big Salt Road and North Island Road.

16.6 (26.7 km) Eagle's Nest USFS campground; 12 sites, tables, water, toilet and canoe launch. Camping fee $5. **Balls Lake**, cutthroat; Dolly Varden; red, pink and silver salmon. ▲

13 (20.9 km) Bridge. **Rio Roberts** and **Rio Beaver creeks**, cutthroat; pink and silver salmon. A 0.7-mile/1.1-km cedar chip and shingle plank boardwalk leads to a viewing deck overlooking falls and Rio Roberts Fish Pass.

10.7 (17.2 km) Rio Beaver Creek bridge.

6.7 (10.8 km) **Goose Creek**, cutthroat; pink and silver salmon. Excellent spawning stream. Good run of pink salmon in mid-August. Lake Ellen Road on right leads 4.5 miles/7.2 km south to Lake No. 3 USFS campsite; two RV sites, pit toilet, two fire rings and two picnic tables. No water or garbage. Road continues beyond campsite to lake and hiking trail to Salt Chuck. Abandoned Salt Chuck Mine is located here. ▲

6.5 (10.5 km) **Thorne River** runs beside road for the next 0.5 mile/0.8 km. Cutthroat; Dolly Varden; steelhead; rainbow; red, pink, dog and silver salmon. Excellent fishing reported at **Milepost 4.9** to **2.1.**

4.9 (7.9 km) Thorne River bridge. Thorne River now follows road on right.

4.1 (6.6 km) Falls Creek.

4 (6.4 km) Gravelly Creek USFS picnic area; walk in to picnic area on the bank of Thorne River at the mouth of Gravelly Creek; three tables, fire rings, vault toilet and open-sided shelter. This site was logged in 1918. Note the large stumps with notches. Notches were used by old-time loggers for spring boards to stand on while sawing or chopping.

3.7 (5.9 km) Gravelly Creek.

2.1 (3.4 km) Right, mouth of Thorne River.

1.7 (2.7 km) Hill on right is an example of a logging cut.

1.3 (2.1 km) Log sorting area. Here different species of logs are sorted for rafting and transporting to mills or for export.

1.2 (1.9 km) Log raft holding area. After logs are sorted and tied into bundles, the bundles are chained together into a raft suitable for towing by tugboat.

0 THORNE BAY. The road extends about 10 miles/16 km beyond the community to Sandy Beach day-use area with picnic shelter, six tables, fire rings, vault toilet and RV parking. Good view of Clarence Strait.

Hydaburg Road Log

The Hydaburg Road is 24.6 miles/39.6 km long and begins 11 miles/17.7 km west of the Hollis main ferry terminal on the Hollis–Klawock–Craig Highway. Opened in 1983, the road has been much improved. Road construction may be under way. Some sections of the road are heavily used by logging trucks.

0 Junction with Hollis–Klawock–Craig Highway.

0.5 (0.8 km) Harris River bridge.

2 (3.2 km) Trailhead for One Duck trail to alpine area and cabin. Contact the USFS office for more information.

4.1 (6.6 km) Bridge.

9.8 (15.8 km) Fork in road, keep right for Hydaburg.

11 (17.7 km) Road on left leads to Twelvemile Arm. This logging road leads to Polk Inlet. Watch for logging and construction activity.

11.8 (19 km) Fork in road, keep right for Hydaburg.

13.9 (22.4 km) View of South Pass.

16.9 (27.2 km) Bridge. Take right fork just after crossing bridge for Hydaburg.

23.5 (37.8 km) Keep right at junction.

23.9 (38.5 km) Take right at junction for Hydaburg, left for Saltery.

24.6 (39.6 km) **HYDABURG.**

North Island Road Log

Signed as USFS Road No. 20, this narrow two-lane road leads north 79.5 miles/127.9 km from its junction with Big Salt and Thorne Bay roads near Control Lake to Labouchere Bay on the northwest corner of the island. The road has a fair to excellent gravel surfacing and some steep grades. Slow down for approaching vehicles. Posted speed is 25 mph/40 kmph. Gas is available at Whale Pass and Coffman Cove.

0 Junction with Big Salt and Thorne Bay roads near Control Lake.

4.8 (7.7 km) USFS Road No. 2050 leads west to upper Staney Creek/Horseshoe Hole and loops back to Road No. 20. Access to Staney Bridge campsite. ▲

7.4 (11.9 km) Rock quarry to east.

10.9 (17.5 km) USFS Road No. 2054 leads west to Staney Creek campsite, Staney Creek cabin and access to salt water. ▲

15.5 (24.9 km) **Junction** with Coffman Cove Road (see log this section).

18.4 (29.6 km) Naukati Creek.

19.2 (30.9 km) View to west of Tuxekan Island and Passage.

21 (33.8 km) Logging road leads west to Naukati Bay.

21.4 (34.4 km) Yatuk Creek bridge.

23.3 (37.5 km) **NAUKATI**, a former logging camp, is 3 miles/4.8 km west; no services.

26.5 (42.6 km) **Sarkar Lake** to east. Fishing and boat launch. USFS public-use cabin at east end of lake.

27.9 (44.9 km) Bridge over Sarkar Lake outlet to salt water.

39.7 (63.9 km) USFS Road No. 25 leads east 7 miles/11.3 km past Neck Lake to small settlement of **WHALE PASS**; groceries and gas available. Whale Pass Road loops back to the main North Island Road at **Milepost 48.6.**

40 (64.4 km) View of Neck Lake to east.

48.6 (78.2 km) Whale Pass loop road to east. Whale Pass is 8 miles/12.9 km from here; Exchange Cove is 16 miles/25.7 km from here.

50.3 (80.9 km) View of El Capitan Passage and Kosciusko Island to west.

51 (82.1 km) Side road leads west 1 mile/1.6 km to USFS field camp; good place to launch cartop boats at salt water.

55.6 (89.5 km) Summit of the North Island Road (elev. 907 feet/276m).

59.5 (95.8 km) Rough road, heavy truck traffic and one-lane bridges north from here.

60.6 (97.5 km) Red Creek one-lane bridge.

61.7 (99.3 km) Big Creek one-lane bridge.

63.9 (102.8 km) View of Red Bay to north; Red Lake is to the south.

67.6 (108.8 km) Buster Creek one-lane bridge.

68.3 (109.9 km) Shine Creek one-lane bridge.

72 (115.9 km) Flicker Creek one-lane bridge.

72.1 (116 km) Memorial Beach picnic area 1.7 miles/2.7 km north; follow signs to parking area. A short trail leads to picnic tables, pit toilet, memorial plaque and beach. Good view of Sumner Strait and Kupreanof Island. This site is a memorial to 12 victims of a 1978 air crash.

79.5 (127.9 km) **LABOUCHERE BAY**, a small logging camp (no facilities) owned and operated by Louisiana–Pacific Corp. The road continues several miles and dead ends at the base of Mount Calder.

Coffman Cove Road Log

Coffman Cove Road branches off the North Island Road (No. 20) at **Milepost 15.5** and leads east and north 20.5 miles/33 km to the logging camp of Coffman Cove. Watch for heavy truck traffic; 25 mph/40 kmph. Slow down for approaching vehicles.

0 Junction with North Island Road.

4.4 (7.1 km) Side road on left (USFS Road No. 30) leads 5 miles/8 km through clear-cut and dead ends.

4.5 (7.2 km) **Logjam Creek** bridge; cutthroat, Dolly Varden, steelhead, pink, silver and sockeye salmon.

9.1 (14.6 km) **Hatchery Creek** bridge; fishing same as Logjam Creek. Trailhead for canoe route to Thorne Bay.

9.4 (15.1 km) Bumpy road on right leads 13 miles/20.9 km to USFS access site; parking area and canoe launch (no trailers) on Luck Lake. Side road then loops north along Clarence Strait to Coffman Cove.

12.1 (19.5 km) View of Sweetwater Lake to left. USFS access site: parking area for Sweetwater public-use cabin, located 0.5 mile/0.8 km along west shore of lake.

17 (27.4 km) Coffman Creek bridge.

19.5 (31.4 km) Chum Creek bridge.

20.2 (32.5 km) **Junction** with Luck Lake loop road.

20.3 (32.7 km) Chum Creek bridge.

20.5 (33 km) **COFFMAN COVE**, a logging camp; groceries, gas, cafe and gifts.

Wrangell

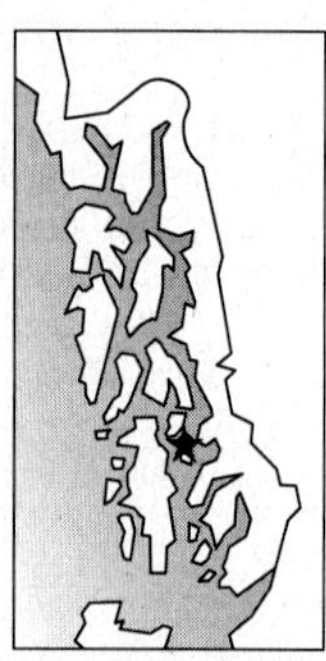

Located at northwest tip of Wrangell Island on Zimovia Strait in central southeastern Alaska; 2.5 miles/4 km south of the Stikine River delta; three hours by ferry or 32 air miles/51.5 km southeast of Petersburg, the closest major community; and six hours by ferry or 85 air miles/136.8 km north of Ketchikan. **Population:** 2,630. **Emergency Services: Police**, phone 874-3304. **Fire Department** and **Ambulance**, phone 874-2000. **Hospital**, Wrangell General, on Bennett Street just off Zimovia Highway, phone 874-3356. **Maritime Search and Rescue**, contact the Coast Guard at 1-800-478-5555.

Visitor Information: Center located in an A-frame building on the corner of Brueger Street and Outer Drive, next to the city hall; phone 874-3901. Write: Chamber of Commerce, Box 49MP, Wrangell, AK 99929. Or contact the Wrangell Convention and Visitors Bureau, Box 1078-MP, Wrangell, AK 99929; phone 874-3770. Information is also available at the Wrangell Museum, one block from the ferry terminal at 122 2nd St.

Elevation: Sea level. **Climate:** Mild and moist with slightly less rain than other Southeast communities. Mean annual precipitation is 79.16 inches, with 63.9 inches of snow. Record monthly precipitation, 20.43 inches in October 1961. Average daily maximum temperature in June is 61°F/16°C; in July 64°F/18°C. Daily minimum in January is 21°F/-6°C. **Radio:** KSTK-FM 101.7. **Television:** Cable and satellite. **Newspaper:** *Wrangell Sentinel* (weekly).

Private Aircraft: Wrangell airport, adjacent northeast; elev. 44 feet/13m; length 6,000 feet/1,829m; paved; fuel 100LL, A.

Wrangell is the only Alaskan city to have existed under four nations and three flags — the Stikine Tlingits, the Russians, British and Americans. Wrangell began in 1834 as a Russian stockade called Redoubt St. Dionysius, built to prevent the Hudson's Bay Co. from fur trading up the rich Stikine River to the east. The Russians, with a change of heart, leased the mainland of southeastern Alaska to Hudson's Bay Co. in 1840. Under the British the stockade was called Fort Stikine.

The post remained under the British flag until Alaska was purchased by the United States in 1867. A year later the Americans established a military post here, naming it Fort Wrangell after the island, which was named by the Russians after Baron von Wrangel, a governor of the Russian–American Co.

Its strategic location near the mouth of the Stikine River, the fastest free-flowing navigable river in North America, made Wrangell an important supply point not only for fur traders but also for gold seekers following the river route to the goldfields. Today, the Stikine River is a popular hunting and recreation area. It is also under study for its potential for hydroelectric power and as a source for copper and other minerals.

Wrangell serves as a hub for goods, services and transportation for outlying fishing villages, and logging and mining camps. Wrangell's economy is also supported by a lumbermill operated by Alaska Pulp Corp., located 6.2 miles/10 km south of town on the Zimovia Highway. The town depended largely on fishing until Japanese interests arrived in the mid-1950s and established a mill downtown (now closed). Fishing is Wrangell's second largest industry, with salmon the major catch.

ACCOMMODATIONS

Wrangell has two motels and three restaurants downtown, as well as service stations, hardware and appliance stores, bakery, fast-food outlets, banks, drugstore, laundromat, grocery stores and gift shops. Bed-and-breakfast accommodations are available. Lodges with restaurants are located on Peninsula Street and at Mile 4.4 Zimovia Highway.

RV camping and picnic area at Shoemaker Bay, **Milepost 4.9** Zimovia Highway. Dump stations located at Shoemaker Bay and downtown at the corner of Front Street and Case Avenue. City Park, at **Milepost 1.9** Zimovia Highway, has tent sites, picnic area with tables, flush toilets, shelters and playground.

TRANSPORTATION

Air: Daily scheduled jet service is provided by Alaska Airlines to other Southeast cities with through service to Seattle and Anchorage. Scheduled commuter air service to Petersburg, Kake and Ketchikan. Charter service available.

Airport terminal is 1.1 miles/1.8 km from ferry terminal or 1.1 miles/1.8 km from Zimovia Highway on Bennett Street.

Ferry: Alaska Marine Highway vessels connect Wrangell with all southeastern Alaska ports plus Prince Rupert, BC, and Bellingham, WA. See MARINE ACCESS ROUTES section for details. Ferry terminal is at the north end of town at the end of Zimovia Highway (also named Church or 2nd Street at this point). Terminal facilities include ticket office, waiting room and vehicle waiting area. Phone 874-3711.

Car Rental: Available.

Taxi: Available to and from airport and ferry terminal.

Highways: Zimovia Highway (see log this section). Logging roads have opened up most of Wrangell Island to motorists. Check with the USFS office at 525 Bennett St. for a copy of the Wrangell Island Road Guide map. (Write USDA Forest Service, Wrangell Ranger District, P.O. Box 51, Wrangell, AK 99929; phone 874-2323.)

Cruise Ships: Wrangell is a regular port of call in summer for several cruise lines.

Private Boats: Transient float located downtown. Reliance Float is located near Shakes Tribal House.

WRANGELL ADVERTISERS

Norris Gift Shop .... Front St.
Stikine Inn and
Dock Side Restaurant .... Stikine Ave.
Tyee Travel, Inc. .... Ph. (907) 874-3383
Wrangell Drug .... Front St.

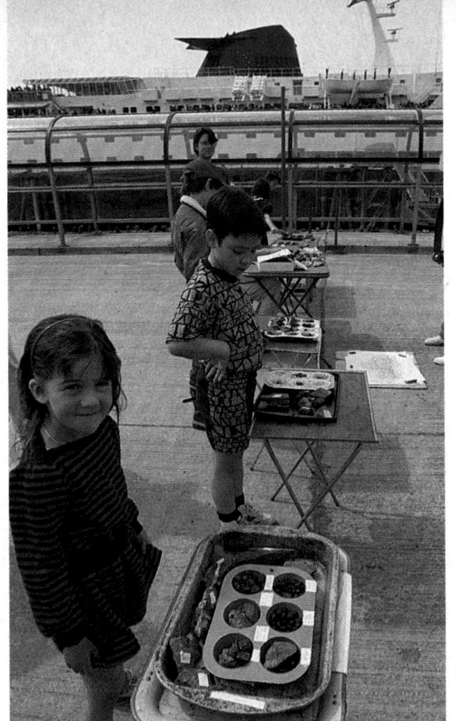

Garnets are sold by children at Wrangell docks. (John W. Warden)

ATTRACTIONS

Shakes Island and Tribal House, in Wrangell Harbor, is reached by boardwalk. It is the site of several excellent totem poles. The replica tribal house contains Indian working tools, an original Chilkat blanket design and other cultural items. It is listed on the National Register of Historic Places. Open irregular hours during summer (May to September) or by appointment; phone 874-3747. Admission $1.

Totem Poles. The last original totems standing in Wrangell were cut down in November 1981 and removed for preservation. A totem restoration project funded by both state and federal agencies was initiated, and replicas of original totems can be found at Kiksadi Totem Park at the corner of Front and Episcopal streets.

Wrangell Museum, at 122 2nd street, two blocks from the ferry terminal, features items from Wrangell's history, including Tlingit artifacts and petroglyphs. The building is a former schoolhouse (on the National Register of Historic Buildings). In summer, the museum is open Monday and Wednesday through Friday 9:30 A.M. to 1 P.M. and 2 to 5 P.M., Saturday and Sunday 1–3:30 P.M., and for at least two hours when cruise ships and most ferries are in port. Open Wednesday in winter 1-4 P.M. and by appointment (phone 874-3770). Admission $1.

Our Collections Museum, located on Evergreen Avenue, is a private collection of antiques and Alaska memorabilia. Open when cruise ships and ferries are in port and by special request. Phone 874-3646. Donations accepted.

Sightseeing Tours of historic attractions and fish bakes are available upon request. Sightseeing buses meet some ferries. Inquire at the visitor center or Wrangell Museum.

The Stikine River delta lies north of Wrangell within the Stikine–LeConte Wilderness. It is accessible by boat or by plane only. The delta is prime habitat for migrating waterfowl, eagles, moose and bear. During the spring run, the second largest concentration of bald eagles in the world can be seen in the Stikine River delta. Also watch for seals resting on ice floes from LeConte Glacier (the glacier is at the head of LeConte Bay, just north of the delta), the southernmost tidewater glacier in North America.

Anan Observatory, managed by the U.S. Forest Service, is located 35 miles/56 km southeast of Wrangell; accessible by boat or plane only. During July and August, visitors can watch bears catch pink salmon headed for the salmon spawning grounds. Bald eagles, ravens, crows and seals are frequently seen feeding on the fish.

AREA FISHING: Fly in to **Thoms Lake, Long Lake, Marten Lake, Salmon Bay, Virginia Lake** and **Eagle Lake.** Thoms Lake and Long Lake are also accessible via road and trail. **Stikine River** near Wrangell (closed to king salmon fishing), Dolly Varden to 22 inches, and cutthroat to 18 inches, best in August; steelhead to 12 lbs., use bait or lures; coho salmon 10 to 15 lbs., use lures, September and October. Saltwater fishing near Wrangell for king salmon, 20 to 40 lbs., best in May and June. Stop by the Dept. of Fish and Game at 215 Front St. for details.

Wrangell Salmon Derby runs from mid-May to Memorial Day weekend. Kings weighing more than 50 lbs. are not unusual.

Petroglyphs are ancient designs pecked into on rock faces, usually found near the high tide marks on beaches. Petroglyph Beach is located 0.7 mile/1.1 km from the ferry terminal; a boardwalk trail leads to the head of the beach from the left of the road. Turn right as you reach the beach and look for petroglyphs between there and a rock outcrop several hundred feet away; at least 20 can be seen. Petroglyphs are also located on the library lawn and are on display in the museum.

Garnet Ledge, a rocky outcrop on the right bank of the Stikine River delta at Garnet Creek, is 7.5 miles/12.1 km from Wrangell Harbor, reached at high tide by small boat. Garnet, a semiprecious stone, can be found embedded in the ledge here. The garnet ledge is on land deeded to the Southeast Council of the Boy Scouts of America by the late Fred Hanford (former mayor of Wrangell). The bequest states that the land shall be used for scouting purposes and the children of Wrangell may take garnets in reasonable quantities (garnets are sold by children at the docks when ships and ferries are in port). Contact the Wrangell Museum (Box 1050-MP, Wrangell 99929; phone 874-3770) for information on digging for garnets.

USFS public-use cabins in the Wrangell district are accessible by air or by boat. The 20 USFS cabins are scattered throughout the region. See Cabins in the GENERAL INFORMATION section, and stop by the USFS office at 525 Bennett St.; phone 874-2323. Visitors may also use the white courtesy phone located in the ferry terminal building. Contact the Wrangell Ranger District at Box 51, Wrangell 99929.

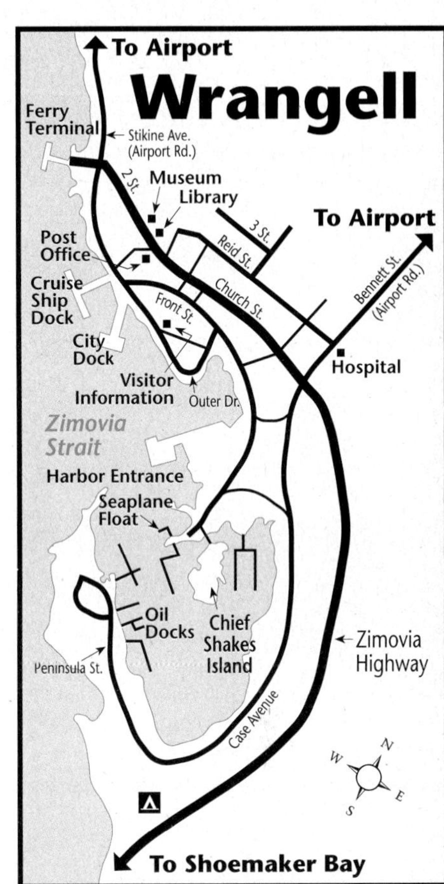

Celebrations in Wrangell include a big Fourth of July celebration that begins with a salmon bake. The annual Tent City Festival, celebrated the first weekend in February, commemorates Wrangell's gold rush days.

Zimovia Highway Log

Zimovia Highway leads south from the ferry terminal to Pat Creek at Mile 11, where it

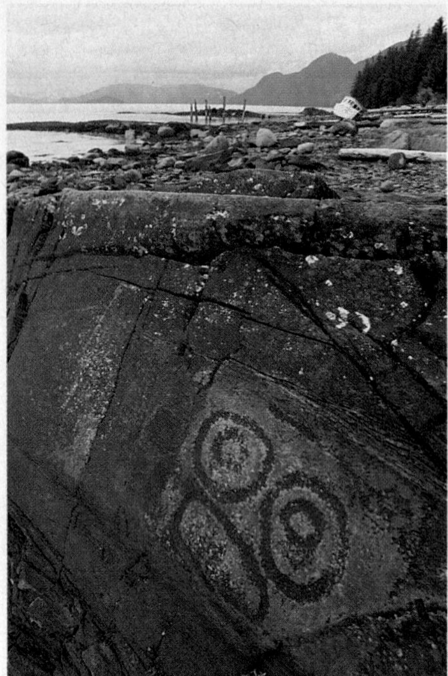

Petroglyphs are found along the beach near Wrangell's ferry terminal. (John W. Warden)

connects with island logging roads.

0 Alaska Marine Highway ferry terminal, ticket office and waiting area. There is a bike path to Mile 1.9.

0.2 (0.3 km) Wrangell Museum and library on left. Two totems stand in front. Post office located across from library.

0.3 (0.5 km) St. Rose of Lima Catholic Church, the oldest Roman Catholic parish in Alaska, founded May 2, 1879.

0.4 (0.6 km) First Presbyterian Church has a red-lighted cross, one of two in the world that serve as navigational aids. This was the first church in Wrangell and is one of the oldest Protestant churches in Alaska (founded in 1877 and built in 1879).

0.6 (1 km) Bennett Street (Airport Road) loops north to the airport and back to the ferry terminal, a distance of 2.2 miles/3.5 km.

0.7 (1.1 km) Public Safety Bldg.

1.9 (3.1 km) City park. Picnic area with shelters, firepits, restrooms, litter barrels. Tent camping only allowed; 24-hour limit. ▲

3.6 (5.8 km) Turnout with beach access. Several turnouts along the highway here offer beach access and good spots for bird watching.

4.4 (7.1 km) Lodge on left with restaurant and lounge.

4.9 (7.9 km) Shoemaker Bay small-boat harbor, boat launch, picnic, camping and parking area. Camping area has tent sites, 29 RV sites ($8 per night, no hookups), water, dump station and restrooms. Tennis court, horseshoe pits and children's playground nearby. Rainbow Falls trailhead; 0.7 mile/1.1 km trail to scenic waterfall. Rainbow Falls trail intersects with Institute Creek trail, which leads 3.5 miles/5.6 km to viewpoint and shelter overlooking Shoemaker Bay. ▲

6.5 (10.5 km) Alaska Pulp Corp.

7.3 (11.7 km) **Milepost 7**, scenic turnout.

8 (12.9 km) Turnout.

8.5 (13.7 km) Turnout, beach access (8 Mile Beach undeveloped recreation area).

10.8 (17.4 km) Access road west to Pat Creek Log Transfer Facility. Road east (Pat Creek Road) leads 0.3 mile/0.5 km to Pat's Lake. This single-lane maintained gravel road continues approximately 6 miles/9.7 km northeast through logging area.

Pat Creek and **Pat's Lake**, cutthroat, Dolly Varden, pink and silver salmon; use bait, spinning gear or flies for Dolly Varden and cutthroat, May to October; use herring, spoon for silvers.

11 (17.7 km) Pat Creek camping area (unmaintained, no facilities); parking for self-contained vehicles. ▲

11.1 (17.9 km) State-maintained highway ends. Begin one-lane Forest Development Road No. 6265 connecting with other Forest Service logging roads (map available from USFS office in Wrangell). Watch for logging trucks.

Petersburg

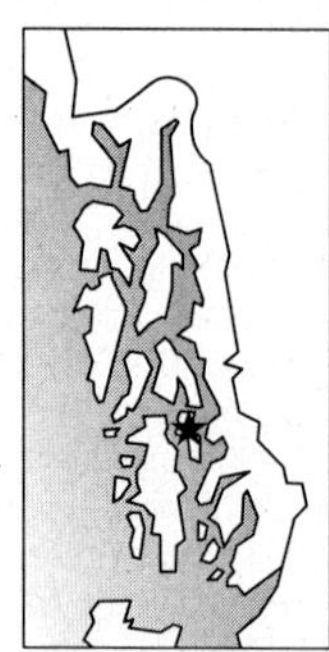

Located on the northwest tip of Mitkof Island at the northern end of Wrangell Narrows, midway between Juneau and Ketchikan. **Population:** 3,620. **Emergency Services:** Phone 911. **Alaska State Troopers**, phone 772-3100. **City Police, Poison Center, Fire Department** and **Ambulance**, phone 772-3838. **Hospital**, Petersburg General, 1st and Excel streets, phone 772-4291. **Maritime Search and Rescue:** contact the Coast Guard at 1-800-478-5555. Harbormaster, phone 772-4688, or CB Channel 9, or VHF Channel 16.

Visitor Information: Chamber of commerce information center located at 1st and Fram streets; open weekdays from 8:30 A.M. to 5 P.M. spring and summer, limited hours during fall and winter. Write: Petersburg Chamber of Commerce, P.O. Box 649MP, Petersburg 99833, phone 772-3646. Petersburg Museum, 2nd and Fram streets. Summer hours 11 A.M. to 5 P.M., Monday, Tuesday, Wednesday; 1-5 P.M. Thursday, Friday, Saturday; 1-8 P.M. Sunday. Phone 772-3598 for winter hours and other information. Alaska Dept. of Fish and Game, State Office Bldg., Sing Lee Alley; open 8 A.M. to 4:30 P.M., Monday through Friday. U.S. Forest Service, in the Federal Bldg.; phone 772-3871 or write P.O. Box 1328, Petersburg 99833.

Elevation: Sea level. **Climate:** Average daily maximum temperature in July, 64°F/18°C; daily minimum in January, 20°F/-7°C. All-time high, 84°F/29°C in 1933; record low, -19°F/-28°C in 1947. Mean annual precipitation, 105 inches; mean annual snowfall, 119 inches. **Radio:** KFSK-FM 100.9, KRSA 580. **Television:** Rural Alaska Television Network, Channel 15; KTOO (PBS) Channel 9 and cable channels. **Newspaper:** *Petersburg Pilot* (weekly).

Private Aircraft: Petersburg airport, 1 mile/1.6 km southeast; elev. 107 feet/33m; length 6,000 feet/1,829m; asphalt; fuel 100, A. Seaplane base 0.5 mile/0.8 km from downtown.

Petersburg was named for Peter Buschmann, who selected the present townsite for a salmon cannery and sawmill in 1897. The sawmill and dock were built in 1899, and the cannery was completed in 1900. He was followed by other Norwegian–Americans who came to fish and work in the cannery and sawmill. Since then the cannery has operated continuously (with rebuilding, expansion and different owners) and is now known as Petersburg Fisheries, a division of Icicle Seafoods Inc.

Today, Petersburg boasts the largest home-based halibut fleet in Alaska and is also well known for its shrimp, crab, salmon, herring and other fish products. Most families depend on the fishing industry for a livelihood. Sportfishing questions should be directed to the Alaska Dept. of Fish and Game's Division of Sportfishing in Ketchikan, phone 225-2859.

ACCOMMODATIONS

Petersburg has a hotel, several motels and bed and breakfasts, many restaurants and several fast-food outlets downtown. The five-block-long commercial area on Main Street (Nordic Drive) has grocery stores, marine and fishing supply stores, hardware, drugstores, travel agency, public showers, banks, gift and variety stores specializing in both Alaskan and Scandinavian items, city hall, post office, gas stations, cocktail bars and a public swimming pool. Petersburg has 17 churches.

There are three RV parks, dump station, hookups, showers, laundry, fee charged. There is a tent campground (known locally as Tent City) on Haugen Drive; it is often filled to capacity in summer with young cannery workers. Public campgrounds are located on Mitkof Highway south of town. ▲

TRANSPORTATION

Air: Daily scheduled jet air service is by Alaska Airlines to major Southeast cities and Seattle, WA, with connections to Anchorage and Fairbanks. Local and charter service available.

The airport, located 1 mile/1.6 km from the Federal Bldg. on Haugen Drive, has a ticket counter and waiting room.

Ferry: Alaska Marine Highway vessels connect Petersburg with all southeastern Alaska cities plus Prince Rupert, BC, and Bellingham, WA. (See MARINE ACCESS ROUTES section for schedules.) Terminal at Milepost 0.9 Mitkof Highway, includes dock, ticket office with waiting room and parking area. Phone 772-3855.

NOTE: RVs arriving late at night are allowed to park free for up to eight hours at the south boat harbor parking lot just north of the ferry terminal.

Car Rental. Available at downtown hotels.

Taxi: There are two taxi companies. Cab service to and from the airport and ferry terminal.

Highways: Mitkof Highway, Sandy Beach Road and Three Lakes Loop Road (see logs this section).

Private Boats: Boaters must check with harbormaster for moorage assignment.

ATTRACTIONS

Clausen Memorial Museum, 203 Fram St., features the world-record king salmon caught in a fish trap commercially (126½ lbs.) and the world-record chum salmon (36 lbs.). It also houses collections of local historical items including a re-creation of the office of colorful local cannery owner Earl Ohmer. Hours are noon-5 P.M. daily from early May to mid-September; call 772-3598 for schedule changes and winter hours.

The Fisk, a 10-foot/3-m bronze sculpture commemorating Petersburg's fishing way of life, stands in a working fountain in front of the museum. It was completed during the Alaska centennial year of 1967 by sculptor Carson Boysen.

Sons of Norway Hall, on the National Register of Historic Places, was built in 1912. Situated on pilings over Hammer Slough (a favorite photography subject), its window shutters are decorated with rosemaling (Norwegian tole painting).

Little Norway Festival is usually scheduled on the weekend closest to Norwegian Independence Day, May 17. Pageantry, old-country dress, contests, Vikings, a Viking ship, dancing and a Norwegian "fish feed" for locals and visitors are featured.

LeConte Glacier, in LeConte Bay, 25 miles/40 km east of Petersburg, is the continent's southernmost tidewater glacier. Fast-moving, the glacier continually "calves," creating thunderous ice falls from its face into the bay. Seals and porpoises are common; whales are often seen. Small aircraft and boats may be chartered in Petersburg or Wrangell to see LeConte Glacier.

Salmon migration and spawning are best observed in the Petersburg area during August and September. Falls Creek bridge and fish ladder is a good location (silver and pink) as are Blind Slough and the Blind River Rapids area, Petersburg Creek and Ohmer Creek (king, silver, pink and chum).

Crystal Lake Fish Hatchery is at Milepost 17.5 Mitkof Highway. This hatchery for coho, king, and steelhead trout is operated by the state of Alaska and used for fish stocking projects in southeastern Alaska. It is open for visits and hatchery personnel will explain the operation, though formal guided tours are not available. Best time to visit is between 8 A.M. and 4 P.M., Monday through Friday.

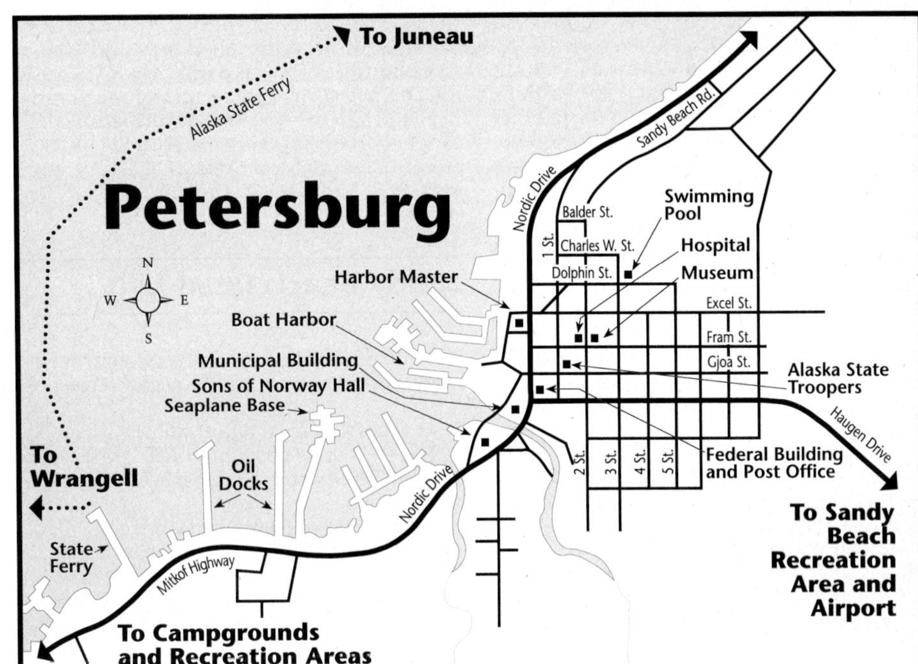

Falls Creek fish ladder is at **Milepost 10.8** Mitkof Highway. The ladder helps migrating salmon bypass difficult falls on the way to spawning grounds in Falls Creek. It can be observed from the creek bank just off the roadside. Best time is late summer and early fall to observe coho and pink salmon.

Petersburg Salmon Derby is scheduled for Memorial Day weekend. Check with the chamber of commerce for details.

Charter a Boat or Plane. There are charter boat services in Petersburg for guided salt- and freshwater fishing trips. Inquire at the chamber of commerce office. Charter floatplanes and helicopters are available for flightseeing, fly-in fishing and transportation.

AREA FISHING: Salmon, steelhead, cutthroat and Dolly Varden at **Falls Creek, Blind Slough** and **Blind River Rapids;** see log of Mitkof Highway this section. Salmon can be caught in the harbor area and **Scow Bay** area. (Rapid tidal currents in front of

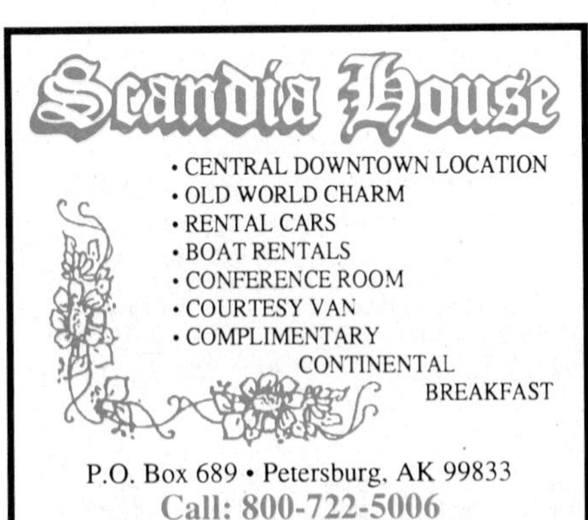

the town necessitate the use of an outboard motor.) **Petersburg Creek,** directly across Wrangell Narrows from downtown within Petersburg Creek–Duncan Salt Chuck Wilderness Area, also offers good fishing. Blind Slough, located 15 miles from the Alaska Marine Highway Ferry Terminal, offers good drive-up fishing for king salmon. Dolly Varden can be caught from the beach north of town and from downtown docks. Sportfishing opportunities for halibut, rockfish, crab and shrimp. Harvest of mussels, clams and the like is not recommended because of the possibility of paralytic shellfish poisoning. Contact the sportfishing division of the Alaska Dept. of Fish and Game (225-2859) for additional information.

Wrangell Narrows is a 23-mile-/37-km-long channel between Mitkof and Kupreanof islands. The channel was dredged in the 1940s to a depth of 26 feet/42m. Extremely narrow in places and filled with rocky reefs, islands and strong currents, the narrows is navigated by ships and ferries with the aid of dozens of markers and flashing lights. The one-and-one-half-hour run through Wrangell Narrows begins on ferries immediately departing Petersburg southbound, or about one and one-half hours after departing Wrangell northbound.

Cabins, canoe and hiking trails managed by the USFS are all within reach of Petersburg, which is the administrative center for the Stikine Area of Tongass National Forest. Stop by the USFS office in the Federal Bldg., or phone 772-3871 for detailed information on cabins and trails. Also consult *The ALASKA WILDERNESS GUIDE*. See also Cabins in the GENERAL INFORMATION section. Information for canoers and kayakers interested in the Stikine River delta or Tebenkof Bay is also available here or at the USFS office in Wrangell.

Sandy Beach Road Log

From Federal Bldg., drive north through town; road leads to Sandy Beach Recreation Area.

0 Federal Bldg. and post office.

0.1 (0.2 km) Petersburg boat harbor one block to left contains one of Alaska's finest fishing fleets.

0.2 (0.3 km) Downtown Petersburg.

0.3 (0.5 km) Petersburg Fisheries Inc., processing plant, Petersburg's largest.

1.2 (1.9 km) Eagle observation point. Eagles can be seen nesting nearby and fishing in Wrangell Narrows. To the northeast is Frederick Sound and the mainland. Icebergs may be spotted in Frederick Sound in the summer.

2.8 (4.5 km) Sandy Beach Recreation Area on left; picnic tables, shelter, toilets, limited parking, no camping. **Junction** with Haugen Road, which loops to airport and back to town.

Mitkof Highway Log

The major road on the island, Mitkof Highway leads 33.8 miles/54.4 km south from the Federal Bldg. to the Stikine River delta at the south end of Mitkof Island. The highway is paved to **Milepost 17.5**; good wide gravel to road end.

0 Federal Bldg. and post office.

0.1 (0.2 km) Bridge over Hammer Slough, an intertidal estuary.

0.5 (0.8 km) Harbor parking and RV staging area (eight-hour RV parking).

0.6 (1 km) Pier and floatplane base.

Petersburg's picturesque Hammer Slough. (Loren Taft)

0.8 (1.3 km) Marine Highway ferry terminal, office and waiting area on right.

2.8 (4.5 km) Muskeg meadows on left. Muskeg is a grassy bog, common in Alaska.

2.9 (4.6 km) **Scow Bay,** a wide portion of Wrangell Narrows with king salmon fishing in spring. Scow Bay is noted traditionally as the first election precinct to report its vote in statewide elections. Scow Bay Loop Road rejoins highway at **Milepost 3.1.**

4 (6.4 km) Lodging on right.

4.3 (6.9 km) Turnout on right with view of Wrangell Narrows.

7.5 (12.1 km) Twin Creek RV Park, private campground and phone.

10.7 (17.2 km) North exit to Three Lakes Loop Road (see log this section).

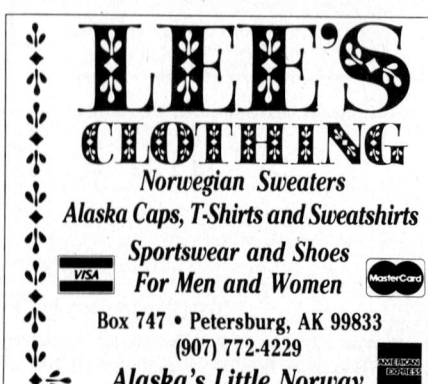

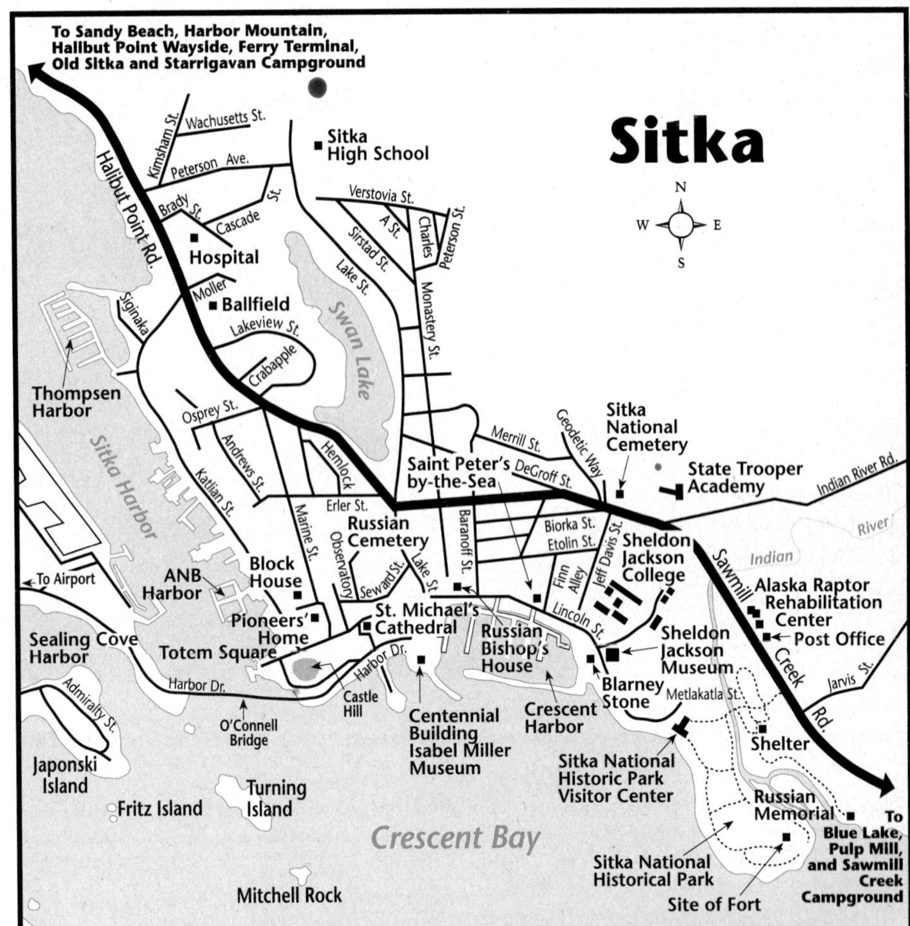

10.8 (17.4 km) **Falls Creek** and fish ladder. Steelhead, April and May; pink salmon below falls in August; coho, August and September; Dolly Varden and cutthroat late summer and fall. No fishing within 300 feet of fish ladder.

11 (17.7 km) Road on right leads 0.5 mile/0.6 km to Papke's Landing; transient boat moorage and boat ramp. USFS Log Transportation Facility.

12.5 (20.1 km) Trailhead.

14.5 (23.3 km) Blind River Rapids parking area and trail. A 0.3-mile/0.4-km boardwalk trail leads through a muskeg meadow to **Blind River Rapids,** hatchery steelhead, mid-April to mid-May; king salmon, June to late July; coho, mid-August to October. Also Dolly Varden and cutthroat.

16.3 (26.2 km) Blind Slough waterfowl viewing area on right. Covered platform with interpretive sign on area waterfowl. Trumpeter swans overwinter in this area.

17.5 (28.2 km) Pavement ends; wide, hard-packed gravel to end of road. Short road leads to Crystal Lake Fish Hatchery and **Blind Slough** Recreation Area with picnic tables, shelter and pit toilets. Hatchery is open for visiting, though no scheduled tours are available. Fishing for steelhead, best in May; cutthroat and Dolly Varden in summer; coho salmon, mid-August to mid-September; king salmon in June and July.

20 (32.2 km) **Manmade Hole** picnic area with tables, firepits, swimming and short trail. Ice-skating in winter. Fishing for cutthroat and Dolly Varden year-round; best in summer and fall.

20.6 (33.1 km) Three Lakes Loop Road begins on left leading to Three Lakes on other side of Mitkof Island, looping back to Mitkof Highway at **Milepost 10.7** near Falls Creek bridge.

21.4 (34.4 km) Woodpecker Cove Road (one-lane) leads about 15 miles/24 km along south Mitkof Island to Woodpecker Cove and beyond. Good views of Sumner Strait. Watch for logging trucks.

21.5 (34.6 km) Ohmer Creek interpretive trail, 0.1 mile/0.2 km long.

21.7 (34.9 km) Ohmer Creek Campground, 15 sites, pit toilets, parking area, picnic tables and firepits. Set in meadow area among trees.

24 (38.6 km) **Blind Slough** USFS Log Transportation Facility. Excellent fishing from skiff for king salmon in June and July, coho salmon, mid-August to mid-September.

26.1 (42 km) Narrow 0.7-mile/1.1-km road on right to Sumner Strait Campground (undeveloped); parking for a dozen vehicles but no other facilities.

27 (43.4 km) View of city of Wrangell.

28 (45 km) Wilson Creek state recreation area (undeveloped); picnic tables, parking. Good view of Sumner Strait.

28.6 (46 km) Banana Point, boat ramp.

31 (49.9 km) Stikine River mud flats, visible on right at low tide. Part of the Stikine River delta, this is the area where Dry Strait meets Sumner Strait.

33.8 (54.4 km) Road ends with turnaround.

Three Lakes Loop Road Log

Access to this 21.4-mile-/34.4-km-long, one-lane loop road is from **Mileposts 10.7** and **20.6** on the Mitkof Highway. *CAUTION: No services; use turnouts.*

0 Junction at **Milepost 10.7** Mitkof Highway; turn east.

1.4 (2.3 km) View of Wrangell Narrows to west. Older clear-cuts; this area was logged between 1964 and 1968.

4.4 (7.1 km) Falls Creek bridge.

7 (11.3 km) Second-growth stand of spruce-hemlock. First growth was destroyed by fire or wind throw more than 180 years ago. This second-growth stand serves as an example of what a logging unit could look like a century or two after clear-cutting.

9.7 (15.6 km) Directly south is a 384-acre clear-cut logged in 1973 under a contract predating the current policy, which usually limits clear-cut tracts to 100 acres.

10.2 (16.4 km) **Big Creek**; steelhead in April and May; coho late August and September; cutthroat and Dolly Varden, best late summer and fall.

12.3 (19.8 km) Muskeg; view of Frederick Sound.

14.2 (22.8 km) Sand Lake trail. Short boardwalk trail leads to each of the Three Lakes. Tennis shoes are ideal for these short walks, but for areas around the lakes it is advisable to wear rubber boots. A 0.7-mile/1.1-km connecting trail to Hill Lake.

14.7 (23.6 km) Hill Lake trail.

15.1 (24.3 km) Crane Lake trail, 1.3 miles/2.1 km to lake; connecting trail to Hill Lake. USFS skiffs and picnic platforms are located at Sand, Hill and Crane lakes.

Sand, Hill and **Crane lakes,** cutthroat trout from May through September.

16.4 (26.4 km) Dry Straits Road.

21.4 (34.4 km) Second **junction** with Mitkof Highway, at **Milepost 20.6.**

Sitka

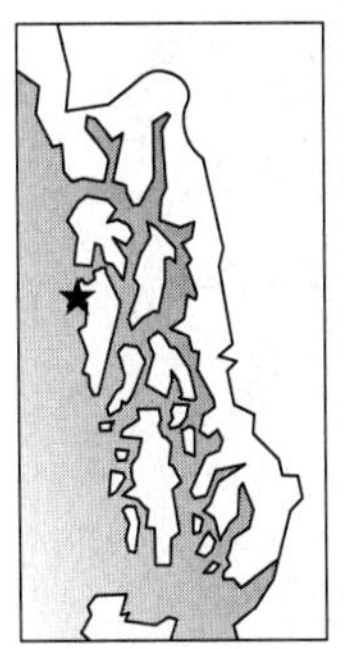

Located on west side of Baranof Island, 95 air miles/153 km southwest of Juneau, 185 air miles/298 km northwest of Ketchikan; two hours flying time from Seattle, WA. **Population:** City and Borough, 8,588. **Emergency Services: Alaska State Troopers, City Police, Fire Department,** and **Ambulance,** phone 911. **Hospital,** Sitka Community, phone 747-3241; Mount Edgecumbe, phone 966-2411. **Maritime Search and Rescue,** phone the Coast Guard at 1-800-478-5555.

Visitor Information: Available at the Isabel Miller Museum in the Centennial Bldg. on Harbor Drive. Museum hours are 8 A.M. to 5 P.M. in summer, extended hours to accommodate ferry passengers; phone 747-6455. Also located in the Centennial Bldg. are the offices of the Sitka Convention and Visitors Bureau and the Greater Sitka Chamber of Commerce. Write the chamber of commerce at Box 638, Sitka 99835; phone 747-8604. Write the Sitka Convention and Visitors Bureau at Box 1226-MP, or phone 747-5940. For U.S. Forest Service information write the Sitka Ranger District at 204 Siginaka Way, or phone 747-6671. For information on Sitka National Historical Park, write Box 738.

Elevation: Sea level. **Climate:** Average daily temperature in July, 55°F/13°C; in Jan-

St. Michael's is in the center of Lincoln Street. (John W. Warden)

uary, 33°F/1°C. Annual precipitation, 95 inches. **Radio:** KIFW 1230, KCAW-FM 104.7, KSBZ-FM 103.1, KRSA-FM 94.9. **Television:** Cable channels. **Newspaper:** *Daily Sitka Sentinel.*

Private Aircraft: Sitka airport on Japonski Island; elev. 21 feet/6m; length 6,500 feet/1,981m; asphalt; fuel 100, A1. Sitka seaplane base adjacent west; fuel 80, 100.

One of the most scenic of southeastern Alaskan cities, Sitka rests on the ocean shore protected at the west by a myriad of small islands and Cape Edgecumbe. Mount Edgecumbe, the Fuji-like volcano (dormant), is 3,201 feet/976m high.

The site was originally occupied by Tlingit Indians. Alexander Baranof, chief manager of the Russian–American Company headquartered in Kodiak, built a trading post and fort (St. Michael's Redoubt) north of Sitka in 1799. Indians burned down the fort and looted the warehouses. Baranof returned in 1804, and by 1808 Sitka was capital of Russian Alaska. Baranof was governor from 1790 to 1818. A statue of the Russian governor was unveiled in 1989; it is located outside of the Centennial Bldg. Castle Hill in Sitka is where Alaska changed hands from Russia to the United States in 1867. Salmon was the mainstay of the economy from the late 1800s until the 1950s, when the numbers of salmon decreased. A pulp mill operated at nearby Silver Bay from 1960 to 1993. Today, tourism, commercial fishing, cold storage plants and government provide most jobs.

ACCOMMODATIONS

Sitka has several hotels/motels, most with adjacent restaurants. Bed and breakfasts are also available.

Sitka Youth Hostel is located at the United Methodist Church, 303 Kimsham St. (one and one-half blocks north from Peterson Avenue and Halibut Point Road). Send correspondence to P.O. Box 2645, Sitka 99835. Open June 1 to Aug. 31; 20 beds, showers, no kitchen facilities. Phone (907) 747-8356.

An array of businesses cluster in the downtown area, which saw its first traffic light installed in 1992. Services in Sitka's downtown area include restaurants, a laundry, drugstore, clothing and grocery stores, and gift shops. Shopping and services are also available along Sawmill and Halibut Point roads. Dump stations are located at the Wastewater Treatment Plant on Japonski Island.

Four campgrounds are available in the Sitka area. From the ferry terminal north they are: the Starrigavan Campground (USFS) at **Milepost 7.8** Halibut Point Road, with 28 sites, six picnic sites, water, tables, pit toilets, 14-day limit, $5 fee; Sitka Sportsman's Assoc. RV Park, located one block south of the ferry terminal on Halibut Point Road, with eight RV sites, water and electrical hookups, $10 fee, reservations accepted (phone 747-6033); Sealing Cove (operated by the City and Borough of Sitka), located adjacent Sealing Cove Boat Harbor on Japonski Island, has overnight parking for 26 RVs, water and electrical hookups, 15-night limit, $10 fee; and Sawmill Creek Campground (USFS) at **Milepost 5.4** Sawmill Creek Road, with eight sites for self-contained RVs and tenting, pit toilets, boil water, unmaintained, no camping fee.

TRANSPORTATION

Air: Scheduled jet service via Alaska Airlines. Charter and commuter service also available. The airport is on Japonski Island, across O'Connell Bridge, 1.7 miles/2.7 km from downtown via Airport Road. Airport facilities include ticket counters, rental cars, small gift shop, restaurant and lounge. Van service to downtown hotels available.

Ferry: Alaska Marine Highway ferry ter-

SITKA ADVERTISERS

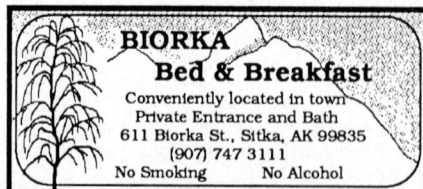

Alaska Ocean View Bed and Breakfast ....1101 Edgecumbe Dr.
Biorka Bed & Breakfast.............611 Biorka St.
Helga's Bed & Breakfast ....2821 Halibut Point Rd.
Karras Bed & Breakfast .....230 Kogwanton St.
Potlatch House, The ....713 Katlian St.
Seafish Alaska ....Ph. (907) 747-5497
Sitka Convention & Visitors Bureau ....Ph. (907) 747-5940
Sitka Hotel..............................118 Lincoln St.
Sitka Sportsman's Assn. RV Park ....Ph. (907) 747-6033
Sitka Super 8 Motel ....Ph. 1-800-800-8000

minal is located at **Milepost 7** Halibut Point Road; phone 747-8737. Buses for downtown meet all ferries. Van and taxi service also available. Sitka is connected via the Marine Highway to other Southeast ports, Prince Rupert, BC, and Bellingham, WA (see MARINE ACCESS ROUTES section).

Bus: Available to downtown hotels.

Taxi: Local service is available.

Car Rental: At airport.

Highways: Halibut Point Road, 7.9 miles/12.7 km, and Sawmill Creek Road, 7.4 miles/11.9 km; see logs this section.

Cruise Ships: Sitka is a popular port of call for several cruise lines.

Private Boats: Transient moorage available at ANB Harbor, located downtown next to the fuel dock; Thomsen Harbor on Katlian Street, 0.6 mile from city center; and Sealing Cove on Japonski Island. Moorage is limited during the summer.

ATTRACTIONS

St. Michael's Cathedral is the focal point of Sitka's history as the capital of Russian Alaska. Built in 1844–48 by Bishop Innocent Veniaminov of the Russian Orthodox Church, this building stood for 118 years as one of the finest examples of rural Russian church architecture. It was destroyed by fire on Jan. 2, 1966. Priceless icons, some dating back before 1800, were saved by townspeople and are now back in place in the rebuilt cathedral (an exact replica).

St. Michael's is located in the center of Lincoln Street downtown; a donation is requested when entering to view icons. Open daily June 1 to Sept. 30, 11 A.M. to 3 P.M. St. Michael's currently serves a Russian Orthodox congregation of about 100 families in Sitka. Visitors are reminded that this is an active parish conducting weekly services.

Castle Hill (Baranof Castle Hill Historic Site) is where Alaska changed hands from Russia to the United States on Oct. 18, 1867. Castle Hill was the site of Baranof's castle. Walkway to site is located on the south side by the bridge (look for sign).

Sitka Pioneers' Home, near the waterfront at Lincoln and Katlian streets, was built in 1934. Pioneers welcome visitors, and handicrafts made by the residents are sold in the gift shop located on the first floor of the west wing.

The Prospector is a 13½-foot/4-m clay and bronze statue in front of the Pioneers' Home. Done by Alonzo Victor Lewis, the statue was dedicated on Alaska Day in 1949. Lewis's model was a real pioneer, William "Skagway Bill" Fonda.

Totem Square is across Katlian Street from the Pioneers' Home and contains a totem, petroglyphs, Russian cannon and three large anchors found in Sitka Harbor and believed to be 18th century English.

Russian Blockhouse beside Pioneers' Home is a replica of the blockhouse that separated Russian and Tlingit sections of Sitka after the Tlingits moved back to the area 20 years after the 1804 battle. (See model of early Sitka in Centennial Bldg.)

New Archangel Russian Dancers, a group of local women, perform authentic Russian dances in authentic costumes. Performances are scheduled to coincide with the arrival of cruise ships. Fee charged. Inquire at the Centennial Bldg. for details.

Old Russian Cemetery is located behind Pioneers' Home and includes graves of such notables as Princess Maksoutoff, wife of Alaska's last Russian governor.

Sitka National Cemetery, at **Milepost 0.5** Sawmill Creek Road, is open 8 A.M. to 5 P.M. daily (maintained by the Veterans Administration). It was known locally as military cemetery. In 1924 Pres. Calvin Coolidge designated the site as Sitka National Cemetery, and until WWII it was the only national cemetery west of the Rockies. Civil War veterans, veterans of the Aleutian Campaign in WWII and many notable Alaskans are buried here. One gravestone is dated December 1867, two months after the U.S. purchase of Alaska from Russia.

Alaska Day Celebration, Oct. 14–18, celebrates the transfer of Alaska from Russia to the United States with a reenactment of the event, complete with Sitka's own 9th (Manchu) Infantry, authentic uniforms and working muskets of the period. Period costumes and beards are the order of the day. Events ranging from pageant to costume ball and parade highlight the affair.

Annual Sitka Summer Music Festival (June 3–24, 1994). Concerts on Tuesday, Friday and some Saturday evenings in the Centennial Bldg., praised for its excellent acoustics. Emphasizing chamber music, an international group of professional musicians gathers to give evening concerts during the festival, plus open rehearsals. Advance tickets are a good idea; the concerts are popular. Dress is informal and concert-goers may have the opportunity to talk with the musicians. Children under 6 years not admitted.

Centennial Building, by the boat harbor on Harbor Drive, is used for Russian dance performances, music festivals, banquets and conventions. Its glass-fronted main hall overlooks Sitka Sound. Chamber of commerce and Sitka Visitors Bureau offices are located here. Nearby is a large hand-carved Tlingit canoe made from a single log.

Isabel Miller Museum, located in the Centennial Bldg., has permanent exhibits highlighting the history of Sitka and its people. Russian tools, paintings from all eras, fishing and forestry exhibits, Alaska Purchase exhibit, and an 8-foot-square scale model of Sitka in 1867 are among the displays. Operated by the Sitka Historical Society; hosts are available to answer questions. Open year-round. Hours are 8 A.M. to 5 P.M. daily in summer; 10 A.M. to noon and 1-4 P.M. weekdays, and by appointment during the winter.

Sitka Lutheran Church, downtown on Lincoln Street, has a small historical display. This was the first organized Lutheran congregation west of the Rockies and one of the first Protestant churches in Alaska.

Sitka is located on the west side of Baranof Island. (Loren Taft)

Sitka National Historical Park reflects both the community's rich Tlingit Indian heritage and its Russian-ruled past. The park consists of two units — the Fort Site, located at the end of Lincoln Street, 0.5 mile/0.8 km from town, and the Russian Bishop's House, located on Lincoln Street near Crescent Harbor.

At the Fort Site stood the Tlingit fort, burned to the ground by Russians after the 1804 Battle of Sitka; this was the last major stand by the Tlingits against Russian settlement. For Alexander Baranof, leader of the Russians, the battle was revenge for the 1802 destruction of Redoubt St. Michael by the Tlingits. There is a visitor center here with audiovisual programs and exhibits of Indian artifacts. The Southeast Alaska Indian Cultural Center has contemporary Tlingit artists demonstrate and interpret various traditional arts for visitors.

There is a self-guiding trail through the park to the fort site and battleground of 1804. The National Park Service conducts guided walks; check for schedule. The park's totem pole collection stands near the visitor center and along the trail. The collection includes original pieces collected in 1901–03, and copies of originals lost to time and the elements. The pieces, primarily from Prince of Wales Island, were collected by Alaska governor John Brady (now buried in Sitka National Cemetery). The originals were exhibited at the 1904 St. Louis Exposition.

The Russian Bishop's House was built by the Russian–American Co. in 1842 for the first Russian Orthodox Bishop to serve Alaska. It was occupied by the church until 1969, and was added to Sitka National Historical Park in 1972. The house is one of the last major Russian log structures remaining in Sitka, and one of the few remaining in North America.

The park's visitor center is open daily except weekends, 8 A.M. to 5 P.M., October to May; daily, 8 A.M. to 6 P.M., June to September. The park grounds and trails are open daily, 5 A.M. to 10 P.M. in summer, shorter hours in winter. The Russian Bishop's House is open 8:30 A.M. to 4:30 P.M. daily in summer; other times by appointment. The visitor center is closed Thanksgiving, Christmas and New Year's. No admission fee. Phone 747-6281 for more information.

Sheldon Jackson Museum, 104 College Dr., on the Sheldon Jackson College campus, contains some of the finest Native arts and crafts found in Alaska. Much of it was collected by missionary Sheldon Jackson and is now owned by the state of Alaska. Admission $2, students under 18 free, annual pass $5. Open in summer 8 A.M. to 5 P.M. daily. Winter hours: Tuesday through Saturday, 10 A.M. to 4 P.M. Free on Saturdays.

All–Alaska Logging Championships (June 25–26, 1994) features loggers from Alaska and the Pacific Northwest competing in splicing, stock power saw bucking, double-hand bucking, horizontal and vertical ax chopping, tree topping and choker setting among other events. Women's events include the rolling pin toss and sawing events. While the contestants are all professional and experienced loggers, there are a few events for amateurs and the general public, such as amateur chopping and Jack-and-Jill bucking (two contestants use a handsaw to cut through a 24-inch spruce).

Blarney Stone, across from Sheldon Jackson College. Believed to originally have been called Baranof's stone and used as a resting stop by Russian–American Co. chief manager Alexander Baranof.

O'Connell Bridge, 1,225 feet/373m long, connecting Sitka with Japonski Island, was the first cable-stayed, girder-span bridge in the United States. It was dedicated Aug. 19, 1972. You'll get a good view of Sitka and the harbors by walking across this bridge.

Old Sitka, at **Milepost 7.5** Halibut Point Road, is a registered national historic landmark and the site of the first Russian settlement in the area in 1799, known then as Fort Archangel Michael. In 1802, in a surprise attack, the Tlingit Indians of the area destroyed the fort and killed most of its occupants, driving the Russians out until Baranof's successful return in 1804.

Visit the Alaska Raptor Rehabilitation Center, located at 1101 Sawmill Creek Road (**Milepost 0.9**) just across Indian River, within easy walking distance of downtown Sitka. This unique facility treats injured eagles, hawks, owls and other birds of prey. Visitors will have the opportunity to see American bald eagles and other raptors close up, review case histories of birds treated at the center and observe medical care being administered to current patients. The facility is open several days a week year-round for self-guided tours, or attend one of the center's education programs. The schedule is subject to ferry and cruise ship arrivals. These guided interpretive tours are scheduled frequently during the summer; phone 747-8662 for times. Admission fee charged for guided tours; donations accepted for self-guided tours.

Hiking Trails. The Sitka Ranger District office at 204 Siginaka Way can provide information sheets and maps for area trails and remote cabins. Trails accessible from the road include Harbor Mountain Ridge trail; Mount Verstovia trail; the easy 5-mile/8-km Indian River trail; and the short Beaver Lake trail off Sawmill Creek Road on Blue Lake Road.

AREA FISHING: Sitka holds an annual salmon derby (May 28–30 and June 4–5, 1994). Saltwater fishing charters available locally. There are also many lakes and rivers on Baranof Island with good fishing; these range from **Katlian River**, 11 miles/17.7 km northeast of Sitka by boat, to more remote waters such as **Rezanof Lake**, which is 40 air miles/64 km southeast of Sitka. USFS public-use cabins at some lakes (see Cabins in the GENERAL INFORMATION section). Stop by the Dept. of Fish and Game office at 304 Lake St. for details on fishing.

Sawmill Creek Road Log

Sawmill Creek Road is a 7.4-mile/11.9-km road, paved for the first 5.4 miles/8.7 km, which begins at Lake Street and ends beyond the pulp mill at Silver Bay.

0 Intersection of Lake Street (Halibut Point Road) and Sawmill Creek Road.

0.5 (0.8 km) Sitka National Cemetery.

0.7 (1.1 km) Indian River bridge. Beginning of Indian River trail on left.

0.9 (1.4 km) Alaska Raptor Rehabilitation Center.

1 (1.6 km) Post office.

1.7 (2.7 km) Mount Verstovia trail on left next to supper club.

3.6 (5.8 km) Thimbleberry Creek bridge.

3.7 (6 km) On left past bridge is start of Thimbleberry Lake and Heart Lake trail. Hike in 0.5 mile/0.8 km to **Thimbleberry Lake,** brook trout to 12 inches, use eggs, May to September. Trail continues 1 mile/1.6 km past Thimbleberry Lake to **Heart Lake**, brook trout.

4.4 (7.1 km) Scenic viewpoint turnout.

5.3 (8.5 km) Alaska Pulp Corp.

5.4 (8.7 km) Blue Lake Road on left. Pavement ends on Sawmill Creek Road. Blue Lake Road (narrow dirt) leads 2.2 miles/3.5 km to small parking area and short downhill trail to Blue Lake (no recreational

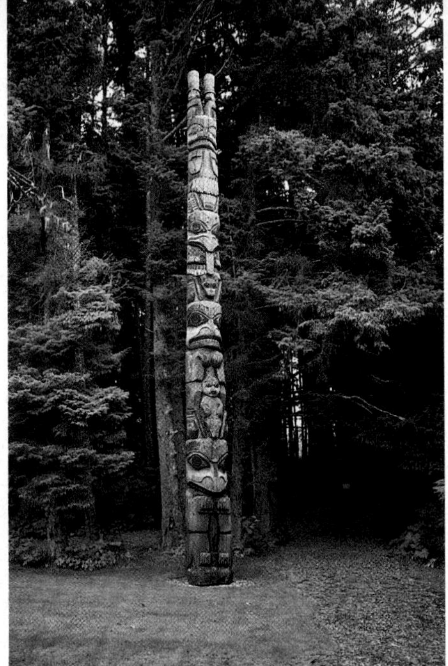

Self-guiding trail through Sitka National Historical Park. (Lee Foster)

facilities; check with city for information). At Mile 1.5 on right is Sawmill Creek USFS campground (unmaintained). **Blue Lake,** rainbow, May to September, use flies, lure or bait. Lightweight skiff or rubber boat recommended.

5.7 (9.2 km) Sawmill Creek and bridge.

7.2 (11.6 km) Public road ends at Herring Cove near mouth of Silver Bay (boat tours of the bay available in Sitka). City road to hydroelectric power plant continues.

7.4 (11.9 km) Gate marking boundary of city road. Road closed to vehicles beyond this point; access for hikers and bicyclists only. No guardrails or road signs to road end.

10.5 (16.9 km) Fish hatchery and gate. Steep grades; watch for rocks on road.

13.7 (22 km) Road end. Green Lake Power Plant.

Halibut Point Road Log

Halibut Point Road (paved) leads northwest from the intersection of Harbor Drive and Lincoln Street past Old Sitka to Starrigavan Creek Campground.

0 Harbor Drive and Lincoln Street. Proceed northwest (road is now Lake Street).

0.1 (0.2 km) Fire station. Intersection with Sawmill Creek Road; keep left.

0.3 (0.5 km) **Swan Lake** to right of road, rainbow from 12 to 14 inches.

0.6 (1 km) Katlian Street on left leads to boat ramp and then to downtown. Hospital to the right.

1.8 (2.9 km) Pioneer Park picnic and day-use area with beach access; parking available.

2.2 (3.5 km) Cascade Creek bridge.

2.3 (3.7 km) Tongass National Forest work center.

2.4 (3.9 km) Sandy Beach; good swimming beach, ample parking, view of Mount Edgecumbe. Whales are sometimes sighted from here.

3.8 (6.1 km) Viewpoint. On a clear day you can see for 50 miles/80 km.

4.2 (6.8 km) Harbor Mountain Road on right. Steep gravel, accessible to cars. Road leads 5 miles/8 km to road end and Harbor Mountain Ridge trail to lookout at 2,300 feet/701m.

4.4 (7.1 km) Granite Creek bridge. Just beyond the bridge on left is Halibut Point state recreation site with swimming beach, shelters, tables, fireplaces and toilets.

7 (11.3 km) Alaska Marine Highway ferry terminal on left.

7.3 (11.7 km) Boat ramp, litter barrel and pit toilet to left.

7.5 (12.1 km) Old Sitka State Historical Site at left, and Starrigavan Creek bridge just ahead. Old Sitka was the site of the Russian Fort Archangel Michael, established in 1799. Commemorative plaque and historical markers. The site is a registered national historic landmark.

7.6 (12.2 km) Narrow road on right runs along the bank of Starrigavan Creek, where pink salmon spawn in August and September, and continues several miles through Starrigavan River valley. Off-road vehicles permitted.

7.8 (12.6 km) Starrigavan Campground and picnic area. Access to beach. **Starrigavan Bay,** Dolly Varden, pink and silver salmon, May to October.

7.9 (12.7 km) Road ends.

Kake

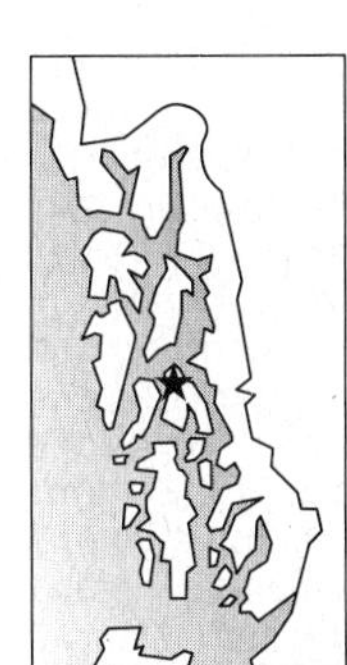

Located on northwest coast of Kupreanof Island in central southeastern Alaska; Petersburg is 40 air miles/64 km or 65 miles/105 km by boat to the southeast; Juneau is 95 air miles/153 km northeast. **Population:** 789 (approximately 85 percent Native). **Emergency Services: Police,** phone 785-3393. **Public Health Center,** phone 785-3333. **Maritime Search and Rescue,** phone the Coast Guard at 1-800-478-5555.

Visitor Information: City of Kake, Box 500, Kake 99830.

Elevation: Sea level. **Climate:** Less than average rainfall for southeastern Alaska, approximately 50 inches annually. Mild temperatures. January average temperatures are around freezing. Slightly warmer than nearby Petersburg. Kake is noted for being in the "banana belt" of Southeast.

Private Aircraft: Kake seaplane base, located adjacent southeast; fuel 100. Airstrip 1 mile/1.6 km west; elev. 148 feet/45m; length 4,000 feet/1,219m; asphalt; unattended.

Transportation: Air–Scheduled service from Petersburg (15-minute flight), Juneau (45 minutes), Wrangell and Sitka. Scheduled daily charter service provided by LAB Flying and Wings of Alaska. **Ferry**–Alaska Marine Highway vessel from Petersburg and Sitka. See MARINE ACCESS ROUTES section for schedule.

Accommodations at local inn and bed and breakfast. There are general, variety and video stores, a cafe and other services. Church groups include Baptist, Salvation Army, Presbyterian and Assembly of God. Kake has an accredited high school, junior high school and elementary.

The town is permanent village of the Kake (pronounced cake) tribe of the Tlingit Indians. The Tlingits from Kake had a well-earned reputation for aggression in the 18th and 19th centuries. In 1869, the Kakes murdered two Sitka traders in revenge for the shooting of a Native by a Sitka sentry. Reprisals taken by the United States resulted in the shelling and destruction of three Kake villages. The tribe eventually settled at the present-day site of Kake, where the government established a school in 1891. Residents have historically drawn ample subsistence from the sea. However, with the advent of a cash economy, the community has come to depend on commercial fishing, fish processing (there is a cannery) and logging. The post office was established in 1904 and the city was incorporated in 1952. The city's claim to fame is its totem, reputedly the world's tallest at 132 feet, 6 inches. It was carved for the 1967 Alaska Purchase Centennial Celebration.

Angoon

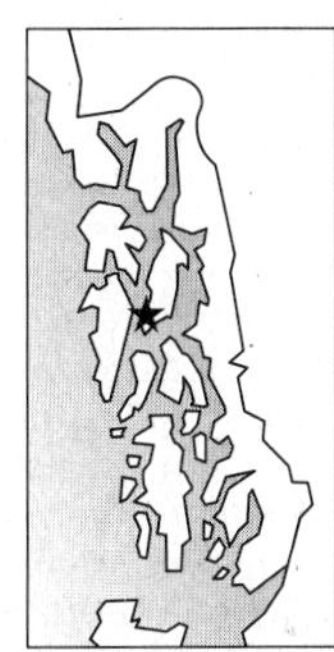

Located on west coast of Admiralty Island on Chatham Strait, at the mouth of Kootznahoo Inlet. The east end of Peril Strait is directly across Chatham Strait from Angoon. Juneau is 60 air miles/96.6 km northeast. Sitka is 41 miles/66 km southwest. **Population:** 638. **Emergency Services: Police,** phone 788-3631. **Clinic,** phone 788-3633.

Visitor Information: Local people are happy to help. You may also contact the U.S. Forest Service's Admiralty Island National Monument office in Angoon (phone 788-3166) or the city of Angoon (phone 788-3653).

Elevation: Sea level. **Climate:** Moderate weather with about 40 inches of annual rainfall and mild temperatures.

Private Aircraft: Angoon seaplane base; 0.9 mile/1.4 km southeast; unattended.

Transportation: Air–Scheduled seaplane service from Juneau. **Ferry**–Alaska Marine Highway service. See MARINE ACCESS ROUTES section for schedule.

Accommodations available at a motel and a bed and breakfast. There is a general store. Fuel service available. There are no RV facilities. Charter fishing boats and canoes are available. Transient moorage for private boats available.

Angoon is a long-established Tlingit Indian settlement at the entrance to Kootznahoo Inlet. It is the only permanent community on Admiralty Island. On Killisnoo Island, across the harbor from the state ferry landing, a community of mostly summer homes has grown up along the island beaches. The lifestyle of this primarily Tlingit community is heavily subsistence: fish, clams, seaweed, berries and venison. Fishing, mostly hand trolling for king and coho salmon, is the principal industry.

The scenery of Admiralty Island draws many visitors to Angoon. All but the northern portion of the island was declared a national monument in December 1980 and is jointly managed by the

Hiker examines old growth Sitka spruce on Admiralty Island. (George Wuerthner)

U.S. Forest Service and Kootznoowoo Inc. Kootznahoo Inlet and Mitchell Bay near Angoon offer a network of small wooded islands, reefs and channels for kayaking. Mitchell Bay and Admiralty Lakes Recreational Area are the two major recreational attractions within the monument. Wildlife includes many brown bears (Admiralty Island's Indian name *Kootznoowoo* means "Fortress of Bears"), Sitka black-tailed deer and bald eagles. There are 12 USFS cabins available for public use in the monument; reservations and fee are required. Contact the U.S. Forest Service in Angoon. Also see Cabins in the GENERAL INFORMATION section.

Local residents can provide directions to the interesting old Killisnoo graveyards, located both on the island and on the Angoon shore of the old Killisnoo settlement, which once was one of the larger communities in southeastern Alaska.

Fishing for salmon is excellent in the Angoon area. (Record kings have been caught in nearby Kelp Bay and in Angoon harbor.) There is also excellent halibut and other bottom fish fishing. Trout (cutthroat and Dolly Varden) fishing in the lakes and streams on Admiralty Island; fair but scattered.

Tenakee Springs

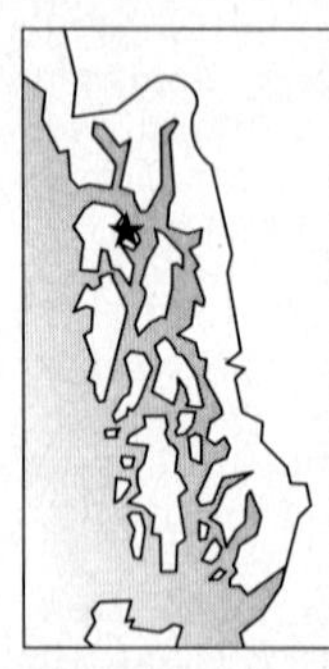

Located on the north shore of Tenakee Inlet on Chichagof Island, 50 miles/80.5 km northeast of Sitka. **Population:** 106. **Visitor Information:** Can be obtained from city hall, phone 736-2207, or from the town's store, phone 736-2205. **Elevation:** Sea level. **Climate:** Average rainfall 63.2 inches annually, with moderate snowfall. **Private Aircraft:** Seaplane base.

Transportation: Air–Scheduled and charter service available through Wings of Alaska out of Juneau. **Ferry**–Alaska Marine Highway service from Sitka and Juneau. See MARINE ACCESS ROUTES section for schedule.

Tenakee Springs has one street — Tenakee Avenue — which is about 3 miles/4.8 km long and 4 to 12 feet wide. Many residents use three-wheel motor bikes for transportation, some ride bicycles, but most walk the short distances between buildings. There are a store, cafe, clinic, post office, library, sawmill and city hall. Accommodations at seven rental cabins (bring your sleeping bag) are available at Snyder Merchantile, and Tenakee Hot Springs Lodge offers rooms and guided sportfishing and sightseeing; phone 736-2400. Tenakee Springs became a city in 1971 and has a mayor, council and planning commission. The city has limited TV and radio reception.

The word Tenakee comes from the Tlingit word *tinaghu,* meaning "Coppery Shield Bay." This refers to three copper shields, highly prized by the Tlingits, lost in a storm.

The hot springs (temperature from 106°F to 108°F/41°C to 42°C) brought people to Tenakee at the turn of the century. A bathhouse, completed in 1940, is located on the waterfront and has posted times of use for men and women. The facility is maintained by contributions from residents and visitors.

The major industry at Tenakee might be described as relaxation, as many retirees have chosen to live here, away from the bustle of other Southeast cities. There are many summer homes along Tenakee Avenue. During the summer, watch for whales in Tenakee Inlet, which are sometimes spotted from town.

Some logging is under way in the area around Tenakee. Tenakee Inlet produces salmon, halibut, Dungeness and king crab, red snapper and cod. A small fleet of fishing vessels is home-ported in Tenakee's harbor, located about 0.5 mile/0.8 km east of town. Although many visitors come to Tenakee to hunt and fish, there are no hunting guides or rental boats available locally. There are three fishing and sightseeing charter services.

Pelican

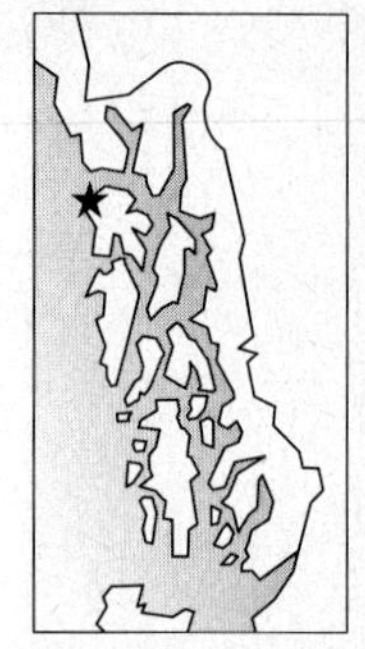

Located on Lisianski Inlet on the northwest coast of Chichagof Island. **Population:** 265. **Emergency Services: Public Safety Officer** and **Fire Department,** phone 911. **Clinic,** phone 735-2250. **Elevation:** Sea level. **Climate:** Average winter temperatures from 21°F/-6°C to 39°F/4°C; summer temperatures from 51°F/11°C to 62°F/17°C. Total average annual precipitation is 127 inches, with 120 inches of snow.

Private Aircraft: Seaplane base; fuel 80, 100.

Transportation: Air–Scheduled air service from Juneau via Glacier Bay Airlines and Wings of Alaska. Also scheduled service from Sitka via Bell Air. **Ferry**–Alaska Marine Highway vessel serves Pelican. See MARINE ACCESS ROUTES section for schedules.

Pelican has two bar-and-grills (one with four rooms for rent), a bed and breakfast, a cafe, grocery and dry goods stores, laundromats and two liquor stores. There is a small-boat harbor, marine repair and a fuel dock.

Established in 1938 by Kalle (Charley) Raataikainen, and named for Raataikainen's fish packer, *The Pelican,* Pelican relies on commercial fishing and seafood processing. The cold storage plant processes salmon, halibut, crab, herring and black cod, and is the primary year-round employer. Pelican has dubbed itself "closest to the fish," a reference to its close proximity to the rich Fairweather salmon grounds. Nonresident fishermen swell the population during the salmon trolling season, from about June to mid-September, and the king salmon winter season, from October through April. Pelican was incorporated in 1943. Most of Pelican is built on pilings over tidelands. A wooden boardwalk extends the length of the community, and there are about 2 miles of gravel road.

Local recreation includes kayaking, hiking, fishing, and watching birds and marine mammals.

Hoonah

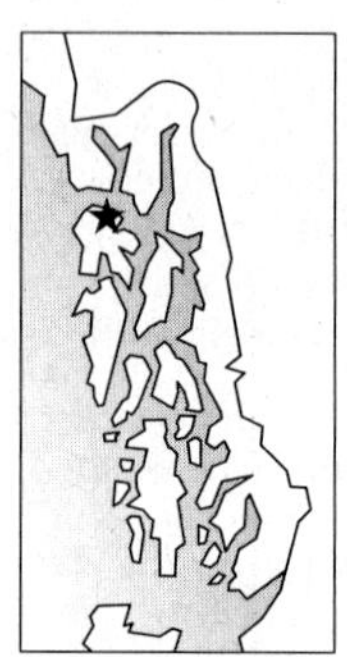

Located on the northeast shore of Chichagof Island, about 40 miles/64 km west of Juneau and 20 miles/32 km south across Icy Strait from the entrance of Glacier Bay. **Population:** 795. **Emergency Services: Alaska State Troopers** and **Hoonah City Police,** phone 945-3655; emergency only phone 911. **Maritime Search and Rescue,** call the Coast Guard at 1-800-478-5555.

Visitor Information: Local business people, city office staff (945-3663, weekdays 8 A.M. to 4:30 P.M.) and the postmaster are happy to help. The U.S. Forest Service office in Hoonah (P.O. Box 135, Hoonah 99829, phone 945-3631) also has visitor informa-

Hoonah is located on the northeast shore of Chichagof Island. (John W. Warden)

tion, including a Hoonah area road guide showing forest roads on Chichagof Island.

Elevation: Sea level. **Climate:** Typical southeastern Alaska climate, with considerable rainfall (100 inches annually). Average daily temperature in July, 57°F/13°C; in January, 35°F/1°C. Prevailing winds are southeasterly.

Private Aircraft: Hoonah airport, adjacent southeast; elev. 30 feet/9m; length 3,000 feet/914m; paved. Seaplane base adjacent.

Transportation: Air–Scheduled and charter service from Juneau. Airport is located about 3 miles from town. **Ferry**–Alaska Marine Highway vessel serves Hoonah. See MARINE ACCESS ROUTES section for schedule.

A lodge offers accommodations. Occasional room rentals and bed-and-breakfast lodging are also available. Hoonah has three restaurants, a grocery, three general stores, a gift shop, a variety store, bank, two marine fuel docks, two gas pumps and a flying service. The marina here, which has showers and a laundromat, is a popular layover for boaters awaiting permits to enter Glacier Bay.

Hoonah is a small coastal community with a quiet harbor for the seining and trolling fleets. The most prominent structures are a cold storage facility, the lodge, bank, post office and the public school. The village has been occupied since prehistory by the Tlingit people. In the late 1800s, missionaries settled here. Canneries established in the area in the early 1900s spurred the growth of commercial fishing, which remains the mainstay of Hoonah's economy. During the summer fishing season, residents work for nearby Excursion Inlet Packing Co. or Hoonah Cold Storage in town. Halibut season begins in May and salmon season opens in midsummer and runs through September. Logging also contributes to the economy, with employment loading log ships and other industry-related jobs. Subsistence hunting and fishing remain an important lifestyle here, and many families gather food in the traditional way: catching salmon and halibut in summer, shellfish and bottom fish year-round; hunting deer, geese and ducks; berry picking in summer and fall.

Hunting and fishing are the main attractions for visitors. Charter fishing is available locally, with good seasonal king and coho (silver) salmon and halibut fishing as well as crabbing. Guide services are available.

Hoonah is the starting point for an extensive logging and forest road system for northwest Chichagof Island. Island road maps ($2) are available through the USFS in Hoonah, Sitka and Juneau.

Juneau

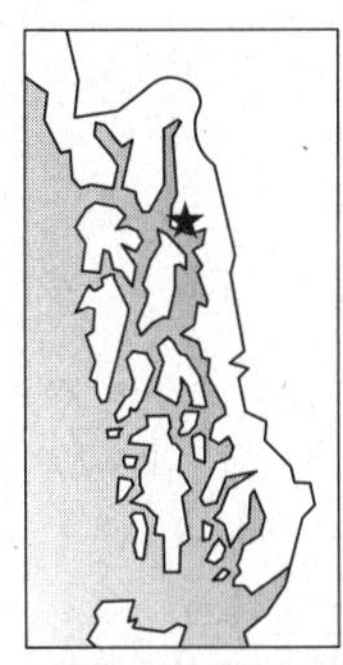

Located in mainland southeastern Alaska on Gastineau Channel opposite Douglas Island; 900 air miles/1,448 km (two hours, 10 minutes flying time) from Seattle, WA, 650 air miles/1,046 km (one hour, 25 minutes by jet) from Anchorage. **Population:** Borough 29,251. **Emergency Services:** Phone 911 for all emergencies. **Police,** phone 586-2780. **Fire Department,** phone 586-5245. **Alaska State Troopers,** phone 789-2161. **Poison Center** and **Hospital,** Bartlett Memorial, phone 586-2611. **Maritime Search and Rescue,** Coast Guard, phone 463-2000 or 1-800-478-5555.

Visitor Information: Juneau Convention & Visitors Bureau, Davis Log Cabin Information Center, 134 3rd St., phone 586-2201 or 586-2284; open year-round 8 A.M. to 5 P.M. Monday through Friday; additional hours during the summer, 9 A.M. to 5 P.M. Saturday, Sunday and holidays. To find out about current events in Juneau, phone 586-JUNO for a recorded message. Visitor information kiosk located in Marine Park on waterfront near Merchants Wharf, usually open daily 8:30 A.M. to 6 P.M., from about June 1 to Sept. 15. Information booth at the airport terminal. Visitor information is also available at the cruise ship terminal on S. Franklin St. when cruise ships are in port, and at the Auke Bay ferry terminal. Large groups contact the Davis Log Cabin Information Center in advance for special assistance.

U.S. Forest Service Information Center at Centennial Hall, 101 Egan Dr.; open 8 A.M. to 5 P.M. daily from Memorial Day to mid-September; 8 A.M. to 5 P.M. Monday through Friday the rest of the year. Phone 586-8751. U.S. Park Service office here open in summer. The center has seasonal exhibits and natural history films. USFS cabins may also be reserved here. Juneau Ranger District (USFS), **Milepost 9.4** Glacier Highway (airport area), phone 586-8800, open 8 A.M. to 5 P.M. weekdays. Mendenhall Glacier Visitor Center (USFS), phone 789-0097, open 9 A.M. to 6 P.M. daily in summer, weekends only in winter.

Elevation: Sea level. **Climate:** Mild and wet. Average daily maximum temperature in July, 63°F/17°C; daily minimum in January, 20°F/-7°C. Highest recorded temperature was 90°F/32°C in July 1975; the lowest -22°F/-30°C in January 1972. Average annual precipitation, 56.5 inches (airport), 92 inches (downtown); 103 inches of snow annually. Snow on ground intermittently from mid-November to mid-April. Prevailing winds are east-southeasterly. **Radio:** KINY-AM 800, KJNO-AM 630, KTOO-FM 104.3, KTKU-FM 105.1, KSUP-FM 106. **Television:** KJUD Channel 8; JATV cable; KTOO (public television). **Newspaper:** *Juneau Empire* (Sunday through Friday).

Private Aircraft: Juneau International Airport, 9 miles/14.5 km northwest; elev. 18 feet/5m; length 8,456 feet/2,577m; asphalt; fuel 100LL, Jet A. Juneau harbor seaplane base, adjacent north; restricted use, no fuel. International seaplane base, 7 miles/11.3 km northwest; 5,000 feet/1,524m by 450 feet/137m. For more information, phone the Juneau Flight Service Station at 789-6124.

HISTORY AND ECONOMY

In 1880, nearly 20 years before the great gold rushes to the Klondike and to Nome, two prospectors named Joe Juneau and Dick Harris found "color" in what is now called Gold Creek, a small, clear stream that runs through the center of present-day Juneau. What they found led to the discovery of one of the largest lodes of gold quartz in the world. Juneau (called Harrisburg the first year) quickly boomed into a gold rush town as claims and mines sprang up in the area.

For a time the largest mine was the Treadwell, across Gastineau Channel south of Douglas (which was once a larger town than Juneau), but a cave-in and flood closed the mine in 1917. In 36 years of operation,

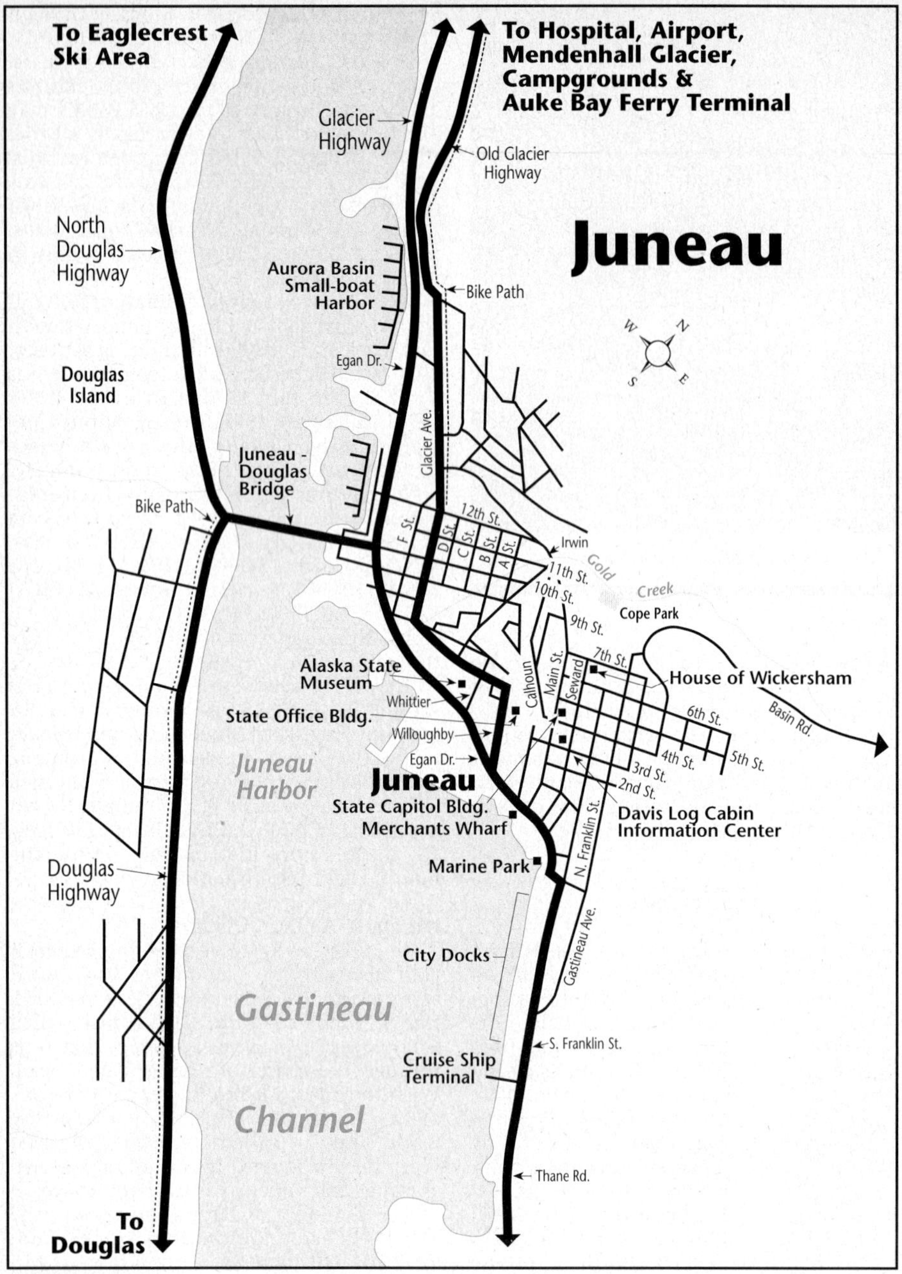

Treadwell produced $66 million in gold. The Alaska–Gastineau Mine, operated by Bart Thane in 1911, had a 2-mile shaft through Mount Roberts to the Perseverance Mine near Gold Creek. The Alaska–Juneau (A–J) Mine was constructed on a mountain slope south of Juneau and back into the heart of Mount Roberts. It operated until 1944, when it was declared a nonessential wartime activity after producing over $80 million in gold. Post–WWII wage and price inflation and the fixed price of gold prevented its reopening.

In 1900, the decision to move Alaska's capital to Juneau was made because of the city's growth, mining activity and location on the water route to Skagway and the Klondike, and because of the decline of Sitka after the Russians left and whaling and fur trade fell off. Actual transfer of government functions did not occur until 1906.

Congress first provided civil government for Alaska in 1884. Until statehood in 1959 Alaska was governed by a succession of presidential appointees, first as the District of Alaska, then as the Territory of Alaska. Between 1867 (when the United States purchased Alaska from Russia) and 1884, the military had jurisdiction over the Dept. of Alaska, except for a three-year period (1877–79) when Alaska was put under control of the U.S. Treasury Dept. and governed by U.S. Collectors of Customs.

With the coming of Alaska statehood in 1959, Juneau's governmental role increased even further. In 1974, Alaskans voted to move the capital from Juneau to a site between Anchorage and Fairbanks, closer to the state's population center. In 1976 Alaska voters selected a new capital site near Willow, 65 road miles/105 km north of Anchorage on the George Parks Highway. However, in November 1982, voters defeated funding for the capital move.

Today, government (federal, state and local) comprises an estimated half of the total basic industry. Tourism is the largest employer in the private sector.

DESCRIPTION

Juneau, often called "a little San Francisco," is nestled at the foot and on the side of Mount Juneau (elev. 3,576 feet/1,091m) with Mount Roberts (elev. 3,819 feet/1,164m) rising immediately to the right as you approach up Gastineau Channel. The residential community of Douglas is south of Juneau on Douglas Island; Juneau and Douglas are connected by a bridge. Neighboring residential areas at the airport, Mendenhall Valley and Auke Bay lie north of Juneau on the mainland.

Shopping is in the downtown area and at suburban malls in the airport and Mendenhall Valley areas.

Juneau's skyline is dominated by several government buildings, including the Federal Bldg. (1962), the massive State Office Bldg. (1974), the State Court Bldg. (1975) and the older brick and marble-columned Capitol Bldg. (1931). The modern Sealaska Plaza is headquarters for Sealaska Corp., one of the 13 regional Native corporations formed after congressional passage of the Alaska Native Claims Settlement Act in 1971.

To explore downtown Juneau, it is best to park and walk; distances are not great. The streets are narrow and congested with pedestrians and traffic (especially rush hours), and on-street parking is scarce. Free visitor parking permits are available at Davis Log Cabin and at the police station to allow visitors extended parking in timed zones. Public parking lots are located across from Wharf Mall at

Main Street and Egan Drive and south of Marine Park at the Marine Park parking garage; fee required.

The Juneau area supports 35 churches, a high school, two middle schools, several elementary schools and the University of Alaska–Southeast campus at Auke Lake. There are three municipal libraries and the state library.

The area is governed by the unified city and borough of Juneau, which encompasses 3,108 square miles/8,060 square km. It is the first unified government in the state, combining the former separate and overlapping jurisdictions of the city of Douglas, city of Juneau and greater Juneau borough.

ACCOMMODATIONS

Juneau has 13 hotels and motels, most of them downtown. There are also several bed and breakfasts. The Juneau International Hostel is located at 614 Harris St. (Juneau 99801), four blocks northeast of the Capitol Bldg. All ages are welcome. Check-in time is 5-11 P.M. during summer, 5–10:30 P.M. the rest of the year. Showers, cooking, laundry and storage facilities are available. Adults $10, children accompanied by parent $5. Groups welcome. Open year-round. Phone 586-9559.

More than 60 restaurants offer a wide variety. Also watch for sidewalk food vendors downtown in summer.

Juneau also has a microbrewery. The Alaskan Brewing Co., located at 5429 Shaune Dr. in the Lemon Creek area, produces Alaskan Amber Beer and Alaskan Pale Ale. Free tours available. Phone 780-5866 for more information.

Pearson's Pond Luxury B & B Inn. If you want spectacular scenery and quality lodging, you'll find it here at an affordable price. Your suite retreat has all the private comforts of home, away from the crowds, yet close to famous attractions. Soothe your cares in a starlit spa amid lush gardens, wild berries and a glacial duck pond. Dine alfresco on your adjoining deck with the healing sounds of nature and the Mendenhall Glacier as a majestic backdrop. Guests say it is the highest combination of privacy, beauty, comfort and warmth. A year-round, smoke- and pet-free experience. Book far ahead for summer, and plan to stay a week or more. Winner of AAA/ABBA 3-diamond/ crown award for excellence. 4541-MP Sawa Circle, Juneau, AK 99801-8723; (907) 789-3772. Great value. A definite 10! [ADVERTISEMENT]

There are two U.S. Forest Service campgrounds: Mendenhall Lake (turn off Glacier Highway at **Milepost 9.4** or **12.2** and continue to Montana Creek Road) and Auke Village (**Milepost 15.4** Glacier Highway). Mendenhall Lake has 60 sites (RVs to 22 feet), water, pit toilets, dump station. Mendenhall campground is on the Mistix Reservation System; phone 1-800-283-

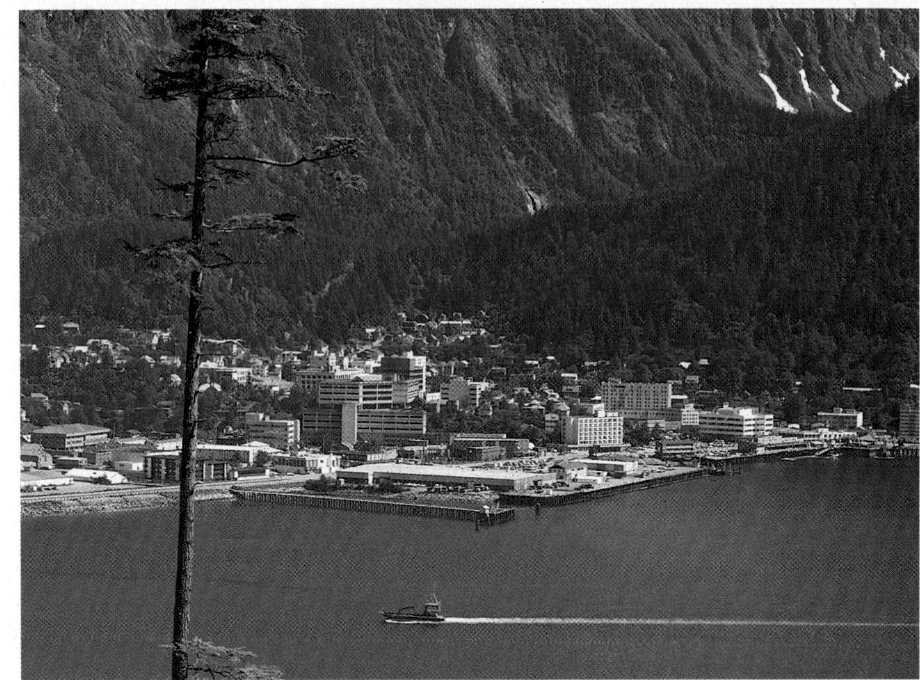

Juneau lies nestled at the foot of Mount Juneau on Gastineau Channel. (Loren Taft)

JUNEAU ADVERTISERS

Alaskan Hotel & Bar, The ....167 S. Franklin St.
Bed & Breakfast Inn—Juneau ....1801 Old Glacier Hwy.
Blueberry Lodge ....Ph. (907) 463-5886
Dawson's Bed & Breakfast..1941 Glacier Hwy.
Driftwood Lodge, The.......................435 Willoughby Ave. W.
Era Helicopters.................Ph. (907) 586-2030
Fiddlehead Restaurant & Bakery, The...........429 W. Willoughby Ave.
Gastineau Salmon Hatchery........................2697 Channel Dr.
Glacier Bay Tours and Cruises ....Ph. (907) 463-5510
Jan's View Bed & Breakfast.......................1670 Glacier Hwy.
Juneau Convention & Visitors Bureau.........................134 3rd St.
Lady Lou Revue................Ph. (907) 586-3686
Loken Aviation, Inc. ....Ph. (907) 789-3331
Lost Chord, The ....2200 Fritz Cove Rd.
Nugget Mall, The.............Ph. (907) 789-2877
Pearson's Pond Luxury B & B Inn ....Ph. (907) 789-3772
Pot Belly Bed & Breakfast, The.............Ph. (907) 586-1279
Super 8 Motel ....Ph. 1-800-800-8000
Thane Ore House.............Ph. (907) 586-3442
Tracy Arm Reservations Center.........................Ph. 1-800-451-5952
Windsock Inn B & B..........Ph. (907) 364-2431

CAMP. Auke Village Campground, 1.5 miles west of the ferry terminal, has 12 campsites. There is a private campground with RV hookups located at **Milepost 12.3** Glacier Highway. The City and Borough of Juneau offers limited RV overnight parking spaces at the Juneau Yacht Club for $5 per space, per night, paid at the harbormaster's office (turnoff at **Milepost 1.7** Egan Drive/Glacier Highway), and at Savikko Park/Sandy Beach (**Milepost 2.5** Douglas Highway). Contact the visitor information center (586-2201) for a brochure on RV facilities. Dump stations are located at Mendenhall Lake campground, Valley Chevron at Mendenhall Center shopping mall in the Mendenhall Valley, and Savikko Park. ▲

TRANSPORTATION

Air: Juneau Municipal Airport turnoff is at **Milepost 8.8** Egan Drive (Glacier Highway). Airport terminal contains ticket counters, lockers, waiting area, gift shop, rental cars, restaurant, lounge and information booth.

The city express bus stops at the airport daily except weekends. Taxi service and van service to downtown are also available. Courtesy vans to some hotels.

Alaska Airlines serves Juneau daily from Seattle, WA, Anchorage, Fairbanks, Ketchikan, Sitka, Yakutat, Cordova, Petersburg and Wrangell. Delta Airlines serves Juneau from Seattle and Fairbanks. Scheduled commuter service to Haines, Skagway, Sitka, Angoon and other points via several air services. Scheduled service between Juneau and Whitehorse, YT, and between Juneau and Atlin, BC, is available in summer.

Charter air service (wheel and floatplanes and helicopters) for hunting, fishing, sightseeing and transportation to other communities (see ads in this section).

Loken Aviation, Inc. provides experienced floatplane service to wilderness cabins, Native villages, and fishing lodges in Southeast Alaska. Thirty years of flying experience guarantee personalized, professional sightseeing and wildlife tours. Visit our ticket counter in the Juneau International Airport or phone (907) 789-3331 for further information. [ADVERTISEMENT]

Ferry: Juneau is served by Alaska Marine Highway ferries. See MARINE ACCESS ROUTES section for schedule and fares.

Alaska state ferries dock at the Auke Bay terminal at **Milepost 13.9** Glacier Highway; phone 465-3941 or 789-7453. Taxi service and private shuttle bus is available from Auke Bay terminal to downtown Juneau.

Bus: Capital Transit city bus system runs from the cruise ship terminal downtown and includes Juneau, Douglas, Lemon Creek, Mendenhall Valley and airport area, Auke Bay (the community, which is about 1.5 miles/2.4 km south of the ferry terminal). Hourly service Monday through Saturday, year-round, limited service on Sundays. Route map and schedule available at the visitor information center. Flag buses at any corner except in downtown Juneau, where bus uses marked stops only.

Highways: Longest road is Glacier Highway, which begins in downtown Juneau and leads 40.2 miles/64.7 km north to Echo Cove. Other major roads are Mendenhall Loop Road and Douglas and North Douglas highways. See logs this section.

Taxi: Two companies.

Cruise Ships: Juneau is southeastern Alaska's most frequent port of call. There were 355 port calls by cruise ships in 1993.

The tour boat MV *Fairweather* offers cruises between Juneau and Skagway mid-May to mid-September. Offered on package tours by Gray Line of Alaska, seats are sold on a space available basis to visitors not on a package tour. Contact their Juneau office in the Baranof Hotel lobby, phone 586-3773. The MV *Fairweather* departs from Yankee Cove, **Milepost 33** Glacier Highway.

Car Rental: Nine car rental agencies are available at the airport and vicinity; there are none downtown, but most rental agencies will take you to their offices. Best to reserve ahead of time because of the great demand for cars.

Private Boats: Transient moorage is available downtown at Harris and Douglas floats and at Auke Bay. Most boaters use Auke Bay. For more information call the Juneau harbormaster at 586-5255 or hail on Channel 16 UHF.

ATTRACTIONS

Juneau walking tour map (in English, French, Spanish, German, or Japanese) is available from the Davis Log Cabin Information Center at 134 3rd St. and from other visitor information sites and from hotels. See Juneau's many attractions — the Russian church, totems, Capitol Bldg., Governor's Mansion, historic graves, monuments, state museum, city museum, and others.

Charter a Boat for salmon and halibut fishing or sightseeing. The visitor information center can provide a list of charter operators; also see ads in this section.

Charter a Plane for fly-in fishing, hunting, transportation to remote lodges and longer flightseeing trips.

Take a Tour. Tours of Juneau and area attractions — by boat, bus, plane and helicopter — can be arranged. These tours range from sightseeing trips out to Mendenhall Glacier to river trips on the Mendenhall River.

Era Helicopters. Soar over the massive Juneau Icefield, viewing four unique and distinctive glaciers. Land on a glacier and walk on ice centuries of years old. Fly past historical gold mining areas. Personalized tour with Alaska's oldest and largest helicopter company. Phone (907) 586-2030 or outside Alaska 1-800-843-1947. Tours also available in Anchorage, Mount McKinley and Valdez. [ADVERTISEMENT]

The Governor's Mansion. (David Job)

Glacier Bay Tours and Cruises. Special packages, Juneau to Glacier Bay National Park, feature round-trip air, lodging, one-day and three-day glacier cruises, sportfishing and more. See Glacier Bay Lodge advertisement in the Glacier Bay section. Contact Glacier Bay Tour Center, 76 Egan Dr., downtown Juneau, 463-5510. For brochure, call toll free 1-800-451-5952. [ADVERTISEMENT]

Visit the Juneau Library. Built on top of the four-story public parking garage in downtown Juneau, this award-winning library designed by Minch Ritter Voelckers Architects is well worth a visit. Take the elevator to the fifth floor and spend a morning or afternoon reading in this well-lighted and comfortable space with a wonderful view of Juneau, Douglas and Gastineau Channel. Located at South Franklin and Admiralty Way, between Marine Park and the cruise ship terminal.

Juneau Douglas City Museum, located in the Veteran's Memorial Bldg. next to the State Capitol Bldg. at 4th and Main, offers exhibits and audiovisual presentations on the Juneau Douglas area, featuring gold mining and local cultural history. Displays include a turn-of-the-century store and kitchen, a large relief map, and a hands-on history room that's fun for kids of all ages. 1994 summer exhibit will feature early voyages of exploration and discovery in Alaska. Free historical walking-tour maps of Juneau are available. Museum gift shop. Summer hours are 9 A.M. to 5 P.M. weekdays, 11 A.M. to 5 P.M. weekends, mid-May to mid-September. Limited hours in winter. Admission $1. Phone 586-3572 or write Parks and Recreation, Attn: Juneau Douglas City Museum, 155 S. Seward St., Juneau 99801, for more information.

State Capitol Building, at 4th and Main, contains the legislative chambers and the governor's office. Free tours available from capitol lobby; daily on the half-hour from 8:30 A.M. to 5 P.M. in summer. The **State Office Building,** one block west, houses the State Historical Library and Kimball theatre organ (free organ concerts at noon Fridays).

Alaska State Museum, is located at 395 Whittier St., just off Egan Drive. Exhibits include the Bald Eagle Nesting Tree and the Lincoln Totem and portray the culture of Native groups in Alaska. Other exhibitions present Alaska's wildlife, mining, the Russian-American period, statehood and arts. The Children's Discovery Area presents a hands-on opportunity to learn about "The Last Frontier." A marine aquarium features Southeast Alaska plants and animals. Native costumes are available to wear for picture taking, etc. Free docent tours are available during the summer season. The Museum Shop carries a full line of Alaska items. Summer hours: 9 A.M. to 6 P.M. weekdays and 10 A.M. to 6 P.M. weekends. Winter hours: 10 A.M. to 4 P.M. Tuesday through Saturday. General admission: $2 for adults. Visitors under age 18 and students with current I.D. are admitted free. Annual Pass holders and members of the Museum's Friends organizations are also free. Phone 465-2901 for more information.

The **House of Wickersham,** 213 7th St., has an important historical collection dating to the days of the late Judge James Wickersham, one of Alaska's first federal judges, who collected Native artifacts, baskets, many photographs and historical documents during his extensive travels throughout the territory early in the century. Phone 586-9001 for more information. (House requires steep climb up to Seventh Street.)

The **Governor's Mansion** at 716 Calhoun Ave. has been home to Alaska's chief executives since it was completed in 1913. The two-and-one-half-story structure, containing 12,900 square feet of floor space, took nearly a year to build. Group tours by advance arrangement. Phone 465-3500.

The Gastineau Salmon Hatchery, operated by Douglas Island Pink and Chum, Inc., is located on Channel Drive 3 miles from downtown. The hatchery offers visitors a chance to see four of the five kinds of Pacific salmon, a fish ladder and incubation areas. The visitor center features interpretive displays, saltwater aquariums with adult salmon and other sea life. Salmon runs return starting in mid-July. Visitor center open 10 A.M. to 6 P.M. in summer. Educational tours provided, nominal admission fee. Phone 463-4810.

See Old Mine Ruins. Remnants from the Treadwell Mine may be seen from Sandy Beach on the Douglas Highway. Ruins from the Alaska–Juneau (A–J) Mine are found

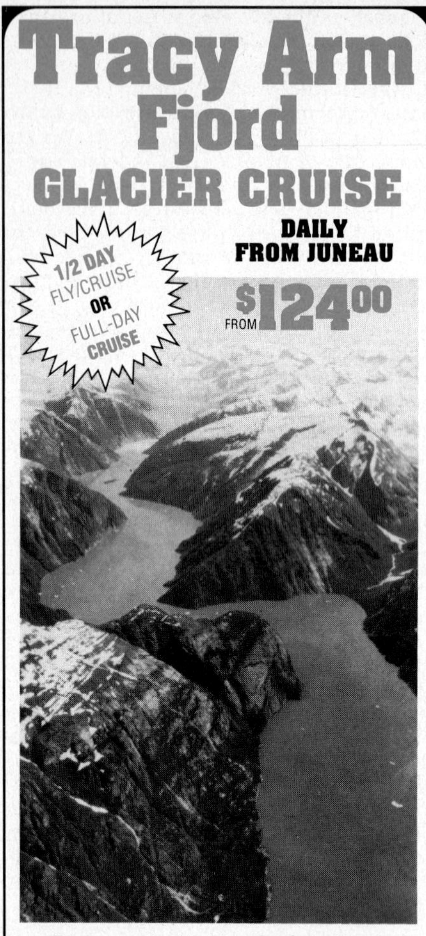

along Basin Road. The impressive remains of the A–J mine stamp mill are located on the hillside along Gastineau Channel just south of Juneau; good views from Douglas Island and from the water. Evidence of the Alaska–Gastineau Mine can be seen south of town on Thane Road. Walking tour maps of the Treadwell Mine and Last Chance Basin mining areas are available from the city museum.

Thane Ore House, Mile 4.4 Thane Road, home of the *Gold Nugget Revue,* featuring the adventures of Joe Juneau, lively cancan dancers and a red hot mama! Enjoy a sumptuous all-you-can-eat buffet of halibut, salmon and BBQ beef ribs, homemade baked beans, corn bread, salad bar and coffee or soft drink. Beer and wine available. Enjoy the indoor/outdoor beachfront facility, a mining museum, horseshoes, beachcombing, nearby fish hatchery, or sitting by the fireplace. The Thane Ore House is open from noon 'til 9 P.M., daily from May through September. The *Gold Nugget Revue,* a Janice D. Holst production, is great family entertainment. 6:30 P.M. showtime! Bring your camera! Information (907) 586-3442/586-1462. [ADVERTISEMENT]

Thane Road is a wide, straight paved road beginning just south of downtown Juneau and extending 5.5 miles/8.9 km along Gastineau Channel. Good views of the channel and old mines. Excellent viewpoint for spawning salmon at Sheep Creek bridge and falls, Mile 4.3, in summer.

Marine Park, located at foot of Seward Street, has tables, benches, information kiosk, sculpture of hard-rock miners and lightering facilities for tour ship launches. Free concerts on Friday evenings in summer.

Mount Juneau Waterfall, scenic but difficult to photograph, descends 3,576 feet/1,091m from Mount Juneau to Gold Creek behind the city. Best view is from Basin Road. The waterfall is also visible from Marine Park.

Mount Roberts Trail Observation Point offers an elevated view of Juneau. Though the trail extends to the 3,819-foot/1,164-m summit, an excellent observation point above Juneau is reached by a 20-minute hike from the start of Mount Roberts trail at the top of Starr Hill (6th Street).

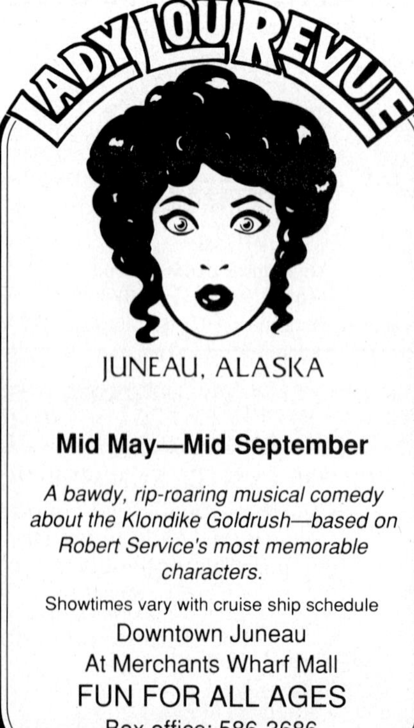

Mendenhall Glacier is about 13 miles/21 km from downtown Juneau at the end of Mendenhall Glacier Spur Road. Turn right northbound at **Milepost 9.4** Egan Drive (Glacier Highway), and then drive straight for 3.6 miles/5.8 km to the glacier and visitor center. There is a large parking area, and trails lead down to the edge of the lake (a sign warns visitors to stay back; falling ice can create huge waves). The visitor center, a short walk up a paved switchback path (accessible, although steep, for wheelchairs) from the parking area, is open daily from Memorial Day week through September, 8:30 A.M. to 5:30 P.M.; weekends only October to May. The visitor center has glacier view, guided hikes and daily video programs in summer; phone 789-0097 or 586-8800. A 0.5-mile/0.8-km self-guiding nature trail starts behind the visitor center. Trailheads for two longer trails — East Glacier and Nugget Creek — are a short walk from the visitor center. Programs and guided hikes with Forest Service interpreters are offered in summer.

Bike Paths. There are designated bike routes to Douglas, to Mendenhall Valley and Glacier, and to Auke Bay. The Mendenhall Glacier bike route starts at the intersection of 12th Street and Glacier Avenue; total biking distance is 15 miles/24.1 km. Bikes can be rented downtown.

Juneau Icefield lies immediately to the east of Juneau over the first ridge of mountains, a 1,500-square-mile expanse of mountains and glaciation that is the source of all the glaciers in the area, including Mendenhall, Taku, Eagle and Herbert. Best way to experience and photograph it is via charter flightseeing. Flights usually take 30 to 60 minutes. Helicopter tours, which land on the glacier, are also available. Helicopter tours last from about 45 minutes to one and one-half hours.

Ski Eaglecrest, Juneau's downhill and cross-country ski area on Douglas Island. Built and maintained by the city of Juneau, the area features a day lodge, cafeteria, ski rental shop, two chair lifts, a tow and runs for experienced, intermediate and beginning skiers. Eight kilometers of maintained cross-country trails available. Open five days a week, late November to early April. The view from the top of the chair lift (operating during ski season only) is worth the visit — Mendenhall Glacier, Juneau Icefield, Lynn Canal, Stephens Passage and more. Drive

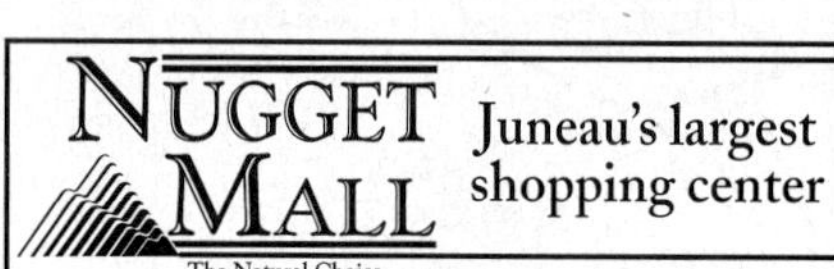

North Douglas Highway to **Milepost 6.9,** then 5.3 miles/8.5 km up the Eaglecrest access road to the lodge. For more information phone 586-5284, or phone 586-5330 for a recorded message about ski conditions.

Perseverance Theatre presents Duffey and Chapman's *Lady Lou Revue,* a musical based on Robert Service's infamous characters. Performances mid-May to mid-September on the Voices Stage in the Merchants' Wharf Mall. Phone 586-3686 (May–Sept.) for schedule and ticket information. Perseverance Theatre was begun in 1978 by Molly Smith and has established a reputation for artistic excellence with its production of both classics and original works. Main stage season runs from September through May.

St. Nicholas Russian Orthodox Church, 5th and Gold streets, a tiny structure built in 1894, is now the oldest original Russian church in southeastern Alaska. Visitors are welcome to Sunday services; open daily for summer tours. Phone 586-1023.

Chapel-by-the-Lake (Presbyterian), **Milepost 11.6** Glacier Highway, is a log structure perched above Auke Lake. Its front, entirely of glass, frames the scenic lake, Mendenhall Glacier and mountains. Popular marriage chapel.

Shrine of St. Terese (Catholic), **Milepost 22.8** Glacier Highway, is a natural stone chapel building on its own island connected to shore by a gravel causeway. A 1 P.M. Sunday mass is said during the summer.

Golden North Salmon Derby is a three-day derby held in early August, offering more than $100,000 in prizes with a $12,000 first prize for the largest king salmon.

Hiking Trails. *Juneau Trails,* a guidebook of 20-plus area hikes, can be purchased for $3 at Davis Log Cabin Information Center or USFS Information Center. Juneau Parks and Recreation Dept. offers free organized hikes; phone 586-5226 for information and schedule.

AREA FISHING: (Several special sportfishing regulations are in effect in the Juneau area; consult current regulations booklet.) Good Dolly Varden fishing available along most saltwater shorelines in Juneau area; pink salmon available about mid-July through August. Good fishing by boat from Juneau, Auke Bay or Tee Harbor in **Favorite** and **Saginaw channels, Chatham Strait** and near mouth of **Taku Inlet,** for salmon, Dolly Varden, halibut and rockfish. Boat in and hike or fly in to **Turner Lake,** 25 miles/40 km east of Juneau, for kokanee and cutthroat; USFS public-use cabins available (see Cabins in the GENERAL INFORMATION section).

For up-to-date angling data for Juneau area, phone 465-4116 for recorded Alaska Dept. of Fish and Game message (April through October). For specific angling information contact the ADF&G, Division of Sport Fish, Area Management Biologist, P.O. Box 20, Douglas 99824; phone 465-4270. A list of charter boats available is maintained at the visitor center.

Egan Drive and Glacier Highway/Juneau Veterans' Memorial Highway Log

Egan Drive from downtown Juneau proceeds north to **Milepost 9.4,** then becomes Glacier Highway. Egan Drive is named for William A. Egan (1914–84), first governor of the state of Alaska. From **Milepost 12.2** to road end, Glacier Highway has been renamed the Juneau Veterans' Memorial Highway. The highway ends 40.5 miles/65.3 km north of Juneau near Echo Cove on Berners Bay. It is a scenic drive northward along Favorite Channel.

Distance from the cruise ship terminal downtown is followed by the distance from road end (RE).

0 RE 40.5 (65.3 km) Cruise ship terminal.

0.3 (0.5 km) **RE 40.2** (64.7 km) Parking garage, three-hour limit.

0.5 (0.8 km) **RE 40** (64.2 km) Stoplight. Marine Way and Main Street. Egan Drive begins here.

0.7 (1.1 km) **RE 39.8** (63.9 km) Alaska State Museum, exit east onto Whittier Street.

1.2 (1.9 km) **RE 39.3** (63.4 km) Stoplight. Tenth Street exit east. For access to Douglas Highway and North Douglas Highway, turn west across Juneau–Douglas bridge (see logs this section).

1.3 (2.1 km) **RE 39.2** (63.1 km) Harris Harbor for small boats.

1.5 (2.4 km) **RE 39** (62.8 km) Juneau–Douglas High School.

1.7 (2.7 km) **RE 38.8** (62.6 km) Aurora Basin small-boat harbor. Access to Juneau Yacht Club on Harbor Way Road; overnight RV parking.

3.9 (6.3 km) **RE 36.6** (59 km) Stoplight. Picnic tables at Twin Lakes to east. Also exit east for Bartlett Memorial Hospital and Alaska Native Health Center; access to Old Glacier Highway and residential area. Gastineau salmon hatchery to west.

5.5 (8.9 km) **RE 35** (56.4 km) Stoplight. Lemon Creek area.

5.9 (9.5 km) **RE 34.6** (55.8 km) Lemon Creek passes beneath highway.

6.1 (9.8 km) **RE 34.4** (55.5 km) Southbound traffic, view area of tide lands; great place to see eagles and waterfowl.

6.7 (10.7 km) **RE 33.8** (54.5 km) Access to Old Glacier Highway and Switzer Creek; exit east.

8.1 (13 km) **RE 32.4** (52.3 km) Airport access road.

8.2 (13.2 km) **RE 32.3** (52.1 km) Fred Meyer shopping center.

8.8 (14.2 km) **RE 31.7** (51.1 km) Stoplight; McDonalds. Airport turnoff and access to Nugget Mall and Airport Shopping Center to west. A 0.3-mile/0.5-km loop road (Old Glacier Highway) provides access to malls and to Juneau Municipal Airport. Loop road rejoins Egan Drive at **Milepost 9.4.**

9.4 (15.1 km) **RE 31.1** (50.1 km) Stoplight. **Junction** with Mendenhall Loop Road. Turn west for airport. Turn east for Mendenhall Center shopping mall and post office (just east of junction), and Mendenhall Glacier and visitor center (3.6 miles/5.8 km from junction).

Mendenhall Loop Road is a paved 6.8-mile/10.9-km loop that rejoins Glacier Highway at **Milepost 12.2.** To reach Mendenhall Glacier from here, drive east 2.2 miles/3.5 km and take spur road another 1.4 miles/2.2 km to the glacier and visitor center. The visitor center is open daily in summer from 9 A.M. to 6:30 P.M.; weekends only in winter.

Continue on Mendenhall Loop Road past glacier spur road turnoff for Montana Creek Road (3.7 miles/6 km from junction) and access to Mendenhall Lake USFS campground, at Mile 0.4 Montana Creek Road. The campground has 60 sites, tables, fireplaces, water, pit toilets and dump station. Reservations not available. Fee charged. Montana Creek Road dead ends 3.5 miles/5.6 km from Mendenhall Loop Road. ▲

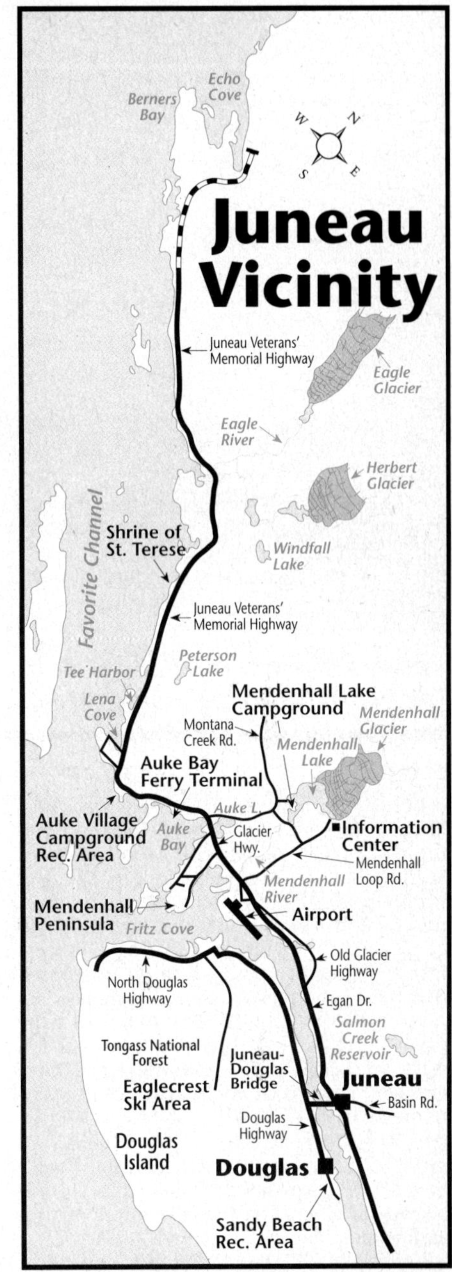

9.7 (15.6 km) **RE 30.8** (49.7 km) Airport area access for southbound travelers via Old Glacier Highway.

9.9 (15.9 km) **RE 30.6** (49.4 km) Mendenhall River and Brotherhood Bridge. The bridge was named in honor of the Alaska Native Brotherhood and is lined by bronze plaques symbolizing the Raven and Eagle clans.

10 (16.1 km) **RE 30.5** (49.2 km) Mendenhall Glacier viewpoint to east; parking area with sign about Brotherhood Bridge and short walking trail.

10.5 (16.9 km) **RE 30** (48.4 km) State troopers office.

10.8 (17.4 km) **RE 29.7** (47.9 km) The 2.1-mile/3.4-km Mendenhall Peninsula Road, a two-lane gravel road, to west. About halfway along this road, Engineer's Cutoff leads 0.3 mile/0.5 km to Fritz Cove Road.

Late evening fishing off Douglas Island. (David Job)

11.4 (18.3 km) **RE 29.1** (46.9 km) Auke Lake scenic wayside to east; limited overnight RV parking spaces. Good view of Mendenhall Glacier reflected in the still waters of the lake. This is one of the most photographed spots in Alaska. Red, pink and coho salmon spawn in Auke Lake system July to September. Chum salmon are primarily from Auke Creek hatchery program.

11.5 (18.5 km) **RE 29** (46.8 km) Fritz Cove Road (paved) leads 2.6 miles/4.2 km west and dead ends at Smuggler's Cove; excellent small-boat anchorage. Scenic viewpoint on Fritz Cove Road at Mile 1.2; Engineer's Cutoff at Mile 1.9 extends 0.3 mile/0.5 km to Mendenhall Peninsula Road.

11.6 (18.7 km) **RE 28.9** (46.6 km) Turnoff to east for Chapel-by-the-Lake and to southeastern branch of University of Alaska.

11.8 (19 km) **RE 28.7** (46.3 km) Short road west to National Marine Fisheries Service biological laboratory (self-guided walking tours between 8 A.M. and 4:30 P.M. Monday through Friday) and University of Alaska–Juneau campus.

12.2 (19.6 km) **RE 28.3** (45.7 km) **Junction** with Mendenhall Loop Road to west. Glacier Highway becomes Juneau Veterans' Memorial Highway and curves around Auke Bay to west. A small-boat harbor with snack shop, skiff and tackle rentals, and boat launch located at the head of the bay. Large schools of herring enter the bay to spawn in the spring.

The 6.8-mile/10.9-km Mendenhall Loop Road rejoins Glacier Highway at **Milepost 9.4.** Motorists may turn east here and follow loop road 3.1 miles/5 km to Montana Creek Road and access to Mendenhall Lake USFS campground, or drive 4.6 miles/7.4 km and turn off on Mendenhall Glacier spur road, which leads another 1.4 miles/2.2 km to the glacier and visitor center. Parking area at Mendenhall Glacier, short steep path to visitor center. The center is open daily in summer from 9 A.M. to 6:30 P.M. ▲

12.3 (19.8 km) **RE 28.2** (45.5 km) Private RV park.

12.4 (20 km) **RE 28.1** (45.3 km) Auke Bay post office to west.

12.6 (20.3 km) **RE 27.9** (45 km) Spaulding trailhead to east; 3.5 miles/5.6 km long. Access to John Muir USFS cabin.

12.8 (20.6 km) **RE 27.7** (44.8 km) Waydelich Creek and bridge.

13.8 (22.2 km) **RE 26.7** (43.1 km) Auke Bay ferry terminal exit.

13.9 (22.4 km) **RE 26.6** (42.9 km) Auke Bay ferry terminal entrance. *LeConte* ferry passengers use parking area and terminal on right; all others use parking area and large terminal on left. Visitor information counter staffed during ferry arrival.

15.1 (24.3 km) **RE 25.4** (41 km) Auke Village Recreation Area begins northbound; five beachside picnic shelters accessible to west of highway (park on highway shoulder).

15.3 (24.6 km) **RE 25.2** (40.7 km) Auke Village totem pole to east.

15.4 (24.8 km) **RE 25.1** (40.5 km) Auke Village USFS campground; 14 picnic units, 12 campsites, tables, fireplaces, water, flush and pit toilets. Fee charged. Open May 1 to Sept. 30. ▲

16.5 (26.4 km) **RE 24.1** (38.9 km) Lena Point Road, south entrance to loop road.

17 (27.3) **RE 23.5** (37.9 km) Lena Point Road, north entrance to loop road.

17.4 (28.1 km) **RE 23.1** (37.3 km) Lena Beach picnic area.

18.4 (29.6 km) **RE 22.1** (35.7 km) Tee Harbor–Point Stevens Road (gravel) leads 0.3 mile/0.6 km west to public parking area and a private marina and fuel float.

19.2 (30.9 km) **RE 21.3** (34.4 km) Inspiration Point turnout to west with view of the Chilkat Range, and over Tee Harbor and Shelter Island across Favorite Channel. Once a "bread-and-butter" commercial fishing area, particularly for halibut fishermen, it is now a popular sportfishing area.

23.1 (37.3 km) **RE 17.4** (28.1 km) Short road west to Catholic Shrine of St. Terese, located on a small island reached by a causeway.

23.3 (37.5 km) **RE 17.2** (27.8 km) Turnout to west and view of island on which Shrine of St. Terese is situated.

23.9 (38.5 km) **RE 16.6** (26.8 km) Peterson Lake trailhead to east; 4 miles/6.4 km long. Access to Peterson Lake USFS cabin. This trail connects with the Spaulding Trail (see **Milepost 12.6**).

24.2 (39 km) **RE 16.3** (26.3 km) **Peterson Creek** bridge. View spawning salmon here in late summer and early fall. Trout fishing. Black and brown bears in area.

24.8 (40 km) **RE 15.7** (25.3 km) Gravel road leads 0.6 mile/1 km west to Amalga Harbor; dock, boat launch, bait casting area. Fireplace and chimney near end of road are remains of an old trapper's cabin.

27.1 (43.7 km) **RE 13.4** (21.6 km) Windfall Lake trailhead to east; 3 miles/4.8 km long.

27.2 (43.9 km) **RE 13.3** (21.4 km) Herbert River bridge.

27.4 (44.2 km) **RE 13.1** (21.1 km) Herbert Glacier trailhead to east; 5 miles/8 km long.

27.7 (44.7 km) **RE 12.8** (20.6 km) Eagle River bridge. Amalga trailhead just across bridge to east; 4 miles/6.4 km long.

28.4 (45.8 km) **RE 12.1** (20.2 km) Eagle Beach picnic area with beachside picnic shelter and eight picnic sites. View of Chilkat Range across Lynn Canal. Duck hunting on flats in low tide during open season.

28.7 (46.2 km) **RE 11.8** (19.1 km) Scenic viewpoint to west.

29.3 (47.2 km) **RE 11.2** (18.1 km) Scenic viewpoint to west.

32.7 (52.8 km) **RE 7.8** (12.6 km) Turnout to west with view of Benjamin Island to southwest; just beyond it is Sentinel Island lighthouse. Visible to the northwest is North Island and northwest of it is Vanderbilt Reef, site of a great sea disaster. The SS *Princess Sophia,* carrying 288 passengers and 61 crew, ran aground on the Vanderbilt Reef in the early morning hours of Oct. 24, 1918. All aboard perished when a combination of stormy seas and a high tide forced the *Sophia* off the reef and she sank early in the evening of Oct. 25. The Vanderbilt Reef is now marked by a navigation light.

32.8 (52.9 km) **RE 7.7** (12.5 km) Pavement ends northbound; two-lane gravel extension of the Glacier Highway begins.

33 (53.1 km) **RE 7.5** (12.1 km) Scenic viewpoint to west. Yankee Cove and beach below this point. The MV *Fairweather* docks at Yankee Cove.

35.4 (57.1 km) **RE 5.1** (8.2 km) Sunshine Cove public beach access.

37.6 (60.7 km) **RE 2.9** (4.7 km) North Bridget Cove trailhead, Point Bridget State Park. The 2,850-acre park offers meadows, forests, rocky beaches, salmon streams and a trail system. Area is popular for cross-country skiing. Fires allowed on beach.

38.8 (61.3 km) **RE 1.7** (2.8 km) Point Bridget trailhead.

39.4 (63.5 km) **RE 1.1** (1.8 km) Kowee Creek bridge. Large parking area to west.

40.4 (65 km) **RE 0.1** (0.3 km) Access left to Echo Cove beach. Park area.

40.5 (65.3 km) **RE 0** Road dead ends near Echo Cove on Berners Bay.

Douglas Highway Log

Douglas Highway is a 3-mile/4.8-km paved road beginning on the Juneau side of the Douglas Bridge, crossing to Douglas Island, turning southeast, passing through the city of Douglas to road end and beginning of Treadwell Mine area.

0 Intersection of Egan Drive and Douglas Bridge.

0.5 (0.8 km) Right, Cordova Street leads to Dan Moller trail.

1.5 (2.4 km) Lawson Creek bridge.

2 (3.2 km) Tlingit Indian cemetery and grave houses.

2.5 (4 km) Turn left to boat harbor; dump station and Savikko Park with five overnight RV parking spaces. Short gravel road leads to Juneau Island U.S. Bureau of Mines headquarters. Sandy Beach Recreation Area with water, toilets, play area, tennis courts, track, two ball fields, picnic tables, shelters and children's playground. Aptly named, this is one of the few sandy beaches in southeastern Alaska. Highway becomes St. Ann's Avenue.

3 (4.8 km) Road end.

North Douglas Highway Log

North Douglas Highway begins after crossing Douglas Bridge from Juneau and immediate right turn northwest. **Milepost 1** appears at small bridge on this turn.

0 Douglas Bridge.

0.3 (0.5 km) **Junction** of Douglas Highway and North Douglas Highway.

4.4 (7.1 km) Heliport to right.

6.9 (11.1 km) Eaglecrest Ski Area turnoff on left; drive 5.3 miles/8.5 km on gravel road to ski area. Good blueberry picking in August.

8.3 (13.5 km) Fish Creek bridge. Large parking area on right of bridge.

8.6 (13.9 km) Ninemile trail on right; small parking area.

9.5 (15.3 km) Scenic turnout and parking area with excellent view of Mendenhall Glacier; litter barrel. Boat ramp; launch permit required (contact harbormaster before arrival).

10.3 (16.6 km) Small waterfall on left.

11.4 (18.4 km) False Outer Point public beach access. Scenic view of Favorite Channel and Lynn Canal; parking area on right. Near the northern tip of Douglas Island, this is an excellent spot to observe marine activity and eagles.

12.3 (19.8 km) Outer Point trailhead on right.

13.1 (21 km) Road end.

Glacier Bay National Park naturalist leads a nature walk on Bartlett Cove beach trail. (Marion Stirrup)

Glacier Bay National Park and Preserve

What Tlingit Indians called "Big Ice-Mountain Bay" in John Muir's day (1879) is today one of southeastern Alaska's most dramatic attractions, Glacier Bay National Park and Preserve. Muir described Glacier Bay as "a picture of icy wildness unspeakably pure and sublime."

There are no roads to Glacier Bay National Park, except for a 10-mile/16-km stretch of gravel road connecting Bartlett Cove with Gustavus airport. Bartlett Cove is the site of a ranger station and Glacier Bay Lodge. Park naturalists conduct daily hikes and other activities from the lodge, and the excursion boats depart from there. Airlines land at Gustavus airport. See Accommodations and Transportation under Gustavus in this section.

Visitors should contact the Superintendent, Glacier Bay National Park and Preserve, Gustavus, AK 99826-0140 for more information, or check with Glacier Bay tour operators. The national park's headquarters is at Bartlett Cove; phone 697-2230.

Situated at the northwest end of the Alexander Archipelago, Glacier Bay National Park includes not only tidewater glaciers but also Mount Fairweather in the Fairweather Range of the St. Elias Mountains, the highest peak in southeastern Alaska, and also the United States portion of the Alsek River.

With passage of the Alaska National Interest Lands Conservation Act in December 1980, Glacier Bay National Monument, established in 1925 by Pres. Calvin Coolidge, became a national park. Approximately 585,000 acres were added to the park/preserve to protect fish and wildlife habitat and migration routes in Dry Bay and along the lower Alsek River, and to include the northwest slope of Mount Fairweather. Total acreage is 3,328,000 (3,271,000 in park, 57,000 in preserve) with 2,770,000 acres designated wilderness.

When the English naval explorer Capt. George Vancouver sailed through the ice-choked waters of Icy Strait in 1794, Glacier Bay was little more than a dent in the coastline. Across the head of this seemingly minor inlet stood a towering wall of ice marking the seaward terminus of an immense glacier that completely filled the broad, deep basin of what is now Glacier Bay. To the north, ice extended more than 100 miles/160 km into the St. Elias Mountains, covering the intervening valleys with a 4,000-foot-/1,219-m-deep mantle of ice.

During the century following Vancouver's pioneer explorations, the glacier retreated some 40 miles/64 km back into the bay, permitting a spruce–hemlock forest to gradually colonize the land. By 1916, Tarr Inlet, at one of the heads of Glacier Bay, was free of ice, and the Grand Pacific Glacier, which once had filled the entire bay, had retreated some 65 miles/105 km from the position observed by Captain Vancouver in 1794. Nowhere else in the world have glaciers receded at such a rapid pace in recent time.

Today, few of the many tributary glaciers that once supplied the huge ice sheet extend to the sea. Glacier Bay National Park encloses 16 active tidewater glaciers, including several on the remote and seldom visited western edge of the park along the Gulf of Alaska and Lituya Bay. Icebergs, cracked off from near-vertical ice cliffs, dot the waters of Glacier Bay.

A decline in the number of humpback whales using Glacier Bay for feeding and calf-rearing led the National Park Service to limit the number of boats visiting Glacier Bay between June and September. These regulations affect all motorized vessels. Check with the National Park Service for current regulations.

Glacier Bay is approximately 100 miles/160 km from Juneau by boat. Park rangers at Bartlett Cove are available to assist in advising visitors who wish to tour Glacier Bay in private boats or by kayak. Permits are required for motorized pleasure boats between June 1 and Aug. 31. The permits are free. A limited number are available, but rarely are boaters turned away. Permits must be obtained prior to entry into Glacier Bay and Bartlett Cove. Request permits no more than two months in advance by writing the National Park Service, Gustavus, AK 99826-0140. For more information, phone 697-2268 (May 1 to Sept. 7).

Glacier Bay Lodge is the only accommodation within the national park, although nearby Gustavus (see description this section) has a number of lodges, inns, bed and breakfasts and rental cabins. Contact Glacier Bay Lodge Inc., 1-800-451-5952, for more information on the concessionaire-operated Glacier Bay Lodge and excursion boat cruises offered from the lodge.

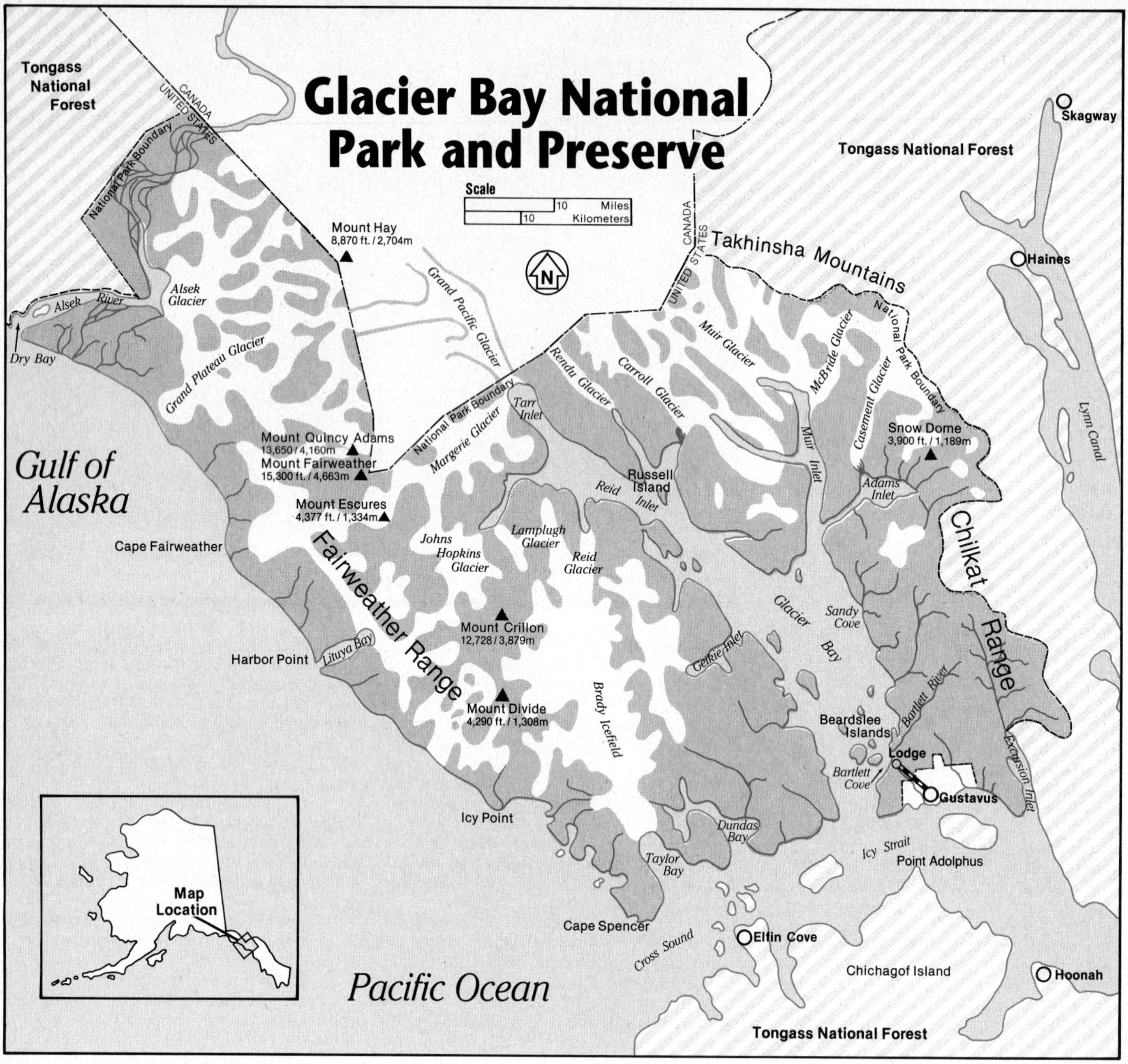

Glacier Bay National Park and Preserve

Tongass National Forest
Scale
10 Miles
10 Kilometers
Mount Hay 8,870 ft. / 2,704m
CANADA UNITED STATES
National Park Boundary
Alsek Glacier
Alsek River
Dry Bay
Grand Plateau Glacier
Grand Pacific Glacier
Takhinsha Mountains
Skagway
Haines
Tongass National Forest
Muir Glacier
McBride Glacier
Rendu Glacier
Carroll Glacier
Tarr Inlet
Margerie Glacier
Mount Quincy Adams 13,650 / 4,160m
Mount Fairweather 15,300 ft. / 4,663m
Mount Escures 4,377 ft. / 1,334m
Gulf of Alaska
Cape Fairweather
Casement Glacier
Snow Dome 3,900 ft. / 1,189m
Muir Inlet
Adams Inlet
Lynn Canal
Russell Island
Reid Inlet
Johns Hopkins Glacier
Lamplugh Glacier
Reid Glacier
Chilkat Range
Fairweather Range
Mount Crillon 12,728 / 3,879m
Glacier Bay
Sandy Cove
Harbor Point
Lituya Bay
Geikie Inlet
Mount Divide 4,290 ft. / 1,308m
Brady Icefield
Bartlett River
Beardslee Islands
Lodge
Bartlett Cove
Gustavus
Excursion Inlet
Icy Point
Dundas Bay
Taylor Bay
Icy Strait
Point Adolphus
Map Location
Cape Spencer
Cross Sound
Elfin Cove
Chichagof Island
Hoonah
Pacific Ocean
Tongass National Forest

Gasoline and diesel fuel may be purchased at Bartlett Cove, where a good anchorage is available. There are no other public facilities for boats within park boundaries; Sandy Cove, about 20 miles/32 km from Bartlett Cove, is a popular anchorage. Gustavus has a dock and small-boat harbor.

CAUTION BOATERS: No attempt should be made to navigate Glacier Bay without appropriate charts, tide tables and local knowledge. Floating ice is a special hazard. Because of the danger from waves caused by falling ice, small craft should not approach closer than 0.5 mile/0.8 km from tidewater glacier fronts.

Wildlife in the national park area is protected and hunting is not allowed. Firearms are illegal. *CAUTION: Brown and black bears are present.*

Fishing for silver and king salmon, Dolly Varden and halibut is excellent. A valid Alaska fishing license is required. Charter fishing trips are available.

GLACIER BAY ADVERTISERS

Alaska's Glacier Bay Tours and Cruises ....Ph. (800) 451-5952
Annie Mae Lodge ....Ph. (907) 697-2346
Glacier Bay Country Inn ...Ph. (907) 697-2288
Glacier Bay—Your Way! ...Ph. (907) 697-2288
Grand Pacific Charters......Ph. (907) 697-2288
Gustavus Inn.....................Ph. (907) 697-2254
Puffin, The ....Ph. (907) 697-2260
Puffin Travel......................Ph. (907) 697-2260
Spirit Walker Expeditions..................Ph. (907) 697-2266

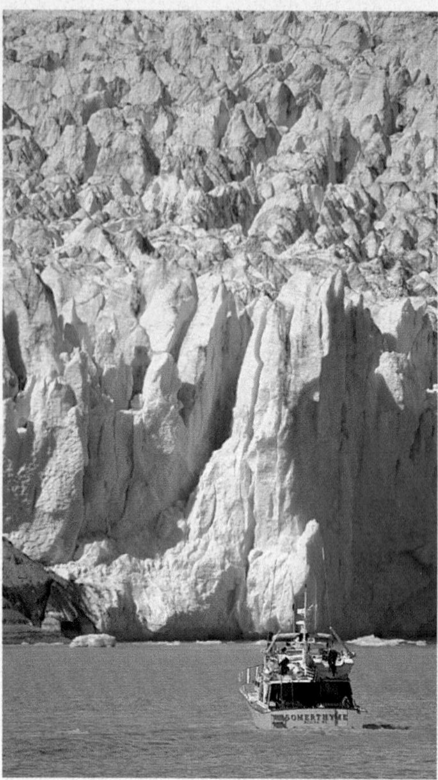

Private boat approaches glacier face in the west arm. (David Job)

There is an established campground at Bartlett Cove with 25 sites. Wilderness camping is also available throughout the park. ▲

Gustavus

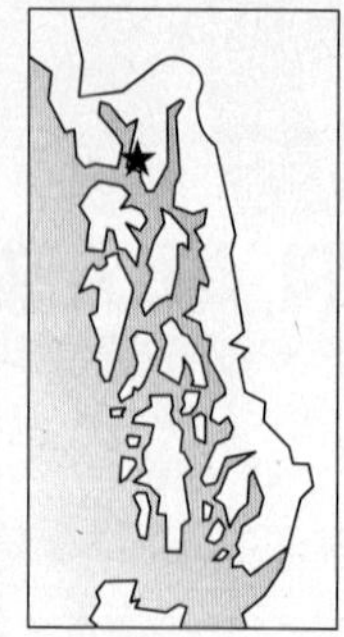

Gateway to Glacier Bay National Park and Preserve, the small community of Gustavus is located just outside the park boundary at the mouth of the Salmon River on the north shore of Icy Passage, 48 miles northwest of Juneau. It is 10 miles/16 km by road from Gustavus to Bartlett Cove within the park. **Population:** approximately 200. **Emergency Services:** Phone 911. **Visitor Information:** Write the Gustavus Visitors Assoc., Box 167, Gustavus 99826.

Surrounded on three sides by the snow-covered peaks of the Chilkat Range and the Fairweather Mountains, Gustavus offers miles of level land with expansive sandy beaches, farmland and forest. Homesteaded in 1914 as a small agricultural community, the area was once named Strawberry Point because of its abundant wild strawberries. Today, most residents maintain gardens and make their living by fishing (commercial and subsistence), fish processing, tourism, arts and crafts, and working for the National Park Service and in various local trades.

Besides its proximity to the national park, Gustavus offers a number of attractions. There is fishing for salmon, halibut and trout; excellent berry picking (strawberries, blueberries, nagoonberries and huckleberries); beachcombing; bird watching; whale-watching tours; hiking; and kayaking. Charter boats offer trips into Icy Strait and Glacier Bay.

ACCOMMODATIONS

Accommodations in Gustavus include several inns, lodges, bed and breakfasts, and self-sufficient cabins. The lodges and inns serve meals for guests (drop-in customers check for space-available reservations for meals). Taxi service is available. Businesses in Gustavus include a grocery store, art gallery, cafe, gift shop, hardware/building supply store, gas station, auto repair shop and fish processing facilities. Fishing supplies and licenses may be purchased locally.

Annie Mae Lodge. Old-fashioned good food and good company. Three fine family-style meals using home-baked bread and pastries, fresh caught seafood, berries off the bush, and garden vegetables. We offer beautiful comfortable rooms, peace, quiet, abundant wildlife, wilderness, sportfishing, kayak trips, whale watching. Glacier Bay boat/plane tours. Box 80, Gustavus, AK 99826. (907) 697-2346. [ADVERTISEMENT]

Glacier Bay Country Inn and Grand Pacific Charters. Peaceful, storybook accommodations, away from the crowds in a wilderness setting. Cozy comforters, warm flannel sheets, private baths. Superb dining features local seafoods, garden-fresh produce, homebaked breads, spectacular desserts. Fishing, whale-watching, sightseeing. Glacier Bay boat/plane tours. Courtesy van, bikes. Box 5MP, Gustavus, AK 99826. Phone (907) 697-2288, fax (907) 697-2289. Winter correspondence (October–April): P.O. Box 2557-MP, St. George, UT 84771. Phone (801) 673-8480, fax (801) 673-8481. [ADVERTISEMENT]

Glacier Bay–Your Way! We arrange unforgettable day or overnight tours of Glacier Bay, whalewatching, sportfishing, kayaking, hiking. Full-service country inn, B&B accommodations and condominium rentals. Transportation arranged. Full meal packages, bicycles. Box 5MP, Gustavus, AK 99826. Phone (907) 697-2288, fax (907) 697-2289. Winter correspondence (October–April): Box 2557-MP, St. George, UT 84771. Phone (801) 673-8480, fax (801) 673-8481. [ADVERTISEMENT]

Gustavus Inn. Country living, family-style gourmet local seafood meals, cozy bar, kitchen garden, bikes, trout fishing poles, courtesy van, afternoon park naturalist trip. Family-run since 1965. Custom fishing and Glacier Bay sightseeing packages arranged. For map, brochures, please write: Gustavus Inn, Box 60-MP, Gustavus, AK 99826 or call (907) 697-2254. [ADVERTISEMENT]

The Puffin. See nearby Glacier Bay and Icy Strait. Stay in your own modern, comfortable, attractively decorated cabin with electricity on quiet wooded homestead. New picturesque central lodge. Complete country breakfast. Bicycles included. Children, pets welcome. Reservations for all charters, Glacier Bay tours. Qualified captains guide fishing, sightseeing charters. Friendly, personal attention; full travel services! (907) 697-2260, fax (907) 697-2258. [ADVERTISEMENT]

Spirit Walker Expeditions. Paddle with whales in Icy Strait! Premium guided sea kayaking trips are the *perfect way* to *really experience* Alaska's wilderness scenery, solitude and wildlife. Superb meals, all gear, instruction included. One to seven days. Beginners, families, custom trips our specialties. Box 240MP, Gustavus, AK 99826. (907) 697-2266 or (800) KAYAKER. [ADVERTISEMENT]

TRANSPORTATION

NOTE: There is no state ferry service to Glacier Bay. Closest port of call for state ferries is Hoonah. (Kayakers getting off at Hoonah can expect a two-day paddle across Icy Strait.)

Air: Glacier Bay may be reached by Alaska Airlines daily jet flights from Juneau and by charter service from Juneau, Sitka, Haines and Skagway to Gustavus airport. Charter air service available in Gustavus. Bus service between the airport and Bartlett Cove is available on jet flights. Taxi service to local facilities and courtesy van service for some lodges are also available.

Rental Cars: Available.

Private Aircraft: Gustavus airport, adjacent northeast; elev. 36 feet/11m; length

6,700 feet/2,042m; asphalt; fuel 100LL, A. Landing within the park is restricted to salt water (Adams Inlet is closed to aircraft landing).

Boat Service: Excursion boats depart daily from Bartlett Cove. You may also charter a boat in Gustavus for sightseeing or fishing. Cruise tours are available from Juneau and Glacier Bay.

Several cruise ships include Glacier Bay cruising in their itineraries.

Yakutat

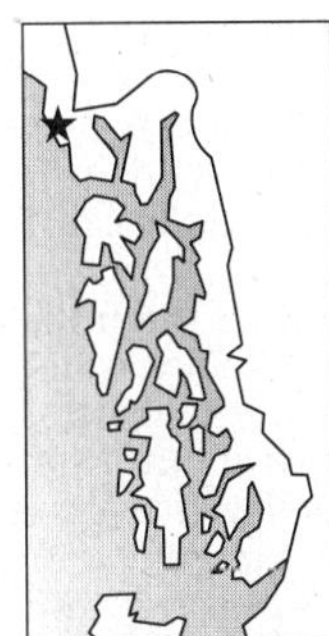

Located on the Gulf of Alaska coast where southeastern Alaska joins the major body of Alaska to the west; 225 miles/362 km northwest of Juneau, 220 miles/354 km southeast of Cordova and 380 miles/611 km southeast of Anchorage. **Population:** 552. **Emergency Services: Dept. of Public Safety,** phone 784-3323. **Fire Department,** phone 911. **Yakutat Health Center,** phone 784-3275. **Maritime Search and Rescue,** contact the Coast Guard at 1-800-478-5555.

Visitor Information: Inquire at one of the lodges, at the city office or the USFS office, or write the city manager at P.O. Box 160, Yakutat, AK 99689. For sportfishing information, stop by the ADF&G office at Mile 0.5 Cannon Beach Road, or write Sport Fish Division, P.O. Box 49, Yakutat 99689, phone 784-3222.

Elevation: Sea level. **Climate:** Similar to the rest of coastal southeastern Alaska: mild in summer, winters are moderate. Average annual snowfall is 216 inches. Total annual precipitation is about 130 inches. Normal daily maximum in August, 60°F/16°C; minimum in January, 17°F/-8°C. Prevailing winds are southeasterly.

Private Aircraft: Yakutat airport, 3 miles/4.8 km southeast; elev. 33 feet/10m; length 7,700 feet/2,347m; asphalt; fuel 100, A1. Seaplane base 1 mile/1.6 km northwest.

Transportation: Air–Daily jet service from Seattle, Juneau, Anchorage and Cordova. Charter air service available.

Yakutat has three lodges, two bed and breakfasts, a restaurant, cafe, gift shop, bank, two grocery stores, post office, clinic and gas station. Boat rentals, car rentals and cab service are available.

Glacier Bear Lodge. See display ad this section.

Yakutat Bay is one of the few refuges for vessels along this long stretch of coast in the Gulf of Alaska. The site was originally the principal winter village of the local Tlingit Indian tribe. Sea otter pelts brought Russians to the area in the 19th century. Fur traders were followed by gold seekers, who came to work the black sand beaches. Commercial salmon fishing developed in this century, and the first cannery was built here in 1904. Today's economy is based primarily on fishing and fish processing. Salmon and some halibut, crab and black cod make up the fishery. Government and local businesses employ most residents. Subsistence activities are primarily fishing (salmon and shellfish), hunting (moose, bear, goats, ducks and small game), and gathering seaweed and berries. The soil is not suitable for agriculture, and a vegetable garden requires a great deal of preparation to produce even small quantities.

While hunting and fishing in particular draw visitors to Yakutat, the surge of Hubbard Glacier in June 1986, which sealed off the mouth of Russell Fiord, drew national attention. Malaspina Glacier, largest on the North American continent, is northwest of town. Nearer to town, Cannon Beach has good beachcombing and a picnic area.

AREA FISHING: Yakutat is considered a world-class sportfishing destination. Steelhead fishing is among the finest anywhere. King and silver (coho) salmon run in abundance in Yakutat area salt water, rivers and streams May through September. The area also boasts red and pink salmon and smelt in season. USFS cabins available on some rivers; check with the Forest Service (586-8751).

Lost River and **Tawah Creek,** 10 miles/16 km south of Yakutat on Lost River Road, silver (coho) salmon to 20 lbs., mid-August through September. **Situk River,** 12 miles/19.3 km south of Yakutat on the Lost River Road (also accessible by Forest Highway 10), is one of Alaska's top fishing spots spring and fall for steelhead and silver salmon and has one of the best sockeye (red) salmon runs in the state, late June through August; steelhead averaging 10 lbs., April 1 to May 30 for spring run, October and November for fall run; king salmon to 45 lbs., mid-June through July; silver salmon to 23 lbs., mid-August through September; pink salmon run in August, yields Dolly Varden also. **Yakutat Bay,** king salmon 30 to 50 lbs., May through June; silver salmon to 20 lbs., late August through September.

Haines

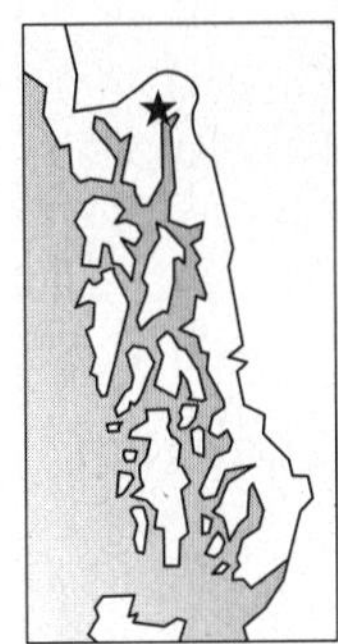

Located on Portage Cove, Chilkoot Inlet, on the upper arm of Lynn Canal, northern southeastern Alaska, 80 air miles/129 km northwest of Juneau; 151 road miles/243 km southeast of Haines Junction, YT. Southern terminus of the Haines Highway. *NOTE: Although Haines is only 13 miles/21 km by water from Skagway, it is 359 miles/578 km by road!* **Population:** 1,238. **Emergency Services: Alaska State Troopers,** phone 766-2552. **City Police,** phone 766-2121. **Fire Department** and **Ambulance,** emergency only phone 911. **Doctor,** phone 766-2521. **Maritime Search and Rescue,** contact the Coast Guard at 1-800-478-5555.

Visitor Information: At 2nd and Willard streets. There are free brochures for all of Alaska and the Yukon. Open daily, 8 A.M. to 8 P.M., June through August; 8 A.M. to 5 P.M. weekdays, September through May. Phone 766-2234 or toll free 1-800-458-3579. Write the Haines Visitor Bureau at P.O. Box 530, Haines 99827.

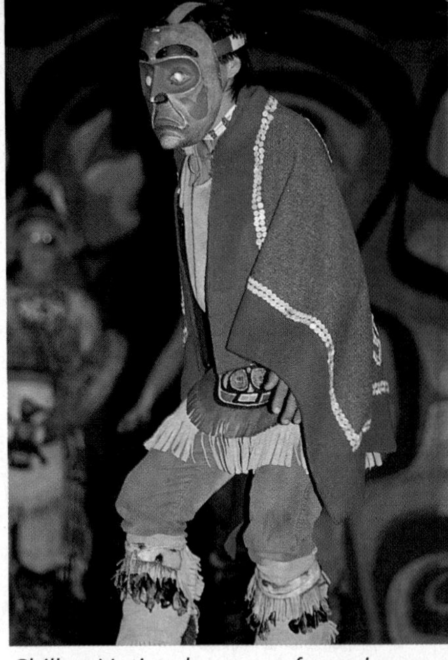

Chilkat Native dancer performs in Haines. (John W. Warden)

Elevation: Sea level. **Climate:** Average daily maximum temperature in July, 66°F/19°C; average daily minimum in January, 17°F/-8°C. Extreme high summer temperature, 90°F/32°C; extreme winter low, -16°F/-27°C; average annual precipitation, 59 inches. **Radio:** KHNS-FM 102.3. **Television:** 12 cable channels. **Newspaper:** *Chilkat Valley News* (weekly).

Private Aircraft: Haines airport, 3 miles/4.8 km west; elev. 16 feet/5m; length 3,000 feet/914m; asphalt; fuel 100; unattended.

The original Indian name for Haines was *Dtehshuh,* meaning "end of the trail." It was a trading post for both Chilkat and Interior Indians. The first white man to settle here was George Dickinson, who came as an agent for the North West Trading Co.

The following year S. Hall Young, a Presbyterian missionary, came into Chilkat Inlet with his friend, naturalist John Muir. They planned to build a Christian town, offering the Chilkat people a missionary and teacher. The site chosen was on the narrow portage between the Chilkat River and Lynn Canal. By 1881, with financial help from Sheldon Jackson, the mission was established. The town was named for Mrs. F.E. Haines, secretary of the Presbyterian National Committee of Home Missions, which raised funds for the new mission.

In 1884 the Haines post office was established, although the settlement was still known locally as Chilkoot. The town became an important outlet for the Porcupine Mining District, producing thousands of dollars' worth of placer gold at the turn of the century. Haines also marked the beginning of the Dalton Trail, which crossed the Chilkat mountain pass to the Klondike goldfields in the Yukon.

Just to the south of Haines city center is Port Chilkoot on Portage Cove. The U.S. government established a permanent military post here in 1904 and called it Fort William H. Seward, in honor of the secretary of state who negotiated the purchase of

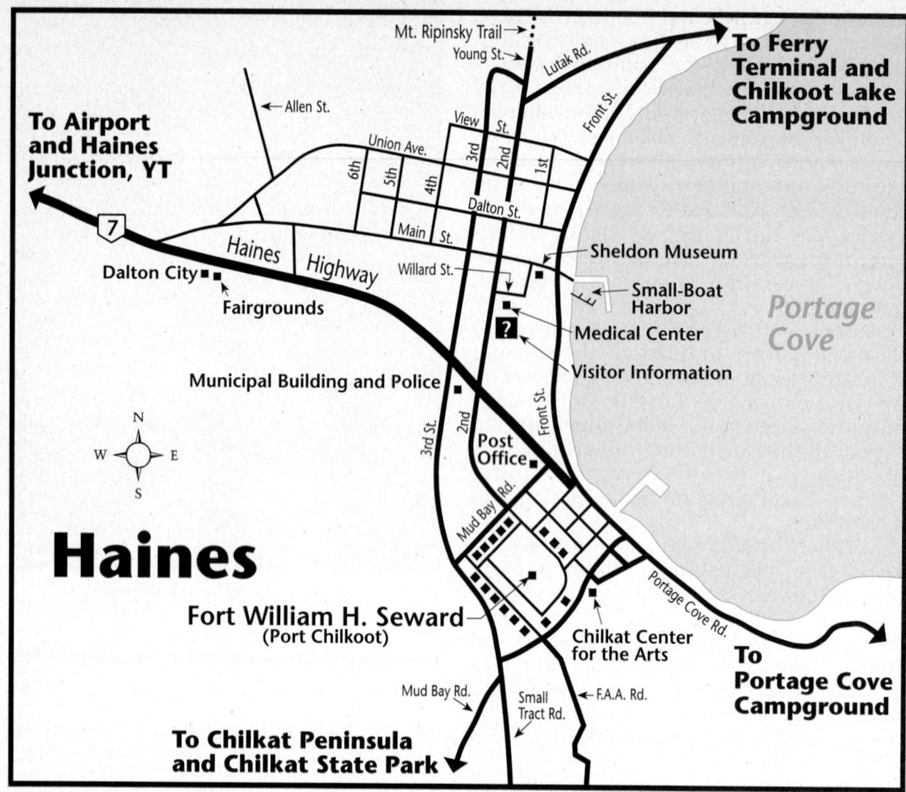

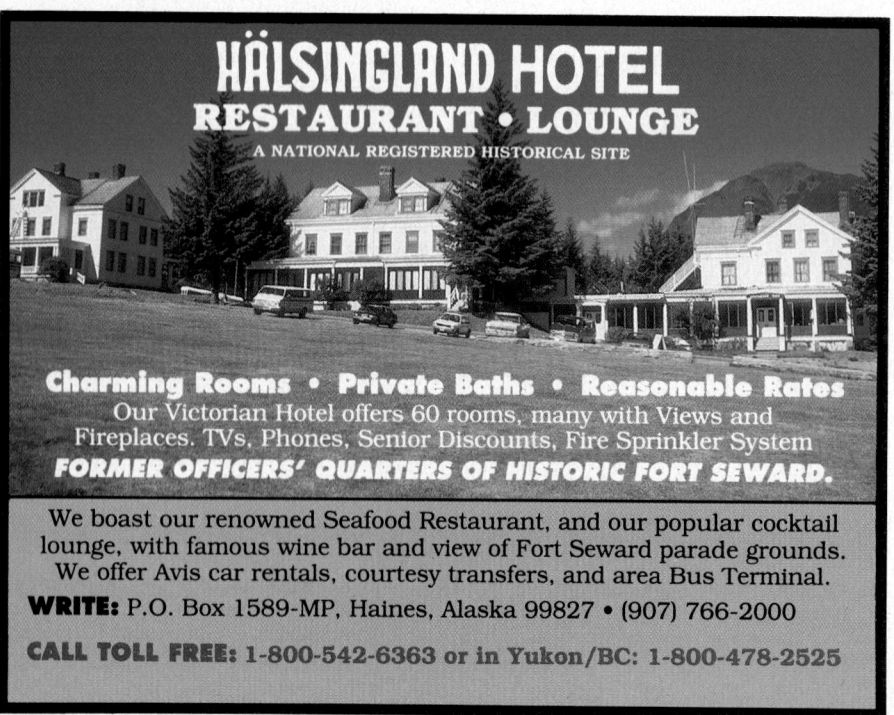

Alaska from Russia in 1867.

In 1922, the fort was renamed Chilkoot Barracks, after the mountain pass and the Indian tribe on the Chilkoot River. (There are two tribes in this area: the Chilkat and the Chilkoot.) Until WWII this was the only U.S. Army post in Alaska. Chilkoot Barracks was deactivated in 1946 and sold in 1947 to a group of enterprising U.S. veterans who had designs of creating a business cooperative on the site. Their original plans were never fully realized, but a few stayed on to convert some of the houses on Officers' Row into homes.

In 1970, Port Chilkoot merged with Haines to become one municipality, the city of Haines. Two years later, the post was designated a national historic site and became officially known, again, as Fort William H. Seward (although many people still call it Port Chilkoot).

Fishing and gold mining were the initial industries of the Haines area. Haines is also remembered for its famous strawberries, developed by Charles Anway about 1900. His Alaskan hybrid, *Burbank,* was a prize winner at the 1909 Alaska–Yukon–Pacific Exposition in Seattle, WA. A strawberry festival was held annually in Haines for many years, and this local event grew into the Southeast Alaska State Fair, which each

HAINES ADVERTISERS

Alaska Nature Tours ....Ph. (907) 766-2876
Captain's Choice Motel ....Ph. (907) 766-3111
Chilkat Restaurant and Bakery, The ....5th Ave.
Chilkoot Lake Tours ....Ph. (907) 766-2891
Chilkoot Sled Dog Adventures ....Ph. (907) 766-3242
Dalton City........................Ph. (907) 766-2476
Don's Camp ....Ph. (907) 766-2303
Eagle Camper RV Park ....751 Union St.
Eagle's Nest Motel and Car Rental............Ph. (907) 766-2891
First Out, Last In Fishing Charters ....Ph. (907) 766-2854
Fort Seward Lodge ....Fort Seward
Haines Chamber of Commerce ....Ph. 1-800-458-3579
Haines Hitch-up RV Park ....Ph. (907) 766-2882
Haines Quick Laundry ....Behind Haines Quick Shop
Haines Quick Shop...........Ph. (907) 766-2330
Haines-Skagway Water Taxi ....Ph. (907) 766-3395
Hälsingland Hotel, Restaurant and Lounge.............................Fort Seward
Helen's Shop...................................Main St.
Howsers Supermarket ....Main St.
King's Store ....Main St.
L.A.B. Flying Service, Inc. ....Main St.
Mt. View Motel.................Ph. (907) 766-2900
Oceanside R.V. Park ....Front St.
Officers Inn Bed & Breakfast ....Fort Seward
Outfitter Liquor Store.......Ph. (907) 766-3220
Outfitter Sporting Goods .Ph. (907) 766-2330
Port Chilkoot Camper Park..........Fort Seward
Port Chilkoot Potlatch ....Fort Seward
River Adventures ....Ph. (907) 766-2050
Sheldon Museum and Cultural Center, The ....25 Main St.
Sheltered Harbor Bed & Breakfast...........Ph. (907) 766-2741
Summer Inn Bed & Breakfast, The.......................247 2nd Ave.
Thunderbird Motel ....242 Dalton St.

Gill-net salmon fishing is part of Haines economy. *(John W. Warden)*

summer draws thousands of visitors. Today, halibut and gill-net salmon fishing, lumbering and tourism are the basis of the economy. Haines is an important port on the Alaska Marine Highway System as the southern terminus of the Haines Highway, one of the two year-round roads linking southeastern Alaska with the Interior.

ACCOMMODATIONS

Haines offers travelers comfortable accommodations with seven hotels/motels and seven bed and breakfasts. There is a youth hostel (families welcome) with cabin accommodations on Small Tract Road.

Haines has all traveler facilities, including hardware and grocery stores, gift shops and art galleries, automotive repair, laundry, post office and bank. Gift shops and galleries feature the work of local artisans. There are several restaurants, cafes and taverns.

State campgrounds in the area include Portage Cove Campground with nine tent sites (backpackers and bicyclists only), 2 miles/3.2 km from Haines on Portage Cove (take beach road south of Fort William H. Seward). Chilkat State Park, with 32 RV sites and three tent sites, is about 7 miles/11 km from Haines on Mud Bay Road (from the Haines Highway, bear right at the Y by the Welcome to Haines sign; continue straight ahead past the high school and up the hill, where road bends to the right; follow signs from hill to Chilkat State Park). Chilkoot Lake Campground (32 sites) is approximately 8 miles/13 km from Haines on Lutak Road (5 miles/8 km past the ferry terminal; turn right when exiting the ferry for Chilkoot Lake). There are five private campgrounds in Haines. ▲

TRANSPORTATION

Air: Haines is served regularly by L.A.B. Flying Service, Haines Airways and Wings of Alaska. Haines airport is 3.5 miles/5.6 km from downtown. Commercial airlines provide transportation to and from motels, and some motels offer courtesy car pickup.

Ferry: Alaska Marine Highway vessels serve Haines from southeastern Alaska, British Columbia and Bellingham, WA. Alaska state ferries run year-round; phone 766-2111. See MARINE ACCESS ROUTES section for details. Ferries unload at the terminal on Lutak Road, 4.5 miles/7.2 km from downtown Haines. Bus/van service meets all ferries in summer.

A local company provides water-taxi service to Skagway twice daily during the summer; phone 766-3395.

Cruise Ships: Seven cruise ships make Haines a port of call.

Private Boats: Transient moorage is available at Letnikof Cove and at the small-boat harbor downtown. Contact the harbormaster, phone 766-2448.

Bus: Local bus service to ferry terminal and guided sightseeing tours are available. Two companies also offer service to and

HAINES

Valley of the Eagles

The beauty of Southeast Alaska is waiting for you in Haines. Enjoy unique cultural attractions such as the Chilkat Bald Eagle Preserve, Fort William H. Seward——a National Historic Landmark, the Chilkat Indian Dancers, Totem Pole Carvers, Dalton City——where the movie "White Fang" was filmed, and many talented Alaskan Artists.

ACCOMMODATIONS/RESTAURANTS

① **ALASKA THUNDERBIRD MOTEL** Downtown motel, all ground floor. Clean, comfortable, direct dial phones, color TV, some kitchenettes. (907) 766-2131, or 800-327-2556.

② **BAMBOO ROOM RESTAURANT** Famous for our halibut fish 'n chips, homemade soups & pies. Daily specials. Seafood & Steaks. Open 6 a.m. year round. Full service bar & liquor store. Second Avenue. (907) 766-2800 or 766-2474.

③ **CAPTAIN'S CHOICE MOTEL** Haines' newest, finest, & most comfortable lodging. Car rentals; courtesy transfers; centrally located. See our display ad. 766-3111 or 800-247-7153 or 800-478-2345 Alaska & Yukon. AAA Approved.

④ **CHILKAT BAKERY & RESTAURANT** Bakery products fresh daily. Breakfast-Lunch-Dinner. 7 a.m. - 9 p.m. Plenty of parking. 5th Avenue.

⑤ **EAGLE'S NEST MOTEL & CAR RENTAL** Fully modern, quiet rooms, AAA approved. Featuring Chilkoot Lake Tours, fishing & sightseeing trips. POB 250, Haines, AK 99827, (907) 766-2891 or 800-354-6009.

⑥ **FORT SEWARD CONDOS** Completely furnished, spacious apartments overlooking the bay. 1 and 2 bedrooms, will sleep 5, 2 day minimum. Reasonable. POB 75, Haines, AK 99827, (907) 766-2425.

⑦ **FT. SEWARD LODGE & RESTAURANT** Affordable lodging, ocean view kitchenettes, restaurant-saloon, Alaskan cuisine and decor. Military & senior discounts. (907) 766-2009. See our display ad.

⑧ **HOTEL HALSINGLAND** Gracious Victorian Hotel. Renowned Seafood Restaurant. Cocktail lounge. Reasonable rates. See our display ad. (800) 542-6363 or Canada (800) 478-2525.

⑨ **MOUNTAIN VIEW MOTEL** Modern, quiet, view units. Reasonable rates, kitchenettes, color TV. Located adjacent to Ft. Seward on Second Ave. (907) 766-2900 or 800-478-2902 BC, Yukon & AK.

⑩ **SUMMER INN BED & BREAKFAST** Open year round. Full, homemade breakfast, centrally located, clean comfortable rooms, nice views, reasonable rates. See our display ad. 247 Second Ave. (907) 766-2970.

ART GALLERIES/GIFT SHOPS

⑪ **BELL'S STORE** For the very best Alaskan gifts and a unique shopping experience. FTD service and Fresh Flowers too. OPEN ALL YEAR. Second Ave.

⑫ **CHILKOOT GARDENS** Quality and varied selection of gifts, jewelry, printwear, books, FTD Florist, Greenhouses, and Hallmark. Open all year. 2nd & Main St. (907) 766-2703 "A shopper's delight."

⑬ **HELEN'S SHOP** Quality Alaskan jewelry and gifts. Open year round. Main Street, POB 284, Haines, AK 99827.

⑭ **KING'S STORE** "Same day" Photo Center. Unique printwear, necessities & gifts. A browser's paradise. Main St. across from museum.

⑮ **WHALE RIDER GALLERY** Artists at work at this fine studio-gallery. Wood carving, prints, & jewelry by local artist, Tresham Gregg.

ATTRACTIONS

⑯ **ALASKA INDIAN ARTS/CHILKAT DANCERS** Traditional Northwest Coast totem carvers, silversmiths & printmakers at work. Home of the Chilkat Dancers who perform several times each week during the summer. At Fort Seward. Box 271, Haines, AK 99827 (907) 766-2160.

⑰ **FORT WILLIAM H. SEWARD NATIONAL HISTORIC LANDMARK** First Army Post built in Alaska. Totem Village & Arts and Cultural Center. Walking tours available.

⑱ **SHELDON MUSEUM & CULTURAL CENTER** History of the Chilkat Valley and culture of the Tlingit Indian People, Dalton Trail, Ft. Seward and more. Bookstore. POB 269, Haines, AK 99827, (907) 766-2366.

⑲ **SOUTHEAST ALASKA STATE FAIR & ALASKAN BALD EAGLE MUSIC FESTIVAL** August 10-14, 1994. Great music, parade, horse show, exhibits, logging show, pig races, food & trade booths.

⑳ **DALTON CITY** The set for the movie "White Fang." Experience the drama of the Gold Rush Era; native artisans, gold panning, sleddog demonstrations and more. See our display ad.

AUTO SERVICE

㉑ **THE PARTS PLACE** Auto-RV-Marine. If you need it, we have it or will get it. 206 3rd Ave. S. 766-2940.

㉒ **BIGFOOT AUTO SERVICE** NAPA Parts, RV Service & Towing; A.S.E. Technicians, Gas, Diesel, Goodyear Sales & Service. (907) 766-2458/2459.

㉓ **BUSHMASTER SERVICE & REPAIR** Four wheel alignment, suspension, brakes, major engine & driveline work, electronic engine controls. Guaranteed service. 4th & Union St. 766-3217.

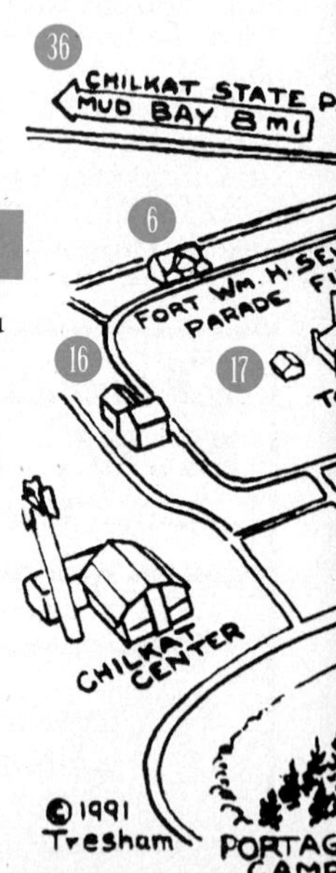

TOURS WILDLIFE VIEWING MUSEUMS HISTORICAL SITES

(24) **WHITE PASS ALASKA'S EAGLE CHEVRON** Providing Gas & Diesel. Free RV Water & Dump; Propane and volume discounts. 766-2338.

CAMPER PARKS

(25) **EAGLE CAMPER PARK** 30 Full Hookups w/ cable TV. Electric Hookups. Tents welcome. Showers, Laundry, Propane. Good Sam & Senior DISCOUNTS. (907) 766-2335. FAX 766-2339.

(26) **HITCH-UP RV PARK** 92 full & partial hook-ups, 20 pull-thrus. Immaculate showers and restrooms, laundromat, gift shop, propane. (907) 766-2882.

(27) **PORT CHILKOOT CAMPER PARK** Lovely wooded area; full & partial hook-ups; showers, laundry; tent welcome. 800-542-6363 or 800-478-2525 AK & Yukon.

FISHING CHARTERS/LODGES

(28) **DON'S CAMP** Chilkat Lake, where great cutthroat trout fishing and good times are found. All gear provided. POB 1276, Haines, AK 99827 (907) 766-2303.

GROCERIES

(29) **HAINES QUICK SHOP/OUTFITTER SPORTING GOODS** Groceries, Videos, Ice, Fishing Licenses, Tackle & Sporting Goods. Next to Post Office. Open daily 7 a.m. to Midnight.

(30) **HOWSERS SUPERMARKET** One Stop Shopping. Groceries, Fresh Meat, Dairy, ICE. Deli Cafe & Salad Bar. NEW: Fresh Bakery Shoppe. Main Street.

(31) **OUTFITTER LIQUOR STORE** Cold beer, wide variety of liquors & wines. Ice. Open daily 8 a.m. to midnight. Next to Post Office.

SERVICES

(32) **E. D. & D.** Cable TV, Computers, Video Tapes, Electronic Parts and Service. Radio Shack Dealer. Mile 1 Haines Highway.

SIGHTSEEING/TRANSPORTATION

(33) **ALASKA NATURE TOURS** Coastal beach to mountain rainforest. Interpretive, bus and walking tours. Bald eagles our specialty. See our display ad. (907) 766-2876.

(34) **CHILKAT GUIDES** Daily 3 1/2 hour float trips through the Bald Eagle Preserve. Also overnight float trips & hiking adventures (907) 766-2491.

(35) **HAINES AIRWAYS** Spectacular flightseeing tours from Haines and Juneau. Scheduled service to Juneau, Haines, Gustavus & Hoonah. (907) 766-2646 or 789-2336.

(36) **HANSON'S NORTH COUNTRY CANOE OUTFITTERS** Wilderness Backpacking & Canoe Trips. Fish for Trout & Salmon. Look for Grizzly Bear, Mountain Goats, Moose, Wolves & Bald Eagles. PO Box 781, Haines, AK 99827.

(37) **L.A.B. FLYING SERVICE** Explore Glacier Country. Scheduled Service and Charters. Flightsee Glacier Bay. (907) 766-2222.

(38) **HAINES-SKAGWAY WATER TAXI** Two roundtrips daily between downtown Haines & Skagway. $29 RT; $18 OW (907) 766-3395.

(39) **SOCKEYE CYCLE/ALASKA BICYCLE TOURS** Rentals, sales, service. Daily 1-3 hour guided tours around the Chilkat Valley, also multi-day fully supported mountain bike tours in British Columbia and the Yukon. Brochure. Box 829, Haines, AK 99827. (907) 766-2869.

(40) **TICKETS, TOURS, TRIPS & THINGS** Water Taxi & Train Trips, Jet Boat & River Rafting in the Chilkat Bald Eagle Preserve, Chilkoot Lake Excursions, Glacier Bay Flightseeing, Salmon Bake, Chilkat dancers, Ferry Reservations, Hotel/Motel Reservations. Box 97, Haines, AK 99827, (907) 766-2665 Down the street from The Visitor's Center.

(41) **THE TRAVEL CONNECTION** See us for ferry reservations, sightseeing, Glacier Bay tours, independent trip planning. Across from the Visitor's Center. (907) 766-2681 or 800-572-8006.

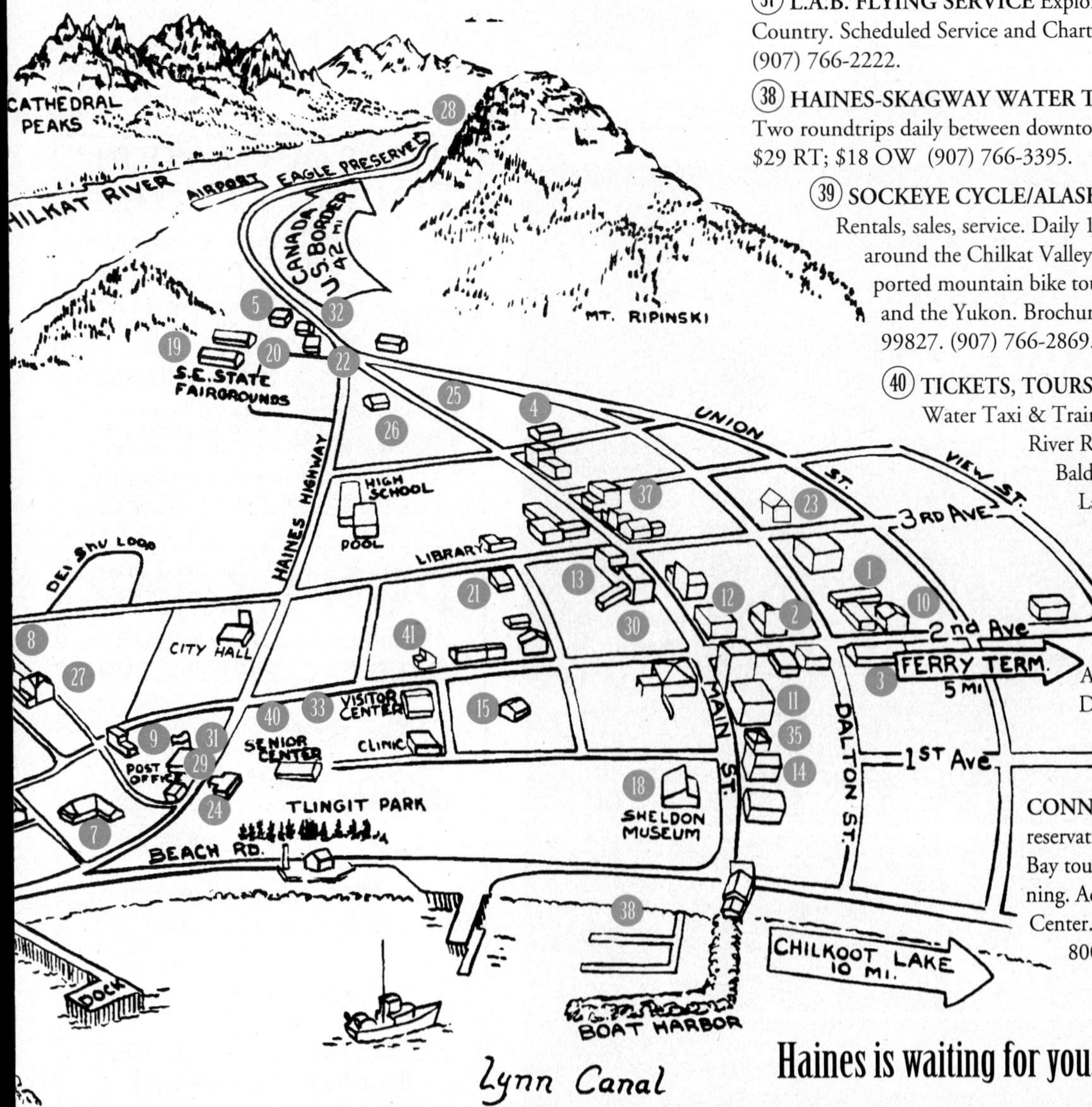

Haines is waiting for you... (800) 458-3579

from Anchorage, Fairbanks and Whitehorse, YT, via the Alaska Highway.

Taxi: 24-hour service to ferry terminal and airport.

Car Rental: Available at Thunderbird Motel, Captain's Choice Motel, Eagle's Nest Motel and Halsingland Hotel.

Highways: The Haines Highway connects Haines, AK, with Haines Junction, YT. It is maintained year-round. See HAINES HIGHWAY section for details.

ATTRACTIONS

Take the walking tour of historic Fort William H. Seward; details and map are available at the visitor information center and at other businesses. Historic buildings of the post include the former cable office; warehouses and barracks; "Soapsuds Alley," the housing for noncommissioned officers whose wives did washing for the soldiers; the former headquarters building, now a residence, fronted by a cannon and a totem depicting a bear and an eagle; Officers' Row at the "Top O' the Hill," restored houses now rented as apartments; the commanding officers' quarters, now the Halsingland Hotel, where Elinor Dusenbury (who later wrote the music for "Alaska's Flag," which became the state song) once lived; the fire hall; the guard house (jail); the former contractor's office, then plumber's quarters, now a motel; the post exchange (now a lodge), gymnasium and movie house; and the mule stables.

Visit the Chilkat Center for the Arts at the auditorium at Fort William H. Seward.

Here, the Chilkat Dancers interpret ancient Tlingit Indian legends, and the production *Smell of the Yukon,* a historically based local melodrama, is performed by the Lynn Canal Community Players. Check with the visitor information center or Alaska Indian Arts Inc. for schedule of performances.

Totem Village, on the former post parade ground, includes a replica of a tribal ceremonial house and a trapper's cabin and cache. There is a salmon bake, the Port Chilkoot Potlatch, held nightly in summer next to the tribal house; reservations recommended. Prior to the establishment of the fort, this area was part of an ancient portage route for Tlingit Indians transporting canoes from the Chilkat River to Lynn Canal.

See the Welcome Totems located at the Y on the Haines Highway. These poles were created by carvers of Alaska Indian Arts Inc. *The Raven* pole is symbolic of Raven, as founder of the world and all his great powers. The second figure is *The Whale,* representing Alaska and its great size. The bottom figure is the head of *The Bear,* which shows great strength. *The Eagle* pole tells of his feeding grounds (the Haines area is noted for its eagles). Top figure is *The Salmon Chief,* who provides the late run of salmon to the feeding grounds. *The Eagle Chief,* head of the Eagle clan, is the third figure, and the bottom figure is *The Brown Bear,* which also feeds on salmon and is a symbol of strength and great size. Inquire at the visitor information center about location of poles.

The Sheldon Museum and Cultural Center, at the end of Main Street near the small-boat harbor, serves Russian tea and has exhibits of Tlingit artifacts, Russian items, Jack Dalton's old sawed-off shotgun and other pioneer items. Children enjoy the mounted animals and old telephones. Film on eagles. A fascinating history lesson. Open 1-5 P.M. (other hours as posted) daily in summer. Admission fee $2.50; children free when accompanied by parents.

Enjoy the Fourth of July celebration, which includes canoe and kayak races on Chilkoot Lake, logging events, bicycle and foot races, pie-eating and other contests, parades and performances at the Chilkat Center for the Arts.

The Southeast Alaska State Fair, held at the fairgrounds in Haines (Aug. 10–14, 1994), features agriculture, home arts, and fine arts and crafts. A big event at the fair is the Bald Eagle Music Festival. There are exhibits of flowers, livestock, baked goods, beer and wine, needlework, quilting, woodworking and a dozen other categories. There are also a parade, horse show and other events, including pig racing for cookies.

Dalton City, a newly opened (1992) visi-

There's a good view of Rainbow Glacier from Mud Bay Road. (Barb Michaels)

tor attraction, is housed in the *White Fang* Disney film set. It is located at the fairgrounds.

Visit the small-boat harbor at the foot of Main Street for a fascinating afternoon outing. Watch gill-net and crab fishermen setting out from here. Good views from Lookout Park and also from the shoreline between Haines and Portage Cove Campground.

Visit State Parks. Chilkoot Lake, at the end of Lutak Road, is worth a visit. Beautiful setting with a picnic area, campground and boat launch. Watch for brown bears in nearby waters in the fall, attracted by spawning salmon. (Private boat tours of Chilkoot Lake are available; check in town.) Chilkat State Park out Mud Bay Road is also a scenic spot with hiking trails, beach access, views of glaciers (Rainbow and Davidson), fishing, camping and picnicking. Both parks are within 10 miles/16 km of downtown Haines.

Go Flightseeing. Local air charter operators offer flightseeing trips for spectacular close-up views of glaciers, ice fields, mountain peaks and bald eagles. Glacier Bay is just west of Haines.

Charter boat operators in Haines offer fishing, sightseeing and photography trips.

Watch totem carvers at the Alaska Indian Arts Inc. workshop, located in the restored hospital at Fort William H. Seward. This nonprofit organization is dedicated to the revival of Tlingit Indian art. Craftsmen also work in silver and stone, and sew blankets. Visitor hours 9 A.M. to noon and 1-5 P.M. weekdays year-round.

Hike Area Trails. Mount Ripinski trail is a strenuous all-day hike, with spectacular views from the summit of mountains and tidal waters. Start at the end of 2nd and Young streets; follow pipeline right-of-way about 1.3 miles/2.1 km to trail, which climbs 3.6 miles/5.8 km to the 3,610-foot/1,100-m summit.

Battery Point trail starts 1 mile/1.6 km beyond Portage Cove Campground and leads about 2 miles/3 km to a primitive camping site on Kelgaya Point overlooking Lynn Canal.

Mount Riley (elev. 1,760 feet/536m) has three routes to the summit. The steepest trail starts at Mile 3 Mud Bay Road and climbs 2.1 miles/3.4 km to the summit. A second route starts at the end of F.A.A. Road and leads 2 miles/3.2 km along the city water supply route to connect with the trail from Mud Bay Road to the summit. A third route follows the Battery Point trail for approximately 2 miles/3.2 km, then forks right for a fairly steep climb through underbrush and over Half Dome to summit of Mount Riley.

Seduction Point, at the southern tip of the Chilkat Peninsula, is accessible from Chilkat State Park via a 6-mile/9.7-km trail.

Count eagles when the world's greatest concentration of American bald eagles takes place October through January on Chilkat River flats below Klukwan. The eagle viewing area begins at **Milepost H 17** on the Haines Highway. The 48,000-acre Alaska Chilkat Bald Eagle Preserve was established in 1982. The Chilkat Valley at Haines is the annual gathering site of more than 3,000 bald eagles, which gather to feed on the late run of chum salmon in the Chilkat River.

AREA FISHING: Local charter boat operators and freshwater fishing guides offer fishing trips. A sportfishing lodge at Chilkat Lake offers good fishing in a semi-remote setting. Good fishing in the spring for king salmon in **Chilkat Inlet**. Halibut best in summer in **Chilkat**, **Lutak** and **Chilkoot inlets**. Dolly Varden fishing good in all lakes and rivers, and along marine shorelines from early spring to late fall. Great pink salmon fishing in August along the marine shoreline of **Lutak Inlet** and in the **Chilkoot River**. Sockeye salmon in the **Chilkoot River**, late June through August. Coho salmon in the **Chilkoot** and **Chilkat rivers**, mid-September through October. Cutthroat trout year-round at **Chilkat** and **Mosquito Lakes**. **Herman Lake** is full of hungry grayling stocked there in the mid-1970s. The lake is located off the Sunshine Mountain Road (watch out for logging trucks) accessed from the steel bridge across the Klehini River at **Milepost H 26.3** Haines Highway; get directions locally. For more information, contact the ADF&G at 766-2625.

Mud Bay Road Log

Mileposts on Mud Bay Road measure distance from its junction with the Haines Highway near Front Street to road end at Mud Bay, a distance of 8 miles/13 km. This road, first paved, then wide gravel, leads to Chilkat State Park, following the shoreline of Chilkat Inlet to Mud Bay on Chilkoot Inlet. **Distance is measured from junction with Haines Highway.**

0.1 (0.2 km) Hotel on left, motel and private camper park on right. ▲

0.2 (0.3 km) **Junction** with 3rd Street, which leads back to town.

0.5 (0.8 km) Small Tract Road on left, a 1.9-mile/3.1-km loop road which rejoins Mud Bay Road at **Milepost 2.3.** Small Tract Road leads to private residences and to Bear Creek Camp and Youth Hostel (dorms, cabins and tent camping).

Mud Bay Road leads to the right, following the shoreline of Chilkat Inlet, with views of Pyramid Island. Excellent area for eagle pictures.

2.3 (3.7 km) Stop sign at T intersection: go right for state park, left to return to town via Small Tract Road.

3 (4.8 km) Mount Riley trail on left, parking area on right.

3.9 (6.3 km) View of Pyramid Island and Rainbow Glacier across Chilkat Inlet. Rainbow Glacier, so named because someone once saw a rainbow over it, is a hanging glacier. The ice field moved out over a cliff rather than moving down a valley to the sea. Davidson Glacier is about 2 miles/3.2 km south of Rainbow Glacier.

4.9 (7.9 km) Boat dock on right for small

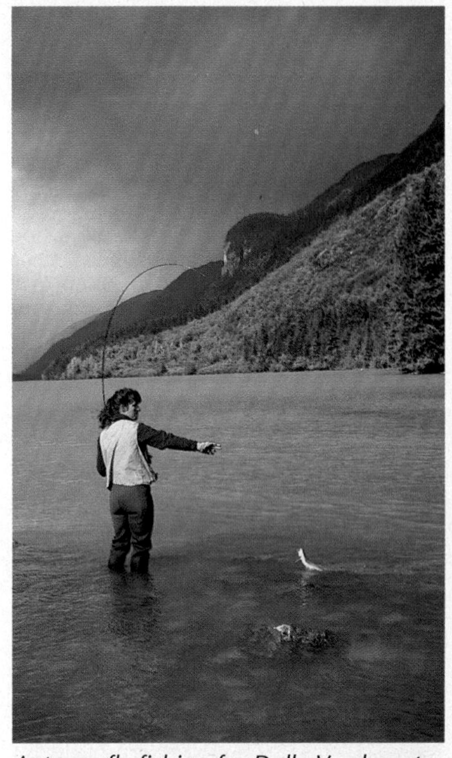

Autumn fly fishing for Dolly Varden at Chilkoot Lake. *(Michael DeYoung)*

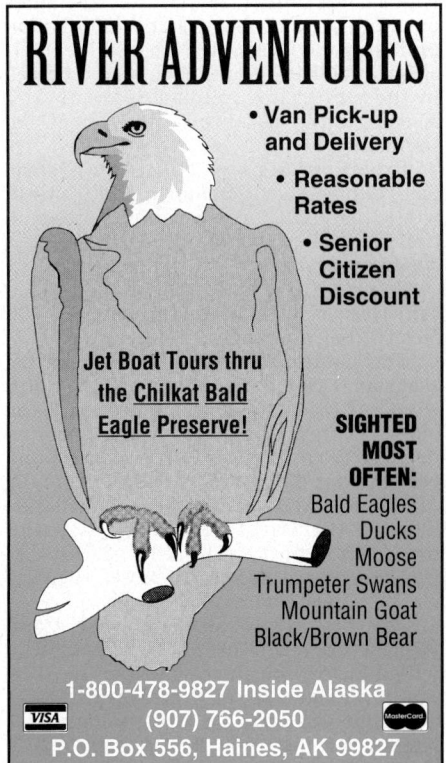

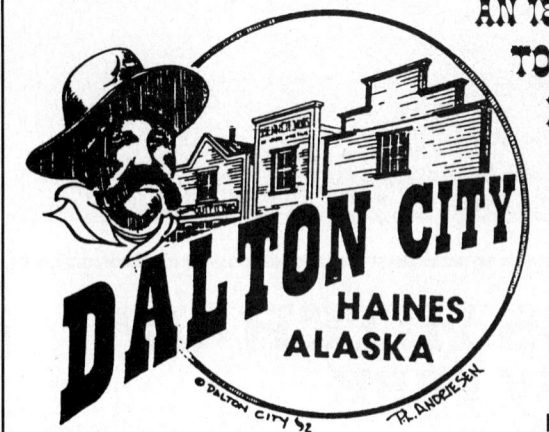

boats (summer tie-off only), boat ramp and pit toilets.

5.2 (8.4 km) Pavement ends, gravel begins.

5.3 (8.5 km) Private road on right to cannery on Letnikof Cove.

6.7 (10.8 km) Turn right and drive in 1.2 miles/1.9 km to entrance of Chilkat State Park (camping area 0.5 mile/0.8 km beyond entrance): 32 campsites, three tent sites on beach, $6 nightly fee or annual pass, picnic sites, pit toilets and boat launch. Access road paved and gravel, grades to 11 percent. Drive carefully. Beach access, view of glaciers and hiking trail to Seduction Point at southern tip of Chilkat Peninsula. ▲

8 (12.9 km) Mud Bay Road turns east and crosses Chilkat Peninsula to Flat Bay (commonly called Mud Bay) on Chilkoot Inlet. Road ends at Mud Bay; short walk to rocky beach.

Lutak Road Log

Lutak Road begins at Front Street, and leads north along Chilkoot Inlet past the Alaska State ferry terminal, then northwest along Lutak Inlet past Chilkoot Lake Campground to road end, a distance of 10 miles/16 km.

Distance is measured from the junction of Front Street with Lutak Road.

0 Junction, Front Street and Lutak Road.

0.1 (0.2 km) Turnout on right with view of Fort Seward and Lynn Canal.

1.6 (2.6 km) Turnouts along road from here to Mile 7 allow good view of gill-net fleet, July through September.

2.4 (3.9 km) Government tank farm, petroleum distribution terminal and beginning of an oil pipeline to Fairbanks. No entry.

3.2 (5.1 km) Dock for oil tankers on right.

3.6 (5.8 km) Alaska State ferry terminal on right.

3.8 (6.1 km) City dock on right is used for shipping lumber and also for docking cruise ships and barges.

4.4 (7.1 km) Sawmill.

8.3 (13.4 km) Road on left follows a wide stretch of the Chilkoot River for 1 mile/1.6 km to Chilkoot Lake picnic area and boat launch; state campground with 32 sites just beyond picnic area, seven-day limit, $8 nightly fee or annual pass. ▲

8.4 (13.5 km) Bridge over the mouth of the **Chilkoot River.** Good salmon fishing in June, July and August. Watch for bears.

In 1983, the Chilkoot tribe dedicated Deer Rock here as a historic reminder of the original location of their village.

Road continues to private homes and deadends; no turnaround.

Skagway

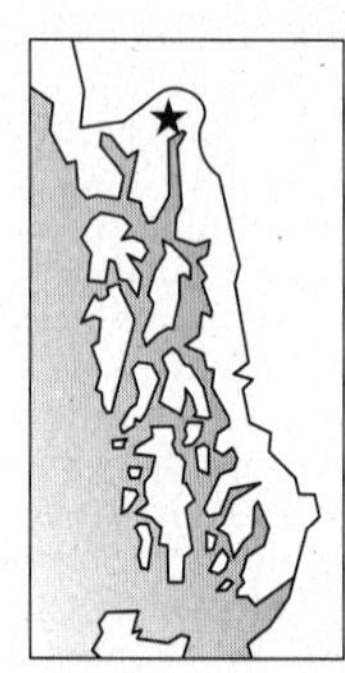

Located on the north end of Taiya Inlet on Lynn Canal, 90 air miles/145 km northwest of Juneau; 108 road miles/174 km south of Whitehorse, YT. The northern terminus of the Alaska Marine Highway Southeast ferry system and southern terminus of Klondike Highway 2 which connects with the Alaska Highway. *NOTE: Although Skagway is only 13 miles/21 km by water from Haines, it is 359 miles/578 km by road!* **Population:** 712. **Emergency Services: Skagway Police Department,** phone 983-2232. **Fire Department** and **Ambulance,** phone 911. **Clinic,** phone 983-2255. **Maritime Search and Rescue,** contact the Coast Guard at 1-800-478-5555.

Visitor Information: Write the Skagway Convention and Visitors Bureau, Box 415MP, Skagway 99840. Phone 983-2854, fax 983-2151. The bureau operates a walk-in information center from May through September in the historic Arctic Brotherhood Hall on Broadway between 2nd and 3rd.

Klondike Gold Rush National Historical Park Visitor Center has exhibits and films on the history of the area and information on hiking the Chilkoot Trail; write Box 517, Skagway 99840; phone 983-2046. Located in the refurbished railroad depot on 2nd Avenue and Broadway, it is open in summer.

Elevation: Sea level. **Climate:** Average daily temperature in summer, 57°F/14°C; in winter, 23°F/-5°C. Average annual precipitation is 29.9 inches. **Radio:** KHNS-FM 91.9. **Newspaper:** *Skagway News* (biweekly).

Private Aircraft: Skagway airport, adjacent west; elev. 44 feet/13m; length 3,700 feet/1,128m; asphalt; fuel 100LL; attended.

The name Skagway (originally spelled Skaguay) is said to mean "home of the north wind" in the local Tlingit dialect. It is the oldest incorporated city in Alaska (incorporated in 1900). Skagway is also a year-round port and one of the two gateway cities to the Alaska Highway in southeastern Alaska: Klondike Highway 2 connects Skagway with the Alaska Highway. (The other gateway city is Haines, connected to the Alaska Highway via the Haines Highway.)

The first white residents were Capt. William Moore and his son, J. Bernard, who settled in 1887 on the east side of the Skagway River valley (a small part of the Moore homesite was sold for construction of a Methodist college, now the city hall).

But Skagway owes its birth to the

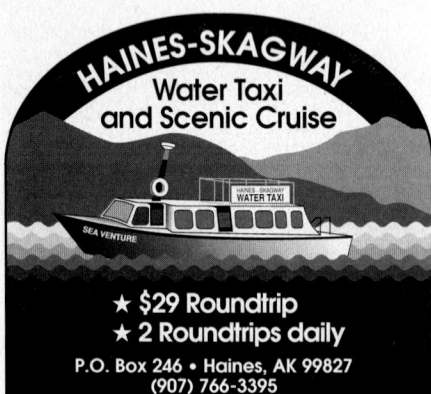

Klondike gold rush. Skagway, and the once-thriving town of Dyea, sprang up as thousands of gold seekers arrived to follow the White Pass and Chilkoot trails to the Yukon goldfields.

In July 1897, the first boatloads of stampeders bound for the Klondike landed at Skagway and Dyea. By October 1897, according to a North West Mounted Police report, Skagway had grown "from a concourse of tents to a fair-sized town, with well-laid-out streets and numerous frame buildings, stores, saloons, gambling houses, dance houses and a population of about 20,000." Less than a year later it was reported that "Skagway was little better than a hell on earth." Customs office records for 1898 show that in the month of February alone 5,000 people landed at Skagway and Dyea.

By the summer of 1899 the stampede was all but over. The newly built White Pass & Yukon Route railway reached Lake Bennett, supplanting the Chilkoot Trail from Dyea. Dyea became a ghost town. Its post office closed in 1902, and by 1903 its population consisted of one settler. Skagway's population — once estimated at 20,000 — dwindled to 500. But Skagway persisted, both as a port and as terminus of the White Pass & Yukon Route railway, which connected the town to Whitehorse, YT, in 1900. Cruise ships, and later the Alaska State Ferry System, brought tourism and business to Skagway. Scheduled state ferry service to southeastern Alaska began in 1963.

Today, tourism is Skagway's main economic base, with Klondike Gold Rush National Historical Park Skagway's major visitor attraction. Within Skagway's downtown historical district, false-fronted buildings and boardwalks dating from gold rush times line the streets. The National Park Service, the city of Skagway and local residents have succeeded in retaining Skagway's Klondike atmosphere.

Skagway has modern schools, churches, a clinic, bank and post office. A U.S. customs office and branch of the U.S. Immigration and Naturalization Service are located in the White Pass depot. The boat harbor and seaplane base has space for cruisers up to 100 feet/30m. Gas, diesel fuel and water are available.

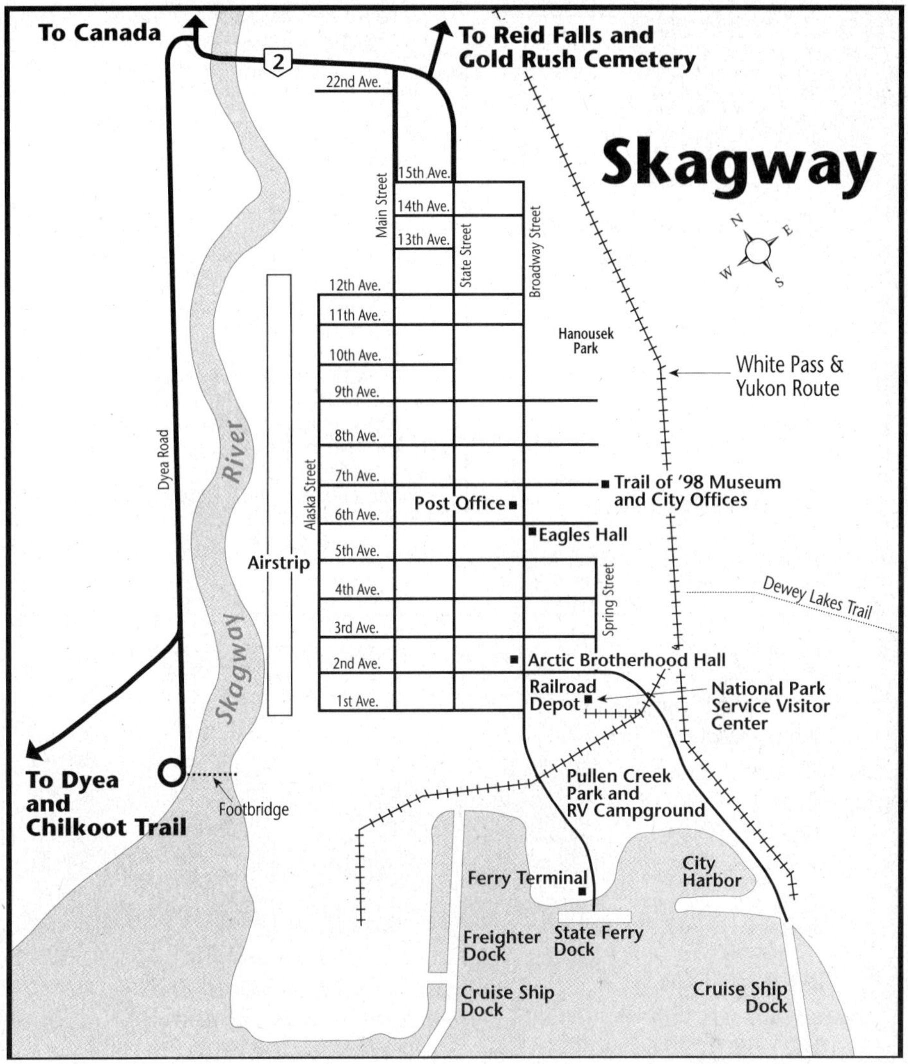

ACCOMMODATIONS

Skagway offers a variety of sleeping accommodations, from gold rush-style hotels and inns to modern motels (reservations are advised in summer). See ads this section.

Historic Skagway Inn Bed & Breakfast, est. 1897, located at 7th and Broadway in historic district. Once a Gold Rush brothel, each Victorian-style room is comfortable and includes full breakfast with homemade muffins and fresh-ground coffee. Walking distance to shops, museums and trails. Friendly innkeepers can make your reservations for railroad, shows, tours plus arrange transportation to Chilkoot trailhead. (907) 983-2289. (800) 478-2290 (inside Alaska), fax (907) 983-2713. [ADVERTISEMENT]

Sergeant Preston's Lodge. "We overnighted at Sergeant Preston's Lodge in the heart of historic Skagway and we highly recommend it. When they say 'we don't relax until you do,' they mean it. It's the friendliest place in town, the most comfortable and the best value for your dollar around. Rooms start at $55. Phone (907) 983-2521." [ADVERTISEMENT]

There are several restaurants, cafes and bars, grocery, hardware and clothing stores, and many gift and novelty shops offering Alaska and gold rush souvenirs, photos, books, records, gold nugget jewelry, furs and ivory. Propane, marine and automobile gas are available, as is diesel fuel.

Lynch & Kennedy Dry Goods, est. 1908. This historic structure is an original gold rush-era business, restored by the National Park Service and reopened in 1993 by Rosemary & Karl Klupar. Stop by and see the restoration and imagine the hustle and bustle of years gone by. Today the Lynch & Kennedy Dry Goods recreates that excitement of yesteryear and is a fun place to visit. Several times a week but always on Tuesday, Lynch & Kennedy Dry Goods presents a visiting artist in action. Every day they feature hand-painted T-shirts, where you can design, create and silk-screen your own shirt. Enjoy the thrill of printing a custom shirt for yourself or as a gift. At the Lynch & Kennedy Dry Goods you will find Native art, custom jewelry, high quality sweatshirts, a children's department and gourmet and home accessories. The Klupars have a special interest in Native art. Rosemary has been on buying trips out to most of the remote Native villages, and knows personally the artists she represents in the shop. Everyone at Lynch & Kennedy Dry Goods is there to help you make an informed buying decision; ask for "Little Known Facts about Native Art" buying guide. Each art piece comes with a biography of the artist and details on how and where the piece was made. The Lynch & Kennedy has made a point of finding quality merchandise not found in every curio shop; many items are handcrafted by local artisans (worthy to be a remembrance of your once-in-a-lifetime trip to the Greatland). The staff is trained to assist you in finding something special or answering your questions about their products or Alaska in general. If they don't have what you're looking for, they will find it or refer you to someone who does. All items in the store are available by mail order. Gift wrapping and shipping available. Lynch & Kennedy Dry Goods is open all year. From May 15–Sept. 15, seven days a week (9 A.M.-10 P.M.). Located at 350 Broadway, just north of The Sourdough Cafe. Lynch & Kennedy Dry Goods, P.O. Box 3, Skagway, AK 99840. Telephone (907) 983-3034. Fax (907) 983-3035. [ADVERTISEMENT]

SKAGWAY ADVERTISERS

Back Track Camper Park ......12th & Broadway
Dedman's Photo Shop & Art Gallery ......Broadway
Door Knob, The ......Broadway
Fairway Market ......4th & State
Gift Corner, The ......4th & Broadway
Gold Rush Lodge ......6th & Alaska
Gold Rush Productions ......Eagles Hall
Gold Rush Repair ......6th & Alaska
Golden North Hotel ......2nd & Broadway
Gray Line of Alaska ......Ph. (907) 983-2241
Historic Skagway Inn Bed & Breakfast ......Ph. (907) 983-2289
Irene's Inn ......6th & Broadway
Klothes Rush Gifts ......5th & Broadway
Lynch & Kennedy Dry Goods ......Ph. (907) 983-3034
McFarlane Trading Co. Alaska ......Ph. (907) 983-2774
Native Carvings & Gifts ......Broadway
Prospector's Sourdough Restaurant ......4th & Broadway
Sergeant Preston's Lodge ......6th & State St.
Skaguay News Depot ......Broadway
Skagway Air Service ......4th & Broadway
Skagway Convention & Visitors Bureau ......Ph. (907) 983-2854
Skagway Hardware ......4th & Broadway
Skagway Inn Bed & Breakfast ......7th & Broadway
Skagway RV & Camping Parks ......Ph. (907) 983-2768
Skagway Sports Emporium ......4th Ave.
Southeast Tours & Fishing Charters ......Ph. 1-800-478-2990
Taiya River Jewelry ......252 Broadway
Trail Bench, The ......2nd & Broadway
Westmark Inn 1-800-544-0970
White Pass & Yukon Route ......Ph. (907) 983-2217
Wind Valley Lodge ......22nd & State St.

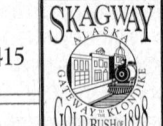

There is one bank in town (National Bank of Alaska), located at 6th and Broadway; open 10 A.M. to 5 P.M. Monday through Friday in summer.

There are several private campgrounds in Skagway offering hookups, tent sites, restrooms and showers, dump stations and laundromats. A campground for backpackers is located at the Chilkoot Trail trailhead near Dyea. ▲

TRANSPORTATION

Air: Daily scheduled service between Skagway and Haines and Juneau via L.A.B. Flying Service, Skagway Air and Wings of Alaska. Charter service also available between towns and for flightseeing via Skagway Air. Temsco provides helicopter tours. Transportation to and from the airport is provided by the flight services and local hotels.

Bus: Bus/van service to Anchorage, Fairbanks, Haines and Whitehorse, YT.

Taxi: Operate year-round and also offer sightseeing service and transportation to Chilkoot Trail trailhead.

Car Rental: Two companies.

Highway: Klondike Highway 2 was completed in 1978 and connects Skagway to the Alaska Highway. It is open year-round. See KLONDIKE HIGHWAY 2 section.

Railroad: White Pass & Yukon Route offers three-hour excursions from Skagway to White Pass Summit and return. Through rail/bus connections are also available daily between Skagway and Whitehorse, with rail motorcar service to Lake Bennett. See WHITE PASS & YUKON ROUTE section for details.

Ferry: Alaska Marine Highway vessels call regularly year-round, as Skagway is the northern terminus of the Southeast ferry system. See MARINE ACCESS ROUTES section for schedules. The ferry terminal is in the large building on the waterfront (see city map this section); restrooms, pay phone and lockers inside. Ferry terminal office hours vary: opening hours are usually posted at the front door. Phone 983-2941 or 983-2229.

Water taxi service is available between Haines and Skagway. For schedules and rates, phone (907) 983-2083 in Skagway; 766-3395 in Haines.

Ships: Skagway is a regular port of call for cruise ships from U.S. and Canadian ports.

The excursion boat MV *Fairweather* cruises to Juneau daily, mid-May to mid-September. Operated by Gray Line of Alaska for their package tours, seats may be purchased by the general public on a space-available basis. Contact their Skagway office at the Westmark Hotel (phone 983-6000).

Private Boats: Transient moorage is available at the Skagway small-boat harbor. Contact the harbormaster at 983-2628.

ATTRACTIONS

Trail of '98 Museum, owned and operated by the citizens of Skagway, is located on the second floor of city hall, corner of 7th Avenue and Spring Street; open 9 A.M. to 5 P.M. daily in summer (mid-May to mid-September), in winter by appointment; admission is $2 for adults, $1 for students

For more details on the Chilkoot Trail, see *The ALASKA WILDERNESS GUIDE*. To order, phone 1-800-726-4707.

and children. The building is the first granite building constructed in Alaska. It was built by the Methodist Church as a school in 1899–1900 to be known as McCabe College, but public school laws were passed that made the enterprise impractical and it was sold to the federal government. For decades it was used as U.S. District Court No. 1 of Alaska, but as the population of the town declined, the court was abandoned and in 1956 the building was purchased by the city. Since May 1961, the second floor has been open as a museum; the main floor is occupied by city of Skagway offices. The museum's main interest is to help preserve Alaskan historical material and to display Alaskan pioneer life. The decor of the old courtroom has been preserved, including the judge's bench and chair and some of Soapy Smith's personal items. For more information, phone 983-2420.

Arctic Brotherhood Hall. Located on Broadway between 2nd and 3rd, some 20,000 pieces of driftwood adorn the false front of this 1899 fraternal meeting hall, used as a visitor information center during the summer. Multimedia presentations are given here. Admission fee charged.

See the show *The Days of 1898 Show With Soapy Smith*. This show, produced by Gold Rush Productions, is put on several times each day; evening performances (subject to cruise ship arrivals) in summer in Eagles Hall. Check the billboard in front of the hall for show times. The show relates the history of Skagway, from the days of the notorious Soapy Smith. Phone 983-2545.

This show is good family entertainment; bring your camera, gamble with funny money (during evening show only), and enjoy this well-done historical musical comedy. Admission fee charged.

Klondike Gold Rush National Historical Park was authorized in 1976 to preserve and interpret the history of the Klondike gold rush of 1897–98. The park, managed by the National Park Service, consists of four units: a six-block historical district in Skagway's business area; a 1-mile-/1.6-km-wide, 17-mile-/27.4-km-long corridor of land comprising the Chilkoot Trail; a 1-mile-/1.6-km-wide, 5-mile-/8-km-long corridor of land comprising the White Pass Trail; and a visitor center at 117 S. Main St. in Seattle, WA.

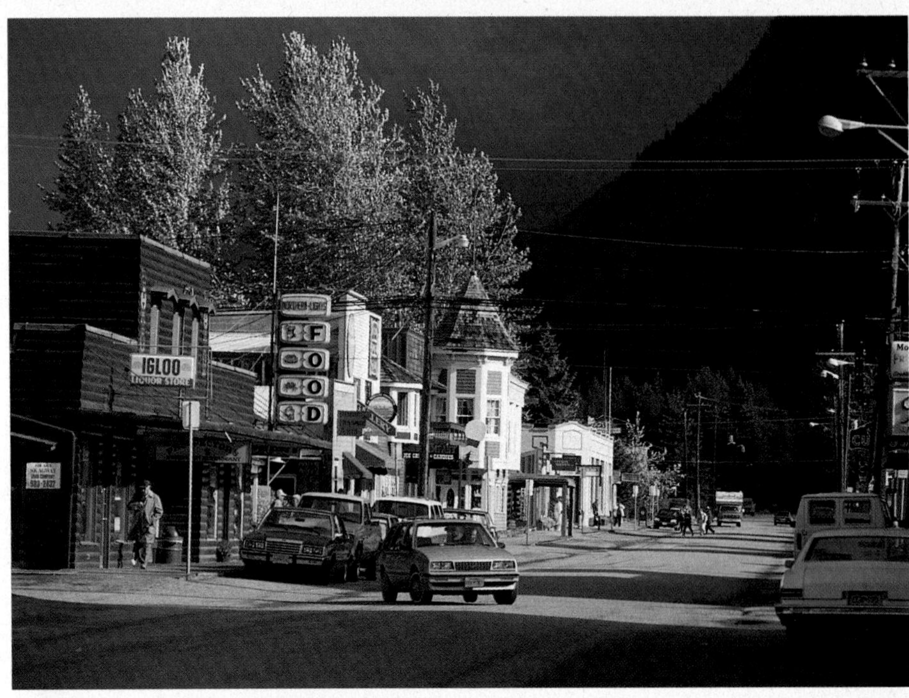

Historic buildings help downtown Skagway retain its frontier atmosphere. (Ron Levy)

In Skagway, the National Park Service offers a variety of free programs in summer. There are daily guided walking tours of downtown Skagway and ranger talks on a variety of topics. Films are also shown. Check with the Park Service's visitor center in the restored railroad depot on 2nd Avenue and Broadway. Summer hours at the center are 8 A.M. to 6 P.M.

McFarlane Trading Co. Alaska. Just two doors from Skagway's incredible ice cream shop, you'll find McFarlane Trading Co. Alaska — a gift shop you must not miss! They have a wide range of genuine Alaskan gifts, usually with printed information to go with them. You'll see a fantastic collection of scrimshaw, refined from the early American whaler's folk art, to today's fine art on Alaskan fossilized walrus or mammoth ivory. Then, there are masks and carvings by Alaskan artists made of ancient whalebone excavated from remote St. Lawrence Island. And don't miss their traditionally created Eskimo dolls, a truly ancient art. Finally, among the Northwest Indian cedar plaques, you'll find dog fur sweaters, created by Tagish's Claudia McPhee. McFarlane's also has jewelry, needlework, art cards and other gifts — all with an Alaskan flair. It is a fact that Skagway is the best "shopping" town in southeast Alaska. It presents an incredible choice of Alaskan arts and crafts at reasonable prices. McFarlane's, in this great little town, is a definite must. (Finally, if you are related to the McFarlane clan, this shop has information on U.S. Clan McFarlane societies.) [ADVERTISEMENT]

Hike the Chilkoot Trail. This 33-mile/53-km trail begins on Dyea Road (see log this section) and climbs Chilkoot Pass (elev. 3,739 feet/1,140m) to Lake Bennett, following the historic route of the gold seekers of '98. The trail is arduous but offers both spectacular scenery and historical relics. There are several campgrounds and shelters along the route. Hikers planning to take the Chilkoot Trail should check with Parks Canada in Whitehorse, phone (403) 668-2116. White Pass & Yukon Route offers hiker rail service from Lake Bennett back to Skagway (see WHITE PASS & YUKON ROUTE section). Detailed information and maps of the trail are available from the National Park Service (Box 517, Skagway 99840). *The ALASKA WILDERNESS GUIDE* also has details on the Chilkoot Trail, and *Chilkoot Pass* by Archie Satterfield is a good hiking and history guide to the trail.

Corrington Museum of Alaska History, located at 5th and Broadway, offers a unique record of events from prehistory to the present. Each of the 40 exhibits at the museum features a scene from Alaska history hand-engraved (scrimshawed) on a walrus tusk. The museum is open in summer. Free admission.

Picnic at Pullen Creek Park. This attractive waterfront park has a covered picnic shelter, two footbridges and two small docks. It is located between the cruise ship and ferry docks, behind the White Pass & Yukon Route depot. Watch for pink salmon in the intertidal waters in August, silver salmon in September.

Helicopter and airplane tours of Skagway and White Pass are available in summer.

Gold Rush Cemetery is 1.5 miles/2.4 km from downtown and makes a nice walk. Go

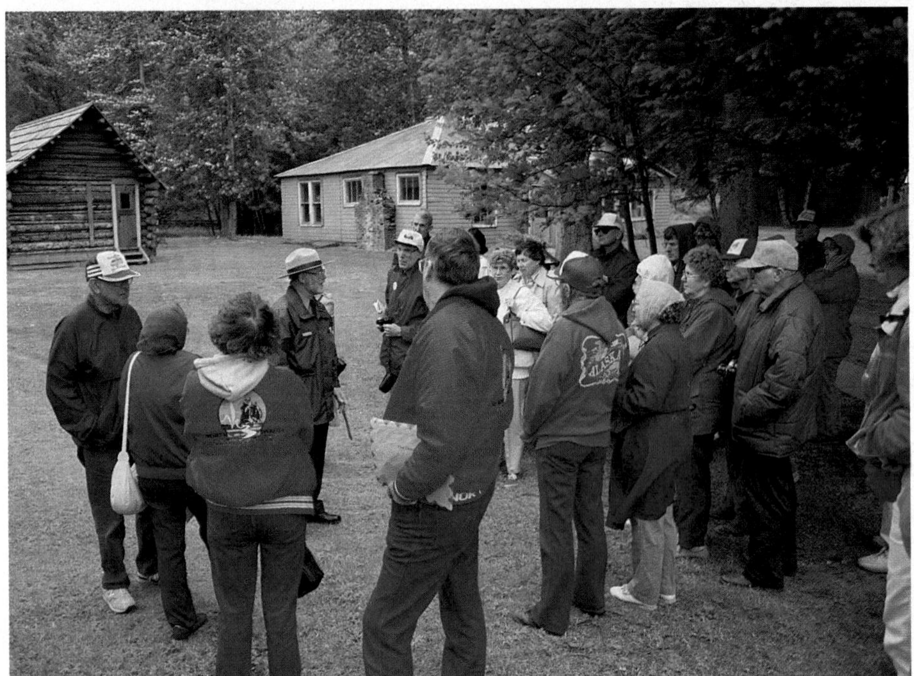

The National Park Service offers guided walking tours of Skagway. (John W. Warden)

north on State Street to a sign pointing to the cemetery. Follow dirt road across tracks into railroad yard, follow posted direction signs, then continue about 0.4 mile/0.6 km farther to the cemetery. If you drive in, a circular road around the cemetery eliminates having to back up to get out. A path on left at the end of the road leads to the cemetery where the graves of both "bad guy" Soapy Smith and "good guy" Frank Reid are located (both men died in a gunfight in July 1898). Smith's original gravestone was whittled away by souvenir hunters and the resting place of the feared boss of Skagway is now marked by a metal marker.

Reid Falls are located near Gold Rush Cemetery, and it is only a short hike from Frank Reid's grave to view them.

Cruise Lynn Canal. Board the MV *Fairweather* for a scenic cruise of beautiful 75-mile Lynn Canal. View marine and wildlife, cascading waterfalls and snow-capped mountains. Cruise to quaint Juneau and enjoy a Gray Line of Alaska tour of the mighty Mendenhall Glacier. Return flight to Skagway over the Juneau Ice Cap. This two-day tour price is $389 ppdo, or enjoy a one-way day cruise between Skagway and Juneau for only $145 per person. Call (907) 983-2241. [ADVERTISEMENT]

AREA FISHING: Local charter boat operators offer fishing trips. The ADF&G Sport Fish Division recommends the following areas and species. Dolly Varden: Fish the shore of **Skagway Harbor, Long Bay** and **Taiya Inlet**, May through June. Try the **Taiya River** by the steel bridge in Dyea in early spring or fall; use red and white spoons or salmon eggs. Pink salmon fishing is good at the small local hatchery. Fish **Skagway Harbor** and **Pullen Creek** in town, July and August; use flashing lures. Coho and chum salmon near the steel bridge on the **Taiya River**, mid-September through October. Trolling in the marine areas is good but often dangerous for small boats. Trout: A steep trail near town will take you to Dewey lakes, which were stocked with Colorado brook trout in the 1920s. **Lower Dewey Lake**, one-half hour to one-hour hike; heavily wooded shoreline, use raft. The brook trout are plentiful and grow to 16 inches but are well fed, so fishing can be frustrating. **Upper Dewey Lake**, a steep two-and-one-half-hour to four-hour hike to above tree line, is full of hungry brook trout to 11 inches. Use salmon eggs or size #10 or #12 artificial flies. **Lost Lake** is reached via a rough trail near Dyea (ask locals for directions). The lake lies at about 1,300 feet elevation and has a good population of rainbow trout. Use small spinners or spoons. For more information, contact the ADF&G office in Haines at 766-2625.

Dyea Road Log

The Dyea Road begins at **Milepost S 2.3** on Klondike Highway 2. It leads southwest toward Yakutania Point, then northwest past Long Bay and the Taiya River to the beginning of the Chilkoot Trail and to a side road leading to the old Dyea townsite and Slide Cemetery. The Dyea Road is a narrow winding gravel road.

Distance is from the junction with Klondike Highway 2.

0 Junction.

0.1 (0.2 km) Old cemetery on right.

0.4 (0.6 km) View of Reid Falls east across the Skagway River.

1.4 (2.3 km) A scenic wayside with platform on left southbound affords view of Skagway, Taiya Inlet and the Skagway River.

1.7 (2.7 km) A steep, primitive road on left southbound descends 0.4 mile/0.6 km toward bank of the Skagway River, with a view of the Skagway waterfront and Taiya Inlet.

Drive to parking area and walk 0.2 mile/0.3 km to Yakutania Point; horse trail beyond parking area. Bridge at base of hill leads to a short trail back to town. Dyea Road turns northwest along Long Bay at this point.

1.9 (3.1 km) Skyline trailhead (poorly signed). This trail leads to top of AB Mountain (elev. 5,000 feet/1,524m).

2.1 (3.4 km) Head of Long Bay.

4 (6 km) City dump.

4.3 (6.9 km) Taiya Inlet comes into view on left northbound as the road curves away from Long Bay.

5.1 (8.2 km) View of the old pilings in Taiya Inlet. The docks of Dyea used to stretch from the trees out and beyond the pilings that are still visible. These long docks were needed to reach deep water because of the great tidal range in this inlet.

5.7 (9.2 km) Hooligan (smelt) run here in the Taiya River in May and early June. Local swimming hole across the road.

6.5 (10.5 km) Dyea information display.

6.7 (10.8 km) Chilkoot Trail trailhead campground, parking area and ranger station.

7.2 (11.6 km) The Chilkoot Trail begins on right northbound. Bridge over Taiya River.

7.4 (11.9 km) A primitive road on left northbound leads southwest to Slide Cemetery (keep right at forks and follow signs) and old Dyea townsite. The cemetery, reached by a short unmarked path through the woods, contains the graves of men killed in the Palm Sunday avalanche, April 3, 1898, on the Chilkoot Trail. At Dyea townsite, covered with fireweed and lupine in summer, hardly a trace remains of the buildings that housed 8,000 people here during the gold rush. About 30 people live in the valley today.

8.4 (13.5 km) Steel bridge across West Creek. Four-wheel drive recommended beyond this point.

WHITE PASS & YUKON ROUTE

The WP&YR has one of the steepest railroad grades in North America. (Loren Taft)

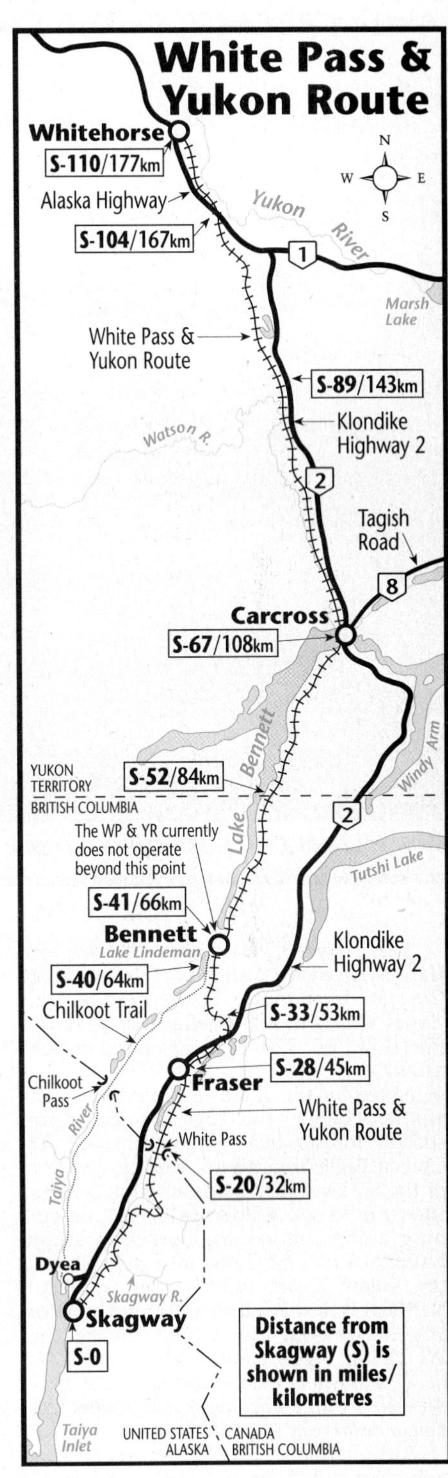

The White Pass & Yukon Route (WP&YR) is a narrow-gauge (36-inch) privately owned railroad built in 1898 at the height of the Klondike gold rush. Between 1900 and 1982, the WP&YR provided passenger and freight service between Skagway, AK, and Whitehorse, YT. After closing for six years, the line re-opened in the summer of 1988 for passenger service. The WP&YR now operates a three-hour round-trip train excursion between Skagway and the White Pass Summit. Other travel options include a 28-mile train trip to Fraser, BC, with connecting motorcoach service to Whitehorse and Chilkoot Trail rail service from Lake Bennett. The WP&YR no longer offers rail service to Whitehorse.

Construction of the White Pass & Yukon Route began in May 1898. It was the first railroad in Alaska and at the time the most northern of any railroad in North America. The railroad reached White Pass in February 1899 and Whitehorse in July 1900.

The railroad follows the old White Pass trail. The upper section of the old "Deadhorse" trail near the summit (Mile 19 on the WP&YR railway) is visible right beside the tracks. During the Klondike gold rush, thousands of men took the 40-mile White Pass trail from Skagway to Lake Bennett, where they built boats to float down the Yukon River to Dawson City and the goldfields.

The White Pass & Yukon Route has one of the steepest railroad grades in North America. From sea level at Skagway the railroad climbs to 2,885 feet/879m at White Pass in only 20 miles of track. Currently, the railroad offers train service on 28 miles of track between Skagway and Fraser, plus an additional 13 miles for motorcar service to Bennett.

Following are services, schedules and fares available on the White Pass & Yukon Route from mid-May to mid-September 1994. All times indicated in schedules are local times. Children 12 and under are half fare when accompanied by an adult. Children under 2 years ride free if not occupying a seat; half fare for separate seat. Reservations are required. For reservations and information, contact the White Pass & Yukon Route, P.O. Box 435, Skagway, AK 99840. Phone toll free in the United States 1-800-343-7373 or (907) 983-2217 in Skagway.

SUMMIT EXCURSION

This approximately three-hour round-trip excursion features the most spectacular part of the WP&YR railway, including the steep climb to White Pass Summit, Bridal Veil Falls, Inspiration Point and Dead Horse Gulch. Offered twice daily, the morning train departs Skagway at 8:45 A.M. and returns at 11:45 A.M.; the afternoon train departs Skagway at 1:15 P.M. and returns at 4:15 P.M. Fares are $72 for adults and $36 for children 12 and under.

THROUGH–SERVICE ("The International")

Through–service between Skagway, AK, and Whitehorse, YT, is offered daily. Through passengers travel by train between Skagway, AK, and Fraser, BC, and by motorcoach between Fraser and Whitehorse, YT. Northbound service departs Skagway at 12:45 P.M., arrives Fraser at 2:30 P.M., and arrives Whitehorse at 6:30 P.M. Southbound service departs Whitehorse at 8:15 A.M., departs Fraser at 10:20 A.M., and arrives Skagway at noon. One-way fares are $92 for adults and $46 for children 12 and under.

LAKE BENNETT RAIL JOURNEY

The Lake Bennett rail journey takes you 20 miles beyond the White Pass summit to historic Lake Bennett. After hiking the treacherous Chilkoot Pass, nearly 20,000 stampeders set up camp here, built boats and traveled down the Yukon River to Dawson City and the goldfields. Five-and-a-half-hour excursion allows time for exploration at the lake, departs Skagway daily. Call for 1994 schedule and prices.

CHILKOOT HIKERS SHUTTLE

For hikers completing the 33-mile Chilkoot Trail, the train offers daily rail service from Lake Bennett back to Skagway or out to Fraser Customs on the Klondike Highway. Advance tickets required. Operates from June through mid-September. (Hikers planning to do the Chilkoot Trail should check with Parks Canada in Whitehorse, phone (403) 668-2116.)

HAINES HIGHWAY

Haines, Alaska, to Haines Junction, Yukon Territory
Alaska Route 7, British Columbia Highway 4 and Yukon Highway 3

View south at Chilkat Pass showing upper limit of coastal spruce forest. (Michael DeYoung)

The paved 151.6-mile-/244-km-long Haines Highway connects Haines, AK (on the state ferry route), at the head of Lynn Canal with the Alaska Highway at Haines Junction, YT. The highway is open year-round.

Noted for the grandeur and variety of its alpine scenery, the highway leads from coastal forests near Haines through the Chilkat Eagle Preserve up over the backbone of the St. Elias Mountains, skirting BC's Tatshenshini-Alsek Wilderness Park, and running along the eastern border of Kluane National Park and down into the valleys of the Yukon basin. Information on Kluane National Park is available in Haines Junction, YT. Allow about four hours' driving time. Watch for logging and fuel trucks. *NOTE: Between May and October there is no gas service between 33 Mile Roadhouse and Haines Junction, a distance of 118 miles/190 km.*

Part of what is now the Haines Highway was originally a "grease trail" used by the coastal Chilkat Indians trading eulachon oil for furs from the Interior. In the late 1880s, Jack Dalton developed a packhorse trail to the Klondike goldfields along the old trading route. The present road was built in 1943 as a military access highway during WWII to provide an alternative route from the Pacific tidewater into Yukon Territory.

This historic corridor is celebrated each year during Dalton Trail Days, July 1–4. Watch for bikes on the highway the first weekend in July during the Kluane/Chilkat International Bike Race.

U.S. and Canada customs stations are located about 40 miles/64 km north of Haines. U.S. customs is open from 7 A.M. to 11 P.M. (Alaska time); Canada customs open from 8 A.M. to midnight (Pacific time). There are no facilities or accommodations at the border. All travelers must stop.

A valid Alaska fishing license is required for fishing along the highway between Haines and the international border at **Milepost H 40.7.** The highway then crosses the northern tip of British Columbia into Yukon Territory. You must have valid fishing licenses for both British Columbia and Yukon Territory if you fish these areas, and a national park fishing license if you fish waters in Kluane National Park.

If you plan to drive the Haines Highway in winter, check road conditions before starting out and carry adequate emergency equipment. In Haines Junction check with the maintenance garage (634-2227) or the RCMP (634-5555).

Emergency medical services: Between Haines and the U.S.–Canada border at **Milepost H 40.7**, phone 911. Between the U.S.–Canada border and Haines Junction, phone the RCMP at 634-5555.

Haines Highway Log

ALASKA ROUTE 7

Driving distance is measured in miles from Haines, AK. Mileposts are up along the Alaska portion of the highway. The kilometre figures on the Canadian portion of the highway reflect the physical kilometreposts and are not an accurate metric conversion of the mileage figure.

Distance from Haines (H) is followed by distance from Haines Junction (HJ).

H 0 HJ 151.6 (244 km) **HAINES.** See HAINES section for accommodations and facilities.

H 0.2 (0.3 km) **HJ 151.4** (243.7 km) Front Street.

H 0.4 (0.6 km) **HJ 151.2** (243.4 km) Second Street. Turn right northbound (left southbound) for visitor information center and downtown Haines.

H 0.5 (0.8 km) **HJ 151.1** (243.2 km) Third Street. Turn right northbound (left southbound) for downtown Haines.

H 1 (1.6 km) **HJ 150.6** (242.4 km) Haines Hitch–Up RV Park. ▲

H 1.2 (1.9 km) **HJ 150.4** (242.1 km) Main Street Y. If southbound, turn right to Fort William H. Seward, left to downtown Haines.

H 1.3 (2.1 km) **HJ 150.3** (241.9 km) Eagle's Nest Motel.

H 3.3 (5.3 km) **HJ 148.3** (238.7 km) Indian graveyard on the right northbound.

H 3.5 (5.6 km) **HJ 148.1** (238.3 km) **Private Aircraft**: Haines airport; elev. 16 feet/5m; length 3,000 feet/914m; asphalt; fuel 100; unattended.

The Chilkat River estuary, which the highway parallels for the next 15 miles/24 km, flows into Chilkat Inlet of Lynn Canal, a massive fjord about 60 miles/96.5 km long. Lynn Canal was named by English explorer Captain Vancouver for his birthplace (King's Lynn) in England. The yellow signs along the highway indicate mileages on the U.S. Army oil pipeline. The pipeline formerly pumped oil from Haines over the St. Elias Mountains to the Alaska Highway at Haines Junction, YT. These signs were used for aerial checking and monitoring of the line.

H 4.3 (6.9 km) **HJ 147.3** (237 km) Turnout along river.

H 6 (9.6 km) **HJ 145.6** (234.3 km) Picnic spot next to Chilkat River and a clear creek.

H 6.6 (10.6 km) **HJ 145** (233.3 km) Mount Ripinski trailhead.

H 8 (12.8 km) **HJ 143.6** (231.1 km) Watch for subsistence fish camps along the highway in June. Also watch for fish wheels on the river.

H 9.2 (14.8 km) **HJ 142.4** (229.2 km) Entering Alaska Chilkat Bald Eagle Preserve northbound. Established in 1982, the 48,000-acre preserve is the seasonal home to more than 3,000 bald eagles, which gather each year to feed on the late run of chum

HAINES HIGHWAY *Haines, AK, to Haines Junction, YT*

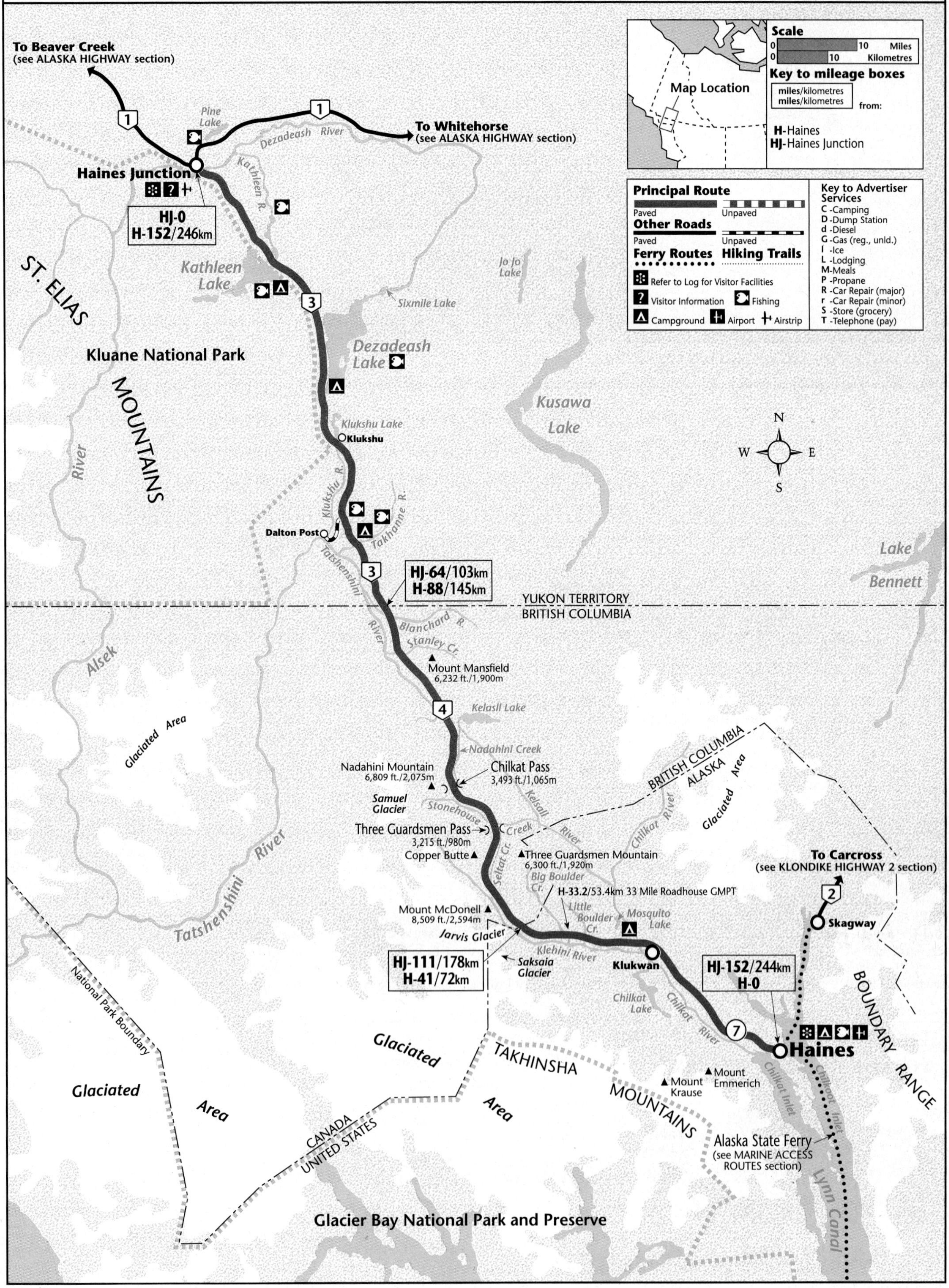

Scale
0 10 Miles
0 10 Kilometres

Key to mileage boxes
miles/kilometres
miles/kilometres
from:
H-Haines
HJ-Haines Junction

Map Location

Principal Route
Paved
Unpaved
Other Roads
Paved
Unpaved
Ferry Routes
Hiking Trails
Refer to Log for Visitor Facilities
Visitor Information
Fishing
Campground
Airport
Airstrip

Key to Advertiser Services
C -Camping
D -Dump Station
d -Diesel
G -Gas (reg., unld.)
I -Ice
L -Lodging
M -Meals
P -Propane
R -Car Repair (major)
r -Car Repair (minor)
S -Store (grocery)
T -Telephone (pay)

To Beaver Creek
(see ALASKA HIGHWAY section)

To Whitehorse
(see ALASKA HIGHWAY section)

Pine Lake
Dezadeash River
Kathleen R.
Haines Junction
HJ-0
H-152/246km
Kathleen Lake
ST. ELIAS MOUNTAINS
Kluane National Park
Jo Jo Lake
Sixmile Lake
Dezadeash Lake
Kusawa Lake
Klukshu Lake
Klukshu
River
Klukshu R.
Takhanne R.
Dalton Post
Tatshenshini River
HJ-64/103km
H-88/145km
Lake Bennett
YUKON TERRITORY
BRITISH COLUMBIA
Blanchard R.
Stanley Cr.
Alsek
Mount Mansfield
6,232 ft./1,900m
Kelasll Lake
Glaciated Area
Nadahini Creek
Nadahini Mountain
6,809 ft./2,075m
Chilkat Pass
3,493 ft./1,065m
Samuel Glacier
Stonehouse Creek
Kelsall River
BRITISH COLUMBIA
ALASKA
Chilkat River
Glaciated Area
Three Guardsmen Pass
3,215 ft./980m
Copper Butte
Seltat Cr.
Three Guardsmen Mountain
6,300 ft./1,920m
Big Boulder Cr.
H-33.2/53.4km 33 Mile Roadhouse GMPT
Tatshenshini River
To Carcross
(see KLONDIKE HIGHWAY 2 section)
Mount McDonell
8,509 ft./2,594m
Little Boulder Cr.
Mosquito Lake
Skagway
Jarvis Glacier
Klehini River
Saksaia Glacier
Klukwan
HJ-111/178km
H-41/72km
HJ-152/244km
H-0
BOUNDARY RANGE
National Park Boundary
Chilkat Lake
Chilkat River
Haines
Glaciated Area
TAKHINSHA MOUNTAINS
Glaciated Area
Mount Krause
Mount Emmerich
Chilkat Inlet
Chilkoot Inlet
CANADA
UNITED STATES
Alaska State Ferry
(see MARINE ACCESS ROUTES section)
Lynn Canal
Glacier Bay National Park and Preserve

Eagle feeds on salmon carcass along the Chilkat River. (Bill Sherwonit)

salmon. Eagle-viewing area begins at **Milepost H 19**; best viewing is mid-October to January.

H 9.6 (15.4 km) **HJ 142** (228.5 km) Magnificent view of Takhinsha Mountains across Chilkat River. This range extends north from the Chilkat Range; Glacier Bay is on the other side. Prominent peaks are Mount Krause and Mount Emmerich (elev. 6,405 feet/1,952m) in the Chilkat Range.

H 14.7 (23.6 km) **HJ 136.9** (220.3 km) Watch for mountain goats on the ridges.

H 17.6 (28.3 km) **HJ 134** (215.6 km) Rustic barn and old cabins. Good photo shots.

H 18.8 (30.3 km) **HJ 132.8** (213.7 km) Slide area.

H 19 (30.6 km) **HJ 132.6** (213.4 km) Begin eagle viewing area (northbound) on Chilkat River flats. Best viewing is mid-October to January. *CAUTION: Eagle watchers, use turnouts and park well off highway!*

H 21.4 (34.4 km) **HJ 130.2** (209.5 km) Turnoff to Indian village of **KLUKWAN**. Gravel access road dead ends at village. No visitor facilities.

H 22 (35.4 km) **HJ 129.6** (208.5 km) Second access northbound to Klukwan (steep grade).

H 23.8 (38.3 km) **HJ 127.8** (205.6 km) Chilkat River bridge. Highway now follows Klehini River. Watch for eagles beginning in late summer.

H 26.3 (42.3 km) **HJ 125.3** (201.6 km) Road west leads across Klehini River; turn off here for Don's Camp on Chilkat Lake.

H 27.3 (43.9 km) **HJ 124.3** (200 km) Mosquito Lake State Recreation Site campground; 10 sites, tables, water, toilets, $6/night or annual pass. Mosquito Lake general store. ▲

H 28.8 (46.3 km) **HJ 122.8** (197.6 km) Muncaster Creek bridge.

H 30.9 (49.7 km) **HJ 120.7** (194.2 km) Leaving Alaska Chilkat Bald Eagle Preserve northbound.

H 31.6 (50.9 km) **HJ 120** (193.1 km) Bridge over Little Boulder Creek.

H 33.2 (53.4 km) **HJ 118.4** (190.5 km) Roadhouse with food, gas and phone. Store. *NOTE: Last available gas northbound until Kathleen Lake Lodge. Check your gas tank.*

33 Mile Roadhouse. See display ad this section.

H 33.8 (54.4 km) **HJ 117.8** (189.6 km) Bridge over Big Boulder Creek. Watch for salmon swimming upstream during spawning season. Closed to salmon fishing.

H 36.2 (58.3 km) **HJ 115.4** (185.7 km) View of Saksaia Glacier.

H 40.4 (65 km) **HJ 111.2** (179 km) U.S. customs, Dalton Cache station. All travelers entering United States MUST STOP. Open year-round 7 A.M. to 11 P.M., Alaska time. Restrooms, large parking area.

Jarvis Glacier moraine is visible from the old Dalton Cache (on the National Register of Historic Places), located behind the customs building.

H 40.7 (65.5 km) **HJ 110.9** (178.5 km) U.S.–Canada border. Last milepost marker is Mile 40, first kilometrepost marker is Kilometrepost 74, northbound.

TIME ZONE CHANGE: Alaska observes Alaska time, Canada observes Pacific time. See Time Zones in the GENERAL INFORMATION section.

BC HIGHWAY 4

H 40.8 (71.8 km) **HJ 110.8** (178.3 km) Canada Customs and Immigration office at Pleasant Camp. All travelers entering Canada MUST STOP. Office is open year-round 8 A.M. to midnight, Pacific time. No public facilities.

H 44.9 (78.5 km) **HJ 106.7** (171.7 km) Bridge over Fivemile Creek.

H 49.7 (86 km) **HJ 101.9** (164 km) Highway crosses Seltat Creek. This is eagle country; watch for them soaring over the uplands. Three Guardsmen Mountain (elev. 6,300 feet/1,920m) to the east.

H 53.9 (92 km) **HJ 97.7** (157.2 km) Three Guardsmen Lake to the east. Glave Peak, part of Three Guardsmen Mountain, rises directly behind the lake.

H 55.1 (94.6 km) **HJ 96.5** (155.3 km) Three Guardsmen Pass to the northeast, hidden by low hummocks along the road. Stonehouse Creek meanders through a pass at the base of Seltat Peak to join the Kelsall River about 6 miles/10 km to the east. To the north is the Kusawak Range; to the south is Three Guardsmen Mountain. The tall poles along the highway indicate the edge of the road for snowplows.

H 55.8 (95.8 km) **HJ 95.8** (154.2 km) Stonehouse Creek culvert.

H 56.2 (96.3 km) **HJ 95.4** (153.5 km) Clear Creek culvert.

H 59.8 (102.1 km) **HJ 91.8** (147.7 km) Double-ended paved turnout on west side of highway at Chilkat Pass, highest summit on this highway (elev. 3,493 feet/1,065m). White Pass Summit on Klondike Highway 2 is 3,290 feet/1,003m. The wind blows almost constantly on the summit and causes drifting snow and road closures in winter. The summit area is a favorite with snow machine and cross-country ski enthusiasts in winter. Snow until late May.

The Chilkat Pass was one of the few mountain passes offering access into the Yukon from the coast. The Chilkat and the Chilkoot passes were tenaciously guarded by Tlingit Indians. These southern Yukon Indians did not want their lucrative fur-trading business with the coastal Indians and Russians jeopardized by white strangers. But the gold rush of 1898, which brought thousands of white people inland, finally opened Chilkat Pass, forever altering the lifestyle of the Interior Natives.

From the Chilkat Pass over Glacier Flats to Stanley Creek, the highway crosses silt-laden streams flowing from the Crestline Glacier. Nadahini Mountain (elev. 6,809 feet/2,075m) to the northwest. Three Guardsmen Mountain to the southeast.

H 63 (107 km) **HJ 88.6** (142.6 km) Chuck Creek culvert.

H 64.4 (109.3 km) **HJ 87.2** (140.3 km) Nadahini River culvert.

H 67.8 (114.7 km) **HJ 83.8** (134.8 km) **Private Aircraft:** Mule Creek airstrip; elev. 2,900 feet/884m; length 4,000 feet/1,219m; gravel. No services.

H 68.9 (116.4 km) **HJ 82.7** (133 km) Mule Creek.

H 73.6 (124.2 km) **HJ 78** (125.5 km) Goat Creek bridge. Watch for horses on road.

H 75.7 (127.3 km) **HJ 75.9** (122.1 km) Holum Creek.

H 81.3 (136.3 km) **HJ 70.3** (113.1 km) Stanley Creek bridge.

H 86.5 (143.6 km) **HJ 65.1** (104.8 km) Blanchard River bridge.

H 87.1 (144.5 km) **HJ 64.5** (103.8 km) Welcome to Yukon sign.

H 87.4 (145 km) **HJ 64.2** (103.3 km) Entering Kluane Game Sanctuary northbound.

H 87.5 (145.2 km) **HJ 64.1** (103.1 km) BC–YT border. Former U.S. Army Alaska–Blanchard River Petroleum pump station, now a highway maintenance camp.

YUKON HIGHWAY 3

H 90.7 (150.7 km) **HJ 60.9** (98 km) Blanchard River Gorge to west.

H 96.2 (159.4 km) **HJ 55.4** (89.1 km) Yukon government Million Dollar Falls Campground on opposite side of Takhanne River; follow access road 0.7 mile/1.1 km west. Boardwalk trail and viewing platform of scenic falls. View of the St. Elias Mountains. Two kitchen shelters, tenting and group firepit, 27 campsites, $8 fee, playground and drinking water (boil water). Walk-in tent sites available. ▲

Good fishing below **Takhanne Falls** for grayling, Dolly Varden, rainbow and salmon. **Takhanne River**, excellent king salmon fishing in early July.

CAUTION: The Takhanne, Blanchard, Tatshenshini and Klukshu rivers are grizzly feeding areas. Exercise extreme caution when fishing or exploring in these areas.

H 96.3 (159.5 km) **HJ 55.3** (89 km) Takhanne River bridge.

H 96.4 (159.7 km) **HJ 55.2** (88.8 km) Parking area at Million Dollar Falls trailhead to west.

H 97.2 (160.8 km) **HJ 54.4** (87.5 km) Second Million Dollars Falls trailhead to west.

H 98.3 (162.6 km) **HJ 53.3** (85.8 km) Good view of Kluane Range.

H 99.5 (164.5 km) **HJ 52.1** (83.8 km) Turnoff to historic Dalton Post, a way point on the Dalton Trail. Steep, narrow, winding access road; four-wheel drive recommended in wet weather. Road not recommended for large RVs or trailers at any time. Several old abandoned log cabins and buildings are located here. Indians once formed a human barricade at Dalton Post to harvest the Klukshu River's run of coho salmon.

Fishing for chinook, coho, sockeye salmon in **Village Creek**. Grayling, Dolly Varden and salmon in **Klukshu River**. Fishing restrictions posted. *CAUTION: Watch for bears.*

H 103.4 (169.7 km) **HJ 48.2** (77.5 km) Viewpoint with information sign to east. Alsek Range to southwest.

H 104 (170.7 km) **HJ 47.6** (76.6 km) Motheral Creek culvert.

H 106.1 (174 km) **HJ 45.5** (73.2 km) Vand Creek.

H 110.8 (181.6 km) **HJ 40.8** (65.6 km) Klukshu Creek.

H 111.6 (183 km) **HJ 40** (64.4 km) Turnoff for **KLUKSHU**, an Indian village, located 0.5 mile/0.8 km off the highway via a gravel road. This summer fish camp and village on the banks of the Klukshu River is a handful of log cabins, meat caches and traditional fish traps. Steelhead, king, sockeye and coho salmon are taken here. Each autumn families return for the annual catch. The site is on the old Dalton Trail and offers good photo possibilities. Museum, picnic spot, Indian souvenirs for sale.

Kluane National Park borders the highway to the west from here to Haines Junction (the visitor centre there has information on the park). Watch for signs for hiking trails, which are posted 3.1 miles/5 km before trailheads. For more information on the park, contact Kluane National Park Reserve, Parks Canada, Box 5495, Haines Junction, YT Y0B 1L0, phone (403) 634-2251, fax (403) 634-2686. Also visit the park information centre in Haines Junction. Open daily, May to September, the centre has excellent interpretive displays.

H 112.8 (185 km) **HJ 38.8** (62.4 km) Gribbles Gulch.

H 114 (187 km) **HJ 37.6** (60.5 km) Parking area at St. Elias Lake trailhead (4-mile/6.4-km round-trip). Novice and intermediate hiking trail winds through subalpine meadow. Watch for mountain goats.

H 117.8 (193 km) **HJ 33.8** (54.4 km) Dezadeash Lodge (closed in 1993, current status unknown). Historically, this spot was known as Beloud Post and is still noted as such on some maps. Mush Lake trail (13.4 miles/21.6 km long) begins behind lodge. It is an old mining road.

NOTE: Watch for horses on highway.

H 119.3 (195 km) **HJ 32.3** (52 km) Turnout along Dezadeash Lake, one of the earliest known features in the Yukon, which parallels the highway for 9 miles/14.5 km northbound, and Dezadeash mountain range. Dezadeash (pronounced DEZ-dee-ash) is said to be the Indian word describing their fishing method. In the spring, the Indians built small fires around the bases of large birch trees, peeled the heat-loosened bark and placed it, shiny white side up, on the bottom of the lake near shore, weighted with stones. From log wharfs built over the white bark Indians waited with spears for lake trout to cross the light area. Another interpretation of Dezadeash relates that Chilkat Indians referred to it as *Dasar-ee-ASH,* meaning "Lake of the Big Winds." Entire tribes were annihilated during mid-19th century Indian wars here.

Dezadeash Lake offers good trolling, also fly-fishing along the shore where feeder streams flow into the lake. There are northern pike, lake trout and grayling in Dezadeash Lake. *CAUTION: This is a mountain lake and storms come up quickly.*

H 119.7 (195.7 km) **HJ 31.9** (51.3 km) Entrance to Yukon government Dezadeash Lake Campground; 20 campsites, $8 fee, kitchen shelter, picnic area, boat launch, no drinking water, pit toilets. ▲

H 123.9 (202.3 km) **HJ 27.7** (44.6 km) Rock Glacier trailhead to west; short 0.5-mile/0.8-km self-guiding trail, partially boardwalk. Interesting and easy walk. Parking area and viewpoint.

H 126.2 (206.9 km) **HJ 25.4** (40.8 km) Dalton Trail Lodge to east with food, lodging and boat rentals.

H 134.8 (219 km) **HJ 16.8** (27 km) Access road west to Kathleen Lake, a glacier-fed turquoise-blue lake, nearly 400 feet/122m deep. Access to bed and breakfast. Access to Kathleen Lake Campground, the only established campground within Kluane National Park. 42 sites, flush toilets and a kitchen area; day-use area with boat launch at lake; campfire programs by park staff. Camping fee $8. The 53-mile/85-km Cottonwood loop trail begins here. ▲

NOTE: National parks fishing license required. **Kathleen Lake**, lake trout average

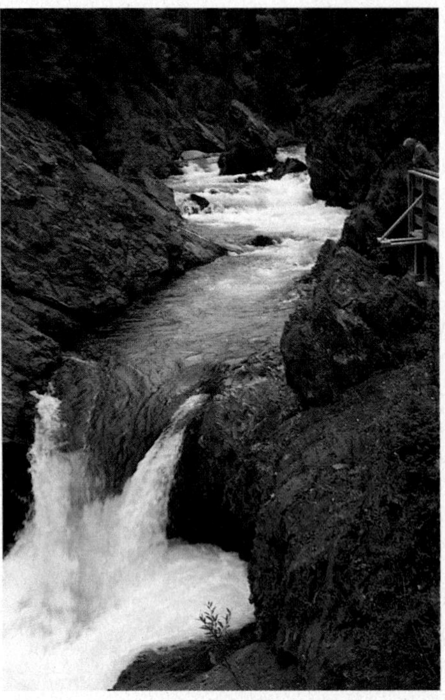

Viewing platform overlooks Million Dollar Falls. (Barb Michaels)

10 lbs., use lures, June and July; kokanee average 2 lbs., June best; grayling to 18 inches, use flies, June to September. **Kathleen River**, rainbow to 17 inches, June to September; grayling to 18 inches, July and August; lake trout average 2 lbs., best in September.

H 135.2 (220.3 km) **HJ 16.4** (26.4 km) Kathleen Lake Lodge.

H 135.8 (220.5 km) **HJ 15.8** (25.4 km) **Kathleen River** bridge; a popular spot for rainbow, lake trout and grayling fishing. Some kokanee.

H 139.2 (227 km) **HJ 12.4** (20 km) Turnout to west. Good view of Kathleen Lake. Information plaque on Kluane and Wrangell–St. Elias national parks.

H 143.4 (233.5 km) **HJ 8.2** (13.2 km) Quill Creek trailhead to west (7-mile/11-km trail).

H 147.1 (239.1 km) **HJ 4.5** (7.2 km) Parking area to west at Auriol trailhead (12-mile/19-km loop trail); skiing and hiking.

H 148.8 (241.1 km) **HJ 2.8** (4.5 km) Rest stop to east with litter barrels and pit toilets. View of community of Haines Junction and Shakwak Valley.

H 151 (245 km) **HJ 0.6** (1 km) Bridges over Dezadeash River. This river is part of the headwaters system of the Alsek River, which flows into the Pacific near Yakutat, AK.

H 151.3 (245.5 km) **HJ 0.3** (0.5 km) Weigh station to west.

H 151.6 (246 km) **HJ 0 HAINES JUNCTION**, turn left for Alaska, keep right for Whitehorse. Turn to Haines Junction (page 133) in the ALASKA HIGHWAY section for description of town and highway log. Whitehorse-bound travelers read log back to front, Alaska-bound travelers read log front to back.

Approximate driving distances from Haines Junction are: Whitehorse 100 miles/161 km; Tok 298 miles/480 km; Fairbanks 504 miles/811 km; and Anchorage 626 miles/1008 km.

KLONDIKE HIGHWAY 2

Skagway, Alaska, to Alaska Highway Junction

The community of Carcross is located on Lake Bennett. (*Earl L. Brown, staff*)

The 98.8-mile-/159-km-long Klondike Highway 2 (also known as the Skagway–Carcross Road and South Klondike Highway) connects Skagway, AK, with the Alaska Highway south of Whitehorse. The highway between Skagway and Carcross (referred to locally as the Skagway Road) was built in 1978 and formally dedicated on May 23, 1981. The highway connecting Carcross with the Alaska Highway (referred to locally as the Carcross Road) was built by the U.S. Army in late 1942 to lay the gas pipeline from Skagway to Whitehorse.

Klondike Highway 2 is a two-lane, asphalt-surfaced road, open year-round. The road has been improved in recent years and is fairly wide. There is a steep 11.5-mile/18.5-km grade between Skagway and White Pass.

IMPORTANT: If you plan to cross the border between midnight and 8 A.M., call ahead or inquire locally regarding customs stations' hours of operation.

Klondike Highway 2 is one of the two highways connecting ferry travelers with the Alaska Highway; the other is the Haines Highway out of Haines. Klondike Highway 2 offers some spectacular scenery and adds only about 55 miles/89 km to the trip for Alaska-bound motorists compared with the Haines Highway. (The distance from Haines to Tok, AK, is approximately 445 miles/716 km; the distance from Skagway to Tok is 500 miles/805 km.) Klondike Highway 2, like the Haines Highway, crosses from Alaska into British Columbia, then into Yukon Territory.

Klondike Highway 2 continues north of Whitehorse, turning off the Alaska Highway to Dawson City. See the KLONDIKE LOOP section for the log of Klondike Highway 2 between the Alaska Highway and Dawson City.

CAUTION: Watch for ore trucks, 85-foot-long, eight-axle vehicles carrying up to 50 tons of lead–zinc concentrates from Faro mine on the Campbell Highway to Skagway. (Mine closed 1993; current status unknown.)

Emergency medical services: Between Skagway and the BC–YT border, phone the Skagway Fire Department at (907) 983-2300. Between the border and the Alaska Highway, phone the Whitehorse ambulance at 1-667-3333, RCMP at 1-667-5555. Police monitor CB Channel 9.

Klondike Highway 2 Log

Mileposts in Alaska and kilometreposts in Canada reflect distance from Skagway. The kilometre distance from Skagway in *The MILEPOST®* log reflects the location of the physical kilometreposts, and is not necessarily an accurate conversion of the mileage figure.

Distance from Skagway (S) is followed by distance from Alaska Highway (AH).

S 0 AH 98.8 (159 km) Ferry terminal in Skagway. See SKAGWAY section for details.

S 1.6 (2.6 km) **AH 97.2** (156.4 km) Skagway River bridge.

S 2.3 (3.7 km) **AH 96.5** (155.3 km) **Junction** with Dyea Road.

S 2.6 (4.2 km) **AH 96.2** (154.8 km) Highway maintenance camp.

S 2.8 (4.5 km) **AH 96** (154.5 km) Plaque to east honoring men and women of the Klondike gold rush, and access to parklike area along Skagway River.

S 2.9 (4.7 km) **AH 95.9** (154.3 km) Access road east to Skagway River. Highway begins steep 11.5-mile/18.5-km ascent northbound from sea level to 3,290 feet/1,003m at White Pass. The huge valleys seen along this stretch of highway were carved by glaciers.

S 4.7 (7.6 km) **AH 94.1** (151.4 km) Turnout to west.

S 5 (8 km) **AH 93.8** (151 km) Turnout to east with view across canyon of White Pass & Yukon Route railway tracks and bridge. The narrow-gauge WP&YR railway was completed in 1900. See the WHITE PASS & YUKON ROUTE section for details on the railway.

S 5.5 (8.8 km) **AH 93.3** (150.1 km) Turnout to west with historical information signs.

S 6 (9.6 km) **AH 92.8** (149.3 km) Turnout to east.

S 6.1 (9.8 km) **AH 92.7** (149.2 km) U.S. customs station; open 24 hours in summer (hours are subject to change). All travelers entering the United States must stop. See Customs Requirements in the GENERAL INFORMATION section.

S 7.4 (11.9 km) **AH 91.4** (147.1 km) View to east of White Pass & Yukon Route railway line.

S 7.7 (12.4 km) **AH 91.1** (146.6 km) Good photo stop for Pitchfork Falls, visible across the canyon. One of Alaska's many spectacular falls, and one of several in this canyon, Pitchfork Falls flows from Goat Lake.

S 8.1 (13 km) **AH 90.7** (146 km) Turnout to east.

S 9.1 (14.6 km) **AH 89.7** (144.4 km) Turnout to east with historical interest signs about the Klondike gold rush trail. Viewpoint looks across the gorge to the White Pass & Yukon Route railway tracks and the canyon leading up to Esk Glacier.

S 9.9 (15.9 km) **AH 88.9** (143.1 km) Truck runout ramp to west for large transport units that may lose air brakes on steep descent southbound.

S 11.1 (17.9 km) **AH 87.7** (141.1 km) Captain William Moore Bridge. This unique cantilever bridge over Moore Creek spans a 110-foot-/34-m-wide gorge. Just north of the bridge to the west is a large waterfall. The bridge is named for Capt. Billy Moore, a riverboat captain and pilot, prospector, packer and trader, who played an important role in settling the town of Skagway. Moore discovered this route over White Pass into the Yukon and was among the first to realize the potential of a railroad across the pass.

S 11.6 (18.7 km) **AH 87.2** (140.3 km) Turnouts to east with view of Skagway River gorge, Captain William Moore Bridge and waterfalls, next 0.1 mile/0.2 km northbound.

S 12 (19.3 km) **AH 86.8** (139.7 km) Truck runout ramp to west.

S 12.6 (20.3 km) **AH 86.2** (138.7 km) Posts on east side of road mark highway shoulders and guide rails for snowplows.

S 14.4 (23.2 km) **AH 84.4** (135.8 km)

KLONDIKE HIGHWAY 2

Skagway, AK, to Junction with Alaska Highway (includes Tagish and Atlin Roads)

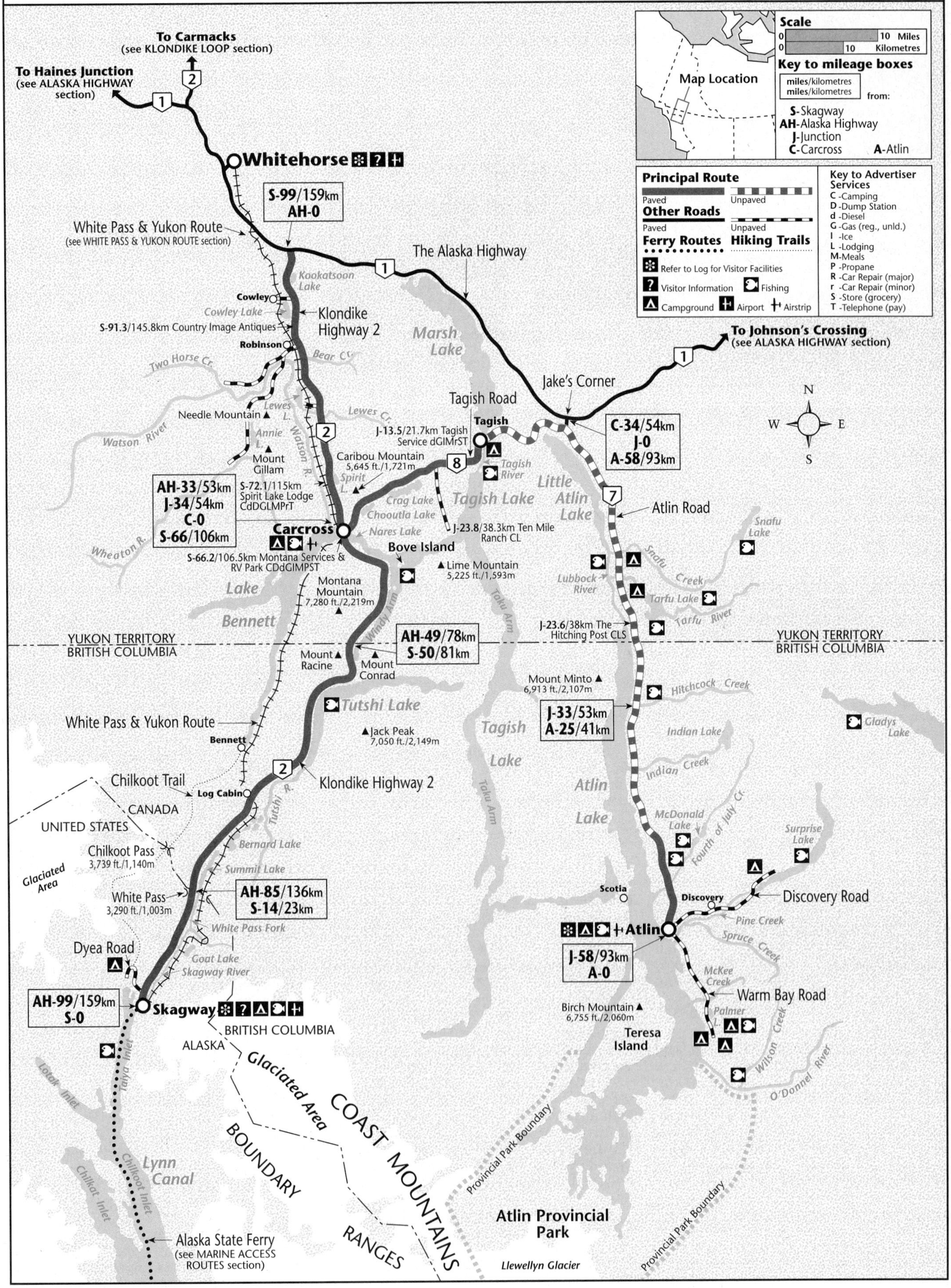

Scale
0 10 Miles
0 10 Kilometres

Map Location

Key to mileage boxes
miles/kilometres
miles/kilometres
from:
S-Skagway
AH-Alaska Highway
J-Junction
C-Carcross
A-Atlin

Principal Route
Paved
Unpaved
Other Roads
Paved
Unpaved
Ferry Routes
Hiking Trails
Refer to Log for Visitor Facilities
Visitor Information
Fishing
Campground
Airport
Airstrip

Key to Advertiser Services
C -Camping
D -Dump Station
d -Diesel
G -Gas (reg., unld.)
I -Ice
L -Lodging
M-Meals
P -Propane
R -Car Repair (major)
r -Car Repair (minor)
S -Store (grocery)
T -Telephone (pay)

To Carmacks
(see KLONDIKE LOOP section)
To Haines Junction
(see ALASKA HIGHWAY section)
Whitehorse
S-99/159km
AH-0
White Pass & Yukon Route
(see WHITE PASS & YUKON ROUTE section)
The Alaska Highway
Kookatsoon Lake
Cowley
Cowley Lake
Klondike Highway 2
S-91.3/145.8km Country Image Antiques
Robinson
Marsh Lake
To Johnson's Crossing
(see ALASKA HIGHWAY section)
Two Horse Cr.
Bear Cr.
Jake's Corner
Tagish Road
Needle Mountain
Lewes L.
Lewes Cr.
Tagish
C-34/54km
J-0
A-58/93km
N
W
E
S
Watson River
Annie L.
Watson R.
J-13.5/21.7km Tagish Service dGIMrST
Mount Gillam
Caribou Mountain
5,645 ft./1,721m
Tagish River
AH-33/53km
J-34/54km
C-0
S-66/106km
S-72.1/115km Spirit Lake Lodge CdDGLMPrT
Spirit L.
Crag Lake
Tagish Lake
Little Atlin Lake
Atlin Road
Snafu Lake
Choutla Lake
Carcross
Nares Lake
J-23.8/38.3km Ten Mile Ranch CL
Wheaton R.
S-66.2/106.5km Montana Services & RV Park CDdGIMPST
Bove Island
Lime Mountain
5,225 ft./1,593m
Snafu Creek
Lubbock River
Lake Bennett
Montana Mountain
7,280 ft./2,219m
Windy Arm
Taku Arm
Tarfu Lake
Tarfu River
J-23.6/38km The Hitching Post CLS
YUKON TERRITORY
BRITISH COLUMBIA
AH-49/78km
S-50/81km
Mount Racine
Mount Conrad
Mount Minto
6,913 ft./2,107m
Hitchcock Creek
Tutshi Lake
J-33/53km
A-25/41km
Gladys Lake
White Pass & Yukon Route
Jack Peak
7,050 ft./2,149m
Tagish Lake
Indian Lake
Bennett
Indian Creek
Chilkoot Trail
Klondike Highway 2
Atlin Lake
Log Cabin
Tutshi R.
Taku Arm
CANADA
UNITED STATES
McDonald Lake
Fourth of July Cr.
Surprise Lake
Bernard Lake
Chilkoot Pass
3,739 ft./1,140m
Glaciated Area
Summit Lake
AH-85/136km
S-14/23km
Scotia
Discovery
Discovery Road
White Pass
3,290 ft./1,003m
White Pass Fork
Atlin
Pine Creek
Spruce Creek
Dyea Road
Goat Lake
Skagway River
J-58/93km
A-0
McKee Creek
Warm Bay Road
AH-99/159km
S-0
Skagway
BRITISH COLUMBIA
ALASKA
Birch Mountain
6,755 ft./2,060m
Palmer L.
Teresa Island
Wilson Creek
O'Donnel River
Taiya Inlet
Lutak Inlet
Glaciated Area
COAST MOUNTAINS
BOUNDARY RANGES
Provincial Park Boundary
Lynn Canal
Chilkoot Inlet
Chilkat Inlet
Atlin Provincial Park
Alaska State Ferry
(see MARINE ACCESS ROUTES section)
Llewellyn Glacier

Traveler stops to read about Bove Island at Milepost S 59.5 turnout. (Barb Michaels)

White Pass Summit (elev. 3,290 feet/ 1,003m). Turnout to west.

CAUTION: Southbound traffic begins steep 11.5-mile/18.5-km descent to Skagway.

Many stampeders on their way to the Klondike goldfields in 1898 chose the White Pass route because it was lower in elevation than the famous Chilkoot Pass trail, and the grade was not as steep. But the White Pass route was longer and the final ascent to the summit treacherous. Dead Horse Gulch (visible from the railway line) was named for the thousands of pack animals that died on this route during the gold rush.

The North West Mounted Police were stationed at the summit to meet every stampeder entering Canada and ensure that each carried at least a year's provisions (weighing about a ton).

S 14.5 (23.3 km) **AH 84.3** (135.7 km) Turnout to west.

S 14.9 (24 km) **AH 84** (135.2 km) U.S.–Canada (AK–BC) border. Turnout to west. Monument to east.

TIME ZONE CHANGE: Alaska observes Alaska time; British Columbia and Yukon Territory observe Pacific time. See Time Zones in the GENERAL INFORMATION section.

S 16.2 (26.1 km) **AH 82.6** (133 km) Highway winds through rocky valley of Summit Lake (visible to east).

S 18.1 (29.1 km) **AH 80.7** (129.9 km) Short bridge with four red pole markers.

S 18.4 (29.6 km) **AH 80.4** (129.4 km) Summit Lake to east.

S 19.3 (31.1 km) **AH 79.5** (128 km) North end of Summit Lake.

S 21.4 (34.4 km) **AH 77.4** (124.5 km) Creek and railroad bridge to east.

S 22.5 (36.2 km) **AH 76.3** (122.8 km) Canada customs at Fraser, open 24 hours. Pay phone. All travelers entering Canada must stop. See Customs Requirements in the GENERAL INFORMATION section.

Old railroad water tower to east, highway maintenance camp to west.

S 22.6 (36.4 km) **AH 76.2** (122.7 km) Beautiful deep-green Bernard Lake to east.

S 24.2 (38.9 km) **AH 74.6** (120.1 km) Turnout to east.

S 25.1 (40.4 km) **AH 73.7** (118.6 km) Shallow Lake to east.

S 25.5 (41 km) **AH 73.3** (118 km) Old cabins and buildings to east.

S 25.9 (41.7 km) **AH 72.9** (117.3 km) A-frame structure to east.

S 26.6 (42.8 km) **AH 72.2** (116.2 km) Turnout to east. Beautiful view of Tormented Valley, a rocky desolate "moonscape" of stunted trees and small lakes east of the highway.

S 27.3 (43.9 km) **AH 71.5** (115 km) Highway crosses tracks of the White Pass & Yukon Route at Log Cabin. With completion of the railway in 1900, the North West Mounted Police moved their customs checkpoint from the summit to Log Cabin. There is nothing here today.

NOTE: There are numerous turnouts along the highway between here and Carcross. Turnouts may be designated for either commercial ore trucks or passenger vehicles.

S 30.7 (49.4 km) **AH 68.1** (109.6 km) Tutshi (too-shy) River visible to east.

S 31.1 (50 km) **AH 67.7** (108.9 km) **Tutshi Lake.** Highway parallels the lake for several miles northbound. Excellent fishing for lake trout and grayling early in season. Be sure you have a British Columbia fishing license.

S 40.1 (64.5 km) **AH 58.7** (94.5 km) Short narrow gravel access road to picnic area with pit toilet on Tutshi Lake. Large vehicles check turnaround space before driving in.

S 40.7 (65.5 km) **AH 58.1** (93.5 km) Good views of Tutshi Lake along here.

S 43.7 (70.5 km) **AH 55.1** (88.7 km) Turnout to east with view of Tutshi Lake.

S 46.4 (75.1 km) **AH 52.4** (84.3 km) To the east is the Venus Mines concentrator, with a capacity of 150 tons per day. A drop in silver prices caused the Venus mill's closure in October 1981. Venus Mines is owned by United Keno Hill Mines (a Falconbridge Nickel company), which operates the silver mines at Elsa, YT.

S 48.5 (78.1 km) **AH 50.3** (81 km) South end of Windy Arm, an extension of Tagish Lake.

S 49.2 (79.2 km) **AH 49.6** (79.9 km) Viewpoint to east.

S 49.9 (80.5 km) **AH 48.9** (78.7 km) Dall Creek.

S 50.2 (81 km) **AH 48.6** (78.2 km) BC–YT border. Turnout with picnic table and litter barrel to east overlooking Windy Arm.

S 51.9 (83.5 km) **AH 46.9** (75.5 km) Large turnout to east with litter barrel, picnic table and historical information sign about Venus Mines.

The first claim on Montana Mountain was staked by W.R. Young in 1899. By 1904 all of the mountain's gold veins had been claimed. In 1905, New York financier Col. Joseph H. Conrad acquired most of the Montana Mountain claims, formed Conrad Consolidated Mines, and began exploration and mining. A town of about 300 people sprang up along Windy Arm and an aerial tramway was built from the Conrad townsite up the side of Montana Mountain to the Mountain Hero adit. (This tramline, visible from the highway, was completed in 1906 but was never used to ship ore because the Mountain Hero tunnel did not find a vein.) More tramways and a mill were constructed, but by 1911 Conrad was forced into bankruptcy: The ore was not as rich as estimated and only a small quantity of ore was milled before operations ceased.

Small mining operations continued over the years, with unsuccessful startups by various mining interests. United Keno Hill Mines (Venus Division) acquired the mining claims in 1979, constructed a 100-ton-per-day mill and rehabilitated the old mine workings in 1980.

S 52.9 (85.1 km) **AH 45.9** (73.8 km) Pooly Creek and canyon, named for J.M. Pooly who staked the first Venus claims in 1901.

Access road east to Pooly Point and Venus Mines maintenance garage, trailers, and security station. No services, facilities or admittance.

S 54.2 (87.2 km) **AH 44.6** (71.8 km) Venus Mines ore storage bin and foundation of old mill to east. The mill was built in the late 1960s and disassembled and sold about 1970. A sign here warns of arsenic being present: Do not pick or eat berries.

S 55.7 (89.6 km) **AH 43.1** (69.4 km) Tramline support just east of highway.

S 59.5 (95.8 km) **AH 39.3** (63.3 km) Turnout with historic information sign about Bove Island. Magnificent views along here of Windy Arm and its islands (the larger island is Bove Island). Windy Arm is an extension of Tagish Lake. Lime Mountain (elev. 5,225 feet/1,593m) rises to the east beyond Bove Island.

S 63.5 (102.2 km) **AH 35.3** (56.8 km) Sections of the old government wagon roads that once linked Carcross, Conrad and other mining claims, visible on either side of the highway.

S 65.3 (105.1 km) **AH 33.5** (53.9 km) Access road west to homes, Carcross Tagish First Nation's Band office and Carcross cemetery. Buried at the cemetery are the famous gold discoverers, Skookum Jim, Dawson (or Tagish) Charlie and Kate Carmack; pioneer missionary Bishop Bompas; and Polly the parrot. (Cemetery is closed to visitors during services.)

S 65.9 (106 km) **AH 32.9** (52.9 km) Access road west to Montana Mountain.

S 66 (106.2 km) **AH 32.8** (52.7 km) Nares Bridge crosses the narrows between Lake Bennett to the west and Tagish Lake to the east. Nares Lake remains open most winters, despite air temperatures that drop well below -40°F/-40°C. The larger lakes freeze to an ice depth of more than 3 feet/1m.

Caribou Mountain (elev. 5,645 feet/ 1,721m) is visible to the east.

S 66.2 (106.5 km) **AH 32.6** (52.4 km) Turnoff west for Carcross (description follows).

Montana Services & RV Park. See display ad this section. ▲

Carcross

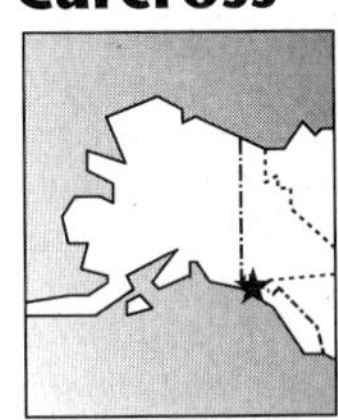

On the shore of Lake Bennett, 44 miles/71 km southeast of Whitehorse. **Population:** 350. **Emergency Services: Police,** phone 821-5555. **Fire Department,** phone 821-2222. **Ambulance,** phone 821-3333. **Health Centre,** phone 821-4444.

Visitor Information: Carcross Visitor Reception Centre is located in the old White Pass & Yukon Route train station. The centre operates daily from 8:30 A.M. to 8:30 P.M., mid-May to mid-September; phone 821-4431. Ferry schedules, maps and information on Yukon, British Columbia and Alaska available.

Elevation: 2,175 feet/663m. **Climate:** Average temperature in January, -4.2°F/ -20.1°C; in July, 55.4°F/13°C. Annual rainfall 11 inches, snowfall 2 to 3 feet. Driest month is April, wettest month August. **Radio:** CKRW, CBC, CKYN-FM 96.1 visitor information station. **Television:** CBC. **Transportation:** Scheduled bus service. Atlin Express Service runs between Atlin and Whitehorse via Tagish and Carcross three times weekly.

Private Aircraft: Carcross airstrip, 0.3 mile/0.5 km north of town via highway; elev. 2,161 feet/659m; length 2,000 feet/610m.

There are a hotel, general store, gift shops with Native handicrafts, snack bar and RV park. Gas station with gifts, groceries and cafe located on the highway by the airstrip. ▲

Carcross was formerly known as Caribou Crossing because of the large numbers of caribou that traversed the narrows here between Bennett and Nares lakes. It became a stopping place for gold stampeders on their way to the Klondike goldfields. Carcross was a major stop on the White Pass & Yukon Route railroad from 1900 until 1982, when the railroad ceased operation. (The WP&YR currently operates a limited excursion service; see WHITE PASS & YUKON ROUTE section for details.) Passengers and freight transferred from rail to stern-wheelers at Carcross. One of these stern-wheelers, the SS *Tutshi* (too-shy), was a historic site here in town until it burned down in July 1990.

A cairn beside the railroad station marks the site where construction crews laying track for the White Pass & Yukon Route from Skagway met the crew from Whitehorse. The golden spike was set in place when the last rail was laid at Carcross on July 29, 1900. The construction project had begun May 27, 1898, during the height of the Klondike gold rush.

Other visitor attractions include St. Saviour's Anglican Church, built in 1902; the Royal Mail Carriage; and the little locomotive *Duchess,* which once hauled coal on Vancouver Island. Frontierland, 2 miles/ 3.2 km north of town on the highway, is also a popular attraction. On sunny days you may sunbathe and picnic at Sandy Beach on Lake Bennett. Since the water is only a few degrees above freezing, swimming is not recommended. Behind the post office there is a footbridge across Nares Lake. This small body of water joins Lake Bennett and Tagish Lake. Check locally for boat tours and boat service on Bennett Lake. A Yukon skydiving school operates here in summer.

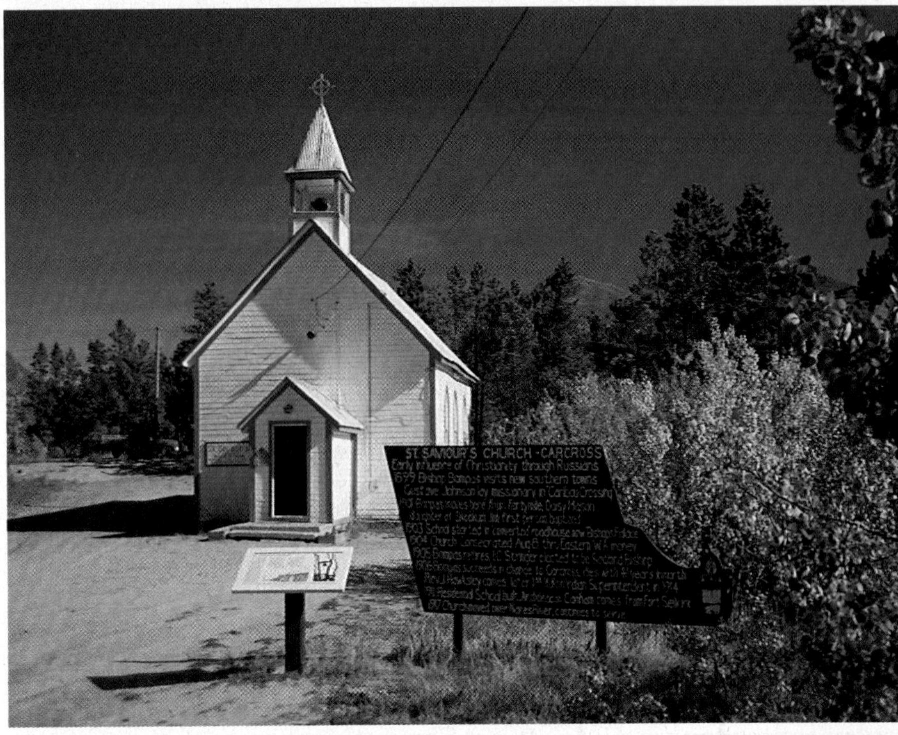

St. Saviour's Anglican Church was built in 1902. (Earl L. Brown, staff)

Fishing in **Lake Bennett** for lake trout, northern pike, arctic grayling, whitefish and cisco.

Caribou Crossing Emporium. A distinctive gift store snuggled in picturesque Carcross, Yukon. Everything about us is unique including our location, which was the original "outhouses" for the White Pass Yukon Rail Depot. Come see our exclusive collection of Yukon designed sweatshirts and T-shirts, as well as other original products. While you are with us, don't forget to get your picture taken with our caribou! Our staff looks forward to seeing you this summer. [ADVERTISEMENT]

Klondike Highway 2 Log

(continued)

S 66.4 (106.9 km) **AH 32.4** (52.1 km) Gas station with gifts, groceries and cafe, and airstrip to east. Turn on access road directly north of airstrip for Carcross Yukon government campground; 14 sites, picnic tables, firewood, drinking water, outhouses, camping fee. ▲

S 66.5 (107 km) **AH 32.3** (52 km) **Junction** with Yukon Highway 8 which leads east to Tagish, Atlin Road and the Alaska Highway at Jake's Corner (see TAGISH ROAD section). Turn east here for alternate access to Alaska Highway and for Yukon government campground on Tagish Road.

S 67.3 (108.3 km) **AH 31.5** (50.7 km) Turnout with point of interest sign about Carcross desert. This unusual desert area of sand dunes, seen east of the highway between Kilometreposts 108 and 110, is the

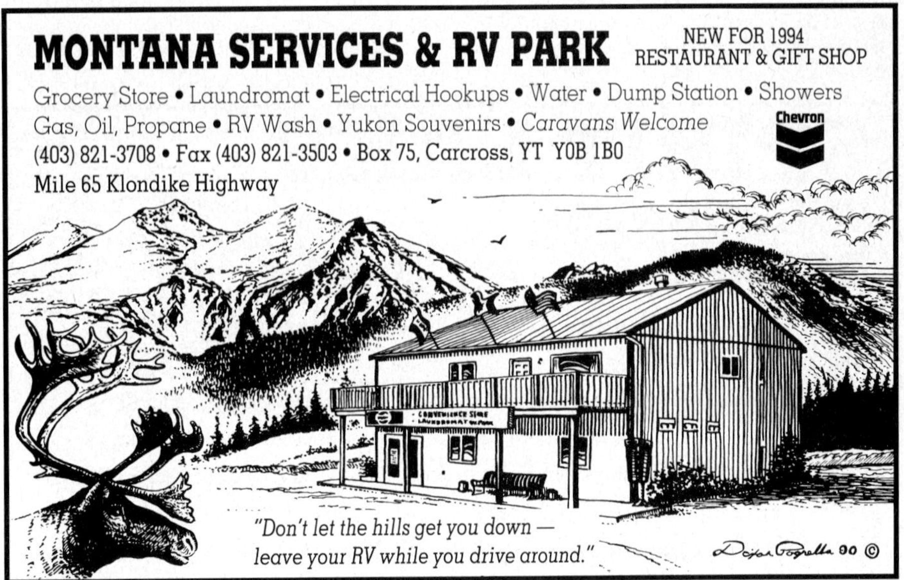

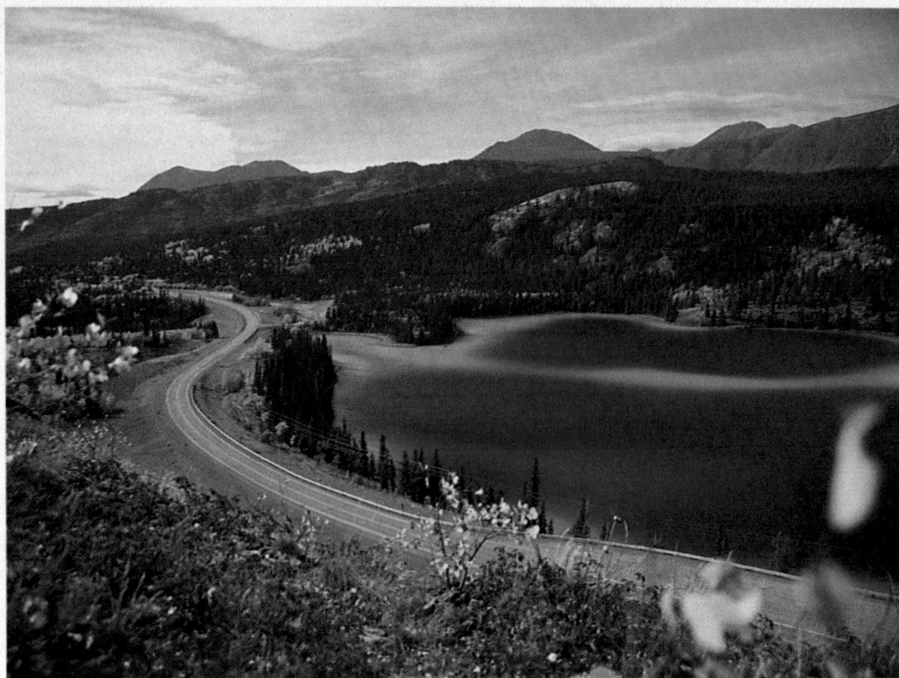

Aptly named Emerald Lake at Milepost S 73.5. (Earl L. Brown, staff)

world's smallest desert and an International Biophysical Programme site for ecological studies. The desert is composed of sandy lake-bottom material left behind by a large glacial lake. Strong winds off Lake Bennett have made it difficult for vegetation to take hold here; only lodgepole pine and kinnikinnick survive. (Kinnikinnick is a low trailing evergreen with small leathery leaves; used for tea.)

S 67.9 (108.6 km) **AH 30.9** (49.7 km) Frontierland (formerly the Museum of Yukon Natural History) features a Yukon wildlife museum, gift shop and coffee house. Among their displays is what is reputedly the world's largest mounted bear — a polar bear.

S 70.3 (112.3 km) **AH 28.5** (45.9 km) Dry Creek.

S 71.2 (113.8 km) **AH 27.6** (44.4 km) Carl's Creek.

S 72.1 (115 km) **AH 26.7** (43 km) Spirit Lake Wilderness Resort east side of road with food, gas, propane, repairs, lodging, camping and ice cream. Access road east to public use area on Spirit Lake. ▲

Spirit Lake Wilderness Resort. See display ad this section. ▲

S 73.2 (116.8 km) **AH 25.6** (41.2 km) Spirit Lake is visible to the east.

S 73.5 (117.3 km) **AH 25.3** (40.7 km) Turnout with point of interest sign to west overlooking beautiful Emerald Lake (also called Rainbow Lake by Yukoners). The rainbowlike colors of the lake result from blue-green light waves reflecting off the white sediment of the lake bottom. This white sediment, called marl, consists of fragments of decomposed shell mixed with clay; it is usually found in shallow, freshwater lakes that have low oxygen levels during the summer months.

S 75.4 (120.3 km) **AH 23.4** (37.7 km) Highway follows base of Caribou Mountain (elev. 5,645 feet/1,721m). View of Montana Mountain to south, Caribou Mountain to east and Gray Ridge Range to the west between Kilometreposts 122 and 128. Flora consists of jack pines and lodgepole pines.

S 79.8 (127.1 km) **AH 19** (30.6 km) Highway crosses Lewes Creek.

S 85.4 (136.3 km) **AH 13.4** (21.6 km) Access road west leads 1 mile/1.6 km to Lewes Lake.

S 85.6 (136.5 km) **AH 13.2** (21.2 km) Rat Lake to west.

S 86.7 (138.2 km) **AH 12.1** (19.4 km) Bear Creek.

S 87.3 (139.1 km) **AH 11.5** (18.5 km) Access road west to large gravel pull-through with historic information sign about Robinson and view of Robinson. In 1899, the White Pass & Yukon Route built a railroad siding at Robinson (named for Stikine Bill Robinson). Gold was discovered nearby in the early 1900s and a townsite was surveyed. A few buildings were constructed and a post office — manned by Charlie McConnell — operated from 1909 to 1915. Low mineral yields caused Robinson to be abandoned, but postmaster Charlie McConnell stayed and established one of the first ranches in the Yukon. Robinson is accessible from Annie Lake Road (see next milepost).

S 87.5 (139.4 km) **AH 11.3** (18.2 km) Road west to Annie Lake (turn left after crossing the railroad tracks to reach Robinson).

Annie Lake Road (can be rough) leads 0.8 mile/1.4 km to Annie Lake golf course, 1.9 miles/3.1 km to McConnell Lake, and 11 miles/17.7 km to Annie Lake. Beyond Annie Lake the road crosses the Wheaton River. The Wheaton Valley–Mount Skukum area has seen a surge of mineral exploration by private prospectors and mining companies in recent years. For the adventuresome, this is beautiful and interesting country. There are no facilities along Annie Lake Road. *CAUTION: Annie Lake Road can be very muddy during spring breakup or during rain.*

S 91.3 (145.8 km) **AH 7.5** (12.1 km) **Country Image Antiques**. See display ad this section.

S 93 (148.5 km) **AH 5.8** (9.4 km) Turnoff west for Cowley and for access to Cowley Lake (1.6 miles/2.6 km).

S 95.5 (154.2 km) **AH 3.3** (5.3 km) Turnoff east for Kookatsoon Lake. There is a Yukon government picnic area at Kookatsoon Lake (day use only). The lake is shallow and usually warm enough for swimming in summer. Picnic tables, firepits and pit toilets. Canoe launch.

S 98.4 (156.5 km) **AH 0.4** (0.7 km) Rock shop on east side of road.

S 98.8 (157.1 km) **AH 0** **Junction** with the Alaska Highway. Turn left (north) for Whitehorse, right (south) for Watson Lake. Turn to **Milepost DC 874.4** (page 116) in the ALASKA HIGHWAY section: Whitehorse-bound travelers continue with that log; travelers heading south down the Alaska Highway read that log back to front.

ATLIN ROAD

Tagish Road Junction, Yukon Territory, to Atlin, British Columbia
Yukon/BC Highway 7
(See map, page 629)

This 58-mile/93.3-km all-weather gravel road leads south to the pioneer gold mining town of Atlin. Built in 1949 by the Canadian Army Engineers, Atlin Road is a good road, usually in excellent condition, with some winding sections. The first 50 miles/80 km are gravel, with the remaining 8 miles/13 km into Atlin paved. Watch for slippery spots in wet weather.

To reach Atlin Road, turn south at Jake's Corner on the Alaska Highway; drive 1.1 miles/1.8 km to the junction of Atlin Road (Highway 7) and Tagish Road (Highway 8); turn left (south) for Atlin.

It is about a two-and-one-half-hour drive to Atlin from Whitehorse and the lake scenery from the village is well worth the trip.

Hiker pauses to take in view of Atlin Lake. (David Job)

Atlin Road Log

Physical kilometreposts in Yukon Territory and mileposts in British Columbia show distance from Tagish Road junction.
Distance from Tagish Road junction (J) is followed by distance from Atlin (A).

J 0 A 58 (93.3 km) **Junction** of Tagish and Atlin roads.

J 1.4 (2.3 km) A 56.6 (91 km) Fish Creek crossing. The road is bordered by many low-lying, boggy areas brilliant green with horsetail *(equisetium)*.

J 1.8 (2.9 km) A 56.2 (90.4 km) Side road west to Little Atlin Lake. Atlin Road descends along east shoreline of Little Atlin Lake approximately 7.6 miles/12.2 km southbound. During midsummer, the roadsides are ablaze with fireweed and wild roses.

J 2.4 (3.9 km) A 55.6 (89.4 km) Large turnout to west on Little Atlin Lake; informal boat launch and camping area. Mount Minto (elev. 6,913 feet/2,107m) can be seen to the southwest. Road climbs southbound.

J 2.8 (4.5 km) A 55.2 (88.8 km) Turnout to west. Watch for bald eagles.

J 5 (8 km) A 53 (85.3 km) Information sign to east about 1983–84 mountain goat transplant. The 12 goats were brought from Kluane National Park. They may be observed on the mountainsides.

J 8.1 (13 km) A 49.9 (80.3 km) Haunka Creek. Turnout to west.

J 8.9 (14.3 km) A 49.1 (79 km) Good view of Mount Minto ahead southbound.

J 13.8 (22.2 km) A 44.2 (71.1 km) Unmarked side road leads 2.4 miles/3.9 km to **Lubbock River**, which connects Little Atlin Lake with Atlin Lake. Excellent for grayling from breakup to mid-September.

J 15.5 (24.9 km) A 42.5 (68.4 km) Snafu Creek. Turnout to west, north of bridge. According to R. Coutts, author of *Yukon Places & Names*, the creek name is an acronym bestowed by army crews who built the road. It stands for Situation Normal — All Fouled Up. (Mr. Coutts resides in Atlin.)

J 16.4 (26 km) A 41.6 (66.9 km) Access road leads 0.7 mile/1.1 km to **Snafu Lake** Yukon government campground; four sites, $8 camping fee, pit toilets, tables, gravel boat ramp, good fishing. ▲

J 18.6 (29.9 km) A 39.4 (63.4 km) Tarfu Creek. Small turnout to east, north of bridge. Creek name is another army acronym. This one stands for Things Are Really Fouled Up.

J 18.7 (30 km) A 39.3 (63.2 km) Abandoned cabin and turnout to west.

J 20.4 (32.8 km) A 37.6 (60.5 km) Turnoff to east for **Tarfu Lake** Yukon government campground via 2.4-mile/3.8-km side road; six sites, $8 camping fee, pit toilets, fishing. Steep grade near campground; not recommended for large RVs or trailers. ▲

J 20.5 (33 km) A 37.5 (60.3 km) Short narrow side road leads east to Marcella Lake; good lake for canoeing.

J 21.8 (35.1 km) A 36.2 (58.2 km) Turnout to west with view of Atlin Lake, which covers 307 square miles/798 square km and is the largest natural lake in British Columbia. Coast Mountains to the southwest.

J 23.6 (38 km) A 34.4 (55.3 km) **The Hitching Post**. See display ad this section. ▲

J 25.8 (41.5 km) A 32.2 (51.8 km) BC–YT border. Road follows east shoreline of Atlin Lake into Atlin.

J 26.8 (43.1 km) A 31.2 (50.2 km) Survival shelter to east.

J 27 (43.5 km) A 31 (49.9 km) Mount Minto to west, Black Mountain to east, and Halcro Peak (elev. 5,856 feet/1,785m) to the southeast.

J 28.5 (45.8 km) A 29.5 (47.5 km) Slow down for sharp curve.

J 32 (51.5 km) A 26 (41.9 km) Excellent views of Coast Mountains, southwest across Atlin Lake, next 6 miles/9.7 km southbound.

J 32.7 (52.6 km) A 25.3 (40.7 km) **Hitchcock Creek**, grayling to 2 lbs. Survival shelter to east.

J 32.8 (52.7 km) A 25.2 (40.5 km) Campground on Atlin Lake; six sites, pit toilets, tables, ramp for small boats. ▲

Discovery Road Log

Discovery Road begins 0.4 mile/0.6 km from Atlin's business district at junction with Atlin Road and leads east 13 miles/20.9 km. This is a good, wide, gravel road, bumpy in spots. Posted speed limit is 50 mph/80 kmph, but 40 mph/60 kmph or less is recommended. There is active gold mining under way along the road; watch for large trucks. Beyond Surprise Lake Dam bridge, the road becomes steep and winding for 1.2 miles/1.9 km to road end (large RVs use caution).

Distance is measured from junction with Atlin Road (J).

J 0 Junction of Atlin Road and Discovery Avenue.

J 0.3 (0.5 km) **Junction** with Warm Bay Road.

J 1.1 (1.8 km) Atlin airport to east. Pioneer cemetery to west contains grave markers and monuments to many of Atlin's historical figures.

J 2.3 (3.7 km) Dump station to south.

J 3.5 (5.6 km) Turnout to south with view of Pine Creek and falls.

J 3.6 (5.8 km) Spruce Creek Road leads south 0.9 mile/1.4 km to recreational gold panning access and 1.5 miles/2.4 km to active gold mining on Spruce Creek (no tours but operations can be photographed from the road). This side road is signed as rough and narrow; suitable for cars, vans and pickups.

J 3.9 (6.3 km) Winding road next 1 mile/1.6 km.

J 5.4 (8.7 km) Former townsite of **Discovery**, originally called Pine Creek, now a ghost town. In its boom days, the town supplied miners working in the area.

J 7 (11.2 km) Active gold mining operation to south can be photographed from the road.

J 8.6 (13.8 km) Slow down for Pine Creek one-lane bridge. Road follows creek drainage from here to Surprise Lake.

J 9.2 (14.8 km) Small lake to east usually has waterfowl.

J 10.7 (17.2 km) View west of mining road switchbacks on mountainside.

J 11.2 (18 km) Road forks: bear to left. Small lake to west.

J 11.8 (19 km) Surprise Lake Dam bridge. Turnout east side of bridge with litter barrel and view of Surprise Lake.

CAUTION: Steep and winding road next 1.2 miles/1.9 km eastbound to road end.

J 12 (19.3 km) **Surprise Lake** recreation site. One campsite near main road. Steep, bumpy access road leads to more campsites near lake. Pit toilets, picnic tables, firepits. Boat launch for cartop boats and canoes. A gold mining operation is visible across the lake. Fishing for arctic grayling. ▲

J 13 (20.9 km) Road forks and both forks deadend along Boulder Creek. Ample turnaround space for vehicles.

Warm Bay Road Log

Warm Bay Road leads south 16.5 miles/26.5 km to numerous points of interest and five camping areas. Warm Bay Road begins at **Milepost J 0.3** Discovery Road, 0.7 mile/1.1 km east of Atlin business district.

Distance is measured from junction with Discovery Road (J).

J 0 Junction with Discovery Road.

J 0.3 (0.5 km) Atlin School.

J 1.5 (2.4 km) Pine Creek one-lane bridge.

J 1.6 (2.6 km) Pine Creek Campground and picnic area; 14 campsites, tenting area, pit toilets, picnic tables, firepits, some firewood and water. Camping fee: $5/RV, $3/tent; pay at any Atlin business. Short trail to Pine Creek and Pine Creek Falls. ▲

J 2 (3.2 km) Atlin Centre for the Arts (see Attractions in Atlin).

J 2.3 (3.7 km) Trailheads either side of road. Monarch trail is a moderately strenuous 3-mile/4.8-km hike through meadows to scenic vista of Atlin area. Some steep sections; summit of Monarch Mountain at elev. 4,723 feet/1,439m. Beach trail is short and easy.

J 2.5 (4 km) Drinking water from pipe beside road.

J 5.7 (9.2 km) Lina Creek.

J 7 (11.2 km) Viewpoint with litter barrel. Llewellyn Glacier and Atlin Lake are to the southwest.

J 9.5 (15.3 km) McKee Creek one-lane bridge. The McKee Creek area has been mined since the 1890s. In July 1981, two area miners found what has been dubbed the "Atlin nugget," a 36.86-troy-ounce, hand-sized piece of gold.

J 11.3 (18.2 km) Palmer Lake to east.

J 11.9 (19.1 km) **Palmer Lake** recreation site to east; camping, fishing, picnic tables, pit toilets. No camping fee. ▲

J 13.9 (22.3 km) Warm Bay recreation site on **Atlin Lake**; camping, fishing, picnic tables, pit toilets. No camping fee. Boat launch for small boats. ▲

J 14.4 (23.2 km) Warm Springs to north. This is a small and shallow spring, good for soaking road-weary bones. Large grassy camping area, picnic tables, pit toilets. No camping fee. The meadow streams, lined with watercress, are a breeding ground for toads and chub. ▲

J 16.3 (26.2 km) Grotto recreation site; two campsites, picnic tables, pit toilets, firepits, litter barrel. ▲

J 16.4 (26.4 km) "The Grotto" to north. Large turnaround. Water flows through a hole in the rocks from an underground stream. Locals report this is a good place to obtain drinking water.

J 16.5 (26.5 km) Maintained road ends. Steep, bumpy and narrow road continues beyond this point; not recommended for travel.

J 36.3 (58.4 km) **A 21.7** (35 km) Turnout with litter barrel to west, south side of Base Camp Creek.

J 36.8 (59.2 km) **A 21.2** (34.1 km) Old Milepost 38.

J 40 (64.4 km) **A 18** (29 km) Indian River. Pull-through turnout south of creek.

J 40.2 (64.7 km) **A 17.8** (28.7 km) Big-game outfitter/guest ranch to east.

J 45.2 (72.7 km) **A 12.8** (20.6 km) Survival shelter to east.

J 45.3 (72.9 km) **A 12.7** (20.5 km) Turnout to west.

J 49.8 (80.1 km) **A 8.2** (13.2 km) Burnt Creek. Gravel ends, pavement begins, southbound.

J 49.9 (80.3 km) **A 8.1** (13.1 km) Davie Hall Lake and turnout to west. Waterfowl are plentiful on lake.

J 51.2 (82.4 km) **A 6.8** (11 km) Watch for horses.

J 51.6 (83 km) **A 6.4** (10.3 km) Ruffner Mine Road leads east 40 miles/64.4 km. Access to **MacDonald Lake**, 2 miles/3.2 km east; bird watching and lake trout fishing from spit.

J 52.8 (85 km) **A 5.2** (8.4 km) Fourth of July Creek.

J 53.4 (85.9 km) **A 4.6** (7.4 km) Spruce Mountain (elev. 5,141 feet/1,567m) to west.

J 55.1 (88.7 km) **A 2.9** (4.7 km) Road skirts east shore of Como Lake next 0.6 mile/1 km southbound.

J 55.2 (88.8 km) **A 2.8** (4.5 km) Turnout with litter barrel to west on Como Lake; good lake for canoeing.

J 55.7 (89.6 km) **A 2.3** (3.7 km) South end of Como Lake; boat ramp.

J 57.1 (91.9 km) **A 0.9** (1.4 km) Atlin city limits.

J 58 (93.3 km) **A 0 Junction** of Atlin Road with Discovery Road. Turn right (west) on Discovery Avenue for town of Atlin; description follows. Turn left (east) for Discovery Road and access to Warm Bay Road; see side road logs this page.

Atlin

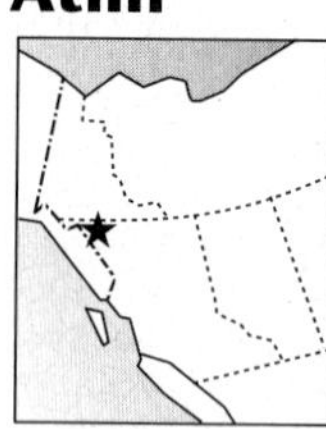

The most northwesterly town in British Columbia, located about 112 miles/180 km southeast of Whitehorse, YT. **Population:** 500. **Emergency Services: Police,** phone 651-7511. **Fire Department,** phone 651-7666. **Ambulance,** phone 651-7700. Red Cross outpost clinic, phone 651-7677.

Visitor Information: Contact the Atlin Visitors Assoc., P.O. Box 365-M, Atlin, BC

Houseboats, boats and planes dock at Atlin waterfront. (Earl L. Brown, staff)

V0W 1A0, fax 651-7696.

Elevation: 2,240 feet/683m. **Radio:** CBC on FM-band. **Television:** Three channels (CBC, BCTV and the Knowledge Network).

Private Aircraft: Peterson Field, 1 mile/1.6 km northeast; elev. 2,348 feet/716m; length 3,950 feet/1,204m; gravel.

Transportation: Air–Regular service from Juneau via Summit Aviation. **Bus**–Service from Whitehorse three times a week.

Referred to by some visitors as Shangri-la, the village of Atlin overlooks the crystal clear water of 90-mile-/145-km-long Atlin Lake and is surrounded by spectacular mountains. On Teresa Island in Atlin Lake is Birch Mountain (elev. 6,755 feet/2,060m), the highest point in fresh water in the world.

Atlin was founded in 1898. The name was taken from the Indian dialect and means Big Water. The Atlin Lake area was one of the richest gold strikes made during the great rush to the Klondike in 1897–98. The first claims were registered here on July 30, 1898, by Fritz Miller and Kenneth McLaren.

ACCOMMODATIONS

The village has a hotel, inns, cottages, bed and breakfasts, laundromat (with showers), restaurants, gas stations (propane, diesel and unleaded available), grocery and general stores. Dump station at Mile 2.3 Discovery Road. The museum and several shops feature local gold nugget jewelry, arts and crafts, and other souvenirs. Air charter service for glacier tours and fly-in fishing trips. Charter boats and fishing charters available.

Bus tours are welcome, but phone ahead so this small community can accommodate you.

The Noland House. This historic home has been restored to provide luxurious accommodations for four guests. Host residence is next-door. Private baths and sitting rooms, complimentary wine and snacks, fully equipped kitchen, lake and mountain views, airport and floatplane dock pickup. $85 double, open May–October. Box 135, Atlin, BC V0W 1A0. (604) 651-7585. [ADVERTISEMENT]

RV park with electric and water hookups, pay phone and boat moorage downtown on lake. There are several camping areas on Atlin Road, Discovery Road and Warm Bay Road (see logs this section). ▲

Sunset on Little Atlin Lake. (Earl L. Brown, staff)

ATTRACTIONS

The MV *Tarahne* (Tah-ron) sits on the lakeshore in the middle of town. Built at Atlin in 1916 by White Pass & Yukon Route, she carried passengers and freight from Atlin to Scotia Bay until 1936. (Scotia Bay is across the lake from Atlin and slightly north.) A 2-mile/3.2-km railway connected Scotia Bay on Atlin Lake to Taku Landing on Tagish Lake, where passengers arrived by boat from Carcross, YT. The *Tarahne* was the first gas-driven boat in the White Pass fleet. After she was lengthened by 30 feet in 1927, she could carry up to 198 passengers. In recent years, Atlin residents have launched a drive to restore the boat; they hope to eventually refloat the vessel and offer tours of Atlin Lake.

Visit the mineral springs at the north end of town, where you may have a drink of sparkling cold mineral water. The gazebolike structure over the springs was built by White Pass in 1922. Picnic area nearby.

Atlin Historical Museum, open weekends during June and September, daily July through August. Located in Atlin's original one-room schoolhouse, the museum has mining artifacts and photo exhibits of the Atlin gold rush; admission fee; phone 651-7522.

The Pioneer Cemetery, located at **Milepost J 1.1** Discovery Road, contains the weathered grave markers of early gold seekers, including Fritz Miller and Kenneth McLaren, who made the first gold discovery in the Atlin area in July 1898. Also buried here is Walter Gladstone Sweet, reputed to have been a card dealer for Soapy Smith in Skagway.

Take a Hike. At **Milepost J 2.3** Warm Bay Road are two trails: the 3-mile/4.8-km Monarch trail and the short, easy Beach trail. The Monarch trail is a moderately strenuous hike with a steep climb at the end to a bird's-eye view of the area.

Tours and Rentals. Motorbike rentals, houseboat rentals, boat tours of Atlin and Tagish lakes, guided fishing trips and marine gas are available. Helicopter service, floatplanes for charter hunting and fishing trips and flightseeing trips of Llewellyn Glacier and the Atlin area are also available.

Atlin Provincial Park, accessible by boat or plane only (charters available in Atlin). Spectacular wilderness area; varied topography; exceptional wildlife habitat.

Take a Drive. 13-mile/21-km Discovery Road and 16.5-mile/26.5-km Warm Bay Road are both suitable for passenger cars and RVs, and both offer sightseeing and recreation. See side road logs this section for details.

Atlin Centre for the Arts, located at **Milepost J 2** Warm Bay Road, is a summer school and retreat for artists and students run by Gernot Dick. The centre is designed to allow participants to distance themselves from urban distractions and focus on the creative process. Contact Atlin Centre for the Arts, 19 Elm Grove Ave., Toronto, ON M6K 2H9, for more information. Currently, a number of talented artists, authors and other creative people make their home in Atlin.

AREA FISHING: The Atlin area is well known for its good fishing. Fly-in fishing for salmon, steelhead and rainbow, or troll locally for lake trout. Grayling can be caught at the mouths of most creeks and streams or off Atlin docks. Public boat launch on Atlin Lake, south of the MV *Tarahne*. Boat charters available. For information on fishing in the area contact local businesses. British Columbia fishing licenses are available from the government agent and local outlets. Fresh and smoked salmon may be available for purchase locally in the summer. Annual fishing derby held in June.

TAGISH ROAD

Alaska Highway (Jake's Corner) to Carcross, Yukon Territory
Yukon Highway 8
(See map, page 629)

The Tagish Road was built in 1942 to lay a gas pipeline. It leads south from the Alaska Highway through the settlement of Tagish to Carcross. This 33.8-mile/54.4-km road connects the Alaska Highway with Klondike Highway 2. The road is good gravel from the Alaska Highway junction to Tagish, asphalt-surfaced between Tagish and Carcross.

If you are traveling Klondike Highway 2 between Skagway and Whitehorse, Tagish Road provides access to Atlin Road and also makes a pleasant side trip. Travelers may wish to use Tagish Road as an alternate route if there is road construction on Klondike Highway 2 between Carcross and the Alaska Highway.

Emergency medical services: phone the RCMP, 1-667-5555; ambulance, phone 1-667-3333.

Tagish Road Log

Kilometreposts measure east to west from Alaska Highway junction to Carcross turnoff; posts are up about every 2 kilometres. **Distance from the junction (J) is followed by distance from Carcross (C).**

J 0 C 33.8 (54.4 km) **Junction** with the Alaska Highway at Jake's Corner. Drive south 1.1 miles/1.8 km to junction of Tagish Road and Atlin Road (Highway 7).

J 1.1 (1.8 km) **C 32.7** (52.6 km) **Junction** of Tagish and Atlin roads. Turn southeast for Atlin, BC (see ATLIN ROAD section); head west for Tagish and Carcross.

J 8.8 (14.2 km) **C 25** (40.2 km) For several miles, travelers may see the NorthwesTel microwave tower on Jubilee Mountain (elev. 5,950 feet/1,814m) to the south between Little Atlin Lake and Tagish River.

J 12.8 (20.6 km) **C 21** (33.8 km) Tagish Yukon government campground, on **Six Mile River** between Marsh Lake to the north and Tagish Lake to the south. Good fishing, boat launch, picnic area, playground, kitchen shelter, 28 campsites with firepits and tables, drinking water and toilets. Camping fee $8. *CAUTION: Watch for black bears.*

J 13 (20.9 km) **C 20.8** (33.5 km) **Tagish Service**. See display ad this section.

J 13.1 (21 km) **C 20.7** (33.3 km) Tagish bridge. Good fishing is a tradition here; Tagish bridge has an anglers' walkway on the north side. **Tagish River**, lake trout, arctic grayling, northern pike, whitefish and cisco. Marina on north side of road at east end of bridge has bait, tackle, fishing licenses, boat rental. Gas, oil, minor repairs, snacks and post office. Pay phone on road.

Gravel ends, pavement begins, westbound.

J 13.5 (21.7 km) **C 20.3** (32.6 km) Improved gravel road leads through parklike area to tiny settlement of **TAGISH** on Tagish River between Marsh and Tagish lakes. Express bus service between Atlin and Whitehorse stops here and in Carcross three times weekly. Tagish means "fish trap" in the local Indian dialect. It was traditionally an Indian meeting place in the spring on the way to set up fish camps and again in the fall to celebrate the catch. Post office at Tagish Service.

Two miles/3.2 km south of Tagish on the Tagish River is **TAGISH POST**, originally named Fort Sifton, the Canadian customs post established in 1897. Two of the original five buildings still stand. The North West Mounted Police and Canadian customs collected duties on thousands of tons of freight carried by stampeders on their way to the Klondike goldfields between September 1897 and February 1898.

J 16.3 (26.2 km) **C 17.5** (28.1 km) Side road leads 1.2 miles/2 km to Tagish Lake and homes.

J 23 (37 km) **C 10.8** (17.4 km) Bryden Creek.

J 23.8 (38.3 km) **C 10** (16.1 km) **Ten Mile Ranch,** located 8 miles south on a maintained gravel road, is a wilderness ranch with rustic log cabins and large RV and tent sites right along the shore of Tagish Lake. A variety of activities include wildlife watching, canoeing, boating, fishing, guided adventure tours from one to four weeks, or just relaxing surrounded by the quiet splendor of mountains and lakes. We look forward to seeing you. Phone (403) 667-1009. [ADVERTISEMENT]

J 24.8 (39.9 km) **C 9** (14.4 km) Crag Lake. Road now enters more mountainous region westbound. Caribou Mountain (elev. 5,645 feet/1,721m) on right.

J 27.2 (43.8 km) **C 6.6** (10.6 km) Porcupine Creek.

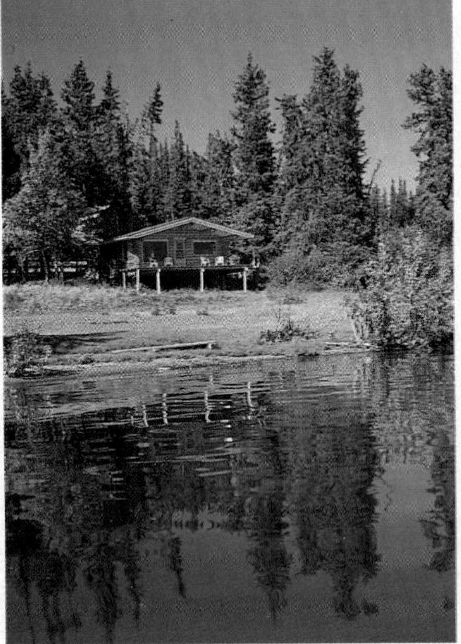

Log cabin at a local ranch on Tagish Lake. (Earl L. Brown, staff)

J 28.4 (45.7 km) **C 5.4** (8.7 km) Pain Creek.

J 30.2 (48.6 km) **C 3.6** (5.8 km) Side road to Choootla Lake.

J 31 (49.9 km) **C 2.8** (4.5 km) First glimpse westbound of Montana Mountain (elev. 7,230 feet/2,204m) across narrows at Carcross.

J 33.8 (54.4 km) **C 0 Junction** with Klondike Highway 2. Westbound travelers turn left for Carcross, right for Whitehorse. See **Milepost S 66.5** (page 631) in the KLONDIKE HIGHWAY 2 section.

NORTHERN WOODS & WATERS ROUTE

Saskatchewan Border to Dawson Creek, British Columbia
Alberta Highways 55, 2 and 49
Includes Alberta Highways 63 and 64
(See maps, pages 639-640)

Marshy lakes and boreal forests characterize this region. (Brian Calkins)

The Northern Woods & Waters Route is a scenic 489.5-mile/787.8-km route originating at the Saskatchewan–Alberta border that passes the lakes, forests and prairies of northern Alberta before terminating at Dawson Creek, British Columbia.

The Northern Woods & Waters Route follows three different highway numbers in Alberta: Highway 55 from the border to Athabasca, Highway 2 from Athabasca to Donnelly Corners, and Highway 49 from Donnelly Corners to Dawson Creek, BC. With the upgrading and paving of a gravel section near Rich Lake in the summer of 1993, the highway is now paved in its entirety and is in good to excellent condition. The only rough area is near the crossing of the Smoky River between Girouxville and Watino. In the summer of 1993 construction was under way on this stretch of highway. Completion is expected by the summer of 1994.

A full array of visitor facilities is available at the larger communities: Grand Centre, Cold Lake, Lac La Biche, Athabasca, Slave Lake, High Prairie, McLennan and Spirit River. Other visitor facilities are available in most of the smaller communities along the route.

Northern Woods & Waters Route Log

ALBERTA HIGHWAY 55
Distance from the Alberta–Saskatchewan border (B) is followed by distance from Dawson Creek (DC).

B 0 DC 489.5 (787.8 km) Alberta–Saskatchewan border. Head west on Highway 55.

B 2 (3.2 km) **DC 487.5** (784.5 km) Cherry Hill Estates to north.

B 3.2 (5.1 km) **DC 486.4** (782.8 km) Cherry Grove (pop. 115) to north.

B 8 (12.8 km) **DC 481.6** (775 km) **Junction** with Highway 897 south to Elizabeth Metis settlement.

B 8.5 (13.6 km) **DC 481.1** (774.2 km) **Junction** with Alberta Highway 28 at Beaver Crossing. Tourist information centre for the region is located on the southeast corner of the junction.

B 9.4 (15.2 km) **DC 480.1** (772.6 km) Side road east 1.8 miles/3 km to Grand Centre Golf and Country Club. The course has nine holes, pro shop, carts for rent and licensed restaurant.

B 10.6 (17.1 km) **DC 478.9** (770.7 km) Entering Grand Centre northbound.

Grand Centre

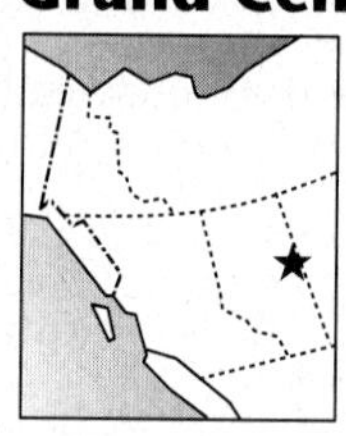

B 11.3 (18.2 km) **DC 478.2** (769.6 km) Located 180 miles/290 km northeast of Edmonton. **Population:** 3,880. **Emergency Services: RCMP**, phone 594-3301. **Hospital and Ambulance**, phone 639-3322. **Fire Department**, phone 594-3100.

Visitor Information: Tourist information centre 3 miles/5 km south at the junction of Highways 55 and 28.

Situated beside one of the largest military bases in Canada (CFB Cold Lake) and immediately south of the community of Cold Lake, Grand Centre is the economic and commercial base of northeast Alberta. Grand Centre, Cold Lake and the military base make up the tri-cities area.

Visitor facilities include two hotels, five motels, many restaurants, retail and grocery stores, and service stations with major-repair facilities. Recreational facilities include a large sports arena, curling rink, tennis courts, public library, ball diamonds and a golf course, 3.6 miles/6 km southeast of town.

Northern Woods & Waters Route Log
(continued)

B 11.7 (18.8 km) **DC 477.8** (769 km) **Junction** with access road west 1.2 miles/2 km to the Cold Lake Air Force Base.

B 11.8 (18.9 km) **DC 477.7** (768.8 km) **Junction** with side road east 11.2 miles/18 km to French Bay Provincial Recreation

NORTHERN WOODS & WATERS ROUTE

Saskatchewan Border to Slave Lake, AB

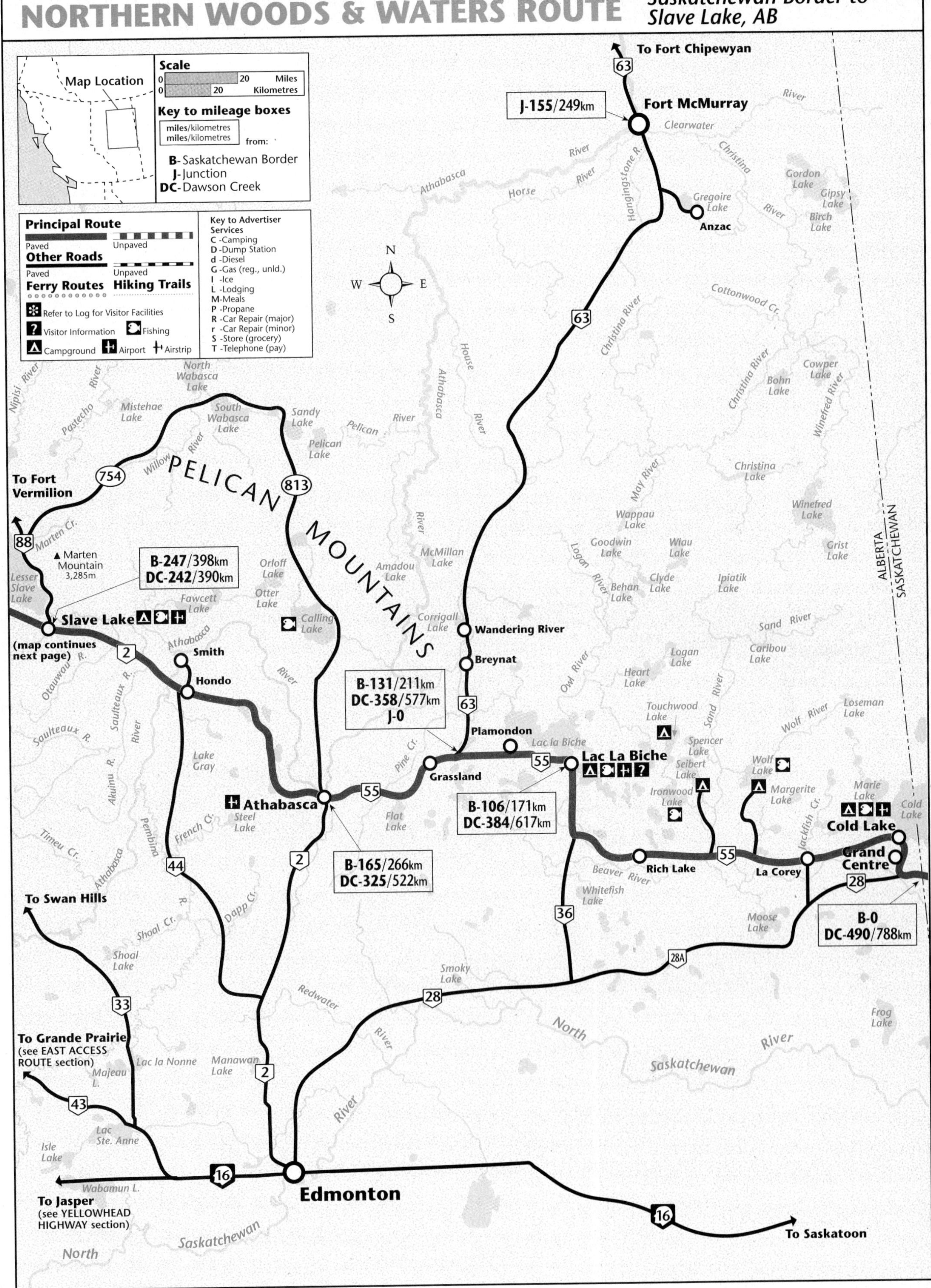

NORTHERN WOODS & WATERS ROUTE

Slave Lake, AB, to Dawson Creek, BC

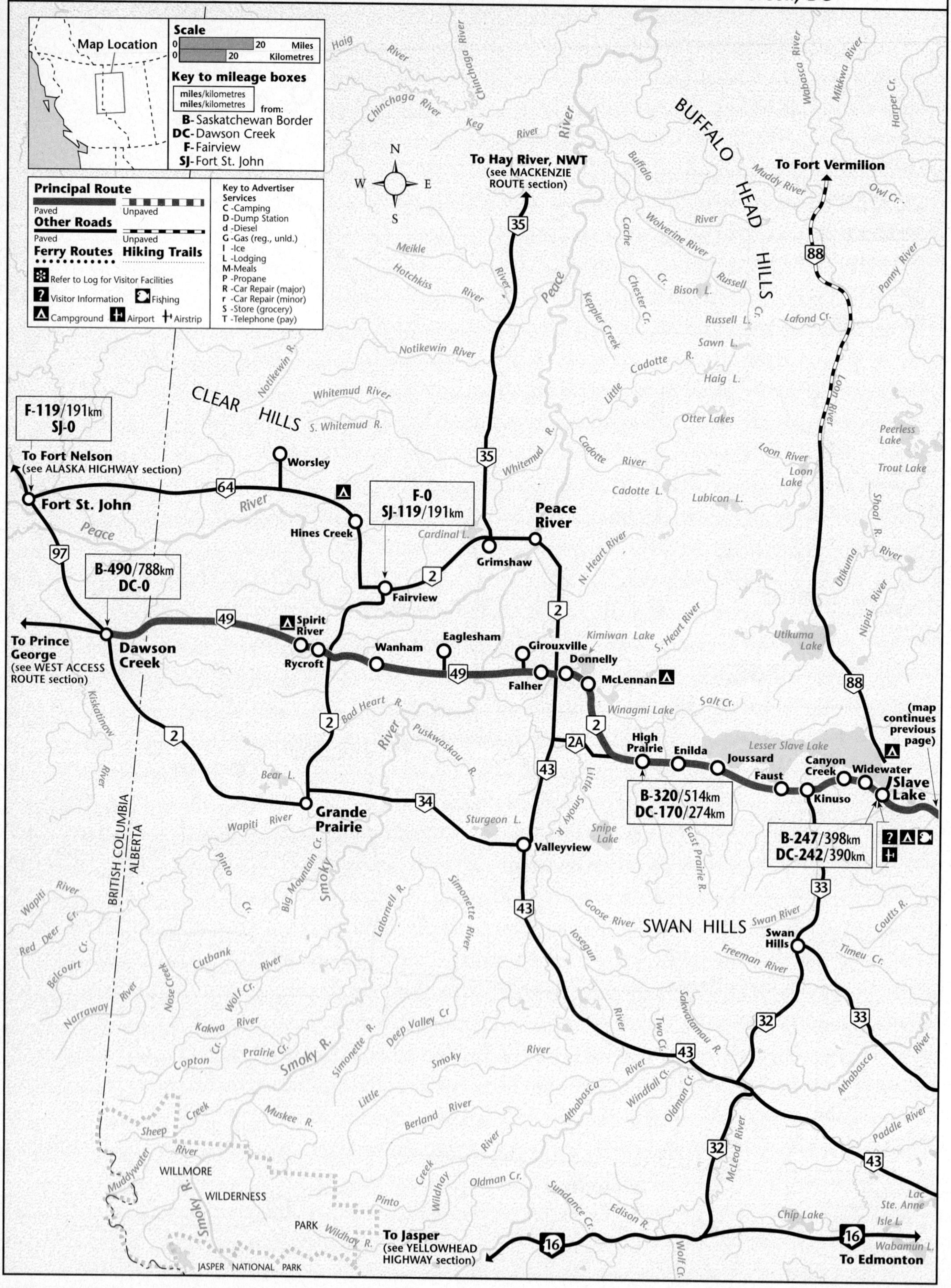

Map Location

Scale
0 — 20 Miles
0 — 20 Kilometres

Key to mileage boxes

miles/kilometres
miles/kilometres
from:
B-Saskatchewan Border
DC-Dawson Creek
F-Fairview
SJ-Fort St. John

Principal Route
Paved
Unpaved
Other Roads
Paved
Unpaved
Ferry Routes
Hiking Trails
Refer to Log for Visitor Facilities
Visitor Information
Fishing
Campground
Airport
Airstrip

Key to Advertiser Services
C -Camping
D -Dump Station
d -Diesel
G -Gas (reg., unld.)
I -Ice
L -Lodging
M-Meals
P -Propane
R -Car Repair (major)
r -Car Repair (minor)
S -Store (grocery)
T -Telephone (pay)

N
W E
S

F-119/191km
SJ-0

To Fort Nelson
(see ALASKA HIGHWAY section)

Fort St. John

B-490/788km
DC-0

F-0
SJ-119/191km

To Prince George
(see WEST ACCESS ROUTE section)

Dawson Creek

To Hay River, NWT
(see MACKENZIE ROUTE section)

To Fort Vermilion

CLEAR HILLS

BUFFALO HEAD HILLS

SWAN HILLS

Worsley
Hines Creek
Fairview
Grimshaw
Peace River
Spirit River
Rycroft
Wanham
Eaglesham
Girouxville
Donnelly
Falher
McLennan
High Prairie
Enilda
Joussard
Faust
Canyon Creek
Widewater
Kinuso
Slave Lake
Grande Prairie
Valleyview
Swan Hills

B-320/514km
DC-170/274km

B-247/398km
DC-242/390km

(map continues previous page)

BRITISH COLUMBIA
ALBERTA

Haig River
Chinchaga River
Keg River
Peace River
Buffalo
Muddy River
Wolverine River
Cache Cr.
Chester Cr.
Bison L.
Russell
Russell Cr.
Russell L.
Lafond Cr.
Sawn L.
Haig L.
Cadotte R.
Little Cadotte R.
Keppler Creek
Meikle
Hotchkiss River
Notikewin River
Notikewin R.
Whitemud River
S. Whitemud R.
Whitemud R.
Otter Lakes
Cadotte River
Cadotte L.
Loon River
Loon Lake
Lubicon L.
Peerless Lake
Trout Lake
Shoal R.
River
Utikuma
Utikuma Lake
Nipisi River
Wabasca River
Mikkwa River
Harper Cr.
Owl Cr.
Panny River
Loon River
Cardinal L.
N. Heart River
S. Heart River
Kimiwan Lake
Salt Cr.
Winagmi Lake
Lesser Slave Lake
Bad Heart R.
Puskwaskau R.
Kiskatinaw River
Bear L.
Wapiti River
Sturgeon L.
Little Smoky R.
Snipe Lake
East Prairie R.
Pinto Cr.
Big Mountain Cr.
Smoky
Latornell R.
Simonette River
Goose River
Iosegun
Swan River
Freeman River
Timeu Cr.
Coutts R.
Red Deer Cr.
Belcourt Cr.
Narraway River
Nose Creek
Cutbank River
Wolf Cr.
Kakwa River
Prairie Cr.
Copton Cr.
Smoky R.
Simonette R.
Deep Valley Cr
Smoky River
Little Smoky
Sakwatamau R.
Two Cr.
River
Athabasca River
Windfall Cr.
Oldman Cr.
Athabasca River
Paddle River
Sheep Creek
Muskee R.
Berland River
Muddywater River
WILLMORE WILDERNESS PARK
Smoky R.
Wildhay R.
Pinto
Creek
Wildhay River
Oldman Cr.
Sundance Cr.
Edison R.
McLeod River
Wolf Cr.
Chip Lake
Lac Ste. Anne
Isle L.
Wabamun L.
JASPER NATIONAL PARK

To Jasper
(see YELLOWHEAD HIGHWAY section)

To Edmonton

Area; 10 sites, water pump, partial hookups, public phone, beach, fishing, informal boat launch. Camping fee $5.50. The Kinusoo Lodge Ski Area has 10 runs, artificial snow, equipment rentals and ski lessons.

B 14.8 (23.9 km) **DC 474.7** (764 km) **Junction** of Highways 55 and 28. The highways combine until Highway 28 goes north 1.8 miles/3 km to the community of Cold Lake. If not stopping in Cold Lake, continue on Alberta Highway 55 westbound.

Cold Lake

Located at the end of Alberta Highway 28. **Population**: 4,000. **Emergency Services: RCMP**, phone 594-3301. **Hospital and Ambulance**, phone 639-3322. **Fire Department**, phone 639-3131. **Visitor Information**: Tourist information booth located on top of a hill in an A-frame overlooking the lake, downtown and marina area. Open May to September.

Elevation: 1,780 feet/543m. **Private Aircraft**: Cold Lake Municipal Airport, located 3.7 miles/6 km west of town; elev. 1,787 feet/546m; length 2,953 feet/900m; asphalt; fuel 80, 100, Jet B.

Cold Lake was incorporated in 1957 as a result of construction of the nearby Canadian Forces base. The town is one of the fastest growing communities in the area.

Visitor facilities include three motels, several restaurants, retail and grocery stores, and service stations with major-repair facilities. Recreational facilities include an ice arena, ball diamonds, tennis courts and public library. **Cold Lake** Provincial Park, 3 miles/5 km east of town via an access road, has 117 campsites, pump and tap water, full hookups, dump station, showers, public phone, beach, fishing and boat launch. Camping fee $13 and up.

Cold Lake M.D. Park in town has 50 sites, tap water, full hookups, dump station, showers, public phone, beach, fishing, boat launch. Camping fee $9 and up.

Northern Woods & Waters Route Log

(continued)

B 17.5 (28.2 km) **DC 471.8** (759.2 km) Cold Lake Municipal Airport to north 2.4 miles/4 km via access road.

B 18.4 (29.6 km) **DC 470.9** (757.8 km) Bridge over Marie Creek.

B 20.6 (33.1 km) **DC 469** (754.7 km) **Junction** with side road north 15 miles/25 km to the Cold Lake fish hatchery and to **English Bay** Provincial Recreation Area; 30 sites, water pump, beach, fishing, boat launch. Camping fee $5.50.

B 21.5 (34.6 km) **DC 468** (753.2 km) **Junction** with Highway 897 (Primrose Lake Road) north 12 miles/20 km to **Ethel Lake** Provincial Recreation Area; 12 sites, water pump, public phone, beach, fishing, boat launch. Camping fee $5.50.

B 21.6 (34.7 km) **DC 467.9** (753.1 km) Small community of Riverhurst (no services).

B 26.7 (42.9 km) **DC 462.9** (744.9 km) **Junction** with Highway 892 south 11 miles/18 km to Ardmore and to Alberta Highway 28. **Junction** with side road north 4 miles/6.4 km to **Crane Lake** East Provincial Recreation Area; 28 sites, water pump, beach, fishing and boat launch.

B 29.8 (47.9 km) **DC 459.8** (739.9 km) **Junction** with side road north 3 miles/5 km to **Crane Lake** West Provincial Recreation Area; 27 sites, water pump, public phone, beach, fishing and boat launch.

B 32.6 (52.5 km) **DC 456.9** (735.3 km) Side road south 1.2 miles/2 km to Lessard.

B 36.5 (58.8 km) **DC 453** (729 km) Bridge over Jackfish Creek.

B 38.3 (61.7 km) **DC 451.2** (726.1 km) **LA COREY** (pop. 62) and **junction** with Alberta Highway 41 south 12 miles/20 km to Bonnyville. La Corey has a small store and service station.

B 42.4 (68.2 km) **DC 447.2** (719.6 km) **Junction** with side road south 1.8 miles/3 km to a large (pick your own) strawberry farm.

B 44.2 (71.1 km) **DC 445.3** (716.7 km) Iron River (no services).

B 44.4 (71.4 km) **DC 445.1** (716.3 km) **Junction** with access road north 6 miles/10 km to **Manatokan Lake** Provincial Recreation Area; 11 sites, partial hookups, water pump, fishing, boat launch.

B 44.5 (71.6 km) **DC 445** (716.2 km) Entering Improvement District 18 and Lac La Biche National Forest westbound.

B 45.7 (73.5 km) **DC 443.9** (714.3 km) Bridge over Manatokan Creek.

B 47.9 (77.1 km) **DC 441.6** (710.7 km) **Junction** with side road 24 miles/40 km north to **Wolf Lake** and campground; 64 sites, partial hookups, water pump, fishing, boat launch. Camping fee $7.50.

B 49.4 (79.5 km) **DC 440.1** (708.3 km) Picturesque old church to south.

B 56.4 (90.8 km) **DC 433.1** (697 km) Bridge over the Sand River.

B 57.1 (91.9 km) **DC 432.4** (695.9 km) Side road south to Glendon.

B 59.5 (95.8 km) **DC 430** (692 km) **Junction** with access road north 20 miles/32 km to **Seibert Lake** and campground; 43 sites, water pump, partial hookups, fishing, boat launch. Camping fee $5.50.

B 61.2 (98.5 km) **DC 428.3** (689.3 km) **Junction** with Highway 881 south to the communities of Goodridge and Mallaig, and to Alberta Highway 28A.

B 64.1 (103.1 km) **DC 425.5** (684.7 km) Entering Beaver Lake Ranger District westbound.

B 64.2 (103.3 km) **DC 425.3** (684.5 km) Small store, gas station and pay phone to south.

B 65.1 (104.8 km) **DC 424.4** (683 km) Highway maintenance yard and stockpiles to north.

B 69.2 (111.3 km) **DC 420.4** (676.5 km) Access road north 4 miles/6.4 km to Frenchman Lake.

B 70.1 (112.8 km) **DC 419.4** (675 km) **Private Aircraft**: Grass airstrip to south; elev. 1,890 feet/600m; length 1,750 feet/563m; unattended.

B 72.3 (116.3 km) **DC 417.3** (671.5 km) **Junction** with Highway 867, which leads 2.5 miles/4 km to the community of Fork Lake (no services).

B 74.5 (119.9 km) **DC 415.1** (667.9 km) Fork Lake visible to south.

B 74.6 (120 km) **DC 415** (667.8 km) **Fork Lake** Campground to south; 46 sites, partial hookups, water pump, phone, beach, fishing, boat launch. Camping fee $7.50.

B 75 (120.7 km) **DC 414.5** (667.1 km) Community of **RICH LAKE** to north. Rich Lake has a small grocery store/confectionery and gas station.

Access road north to Lakeland Provincial Park and Recreation Area, Alberta's third largest park. **Ironwood Lake** Campground, 10 miles/16 km north, has 20 sites, partial hookups, water pump, fishing and boat launch. Camping fee $5.50. **Pinehurst Lake** Campground, located 16 miles/26 km north, has 70 sites, partial hookups, water pump, picnic tables, shelter, beach, fishing and boat launch. Camping fee $5.50. The recreation area is also accessible from **Milepost B 90.1** and from **Milepost B 96.**

B 76 (122.3 km) **DC 413.5** (665.5 km) Rich Lake Community Centre to north.

B 82.6 (133 km) **DC 406.9** (654.8 km) **Junction** with Highway 866 south to the communities of McRae and Boyne Lake.

B 90.1 (145 km) **DC 399.4** (642.8 km) **Junction** with access road that leads north 3.6 miles/6 km and then east 20 miles/32 km to Lakeland Provincial Park and Recreation Area.

B 91.5 (147.3 km) **DC 398** (640.5 km) Craigend Community Hall to south.

B 93.5 (150.5 km) **DC 396** (637.3 km) **Junction** with Alberta Highway 36 south 11 miles/18 km to the Kikino Metis settlement and then 34 miles/54 km to Alberta Highway 28A.

B 96 (154.5 km) **DC 393.5** (633.3 km) **Junction** with secondary road west to Hylo. A secondary access road to east leads 22 miles/35 km to Lakeland Provincial Park.

B 98.1 (157.8 km) **DC 391.5** (630 km) Bridge over the Beaver River.

B 99.7 (160.5 km) **DC 389.8** (627.3 km) Second bridge over the Beaver River.

B 100.5 (161.8 km) **DC 389** (626 km) **Junction** with access road east 7 miles/12 km to the Spruce Point Campground on **Beaver Lake**; 265 sites, full hookups, water pump, showers, dump station, public phone, teepee rentals, picnic tables, shelter, beach, fishing, boat launch and boat rentals.

B 101.7 (163.7 km) **DC 387.8** (624.1 km) Third bridge over the Beaver River.

B 104.5 (168.1 km) **DC 385.1** (619.7 km) Roadside turnout with litter barrels and historic plaque.

B 104.7 (168.5 km) **DC 384.8** (619.3 km) Entering Lac La Biche westbound.

B 105 (169 km) **DC 384.5** (618.8 km) **Junction** with side road east 2.5 miles/4 km to **Beaver Lake** Provincial Recreation Area; 100 sites, partial hookups, water pump, fishing, boat launch. Camping fee $7.50.

B 105.9 (170.5 km) **DC 383.6** (617.3 km) **Junction** with Highway 881 north 7 miles/11 km to Sir Winston Churchill Provincial Park and Campground; 72 sites, full hookups, pump and tap water, showers, dump station, beach, fishing, boat launch. Camping fee $10.75. **Touchwood Lake** Campground is located 8 miles/30 km north and east on Highway 881 and then 18 miles/30 km east on an access road; 75 sites, partial hookups, water pump, beach, fishing, boat launch. Camping fee $7.50.

Downtown Lac La Biche is just east of the Highway 881 junction.

Lac La Biche

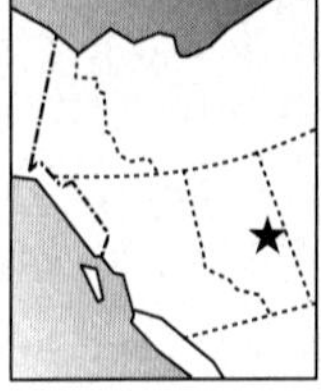

B 106 (170.6 km) **DC 383.5** (617.2 km) Located 134 miles/215 km northeast of Edmonton on Alberta Highway 55. **Population**: 2,550. **Emergency Services: RCMP**, phone 623-4380. **Hospital**, phone 623-4404. **Ambulance**, phone 623-2142. **Fire Department**, phone 623-4311.

Visitor Information: Tourist information booth at the west end of town on Highway 55, phone 623-4804. Open during the summer months only. Town office, located in McArthur Place, phone 623-4323.

Elevation: 1,840 feet/561m. **Private Aircraft**: Lac La Biche Municipal Airport, 1.8 miles/3 km west of town; elev. 1,825 feet/556m; length 3,500 feet/1,067m; asphalt; fuel 80, 100, Jet B.

Lac La Biche's roots go back to 1798 and establishment of a Hudson's Bay Co. trading post. In 1853, Father Albert La Comb built a mission in the area. In 1855 the mission was moved 7 miles east to its present site on the south shore of the lake. Located between the Athabasca, Mackenzie and Churchill river systems, the mission became the transportation centre of the north. Today, Lac La Biche is a major jumping-off point for the surrounding area.

Lakeland Provincial Park is a 15- to 29-mile/24- to 47-km drive east of town. The park became Alberta's third largest park in 1992 and showcases some of Alberta's finest wilderness lakes. Alberta is emphasizing non-consumptive recreational opportunities in the park, and camping areas are located near, rather than within, the park (see **Milepost B 75** and **Milepost B 105.9**).

Two of the park's special features appeal to canoeists and cross country skiers. Alberta's first circle-tour canoe route is expected to be completely developed by summer 1994 around a cluster of lakes in the park, and the Shaw Lake Nordic Ski Area offers 12 miles/20 km of the most scenic groomed trails in Alberta. The adjacent recreation area contains four provincial campgrounds, numerous sandy beaches and a designated trophy lake; **Seibert Lake** is accessible by four-wheel drive only. ▲

Sir Winston Churchill Provincial Park is located on an island in Lac La Biche, joined to the mainland by a causeway (see **Milepost B 105.9**). This island features an old-growth forest that escaped the fires that destroyed the boreal forest growth around the lake. In 1920 the island and the shores of Lac La Biche were designated as a bird sanctuary. Today, bird watchers can view more than 200 species of birds. ▲

Syncrude oil sands outside Fort McMurray. *(Alberta Tourism)*

Northern Woods & Waters Route Log

(continued)

B 107.4 (172.8 km) **DC 382.2** (615 km) Turnoff to north to Lac La Biche airport.

B 108.7 (174.9 km) **DC 380.8** (612.9 km) **Junction** with Highway 633 southwest 9.3 miles/15 km to **Missawawi Lake** Campground; 20 sites, partial hookups, water pump, fishing, boat launch. Camping fee $5.50. ▲

B 112.4 (180.9 km) **DC 377.1** (606.9 km) Access road north 1.8 miles/3 km to Lac La Biche mission historic site.

B 116 (186.6 km) **DC 373.6** (601.2 km) Old mission road to the north.

B 122.1 (196.5 km) **DC 367.4** (591.3 km) **Junction** with Highway 858 north 1.6 miles/2.6 km to **PLAMONDON** (pop. 260). Plamondon has a hotel, restaurants, service stations with minor-repair facilities, car wash, curling rink and museum. The museum, a church built in 1911, has many artifacts that depict the history of the Plamondon area.

Highway 858 continues north 7.5 miles/12 km beyond a bird sanctuary to Plamondon Beach Provincial Recreation Area; 69 sites, partial hookups, shelter, water pump, beach, fishing. Camping fee $5.50. ▲

A side road leads south from this junction to Venice.

B 129.2 (207.9 km) **DC 360.3** (579.9 km) Entering Athabasca County westbound.

B 129.3 (208 km) **DC 360.2** (579.8 km) Access road north to Charron Lake County Recreation Area.

B 130.2 (209.5 km) **DC 359.3** (578.3 km) Atmore; cafe, service station, small store.

B 131.2 (211.2 km) **DC 358.3** (576.6 km) **Junction** with Alberta Highway 63 north 150 miles/250 km to Fort McMurray. (See side road log of HIGHWAY 63 on page 647).

B 134.2 (216 km) **DC 355.3** (571.8 km) Side road north 4 miles/7 km to a landfill.

B 135.6 (218.2 km) **DC 353.9** (569.6 km) **GRASSLAND** (pop. 66); motel, restaurants, service stations with repair facilities, store.

B 136 (218.8 km) **DC 353.6** (569 km) Small ornate Ukrainian Orthodox church to south.

B 136.3 (219.3 km) **DC 353.3** (568.5 km) Side road north 5 miles/8 km to a landfill.

B 138.9 (223.5 km) **DC 350.6** (564.3 km) **Junction** with access road west and north to a large pulp mill.

B 142.3 (229 km) **DC 347.2** (558.8 km) Spruce Valley Road to north.

B 144.4 (232.4 km) **DC 345.1** (555.4 km) Hamlet of Donatville; small store, gas, pay phone. Side road east 12 miles/20 km to North Buck Lake.

B 145.5 (234.1 km) **DC 344.1** (553.7 km) **Junction** with Alberta Highway 63 south 11 miles/17 km to Boyle and 55 miles/89 km to Alberta Highway 28. Hope Lake Campground, located 2 miles/3.2 km south and 2 miles/3.2 km east, has 40 sites, partial hookups, shelter and water pump. ▲

B 147 (236.5 km) **DC 342.6** (551.3 km) Railroad crossing.

B 148 (238.2 km) **DC 341.5** (549.6 km) Construction and paving of a new side road north 6 miles/10 km to the Alberta Pacific (ALPAC) sawmill complex. Completion of road expected summer 1994.

B 148.8 (239.4 km) **DC 340.8** (548.4 km) Bridge over Flat Bed Creek.

B 149.8 (241.1 km) **DC 339.7** (546.7 km) Roadside turnout with a historical plaque describing the former community of Amber Valley to north.

B 150.5 (242.2 km) **DC 339** (545.6 km) Amber Valley Road to south. Old community centre to north.

B 150.6 (242.3 km) **DC 338.9** (545.5 km) Bridge over Pine Creek.

B 154.5 (248.7 km) **DC 335** (539.1 km) Furguson Road to south.

B 156.6 (252 km) **DC 332.9** (535.8 km) Babette Road to south.

B 158.5 (255.2 km) **DC 330.9** (532.6 km) **Junction** with forestry access road.

B 161.9 (260.6 km) **DC 327.6** (527.2 km) **Junction** with Highway 827 south. Access road north 9 miles/15 km to **Jackfish Lake** Campground; 26 sites, partial hookups, water pump, fishing, boat launch. Camping fee $7. ▲

B 163.9 (263.8 km) **DC 325.6** (524 km) **Junction** with Wood Heights Road.

B 164.7 (265 km) **DC 324.9** (522.8 km) **Junction** with Highway 813 north 38 miles/62 km to the community of Calling Lake and **Calling Lake** Provincial Park; 25 sites, boat launch, firewood, fishing. **Rock Island Lake** and Tanasiuk Campground are located 59 miles/96 km north of this junction; 51 sites, fishing, boat launch. ▲

B 164.9 (265.3 km) **DC 324.7** (522.5 km) Athabasca River visible to north. Athabasca Rivers Edge Campground has 25 sites, partial hookups, tap water, public phone and picnic tables. Camping fee $7. ▲

Athabasca

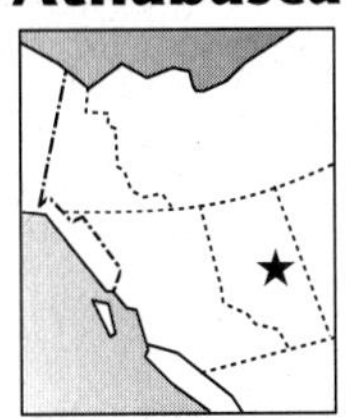

B 165 (265.5 km) **DC 324.5** (522.3 km) Located 91 miles/147 km north of Edmonton at the junction of Highways 55 and 2. **Population:** 2,000. **Emergency Services: RCMP,** phone 675-4252. **Hospital and Ambulance,** phone 675-2261. **Fire Department,** phone 675-2200.

Visitor Information: Tourist information booth along the Athabasca River near the grain elevators in an old train caboose. Open during the summer months only.

Elevation: 1,750 feet/527m. **Private Aircraft:** Athabasca Municipal Airport, 3 miles/5 km east at the junction of Highways 2 and 827; elev. 1,880 feet/574m; length 3,000 feet/914m; asphalt; fuel 80, 100.

Visitor facilities include a hotel, three motels, many restaurants, retail and grocery outlets, public library, hockey and curling rink, tennis courts and a swimming pool. A nine-hole golf course is 1.2 miles/2 km north on Highway 813. The course has a clubhouse, driving range and grass greens.

Athabasca Landing was founded by the Hudson's Bay Co. in 1874, when the Athabasca Landing Trail was established and a trading post was constructed. In its early years, Athabasca was a busy transshipment point for freight movement in northwestern Canada. The Athabasca Landing Trail, running from Athabasca south 99 miles/160 km to Edmonton, became in 1880 the first registered highway in Alberta. The railroad arrived in Athabasca in 1912.

The Athabasca Landing Trail, a 76-mile/121-km corridor from Gibbons to Athabasca, runs roughly parallel to Highway 2 and served the Indians long before the arrival of the Europeans. It became the overland route connecting the Athabasca and north Saskatchewan rivers. The Hudson's Bay Co. developed the trail in 1875, and for the next 35 years it played a vital role in the development of the North. The first part of the old trail has been lost to the plough, and today the trail begins 24 miles/40 km north of Edmonton.

Northern Woods & Waters Route Log

(continued)

ALBERTA HIGHWAY 2

B 165.1 (265.7 km) **DC 324.4** (522.1 km) Bridge over the Tawatinaw River.

B 165.8 (266.8 km) **DC 323.7** (521 km) Entrance to Athabasca University to south.

B 173.9 (279.8 km) **DC 315.7** (508 km) **Junction** with side road west to the communities of Baptiste Lake and Sunset Beach.

B 176 (283.2 km) **DC 313.6** (504.6 km) Side road to west 1.2 miles/2 km to a landfill.

B 176.3 (283.8 km) **DC 313.2** (504 km) Bridge over Baptiste Creek.

B 178.2 (286.8 km) **DC 311.3** (501 km) White Gull to west via Groesmont Road.

B 179.3 (288.5 km) **DC 310.3** (499.3 km) Access road east 2.5 miles/4 km and then north 5 miles/8 km to **Island Lake** Provincial Recreation Campground; 11 sites, water pump, partial hookups, fishing, boat launch. Camping fee $7. **Chain Lakes** Campground, located another 7 miles/12 km north, has 20 sites, partial hookups, water pump, fishing and boat launch. Electric motors only. Camping fee $5.50.

B 180.6 (290.6 km) **DC 309** (497.2 km) Community of Island Lake South (pop. 122) to east.

B 181.1 (291.4 km) **DC 308.5** (496.4 km) Island Lake visible to east.

B 181.4 (292 km) **DC 308** (495.6 km) North entrance east into Island Lake Recreation Area (see **Milepost B 179.3**).

B 182 (293 km) **DC 307.5** (494.8 km) Island Lake store and gas station to east.

B 183.2 (294.8 km) **DC 306.3** (493 km) Access road east 12 miles/20 km to Chain Lakes.

B 185.6 (298.7 km) **DC 303.9** (489.1 km) Access road west 1.2 miles/2 km to Ghost Lake.

B 186.7 (300.4 km) **DC 302.8** (487.3 km) Lawrence Lake visible to west.

B 193.7 (311.8 km) **DC 295.8** (476 km) **Lawrence Lake** Campground to west; 27 sites, partial hookups, water pump, fishing, boat launch. Camping fee $7.50.

B 193.9 (312 km) **DC 295.7** (475.8 km) Lawrence Lake visible to south.

B 199.7 (321.3 km) **DC 289.9** (466.5 km) Creek crossing.

B 201.1 (323.7 km) **DC 288.4** (464.1 km) Secondary side road north 14 miles/23 km to Smith.

B 206.1 (331.7 km) **DC 283.4** (456.1 km) Secondary side road north 5.5 miles/9 km to Hondo.

B 210.2 (338.3 km) **DC 279.3** (449.5 km) **Junction** with Alberta Highway 44 south 66 miles/105 km to Westlock and to Alberta Highway 18. Chisholm Provincial Recreation Area is 6 miles/10 km south; eight sites, picnic tables, no hookups, no camping fee.

B 210.8 (339.3 km) **DC 278.7** (448.5 km) Roadside turnout for large trucks on both sides of highway.

B 212.3 (341.6 km) **DC 277.3** (446.2 km) **Junction** with Highway 2A north 1.8 miles/3 km to Hondo (no services) and 9 miles/15 km to **SMITH** (pop. 250). Smith has a hotel, restaurant, small store and service station with minor-repair facilities. A secondary road continues north and west out of Smith, along the Slave River, and rejoins the highway at **Milepost B 236.1**. **Fawcett Lake** Resort is 24 miles/39 km northeast of Smith; 324 sites, dump station, tap water, showers, public phone, laundry, beach, boat launch, fishing, boat and canoe rentals, store, concession/food service. **West Fawcett Lake** Campground, 15 miles/25 km north of Smith, has 28 sites, partial hookups, water pump, fishing and boat launch. Camping fee $7.50.

B 212.5 (341.9 km) **DC 277.1** (445.9 km) Railroad crossing.

B 214.1 (344.6 km) **DC 275.4** (443.2 km) Bridge over the Athabasca River. Entering Slave Lake Ranger District westbound.

B 215 (346 km) **DC 274.5** (441.8 km) Highway maintenance yard to north.

B 222.8 (358.6 km) **DC 266.7** (429.2 km) Bridge over the Saulteaux River.

B 226 (363.7 km) **DC 263.5** (424.1 km) Forest cutline to south.

B 230.4 (370.8 km) **DC 259.1** (417 km) Bridge over the Otauwau River.

B 235.5 (379 km) **DC 254** (408.8 km) Divided highway begins westbound.

B 236.1 (380 km) **DC 253.4** (407.8 km) **Junction** with loop road from Smith. **Lesser Slave River** Provincial Recreation Area located 5.5 miles/9 km north on the return road has 11 sites, partial hookups, water pump, fishing and picnic area. Camping fee $5.50.

B 239.5 (385.5 km) **DC 250** (402.3 km) Mitsue Provincial Recreation Area to north; 12 sites, water pump, fishing and picnic tables.

B 243.4 (391.7 km) **DC 246.1** (396.1 km) Mitsue Lake industrial and logging road.

B 245.1 (394.5 km) **DC 244.4** (393.3 km) Poplar Lane to north.

B 245.7 (395.5 km) **DC 243.8** (392.3 km) Heavy-truck inspection and weigh station to south.

B 246.6 (396.8 km) **DC 243** (391 km) **Junction** with Alberta Highway 88 (Bicentennial Highway), which leads north to Lesser Slave Lake Provincial Park (see description following); 105 miles/168 km to the community of Red Earth Creek; and 255 miles/410 km to Fort Vermilion. Highway 88 is paved to Red Earth Creek; the remainder of the road to Fort Vermilion is gravel and in poor condition. In wet weather the road can be slippery, muddy and rutted.

Lesser Slave Lake Provincial Park, along the east shore of Lesser Slave Lake, is divided into three different recreational areas. Devonshire Beach day-use area is 3.6 miles/6 km north on Highway 88. Northshore day-use area, 7 miles/11 km north on Highway 88, has 14 picnic sites, shelter, water pump and a fish-cleaning stand. Martin River Campground, 18 miles/30 km north on Highway 88, has 113 sites, dump station, public phone, ski trails, hiking trails, beach, fishing and tap water.

B 247.2 (397.8 km) **DC 242.3** (390 km) Bridge over Sawridge Creek.

Slave Lake

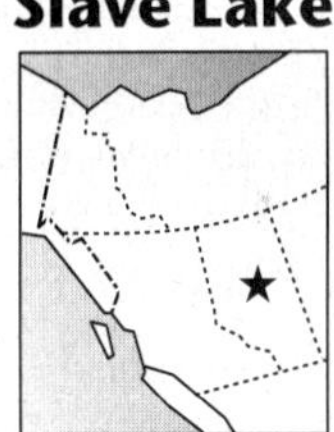

B 247.4 (398.1 km) **DC 242.2** (389.7 km) Located on the southeast shore of Lesser Slave Lake, 152 miles/245 km northwest of Edmonton. **Population:** 5,800. **Emergency Services: RCMP,** phone 849-3045. **Hospital,** phone 324-3732. **Ambulance,** phone 849-3614. **Fire Department,** phone 849-3511.

Visitor Information: In a small building on the service road just off Highway 2, phone 849-4611. Open mid-May to mid-September. The town office is located at 328 2nd St. NE, phone 849-3606.

Elevation: 1,900 feet/581m. **Private Aircraft:** Slave Lake Airport; elev. 1,900 feet/581m; length 5,000 feet/1,524m; asphalt; fuel 80, 100, Jet B.

Originally known as Sawridge when it was founded in the 1880s, Slave Lake was an important jumping-off point for steamboat traffic that carried prospectors bound for the Yukon and the Klondike gold rushes. Early settlers included the Metis and Cree Indians. Today, their descendants contribute to the rich cultural heritage of this well-integrated community.

Visitor facilities include a hotel, two motels, several restaurants and fast-food outlets, numerous stores, service stations with major-repair facilities and car washes.

Recreational facilities include a public library, movie theatre, curling rink, ball diamonds, racquetball and tennis courts, soccer field, parks, miniature golf course and cross-country ski trails. The Gilwood Golf and Country Club, 6 miles/10 km north on Highway 88, has nine holes, clubhouse, licensed restaurant, driving range, practice greens, and cart and club rentals.

Lesser Slave Lake Provincial Park,

Lesser Slave Lake offers good fishing and camping opportunities. (Alberta Tourism)

located north of Slave Lake on Highway 88, stretches along the northeastern shore of Lesser Slave Lake, with 5 miles/8 km of beautiful sandy beaches against a backdrop of rolling hills and luxurious growth of spruce, pine and poplar trees. The park consists of a number of campsites and day-use areas (see **Milepost B 246.6**).

Northern Woods & Waters Route Log

(continued)

B 248.2 (399.4 km) **DC 241.3** (388.4 km) Turnoff to Slave Lake industrial area and Sawridge Recreation Area to north. The Sawridge Campground has 32 sites with partial hookups, water pump, showers, picnic tables, fireplaces, firewood, stove, beach, fishing, boat rentals and hiking trails.

B 249.5 (401.6 km) **DC 240** (386.2 km) Creek crossing.

B 250.2 (402.7 km) **DC 239.3** (385.1 km) Entering Sawridge Indian Reserve westbound.

B 253.1 (407.3 km) **DC 236.4** (380.5 km) Turnout with litter barrels to north. Leaving Sawridge Indian Reserve westbound.

B 255.2 (410.7 km) **DC 234.3** (377.1 km) Wagner to north. Landfill to south.

B 257.6 (414.5 km) **DC 232** (373.3 km) Creek crossing. Entering Kinuso Ranger District westbound.

B 257.9 (415.1 km) **DC 231.6** (372.7 km) Secondary road north to Wagner.

B 259.1 (417 km) **DC 230.4** (370.8 km) Access road north 0.6 mile/1 km to **WIDEWATER** (pop. 203). Widewater has a small store, gas station and pay phone.

B 261.2 (420.4 km) **DC 228.4** (367.6 km) **CANYON CREEK** (pop. 164) to north. Canyon Creek has a hotel, grocery store, gas station and pay phone.

B 265.6 (427.4 km) **DC 223.9** (360.4 km) Access road north 1.8 miles/3 km to Assineau (no services).

B 266.1 (428.3 km) **DC 223.4** (359.5 km) Assineau River Campground to north; 21 sites, partial hookups, water pump, picnic tables and firewood. Camping fee $5.50.

B 266.2 (428.5 km) **DC 223.3** (359.3 km) Bridge over the Assineau River.

B 272.5 (438.6 km) **DC 217** (349.2 km) Bridge over Eula Creek.

B 273.3 (439.8 km) **DC 216.2** (348 km) **Junction** with Alberta Highway 33 (Grizzly Trail), which leads south to Swan Hills (45 miles/72 km) and Barrhead (108 miles/174 km) to junction with Alberta Highway 43 (136 miles/219 km).

B 275.5 (443.3 km) **DC 214.1** (344.5 km) Bridge over the Swan River.

B 275.8 (443.9 km) **DC 213.7** (343.9 km) **Junction** with side road north 1.2 miles/2 km to **KINUSO** (pop. 282); hotel, cafe, store, service station and museum.

B 276.5 (444.9 km) **DC 213.1** (342.9 km) Side road north to Kinuso ranger station.

B 277 (445.7 km) **DC 212.6** (342.1 km) Bridge over Strawberry Creek.

B 278.4 (448 km) **DC 211.1** (339.8 km) Access road north 7 miles/11 km to Spruce Point Park Campground; 126 sites, partial hookups, dump station, water pump, showers, wheelchair-accessible washroom, shelter, store, concession, beach, boat launch, boat rentals, fishing, fireplaces and firewood. Camping fee $10.

B 279.3 (449.5 km) **DC 210.2** (338.3 km) Strawberry Creek Cafe and service station to north.

B 279.4 (449.7 km) **DC 210.1** (338.1 km) Landfill to south.

B 283 (455.5 km) **DC 206.5** (332.3 km) Creek crossing.

B 284 (457 km) **DC 205.6** (330.8 km) **FAUST** (pop. 344) to north. Faust has a hotel, restaurant, gas, two stores and a laundromat.

B 284.7 (458.2 km) **DC 204.8** (329.6 km) Side road north to the Faust RCMP detachment.

B 289.1 (465.2 km) **DC 200.4** (322.5 km) Creek crossing. Entering Driftpile Indian Reserve westbound.

B 290 (466.4 km) **DC 199.7** (321.4 km) Small cafe and gas station to north.

B 291.3 (468.8 km) **DC 198.2** (319 km) Bridge over the Driftpile River.

B 293 (471.6 km) **DC 196.5** (316.2 km) Leaving Driftpile Indian Reserve westbound.

B 296 (476.7 km) **DC 193.3** (311.1 km) Turnouts with litter barrels on both sides of highway.

B 298 (479.5 km) **DC 191.6** (308.3 km) **JOUSSARD** (pop. 270) to north on access road. Joussard has a small store, service station and cafe. Joussard Lakeshore Campground, located on the south shore of **Lesser Slave Lake,** has 25 sites, full hookups, dump station, tap water, showers, picnic tables, firewood, fishing and boat launch. Camping fee $8 and up.

B 299.9 (482.7 km) **DC 190** (305.1 km) Entering High Prairie Ranger District westbound.

B 304.4 (489.8 km) **DC 185.2** (298 km) Entering Sucker Creek Indian Reserve westbound.

B 305.3 (491.3 km) **DC 184.2** (296.5 km) Bridge over Sucker Creek.

B 306.3 (492.9 km) **DC 183.2** (294.9 km) Sucker Creek Cafe to north.

B 308.3 (496.2 km) **DC 181.3** (291.7 km) Small cafe and gas station to north.

B 309 (497.2 km) **DC 180.6** (290.7 km) Roadside turnout to north with litter barrels and historical point of interest.

B 309.3 (497.8 km) **DC 180.2** (290 km) **Junction** with Highway 750 northeast to Alberta Highway 88 (Bicentennial Highway), 103 miles/165 km. Highway 750 also provides access to Grouard, 13 miles/21 km north, site of St. Bernard Mission Church and the Native Cultural Arts Museum. Hilliard's Bay Provincial Park, 8 miles/13 km east of Grouard on **Lesser Slave Lake,** has 189 sites, water, phone, beach and fishing.

B 309.8 (498.6 km) **DC 179.7** (289.2 km) Small store and gas to north.

B 312.4 (502.8 km) **DC 177.1** (285 km) **ENILDA** (pop. 128); small store and gas station.

B 313.5 (504.5 km) **DC 176** (283.3 km) East Prairie settlement and sawmill to south. Turnouts on both sides of highway.

B 313.7 (504.8 km) **DC 175.9** (283 km) Bridge over the East Prairie River.

B 318.2 (512 km) **DC 171.4** (275.8 km) High Prairie Lions Campground to north; 14 sites, partial hookups, pump, picnic tables, shelter and firewood. Camping fee $5.

B 318.6 (512.8 km) **DC 170.9** (275 km) Entering High Prairie westbound.

High Prairie

B 319.6 (514.3 km) **DC 169.9** (273.5 km) Located 230 miles/370 km northwest of Edmonton, 78 miles/126 km southeast of Peace River. **Population:** 2,970. **Emergency Services: RCMP,** phone 523-3378. **Hospital and Ambulance,** phone 523-3341. **Fire Department,** phone 523-3388.

Visitor Information: Tourist information centre in the centre of town on the north side of Highway 2. Open summer months only. The High Prairie town office is downtown, phone 523-3388.

Elevation: 1,850 feet/602m. **Private Aircraft:** High Prairie Regional Airport, 3 miles/5 km south on Highway 749; elev. 1,850 feet/602m; length 3,000 feet/914m;

asphalt; fuel 80, 100.

While the High Prairie area was being settled by homesteaders in the late 19th century, the arrival of the railroad in 1914 heralded the beginning of High Prairie as a town. A busy agricultural center, this picturesque community of almost 3,000 people also serves the surrounding forest and oil field industries.

Visitor facilities include four motels, restaurants, retail and grocery stores, service stations with major-repair facilities, a library, an art gallery and the High Prairie District Museum, located in the centre of town on Highway 2 and part of the library complex. The museum features pioneer artifacts depicting the history of the region. Visitors welcome. Open Tuesday through Saturday 9 A.M. to 5 P.M.; extended hours during the summer.

Recreational facilities include a swimming pool, tennis courts, skating rink, curling rink, hockey arena and ball diamonds. The High Prairie Golf Course, located 5 miles/8 km west of town and south of Highway 2, has nine holes, driving range, clubhouse with licensed dining, pro shop and carts for rent.

Northern Woods & Waters Route Log

(continued)

B 319.7 (514.5 km) **DC 169.8** (273.3 km) **Junction** with Highway 749 south 20 miles/32 km to Banana Belt Park on the West Prairie River; six campsites, picnic tables and water pump. No camping fee. ▲

Highway 749 leads north out of High Prairie 12 miles/20 km and then becomes Highway 679, which leads west 18 miles/30 km and rejoins Highway 2 at **Milepost B 341.9**. **Winagami Lake** Provincial Park, 20 miles/32 km northwest of High Prairie off Highway 679, is a day-use area and campground. The campground has 63 sites, one site and facility for disabled use, dump station, fishing, boat launch, wading pool, paved trails, bird-viewing platforms with scopes, fireplaces, firewood, shelter and tap water. ♿▲

Hart River Provincial Recreation Area, 24 miles/40 km northwest of High Prairie, is a day-use area with picnic tables, beach, fishing and boat launch.

B 320.2 (515.3 km) **DC 169.3** (272.5 km) Bridge over the West Prairie River.

B 321.1 (516.8 km) **DC 168.4** (271 km) Railroad crossing.

B 324.1 (521.5 km) **DC 165.5** (266.3 km) Creek crossing.

B 324.7 (522.5 km) **DC 164.9** (265.3 km) High Prairie Golf Course to south.

B 328.8 (529.2 km) **DC 160.7** (258.6 km) **Junction** with Alberta Spur Highway 2A west to Highway 43 (see MACKENZIE ROUTE for Highway 43 log). Continue on Highway 2 north to McLennan.

B 329.3 (530 km) **DC 160.2** (257.8 km) Turnout with litter barrels to east.

B 331.4 (533.3 km) **DC 158.1** (254.5 km) Railroad crossing.

B 341.9 (550.3 km) **DC 147.6** (237.5 km) **Junction** with Highway 679 east 7 miles/11 km to **Winagami Lake** Provincial Park. (see **Milepost B 319.7**). ♿▲

B 343 (552 km) **DC 146.5** (235.8 km) Hamlet of Kathleen (no services).

B 348.5 (560.8 km) **DC 141.1** (227 km) Landfill to west.

B 349.5 (562.4 km) **DC 140.1** (225.4 km) Entering McLennan westbound.

McLennan

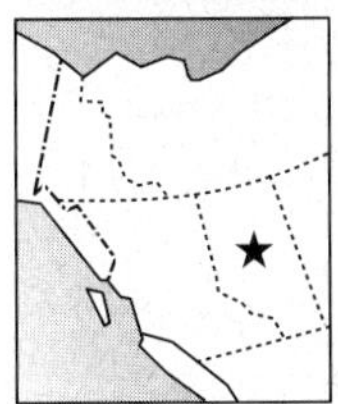

B 350.2 (563.5 km) **DC 139.4** (224.3 km) Located 288 miles/464 km northwest of Edmonton on Highway 2. **Population:** 1,100. **Emergency Services: RCMP**, phone 324-3061. **Hospital and Ambulance**, phone 324-3730. **Fire Department**, phone 324-3811.

Visitor Information: Tourist information centre in town on the north side of Highway 2. Open May to September.

Elevation: 1,920 feet/584m. **Private Aircraft**: Smoky River Regional Airport, 8 miles/13 km west on Highway 2 and 0.6 mile/1 km south on access road, 1.2 miles/2 km south of Donnelly; elev. 1,949 feet/592m; length 2,953 feet/900m; asphalt; fuel 80, 100.

McLennan was founded in 1914 as a divisional point for the Edmonton, Dunvegan and British Columbia railway. It was named after John K. McLennan, then secretary of the railway, by his brother-in-law J.D. McArther, the builder of the railway. In the years since, McLennan has developed from a rustic frontier outpost to a modern community. McLennan is the seat of the Roman Catholic Archdiocese of the Grouard-McLennan area and has a beautiful cathedral. Set on the south shore of Kimiwan Lake, which is at the centre of three major migration flyways (Mississippi, Pacific and Central), the community has chosen the slogan "Bird Capital of Canada."

Visitor facilities include a hotel, motel, restaurants, grocery and retail stores, service stations with major-repair facilities, library, laundromat and a museum housed in an old passenger rail car.

Recreational facilities include an arena, curling rink, tennis courts, ball diamonds and a nine-hole golf course. McLennan Community Campground and Recreation Area, located in town on the south shore of Kimiwan Lake, has 28 sites with hookups, beach, boat launch, licensed dining room and lounge. ▲

Northern Woods & Waters Route Log

(continued)

B 350.8 (564.5 km) **DC 138.8** (223.4 km) Kimiwan Lake visible to north.

B 351 (564.8 km) **DC 138.6** (223 km) Smoky River Regional Golf Course to south; nine holes, pro shop, licensed dining and cart rental. Historical point of interest to north about the Northern Woods & Waters Route.

B 351.5 (565.7 km) **DC 138** (222.1 km) **Junction** with Highway 746 south to Highway 2A.

B 351.6 (565.8 km) **DC 137.9** (222 km) Railroad crossing.

B 358.7 (577.2 km) **DC 130.9** (210.6 km) Donnelly to north, Smoky River Regional Airport to south. **DONNELLY** (pop. 450) has a hotel, restaurants, stores, service stations with repair facilities, and a library. A historic site 3 miles/5 km south of town features a fully operational 1904 Case steam engine.

B 359.7 (578.8 km) **DC 129.9** (209 km) **Junction** of Alberta Highway 49 west, Highway 43 south and Highway 2 north to Peace River and the Mackenzie Highway (see MACKENZIE ROUTE section). The Northern Woods & Waters Route follows Alberta Highway 49 west to Dawson Creek, BC.

ALBERTA HIGHWAY 49

B 361.7 (582.1 km) **DC 127.8** (205.7 km) Large alfalfa-dehydrating plant to the north.

B 362.2 (582.9 km) **DC 127.4** (205 km) Falher Municipal Campground to north; 30 sites, full hookups, tap water, public phone. ▲

B 362.5 (583.3 km) **DC 127.1** (204.5 km) Access road north 1 mile/1.6 km to **FALHER** (pop. 650), named after Father Constant Falher, who arrived in 1912. Falher incorporated in 1929. Falher is known as the "Honey Capital of Canada" and boasts the world's largest replica of a honey bee. The town has a strong agricultural base, with five grain elevators and two alfalfa-processing plants, which produce more than 50,000 tons annually. Visitor facilities include a hotel, motel, stores, restaurants and service stations with major repair. Recreational facilities include an arena, an indoor swimming pool, tennis courts and ball diamonds.

B 367.8 (591.9 km) **DC 121.7** (195.9 km) **Junction** with Highway 744 north 1.8 miles/3 km to Girouxville and on to Peace River. **GIROUXVILLE** (pop. 367) was settled around 1913 and incorporated in 1928. The community has one of the largest museums in Alberta. Opened in 1969, the museum features artifacts recalling Indian life, missionary works, pioneering and trapping, and early machinery and equipment. Open year-round. Small admission fee. Visitor facilities include a hotel, family restaurant, service stations with repair facilities, grocery store, health food store and laundromat.

B 379.4 (610.5 km) **DC 110.2** (177.3 km) *CAUTION: Steep descent westbound and a very rough road (slow down). Construction and rerouting of this 7.5-mile/12-km stretch of road is under way and expected to be completed summer 1994.*

B 381.3 (613.6 km) **DC 108.2** (174.1 km) Access road north to Peavine Creek day-use area; 10 sites, water pump, shelter, picnic area, fireplaces, firewood and boat launch.

B 381.5 (613.9 km) **DC 108.1** (173.9 km) Bridge over the Smoky River.

B 381.7 (614.3 km) **DC 107.8** (173.5 km) Watino to north. Entering Spirit River Ranger District westbound as the highway ascends a steep hill.

B 383.7 (617.5 km) **DC 105.8** (170.3 km) **Junction** with Highway 740 north 5 miles/8 km to Tangent (no services). Highway 740 continues north 30 miles/49.5 km to the Shaftsbury Ferry crossing of the Peace River. North of the crossing, the highway splits, with one way going to Grimshaw and a connection with the Mackenzie Route, and the other to Peace River. (See MACKENZIE ROUTE section.)

B 390.9 (629 km) **DC 98.7** (158.8 km) Access road south 0.6 mile/1 km to Lakeside Golf and Country Club; nine holes and pro shop.

B 391.7 (630.3 km) **DC 97.9** (157.5 km) Eaglesham food and gas station to north.

B 391.9 (630.6 km) **DC 97.7** (157.2 km) **Junction** with Highway 739 north 4 miles/6.4 km to **EAGLESHAM** (pop. 185). Eaglesham has a hotel, motel, restaurant, gas station, library and curling rink. Kieyho Park and day-use area, located 10 miles/16 km north of town on the south shore of the Peace River, has four sites, picnic tables, hiking trails and boat launch.

Agriculture is a key industry in this region. (Brian Calkins)

B 404.6 (651.1 km) **DC 84.9** (136.7 km) Access road north to a small ski slope.

B 411.9 (662.8 km) **DC 77.7** (125 km) **Junction** with Highway 733 south 26 miles/42 km to TeePee Creek and 35.4 miles/57 km to Alberta Highway 34. Access road off Highway 49 leads north 0.6 miles/1 km to **WANHAM** (pop. 250). Settled in 1914, today Wanham is a thriving community with a hotel, restaurant, service station with repair facilities, stores, hockey and curling rink, and museum.

B 413.8 (666 km) **DC 75.7** (121.8 km) Access road south 1.8 miles/3 km to **Dreamers Lake** Campground & Recreation Area; 26 sites, water pump, picnic tables, public phone, boat launch, fishing and a nine hole golf course. Camping fee.

B 416.5 (670.2 km) **DC 73.1** (117.6 km) Railroad crossing.

B 417.8 (672.3 km) **DC 71.8** (115.5 km) Bridge over the Saddle River. Saddle River Campground to south.

B 424.5 (683.2 km) **DC 65** (104.6 km) **Junction** with Alberta Highway 2. Northbound, Highway 2 crosses the Peace River to connect with Alberta Highway 64 to Fort St. John (see side road log page 649) or to Grimshaw at the gateway of the Mackenzie Highway (see MACKENZIE ROUTE section). Southbound, Highway 2 leads through the communities of Sexsmith and Grande Prairie, then west to Dawson Creek (see EAST ACCESS ROUTE section). Continue on Highway 49 for Dawson Creek.

B 425.6 (684.9 km) **DC 63.9** (102.9 km) Bridge over the Spirit River.

B 425.7 (685 km) **DC 63.9** (102.8 km) **Nardham Lake** Campground to north; 15 sites, hookups, picnic tables, water pump, canoeing, fishing. Camping fee $5.

B 426.1 (685.7 km) **DC 63.4** (102.1 km) Entering **RYCROFT** (pop. 534) westbound. Rycroft is located at the crossroads of Highways 49 and 2, en route to "mile zero" of both the Alaska or Mackenzie highways. Rycroft was established with the coming of the railroad in 1912 and was incorporated on March 15, 1944. Visitor facilities include a motel, restaurants, service stations with major-repair facilities, stores, bank, library, ball diamonds, ice arena and tennis courts.

B 427.8 (688.4 km) **DC 61.8** (99.4 km) Access road south 2.4 miles/4 km to golf course; nine holes, licensed dining, clubhouse, pro shop and carts for rent.

B 429.8 (691.7 km) **DC 59.7** (96.1 km) Spirit River Airport entrance, visitor center and St. Elias Ukrainian Church to north.

B 430.5 (692.8 km) **DC 59** (95 km) Entering Spirit River westbound.

Spirit River

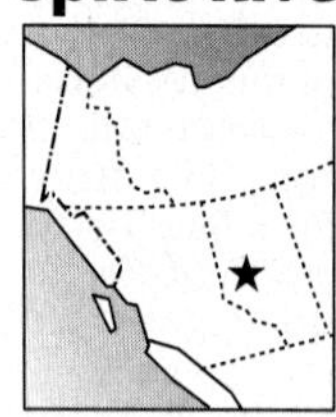

B 430.6 (693 km) **DC 58.9** (94.8 km) Located 221 miles/356 km northwest of Edmonton, 47 miles/76 km north of Grande Prairie, 60 miles/96 km east of Dawson Creek, BC. **Population:** 1,150. **Emergency Services: RCMP**, phone 864-3533. **Hospital**, phone 864-3993. **Ambulance**, phone 864-2453. **Fire Department**, phone 864-3511.

Visitor Information: Tourist information booth located in town on the north side of Highway 49, across from the picturesque St. Elias Ukrainian Orthodox Church. Open summer months only.

Elevation: 2,100 feet/637m. **Private Aircraft**: Spirit River Regional Airport, located on the north side of Highway 49, across from the business district; elev. 2,044 feet/621m; length 3,000 feet/914m; asphalt; fuel 80, 100.

In 1891, a trading post was established along both sides of the original settlement of Spirit River. When the railroad came through in 1913, the community established itself as an agricultural centre. Today, Spirit River is a major trading centre for a large rural population.

Visitor facilities include a hotel, motel, restaurants, retail and grocery stores, service stations, bank and public library. A museum houses artifacts of the early days of Spirit River. Recreational facilities include an arena, curling rink, tennis courts, soccer field and ball diamond. Spirit River Municipal Campground, located in town, has eight sites, partial hookups, tap water, public phone and dump station. Camping fee charged.

Northern Woods & Waters Route Log

(continued)

B 430.9 (693.4 km) **DC 58.7** (94.4 km) **Junction** with Highway 731 south 16 miles/26 km and east 3 miles/5 km to Woking, and then farther east 3 miles/5 km to Alberta Highway 2. Hilltop Recreation Area, located 11.2 miles/18 km south on Highway 731 and then west 7 miles/11 km on Highway 677, and then south 3.6 miles/6 km on Highway 724, has eight sites, water pump and hiking trails. No camping fee.

Chinook Valley Golf Course, 12 miles/20 km south on Highway 741, has nine holes, pro shop and licensed dining.

B 433.9 (698.3 km) **DC 55.6** (89.5 km) **Junction** with Highway 727 north 6 miles/10 km to Devale.

B 436.4 (702.3 km) **DC 53.1** (85.5 km) Creek crossing.

B 441 (709.7 km) **DC 48.5** (78.1 km) Happy Valley Road to south.

B 441.7 (710.9 km) **DC 47.8** (76.9 km) Creek crossing.

B 443.2 (713.3 km) **DC 46.3** (74.5 km) Creek crossing.

B 445.7 (717.2 km) **DC 43.9** (70.6 km) Bridge over Ksituan River.

B 446.1 (717.9 km) **DC 43.4** (69.9 km) Access road north 1.8 miles/3 km to Jackbird day-use area, and 7 miles/11 km to the community of Blueberry Mountain.

B 447.1 (719.5 km) **DC 42.4** (68.3 km) **Junction** with Highway 725 north 4 miles/7 km to **Moonshine Lake** Provincial Park and Campground; 110 sites (23 with power), tap water, dump station, public phone, canoeing, fishing, boat launch, shelter, firewood, ball diamond. Electric motors only. Camping fee $10.75.

B 453.6 (729.9 km) **DC 36** (57.9 km) Forest cutline runs across the highway.

B 454.2 (731 km) **DC 35.3** (56.8 km) Silver Valley Road to north.

B 454.6 (731.6 km) **DC 34.9** (56.2 km) Silver Valley Provincial Recreation Area to north; seven sites, water pump and picnic tables. No camping fee.

B 457.2 (735.8 km) **DC 32.3** (52 km) Microwave tower to north.

B 460.4 (741 km) **DC 29.1** (46.8 km) Gordendale to north (no services).

B 464.1 (746.8 km) **DC 25.5** (41 km) Creek crossing.

B 466.5 (750.8 km) **DC 23** (37 km) Pillsworth Road to north leads 21.7 miles/35 km to Cotillian Campsite; 13 sites, tap water, picnic tables, shelter, firewood and boat launch. No camping fee.

B 468.2 (753.5 km) **DC 21.3** (34.3 km) Small airstrip to south.

B 471.6 (759.1 km) **DC 17.8** (28.7 km) **Junction** with Highway 719 north 5 miles/8 km to Bonanza; gas, food, pay phone.

B 474.9 (764.2 km) **DC 14.7** (23.6 km) Baytree to north; gas, food, pay phone.

B 478.2 (769.6 km) **DC 11.3** (18.2 km) Large roadside turnout with litter barrels and bathrooms to south.

B 480 (772.4 km) **DC 9.6** (15.4 km) Alberta–British Columbia border. NOTE: Alberta observes Mountain standard time. Most of British Columbia observes Pacific standard time. Both observe daylight saving time. See Time Zones in the GENERAL INFORMATION section for details.

B 485.5 (781.3 km) **DC 4.6** (7.4 km) Pouce Coupe River bridge.

B 486.3 (782.7 km) **DC 3.2** (5.1 km) **Junction** with access road north 10 miles/16 km to Rolla and on to the crossing of the Peace River and Clayhurst. South from here, the road leads 3 miles/5 km to Pouce Coupe.

B 487 (783.7 km) **DC 2.5** (4.1 km) Railroad crossing.

B 488.9 (786.8 km) **DC 0.6** (1 km) Railroad crossing.

B 489.5 (787.8 km) **DC 0** Downtown Dawson Creek, BC. (See the ALASKA HIGHWAY section for description.)

Highway 63 Log

Highway 63 provides an interesting and scenic side road for those who want to explore historic Fort McMurray.

Distance from the junction of Alberta Highways 55 and 63 (J) is followed by distance from Fort McMurray (FM).

J 0 FM 154.5 (248.6 km) **Junction** of Highways 55 and 63.

J 0.9 (1.5 km) **FM 153.6** (247.2 km) Turnout with litter barrels to east.

J 1.6 (2.5 km) **FM 152.9** (246.1 km) Charron Lake visible to east.

J 1.9 (3 km) **FM 152.6** (245.6 km) Oil refinery and radio tower to west.

J 2.5 (4 km) **FM 152** (244.6 km) Entering Wandering River Ranger District northbound.

J 7.7 (12.4 km) **FM 146.8** (236.2 km) Side road east and south to Charron Lake and Plamondon.

J 9.2 (14.9 km) **FM 145.3** (233.8 km) Bridge over the La Biche River.

J 15.3 (24.7 km) **FM 139.1** (223.9 km) Microwave tower to east.

J 17.3 (27.8 km) **FM 137.2** (220.8 km) Rest area to east.

J 24 (38.7 km) **FM 130.4** (209.9 km) Side road leads west 0.5 mile/0.8 km to **BREYNAT** (pop. 30); store with gas and pay phone, auto garage with minor-repair facilities, community center, Roman Catholic church and ball diamond.

J 25.7 (41.4 km) **FM 128.8** (207.2 km) Bridge over the Wandering River.

J 27.6 (44.4 km) **FM 126.9** (204.2 km) **WANDERING RIVER** (pop. 70); motel, restaurant, tavern, store, service station with minor-repair facilities, library, ball diamond and school.

J 27.7 (44.5 km) **FM 126.8** (204.1 km) Turnout with litter barrels to east.

J 28 (45.1 km) **FM 126.5** (203.5 km) Access road west 0.6 mile/1 km to the Wandering River Ranger Station.

J 28.1 (45.3 km) **FM 126.3** (203.3 km) Bridge over the Wandering River. Service station to east.

J 28.3 (45.6 km) **FM 126.1** (203 km) Access road west 9 miles/15 km to Round Lake Recreation Area and Campground. ▲

J 29.3 (47.2 km) **FM 125.1** (201.4 km) Lyle Lake visible to west.

J 30.9 (49.7 km) **FM 123.6** (198.9 km) Gravel stockpiles to east.

J 35.4 (56.9 km) **FM 119.1** (191.7 km) Turnout with litter barrels on both sides of highway.

J 36.1 (58.1 km) **FM 118.4** (190.5 km) Bridge over the **Wandering River**. Wandering River Campground to east on the north side of the river; 15 sites, partial hookups, water pump, picnic tables, fishing. Camping fee $5.50. ▲

J 45.9 (73.8 km) **FM 108.6** (174.8 km) Turnout with litter barrels to east.

J 49.6 (79.9 km) **FM 104.8** (168.7 km) Radio tower to west.

J 51.7 (83.2 km) **FM 102.8** (165.4 km) Microwave towers to west.

J 55.9 (89.9 km) **FM 98.6** (158.7 km) Turnout with litter barrels and restrooms on both sides of highway.

J 61.5 (98.9 km) **FM 93** (149.7 km) Bridge over the Bear River.

J 63.7 (102.5 km) **FM 90.8** (146.1 km) Bridge over the House River.

J 63.8 (102.6 km) **FM 90.7** (146 km) **House River** Recreation Area and Campground to east on north side of river; 10 sites, partial hookups, water pump, picnic tables, fishing. Camping fee $5.50. ▲

J 68.4 (110.1 km) **FM 86.1** (138.5 km) Turnout with litter barrels to east.

J 71 (114.2 km) **FM 83.5** (134.4 km) Waskahigan Campground to west; seven sites, partial hookups, picnic tables, shelter, fishing. Camping fee $5.50. ▲

J 71.6 (115.2 km) **FM 82.9** (133.4 km) Bridge over Crow Creek.

J 74.9 (120.5 km) **FM 79.6** (128.1 km) **Crow Lake** Campground to east; 17 sites, partial hookups, boat launch, fishing, canoeing and walk-in tenting. Camping fee $5.50. ▲

J 75.2 (121 km) **FM 79.3** (127.6 km) Turnouts with litter barrels on both sides of highway.

J 78.6 (126.5 km) **FM 75.9** (122.1 km) Microwave tower to west.

J 82.3 (132.4 km) **FM 72.2** (116.2 km) Forest cutline crosses the highway.

J 86.4 (139.1 km) **FM 68** (109.5 km) Oil-pumping station to east.

J 87.9 (141.5 km) **FM 66.6** (107.1 km) **Mariana Lakes** Campground to west; 13 sites, partial hookups, water pump, picnic tables, shelter and fishing. Camping fee $5.50. ▲

J 88.4 (142.2 km) **FM 66.1** (106.4 km) Mariana Lakes service station to west; restaurant; diesel and propane; auto and tire repairs; rooms for rent.

J 90.2 (145.2 km) **FM 64.3** (103.4 km) Mariana Lake visible to west.

J 97.9 (157.6 km) **FM 56.5** (91 km) Entering Fort McMurray Ranger District northbound.

J 98.4 (158.3 km) **FM 56.1** (90.3 km) Turnouts with litter barrels on both sides of the highway.

J 99.4 (159.9 km) **FM 55.1** (88.7 km) Microwave tower to west.

J 106.9 (172 km) **FM 47.5** (76.6 km) Turnouts with litter barrels on both sides of highway.

NOTE: Road narrows and becomes rough in spots for the next 12 miles/19 km northbound.

J 113 (181.8 km) **FM 41.5** (66.8 km) Radio tower to east.

J 115.7 (186.2 km) **FM 38.8** (62.4 km) Turnouts with litter barrels and restrooms on both sides of highway.

J 119.8 (192.8 km) **FM 34.7** (55.8 km) Bridge over Horse Creek.

J 120.4 (193.7 km) **FM 34.1** (54.9 km) Microwave towers to west.

J 121 (194.7 km) **FM 33.5** (53.9 km) Turnout with litter barrels to east.

J 122.2 (196.7 km) **FM 32.3** (51.9 km) Turnout with litter barrels to west.

J 127.1 (204.6 km) **FM 27.5** (44.2 km) Greyling Campground to east; 34 sites, partial hookups, water pump, picnic tables, fishing, hiking. Camping fee $7.50. ▲

J 131.1 (211 km) **FM 23.4** (37.6 km) Bridge over the Hangingstone River.

J 131.5 (211.6 km) **FM 23** (37 km) **Hangingstone River** Provincial Recreation Area to west; 60 sites, water pump, public phone, picnic tables, shelter, fishing. No camping fee. River usually closed in spring to allow fish to spawn. ▲

J 133.8 (215.3 km) **FM 20.7** (33.3 km) Stony Mountain Road to east.

J 140.3 (225.8 km) **FM 14.2** (22.8 km) **Junction** with Highway 881 southeast 14 miles/23 km to **ANZAC** (pop. 280). The community was named Anzac, an acronym for the Australian and New Zealand Army Corps, by railroad workers in 1919. Anzac has a motel, two restaurants, service station, store and community hall.

Gregoire Lake Provincial Park, 5.5 miles/9 km east of Highways 63 and 881, has 140 sites, tap water, public phone, group camping, picnic tables, beach and boat launch. Camping fee. ▲

J 142.2 (228.8 km) **FM 12.3** (19.8 km) Fort McMurray Gun Club and Shooting Range to west.

J 143.7 (231.2 km) **FM 10.8** (17.4 km) Turnouts with litter barrels on both sides of the highway.

J 148.8 (239.4 km) **FM 5.7** (9.2 km) Highway divides into four lanes northbound.

J 149.4 (240.4 km) **FM 5.1** (8.2 km) Landfill to west.

J 150.3 (241.8 km) **FM 4.2** (6.8 km) **Junction** with Highway 69 east 4 miles/7 km to the Fort McMurray Airport and then another 6 miles/10 km to Spruce Valley ski hill.

J 150.4 (242 km) **FM 4.1** (6.6 km) Fort McMurray city limit.

J 151.3 (243.5 km) **FM 3.2** (5.1 km) McKenzie Avenue and the Oil Sands Interpretive Centre to east.

J 151.6 (244 km) **FM 2.9** (4.6 km) Centennial Park to west.

J 151.7 (244.1 km) **FM 2.8** (4.5 km) Fort McMurray Visitor Centre to east.

J 152.3 (245.1 km) **FM 2.2** (3.5 km) Gregoire Drive to east. Beacon Hill Drive to west.

J 153.8 (247.5 km) **FM 0.6** (1 km) King Street to east.

J 154 (247.9 km) **FM 0.4** (0.7 km) Bridge over the Hangingstone River.

Fort McMurray

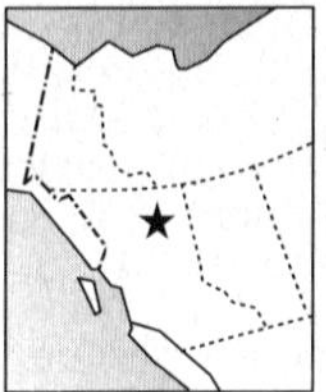

J 154.5 (248.6 km) **FM 0** Located 275 miles/442 km northeast of Edmonton. **Population**: 34,706. **Emergency Services: RCMP**, phone 791-7267. **Hospital**, phone 791-6161. **Ambulance**, phone 743-3311. **Fire Department**, phone 743-7050.

Visitor Information: Tourist information centre on the south end of town.

Elevation: 830 feet/253m. **Private Aircraft**: Fort McMurray Airport, 9 miles/15 km south and east of the city;

elev. 1,224 feet/373m; length 6,000 feet/1,829m; asphalt; fuel 80, 100, Jet B.

Transportation: Air–Fort McMurray is served with 45 scheduled flights from Pacific Western, Canadian Airlines, Air BC, Time Air and Northwestern Air. Charter service available. **Bus**–Fort McMurray is served daily by Red Arrow, Greyhound and Diversified bus lines. The city also has a transit system. **Taxi** and **Rental Cars**–Available.

The Cree have lived in this area for centuries. Explorer and fur trader Peter Pond became the first white man to view the current site of Fort McMurray when he traveled the Clearwater to its junction with the Athabasca in 1778.

The site's original attraction was its strategic location among the rich fur areas of the north. In 1790, the North West Trading Co. established a trading post on the west side of the Athabasca, opposite the present site of Fort McMurray, and called it "Fort of the Forks." The post was abandoned some 50 years later when a smallpox epidemic struck.

In 1870, H.J. Moberly chose a new site on the east bank of the Athabasca, near the Clearwater River, for the construction of a Hudson's Bay Co. trading post named in honour of William McMurray, who was in charge of the company's Athabasca district. The new post survived a fire and three severe floods to become the major depot on the supply route from northern Saskatchewan to Lake Athabasca via the Athabasca River.

Today, Fort McMurray's economy is driven by its two oil-sands plants, which produce more than 200,000 barrels daily. Fort McMurray became a city in September 1980.

A major attraction in Fort McMurray is the Oil Sands Interpretive Centre on Highway 63 at the entrance to town. The centre features the history, development and technology of Alberta's oil sands industry. Both guided and self-guided tours available. Open year-round; phone (403) 743-7167.

Fort McMurray has nine motels, three bed and breakfasts, many restaurants, fast-food outlets, cocktail lounges and taverns, several shopping malls, banks, numerous service stations and garages, libraries, schools and churches.

Recreational facilities include an indoor sports complex, an arena, curling rinks, bowling alleys, tennis courts, soccer fields, racquetball courts, billiard hall, ball diamonds and two golf courses. Fort McMurray Golf Club has 18 holes, pro shop, licensed dining and lounge, driving range, and carts for rent.

Fort McMurray has two campgrounds: Fort McMurray Centennial Park has 41 sites, partial hookups, dump station, tap water, public phone and walking trails. Camping fee $7. Rotary Park Campground, located near the airport entrance, has 45 sites, public phone, full hookups, tap water, showers and hiking trails. Camping fee $7 and up. ▲

Highway 63 Log

(continued)

HIGHWAY 63 NORTH

Highway 63 north from Fort McMurray is paved to the Fort Chipewyan access road. **Distance from downtown Fort McMurray (FM) is shown.**

FM 0 Downtown Fort McMurray. Intersection of Highway 63 and Hospital Street.

FM 1.6 (2.5 km) Athabasca River bridge.

FM 4.6 (7.4 km) Divided highway ends northbound.

FM 5.3 (8.6 km) Fort McMurray city limit.

FM 11.9 (19.2 km) Northland Forest Products sawmill to east.

FM 13.8 (22.2 km) Highway maintenance yard to east.

FM 14.1 (22.7 km) Fort McMurray Race Track to east.

FM 15 (24.1 km) Bridge over Poplar Creek.

FM 15.2 (24.4 km) Passing lane begins as the highway ascends a steep hill northbound.

FM 16 (25.8 km) Turnout to west for wildlife lookout area.

FM 16.1 (25.9 km) Microwave tower to west.

FM 16.2 (26 km) End passing lane northbound.

FM 18.6 (30 km) Turnoff into the Suncor oil-sands refinery to east. Constructed in the mid-1960s, this refinery extracts the valuable bitumen from Canada's vast oil sands. Suncor was the pioneer of the oil-sands business and the first company to operate a commercially successful oil-sands plant.

FM 18.8 (30.2 km) Radio tower to east.

FM 20.3 (32.7 km) Turnout and parking area to east.

FM 21.5 (34.6 km) Large oil-dumping station and radio tower to east.

FM 22.6 (36.4 km) Access road east 0.4 mile/0.7 km up a steep hill to the oil-sands viewpoint. From here you can view through binoculars the open-pit mine operations of the Suncor plant.

FM 23.2 (37.4 km) Oil-processing and recycling plant to east.

FM 23.9 (38.4 km) Syncrude oil refinery visible to west.

FM 25.2 (40.6 km) Entering Fort MacKay Ranger District northbound.

FM 25.4 (40.8 km) Turnoff to the Syncrude oil refinery to west. Syncrude Canada Ltd. operates the largest synthetic crude-oil-production facility in the world. This oil-sands plant produces more than 100,000 barrels a day, which is about 10 percent of Canada's oil requirements.

FM 25.5 (41 km) Pavement changes to a black shale chip-seal surface northbound.

FM 25.7 (41.4 km) Turnoff into the Syncrude lower camp complex to east.

FM 26.3 (42.4 km) Private airstrip to east.

FM 26.5 (42.7 km) Microwave tower to west.

FM 27 (43.5 km) Mildred Lake, large equipment service center to west. (Private property; authorized personnel only).

FM 27.8 (44.7 km) Turnoff to the north end of the Syncrude oil-mining pit on both sides of the highway.

FM 28.6 (46.1 km) Short side road east to the Fort MacKay Ranger Station.

FM 31.2 (50.2 km) Small radio tower to east.

FM 32.3 (52 km) Access road west 3.7 miles/6 km to **FORT MACKAY** (pop. 268); store, gas, laundromat, post office, school and pay phone.

FM 33.2 (53.5 km) Bridge over the Athabasca River.

FM 33.6 (54.1 km) Pavement ends, gravel begins northbound.

FM 38 (61.1 km) Access road west 1 mile/0.6 km to the barge terminal on the Athabasca River.

FM 38.2 (61.4 km) Highway 63 ends. A gravel-dirt winter road/summer trail leads north along the Athabasca River approximately 99 miles/160 km to Fort Chipewyan (description follows). There are no services beyond this point, and there are no permanent bridge or ferry crossings at any of the rivers south of Fort Chipewyan.

FORT CHIPEWYAN (pop. 967) is the oldest permanently inhabited settlement in Alberta. Founded in 1788 when Roderick Mackenzie, a cousin of explorer Alexander Mackenzie, built a trading post at Fort Point on the south shore of Lake Athabasca's west end. The trading post was moved to its present site on the north shore in 1800. Initially belonging to the North West Trading Co., Fort Chipewyan came under the control of the Hudson's Bay Co. in 1821 when the two companies merged. As the richest and most established outpost of the Northwest, Fort Chipewyan received all furs from the Pacific Northwest as they were transported east, and all of the Eastern supplies were redistributed north and west from this vital depot.

The cultural traditions of the Cree, Chipewyan and Metis are still part of the daily lives of Fort Chipewyan residents. A traditional lifestyle of hunting, trapping and fishing is blended with wage labor and administrative positions.

Fort Chipewyan, often referred to as "Fort Chip" or just "Chip" by the locals, has a tourist lodge with 10 rooms, dining room with a fireplace overlooking the lake, and a lounge.

Other visitor facilities include restaurants, service stations, stores, bed and breakfast and a museum. The Fort Chipewyan Bicentennial Museum, opened in 1990, is a replica of the Hudson's Bay Co.'s 1870 stores building. The museum was built as part of the 1788–1988 bicentennial celebrations in Fort Chipewyan. Native and historical displays depict the key role Fort Chipewyan played in Canada's early exploration and the fur trade. Included in the exhibits is a model of the fort from the late 1800s.

Highway 64 Log

Fairview, on Highway 2, is 28 miles from the junction of Highway 2 and Highway 49, the Northern Woods & Waters Route.
Distance from Fairview (F) is followed by distance from Fort St. John (SJ).

F 0 SJ 118.7 (191 km) **Junction** of Highways 2 and 64A at Fairview. See the MACKENZIE ROUTE section for description of Fairview.

F 2.1 (3.3 km) **SJ 116.7** (187.8 km) Fairview Airport to north.

F 4 (6.5 km) **SJ 114.6** (184.5 km) **Junction** of Highways 64 and 64A.

F 6.3 (10.1 km) **SJ 112.4** (180.9 km) Access road west to a small ski slope.

F 7.8 (12.5 km) **SJ 110.9** (178.5 km) Creek crossing.

F 8.3 (13.4 km) **SJ 110.4** (177.6 km) Railroad crossing.

F 10.4 (16.8 km) **SJ 108.2** (174.2 km) Entering Improvement District 21 northbound. Fairview Municipal District southbound.

F 14.4 (23.1 km) **SJ 104.3** (167.9 km) Bridge over Hines Creek.

F 14.5 (23.3 km) **SJ 104.2** (167.7 km) Side road west 2.5 miles/4 km to the Hines Creek Golf and Country Club; nine holes, pro shop, clubhouse, licensed dining and carts for rent.

F 14.7 (23.7 km) **SJ 104** (167.3 km) Access road east 1.2 miles/2 km to George Lake Campground on the north shore of Hines Creek; 18 sites, picnic tables, public phone, horseshoe pits, beach and boat launch. No camping fee. ▲

F 15.8 (25.4 km) **SJ 102.8** (165.6 km) George Lake.

F 17.6 (28.3 km) **SJ 101.1** (162.7 km) **Junction** with Highway 685 and the community of **HINES CREEK** (pop. 550) to west. Hines Creek is the second largest grain delivery point in the Peace River District. The community has a motel, restaurant, service station with major repair and grocery store. The "End of Steel" Museum, located at the edge of the village, tells the story of the railroad's journey west, and what it meant to the pioneers. Carter Campground, 17.4 miles/28 km west on Highway 685, has 24 sites, group camping, viewpoint and boat launch. No camping fee. ▲

F 18.6 (30 km) **SJ 100** (160.9 km) Bridge over Jack Creek.

F 23 (37 km) **SJ 95.7** (154 km) Montagneuse Valley Road to north.

F 25.2 (40.6 km) **SJ 93.5** (150.4 km) Bridge over Montagneuse Creek.

F 26.3 (42.4 km) **SJ 92.3** (148.6 km) **Junction** with Highway 730 north 8.1 miles/13 km to the community of Eureka River. From Eureka River an access road leads northeast 14.3 miles/23 km to **Stanley Lake** Campground; 15 sites, partial hookups, water pump, boat launch (electric motor boats only), fishing. Camping fee $7.50.

F 29.8 (48 km) **SJ 88.9** (143 km) Clear Hills visible to north.

F 35.5 (57.2 km) **SJ 83.1** (133.8 km) Side road north 23 miles/37 km to **Running Lake** Campground; 19 sites, partial hookups, water pump, boat launch (electric motors only), fishing. Camping fee $7.50.

Fairview is an agricultural centre and has a college. (Brian Calkins)

F 39.6 (63.7 km) **SJ 79.1** (127.3 km) **Junction** with Highway 726 south 5 miles/8 km to Many Islands Campground on the north shore of the **Peace River**; 27 sites, water pump, boat launch, fishing, day-use area and hiking trails. No camping fee.

F 40.6 (65.4 km) **SJ 78** (125.6 km) **Junction** with Highway 726 north 9.9 miles/16 km to **WORSLEY** (pop. 51). Worsley serves as the business center for the surrounding farming and agricultural area. Visitor facilities include a hotel, restaurant, service station with minor-repair facilities, grocery store, laundromat and tavern. Running Lake Campground is located 19.9 miles/32 km east and north of Worsley. (See **Milepost F 35.5** for description). The Whispering Pines Ski Slope, 14.9 miles/24 km northwest of Worsley, has three runs, tee rope, tee bar and restaurant.

F 43.7 (70.4 km) **SJ 74.9** (120.6 km) Creek crossing.

F 54.4 (87.6 km) **SJ 64.3** (103.4 km) Cleardale to north; gas station, cafe, small store, car/truck wash, pay phone.

F 58.3 (93.9 km) **SJ 60.3** (97.1 km) Golf course to south via access road.

F 60.5 (97.4 km) **SJ 58.2** (93.6 km) Steep descent into the Clear River Valley westbound.

F 62.6 (100.7 km) **SJ 56.1** (90.3 km) Bridge over the Clear River.

F 68.9 (110.9 km) **SJ 49.8** (80.1 km) **Junction** with Highway 717. South, the highway leads 6.2 miles/10 km to the community of Bear Canyon, which has a gas station, grocery store and pay phone. The highway continues southwest to Cherry Point and the Alberta–British Columbia border. North, the highway leads 24.9 miles/40 km to Clear Prairie.

F 71.1 (114.4 km) **SJ 47.6** (76.6 km) Access road north 1.8 miles/3 km to **Ole's Lake** Campground; 16 sites, partial hookups, water pump, boat launch (electric motors only), fishing. Camping fee $7.50.

F 75.7 (121.9 km) **SJ 42.9** (69.1 km) Turnout to south.

F 76.7 (123.5 km) **SJ 41.9** (67.5 km) Alberta–British Columbia border.

F 80.8 (130.1 km) **SJ 37.8** (60.9 km) **Junction** with secondary access road south 15 miles/25 km to Clayhurst.

F 82.7 (133.1 km) **SJ 36** (57.9 km) Goodlow; gas, food and groceries.

F 83.6 (134.6 km) **SJ 35** (56.4 km) Bridge over Alces Creek.

F 89.1 (143.4 km) **SJ 29.6** (47.6 km) Flatrock School to south.

F 101.5 (163.4 km) **SJ 17.2** (27.6 km) Community of Cecil Lake; grocery store and gas station.

F 106.5 (171.4 km) **SJ 12.2** (19.5 km) Steep descent into the Beatton River Canyon westbound.

F 108.9 (175.3 km) **SJ 9.8** (15.7 km) Narrow one-lane bridge over the Beatton River.

CAUTION: Road ascends a steep hill with rough spots. Intermittent pavement breaks and hairpin turns for the next 2.1 miles/3.3 km westbound.

F 111.2 (178.9 km) **SJ 7.5** (12.1 km) Road straightens out westbound. Good road into Fort St. John.

F 112.2 (180.6 km) **SJ 6.5** (10.4 km) **Junction** with side road south to the Alaska Highway and the community of Taylor.

F 112.9 (181.7 km) **SJ 5.8** (9.3 km) Access road south to the Fort St. John Airport.

F 115.6 (186.1 km) **SJ 3** (4.9 km) Railroad crossing. Entering Fort St. John westbound.

F 117.4 (189 km) **SJ 1.2** (2 km) Downtown Fort St. John (see ALASKA HIGHWAY section for description).

F 117.7 (189.4 km) **SJ 1** (1.6 km) 100th Street.

F 118.7 (191 km) **SJ 0 Junction** with the Alaska Highway.

SILVER TRAIL HIGHWAY

Klondike Highway Junction to Keno City, YT
Yukon Highway 11

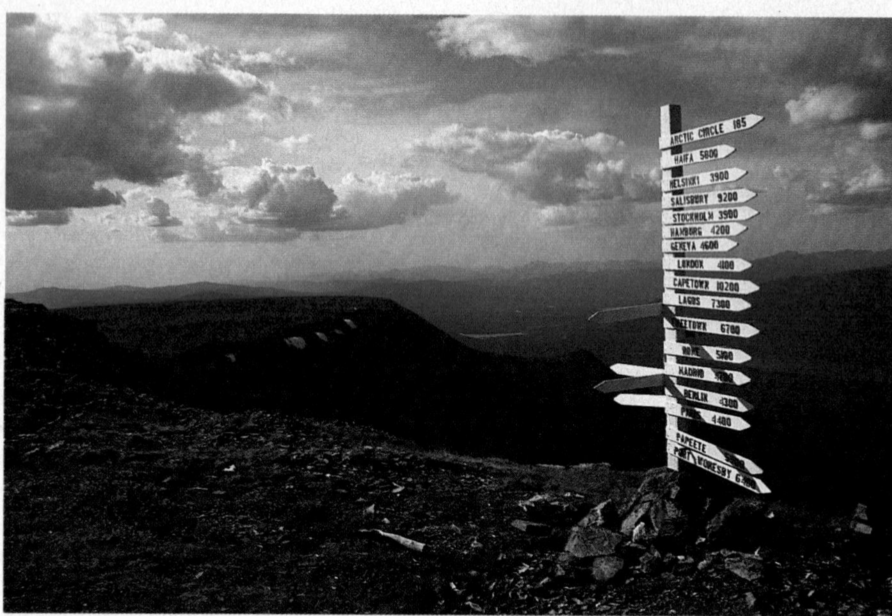

Milepost sign atop Keno Hill at Keno City on the Silver Trail. (Rollo Pool)

The Silver Trail leads northeast from the Klondike Highway (see **Milepost J 214.4** in the KLONDIKE LOOP section) to Mayo, Elsa and Keno City. From its junction with the Klondike Highway (Yukon Highway 2), the Silver Trail (Yukon Highway 11) leads 31.9 miles/51.3 km to Mayo; 60.3 miles/97 km to Elsa; and 69.1 miles/111.2 km to Keno City. The Silver Trail also provides access to Duncan Creek Road, the original Silver Trail. It is approximately 140 miles/225 km round-trip to Keno City and an easy day trip for motorists. The road is asphalt-surfaced to Mayo, hard-packed gravel from Mayo to Keno. Watch for soft shoulders, especially in wet weather. Gas is available only at Mayo and at Stewart Crossing on the Klondike Highway.

There is an information kiosk on the Klondike Highway at the south end of Stewart River bridge. Stop at the kiosk for information on the Silver Trail, or visit Binet House Interpretive Centre in Mayo (open 10:30 A.M. to 6 P.M. in summer), phone 996-2926. Or write Silver Trail Tourism, Box 268, Mayo, YT Y0B 1M0; phone (in summer) 996-2926, winter phone 996-2024.

The Silver Trail to Mayo follows the Stewart River through what has been one of the richest silver mining regions in Canada.

Emergency medical services: In Mayo, phone (403) 996-4444; or phone the RCMP toll free, Yukon-wide, at 1-667-5555.

Silver Trail Log

Distance is measured from the junction with the Klondike Highway (J).

J 0 **Junction** of Silver Trail (Yukon Highway 11) and Klondike Highway.

J 0.2 (0.3 km) Marker shows distance to Mayo 51 km, Elsa 97 km, Keno 110 km.

J 1.2 (2 km) Stewart River to the south.

J 3 (4.8 km) Bad curve. Turnout to south.

J 9.6 (15.4 km) Large gravel pit turnout to south.

J 27.4 (44.1 km) Pull-through rest area with outhouses, litter barrel and picnic tables.

J 30.7 (49.5 km) Winding descent for northeast-bound traffic; good view of valley.

J 31.2 (50.2 km) McIntyre Park picnic area to south on banks of the Mayo River.

J 31.3 (50.3 km) **Mayo River** bridge. Good fishing from bridge for grayling.

J 31.9 (51.3 km) **Junction** with access road to Mayo (description follows). Turn right (south) for Mayo, keep left (north) for road to Elsa and Keno City.

Mayo

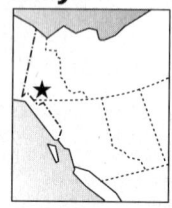

Located on the bank of the Stewart River near its confluence with the Mayo River. **Population:** 500. **Emergency Services: RCMP**, phone 996-5555. **Ambulance,** phone 996-2345. **Elevation:** 1,650 feet/503m. **Radio:** CBC 1230. **Television:** CBC Anik, Channel 7.

Climate: Residents claim it's the coldest and hottest spot in Yukon. Record low, -80°F/-62.2°C (February 1947); record high, 97°F/36.1°C (June 1969).

Private Aircraft: Mayo airstrip, 4 miles/6.5 km north; elev. 1,653 feet/504m; length 4,850 feet/1,478m; gravel; fuel 100, Jet B.

Mayo has most traveler facilities including two motels, two bed and breakfasts, cafe, laundromat, gas station, hardware, grocery and variety stores (closed Sunday). Tire repair and minor vehicle repair are available. Post office, liquor store and

SILVER TRAIL HIGHWAY *Klondike Highway Junction to Keno City, YT*

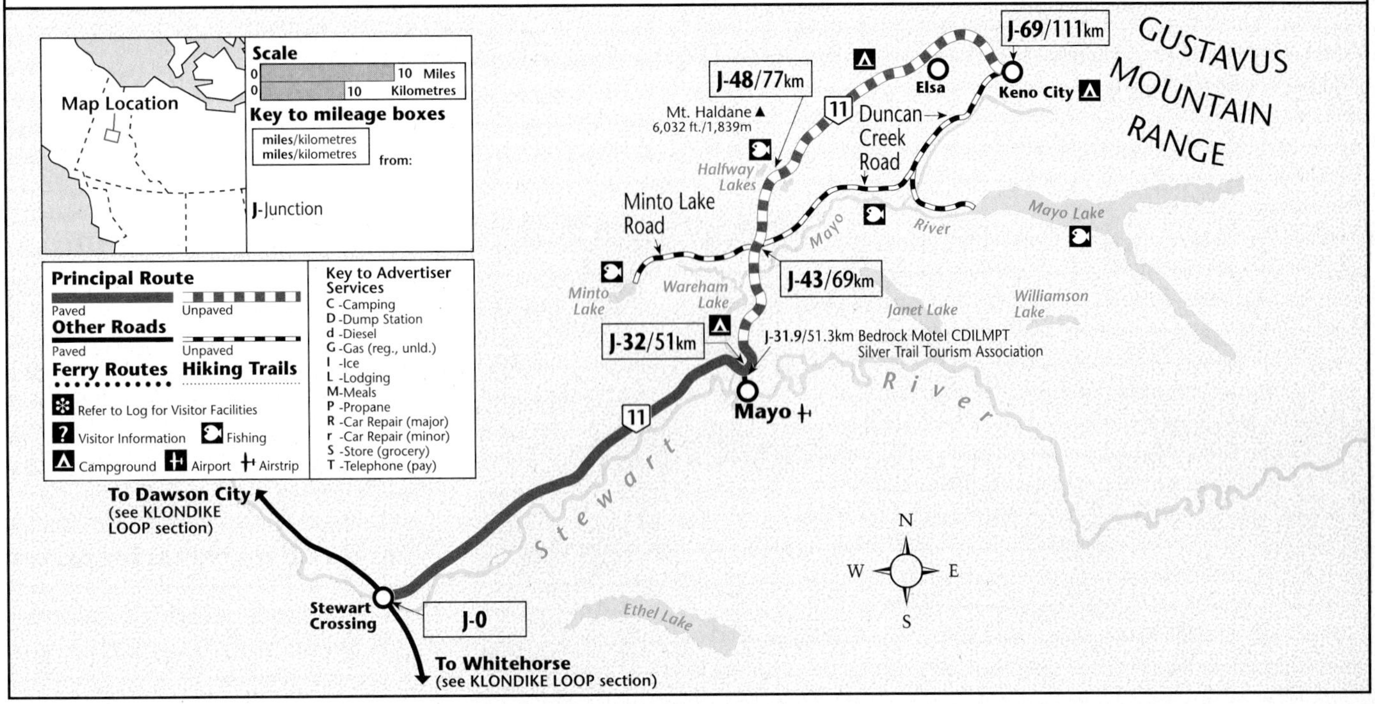

library located in the Territorial Bldg. Bank service available 10 A.M. to 1 P.M. Monday, Wednesday and Friday.

Scheduled air service to Whitehorse and Dawson City. Charter floatplane and helicopter service available. Scheduled bus service. Canoeists can put in at Mayo on the Stewart River for a paddle to Stewart Crossing.

Mayo was formerly known as Mayo Landing and began as a river settlement and port for silver ore shipments to Whitehorse. It is now a service centre for mineral exploration in the area. Yukon Electrical Co. Ltd. operates a hydroelectric project here.

The Silver Trail Tourism Association. See display ad this section.

Silver Trail Log

(continued)

J **32.8** (52.8 km) Mayo airport, built in 1928 by the Treadwell Mining Co. Pavement ends, gravel begins, northbound.

J **34.9** (56.2 km) Side road to Mayo hydro dam, built in 1951 and completed in 1952.

J **35.8** (57.6 km) Turnoff to west for Five Mile Lake Yukon government campground; 20 sites, boat launch, picnic tables, firepits. ▲

J **36.1** (58.1 km) Five Mile Lake day-use area.

J **36.2** (58.2 km) Small lake to east.

J **37.6** (60.5 km) Wareham Lake to east, created by the Mayo River power project. This lake is not good for fishing.

J **38.2** (61.4 km) Survival shelter to east.

J **42.9** (69 km) **Junction** of Yukon Highway 11 with Minto Lake Road and Duncan Creek Road. Turn west (left) and drive 12 miles/19 km for **Minto Lake;** good fishing for lake trout and grayling. Also access to Highet Creek.

Turn east (right) at junction for Duncan Creek Road, which leads to Mayo Lake and Keno City. The original Silver Trail, Duncan Creek Road was used by Treadwell Yukon during the 1930s to haul silver ore from Keno into Mayo, where it was loaded onto riverboats. This 25-mile/40-km back road is mostly good hard-packed gravel. Motorists note, however, that the last 10 miles/16 km into Keno City via Duncan Creek Road are narrow and winding, slippery when wet, and not recommended for large vehicles or trailers. Heading northeast on Duncan Creek Road, travelers will see the site of Fields Creek Roadhouse at Mile 5, and Stones Roadhouse at Mile 11. At Mile 14 Duncan Creek Road junctions with a 6-mile/10-km side road which leads to **Mayo Lake;** there is good fishing along the **Mayo River** to the dam at the west end of Mayo Lake. At Mile 14.2 there is a private gold mine, Duncan Creek Golddusters, with guided tours and gold panning (fee charged). At Mile 18 are the remains of the Van Cleaves Roadhouse. At Mile 25 Duncan Creek Road junctions with Highway 11 at Keno City.

J **48** (77.2 km) **Halfway Lakes;** fishing for northern pike. Silver Trail Inn; food and lodging in summer.

J **49** (78.8 km) Mount Haldane Lions survival shelter. Watch for turnoff for Mount Haldane trail; follow gravel road 2 miles/3.2 km to trailhead. This 4-mile-/6.4-km-long trail leads to summit.

J **54.9** (88.3 km) South McQuesten River Road; drive northwest 5 miles/8 km for Silver Centre Campsite, a public campground built by the people of Elsa. ▲

J **60.3** (97 km) **ELSA** (pop. 10) was a company town for United Keno Hill Mines, formerly one of the largest silver mines in North America and one of the Yukon's oldest, continuously operating hardrock mines until its closure in 1989. The Elsa claim is a well-mineralized silver vein, located on Galena Hill and named for the sister of prospector Charlie Brefalt, who received $250,000 for Treadwell Yukon's richest mine. A plaque here commemorates American engineer Livingston Wernecke, who came to the Keno Hill area in 1919 to investigate the silver–lead ore discoveries for Treadwell–Yukon Mining Co.

Rock hounds request permission from the mine security office to look for galena, quartz crystals, pyrite and other minerals.

J **63.8** (102.6 km) Side road leads north to Hanson Lakes and McQuesten Lake. Galena Mountains to east. An information sign marks the Wind River trail, a former winter road to oil exploration sites, which leads 300 miles/483 km north to the Bell River. The twin towers are abandoned telephone relays.

J **69.1** (111.2 km) **KENO CITY** (pop. about 50). Originally called Sheep Hill by the early miners, it was renamed Keno — a gambling game — after the Keno mining claim that was staked by Louis Bouvette in July 1919. This enormously rich discovery of silver and galena sparked the interest of two large mining companies, the Guggenheims and Treadwell Yukon, who set up camps in the area. During the 1920s, Keno City was a boom town.

Keno has a hotel with a bar (no food service available), a coffee shop, and washers, dryers and showers available for the public. There is a city campground located on Lightning Creek. ▲

Well worth a visit here is the Keno Mining Museum, phone 995-2792. Photographs and tools recall the mining history of the area. It is open 10 A.M. to 6 P.M. in summer. Be sure to get your Yukon Gold Explorer's Passport stamped at the museum — its location makes it the most exclusive of the 13 passport stamps.

There are a number of hiking trails in the Keno area; inquire at the museum. The Summit trail (can be driven) leads 6.5 miles/10.5 km to the milepost sign on top of Keno Hill.

CAMPBELL HIGHWAY

Watson Lake, Yukon Territory, to Junction with Klondike Loop
Yukon Highway 4

Campbell Highway winds through Pelly River valley near Ross River. (Earl L. Brown, staff)

Named for Robert Campbell, the first white man to penetrate what is now known as Yukon Territory, this all-weather gravel road leads 373 miles/600.2 km northwest from the Alaska Highway at Watson Lake, to junction with the Klondike Highway 2 miles/3.2 km north of Carmacks (see the KLONDIKE LOOP section). Gas is available at Watson Lake, Ross River, Faro and Carmacks.

The highway is gravel with the exception of some paved portions between Faro and Carmacks. Should the mine at Faro reopen, watch for large ore trucks between Faro and Carmacks. Drive with your headlights on at all times.

The Campbell Highway is an alternative route to Dawson City. It is about 20 miles/32 km shorter than driving the Alaska Highway through to Whitehorse, then driving up the Klondike Highway to Dawson City.

The Robert Campbell Highway was completed in 1968 and closely follows sections of the fur trade route established by Robert Campbell. Campbell was a Hudson's Bay Co. trader who was sent into the region in the 1840s to find a route west into the unexplored regions of central Yukon. Traveling from the southeast, he followed the Liard and Frances rivers, building a chain of posts along the way. His major discovery came in 1843, when he reached the Yukon River, which was to become the major transportation route within the Yukon.

Emergency medical services: Phone the RCMP or ambulance in Watson Lake, Ross River or Carmacks. Or phone toll free, Yukon-wide, the RCMP at 1-667-5555, or the ambulance at 1-667-3333.

Campbell Highway Log

YUKON HIGHWAY 4
Distance from Watson Lake (WL) is followed by distance from junction with the Klondike Highway just north of Carmacks (J). Mileages reflect the location of physical kilometreposts; driving distance may vary from log.

WL 0 J 373 (600.2 km) **Junction** of the Campbell Highway with the Alaska Highway at Watson Lake (see description of Watson Lake in the ALASKA HIGHWAY section). The famous sign forest is located at this junction. In the parking area off the Campbell Highway (also called Airport Road) is a point of interest sign relating the highway's history.

WL 0.6 (1 km) **J 372.4** (599.3 km) Hospital on right northbound.

WL 4.3 (6.9 km) **J 368.7** (593.3 km) Access road on right northbound to Mount Maichen ski hill.

WL 6.3 (10.1 km) **J 366.7** (590.1 km) Airport Road left to Watson Lake airport. Pavement ends, hard-packed gravel begins, northbound.

WL 6.7 (10.8 km) **J 366.3** (589.5 km) Watson Creek. The highway begins to climb to a heavily timbered plateau and then heads north following the east bank of the Frances River. Tamarack is rare in Yukon, but this northern type of larch can be seen along here. Although a member of the pine family, it sheds its needles in the fall.

WL 10.4 (16.7 km) **J 362.6** (583.5 km) MacDonald Creek.

WL 22.5 (36.2 km) **J 350.5** (564.1 km) Tom Creek.

WL 27.3 (44 km) **J 345.7** (556.3 km) Sa Dena Hes Mine access.

WL 36.1 (58.1 km) **J 336.9** (542.2 km) Frances River bridge. Turnout at north end of bridge; picnic spot. The highway crosses to west bank and follows the river northward. Named by Robert Campbell for the wife of Sir George Simpson, governor of the Hudson's Bay Co. for 40 years, the Frances River is a tributary of the Liard River. Robert Campbell ascended the Liard River to the Frances River and then went on to Frances Lake and the Pelly River. The Frances River was part of Hudson's Bay Co.'s route into central Yukon for many years before being abandoned because of its dangerous rapids and canyons.

WL 47.2 (76 km) **J 325.8** (524.3 km) Lucky Creek.

WL 49.6 (79.8 km) **J 323.4** (520.4 km) Simpson Creek.

WL 51.8 (83.4 km) **J 321.2** (516.9 km) Access road leads west 1 mile/1.6 km to **Simpson Lake** Yukon government campground: 19 campsites, $8 fee, boat launch, dock, swimming beach, playground, kitchen shelter and drinking water (boil water). Excellent fishing for lake trout, arctic grayling and northern pike.

WL 58.5 (94.2 km) **J 314.5** (506.1 km) Large turnout with litter barrels.

WL 58.7 (94.5 km) **J 314.3** (505.8 km) Access road west to Simpson Lake.

WL 68.5 (110.2 km) **J 304.5** (490 km) **Miner's Junction**, junction with Nahanni Range Road (formerly known as Cantung Junction); no services. Nahanni Range Road leads 125 miles/201.2 km northeast to Tungsten (see NAHANNI RANGE ROAD section). The road is not maintained and is not recommended for tourist traffic.

WL 70.3 (113.2 km) **J 302.7** (487.1 km) Yukon government Tuchitua River maintenance camp to east.

WL 70.5 (113.4 km) **J 302.5** (486.8 km) One-lane bridge over Tuchitua River.

WL 91.7 (147.6 km) **J 281.3** (452.7 km) Jules Creek.

WL 100 (160.9 km) **J 273** (439.3 km) 99 Mile Creek.

WL 106.6 (171.6 km) **J 266.4** (428.7 km) Caesar Creek.

WL 107.1 (172.4 km) **J 265.9** (427.9 km)

CAMPBELL HIGHWAY

Watson Lake, YT, to Junction with Klondike Loop (includes Nahanni Range Road)

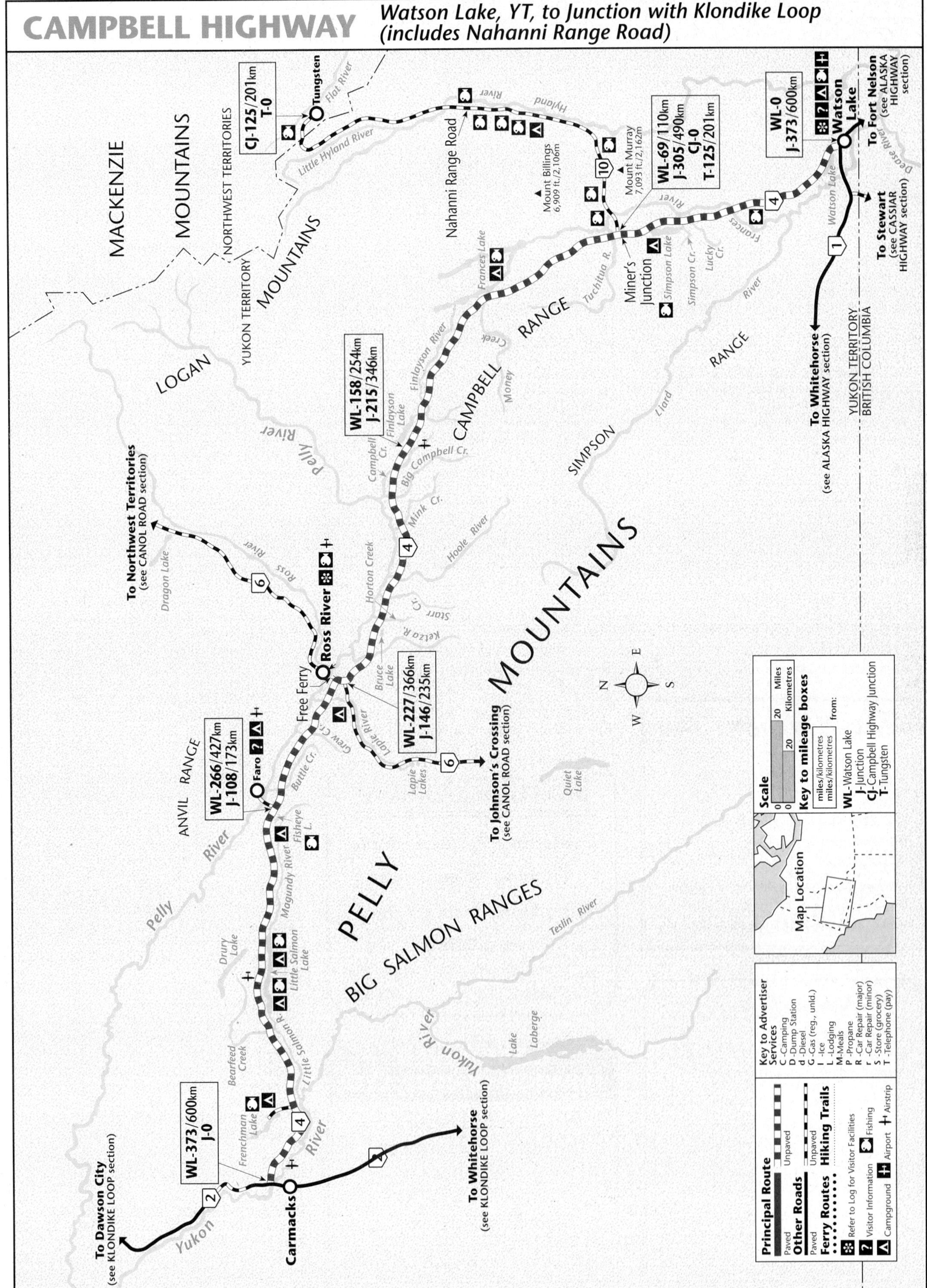

MACKENZIE MOUNTAINS
NORTHWEST TERRITORIES
YUKON TERRITORY
MOUNTAINS
LOGAN
CAMPBELL RANGE
SIMPSON RANGE
PELLY MOUNTAINS
BIG SALMON RANGES
ANVIL RANGE
CJ-125/201km T-0
Tungsten
Flat River
Little Hyland River
Hyland River
Nahanni Range Road
Mount Billings 6,909 ft./2,106m
Mount Murray 7,093 ft./2,162m
WL-69/110km J-305/490km CJ-0 T-125/201km
WL-0 J-373/600km
Watson Lake
To Fort Nelson (see ALASKA HIGHWAY section)
To Stewart (see CASSIAR HIGHWAY section)
To Whitehorse (see ALASKA HIGHWAY section)
YUKON TERRITORY
BRITISH COLUMBIA
Miner's Junction
Simpson Lake
Simpson Cr.
Lucky Cr.
Tuchitua R.
Frances River
Frances Lake
Finlayson River
Finlayson Lake
Money Creek
Liard River
WL-158/254km J-215/346km
Campbell Cr.
Big Campbell Cr.
Mink Cr.
Hoole River
Pelly River
Horton Creek
Starr Cr.
Ketza R.
Bruce Lake
To Northwest Territories (see CANOL ROAD section)
Dragon Lake
Ross River
Ross River
Free Ferry
WL-227/366km J-146/235km
Lapie River
Lapie Lakes
To Johnson's Crossing (see CANOL ROAD section)
Grew Cr.
Buttle Cr.
WL-266/427km J-108/173km
Faro
Fisheye L.
Magundy River
Quiet Lake
Teslin River
Drury Lake
Little Salmon Lake
Little Salmon R.
Bearfeed Creek
Frenchman Lake
Lake Laberge
Yukon River
WL-373/600km J-0
To Dawson City (see KLONDIKE LOOP section)
Carmacks
To Whitehorse (see KLONDIKE LOOP section)
N E S W
Scale
0 20 Miles
0 20 Kilometres
Key to mileage boxes
miles/kilometres
miles/kilometres from:
WL-Watson Lake
J-Junction
CJ-Campbell Highway Junction
T-Tungsten
Map Location
Principal Route
Paved Unpaved
Other Roads
Paved Unpaved
Ferry Routes
Hiking Trails
Refer to Log for Visitor Facilities
Visitor Information
Fishing
Campground
Airport
Airstrip
Key to Advertiser Services
C-Camping
D-Dump Station
d-Diesel
G-Gas (reg., unld.)
I-Ice
L-Lodging
M-Meals
P-Propane
R-Car Repair (major)
r-Car Repair (minor)
S-Store (grocery)
T-Telephone (pay)

View of Frances Lake to east, Campbell Range of the Pelly Mountains to west.

WL 108.9 (175.3 km) **J 264.1** (425 km) Access road east leads 0.6 mile/1 km to **Frances Lake** Yukon government campground: 19 campsites, $8 fee, boat launch, kitchen shelter, drinking water (boil water). The solitary peak between the two arms of Frances Lake is Simpson Tower (elev. 5,500 feet/1,676m). It was named by Robert Campbell for Hudson's Bay Co. governor Sir George Simpson. Fishing for lake trout, grayling and northern pike.

WL 109.1 (175.5 km) **J 263.9** (424.7 km) Money Creek, which flows into the west arm of Frances Lake, one of the Yukon's largest lakes. The creek was named for Anton Money, a mining engineer and prospector who found and mined placer gold in this area between 1929 and 1946. Money later operated "The Village" service station at Mile 442 on the Alaska Highway. He died in 1993, in Santa Barbara, CA.

WL 109.4 (176 km) **J 263.6** (424.2 km) Gravel turnout. View southbound of Frances Lake.

WL 113.8 (183.2 km) **J 259.2** (417.1 km) Dick Creek.

WL 123.8 (199.2 km) **J 249.2** (401 km) Highway descends Finlayson River valley, swinging west away from Frances Lake and following the Finlayson River that may be seen occasionally to the east for about the next 20 miles/32 km. Mountains to the west are part of the Campbell Range.

WL 126.4 (203.5 km) **J 246.6** (396.9 km) Light Creek.

WL 129.1 (207.7 km) **J 243.9** (392.5 km) Van Bibber Creek.

WL 134.1 (215.8 km) **J 238.9** (384.5 km) Wolverine Creek.

WL 147.5 (237.4 km) **J 225.5** (362.9 km) Finlayson Creek, which flows into the river of the same name, drains Finlayson Lake into Frances Lake. Named by Robert Campbell in 1840 for Chief Factor Duncan Finlayson, who later became director of the Hudson's Bay Co. Placer gold mined at the mouth of Finlayson River in 1875 is believed to be some of the first gold mined in the territory. Finlayson Lake (elev. 3,100 feet/945m), on the Continental Divide, separates watersheds of Mackenzie and Yukon rivers.

WL 148.1 (238.4 km) **J 224.9** (361.9 km) Access road north to Finlayson Lake picnic area; litter barrels. To the southwest are the Pelly Mountains.

WL 149 (239.8 km) **J 224** (360.5 km) Turnout with observation platform and information panel on Finlayson caribou herd.

WL 158.1 (254.5 km) **J 214.9** (345.8 km) **Private Aircraft:** Finlayson Lake airstrip to south; elev. 3,300 feet/1,006m; length 2,100 feet/640m; gravel.

WL 163.7 (263.5 km) **J 209.3** (336.8 km) Nancy J. Creek.

WL 164.4 (264.5 km) **J 208.6** (335.7 km) Little Campbell Creek. Robert Campbell followed this creek to the Pelly River in 1840.

WL 170.4 (274.2 km) **J 202.6** (326 km) Bridge over Big Campbell Creek, which flows into Pelly River at Pelly Banks. Robert Campbell named the river and banks after Hudson's Bay Co. governor Sir John Henry Pelly. Campbell built a trading post here in 1846; never successful, it burned down in 1849. Isaac Taylor and William S. Drury later operated a trading post at Pelly Banks, one of a string of successful posts established by their firm in remote spots throughout the Yukon from 1899 on.

The highway follows the Pelly River for the next 90 miles/145 km.

WL 179 (288.1 km) **J 194** (312.2 km) Mink Creek culvert.

WL 193.9 (312 km) **J 179.1** (288.2 km) Bridge over Hoole Canyon; turnout to north. Confluence of the Hoole and Pelly rivers. Campbell named the Hoole River after his interpreter, Francis Hoole, a half-Iroquois and half-French Canadian employed by the Hudson's Bay Co. Dig out your gold pan — this river once yielded gold.

WL 199.8 (321.6 km) **J 173.2** (278.7 km) Starr Creek culvert.

WL 206.5 (332.3 km) **J 166.5** (267.9 km) Horton Creek.

WL 210.7 (339 km) **J 162.3** (261.2 km) Bruce Lake to south.

WL 211.8 (340.8 km) **J 161.2** (259.4 km) Bruce Creek.

WL 215.4 (346.6 km) **J 157.6** (253.6 km) Private side road leads south 27.3 miles/44 km to Ketza River Project. The first gold bar was poured at Ketza River mine in 1988. The Ketza River hard-rock gold deposit was first discovered in 1947, but the mine was only recently developed. No visitor facilities.

WL 217.9 (350.7 km) **J 155.1** (249.6 km) Ketza River. St. Cyr Range to southwest.

WL 219.4 (353 km) **J 153.6** (247.2 km) Ketza Creek.

WL 221.4 (356.3 km) **J 151.6** (244 km) Beautiful Creek culvert.

WL 224.8 (361.8 km) **J 148.2** (238.5 km) **Coffee Lake** to south; local swimming hole, picnic tables, trout fishing (stocked).

WL 227.3 (365.8 km) **J 145.7** (234.5 km) **Junction** with South Canol Road (see CANOL ROAD section) which leads south 129 miles/207 km to Johnson's Crossing and the Alaska Highway. Ross River Flying Service; floatplane base on Jackfish Lake here.

WL 227.5 (366.1 km) **J 145.5** (234.1 km) Unmaintained side road on right westbound is continuation of Canol Road to Ross River. Use main Ross River access road next milepost.

WL 232.3 (373.8 km) **J 140.7** (226.4 km) Access road leads 7 miles/11.2 km to Ross River (description follows). Rest area with toilets on highway just north of this turnoff.

Ross River

Located on the southwest bank of the Pelly River. **Population:** 376. **Emergency Services: RCMP,** phone 969-5555. **Hospital,** phone 969-2221. **Radio:** CBC 990, local FM station. **Transportation:** Scheduled air service via Trans North Air.

Private Aircraft: Ross River airstrip; elev. 2,408 feet/734m; length 5,500 feet/1,676m; gravel; fuel 40.

A point of interest sign on the way into Ross River relates that in 1843, Robert Campbell named Ross River for Chief Trader Donald Ross of the Hudson's Bay Co. From 1903, a trading post called Nahanni House (established by Tom Smith and later owned by the Whitehorse firm of Taylor and Drury) located at the confluence of the Ross and Pelly rivers supplied the Indians of the area for nearly 50 years. With the building of the

ROSS RIVER ADVERTISERS

Dena General Store ....Ph. (403) 969-2280
Leprechaun Hideaway......Ph. (403) 969-2905
Ross River Service Centre Ltd. .... Ph. (403) 969-2212
Welcome Inn, The ....Ph. (403) 969-2218

Ferry and footbridge cross the Pelly River at Ross River. (Earl L. Brown, staff)

Canol pipeline service road in WWII and the completion of the Robert Campbell Highway in 1968, the community was linked to the rest of the territory by road. Originally situated on the north side of the Pelly River, the town has been in its present location since 1964. Today, Ross River is a supply and communication base for prospectors testing and mining mineral bodies in this region.

Ross River has gas stations with diesel, full mechanical and tire repair, grocery stores, two motels with dining, and a bed and breakfast. The nearest campground is Lapie Canyon (see **Milepost WL 233.5**). Self-contained RVs may overnight at the gravel parking lot at the end of the pedestrian suspension bridge on the Ross River side.

Ross River is also a jumping-off point for big game hunters and canoeists. There are two registered hunting outfitters here. Canoeists traveling the Pelly River can launch just downriver from the ferry crossing. Experienced canoeists recommend camping on the Pelly's many gravel bars and islets to avoid bears, bugs and the danger of accidentally setting tundra fires. The Pelly has many sweepers, sleepers and gravel shallows, some gravel shoals, and extensive channeling. There are two sets of rapids between Ross River and the mouth of the Pelly: Fish Hook and Granite Canyon. Water is potable (boil), firewood available and wildlife plentiful. Inquire locally about river conditions before setting out.

Rock hounds watch for coal seams on the access road into Ross River. Also check Pelly River gravels for jaspers and the occasional agate.

The suspension footbridge at Ross River leads across the Pelly River to the site of an abandoned Indian village 1 mile/1.6 km upstream at the mouth of the Ross River.

A government ferry crosses the Pelly River daily in summer, from 8 A.M. to noon and 1-5 P.M. Across the river, the North Canol Road leads 144 miles/232 km to Macmillan Pass at the Northwest Territories border. See the CANOL ROAD section for details.

Campbell Highway Log

(continued)

WL 232.3 (373.8 km) **J 140.7** (226.4 km) Access road leads 7 miles/11.2 km to Ross River (see preceding description).

WL 232.5 (374.2 km) **J 140.5** (226.1 km) Rest area with toilets.

WL 233.4 (375.6 km) **J 139.6** (224.6 km) Lapie River bridge crosses deep gorge of Lapie River, which flows into the Pelly River from Lapie Lakes on the South Canol Road. Highway continues to follow the Pelly River and Pelly Mountains.

WL 233.5 (375.8 km) **J 139.5** (224.5 km) Turnoff to left (south) to Lapie Canyon Yukon government campground adjacent Lapie River: short scenic trails, viewpoint, picturesque canyon; kitchen shelters, firewood, group firepit and picnic area; walk-in tent sites, 14 campsites, $8 fee, drinking water (boil water); boat launch. ▲

WL 236.3 (380.3 km) **J 136.7** (220 km) Danger Creek. In 1905, naturalist Charles Sheldon named this creek after his horse, Danger, supposedly the first horse in this area.

WL 239.9 (386 km) **J 133.1** (214.2 km) Panoramic view of the Pelly River valley just ahead westbound.

WL 243.6 (392 km) **J 129.4** (208.2 km) *CAUTION: Hill and bad corner.*

WL 244.2 (393 km) **J 128.8** (207.3 km) Highway narrows over Grew Creek, no guide rails. This creek was named for Hudson's Bay Co. trader Jim Grew, who trapped this area for many years before his death in 1906.

WL 251 (404 km) **J 122** (196.3 km) Turnout to north.

WL 260.4 (419 km) **J 112.6** (181.2 km) Buttle Creek, named for Roy Buttle, a trapper, prospector and trader who lived here in the early 1900s, and at one time owned a trading post at Ross River.

WL 264.7 (426 km) **J 108.3** (174.3 km) Across the wide Pelly River valley to the north is a view of the mining community of Faro.

WL 265.5 (427.3 km) **J 107.5** (173 km) Access road on right westbound leads 5.6 miles/9 km to Faro. Point of interest sign about Faro at intersection. Rest area with toilets and litter barrels to south just west of this junction.

Southbound travelers note: The highway is gravel from here to Watson Lake.

Faro

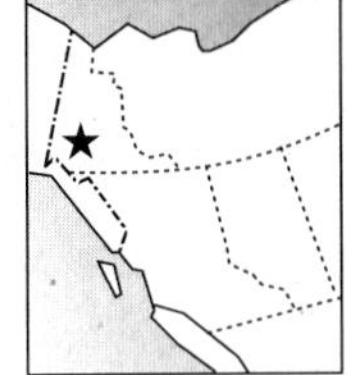

Located in east-central Yukon Territory, 220 road miles/354 km from Whitehorse. **Population:** 500 to 600. **Emergency Services: RCMP**, phone 994-5555. **Fire Department**, phone 994-2222. **Hospital**, phone 994-2736.

Climate: Temperatures range from -51°F/-46°C in winter to a summer maximum of 84°F/29°C. **Radio:** CBC-FM 100.3, CKRW 97.5, CHON 98.7. **Television:** CBC and seven cable channels. **Transportation:** Scheduled air service to Whitehorse and Ross River via Alcan Air.

Private Aircraft: Faro airstrip; 1.5 miles/2.4 km south; elev. 2,351 feet/717m; length 3,000 feet/914m; gravel; fuel 100.

Faro is named after the card game. The Cyprus Anvil mining and milling operation began producing lead–silver and zinc concentrates in 1969; operation was shut down in 1982 because of depressed metal prices and a poor economic market. A limited waste stripping operation was begun in June 1983. Mothballing of the mine began in the spring of 1985, but the mine was reopened in 1986 by Curragh Resources Inc. It closed down again in 1993. This mine was one of the biggest lead producers in the world.

Faro has a visitor information centre, open June through August. Food, gas, store, lodging and private campground available.

Campbell Highway Log

(continued)

WL 268.4 (432 km) **J 104.6** (168.3 km) Johnson Lake Yukon government campground; 15 sites (seven pull-throughs), $8 fee, toilets, water pump, firewood, picnic shelter, boat launch. ▲

The Campbell Highway now follows the valley of the Magundy River. There are several turnouts.

Northbound travelers note: The highway alternates between paved and gravel surfacing between Faro and Carmacks.

WL 285.8 (460 km) **J 87.2** (140.3 km) Magundy River airstrip to north; summer use only. Watch for livestock.

WL 288.1 (463.7 km) **J 84.9** (136.6 km) First glimpse of 22-mile-/35-km-long Little Salmon Lake westbound.

WL 299.3 (481.7 km) **J 73.7** (118.6 km) East end of Little Salmon Lake. Food and lodging at Lena's Place; open year-round. Highway follows north shore.

WL 300.1 (483 km) **J 72.9** (117.3 km) Short access road south to Drury Creek Yukon government campground, situated on the creek at the east end of **Little Salmon Lake:** boat launch, fish filleting table, kitchen shelter, group firepit, 18 campsites, $8 fee, drinking water. Good fishing for northern pike, grayling, whitefish, lake trout 2 to 5 lbs., June 15 through July. ▲

WL 300.4 (483.5 km) **J 72.6** (116.8 km) Turnout at east end Drury Creek bridge. Yukon government maintenance camp to north.

WL 308.2 (496 km) **J 64.8** (104.3 km) Turnout overlooking lake.

WL 311.3 (501 km) **J 61.7** (99.3 km) *CAUTION: Slow down for curves.* Highway follows lakeshore; no guide rails. Turnouts overlooking Little Salmon Lake next 8.5 miles/13.6 km westbound.

WL 316.9 (510 km) **J 56.1** (90.3 km) **Private Aircraft**: Little Salmon airstrip; elev. 2,200 feet/671m; length 1,800 feet/549m; sand and silt.

WL 321.4 (517.3 km) **J 51.6** (83 km) Steep, narrow, winding road south leads to Yukon government **Little Salmon Lake** campground; boat launch, fishing, 12 campsites, $8 fee, drinking water, picnic tables, outhouses, firepits and kitchen shelter. ▲

WL 324.7 (522.6 km) **J 48.3** (77.7 km) Bearfeed Creek, a tributary of Little Salmon River, named because of the abundance of bears attracted to the berry patches in this area. Access to creek to north at west end of bridge.

Highway follows Little Salmon River (seen to south) for about 25 miles/40 km westbound.

WL 341 (548.7 km) **J 32** (51.5 km) *CAUTION: Slow down for hill.*

WL 343.8 (553.2 km) **J 29.2** (47 km) Picnic spot on Little Salmon River, which flows into the Yukon River.

WL 347.3 (559 km) **J 25.7** (41.4 km) Access road leads 4.9 miles/8 km north to **Frenchman Lake** Yukon government campground (10 sites), 5.6 miles/9 km to photo viewpoint of lake, and 9.3 miles/15 km to Nunatak Yukon government campground (10 sites, $8 fee). Access road narrows and surface deteriorates beyond Frenchman Lake Campground. South end of this 12-mile-/19-km-long lake offers good fishing for trout, pike and grayling.

WL 349.5 (562.4 km) **J 23.5** (37.8 km) Turnoff to south for 0.9-mile/1.4-km gravel road to Little Salmon Indian village near confluence of Little Salmon River and Yukon River. There are some inhabited cabins in the area and some subsistence fishing. Private lands, no trespassing.

WL 356.2 (573.2 km) **J 16.8** (27 km) Turnout with point of interest sign overlooking Eagles Nest Bluff (formerly called Eagle Rock), well-known marker for river travelers. One of the worst steamboat disasters on the Yukon River occurred near here when the paddle-wheeler *Columbian* blew up and burned after a crew member accidentally fired a shot into a cargo of gunpowder.

WL 356.7 (574 km) **J 16.3** (26.2 km) View of the Yukon River. At this point Whitehorse is about 160 miles/258 km upstream and Dawson City is about 300 miles/483 km downriver.

WL 360.4 (580 km) **J 12.6** (20.3 km) Northern Canada Power Commission's transmission poles and lines can be seen along highway. Power is transmitted from Aishihik dam site via Whitehorse dam and on to Cyprus Anvil mine and Faro. Orange balls mark lines where they cross river as a hazard to aircraft.

WL 370 (595.4 km) **J 3** (4.8 km) **Private Aircraft**: Carmacks airstrip to south; elev. 1,770 feet/539m; length 5,200 feet/1,585m; gravel.

WL 370.7 (596.5 km) **J 2.3** (3.7 km) Tantalus Butte coal mine on hill to north overlooking junction of Campbell and Klondike highways. The butte was named by U.S. Army Lt. Frederick Schwatka in 1883, because of its tantalizing appearance around many bends of the river before reaching it.

The Tantalus coal seam was discovered in 1887 by George Carmack. Yukon Coal Co.'s Tantalus mine was used as the main source of heating material at United Keno Hill mine as well as the communities of Carmacks, Dawson City and Mayo for some 20 years. Cyprus Anvil Mining Corp. reactivated the coal mine in 1969 to feed its one coal-fired kiln used to dry concentrates. In the mid-1970s, Cyprus Anvil began open-pitting the coal mine.

WL 373 (600.2 km) **J 0 Junction** with the Klondike Highway (Yukon Highway 2), which leads south 2 miles/3.2 km to Carmacks, 103 miles/166 km to the Alaska Highway, and north 221 miles/355 km to Dawson City. (See the KLONDIKE LOOP section.)

Eastbound travelers note: Highway surfacing alternates between paved and gravel from here to Faro.

NAHANNI RANGE ROAD

Campbell Highway Junction to Tungsten, NWT
Yukon Highway 10
(See map, page 653)

Roadside sign. (Earl L. Brown, staff)

The Nahanni Range (Tungsten) Road branches off the Campbell Highway 68.5 miles/110.2 km north of Watson Lake and leads 125 miles/201.2 km northeast to the former mining town of Tungsten, NWT.

Nahanni Range Road is maintained by the Yukon government from the Campbell Highway junction to **Milepost CJ 82**. The remaining 43 miles/69 km to Tungsten are unmaintained and not recommended for travel. The road to Mile 82 is gravel surfaced with some small washouts and soft steep shoulders. *NOTE: The Yukon government does not recommend this road for general tourist travel due to lack of services and maintenance.*

Construction of the Nahanni Range Road was begun in 1961 to provide access to the mining property. The road was completed in 1963 with the bridging of the Frances and Hyland rivers.

Nahanni Range Road Log

Distance from Campbell Highway junction (CJ) is followed by distance from Tungsten (T).

CJ 0 T 125 (201.2 km) **Miner's Junction**; formerly known as Cantung Junction; no services.

CJ 5.1 (8.2 km) **T 119.9** (193 km) **Upper Frances River** bridge; good grayling fishing in stream on southeast side.

CJ 7.4 (11.9 km) **T 117.6** (189.2 km) Good grayling fishing at confluence of **Sequence Creek** and **Frances River**.

CJ 11.8 (19 km) **T 113.2** (182.2 km) Queen Creek.

CJ 13.1 (21.1 km) **T 111.9** (180.1 km) King Creek.

CJ 14.2 (22.8 km) **T 110.8** (178.3 km) Road passes between Mount Billings to the north (elev. 6,909 feet/2,106m) and Mount Murray to the south (elev. 7,093 feet/2,162m).

CJ 20.3 (32.7 km) **T 104.7** (168.5 km) Short access road to **Long Lake**, grayling fishing.

CJ 21.5 (34.6 km) **T 103.5** (166.5 km) Long Lake Creek. There are a few private log cabins along here.

CJ 24.1 (38.8 km) **T 100.9** (162.4 km) Dolly Varden Creek.

CJ 28.4 (45.7 km) **T 96.6** (155.4 km) French Creek.

CJ 28.9 (46.5 km) **T 96.1** (154.6 km) Road enters the narrow Hyland River valley through the Logan Mountains.

CJ 32.6 (52.4 km) **T 92.4** (148.7 km) South Bridge Creek.

CJ 33.2 (53.4 km) **T 91.8** (147.7 km) North Bridge Creek.

CJ 38.1 (61.3 km) **T 86.9** (139.8 km) Jackpine Creek.

CJ 40.6 (65.3 km) **T 84.4** (135.8 km) **Spruce Creek**, good glides and broken pools upstream for grayling fishing.

CJ 42.8 (68.9 km) **T 82.2** (132.3 km) Short access road to Hyland River.

CJ 45.8 (73.7 km) **T 79.2** (127.4 km) **Conglomerate Creek**, scenic spot to picnic. Good grayling fishing near small waterfall.

CJ 48 (77.2 km) **T 77** (123.9 km) Mining road to west.

CJ 52.1 (83.8 km) **T 72.9** (117.3 km) South Moose Creek.

CJ 52.2 (84 km) **T 72.8** (117.1 km) Yukon government campground; 10 sites, kitchen shelter, picnic tables.

CJ 52.5 (84.5 km) **T 72.5** (116.6 km) North Moose Creek.

CJ 62.4 (100.4 km) **T 62.6** (100.7 km) **Flood Creek**, good grayling fishing.

CJ 68.4 (110.1 km) **T 56.6** (91 km) Hyland River bridge; turnout with litter barrel.

CJ 71 (114.2 km) **T 54** (86.9 km) Emergency airstrip to west.

CJ 75.9 (122.1 km) **T 49.1** (79 km) Ostensibility Creek.

CJ 82 (132 km) **T 42.9** (69 km) **Piggott Creek**, good grayling fishing. Outhouse.

NOTE: Yukon government road maintenance ends. Road not recommended for travel beyond this point.

CJ 116.8 (188 km) **T 8.2** (13.2 km) YT–NWT border.

CJ 125 (201.2 km) **T 0 TUNGSTEN**, which was the company town for one of the richest mines in the world and Canada's only tungsten producer, was originally called Cantung (Canada Tungsten Mining Corp. Ltd.). Open-pit mining began here in the early 1960s with the discovery of scheelite in the Flat River area. Scheelite is an ore of tungsten, an oxide used for hardening steel and making white gold. The mine shut down in 1986, and the population of 500 moved out. Only a security staff remains.

CANOL ROAD

Alaska Highway Junction to NWT Border
Yukon Highway 6
(See map, page 658)

Narrow and winding North Canol Road along the Ross River. (Earl L. Brown, staff)

The 513-mile-/825-km-long Canol (Canadian Oil) Road was built to provide access to oil fields at Norman Wells, NWT, on the Mackenzie River. Conceived by the U.S. War Dept. to help fuel Alaska and protect it from a Japanese invasion, the road and a 4-inch-diameter pipeline were constructed from Norman Wells, NWT, through Macmillan Pass, past Ross River, to Johnson's Crossing on the Alaska Highway. From there the pipeline carried oil to a refinery at Whitehorse.

Begun in 1942 and completed in 1944, the Canol Project included the road, pipeline, a telephone line, the refinery, airfields, pumping stations, tank farms, wells and camps. Only about 1 million barrels of oil were pumped to Whitehorse before the war ended in 1945 and the $134 million Canol Project was abandoned. (Today, Norman Wells, pop. 757, is still a major supplier of oil with a pipeline to Zama, AB, built in 1985.)

Since 1958, the Canol Road between Johnson's Crossing on the Alaska Highway and Ross River on the Campbell Highway (referred to as the South Canol Road) and between Ross River and the YT–NWT border (referred to as the North Canol Road) has been rebuilt and is open to summer traffic. It is maintained to minimum standards.

The 136.8-mile/220.2-km South Canol Road is a narrow winding road which crests the Big Salmon Range and threads its way above Lapie Canyon via a difficult but scenic stretch of road. Construction on the South Canol has replaced many old bridges with culverts, but there are still a few one-lane wooden bridges. Driving time is about four hours one way. Watch for steep hills and bad corners. There are no facilities along the South Canol Road and it is definitely not recommended for large RVs or trailers. Not recommended for any size vehicle in wet weather. Inquiries on current road conditions should be made locally or with the Yukon Dept. of Highways in Whitehorse before driving this road.

The 144.2-mile/232-km North Canol Road is also a narrow, winding road which some motorists have compared to a roller coaster. All bridges on the North Canol are one-lane, and the road surface can be very slippery when wet. Not recommended during wet weather and not recommended for large RVs or trailers. If mining is under way along the North Canol, watch for large transport trucks.

Our log of the North Canol ends at the YT–NWT border, where vehicles may turn around. Road washouts prohibit travel beyond this point. From the border to Norman Wells it is 230 miles/372 km of unusable road that has been designated the Canol Heritage Trail by the NWT government. Some adventurous travelers have hiked it and report that there are no facilities and river crossings are hazardous, but the route through the Mackenzie Mountains is scenic and there are many relics of the Canol Project.

WARNING: The only facilities on the Canol Road are at Ross River and at Johnson's Crossing on the Alaska Highway.

Emergency medical services: In Ross River, phone (403) 969-2221; or phone the RCMP, (403) 969-5555, or 1-667-5555.

South Canol Road Log

Distance from the junction with the Alaska Highway (J) is followed by distance from the Campbell Highway junction (C).

J 0 C **136.8** (220.2 km) **Junction** of the Canol Road (Yukon Highway 6) with the Alaska Highway. Food, gas and camping at Johnson's Crossing at the southwest end of the Teslin River bridge, 0.7 mile/1.1 km from Canol Road turnoff.

NOTE: Kilometreposts are up along the South Canol and reflect distance in kilometres from the Alaska Highway.

J **3.9** (6.2 km) C **132.9** (213.8 km) Fourmile Creek. Road begins ascent across the Big Salmon River to the summit (elev. about 4,000 feet/1,219m). Snow possible at summit early October to late spring.

J **6.2** (10 km) C **130.6** (210.1 km) Beaver Creek.

J **13.9** (22.4 km) C **122.9** (197.8 km) Moose Creek.

J **17.2** (27.6 km) C **119.6** (192.4 km) Seventeenmile Creek.

J **19.4** (31.2 km) C **117.4** (188.9 km) Murphy Creek.

J **19.8** (31.8 km) C **117** (188.3 km) Kilometrepost 32. Pelly Mountains can be seen in distance northbound.

J **27** (43.4 km) C **109.8** (176.7 km) One-lane wooden bridge over Evelyn Creek.

J **28.7** (46.2 km) C **108.1** (174 km) Two-lane bridge over Sidney Creek.

J **30.6** (49.2 km) C **106.2** (170.9 km) Access road on right northbound leads to Sidney Lake. Nice little lake and good place to camp.

From here northbound the South Canol follows the Nisutlin River, which is to the east and can be seen from the road the next 30 miles/48 km until the road crosses the Rose River beyond Quiet Lake.

J **30.9** (49.7 km) C **105.9** (170.4 km) Turnout with litter barrel to east.

J **36.7** (59 km) C **100.1** (161.1 km) Coyote Creek, culverts.

J **39.1** (62.9 km) C **97.7** (157.2 km) Good view of Pelly Mountains ahead. Road crosses Cottonwood Creek.

J **42** (67.6 km) C **94.8** (152.5 km) Access road on right northbound leads to Nisutlin River. Good place to camp with tables and outhouse.

J **47.8** (76.9 km) C **89** (143.2 km) Quiet Lake Yukon government campground; 20 sites, $8 fee, boat launch, picnic tables, kitchen shelter. Watch for steep hills northbound to Quiet Lake. ▲

J **54.7** (88 km) C **82.1** (132.1 km) Lake Creek. Road now follows **Quiet Lake** to west; good fishing for lake trout, northern pike and arctic grayling.

J **56** (90.1 km) C **80.8** (130 km) Turnout with point of interest sign overlooking Quiet Lake. This is the largest of three lakes

CANOL ROAD *Alaska Highway Junction, YT, to NWT Border*

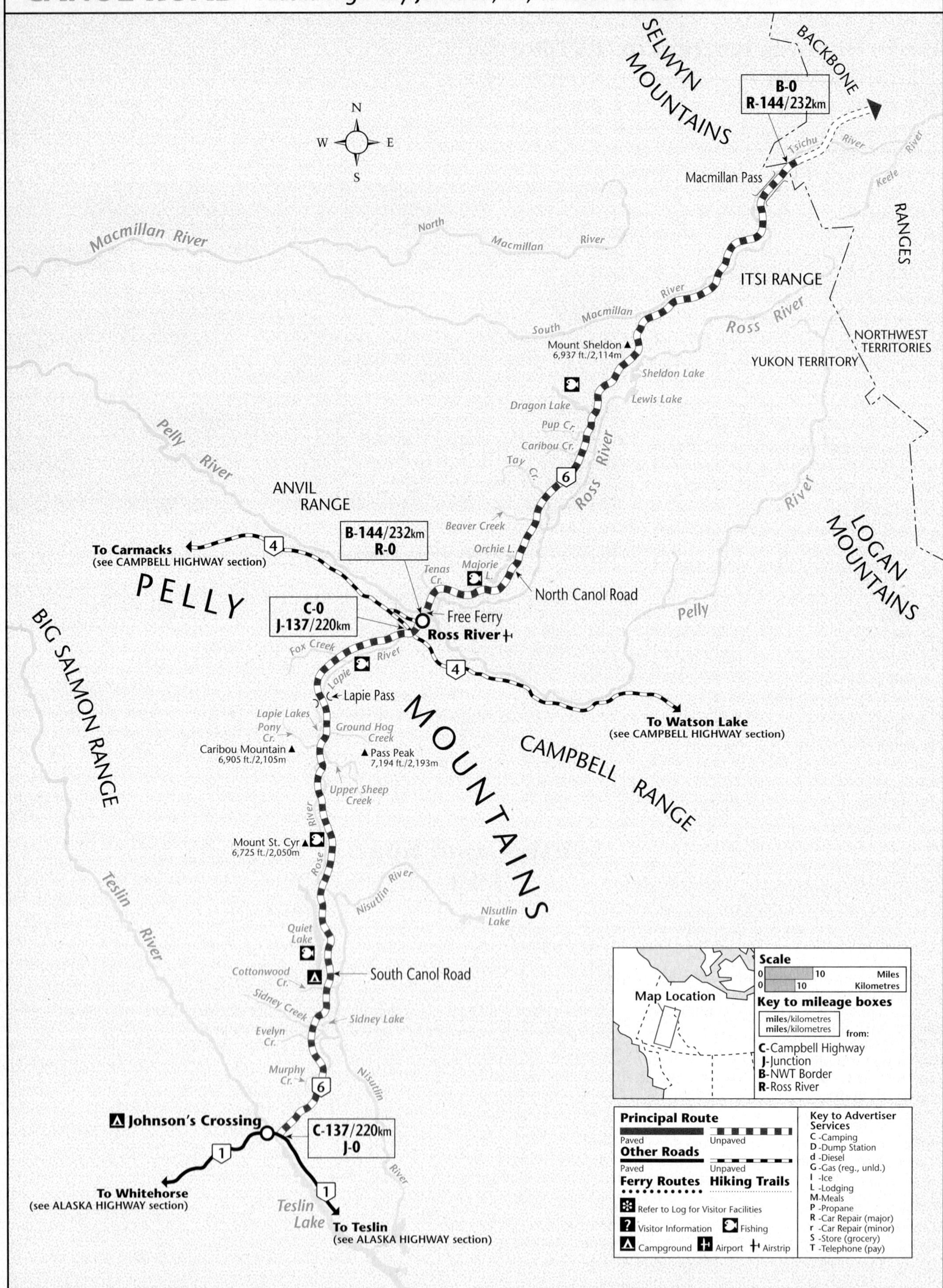
SELWYN MOUNTAINS
BACKBONE RANGES
B-0
R-144/232km
Tsichu River
Keele River
Macmillan Pass
N
W
E
S
Macmillan River
North Macmillan River
ITSI RANGE
South Macmillan River
Ross River
NORTHWEST TERRITORIES
YUKON TERRITORY
Mount Sheldon
6,937 ft./2,114m
Sheldon Lake
Lewis Lake
Dragon Lake
Pup Cr.
Caribou Cr.
Tay Cr.
6
Pelly River
ANVIL RANGE
Beaver Creek
B-144/232km
R-0
To Carmacks
(see CAMPBELL HIGHWAY section)
4
Orchie L.
Majorie L.
Tenas Cr.
North Canol Road
LOGAN MOUNTAINS
PELLY
C-0
J-137/220km
Free Ferry
Ross River
Pelly
Fox Creek
Lapie River
Lapie Pass
To Watson Lake
(see CAMPBELL HIGHWAY section)
BIG SALMON RANGE
Lapie Lakes
Pony Cr.
Ground Hog Creek
Caribou Mountain
6,905 ft./2,105m
Pass Peak
7,194 ft./2,193m
MOUNTAINS
CAMPBELL RANGE
Upper Sheep Creek
Rose River
Mount St. Cyr
6,725 ft./2,050m
Teslin River
Nisutlin River
Nisutlin Lake
Quiet Lake
Cottonwood Cr.
South Canol Road
Sidney Creek
Sidney Lake
Evelyn Cr.
Murphy Cr.
Johnson's Crossing
C-137/220km
J-0
To Whitehorse
(see ALASKA HIGHWAY section)
Teslin Lake
To Teslin
(see ALASKA HIGHWAY section)
Map Location
Scale
0 10 Miles
0 10 Kilometres
Key to mileage boxes
miles/kilometres
miles/kilometres
from:
C-Campbell Highway
J-Junction
B-NWT Border
R-Ross River
Principal Route
Paved
Unpaved
Other Roads
Paved
Unpaved
Ferry Routes
Hiking Trails
Refer to Log for Visitor Facilities
Visitor Information
Fishing
Campground
Airport
Airstrip
Key to Advertiser Services
C -Camping
D -Dump Station
d -Diesel
G -Gas (reg., unld.)
I -Ice
L -Lodging
M -Meals
P -Propane
R -Car Repair (major)
r -Car Repair (minor)
S -Store (grocery)
T -Telephone (pay)

that form the headwaters of the Big Salmon River system. The 17-mile-/28-km-long lake was named in 1887 by John McCormack, one of four miners who prospected the Big Salmon River from its mouth on the Yukon River to its source. Although they did find some gold, the river and lakes have become better known for their good fishing and fine scenery. Until the completion of the South Canol Road in the 1940s, this area was reached mainly by boating and portaging hundreds of miles up the Teslin and Nisutlin rivers.

J 61.2 (98.5 km) **C 75.6** (121.6 km) Turnoff on left northbound (west) for **Quiet Lake**, day-use area with picnic sites, water, boat launch and fishing. Entry point for canoeists on the Big Salmon River.

J 61.5 (99 km) **C 75.3** (121.2 km) Yukon government Quiet Lake maintenance camp on left northbound.

J 62.6 (100.7 km) **C 74.2** (119.4 km) Distance marker indicates Ross River 126 km.

J 63.7 (102.5 km) **C 73.1** (117.6 km) Steep hill and panoramic view of mountains and valley at Kilometrepost 102.

J 65.5 (105.4 km) **C 71.3** (114.7 km) One-lane Bailey bridge across Rose River No. 1. The road now follows the valley of the Rose River into Lapie Pass northbound.

J 70.4 (113.3 km) **C 66.4** (106.8 km) Canol Creek culvert.

J 71.9 (115.7 km) **C 64.9** (104.4 km) Deer Creek.

J 75.7 (121.8 km) **C 61.1** (98.3 km) Gravel Creek culvert.

J 81.1 (130.5 km) **C 55.7** (89.6 km) Road crosses creek (name unknown) in culvert just south of Kilometrepost 130.

J 83.7 (134.7 km) **C 53.1** (85.4 km) Dodge Creek culvert at Kilometrepost 134.

J 87.1 (140.2 km) **C 49.7** (80 km) Rose River No. 2 culvert just south of Kilometrepost 140.

J 89.7 (144.3 km) **C 47.1** (75.8 km) Rose River No. 3 culverts.

J 91.5 (147.2 km) **C 45.3** (72.9 km) Rose River No. 4 culverts.

J 93.8 (151 km) **C 43** (69.2 km) Rose River No. 5 culverts.

J 94.1 (151.4 km) **C 42.7** (68.7 km) Distance marker indicates Ross River 76 km.

J 95.1 (153 km) **C 41.7** (67.1 km) Upper Sheep Creek joins the Rose River here. To the east is Pass Peak (elev. 7,194 feet/2,193m).

J 96.4 (155.1 km) **C 40.4** (65 km) Rose River No. 6.

J 97.1 (156.2 km) **C 39.7** (63.9 km) Rose Lake to east.

J 97.5 (156.9 km) **C 39.3** (63.2 km) Pony Creek. Caribou Mountain (elev. 6,905 feet/2,105m) to west.

J 101.1 (162.7 km) **C 35.7** (57.4 km) Lakes to west are part of Lapie Lakes chain, headwaters of the Lapie River. These features were named by Dr. George M. Dawson of the Geological Survey of Canada in 1887 for Lapie, an Iroquois Indian companion and canoeman of Robert Campbell, who was the first to explore the Pelly River area in 1843 for the Hudson's Bay Co.

J 101.2 (162.8 km) **C 35.6** (57.3 km) Ground Hog Creek.

J 102.5 (165 km) **C 34.3** (55.2 km) Access road on left northbound leads west a short distance to Lapie Lakes. Good place to camp.

J 107.4 (172.8 km) **C 29.4** (47.3 km) Lapie River No. 1 culverts. Ponds reported good for grayling fishing.

J 107.5 (173 km) **C 29.3** (47.1 km) Ahead northbound is Barite Mountain (elev. about 6,500 feet/1,981m).

J 110 (177 km) **C 26.8** (43.1 km) Gold Creek.

J 111.4 (179.2 km) **C 25.4** (40.8 km) Bacon Creek.

J 113.4 (182.5 km) **C 23.4** (37.6 km) Boulder Creek.

J 115.6 (186 km) **C 21.2** (34.1 km) Road runs to the east side of Barite Mountain.

J 120.2 (193.4 km) **C 16.6** (26.7 km) Fox Creek culverts.

J 120.7 (194.2 km) **C 16.1** (25.9 km) The road follows the Lapie River Canyon for about the next 11 miles/18 km, climbing to an elevation of about 500 feet/152m above the river. Narrow road, watch for rocks.

J 123.3 (198.4 km) **C 13.5** (21.7 km) Kilometrepost 200. Distance marker indicates Ross River 26 km. Lapie River runs to right side of road northbound.

J 124.7 (200.6 km) **C 12.1** (19.4 km) Glacier Creek.

J 126.3 (203.2 km) **C 10.5** (16.9 km) Turnouts on right side of road northbound overlooking Lapie River Canyon.

J 132.3 (212.9 km) **C 4.5** (7.2 km) Narrow one-lane bridge over Lapie River No. 2. Point of interest sign on north end of bridge about the Lapie River Canyon. Approximately 100 million years ago, flat horizontal layers of rock were buried several kilometres below the surface of the earth. Movement by rigid plates of the earth's crust subjected the rock to massive compression and strain, and it was deformed into folds. Over millions of years, the rocks rose, exposing the folds in the canyon wall.

J 133 (214 km) **C 3.8** (6.1 km) Erosional features called hoodoos can be seen in the clay banks rising above the road.

J 133.3 (214.5 km) **C 3.5** (5.6 km) Ash layer can be seen in clay bank on right side of road.

J 135.6 (218.2 km) **C 1.2** (1.9 km) Jackfish Lake, below on left northbound, is used for docking floatplanes.

J 136.8 (220 km) **C 0 Junction** of South Canol Road with the Campbell Highway. Approximately straight ahead northbound, across the Campbell Highway, a poorly maintained section of the Canol Road continues to Ross River. Motorists bound for Ross River or the North Canol Road are advised to turn left (west) on the Campbell Highway from the South Canol and drive about 5 miles/8 km to the main Ross River access road (see map).

North Canol Road Log

Distance from Ross River (R) is followed by distance from NWT border (B).

R 0 B 144.2 (232 km) **ROSS RIVER** (see description in the CAMPBELL HIGHWAY section). Yukon government Ross River ferry (free) crosses the Pelly River. Ferry operates from 8 A.M. to noon and 1-5 P.M. daily from late May to mid-October. Those who miss the last ferry crossing of the day may leave their vehicles on the opposite side of the river and use the footbridge to walk into Ross River; vehicles can be brought over in the morning.

R 0.4 (0.6 km) **B 143.8** (231.4 km) Stockpile to west is barite from the Yukon Barite Mine.

R 0.6 (1 km) **B 143.6** (231.1 km) Road to east leads to original site of Ross River and Indian village.

R 0.9 (1.4 km) **B 143.3** (230.6 km) Second access road east to old Ross River and Indian village. Canol Road follows the Ross River.

R 2.1 (3.4 km) **B 142.1** (228.7 km) *CAUTION: Slide area, watch for falling rocks.*

R 3.9 (6.2 km) **B 140.3** (225.8 km) Kilometrepost 236. Kilometreposts on the North Canol reflect distance from the Alaska Highway.

R 4.7 (7.6 km) **B 139.5** (224.5 km) Raspberry patch. Good pickings.

R 6.8 (10.9 km) **B 137.4** (221.1 km) One-lane bridge over Tenas Creek.

R 10.3 (16.5 km) **B 133.9** (215.5 km) Kilometrepost 246.

R 10.6 (17 km) **B 133.6** (215 km) Gravel pit to west.

R 15.5 (24.9 km) **B 128.7** (207.1 km) Kilometrepost 254.

R 17 (27.3 km) **B 127.2** (204.7 km) Deep Creek.

R 20.9 (33.6 km) **B 123.3** (198.4 km) **Marjorie Creek.** Locals report good grayling fishing.

R 21 (33.8 km) **B 123.2** (198.2 km) Access road to west leads to Marjorie Lake. Access road not recommended for large RVs.

R 21.7 (34.9 km) **B 122.5** (197.1 km) Marjorie Lake to west.

R 27 (43.4 km) **B 117.2** (188.6 km) Kilometrepost 272. Unnamed lake to east.

R 28.1 (45.2 km) **B 116.1** (186.8 km) Boat launch on Orchie Lake to west.

R 29.8 (48 km) **B 114.4** (184.1 km) Distance marker indicates NWT border 195 km, Ross River 50 km.

R 30.9 (49.7 km) **B 113.3** (182.3 km) Kilometrepost 278.

R 31.9 (51.3 km) **B 112.3** (180.7 km) One-lane bridge over Gravel Creek. The next 15 miles/24 km are excellent moose country.

R 33.4 (53.7 km) **B 110.8** (178.3 km) One-lane bridge over Flat Creek.

R 34.6 (55.7 km) **B 109.6** (176.3 km) Kilometrepost 284.

R 37 (59.5 km) **B 107.2** (172.5 km) One-lane bridge over Beaver Creek.

R 40.7 (65.5 km) **B 103.5** (166.5 km) Kilometrepost 294.

R 41.8 (67.2 km) **B 102.4** (164.8 km) One-lane bridge over 180 Mile Creek.

R 43.9 (70.6 km) **B 100.3** (161.4 km) One-lane bridge over Tay Creek.

R 44.4 (71.4 km) **B 99.8** (160.6 km) Kilometrepost 300.

R 46.3 (74.5 km) **B 97.9** (157.5 km) One-lane bridge over Blue Creek.

R 48.1 (77.4 km) **B 96.1** (154.6 km) Kilometrepost 306. Flood Creek culvert.

R 57.6 (92.7 km) **B 86.6** (139.3 km) Clifford's Slough to the east.

R 58.6 (94.3 km) **B 85.6** (137.7 km) Steep hill to one-lane bridge over Caribou Creek.

R 61.1 (98.3 km) **B 83.1** (133.7 km) Distance marker indicates NWT border 145 km, Ross River 100 km.

R 61.8 (99.4 km) **B 82.4** (132.6 km) One-lane bridge over Pup Creek.

R 62.8 (101 km) **B 81.4** (131 km) Kilometrepost 330.

R 64.8 (104.3 km) **B 79.4** (127.7 km) Turnout to west. Steep hill.

R 65.1 (104.7 km) **B 79.1** (127.3 km) Turnout to **Dragon Lake**; overnight parking, litter barrels. Locals report that early spring is an excellent time for pike and trout in the inlet. Rock hounds check roadsides and borrow pits for colorful chert, which can be worked into jewelry.

R 65.4 (105.2 km) **B 78.8** (126.8 km) Kilometrepost 334. Large, level, gravel turnout to west overlooking Dragon Lake; boat launch.

R 68.9 (110.8 km) **B 75.3** (121.2 km) Kilometrepost 340.

R 69.6 (112 km) **B 74.6** (120 km) Wreckage of Twin Pioneer aircraft to west. WWII remnants can be found in this area.

R 69.9 (112.5 km) **B 74.3** (119.5 km) Road to Twin Creek.

R 70.8 (113.9 km) **B 73.4** (118.1 km) Airstrip.

R 71 (114.2 km) **B 73.2** (117.8 km) One-lane bridge over Twin Creek No. 1. Yukon government maintenance camp.

R 71.1 (114.4 km) **B 73.1** (117.6 km) One-lane bridge over Twin Creek No. 2. Good views of Mount Sheldon.

R 75.1 (120.8 km) **B 69.1** (111.2 km) Kilometrepost 350. Mount Sheldon ahead, located 3 miles/4.8 km north of Sheldon Lake; a very beautiful and distinguishable feature on the Canol Road (elev. 6,937 feet/2,114m). In 1900, Poole Field and Clement Lewis, who were fans of writer Rudyard Kipling, named this peak Kipling Mountain and the lake at its base Rudyard. In 1907, Joseph Keele of the Geological Survey of Canada renamed them after Charles Sheldon, a well-known sheep hunter and naturalist who came to the area to collect Stone sheep specimens for the Chicago Natural History Museum in 1905.

R 76.4 (123 km) **B 67.8** (109.1 km) Kilometrepost 352. Of the three-lake chain, Sheldon Lake is farthest north, then Field Lake and Lewis Lake, which is just visible from here. Lewis Lake is closest to the confluence of the Ross and Prevost rivers.

Field Lake and Lewis Lake were named in 1907 by Joseph Keele of the Geological Survey of Canada after Poole Field and Clement Lewis. The two partners, who had prospected this country, ran a trading post called Nahanni House at the mouth of the Ross River in 1905.

R 77.6 (124.9 km) **B 66.6** (107.2 km) Kilometrepost 354. One-lane bridge over Riddell Creek. Tip of Mount Riddell (elev. 6,101 feet/1,859m) can be seen to the west.

R 78.8 (126.8 km) **B 65.4** (105.2 km) View of Sheldon Lake ahead, Field Lake to right northbound.

R 79.8 (128.4 km) **B 64.4** (103.6 km) Access road east to Sheldon Lake.

R 82.7 (133.1 km) **B 61.5** (99 km) One-lane bridge over Sheldon Creek. Road climbs, leaving Ross River valley and entering Macmillan Valley northbound.

R 89.3 (143.7 km) **B 54.9** (88.3 km) Height of land before starting descent northbound into South Macmillan River system.

R 89.7 (144.3 km) **B 54.5** (87.7 km) Steep hill. Road may wash out during heavy rains. Deep ditches along roadside help channel water.

R 91.4 (147.1 km) **B 52.8** (85 km) One-lane bridge over Moose Creek.

R 91.6 (147.4 km) **B 52.6** (84.6 km) Milepost 230.

R 92.3 (148.5 km) **B 51.9** (83.5 km) Kilometrepost 378. Peaks of the Itsi Range ahead. Rugged, spectacular scenery northbound.

R 92.7 (149.1 km) **B 51.5** (82.9 km) Distance marker indicates NWT border 95 km, Ross River 150 km.

R 93.5 (150.4 km) **B 50.7** (81.6 km) Kilometrepost 380.

R 93.8 (151 km) **B 50.4** (81.1 km) First of several WWII vehicle dumps to west. To the east is a wannigan, or skid shack, used as living quarters by Canol Road workers during construction of the road. It was too far to return to base camp; these small buildings were strategically located along the route so the workers had a place to eat and sleep at night.

R 94 (151.3 km) **B 50.2** (80.8 km) To east are remains of a maintenance depot where heavy equipment was repaired. Concrete foundations to west. First glimpse of the South Macmillan River northbound.

R 94.7 (152.4 km) **B 49.5** (79.6 km) Kilometrepost 382. Another Canol project equipment dump to explore. Watch ditches for old pieces of pipeline.

R 97.8 (157.4 km) **B 46.4** (74.6 km) One-lane bridge over Boulder Creek.

R 98.4 (158.3 km) **B 45.8** (73.7 km) Kilometrepost 388.

R 98.5 (158.5 km) **B 45.7** (73.5 km) Access road west to South Macmillan River where boats can be launched. Locals advise launching boats here rather than from the bridge at **Milepost R 113.6**, which washes out periodically and leaves dangerous debris in the river.

R 100.8 (162.2 km) **B 43.4** (69.8 km) Kilometrepost 392.

R 101 (162.5 km) **B 43.2** (69.5 km) View of Itsi Range ahead northbound. Itsi is said to be an Indian word meaning "wind" and was first given as a name to Itsi Lakes, headwaters of the Ross River. The road dips down and crosses an unnamed creek.

R 102.1 (164.3 km) **B 42.1** (67.7 km) Milepost 240. Kilometrepost 394.

R 104.5 (168.2 km) **B 39.7** (63.9 km) Kilometrepost 398. View of the South Macmillan River from here.

R 105.3 (169.4 km) **B 38.9** (62.6 km) View of Selwyn Mountains, named in 1901 by Joseph Keele of the Geological Survey of Canada for Dr. Alfred Richard Selwyn (1824–1902), a distinguished geologist in England. Dr. Selwyn later became director of the Geological Survey of Australia and then director of the Geological Survey of Canada from 1869 until his retirement in 1895.

R 108.2 (174.1 km) **B 36** (57.9 km) Kilometrepost 404.

R 111 (178.6 km) **B 33.2** (53.4 km) One-lane bridge over Itsi Creek.

R 112.2 (180.5 km) **B 32** (51.5 km) One-lane bridge over Wagon Creek.

R 113.1 (182 km) **B 31.1** (50 km) Kilometrepost 412.

R 113.6 (182.8 km) **B 30.6** (49.2 km) Turnout to east on South Macmillan River. Good place for a picnic but not recommended as a boat launch. One-lane Bailey bridge over South Macmillan River No. 1.

Robert Campbell, a Hudson's Bay Co. explorer on a journey down the Pelly River in 1843, named this major tributary of the Pelly after Chief Factor James McMillan, who had sponsored Campbell's employment with the company.

R 114.3 (183.9 km) **B 29.9** (48.1 km) Kilometrepost 414.

R 115.1 (185.2 km) **B 29.1** (46.8 km) Access road on left northbound leads about 7 miles/11 km to Yukon Barite Mine. Barite is a soft mineral that requires only crushing and bagging before being shipped over the Dempster Highway to the Beaufort Sea oil and gas wells, where it is used as a lubricant known as drilling mud.

R 115.6 (186 km) **B 28.6** (46 km) Kilometrepost 416.

R 117.2 (188.6 km) **B 27** (43.4 km) Access road on right northbound to gravel pit.

R 118.8 (191.2 km) **B 25.4** (40.8 km) Dept. of Public Works maintenance camp; status unknown.

R 118.9 (191.3 km) **B 25.3** (40.7 km) One-lane bridge over Jeff Creek.

R 121.2 (195 km) **B 23** (37 km) One-lane bridge over Hess Creek. Bears in area.

R 123 (197.9 km) **B 21.2** (34.1 km) Kilometrepost 428.

R 123.2 (198.3 km) **B 21** (33.8 km) Gravel turnout on left northbound with RCMP trailer. Distance marker indicates NWT border 45 km, Ross River 200 km. One-lane bridge over Dewhurst Creek.

R 126.6 (203.7 km) **B 17.6** (28.3 km) Kilometrepost 434.

R 127.5 (205.2 km) **B 16.7** (26.9 km) Entering Macmillan Pass. At "Mac Pass," the road climbs to elevations above 4,480 feet/1,366m.

R 129.4 (208.2 km) **B 14.8** (23.8 km) One-lane bridge over Macmillan River No. 2.

R 129.5 (208.4 km) **B 14.7** (23.6 km) Abandoned Army vehicles from the Canol Project on left northbound.

R 129.6 (208.6 km) **B 14.6** (23.5 km) Abandoned Army vehicles from the Canol Project on right northbound.

R 131.5 (211.6 km) **B 12.7** (20.4 km) Kilometrepost 442.

R 133.6 (215 km) **B 10.6** (17 km) To the west is Cordilleran Engineering camp, managers of the mining development of Ogilvie Joint Venture's Jason Project. The Jason deposit is a zinc, lead, silver, barite property. The deposit's size is still uncertain.

One-lane bridge over Sekie Creek No. 1.

R 133.9 (215.5 km) **B 10.3** (16.6 km) Kilometrepost 446.

R 134.4 (216.3 km) **B 9.8** (15.8 km) Fuel tanks on left northbound.

R 136.3 (219.3 km) **B 7.9** (12.7 km) Sekie Creek No. 2 culvert.

R 136.4 (219.5 km) **B 7.8** (12.5 km) Access to Macmillan airstrip on left northbound. Access road to right to Hudson Bay Mining & Smelting's Tom lead–zinc mineral claims. The Tom is a stratabound silver–lead–zinc deposit and the size is yet to be determined. At one time it was considered to be 9 million tons of 16 percent combined lead–zinc.

R 137.6 (221.4 km) **B 6.6** (10.6 km) Kilometrepost 452.

R 137.7 (221.6 km) **B 6.5** (10.5 km) One-lane bridge over Macmillan River No. 3.

R 141.8 (228.2 km) **B 2.4** (3.8 km) One-lane bridge over Macmillan River No. 4.

R 142.9 (230 km) **B 1.3** (2.1 km) One-lane bridge over Macmillan River No. 5.

R 144.1 (231.9 km) **B 0.1** (0.2 km) One-lane bridge over Macmillan River No. 6.

R 144.2 (232 km) **B 0** YT–NWT border. Sign cautions motorists to proceed at their own risk. The road is not maintained and bridges are not safe beyond this point. Vehicles turn around here.

Ahead is the Tsichu River valley and the Selwyn Mountains. The abandoned North Canol Road continues another 230 miles/372 km from the YT–NWT border to Norman Wells, NWT. Designated the Canol Heritage Trail, it is suitable for hiking, bicycles or motorcycles. There are some river crossings. It is prime grizzly and caribou habitat with exceptional mountain scenery.

DEMPSTER HIGHWAY

Milepost D 25 Klondike Highway 2 to Inuvik, NWT
Yukon Highway 5, NWT Highway 8

(See map, page 662)

Dempster Highway winds toward Richardson Mountains on elevated berm.
(Earl L. Brown, staff)

The Dempster Highway begins 25 miles/40.2 km east of Dawson City, YT, at its junction with Klondike Highway 2, and leads 456.3 miles/734.3 km northeast to Inuvik, NWT.

The highway is named for Inspector W.J.D. Dempster. Dempster was sent to look for a missing RCMP patrol that had set out for Dawson City by dog team from Fort McPherson in December of 1910. He discovered their frozen bodies on March 22, 1911, only 26 miles from where they had started. Lack of knowledge of the trail, coupled with too few rations, had doomed the four-man patrol. The "lost patrol" is buried at Fort McPherson.

Construction of the Dempster Highway began in 1959, under the Road to Resources program, and was completed in 1978. A five-year major reconstruction and surfacing program on the highway concluded in 1988, although freezing weather and heavy truck traffic may erode both road base and surfacing in areas. Calcium chloride is used in some areas to reduce dust and as a bonding agent; wash your vehicle as soon as practical.

The Dempster is a gravel road. There are stretches of clay surface that can be slippery in wet weather. Summer driving conditions on the Dempster vary depending on weather and maintenance. Generally, road conditions range from fair to excellent, with highway speeds attainable on some sections.

Facilities are still few and far between on the Dempster. Full auto services are available at Klondike River Lodge at the Dempster Highway turnoff on Klondike Highway 2. Gas, propane, food and lodging, and car repair are also available at Eagle Plains Hotel, located at about the halfway point on the Dempster. Gas is also available in Fort McPherson. Gas up whenever possible.

The Dempster is open year-round. The highway is fairly well-traveled in summer: A driver may not see another car for an hour, and then pass four cars in a row. Locals say the highway is smoother and easier to drive in winter, but precautions should be taken against cold weather, high winds and poor visibility; check road conditions before proceeding in winter. DRIVE WITH YOUR HEADLIGHTS ON!

There are two ferry crossings on the Dempster, at **Milepost J 334.9** (Peel River crossing) and **J 377.9** (Mackenzie River and Arctic Red River crossings). Free government ferry service is available 15 hours a day (9 A.M. to 1 A.M. Northwest Territories time, 8 A.M. to midnight Yukon time) during summer (from about June to mid-October). Cross by ice bridge in winter.

General information on Northwest Territories is available by calling the Arctic Hotline at 1-800-661-0788. For recorded messages on ferry service, road and weather conditions, phone 1-800-661-0750 or 0752. If you are in Dawson City, the Western Arctic Visitor Centre has information on Northwest Territories and the Dempster Highway. Located in the B.Y.N. Bldg. on Front Street, across from the Yukon Visitor Centre, it is open 9 A.M. to 9 P.M., June to September; phone (403) 993-6167. Or write the Western Arctic Tourism Assoc., Box 2600MP, Inuvik, NT X0E 0T0; phone (403) 979-4321, fax (403) 979-2434 for more information.

Dempster Highway Log

YUKON HIGHWAY 5

Driving distance is measured in miles. The kilometre figure on the Yukon portion of the highway reflects the physical kilometreposts and is not necessarily an accurate metric conversion of the mileage figure. Kilometreposts are green with white lettering and are located on the right-hand side of the highway, northbound.

Distance from junction with Klondike Highway 2 (J) is followed by distance from Inuvik (I).

J 0 I 456.3 (734.3 km) **Junction** of Yukon Highways 2 and 5, 25 miles/40.2 km east of Dawson City, also known as Dempster Corner. Lodge with food, gas, propane, lodging, camping and tire repairs; open all year. Vehicle storage.

Klondike River Lodge. See display ad this section.

J 0.1 (0.2 km) **I 456.2** (734.2 km) Dempster Highway monument with information panels on history and culture, wildlife, ecology and driving tips.

J 0.2 (0.3 km) **I 456.1** (734 km) One-lane wood-planked bridge over Klondike River. The road follows the wooded (spruce and poplar) North Klondike River valley.

J 0.9 (1.4 km) **I 455.4** (732.9 km) Distance marker shows Eagle Plains 363 km (226 miles), Inuvik 735 km (457 miles).

J 3 (5 km) **I 453.3** (729.5 km) Forest fire burn area from summer 1991 fire that burned for two months and covered 5,189 acres/2,100 hectacres.

J 4 (6.4 km) **I 452.3** (727.9 km) The North Fork Ditch channeled water from the North Klondike River to a power plant 15.5 miles/25 km farther west for nearly 60 years, until the 1960s, and it helped to provide electricity and water for huge gold-dredging operations farther down the valley.

J 6.5 (10.5 km) **I 449.8** (723.9 km) 6,693-foot Antimony Mountain, about 18.5

DEMPSTER HIGHWAY *Klondike Highway Junction to Inuvik, NWT*

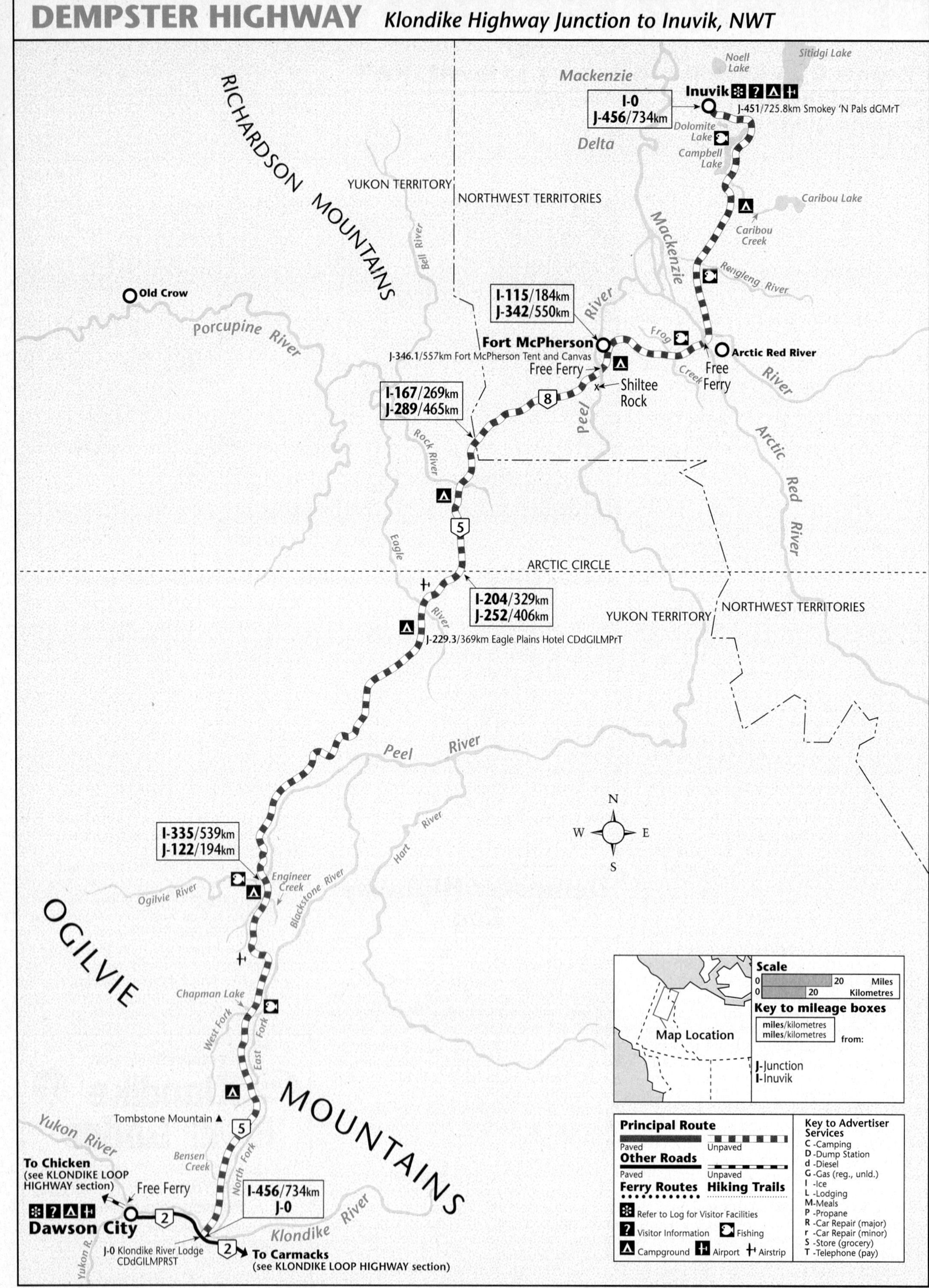
Inuvik
I-0
J-456/734km
J-451/725.8km Smokey 'N Pals dGMrT
Noell Lake
Sitidgi Lake
Mackenzie
Delta
Dolomite Lake
Campbell Lake
Caribou Lake
Caribou Creek
Rengleng River
RICHARDSON MOUNTAINS
YUKON TERRITORY
NORTHWEST TERRITORIES
Bell River
Mackenzie
Old Crow
Porcupine River
I-115/184km
J-342/550km
Fort McPherson
J-346.1/557km Fort McPherson Tent and Canvas
Free Ferry
Shiltee Rock
Frog Creek
Arctic Red River
Free Ferry
River
Peel
I-167/269km
J-289/465km
Rock River
Arctic Red River
Eagle River
ARCTIC CIRCLE
I-204/329km
J-252/406km
J-229.3/369km Eagle Plains Hotel CDdGILMPrT
Peel River
Hart River
N
W
E
S
I-335/539km
J-122/194km
Engineer Creek
Ogilvie River
Blackstone River
OGILVIE MOUNTAINS
Chapman Lake
West Fork
East Fork
Tombstone Mountain
Yukon River
Bensen Creek
North Fork
To Chicken
(see KLONDIKE LOOP HIGHWAY section)
Free Ferry
I-456/734km
J-0
Dawson City
J-0 Klondike River Lodge CDdGILMPRST
Klondike River
Yukon R.
To Carmacks
(see KLONDIKE LOOP HIGHWAY section)
Scale
0 20 Miles
0 20 Kilometres
Map Location
Key to mileage boxes
miles/kilometres
miles/kilometres
from:
J-Junction
I-Inuvik
Principal Route
Paved
Unpaved
Other Roads
Paved
Unpaved
Ferry Routes
Hiking Trails
Refer to Log for Visitor Facilities
Visitor Information
Fishing
Campground
Airport
Airstrip
Key to Advertiser Services
C -Camping
D -Dump Station
d -Diesel
G -Gas (reg., unld.)
I -Ice
L -Lodging
M -Meals
P -Propane
R -Car Repair (major)
r -Car Repair (minor)
S -Store (grocery)
T -Telephone (pay)

miles/30 km away, is one peak of the Ogilvie Mountains and part of the Snowy Range.

J 12.4 (20 km) **I 443.9** (714.4 km) North Klondike Range, Ogilvie Mountains to the west of the highway lead toward the rugged, interior Tombstone Range. These mountains were glaciated during the Ice Age.

J 15.4 (24.5 km) **I 440.9** (709.5 km) Glacier Creek.

J 16.6 (26.7 km) **I 439.7** (707.6 km) Pullout to west.

J 18.1 (29 km) **I 438.2** (705.2 km) Bensen Creek.

J 25.6 (41 km) **I 430.7** (693.1 km) Pea Soup Creek.

J 29.8 (48 km) **I 426.5** (686.4 km) Scout Car Creek.

J 31.7 (51 km) **I 424.6** (683.3 km) Wolf Creek. Trapper's cabin beside creek.

J 34.7 (55.8 km) **I 421.6** (678.5 km) Highway follows North Fork Klondike River.

J 36.6 (58.9 km) **I 419.7** (675.4 km) Grizzly Creek. Mount Robert Service to right northbound.

J 39.6 (63.7 km) **I 416.7** (670.6 km) Mike and Art Creek.

J 40.4 (65 km) **I 415.9** (669.3 km) Klondike Camp Yukon government highway maintenance station. No visitor services but may provide help in an emergency.

J 41.8 (67.3 km) **I 414.5** (667.1 km) First crossing of the North Fork Klondike River. The highway now moves above tree line and on to tundra northbound. At an elevation of approximately 4,003 feet/1,220m, you'll cross the watershed between the Yukon and Mackenzie basins.

J 43 (69.2 km) **I 413.3** (665.2 km) Spectacular first view of Tombstone Range northbound.

J 44.4 (71.5 km) **I 411.9** (662.9 km) Tombstone Mountain Yukon government campground (3,392 feet/1,034m above sea level) with 22 sites, $8 fee, shelter, fireplaces, water, tables, pit toilets. Interpretive centre located at campground during July and August has displays, a resource library and handouts with area information, and conducts campfire talks and nature walks. Good hiking trail begins past the outhouses and leads toward the headwaters of the North Fork Klondike River. ▲

J 46 (74 km) **I 410.3** (660.3 km) Large double-ended pullout. Good views of North Fork Pass and river. To the southwest is Tombstone Mountain (7,195 feet/2,193m). Outstanding aerial view of the mountain available through flightseeing trip out of Dawson City. To the north is the East Fork Blackstone River valley; on each side are the Ogilvie Mountains, which rise to elevations of 6,890 feet/2,100m.

J 48.4 (77.9 km) **I 407.9** (656.4 km) Blackstone River culvert. Tundra in the region indicates permafrost.

J 51 (82 km) **I 405.3** (652.2 km) North Fork Pass Summit. Wildflowers abundant late June-early July. Descent to the Blackstone River. Good bird-watching area (eagles, jaegers, ravens, robins, ptarmigan, swallows, short-eared owls and the rarely seen gyrfalcon). A hike up to the lower knoll to the right of the main mountain increases chances of seeing pika and marmots.

J 52.2 (84 km) **I 404.1** (650.3 km) Anglecomb Peak (also called Sheep Mountain) is a lambing and nursery habitat for Dall sheep during May and June, as well as a frequent nesting area for a pair of golden eagles.

J 54.2 (87.2 km) **I 402.1** (647.1 km) First crossing of East Fork Blackstone River.

Iron oxide gives Engineer Creek its distinctive colour. (Earl L. Brown, staff)

J 56.5 (91 km) **I 399.8** (643.4 km) The Blackstone Uplands, stretching from North Fork Pass to Chapman Lake, are a rich area for birdlife (long-tailed jaegers, gyrfalcons, peregrine falcons, red-throated loons and oldsquaw ducks). Big game hunting is also available in the region. Focusing on Dall sheep and grizzly bears, two outfitters work out of the Dempster corridor.

J 63.4 (102 km) **I 392.9** (632.3 km) Distance marker shows Eagle Plains 261 km (162 miles), Inuvik 633 km (393 miles), Dawson 142 km (88 miles), Whitehorse 600 km (373 miles).

J 66.9 (107.6 km) **I 389.4** (626.7 km) Large gravel pullout with litter barrels. Access to Blackstone River.

J 71.5 (115 km) **I 384.8** (619.3 km) First crossing of West Fork Blackstone River. Watch for arctic terns. Good fishing for Dolly Varden and grayling a short distance downstream where the west and east forks of the Blackstone join to form the **Blackstone River**, which the road now follows. After the river crossing, two low, cone-shaped mounds called pingos are visible upriver about 5 miles/8 km.

J 72.1 (116 km) **I 384.2** (618.3 km) Commemorative road sign about sled dog patrols of the Royal North–West Mounted Police. Also a sign: Watch for horses. View over Chapman Lake, one of the few lakes close to the highway that is large enough to permit floatplane operations. Porcupine caribou herd often crosses highway in this area in mid-October.

J 77.3 (124.4 km) **I 379** (609.9 km) **Private Aircraft:** Government airstrip (road is part of the strip); elev. 3,100 feet/945m; length 3,000 feet/914m.

J 96 (154.5 km) **I 360.3** (579.8 km) Northbound, highway passes through barren gray hills of Windy Pass. The Windy Pass summit area is much the same as it was when prehistoric humans entered it. The mountain ridges are the breeding habitat for some species of butterflies and moths not known to exist anywhere else.

J 106 (169.7 km) **I 350.3** (563.7 km) Creek culvert. Sulfurous smell is from the creek, which is red from iron oxide. Watch for interesting geological features in hills along road.

J 108.1 (173 km) **I 348.2** (560.4 km) Views of red-coloured Engineer Creek, and also erosion pillars and red rock (iron oxide) of nearby hills between here and Kilometrepost 182.

J 121.7 (194 km) **I 334.6** (538.5 km) Sapper Hill, named in 1971 in honour of the 3rd Royal Canadian Engineers who built the Ogilvie River bridge. "Sapper" is a nickname for an army engineer. **Engineer Creek** Yukon government campground; some sites washed out in '93; expected to reopen with approximately a dozen sites in 1994. $8 fee, fireplaces, water, tables, pit toilets. Grayling fishing. ▲

J 122.9 (195.7 km) **I 333.4** (536.5 km) The 360-foot/110-m Jeckell Bridge spans the Ogilvie River here. Built by the Canadian Armed Forces Engineers as a training exercise, it is named in honour of Allan Jeckell, controller of the Yukon from 1932 to 1946. Fossil coral may be visible in limestone outcrops to the northeast of the bridge.

The Ogilvie River and Ogilvie Mountains were named in honour of William Ogilvie, a highly respected Dominion land surveyor and commissioner of the Yukon during the Klondike gold rush.

J 123 (195.8 km) **I 333.3** (536.4 km) Ogilvie grader station, Yukon government maintenance camp is on north side of the river. Emergency-only gas and minor repairs may be available (not guaranteed).

For the next 25 miles/40 km, the highway follows the narrow valley of the Ogilvie River. For the first 12 miles/20 km, talus slopes edge the road, and game trails are evident along their precipitous sides.

J 124.3 (197.7 km) **I 332** (534.3 km) View of castlelike outcroppings of rock, known as tors, on mountaintops to north.

J 131.9 (209.5 km) **I 324.4** (522.1 km) Between here and Kilometrepost 216, watch for bird nests in the shale embankments along the highway and unusual rock outcroppings and erosion pillars in surrounding hills. Highway crosses rolling plateau country near Kilometrepost 218.

J 137.5 (221.2 km) **I 318.8** (513 km) Small turnout with litter barrels. Easy access to **Ogilvie River**. Good grayling fishing. Elephant Rock may be viewed from right side of road northbound. Fascinating mountain of broken rock and shale near Kilometrepost 224.

J 137.6 (221.5 km) **I 318.7** (512.9 km) Davies Creek.

J 149.1 (235.8 km) **I 307.2** (494.4 km) Ogilvie airstrip, status unknown. The great gray owl, one of Canada's largest, is known to nest as far north as this area.

J 154.4 (244 km) **I 301.9** (485.8 km) Highway climbs above and away from the

Ogilvie River, following a high ridge to the Eagle Plains plateau. One of the few unglaciated areas in Canada, this country is shaped by wind and water erosion rather than by the grinding action of ice. Views of Mount Cronkhite and Mount McCullum to the east.

Seismic lines next 62 miles/100 km provide hiking paths across the tundra. This was the major area of oil and gas exploration activity for which the road was originally built. In season, fields of cotton grass and varieties of tundra plants make good photographic subjects. The road continues to follow a high ridge (elev. 1,969 feet/600m) with broad sweeps and easy grades to give the traveler the feeling of being on top of the world.

J 160.9 (259 km) **I 295.4** (475.4 km) Large double-ended turnout. Panoramic Ogilvie-Peel viewpoint. Lowbush cranberries in August. Outhouse, litter barrels.

J 171.7 (270.6 km) **I 284.6** (458 km) Highway begins descent northbound and crosses fabulous high rolling country above tree line.

J 175.6 (276.7 km) **I 280.7** (451.7 km) Gravel pit full of old oil drums.

J 187.7 (302 km) **I 268.6** (432.3 km) Forest fire burn area; 13,590 acres/5,500 hectacres burned in July-August 1991.

J 204.5 (321 km) **I 256.3** (412.5 km) Road widens to become part of an airstrip.

J 215.6 (347 km) **I 240.7** (387.4 km) Richardson Mountains to the northeast. The thick blanket of rock and gravel that makes up the roadbed ahead is designed to prevent the underlying permafrost from melting. Much of the highway was built in winter, with the roadbed being dumped on top of the moss-covered permafrost. The roadbed conducts heat more than the surrounding vegetation does and must be extra thick to compensate.

J 229.3 (369 km) **I 227** (365.3 km) **Mile 231. EAGLE PLAINS;** hotel, phone (403) 979-4187, fax (403) 979-4187; food, gas, propane, aviation fuel, diesel and lodging. Open year-round.

Built in 1978, just before completion of the Dempster Highway, the hotel here was an engineering challenge. Engineers considered the permafrost in the area and found a place where the bedrock was at the surface. The hotel was built on this natural pad, thus avoiding the costly process of building on pilings as was done at Inuvik.

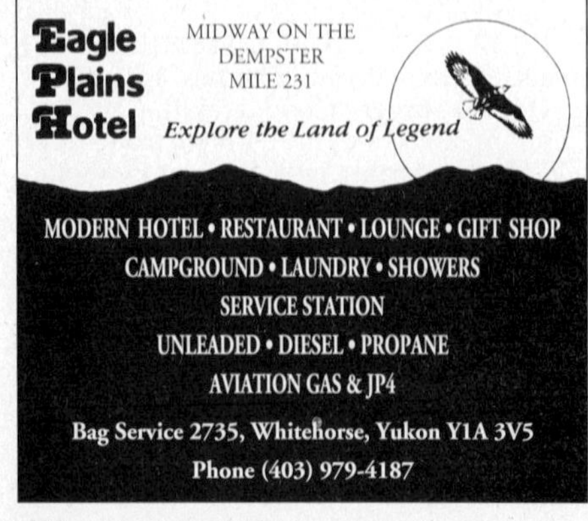

J 234.8 (377.8 km) **I 221.5** (356.5 km) Short side road to picnic site with information sign about Albert Johnson, "The Mad Trapper of Rat River." Something of a mystery man, Johnson wounded a constable who had come to question him about a trapline dispute. The ensuing manhunt became famous in the North, as Johnson eluded Mounties for 48 days during the winter of 1931–32. Johnson was killed in a shoot-out on Feb. 17, 1932. He was buried at Aklavik, a community located 36 miles/58 km by air west of Inuvik.

Dick North, author of two books on Johnson (and also author of *The Lost Patrol*), was quoted in the *New York Times* (June 3, 1990) as being 95 percent certain that Johnson, whose true identity has not been known, was a Norwegian–American bank robber named Johnson. Dick North is currently curator of the Jack London exhibit in Dawson City.

J 234.9 (378 km) **I 221.4** (356.3 km) **Eagle River** bridge. Like the Ogilvie bridge, it was built by the Dept. of National Defence as a training exercise. In contrast to the other rivers seen from the Dempster, the Eagle is a more sluggish, silt-laden stream with unstable banks. It is the main drainage channel for the western slopes of the Richardson Mountains. It and its tributaries provide good grayling fishing. Canoeists leave here bound for Alaska via the Porcupine and Yukon rivers.

J 239.4 (385.3 km) **I 216.9** (349.1 km) Views of the Richardson Mountains (elev. 3,937 feet/1,200m) ahead. Named for Sir John Richardson, surgeon and naturalist on both of Sir John Franklin's overland expeditions to the Arctic Ocean.

J 241.7 (389 km) **I 214.6** (345.4 km) **Private Aircraft:** Emergency airstrip; elev. 2,365 feet/721m; length 2,500 feet/762m; gravel. Used regularly by aircraft hauling freight to Old Crow, a Kutchin Indian settlement on the Porcupine River and Yukon's most northerly community.

J 252 (405.5 km) **I 204.3** (328.8 km) Large double-ended turnout. On June 22 here the sun does not fall below the horizon for 24 hours. Picnic tables, litter barrels, outhouses nearby. Sign marks Arctic Circle crossing, 66°33′N. The road now crosses arctic tundra on an elevated berm beside the Richardson Mountains with sweeping views in all directions.

J 277 (445.8 km) **I 179.3** (288.5 km) Rock River Yukon government campground; 18 sites, $8 fee, tables, kitchen shelter, water, firepits, outhouses. Black flies prevalent; bring repellent. ▲

J 280.1 (450.8 km) **I 176.2** (283.6 km) Turnout. Highway winds toward the Richardson Mountains, crossing them at George's Gap near the YT–NWT border. Good hiking area and excellent photographic possibilities.

J 288 (463.5 km) **I 168.3** (270.8 km) Turnout; good overnight spot for self-contained vehicles.

J 288.5 (464.3 km) **I 167.8** (270 km) Plaque about Wright Pass, named for Al Wright, a highway engineer with Public Works Canada who was responsible for the routing of the Dempster Highway.

J 288.9 (465 km) **I 167.4** (269.4 km) YT–NWT border. Historical marker. Continental Divide in the Richardson Mountains: West of here, water flows to the Pacific Ocean. East of here, water flows to the Arctic Ocean. Good photo spot.

TIME ZONE CHANGE: Yukon Territory observes Pacific standard time; Northwest Territories is on Mountain time. See Time Zones in the GENERAL INFORMATION section for details.

NWT HIGHWAY 8

IMPORTANT: New (1993) kilometreposts northbound (with white letters on a blue background) indicate distance from YT–NWT border and are indicated at intervals in our log. Highway descends northbound.

NOTE: Northbound travelers watch for change to narrower road surface.

J 297.6 (479 km) **I 158.7** (255.4 km) Kilometrepost 14. **James Creek;** good fishing. Highway maintenance camp. Good spot to park overnight.

J 299 (481.2 km) **I 157.3** (253.1 km) Sign advises no passing next 4.3 miles/7 km; climb to Wright Pass summit.

J 303.7 (488.7 km) **I 152.6** (245.6 km) Wright Pass Summit. From here northbound, the Dempster Highway descends a somewhat rocky, narrow track some 2,300 feet/853m to the Peel River crossing, 32 miles/51 km away.

J 316.3 (509 km) **I 140** (225.3 km) Kilometrepost 44. Side road leads down to Midway Lake. The Midway Lake Music Festival is staged here in June 1994. Call (403) 952-2226 for exact dates.

J 319.4 (514 km) **I 136.9** (220.3 km) **Private Aircraft:** Highway widens to form Midway airstrip; length 3,000 feet/914m.

J 329.3 (530 km) **I 127** (204.4 km) View of Peel River Valley and Fort McPherson to north. Litter barrels.

J 332.4 (535 km) **I 123.9** (199.4 km) Kilometrepost 70. Highway begins descent northbound to Peel River.

J 334.9 (539 km) **I 121.4** (195.4 km) Peel River crossing, called locally Eightmile because it is situated 8 miles/12.8 km south of Fort McPherson. Free government ferry service 15 hours a day during summer (from about early or mid-June to mid-October). Double-ended cable ferry: Drive on, drive off. Light vehicles cross by ice bridge in late November; heavier vehicles cross as ice thickens. *No crossing possible during freezeup or breakup.* Phone (toll free) 1-800-661-0752 for information on ferry crossings, road conditions and weather.

The level of the Peel River changes rapidly in spring and summer in response to meltwater from the mountains and ice jams on the Mackenzie River. The alluvial flood plain is covered by muskeg on the flats, and scrubby alder and stunted black spruce on the valley sides.

Indians from Fort McPherson have summer tent camps on the Peel River. The Indians net whitefish and sheefish (inconnu) then dry them on racks or in smokehouses for the winter.

About 4 miles/6.4 km south upstream is a trail leading to Shiltee Rock, which gives excellent views of the Peel River and the southern end of the Mackenzie.

J 335.9 (540.6 km) **I 120.4** (193.8 km) Nutuiluie territorial campground with 20 sites. (Campground name is from the Gwich'in term *Noo-til-ee,* meaning "fast flowing waters." Information centre open daily June to September. Camping permits, potable water, firewood, pit toilets available. ▲

J 337.4 (543 km) **I 118.9** (191.3 km) Kilometrepost 78.

J 340.4 (547.8 km) **I 115.9** (186.5 km) Access road right to Fort McPherson airport.

J 341.8 (550 km) **I 114.5** (184.3 km) Side road on left to Fort McPherson (description follows).

Fort McPherson

Located on a flat-topped hill about 100 feet/30m above the Peel River, 24 miles/38 km from its junction with the Mackenzie River; 100 miles/160 km southwest of Aklavik by boat along Peel Channel, 31 miles/50 km directly east of the Richardson Mountains. **Population:** 632. **Emergency Services: RCMP**, phone 952-2551. **Health Center**, phone 952-2586. **Radio:** CBC 680.

Private Aircraft: Fort McPherson airstrip; 67°24'N 134°51'W; elev. 142 feet/43m; length 3,500 feet/1,067m; gravel.

This Déné Indian settlement has a public phone, cafe, two general stores and two service stations (one with tire repair). A co-op hotel here offers eight rooms and a restaurant. Arts and crafts include beadwork and hide garments.

Wildlife watching and canoe trips are popular along the Peel River.

Aklak Air provides scheduled air service from Inuvik.

Fort McPherson was named in 1848 for Murdoch McPherson, chief trader of the Hudson's Bay Co., which had established its first posts in the area eight years before. Between 1849 and 1859 there were frequent feuds with neighboring Inuit, who later moved farther north to the Aklavik area, where they established a fur-trading post.

In addition to subsistence fishing and hunting, income is earned from trapping (mostly muskrat and mink), handicrafts, government employment, and commercial enterprises such as Fort McPherson Tent and Canvas factory, which specializes in nylon bags, tents and tepees. Tours during business hours, 9 A.M. to 5 P.M. weekdays; (403) 952-2179 or (800) 661-0888.

Buried in the cemetery outside the Anglican church are Inspector Fitzgerald and three other men of the Royal North-West Mounted Police. The four men left Fort McPherson by dog team Dec. 21, 1910, on their ill-fated patrol, carrying mail and dispatches from Herschel Island to Dawson City. Corporal W.J.D. Dempster found their bodies on March 22, 1911. A vivid account of their journey is found in Dick North's *The Lost Patrol*. One of the last entries in Fitzgerald's diary read: "We have now only 10 pounds of flour and 8 pounds of bacon and some dried fish. My last hope is gone. ... We have been a week looking for a river to take us over the divide, but there are dozens of rivers and I am at a loss."

Photos and artifacts depicting the history and way of life of the community are displayed in the Chief Julius School.

Fort McPherson Tent & Canvas. See display ad this section.

Dempster Highway Log

(continued)

J 342.4 (551 km) **I 113.9** (183.3 km) Kilometrepost 86.

J 365.1 (587.6 km) **I 91.2** (146.8 km) **Frog Creek.** Grayling and pike. Road on right northbound leads to picnic area.

J 377.1 (606.8 km) **I 79.2** (127.5 km) Mackenzie River wayside area.

J 377.9 (608.2 km) **I 78.4** (126.2 km) Mackenzie River crossing. Free government ferry service available 15 hours a day during summer (from about early or mid-June to early October). Double-ended ferry: Drive on, drive off. Light vehicles may cross by ice bridge in late November; heavier vehicles can cross as ice thickens. *No crossing possible during freezeup and breakup.*

The ferry travels between landings on either side of the Mackenzie River. If you wish to go to Arctic Red River, you must tell the crewmen. **ARCTIC RED RIVER** (pop. 120) is a Déné Indian settlement situated above the confluence of the Mackenzie and Arctic Red rivers. Limited visitor services available: two rooms, gas (not always available), some groceries.

J 399.6 (643 km) **I 56.7** (91.2 km) **Rengling River**, grayling fishing.

J 404.4 (650.8 km) **I 51.9** (83.5 km) Beginning of 13-mile/21-km straight stretch.

J 409.7 (659.3 km) **I 46.6** (75 km) Distance marker shows Inuvik 75 km.

J 426.3 (686 km) **I 30** (48.3 km) Caribou Creek picnic and camping area. ▲

J 431.4 (694.3 km) **I 24.9** (40.1 km) Campbell Lake and Campbell escarpment ahead northbound. Good place to glass for peregrine falcons.

J 440.6 (709 km) **I 15.7** (25.3 km) Cabin Creek picnic spot; pit toilets.

J 442.4 (712 km) **I 13.9** (22.4 km) **Campbell Creek** picnic area; pit toilets. Good fishing for pike and whitefish, some sheefish (inconnu). Creek leads a short distance to Campbell Lake. Boat launch. Bring mosquito repellent.

J 449.9 (724 km) **I 6.4** (10.3 km) Airport Road turnoff; pavement begins.

J 451 (725.8 km) **I 5.3** (8.5 km) Food, gas, and lodging.

Smokey n' Pals. See display ad this section.

J 451.7 (727 km) **I 4.6** (7.4 km) Kilometrepost 262.

J 454 (730.6 km) **I 2.3** (3.7 km) Chuk Park territorial campground; 38 campsites, 20 pull-through, electric hookups, firewood, water, showers, $10 fee. Lookout tower. ▲

J 456.3 (734.3 km) **I 0** Turn left northbound for Inuvik town centre (description follows).

Inuvik

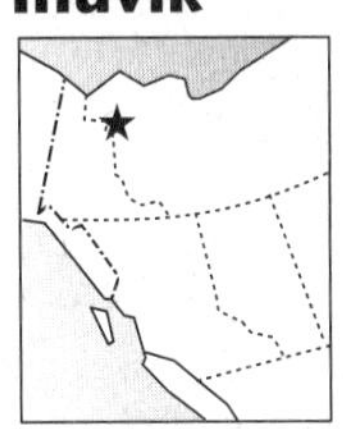

Situated on a flat wooded plateau that runs parallel to the east channel of the Mackenzie River, some 60 air miles/88 km south of the Beaufort Sea, 36 air miles/58 km and 70 water miles/113 km from Aklavik on the western edge of the delta. **Population:** 3,400, Déné, White and Inuvialuit.

Emergency Services: RCMP, phone 979-2935. **Hospital**, Inuvik General, phone 979-2955.

Visitor Information: Tourist booth on Mackenzie Road at stoplight, open May through September. Phone (403) 979-4321. Or contact the Western Arctic Tourism Assoc., Box 2600, Inuvik, NT X0E 0T0, phone 979-4321, fax 979-2434.

Elevation: 224 feet/68m. **Climate:** May 24 marks 57 days of midnight sun. The sun begins to set on July 19; on Dec. 6, the sun sets and does not rise until Jan. 6. Average annual precipitation 4 inches rainfall, 69 inches snowfall. July mean high 67°F/19°C, mean low 45°F/7°C. January mean high -11°F/-24°C, mean low -30°F/-35°C. **Radio** and **Television:** CBC and local. **Newspaper:** *The Drum* (weekly).

Private Aircraft: Inuvik airstrip; elev. 224 feet/68m; length 6,000 feet/1,829m; asphalt; fuel 80, 100. Townsite airstrip; elev. 10 feet/3m; length 1,800 feet/549m; gravel; fuel 80, 100, Jet B, F40. High pressure refueling.

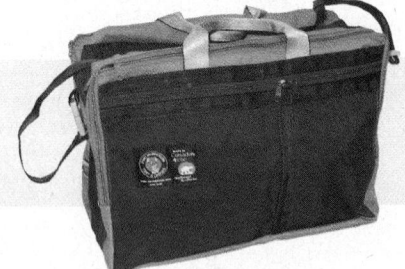

Inuvik, meaning "The Place of Man," is the largest Canadian community north of the Arctic Circle, and the major government, transportation and communication centre for Canada's western arctic. Construction of the town began in 1955 and was completed in 1961. It was the main supply base for the petrochemical exploration of the delta until Tuktoyaktuk took over that role as activity centered in the Beaufort Sea. In Inuvik some hunting, fishing and trapping is done, but most people earn wages in government and private enterprises, particularly in transportation and construction. With the delta one of the richest muskrat areas in the world, Inuvik is the western centre for shipping furs south.

The town's official monument says, in part, that Inuvik was "the first community north of the Arctic Circle built to provide the normal facilities of a Canadian town."

TRANSPORTATION

Air: Aklak Air provides scheduled service between Inuvik and Aklavik, Tuktoyaktuk, Sachs Harbour, Fort McPherson and Paulatuk. Scheduled service to Whitehorse and Old Crow, YT, via Alkan Air. Scheduled service to Edmonton, AB, and to Yellowknife, NWT, via NWT Air and Canadian Airlines International. Scheduled service to Aklavik and Tuktoyaktuk via Arctic Wings. Several air charter services operate out of Inuvik, offering flights to delta communities and charter service for hunting, fishing and camping trips. **Highways:** Dempster Highway from Dawson City. Winter roads (December into April) to Aklavik and Tuktoyaktuk. **Bus**: Service from Dawson City to Inuvik three times a week via Arctic Tour Co., phone 979-4100. **Taxi** and **rental cars:** Available.

ACCOMMODATIONS

Visitors will find most facilities available, although accommodations should be reserved in advance. Inuvik has three hotels, all with dining lounges, and three bed and breakfasts. There are also a laundry, post office, territorial liquor store, banks and churches. There are three gas stations and a car wash; propane, auto repair and towing are available. Hardware, grocery and general stores and gift shops are here.

Finto Motor Inn, located on the corner of Bypass Road and Mackenzie Road as you enter town. Modern facilities include: large rooms, laundry services (for guests), cable TV, kitchenettes, dining room, quiet lounge, crafts, carvings, and local artwork for sale. VISA, MasterCard, En Route, Diner's Club, American Express accepted. Reservations recommended. For reservations or more information, call (403) 979-2647, fax (403) 979-3442. Take advantage of our weekend $25 discount coupon! Write Box 1925, Inuvik, NT X0E 0T0. [ADVERTISEMENT]

Happy Valley territorial campground; 20 RV sites, electrical hookups, 10 tent pads, hot showers, firewood, water, dump station, fee. Chuk Park territorial campground; 20 sites, electrical hookups, firewood, water, showers, $10 fee. ▲

ATTRACTIONS

Igloo Church, painted white with lines to simulate snow blocks, is on Mackenzie Road as you drive in to Inuvik. Inside the church is Inuit painter Mona Thrasher's interpretation of the Stations of the Cross. Visitors are welcome.

Ingamo Hall is a three-story log community hall that serves the social and recreational needs of Native families. The hall was built by Allan Crich over a three-year period, using some 1,020 logs that were cut from white spruce trees in the southern part

INUVIK ADVERTISERS

Arctic Esso Service	29 Distributor St.
Boreal Books	Ph. (403) 979-2260
Eskimo Inn Ltd.	Ph. (403) 979-2801
Finto Motor Inn	Ph. (403) 979-2647
Great Northern Arts Festival, The	Ph. (403) 979-3536
Inuvik Visitors' Assoc.	Ph. (403) 979-4321
Mackenzie Hotel, The	Ph. (403) 979-2861
Robertson's Bed & Breakfast	Ph. (403) 979-3111
Western Arctic Nature Tours	Ph. (403) 979-3300
Western Arctic Tourism Assoc.	Ph. (403) 979-4321

of the Mackenzie River valley and floated down the river to Inuvik.

Tour Western Arctic Communities: Air charter service is available to **AKLAVIK** (pop. 800), an important centre for muskrat harvesting; **TUKTOYAKTUK** (pop. 950), an Inuit village on the Arctic coast and site of oil development; **SACHS HARBOUR** (pop. 158) on Banks Island, an Inuit settlement supported by trapping and some big game outfitters; **PAULATUK** (pop. 95), an Inuit settlement supported by hunting, fishing, sealing and trapping; and **HOLMAN** (pop. 300), an Inuit community on the west coast of Victoria Island, famous for its print-making. Scheduled air service is also available to **OLD CROW** (pop. 267), an Indian settlement on the Porcupine River in Yukon Territory.

The **Mackenzie River delta**, one of the largest deltas in North America and an important wildlife corridor to the Arctic, is 40 miles/64 km wide and 60 miles/97 km long. A maze of lakes, channels and islands, the delta supports a variety of bird life, fish and muskrats. Boat tours of the Mackenzie River are available.

Western Arctic Nature Tours, beside the Igloo Church, has Arctic wildlife displays, local artwork and crafts. Touch the Arctic Ocean? Lifelong resident Fred Carmichael and staff have a tour for you. Fly and/or boat to Tuktoyaktuk on the Arctic coast for a guided tour. Wildlife viewing? Fly to Herschel Island Yukon Park, rich in history and a naturalist's delight. Toast the midnight sun while cruising the Mackenzie River. Enjoy a meal at a camp. Try fishing. Interested? Call (403) 979-3300, fax (403) 979-3400 or write Box 1530(M), Inuvik, NWT X0E 0T0. [ADVERTISEMENT]

Special Events. The annual Northern Games are held in Inuvik or other western Arctic communities in summer. Traditional Inuit and Déné sports, dances, competitions, crafts and Good Woman Contest (where northern women show their talent at animal skinning, bannock baking and other bush skills) are part of the festival. Visitors are welcome to join northerners from Alaska, Yukon Territory, Labrador and the Northwest Territories. For more information, write Northern Games Assoc., Box 1184, Inuvik, NT X0E 0T0.

The sixth annual Great Northern Arts Festival is scheduled for July 22–31, 1994. For more information contact the Arts Festival, Box 2921, Inuvik, NT X0E 0T0; phone 979-3536.

Boreal Books carries a full range of northern books on history, Native studies, exploration and wildlife. Full selection of area postcards, northern posters and local music. Authorized agent for topo maps, marine charts and air charts. Heritage books. Catalogue available. Mail orders welcome. Open all week. Phone (403) 979-2260, fax (403) 979-4429. [ADVERTISEMENT]

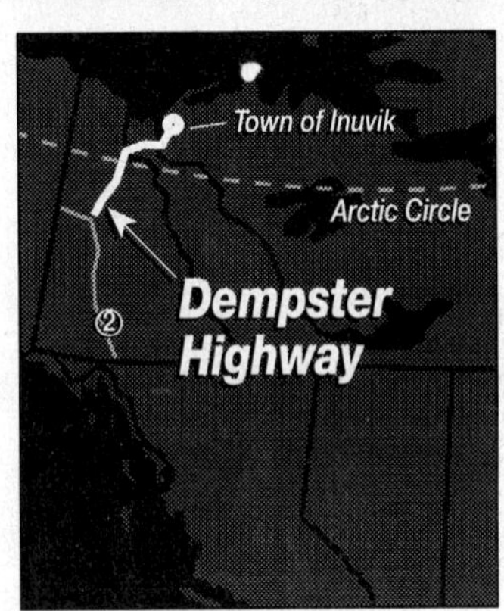

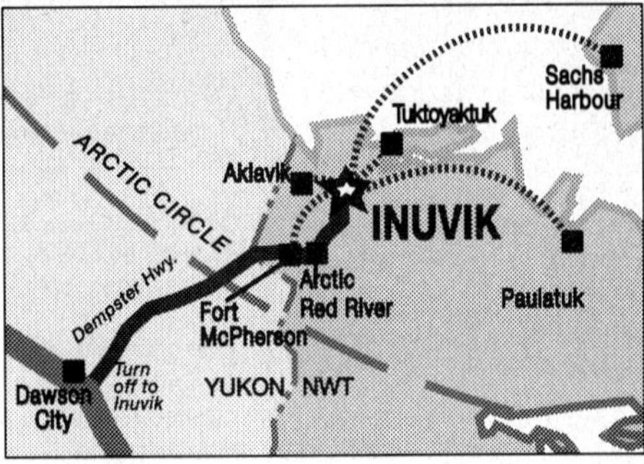

DALTON HIGHWAY

(Formerly the North Slope Haul Road)
Milepost F 73.1 Elliott Highway to Deadhorse, Alaska
Alaska Route 11

The 414-mile/666.3-km Dalton Highway (still referred to as the "Haul Road") begins at **Milepost F 73.1** on the Elliott Highway and ends — for the general public — at Deadhorse, a few miles from Prudhoe Bay and the Arctic Ocean. (Access to Prudhoe Bay, site of oil drilling operations, is restricted by the oil companies.) Maintenance and operation of the state-owned highway is the responsibility of the Dept. of Transportation in Fairbanks, 2301 Peger Road, Fairbanks 99701; phone (907) 451-2209.

The highway is named for James William Dalton, an arctic engineer involved in early oil exploration efforts on the North Slope. It was built as a haul road between the Yukon River and Prudhoe Bay during construction of the trans-Alaska pipeline, and was originally called the North Slope Haul Road. Construction of the road began April 29,

Oil company roads and operations complex at Prudhoe Bay. (George Wuerthner)

DALTON HIGHWAY *Milepost F 73.1 Elliott Highway to Deadhorse, AK*

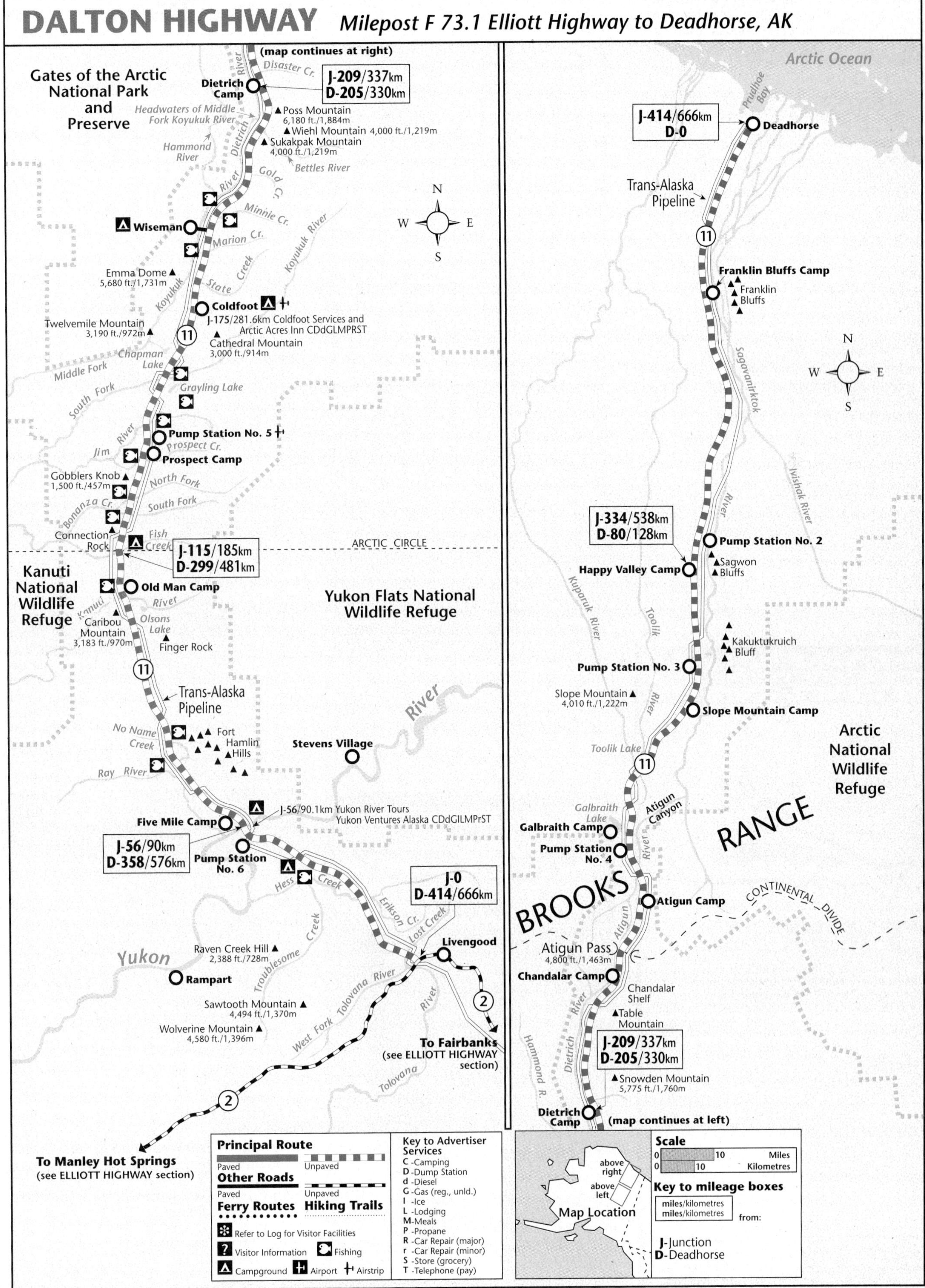

1974, and was completed five months later. The road is 28 feet/9m wide with 3 to 6 feet/1 to 2m of gravel surfacing. Some sections of road are underlain with plastic foam insulation to prevent thawing of the permafrost.

Construction of the 800-mile-/1,287-km-long pipeline between Prudhoe Bay and Valdez took place between 1974 and 1977. The 48-inch-diameter pipeline, of which slightly more than half is aboveground, has 10 operating pump stations. The control center is in Valdez. For additional information on the pipeline, contact: Public Affairs Dept., Alyeska Pipeline Service Co., 1835 S. Bragaw St., Anchorage, AK 99512.

The Bureau of Land Management (BLM) manages 2.7 million acres of public land along the Dalton Highway between the Yukon and Pump Station No. 2. For information on BLM lands, contact: Arctic District, BLM, 1150 University Ave., Fairbanks, AK 99709; phone (907) 474-2301.

Public travel on the Dalton Highway was originally restricted to the first 55 miles/ 89 km of the highway to the Yukon River bridge. In recent years, the public has been able to drive the Dalton Highway 211 miles/340 km to Disaster Creek without a permit. Gov. Walter J. Hickel moved to open the Dalton Highway to Deadhorse in July 1991, but the opening was postponed pending the outcome of several issues. Contact the DOT regarding current status of highway beyond Disaster Creek.

Services along the Dalton Highway are limited. Gas, diesel fuel, tire repair, restaurant, motel, phone and emergency communications, and dump station are available at **Milepost J 56**, just past the Yukon River bridge. Gas, tire repair, restaurant, motel and phone are also available at Coldfoot, **Milepost J 175.** (Phones at both locations are for credit card and collect calls only.) Public phone at Wiseman.

Helicopters fly low over the pipeline both for surveillance and for moving Alyeska Pipeline Service Co. personnel and equipment. The road is patrolled by Alaska State Troopers. For emergency services contact the Alaska State Troopers via CB radio, Channel 19, or ask that a message be relayed via the Alyeska facility or any state highway maintenance camp. Towing fees by private wrecker service have ranged as high as $5 a mile, each way.

Road conditions vary depending on weather, maintenance and time of year, but in general the road has a reputation for being rough. Watch for ruts, rocks, dust, soft shoulders and trucks. There are several steep (10 percent) grades. Drive with your headlights on at all times.

The Dalton Highway is unique in its scenic beauty, wildlife and recreational opportunities. Travelers are requested to use the formal turnouts and campgrounds provided to avoid permanently scarring the landscape with footpaths, "tent rings" and other signs of use.

All waters between the Yukon River bridge and Dietrich River are part of the Yukon River system, and most are tributaries of the Koyukuk River. Fishing for arctic grayling is especially good in rivers accessible by foot from the highway. The larger rivers also support burbot, salmon, pike and whitefish. Small Dolly Varden are at higher elevations in streams north of Coldfoot. According to the Dept. of Fish and Game, anglers should expect high, turbid water conditions throughout much of June as the snowpack melts in the Brooks Range, with the best fishing occurring during July and August.

Dalton Highway Log

Distance from junction with Elliott Highway (J) is followed by distance from Deadhorse (D).

J 0 D 414 (666.3 km) **Junction** with Elliott Highway at **Milepost F 73.1.**

J 4 (6.4 km) **D 410** (659.8 km) Highway descends steeply into the Lost Creek valley. Lost Creek flows into the West Fork Tolovana River. Pipeline is visible stretching across the ridges of the distant hills.

J 5.6 (9 km) **D 408.4** (657.2 km) Lost Creek culvert. Steep hills north- and southbound. Pipeline access road; no public admittance. There are many of these access roads along this highway; all are posted as closed to the public.

J 9.8 (15.8 km) **D 404.2** (650.5 km) Road follows a high ridge with spectacular view of Erickson Creek area and pipeline.

J 12 (19.3 km) **D 402** (646.9 km) Small gravel turnouts.

J 12.1 (19.5 km) **D 401.9** (646.8 km) Erickson Creek culvert.

J 20.9 (33.6 km) **D 393.1** (632.6 km) Steep double-ended turnout at gravel pit to west.

J 21 (33.8 km) **D 393** (632.5 km) Descent to Hess Creek begins northbound.

J 23.6 (38 km) **D 390.4** (628.3 km) Pipeline access road, pond.

J 23.8 (38.3 km) **D 390.2** (627.9 km) **Hess Creek** bridge. Campsite in trees. Large gravel bar along creek at north end of bridge. *CAUTION: Sandpit at entrance to gravel bar is an easy place to get stuck.* Bring your mosquito repellent. Whitefish and grayling fishing. Hess Creek, known for its colorful mining history, is the largest stream between the junction and the Yukon River bridge.

J 23.9 (38.5 km) **D 390.1** (627.8 km) Road to west leads 0.2 mile/0.3 km to pond with parking space adequate for camping.

J 25 (40.2 km) **D 389** (626 km) Double-ended rough turnout. Good view of pipeline and remote-operated valve site as the highway crosses Hess Creek and valley.

J 26 (41.8 km) **D 388** (624.4 km) Pipeline parallels highway about 250 feet/76m away.

J 26.3 (42.3 km) **D 387.7** (623.9 km) Turnout with litter barrel.

J 27 (43.4 km) **D 387** (622.8 km) Evidence of 1971 lightning-caused forest fire.

J 28.4 (45.7 km) **D 385.6** (620.5 km) Gravel pit road and pipeline access road to west.

J 33.7 (54.2 km) **D 380.3** (612 km) Turnout at tributary of Hess Creek.

J 35.5 (57.1 km) **D 378.5** (609.1 km) Rough turnout at gravel pit.

J 38.1 (61.3 km) **D 375.9** (604.9 km) Pipeline goes under road. Evidence of the revegetation project undertaken by the oil companies.

J 40.7 (65.5 km) **D 373.3** (600.7 km) Double-ended turnout with litter barrel. Overview of Troublesome and Hess creeks areas. Brush obscures sweeping views.

J 43.1 (69.4 km) **D 370.9** (596.9 km) Isom Creek culvert. Steep ascent from valley north- and southbound.

J 44.6 (71.8 km) **D 369.4** (594.5 km) Turnout with litter barrel.

J 47.9 (77.1 km) **D 366.1** (589.2 km) Highway begins descent to Yukon River.

J 48.5 (78.1 km) **D 365.5** (588.2 km)

Pipeline access road. Goalpostlike structures, called "headache bars," guard against vehicles large enough to run into and damage the pipeline.

J 50.1 (80.6 km) **D 363.9** (585.6 km) Turnout.

J 53.2 (85.6 km) **D 360.8** (580.6 km) First view northbound of the Yukon River. As road drops, you can see the pipeline where it crosses the river. Fort Hamlin Hills are beyond the pipeline.

J 54 (86.9 km) **D 360** (579.3 km) **PUMP STATION NO. 6.**

J 54.5 (87.7 km) **D 359.5** (578.5 km) Turnout to west.

J 55.6 (89.5 km) **D 358.4** (576.8 km) Yukon River bridge (formally the E.L. Patton Bridge, named for the president of the Alyeska Pipeline Service Co. after his death in 1982). This wood-decked bridge, completed in 1975, is 2,290 feet/698m long and has a 6 percent grade.

J 56 (90.1 km) **D 358** (576.1 km) Gas, diesel, tire repair, restaurant, motel, phone and emergency communications available at Yukon Ventures Alaska. Daily trips to working Native fish camp offered through Yukon River Tours.

This is the southern boundary of BLM-managed lands. The Yukon Crossing Visitor Contact Station here, managed and staffed by the BLM, is open seven days a week, June through August. There is also an Alyeska pipeline interpretive display here with information on the Yukon River, pipeline construction and related subjects. East of the highway is a camping area with litter barrels. Road closed east of campsite. ▲

Yukon River Tours. See display ad this section.

Yukon Ventures Alaska. See display ad this section.

J 60.6 (97.5 km) **D 353.4** (568.7 km) Site of **FIVE MILE CAMP**, a former pipeline construction camp. No structures remain at these former construction camps. There is an undeveloped campsite here and an outhouse. Water is available from an artesian well. Highway crosses over buried pipeline.

J 60.8 (97.8 km) **D 353.2** (568.4 km) Five Mile airstrip (length 3,500 feet/1,067m); controlled by Alyeska Security. *CAUTION: Be prepared to stop at control gates at both ends of airstrip.*

J 61.6 (99.1 km) **D 352.4** (567.1 km) View of Fort Hamlin Hills to north, pump station No. 6 to south.

J 61.9 (99.6 km) **D 352.1** (566.6 km) Sevenmile DOT/PF highway maintenance camp and Alaska State Trooper.

J 68.4 (110.1 km) **D 345.6** (556.2 km) Highway crosses over buried pipeline.

J 69.2 (111.4 km) **D 344.8** (554.9 km) Double-ended turnout at crest of hill overlooking the Ray River to the north.

J 70 (112.7 km) **D 344** (553.6 km) **Ray River** overlook and turnout. Scenic view of the Ray Mountains to the west. Burbot, grayling and northern pike fishing.

J 72.6 (116.8 km) **D 341.4** (549.4 km) Fort Hamlin Hills Creek bridge and turnout. Winter trail scars are visible here.

J 74.8 (120.4 km) **D 339.2** (545.9 km) Steep descent northbound followed by steep ascent; dubbed the Roller Coaster.

J 79.1 (127.3 km) **D 334.9** (539 km) **No Name Creek** and turnout; burbot, grayling and whitefish.

J 81.6 (131.3 km) **D 332.4** (534.9 km) Fort Hamlin Hills are visible to the southeast. Tree line on surrounding hills is about 2,000 feet/610m.

J 86.5 (139.2 km) **D 327.5** (527 km) Scenic overlook 1 mile/1.6 km west with view of tors to northeast, Yukon Flats Wildlife Refuge to east and Fort Hamlin Hills to southeast. Tors are high, isolated pinnacles of jointed granite jutting up from the tundra and are a residual feature of erosion.

J 88.5 (142.4 km) **D 325.5** (523.8 km) Mackey Hill. Entering Game Management Unit 25D northbound, Unit 20F southbound. The high, unnamed hill east of the road is 2,774 feet/846m in elevation.

J 90.2 (145.2 km) **D 323.8** (521.1 km) Double-ended turnouts both sides of highway. A good photo opportunity of the road and pipeline to the north. The small green structure over the buried pipe is a radio-controlled valve, allowing the pipeline oil flow to be shut down when necessary. *NOTE: Expect road construction next 10 miles/16 km northbound in 1994.*

J 91.1 (146.6 km) **D 322.9** (519.6 km) Culvert directs water from branch of West Fork of Dall River. Watch for soft spots in road.

J 94 (151.3 km) **D 320** (515 km) Turnout at former gravel pit road to west.

J 96 (154.5 km) **D 318** (511.8 km) The road lies above tree line for about 5 miles/8 km. Good opportunities for photos, berry picking (blueberries, lowbush cranberries), wildflower viewing and hiking. Northbound, the terrain becomes more rugged and scenic.

J 97.5 (156.9 km) **D 316.5** (509.3 km) Finger Rock (signed Finger Mountain), a tor, is visible east of the road and most easily seen to the south. Tors are visible for the next 2 miles/3.2 km.

Prehistoric hunting sites are numerous in this region. Please do not collect or disturb artifacts.

J 98.2 (158 km) **D 315.8** (508.2 km) High viewpoint; Caribou Mountain is in the distance to the northwest. Olsens Lake, Kanuti Flats, Kanuti River drainage and site of former Old Man Camp are visible ahead northbound. The road descends and passes through several miles of valley bottom with excellent mountain views.

J 100.7 (162.1 km) **D 313.3** (504.2 km) Pipeline passes under highway. *NOTE: Expect road construction next 10 miles/16 km southbound in 1994.*

J 105.8 (170.3 km) **D 308.2** (496 km) **Kanuti River**, crossing and turnout; burbot, grayling. Abandoned airstrip.

J 107 (172.2 km) **D 307** (494.1 km) Site of **OLD MAN CAMP**, a former pipeline construction camp.

J 109.1 (175.6 km) **D 304.9** (490.7 km) Turnout to west.

J 109.8 (176.7 km) **D 304.2** (489.5 km) Turnout at Beaver Slide. *CAUTION: Road descends very steeply northbound. Watch for soft spots. Slippery when wet.*

J 110 (177 km) **D 304** (489.2 km) Visible against the hillside to the east are water bars constructed to prevent erosion above the buried pipeline.

J 111.5 (179.4 km) **D 302.5** (486.8 km) View of valley and Fish Creek to the north.

J 112.2 (180.6 km) **D 301.8** (485.7 km) Turnout at pipeline access road. Moose and bear frequent willow thickets here.

J 113.9 (183.3 km) **D 300.1** (483 km) Evidence of old winter trail to Bettles is visible here.

View of highway and pipeline, looking south from Chandalar Shelf. (Bruce M. Herman)

J 114 (183.5 km) **D 300** (482.8 km) **Fish Creek** bridge and turnout; burbot, grayling 12 to 18 inches.

J 115.3 (185.5 km) **D 298.7** (480.7 km) The Arctic Circle, north latitude 66°33'. BLM wayside with tables, restrooms and interpretive display. Stop and have your picture taken with the sign. This is also a good photo point, with views to the south and to the west. Follow road off turnout 0.6 mile/1 km for undeveloped campsite. If you reach the Alyeska access gate you've gone too far.

J 124.7 (200.7 km) **D 289.3** (465.6 km) Turnout to east at **South Fork Bonanza Creek;** burbot, grayling, whitefish.

J 125.7 (202.3 km) **D 288.3** (464 km) Turnout to east at **North Fork Bonanza Creek;** burbot, grayling, whitefish.

J 127.1 (204.5 km) **D 286.9** (461.7 km) Turnout.

J 127.7 (205.5 km) **D 286.3** (460.7 km) Paradise Hill; blueberries and lowbush cranberries in season.

J 128.9 (207.4 km) **D 285.1** (458.8 km) Gravel pit.

J 129.3 (208.1 km) **D 284.7** (458.2 km) *CAUTION: Long ascent northbound with a short stretch that is very steep. Give trucks plenty of room here!*

J 131.3 (211.3 km) **D 282.7** (454.9 km) Solar-powered communications tower.

J 131.5 (211.6 km) **D 282.5** (454.6 km) View of pump station No. 5 to north.

J 132 (212.4 km) **D 282** (453.8 km) Turnout with litter barrels and toilets at Gobblers Knob (elev. 1,500 feet/457m) overlooking the Jack White Range, Pope Creek Dome (the dominant peak to the northwest), Prospect Creek drainage, pump station No. 5, Jim River drainage, South Fork Koyukuk drainage and the Brooks Range on the northern horizon.

J 134.7 (216.8 km) **D 279.3** (449.5 km) Pipeline access road.

J 135.1 (217.4 km) **D 278.9** (448.8 km) **Prospect Creek**; grayling, whitefish and pike. Active gold mining area.

J 135.7 (218.4 km) **D 278.3** (447.9 km) Turnout with outhouse. Old winter road goes up creek to mines. Turn left for site of **PROSPECT CAMP**, which holds the record for lowest recorded temperature in Alaska (-80°F/-62°C, Jan. 23, 1971). Rough road leads 0.5 mile/0.8 km to Claja Pond; beaver, ducks. Undeveloped campsite on Jim River. Old winter road to Bettles crosses river here.

J 137.1 (220.6 km) **D 276.9** (445.6 km) **PUMP STATION NO. 5** (signed incorrectly as Prospect Camp). No public access. Side road leads to well. Pump station No. 5 is not actually a pump station, but a "drain down" or pressure relief station.

Private Aircraft: Airstrip; length 5,000 feet/1,524m; lighted runway. This airstrip is used as a BLM fire fighting staging area.

J 138.1 (222.2 km) **D 275.9** (444 km) Jim River DOT/PF highway maintenance camp EMT squad. Site of 1988 burn.

J 139 (223.7 km) **D 275** (442.6 km) Road to gravel pit.

J 140.1 (225.5 km) **D 273.9** (440.8 km) Turnout at **Jim River,** bridge No. 1; burbot, chum and king salmon, grayling, pike, whitefish. *CAUTION: Bears here for fall salmon run.*

J 141 (226.9 km) **D 273** (439.3 km) Turnout to east at Jim River, bridge No. 2.

J 141.8 (228.2 km) **D 272.2** (438.1 km) Douglas Creek; blueberries and lowbush cranberries in season.

J 144.1 (231.9 km) **D 269.9** (434.4 km) Bridge No. 3 across main channel of **Jim River;** turnout to east at south end of bridge. See **Milepost J 140.1** for fishing.

J 145 (233.3 km) **D 269** (432.9 km) Road to refuse dump (locked).

J 145.6 (234.3 km) **D 268.4** (431.9 km) Pipeline passes under road. First views northbound of Brooks Range foothills to the north.

J 150.3 (241.9 km) **D 263.7** (424.4 km) **Grayling Lake** to east has good grayling fishing in open water season.

J 150.8 (242.7 km) **D 263.2** (423.6 km) Turnout on Grayling Lake. The road is passing through the foothills of the Brooks Range. There is an active gold mining area behind the hills to the west.

J 155.2 (249.8 km) **D 258.8** (416.5 km) Overlook for the South Fork Koyukuk River valley.

J 156 (251.1 km) **D 258** (415.2 km) Turnout with outhouse at the **South Fork Koyukuk River** bridge; grayling, whitefish, chum and king salmon.

This large river flows past the villages of Bettles, Allakaket, Hughes and Huslia before draining into the Yukon River near Koyukuk.

J 159.1 (256 km) **D 254.9** (410.2 km) Bridge over pipeline.

J 160 (257.5 km) **D 254** (408.8 km) Good view of Chapman Lake 0.5 mile/0.8 km west of road. Old mine trail is visible from the road.

The two mountains visible to the north are Twelvemile Mountain (elev. 3,190 feet/972m), left, and Cathedral Mountain (elev. 3,000 feet/914m), on right. The foothills of the Brooks Range are also to the north.

J 163.3 (262.8 km) **D 250.7** (403.5 km) Turnout to west.

J 165.1 (265.7 km) **D 248.9** (400.6 km) Turnout to west with view of pipeline.

J 165.7 (266.7 km) **D 248.3** (399.6 km) Turnout on west side of road overlooking Middle Fork Koyukuk River.

J 167.2 (269.1 km) **D 246.8** (397.2 km) Old winter trail to Tramway Bar.

J 175 (281.6 km) **D 239** (384.6 km) **COLDFOOT,** site of a historic mining camp at the mouth of Slate Creek on the east bank of the Middle Fork Koyukuk River. Food, gas, diesel, phone, lodging, RV park, dump station and post office available at Coldfoot Services (phone 678-5201). There is a 3,500-foot/1,067-m runway to west, maintained by the state. An Alaska State Trooper, a Fish and Wildlife officer and BLM field station are located at Coldfoot. A visitor center here, operated by the BLM, USF&WS and National Park Service, offers travel information and nightly presentations on the natural and cultural history of the Arctic. It is open from June 1 through September. Topographic maps for sale.

Originally named Slate Creek, Coldfoot reportedly got its name in 1900 when gold stampeders got as far up the Koyukuk as this point, then got cold feet, turned and departed. The old cemetery still exists.

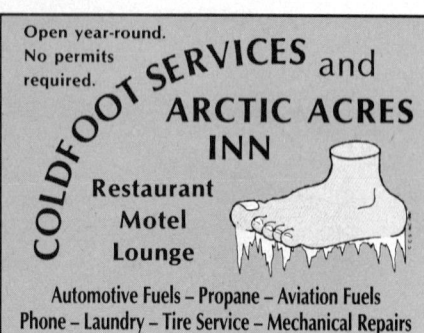

Emma Dome (elev. 5,680 feet/1,731m) is to the west.

Coldfoot Services & Arctic Acres Inn. See display ad this section.

J **179.9** (289.5 km) D **234.1** (376.7 km) Marion Creek Campground; 26 sites, tables, toilets, firepits, water, litter barrels, information kiosk. Marion Creek trailhead, RV parking. ▲

J **184.4** (296.7 km) D **229.6** (369.5 km) Scenic overlook. Excellent view of Middle Fork Koyukuk River and rock slide on adjacent mountain.

J **186** (299.3 km) D **228** (366.9 km) The historic mining community of Wiseman can be seen across the Koyukuk River to the west. Access to Wiseman from **Milepost J 188.6.**

J **186.7** (300.5 km) D **227.3** (365.8 km) Turnouts both sides of highway.

J **187.2** (301.3 km) D **226.8** (365 km) Turnout to west at **Minnie Creek;** burbot, grayling, whitefish.

J **188.5** (303.4 km) D **225.5** (362.9 km) Turnout at **Middle Fork Koyukuk River** bridge No. 1; Dolly Varden, grayling, whitefish.

J **188.6** (303.5 km) D **225.4** (362.7 km) Improved (1991) access road to **WISEMAN,** a historic mining town. The heyday of Wiseman came in about 1910, after gold seekers abandoned Coldfoot. The Wiseman Trading Co. still stands and houses the town's museum, featuring old photos and mining equipment. About 25 residents live here year-round today, and the population increases in the summer with the arrival of miners. (Note that this is an active mining area and all buildings are privately owned.) Wiseman has a general store, public phone and campground. ▲

J **189** (304.2 km) D **225** (362.1 km) Finger dikes keep river away from highway and pipeline.

J **190.5** (306.6 km) D **223.5** (359.7 km) Narrow bridge over Hammond River.

J **190.8** (307.1 km) D **223.2** (359.2 km) Middle Fork Koyukuk River bridge No. 2.

J **192.8** (310.3 km) D **221.2** (356 km) Link Up, where two sections of pipeline constructed by different crews were joined.

J **194** (312.2 km) D **220** (354 km) First view northbound of Sukakpak Mountain (elev. 4,000 feet/1,219m) to north. Sukakpak Mountain is believed to mark the traditional boundary between Eskimo and Athabascan Indian territories. Wiehl Mountain (elev. 4,000 feet/1,219m) is east of Sukakpak. The high mountain just to the west of the road is unnamed.

J **197** (317 km) D **217** (349.2 km) Old cabin just west of road is reported to have been constructed in the early 1900s; private property. Gold Creek bridge.

J **197.3** (317.5 km) D **216.7** (348.7 km) Cat trail to gold mining area.

J **197.7** (318.2 km) D **216.3** (348.1 km) Turnout to east and view of Wiehl Mountain.

J **200** (321.9 km) D **214** (344.4 km) View of the Middle Fork Koyukuk River, a typical braided river exhibiting frequent changes of the streambed during high water.

J **203.5** (327.5 km) D **210.5** (338.7 km) Turnout and 0.5-mile/0.8-km footpath to Sukakpak Mountain. The short mounds of earth between the road and Sukakpak are palsas, formed by ice beneath the soil pushing the vegetative mat and soil upward.

J **203.8** (328 km) D **210.2** (338.3 km) Turnouts next 0.6 mile/1 km northbound.

J **204.3** (328.8 km) D **209.7** (337.5 km) Middle Fork Koyukuk River bridge No. 3; turnout with toilets and litter barrels to east.

J **204.5** (329.1 km) D **209.5** (337.1 km) Middle Fork Koyukuk River bridge No. 4.

J **205.3** (330.4 km) D **208.7** (335.9 km) Turnout to west. Good view of north side of Sukakpak Mountain.

J **207** (333.1 km) D **207** (333.1 km) **Dietrich River** bridge, turnout to west at south end; burbot, grayling, whitefish and Dolly Varden.

J **207.5** (333.9 km) D **206.5** (332.3 km) Small, unnamed lake on east side of road with nice view of Sukakpak Mountain. Dillon Mountain (proposed name) is just to the north.

J **209** (336.3 km) D **205** (329.9 km) Drag reducing injection site at pipeline Mile 203. Injected substance facilitates oil flow.

J **209.1** (336.5 km) D **204.9** (329.7 km) Site of **DIETRICH CAMP,** a former pipeline construction camp.

J **211** (339.6 km) D **203** (326.7 km) Disaster Creek. Turnout with litter barrel to east.

J **216** (347.6 km) D **198** (318.6 km) Snowden Creek culvert. Panorama of Dietrich River valley and Brooks Range north and west of the road.

J **217.1** (349.4 km) D **196.9** (316.9 km) Rock spire to east is Snowden Mountain (elev. 5,775 feet/1,760m).

J **221.6** (356.6 km) D **192.4** (309.6 km) Turnout to west is quarry of black marble with white calcite veins.

J **221.8** (356.9 km) D **192.2** (309.3 km) Turnout at gravel pit to east.

J **224** (360.5 km) D **190** (305.8 km) Turnout at gravel pit.

J **226** (363.7 km) D **188** (302.5 km) Pipeline remote valve just west of road. The arch-shaped concrete structures keep pipeline buried in areas of possible flooding.

J **227.3** (365.8 km) D **186.7** (300.5 km) Nutirwik Creek culvert.

J **228** (366.9 km) D **186** (299.3 km) Highway parallels Dietrich River.

J **231.4** (372.4 km) D **182.6** (293.9 km) Small turnouts both sides of highway.

J **234.9** (378 km) D **179.1** (288.2 km) North Slope Borough boundary. Borough offices are located in Barrow.

J **235.3** (378.7 km) D **178.7** (287.6 km) Large turnout with litter barrel at foot of Chandalar Shelf and beginning of a long, steep (10 percent) grade. The farthest north spruce tree along the highway is located just south of the turnout. No trees beyond here.

J **236.3** (380.3 km) D **177.7** (286 km) Turnouts and view of the Dietrich River valley to the south next 0.3 mile/0.5 km.

J **237.1** (381.6 km) D **176.9** (284.7 km) Turnout at top of Chandalar Shelf; DOT/PF checkpoint. Headwaters of the Chandalar River are to the east. Table Mountain (elev. 6,425 feet/1,958m) is to the southeast. Dietrich River valley to south.

J **239** (384.6 km) D **175** (281.6 km) Brown net structure west of road is called a Wyoming Gage; it is used to measure precipitation. Sponsored by the Soil and Water Conservation Service.

J **239.2** (384.9 km) D **174.8** (281.3 km) Site of **CHANDALAR CAMP,** a former pipeline construction camp, now used as a BLM field station.

J **239.4** (385.3 km) D **174.6** (281 km) Chandalar highway maintenance station on west side of highway.

J **242.2** (389.8 km) D **171.8** (276.5 km) West Fork Chandalar River bridge.

J **242.5** (390.2 km) D **171.5** (276 km) Begin long, steep climb northbound toward Atigun Pass. Winter avalanche area.

J **244.7** (393.8 km) D **169.3** (272.5 km) Turnout at top of Atigun Pass (elev. 4,800 feet/1,463m), highest highway pass in Alaska; Continental Divide. A Wyoming Gage is located here. Nice example of a cirque, an amphitheater-shaped bowl or depression caused by erosion, in mountain east of road. Endicott Mountains are to the west, Phillip Smith Mountains to the east. James Dalton Mountain is to the left ahead northbound.

Highway descends steeply toward the North Slope. Many mountains in the area

Caribou herds migrate across the North Slope. (Jerrianne Lowther, staff)

exceed 7,000 feet/2,134m in elevation. The pipeline is in a buried, insulated concrete cribbing to the east. Construction in this area was extremely complex, difficult and dangerous.

J 248.4 (399.8 km) **D 165.6** (266.5 km) Turnouts both sides of highway. Good spot to view Dall sheep.

J 249.3 (401.2 km) **D 164.7** (265.1 km) Bridge over Spike Camp Creek. Highway crosses buried pipeline.

J 249.7 (401.8 km) **D 164.3** (264.4 km) Site of **ATIGUN CAMP**, a former pipeline construction camp. Turnouts both sides of highway. View of Atigun River valley. Another Wyoming Gage is located here.

J 251.5 (404.7 km) **D 162.5** (261.5 km) Turnouts next 0.3 mile/0.5 km northbound.

J 253.1 (407.3 km) **D 160.9** (258.9 km) Atigun River crossing No. 1. Highway crosses buried pipeline. *CAUTION: Grizzly bears in area.*

J 258.4 (415.8 km) **D 155.6** (250.4 km) Trevor Creek bridge.

J 258.6 (416.2 km) **D 155.4** (250.1 km) Turnout.

J 261.4 (420.7 km) **D 152.6** (245.6 km) Turnout.

J 265 (426.5 km) **D 149** (239.8 km) Roche Moutonnee Creek bridge.

J 267.5 (430.5 km) **D 146.5** (235.8 km) Bridge over Holden Creek.

J 268 (431.3 km) **D 146** (235 km) Good view of pump station No. 4.

J 269.3 (433.4 km) **D 144.7** (232.9 km) **PUMP STATION NO. 4.** This station has the highest elevation of all the pipeline stations (2,760 feet/841m), and is also a launching and receiving station for special devices called "pigs." A pig consists of spring-mounted scraper blades and/or brushes on a central body which moves through the pipe, cleaning accumulated wax from interior walls and monitoring conditions inside the pipe.

J 269.5 (433.7 km) **D 144.5** (232.5 km) Highway bridge passes over pipeline.

J 270.9 (436 km) **D 143.1** (230.3 km) Atigun River crossing No. 2. The Arctic National Wildlife Refuge boundary is located 3 miles/4.8 km east along the Atigun gorge. Galbraith Lake may be seen to the west. There are a large number of archaeological sites in this vicinity.

J 274 (440.9 km) **D 140** (225.3 km) View of Galbraith Lake and Galbraith camp.

J 274.7 (442.1 km) **D 139.3** (224.2 km) Road access to **GALBRAITH CAMP**, a construction camp; outhouse, litter barrel. BLM and USF&WS field stations located here.

J 276.5 (445 km) **D 137.5** (221.3 km) Island Lake.

J 284.3 (457.5 km) **D 129.7** (208.7 km) Toolik Lake west of road. A former construction camp, Toolik Lake is now the site of a University of Alaska research camp.

J 286.2 (460.6 km) **D 127.8** (205.7 km) Turnout to east at high point in road. View of Brooks Range south and east.

J 288.8 (464.8 km) **D 125.2** (201.5 km) Kuparuk River bridge.

J 289.3 (465.6 km) **D 124.7** (200.7 km) Pipeline crossing. Short, buried section of pipeline to west is called a sag bend and is to allow for wildlife crossing. Watch for caribou northbound.

J 290.4 (467.3 km) **D 123.6** (198.9 km) Turnout to east.

J 294.4 (473.8 km) **D 119.6** (192.5 km) Second sag bend northbound.

J 297.8 (479.2 km) **D 116.2** (187 km) Oxbow Creek culvert. Small turnout to east.

J 301 (484.4 km) **D 113** (181.8 km) Turnout. Slope Mountain (elev. 4,010 feet/ 1,222m) is just west of road. Watch for Dall sheep. This is the northern boundary of BLM-managed land. Land north of here is managed by the state.

J 305.7 (492 km) **D 108.3** (174.3 km) Site of **SLOPE MOUNTAIN CAMP**, a former pipeline construction camp, now Sag River highway maintenance station.

J 309 (497.3 km) **D 105** (169 km) Highway parallels Sagavanirktok River.

J 311.8 (501.8 km) **D 102.2** (164.5 km) **PUMP STATION NO. 3.**

J 319.8 (514.7 km) **D 94.2** (151.6 km) Turnout to east at Oil Spill Hill.

J 320 (515 km) **D 94** (151.3 km) The long range of hills east of the road is the Kakuktukruich Bluff.

J 325.3 (523.5 km) **D 88.7** (142.7 km) Turnout with litter barrel to east at the top of a steep grade called Ice Cut.

J 326.2 (525 km) **D 87.8** (141.3 km) Pipeline crossing.

J 330.7 (532.2 km) **D 83.3** (134.1 km) Dan Creek bridge.

J 334.4 (538.1 km) **D 79.6** (128.1 km) Site of **HAPPY VALLEY CAMP**, a former pipeline construction camp.

J 347.6 (559.4 km) **D 66.4** (106.9 km) Sagwon airstrip. The airstrip is currently not in use in order to protect nesting peregrine falcons in the area.

J 350.5 (564.1 km) **D 63.5** (102.2 km) View of Sagwon Bluffs to the east. The road passes over several low hills that offer views of the surrounding terrain.

J 353 (568 km) **D 61** (98.2 km) Wyoming Gage west of road.

J 355.1 (571.5 km) **D 58.9** (94.8 km) Turnout with litter barrel to east.

J 358.8 (577.4 km) **D 55.2** (88.8 km) **PUMP STATION NO. 2** to the east.

NOTE: The worst winter weather conditions on the Dalton Highway are experienced the next 38 miles/61 km northbound. Blowing snow may obscure visibility and block road.

J 364 (585.8 km) **D 50** (80.5 km) Low hills to the north are the Franklin Bluffs. East of the road, the Ivishak River empties into the Sagavanirktok River on its journey to the Arctic Ocean.

J 365.1 (587.6 km) **D 48.9** (78.7 km) Turnout with litter barrel by pond to west; watch for nesting waterfowl.

J 366 (589 km) **D 48** (77.2 km) Large animal crossing in pipeline for caribou.

J 376 (605.1 km) **D 38** (61.2 km) The small hill that rises abruptly on the horizon about 5 miles/8 km west of the road is called a pingo. Pingos often form from the bed of a lake that has been covered by vegetation. Freezing of the water can raise the surface several hundred feet above the surrounding terrain.

J 377.3 (607.2 km) **D 36.7** (59.1 km) Turnout with litter barrel to east at site of **FRANKLIN BLUFFS CAMP**, a former pipeline construction camp. *CAUTION: Watch for loose, coarse gravel on road.*

J 383 (616.4 km) **D 31** (49.9 km) Franklin Bluffs to the east and a pingo to the west.

J 398.7 (641.6 km) **D 15.3** (24.6 km) Underground pipeline crossing.

J 413.3 (665.1 km) **D 0.7** (1.1 km) Turnout at former highway checkpoint. Oil field activity and equipment become visible along the horizon.

J 414 (666.3 km) **D 0** Northern limit of state-owned highway at **DEADHORSE** (description follows). Access to the Arctic Ocean is on roads owned by the oil companies; permission must be obtained. Airport is 2 miles/3.2 km ahead.

Deadhorse was established to accommodate Prudhoe Bay oil operations. The area population, which includes oil and airline-related personnel, varies between 3,500 and 8,600. For security purposes, visitors are not allowed on the docks or on area roads.

Accommodations are available at several camps, but reservations should be made well in advance, as increased oil drilling activity will result in a shortage of available rooms.

Scheduled air service from Fairbanks and Anchorage (flying time from Anchorage: one hour, 35 minutes). Air taxi service is available at the airport. Packaged tours to the North Slope area are available.

GENERAL INFORMATION

Air Travel

SCHEDULED AIR SERVICE TO ALASKA

Alaska Airlines, MarkAir, Morris Air, Delta Airlines, Northwest Orient Airlines, United Airlines and Hawaiian Air all provide scheduled jet service between Alaska and the Lower 49. Air France, British Airways, China Airlines, Japan Air Lines, KLM Royal Dutch Airlines, Korean Air Lines, Lufthansa, Northwest Orient Airlines (Japan), Sabena Belgian World Airlines, Swissair and SAS (Scandinavian Airlines System) serve Anchorage from other countries. Contact your travel agent for current schedules and fares.

SCHEDULED AIR SERVICE WITHIN ALASKA

Following are listed many of the carriers offering interstate scheduled air service. Interline service available to most rural Alaska points; check with carriers. Also check local air taxi operators for charter and commuter service to Alaskan communities.

From ANCHORAGE

Alaska Airlines, 4750 International Airport Road, Anchorage 99502 — To Fairbanks, Prudhoe Bay, Cordova, Yakutat, Juneau, Sitka, Wrangell, Petersburg, Ketchikan, Nome, Kotzebue, Aniak, St. Mary's, Bethel, Dillingham, Dutch Harbor, King Salmon, Kodiak, Barrow and Gustavus/Glacier Bay (summer only).

Delta Airlines — Serves Fairbanks.

Era Aviation (Alaska Airlines commuter), 6160 S. Airpark Dr., Anchorage 99502 — To Kenai, Homer, Kodiak, Valdez and Iliamna plus 17 western Alaska villages from hub in Bethel.

MarkAir, Inc., 4100 W. International Road, Box 196769, Anchorage 99519-6769 — To Aniak, Barrow, Bethel, Cold Bay, Cordova, Dillingham, Fairbanks, Homer, Kenai, Dutch Harbor/Unalaska, Galena, King Salmon, Nome, Kotzebue, Kodiak, McGrath, Port Heiden, Prudhoe Bay/Deadhorse, St. George, St. Mary's, St. Paul, Sand Point, Unalakleet, Valdez.

PenAir (Alaska Airlines commuter), 4851 Aircraft Dr., Anchorage 99502, phone (907) 243-2485 — To McGrath, Unalakleet, Dillingham, King Salmon, Dutch Harbor, Akutan and the Pribilof Islands.

Reeve Aleutian Airways (Alaska Airlines commuter), 4700 W. International Airport Road, Anchorage 99502 — To points on the Alaska Peninsula, on the Aleutian Islands and on the Pribilof Islands.

United Airlines, Anchorage International Airport, phone toll free (800) 241-6522 — To Fairbanks.

From BARROW

Cape Smythe Air Service, Box 549, Barrow 99723, phone (907) 852-8333 — Barrow service to Atqasuk, Wainwright, Point Lay, Point Hope, Nuiqsut, Deadhorse (Prudhoe Bay) and Barter Island. Also offices in Kotzebue with service to Buckland, Deering, Ambler, Kiana, Kivalina, Kobuk, Noatak, Noorvik, Point Hope, Selawik and Shungnak. Offices in Nome with service to St. Michael, Shishmaref, Stebbins, Teller, Unalakleet, Wales, Shaktoolik, White Mountain, Koyuk, Golovin, Elim, Brevig Mission, Gambell and Savoonga.

From FAIRBANKS

Frontier Flying Service, 3820 University Ave., Fairbanks 99709 — To 23 Interior and Arctic villages including Gates of the Arctic National Park and the Arctic National Wildlife Refuge.

Larry's Flying Service Inc., 3822 University Ave., Fairbanks 99709 — To Anaktuvuk Pass, Bettles, Fort Yukon and 12 more villages.

From GLENNALLEN

Gulkana Air Service, Box 342, Glennallen 99588 — Serves Wrangell–St. Elias National Park and all the Copper River Basin.

From GUSTAVUS (Glacier Bay)

Glacier Bay Airways, Box 1, Gustavus 99826 — To Juneau, Hoonah, Excursion Inlet, Skagway, Haines and other Southeast points.

From HAINES

Haines Airways, Box 470, Haines 99827, phone (907) 766-2646 — To Juneau, Hoonah and Gustavus/Glacier Bay.

L.A.B. Flying Service (Alaska Airlines commuter), Box 272, Haines 99827 — To Juneau, Hoonah, Skagway and Gustavus/Glacier Bay.

From JUNEAU

Air North, 1873 Shell Simons Dr., Juneau 99801 — To Whitehorse, YT.

L.A.B. Flying Service (Alaska Airlines commuter), Box 2201, Juneau 99803 — To Haines, Hoonah, Skagway and Gustavus/Glacier Bay.

Loken Aviation, 8995 Yandukin Dr., Juneau 99801, phone (907) 789-3331 — To all Southeast points.

Wings of Alaska Flightseeing and Charters, 1873 Shell Simmons Dr., Juneau 99801 — To Haines, Hoonah, Skagway, Pelican, Elfin Cove, Angoon, Tenakee, Petersburg, Kake and Gustavus/Glacier Bay.

From KETCHIKAN

Ketchikan Air Service, 1600 International Airport, Ketchikan 99901, phone (907) 225-6608, fax (907) 247-6608 — To Craig, Klawock, Wrangell, Petersburg, Prince Rupert, Metlakatla, Coffman Cove, Long Island, Thorne Bay and other Southeastern points.

From NOME

Bering Air, Inc., Box 1650, Nome 99762 — From Nome and Kotzebue to western Alaska points and Russian Far East.

From PETERSBURG

Alaska Island Air, Box 508, Petersburg 99833 — To Kake and Rowan Bay.

From SKAGWAY

Skagway Air Service, Box 357, Skagway 99840 — To Juneau, with flag stops in Haines, Hoonah and Gustavus/Glacier Bay.

From WRANGELL

Ketchikan Air Service, Box 847, Wrangell 99929 — To Petersburg, Ketchikan and Kake.

SCHEDULED AIR SERVICE TO/IN YUKON AND WESTERN CANADA

Air North, P.O. Box 4998, Whitehorse, YT Y1A 4S2, phone (403) 668-2228 — Between Whitehorse, Dawson City, Fairbanks, Juneau and Old Crow.

AirBC, 4740 Agar Dr., Richmond, BC V7B 1A6, for reservations phone Air Canada (604) 688-5515 — Interprovincial service and service from Vancouver to U.S. destinations of Seattle and Portland.

Alkan Air, P.O. Box 4008, Whitehorse, YT Y1A 3S9, phone (403) 668-2107, fax (403) 667-6117 — Between Whitehorse, Dawson City, Mayo, Faro, Ross River, Watson Lake, Old Crow and Inuvik, NWT.

Canadian Airlines International, 206-1030 W. Georgia St., Vancouver, BC V6E 2Y2, phone (604) 279-6611 — To Calgary, Edmonton, Vancouver, Prince George, Prince Rupert, Fort St. John, Fort Nelson, Watson Lake, Whitehorse and other points.

North Coast Air Services, Box 610, Prince Rupert, BC V8J 3R5, phone (604) 627-1351, fax (604) 627-1356 — From Prince Rupert to Queen Charlotte Islands. Local and scheduled services.

PRIVATE AIRCRAFT

The MILEPOST® logs include the location of most airstrips along the Alaska Highway, on other highways in Alaska and in Alaskan communities, and along highways in northwestern Canada. Airstrips in British Columbia and Alberta are too numerous to be included. Aircraft symbols corresponding to airstrip locations are included on the highway strip maps. The map symbols are a white plane for airports with scheduled service, and a black plane for airstrips with no scheduled service and limited facilities.

Private aircraft information in these logs includes only the name and location of the airstrip, the elevation, length and surface material of the longest runway and the availability of fuel. Many Northland pilots fly jet craft and jet and other fuel is available at many airports.

There are literally thousands of landing areas in the North for amphibious aircraft; *The MILEPOST®* does not include these in the log copy. A Water Aerodrome Supplement is available from the Canada Map Office.

CAUTION: The brief description of airstrips given in The MILEPOST® *is in no way intended as a guide for pilots flying in the North.* Up-to-date information on airstrips, fuel and service, and radio facilities is published every eight weeks in accordance with specifications and agreements by the U.S. Dept. of Defense, the Federal Aviation Administration and the Dept. of Commerce, and in Canada by the Minister of Transport and the Chief of the Defence Staff.

Pilots should have the latest U.S. government flight information publication, *Alaska Supplement*, and the Canadian DND flight information publication, *Canada Flight Supplement*. Also suggested are the World Aeronautical Charts for the appropriate areas. Sectional maps are usually available at aviation stores along the way. A catalog of aeronautical charts and related publications is available from the NOAA offices. If there are no regional offices in your area, write: U.S. Dept. of Commerce, NOAA National Ocean Survey Distribution Division (C44), 6501 Lafayette Ave., Riverdale, MD 20840. Request a Canadian aeronautical chart catalog from the Canada Map Office, Dept. of Energy, Mines and Resources, 615 Booth St., Ottawa, ON K1A 0E9.

Pilots may also get in touch with the Alaska Airmen's Assoc., Inc., (907) 272-1251, for a copy of the *Alaska Airmen's Logbook for Alaska, Northwest Canada and Russia*.

Two free Canadian publications of interest are *Air Tourist Information — Canada* and *Flying the Alaska Highway In Canada*. Both are available from Transport Canada, AAN DHD, Ottawa, ON K1A 0N8.

Alcoholic Beverages

Alaska: Legal drinking age is 21. Packaged liquor, beer and wine are sold by licensed retailers rather than in state liquor stores. The sale and/or importation of alcoholic beverages is prohibited in some 70 Bush communities.

Alberta: Legal age is 18. Packaged liquor, beer and wine are sold in government liquor stores (open daily except Sunday and holidays) and beer (to take out) is also sold in some taverns. On Sunday, liquor is served only with food in licensed dining rooms.

British Columbia: Legal age is 19. Packaged liquor, beer and wine are sold only in government liquor stores (open daily except Sunday and holidays). Sunday serving laws in licensed premises vary from community to community.

Northwest Territories: Legal age is 19. Packaged liquor, beer and wine are sold in government liquor stores at Hay River, Pine Point, Fort Simpson, Fort Smith, Yellowknife, Norman Wells and Inuvik. Beer only agencies are located in some other places. You can purchase liquor in most hotels for consumption on the premises. The sale and possession of alcohol is prohibited in several communities.

Yukon Territory: Legal age is 19. Packaged liquor, beer and wine are sold in government liquor stores at Watson Lake, Whitehorse, Dawson City and Haines Junction. Some licensed premises have beer and wine for take-out sale.

Arctic Circle

The latitude of the Arctic Circle is approximately 66°33' north from the equator. We say "approximately" because the Arctic Circle varies a few seconds in latitude from year to year.

During summer solstice, June 20 or 21, the sun does not set at the Arctic Circle (it appears not to set for four days because of refraction). Farther north, at Barrow, the sun does not set from May 10 to Aug. 2.

At winter solstice, Dec. 21 or 22, the sun does not rise for one day at the Arctic Circle. At Barrow, the sun does not rise for 67 days.

Two highways cross the Arctic Circle. The Dalton Highway starts near Fairbanks and ends at Prudhoe Bay on the Arctic Ocean. The public may travel as far north as Dietrich, 100 miles/161 km north of the Arctic Circle. The Dempster Highway starts near Dawson City, YT, crosses the Arctic Circle after 250 miles/402 km, and ends at Inuvik, NT, 200 miles/322 km north of the Arctic Circle.

Bears

In Alaska, you are treading on bear territory. A true part of this wild country, bears can be a fearsome foe — never a friend.

There are three types of bears found in Alaska: the black bear, brown/grizzly bear and polar bear. Black bears range throughout most of the state, with highest densities in Southeast, Prince William Sound and Southcentral. Black bears can be brown in color, and may be confused with a grizzly, although they are normally smaller than a grizzly, with a more pointed head. Brown/grizzly bears range in color from black to blond, and range over most of the state. Alaska's coastal brown/grizzly bears are the world's largest carnivorous land mammal. (While polar bears are as large or larger, they actually live at sea on the ice, rather than on land.) Grizzlies have a distinct shoulder hump and larger head than black bears. Visitors are most likely to see grizzlies in areas such as Denali National Park, McNeil River or Katmai National Park.

Bears are large, powerful animals, both unpredictable and dangerous. They will defend their territory, themselves and their young. Like any animal, survival is their most compelling instinct. Avoid surprising them. Avoid close encounters.

They may be any place — in campgrounds, highway rest stops or along hiking trails — so you must always be cautious and alert. Each bear has individual characteristics and behavior and there are no formulas that apply to all bears.

If you are careless and disrespectful you increase the possibility of conflict between people and bears. If you use reasonable judgment and precaution you can reduce the risk to yourself and to the bear.

When hiking, make a lot of noise and avoid dense brush. Hike in the open if possible. Let the bears know where you are. Bears will normally avoid people. Even though their vision is poor, their senses of smell and hearing are excellent. Surprise meetings can occur. Wind and rivers may muffle your noises and you could surprise a bear.

Make noise by talking, ringing a bell or shaking a few pebbles in a can. Make a variety of noises. Talking or singing out loud is one of the best ways to let a bear know you are around.

Dogs are not permitted in national park backcountry. In bear country they can be a liability. Even wolves have difficulty driving bears away. Your pet, when hard pressed, may run to you with a grizzly in close pursuit.

Trouble between you and the grizzly bear can be caused by:

1. Cubs — A small, cuddly looking cub means that a protective mother is usually nearby. She aggressively protects her young, so don't approach.

2. Photography — Taking a close-up photo could lead to disaster. Keep your distance and use a telephoto lens.

3. Camps — Keep your campsite clean. Bears are omnivorous — they eat almost anything. Food and the accompanying odors attract bears. Do not bury trash — carry out everything you carry in.

In campgrounds, store food in vehicles or storage lockers (where provided). When in the backcountry, use bear-resistant food containers for all food and trash. Do not store food in your tent. Eliminate food odor from your camp and from yourself. Wash hands and face before retiring. *(Based on a National Park Service publication.)*

Bicycling in Alaska

Road conditions vary throughout Alaska, from newly paved highways to unimproved dirt roads. In planning your bicycling routes, read the highway logs in *The MILEPOST®* carefully. Abrupt changes in road conditions are generally noted in the log, as are steep grades and whether or not there are shoulders. With the recent popularity of the "mountain bike," additional routes are available to the rider who can travel on unimproved dirt roads and trails. Bicyclists will have to share the highways with vehicles, but you can avoid traffic by riding in the early morning and on weekdays. One advantage of Alaska touring in summer are the long daylight hours.

At press time, there were no laws governing bicyclists other than normal vehicle laws. Helmets are recommended.

Bicyclists stop in Eagle to phone home. (Jerrianne Lowther, staff)

Boating, Canoeing and Kayaking

Thousands of miles of waterways for both marine boating and lake and riverboating are available to visitors to the North.

For marine sailors, southeastern Alaska's Inside Passage offers both recreational boating and a sheltered transportation route. There are numerous marine charter services throughout Southeast for visiting boaters, most offering sportfishing or sightseeing tours, others with marine craft for charter (most skippered, some bare-boat). Boaters wishing to sail their own craft to Southeast should have the appropriate nautical charts and pilot guides. For U.S. waters, check locally for authorized nautical chart dealers or contact NOAA (National Oceanic & Atmospheric Administration); local offices should be listed in the phone book under United States Government, Dept. of Commerce, or write the National Ocean Survey Distribution Division (C44), 6501 Lafayette Ave., Riverdale, MD 20840. For Washington and Alaska waters you'll also need the *United States Coast Pilot* (Books 8 and 9). For British Columbia waters you'll need the *British Columbia Coast Pilot* (Volumes I and II), available from authorized dealers or the Government of Canada Fisheries & Oceans Scientific Information and Publications Branch, Ottawa. Charts of Canadian coastal waters are available from authorized dealers or from the Chart Distribution Office, Dept. of Fisheries and Oceans, Box 8080, 1675 Russell Road, Ottawa, ON K1G 3H6.

Marine travelers may also check local bookstores for Alaska cruising titles. Bluewater paddlers should have with them current NOAA Tidal Current Tables. Contact the DOT/PF (Box 3-1000, Juneau AK 99802) for a directory of harbor facilities.

Keep in mind that U.S. visitors entering Canada by private boat must report to Canadian customs immediately on arrival.

It is possible to travel thousands of miles on Northland river systems by boat, canoe, kayak or raft. In Alaska and Yukon Territory, the Yukon River system provides such opportunity. In Northwest Territories, the Mackenzie River system provides endless waterways to explore.

River travelers keep in mind that proper planning, good skills and common sense can help lessen the chance of capsize and possible injury or loss of equipment. It is always a good idea to check with local sources, such as sporting goods stores or state and federal agencies, for current information on river conditions.

Canoe trails have been established on rivers and lakes near Fairbanks, Anchorage, on Prince of Wales Island and on the Kenai Peninsula in Alaska.

Canoeing on the Kenai Peninsula's Swan Lake and Swanson River canoe trails starts about late May and continues until late October. For details on the trails write the Refuge Manager, Kenai National Wildlife Refuge, Box 2139, Soldotna 99669.

The Bureau of Land Management has established river trails near Fairbanks and Anchorage. The Anchorage (southern) region has seven river trails; the Fairbanks (northern) region also has seven river trails, including the Kobuk and Fortymile rivers. For details on these trails, write the Bureau of Land Management, 1150 University Ave., Fairbanks 99709, phone (907) 474-2200. BLM brochures on river trails include access points, portages and scale of difficulty.

The Alaska Public Lands Information Centers in Tok, Fairbanks, and Anchorage have information on many of Alaska's navigable rivers. Paddling guides, river logs and maps are available. Visit the centers or contact the Alaska Public Lands Information Center at: 250 Cushman St., Suite 1A, Fairbanks 99701, phone (907) 456-0527; 605 W. 4th Ave., Suite 105, Anchorage 99501, phone (907) 271-2737; or P.O. Box 359, Tok 99780, phone (907) 883-5667.

Canoe trails have been established on Prince of Wales Island along the Honker Divide and at Sarkar Lakes. Outstanding sea kayaking opportunities are also available on the west coast of Prince of Wales Island. Contact Craig Ranger District, Tongass National Forest, P.O. Box 145, Craig 99921, phone (907) 826-3271. For maps and information contact the Thorne Bay Ranger District, Tongass National Forest, Box 1, Thorne Bay 99950, phone (907) 828-3304.

Sea kayaking/camping map and brochure for Misty Fiords National Monument is available from Misty Fiords National Monument, Tongass National Forest, 3031 Tongass Ave., Ketchikan 99901, phone (907) 225-2148.

In Yukon Territory there are more than a dozen rivers and lakes suitable for canoeing. Write Tourism Yukon, Box 2703, Whitehorse, YT Y1A 2C6.

For information on canoeing in the tundra and subarctic regions of Northwest Territories and the Mackenzie River system write to TravelArctic, Yellowknife, NT X1A 2L9.

Bus Lines

Independent travelers wishing to travel by public bus within Alaska and Yukon Territory will generally find routes and services much more limited than in the Lower 48. Scheduled bus service is available within Alaska and Yukon Territory, but scheduled direct bus service to Alaska from the Lower 48 is not available, unless you wish to join an escorted motorcoach tour. If your schedule allows, you can travel from the Lower 48 to Alaska via public bus service by using several carriers. Most scheduled bus service in the North is seasonal.

Contact the following companies for current schedules:

Alaska Direct Bus Line, 125 Oklahoma St., Anchorage 99504, phone (800) 770-6652 or (907) 277-6652. Service from Anchorage to Fairbanks, Tok, Whitehorse, Haines, Skagway and Dawson City.

Alaska Sightseeing/Cruise West, 4th and Battery Bldg., Suite 700, Seattle, WA 98121, phone (907) 276-1305 (summer) or (800) 426-7702 year-round. Motorcoach trips connect Anchorage, Denali Park and Valdez.

Alaskon Express, 300 Elliott Ave. W., Seattle, WA 98119, phone (800) 544-2206. Scheduled service from Anchorage, Fairbanks, Haines, Skagway, Whitehorse and most communities en route.

Caribou Express–Bus, 700 W. 6th Ave., Suite 129, Anchorage 99501, phone (907) 278-5776. Coach service to Anchorage, Denali Park, Fairbanks, Tok, Alyeska, Portage Glacier, Homer, Valdez and Seward.

Denali Express, 405 L St., Anchorage 99501, phone (800) 327-7651 or (907) 274-8539. Service between Anchorage and Fairbanks.

Gray Line of Alaska, 300 Elliott Ave. W., Seattle, WA 98119, phone (800) 544-2206. Scheduled service to Skagway, Whitehorse and Haines. Motorcoach tours to Anchorage, Denali Park, Fairbanks, Prince William Sound, Seward and Portage Glacier.

Greyhound Lines of Canada, 4121 2nd Ave., Whitehorse, YT Y1A 3T8, phone (403) 667-2223. Scheduled service to Whitehorse from all U.S.–Canada border crossings; also between Whitehorse and Anchorage, Fairbanks, Skagway and Dawson Creek.

Norline Coaches (Yukon) Ltd., 2191 2nd Ave., Whitehorse, YT Y1A 4T8, phone (403) 668-3355. Service between Whitehorse, Mayo, Carmacks and Dawson City.

Northwest Stage Lines, Box 4932, Whitehorse, YT Y1A 4S2, phone (403) 668-6975. Service to Faro, Ross River, Haines Junction, Burwash and Beaver Creek.

Princess Tours®, 2815 2nd Ave., Suite 400, Seattle, WA 98121, phone (206) 728-4202. Motorcoach tours include the Klondike in Yukon, Anchorage, the Kenai Peninsula, Denali National Park, Fairbanks and Prudhoe Bay.

Seward Bus Line, P.O. Box 1338, Seward 99664, phone (907) 224-3608. Service between Anchorage, Homer and Seward.

Cabins

If you've ever wanted to try living in a log cabin in the wilderness, the USDA Forest Service gives you the opportunity for $20 per night per cabin through June; the fee goes up to $30 as of July 1, 1994. There are approximately 200 of these public-use cabins scattered throughout Tongass and Chugach national forests.

Cabins are accessible by air, boat, or trail. Average size is 12 by 14 feet. Most cabins have wood stoves, some have oil stoves. Check with the Forest Service to determine what type of stove is provided. All cabins have tables and sleeping room for four or more people. You must supply bedding, cookware, stove oil if necessary, and food. Splitting mauls are provided on site for cutting firewood. There are pit toilets but no garbage dumps (pack garbage out). Skiffs are provided at some cabins.

Permits for use of recreation cabins are issued on either a first-come first-serve basis, or by drawing. Applications for permits may be made in person or by mail up to 180 days in advance. You must have a permit for the specific length of occupancy. There is a three-day limit May 15 to Aug. 31 on hike-in cabins in the Chugach National Forest. There is a seven-day limit on other cabins in the Tongass National Forest from April 1 to Oct. 31, 10-day limit Nov. 1 through March 31.

For reservations and information on Chugach National Forest cabins, contact the Alaska Public Lands Information Center, 605 W. 4th Ave., Suite 105, Anchorage, AK 99501, phone 271-2737.

For reservations and information on Tongass National Forest cabins, contact one of the following area offices: Ketchikan Ranger District, Federal Bldg., Ketchikan 99901, phone 225-3101; Petersburg Ranger District, Box 309, Petersburg 99833, phone 772-3841; or Sitka Ranger District, 204 Siginaka Way, Sitka 99833, phone 747-6671.

The Bureau of Land Mangement has public-use cabins in Alaska, all within 75 miles of Fairbanks. Cabins must be reserved prior to use and a fee is required. Contact the Fairbanks Support Center Public Room at 1150 University Ave., Fairbanks 99709, phone 474-2250.

The U.S. Fish & Wildlife Service maintains public-use cabins within Kodiak National Wildlife Refuge. Contact the refuge manager, 1390 Buskin River Road, Kodiak 99615.

The Alaska Division of Parks and Outdoor Recreation maintains several public-use cabins scattered throughout the state. For reservations and information contact the following regional offices: Southcentral, Box 107001, Anchorage 99510, phone 762-2617; Southeast, 400 Willoughby Ave., Juneau 99801, phone 465-4563; and Northern Region, 3700 Airport Way, Fairbanks 99709-4613, phone 451-2695.

Calendar of Events—1994

Travelers may wish to take into account some of the North's major celebrations when planning their visit. Following are some of these events listed by month and by place. Additional events are detailed under Attractions under the communities covered in the highway logs.

FEBRUARY

Anchorage — Fur Rendezvous. **Cordova** — Iceworm Festival. **Fairbanks** — Yukon Quest Sled Dog Race. **Nenana** — Tripod Raising Festival. **Whitehorse, YT** — Yukon Quest Sled Dog Race; Sourdough Rendezvous.

MARCH

Anchorage — Iditarod Trail Sled Dog Race. **Bethel** — Camai Native Dance Festival. **Fairbanks** — Winter Carnival; North American Sled Dog Championships. **Nome** — Bering Sea Ice Classic Golf Tournament; month of Iditarod events. **North Pole** — Winter Carnival.

APRIL

Girdwood — Alyeska Spring Carnival. **Juneau** — Alaska Folk Festival.

MAY

This month is a busy one for fishing derbies for halibut (Homer, Seldovia and Valdez) and salmon (Ketchikan, Petersburg, Seldovia and Sitka).

Delta Junction — Buffalo Wallow Square Dance Jamboree. **Kodiak** — Crab Festival. **Nome** — Polar Bear Swim. **Petersburg** — Little Norway Festival. **Talkeetna** — Miners Day Festival.

JUNE

Anchorage — Mayor's Midnight Sun Marathon. **Fairbanks** — Midnight Sun Baseball Game. **Nenana** — River Daze. **Nome** — Midnight Sun Festival. **Palmer** — Colony Days. **Sitka** — All-Alaska Logging Championships; Summer Music Festival.

JULY

Chugiak–Eagle River — Bear Paw Festival. **Dawson City, YT** — International Midnight Dome Race; Yukon Gold Panning Championships. **Delta Junction** — Deltana Fair. **Fairbanks** — Golden Days; World Eskimo–Indian Olympics. **Inuvik, NT** — Great Northern Arts Festival. **Seward** — Mount Marathon Race. **Soldotna** — Progress Days. **Talkeetna** — Moose Dropping Festival.

AUGUST

Dawson City, YT — Discovery Days. **Fairbanks** — Tanana Valley State Fair. **Haines** — Southeast Alaska State Fair. **Kodiak** — State Fair and Rodeo. **Ninilchik** — Kenai Peninsula State Fair. **Palmer**—Alaska State Fair. **Seward** — Silver Salmon Derby.

SEPTEMBER

Dawson City, YT — Great Klondike Outhouse Race. **Fairbanks** — Equinox Marathon. **Nome** — Great Bathtub Race. **Seldovia** — Blueberry Festival. **Skagway** — Trail of '98 Road Relay to Whitehorse, YT.

OCTOBER

Anchorage — Oktoberfest. **Sitka** — Alaska Day Festival.

NOVEMBER

Anchorage — Great Alaska Shootout.

Camping

The MILEPOST® indicates both private and public campgrounds with tent symbols in the highway logs and on the strip maps for Alaska, Yukon Territory, Northwest Territories and parts of Alberta and British Columbia. Federal, state and provincial agencies offering camping areas are listed here. Reservations are not accepted at any provincial, state or federal campgrounds. Keep in mind that government campgrounds do not maintain dump stations (excepting a few British Columbia provincial parks) and few offer electrical hookups. Season dates for most campgrounds in the North depend on weather. Check the highway logs for commercial campgrounds in the North. *NOTE: Campers are urged to use established campgrounds. Overnighting in rest areas and turnouts is illegal unless otherwise posted, and may be unsafe.* ▲

ALASKA

The **Alaska Public Lands Information Centers** in Fairbanks, Anchorage and Tok provide information on all state and federal campgrounds in Alaska, along with state and national park passes and details on wilderness camping. Visit the centers, or contact the Alaska Public Lands Information Center at: 605 W. 4th Ave., Suite 105, Anchorage 99501, phone (907) 271-2737; 250 Cushman St., Suite 1A, Fairbanks 99701, phone (907) 456-0527; or P.O. Box 359, Tok 99780, phone (907) 883-5667.

The **Alaska Division of Parks and Outdoor Recreation** maintains an extensive system of roadside campgrounds and waysides. All are available on a first-come, first-served basis. There is a $6 to $8 per night camping fee charged at all developed state campgrounds, except for $10 at Eklutna Lake and Willow Creek, and $12 at Eagle River and Chena River campgrounds. *(NOTE: Rates are subject to change.)* An annual pass, good for unlimited camping in a calendar year, is available for $75. The pass is in the form of a nontransferable windshield decal. Beginning in 1994, there is a day-use parking fee of $2 per vehicle at a small number of state park facilities, including some picnic sites, trailheads and fishing access sites. A full-year parking pass may be purchased for $25. To obtain camping or parking passes, send check or money order payable to the State of Alaska to Alaska Camping Pass, Division of Parks and Outdoor Recreation, P.O. Box 107001, Anchorage 99510-7001.

The **USDA Forest Service** provides numerous camping areas in Chugach and Tongass national forests. Most USFS campgrounds charge a fee of from $6 to $8 per night depending on facilities. There is a 14-day limit at most campgrounds; this regulation is enforced. For further information write the Office of Information, USDA Forest Service, Box 1628, Juneau 99802.

The **Bureau of Land Management** maintains about 25 free camping areas in the state. Write to the Bureau of Land Management, Attn: The Public Rooms, 1150 University Ave., Fairbanks 99709, phone 474-2200.

The **National Park Service** maintains seven campgrounds in Denali National Park and Preserve. There are established hike-in campgrounds at Glacier Bay and Katmai national parks and preserves, and wilderness camping in other national parks and preserves in Alaska. For further information contact the Alaska Public Lands Information Center, 605 W. 4th, Suite 105, Anchorage 99501, phone 271-2737.

The **U.S. Fish & Wildlife Service** manages several camping areas within Kenai National Wildlife Refuge. Contact the Refuge Manager, Kenai National Wildlife Refuge, Box 2139, Soldotna 99669.

Two special passes for federal recreation areas are available to U.S. citizens. The Golden Age Passport is for persons age 62 and older, and the Golden Access Passport is for blind and disabled persons. Both provide free lifetime admittance to federally-operated parks, monuments, historic sites, recreation areas and wildlife refuges that charge entrance fees. Accompanying passengers in a private car enter without charge as well. The passport bearer also receives a 50 percent discount on federal use fees charged for facilities and services such as camping, boat launching and parking. These passes must be obtained in person by showing proof of age for a Golden Age Passport, or proof of being medically determined to be blind or permanently disabled for the Golden Access Passport. The passports are available at most of the federal recreation areas where they may be used, so travelers do not need to obtain them in advance.

CANADA

National park campgrounds generally have a per night fee. Per night fees range from $6.50 for a tent site to $17 for a full-service site with individual water, sewer and electrical hookups. In addition, a park motor license sticker is required for motorists staying overnight in the national parks. Electrical service is standard 60 cycle. Wood for campfires is supplied free to all camping and picnicking grounds. Bring your own ax to split kindling. "Serviced" campgrounds have caretakers.

Alberta has 67 **provincial park campgrounds**, some with limited facilities, others with picnic tables, electrical hookups, flush toilets, barbecues and nature programs. There is a fee ranging from $7 to $15 per night for provincial parks. There are also limited facilities at roadside campsites provided by Alberta Parks Service and at campsites in the **Forest Recreation Areas**. A nominal fee is charged. Private and public campgrounds are listed in *Campgrounds in Alberta*, available from Travel Alberta.

In British Columbia, **provincial park campgrounds** are indicated 1.2 miles/2 km and 1,312 feet/400m before the entrance along the highways by blue-and-white signs. They are serviced from spring to early fall (however, they may be used throughout the year). Fees range from $6 to $15.50 per night. Gates close from 11 P.M. to 6 A.M. in some parks.

In Northwest Territories: **Territorial campground** fees are $5 or $10 per night, depending upon the site, in attended campgrounds and parks with facilities. Free firewood is supplied for use in campground.

Yukon Territory has more than 40 **Yukon government campgrounds** located along its road system. There is a per night fee charged for nonresidents. These well-maintained government campgrounds often have kitchen shelters (which may not be used as sleeping accommodations) and free firewood for use at the campground. There is a 14-day limit.

Customs Requirements

Crossing the border into Canada or reentering the United States is a fairly straightforward procedure. However, there are a few items which Alaska-bound travelers should be alerted to.

The first is firearms. Canada has very specific and strict requirements on what firearms may be brought into Canada. If you plan to travel with a firearm, read these requirements carefully.

Certain items, mainly crafts and souvenirs made from parts of wild animals, have caused some problems for travelers to the North in recent years. An item which may be purchased legally in Alaska, for example carved ivory, can be brought back into the Lower 49 but may not be permitted transit through Canada without a permit. Some items which may be purchased legally in parts of Canada may not be allowed into the United States. For example, a seal fur doll purchased in Inuvik, NWT, would be confiscated by U.S. customs because the import of seal products is restricted except by special permit.

IMPORTANT: You cannot cross the border unless the customs office for the country you are entering is open. Severe fines are levied for crossing without clearing customs. Officials at Canadian customs are concerned about child abductions. If you are traveling with children, remember to bring identification for them.

Read through the following information and contact Canadian or U.S. customs offices directly.

ENTRY INTO CANADA
FROM THE UNITED STATES

Your best source of general information on this subject is the Canadian Government Office of Tourism's travel information brochure. To obtain a copy write Tourism Canada, 235 Queen St., Ottawa, ON K1A 0H5. Revenue Canada can also answer travel questions, phone (613) 957-0275. Here are excerpts from the travel brochure.

Citizens or permanent residents of the United States can usually cross the U.S.–Canada border either way without difficulty or delay. They do not require passports or visas. However, to assist officers of both countries in speeding the crossing, native-born U.S. citizens should carry some identifying paper that shows their citizenship, just in case they are asked for it. This would include a driver's license, voters registration, passport with photo, or some employment cards with description and photo. Social security cards are not positive identification. Birth certificates of children are sometimes required. Proof of residence may also be required. Naturalized U.S. citizens should carry a naturalization certificate or some other evidence of citizenship. Permanent residents of the United States who are not U.S. citizens are advised to have their Resident Alien Card (U.S. Form 1-151 or Form 1-551).

All persons other than U.S. citizens or legal residents, and residents of Greenland, require a valid passport or an acceptable travel document.

Visitors of the United States who have a single entry visa to that country should check with an office of the U.S. Immigration and Naturalization Service to make sure that they have all the papers they need to get back into the United States.

Persons temporarily in the United States who would require visas if coming to Canada directly from their countries of origin should contact the Canadian Embassy, Consulate or Office of Tourism in their home country before departure for the United States.

Persons under 18 years of age who are not accompanied by an adult should bring a letter with them from a parent or guardian giving them permission to travel into Canada. A divorced parent may find a copy of the divorce/custody papers helpful.

Although there is no set standard for monies required for entrance into Canada, the visitor must have sufficient funds to cover his cost of living per day for the planned length of stay. Consideration in assessing "sufficient funds" includes the locale in which the visitor plans to stay and whether he will be staying with a friend or relative. (Readers report being turned back for lacking $150 in cash; one customs official suggests $500 as an appropriate amount.) The visitor must also have return transportation fare to his country of origin.

Vehicles: The entry of vehicles and trailers into Canada for touring purposes, for periods up to 12 months, is generally a quick, routine matter, without payment of a customs assessment, and any necessary permits are issued at the port of entry. Rental trailers of the U-Haul luggage variety may be subject to a nominal deposit, which is refundable on proof of exportation of trailer. Motor vehicle registration forms should be carried and, if the vehicle is rented from a car rental company, a copy of the rental contract stipulating use in Canada. If a tourist enters Canada using a vehicle not registered in his name, it is suggested that he carry a letter from its registered owner authorizing the use of the vehicle.

U.S. motorists planning to travel in Canada are advised to obtain a Canadian Nonresident Interprovincial Motor Vehicle Liability Insurance Card, which provides evidence of financial responsiblity. This card is available only in the United States through U.S. insurance companies or their agents. All provinces in Canada require visiting motorists to produce evidence of financial responsibility should they be involved in an accident. Financial responsibility limits vary by province.

All national driver's licenses are valid in Canada.

Trailers: If you plan to leave your vacation trailer in Canada for a season while returning home from time to time, ask Canada customs for a wallet-sized special permit — an E-99. Post the permit inside the trailer so that it can be seen easily from outside. You may not store a vacation trailer in Canada during the off-season.

Entry by private boat: Visitors planning to enter Canada by private boat should contact customs in advance for a list of ports of entry that provide customs facilities and their hours of operation. Immediately upon arrival, visitors must report to customs and complete all documentation. In emergency situations, visitors must report their arrival to the nearest regional customs office or office of the RCMP.

Baggage: The necessary wearing apparel and personal effects in use by the visitor are admitted free of duty. Up to 50 cigars, 200 cigarettes (one carton) and 14 ounces of manufactured tobacco and up to 40 ounces of spiritous liquor or wine *OR* 24 12-ounce cans or bottles of beer or ale may be allowed entry in this manner. Additional quantities of alcoholic beverages up to a maximum of 2 gallons may be imported into Canada (except the Northwest Territories) on a payment of duty and taxes plus charges for a provincial permit at port of entry. To import tobacco products a person must be 18 years of age or over and to import alcoholic beverages the importer must have reached the legal age established by authorities of the province or territory into which the alcoholic beverages are being entered.

Recreational Equipment: Visitors may also bring in sporting outfits and other equipment for their own use by declaring them at entry. These can include fishing tackle, portable boats, outboard motors, snowmobiles, equipment for camping, golf, tennis and other games, radios and portable or table-model television sets used for the reception of sound broadcasting and television programs, musical instruments, typewriters and cameras (with a reasonable amount of film and flashbulbs) in their possession on arrival. Although not a requirement, it may facilitate entry if visitors have a list (in duplicate) of each item, including serial numbers when possible. All such articles must be identified and reported when leaving Canada. ▲

Transporting goods through Canada: U.S. citizens from the Lower 49 who wish to transport personally their household or personal effects to Alaska when such goods are not intended for use in Canada, may obtain a temporary admission permit at the border to facilitate the in-transit movements of goods through Canada. A refundable security deposit may be required at time of entry. The traveler should prepare a list of the goods in triplicate, indicating values and serial numbers where applicable.

Firearms: Firearms are divided into three categories — prohibited, restricted and long guns.

A nonresident importing a "long gun" or moving in transit through Canada with a "long gun" does not require a Firearms Acquisition Certificate nor a Permit to Transport providing the visitor is 16 years of age or older and the firearm is for sporting or competition use. A "long gun" means a regular hunting rifle or shotgun as so described by the manufacturer, and which does not fall into the category of a prohibited or restricted firearm.

A prohibited firearm includes any firearm that is capable of firing bullets in rapid succession during one pressure of the trigger, or any firearm adapted from a rifle or shotgun whether by sawing, cutting or other alteration or modification, that as so adapted, has a barrel that is less than 18 inches/46 cm in length, or that is less than 26 inches/66 cm in overall length. Such weapons are not permitted entry into Canada.

A restricted firearm includes any firearm that is not a prohibited weapon, has a barrel less than 18½ inches/47 cm in length and is capable of discharging center-fire ammunition in a semiautomatic manner, or is designed or adapted to be fired when reduced to a length less than 26 inches/66 cm by folding, telescoping or otherwise. Also included would be any firearm designed, altered or intended to be aimed and fired by the action of one hand, such as revolvers and handguns.

Restricted firearms may only enter Canada when accompanied by a Permit to Transport or a Permit to Carry issued by a Canadian Local Registrar of Firearms. These permits are rarely issued.

The following quantities of explosives (not including hollow-point handgun ammunition) may enter Canada for personal use by hunters and competitive marksmen without a permit issued by the Explosives Branch of the Dept. of Energy, Mines and Resources: 5,000 safety cartridges; 5,000 primers for safety cartridges; 5,000 empty primed safety cartridge cases; 17.6 pounds/8 kg smokeless powder (small-arms nitro compound).

Nonresidents arriving at a Canada Customs port must declare all their firearms. Anyone who illegally carries a firearm into Canada is subject to a number of penalties, including seizure of the weapon and the vehicle in which it is carried.

Plants, fruit and vegetables: House plants may be imported without a permit. Some fruits and vegetables may be restricted entry into Canada and all are subject to inspection at the border.

Animals: Dogs and cats (over three months of age) from the United States must be accompanied by a certificate issued by a licensed veterinarian of Canada or the United States certifying that the animal has been vaccinated against rabies during the preceding 36 months; such a certificate shall describe the animal and date of vaccination and shall be initialed by inspectors and returned to the owner.

Up to two pet birds per family may be imported into Canada. Birds of the parrot family and song birds may be admitted when accompanied by the owner, if the owner certifies in writing that, upon entering the country, the birds have not been in contact with any other birds during the preceding 90 days and have been in the owner's possession for the entire period. All birds of the parrot family, except budgies, cockatiels and Rose-ringed parakeets, are on the CITES endangered species list and require at the minimum a U.S. CITES export permit with some species requiring an additional Canadian CITES import permit. The temporary movement of all parrots through Canada requires a CITES Temporary Import Certificate from the Canadian Wildlife Service. Contact Canadian Wildlife Service, Ottawa, ON K1A 0H3, phone (819) 997-1840.

Endangered species: The importation of certain animals and plants that are on the endangered species list is prohibited. This applies to any recognizable by-product made of the fur, skin, feathers, bone, etc., of these creatures. For example, U.S. citizens transporting carved ivory or parts of lynx, otter, brown/grizzly bear or wolf through Canada must first obtain an export and/or transit permit from the U.S. Fish and Wildlife Service. (Permits are available at 1412 Airport Way in Fairbanks or at any U.S. Fish and Wildlife Refuge office.) Many ivory sellers will furnish a permit upon request. To avoid the need for a permit, either mail the items or travel directly back to the Lower 48. Request a list of restricted items from Convention Administrator, Canadian Wildlife Service, Environment Canada, Ottawa, ON K1A 0H3.

REENTRY INTO THE UNITED STATES

It is, of course, the responsibility of the traveler to satisfy U.S. immigration authorities of his right to reenter the United States.

Canadian immigration officers may caution persons entering from the United States if they may have difficulty in returning.

Reentry to the United States can be simplified if you list all your purchases before you reach the border, keep sales receipts and invoices handy, and pack purchases separately.

Within 48 Hours: Residents of the United States visiting Canada for less than 48 hours may take back for personal or household use merchandise to the fair retail value of $25, free of U.S. duty and tax. Any or all of the following may be included, so long as the total value does not exceed $25; 50 cigarettes, 10 cigars (non-Cuban in origin), 4 ounces/150 ml of alcoholic beverage or alcoholic perfume.

If any article brought back is subject to duty or tax, or if the total value of all articles exceeds $25, no article may be exempted from duty or tax. Members of a family household are not permitted to combine the value of their purchases under this exemption.

Persons crossing the International Boundary at one point and reentering the United States in order to travel to another part of Canada should inquire at U.S. customs regarding special exemption requirements.

After More Than 48 Hours: U.S. residents returning from Canada may take back, once every 30 days, merchandise for personal or household use to the value of $400 free of U.S. duty and tax, provided they have remained in Canada 48 hours. The exemption will be based on the fair retail value of the article acquired and goods must accompany the resident upon arrival in the United States. Members of a family household traveling together may combine their personal exemptions — thus a family of five could be entitled to a total exemption of $2,000. Up to 100 cigars (non-Cuban in origin) per person may be imported into the United States by U.S. residents, and also 1 liter of alcoholic beverages if the resident has attained the age of 21 years, and up to 200 cigarettes.

Federal wildlife laws affect what U.S. citizens may bring back into the United States from Canada. The list is extensive, and U.S. visitors to Canada should be particularly aware that the import of the following is restricted except by special permit: products made from sealskin, whalebone and whale and walrus ivory, sea otter, or polar bear, and most wild bird feathers, mounted birds and skins. Thus, an item that may be purchased legally in parts of Canada, such as a seal fur doll, may not be allowed into the United States. For a complete list of restricted items and information on import permits, contact the nearest U.S. Fish and Wildlife Service office.

Pets: Domestic dogs, including those taken out of the country and being returned, must have a valid rabies vaccination certificate identifying the dog and date of vaccination and bearing the signature of a licensed veterinarian. A date of expiration should be included. If no date of expiration is specified, the certificate is acceptable if the date of vaccination is no more than 12 months before the date of arrival. Vaccination against rabies is not required for cats.

For further information contact the nearest U.S. customs office or write U.S. Customs Service, Washington, DC 20229.

Daylight Hours

	SUMMER MAXIMUM		
	Sunrise	Sunset	Hrs. of daylight
Barrow	May 10	Aug. 2	84 days continuous
Fairbanks	2:59 A.M.	12:48 P.M.	21:49 hours
Anchorage	4:21 A.M.	11:42 P.M.	19:21 hours
Juneau	3:51 A.M.	10:09 P.M.	18:18 hours
Ketchikan	4:04 A.M.	9:32 P.M.	17:28 hours
Adak	6:27 A.M.	11:10 P.M.	16:43 hours

	WINTER MINIMUM		
	Sunrise	Sunset	Hrs. of daylight
Barrow	Jan. 24 noon	Nov. 18 noon	none
Fairbanks	10:59 A.M.	2:41 P.M.	3:42 hours
Anchorage	10:14 A.M.	3:42 P.M.	5:28 hours
Juneau	8:46 A.M.	3:07 P.M.	6:21 hours
Ketchikan	8:12 A.M.	3:18 P.M.	7:05 hours
Adak	9:52 A.M.	5:38 P.M.	7:46 hours

Disabled Visitor Services

Accommodations and other facilities (public and private) that are equipped for the disabled traveler are noted with the wheelchair icon ♿. Travelers should be aware, however, that not all facilities carrying this symbol may indeed be wheelchair accessible, and that facilities not carrying this icon may be wheelchair accessible. Disabled visitors should call ahead to businesses for specific information on the accessibility of services. *The MILEPOST*® is in the process of adding this information to the logs and we do not expect to have complete information this year. Readers can help by letting us know about disabled visitor services.

Relay Alaska is a service of GCI. Deaf, hard-of-hearing and speech-impaired persons may contact GCI, a long-distance telephone carrier certified by the Alaska Public Utilities Commission to provide Telecommunications Relay Service in Alaska. Relay Alaska allows text telephone users and voice phone users to communicate with each other through specially trained GCI assistants. For additional information, phone GCI (800) 770-2234 V/TTY or Alascom (800) 252-7266.

Driving Information

Driving to the North is no longer the ordeal it was in the early days. Those early images of the Alaska Highway with vehicles sunk in the mud up to their hubcaps are far removed from the asphalt-surfaced Alaska Highway of today.

Highways in the North range from four-lane paved freeways to one-lane dirt and gravel roads. Major highways in Alaska are paved with the exception of the following highways which are gravel: Steese Highway (Alaska Route 6), Taylor Highway (Alaska Route 5), Elliott Highway (Alaska Route 2), Dalton Highway and Denali Highway (Alaska Route 8).

In Yukon Territory, all of the Alaska Highway and most of the Klondike Highway from Skagway to Dawson City are asphalt-surfaced. All other roads are gravel.

Major routes through Alberta and British Columbia are paved, with the exception of the Cassiar Highway, which has both gravel and asphalt surfacing. The Cassiar Highway (BC Highway 37) is becoming a popular route North.

All highways within Northwest Territories are gravel. Most gravel roads in the North are well-maintained and treated with calcium chloride as a dust-control measure (wash your vehicle as soon as practical).

RV owners should be aware of the height of their vehicles in metric measurements, as bridge heights in Canada are noted in meters.

Know your vehicle and its limitations. Some Northern roads may not be suitable for a large motorhome or trailer, but most roads will present no problem to a motorist who takes his time and uses common sense.

Auto Preparation: The following recommendations for driving in the North Country in summer are from our MILEPOST field editors. One thing to keep in mind is the variable nature of road conditions: Some sections of road may be in poor condition because of construction or weather; other highways — particularly gravel roads closed in winter — may be either very rough or very smooth, depending on when maintenance crews last worked on the road. Another thing to remember is the wide range of roads in the North, from four-lane freeway to narrow gravel roads. For example, the Alaska Highway is surfaced almost its entire length and the greatest distance between services is only about 100 miles/160 km. Although there still can be some rough spots on the Alaska Highway, either because of construction or because the surfacing has deteriorated, it is generally a good highway. The more remote roads, such as the Dempster or Dalton highways, are gravel and motorists are much farther from assistance. More preparation is required for these roads.

There are some simple preparations motorists can make for their trip North which can make driving easier. First make sure your vehicle and tires are in good condition before starting out. An inexpensive and widely available item to include are clear plastic headlight covers (or black metal matte screens). These protect your headlights from flying rocks and gravel. You might also consider a wire-mesh screen across the front of your vehicle to protect paint, grill and radiator from flying rocks. The finer the mesh, the more protection from flying gravel. For those of you hauling trailers, a piece of quarter-inch plywood fitted over the front of your trailer offers protection.

There is practically no way to protect the windshield, although some motorists have experimented with screen shields that do not seriously impair their vision. However, these may make you feel like you're driving a hamster cage. These are not recommended nor do you see many of them in the North, but it is, of course, up to the individual motorist whether these are worthwhile.

Many motorists find bug screens a worthwhile investment.

Crankcases are seldom damaged, but gas tanks can be on rough gravel roads. Sometimes rocks work their way in between the plate and gas tank, wearing a hole in the tank. You may wish to insert a rubber mat of some kind between gas tank and securing straps. However, drivers maintaining safe speeds should have no problems with punctured gas tanks. The higher the clearance on your vehicle the better on some of the rougher gravel roads.

Also keep in mind the simple precautions that make driving easier. A visor or tinted glass helps when you're driving into the sun. Good windshield wipers and a full windshield washer (or a bottle of wash and a squeegee) make life easier.

Dust and mud are generally not a major problem on Northern roads, though you may run into both. Heavy rains combined with a gravel road or roadbed torn up for construction make mud. Mud flaps are suggested. Many gravel roads in the North (such as the Dalton Highway) are treated with calcium chloride as a dust-control measure. Because calcium chloride tends to eat into paint and metal parts on your vehicle, be sure to thoroughly wash your vehicle. Dust can seep into everything and it's difficult if not impossible to keep it out. Remember to close the windows on your trailer or camper when on a dusty road. It also helps to keep clothes, food and bedding in sealed plastic bags. Also check your air filter periodically.

Driving at slow, safe speeds not only keeps down the dust for drivers in back of you, it also helps prevent you from spraying other vehicles with gravel.

Although auto shops in Northern communities are generally well-stocked with parts, do carry the following for emergencies and on-the-spot repairs: flares; first-aid kit; trailer bearings; good bumper jack with lug wrench; a simple set of tools, such as crescent wrenches, socket and/or open-end wrenches, hammer, screwdrivers, pliers, wire, prybar (for changing that fan belt); electrician's tape; small assortment of nuts and bolts; fan belt; and one or two spare tires (two spares for remote roads).

If you are driving a vehicle which may require parts not readily available up North, add whatever you think necessary. You may wish to carry an extra few gallons of gas and also water, especially on remote roads. You may also wish to carry a can of fluid for brakes, power steering and automatic transmissions.

If your vehicle should break down on the highway and tow truck service is needed, normally you will be able to flag down a passing motorist. Travelers in the Northland are generally helpful in such situations (traditionally, the etiquette of the country requires one to stop and provide assistance). If you are the only person traveling in the disabled vehicle, be sure to leave a note on your windshield indicating when you left the vehicle and in what direction you planned to travel.

Gasoline: Unleaded gas is widely available in Alaska and is the rule in Canada. Diesel gas is also commonly available. In Alaska, check with the Alaska State Troopers, and in Canada the RCMP, about gas availability. Good advice for Northern travelers: gas up whenever possible.

Gas prices in the North, as elsewhere, vary. Generally, gas prices are slightly higher in Canada and Alaska than the Lower 48, but this is not a hard and fast rule. You may find gas in Anchorage or elsewhere at the same price — or even lower — than at home. A general rule of thumb is the more remote the gas station, the higher the price. And gas prices may vary considerably from service station to service station within the same community.

It is a good idea to carry cash, since some gas stations in Alaska are independents and do not accept credit cards. Most Chevron, Texaco and Tesoro stations will accept VISA or MasterCard. Also watch for posted gas prices that are for *cash,* but not noted as such. Besides double-checking the posted price before filling up, also check with the attendant to make sure you have the correct pump for unleaded, regular or diesel, depending on what you want.

Keep in mind that Canadian gas stations have converted to the metric system; quantity and price are based on liters. There are 3.785 liters per U.S. gallon, 4.5 liters per imperial gallon. See Metric System this section for conversion chart.

Insurance: Auto insurance is mandatory in all Canadian provinces and territories. Drivers should carry adequate car insurance before entering the country. Visiting motorists are required to produce evidence of financial responsibility should they be involved in an accident. There is an automatic fine if visitors are involved in an accident and found to be uninsured, and your car can be impounded. Your insurance company should be able to provide you with proof of insurance coverage (request a Canadian Nonresident Interprovincial Motor Vehicle Liability Insurance Card), which is accepted as evidence of financial responsibility.

The minimum liability insurance requirement in Canada is $200,000 Canadian, except in the Province of Quebec where the limit is $50,000 Canadian. Further information regarding automobile insurance in Canada may be obtained from The Insurance Bureau of Canada, 181 University Ave., Toronto, ON M5H 3M7.

Tires: On gravel, the faster you drive, the faster your tires will wear out. So take it easy.

If you take it easy, you should have no problems with your tires, provided you have the right size for your vehicle, with the right pressure, not overloaded, and not already overly worn. Belted bias or radial ply tires are recommended for gravel roads.

Carry one good spare. Consider two spares if you are traveling remote gravel roads such as the Dempster or Dalton highways. The space-saver doughnut spare tires found in some passenger cars are not adequate for travel on gravel roads.

In Alaska, studded tires are permitted from Sept. 15 to May 1 (Sept. 30 to April 15 south of 60°N).

Emergency Medical Services

Phone numbers of emergency medical services (if available), such as ambulance and hospital, are listed along with police and fire departments at the beginning of each town or city description in *The MILEPOST*®. Emergency medical services along highways are listed in the highway introductions.

In addition, travelers should note that CB Channels 9 and 11 are monitored for emergencies in most areas, Channels 14 and 19 in some areas. Recommendations for emergency equipment and a list of emergency medical services on Alaska's highways are detailed in a brochure called *Help Along The Way,* available from the Emergency Medical Services Section, Division of Public Health, Dept. of Health & Social Services, P.O. Box 110616, Juneau 99811-0616.

Fires

Travelers are asked to refrain from building campfires on the tundra. Campfires are a source for peat burns and forest fires, and peat burns are nearly impossible to extinguish. When wildfires threaten inhabited areas, the BLM's Alaska Fire Service (in the northern half of the state) and the State of Alaska Division of Forest (in the southern half of the state) provide fire protection to lands managed by the BLM, National Park Service, U.S. Fish and Wildlife Service, Native corporations and the state.

All land management agencies in Alaska have placed their lands in one of four protection categories — critical, full, modified and limited. These protection levels set priorities for fire fighting. Most of Alaska's 586,000 square miles of land is a vast area with no roads. Fire fighters must be brought in to the fire by airplane or helicopter and they must communicate by portable radio in dangerous conditions.

Unusually dry weather in 1990 made it the most severe fire season on record in Alaska. Lightning was the primary cause of fires with an average of 2,000 strikes a day occurring between June 26 and July 5.

Fishing

Throughout *The MILEPOST*® you will find this ➻ friendly little symbol. Wherever you see one, you will find a description of the fishing at that point.

Following is a brief summary of fishing license fees, rules and regulations for Alaska and Canada. It is not possible to list all the latest regulations in *The MILEPOST*®, so we urge you to obtain up-to-date information.

Alaska: A nonresident fishing license, valid for the calendar year issued, costs $50. A special three-day nonresident fishing license may be purchased for $15. A 14-day nonresident permit is $30. A one-day nonresident fishing license may also be purchased for $10. All anglers fishing for king salmon must also purchase a current year's king salmon tag, which costs $20 for nonresidents. Nonresidents under 16 years of age do not need a fishing license, although they must have the required tag in their possession if sportfishing for king salmon.

Resident sportfishing licenses cost $15; the king salmon tag is $10 for residents. A resident is a person who has maintained a permanent place of abode within the state for the previous 12 consecutive months and has continuously maintained his voting residence in the state, and any member of the military service who has been stationed in the state for the immediately preceding 12 months.

Nearly all sporting goods stores in Alaska sell fishing licenses.

The Alaska Dept. of Fish and Game publishes a variety of materials for fishermen. For a price list and free pamphlets, write the Alaska Dept. of Fish and Game, Public Communications Section, P.O. Box 25526, Juneau 99802-5526, phone 465-4112, or contact any regional office of the Dept. of Fish and Game. Be sure you have the most recent edition of the ADF&G regulations booklet for information on bag limits and special permits.

Canada: A special fishing license is necessary for fishing in Canadian national parks and is good for the entire season in all national parks. These are on sale at park gates.

Alberta: Annual nonresident license (season), $30; limited (five-day) nonresident, $20. Licenses not required for anglers under 16 or residents 65 years of age or more.

British Columbia: Annual nonresident, non-Canadian angler's license, $27; nonresident short-term fishing license, valid for six consecutive days and not valid for steelhead fishing, $15. Licenses not required for anglers under 16 years of age. Special permits required for steelhead and for nonresident fishing lakes and streams classified as "Special Water." Freshwater and saltwater fishing licenses are required of all anglers 16 and older; both are renewable on March 31.

Northwest Territories: Annual nonresident fishing license (season), $40; three-day nonresident license, $30. Nonresident anglers under 16 years of age do not need a license when accompanied by a licensed angler. Fishing licenses are available from the visitor information center at the Alberta–Northwest Territories border on the Mackenzie Highway and in most communities from hardware and sporting goods stores, fishing lodges, RCMP and government wildlife offices.

Yukon Territory: Season fishing license fee for a nonresident is $35, or $20 for six days. A one-day nonresident license is also available for $5. Canadian resident season fee is $25. All persons 16 years of age or over must have a license.

Gold Panning

If you are interested in gold panning, sluicing or suction dredging in Alaska — whether for fun or profit — you'll have to know whose land you are on and familiarize yourself with current regulations. Recreational gold panning is allowed on some state and federal lands. Regulations on use of gold pans and hand shovels, nonmechanized sluice boxes and suction dredges vary depending on where you are.

Throughout Alaska, there are two sets of mining regulations to be familiar with — state and federal. Free pamphlets describing the respective requirements of each can be obtained from mining information offices of the State Division of Mining or the Bureau of Land Management. Contact them at: State Division of Mining, P.O. Box 107016, Anchorage 99510-7016, phone 762-2518; Bureau of Land Management, 222 W. 7th Ave. #13, Anchorage 99513-7599, phone 271-5960; State Divison of Mining, 3700 Airport Way, Fairbanks 99709, phone 451-2788; Bureau of Land Management, 1150 University Ave., Fairbanks 99709-3844, phone 474-2200.

Panning, sluicing and suction dredging on private property, established mining claims and Native lands is considered trespassing unless you have the consent of the owner.

You can pan for gold for a small fee by visiting one of the commercial gold panning resorts in Alaska and the Yukon. These include Crow Creek Mine (off Alyeska Access Road, see SEWARD HIGHWAY section); Gold Dredge No. 8 near Fairbanks (see STEESE HIGHWAY section); Little Eldorado, also near Fairbanks (see ELLIOTT HIGHWAY section); and Guggieville and commercial operations on Bonanza Creek Road outside Dawson City, YT (see the KLONDIKE LOOP section). These resorts rent gold pans and let you try your luck on gold-bearing creeks and streams on their property.

Hiking

The National Park Service (605 W. 4th, Anchorage 99501) has general information on hiking in all of the NPS-administered national parks, preserves and monuments in Alaska.

For details on hiking in Chugach State Park, contact Alaska State Division of Parks, Pouch 7-001, Anchorage 99510. Two excellent brochures, one a summer guide to Chugach State Park, the other a winter guide to the park, are available from the park office. Both brochures include a map of the park showing access to trailheads, campgrounds, picnic areas, snow machine and cross-country ski trails, off-road vehicle areas and boating sites from the Glenn Highway, from downtown Anchorage and from the Seward Highway. For visitors to Anchorage, Chugach State Park offers nearby, easily accessible wilderness for day hikes and wildlife viewing.

U.S. Fish and Wildlife Service, 1011 E. Tudor Road, Anchorage 99503, has brochures about the many wildlife refuges and ranges.

The Bureau of Land Management, 1541 Gaffney Road, Fairbanks 99703, has brochures on hiking trails and recreation areas.

The USDA Forest Service Supervisor and District Ranger offices have trail maps and detailed information on hiking trails in Tongass and Chugach national forests.

An extensive system of hiking trails on the Kenai Peninsula is maintained by the Anchorage and Seward Ranger districts of the Chugach National Forest. The most popular trail is the Resurrection Pass trail, a 38.6-mile/62.1-km trail that follows Resurrection Creek from Hope up Resurrection Pass then down Juneau Creek to the Sterling Highway. Other popular Kenai Peninsula trails are Johnson Pass, Crow Pass, Russian Lakes and Ptarmigan Creek. There are public-use cabins along many of the trails; these must be reserved in advance. For general information, write Chugach National Forest, 201 E. 9th Ave., Suite 100, Anchorage 99501. (For specific information on trails and cabins in Chugach and Tongass national forests, see area office addresses in Cabins this section.)

Yukon Territory has established wilderness trails, too. Information about hiking in Kluane National Park is available from the Superintendent, Kluane National Park, Box 5495, Haines Junction, YT Y0B 1L0. For other hiking trails in the Yukon contact Tourism Yukon, Box 2703, Whitehorse, YT Y1A 2C6.

Holidays—1994

The following list of observed holidays in Alaska and Canada can help you plan your trip. Keep in mind that banks and other agencies may be closed on these holidays and traffic may be heavier.

ALASKA	
New Year's Day	Jan. 1
Martin Luther King Day	Jan. 17
Presidents' Day	Feb. 21
Seward's Day	March 28
Easter Sunday	April 3
Memorial Day	May 30
Independence Day	July 4
Labor Day	Sept. 5
Columbus Day	Oct. 10
Alaska Day	Oct. 18
Veterans Day	Nov. 11
Thanksgiving Day	Nov. 24
Christmas Day	Dec. 25

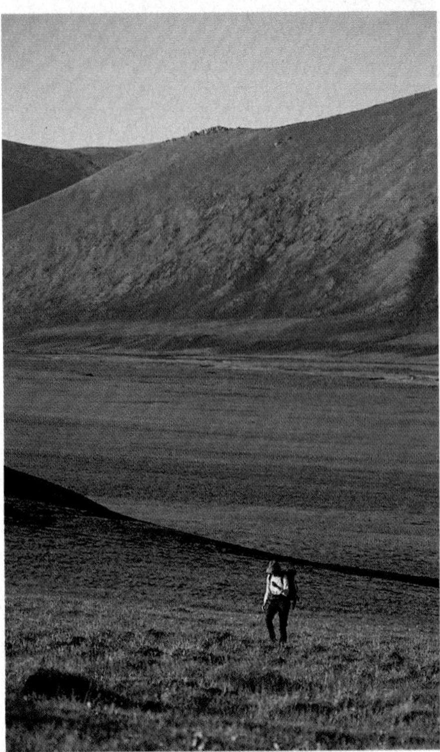

Hiker finds solitude in the Brooks Range. (Bill Sherwonit)

CANADA	
New Year's Day	Jan. 1
Good Friday	April 1
Easter Monday	April 4
Victoria Day	May 23
Canada Day	July 1
Alberta Heritage Day	Aug. 1
British Columbia Day	Aug. 1
Discovery Day (YT)	Aug. 15
Labour Day	Sept. 5
Thanksgiving Day	Oct. 10
Remembrance Day	Nov. 11
Christmas Day	Dec. 25
Boxing Day	Dec. 26

Hunting

Obtain up-to-date information on fees, licenses, seasons, bag limits and regulations from the following government agencies for Alaska, Alberta, British Columbia, Northwest Territories and Yukon Territory.

Alaska: Alaska Dept. of Fish and Game, Box 25526, Juneau, AK 99802. A complete list of registered Alaska guides is available for $5 from the Dept. of Commerce, Occupational Licensing/Big Game Board, Box 110806, Juneau, AK 99811-0806.

Alberta: Alberta Forest, Lands and Wildlife, 9920 108 St., Edmonton, AB T5K 2M4.

British Columbia: Fish and Wildlife Branch, Ministry of Environment, 810 Blanchard St., Victoria, BC V8V 1K5.

Northwest Territories: Department of Economic Development and Tourism, Box 1320, Yellowknife, NT X1A 2L9.

Yukon Territory: Tourism Yukon, Box 2703, Whitehorse, YT Y1A 2C6.

Information Sources

Contact the following state and provincial tourism agencies for free maps and brochures and for travel-related questions.

Alaska: Alaska Division of Tourism, P.O. Box 110801, Juneau, AK 99811-0801, phone (907) 465-2010.

Alberta: Travel Alberta, 3rd Floor, 10155 102 St., Edmonton, AB T5J 4L6, phone 1-800-661-8888.

British Columbia: Tourism British Columbia, Parliament Buildings, Victoria, BC V8V 1X4, phone 1-800-663-6000.

Northwest Territories: Dept. of Economic Development and Tourism, Box 1320, Yellowknife, NT X1A 2L9, phone 1-800-661-0788.

Yukon Territory: Tourism Yukon, Box 2703, Whitehorse, YT Y1A 2C6, phone (403) 667-5340.

Maps

Visitors to Alaska may want more detailed maps of Alaska's backcountry than the highway strip maps and "Plan-A-Trip" Map included in *The MILEPOST®*. Your best source for topographic maps is the U.S. Geological Survey. USGS topographic maps are available in scales. For Alaska, the standard scale is 1:63, 360, 15 minute series, 1-inch to 1 mile. Maps are available by mail from the USGS Distribution Section, Box 25286, Federal Center, Denver, CO 80225. Write for an index of maps for Alaska; the index shows published topographic maps available, quadrangle location, name and survey date. (The index and a booklet describing topographic maps are free.)

Sales counters are maintained at USGS offices throughout the country; check the phone book to see if there's an office near you. In Alaska, USGS maps may be purchased over the counter (no mail order) at USGS offices located at: Federal Bldg., 701 C St., Room F-146, Anchorage 99513, or 4230 University Dr., Room 101, Anchorage 99508-4664; 441 Federal Bldg., 709 W. 9th St., Juneau; and Box 12, New Federal Bldg., 101 12th Ave., Room 126, Fairbanks, 99701. Many commercial dealers also sell USGS maps.

Chugach National Forest maps are available for a small fee from the USDA Forest Service, 201 E. 9th Ave., Suite 100, Anchorage 99501. Tongass National Forest maps are available from the USDA Forest Service, P.O. Box 21628, Juneau 99802, and the Alaska Natural History Association, 605 W. 4th Ave. Suite 120, Anchorage 99501. For details on other federal or state lands, contact the appropriate government agency, listed under Information Sources.

Topographic maps of Canada are available from the Canada Map Office, 615 Booth St., Ottawa, ON K1A 0E9. Index maps showing the published topographic maps are available free of charge: Eastern Canada–Index 1, Western Canada–Index 2, Northern Canada–Index 3. Also available is a list of authorized topographic map dealers for each province.

Metric System

Canada has converted to the metric system. Inches have been replaced with centimetres, feet and yards with metres, miles with kilometres and Fahrenheit with Celsius. Miles, feet, yards and temperatures in all sections of *The MILEPOST®* are followed by the equivalent metric measure. (Equivalents are: 1 mile=1.609 kilometres; 1 kilometre=0.62 miles; 1 yard=0.9144 metres; 1 metre=39.37 inches.) See conversion table for liters and gallons.

LITERS TO GALLONS CONVERSION TABLE

Liters	Gallons	Liters	Gallons	Liters	Gallons
1	.3	21	5.5	41	10.8
2	.5	22	5.8	42	11.1
3	.8	23	6.1	43	11.4
4	1.1	24	6.3	44	11.6
5	1.3	25	6.6	45	11.9
6	1.6	26	6.9	46	12.2
7	1.8	27	7.1	47	12.4
8	2.1	28	7.4	48	12.7
9	2.4	29	7.7	49	12.9
10	2.6	30	7.9	50	13.2
11	2.9	31	8.2	51	13.5
12	3.2	32	8.5	52	13.7
13	3.4	33	8.7	53	14.0
14	3.7	34	9.0	54	14.3
15	4.0	35	9.2	55	14.5
16	4.2	36	9.5	56	14.8
17	4.5	37	9.8	57	15.0
18	4.8	38	10.0	58	15.3
19	5.0	39	10.3	59	15.6
20	5.3	40	10.6	60	15.9

For more precise conversion: 1 liter equals .2642 gallons; 1 gallon equals 3.785 liters.

Money/Credit Cards

The money system in Canada is based on dollars and cents, but the Canadian dollar and the American dollar are two separate currencies and the rate of exchange varies. U.S. currency is accepted as payment in Canada, but the best advice for visitors is: exchange your currency for Canadian funds at a bank in Canada. The visitor is then assured of receiving the rate of exchange prevailing on that day. Although businesses in Canada will accept American dollars, they will often give a lesser rate of exchange than banks or no exchange rate.

As you travel north away from the more populated areas you will find banks located only in the major cities or at best the smaller communities will be served by traveling banks or banks open only one to three days a week for limited hours. Banks in Whitehorse and Dawson City, YT, Yellowknife, NWT, and major Alaskan cities are open generally 10 A.M. to 3 P.M. weekdays (open until 6 P.M. on Friday). Also, some Canadian holidays differ from U.S. holidays, see list under Holidays in this section.

Major American bank and credit cards, including most oil company cards and those of retailers who do business in both countries, are accepted in Canada, too. Credit card purchases are billed at the U.S. dollar equivalent of the Canadian price at the full exchange rate for the day of billing.

It is a good idea to carry cash, since some gas stations in Alaska are independents and do not accept oil company credit cards or major bank credit cards.

Tourists to Canada may be eligible for a rebate on the Goods and Services Tax (GST) paid on certain goods and short-term accommodation. Short-term means accommodation for no more than 30 days at any one location. The purchase must be for a minimum of $100 to qualify for a refund. Check with tourism or customs authorities for more information.

Mosquitoes

Mosquitoes emerge from hibernation before the snow has entirely disappeared. They peak in about June but continue to harass humans through the fall. Mosquitoes are especially active in the early morning and at dusk. Mosquitoes hatch their eggs in water, so the North — with its marshy tundra and many lakes — is a good breeding ground.

The female mosquito penetrates the skin with a hollow snout to draw blood to nourish her eggs. Mosquito saliva, injected into the wound, is what causes the itch, redness and swelling. Mosquitoes rely on their antennae to smell and are attracted to warmth, moisture, carbon dioxide and dark colors, among other things. Mosquitoes fly into the wind, relying on their senses to pick up a potential meal. They then must home in to within a few inches of the object to determine if it is a good meal. Insect repellents work by jamming the mosquitoes' sensors so that they can't tell if you are a meal.

You can't plan your summer vacation around the mosquito. You can take steps to avoid them. The USDA recommends a lightweight hooded parka, tight fitting at the wrists, with a drawstring hood so it fits snugly around the face, and trousers tucked securely in socks, to reduce biting. Mosquitoes can bite through thin material (such as a cotton shirt), so wear some heavier protection when and where mosquitoes are active. Choose a campsite away from mosquito-breeding areas. According to the USDA, a 5 mph wind velocity grounds most mosquitoes, so locating your campsite where you'll catch a breeze also helps.

According to the USDA, mosquito repellents containing diethyl-meta-toluamide (DEET) are most effective. Make sure you apply repellent to all exposed skin, including hands, ears and feet.

National Parks, Preserves and Monuments

The Alaska National Interest Lands Conservation Act, passed in December 1980, placed more than 97 million acres into new or expanded national parks, monuments, preserves and wildlife refuges. Denali and Glacier Bay national parks and preserves are covered in detail in *The MILEPOST®*. For general information on all of Alaska's national and state parks, refuges and forests, contact the Alaska Public Lands Information Centers either in Anchorage at 605 W. 4th Ave., Suite 105, Anchorage 99510, phone (907) 271-2737; Fairbanks at 250 Cushman, Suite 1A, Fairbanks 99701, phone (907) 456-0527; or Tok at Box 359, Tok 99780, phone (907) 883-5667.

Pets

Many people travel to the North with their pets and it is generally not a problem. Pet food is available at local grocery stores and there are pet stores and kennels in the larger cities.

You must have a certificate of rabies vaccination for your pet to cross the U.S.–Canada border. See Customs Requirements in this section.

Unless you have one of those unusual dogs that comes when you call, keep your dog on a leash, both for his own safety and as a courtesy to other travelers. Dogs are not allowed on national park hiking trails and must be on a leash near your vehicle or confined in your vehicle elsewhere in national parks. Some hotels and motels accept pets, others do not.

Do have identification on your pet should he get lost. However, the best idea is to keep your pet on a leash. There is a great deal of wilderness up North and the chances of recovering a lost dog are slim.

Also keep in mind that not all communities in the North have a resident veterinarian. Pet emergency phone numbers are listed in some places in *The MILEPOST®*.

If you are traveling with your pet on the Alaska state ferry, read the information on pets in the MARINE ACCESS ROUTES section.

Police

Alaska: The Alaska State Troopers are the primary police force in Alaska, and there are city police departments in each of the towns. You will find their phone numbers listed throughout *The MILEPOST®*.

Canada: The Royal Canadian Mounted Police (RCMP) is the primary police force and public safety organization throughout western Canada, although cities and towns in Alberta and British Columbia have their own city or municipal police department. If you are involved in an automobile accident within the city limits of a town in British Columbia, for instance, report the accident to the city police. Outside a city, you should report to the RCMP.

The RCMP is the only police force in Yukon Territory and Northwest Territories. (The RCMP will celebrate its 100th anniversary in 1995.)

The RCMP plays a major role in relaying urgent messages to visitors; if you need to locate someone in Canada, contact them.

Postal Rates

Alaska: Rates are the same as for all other U.S. states.

Canada: Rates at press time were 43¢ first class (30 grams, about 1 ounce) within Canada, and 49¢ (30 grams) to the United States. U.S. postage stamps may not be used for mailings sent from Canada.

Shipping

Vehicles: Carriers that will ship cars, truck campers, house trailers and motorhomes from Anchorage to Seattle include: Sea–Land Freight Service, Inc., 1717 Tidewater Ave., Anchorage 99501, phone (907) 274-2671; Alaska Railroad, Box 107500, Anchorage 99510, phone (907) 265-2490; and Totem Ocean Trailer Express, 2511 Tidewater, Anchorage 99501, phone (907) 276-5868.

In the Seattle, WA, area, contact Sea–Land Service, Inc., 3600 Port of Tacoma Road, Tacoma 98424, phone (206) 922-3100 or 1-800-426-4512 (outside Washington); Alaska Railroad, 2203 Airport Way S., Suite

215, Seattle 98134, phone (206) 624-4234; Totem Ocean Trailer Express, P.O. Box 24908, Seattle 98124, phone (206) 628-9280 or 1-800-426-0074 (except from Washington, Alaska or Hawaii); or A.A.D.A. Systems, P.O. Box 2323, Auburn 98071, phone (206) 762-7840.

Vehicle shipment between southeastern Alaska and Seattle is provided by Boyer Alaska Barge Line, 7318 4th Ave. S., Seattle 98108, phone (206) 763-8575 (serves Ketchikan, Metlakatla, Prince of Wales Island and Wrangell); and Alaska Marine Lines, 5615 W. Marginal Way SW, Seattle 98106, phone (206) 763-4244 or toll free (800) 443-4343 (direct service to Ketchikan, Wrangell, Petersburg, Sitka, Juneau, Haines, Skagway, Yakutat, Excursion Inlet and Hawk Inlet).

Persons shipping vehicles between Seattle and Anchorage are advised to shop around for the carrier that offers the services and rates most suited to the shipper's needs. Not all carriers offer year-round service and freight charges vary greatly depending upon the carrier and the length and height of the vehicle. Rates quoted here are only approximate. Sample fares per unit: northbound, Seattle to Anchorage, under 66 inches in height, $1,225; over 66 inches and under 84 inches in height, $1,785; southbound, Anchorage to Seattle, any unit under 84 inches, $640. Over 17 feet to 21 feet, northbound, $2,160; southbound, $65 per foot. Rates increase frequently and the potential shipper is cautioned to call carriers' rate departments for those rates in effect at shipping time.

Not all carriers accept rented moving trucks and trailers, and a few of those that do require authorization from the rental company to carry its equipment to Alaska. Check with the carrier and your rental company before booking service.

Book your reservation at least two weeks in advance and three weeks during summer months, and prepare to have the vehicle at the carrier's loading facility two days prior to sailing. Carriers differ on what nonvehicle items they allow to travel inside, from nothing at all to goods packaged and addressed separately. Coast Guard regulations forbid the transport of vehicles holding more than one-quarter tank of gas, and none of the carriers listed above allow owners to accompany their vehicles in transit. Remember to have fresh antifreeze installed in your car or truck prior to sailing!

You may ship your vehicle aboard a state ferry to southeastern ports (at a lesser rate), however, you must accompany your vehicle or arrange for someone to drive it on and off the ferry at departure and arrival ports. See MARINE ACCESS ROUTES section.

Household Goods and Personal Effects: Most moving van lines have service to and from Alaska through their agency connections in most Alaska and Lower 48 cities. To initiate service contact the van line agents nearest your origin point.

Northbound goods are shipped to Seattle and transferred through a port agent to a water vessel for carriage to Alaska. Few shipments go over the road to Alaska. Southbound shipments are processed in a like manner through Alaska ports to Seattle, then on to destination.

U-Haul provides service into the North Country for those who prefer to move their goods themselves. At press time, there were 53 U-Haul dealerships in Alaska and northwestern Canada for over-the-road service. In Alaska, there were eight dealerships in Anchorage, six in Fairbanks and one in each of the following communities: Homer, Juneau, Ketchikan, Delta Junction, Haines, Kenai, Glennallen, Palmer, Seward, Soldotna, Tok, Valdez, Wasilla, Eagle River, Sitka and North Pole. In Canada, there were dealerships and ready stations in Dawson Creek, Fort St. John, Fort Nelson, Whitehorse and at other locations along the Alaska Highway. There were also breakdown stations for service of U-Haul vehicles in Beaver Creek, Swift River and the Kluane Wilderness Area.

It's also possible to ship a rented truck or trailer into southeastern Alaska aboard the water carriers that accept privately owned vehicles (see Shipping Vehicles). A few of the water carriers sailing between Seattle and Anchorage also carry rented equipment. However, shop around for this service, for this has not been common practice in the past, and rates can be very high if the carrier does not yet have a specific tariff established for this type of shipment. You will not be allowed to accompany the rented equipment.

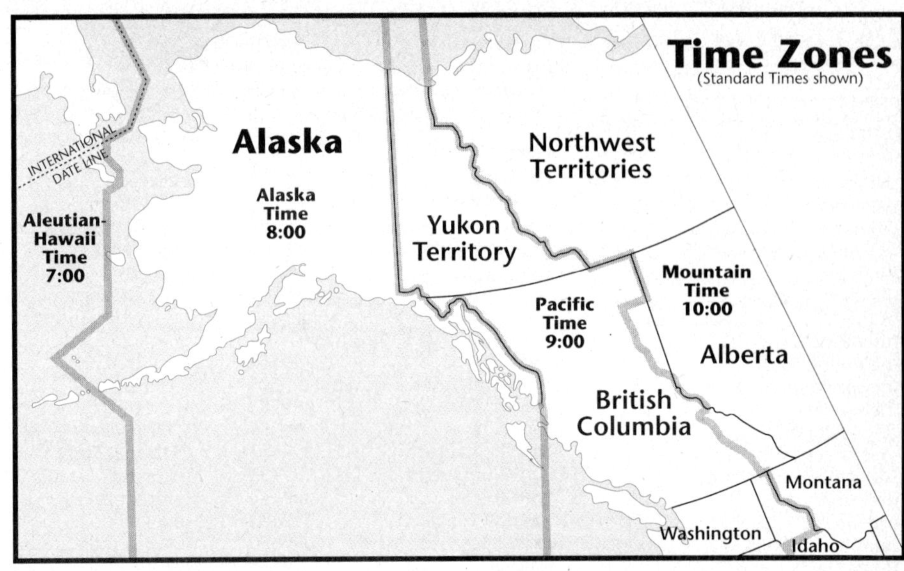

Telephone, Telegraph, Money Orders

Alaska: All of Alaska uses the 907 area code.

Telegrams, cablegrams, mailgrams, telex and fax can be sent by telephone from anywhere in Alaska through Western Union. Money transfers can also be sent and received within 15 minutes through Western Union agencies, many with extended hours of operation. Western Union branch offices are located throughout the state and continental United States. To find the Western Union location nearest you, and for hours of operation, phone 1-800-325-6000.

Alberta: All of the province shares the area code 403.

British Columbia: All of the province shares the area code 604.

Northwest Territories: The territory has three area codes. The area code for all communities included in *The MILEPOST®* is 403.

Yukon Territory: All of the territory shares the area code 403 (same as Alberta).

Persons wishing to send telegrams to or from Canada, as well as needing money transfer services, should contact the offices of the Canadian Western Union affiliate, Unitel–Transdollar. To find the location nearest you, phone 1-800-361-1877.

Time Zones

At Alaska's request, the federal government reduced the state's time zones from four to two, effective Oct. 30, 1983. The state now is operating on Alaska time, or one hour earlier than Pacific time. The only residents of the state not setting their clocks on Alaska time are in the four western Aleutian Island communities of Atka, Adak, Shemya and Attu, which moved from Bering time to Aleutian–Hawaii time.

British Columbia is on Pacific standard time (daylight saving time in summer), the same as Yukon Territory, except for the area around Dawson Creek and Fort St. John and south from Valemount through Cranbrook, which are on mountain time. All of Alberta and western Northwest Territories are on mountain time and both observe daylight saving time.

Water

Purify all surface water that is to be used for drinking or cooking. Northern lakes, streams and rivers may be contaminated by the Giardia organism, which can cause the intestinal disorder giardiasis. Giardiasis is characterized by diarrhea, gas, loss of appetite, abdominal cramps and bloating. These symptoms may appear from a few days to a few weeks after ingestion of the organism. To purify water, boil for at least one minute at a full rolling boil. It is a good idea to treat even piped water at campgrounds to be on the safe side.

It is also recommended that travelers carry drinking water, and refill containers at safe sources whenever available. RV travelers should consider carrying buckets and funnels to use to fill tanks at campgrounds with non-standard water faucets.

Swimmers should inquire locally before taking a dip in any gravel pits or roadside lakes. Some of the Northern ponds are host to the larvae of schistosomes, which cause "swimmer's itch." Symptoms are redness and itching of the skin, beginning immediately and lasting up to a week.

Zip Codes in Alaska

Afognak 99697
Akhiok 99615
Akiachak 99551
Akiak 99552
Akutan 99553
Alakanuk 99554
Aleknagik 99555
Alexander Creek 99695
Alifak 99697
Allakaket 99720
Ambler 99786
Amook 99697
Anaktuvuk Pass 99721
Anchor Point 99556
Anchorage:
  General Delivery 99501
  See street listings in official zip code directory.
Anderson 99744
Angoon 99820
Aniak 99557
Anvik 99558
Arctic Village 99722
Atka 99547
Atmautluak 99559
Attu 99502
Auke Bay 99821
Baranof 99850
Barrow 99723
Beaver 99724
Bell Island 99950
Bethel 99559
Bettles Field 99726
Big Lake 99652
Bird Creek 99540
Border 99780
Brevig Mission 99785
Buckland 99727
Cantwell 99729
Cape Pole 99950
Cape Yakataga 99695
Central 99730
Chalkyitsik 99788
Chatham 99850
Chefornak 99561
Chevak 99563
Chickaloon 99674
Chicken 99732
Chignik 99564
Chignik Lagoon 99565
Chignik Lake 99548
Chisana 99790
Chitina 99566
Chuathbaluk 99557
Chugiak 99567
Circle 99733
Clam Gulch 99568
Clarks Point 99569
Clear 99704
Coffman Cove 99918
Cold Bay 99571
Coldfoot 99701
College 99701
  P.O. Boxes 99708
Cooper Landing 99572
Copper Center 99573
Cordova 99574
Craig 99921
Crooked Creek 99575
Deep Bay 99950
Deering 99736
Delta Junction 99737
Denali National Park 99755
Dillingham 99576
Dolomi 99950
Dot Lake 99737
Douglas 99824
Driftwood Bay 99695
Dutch Harbor 99692
Eagle 99738
Eagle River 99577
Eek 99578
Egegik 99579
Eielson AFB 99702
Ekuk 99695
Ekwok 99580
Elfin Cove 99825
Elim 99739
Elmendorf AFB 99506
Emmonak 99581
English Bay 99603
Ester 99725
Excursion Inlet 99850
Fairbanks:
  General Delivery 99701
  See street listings in official zip code directory.
False Pass 99583
Farewell 99695
Fire Cove 99950
Flat 99584
Fort Richardson 99505
Fort Wainwright 99703
Fort Yukon 99740
Fortuna Ledge 99585
Funter Bay 99850
Gakona 99586
Galena 99741
Gambell 99742
Girdwood 99587
Glennallen 99588
Gold Creek 99695
Golovin 99762
Goodnews Bay 99589
Grayling 99590
Gulkana 99695
Gustavus 99826
Haines 99827
Halibut Cove 99603
Happy Harbor 99950
Hawk Inlet 99850
Healy 99743
Holy Cross 99602
Homer 99603
Hoonah 99829
Hooper Bay 99604
Hope 99605
Houston 99694
Hughes 99745
Huslia 99746
Hydaburg 99922
Hyder 99923
Icy Bay 99695
Igiugig 99613
Iliamna 99606
Indian 99540
Ivanoff Bay 99695
Juneau:
  General Delivery 99801
  See street listings in official zip code directory.
Kake 99830
Kaktovik 99747
Kalskag 99607
Kaltag 99748
Karluk 99608
Kasaan 99950
Kasigluk 99609
Kasilof 99610
Kasitsna Bay 99695
Kenai 99611
Kenny Cove 99695
Ketchikan 99901
Kiana 99749
King Cove 99612
King Salmon 99613
Kipnuk 99614
Kitoi Bay 99697
Kivalina 99750
Klawock 99925
Kobuk 99751
Kodiak 99615
Kokhanok 99606
Koliganek 99576
Kongiganak 99559
Kotlik 99620
Kotzebue 99752
Koyuk 99753
Koyukuk 99754
Kwethluk 99621
Kwigillingok 99622
Lab Bay 99950
Lake Minchumina 99757
Larsen Bay 99624
Levelock 99625
Lime Village 99695
Little Diomede 99762
Long Island 99950
Loring 99950
Lower Kalskag 99626
Manley Hot Springs 99756
Manokotak 99628
May Creek 99695
McCarthy 99695
McGrath 99627
McKinley Park (see Denali National Park)
Mekoryuk 99630
Mentasta Lake 99780
Metlakatla 99926
Meyers Chuck 99903
Minto 99758
Moose Pass 99631
Moser Bay 99697
Mountain Village 99632
Naknek 99633
Napakiak 99634
Napaskiak 99559
Neets Cove 99950
Nelson Lagoon 99571
Nenana 99760
New Stuyahok 99636
Newtok 99559
Nickolaevsk 99556
Nightmute 99690
Nikiski 99635
Nikolai 99691
Nikolski 99638
Ninilchik 99639
Noatak 99761
Nome 99762
Nondalton 99640
Noorvik 99763
North Pole 99705
Northway 99764
Noyes Island 99950
Nuiqsut 99789
Nulato 99765
Nunapitchuk 99641
Nyac 99642
Old Harbor 99643
Olga Bay 99697
Ophir Bay 99695
Ouzinkie 99644
Palmer 99645
Paxson 99737
Pedro Bay 99647
Pelican 99832
Perryville 99648
Petersburg 99833
Pilot Point 99649
Pilot Station 99650
Platinum 99651
Point Baker 99927
Point Hope 99766
Point Lay 99723
Pope Vancy Landing 99695
Port Alexander 99836
Port Alice 99950
Port Alsworth 99653
Port Ashton 99695
Port Bailey 99697
Port Clarence 99790
Port Graham 99603
Port Heiden 99549
Port Johnson 99950
Port Lions 99550
Port Moller 99695
Port Protection 99950
Port San Juan 99695
Port Walter 99850
Port William 99697
Portage Creek 99695
Prudhoe Bay 99734
Quinhagak 99655
Rampart 99767
Red Devil 99656
Red Mountain 99695
Rowan Bay 99850
Ruby 99768
Russian Mission 99657
Saint George Island 99591
Saint Marys 99658
Saint Michael 99659
Saint Paul Island 99660
Salcha 99714
Sand Point 99661
Savoonga 99769
Scammon Bay 99662
Seal Bay 99697
Selawik 99770
Seldovia 99663
Seward 99664
Shageluk 99665
Shaktoolik 99771
Sheldon Point 99666
Shishmaref 99772
Shungnak 99773
Sitka 99835
Skagway 99840
Skwentna 99667
Slana 99586
Sleetmute 99668
Soldotna 99669
Solomon 99790
South Naknek 99670
Sparrevohn 99502
Stebbins 99671
Sterling 99672
Stevens Village 99774
Stony River 99557
Sutton 99674
Takotna 99675
Talkeetna 99676
Tanacross 99776
Tanana 99777
Tatitlek 99677
Telida 99695
Teller 99778
Tenakee Springs 99841
Terror Bay 99697
Tetlin 99779
Thorne Bay 99919
Togiak 99678
Tok 99780
Tokeen 99950
Toksook Bay 99637
Trapper Creek 99683
Tuluksak 99679
Tuntutuliak 99680
Tununak 99681
Twin Hills 99576
Tyonek 99682
Uganik Bay 99697
Ugashik 99695
Unalakleet 99684
Unalaska 99685
Utopia 99790
Uyak 99697
Valdez 99686
Venetie 99781
View Cove 99950
Wainwright 99782
Wales 99783
Ward Cove 99928
Wasilla 99687
Waterfall 99950
West Point 99697
Whale Pass 99950
White Mountain 99784
Whittier 99693
Willow 99688
Wiseman 99790
Wrangell 99929
Yakutat 99689
Yes Bay 99950
Zackar Bay 99697

INDEX OF PLACE NAMES

Communities, Highways, National Parks (NP), National Wildlife Refuges (NWR) and other attractions.

***A detailed map is included.**